PSYCHOLOGY

THE SCIENCE OF

SECOND EDITION IN MODULES

LAURA A. KING

University of Missouri, Columbia

McGraw Hill

Connect
Learn
Succeed™

McGraw-Hill Higher Education
A Division of The McGraw-Hill Companies

1 2 3 4 5 6 7 8 9 0 QVR/QVR 9 8 7 6 5 4 3 2 1

ISBN: 978-0-07-803549-4
MHID: 0-07-803549-X

Sponsoring Editor: *Allison McNamara*
Executive Marketing Manager: *Julia Flohr Larkin*
Executive Market Development Manager: *Sheryl Adams*
Developmental Editor: *Cara Labell*
Production Editor: *Catherine Morris*
Manuscript Editor: *Barbara Hacha*
Art Manager: *Robin Mouat*
Design Manager: *Cassandra Chu*
Text and Cover Designer: *Linda Beaupré*
Illustrators: *John and Judy Waller*
Lead Photo Research Coordinator: *Alexandra Ambrose*
Photo Researcher: *David Tietz*
Buyer II: *Tandra Jorgensen*
Media Project Manager: *Andrea Helmbolt*
Digital Product Manager: *Jay Gubernick*
Composition: *10.5/12 Adobe Garamond by Aptara®, Inc.*
Printing: *45# Orion Satin, Quad/Grahics*

Vice President Editorial: *Michael Ryan*
Publisher: *Mike Sugarman*
Director of Development: *Dawn Groundwater*

Cover: ©Foodcollection RF

Credits: The credits section for this book begins on page C1 and is considered an extension of the copyright page.

Library of Congress Cataloging-in-Publication Data

King, Laura A. (Laura Ann)
  The science of psychology: modules/Laura King, John Santrock.—2nd ed.
    p. cm.
  Includes bibliographical references and index.
  ISBN-13: 978-0-07-803549-4 (alk. paper)
  ISBN-10: 0-07-803549-X (alk. paper)
  1. Psychology–Textbooks. I. Santrock, John W. II. Title.
  BF121.K538 2011
  150—dc23

                                    2011027468

www.mhhe.com

LAURA A. KING

Laura King majored in English at Kenyon College, but in the second semester of her junior year she declared a second major in psychology. She completed her bachelor's degree in English with high honors and distinction and in psychology with distinction in 1986. Laura then did graduate work at Michigan State University and the University of California, Davis, receiving her Ph.D. in personality psychology in 1991.

Laura began her career at Southern Methodist University in Dallas, moving to the University of Missouri, Columbus, in 2001, where she is now the Frederick A. Middlebush Professor of Psychological Sciences. In addition to seminars in the development of character, social psychology, and personality psychology, she has taught undergraduate introductory psychology, introduction to personality psychology, and social psychology. At SMU, she received six different teaching awards, including the M Award for "sustained excellence" in 1999. At the University of Missouri, she received the Chancellor's Award for "outstanding research and creative activity" in 2004.

Her research, which has been funded by the National Institute of Mental Health, has focused on a variety of topics relevant to the question of what it is that makes for a good life. She has studied goals, life stories, happiness, well-being, and meaning in life. In general, her work reflects an enduring interest in studying what is good and healthy in people. In 2001, her research accomplishments were recognized by a Templeton Prize in positive psychology. Laura's research (often in collaboration with undergraduate and graduate students) has been published in the *American Psychologist,* the *Journal of Personality and Social Psychology, Psychological Science,* and other publications. Currently editor-in-chief of the personality and individual differences section of the *Journal of Personality and Social Psychology,* Laura has also served as the editor-in-chief of the *Journal of Research in Personality* and as an associate editor for the *Personality and Social Psychology Bulletin,* as well as on numerous grant panels. She has edited or co-edited special sections of several journals, including the *American Psychologist.* In "real life," Laura is an accomplished cook and enjoys listening to music (mostly jazz vocalists and singer-songwriters), gardening, and chasing Sam, her 6-year-old son.

BRIEF CONTENTS

CONTENTS

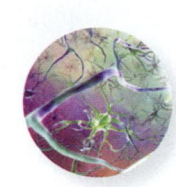

5
States of
Consciousness   148

6
Learning   188

7
Memory   226

8
Thinking, Intelligence, and Language 266

9
Human Development 304

10
Motivation and Emotion 348

11
Gender, Sex, and Sexuality   384

12
Personality   428

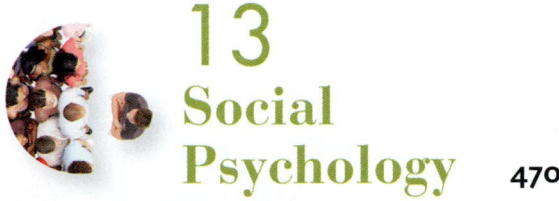

13
Social Psychology   470

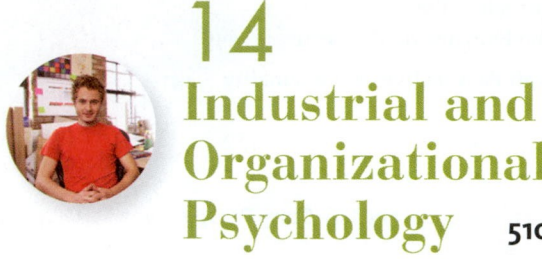

14
Industrial and Organizational Psychology 510

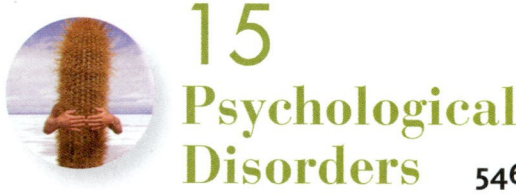

15
Psychological Disorders 546

16
Therapies 584

17 Health Psychology **620**

1 KNOWLEDGE BASE OF PSYCHOLOGY
Demonstrate familiarity with the major concepts, theoretical perspectives, empirical findings, and historical trends in psychology.

1.1 Characterize the nature of psychology as a discipline.
1.2 Demonstrate knowledge and understanding, representing appropriate breadth and depth in selected content areas of psychology.
1.3 Use the concepts, language, and major theories of the discipline to account for psychological phenomena.
1.4 Explain major perspectives of psychology (e.g., behavioral, biological, cognitive, evolutionary, humanistic, psychodynamic, and sociocultural).

- Module 1: 1.1, 1.2, 1.3
- Module 6: 6.1, 6.2, 6.3
- Module 7: 7.1, 7.2, 7.3, 7.4, 7.5, 7.6
- Module 8: 8.1, 8.2
- Module 17
- *Human Development and Health and Wellness* (p. 345)
- Module 35: 35.1, 35.2, 35.4, 35.5
- Module 44: 44.1
- Module 42: 42.2, 42.3
- Module 45: 45.1, 45.2
- Module 48: 48.1
- Module 49: 49.1
- Module 50: 50.3
- Module 58: 58.1
- Module 60: 60.1
- Module 62: 62.2
- Module 65: 65.1, 65.3, 65.4, 65.5

2 RESEARCH METHODS IN PSYCHOLOGY
Understand and apply basic research methods in psychology, including research design, data analysis, and interpretation.

2.1 Describe the basic characteristics of the science of psychology.
2.2 Explain different research methods used by psychologists.
2.3 Evaluate the appropriateness of conclusions derived from psychological research.
2.4 Design and conduct basic studies to address psychological questions using appropriate research methods.
2.5 Follow the APA Codes of Ethics in the treatment of human and nonhuman participants in the design, data collection, interpretation, and reporting of psychological research.
2.6 Generate research conclusions appropriately based on the parameters of particular research methods.

- Module 1: *Critical Controversy: Are Young Americans in the Middle of a Narcissism Epidemic?* (p. 6)
- Module 2: *Intersection: Social Psychology and Cross-Cultural Psychology: Is Success Always Sweeter Than Failure?* (p. 22)
- *The Science of Psychology and Health and Wellness* (p. 24)
- Module 3: 3.1, 3.2
- Module 4: 4.1, 4.2, 4.3, 4.4: *Intersection: Social Psychology and Developmental Psychology: Is High Self-Esteem Such a Good Thing?* (p. 42)
- Module 5: 5.1, 5.2, 5.3: *Critical Controversy: Would Reality TV Pass the Institutional Review Board?* (p. 56)
- *The Scientific Method and Health and Wellness* (p. 58)
- Module 7: *Critical Controversy: Are Human Brains Uniquely Wired to Recognize Faces?* (p. 85); *Intersection: Emotion and Neuroscience: Is Your Brain Happy?* (p. 91)
- Module 8: 8.2
- Module 9: *Intersection: Perception and Social Psychology: Was That a Gun or Car Keys?* (p. 116)
- Module 11: *Critical Controversy: Are Cochlear Implants a "Cure" for Deafness?* (p. 135)
- *Sensation, Perception, and Health and Wellness* (p. 146)
- Module 13: *Intersection: Consciousness and Developmental Psychology: How Do We Develop a Sense of the Minds of Others?* (p. 154)
- Module 14: 14.2
- Module 15: *Critical Controversy: Should Illicit Psychoactive Drugs Be Legalized for Medical Use?* (p. 179)
- Module 16: 16.3
- *Consciousness and Health and Wellness: Meditation* (p. 185)
- Module 18: 18.1, 18.2
- Module 19: *Intersection: Behaviorism and Cognitive Neuroscience: If It Feels Good, Is It Rewarding?* (p. 204); *Critical Controversy: Will Sparing the Rod Spoil the Child?* (p. 210)
- *Learning and Health and Wellness* (p. 223)
- Module 23: *Intersection: Memory and Sensation: Why Is Smell Specially Connected with Memory?* (p. 243)

2   RESEARCH METHODS IN PSYCHOLOGY, *continued*
Understand and apply basic research methods in psychology, including research design, data analysis, and interpretation.

3   CRITICAL THINKING SKILLS IN PSYCHOLOGY
Respect and use critical and creative thinking, skeptical inquiry, and, when possible, the scientific approach to solving problems related to behavior and mental processes.

3.1   Use critical thinking effectively.
3.2   Engage in creative thinking.
3.3   Use reasoning to recognize, develop, defend, and criticize arguments and other persuasive appeals.
3.4   Approach problems effectively.

3 CRITICAL THINKING SKILLS IN PSYCHOLOGY, *continued*
Respect and use critical and creative thinking, skeptical inquiry, and, when possible, the scientific approach to solving problems related to behavior and mental processes.

- Module 7: 7.3; *Critical Controversy: Are Human Brains Uniquely Wired to Recognize Faces?* (p. 85); *Intersection: Emotion and Neuroscience: Is Your Brain Happy?* (p. 91)
- Module 8: 8.2
- Module 9: *Intersection: Perception and Social Psychology: Was That a Gun or Car Keys?* (p. 116)
- Module 11: *Critical Controversy: Are Cochlear Implants a "Cure" for Deafness?* (p. 135)
- Module 13: *Intersection: Consciousness and Developmental Psychology: How Do We Develop a Sense of the Minds of Others?* (p. 154)
- Module 14: 14.2, 14.6
- Module 15: *Critical Controversy: Should Illicit Psychoactive Drugs Be Legalized for Medical Use?* (p. 179)
- Module 26
- Module 28: 28.2, 28.3, 28.4; *Intersection: Emotion and Cognition: How Are You Feeling and Thinking Today?* (p. 278)
- Module 29: 29.3, 29.4
- Module 30: 30.3
- *Thinking, Problem Solving, and Health and Wellness* (p. 301)
- Module 31
- Module 38: 38.4, 38.5
- Module 40: 40.3
- Module 41: 41.3
- Module 42: 42.2; *Critical Controversy: Can Abstinence-Only Sex Education Be Effective?* (p. 417)
- Module 45: 45.3
- Module 46: 46.3
- Module 47: 47.3
- Module 50: *Intersection: Personality and Organizational Psychology: Hey, What's Your Type?* (p. 462)
- Module 51: 51.3
- Module 52: *Critical Controversy: Do Violent Video Games Lead to Violence?* (p. 490)
- Module 53: 53.2; *Intersection: Social Psychology and Cognitive Neuroscience: Is the Brain Wired for Conformity?* (p. 494)
- Module 54: *Critical Controversy: Is a Happy Worker a More Productive Worker?* (p. 532)
- Module 56: 56.4
- Module 57: 57.2
- Module 58: 58.2; *Critical Controversy: Are Psychological Disorders a Myth?* (p. 552)
- Module 61: 61.2
- Module 64: *Critical Controversy: Do Antidepressants Increase Suicide Risk in Children?* (p. 589)

4 APPLICATION OF PSYCHOLOGY
Understand and apply psychological principles to personal, social, and organizational issues.

4.1 Describe major applied areas (e.g., clinical, counseling, industrial/organizational, and school) and emerging (e.g., health, forensics, media, and military) applied areas of psychology.

4.2 Identify appropriate applications of psychology in solving problems.

4.3 Articulate how psychological principles can be used to explain social issues and inform public policy.

- Module 1: 1.2; *Critical Controversy: Are Young Americans in the Middle of a Narcissism Epidemic?* (p. 6)
- Module 2: 2.2
- *The Science of Psychology and Health and Wellness* (p. 24)
- Module 4: 4.4
- Module 5: 5.2; *Critical Controversy: Would Reality TV Pass the Institutional Review Board?* (p. 56)
- *The Scientific Method and Health and Wellness* (p. 58)

4 APPLICATION OF PSYCHOLOGY, *continued*
Understand and apply psychological principles to personal, social, and organizational issues.

4.4 Apply psychological concepts, theories, and research findings as these relate to everyday life.

4.5 Recognize that ethically complex situations can develop in the application of psychological principles.

- Module 7: 7.6; *Critical Controversy: Are Human Brains Uniquely Wired to Recognize Faces?* (p. 85); *Intersection: Emotion and Neuroscience: Is Your Brain Happy?* (p. 91)
- Module 8: 8.2, 8.3
- *Psychology's Biological Foundations and Health and Wellness* (p. 101)
- Module 9: *Intersection: Perception and Social Psychology: Was That a Gun or Car Keys?* (p. 116)
- Module 11: *Critical Controversy: Are Cochlear Implants a "Cure" for Deafness?* (p. 135)
- *Sensation, Perception, and Health and Wellness* (p. 146)
- Module 14: 14.2, 14.3, 14.4, 14.5, 14.6
- Module 15: *Critical Controversy: Should Illicit Psychoactive Drugs Be Legalized for Medical Use?* (p. 179)
- Module 16: 16.3
- Module 17
- Module 18: 18.2
- Module 19: *Intersection: Behaviorism and Cognitive Neuroscience: If It Feels Good, Is It Rewarding?* (p. 204)
- *Learning and Health and Wellness* (p. 223)
- Module 23: *Intersection: Memory and Sensation: Why Is Smell Specially Connected with Memory?* (p. 243)
- Module 24: 24.3
- Module 26
- Module 28: 28.2, 28.3, 28.4; *Intersection: Emotion and Cognition: How Are You Feeling and Thinking Today?* (p. 278)
- Module 30: 30.3; *Critical Controversy: Does Gender Influence Language?* (p. 295)
- Module 31: 31.1; *Critical Controversy: Genes or Superparents: Which Matters More to Kids?* (p. 309)
- Module 32: *Intersection: Developmental Psychology and Clinical Psychology: Is "Girl Talk" Always a Good Thing?* (p. 327)
- Module 33
- Module 34: 34.1, 34.3, 34.4
- *Human Development and Health and Wellness* (p. 345)
- Module 35: 35.7; *Critical Controversy: Does Extrinsic Motivation Undermine Intrinsic Motivation?* (p. 355)
- Module 37: 37.4
- *Motivation, Emotion, and Health and Wellness: The Pursuit of Happiness* (p. 380)
- Module 38: 38.4, 38.5; *Intersection: Gender and Neuroscience: Are There His and Hers Brains?* (p. 389)
- Module 40: 40.2, 40.3
- Module 41: 41.3, 41.4
- Module 42: 42.2; *Critical Controversy: Can Abstinence-Only Sex Education Be Effective?* (p. 417)
- Module 43: 43.5
- *Sexuality and Health and Wellness* (p. 424)
- Module 46: 46.2, 46.3
- Module 49: *Critical Controversy: Can Personality Change?* (p. 458)
- Module 50: *Intersection: Personality and Organizational Psychology: Hey, What's Your Type?* (p. 462)
- Module 51: 51.1, 51.2, 51.3
- Module 52: 52.1, 52.2; *Critical Controversy: Do Violent Video Games Lead to Violence?* (p. 490)
- Module 53: 53.1, 53.2; *Intersection: Social Psychology and Cognitive Neuroscience: Is the Brain Wired for Conformity?* (p. 494)
- Module 54: 54.1, 54.2
- Module 55: 55.3
- Module 56: 56.1, 56.2, 56.3
- Module 57: 57.1; *Intersection: Personality Psychology and Organizational Psychology: Who's in Charge?* (p. 535)
- *I/O Psychology and Health and Wellness* (p. 542)

4 APPLICATION OF PSYCHOLOGY, *continued*
Understand and apply psychological principles to personal, social, and organizational issues.

- Module 58: *Critical Controversy: Are Psychological Disorders a Myth?* (p. 552)
- Module 60: 60.3; *Intersection: Child Psychology and Developmental Psychology: Will New Discoveries Bring Depressed Children a Happier Future?* (p. 564)
- Module 64: 64.1, 64.2, 64.3; *Critical Controversy: Do Antidepressants Increase Suicide Risk in Children?* (p. 589)
- Module 65: 65.1, 65.2, 65.3, 65.4, 65.6; *Intersection: Clinical Psychology and Neuroscience: How Does Therapy Change the Brain?* (p. 606)
- *Therapies and Health and Wellness* (p. 617)
- Module 69: 69.1, 69.2, 69.3, 69.4, 69.5
- Module 70: 70.1, 70.2, 70.3

5 VALUES IN PSYCHOLOGY
Value empirical evidence, tolerate ambiguity, act ethically, and reflect other values that are the underpinnings of psychology as a science.

5.1 Recognize the necessity for ethical behavior in all aspects of the science and practice of psychology.
5.2 Demonstrate reasonable skepticism and intellectual curiosity by asking questions about causes of behavior.
5.3 Seek and evaluate scientific evidence for psychological claims.
5.4 Tolerate ambiguity and realize that psychological explanations are often complex and tentative.
5.5 Recognize and respect human diversity.
5.6 Assess and justify their engagement with respect to civic, social, and global responsibilities.
5.7 Understand the limitations of their psychological knowledge and skills.

- Module 1: 1.1, 1.2; *Critical Controversy: Are Young Americans in the Middle of a Narcissism Epidemic?* (p. 6)
- Module 2: *Intersection: Social Psychology and Cross-Cultural Psychology: Is Success Always Sweeter Than Failure?* (p. 22)
- Module 9: *Intersection: Perception and Social Psychology: Was That a Gun or Car Keys?* (p. 116)
- Module 11: *Critical Controversy: Are Cochlear Implants a "Cure" for Deafness?* (p. 135)
- Module 13: *Intersection: Consciousness and Developmental Psychology: How Do We Develop a Sense of the Minds of Others?* (p. 154)
- Module 14: 14.6
- Module 15: *Critical Controversy: Should Illicit Psychoactive Drugs Be Legalized for Medical Use?* (p. 179)
- Module 16: 16.1, 16.2
- Module 17
- Module 18
- Module 19: *Intersection: Behaviorism and Cognitive Neuroscience: If It Feels Good, Is It Rewarding?* (p. 204); *Critical Controversy: Will Sparing the Rod Spoil the Child?* (p. 210)
- *Learning and Health and Wellness* (p. 223)
- Module 21: 21.4
- Module 32: 32.3, 32.11; *Intersection: Developmental Psychology and Clinical Psychology: Is "Girl Talk" Always a Good Thing?* (p. 327)
- Module 34: 34.4
- Module 35: 35.5
- Module 36: 36.3
- Module 37: 37.4
- Module 38: 38.4, 38.5
- Module 40: 40.2, 40.3, 40.4
- Module 42: 42.2, 42.4; *Critical Controversy: Can Abstinence-Only Sex Education Be Effective?* (p. 417)
- Module 46: 46.2
- Module 51: 51.1, 51.2, 51.3
- Module 53: 53.1, 53.2, 53.3
- Module 54: 54.2
- Module 56: 56.1, 56.4
- Module 57: 57.2
- Module 58
- *Therapies and Health and Wellness* (p. 617)
- Module 68: 68.3

6 INFORMATION AND TECHNOLOGICAL LITERACY
Demonstrate information competence and the ability to use computers and other technology for many purposes.

6.1 Demonstrate information competence at each stage in the following process:
 a. *Formulate a researchable topic that can be supported by database search strategies.*
 b. *Locate and choose relevant sources from appropriate media, which may include data and perspectives outside traditional psychology and Western boundaries.*
 c. *Use selected sources after evaluating their suitability based on*
   (1) *Appropriateness, accuracy, quality, and value of the source.*
   (2) *Potential bias of the source.*
   (3) *The relative value of primary versus secondary sources, empirical versus nonempirical sources, and peer-reviewed versus non-peer-reviewed sources.*
 d. *Read and accurately summarize the general scientific literature of psychology.*
6.2 Use appropriate software to produce understandable reports of the psychological literature, methods, and statistical and qualitative analyses in APA or other appropriate style, including graphic representations of data.
6.3 Use information and technology ethically and responsibly.
6.4 Demonstrate these computer skills:
 a. *Use basic word processing, database, e-mail, spreadsheet, and data analysis programs.*
 b. *Search the web for high-quality information.*
 c. *Use proper etiquette and security safeguards when communicating through e-mail.*

- Module 3
- Module 4
- Module 5

7 COMMUNICATION SKILLS
Communicate effectively in a variety of formats.

7.1 Demonstrate effective writing skills in various formats (e.g., essays, correspondence, technical papers, note taking) and for various purposes (e.g., informing, defending, explaining, persuading, arguing, teaching).
7.2 Demonstrate effective oral communication skills in various formats (e.g., group discussion, debate, lecture) and for various purposes (e.g., informing, defending, explaining, persuading, arguing, teaching).
7.3 Exhibit quantitative literacy. Demonstrate interpersonal communication skills.
7.4 Exhibit the ability to collaborate effectively.

- Module 51: 51.4
- Module 53: 53.2
- "Apply Your Knowledge" questions

8 SOCIOCULTURAL AND INTERNATIONAL AWARENESS
Recognize, understand, and respect the complexity of sociocultural and international diversity.

8.1 Interact effectively and sensitively with people from diverse backgrounds and cultural perspectives.

8.2 Examine the sociocultural and international contexts that influence individual differences.

8.3 Explain how individual differences influence beliefs, values, and interactions with others and vice versa.

8.4 Understand how privilege, power, and oppression may affect prejudice, discrimination, and inequity. Recognize prejudicial attitudes and discriminatory behaviors that might exist in themselves and others.

- Module 1: 1.1, 1.2
- *The Science of Psychology and Health and Wellness* (p. 24)
- Module 15: *Critical Controversy: Should Illicit Psychoactive Drugs Be Legalized for Medical Use?* (p. 179)
- Module 21: 21.4
- Module 32: 32.3
- Module 35: 35.5
- Module 36: 36.3
- Module 37: 37.2, 37.4
- Module 38: 38.5
- *Sexuality and Health and Wellness* (p. 424)
- Module 46: 46.2
- Module 51: 51.1, 51.2, 51.3
- Module 53: 53.2
- Module 54: 54.1, 54.2
- Module 56: 56.2, 56.3, 56.4
- Module 57: 57.1, 57.2

9 PERSONAL DEVELOPMENT
Develop insight into their own and others' behavior and mental processes and apply effective strategies for self-management and self-improvement.

9.1 Reflect on their experiences and find meaning in them.

9.2 Apply psychological principles to promote personal development.

9.3 Enact self-management strategies that maximize health outcomes.

9.4 Display high standards of personal integrity with others.

9.5 Seek input from and experiences with diverse people to enhance the quality of solutions.

- *The Science of Psychology and Health and Wellness* (p. 24)
- *The Scientific Method and Health and Wellness* (p. 58)
- Module 7: *Intersection: Emotion and Neuroscience: Is Your Brain Happy?* (p. 91)
- Module 11: *Critical Controversy: Are Cochlear Implants a "Cure" for Deafness?* (p. 135)
- *Learning and Health and Wellness* (p. 223)
- Module 35: 35.6, 35.7; *Critical Controversy: Does Extrinsic Motivation Undermine Intrinsic Motivation?* (p. 355)
- *Motivation, Emotion, and Health and Wellness: The Pursuit of Happiness* (p. 380)
- Module 42: 42.2
- Module 43: 43.5
- *Sexuality and Health and Wellness* (p. 424)
- Module 50: *Intersection: Personality and Organizational Psychology: Hey, What's Your Type?* (p. 462)
- Module 56: 56.2, 56.3, 56.4
- Module 57: 57.1
- *I/O Psychology and Health and Wellness* (p. 542)
- Module 65: 65.2
- Module 68: 68.1, 68.2, 68.3; *Intersection: Health Psychology and Motivation: Why Do We Do the Things We Shouldn't Do?* (p. 629)
- Module 69: 69.1, 69.2, 69.4, 69.5
- Module 70: 70.1, 70.2, 70.3

10 CAREER PLANNING AND DEVELOPMENT
Pursue realistic ideas about how to implement their psychological knowledge, skills, and values in occupational pursuits in a variety of settings.

10.1 Apply knowledge of psychology (e.g., decision strategies, life span processes, psychological assessment, types of psychological careers) when formulating career choices.

10.2 Identify the types of academic experience and performance in psychology and the liberal arts that will facilitate entry into the workforce, postgraduate education, or both.

10.3 Describe preferred career paths based on accurate self-assessment of abilities, achievement, motivation, and work habits.

10.4 Identify and develop skills and experiences relevant to achieving selected career goals.

10.5 Articulate how changing societal needs can influence career opportunities and foster flexibility about managing changing conditions.

10.6 Demonstrate an understanding of the importance of lifelong learning and personal flexibility to sustain personal and professional development as the nature of work evolves.

- Module 35: 35.7
- Module 50: 50.2; *Intersection: Personality and Organizational Psychology: Hey, What's Your Type?* (p. 462)
- Module 55: 55.3
- Module 56: 56.1, 56.2, 56.3
- Module 57: 57.1; *Intersection: Personality Psychology and Organizational Psychology: Who's in Charge?* (p. 535)
- *I/O Psychology and Health and Wellness* (p. 542)

THE SCIENCE OF
PSYCHOLOGY

SECOND EDITION IN MODULES

*The Science of Psychology, Second Edition **in Modules*** offers instructors flexibility in teaching and gives students a manageable framework for course success.

HOW MODULES WORK FOR YOU

Each section is broken down into modules, giving you the **flexibility** to assign the content you want, in the order you prefer.

McGraw-Hill ***Create*™** provides a simple way for you to customize texts and eBooks for your course.

***Connect* Psychology™** provides a groundbreaking digital learning solution that makes managing assignments easier and improves student performance.

Real-time reports within Connect show how well each student is performing on each course assignment. Use this feature to spot problem areas *before* they crop up on an exam.

HOW MODULES WORK FOR YOUR STUDENTS

The **modular format** promotes student learning and success by presenting content in small, manageable chunks.

The "**appreciative view**" puts function before dysfunction and treats psychology as an integrated science. Students come to understand the true breadth of the discipline and to apply what they learn to their own daily experiences.

The **adaptive learning system** helps students identify what they "know and don't know." Then it guides them to focus on the areas that need improvement through interactivities, exercises, and readings.

SUCCESS

POWERED BY *CONNECT* PSYCHOLOGY

Connect Psychology is a response to today's student. The groundbreaking adaptive learning system helps students "know what they know" while guiding them to experience and learn what they don't know through engaging interactivities, exercises, and readings. Instructors teaching with *Connect* report their students' performance has jumped by a letter grade or more.

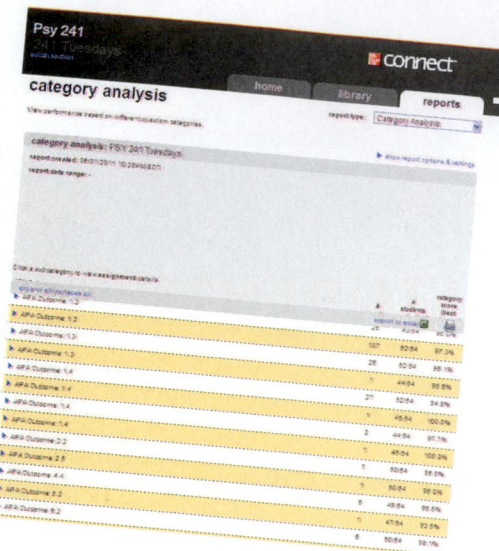

■ *Adaptive learning system:* Students come to class with a range of preparedness. With a focus on course crucial concepts, LearnSmart is like a personal tutor guiding students to spend less time on what they already know and more on what they don't.

■ *Real-time reports:* These printable, exportable reports show how well each student (or section) is performing on assignments. Instructors can use this feature to easily spot problem areas for the class as a whole or for individual students *before* they crop up on an exam.

■ *Learning objectives:* Every assignment and course resource can be sorted by learning objective, with point-and-click flexibility. Instructors can use this feature to customize content, assignments, and assessments.

■ *Assignable and assessable activities:* Instructors can deliver assignments and tests easily online, and students can practice skills that fulfill learning objectives at their own pace and on their own schedule.

■ *Correlation to APA learning goals and outcomes:* All assignable and assessable activities within *Connect* are correlated to the *APA Guidelines for the Undergraduate Major in Psychology*. Measure and evaluate student progress toward the learning goals and outcomes by the APA with customized reporting with *Connect*.

McGraw-Hill Higher Education and Blackboard have teamed up. What does this mean for you?

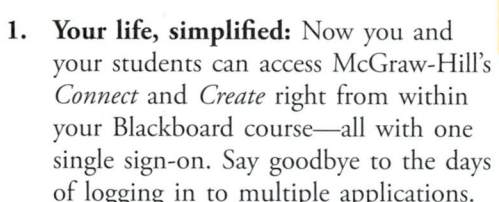

1. **Your life, simplified:** Now you and your students can access McGraw-Hill's *Connect* and *Create* right from within your Blackboard course—all with one single sign-on. Say goodbye to the days of logging in to multiple applications.

2. **Deep integration of content and tools:** Not only do you get single sign-on with *Connect* and *Create*, you also get deep integration of McGraw-Hill content and content engines right in Blackboard. Whether you're choosing a book for your course or building *Connect* assignments, all the tools you need are right where you want them—inside of Blackboard.

3. **Seamless grade books:** Are you tired of keeping multiple grade books and manually synchronizing grades into Blackboard? We thought so. When a student completes an integrated *Connect* assignment, the grade for that assignment automatically (and instantly) feeds your Blackboard grade center.

4. **A solution for everyone:** Whether your institution is already using Blackboard or you just want to try Blackboard on your own, we have a solution for you. McGraw-Hill and Blackboard now offer you easy access to industry-leading technology and content, whether your campus hosts it or we do. Be sure to ask your local McGraw-Hill representative for details.

THE POWER OF CUSTOMIZATION: *CREATE*

Craft your teaching resources to match the way you teach. The flexibility of **The Science of Psychology, Second Edition in Modules** provides the perfect opportunity to create the book you've always wanted. With McGraw-Hill *Create*, **www.mcgrawhillcreate.com,** you can easily rearrange modules, combine material from other content sources, and quickly upload content you have written, such as your course syllabus or teaching notes. *Create* even allows you to personalize your book's appearance by selecting the cover and adding your name, school, and course information. Order a *Create* book and you'll receive a complimentary print review copy in three to five business days or a complimentary **electronic review copy** via e-mail in **about an hour.** Go to **www.mcgrawhillcreate.com** today and register. Experience how McGraw-Hill *Create* empowers you to teach *your* students *your* way.

FLEXIBILITY

PREFACE

In Appreciation

When I set out to write the first edition of *The Science of Psychology: An Appreciative View,* I could not have imagined how well it would be received by instructors and students alike. Who knew that the focus on *why things go right* would strike such a strong chord in the classroom? Over the past three years I have met dozens of faculty members across the country, and I continue to be awestruck by the hard work, dedication, and enthusiasm of introductory psychology instructors. So, I wanted to say thank you. You all continue to inspire me—to be a better teacher myself, to develop the best learning solutions for the introductory psychology course, and to make our field fun and relevant to today's students. Thank you!

Appreciating Why Things Go Right

The Science of Psychology, Second Edition in Modules places **function and dysfunction in balance.** Rather than focusing first on why things go wrong, the focus is first on why things go right.

One of the challenges instructors face in focusing on function first is going against the grain of human nature. Research in psychology itself tells us that the negative captures our attention more readily than the positive. There is no question that bad news makes headlines. A global recession, disturbing climate changes, a catastrophic oil spill, and the everyday demands of juggling work, family, and finances—these and other issues loom large for us all. We strive and struggle to find balance and to sculpt a happy life. The science of psychology has much to offer in terms of helping us understand the choices we make and the implications of these choices for ourselves and for others around the world.

The Science of Psychology, Second Edition in Modules communicates the nature and breadth of psychology and its value as a science with an appreciative perspective. Its primary goal is to help students think like psychological scientists, which includes asking questions about their own life experiences. Throughout, students' curiosity is nurtured through timely, applied examples and a focus on what psychological science means for people going about daily life.

Psychological Inquiry selections stimulate students' analytical thinking about psychology's practical applications. The features reinforce student understanding of central aspects of research design, such as the difference between correlational and experimental studies and the concepts of independent and dependent variables. These selections give students an opportunity to analyze a figure, graph, or other illustration and also include a set of critical thinking questions. For example, the Psychological Inquiry feature in Module 19 on classical conditioning prompts students to analyze graphical schedules of reinforcement and different patterns of responding to them.

psychological inquiry

Schedules of Reinforcement and Different Patterns of Responding
This figure shows how the different schedules of reinforcement result in different rates of responding. The graph's X or horizontal axis represents time. The Y or vertical axis represents the cumulative responses. That means that as the line goes up, the total number of responses are building and building. In the figure, each hash mark indicates the delivery of reinforcement. That is, each of those little ticks indicates that a reward is being given.

Look closely at the pattern of responses over time for each schedule of reinforcement. On the fixed-ratio schedule, notice the dropoff in responding after each response; on the variable-ratio schedule, note the high, steady rate of responding. On the fixed-interval schedule, notice the immediate dropoff in responding after reinforcement and the increase in responding just before reinforcement (resulting in a scalloped curve); and on the variable-interval schedule, note the slow, steady rate of responding.

1. Which schedule of reinforcement represents the "most bang for the buck"? That is, which one is associated with the most responses for the least amount of reward?
2. Which schedule of reinforcement is most like pop quizzes?
3. Which is most like regular tests on a course syllabus?
4. Which schedule of reinforcement would be best if you have very little time for training?
5. Which schedule of reinforcement do you think is most common in your own life? Why?

Appreciating Psychology as an Integrated Whole

A goal of *The Science of Psychology, Second Edition in Modules* is to present psychology as an integrated field in which the whole is greater than the sum of its parts, but the parts are essential to the whole. Accordingly, areas where specialized subfields overlap and where research findings in one subfield support important studies and exciting discoveries in another are illuminated. Students come to appreciate, for example, how neuroscientific findings inform social psychology and how discoveries in personality psychology relate to leadership in organization settings. **Intersections** showcase research at the crossroads of two areas and shed light on these intriguing connections. This second edition includes many new Intersections showing the influence of work in one field of psychology on another. For example, the Intersection in Module 32 in the section on human development links work in developmental psychology with clinical psychology to explore the topic "Is 'Girl Talk' Always a Good Thing?"

Appreciating Psychology as a Science

The second edition's attention to function before dysfunction, up-to-date coverage, and broad scope reflect the field of psychology *today*. These qualities underscore psychology's vital and ongoing role as a **science that ever advances knowledge** about ourselves and our interactions in the world. Psychology is a vigorous young science and one that changes quickly. The text narrative interweaves the most current research with classic findings to give students an appreciation of this vitality. In Module 53, for instance, the treatment of Milgram's classic study on obedience is complemented by analysis of Burger's recent attempts to re-create the study.

In conjunction with creating current and contemporary course materials, *The Science of Psychology, Second Edition in Modules* includes citations that bring the most important recent and ongoing research into the text. These updated references give students and instructors the very latest that psychology has to offer on each topic.

Appreciating science also means appreciating disagreements in the field. Each section contains a **Critical Controversy** feature highlighting current psychological debates and posing thought-provoking questions that encourage students to examine the evidence on both sides. For example, Module 42's Critical Controversy investigates whether abstinence-only sex education can be effective.

Finally, appreciating science also means helping students master challenging scientific concepts. Two special inserts, **Touring the Nervous System and the Brain** and **Touring the Senses,** feature detailed full-color transparency overlays of important figures. Conceived and developed with the input of an expert consultant, the overlays offer students hands-on practice in grasping key biological structures and processes that are essential to an appreciation of the role of science in psychology and success in the course. Finally, **Test Yourself and Apply Your Knowledge** questions appear at the end of every module to help students check what they know before moving on.

Appreciating Flexibility: A Modular Organization

The modular format of *The Science of Psychology, Second Edition in Modules* allows instructors to assign topics in "chunks," so they can easily adapt the material for their courses. For students, the modular format presents content in a manageable framework that encourages focused learning and course mastery.

ACKNOWLEDGMENTS

The quality of *The Science of Psychology, Second Edition in Modules* is a testament to the skills and abilities of so many people, and I am tremendously grateful to the following individuals for their insightful contributions during the project's development and production.

Board of Advisors

Mike Devoley, *Arizona State University*
Olga Lazareva, *Drake University*
Irv Lichtman, *Lone Star College, Montgomery*
Laura Montgomery, *Lone Star College, Montgomery*
Eva Szeli, *Arizona State University*
Annette Towler, *DePaul University*
Lucy Troup, *Colorado State University*

Manuscript Reviewers

Cheryl Anagnopoulos, *Black Hills State University*
David Andresen, *Metropolitan State College of Denver*
Lindette Baas, *Arizona Western College-Yuma*
Mita Banerjee, *Pitzer College*
Michael Barber, *Santa Fe College*
Ted A. Barker, *Northwest Florida State College*
Richard Bernstein, *Broward College-South*
Kenneth G. Brewer, *Northeast State Community College*
Deborah S. Briihl, *Valdosta State University*
Victor Broderick, *Lincoln Land Community College*
Ellen Broom, *Texas Christian University*
Susan D. Burleson, *Davidson County Community College*
Jarrod N. Calloway, *Northwest Mississippi Community College*
Lorelei A. Carvajal, *Triton Community College*
David Cavalleri, *Santa Fe College*
Sharon E. Chacon-Mineau, *Northeast Wisconsin Technical College*
Wanda Clark, *South Plains College*
Verne Cox, *University of Texas-Arlington*
Trina Cyterski, *University of Georgia*
Meliksah Demir, *Northern Arizona University*
Mike Devoley, *Lone Star College, Montgomery*
Rock Doddridge, *Asheville-Buncombe Tech Community College*
Sundi Donovan, *Liberty University*
Evelyn N. Doody, *College of Southern Nevada*
Michael G. Dudley, *Southern Illinois University, Edwardsville*
Kristin S. Edwards, *Ohio State University-Columbus*
Kathy Erickson, *Pima Community College*
Diane K. Feibel, *University of Cincinnati-Raymond Walters College*

Debra L. Frame, *University of Cincinnati-Raymond Walters College*
Betty Jane Fratzke, *Indiana Wesleyan University*
Laura Gaudet, *Chadron State College*
Katherine Gibbs, *University of California-Davis*
Gregg Gold, *Humboldt State University*
Nicholas Greco, *College of Lake County*
Gladys S. Green, *Manatee Community College*
Jerry Green, *Tarrant County College*
Laura Gruntmeir, *Redlands Community College*
Shawn M. Haake, *Iowa Central Community College*
Carrie E. Hall, *Miami University of Ohio*
Sheryl M. Hartman, *Miami Dade College*
Lesley Hathorn, *Metropolitan State College of Denver*
Kimberly Henderson, *Boise State University*
John Hensley, *Tulsa Community College*
Rebecca Henthorn, *Murray State College*
Jennifer K. Higa-King, *Honolulu Community College*
Martha J. Hinkle, *Oakton Community College*
James Hunsicker, *Southwestern Oklahoma State University*
Joni Jecklin, *Heartland Community College*
Wendy Johnson, *Borough of Manhattan Community College*
Linda Jones, *Blinn College*
Diana Joy, *Community College of Denver*
Hilary Kalagher, *Indiana University*
Patty M. Keller, *Saint Louis Community College-Kirkwood*
Shelia Kennison, *Oklahoma State University*
Yuthika Kim, *Oklahoma City Community College*
Kevin M. King, *University of Washington*
Cherie L. Kittrell, *State College of Florida*
Larry Kollman, *Northern Iowa Area Community College*
David Kreiner, *University of Central Missouri*
Jeff Lawley, *Louisiana State University-Shreveport*
Cathy Lawrenz, *Johnson County Community College*
Kristin Lazarova, *Northeast State Community College*
Juliet Lee, *Cape Fear Community College*
Kenneth J. Leising, *Texas Christian University*
Heather Lench, *Texas A&M University*
Irv Lichtman, *Lone Star College, Montgomery*
Eric Limegrover, *Miami University of Ohio*

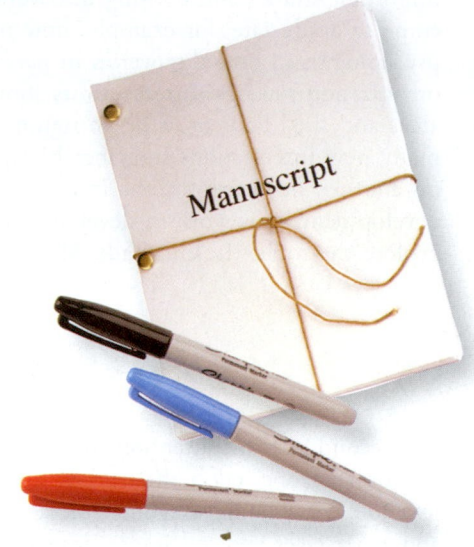

Amy Lindsey, *Utica College*
Tammy Lochridge, *Itawamba Community College*
Ann Madden, *Florida State College-South Campus*
Betty Magjuka, *Gloucester County College*
Debra Matchinsky, *North Hennepin Community College*
Christopher Mayhorn, *North Carolina State University*
Dawn M. McBride, *Illinois State University*
Shawn Mikulay, *Elgin Community College*
Laura K. Montgomery, *Lone Star College, Montgomery*
Kristie Morris, *Rockland Community College*
Judith Ann Nichols, *Lincoln Land Community College*
Fabian Novello, *Clark State Community College*
Bernadette A. O'Leary, *California State University-Long Beach*

Debbie Palmer, *University of Wisconsin-Stevens Point*

Lisa L. Poole, *Northeast State Community College*

Helen J. Powell, *Baker College*

Marianna Rader, *Florida State College-Downtown*

Michael Rader, *Northern Arizona University*

Cynthia K. Shinabarger Reed, *Tarrant County College-NE*

Karen Clay Rhines, *Northampton Community College*

Michael C. Rhoads, *University of Northern Colorado*

Carol P. Russell, *Owens Community College*

Kristina L. Schaefer, *Moorpark College*

Nick Schmitt, *Heartland Community College*

Chris Scribner, *Lindenwood University*

David Shepard, *South Texas College*

Barry Silber, *Hillsborough Community College*

Jason S. Spiegelman, *Community College of Baltimore County*

Kim Stark-Wroblewski, *University of Central Missouri*

Wayne S. Stein, *Brevard Community College*

Krishna S. Stilianos, *Oakland Community College*

Kevin Sumrall, *Lone Star College, Montgomery*

Michael W. Torello, *Capital University*

Annette Towler, *DePaul University*

Lucy J. Troup, *Colorado State University*

Alicia Uddin, *Tulsa Community College*

Glenn Valdez, *Grand Valley State University*

Maria G. Valdovinos, *Drake University*

Thomas E. Van Canfort, *Fayetteville State University*

Jennifer Vaughn, *Metropolitan Community College*

Jacqueline J. von Spiegel, *Ohio State University-Columbus*

Jeff Wachsmuth, *Napa Valley College*

Andrew S. Walters, *Northern Arizona University*

Roger Ward, *University of Cincinnati-Raymond Walters College*

Guillermo Wated, *Barry University*

Shannon Welch, *University of Idaho*

Steve J. Withrow, *Guilford Tech Community College-Jamestown*

Design Reviewers

David Cavalleri, *Santa Fe College*

Gregg Gold, *Humboldt State University*

Gladys S. Green, *Manatee Community College*

Carrie E. Hall, *Miami University of Ohio*

Sheryl M. Hartman, *Miami Dade College*

Hilary Kalagher, *Indiana University*

Cheri L. Kittrell. *State College of Florida*

Heather Lench, *Texas A&M University*

Debbie Palmer, *University of Wisconsin-Stevens Point*

Marianna Rader, *Florida State College-Downtown*

Glenn Valdez, *Grand Valley State University*

Jeff Wachsmuth, *Napa Valley College*

Connect and LearnSmart Consultants

Ted A. Barker, *Northwest Florida State College*

Lorelei A. Carvajal, *Triton Community College*

Jenel Cavazos, *University of Oklahoma*

Rock Doddridge, *Asheville-Buncombe Tech Community College*

Dawn Echols, *Gainesville State College*

Regina Hughes, *Collin College*

Joni Jecklin, *Heartland Community College*

Cheri Kittrell, *Manatee Community College*

Michael Rader, *Northern Arizona University*

Kristina L. Schaefer, *Moorpark College*

Nick Schmitt, *Heartland Community College*

Laurie A. Wolfe, *Anoka-Ramsey Community College*

Test Bank Reviewers

Jeff Henriques, *University of Wisconsin, Madison*

Jason Spiegelman, *Community College of Baltimore City*

Expert Reviewers

Barbara Sayad, *California State University-Monterey Bay*

William Yarber, *Indiana University-Bloomington*

PsychInteractive Advisory Board

Melissa Acevedo, *Westchester Community College*

Jennifer Brooks, *Collin County Community College*

Jeffrey Green, *Virginia Commonwealth University*

Julie Bauer Morrison, *Glendale Community College*

Phil Pegg, *Western Kentucky University*

Tanya Renner, *Kapi'olani Community College; University of Hawaii*

Carla Strassle, *York College of Pennsylvania*

Jim Stringham, *University of Georgia*

Introductory Psychology Symposia Participants

Every year, McGraw-Hill conducts several Introductory Psychology Symposia that are attended by instructors from across the country.

These events are an opportunity for editors from McGraw-Hill to gather information about the needs and challenges of instructors teaching the introductory psychology course. The symposia also offer a forum for the attendees to exchange ideas and experiences with colleagues whom they might not have otherwise met. The feedback we have received has been invaluable and has contributed to the development of *The Science of Psychology, Second Edition in Modules.*

Melissa Acevedo, *Westchester Community College*

Terry Scott Adcock, *Parkland College*

Carol Anderson, *Bellevue College*

Susan A. Anderson, *University of South Alabama*

Diane Davis Ashe, *Valencia Community College*

Thomas C. Bailey, *University of Maryland University College*

Steven Barnhart, *Middlesex County College*

David E. Baskind, *Delta College*

Shirley Bass-Wright, *St. Philip's College*

Scott C. Bates, *Utah State*

Jennifer Beck, *Austin Community College*

James L. Becker, *Pulaski Technical College*

Aileen M. Behan-Collins, *Chemeketa Community College*

Andrew Berns, *Milwaukee Area Tech Community College*

Joy L. Berrenberg, *University of Colorado-Denver*

Ginette Blackhart, *East Tennessee State University*

Stephen Blessing, *University of Tampa*

Susan Boatright, *University of Rhode Island*

Deborah S. Briihl, *Valdosta State University*

Tamara Brown, *University of Kentucky*

Brad Brubaker, *Indiana State University*

Carrie Canales, *West Los Angeles College*

Jessica Carpenter, *Elgin Community College*

Lorelei A. Carvajal, *Triton Community College*

Karen Christoff, *University of Mississippi*

Jack Chuang, *San Jacinto College-Central*

Douglas L. Chute, *Drexel University*

Diana Ciesko, *Valencia Community College-East*

Marsha G. Clarkson, *Georgia State University*

Doreen Collins-McHugh, *Seminole State College of Florida*

Laurie L. Couch, *Morehead State University*

Michaela DeCataldo, *Johnson & Wales University*

Bonnie Dennis, *Virginia Western Community College*

Anne Marie Donohue, *Montgomery County Community College*

Katherine Dowdell, *Des Moines Area Community College*

Laura Duvall, *Heartland Community College*

David Echevarria, *University of Southern Mississippi*

Penny Edwards, *Tri-County Technical College*

Andrea Ericksen, *San Juan College*

Michael Erickson, *University of California-Riverside*

Acknowledgments   **xxvii**

Barbara Etzel, *Finger Lakes Community College*
Dan Fawaz, *Georgia Perimeter College*
Greg J. Feist, *San Jose State University*
Dave Filak, *Joliet Junior College*
Beth Finders, *Saint Charles Community College*
Tom Fischer, *Wayne State University*
Paul A. Fox, *Appalachian State University*
Debra L. Frame, *University of Cincinnati-Raymond Walters College*
Paula Frioli, *Truckee Meadows Community College*
Dale Fryxell, *Chaminade University*
Ellen Furlong, *Ohio State University*
Lynne Gabriel, *Lakeland Community College*
John Gambon, *Ozarks Technical and Community College*
Travis Gibbs, *Riverside Community College-Moreno Valley Campus*
Charles W. Ginn, *University of Cincinnati*
Robert L. Gordon, *Wright State University*
Sam Gosling, *University of Texas-Austin*
Bonnie Gray, *Scottsdale College*
Jeff Green, *Virginia Commonwealth University*
Jerry Green, *Tarrant County College*
Daine Grey, *Middlesex Community College*
Mark Griffin, *Georgia Perimeter College*
Paul Grocoff, *Scottsdale College*
Robert Guttentag, *University of North Carolina-Greensboro*
David T. Hall, *Baton Rouge Community College*
Ericka Hamilton, *Moraine Valley Community College*
Lora Harpster, *Salt Lake Community College*
Gregory Eugene Harris, *Polk Community College-Winter Haven, Florida*
Lesley Hathorn, *Metropolitan State College of Denver*
Rose Hattoh, *Austin Community College*
Traci Haynes, *Columbus State Community College*
Brett Heintz, *Delgado Community College*
Carmon Weaver Hicks, *Ivy Tech Community College*
Natalie W. Hopson, *Salisbury University*
Rachel Hull, *Texas A&M University*
Mayte Insua-Auais, *Miami Dade College-North Campus*
Linda A. Jackson, *Michigan State University*
Nita Jackson, *Butler Community College*
Margaret Jenkins, *Seminole State College*
Sean P. Jennings, *Valencia Community College*

Joan Batelle Jenson, *Central Piedmont Community College*
Robin Joynes, *Kent State University*
Barbara Kennedy-Stein, *Brevard Community College-Palm Bay Campus*
Shelia Kennison, *Oklahoma State University*
Yuthika Kim, *Oklahoma City Community College*
Christina Knox, *College of the Sequoias*
Dana Kuehn, *Florida Community College-Deerwood Center*
Eric Landrum, *Boise State University*
Ladonna Lewis, *Glendale Community College*
Mary Lewis, *Oakland University*
Deborah Licht, *Pikes Peak Community College*
Maria Lopez, *Mt. San Jacinto College-San Jacinto Campus*
Sonya L. Lott-Harrison, *Community College of Philadelphia*
Jeff Love, *Penn State University*
Lea Ann Lucas, *Sinclair Community College*
Wade Lueck, *Mesa Community College*
Lynda Mae, *Arizona State University*
Mike Majors, *Delgado Community College*
Karen Marsh, *University of Minnesota-Duluth*
Diane Martichuski, *University of Colorado-Boulder*
Wanda C. McCarthy, *University of Cincinnati-Clermont College*
Sean Meegan, *University of Utah*
Kathleen Mentink, *Chippewa Valley Technical College*
Steven P. Mewaldt, *Marshall University*
Shawn Mikulay, *Elgin Community College*
Michelle D. Miller, *Northern Arizona University*
Joel Morgovsky, *Brookdale Community College*
Kathy Morrow, *Wayne County Community College*
Patricia Nation, *Bluegrass Community and Technical College*
Jeff Neubauer, *Pima Community College-Northwest Campus*
Glenda Nichols, *Tarrant County College-South Campus*
Jane Noll, *University of Southern Florida*
Eileen O'Brien, *University of Maryland-Baltimore County*
Donald Orso, *Anne Arundel Community College*
Jack A. Palmer, *University of Louisiana-Monroe*
Jeff Parsons, *Hunter College-CUNY*
David Perkins, *University of Louisiana-Lafayette*
Julie A. Penley, *El Paso Community College*

Frank Provenzano, *Greenville Technical College*
Reginald Rackley, *Southern University*
Cynthia K. S. Reed, *Tarrant County College*
Tanya Renner, *Kapi'olani Community College*
Vicki Ritts, *Saint Louis Community College-Meramec*
Alan Roberts, *Indiana University*
Caton F. Roberts, *University of Wisconsin-Madison*
Steven Ross, *Owens Community College*
Debra Rowe, *Oakland Community College*
Larry Rudiger, *University of Vermont*
Phyllis Rundhaug, *San Jacinto College*
Traci Sachteleben, *Southwestern Illinois College*
Sharleen Sakai, *Michigan State University*
Donna Love Seagle, *Chattanooga State Technical Community College*
James Shannon, *Citrus College*
Elizabeth Sheehan, *Georgia State University*
Maria Shpurik, *Florida International University*
Barry Silber, *Hillsborough Community College*
Peggy Skinner, *South Plains College*
Chris Smith, *Tyler Community College*
Lilliette Johnson Smith, *Southwest Tennessee Community College*
Wayne S. Stein, *Brevard Community College-Melbourne Campus*
Genevieve Stevens, *Houston Community College-Central*
Rick Stevens, *University of Louisiana-Monroe*
Richard Suplita, *University of Georgia*
Eva Szeli, *Arizona State University*
Shawn Talbot, *Kellogg Community College*
Helen Taylor, *Bellevue Community College*
Sheila E. Ten Eyck, *Pittsburgh Technical Institute*
Felicia Friendly Thomas, *California State Polytechnic University-Pomona*
Lisa Thomassen, *Indiana University-Bloomington*
Karen Tinker, *North West Arkansas Community College*
Isabel Trombetti, *Community College of Rhode Island*
Margot Underwood, *Joliet Junior College*
Barbara Van Horn, *Indian River Community College*
Andrew Walters, *Northern Arizona University*
Martin Wolfger, *Ivy Tech Community College-Bloomington*
Andrew Woster, *South Dakota State University*
John W. Wright, *Washington State University*
Matt Yeazel, *Anne Arundel Community College*

INSTRUCTOR AND STUDENT RESOURCES

Appreciating Course Materials and Management

Create. Craft your teaching resources to match the way you teach! With McGraw-Hill *Create*, www.mcgrawhillcreate.com, you can easily rearrange modules, combine material from other content sources, and quickly upload content you have written, like your course syllabus or teaching notes. Find the content you need in *Create* by searching through thousands of leading McGraw-Hill textbooks. Arrange your book to fit your teaching style. *Create* even allows you to personalize your book's appearance by selecting the cover and adding your name, school, and course information. Order a *Create* book, and you'll receive a complimentary print review copy in three to five business days or a complimentary electronic review copy (eComp) via e-mail in about one hour. Go to www.mcgrawhillcreate.com today and register. Experience how McGraw-Hill *Create* empowers you to teach your students your way.

Blackboard. McGraw-Hill Higher Education and Blackboard have teamed up. What does this mean for you?

- *Your life, simplified:* Now you and your students can access McGraw-Hill's *Connect* and *Create* right from within your Blackboard course—all with one single sign-on. Say goodbye to the days of logging in to multiple applications.
- *Deep integration of content and tools:* Not only do you get single sign-on with *Connect* and *Create,* you also get deep integration of McGraw-Hill content and content engines right in Blackboard. Whether you're choosing a book for your course or building *Connect* assignments, all the tools you need are right where you want them—inside of Blackboard.
- *Seamless grade books:* Are you tired of keeping multiple grade books and manually synchronizing grades into Blackboard? We thought so. When a student completes an integrated *Connect* assignment, the grade for that assignment automatically (and instantly) feeds your Blackboard grade center.
- *A solution for everyone:* Whether your institution is already using Blackboard or you just want to try Blackboard on your own, we have a solution for you. McGraw-Hill and Blackboard can now offer you easy access to industry-leading technology and content, whether your campus hosts it or we do. Be sure to ask your local McGraw-Hill representative for details.

Tegrity. Tegrity Campus is a service that makes class-time instruction available all the time by automatically capturing every lecture in a searchable format for students to review when they study and complete assignments. With a simple one-click start-and-stop process, you capture all computer screens and corresponding audio. Students replay any part of any class with easy-to-use browser-based viewing on a PC or Mac.

Educators know that the more students can see, hear, and experience class resources, the better they learn. With Tegrity Campus, students quickly recall key moments by using the unique search feature of Tegrity Campus. This search helps students efficiently find what they need, when they need it, across an entire semester of class recordings. Help turn all your students' study time into learning moments immediately supported by your lecture.

CourseSmart e-Textbook. This text is available as an eTextbook at **www.CourseSmart.com**. At CourseSmart your students can take advantage of significant savings off the cost of a print textbook, reduce their impact on the environment, and gain access to powerful web tools for learning. Course-Smart eTextbooks can be viewed online or downloaded to a computer. The eTextbooks allow students to do full-text searches, add highlighting and notes, and share notes with classmates. CourseSmart has the largest selection of eTextbooks available anywhere. Visit **www.CourseSmart.com** to learn more and to try a sample module.

Appreciating Instructor Support

What if . . .

- You could re-create the one-on-one experience of working through difficult concepts in office hours with every student without having to invest any office-hour time to do so?
- You could see at a glance how well each of your students (or sections) is performing in each segment of your course?
- You had all of the assignments and resources for your course pre-organized by learning objective and with point-and-click flexibility?

Over the course of developing *The Science of Psychology, Second Edition in Modules,* we asked these questions and many more. We did not stop at simply asking questions either. We visited with faculty across the country and also observed what you do to prepare and deliver your courses. And we observed students as they worked through assignments and studied for exams. The result of these thousands of hours of research and development is a state-of-the-art learning environment tool that bolsters student performance at the same time as it makes instructors' lives easier and more efficient. To experience this environment for yourself, please visit **www.mcgraw-hillconnect.com**.

Online Learning Center for Instructors The password-protected instructor side of the Online Learning Center (**www.mhhe.com/kingmodules**) contains the Instructor's Manual, Test Bank files, PowerPoint slides, Classroom Performance System (CPS or "clicker") Questions, Image Gallery, and other valuable material to help you design and enhance your course. See more information about specific assets below. Ask your local McGraw-Hill representative for password information.

Instructor's Manual by Regina Hughes, Collin College and Lorelei A. Carvajal, Triton Community College

The Instructor's Manual provides a wide variety of tools and resources for presenting the course, including learning objectives, ideas for lectures and discussions, and handouts. The Connections section serves as a roadmap outlining all the other ancillaries for that module and points out all the unique and interesting features available.

Test Bank by Cheri Kittrell, Manatee Community College and Ted A. Barker, Northwest Florida State College

By increasing the rigor of the Test Bank development process, McGraw-Hill has raised the bar for student assessment. Over 1,700 multiple-choice and 85 essay questions were prepared by a coordinated team of subject-matter experts. Each question and set of possible answers were methodically vetted by the team for accuracy, clarity, effectiveness, and accessibility, and each is annotated for level of difficulty, Bloom's taxonomy, APA learning outcomes, and corresponding coverage in the text. Organized by module, the questions are designed to test factual, applied, and conceptual understanding. The Test Bank is compatible with McGraw-Hill's computerized testing program, EZ Test, and most course management systems.

PowerPoint Presentations by Jason S. Spiegelman, Community College of Baltimore County and Victor Broderick, Lincoln Land Community College

The PowerPoint Presentations cover the key points of each module and include figures and charts from the text. The presentations serve as an organizational and a navigational tool integrated with examples and activities from an expert teacher. The slides can be used as is or modified to meet the needs of the individual instructor.

Classroom Performance System (CPS) by Jason S. Spiegelman, Community College of Baltimore County

The Classroom Performance System's mix of factual and opinion questions allows instructors to know what concepts their students are variously mastering and those with which students are having difficulty. CPS, a "clicker" system, is a great way to give interactive quizzes, maximize student participation in class discussions, and take attendance.

Image Gallery

The Image Gallery features the complete set of figures and tables from the text. These images are available for download and can be easily embedded into instructors' PowerPoint slides.

Appreciating How Students Study

Today's students are different, and how they study is different as well. With this in mind, *The Science of Psychology, Second Edition in Modules* takes these changed realities into account in providing students with a roadmap for success.

Adaptive Learning System

This adaptive learning system is an unparalleled, intelligent learning system based on cognitive mapping that *diagnoses* your students' knowledge of a particular subject and then creates an individualized learning path geared toward student success in your course. It offers individualized assessment by delivering appropriate learning material in the form of questions at the right time, helping students attain mastery of the content. Whether the system is assigned by you or used independently by students as a study tool, the results can be recorded in an easy-to-use grade report that allows you to measure student progress at all times and coach your students to success.

As an added benefit, all content covered in this adaptive learning system is tied to learning objectives for your course so that you can use the results as evidence of subject mastery. This tool also provides a personal study plan that allows the student to estimate the time it will take and the number of questions required to learn the subject matter. Your students will learn faster, study more efficiently, and retain more knowledge when using *The Science of Psychology, Second Edition in Modules*.

Online Learning Center for Students by Cheri Kittrell, Manatee Community College and Alisha Janowsky, University of Central Florida

The Student Online Learning Center contains module-by-module quizzes, outlines, learning objectives, and key terms. The multiple-choice, applied multiple-choice, fill-in-the-blank, and true/false quizzes ask questions that build on conscientious reading of the text. To access the Online Learning Center, go to **www. mhhe.com/kingmodules.**

THE SCIENCE OF PSYCHOLOGY

SECOND EDITION IN MODULES

What Is Psychology?

The Mystery That Is You

Do you have a hero? In a December 2009 Gallup poll, the most admired American man was President Barack Obama. The previous president, George W. Bush, was a distant second, followed by Nelson Mandela (Page, 2009). For the most admired woman, Hillary Rodham Clinton edged out Sarah Palin, and Oprah Winfrey was third. These are all famous people who have made significant contributions in public life.

At the right moment, though, an "ordinary" person can become a hero. On January 15, 2009, US Airways Captain Chesley "Sully" Sullenberger was piloting a routine flight out of New York City. A few moments after takeoff, the plane hit a flock of geese, and the engines cut out. With 155 people on board, Captain Sullenberger made a split-second decision to land in the Hudson River. He managed to glide the aircraft into the water with no engine power. Just six minutes after takeoff, all 155 on board began deplaning from the floating craft into waiting rescue boats. Sullenberger had calmly saved everyone on board, becoming a hero to the world (CBS News, 2009).

Even in less extraordinary circumstances, people make choices that might be called heroic. They are generous when they might be selfish. They are forgiving when they could hold a grudge. They work hard when they could slack off. You might not think of psychology as focusing on admirable aspects of everyday human behavior, but in fact the science of psychology is about *all* of human behavior.

Scientists, including psychologists, bring such powerful observations to their efforts. As scientists, moreover, psychologists are passionate about what they study—and what they study is you. As you are reading this book, thousands of dedicated scientists are studying things about you that you might have never considered, such as how your brain responds to a picture flashed on a screen and how your eyes adjust to a sunny day. There is not a single thing about you that is not fascinating to some psychologist somewhere. ●

Defining Psychology: Historical and Contemporary Perspectives

- **psychology** The scientific study of behavior and mental processes.

- **science** The use of systematic methods to observe the natural world, including human behavior, and to draw conclusions.

- **behavior** Everything we do that can be directly observed.

- **mental processes** The thoughts, feelings, and motives that each of us experiences privately but that cannot be observed directly.

What do you think of when you hear the term "psychology"? Do you think of someone laying on a couch talking to a therapist? Do you picture a scientist observing behavior? To introduce the field, this module defines psychology, explores how it developed, and describes its contemporary approaches.

1·1 DEFINING PSYCHOLOGY

Formally defined, **psychology** is the scientific study of behavior and mental processes. Let's consider the three key terms in this definition: *science, behavior,* and *mental processes*.

As a **science,** psychology uses systematic methods to observe human behavior and draw conclusions. The goals of psychological science are to describe, predict, and explain behavior. In addition, psychologists are often interested in controlling or changing behavior, and they use scientific methods to examine interventions that might help, for example, reduce violence or promote happiness.

Researchers might be interested in knowing whether individuals will help a stranger who has fallen down. The researchers could devise a study in which they observe people walking past a person who needs help. Through many observations, the researchers could come to *describe* helping behavior by counting how many times it occurs in particular circumstances. The researchers may also try to *predict* who will help, and when, by examining characteristics of the individuals studied. Are happy people more likely to help? Are women or men more likely to help? After psychologists have analyzed their data, they also will want to *explain* why helping behavior occurred when it did. Finally, these researchers might be interested in changing helping behavior, by devising strategies to increase helping.

Behavior is everything we do that can be directly observed—two people kissing, a baby crying, a college student riding a motorcycle to campus. **Mental processes** are the thoughts, feelings, and motives that each of us experiences privately but that cannot be observed directly. Although we cannot directly see thoughts and feelings, they are nonetheless real. They include *thinking* about kissing someone, a baby's *feelings* when its mother leaves the room, and a student's *memory* of a motorcycle trip.

The Psychological Frame of Mind

What makes for a good job, a good marriage, or a good life? Although there are a variety of ways to come to answer the big questions of life, psychologists approach these questions as scientists. Psychology is a rigorous discipline that tests assumptions, bringing scientific data to bear on the questions of central interest to human beings (Stanovich, 2010). Psychologists conduct research and rely on that research to provide evidence for their conclusions. They examine the available evidence about some aspect of mind and behavior, evaluate how strongly the data (information) support their hunches, analyze disconfirming evidence, and carefully consider whether they have explored all of the possible factors and explanations (Sternberg, Roediger, & Halpern, 2007). At the core of this scientific approach are four attitudes: critical thinking, skepticism, objectivity, and curiosity.

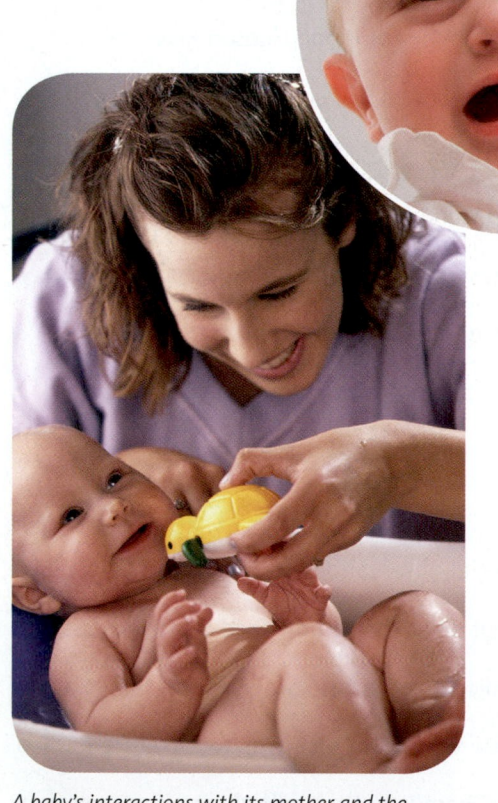

A baby's interactions with its mother and the infant's crying are examples of behavior *because they are observable. The feelings underlying the baby's crying are an example of a* mental process *that is unobservable.*

Like all scientists, psychologists are critical thinkers. **Critical thinking** is the process of reflecting deeply and actively, asking questions, and evaluating the evidence. Thinking critically means asking ourselves *how* we know something. Critical thinkers question and test what some people say are facts. They examine research to see how soundly it supports an idea (McMillan, 2008). Critical thinking reduces the likelihood that conclusions will be based on unreliable personal beliefs, opinions, and emotions. *Thinking critically will be very important as you read this book.* Some of the things you read will fit with your current beliefs, and some will challenge you to reconsider your assumptions. Actively engaging in critical thinking is vital to making the most of psychology. As you read, think about how what you are learning relates to your life experiences and the assumptions you might have about people.

In addition, scientists are characterized by *skepticism* (Stanovich, 2010). Skeptical people challenge whether a supposed fact is really true. Being skeptical can mean questioning what "everybody knows." There was a time when "everybody knew" that women were morally inferior to men, that race could influence a person's IQ, and that the earth was flat. Psychologists, like all scientists, look at such assumptions in new and questioning ways and with a skeptical eye.

Psychology researchers often turn up the unexpected in human behavior. For example, it might seem obvious that couples who live together before marriage have a better chance of making the marriage last. After all, practice makes perfect, right? Yet researchers have found a higher rate of marital success for couples who did *not* live together before marriage (Rhoades, Stanley, & Markham, 2009; Wilson & Smallwood, 2008). You might use scientific skepticism the next time you encounter an infomercial about the latest diet craze that promises to help you lose weight "without diet or exercise." A skeptic knows that if something sounds too good to be true, it probably is.

Related to critical thinking and skepticism is the distinction between science and pseudoscience. *Pseudo* means "fake," and *pseudoscience* refers to information that is couched in scientific terminology but is not supported by sound scientific research. Astrology is an example of a pseudoscience. Although astrologers may present detailed information about an individual, supposedly based on when that person was born, no scientific evidence supports these assumptions and predictions. One way to tell that an explanation is pseudoscience rather than science is to look at how readily proponents of the explanation will accept evidence to the contrary.

Being open to the evidence means thinking *objectively*. Scientists are objective and believe that one of the best ways to be objective is to apply the empirical method to learn about the world (Beins, 2009; Stanovich, 2010). Using the **empirical method** means gaining knowledge through the observation of events, the collection of data, and logical reasoning. Being objective involves seeing things as they really are, *not as we would like them to be.* Objectivity means waiting to see what the evidence tells us rather than going with our hunches. Does the latest herbal supplement truly help relieve depression? An objective thinker knows that we must have sound evidence before answering that question.

Last, scientists are curious. The scientist notices things in the world (a star in the sky, an insect, a happy person) and wants to know what it is and why it is that way. Science involves asking questions, even very big questions, such as where did the earth come from, and how does love between two people endure for 50 years? Thinking like a psychologist means opening your mind and imagination to wondering why things are the way they are. Once you begin to think like a psychologist, you might notice that the world looks like a different place. Easy answers and simple assumptions will not do.

As you can probably imagine, psychologists have many different opinions about many different things, and psychology, like any science, is filled with debate and controversy. Throughout this book, we will survey areas of hot debate in psychology in a feature called Critical Controversy. As the first example, check out this module's Critical Controversy concerning whether the generation of Americans born since the 1980s is experiencing an epidemic of self-love.

Debate and controversy are a natural part of thinking like a psychologist. Psychology has advanced as a field *because* psychologists do not always agree with one another about

● **critical thinking** The process of reflecting deeply and actively, asking questions, and evaluating the evidence.

● **empirical method** Gaining knowledge through the observation of events, the collection of data, and logical reasoning.

"According to this rubbish I'm going on a long journey."

© Roy Nixon. www.CartoonStock.com.

CRITICAL CONTROVERSY

Are Young Americans in the Middle of a Narcissism Epidemic?

In reading status updates posted to Facebook and Twitter, it is easy to get the impression that many young adults think even the smallest details of their lives are fascinating. A lively controversy in psychology concerns whether young adults in the United States today are more likely to think of themselves as special and extraordinary compared to their counterparts in previous generations. Jean Twenge and her colleagues argue that Americans born since the 1980s are different in being unusually self-confident, self-assertive, and self-centered (Twenge, 2006; Twenge & Campbell, 2009; Twenge & Foster, 2008).

Examining evidence from nationally representative surveys of U.S. high school students over 30 years, Twenge and Keith Campbell (2008) found that students in 2006 gave themselves higher ratings as compared to students in 1975 in terms of their positive expectations as spouses, parents, and workers. Indeed, students in 1975 on average rated themselves as likely to be "good" in these roles, whereas students in 2006 rated themselves as likely to be "very good" (Twenge & Campbell, 2008). Imagine—an entire generation of swollen heads. What are the implications for educators trying to teach them and for employers trying to manage them (Twenge & S. M. Campbell, 2010)? Twenge refers to these individuals as Generation Me and suggests that there is an epidemic of *narcissism* (a condition of intense, unhealthy self-love) in this age group (2006). The popular media—including CBS News, National Public Radio, and several major newspapers—have jumped on the bandwagon to cover this "epidemic" (Associated Press, 2007).

Other psychologists sharply disagree with these conclusions. They argue that the positivity of Americans' self-views has remained stable over time (Donnellan, Trzesniewski, & Robins, 2009; Trzesniewski, Donnellan, & Robins, 2008). For example, Kali Trzesniewski and Brent

© Kate Taylor. www.CartoonStock.com.

Donnellan (2009) looked at Twenge and Campbell's data and noted that small differences in the order of the questions could produce the differences in the ratings students made. In most of their analyses, Twenge and Campbell focused on 1975, but 1975 might not have been a representative year, Trzesniewski and Donnellan assert, because the order of the questions was changed after that year. These changes may have rendered 1975 an unusually modest year (Trzesniewski & Donnellan, 2009). Looking at the data for 1975, 1976, and 1977 and comparing these to 2006, Trzesniewski and Donnellan found no evidence that students had developed increasingly positive self-views over time (2009). Thus, Trzesniewski and Donnellan caution against assuming that the young adults of today are especially likely to think of themselves as special or extraordinary (Trzesniewski & Donnellan, 2009, 2010).

This debate illustrates a number of important aspects of the science of psychology. First, solid scientific evidence is a vital part of psychology, and claims must be supported by that evidence. Further, scientists can look at the same data and reach strikingly different conclusions. The lesson here is that no matter how popular a research conclusion might be, it must be evaluated critically and objectively. In their search for answers to fascinating questions, psychologists rely on the empirical method for solid evidence.

WHAT DO YOU THINK?

- Where do you fall in this debate? What kind of research would be needed to change your mind about whether there is a narcissism epidemic among young Americans?

- What problems are inherent in drawing conclusions about the members of an entire generation?

---

why the mind and behavior work as they do. Psychologists have reached a more accurate understanding of human behavior *because* psychology fosters controversies and *because* psychologists think deeply and reflectively and examine the evidence on all sides. A good place to try out your critical thinking skills is by revisiting the definition of psychology.

Psychology as the Science of All Human Behavior

As you consider the definition of psychology as the science of human behavior, you might be thinking, okay, where's the couch? Where's the mental illness? Psychology certainly does include the study of therapy and psychological disorders. *Clinical psychologists* in particular specialize in studying and treating psychological disorders. By definition, though, psychology is a much more *general* science (Ash & Sturm, 2007). Surely, psychological disorders are very interesting, and the media often portray psychologists as therapists. Yet the view of psychology as the science of what is wrong with people started long before television was invented. So how did we end up with the idea that psychology is only about mental illness?

When they think about psychology, many people think of Sigmund Freud (1856–1939). Freud believed that most of human behavior is caused by dark, unpleasant, unconscious impulses pressing for expression. For Freud, even the average person on the street is a mysterious well of unconscious desires. Certainly, Freud has had a lasting impact on psychology and on society; as recently as March 2006, on the occasion of his 150th birthday, Freud was featured on the cover of *Newsweek*. Consider, though, that Freud based his ideas about human nature on the patients whom he saw in his clinical practice— individuals who were struggling with psychological problems. His experiences with these clients, as well as his analysis of himself, colored his outlook on all of humanity. Freud (1996) once wrote, "I have found little that is 'good' about human beings on the whole. In my experience most of them are trash."

Freud's view of human nature has crept into general perceptions of what psychology is all about. Imagine, for example, that you are seated on a plane, having a pleasant conversation with the woman (a stranger) sitting next to you. At some point you ask your seatmate what she does for a living, and she informs you she is a psychologist. You might think to yourself, "Uh oh. What have I already told this person? What secrets does she know about me that I don't know about myself? Has she been analyzing me this whole time?" Would you be surprised to discover that this psychologist studies happiness? Or intelligence? Or the processes related to the experience of vision? The study of psychological disorders is a very important aspect of psychology, but it represents only one part of the science of psychology.

Psychology seeks to understand the truths of human life in *all* its dimensions, including people's best and worst experiences. Psychologists acknowledge that, as in the heroism of Sully Sullenberger, sometimes an individual's best moments emerge amid the most difficult circumstances. Research on the human capacity for forgiveness demonstrates this point (Bono, McCullough, & Root, 2008; Lawler-Row & others, 2008; Legaree, Turner, & Lollis, 2007). Forgiveness is the act of letting go of our anger and resentment toward someone who has harmed us. Through forgiveness we cease seeking revenge or avoiding the person who did us harm, and we might even wish that person well.

A case in point: In October 2006, after Charles Carl Roberts IV took 10 young Amish girls hostage in a one-room schoolhouse in Pennsylvania, eventually murdering 5 of them and wounding 5 others before killing himself, the grief-stricken Amish community focused not on hatred and revenge but on forgiveness. As funds were being set up for the victims' families, the Amish insisted on establishing one for the murderer's family. As they prepared simple funerals for the dead girls, the community invited the killer's wife to attend. The science of psychology has much to offer to our understanding of not only the perpetrator's violence but also the victims' capacity for forgiveness.

The willingness of the Amish community to forgive this horrible crime is both remarkable and puzzling. Can we scientifically understand the human ability to forgive even what might seem to be unforgivable? As it happens, a number of psychologists have taken up the topic of forgiveness in research and clinical practice (Bono & McCullough, 2006; Cohen & others, 2006). Michael McCullough and his colleagues (2007) have shown that the capacity to forgive is an unfolding process that often takes time. For the Amish, their deep religious faith led them to embrace forgiveness, where many people might have been motivated to seek revenge and retribution. Researchers also have explored the relationship between religious commitment and forgiveness (McCullough, Bono, & Root, 2007). More recently, researchers have determined that forgiveness takes mental skills and abilities, not just emotional fortitude (Pronk & others, 2010).

The murder in 2006 of five Amish schoolgirls evoked feelings in the community not of hatred and revenge but of forgiveness.

Some argue that psychology has focused too much on the negative while neglecting qualities that reflect the best of

● **positive psychology** A branch of psychology that emphasizes human strengths.

humanity (Seligman & Csikszentmihalyi, 2000). From these criticisms positive psychology has emerged. **Positive psychology** is a branch of psychology that emphasizes human strengths. Research in positive psychology centers on topics such as hope, optimism, happiness, and gratitude (Snyder & Lopez, 2009). One goal of positive psychology is to bring a greater balance to the field by moving beyond focusing on how and why things go wrong in life to understanding how and why things go right. Positive psychology is not without its own critics, though. Indeed, some psychologists insist that human weaknesses are the most important topics to study (Lazarus, 2003).

To be a truly general science of human behavior, psychology must address *all* sides of human experience. Surely, controversy—such as that concerning positive psychology—is a part of any science. The healthy debate that characterizes the field of psychology can give rise to new psychological perspectives, and this is a sign of a lively discipline.

1·2 PSYCHOLOGY IN HISTORICAL PERSPECTIVE

Psychology seeks to answer questions that people have been asking for thousands of years—for example:

- How do we learn?
- What is memory?
- Why does one person grow and flourish while another struggles?

It is a relatively new idea that such questions might be answered through scientific inquiry. From the time human language included the word *why* and became rich enough to enable people to talk about the past, people have created myths to explain why things are the way they are. Ancient myths attributed most important events to the pleasure or displeasure of the gods. When a volcano erupted, the gods were angry; if two people fell in love, they had been struck by Cupid's arrows. Gradually, myths gave way to *philosophy*—the rational investigation of the underlying principles of being and knowledge. People attempted to explain events in terms of natural rather than supernatural causes.

Western philosophy came of age in ancient Greece in the fourth and fifth centuries B.C.E. Socrates, Plato, Aristotle, and others debated the nature of thought and behavior, including the possible link between the mind and the body. Later philosophers, especially René Descartes, argued that the mind and body were completely separate, and they focused their attention on the mind. Psychology grew out of this tradition of thinking about the mind and body. The influence of philosophy on contemporary psychology persists today, as researchers who study emotion still talk about Descartes, and scientists who study happiness often refer to Aristotle (Biswas-Diener, Kashdan, & King, 2009).

In addition to philosophy, psychology also has roots in the natural sciences of biology and physiology (Johnson, 2008; Pinel, 2009). Read on to trace how the modern field of psychology developed.

William Wundt (1832–1920) Wundt founded the first psychology laboratory (with his co-workers) in 1879 at the University of Leipzig.

Wundt's Structuralism and James's Functionalism

Wilhelm Wundt (1832–1920), a German philosopher-physician, put the pieces of the philosophy–natural science puzzle together to create the academic discipline of psychology. Some historians say that modern psychology was born in December 1879 at the University of Leipzig, when Wundt and his students, especially E. B. Titchener, performed an experiment to measure the time lag between the instant a person heard a sound and the moment he or she pressed a telegraph key to signal having heard it. What was so special about this experiment? Wundt's study was about the workings of the brain: He was trying to measure the time it took the human brain and nervous system to translate information into action.

At the heart of this experiment was the idea that mental processes could be measured. This notion ushered in the new science of psychology.

Wundt and his collaborators concentrated on discovering the basic elements, or "structures," of mental processes. Their approach was thus called **structuralism** because of its focus on identifying the structures of the human mind, and their method of study was *introspection* (literally, "looking inside"). For this type of research, a person in Wundt's lab would be asked to think (introspect) about what was going on mentally as various events took place. For example, the individual might be subjected to a sharp, repetitive clicking sound and then might have to report whatever conscious feelings the clicking produced. What made this method scientific was the systematic, detailed self-reports required of the person in the controlled laboratory setting.

Although Wundt is most often regarded as the founding father of modern psychology, it was psychologist and philosopher William James (1842–1910), perhaps more than anyone else, who gave the field an American stamp. From James's perspective, the key question for psychology is not so much what the mind *is* (that is, its structures) as what it *is for* (its purposes or functions). James's view was eventually named *functionalism.*

In contrast to structuralism, which emphasized the components of the mind, **functionalism** probed the functions and purposes of the mind and behavior in the individual's adaptation to the environment. Whereas structuralists were looking inside the mind and searching for its structures, functionalists focused on human interactions with the outside world and the purpose of thoughts. If structuralism is about the "what" of the mind, functionalism is about the "why." Unlike Wundt, James did not believe in the existence of rigid structures in the mind. Instead, James saw the mind as flexible and fluid, characterized by constant change in response to a continuous flow of information from the world. James called this natural flow of thought a "stream of consciousness."

A core question in functionalism is, why is human thought *adaptive*—that is, why are people better off because they can think than they would be otherwise? When we talk about whether a characteristic is adaptive, we are focusing on how it makes an organism better able to survive. As we will see next, functionalism fit well with the theory of evolution through natural selection proposed by British naturalist Charles Darwin (1809–1882).

Darwin's Natural Selection

In 1859, Darwin published his ideas in *On the Origin of Species.* A centerpiece of his theory was the principle of **natural selection,** an evolutionary process in which organisms that are best adapted to their environment will survive and, importantly, produce offspring.

Darwin noted that the members of any species are often locked in competition for scarce resources such as food and shelter. Natural selection is the process by which the environment determines who wins that competition. Darwin asserted that organisms with biological features that led to survival and reproduction would be better represented in subsequent generations. Over many generations, organisms with these characteristics would constitute a larger percentage of the population. Eventually, this process could change an entire species.

Importantly, a characteristic cannot be passed from one generation to the next unless it is recorded in the *genes,* those collections of molecules that are responsible for heredity. Genetic characteristics that are associated with survival and reproduction are passed down over generations. According to evolutionary theory, species change through random genetic mutation. That means that, essentially by accident, some members of a species are born with genetic characteristics that make them different from other members. If these changes are adaptive (if they help those members compete for food, survive, and reproduce), they become more common in the species. If environmental conditions were to change, however, other characteristics might become favored by natural selection, moving the process in a different direction.

● **structuralism** Wundt's approach to discovering the basic elements, or structures, of mental processes; so called because of its focus on identifying the structures of the human mind.

● **functionalism** James's approach to mental processes, emphasizing the functions and purposes of the mind and behavior in the individual's adaptation to the environment.

● **natural selection** Darwin's principle of an evolutionary process in which organisms that are best adapted to their environment will survive and produce offspring.

William James (1842–1910) James's approach became known as functionalism.

psychological *inquiry*

Explore Evolution from Giraffes to Human Beings

Evolution through natural selection and genetic mutation is a slow process that explains the various characteristics we see in creatures in the natural world. Darwin developed his theory of evolution through natural selection by observing phenomena in nature.

Let's take a look at a familiar creature of our natural world—the giraffe. Giraffes are the tallest mammals on earth, with some reaching a soaring height of 19 feet. Much of that height comes from the giraffe's very long neck. That neck poses a mystery that fascinates scientists: *Why* does the giraffe have such a long neck? Critically explore some possible reasons, below, and answer the questions with each.

1. An evolutionary explanation for the giraffe's neck would begin by assuming that, ages ago, some giraffes were genetically predisposed to have longer necks and others were genetically predisposed to have shorter necks. Take this evolutionary argument one step further: Why do we now see *only* giraffes with long necks?

2. You might reasonably guess that giraffes have long necks in order to reach leaves growing on tall trees—in other words, so that they can eat and survive. However, giraffes often prefer to eat from bushes and relatively low tree branches. Instead, male giraffes use their long necks in fights with other giraffes as they compete over mates. Those that win the fights are more likely to reproduce. Over the course of time, were the winners those with the longer necks or the shorter necks? Explain.

3. The process of evolution sheds light on why members of a particular species share common characteristics. If you were to apply evolutionary theory to human beings, what kinds of characteristics would you focus on, and why? Choose one human characteristic and apply the same kinds of questions you considered about the giraffe's long neck. Why are we humans the way we are?

Evolutionary theory implies that the way we are, at least in part, is the way that is best suited to survival in our environment (Cosmides, 2011). The Psychological Inquiry feature above lets you critically apply the principles of Darwin's theory of evolution.

Darwin's theory continues to influence psychologists today because it is strongly supported by observation. We can make such observations every day. Right now, for example, in your kitchen sink, various bacteria are locked in competition for scarce resources in the form of those tempting food particles from your last meal. When you use an antibacterial cleaner, you are playing a role in natural selection, because you are effectively killing off the bacteria that cannot survive the cleaning agents. However, you are also letting the bacteria that are genetically adapted to survive that cleanser to take over the sink. The same principle applies to taking an antibiotic medication at the first sign of a sore throat or an earache. By killing off the bacteria that may be causing the illness, you are creating an environment where their competitors (so-called antibiotic-resistant bacteria) may flourish. These observations powerfully demonstrate Darwinian selection in action.

If structuralism won the battle to be the birthplace of psychology, functionalism won the war. To this day, psychologists continue to talk about the adaptive nature of human characteristics, although they have branched out to study more aspects of human behavior than Wundt or James might ever have imagined. In a general way, since the days of those pioneers in the field, psychology has defined itself as the science of human behavior. The question of what exactly counts as human behavior, however, has fueled debate throughout the history of the field. For some psychologists, behavior has meant only observable actions; for others, it has included thoughts and feelings; for still others, unconscious processes have been the focal point. Traces of this debate can be seen today in the various contemporary approaches to the science of psychology that we will consider next.

1-3 CONTEMPORARY APPROACHES TO PSYCHOLOGY

In this section we survey seven different approaches that represent the intellectual backdrop of psychological science: biological, behavioral, psychodynamic, humanistic, cognitive, evolutionary, and sociocultural.

The Biological Approach

Some psychologists examine behavior and mental processes through the **biological approach,** which is a focus on the body, especially the brain and nervous system. For example, researchers might investigate the way your heart races when you are afraid or how your hands sweat when you tell a lie. Although a number of physiological systems may be involved in thoughts and feelings, perhaps the largest contribution to physiological psychology has come through the emergence of neuroscience (Koch, 2011; Salzman & Fusi, 2010).

Neuroscience is the scientific study of the structure, function, development, genetics, and biochemistry of the nervous system. Neuroscience emphasizes that the brain and nervous system are central to understanding behavior, thought, and emotion. Neuroscientists believe that thoughts and emotions have a physical basis in the brain. Electrical impulses zoom throughout the brain's cells, releasing chemical substances that enable us to think, feel, and behave. Our remarkable human capabilities would not be possible without the brain and nervous system, which constitute the most complex, intricate, and elegant system imaginable. Although biological approaches might sometimes seem to reduce complex human experience into simple physical structures, developments in neuroscience have allowed psychologists to understand the brain as an amazingly complex organ, perhaps just as complex as the psychological processes linked to its functioning.

B. F. Skinner was a tinkerer who liked to make new gadgets. The younger of his two daughters, Deborah, was raised in Skinner's enclosed Air-Crib. Some critics accused Skinner of monstrous experimentation with his children; however, the early controlled environment has not had any noticeable harmful effects. Deborah, shown here as a child with her parents, is today a successful artist whose work strongly reflects her unique early childhood experience.

The Behavioral Approach

The **behavioral approach** emphasizes the scientific study of observable behavioral responses and their environmental determinants. It focuses on an organism's visible interactions with the environment—that is, behaviors, not thoughts or feelings. The principles of the behavioral approach have been widely applied to help people change their behavior for the better (Miltenberger, 2008). The psychologists who adopt this approach are called *behaviorists.* Under the intellectual leadership of John B. Watson (1878–1958) and B. F. Skinner (1904–1990), behaviorism dominated psychological research during the first half of the twentieth century.

Skinner (1938) emphasized that psychology should be about what people do—their actions and behaviors—and should not concern itself with things that cannot be seen, such as thoughts, feelings, and goals. He believed that rewards and punishments determine our behavior. For example, a child might behave in a well-mannered fashion because her parents have previously rewarded this behavior. We do the things we do, behaviorists say, because of the environmental conditions we have experienced and continue to experience.

● **biological approach** An approach to psychology focusing on the body, especially the brain and nervous system.

● **neuroscience** The scientific study of the structure, function, development, genetics, and biochemistry of the nervous system, emphasizing that the brain and nervous system are central to understanding behavior, thought, and emotion.

● **behavioral approach** An approach to psychology emphasizing the scientific study of observable behavioral responses and their environmental determinants.

Contemporary behaviorists still emphasize the importance of observing behavior to understand an individual, and they use rigorous methods advocated by Watson and Skinner (Cheng & Holyoak, 2011). However, not every behaviorist today accepts the earlier behaviorists' rejection of thought processes, which are often called *cognition* (Shanks, 2010).

The Psychodynamic Approach

The **psychodynamic approach** emphasizes unconscious thought, the conflict between biological drives (such as the drive for sex) and society's demands, and early childhood family experiences. Practitioners of this approach believe that sexual and aggressive impulses buried deep within the unconscious mind influence the way people think, feel, and behave.

Sigmund Freud, the founding father of the psychodynamic approach, theorized that early relationships with parents shape an individual's personality. Freud's (1917) theory was the basis for the therapeutic technique that he called *psychoanalysis,* which involves an analyst's unlocking a person's unconscious conflicts by talking with the individual about his or her childhood memories, as well as the individual's dreams, thoughts, and feelings. Certainly, Freud's views have been controversial, but they remain a part of contemporary psychology. Today's psychodynamic theories tend to place less emphasis on sexual drives and more on cultural and social experiences as determinants of behavior.

Sigmund Freud (1856–1939) Freud was the founding father of the psychodynamic approach.

● **psychodynamic approach** An approach to psychology emphasizing unconscious thought, the conflict between biological drives (such as the drive for sex) and society's demands, and early childhood family experiences.

● **humanistic approach** An approach to psychology emphasizing a person's positive qualities, the capacity for positive growth, and the freedom to choose any destiny.

The Humanistic Approach

The **humanistic approach** emphasizes a person's positive qualities, the capacity for positive growth, and the freedom to choose one's destiny. Humanistic psychologists stress that people have the ability to control their lives and are not simply controlled by the environment (Maslow, 1971; Rogers, 1961). They theorize that rather than being driven by unconscious impulses (as the psychodynamic approach dictates) or by external rewards (as the behavioral approach emphasizes), people can choose to live by higher human values such as *altruism*—unselfish concern for other people's well-being—and free will. Many aspects of this optimistic approach appear in research on motivation, emotion, and personality psychology (Ciani & others, 2010; Sheldon & Gunz, 2009).

The Cognitive Approach

● **cognitive approach** An approach to psychology emphasizing the mental processes involved in knowing: how we direct our attention, perceive, remember, think, and solve problems.

According to cognitive psychologists, the human brain houses a "mind" whose mental processes allow us to remember, make decisions, plan, set goals, and be creative (Grigorenko & others, 2008; Sternberg, 2009). The **cognitive approach,** then, emphasizes the mental processes involved in knowing: how we direct our attention, perceive, remember, think, and solve problems. Many scientists who adopt this approach focus on *information processing,* the ways that the human mind interprets incoming information, weighs it, stores it, and applies it to decision making. Cognitive psychologists seek answers to questions such as how we solve math problems, why we remember some things for only a short time but others for a lifetime, and how we use our imagination to plan for the future.

Cognitive psychologists view the mind as an active and aware problem-solving system. This view contrasts with the behavioral view, which portrays behavior as controlled by external environmental forces. In the cognitive view, an individual's mental processes are in control of behavior through memories, perceptions, images, and thinking.

The Evolutionary Approach

● **evolutionary approach** An approach to psychology centered on evolutionary ideas such as adaptation, reproduction, and natural selection as the basis for explaining specific human behaviors.

Although arguably all of psychology emerges out of evolutionary theory, some psychologists emphasize an **evolutionary approach** that uses evolutionary ideas such as adaptation, reproduction, and natural selection as the basis for explaining specific human behaviors. David Buss (2008) argues that just as evolution molds our physical features, such as body shape, it also influences our decision making, level of aggressiveness, fears, and mating patterns. Thus, evolutionary psychologists argue, the way we adapt is traceable to problems early humans faced in adapting to their environment (Meston & Buss, 2009).

Evolutionary psychologists believe their approach provides an umbrella that unifies the diverse fields of psychology (Cosmides, 2011). Not all psychologists agree with this conclusion, however. For example, some critics stress that the evolutionary approach provides an inaccurate explanation of why men and women have different social roles and does not adequately account for cultural diversity and experiences (Wood & Eagly, 2010). Yet, even psychologists who disagree with applying the evolutionary approach to psychological characteristics still agree with the general principles of evolutionary theory.

The Sociocultural Approach

The **sociocultural approach** examines the ways in which social and cultural environments influence behavior. Socioculturalists argue that understanding a person's behavior requires knowing about the cultural context in which the behavior occurs (Matthews & Gallo, 2011). Researchers who focus on sociocultural influences might compare people from different cultures to see whether they are similar or different in important ways (Kitayama, 2011).

The sociocultural view focuses not only on comparisons of behavior across countries but also on the behavior of individuals from different ethnic and cultural groups within a country (Grigorenko & Takanishi, 2010). Thus, in recent years, there has been increased interest in the United States on the behavior of African Americans, Latinos, and Asian Americans, especially with regard to the factors that have restricted or enhanced their ability to adapt and cope with living in a predominantly Euro-American society (Banks, 2010).

According to humanistic psychologists, warm, supportive behavior toward others helps us to realize our capacity for self-understanding.

● **sociocultural approach** An approach to psychology that examines the ways in which social and cultural environments influence behavior.

Summing Up the Seven Contemporary Approaches

These seven psychological approaches provide different views of the same behavior, and all of them may offer valuable insights that the other perspectives miss. Think about the simple experience of seeing a cute puppy. Looking at that puppy involves physical processes in the eyes, nervous system, and brain—the focus of the biological approach to psychology. The moment you spot that puppy, though, you might smile without thinking and reach down to pet the little guy. That reaction might be a response based on your past learning with your own dog (behavioral perspective), or on unconscious memories of a childhood dog (psychodynamic perspective), or on conscious memories that you especially like this dog breed (cognitive perspective), or even evolutionary processes that promoted cuteness to help offspring survive (evolutionary approach). You might find yourself striking up a conversation with the puppy's owner, based on your shared love of dogs (humanistic perspective). Further, sociocultural factors might play a role in your decision about whether to ask the owner if you could hold the puppy, whether you share those warm feelings about the puppy with others, and even whether (as in some cultures) you might view that puppy as food.

SUMMARY

Psychology is the scientific study of human behavior and mental processes. Psychologists approach human behavior as scientists who think critically and are curious, skeptical, and objective. Behavior includes everything organisms do that can be observed. Mental processes are thoughts, feelings, and motives.

As a truly general science, psychology addresses all sides of human experience—positive and negative, strengths and weaknesses. Psychology is characterized by controversy and debate, and new psychological perspectives sometimes arise when one scientist questions the views of another.

Psychology emerged as a science from the fields of philosophy and physiology. Two founders of the science of psychology are Wilhelm Wundt and William James. Wundt's structuralism emphasized the conscious mind and its structures. James's functionalism focused on the functions of the mind in human adaptation to the environment. The functionalist emphasis on the mind's adaptive character fit well with the new understandings that came from Charles Darwin's theory of evolution.

Different approaches to psychology include biological, behavioral, psychodynamic, humanistic, cognitive, evolutionary, and sociocultural views. All of these consider important questions about human behavior from different but complementary perspectives.

The biological approach focuses on the body, especially the brain and nervous system. Technological advances in brain imaging have allowed researchers to examine the brain in all its complexity. The behavioral approach emphasizes the scientific study of observable behavioral responses and their environmental determinants. John B. Watson and B. F. Skinner were important early behaviorists. The psychodynamic approach emphasizes unconscious thought, the conflict between biological instincts and society's demands, and early family experiences. Sigmund Freud was the founding father of the psychodynamic approach. The humanistic approach emphasizes a person's capacity for positive growth, freedom to choose a destiny, and positive qualities. The cognitive approach emphasizes the mental processes involved in knowing. Cognitive psychologists study attention, thinking, problem solving, remembering, and learning. The evolutionary approach stresses the importance of adaptation, reproduction, and "survival of the fittest." The sociocultural approach focuses on the social and cultural determinants of behavior and encourages us to attend to the ways that our behavior and mental processes are embedded in a social context.

KEY TERMS

psychology 4
science 4
behavior 4
mental processes 4
critical thinking 5
empirical method 5
positive psychology 8
structuralism 9
functionalism 9

natural selection 9
biological approach 11
neuroscience 11
behavioral approach 11
psychodynamic approach 12
humanistic approach 12
cognitive approach 12
evolutionary approach 12
sociocultural approach 13

TEST YOURSELF

1. What makes psychology a science? What are the goals of psychological scientists?

2. What four attitudes are at the core of the scientific approach?

3. Which particular Freudian views of human nature have influenced general perceptions of what psychology is all about?

4. What is structuralism? How does functionalism contrast with structuralism?

5. What is meant when we say that a particular characteristic of an organism is adaptive?

6. In what ways is Darwin's work relevant to psychology?

7. Which approach to psychology is most interested in early childhood relationships?

8. Which approach to psychology focuses on self-fulfillment, altruism, and personal growth?

9. What specific ideas did B. F. Skinner's behaviorist approach emphasize?

APPLY YOUR KNOWLEDGE

1. Ask 10 friends and family members to tell you the first thing that comes to mind when they think of psychology or a psychologist. After hearing their answers, share with them the broad definition of psychology given in this module. How do they react?

2. Visit the website of a major book retailer (such as Amazon) and enter "psychology" as a search term. Read the descriptions of five to seven of the most popular psychology books listed. How well do the themes covered represent your perceptions of what psychology is? How well do they represent the approaches to psychology discussed in the text? Are any perspectives over- or underrepresented? If so, why do you think that is?

3. Human beings evolved long ago in a very different environment than we occupy today. The survivors were those who were most able to endure extremely difficult circumstances, struggling to find food, avoid predators, and create social groups. What do you think were the most adaptive traits for these early humans? Are those traits still adaptive? To what specific environments are humans adapting today?

4. Adopt Wilhelm Wundt's approach to understanding the human mind and behavior. Invite three friends to listen to a piece of music, and then ask them to reflect on the experience. Examine what they each say about various aspects of the music. What does this exercise tell you about the subjectivity of introspection? In what ways do you think the method is worthwhile, and in what ways is it limited?

What Psychologists Do

People who think of themselves as psychologists work in a wide range of settings and engage in many different activities. Figure 2.1 shows the various settings in which psychologists practice their profession. In this section we look at what psychologists do, and then we zoom in on the areas of specialization.

2·1 CAREERS IN PSYCHOLOGY

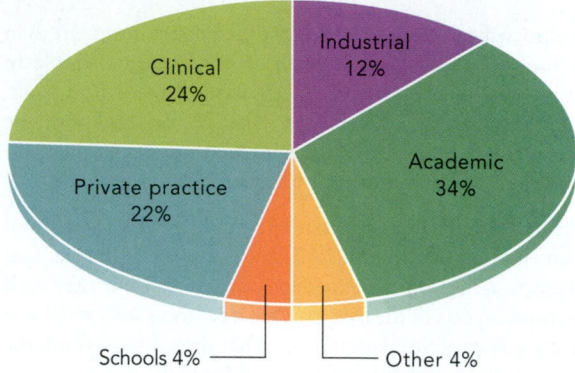

FIGURE 2.1   Settings in Which Psychologists Work More psychologists work in academic environments (34 percent), such as colleges and universities, than in any other setting. However, clinical (24 percent) and private practice (22 percent) settings—both of them contexts in which many psychologists in the mental health professions work—together make up almost half of the total settings.

Individuals with undergraduate training in psychology might use their expertise in occupations ranging from human resources and business consulting to doing casework for individuals struggling with psychological disorders. Those with graduate training in psychology might work as therapists and counselors, researchers and teachers in universities, or as business consultants or marketing researchers.

Individuals who are primarily engaged in helping others are often called *practitioners* of psychology. They spend most of their time in clinical practice, seeing clients and offering them guidance as they work through problems. However, even psychologists who are primarily concerned with clinical practice pay attention to scientific research. For these individuals, rigorous research guides their therapeutic practice and their efforts to make improvements in the lives of their patients. Increasingly, psychologists who primarily provide therapy engage in *evidence-based practice*—that is, they use therapeutic tools whose effectiveness is supported by empirical research (Beidas & Kendall, 2010; Sandler, Wolchik, & Schoenfelder, 2011).

An important distinction that is often not well understood is the difference between a clinical psychologist and a psychiatrist. A clinical psychologist typically has a doctoral degree in psychology, which requires approximately four to five years of graduate work and one year of internship in a mental health facility. In contrast, a psychiatrist is a physician with a medical degree who subsequently specializes in abnormal behavior and psychotherapy. Another difference between a psychiatrist and a clinical psychologist is that a psychiatrist can prescribe drugs, whereas a clinical psychologist generally cannot. Despite these differences, clinical psychologists and psychiatrists are alike in sharing an interest in improving the lives of people with mental health problems.

Many psychologists who are employed at universities divide their time between teaching and doing research. Research in psychology creates the knowledge that is presented in this book and that you will be learning about in your introductory psychology course.

Human behavior is a vast, complex topic. Most psychologists specialize in a particular area of study, as we consider next.

2·2 AREAS OF SPECIALIZATION

Psychology has many areas of specialization. Currently, there are 56 divisions in the American Psychological Association, each focusing on a specific subfield of psychology. Division 1, the Society of General Psychology, seeks to provide a coherent integration of the vast science of psychology. Division 2, the Society for the Teaching of Psychology, is dedicated to devising the best ways to help students learn about this fascinating science. The other main specializations in the field of psychology include the following:

Physiological Psychology and Behavioral Neuroscience

Researchers who study *physiological psychology* are interested in the physical processes that underlie mental operations such as vision and memory. Physiological psychologists may use animal models (that is, they may employ animals, such as rats, to study processes that are difficult or impossible to study in the same way in humans) to examine such topics as the development of the nervous system. The field of *behavioral neuroscience* also focuses on biological processes, especially the brain's role in behavior (Rilling & Sanfey, 2011).

Richard J. Davidson of the University of Wisconsin, Madison, shown with the Dalai Lama, is a leading researcher in behavioral neuroscience.

Sensation and Perception

Researchers who study *sensation and perception* focus on the physical systems and psychological processes that allow us to experience the world—to smell the Thanksgiving turkey in the oven (Yeshurun & Sobel, 2010) and to see the beauty of a sunset (Keen, 2011).

Learning

Learning is the intricate process by which behavior changes to adapt to changing circumstances (Cheng & Holyoak, 2011). Many researchers study the basic principles of learning using animals such as rats and pigeons (Ploog & Williams, 2010). Learning has been addressed from the behavioral and cognitive perspectives (Shanks, 2010).

Cognitive Psychology

Cognitive psychology is the broad name given to the field of psychology that examines attention, consciousness, information processing, and memory. Cognitive psychologists are also interested in skills and abilities such as problem solving, decision making, expertise, and intelligence (Margrett & others, 2010; Sternberg, 2011). Researchers in cognitive psychology and sensation perception are sometimes called *experimental psychologists*.

Developmental Psychology

Developmental psychology is concerned with how people become who they are, from conception to death. In particular, developmental psychologists concentrate on the biological and environmental factors that contribute to human development (Goldsmith, 2011). Developmentalists study child development (Grusec, 2011) but also adult development and aging (Staudinger & Gluck, 2011). Their inquiries range across the biological, cognitive, and social domains of life (Nelson, 2011).

Motivation and Emotion

Researchers from a variety of specializations are interested in *motivation and emotion*, two important aspects of experience. Research questions addressed by scientists who study motivation include how individuals persist to attain a difficult goal and how rewards affect the experience of motivation (Boekaerts, 2010). Emotion researchers delve into such topics as the physiological and brain processes that underlie emotional experience, the role of emotional expression in health, and the possibility that emotions are universal (Izard, 2009).

© Randall McIlwaine. www.CartoonStock.com.

Psychology of Women and Gender

The *psychology of women* studies psychological, social, and cultural influences on women's development and behavior. This field stresses the importance of integrating information about women with current psychological knowledge and beliefs and applying the information to society and its institutions (Martin & Ruble, 2010; Wood & Eagly, 2010). Psychologists are also interested in understanding the broad topic of *gender* and the ways in which our biological sex influences our ideas about ourselves as men and women.

Personality Psychology

Personality psychology studies personality, consisting of the relatively enduring characteristics of individuals. Personality psychologists study such topics as traits, goals, motives, genetics, personality development, and well-being (McAdams & Olson, 2010). Researchers in personality psychology are interested in those aspects of your psychological makeup that make you uniquely you.

Social Psychology

Social psychology deals with people's interactions with one another, relationships, social perceptions, social cognition, and attitudes (Bohner & Dickel, 2011; Erber & Erber, 2011). Social psychologists are interested in the influence of groups on individuals' thinking and behavior and in the ways that the groups to which we belong influence our attitudes. The research questions that concern social psychologists include understanding and working to reduce racial prejudice, determining whether two heads really are better than one, and exploring how the presence of others influences performance. Social psychologists also study the important domain of close interpersonal relationships (Shaver & Mikulincer, 2011).

Industrial and Organizational (I/O) Psychology

Industrial and organizational psychology (I/O psychology) centers on the workplace—both the workers and the organizations that employ them. I/O psychology is often divided into *industrial psychology* and *organizational psychology*. Among the main concerns of industrial psychology are personnel matters and human resource management (Aguinis & Kraiger, 2009). Thus, industrial psychology is increasingly referred to as *personnel psychology*. *Organizational psychology* examines the social influences in organizations (Aquino & Thau, 2009), as well as organizational leadership (Avolio, Walumbwa, & Weber, 2009; Gigerenzer, 2011).

- **psychopathology** The scientific study of psychological disorders and the development of diagnostic categories and treatments for those disorders.

The research of Carol S. Dweck of Stanford University spans developmental and social psychology. Her influential work looks at how our ideas of self play a role in motivation, self-regulation, and achievement.

Clinical and Counseling Psychology

Clinical and counseling psychology is the most widely practiced specialization in psychology. Clinical and counseling psychologists diagnose and treat people with psychological problems (Hersen & Gross, 2008). Counseling psychologists sometimes work with people to help solve practical problems in life (Forrest, 2010). For example, counseling psychologists may work with students, advising them about personal problems and career planning. Clinical psychologists are interested in **psychopathology**—the scientific study of psychological disorders and the development of diagnostic categories and treatments for those disorders.

Health Psychology

Health psychology is a multidimensional approach to human health that emphasizes psychological factors, lifestyle, and

Social psychologists explore the powerful influence of groups (such as, clockwise, Chinese Americans, members of motorcycle clubs, gay Americans, military families, and inner-city youths) on individuals' attitudes, thinking, and behavior.

the nature of the healthcare delivery system (Miller, Chen, & Cole, 2009). Many health psychologists study the roles of stress and coping in people's lives (Carver & Connor-Smith, 2010; Holsboer & Ising, 2010). Health psychologists may work in physical or mental health areas. Some are members of multidisciplinary teams that conduct research or provide clinical services.

This list of specialties cannot convey the extraordinarily rich knowledge you will be gaining as a student in introductory psychology. To whet your appetite for what is to come, check out the Psychological Inquiry feature and try answering some of the questions that fascinate psychologists.

The specialties that we have discussed so far are the main areas of psychology that we cover in this book. However, they do not represent an exhaustive list of the interests of the field. Other specializations in psychology include the following.

Community Psychology

Community psychology concentrates on improving the quality of relationships among individuals, their community, and society at large. Community psychologists are practitioner scientists who provide accessible care for people with psychological problems. Community-based mental health centers are one means of delivering services such as outreach programs to people in need, especially those who traditionally have been underserved by mental health professionals (Trickett, 2009).

psychological *inquiry*

Questions That Psychology Specialists Ask

This table identifies, by module, the topics we will investigate in this book (column 1). For each topic, a question is posed that the module will answer (column 2). What do you think the research will show about each of these questions? In the space provided in the note pad, jot down your guesses. Be bold—there are no right answers (yet)!

Module and Topic		Question
4	Types of Psychological Research	How is self-esteem related to increased aggression?
7	The Brain	How does behavior change the brain?
9	How We Sense and Perceive the World	Is there evidence for the existence of ESP?
14	Sleep and Dreams	What do dreams mean?
19	Operant Conditioning	How do pop quizzes influence studying?
23	Memory Storage	Are you likely to remember what you've learned in intro psychology this year 50 years from now?
30	Language	Who talks more, men or women?
32	Child Development	What kind of parenting is associated with children who are responsible and kind?
37	Emotion	Does pursuing happiness make people happier?
41	Sexual Orientation	Where does sexual orientation come from?
49	Biological Perspectives of Personality	Are personality characteristics genetically determined?
54	Social Relations	How can we best combat racial prejudice?
57	Organizational Psychology and Culture	Are happy workers more productive?
58–60, 62	Defining and Explaining Abnormal Behavior; Anxiety Disorders; Mood Disorders; and Schizophrenia	What role do genes play in psychological disorders?
65	Psychotherapy and Its Effectiveness	Does psychotherapy work?
68	Resources for Effective Life Change	What is the role of religion and spirituality in influencing healthy choices?

Your Hunch

2.

3.

4.

5.

6.

7.

8.

9.

10.

11.

12.

13.

14.

15.

16.

17.

Community psychologists strive to create communities that are more supportive of their residents by pinpointing needs, providing services, and teaching people how to access resources that are already available (Moritsugu, Wong, & Duffy, 2010). Community psychologists are also concerned with prevention. That is, they try to prevent mental health problems by identifying high-risk groups and then intervening with appropriate services and resources in the community.

School and Educational Psychology

School and educational psychology centrally concerns children's learning and adjustment in school. School psychologists in elementary and secondary school systems test children, make recommendations about educational placement, and collaborate on educational planning teams. Educational psychologists work at colleges and universities, teach classes, and do research on teaching and learning (Banks, 2010).

Environmental Psychology

Environmental psychology is the study of the interactions between people and their physical environment. Environmental psychologists explore the effects of physical settings in most major areas of psychology, including perception, cognition, learning, development, abnormal behavior, and social relations (Gifford, 2009; Hartmann & Apaolaza-Ibanez, 2010). Topics that an environmental psychologist might study range from how different building and room arrangements influence behavior to what strategies might be used to reduce human behavior that harms the environment.

Forensic Psychology

Forensic psychology is the field of psychology that applies psychological concepts to the legal system (Campbell & Brown, 2010). Social and cognitive psychologists increasingly conduct research on topics related to psychology and law. Forensic psychologists are hired by legal teams to provide input about many aspects of trials, such as jury selection. Forensic psychologists with clinical training may also testify as experts in trials, such as when they are asked to evaluate whether a person is likely to be a danger to society.

Sport Psychology

Sport psychology applies psychology's principles to improving sport performance and enjoying sport participation (Rotella, 2010). Sport psychology is a relatively new field, but it is rapidly gaining acceptance. It is now common to hear about elite athletes working with a sport psychologist to improve their game.

Cross-Cultural Psychology

Cross-cultural psychology is the study of culture's role in understanding behavior, thought, and emotion (Greenfield, 2009; Kitayama, 2011). Cross-cultural psychologists

Community psychologists provide accessible care to local populations, often through efforts such as the suicide-prevention program advertised in this poster.

Social Psychology and Cross-Cultural Psychology: Is Success Always Sweeter Than Failure?

At one time or another, all of us experience the high of success. At other times we endure the agony of failure. When we succeed, we often want to savor our moment of achievement, perhaps hanging up, for all to see, our hard-won diploma or the treasured essay on which we received an A. When we fail, we might hide the results in a drawer, literally or otherwise. Are these responses natural to all people, or does *culture*—the shared meanings that characterize a particular social group—matter when we are judging success and failure?

To get a feel for how researchers have addressed this question, imagine that you are in a psychological study in which you are asked to solve a number of puzzles. Some of the puzzles are easy, and you complete them with no problem. The other puzzles are difficult; try as you might, you cannot figure them out. After the study, you are left alone with the puzzles, and the researchers inform you that if you would like, you can keep working the puzzles while they prepare the rest of the study materials. Which puzzles will you be likely to choose?

If you are like most U.S. college students, you will gravitate toward the easy puzzles, choosing to work on what you know you are already good at. However, if you are like most Asian students, you will pick up the difficult puzzles and keep working on those that you have not yet solved (Heine, 2005; Heine &

Hamamura, 2007). These cultural differences are thought to emerge out of differing views of the self, goals, and learning. Compared to U.S. students, Asian students may be more likely to view failure as an opportunity to learn. What explains these differences?

Researchers interested in the influence of culture on psychological processes have distinguished individualistic cultures from collectivistic ones (Triandis, 2007). *Individualistic cultures* (such as the United States and western European nations) emphasize the uniqueness of each individual and his or her thoughts, feelings, and choices. Individualistic cultures view the person as having an independent sense of self, separate from his or her social group. In contrast, *collectivistic cultures* (such as those in East Asia) emphasize the social group and the roles the individual plays in that larger group. Collectivistic cultures view the person as embedded in the social network or as having an interdependent sense of self.

Participants from individualistic cultures tend to be more likely to emphasize their strengths and to show a tendency toward self-enhancing. Such individuals feel better about themselves when they are successful, and they enjoy focusing on success (Heine & others, 1999). On the

How does your cultural experience influence your perceptions of success and failure?

other hand, individuals from collectivistic cultures take a more self-critical view. They are more likely to switch away from tasks in which they have been successful and to pursue tasks in which they might instead improve themselves, a pattern that has been shown not only in Asian cultures (Falk & others, 2009; Heine & Hamamura, 2007) but also in Chile (Heine & Raineri, 2009) and among Mexican Americans (Tropp & Wright, 2003) and Native Americans (Fryberg & Markus, 2003).

These differences in responses to failure have prompted some observers to assert that feeling good about oneself is not a universal but rather a culturally specific need that applies only to individualists (Heine & Buchtel, 2009). By examining psychological processes across different cultures, psychologists can investigate whether the world around them is truly representative of human beings or is instead the product of culture.

compare the nature of psychological processes in different cultures with a special interest in whether psychological phenomena are universal or culture-specific.

Keep in mind that psychology is a collaborative science in which psychologists work together to examine a wide range of research questions. It is common for scholars from different specialties within psychology to join forces to study some aspect of human behavior. The Intersection feature reviews research that represents collaboration among scientists from different specialties to probe the same question. See how looking at psychology through the lens of culture can influence our conclusions by checking out this module's Intersection.

SUMMARY

Psychologists work in a wide range of settings and engage in many different activities. Individuals with undergraduate training in psychology hold occupations ranging from human resources and business consulting to doing casework for individuals struggling with psychological disorders. Those with graduate training in psychology might work as therapists and counselors, researchers and teachers in universities, or as business consultants or marketing researchers.

A clinical psychologist typically has a doctoral degree in psychology, whereas a psychiatrist is a medical doctor who specializes in treating people with abnormal behavior. A psychiatrist treats patients with psychotherapy and can prescribe drugs; a clinical psychologist generally cannot prescribe medication.

Main areas of specialization in psychology include physiological psychology and behavioral neuroscience, developmental psychology, sensation and perception, cognitive psychology, learning, motivation and emotion, personality psychology, social psychology, industrial and organizational psychology, clinical and counseling psychology, and health psychology. Other specialties include community psychology, school and educational psychology, environmental psychology, the psychology of women, forensic psychology, sport psychology, and cross-cultural psychology.

KEY TERMS

psychopathology   18

TEST YOURSELF

1. What are some career options for a person with an undergraduate degree in psychology? What careers might someone with a graduate degree in psychology pursue?

2. What important distinctions are there between a clinical psychologist and a psychiatrist?

3. Name five areas of specialization in psychology and describe the primary concerns of each of them.

APPLY YOUR KNOWLEDGE

1. In the directory for your school (or for another institution), look up the psychology faculty. Select several faculty members and see what the areas of specialization are for each person (be careful, they may not be the same as the classes they teach). How do you think their areas of academic training might affect the way they teach their classes?

2. What subfield of psychology most interests you? Why? Use the internet and search for information about that subfield. Identify at least one area of active research in that subfield and explain its strengths and weaknesses.

The Science of Psychology and Health and Wellness

We have reviewed a variety of ways that psychologists approach human behavior. Psychology has learned much about behavior that is relevant to you and your life. In this book, we seek to answer the question, what does psychology have to say about *you,* by tying research in psychology to your physical health and psychological wellness. At the close of each module, we will consider how the topics covered matter to your physical body and your mind. This link between the mind and the body has fascinated philosophers for centuries. Psychology occupies the very spot where the mind and body meet.

HOW THE MIND IMPACTS THE BODY

When you think about psychology, your first thought might be about the mind and the complex feelings—love, gratitude, hate, anger, and others—that emanate from it. Psychology has come to recognize more and more the degree to which that mind is intricately connected to the body. As you will see when we examine neuroscience in Modules 3 and 4, observations of the brain at work reveal that when mental processes change, so do physical processes (Hagner, 2007).

Health psychologists talk about health behavior as just a subset of behaviors that are relevant to physical health. These behaviors might include eating well, exercising, not smoking, performing testicular and breast self-exams, brushing your teeth, and getting enough sleep. But think about it: Is there ever really a time when your behavior is *not* relevant to your body, and therefore to your health? Is there ever a time when you are doing something—thinking, feeling, walking, running, singing—when your physical body is not present? As long as your body is there—with your heart, lungs, blood, and brain activated—your health is affected. In short, *everything* we do, see, think, and feel is potentially important to our health and well-being.

It might be instructive to think concretely about the ways the mind and body relate to each other, even as they are united in the physical reality of a person. Let's say you see a "Buns of Steel" infomercial on TV. You decide to embark on a quest for these legendary buns. Commitment, goal setting, and self-discipline will be among the many mental processes necessary to resculpt your rear. In this example, the mind works on the body by producing behaviors that change its shape and size.

HOW THE BODY IMPACTS THE MIND

FRANK & ERNEST © Thaves/Distributed by Newspaper Enterprise Association, Inc.

Similarly, the body can influence the mind in dramatic ways. Consider how fuzzy your thinking is after you stay out too late and how much easier it is to solve life's problems when you have had a good night's sleep. Also recall your outlook on the first day of true recovery from a nagging cold: Everything just seems better. Your mood and your work improve. Clearly, physical states such as illness and health influence the way we think.

The relationship between the body and mind is illustrated in a major question that psychologists regularly encounter: What is the impact of nature (genetic heritage) versus nurture (social experience) on a person's psychological characteristics? The influence of genetics on a variety of psychological characteristics, and the ways that genetic endowments can themselves be altered by social experience, will be addressed in many of the main topics in this book, from development (Modules 31–34) to personality (Modules 44–50) to psychological disorders (Modules 58–63). You will see that your physical and mental selves are intertwined in ways you may have never considered (Diamond, Casey, & Munakata, 2011).

Throughout this book, we investigate the ways that all of the various approaches to psychology matter to your life. Psychology is crucially about you, essential to your understanding of your life, your goals, and the ways that you can use the insights of thousands of scientists to make your life healthier and happier. In taking introductory psychology, you have an amazing opportunity. You will learn a great deal about human beings, especially one particular human being: you. Whether the psychological research presented is about emotions and motivation or the structures of the nervous system, it is still essentially about the mystery that is you.

SUMMARY

Over time, the field of psychology has come to recognize that the mind and the body are intricately related. The mind can influence the body. The way we think has implications for our nervous system and brain. Our motives and goals can influence our bodies as we strive to be physically fit and eat well. In turn, the body can have an impact on the mind. We think differently when our bodies are rested versus tired, healthy versus unhealthy.

Plan to make the most of your experience in taking introductory psychology by applying your learning to your life. Psychology is, after all, the scientific study of you—your behavior, thoughts, goals, and well-being.

TEST YOURSELF

1. What has psychology increasingly come to recognize about the relationship between the mind and the body?

2. What are some mental processes that might be involved in efforts to change your physical body, as through diet or exercise?

3. What is some real-life evidence of the body's impact on the mind? Give examples that are different from those in the text.

Psychology's Scientific Method

The Thrill of Third

As officials handed out the Olympic medals for the 1,500-meter speed skating event at the 2010 Vancouver Winter Games, Jung-Su Lee of South Korea accepted the gold and Apolo Ohno of the United States took the silver. No one, though, was smiling more broadly than J. R. Celski as he accepted the bronze. Celski, a 19-year-old American, was recovering from an injury and had not expected to win a medal at all.

Psychologist Tom Gilovich and his colleagues noticed Celski's joy as they watched the 1992 Summer Olympic Games in Barcelona: Silver medalists generally looked less happy than the bronze medalists they had just beaten (Medvec, Madey, & Gilovich, 1995). The researchers surmised that these varying reactions came from the different ways in which the athletes thought about "what might have been." Silver medalists might be tortured by the thought "I almost won the gold." In contrast, bronze medalists might take solace in thinking, "I almost missed the medals altogether."

In a series of studies to investigate their theory, the researchers asked individuals who had not watched the 1992 Olympics to look at videos of the games and to rate how happy the athletes looked at two different moments—just as the events ended and as they stood on the medal podium. In support of the researchers' hunches, the silver medalists were rated as appearing less happy than the bronze medalists both right after the event and on the podium. Moreover, in post-event interviews, the silver medalists were more likely to say things might have gone *better,* while the bronze medalists were more likely to consider how things could have been *much worse.*

This example demonstrates how psychologists can take an observation from everyday life, develop a theory that might explain that observation, and then test their ideas systematically using the scientific method. ●

The Scientific Method and Thinking Critically

Being a psychologist means being a scientist who studies psychology. This module begins by explaining the scientific method that psychologists use to study psychology. The scientific method shows how psychologists think critically. However, thinking critically is not something only done when you conduct research. It is also something you need to do when you read, or consume, research. The module concludes by sharing guidelines for how you can think critically about psychological research.

3·1 PSYCHOLOGY'S SCIENTIFIC METHOD

Science is defined not by *what* it investigates but by *how* it investigates. Whether you want to study photosynthesis, butterflies, Saturn's moons, or happiness, the *way* you study your question of interest determines whether your approach is scientific. The scientific method is how psychologists gain knowledge about mind and behavior.

It is the use of the scientific method that makes psychology a science (Langston, 2011; McBurney & White, 2010). Indeed, most of the studies psychologists publish in research journals follow the scientific method, which comprises these five steps (Figure 3.1):

1. Observing some phenomenon
2. Formulating hypotheses and predictions
3. Testing through empirical research
4. Drawing conclusions
5. Evaluating the theory

Step 1. Observing Some Phenomenon

The first step in conducting a scientific inquiry involves observing some phenomenon in the world. The curious, critically thinking psychologist sees something in the world and wants to know why or how it is the way it is. The phenomena that scientists study are called variables, a word related to the verb *to vary*. A **variable** is anything that can change. For example, one variable that interests psychologists is happiness. Some people seem to be generally happier than others. What might account for these differences?

As scientists consider answers to such questions, they often develop theories. A **theory** is a broad idea or set of closely related ideas that attempts to explain observations. Theories tell us about the relationships between variables on a conceptual level. Theories seek to explain why certain things have happened, and they can be used to make predictions about future observations. For instance, some psychologists theorize that the most important human need is the need to belong to a social group (Baumeister & Leary, 2000).

Step 2. Formulating Hypotheses and Predictions

The second step in the scientific method is stating a hypothesis. A **hypothesis** is an educated guess that derives logically from a theory. It is a prediction that can be tested. A theory can generate many hypotheses. If more and more hypotheses related to a theory turn out to be true, the theory gains in credibility. So, a researcher who believes that social belonging is the most important aspect of human functioning might predict that people who belong to social groups will be happier than those who do not. Another hypothesis from the theory that belongingness is important to human functioning might

Science is defined not by what it studies but by how it investigates. Photosynthesis, butterflies, and happiness all can be studied in a scientific manner.

● **variable** Anything that can change.

● **theory** A broad idea or set of closely related ideas that attempts to explain observations and to make predictions about future observations.

● **hypothesis** An educated guess that derives logically from a theory; a prediction that can be tested.

1	**2**	**3**	**4**	**5**
Observing Some Phenomenon	**Formulating Hypotheses and Predictions**	**Testing Through Empirical Research**	**Drawing Conclusions**	**Evaluating the Theory**
We feel good when we give someone a gift. However, do we genuinely feel better giving something away than we might feel if we could keep it? Elizabeth Dunn, Lara Aknin, and Michael Norton (2008) decided to test this question.	These researchers hypothesized that spending money on other people would lead to greater happiness than spending money on oneself.	In an experiment designed to examine this prediction, the researchers randomly assigned undergraduate participants to receive money ($5 or $20) that the students had to spend on either themselves or someone else by 5 P.M. that day. Those who spent the money on *someone else* reported greater happiness that night.	The experiment supported the hypothesis that spending money on others can be a strong predictor of happiness. Money might not buy happiness, the researchers concluded, but spending money in a particular way, that is, on other people, may enhance happiness.	The experimental results were published in the prestigious journal *Science*. Now that the findings are public, other researchers might investigate related topics and questions inspired by this work, and their experiments might shed further light on the original conclusions.

FIGURE 3.1 Steps in the Scientific Method: Is It Better to Give Than to Receive? This figure shows how the steps in the scientific method were applied in a research experiment examining how spending money on ourselves or others can influence happiness (Dunn, Aknin, & Norton, 2008).

be that individuals who have been socially excluded should feel less happy than those who have been socially included.

Step 3. Testing Through Empirical Research

The next step in the scientific method is to test the hypothesis by conducting *empirical research,* that is, by collecting and analyzing data. At this point, it is time to design a study that will test predictions that are based on the theory. To do so, a researcher first needs a concrete way to measure the variables of interest.

An **operational definition** provides an objective description of how a variable is going to be measured and observed in a particular study. Operational definitions eliminate the fuzziness that might creep into thinking about a problem. Imagine, for instance, that everyone in your psychology class is asked to observe a group of children and to keep track of kind behaviors. Do you think that all your classmates will define "kind behaviors" in the same way? Establishing an operational definition ensures that everyone agrees on what a variable means.

To measure personal happiness, for example, prominent psychologist Ed Diener and his students (1985) devised a self-report questionnaire that measures how satisfied a person is with his or her life, called the Satisfaction with Life Scale. (You will get a chance to complete the questionnaire later in this module.) Scores on this questionnaire are then used as measures of happiness. Research using this scale and others like it has shown that certain specific factors—marriage, religious faith, purpose in life, and good health—are strongly related to being happy (Diener, 1999; Pavot & Diener, 2008).

Importantly, there is not just one operational definition for any variable. While Diener and colleagues used a questionnaire, consider that in the study of silver and bronze medalists described at the beginning of this module, researchers used ratings of facial expressions as an operational definition of happiness. In yet another study, one that examined happiness as a predictor of important life outcomes, Lee Anne Harker and Dacher Keltner (2001) looked at the yearbook pictures of college women who had graduated three decades earlier

● **operational definition** A definition that provides an objective description of how a variable is going to be measured and observed in a particular study.

Researchers have identified Duchenne smiling (notice the wrinkles) as a sign of genuine happiness.

and coded the photographs for the appearance of *Duchenne smiling.* This type of smiling is genuine smiling—the kind that creates little wrinkles around the outer corner of the eyes. Duchenne smiling has been shown to be a sign of true happiness. (If you want to see whether someone in a photograph is smiling genuinely, cover the bottom of the person's face. Can you still tell that he or she is smiling? A genuine smile is evident in the eyes, not just the mouth.) So, while Diener and colleagues operationally defined happiness as a score on a questionnaire, Harker and Keltner operationally defined happiness as Duchenne smiling. Harker and Keltner found that happiness, as displayed in these yearbook pictures, predicted positive life outcomes, such as successful marriages and satisfying lives, some 30 years later.

Devising satisfactory operational definitions for the variables in a study is a crucial step in designing psychological research. To study anything, we have to have a way to see it or measure it. Clearly, in order to establish an operational definition for any variable, we first must agree on what we are trying to measure. If we think of happiness as something that people know about themselves, then a questionnaire score might be a good operational definition of the variable. If we think that people might not be aware of how happy they are (or are not), then a facial expression might be a better operational definition. In other words, our definition of a variable must be set out clearly before we operationally define it. You might try your hand at operationally defining the following variables: generosity, love, maturity, exhaustion, and physical attractiveness. What are some things that *you* find interesting? How might you operationally define these variables?

Because operational definitions allow for the measurement of variables, researchers have a lot of numbers to deal with once they have conducted a study. A key aspect of the process of testing hypotheses is *data analysis. Data* refers to all the information (all those numbers) researchers collect in a study—say, the questionnaire scores or the behaviors observed. Data analysis means "crunching" those numbers mathematically to see if they support predictions. We will cover some of the basics of data analysis later.

The following example demonstrates the first three steps in the scientific method. One theory of well-being is *self-determination theory* (Deci & Ryan, 2000; Ryan & Deci, 2009). According to this theory, people are likely to feel fulfilled when their lives meet three important needs: relatedness (warm relations with others), autonomy (independence), and competence (mastering new skills). One hypothesis that follows logically from this theory is that people who value money, material possessions, prestige, and physical appearance (that is, *extrinsic rewards*) over the needs of relatedness, autonomy, and competence (which are *intrinsic rewards*) should be less fulfilled, less happy, and less well adjusted. In a series of studies entitled "The Dark Side of the American Dream," researchers Timothy Kasser and Richard Ryan asked participants to complete self-report measures of values and of psychological and physical functioning (Kasser & Ryan, 1993, 1996; Kasser & others, 2004). Thus, the operational definitions of values and psychological functioning were questionnaire scores. The researchers found that individuals who value material rewards over more intrinsic rewards do indeed tend to suffer as predicted.

Step 4. Drawing Conclusions

Based on the results of the data analyses, scientists then draw conclusions from their research. It is important to keep in mind that usually a theory is revised only after a number of studies produce similar results. Before we change a theory, we want to be sure that the research can be replicated, or repeated, by other scientists using different methods. If a research finding is shown again and again—that is, if it is *replicated*— across different researchers and different specific methods, it is considered reliable. It is a result on which we can depend.

Step 5. Evaluating the Theory

The final step in the scientific method is one that never really ends. Researchers submit their work for publication, and it undergoes rigorous review. Afterward, the published studies are there for all to see, read, and evaluate continually. Scholars go back and consider the theory that started it all. Do the studies really support the theory?

One special type of study involves a meta-analysis. **Meta-analysis** is a statistical procedure that summarizes a large body of evidence from the research literature on a particular topic. For a meta-analysis, a researcher tries to find all of the studies that have been done on a topic of interest. The researcher then compares all the studies and their findings. A meta-analysis allows researchers to conclude whether a result is consistent in the literature and to estimate the magnitude of the relationship between variables (McDonald & others, 2010). An example of a meta-analysis is a study conducted by Sonja Lyubomirsky and her colleagues examining the relationship between happiness and work success (Lyubomirsky, King, & Diener, 2005). They found that across 43 different studies, happy people were less likely to be "burned out" and to think about quitting their jobs and more likely to receive positive evaluations from their supervisors.

● **meta-analysis** A method that allows researchers to combine the results of several different studies on a similar topic in order to establish the strength of an effect.

The research community maintains an active conversation about what scientists know, and this dialogue constantly questions conclusions. From published studies, a scholar may come up with a new idea that will eventually change the thinking on some topic. Steps 3, 4, and 5 in the scientific method are part of an ongoing process. That is, researchers go back and do more research, revise their theories, hone their methods, and draw and evaluate their new conclusions.

3·2 THINKING CRITICALLY ABOUT PSYCHOLOGICAL RESEARCH

Not all psychological information that is presented for public consumption comes from professionals with excellent credentials and reputations at colleges or universities or in applied mental health settings (Stanovich, 2010). Because journalists, television reporters, and other media personnel are not usually trained in psychological research, they often have trouble sorting through the widely varying material they find and making sound decisions about the best information to present to the public. In addition, the media often focus on sensationalistic and dramatic psychological findings to capture public attention. Media reports may go beyond what actual research articles and clinical findings really say. For example, recall from Module 1 the research controversy over the alleged epidemic of narcissism in members of Generation Me. The popular media latched on to this work, although subsequent research has called its conclusions into question.

Snapshots

"This just in from the AMA: New studies reveal that life is bad for you."

© Jason Love. www.CartoonStock.com.

Even when the media present the results of excellent research, they sometimes have trouble accurately informing people about the findings and their implications for people's lives. This entire book is dedicated to carefully introducing, defining, and elaborating on key concepts and issues, research, and clinical findings. The media, however, do not have the luxury of so much time and space to detail and specify the limitations and qualifications of research. In the end, *you* have to take responsibility for evaluating media reports on psychological research. To put it another way, you have to consume psychological information critically and wisely. Five guidelines follow.

Avoid Overgeneralizing Based on Little Information

Media reports of psychological information often leave out details about the nature of the sample used in a given study. Without information about sample characteristics—such as the number of participants, their sex, or their ethnic representation—it is wise to take research results with a grain of salt. For example, research that demonstrated the classic "fight or flight" response to stress has had great impact on how we understand the body's response to threatening situations. Yet the original work on this topic included only male participants (Taylor, 2011).

Distinguish Between Group Results and Individual Needs

Just as we cannot generalize from a small group to all people, we also cannot apply conclusions from a group to an individual. When you learn about psychological research through the media, you might be disposed to apply the results to your life. It is important to keep in mind that statistics about a group do not necessarily represent each individual in the group equally well. Imagine, for example, taking a test in a class and being told that the class average was 75 percent, but you got 98 percent. It is unlikely that you would want the instructor to apply the group average to your score.

Sometimes consumers of psychological research can get the wrong idea about whether their own experience is "normal" if it does not match group statistics. New parents face this issue all the time. They read about developmental milestones that supposedly characterize an entire age group of children; one such milestone might be that most 2-year-olds are conversing with their parents. However, this group information does not necessarily characterize *all* children who are developing normally. Albert Einstein did not start talking until he was the ripe old age of 3.

Look for Answers Beyond a Single Study

The media might identify an interesting piece of research and claim that its conclusions are phenomenal and have far-reaching implications. Although such pivotal studies do occur, they are rare. It is safer to assume that no single study will provide conclusive answers to an important question, especially answers that apply to all people. In fact, in most psychological domains that prompt many investigations, conflicting results are common. Answers to questions in research usually emerge after many scientists have conducted similar investigations that yield similar conclusions. Remember that you should not take one research study as the absolute, final answer to a problem, no matter how compelling the findings.

Avoid Attributing Causes Where None Have Been Found

Correlational studies look for relationships between two or more variables in order to describe how they change together (see Module 4, p. 37). Drawing casual conclusions from correlational studies is one of the most common mistakes the media make. For example, the results of the Nun Study, a correlational study conducted by David Snowdon and his colleagues (Grossi & others, 2007; Mortimer, Snowden, & Markesbery, 2009; Snowdon, 2003) that is described in Module 4 (p. 39) suggests that happy people live longer. However, we cannot state that happiness *caused* them to live longer. When a true experiment has not been conducted—that is, when participants have not been randomly assigned to treatments or experiences—two variables might have only a non-causal relationship to each other. Causal interpretations cannot be made when two or more factors are simply correlated. We cannot say that one causes the other. When you hear about correlational studies, be skeptical of words indicating causation until you know more about the particular research.

Consider the Source of Psychological Information

Studies conducted by psychologists are not automatically accepted by the rest of the research community. The researchers usually must submit their findings to an academic journal for review by their colleagues, who make a decision about whether to publish the paper, depending on its scientific merit. Although the quality of research and findings is not uniform among all psychology journals, in most cases journals submit the findings to far greater scrutiny than do the popular media (Stanovich, 2010).

Within the media, though, you can usually draw a distinction. The reports of psychological research in respected newspapers such as the *New York Times* and the *Washington Post*, as well as in credible magazines such as *Time* and the *Atlantic Monthly*, are far more trustworthy than reports in tabloids such as the *National Enquirer* and *Star.* Yet whatever the source—serious publication, tabloid, or even academic journal—you are responsible for reading the details behind the reported findings and for analyzing the study's credibility.

SUMMARY

Psychologists use the scientific method to address research questions. This method involves starting with a theory and then making observations, formulating hypotheses, testing these through empirical research, drawing conclusions, and evaluating the theory. The science of psychology is an ongoing conversation among scholars.

In your everyday life and in introductory psychology, you will be exposed to psychological research findings. In approaching psychological research in the media, you should adopt the attitude of a scientist and critically evaluate the research presented. This means being careful to avoid overgeneralizing based on little information, realizing that group results may not apply to every individual, looking for answers beyond a single study, and avoiding attributing causation when none has been found. Finally, it is important to consider the source when you encounter research in the popular media.

KEY TERMS

variable   28
theory   28
hypothesis   28

operational definition   29
meta-analysis   31

TEST YOURSELF

1. What are the five steps in the scientific method?
2. What is an operational definition, and what is its value in a study?
3. What is a meta-analysis? Why do researchers use this procedure?
4. For what reasons are media reports on psychological studies often problematic?
5. Why is it wise to look beyond the conclusions of just one research study?
6. How does the submission of research findings to a respectable academic journal aid both researchers and the public?

APPLY YOUR KNOWLEDGE

1. What are some positive and negative correlations that you have observed in your own experience? What are some third variables that might explain these relationships? Do you think these relationships may be causal? How would you design an experiment to test that possibility?
2. In the next few days, look through several newspapers and magazines for reports about psychological research. Also notice what you see and hear on television about psychology. Apply the guidelines for being a wise consumer of information about psychology to these media reports.

TYPES OF PSYCHOLOGICAL RESEARCH

Psychologists commonly use three types of research. *Descriptive research* involves finding out about the basic dimensions of some variable (for example, what the average level of happiness is for men in the United States). *Correlational research* is interested in discovering relationships between variables (for instance, whether being married predicts greater happiness for men). *Experimental research* concerns establishing causal relationships between variables (for example, whether women perceive men as more attractive if the men are smiling). In this module, we examine each of these types of research.

4-1 DESCRIPTIVE RESEARCH

● **descriptive research** Research that determines the basic dimensions of a phenomenon, defining what it is, how often it occurs, and so on.

Just as its name suggests, **descriptive research** is about describing some phenomenon—determining its basic dimensions and defining what this thing is, how often it occurs, and so on. By itself, descriptive research cannot prove what causes some phenomenon, but it can reveal important information about people's behaviors and attitudes (Stake, 2010). Descriptive research methods include observation, surveys and interviews, and case studies.

Observation

Imagine that you are going to conduct a study on how children who are playing together resolve conflicts that arise. The data that are of interest to you concern conflict resolution. As a first step, you might go to a playground and simply observe what the children do—how often you see conflict resolution occur and how it unfolds. You would likely keep careful notes of what you observe.

This type of scientific observation requires an important set of skills (R. A. Smith & Davis, 2010). Unless you are a trained observer and practice your skills regularly, you might not know what to look for, you might not remember what you saw, you might not realize that what you are looking for is changing from one moment to the next, and you might not document and communicate your observations effectively. Furthermore, you might not realize the value of having one or more others do the observations as well, so that you develop a sense of the accuracy of your observations. In short, for observations to be effective, they must be systematic. You must know whom you are observing, when and where you will observe, and how you will make the observations. Also, you need to know in advance in what form you will document them: in writing, by sound recording, or by video.

Surveys and Interviews

Sometimes the best and quickest way to get information about people is to ask them for it. One technique is to interview them directly. A related method that is especially useful when information from many people is needed is the *survey,* or questionnaire. A survey presents a standard set of questions, or *items,* to obtain people's self-reported attitudes or beliefs about a particular topic.

Although surveys can be a straightforward way to measure psychological variables, constructing them requires care (Stangor, 2011). For example, surveys can measure only what people think about themselves. Thus, if we are interested in studying a variable that we think is unconscious, such as a psychodynamic drive, we cannot use a survey. Furthermore, people do not always know the truth about themselves. If you were answering a survey that asked, "Are you a generous person?" how might your answer compare to that of a friend who is asked to make that same rating about you? One particular problem with surveys and interviews is the tendency of participants to answer questions in a way that will make them look good rather than in a way that communicates what they truly think or feel (McMillan & Wergin, 2010).

Another challenge in survey construction is that when a questionnaire is used to define variables operationally, it is crucial that the items clearly probe the specific topic of interest and not some other characteristic. The language used in a survey therefore must be clear and understandable if the responses are to reflect the participants' actual feelings.

Surveys and interviews can examine a wide range of topics, from religious beliefs to sexual habits to attitudes about gun control (Rosnow & Rosenthal, 2008). Some survey and interview questions are unstructured and open-ended, such as "How fulfilling would you say your marriage is?" Such questions allow for unique responses from each person surveyed. Other survey and interview questions are more structured and ask about quite specific things. For example, a structured question might ask, "How many times have you talked with your partner about a personal problem in the past month: 0, 1–2, 3–5, 6–10, 11–30, every day?"

Case Studies

A **case study,** or **case history,** is an in-depth look at a single individual. Case studies are performed mainly by clinical psychologists when, for either practical or ethical reasons, the unique aspects of an individual's life cannot be duplicated and tested in other individuals. A case study provides information about one person's goals, hopes, fantasies, fears, traumatic experiences, family relationships, health, and anything else that helps the psychologist understand the person's mind and behavior. Case studies can also involve in-depth explorations of particular families or social groups.

● **case study or case history** An in-depth look at a single individual.

An example of a case study is the analysis of India's spiritual leader Mahatma Gandhi (1869–1948) by psychodynamic theorist Erik Erikson (1969). Erikson studied Gandhi's life in great depth to discover how his positive spiritual identity developed, especially during his youth. In piecing together Gandhi's identity development, Erikson described the contributions of culture, history, family, and various other factors that might affect the way other people form an identity.

Case histories provide dramatic, detailed portrayals of people's lives, but we must be cautious about applying what we learn from one person's life to other people. The subject of a case study is unique, with a genetic makeup and personal history that no one else shares. Case studies can be very valuable at the first step of the scientific method, in that they often provide vivid observations that can then be tested in a variety of ways in psychological research. However, and importantly, an in-depth study of a single case may not be generalizable to the general population.

Mahatma Gandhi was India's spiritual leader in the mid-twentieth century. Erik Erikson conducted an extensive case study of Gandhi's life to determine what contributed to his identity development.

The Value of Descriptive Research

Descriptive research allows researchers to get a sense of a subject of interest, but it cannot answer questions about how and why things are the way they are. Nevertheless, descriptive research does explore intriguing topics, such as the experience of happiness in different cultures. Before reading about and considering the value of that research, complete the measure below. Specifically, using the 7-point scale, indicate your agreement with each item that follows the scale.

7	6	5	4	3	2	1
Strongly Agree	Agree	Slightly Agree	Neither Agree nor Disagree	Slightly Disagree	Disagree	Strongly Disagree

1. In most ways my life is close to my ideal.

2. The conditions of my life are excellent.

3. I am satisfied with my life.

4. So far I have gotten the important things I want in life.

5. If I could live my life over, I would change almost nothing.

You have just completed the Satisfaction with Life Scale (or SWLS; Diener & others, 1985), one operational definition of happiness. To find out your score, add up your ratings and divide by 5. This average rating could be considered your level of general happiness. A broad range of studies in many different countries have used this scale and others like it to measure happiness levels. Based on such research, Ed and Carol Diener (1996) concluded that most people are pretty happy because they score above the midpoint, 3.5, on the scale you just completed. However, research on happiness in various cultures has generally centered on relatively industrialized countries. What about nonindustrialized societies?

One study examined levels of happiness in groups of people who have not generally been included in psychological studies (Biswas-Diener, Vitterso, & Diener, 2005). The research examined three groups: the Inughuits (Inuits) of Greenland, the Maasai of southern Kenya, and American Old Order Amish. All three groups completed measures essentially the same as the one you just did.

The Inuit tribe studied (the Inughuits) live at 79 degrees latitude (very far north), in the harshest climate inhabited by a traditional human society. Rocks, glaciers, and the sea dominate the landscape. Farming is impossible. The Inughuits have some modern conveniences, but they generally adhere to a traditional hunting culture. It is not uncommon to find an Inughuit hunter carving a seal or caribou on the kitchen floor while children watch TV in the next room. Most of us might feel a little blue in the winter months when gloomy weather seems to stretch on, day after day. For the Inughuits, however, the sun never rises at all throughout the winter months, and in the summer, it never sets. How happy could an individual be in such a difficult setting? Pretty happy, it turns out, as the Inughuits averaged a 5.0 on the Satisfaction with Life Scale.

The Maasai are an indigenous (native) African nomadic group who live in villages of about 20 people, with little exposure to the West. Maasai are fierce warriors, and their culture has many traditional ceremonies built around a boy's passage from childhood to manhood. Boys are circumcised between the ages of 15 and 22, and they are forbidden from moving or making a sound during the procedure. Girls also experience circumcision as they enter puberty, in a controversial rite that involves the removal of the clitoris and that makes childbirth extremely difficult. The Maasai practice child marriage and polygamy. Maasai women have very little power and are generally expected to do most of the work. How happy could an individual be in this context? Maasai men and women who completed the measure orally in their native tongue, Maa, averaged a 5.4 on the life satisfaction scale (Biswas-Diener, Vitterso, & Diener, 2005).

Finally, the Old Order Amish of the midwestern and northeastern United States belong to a strict religious sect that explicitly rejects modern aspects of life. The Amish separate themselves from mainstream society and travel by horse and buggy. The women wear bonnets, and the men sport beards, dark clothes, and dark brimmed hats. The Amish farm without modern machinery and dedicate their lives to simplicity—without radios, TVs, CDs, DVDs, iPods, cell phones, washing machines, and cars. Still, the Amish are relatively happy, averaging 4.4 on the 7-point happiness scale (Biswas-Diener, Vitterso, & Diener, 2005).

Like a host of other studies in industrialized nations, these results indicate that most individuals are pretty happy. Such descriptive findings provide researchers of well-being a valuable foundation for further examining the processes that lead to these feelings of happiness in different cultural settings. If a researcher wanted to extend these findings to investigate predictors of happiness in different cultures, he or she would then turn to a correlational design.

4-2 CORRELATIONAL RESEARCH

We have seen that descriptive research tells us about the basic dimensions of a variable. In contrast, **correlational research** tells us about the relationship between two variables. The purpose of correlational research is to examine whether and how two variables *change together*. That is, correlational research looks at a co-relationship. For instance, if one of the variables increases, what happens to the other one? When two variables change together, we can predict one from the other, and we say that the variables are correlated.

Correlational research is so named because of the statistical technique *correlation* that is typically used to analyze these types of data. The key feature of a correlational study is that the factors of interest are measured or observed to see how they are related (Kiess & Green, 2010; Levin & Fox, 2011). If we wanted to know whether shy people are happy, we might give the same people two questionnaires—one that measures shyness and another that measures happiness. For each person we would have two scores, and we would then see whether shyness and happiness relate to each other in a systematic way.

The degree of relationship between two variables is expressed as a numerical value called a *correlational coefficient,* which is most commonly represented by the letter *r*. The correlation coefficient is a statistic that tells us two things about the relationship between two variables—its strength and its direction. The value of a correlation always falls between −1.00 and +1.00. The number or magnitude of the correlation tells us about the *strength* of the relationship. The closer the number is to ±1.00, the stronger the relationship. The sign (+ or −) tells us about the *direction* of the relationship between the variables. A positive sign means that as one variable increases, the other also increases. A negative sign means that as one variable increases, the other decreases. A zero correlation means that there is no systematic relationship between the variables.

Examples of scatter plots (a type of graph that plots scores on the two variables) showing positive and negative correlations appear in Figure 4.1. Note that every dot in this figure represents both scores for one person.

● **correlational research** Research that examines the relationships between variables, whose purpose is to examine whether and how two variables change together.

● **third variable problem** The circumstance where a variable that has not been measured accounts for the relationship between two other variables. Third variables are also known as confounds.

Correlation Is Not Causation

Look at the terms in bold type in the following newspaper headlines:

Researchers **Link** Coffee Consumption to Cancer of Pancreas

Brain Size Is **Associated** with Gender

Psychologists Discover **Relationship** Between Religious Faith and Good Health

Reading these headlines, one might conclude that coffee causes pancreatic cancer, gender causes differences in brain size, and religious faith causes good health. The boldface words are synonymous only with correlation, however, not with causality.

Correlation does not equal causation. Remember, correlation means only that two variables change together. Being able to predict one event based on the occurrence of another event does not necessarily tell us anything about the cause of either event (Aron, Aron, & Coups, 2011; Heiman, 2011). At times some other variable that has not been measured accounts for the relationship between two others. Researchers refer to this circumstance as the **third variable problem.**

To understand the third variable problem, consider the following example. A researcher measures two variables: the number of ice cream cones sold in a town and the number of violent crimes that occur in that town throughout the year. The researcher finds that ice cream cone sales and violent crimes are positively correlated, to the magnitude of +.50. This high positive correlation would indicate that as ice cream sales increase, so does violent crime. Would it be reasonable for the local paper to run the headline "Ice Cream Consumption Leads to Violence"? Should concerned citizens gather outside the local Frosty Freeze to stop the madness? Probably not. Perhaps you have already thought of the third variable that might explain this correlation—heat. Indeed, when it is hot

FIGURE 4.1 Scatter Plots Showing Positive and Negative Correlations A positive correlation is a relationship in which two factors vary in the same direction, as shown in the two scatter plots on the left. A negative correlation is a relationship in which two factors vary in opposite directions, as shown in the two scatter plots on the right.

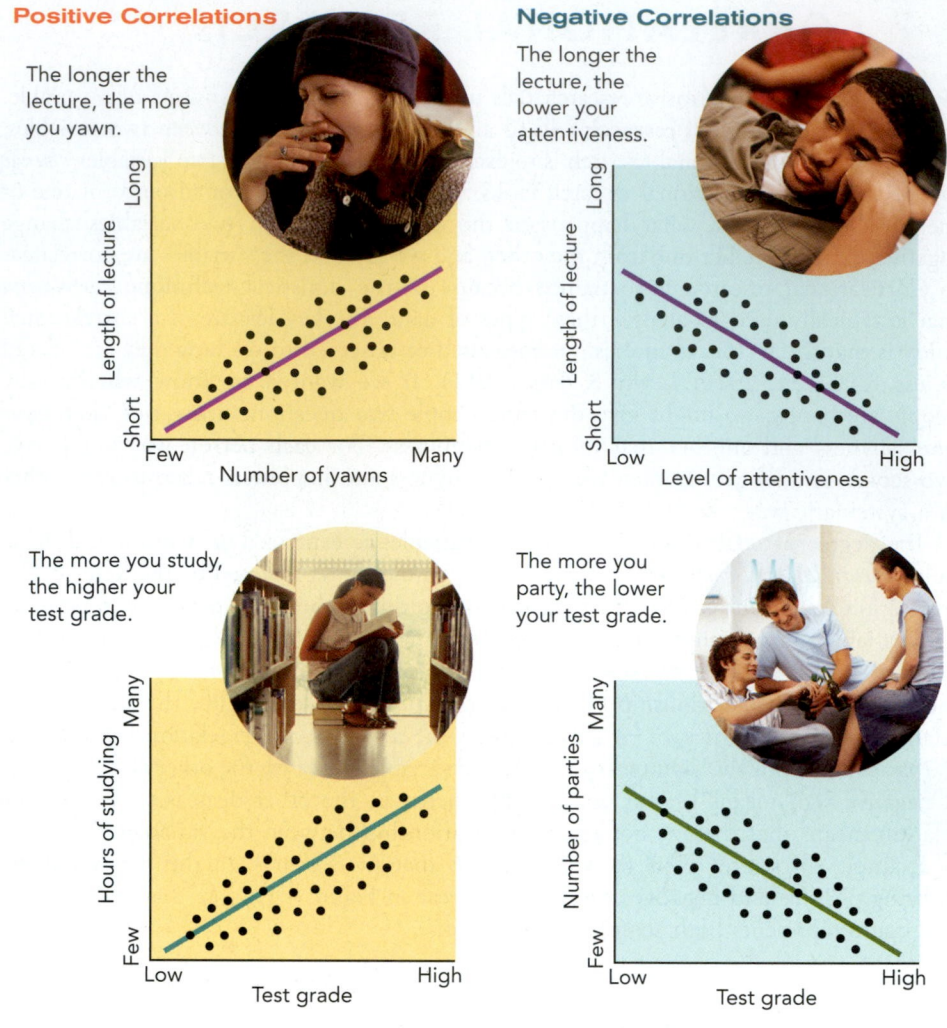

Positive Correlations

The longer the lecture, the more you yawn.

The more you study, the higher your test grade.

Negative Correlations

The longer the lecture, the lower your attentiveness.

The more you party, the lower your test grade.

outside, people are more likely both to purchase ice cream and to act aggressively (Anderson & Bushman, 2002). Such a third variable is also called a *confound*.

The Value of Correlational Research

Given the potential problems with third variables, why do researchers bother to conduct correlational studies? There are several very good reasons. Although correlational studies cannot show a causal relationship between variables, they do allow us to use one variable to predict a person's score on another. This is the reasoning behind tests such as the SAT and ACT, which provide a measure of academic ability that will predict performance in college. In addition, some important questions can be investigated only through correlational studies. Such questions may involve variables that can only be measured or observed, such as biological sex, personality traits, genetic factors, and ethnic background. Another reason why researchers conduct correlational studies is that sometimes the variables of interest are real-world events that influence people's lives, such as Hurricane Katrina in 2005 and the earthquake in Haiti in 2010. Correlational research is also valuable in cases where it would not be ethical to do research in any other way. For example, it would be unethical for an experimenter to direct expectant mothers to smoke varying numbers of cigarettes in order to see how cigarette smoke affects birth weight and fetal activity.

Although we have predominantly focused on relationships between just two variables, researchers often measure many variables in their studies. This way, they can examine whether a relationship between two variables is explained by a third variable (or a fourth or fifth variable). An interesting question that researchers have probed in this fashion is, do happy people live longer? In one study, 2,000 Mexican Americans aged 65 and older were interviewed twice over the course of two years (Ostir & others, 2000). In the first assessment, participants completed measures of happiness but also reported about potential third variables such as diet, physical health, smoking, marital status, and distress. Two years later, the researchers contacted the participants again to see who was still alive. Even with these many potential third variables taken into account, happiness predicted who was still living two years later.

Correlational studies are useful, too, when researchers are interested in studying everyday experience. For example, correlational researchers have begun to use daily journal keeping, known as the *experience sampling method (ESM)*, to study people in their natural settings. ESM studies involve having people report on their experiences in a diary a few times a day or to complete measures of their mood and behavior whenever they are beeped by an electronic organizer. A similar method, *event-contingent responding*, asks participants to complete a report each time they engage in a particular behavior, such as drinking alcohol or having sex (Cooper, 2010). Such methods allow researchers to get close to real life as it happens.

Correlational research is useful for studying the impact on people's lives of events such as the Haitian earthquake of early 2010.

Although the correlation coefficient is often used to express the relationship between two variables, it is important to keep in mind that what makes a study correlational is not the statistic researchers use to analyze the data. Rather, a study is correlational when it relies on measuring variables to see how they are related. To get a sense of this distinction and learn about some clever ways in which psychologists have operationalized variables, check out the Psychological Inquiry.

Longitudinal Designs

One way that correlational researchers can deal with the issue of causation is to employ a special kind of systematic observation called a **longitudinal design.** Longitudinal research involves obtaining measures of the variables of interest in multiple waves over time. This type of research can suggest potential causal relationships because if one variable is thought to cause changes in another, it should at least come before that variable in time.

● **longitudinal design** A special kind of systematic observation, used by correlational researchers, that involves obtaining measures of the variables of interest in multiple waves over time.

One intriguing longitudinal study is the Nun Study, conducted by David Snowdon and his colleagues (Grossi & others, 2007; Mortimer, Snowdon, & Markesbery, 2009; Snowdon, 2003). The study began in 1986 and has followed a sample of 678 School Sisters of Notre Dame (SSND) ever since. The nuns ranged in age from 75 to 103 when the study began. These women complete a variety of psychological and physical measures annually. This sample is unique in many respects. However, certain characteristics render the participants an excellent group for correlational research. For one thing, many potential extraneous third variables are relatively identical for all the women in the group. Specifically, their biological sex, living conditions, diet, activity levels, marital status, and religious participation are essentially held constant, so there is little chance that differences would arise in these variables that might explain the study's results.

Researchers examined the relationship between happiness and longevity using this rich dataset. All of the nuns had been asked to write a spiritual autobiography when they entered the convent (for some, as many as 80 years before). Deborah Danner and her colleagues (2001) were given access to these documents and used them as indicators of happiness earlier in life by counting the number of positive emotions expressed in the autobiographies (note that here we have yet another operational definition of happiness). Higher levels of positive emotion expressed in autobiographies written at an average age of 22 were associated with a 2.5-fold difference in risk of mortality when

psychological *inquiry*

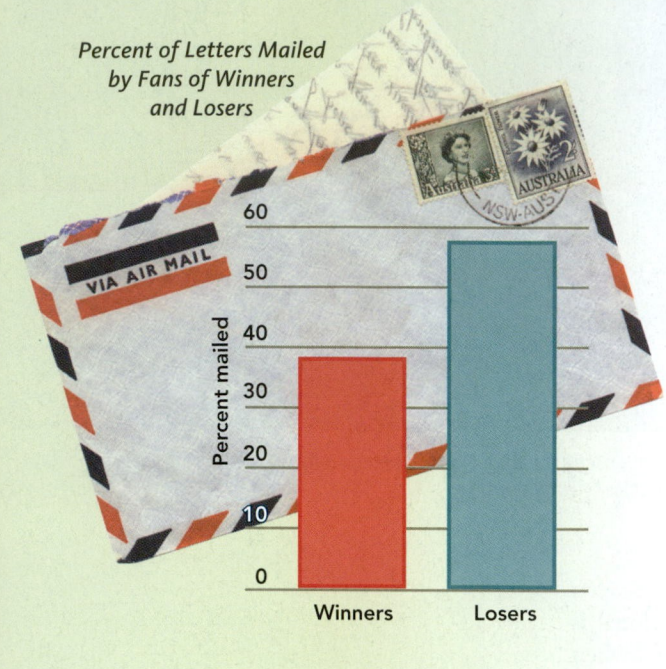

Percent of Letters Mailed by Fans of Winners and Losers

Percent mailed

60
50
40
30
20
10
0

Winners   Losers

Miserable but Helpful?

Many studies have shown that happy individuals are more helpful than people in a negative mood. Social psychologist R. F. Soames Job (1987) was interested in examining how mood relates to helping. In a clever study, he used naturally occurring mood and an unusual measure of helpfulness.

The study took place outside a major rugby match pitting Canterbury-Bankstown against St. George, in Sydney, Australia. Rugby is enormously popular in Sydney, and more than 40,000 people attended the match. While the game was going on, the researchers placed 100 stamped letters on the windshields of cars parked around the sporting grounds. The letters were addressed to the same person, and a handwritten note on each letter said, "Found near your car." Cars belonging to supporters of each team were identified by different colored streamers, team stickers, and posters. Fifty letters were placed on the cars of supporters of each team. The researchers then waited to see which type of fan was most likely to put the letter in the mailbox—a fan of the winning team or of the losing team. The figure shows the results. Try your hand at the questions below.

1. What were the variables of interest in this study?

2. How did the study operationally define these variables?

3. Why is this a correlational study?

4. Job concluded that these data support the notion that negative mood relates to helping. Is this conclusion justified, in your opinion? Why or why not?

5. Identify at least one third variable that might explain the results of this study.

● **experiment** A carefully regulated procedure in which the researcher manipulates one or more variables that are believed to influence some other variable.

the nuns were in their 80s and 90s. That is, women who included positive emotion in their autobiographies when they were in their early 20s were two-and-a-half times more likely to survive some 60 years later.

Longitudinal designs provide ways by which correlational researchers may attempt to demonstrate causal relations among variables (Gibbons, Hedeker, & DuToit, 2010). Still, it is important to be aware that even in longitudinal studies, causal relationships are not completely clear. For example, the nuns who wrote happier autobiographies may have had happier childhood experiences that might be influencing their longevity, or a particular genetic factor might explain both their happiness and their survival. As you read about correlational research studies throughout this book, do so critically, and with a modicum of skepticism; consider that even the brightest scientist may not have thought of all of the potential third variables that could have explained the results. It is easy to assume causality when two events or characteristics are merely correlated. Remember those innocent ice cream cones, and critically evaluate conclusions that may be drawn from simple observation.

4·3 EXPERIMENTAL RESEARCH

To determine whether a causal relationship exists between variables, researchers must use experimental methods (Christensen, Johnson, & Turner, 2011). An **experiment** is a carefully regulated procedure in which the researcher manipulates one or more variables that are believed to influence some other variable. Imagine, for example, that a researcher notices that people who listen to classical music seem to be of above average intelligence. A correlational study on this question would not tell us if listening to classical music *causes*

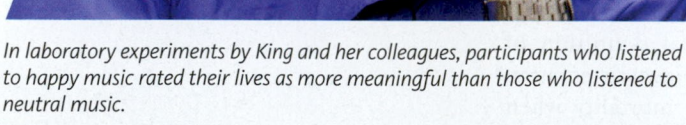

In laboratory experiments by King and her colleagues, participants who listened to happy music rated their lives as more meaningful than those who listened to neutral music.

increases in intelligence. In order to demonstrate causation, the researcher would manipulate whether or not people listen to classical music. He or she might create two groups: one that listens to classical music and one that listens to pop music. To test for differences in intelligence, the researcher would then measure intelligence.

If that manipulation led to differences between the two groups on intelligence, we could say that the manipulated variable *caused* those differences: The experiment has demonstrated cause and effect. This notion that experiments can demonstrate causation is based on the idea that if participants are *randomly assigned* to groups, the only systematic difference between them must be the manipulated variable. **Random assignment** means that researchers assign participants to groups by chance. This technique reduces the likelihood that the experiment's results will be due to any preexisting differences between groups (Graziano & Raulin, 2010).

To get a sense of what experimental studies, as compared to correlational studies, can reveal, consider the following example. Psychologists have long assumed that experiencing one's life as meaningful is an important aspect of psychological well-being (Frankl, 1963/1984; Steger & Frazier, 2005). Because surveys that measure meaning in life and well-being correlate positively (that is, the more meaningful your life, the happier you are), the assumption has been that experiencing meaning in life causes greater happiness. Because the studies involved in exploring this relationship have been correlational, however, the cause is unclear. Meaning in life may lead people to be happier, but the reverse might also be true: Happiness might make people feel that their lives are more meaningful.

To address this issue, Laura King and her colleagues conducted a series of laboratory experiments (King & Hicks, 2010; King & others, 2006). In one study, the researchers put some participants in a positive mood by having them listen to happy music. Other participants listened to neutral music. Participants who listened to happy music rated their lives as more meaningful than did individuals who listened to neutral music. Note that participants were randomly assigned to one of two conditions, happy music or neutral music, and then rated their meaning in life using a questionnaire. In this case happiness was operationally defined by the type of music participants heard, and meaning in life was operationally defined by ratings on a questionnaire. Because participants were randomly assigned to conditions, we can assume that the only systematic difference between the two groups was the type of music they heard. As a result, we can say that the happy music caused people to rate their lives as more meaningful.

> ● **random assignment** Researchers' assignment of participants to groups by chance, to reduce the likelihood that an experiment's results will be due to preexisting differences between groups.

Independent and Dependent Variables

Experiments have two types of variables: independent and dependent. An **independent variable** is a manipulated experimental factor. The independent variable is the variable that the experimenter changes to see what its effects are; it is a potential cause. Any experiment may include several independent variables, or factors that are manipulated, to determine their effect on some outcome. In the study of positive mood and meaning in life, the independent variable is mood (positive versus neutral), operationally defined by the type of music participants heard.

Sometimes the independent variable is the individual's social context. Social psychologists often manipulate the social context with the help of a confederate. A **confederate** is a person who is given a role to play in a study so that the social context can be manipulated. For example, if a researcher is interested in reactions to being treated rudely, he or she might assign a confederate to treat participants rudely (or not).

A **dependent variable** in an experiment is the variable that may change as a result of manipulations of the independent variable. It represents the outcome (effect) in an experiment. As researchers manipulate the independent variable, they measure the dependent variable to test for any effect of the manipulated variable. In the study by King and others of music type and meaning in life, meaning in life was the dependent variable.

Independent and dependent variables are two of the most important concepts in psychological research. Remember that the independent variable is the *cause,* and the dependent variable is the *effect.*

> ● **independent variable** A manipulated experimental factor; the variable that the experimenter changes to see what its effects are.

> ● **confederate** A person who is given a role to play in a study so that the social context can be manipulated.

> ● **dependent variable** The outcome; the factor that can change in an experiment in response to changes in the independent variable.

Social Psychology and Developmental Psychology: Is High Self-Esteem Such a Good Thing?

Low self-esteem is frequently implicated in society's ills, from juvenile delinquency to violent acts of aggression. It often seems as if we could make the world a better place if we could help everyone achieve higher self-esteem. Yet in the late 1990s, psychologist Roy Baumeister presented a provocative idea: He suggested that *high* self-esteem, not low self-esteem, is associated with aggressive acts (Baumeister, 1999; Baumeister, Bushman, & Campbell, 2000; Baumeister & Butz, 2005; Baumeister & others, 2007; Bushman & Baumeister, 2002). In a variety of experimental studies, he showed that individuals who scored very high on a measure of self-esteem were more likely than their counterparts with low self-esteem to behave aggressively toward others when their self-esteem was threatened. For example, individuals with high self-esteem might have been more likely to blast someone with loud noise in the lab after being told that they did not perform well on an intelligence test. These findings conflicted with a long-held belief in psychology that self-esteem was a central component of psychological health.

Following the publication of Baumeister's work, research conducted by developmental psychologists (who study the ways human beings mature from earliest childhood to old age) challenged the notion that high self-esteem was bad. These researchers used longitudinal data collected from a large sample of individuals in Dunedin, New Zealand, to show that contrary to Baumeister's conclusions, low (not high) self-esteem was associated with a variety of negative outcomes, including aggression, delinquency, poor health, and limited economic prospects through the middle adulthood years (Donnellan & others, 2005; Trzesniewski & others, 2006).

How can we resolve this apparent conflict between experimental evidence and longitudinal correlational evidence? One possibility is that individuals with high self-esteem might act aggressively in the artificial setting of a laboratory when given the chance to do so, but would not engage in actual aggressive behavior in real life. Another possibility is that Baumeister was talking about a particular kind of high self-esteem: inflated and unstable high self-esteem (W. K. Campbell & others, 2004; Konrath, Bushman, & Campbell, 2006). Individuals with unrealistically high self-esteem appear to be prone to react aggressively in response to a threat. Such individuals might be best described not as psychologically healthy but rather as narcissistic. For most people, though, it is more likely that low self-esteem rather than high self-esteem is linked to higher levels of aggression.

Do you know anyone who is aggressive? Do you think the person has high or low self-esteem?

Experimental and Control Groups

Experiments can involve one or more experimental groups and one or more control groups. In an experiment, the researcher manipulates the independent variable to create these groups. An **experimental group** consists of the participants in an experiment who receive, say, the drug or other treatment under study—that is, those who are exposed to the change that the independent variable represents. A **control group** in an experiment is as much like the experimental group as possible and is treated in every way like the experimental group except for that change. The control group provides a comparison against which the researcher can test the effects of the independent variable. In the study of meaning in life above, participants who listened to happy music were the experimental group, and those who heard neutral music were the control group.

To see how experimental and correlational research can be applied to the same research question, check out the Intersection.

- **experimental group** The participants in an experiment who receive the drug or other treatment under study—that is, those who are exposed to the change that the independent variable represents.

- **control group** The participants in an experiment who are as much like the experimental group as possible and who are treated in every way like the experimental group except for a manipulated factor, the independent variable.

Some Cautions about Experimental Research

Validity refers to the soundness of the conclusions that a researcher draws from an experiment. Two broad types of validity matter to experimental designs. The first is

external validity, which refers to the degree to which an experimental design actually reflects the real-world issues it is supposed to address. That is, external validity is concerned with the question, do the experimental methods and the results *generalize*—do they apply—to the real world?

Imagine, for example, that a researcher is interested in the influence of stress (the independent variable) on creative problem solving (the dependent variable). The researcher randomly assigns individuals to be blasted with loud noises at random times during the session (the high-stress or experimental group) or to complete the task in relative quiet (the control group). As the task, the researcher gives all participants a chance to be creative by asking them to list every use they can think of for a cardboard box. Counting up the number of uses that people list, the researcher discovers that those in the high-stress group generated fewer uses of the box. This finding might seem to indicate that stress reduces creativity. In considering the external validity of this study, however, we might appropriately ask some questions: How similar are the blasts of loud, random noises to the stresses people experience every day? Is listing uses for a cardboard box really an indicator of creativity? We are asking, in other words, if these operational definitions do a good job of reflecting the real-world processes they are supposed to represent.

The second type of validity is **internal validity,** which refers to the degree to which changes in the dependent variable are genuinely due to the manipulation of the independent variable. In the case of internal validity, we want to know whether the experimental methods are free from biases and logical errors that may render the results suspect. Although experimental research is a powerful tool, it requires safeguards (Leary, 2008). Expectations and biases can, and sometimes do, tarnish results (Ray, 2009; Rosnow & Rosenthal, 2008), as we next consider.

EXPERIMENTER BIAS

Experimenters may subtly (and often unknowingly) influence their research participants. **Experimenter bias** occurs when the experimenter's expectations influence the outcome of the research. No one designs an experiment without wanting meaningful results. Consequently, experimenters can sometimes subtly communicate to participants what they want the participants to do. **Demand characteristics** are any aspects of a study that communicate to participants how the experimenter wants them to behave. The influence of experimenter expectations can be very difficult to avoid.

In a classic study, Robert Rosenthal (1966) turned college students into experimenters. He randomly assigned the participants rats from the same litter. Half of the students were told that their rats were "maze bright," whereas the other half were told that their rats were "maze dull." The students then conducted experiments to test their rats' ability to navigate mazes. The results were stunning. The so-called maze-bright rats were more successful than the maze-dull rats at running the mazes. The only explanation for the results is that the college students' expectations, conveyed in their behaviors, affected the rats' performance.

Often the participants in psychological studies are not rats but people. Imagine that you are an experimenter, and you know that a participant is going to be exposed to disgusting pictures in a study. Is it possible that you might treat the person differently than you would if you were about to show him photos of cute kittens? The reason experimenter bias is important is that it introduces systematic differences between the experimental group and the control groups; this means that we cannot know if those who looked at disgusting pictures were more, say, upset because of the pictures or because of different treatment by the experimenter.

Like third variables in correlational research, these systematic biases are called *confounds*. In experimental research, confounds are factors that "ride along" with the experimental manipulation, systematically and undesirably influencing the dependent variable. Experimenter bias, demand characteristics, and confounds may all lead to biased results.

RESEARCH PARTICIPANT BIAS AND THE PLACEBO EFFECT

Like experimenters, research participants may have expectations about what they are supposed to do and how they should behave, and these expectations may affect the

● **external validity** The degree to which an experimental design actually reflects the real-world issues it is supposed to address.

● **internal validity** The degree to which changes in the dependent variable are due to the manipulation of the independent variable.

● **experimenter bias** Occurs when the experimenter's expectations influence the outcome of the research.

● **demand characteristics** Any aspects of a study that communicate to the participants how the experimenter wants them to behave.

"We close at six!"

Advertisements for prescription drugs usually describe not only the side effects on people taking the actual drug but also the effects experienced by individuals receiving a placebo.

● **research participant bias** Occurs when the behavior of research participants during the experiment is influenced by how they think they are supposed to behave or their expectations about what is happening to them.

● **placebo effect** Occurs when participants' expectations, rather than the experimental treatment, produce an outcome.

● **placebo** In a drug study, a harmless substance that has no physiological effect, given to participants in a control group so that they are treated identically to the experimental group except for the active agent.

● **double-blind experiment** An experimental design in which neither the experimenter nor the participants are aware of which participants are in the experimental group and which are in the control group until the results are calculated.

results of experiments (Christensen, 2007). **Research participant bias** occurs when the behavior of research participants during the experiment is influenced by how they think they are supposed to behave or by what their expectations are about what is happening to them.

One example of the power of participant expectations is the placebo effect. The **placebo effect** occurs when participants' expectations, rather than the experimental treatment, produce a particular outcome. Participants in a drug study might be assigned to an experimental group that receives a pill containing an actual painkiller or to a control group that receives a placebo pill. A **placebo** is a harmless substance that has no physiological effect. This placebo is given to participants in a control group so that they are treated identically to the experimental group except for the active agent—in this case, the painkiller. Giving individuals in the control group a placebo pill allows researchers to determine whether changes in the experimental group are due to the active drug agent and not simply to participants' expectations.

Another way to ensure that neither the experimenter's nor the participants' expectations affect the outcome is to design a **double-blind experiment.** In this design, neither the experimenter administering the treatment nor the participants are aware of which participants are in the experimental group and which are in the control group until the results are calculated. This setup ensures that the experimenter cannot, for example, make subtle gestures signaling who is receiving a drug and who is not. A double-blind study allows researchers to distinguish the specific effects of the independent variable from the possible effects of the experimenter's and the participants' expectations about it.

4-4 APPLICATIONS OF THE THREE TYPES OF RESEARCH

All three types of research—descriptive, correlational, and experimental—can be used to address the same topic (Figure 4.2). For instance, various researchers have used different research methods to explore the role of intensely positive experiences in human functioning, as follows.

Observation
Psychologists are using observational methods to examine President Obama's inaugural address, focusing on the words he used and the themes he stressed to make predictions about his presidency. Other observational data might include facial expressions of the crowd during the inaugural ceremony and the content of various post-election blogs.

Survey and Interview
Researchers can use surveys and telephone interviews to track popular approval of the president and to gauge public support for his various initiatives and programs. Survey research can also probe how different demographic groups (for example, African Americans and Euro-Americans) might differ in their expectations about the president.

Case Study
President Obama has published two autobio-graphical books, *The Audacity of Hope* and *Dreams from My Father*. These works provide valuable data for psychologists who are interested in using case studies to understand his life story and his path to presidential office.

Correlational Research
Correlational research can track the ways that attitudes toward African Americans may have changed with Obama's candidacy and election. In addition, examining the aspirations of children of various ethnicities before and after the election allows psychologists to study the influence of this new role model on American children.

Experimental Research
Psychologists interested in attitudes and behaviors toward different ethnic groups can use images of President Obama in experimental research to examine how visual reminders of the president influence such attitudes and behaviors.

FIGURE 4.2 **Psychology's Research Methods Applied to Studying President Barack Obama** Psychologists can apply very different methods to study the same phenomenon. The historic election of Barack Obama, the first African American president, opened up a host of new research questions for psychologists.

Abraham Maslow believed that people who were the healthiest and the happiest were capable of having intense moments of awe; he used the descriptive case study approach (1971) to examine the role of such "peak experiences" in the lives of such individuals, who seemed to enjoy the best of life. In contrast, Dan McAdams (2001) used correlational research to probe individuals' descriptions of their most powerful positive experiences. He found that individuals who were motivated toward warm interpersonal experiences tended to mention such experiences as the best memories of their lives. Finally, experimental researchers have also investigated this topic by randomly assigning individuals to write about their most intensely positive experiences for a few minutes each day for two or three days. Those who wrote about emotional and happy topics experienced enhanced positive mood as well as fewer physical illnesses two months later, as compared to individuals in control groups who wrote about topics that were not emotional (Burton & King, 2004, 2008). So, researchers coming from many different methodological perspectives can address the same topic, leading to different but valuable contributions to knowledge.

SUMMARY

Three types of research commonly used in psychology are descriptive research (finding out about the basic dimensions of some variable), correlational research (finding out if and how two variables change together), and experimental research (determining the causal relationship between variables). Descriptive research includes observation, surveys, interviews, and case studies. Correlational research often includes surveys and interviews as well as observation. Experimental research often occurs in a lab but can also be done in a natural setting.

In an experiment, the independent variable is manipulated to see if it produces changes in the dependent variable. An experiment involves comparing two groups: the experimental group (the one that receives the treatment or manipulation of the independent variable) and the control group (the comparison group or baseline that is equal to the experimental group in every way except for the independent variable). Experimental research relies on random assignment to ensure that the groups are roughly equivalent before the manipulation of the independent variable.

KEY TERMS

descriptive research   34
case study or case history   35
correlational research   37
third variable problem   37
longitudinal design   39
experiment   40
random assignment   41
independent variable   41
confederate   41
dependent variable   41
experimental group   42

control group   42
external validity   43
internal validity   43
experimenter bias   43
demand characteristics   43
research participant bias   44
placebo effect   44
placebo   44
double-blind experiment   44

TEST YOURSELF

1. Define descriptive, correlational, and experimental research.
2. Explain why correlation is not the same as causation.
3. What is the difference between an experimental group and a control group?

APPLY YOUR KNOWLEDGE

1. It's time to get out those old photos from the prom, wedding, or family reunion and see just how happy people were (or weren't). Look at some pictures from your own life and see who was genuinely smiling and who was faking it. Just cover the mouths with your finger—you can see who is happy from their eyes.

2. Is an old diary of yours hanging around somewhere? Pull it out and take a look at what you wrote. Count up your positive emotion words or negative emotion words. Are there themes in your diary from years ago that are still relevant to your life today? Does looking at your own diary change the way you might think about the results of the Nun Study? Explain.

How Psychological Research Is Conducted

In addition to considering the type of research to be conducted, a psychologist needs to plan for how to collect the data and how to analyze the data. This module takes a close look at both of these activities as well as the role of ethics in conducting research.

5·1 RESEARCH SAMPLES AND SETTINGS

Regardless of whether a study is correlational or experimental, among the important decisions to be made when collecting data are whom to choose as the participants and where to conduct the research. Will the participants be people or animals? Will they be children, adults, or both? Where will the research take place—in a lab or in a natural setting?

The Research Sample

When psychologists conduct a study, they usually want to be able to draw conclusions that will apply to a larger group of people than the participants they actually study. The entire group about which the investigator wants to draw conclusions is the **population.** The subset of the population chosen by the investigator for study is a **sample.** The researcher might be interested only in a particular group, such as all children who are gifted and talented, all young women who embark on science and math careers, or all gay men. The key is that the sample studied must be representative of the population to which the investigator wants to generalize his or her results. That is, the researcher might study only 100 gifted adolescents, but he or she wants to apply these results to all gifted and talented adolescents. A representative sample for the United States would reflect the U.S. population's age, socioeconomic status, ethnic origins, marital status, geographic location, religion, and so forth.

To mirror the population as closely as possible, the researcher uses a **random sample,** a sample that gives every member of the population an equal chance of being selected. Random sampling improves the chances that the sample is representative of the population. In actual practice, however, random sampling typically only *approximates* this

● **population** The entire group about which the investigator wants to draw conclusions.

● **sample** The subset of the population chosen by the investigator for study.

● **random sample** A sample that gives every member of the population an equal chance of being selected.

The research sample might include a particular group, such as all gay men or all women runners.

ideal—for example, by randomly sampling people who have telephones or people who live in a particular town or state. Note that a random sample is *not* the same thing as random assignment. Random assignment is about making sure experimental and control groups are equivalent, and a random sample is about selecting participants from a population so that the sample is representative of that population.

In selecting a sample, researchers must strive to minimize bias, including gender bias. Because psychology is the scientific study of human behavior, it should pertain to *all* humans, and so the participants in psychological studies ought to be representative of humanity as a whole. Early research in the field often included just the male experience—not only because the researchers themselves were often male, but also because the participants too were typically male (Etaugh & Bridges, 2010). For a long time, the human experience studied by psychologists was primarily the male experience.

There is also a growing realization that psychological research needs to include more people from diverse ethnic groups (Swanson, Edwards, & Spencer, 2010; Tamis-LeMonda & McFadden, 2010). Because a great deal of psychological research involves college student participants, individuals from groups that have not had as many educational opportunities have not been strongly represented in that research. Given the fact that individuals from diverse ethnic groups have been excluded from psychological research for so long, we might reasonably conclude that people's real lives are more varied than past research data have indicated.

These issues are important because scientists want to be able to predict human behavior broadly speaking, not just the behavior of non-Latino White, male college students. Imagine if policymakers planned their initiatives for a wide range of Americans based on research derived from only a small group of individuals from a particular background. What might the results be?

The Research Setting

All three types of research we examined in the preceding section can take place in different physical settings. The setting of the research does not determine the type of research it is. Common settings include the research laboratory and natural settings.

Because psychological researchers often want to control as many aspects of the situation as possible, they conduct much of their research in a laboratory—a controlled setting with many of the complex factors of the real world, including potential

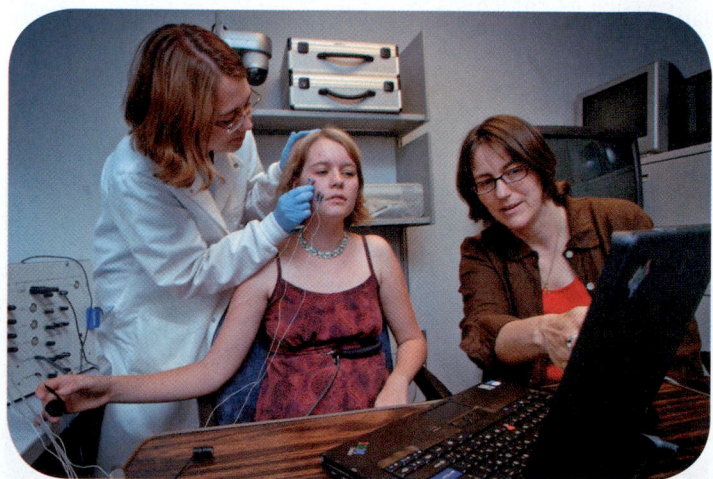

Natural settings and laboratories are common locales for psychological studies. (Left) Jane Goodall, who specializes in animal behavior, has carried out extensive research on chimpanzees in natural settings. Her work has contributed a great deal to our understanding of these intelligent primates. (Right) Barbara L. Fredrickson, a psychologist at the University of North Carolina, Chapel Hill, whose work investigates topics such as positive emotions and human flourishing, conducts a laboratory study.

confounds, removed (Kantowitz, Roediger, & Elmes, 2009). Although laboratory research provides a great deal of control, doing research in the laboratory has drawbacks. First, it is almost impossible to conduct research in the lab without the participants knowing they are being studied. Second, the laboratory setting is not the real world and therefore can cause the participants to behave unnaturally. A third drawback of laboratory research is that individuals who are willing to go to a university laboratory may not be representative of groups from diverse cultural backgrounds. Those who are unfamiliar with university settings and with the idea of "helping science" may be intimidated by the setting. Fourth, some aspects of the mind and behavior are difficult if not impossible to examine in the laboratory.

Research can also take place in a natural setting. **Naturalistic observation** is viewing behavior in a real-world setting (Leedy & Ormrod, 2010). Psychologists conduct naturalistic observations at sporting events, child-care centers, work settings, shopping malls, and other places that people frequent. If you wanted to study the level of civility on your campus for a research project, most likely you would include naturalistic observation of how people treat one another in such gathering places as the cafeteria and the library reading room. In another example of a natural setting, researchers who use survey methods are increasingly relying on web-based assessments that allow participants to complete the measures using the Internet.

● **naturalistic observation** The observation of behavior in a real-world setting.

The type of research a psychologist conducts, the operational definitions of the variables of interest, and the choice of sample and setting are decisions that ideally are guided by the research question itself. However, sometimes these decisions represent a compromise between the psychologist's key objective (for example, to study a representative sample of Americans) and the available resources (for instance, a sample of 100 college students). For a closer look at the process of conducting an experiment in a real-world setting, check out the Psychological Inquiry.

5-2 ANALYZING AND INTERPRETING DATA

Once psychologists collect data, whether they do so in a lab or a natural setting, it is time to analyze and interpret them. For this task they use *statistics,* mathematical methods for reporting data (Howell, 2010). There are two basic categories of statistics: descriptive statistics, which are used to describe and summarize data, and inferential statistics, which are used to draw conclusions about those data.

Psychology students are sometimes surprised to learn that a statistics course is often a requirement for the major. In this section, as we look at how psychologists analyze and interpret research data, you will get a flavor of the ways in which math plays an important role in the science of psychology.

Descriptive Statistics

Most psychological studies generate considerable numerical data. Simply listing all of the scores (or other measures) generated by a study—for each individual in the study—is not very meaningful. **Descriptive statistics** are the mathematical procedures researchers have developed to describe and summarize sets of data in a meaningful way. Descriptive statistics reveal the "big picture"—the overall characteristics of the data and the variation among them.

● **descriptive statistics** Mathematical procedures that are used to describe and summarize sets of data in a meaningful way.

MEASURES OF CENTRAL TENDENCY

A *measure of central tendency* is a single number that indicates the overall characteristics of a set of data. The three measures of central tendency are the mean, the median, and the mode.

psychological *inquiry*

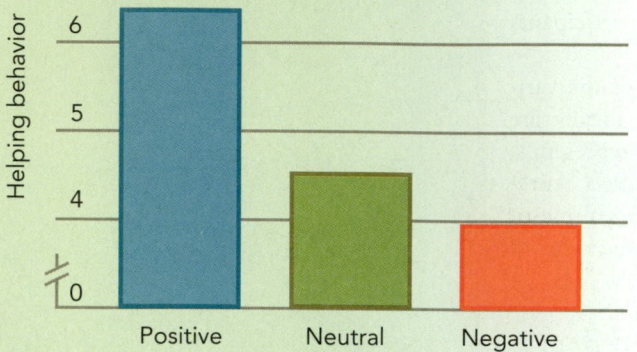

Target Employee Helping as a Function of Mood Condition

Adapted from Forgas, Dunn, & Granland, 2008.

Experimentation in a Natural Setting

A team of social psychologists was interested in examining how mood influences helping behavior in the real world. They hypothesized that, especially among the less experienced members of a sales staff, mood would guide behavior, so that happy salespersons would be most helpful to customers and unhappy salespersons less so. Researchers Joseph Forgas, Elizabeth Dunn, and Stacey Granland (2008) conducted an experiment in a Target department store, as follows.

First, the experimenters trained two confederates. The first confederate was in charge of manipulating the employees' mood. There were three mood conditions:

- In the *positive mood condition,* the confederate said, "I just wanted to let someone know that I am so impressed with the service at this store! The store looks great and the staff is so nice. I was able to get what I wanted and will be coming back to this store again."

- In the *negative mood condition,* the confederate said, "I just wanted to let someone know that I am so disappointed with the service at this store. The store looks terrible and the staff is rude. I couldn't get anything I wanted and won't be coming back here again."

- In the *neutral mood condition,* the confederate simply observed, "Interesting, I have been coming here quite regularly and this store seems always the same, nothing much changes."

Employees were chosen randomly by the confederate and were randomly assigned to the conditions.

Then, after the first confederate left the employees, the second confederate, who was blind to the mood procedure (meaning unaware of the mood condition for each participant), approached the employees individually and asked, "Excuse me, could you tell me where I could find the book *The White Bear*?" This confederate surreptitiously recorded (1) the number of helpful responses, (2) the number of actual attempts to help, and (3) the time spent helping. These three values were averaged to create an overall helpfulness score. (If the staff salesperson saw the confederate jotting things down, the confederate pretended to be checking a shopping list.) The figure shows the results for the less experienced sales staff.

Answer these questions to see how much you remember about experimental design.

1. Despite the natural setting, this was an experiment. Why?

2. What was the independent variable and what was its operational definition?

3. What was the dependent variable and what was its operational definition?

4. Why is it important that the second confederate was "blind" to the mood condition?

5. Why were the employees assigned to mood condition randomly?

6. The store management was aware of the study, but the employees were not. Do you think the experiment was ethical? Why or why not?

Most quantitative techniques in psychological science begin with the mean. The **mean** is what people often call the average. The mean is calculated by adding all the scores in a set of scores and then dividing by the number of scores. As a good indicator of the central tendency for a group of scores, the mean is the measure that is used most often. When your instructor provides students with their exam grades, he or she might mention the test mean, because this average gives the class a general idea of how the group performed.

● **mean** A measure of central tendency that is the average for a sample.

The mean is not so helpful, however, when a group of scores contains a few extreme scores, especially if the number of cases in the group is small. Consider the annual earnings for the two groups of five people shown in the table below.

Group 1	Group 2
$19,000	$19,000
19,000	19,000
23,000	23,000
24,000	24,000
25,000	45,000,000
Mean $22,000	Mean $9,017,000
Median $23,000	Median $23,000
Mode $19,000	Mode $19,000

Group 1 lists the earnings of five ordinary people. Group 2 is composed of the earnings of four ordinary people plus the approximate earnings of movie director Steven Spielberg. Now look at the means that have been calculated for the two groups. The vast difference between them is due to the one extreme score. In such a situation, one of the other two measures of central tendency, the median or the mode, would give a more accurate picture of the data overall.

The **median** is the score that falls exactly in the middle of the distribution of scores after they have been arranged (or ranked) from highest to lowest. When you have an odd number of scores (say, five or seven), the median is the score with the same number of scores above it as below it. In the table above, each group has a median income of $23,000. Notice that, unlike the mean, the median is unaffected by extreme scores. The medians are the same for both groups ($23,000), but their means are extremely different ($22,000 versus $9,017,000). Of course, if there is an even number of scores, there is no "middle" score. This problem is dealt with by averaging the scores that share the middle location.

● **median** A measure of central tendency that is the middle score in a sample.

● **mode** A measure of central tendency that is the most common score in a sample.

The **mode** is the score that occurs most often in a dataset. In our earnings example, the mode is $19,000, which occurs twice in each group. All of the other annual incomes occur only once. The mode is the least used measure of central tendency. Yet the mode can be particularly useful, for example, in cases in which information is desired about preference or popularity. Consider a teacher who wants to know the most popular or least popular child in her classroom. She might create a questionnaire and ask students which of their classmates they like the most or the least. The most frequently nominated child would be the mode in these instances.

MEASURES OF DISPERSION

In addition to revealing the central characteristics of a sample, descriptive statistics can also give us *measures of dispersion,* which describe how much the scores in a sample differ from one another. That is, these measures give us a sense of the spread of scores, or how much variability exists in the data. Let's look at some common ways that researchers measure dispersion.

To begin, suppose that four students rate their positive mood on a scale from 1 (not at all positive) to 7 (extremely positive), as follows:

Positive Mood

Sarah	7
Sun Mee	6
Josh	2
Rodney	5

● **range** A measure of dispersion that is the difference between the highest and lowest scores.

(You might note that the mean for these data is 20/4, or 5.) One common measure of dispersion is the **range,** which is the distance between the highest and the lowest scores. In the example above, the range in positive mood is 5 (that is, the highest score, 7, minus the lowest score, 2). Generally speaking, the range is a rather simplistic estimate of the variability within a group of scores. Because the range takes into account only the lowest and highest scores, it can produce a misleading picture of how different from one another scores in the dataset actually are. Note that for positive mood, most people in the example have fairly similar high scores, but using the range alone gives the impression that scores are very widely dispersed.

● **standard deviation** A measure of dispersion that tells us how much scores in a sample differ from the mean of the sample.

A more informative measure of dispersion, and the one most commonly used in psychological research, is the standard deviation. The **standard deviation** measures how much scores vary, on average, around the mean of the sample. There is a little hitch, however. One of the mathematical properties of the mean is that if you add up each person's difference from the mean, the sum will always be 0. So, we cannot calculate the average difference (or deviation) from the mean and get a meaningful answer.

To get around this problem, we take each person's difference from the mean and multiply it by itself. This removes the negative numbers, and the sum of these differences will no longer equal 0. We add these squared deviations together and then divide by the number of cases (minus 1). Finally, we take the square root of that number. Essentially, then, the standard deviation is the square root of the average squared deviation from the mean. The smaller the standard deviation, the less variability in the dataset. A small standard deviation indicates that, on average, scores are close to the mean.

The following table presents the information needed to calculate the standard deviation for the positive mood ratings given above.

Participant	A Rating	B Difference from the mean (5)	C *Squared* difference from the mean (5)
Sarah	7	2	4
Sun Mee	6	1	1
Josh	2	–3	9
Rodney	5	0	0
MEAN = $\frac{(7 + 6 + 2 + 5)}{4}$ = 5.0		Sum of this column = 0	Sum of these differences = 4 + 1 + 9 + 0 = 14

Column A presents the ratings by each participant. Column B shows the differences of these scores from the mean (5). Notice that if we add up Column B, the answer is 0. Column C shows the squared deviations from the mean for each participant. Adding up those squared differences, we get 14. Next, we divide 14 by the number of participants minus 1, in this case 14 divided by 3 = 4.67, and then we take the square root of that number, which is 2.16. This is the standard deviation of our sample, which, compared to the range of 5, tells us that the group is actually fairly closely arranged around the mean.

The mean and standard deviation together yield a lot of information about a sample. Indeed, given the raw scores, the means, and the standard deviations of two variables, we can calculate the correlation coefficient in no time. The correlation coefficient is not a descriptive statistic but rather an inferential statistic, our next topic.

Inferential Statistics

Imagine that, inspired by the research of Lee Anne Harker and Dacher Keltner on college yearbooks (see p. 29), you conduct a study on the relationship between expressions of positive emotion and interpersonal success. In your project, you video-record job candidates being interviewed, code the videos for Duchenne smiling by the candidates, and document which of the job seekers were called back for a second interview. Let's say you calculate that the mean number of smiles for candidates who were not called back was 3.5, and the mean number of smiles for candidates who were called back was 6.5. So, those who were called back generated, on average, 3 more smiles than those who were not called back. Does that difference matter? It seems pretty big, but is it big enough? Could we have obtained the same difference simply by chance?

To draw conclusions about differences we observe in studies, we want to know that the difference is likely to be one that can be replicated or found consistently in a variety of studies. Inferential statistics are the tools that help us to state whether a difference is unlikely to be the result of chance. More specifically, **inferential statistics** are the mathematical methods used to indicate whether data sufficiently support a research hypothesis (Kiess & Green, 2010).

The logic behind inferential statistics is relatively simple. Inferential statistics yield a statement of probability about the differences observed between two or more groups; this probability statement gives the odds that the observed differences were due simply to chance. In psychological research the standard is that if the odds are 5 out of 100 (or .05) or less that the differences are due to chance, the results are considered *statistically significant*. In statistical language, this is referred to as the .05 level of statistical significance, or the .05 confidence level. Put another way, statistical significance means that the differences observed between two groups are large enough that it is highly unlikely that those differences are merely due to chance. The .05 level of statistical significance is considered the minimum level of probability that scientists will accept for concluding that the differences observed are real, thereby supporting a hypothesis.

Recall that although we study a sample, we typically wish to generalize our findings to a population. Inferential statistics are the bridge between a sample and a population, because they tell us the likelihood that the results we found with a sample reflect differences in the larger population. It makes sense that the larger our sample is, the more likely it is to represent that population. Thus, significance tests are based in part on the number of cases in a sample. The higher the number of cases, the easier it is to get statistical significance. As a result, with a very large sample, even very small differences may be significant.

However, statistical significance is not the same thing as real-world significance. Even if a difference is found to be statistically significant, its real-world value remains to be evaluated by critically thinking scientists.

● **inferential statistics** Mathematical methods that are used to indicate whether results for a sample are likely to generalize to a population.

Being part of a research study can potentially lead to unintended consequences for the participants. After taking part in a study of young dating couples (Rubin & Mitchell, 1976), some participants identified problems in their relationship and ended it.

5-3 CONDUCTING ETHICAL RESEARCH

Ethics is a crucial consideration for all science. This fact came to the fore in the aftermath of World War II, for example, when it became apparent that Nazi doctors had used concentration camp prisoners as unwilling participants in experiments. These atrocities spurred scientists to develop a code of appropriate behavior—a set of principles about the treatment that participants in research have a right to expect. In general, ethical principles of research focus on balancing the rights of the participants with the rights of scientists to ask important research questions (Smith & Davis, 2010).

The issue of ethics in psychological research may affect you personally if at some point you participate in a study. In that event, you need to know your rights as a participant and the researchers' responsibilities in ensuring that these rights are safeguarded. Experiences in research can have unforeseen effects on people's lives.

One investigation of young dating couples asked them to complete a questionnaire that coincidentally stimulated some of the participants to think about potentially troublesome issues in the relationship (Rubin & Mitchell, 1976). One year later, when the researchers followed up with the original sample, 9 of 10 participants said they had discussed their answers with their dating partners. In most instances, the discussions helped to strengthen the relationships. In some cases, however, the participants used the questionnaire as a springboard to discuss problems or concerns previously hidden. One participant said, "The study definitely played a role in ending my relationship with Larry." In this case, the couple had different views about how long they expected to be together. She was thinking of a short-term dating relationship, whereas he was thinking in terms of a lifetime. Their answers to the questions brought the disparity in their views to the surface and led to the end of their relationship. Researchers have a responsibility to anticipate the personal problems their study might cause and, at least, to inform the participants of the possible fallout.

Ethics comes into play in every psychological study. Even smart, conscientious students sometimes think that members of their church, athletes in the Special Olympics, or residents of the local nursing home present great samples for psychological research. Without proper permission, though, the most well-meaning, kind, and considerate researchers still violate the rights of the participants.

Ethics Guidelines

A number of guidelines have been developed to ensure that research is conducted ethically. At the base of all of these guidelines is the notion that a person participating in psychological research should be no worse off coming out of the study than he or she was on the way in.

Today colleges and universities have a review board (typically called the *institutional review board,* or *IRB*) that evaluates the ethical nature of research conducted at their institutions. Proposed research plans must pass the scrutiny of a research ethics committee before the research can be initiated. In addition, the American Psychological Association (APA) has developed ethics guidelines for its members. The code of ethics instructs psychologists to protect their participants from mental and physical harm. The participants' best interests need to be kept foremost in the researcher's mind (Gravetter, 2009; Ray, 2009). The APA's guidelines address four important issues:

- *Informed consent:* All participants must know what their participation will involve and what risks might develop. For example, participants in a study on dating should be told beforehand that a questionnaire might stimulate thoughts about issues in their relationships that they have not considered. Participants also should be informed that in some instances a discussion of the issues might improve their relationships but that in others it might worsen the relationships and even end them. Even after informed consent is given, participants must retain the right to withdraw from the study at any time and for any reason.

- *Confidentiality:* Researchers are responsible for keeping all of the data they gather on individuals completely confidential and, when possible, completely anonymous. Confidential data are not the same as anonymous. When data are confidential, it is possible to link a participant's identity to his or her data.

- *Debriefing:* After the study has been completed, the researchers should inform the participants of its purpose and the methods they used. In most cases, the experimenters also can inform participants in a general manner beforehand about the purpose of the research without leading the participants to behave in a way that they think that the experimenters are expecting. When preliminary information about the study is likely to affect the results, participants can at least be debriefed after the study's completion.

- *Deception:* This is an ethical issue that psychologists debate extensively. In some circumstances, telling the participants beforehand what the research study is about substantially alters the participants' behavior and invalidates the researcher's data. For example, suppose a psychologist wants to know whether bystanders will report a theft. A mock theft is staged, and the psychologist observes which bystanders report it. Had the psychologist informed the participants beforehand that the study intended to discover the percentage of bystanders who will report a theft, the whole study would have been ruined. Thus, the researcher deceives participants about the purpose of the study, perhaps leading them to believe that it has some other purpose. In all cases of deception, however, the psychologist must ensure that the deception will not harm the participants and that the participants will be told the true nature of the study (will be debriefed) as soon as possible after the study is completed.

The federal government also takes a role in ensuring that research involving human participants is conducted ethically. The Office for Human Research Protection is devoted to ensuring the well-being of participants in research studies. Over the years, the office has dealt with many challenging and controversial issues—among them, informed consent rules for research on mental disorders, regulations governing research on pregnant women and fetuses, and ethical issues regarding AIDS vaccine research.

For generations, psychologists have used animals in some research. Animal studies have provided a better understanding of and solutions for many human problems (Pinel, 2009). Neal Miller (1985), who has made important discoveries about the effects of biofeedback on health, listed the following areas in which animal research has benefited humans:

- Psychotherapy techniques and behavioral medicine
- Rehabilitation of neuromuscular disorders
- Alleviation of the effects of stress and pain
- Drugs to treat anxiety and severe mental illness
- Methods for avoiding drug addiction and relapse
- Treatments to help premature infants gain weight so they can leave the hospital sooner
- Methods used to alleviate memory deficits in old age

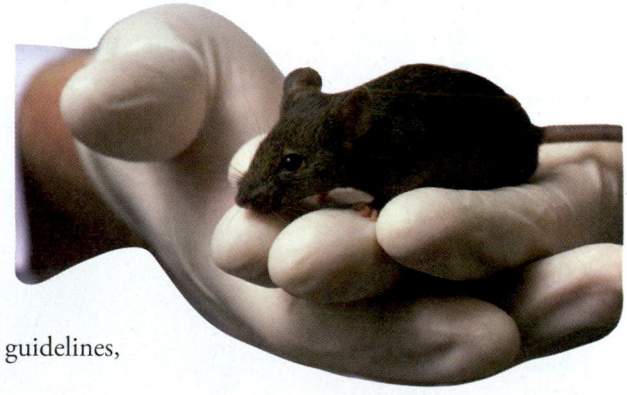

About 5 percent of APA members use animals in their research. Rats and mice account for 90 percent of all psychological research with animals. It is true that researchers sometimes use procedures with animals that would be unethical with humans, but they are guided by a set of standards for housing, feeding, and maintaining the psychological and physical well-being of their animal subjects. Researchers are required to weigh potential benefits of the research against possible harm to the animal and to avoid inflicting unnecessary pain. In short, researchers must follow stringent ethical guidelines, whether animals or humans are the subjects in their studies.

The Place of Values in Psychological Research

Questions are asked not only about the ethics of psychology but also about its values and its standards for judging what is worthwhile and desirable. Some psychologists argue that psychology should be value-free and morally neutral. From their perspective, the psychologist's role as a scientist is to present facts as objectively as possible. Others believe that because psychologists are human, they cannot possibly be value-free. Indeed, some people go so far as to argue that psychologists should take stands on certain issues. For example, psychological research shows that children reared by gay male and lesbian parents are no more likely to be gay than other children and tend to show levels of psychological health that are equal to or higher than those of children reared by heterosexual parents (Patterson & Hastings, 2007). To the extent that some have argued against the rights of gays and lesbians to adopt children or to retain custody of their biological children, psychologists may have a role to play in the debate about these issues.

To explore questions about the ethics of research further, read the Critical Controversy feature about reality TV.

CRITICAL CONTROVERSY

Would Reality TV Pass the Institutional Review Board?

Survivor, American Idol, Big Brother—these are just a few of the many popular reality shows that fill the U.S. television airwaves. While critics debate the quality of these shows, reality TV watchers may think that they are learning a lot about human nature by tuning in to see who will get voted off, who will willingly eat ground-up rats, or who will be ridiculed by the American Idol judges.

For you as a student of psychology, an appropriate question might be, would these reality TV shows ever gain the approval of the IRB of an institution of higher learning? This issue was of interest to Barbara Spellman, a founding member of the American Psychological Society Committee on Human Subject Protection, who examined reality TV programming with an eye toward the ethical issues these shows present. If we were to consider reality TV from the perspective of the APA ethical guidelines, at least five issues that Spellman (2005) identified would come to the fore.

First, how do reality shows achieve informed consent? The principle of informed consent means that all participants must know what their participation will involve and what risks might develop. Yet the very thing that makes reality shows exciting is the element of the unknown—the potential for surprise. Clearly the producers of Survivor are not going to inform contestants upfront that for their particular episode they will be asked to eat live bugs, because the element of shock and the dramatic moment of the decision would diminish greatly if it occurred off camera while the person perused the consent form. On the other hand, we might note that it is highly unlikely that anyone who participates on such a show has not watched a few episodes, and therefore most participants will have a pretty good idea that they must expect the unexpected.

A second, related problem with at least some reality shows is the use of deception. Fooling a group of women into believing that a semi-employed construction worker is actually a millionaire is probably not likely to satisfy APA ethical considerations.

A third issue that might arise is that of risk. Many reality shows pose a great deal of psychological and/or physical risk. Some reality shows include children (for example, Wife Swap), and it is very unlikely that an IRB would consider posing any kind of risk to children justified.

A fourth major stumbling block for reality TV is the potential for huge cash awards to compel people to behave in ways they would not otherwise do. Is it "really" lying if you are doing it in order to win a million dollars? If a person does something to "play the game" that he or she would never do outside of the game, haven't we shown that money has compelled the individual to act in ways he or she might later regret or be judged for?

Remember that ethical considerations involve balancing the rights of participants with the scientist's right to know. Thus, a fifth question pertinent to a study of reality TV is, what is the value of what we can learn from these "experiments"? This brings up the issue of how "natural" reality shows are. Are people truly themselves when the cameras are rolling?

Would Survivor gain the approval of your school's institutional review board?

WHAT DO YOU THINK?

- Do reality TV shows represent natural human behavior? Explain.
- What kind of reality show would you design if you were interested in exploring important psychological processes? What ethical safeguards would you build into the design to protect participants?

SUMMARY

Two important decisions that must be made for psychological research are whom to study and where to study them. A sample is the group that participates in a study; a population is the group to which the researcher wishes to generalize the results. A random sample is the best way of ensuring that the sample reflects the population.

Research settings include both the laboratory and real-world, naturalistic contexts. The laboratory allows a great deal of control, but naturalistic settings may give a truer sense of natural behavior.

Descriptive statistics are used to describe and summarize samples of data in a meaningful way. Two types of descriptive statistics are measures of central tendency and measures of variability. Measures of central tendency are the mean (or mathematical average), the median (the middle score), and the mode (the most common score). Measures of variability include the range (the difference between the highest and lowest scores) and the standard deviation (the square root of the average squared deviation from the mean).

Inferential statistics are used to draw conclusions about data. Inferential statistics aim to uncover statistical significance, which means that the differences observed between groups (or the correlation between variables) are unlikely to be the result of chance.

For all kinds of research, ethical treatment of participants is crucial. Participants should leave a psychological study no worse off than they were when they entered. Some guiding principles for ethical research in psychology include informed consent, confidentiality, debriefing (participants should be fully informed about the purpose of a study once it is over), and explaining fully the use of deception in a study.

KEY TERMS

population   47
sample   47
random sample   47
naturalistic observation   49
descriptive statistics   49
mean   51

median   51
mode   51
range   52
standard deviation   52
inferential statistics   53

TEST YOURSELF

1. With respect to a research study, what is meant by a population? What is a sample?
2. What is the difference between a random sample and random assignment?
3. What are two common physical settings for research?
4. What is meant by a measure of central tendency? Name three measures of central tendency.
5. What do measures of dispersion describe?
6. What does standard deviation measure?
7. What two things do the ethical principles used in research seek to balance?
8. With respect to the participants in a study, what do the various ethical guidelines covering research all fundamentally seek to protect?
9. What four key issues do the APA's ethics guidelines address?

APPLY YOUR KNOWLEDGE

1. The study of the Olympic athletes described earlier was a correlational study. Design an experiment that would test the prediction that those who finish second are likely to be less happy than those who finish third.
2. Pick a topic of interest to you and define the variables. Then list as many ways to operationalize the variables as you can. Come up with at least one behavioral measure of the variable. Would your topic be best studied using a correlational or an experimental method? How would you conduct the study?

The Scientific Method and Health and Wellness

The research of James Pennebaker of the University of Texas, Austin, probes the connections among traumatic life experience, expressive writing, physical and mental health, and work performance.

Throughout this book we examine a host of ways that psychological research has implications for health and wellness. In this concluding section, we focus on a research topic in which the scientific method has played a particularly important role in the conclusions drawn—the power of expressive writing to enhance health and wellness.

James Pennebaker has conducted a number of studies that converge on the same conclusion: that writing about one's deepest thoughts and feelings concerning one's most traumatic life event leads to a number of health and well-being benefits (Pennebaker & Chung, 2007). This research began with a correlational study comparing two groups of individuals—those who had lost a spouse to suicide and those who had lost a spouse to an accident (Pennebaker & O'Heeron, 1984). The results of the study showed that survivors of a suicide were more likely to have become sick in the months after the death, compared to accident survivors. Importantly, the difference was explained by the fact that individuals whose spouses had committed suicide were much less likely to talk about their loss, compared to the other participants.

These correlational findings led Pennebaker to wonder whether it might be possible to manipulate expressing one's thoughts and feelings about a traumatic event *experimentally* and thereby to receive the benefits of socially sharing the trauma. So, in subsequent studies, participants have been randomly assigned to write about one of two topics—either the individual's most traumatic life event or a relatively uninteresting topic (for example, his or her plans for the day). Assignment of the specific topic is meant to control for the act of writing itself so that the control group is as much like the experimental group as possible (Baddeley & Pennebaker, 2009; Pennebaker & Graybeal, 2001).

The participants write about the same topic for three or four consecutive days for about 20 minutes each day. Weeks or months after writing, participants in the trauma writing group have better physical health than those in the control group. Since the first traumatic writing study, a host of researchers have replicated these effects, showing that writing about trauma is associated with superior immune function, better response to a vaccine, higher psychological well-being, better adjustment to coming to college, and more quickly finding employment after being laid off from work (Lepore & Smyth, 2002; Pennebaker, 1997a, 1997b, 2004). Thus, we might conclude that documenting one's deepest thoughts and feelings about traumatic life events is necessary to attain the "healing power" of writing.

Note, however, that the participants in the trauma group were not just writing about a trauma. They were also documenting an important personal experience. Thinking about these results in terms of the internal validity of the conclusions, we might ask if focusing on a trauma is the key ingredient in producing health benefits. Might there be other, less negative aspects of life that are equally meaningful and that might promote good health when they are the subject of personal writing? Indeed, subsequent research shows that health benefits can emerge from writing about a variety of topics, including how one has grown from a negative experience (King & Miner, 2000; Low, Stanton, & Danoff-Burg, 2006), one's life dreams (King, 2001), and one's most intensely positive experiences (Burton & King, 2004, 2009). In a recent study, participants who wrote about either a traumatic life event or an extremely positive event for just two minutes a day over two days reported fewer illnesses a month later (Burton & King, 2008).

The body of evidence for the effects of expressive writing on health is substantial and has been subjected to two meta-analyses, the procedure described in Module 3. These meta-analyses indicate that individuals who write over days that are spaced apart tend to benefit most from writing, and that feeling distressed while writing is not necessary to enjoy these benefits (Frattaroli, 2006; Smyth, 1998).

If you would like to explore the healing power of writing in your own life, use the simple guidelines below:

- Find a quiet place to write.

- Pick just one topic to explore through writing.

- Dedicate yourself to a few minutes of writing each day, perhaps writing once a week for a few weeks.

- While writing, do not worry about punctuation, grammar, or spelling—just let yourself go and write about all of the thoughts, emotions, and feelings associated with the experience you are documenting.

- If you feel that writing about something negative is not for you, try writing about your most positive life experiences, the people you care about, or all the things for which you feel grateful.

The long and growing literature on the effects of expressive writing on health demonstrates how research methods influence the conclusions that scientists reach and how the process of scientific research builds from one study to the next. This literature also demonstrates how psychological research is relevant to the daily life of everyone with a story to write—and how an individual can benefit from writing that story.

SUMMARY

A great deal of psychological research has relevance to health and wellness. An example is research by James Pennebaker on the effects of expressive writing on health and well-being. This research has shown that individuals who are randomly assigned to write about a traumatic life event for a few minutes a day over three or four days show a host of health and well-being benefits compared to those in a control condition. Subsequent research has shown that these health benefits can be obtained by writing about very positive life experiences and even just writing for a couple of minutes.

This research demonstrates how a research question can begin as a correlational study and then move to the laboratory to demonstrate causation. When many studies have been done on a topic, a meta-analysis can provide a sense of the overall importance of the results. This example also shows how psychological research can have important implications for everyday life.

TEST YOURSELF

1. Briefly describe Pennebaker's initial correlational study comparing two groups of individuals who had lost a spouse.

2. What did Pennebaker's subsequent experimental research show?

3. What does the accumulated body of evidence indicate about the effects of expressive writing on health?

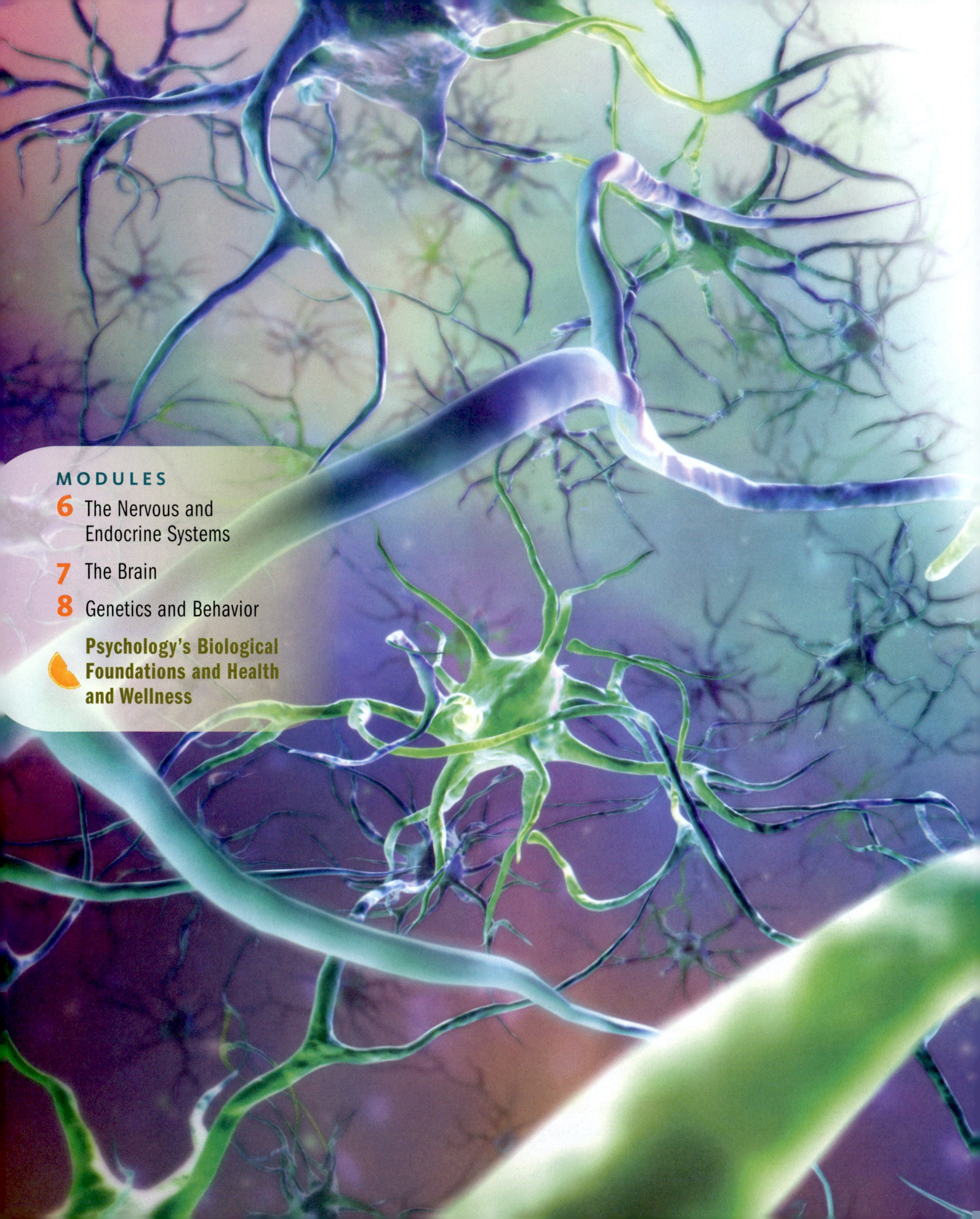

Biological Foundations of Behavior

Extraordinary Engine: The Human Brain

In August 2007, Adam Lepak was a first-year community college student who had spent the previous summer touring the country with his friends as a rock band. Late to class one morning, he sped along on his motorcycle. As he swerved to miss a car, he lost control of his bike and crashed.

After six months of lying unconscious, Adam began to regain awareness. When he did, the world was eerily different. Adam was convinced that his family and friends—who had waited patiently by his bedside, coaxing him to wake up—were impostors. Adam's accident had damaged the regions of his brain responsible for the warm glow of familiarity. Not only did Adam question the identities of his loved ones, but he also struggled to recognize that the young man looking at him in the mirror was himself (Carey, 2009).

Today Adam continues the difficult recovery. He has had to relearn how to walk and talk and struggled to regain the feeling of familiarity that provides human beings with a sense of self. He has to be reminded—and to remind himself repeatedly—that he had a motorcycle accident and that the "impostors" around him are in truth his mother, father, brother, and friends.

Adam's case illuminates the brain's role in the precious human experiences of having an identity and of feeling warmth toward others.

The brain is extraordinarily complex—both the object of study and the reason we are able to study it. ●

The Nervous and Endocrine Systems

As part of an exploration of the biological foundations of behavior, this module focuses on the body's communication systems. It begins by describing our nervous system before taking a closer look at neurons, the specialized cells that make up the communication network of the nervous system. Finally, the module describes the endocrine system, the collection of glands that regulate activities of certain organs by releasing chemical products into the blood stream.

6·1 THE NERVOUS SYSTEM

● **nervous system** The body's electrochemical communication circuitry.

The **nervous system** is the body's electrochemical communication circuitry. The field that studies the nervous system is called *neuroscience,* and the people who study it are *neuroscientists.*

The human nervous system is made up of billions of communicating nerve cells, and it is likely the most intricately organized aggregate of matter on the planet. A single cubic centimeter (about the size of a snack cube of cheese) of the human brain consists of well over 50 million nerve cells, each of which communicates with many other nerve cells in information-processing networks that make the most elaborate computer seem primitive.

Characteristics of the Nervous System

The brain and nervous system guide our interactions with the world around us, move the body through the world, and direct our adaptation to the environment. Several extraordinary characteristics allow the nervous system to command our behavior: complexity, integration, adaptability, and electrochemical transmission.

COMPLEXITY

The human brain and nervous system are enormously complex. The orchestration of the billions of nerve cells in the brain—to allow you to talk, write, sing, dance, and think—is awe inspiring. As you read this book, your brain is carrying out a multitude of functions, including seeing, reading, learning, and (we hope) breathing. Extensive assemblies of nerve cells participate in each of these activities, all at once.

As we dance, write, play sports, talk, think, and connect with the world in countless other ways, the brain and the nervous system guide our every interaction, movement, and adaptation.

INTEGRATION

Neuroscientist Steven Hyman (2001) has called the brain the "great integrator," meaning that the brain does a wonderful job of pulling information together. Think of everything going on around you right now, as well as the multitude of processes happening in your body—like breathing, the digestion of your last meal, the healing of a cut. Somehow, you need to make sense of all of these various stimuli. Similarly, the shapes on this page are not simply splashes of ink but letters, and those letters compose words that make sense. It is your brain that draws your experiences together into a coherent whole. Sounds, sights, touches, tastes, and smells—the brain integrates all of these sensory inputs so that you can function in the world.

The nervous system has different levels and many different parts. Brain activity is integrated across these levels through countless interconnections of brain cells and extensive pathways that link different parts of the brain and body. Each nerve cell communicates, on average, with 10,000 others, making an astronomical number of connections (Bloom, Nelson, & Lazerson, 2001). The evidence for these connections is observable, for example, when a loved one takes your hand. How does your brain know, and tell you, what has happened? Bundles of interconnected nerve cells relay information about the sensation in your hand through the nervous system in a very orderly fashion, all the way to the areas of the brain involved in recognizing that someone you love is holding your hand. Then the brain might send a reply and prompt your hand to give your loved one a little squeeze.

Sometimes the brain's attempts to make sense of experience go awry. Adam Lepak saw his mother's face without recognizing her, and his brain made sense of that experience by concluding that she must be a fake (Carey, 2009).

ADAPTABILITY

The world around us is constantly changing. To survive, we must adapt to new conditions. The brain and nervous system together serve as our agent for adapting to the world. Although nerve cells reside in certain brain regions, they are not unchanging structures. They have a hereditary, biological foundation, but they are constantly adapting to changes in the body and the environment (Coch, Fischer, & Dawson, 2007).

The term **plasticity** refers to the brain's special physical capacity for change. Adam Lepak's slow recovery demonstrates the brain's plasticity. Less dramatic examples of plasticity occur in all of us. For example, you might believe that thinking is a mental process, not a physical one. Yet thinking *is* a physical event, because every thought you have is reflected in physical activity in the brain. Moreover, the brain can be changed by experience. London cab drivers who have developed a familiarity with the city show increases in the size of the area of the brain thought to be responsible for reading maps (Maguire & others, 2000). Think about that: When you change the way you think, you are *literally* changing the brain's physical processes and even its shape. Our daily experiences contribute to the wiring or rewiring of the brain (Nelson, 2011), just as the experiences of those London cab drivers did.

● **plasticity** The brain's special capacity for change.

ELECTROCHEMICAL TRANSMISSION

The brain and the nervous system function essentially as an information-processing system powered by electrical impulses and chemical messengers (Chichilnisky, 2007). When an impulse travels down a nerve cell, or *neuron,* it does so electrically. When that impulse gets to the end of the line, it communicates with the next neuron using chemicals, as we will consider in detail later in this module.

Pathways in the Nervous System

As we interact with and adapt to the world, the brain and the nervous system receive and transmit sensory input (like sounds, smells, and flavors), integrate the information taken in from the environment, and direct the body's motor activities. Information flows into the brain through input from our senses, and the brain makes sense of that information, pulling it together and giving it meaning. In turn, information moves out of the brain to the rest of the body, directing all of the physical things we do (Fox, 2008).

The nervous system has specialized pathways that are adapted for different functions. These pathways are made up of afferent nerves, efferent nerves, and neural networks (discussed later in

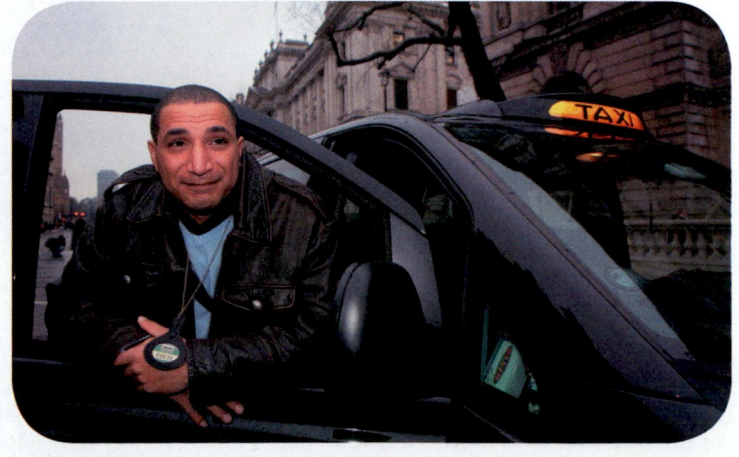

●**afferent nerves** Also called sensory nerves; nerves that carry information about the external environment *to* the brain and spinal cord via sensory receptors.

●**efferent nerves** Also called motor nerves; nerves that carry information *out of* the brain and spinal cord to other areas of the body.

●**central nervous system (CNS)** The brain and spinal cord.

●**peripheral nervous system (PNS)** The network of nerves that connects the brain and spinal cord to other parts of the body.

the module). **Afferent nerves,** or sensory nerves, carry information *to* the brain and spinal cord. These sensory pathways communicate information about the external environment (for example, the sight of a sunrise) and internal conditions (for example, fatigue or hunger) from sensory receptors to the brain and spinal cord. **Efferent nerves,** or motor nerves, carry information *out of* the brain and spinal cord—that is, they carry the nervous system's output. These motor pathways communicate information from the brain and spinal cord to other areas of the body, including muscles and glands, instructing them, in a sense, to get busy.

Divisions of the Nervous System

This truly elegant system is highly ordered and organized for effective function. Figure 6.1 shows the two primary divisions of the human nervous system: the central nervous system and the peripheral nervous system.

The **central nervous system (CNS)** is made up of the brain and spinal cord. More than 99 percent of all nerve cells in our body are located in the CNS (Brooker & others, 2010). The **peripheral nervous system (PNS)** is the network of nerves that connects the brain and spinal cord to other parts of the body. The functions of the peripheral nervous system are to bring information to and from the brain and spinal cord and to carry out the commands of the CNS to execute various muscular and glandular activities.

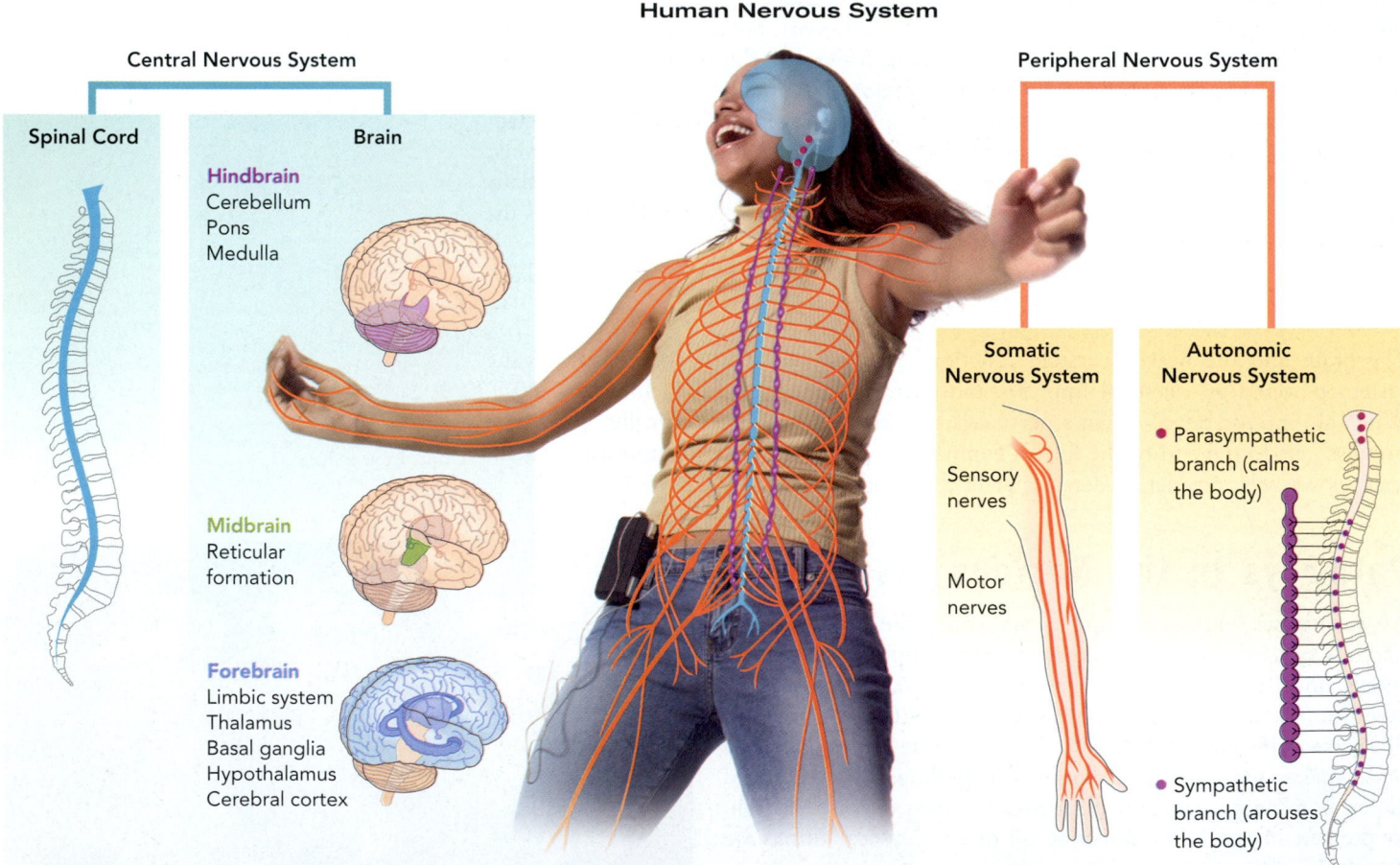

Human Nervous System

FIGURE 6.1 **Major Divisions of the Human Nervous System** The nervous system has two main divisions. One is the *central nervous system* (*left*), which comprises the brain and the spinal cord. The nervous system's other main division is the *peripheral nervous system* (*right*), which itself has two parts—the *somatic nervous system,* which controls sensory and motor neurons, and the *autonomic nervous system,* which monitors processes such as breathing, heart rate, and digestion. These complex systems work together to help us successfully navigate the world.

The peripheral nervous system has two major divisions: the somatic nervous system and the autonomic nervous system. The **somatic nervous system** consists of sensory nerves, whose function is to convey information from the skin and muscles to the CNS about conditions such as pain and temperature, and motor nerves, whose function is to tell the muscles what to do. The function of the **autonomic nervous system** is to take messages to and from the body's internal organs, monitoring such processes as breathing, heart rate, and digestion.

The autonomic nervous system also is divided into two parts. The first part, the **sympathetic nervous system,** arouses the body to mobilize it for action, while the second, the **parasympathetic nervous system,** calms the body. The sympathetic nervous system is involved in the "fight or flight" response, the body's reaction to a threat (an incident that you can either stay and fight or flee). When you feel your heart pounding and your hands sweating under stress, those experiences reveal the sympathetic nervous system in action. If you need to run away from a dangerous situation, the sympathetic nervous system sends blood out to your extremities to prepare you for taking off. The parasympathetic nervous system is responsible for the ways you calm down once you have escaped the danger.

In an emergency, the sympathetic nervous system also triggers the body's release of powerful hormones (Maggio & Segal, 2009). These stress hormones allow you to focus attention on what needs to be done *now*. For example, in an emergency, people sometimes report feeling strangely calm and doing what has to be done, whether calling 911 or applying pressure to a serious wound. Such experiences reveal the benefits of stress hormones for humans in times of acute emergency (Holsboer & Ising, 2010). We will revisit the relationship between the experience of stress and the nervous system in Psychology's Biological Foundations of Health and Wellness.

● **somatic nervous system** The body system consisting of the sensory nerves, whose function is to convey information from the skin and muscles to the CNS about conditions such as pain and temperature, and the motor nerves, whose function is to tell muscles what to do.

● **autonomic nervous system** The body system that takes messages to and from the body's internal organs, monitoring such processes as breathing, heart rate, and digestion.

● **sympathetic nervous system** The part of the autonomic nervous system that arouses the body.

● **parasympathetic nervous system** The part of the autonomic nervous system that calms the body.

6·2 NEURONS

Within each division of the nervous system, much is happening at the cellular level. Nerve cells, chemicals, and electrical impulses work together to transmit information at speeds of up to 330 miles per hour. As a result, information can travel from your brain to your hands (or vice versa) in a matter of milliseconds (Shier, Butler, & Lewis, 2010). Just how fast is 330 miles per hour? Consider that the NASCAR speed record was set in 1987 by Bill Elliott, who completed a lap driving at 212.8 miles per hour.

There are two types of cells in the nervous system: neurons and glial cells. **Neurons** are the nerve cells that handle information processing; we will generally concentrate on neurons in this module. The human brain contains about 100 billion neurons. The average neuron is a complex structure with as many as 10,000 physical connections with other cells. Recently, researchers have been particularly interested in a special type of neuron called a *mirror neuron*. Mirror neurons seem to play a role in imitation and are activated (in primates and humans) both when we perform an action and when we watch someone else perform that same activity (Hickok, 2010). In addition to imitation, mirror neurons are thought to be involved in language, especially speech (Yamazaki & others, 2010); new motor skills (Ferrari & others, 2009); empathy and understanding of others (Cattaneo & Rizzolatti, 2009); and the social behavior of children with autism, who have difficulty with language and social skills (Le Bel, Pineda, & Sharma, 2009).

The other cell type, **glial cells** (or *glia*), provides support, nutritional benefits, and other functions in the nervous system (Kriegstein & Alvarez-Buylla, 2009). Glia keep neurons running smoothly, and recent estimates indicate that there are about as many glia cells as neurons in the brain (Azevedo & others, 2009). You might think of the glial cells as the pit crew in the raceway of the nervous system.

Neuoroscientists know much less about the function of glial cells than neurons, but dramatic new discoveries have shed light on ways in which glial cells might be involved in behavior. Until recently, it was thought that glia do not have synapses or release neurotransmitters, both of which, as we will see, are crucial for neural transmission.

● **neurons** One of two types of cells in the nervous system; neurons are the nerve cells that handle the information-processing function.

● **glial cells** Also called glia; the second of two types of cells in the nervous system; glial cells provide support, nutritional benefits, and other functions and keep neurons running smoothly.

However, research now suggests that some glial cells are not just passive bystanders to neural transmission but may detect neural impulses and send signals to other glial cells (Chakraborty & others, 2010; Gao & Ji, 2010). Glial cells may play roles in memory (Wang & others, 2009); deterioration in Alzheimer disease (Erol, 2010); pain (Dubový & others, 2010; Gao & Ji, 2010); psychological disorders such as schizophrenia (Pantazopoulos & others, 2010) and mood disorders (Huang & others, 2009); and the development of neural stem cells (Lindvall & Kokaia, 2010), which we will examine later in this module. Still, by far the majority of information processing in the brain is done by neurons, not glial cells.

Specialized Cell Structure

Not all neurons are alike, as they are specialized to handle different functions. However, all neurons do have some common characteristics. Most neurons are created very early in life, but their shape, size, and connections can change throughout the life span. The way neurons function reflects the major characteristic of the nervous system described at the beginning of the module: plasticity. That is, neurons can and do change.

Every neuron has a cell body, dendrites, and an axon (Figure 6.2). The **cell body** contains the nucleus, which directs the manufacture of substances that the neuron needs for growth and maintenance. **Dendrites,** treelike fibers projecting from a neuron, receive information and orient it toward the neuron's cell body. Most nerve cells have numerous dendrites, which increase their surface area, allowing each neuron to receive input from many other neurons. The **axon** is the part of the neuron that carries information away from the cell body toward other cells. (Remember that *axon* and *away* both start with the letter *a*). Although extremely thin (1/10,000th of an inch—a human hair by comparison is 1/1,000th of an inch), axons can be very long, with many branches. In fact, some extend more than 3 feet—all the way from the top of the brain to the base of the spinal cord. Finally, covering all surfaces of the neurons, including the dendrites and axons, is a very thin cellular membrane that allows substances to move in and out of the cell. We will examine this membrane and its functions in more detail later.

A **myelin sheath,** a layer of cells containing fat, encases and insulates most axons. By insulating the axons, myelin sheaths speed up transmission of nerve impulses (Diamond, 2009). The sheer size of the human brain and body make the myelin sheaths

● **cell body** The part of the neuron that contains the nucleus, which directs the manufacture of substances that the neuron needs for growth and maintenance.

● **dendrites** Treelike fibers projecting from a neuron, which receive information and orient it toward the neuron's cell body.

● **axon** The part of the neuron that carries information away from the cell body toward other cells.

● **myelin sheath** A layer of fat cells that encases and insulates most axons.

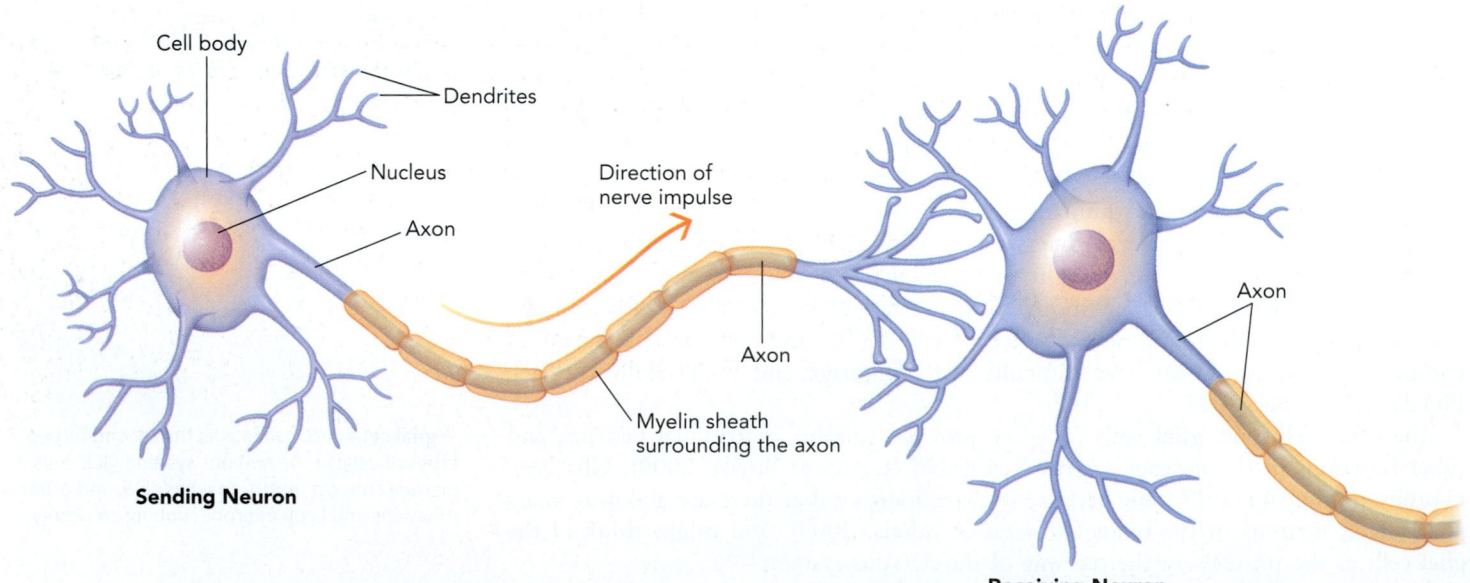

FIGURE 6.2   The Neuron The drawing shows the parts of a neuron and the connection between one neuron and another. Note the cell body, the branching of dendrites, and the axon with a myelin sheath.

Touring the Nervous System and the Brain

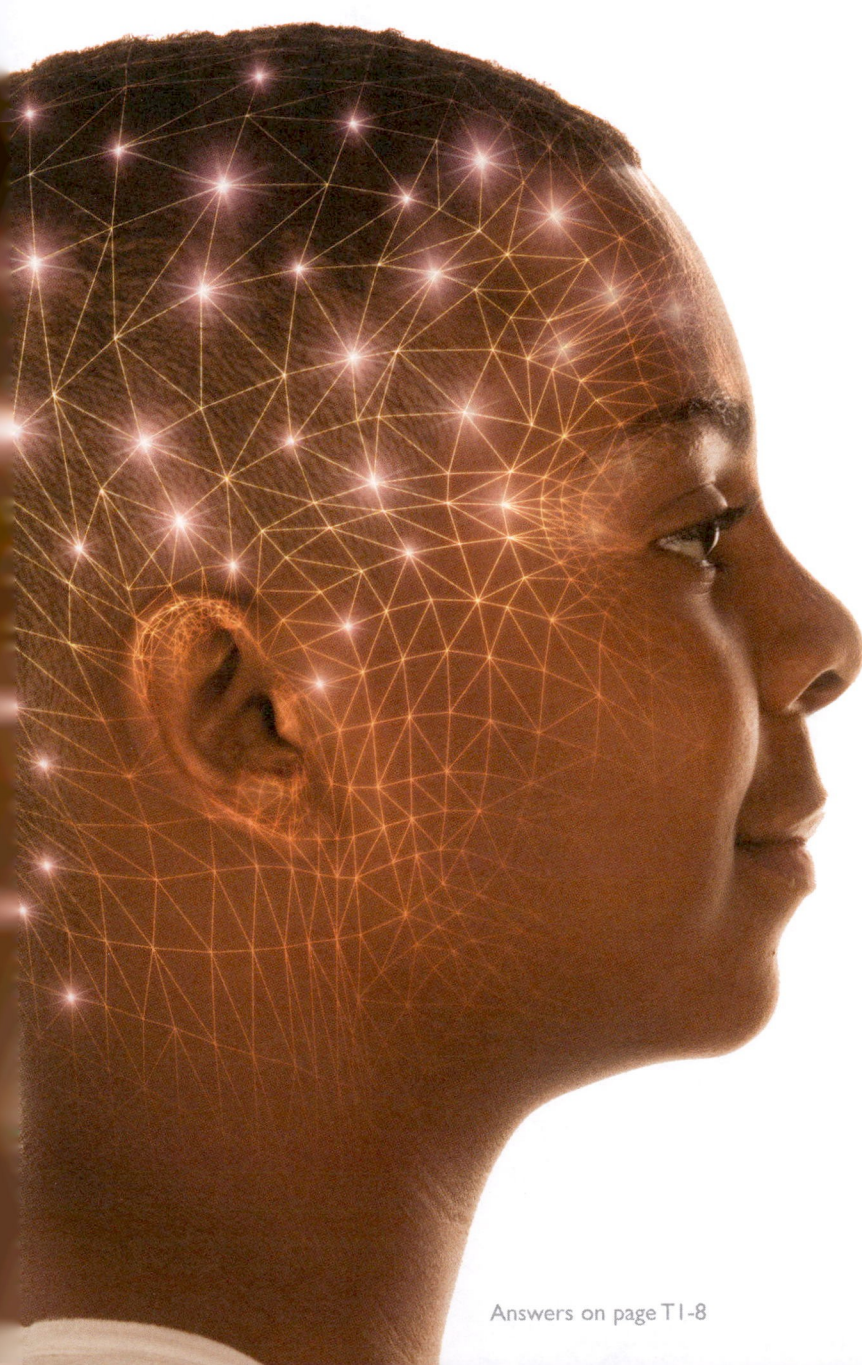

GOALS OF THE TOUR

1 **The Neuron and Synapse.** Identify parts of the neuron and synapse and describe how they communicate information.

2 **The Resting Potential and Action Potential.** Describe the ions used in maintaining the resting potential and in producing the action potential.

3 **Structures and Functions in the Human Brain.** Identify the brain's key structures and functions.

4 **Cerebral Cortex Lobes and Association Areas.** Identify the location and describe the function of the four cerebral lobes.

5 **Visual Information in the Split-Brain.** Describe hemispheric lateralization and communication in the brain.

6 **Central and Peripheral Nervous Systems.** Identify the parts of the central and peripheral nervous systems and describe the body functions they control.

The Neuron and the Synapse

1 Identify parts of the neuron and synapse and describe how they communicate information.

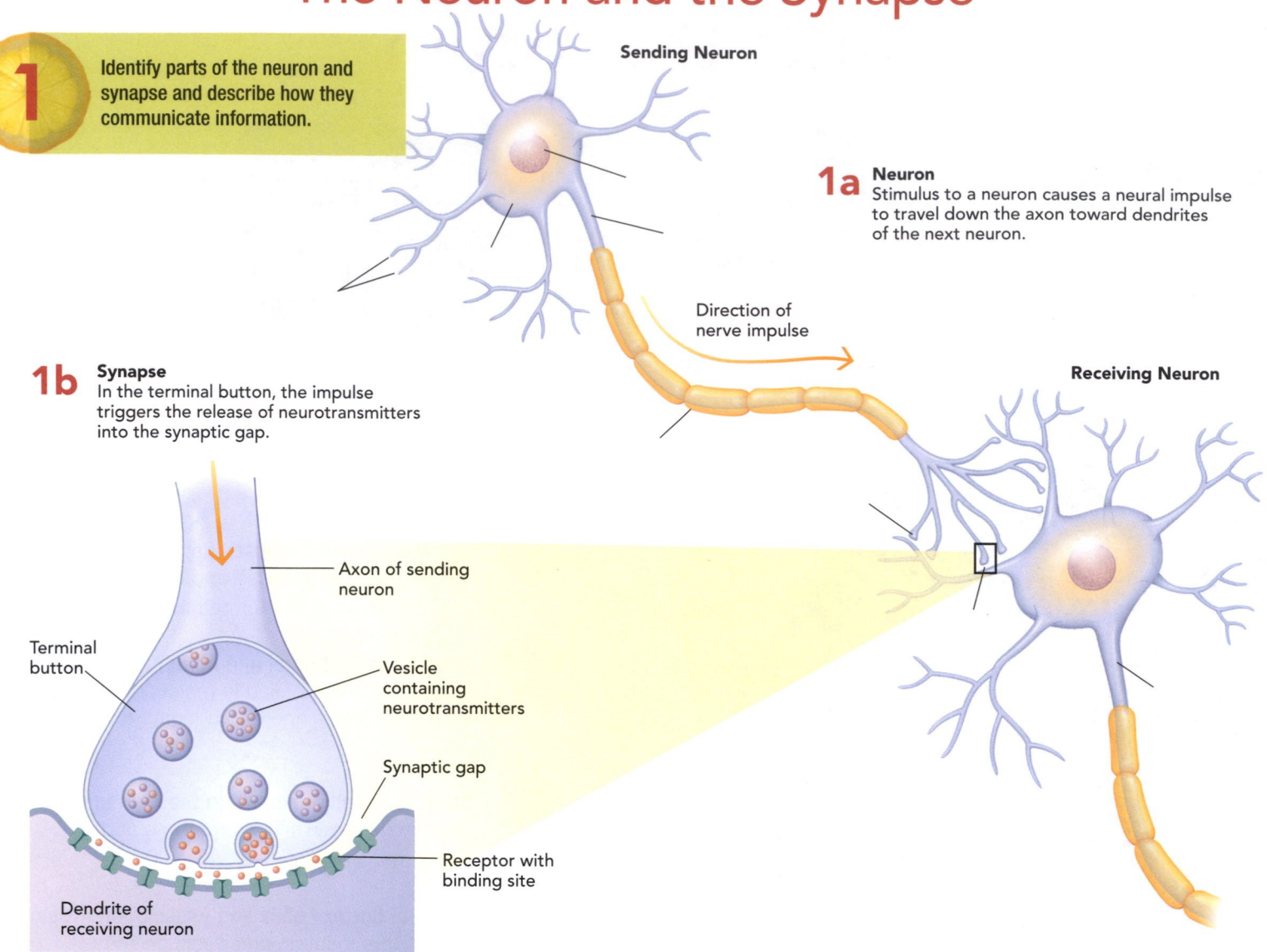

Sending Neuron

1a Neuron
Stimulus to a neuron causes a neural impulse to travel down the axon toward dendrites of the next neuron.

Direction of nerve impulse

Receiving Neuron

1b Synapse
In the terminal button, the impulse triggers the release of neurotransmitters into the synaptic gap.

Axon of sending neuron

Terminal button

Vesicle containing neurotransmitters

Synaptic gap

Receptor with binding site

Dendrite of receiving neuron

The Resting Potential and Action Potential

2a Resting Potential
The electrical potential across the membrane when the neuron is not stimulated. −70 mV inside relative to the outside of the membrane.

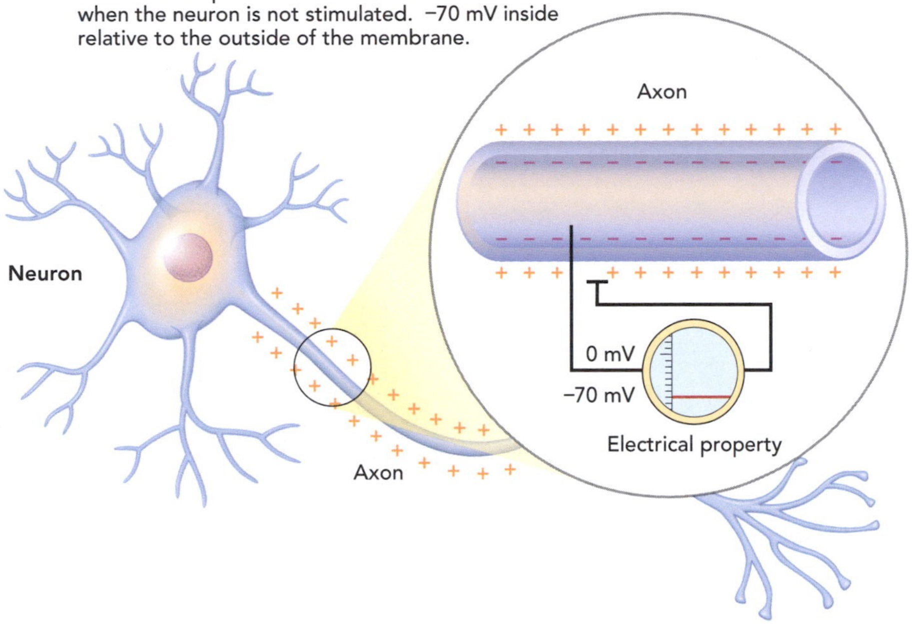

Neuron

Axon

Axon

0 mV

−70 mV

Electrical property

Describe the ions used in maintaining the resting potential and in producing the action potential.

2

2b Action Potential
The action potential is generated by an impulse within a neuron that causes a brief wave of positive electrical charge to sweep down the axon.

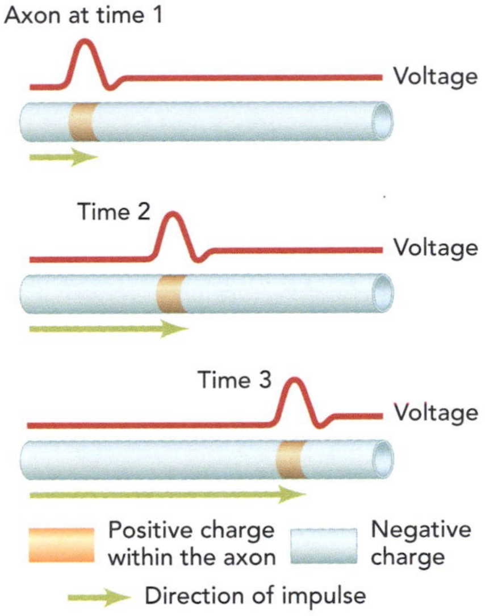

Axon at time 1

Voltage

Time 2

Voltage

Time 3

Voltage

Positive charge within the axon

Negative charge

Direction of impulse

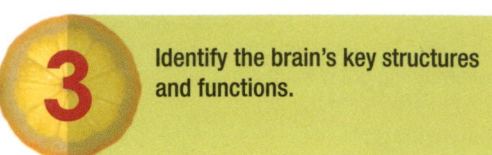

Structures and Functions of the Human Brain

3 Identify the brain's key structures and functions.

3a Brain Stem Structures

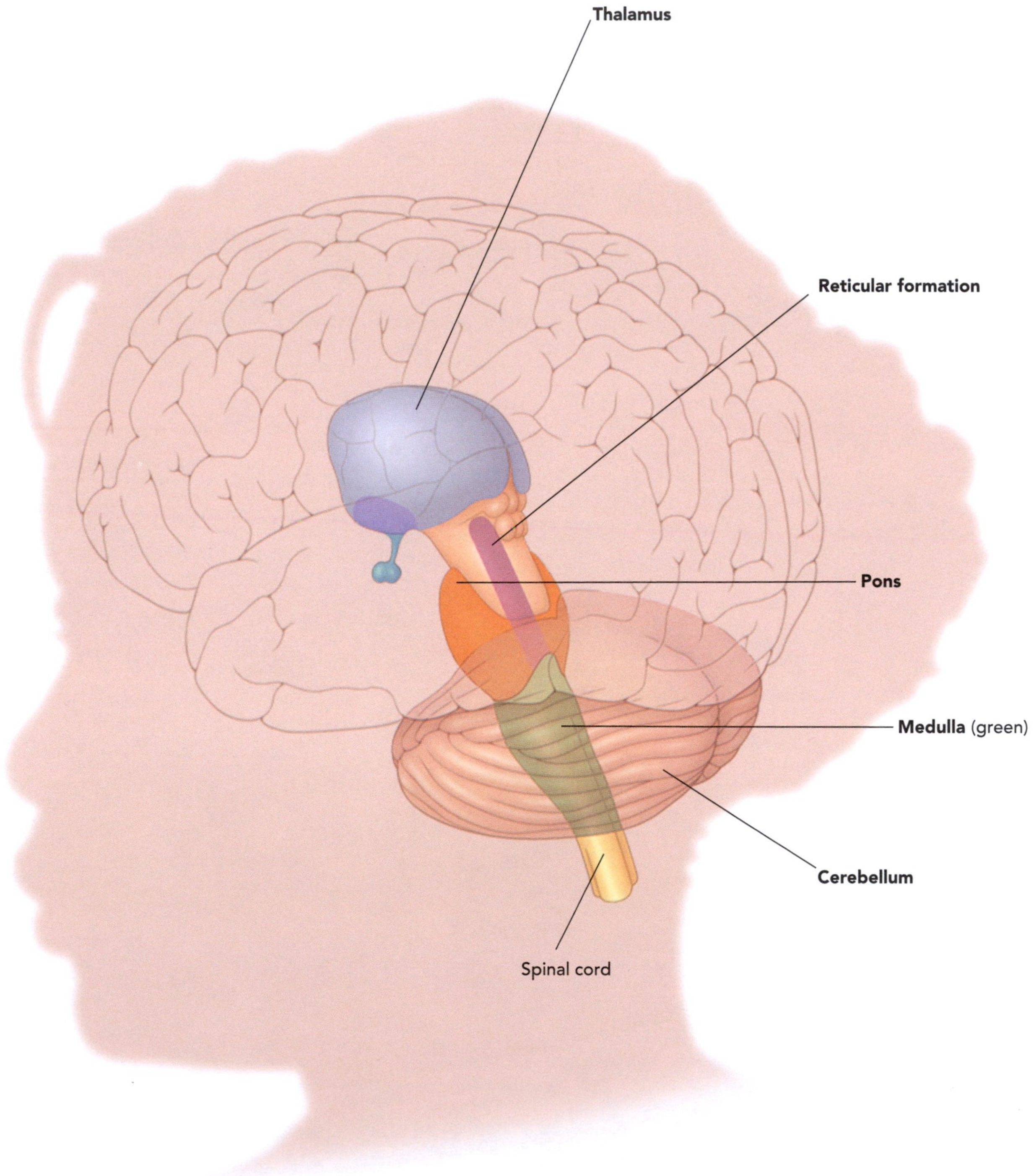

Thalamus

Reticular formation

Pons

Medulla (green)

Cerebellum

Spinal cord

Cerebral Cortex Lobes and Association Areas

Identify the location of the four cerebral cortex lobes and describe their primary functions.

4

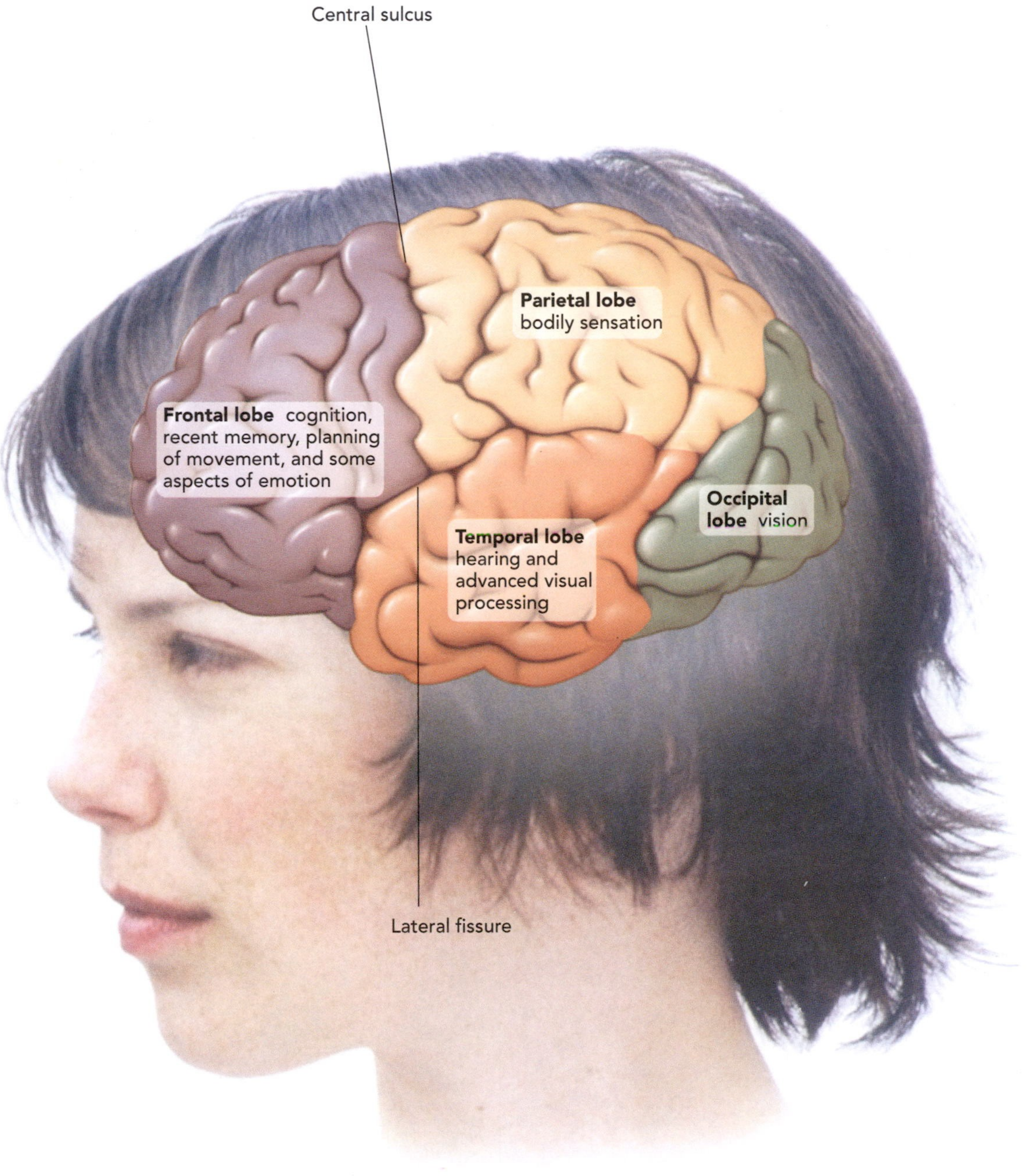

Central sulcus

Parietal lobe bodily sensation

Frontal lobe cognition, recent memory, planning of movement, and some aspects of emotion

Occipital lobe vision

Temporal lobe hearing and advanced visual processing

Lateral fissure

Visual Information in the Split-Brain

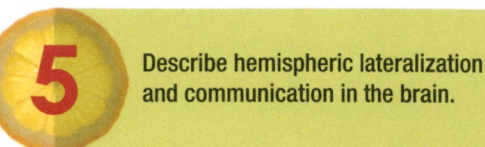

5 Describe hemispheric lateralization and communication in the brain.

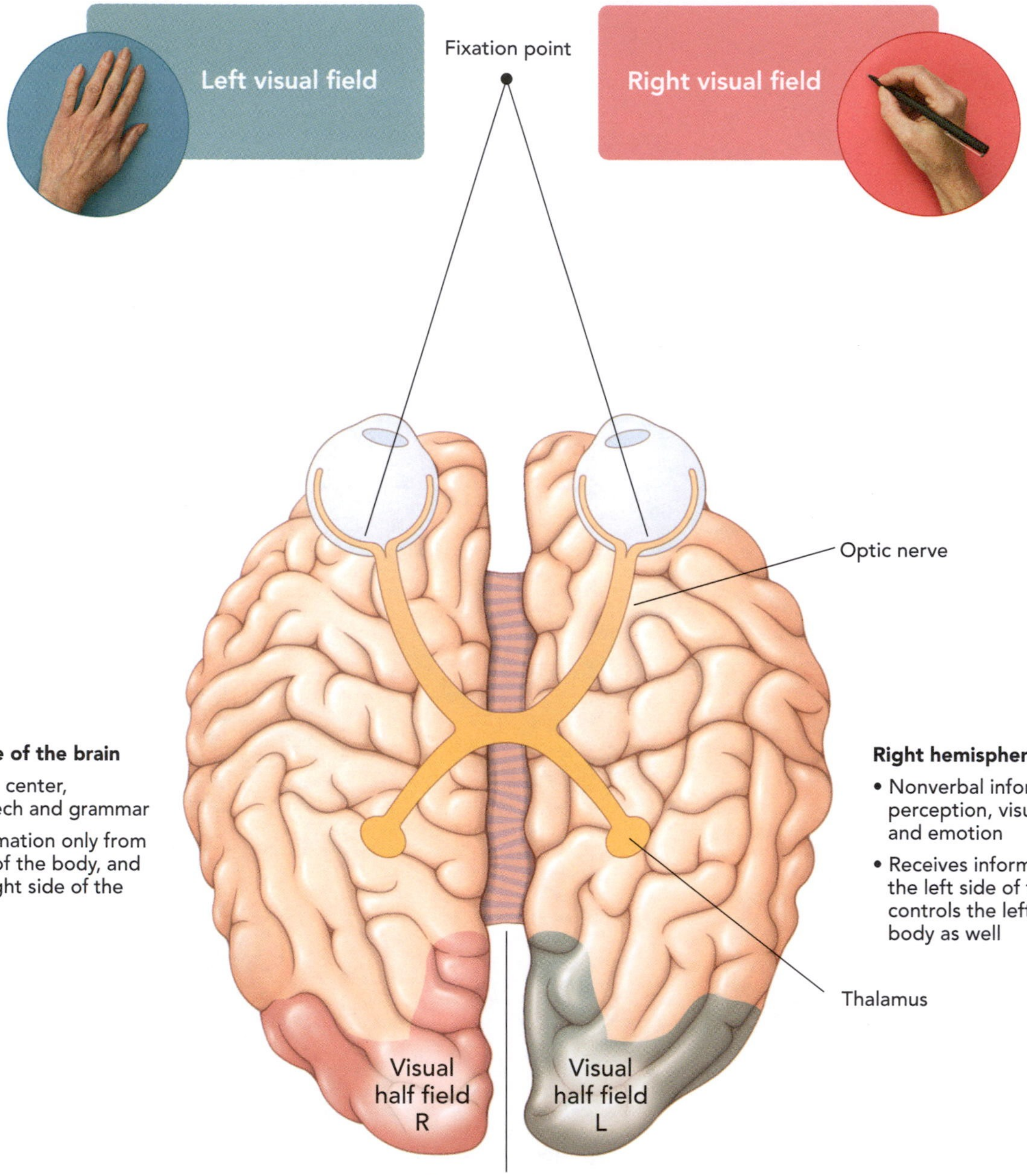

Left visual field

Fixation point

Right visual field

Optic nerve

Left hemisphere of the brain
- Main language center, especially speech and grammar
- Receives information only from the right side of the body, and controls the right side of the body as well

Right hemisphere of the brain
- Nonverbal information, such as perception, visual recognition, and emotion
- Receives information only from the left side of the body, and controls the left side of the body as well

Thalamus

Visual half field R

Visual half field L

Corpus callosum

A thick band of axons that connect brain cells in one hemisphere to the other. In healthy brains, the two sides engage in a continuous flow of information via this neural bridge and share information.

Central and Peripheral Nervous Systems

6a **The Central Nervous System** ●

Brain

Spinal cord

Identify the parts of the central and peripheral nervous systems and describe the bodily functions they control.

6

1. THE NEURON AND SYNAPSE

The *neuron* consists of a *cell body*, *dendrites*, and an *axon*. The cell body is the structure of the neuron that contains the nucleus, which consists of the genetic material including the chromosomes. The dendrites are branches of the neuron that receive information from other neurons. The axon sends information away from the cell body to other neurons or cells.

When a neuron fires, it sends an electrical impulse down the axon, known as the *action potential*. When the impulse arrives at the axon terminal buttons, it causes the release of *neurotransmitter* molecules into the *synapse*. The synapse is the gap junction between two neurons. Neurons communicate with one another by means of chemical signals provided by neurotransmitters that cross the synapse.

The neurotransmitter released by the sending neuron enters the synaptic gap and attaches to a *binding site* located on a *receptor* on the receiving neuron. The receptor contains a channel that is typically closed when the receiving neuron is in the resting state (*resting potential*). When the neurotransmitter binds to the receptor, it causes an opening of the receptor channel that then allows a particular *ion* to enter or leave the receiving neuron. If a neurotransmitter causes the opening of channels on the receiving neuron to a positively charged ion like sodium (Na^+), it will become less negative in charge. The entry of sodium will cause a change in the electrical charge (potential) of the receiving neuron that may make it more likely to generate its own action potential.

2. THE RESTING POTENTIAL AND ACTION POTENTIAL

The neuron maintains electrical properties called an *electrical gradient*, displaying a difference in the electrical charge inside and outside of the cell. The electrical gradient is created because the membrane of the neuron is *selectively permeable*. Some molecules can pass through it more freely than others. The membrane is not permeable to large negatively charged protein molecules that are trapped inside the neuron. Inside and outside of the neuron are various electrically charged particles called *ions* that vary in concentrations. The ions that play an important role in the function of the neuron are sodium (Na^+), potassium (K^+), and chloride (Cl^-). These ions enter or leave the neuron through special channels provided by protein molecules that line the neuron.

The *resting potential* is the electrical property of the neuron when it is not stimulated or not sending a nerve impulse. In a typical neuron this is seen as a -70 mV charge inside relative to the outside of the membrane. During the resting potential, the sodium channels are closed, leaving a higher concentration of sodium ions outside of the neuron membrane. The negative charge of a neuron during the resting state is largely maintained by the negatively charged protein molecules trapped inside the neuron and by the inability of positively charged sodium ions to cross the membrane into the neuron.

The *action potential* occurs when the neuron is stimulated to generate a nerve impulse down the axon. This is often referred to as the firing of the neuron. During the action potential, there is a rapid and slight reversal in the electrical charge from -70 mV to +40 mV. The action potential occurs as a brief wave of positive charge that sweeps down the axon.

3. STRUCTURES AND FUNCTIONS IN THE HUMAN BRAIN

The brain stem structures are embedded within the core of the brain and provide a number of vital functions for survival. These include the medulla, pons, cerebellum, reticular formation, and the thalamus.

The *medulla* is a brain structure just above the spinal cord. It controls a number of life-sustaining reflexes and functions including breathing, coughing, vomiting, and heart rate. The *pons* lies just above the medulla and is involved in functions including sleep and arousal. The *cerebellum* is a large structure at the base of the brain with many folds. It is traditionally known to be involved in motor coordination and balance but also plays a role in attention of visual and auditory stimuli and the timing of movements. The *reticular formation* is an elaborate diffuse network of neurons that runs through the core of the medulla and pons to the base of the thalamus. It plays a role in arousal, attention, sleep patterns, and stereotyped patterns such as posture and locomotion. The *thalamus* is a central structure in the brain that relays auditory, visual, and somatosensory (bodily senses) information to the cerebral cortex.

The limbic system comprises a number of brain structures involved in motivation, emotion, and memory. The *hypothalamus* is a small structure that is located just below the thalamus. It controls the autonomic nervous system as well as the release of hormones from the pituitary gland. It is involved in a number of functions including eating, drinking, and sexual behavior, and plays an important role in the expression of emotions and stress responses. The *hippocampus* is located in the temporal lobe and plays a role in learning and memory. Adjacent to the hippocampus is the amygdala, which is involved in fear and anxiety.

The *cerebral cortex* is the outer layer of the brain and is involved in higher-order functions such as thinking, learning, consciousness, and memory.

4. CEREBRAL CORTEX LOBES AND ASSOCIATION AREAS

The *cerebral cortex* is anatomically divided into four lobes: occipital lobe, parietal lobe, temporal lobe, and frontal lobe. The *occipital lobe* is located in the posterior end (back region) of the cortex and is involved in processing *visual information*. The *parietal lobe* lies between the occipital lobe and the *central sulcus*, which is one of the deepest grooves in the surface of the cortex. The parietal lobe is involved in *bodily senses*. The area just posterior to the central sulcus is called the primary somatosensory cortex because it is the primary target for the *touch senses* of the body and information for muscle-stretch receptors and joint receptors. The *temporal lobe* is the large portion of each hemisphere near the temples and lies behind the frontal lobe and below the *lateral fissure*. It is the primary region of the cortex that processes *auditory information*. The *frontal lobe* extends from the central sulcus to the anterior limit (forward region) of the brain. The region of the frontal lobe immediately adjacent to the central sulcus is called the *motor cortex* because it controls *fine movements*. The most anterior region is called the *prefrontal cortex;* it is involved in higher brain functions including *cognition* (thought processes), recent *memory*, the *planning of movement*, and some aspects of *emotion*.

Association areas are not primarily sensory or motor areas but, rather, associate sensory and motor inputs that give rise to higher mental functions such as perception, learning, remembering, thinking, and speaking.

5. VISUAL INFORMATION IN THE SPLIT-BRAIN

Lateralization refers to the division of labor between the two cerebral hemispheres of the brain. The *left hemisphere* receives sensory information from and controls the movements in the right side of the body. Likewise, images of objects in the right visual field are projected to the left half of the retina of each eye, which in turn sends the information to the visual cortex in the left hemisphere. The left hemisphere also contains the main language area involved in the comprehension and production of language.

The *right hemisphere* receives sensory information from and controls the movements in the left side of the body. Likewise, images of objects in the left visual field are projected to the right half of the retina of each eye, which in turn sends the information to the visual cortex in the right hemisphere. The right hemisphere processes nonverbal information, such as perception, visual recognition, and emotion.

In the healthy brain the two cerebral hemispheres share information with each other across the broad band of axons called the *corpus callosum*. In some instances the corpus callosum is surgically cut, a procedure called the *split-brain*. In the split-brain, information in one cerebral hemisphere is confined to that side of the brain.

6. CENTRAL AND PERIPHERAL NERVOUS SYSTEMS

The nervous system is made up of the *central nervous system* and the *peripheral nervous system*. The central nervous system is comprised of the brain and the spinal cord. The peripheral nervous system consists of all nerve fibers outside of the brain and spinal cord. The peripheral nervous system is made up of two major divisions: the *somatic division* and the *autonomic division*.

The *somatic division* consists of nerve fibers conveying information from the brain and spinal cord to skeletal muscles; this information controls movement and sends information back to the brain via the spinal cord from sensory receptors located in various parts of the body.

The *autonomic division* controls the glands and muscles of the internal organs such as the heart, digestive system, lungs, and salivary glands, and it consists of the sympathetic and the parasympathetic branches. The *sympathetic branch* arouses the body, mobilizes its energy during physical exercise and in stressful situations, and activates the adrenal gland to release epinephrine into the bloodstream. The *parasympathetic branch* calms the body and conserves and replenishes energy.

important—consider how much ground the nervous system must cover quickly. Axons without myelin sheaths are not very good conductors of electricity. However, with the insulation of myelin sheaths, axons transmit electrical impulses and convey information much more rapidly (Diamond, 2009). We can compare the myelin sheath's development to the evolution of freeways as cities grew. A freeway is a shielded road. It keeps fast-moving, long-distance traffic from getting snarled by slow, local traffic.

Numerous disorders are associated with problems in either the creation or the maintenance of myelin. One of them is multiple sclerosis (MS), a degenerative disease of the nervous system in which myelin tissue hardens, disrupting neuronal communication. In MS, scar tissue replaces the myelin sheath. Symptoms of the disease include blurry and double vision, tingling sensations throughout the body, and general weakness.

The Neural Impulse

To transmit information to other neurons, a neuron sends brief electrical impulses (let's call them "blips") through its axon. As you reach to turn this page, hundreds of such impulses will stream down the axons in your arm to tell your muscles when to flex and how quickly. By changing the rate of the signals, or blips, the neuron can vary its message. Those impulses traveling down the axon are electrical. How does a neuron—a living cell—generate electricity? To answer this question, we need to take a moment to examine the axon and the cellular membrane that surrounds it.

The axon is a tube encased in a membrane. There are fluids both inside and outside the axon. Floating in those fluids are electrically charged particles called *ions*. Some of these ions, notably sodium and potassium, carry positive charges. Negatively charged ions of chlorine and other elements also are present. The membrane surrounding the axon prevents negative and positive ions from randomly flowing into or out of the cell. That membrane has thousands of tiny gates in it. These gates are generally closed, but they can open. We call the membrane *semipermeable* because fluids and ions can sometimes flow into and out of it. In fact, the neuron creates electrical signals by moving positive and negative ions back and forth through its outer membrane.

Normally, when the neuron is resting—that is, not transmitting information—the tiny gates in the membrane, called *ion channels,* are closed, and a slight negative charge is present along the inside of the cell membrane. On the outside of the cell membrane, the charge is positive. Because of the difference in charge, the membrane of the resting neuron is said to be *polarized,* with most negatively charged ions on the inside of the cell and most positively charged ions on the outside. This polarization creates a voltage between the inside and outside of the axon wall (Figure 6.3). That voltage, called the

Country music star Clay Walker has multiple sclerosis (MS) and has founded a charity, Band Against MS, to work for a cure for the disease.

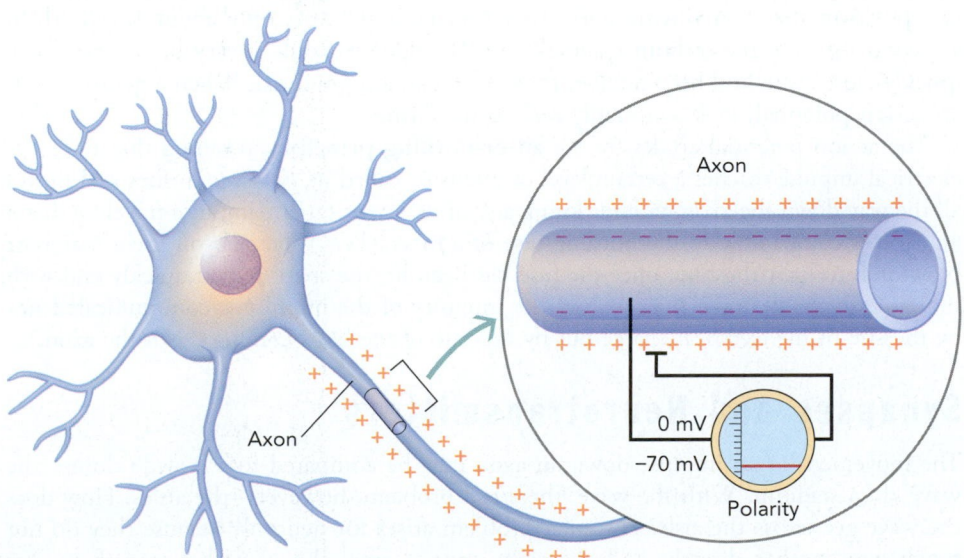

FIGURE 6.3 The Resting Potential
An oscilloscope measures the difference in electrical potential between two electrodes. When one electrode is placed inside an axon at rest and one is placed outside, the electrical potential inside the cell is −70 millivolts (mV) relative to the outside. This potential difference is due to the separation of positive (+) and negative (−) charges along the membrane.

FIGURE 6.4 **The Action Potential**
An action potential is a brief wave of positive electrical charge that sweeps down the axon as the sodium channels in the axon membrane open and close. (*a*) The action potential causes a change in electrical potential as it moves along the axon. (*b*) The movements of sodium ions (Na$^+$) and potassium ions (K$^+$) into and out of the axon cause the electrical changes.

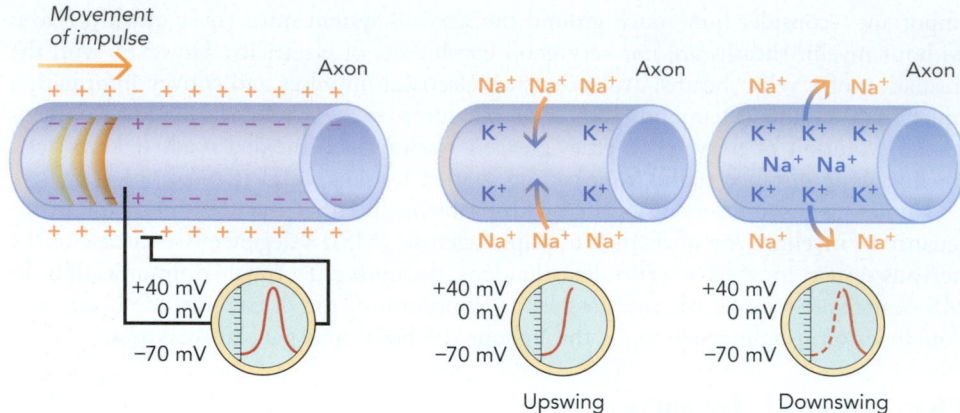

(a) Action potential generated by an impulse within a neuron

(b) Movement of sodium (Na$^+$) and potassium (K$^+$) ions responsible for the action potential

● **resting potential** In an inactive neuron, the voltage between the inside and outside of the axon wall.

neuron's **resting potential,** is between -60 and -75 millivolts. A millivolt is $1/1000$ of a volt.

How does the movement of ions across the membrane occur? Those ion channels open and close to let the ions pass into and out of the cell. For ions, it is true that opposites attract. The negatively charged ions on the inside of the membrane and the positively charged ions on the outside of the membrane will rush to each other if given the chance. Impulses that travel down the neuron do so by opening and closing ion channels, allowing the ions to flow in and out.

A neuron becomes activated when an incoming impulse—a reaction to, say, a pinprick or the sight of someone's face—raises the neuron's voltage, and the sodium gates at the base of the axon open briefly. This action allows positively charged sodium ions to flow into the neuron, creating a more positively charged neuron and *depolarizing* the membrane by decreasing the charge difference between the fluids inside and outside of the neuron. Then potassium channels open, and positively charged potassium ions move out through the neuron's semipermeable membrane. This outflow returns the neuron to a negative charge. Then the same process occurs as the next group of channels flips open briefly. So it goes all the way down the axon, like a long row of cabinet doors opening and closing in sequence. It is hard to imagine, but this system of opening and closing tiny doors is responsible for the beautiful fluid movements of a ballet dancer and the flying fingers of a pianist playing a concerto.

● **action potential** The brief wave of positive electrical charge that sweeps down the axon.

The term **action potential** describes the brief wave of positive electrical charge that sweeps down the axon (Figure 6.4). An action potential lasts only about $1/1,000$th of a second, because the sodium channels can stay open for only a very brief time. They quickly close again and become reset for the next action potential. When a neuron sends an action potential, it is commonly said to be "firing."

● **all-or-nothing principle** The principle that once the electrical impulse reaches a certain level of intensity (its threshold), it fires and moves all the way down the axon without losing any intensity.

The action potential abides by the **all-or-nothing principle,** meaning that once the electrical impulse reaches a certain level of intensity, called its *threshold,* it fires and moves all the way down the axon without losing any of its intensity. The impulse traveling down an axon is comparable to the burning fuse of a firecracker. Whether you use a match or blowtorch to light the fuse, once the fuse has been lit, the spark travels quickly and with the same intensity down the fuse. So, the intensity of the impulse is communicated not by the size of the electrical charge but by the rate of the blips coming down the axon.

Synapses and Neurotransmitters

The movement of an impulse down an axon may be compared to a crowd's doing "the wave" in a stadium. With the wave, there is a problem, however—the aisles. How does the wave get across the aisle? A similar problem arises for neurons, because they do not touch one another directly, and electricity cannot cross the space between them. Yet somehow neurons manage to communicate.

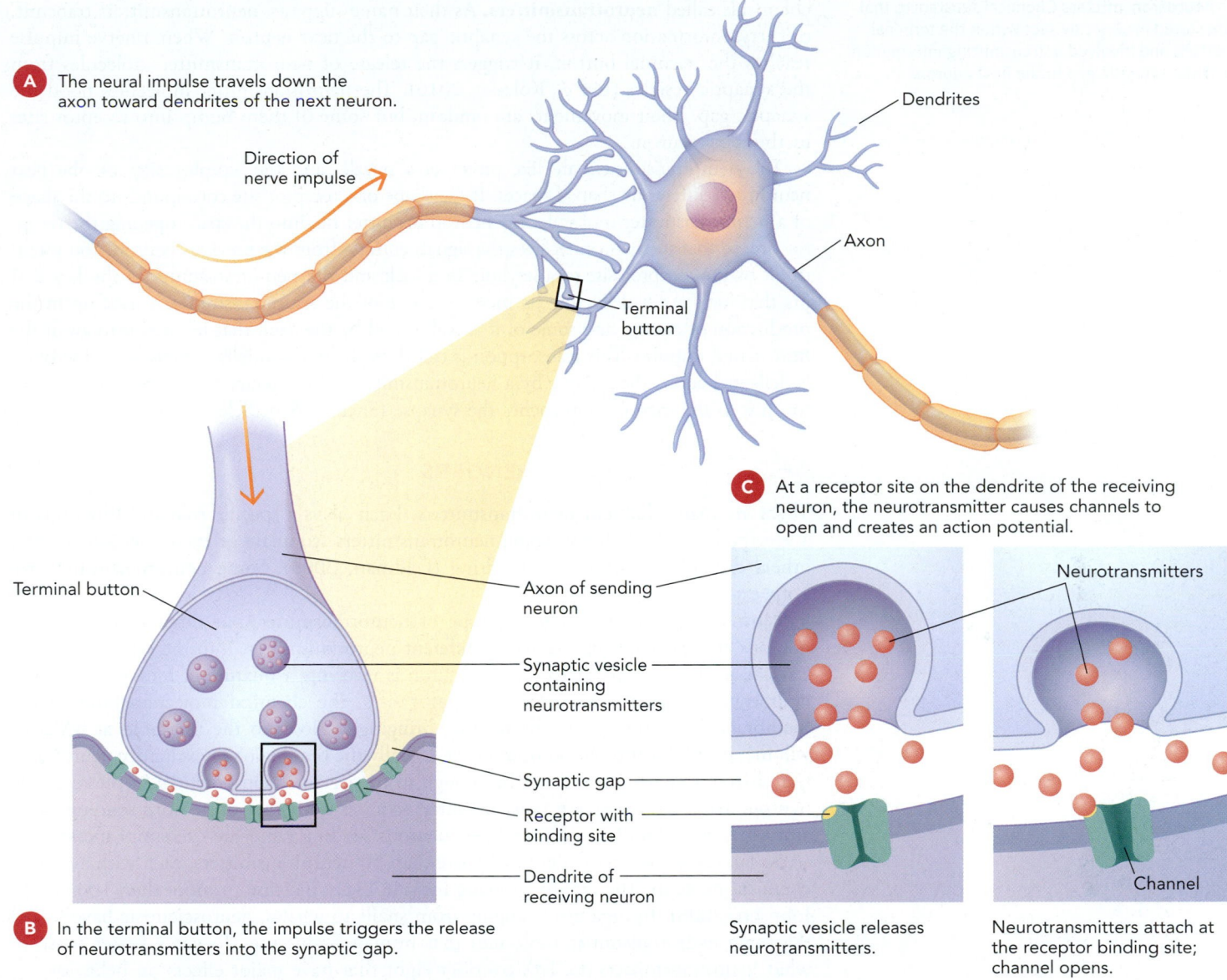

A The neural impulse travels down the axon toward dendrites of the next neuron.

Direction of nerve impulse

Dendrites

Axon

Terminal button

C At a receptor site on the dendrite of the receiving neuron, the neurotransmitter causes channels to open and creates an action potential.

Terminal button

Axon of sending neuron

Synaptic vesicle containing neurotransmitters

Synaptic gap

Receptor with binding site

Dendrite of receiving neuron

Neurotransmitters

Channel

B In the terminal button, the impulse triggers the release of neurotransmitters into the synaptic gap.

Synaptic vesicle releases neurotransmitters.

Neurotransmitters attach at the receptor binding site; channel opens.

FIGURE 6.5 **How Synapses and Neurotransmitters Work** (*A*) The axon of the *presynaptic* (sending) neuron meets dendrites of the *postsynaptic* (receiving) neuron. (*B*) This is an enlargement of one synapse, showing the synaptic gap between the two neurons, the terminal buttons, and the synaptic vesicles containing a neurotransmitter. (*C*) This is an enlargement of the receptor site. Note how the neurotransmitter opens the channel on the receptor site, triggering the neuron to fire.

Here is where the chemical part of electro*chemical* transmission comes in. Neurons communicate with one another through chemicals that carry messages across the space. This connection between one neuron and another is one of the most intriguing and highly researched areas of contemporary neuroscience (Kelsch, Sim, & Lois, 2010). Figure 6.5 gives an overview of how this connection between neurons takes place.

SYNAPTIC TRANSMISSION

Synapses are tiny spaces (the aisle in our stadium analogy) between neurons, and the gap between neurons that the synapses create is referred to as the *synaptic gap.* Most synapses lie between the axon of one neuron and the dendrites or cell body of another neuron (Turriagno, 2010). Before an impulse can cross the synaptic gap, it must be converted into a chemical signal.

Each axon branches out into numerous fibers that end in structures called *terminal buttons.* Stored in very tiny synaptic vesicles (*sacs*) within the terminal buttons are

● **synapses** Tiny spaces between neurons; the gaps between neurons are referred to as synaptic gaps.

● **neurotransmitters** Chemical substances that are stored in very tiny sacs within the terminal buttons and involved in transmitting information across a synaptic gap to the next neuron.

chemicals called **neurotransmitters.** As their name suggests, neurotransmitters transmit, or carry, information across the synaptic gap to the next neuron. When a nerve impulse reaches the terminal button, it triggers the release of neurotransmitter molecules from the synaptic vesicles (Lin & Koleske, 2010). The neurotransmitter molecules flood the synaptic gap. Their movements are random, but some of them bump into receptor sites in the next neuron.

The neurotransmitters are like pieces of a puzzle, and the receptor sites on the next neuron are differently shaped spaces. If the shape of a receptor site corresponds to the shape of a neurotransmitter molecule, the neurotransmitter fits into the space opening the receptor site, so that the neuron receives the signals coming from the previous neuron. You might think of the receptor site as a keyhole in a lock and the neurotransmitter as the key that fits that lock. After delivering its message, some of the neurotransmitter is used up in the production of energy, and some of it is reabsorbed by the axon that released it to await the next neural impulse. This reabsorption is called *reuptake.* Essentially, a message in the brain is delivered across the synapse by a neurotransmitter, which pours out of the terminal button just as the message approaches the synapse (Shen & Scheiffele, 2010).

NEUROCHEMICAL MESSENGERS

There are many different neurotransmitters. Each plays a specific role and functions in a specific pathway. Whereas some neurotransmitters stimulate or excite neurons to fire, others can inhibit neurons from firing (Feldman, 2009). Some neurotransmitters are both excitatory *and* inhibitory.

Most neurons secrete only one type of neurotransmitter, but often many different neurons are simultaneously secreting different neurotransmitters into the synaptic gaps of a single neuron. At any given time, a neuron is receiving a mixture of messages from the neurotransmitters. At the neuron's receptor sites, the chemical molecules bind to the membrane and either excite the neuron, bringing it closer to the threshold at which it will fire, or inhibit the neuron from firing. Usually the binding of an excitatory neurotransmitter from one neuron will not be enough to trigger an action potential in the receiving neuron. Triggering an action potential often requires a number of neurons sending excitatory messages simultaneously, or fewer neurons sending rapid-fire excitatory messages.

So far, researchers have identified more than 50 neurotransmitters, each with a unique chemical makeup. The rapidly growing list will likely increase to more than 100 (G. B. Johnson, 2008). In organisms ranging from snails to whales, neuroscientists have found the same neurotransmitter molecules that human brains use. To get a better sense of what neurotransmitters do, let's consider eight that have major effects on behavior.

Acetylcholine *Acetylcholine (ACh)* usually stimulates the firing of neurons and is involved in muscle action, learning, and memory (Woolf & Butcher, 2010). ACh is found throughout the central and peripheral nervous systems. The venom from the bite of the black widow spider causes ACh to gush out of the synapses between the spinal cord and skeletal muscles, producing violent muscle spasms and weakness. The role of ACh in muscle function also comes to light in the working of Botox, a brand-name product made from botulin. A bacterial poison, botulin destroys ACh, so that when someone gets an injection of Botox, his or her facial muscles—which are activated by ACh—are prevented from moving, with the result that wrinkles do not form (Kuan, 2009).

Individuals with Alzheimer disease, a degenerative brain disorder that involves a decline in memory, have an acetylcholine deficiency (Penner & others, 2010). Some of the drugs that alleviate Alzheimer symptoms do so by compensating for the loss of the brain's supply of acetylcholine.

GABA *GABA (gamma aminobutyric acid)* is found throughout the central nervous system. It is believed to be the neurotransmitter present in as many as one-third of the brain's synapses. GABA plays a key function in the brain by inhibiting many neurons from firing (Uusi-Oukari & Korpi, 2010); indeed, GABA is the brain's brake pedal, helping to regulate neuron firing and control the precision of the signal being carried

The neurotransmitter-like venom of the black widow spider does its harm by disturbing neurotransmission.

from one neuron to the next. Low levels of GABA are linked with anxiety. Valium and other antianxiety drugs increase GABA's inhibiting effects (Zwanzger & others, 2009).

Glutamate   *Glutamate* has a key role in exciting many neurons to fire and is especially involved in learning and memory (Lovinger, 2010). Too much glutamate can overstimulate the brain and trigger migraine headaches or even seizures. Researchers have recently proposed that glutamate also is a factor in anxiety, depression, schizophrenia, Alzheimer disease, and Parkinson disease (Adlard & others, 2010; Garbett & others, 2010; Garcia, Neely, & Deutsch, 2010). Because of the widespread expression of glutamate in the brain, glutamate receptors have increasingly become the targets of drug treatment for a number of neurological and psychological disorders (Niswender & Conn, 2010).

Norepinephrine   Stress stimulates the release of another of the body's neurotransmitters—*norepinephrine* (Katzman, 2009). Norepinephrine (also called *noradrenaline*) inhibits the firing of neurons in the central nervous system, but it excites the heart muscle, intestines, and urogenital tract. This neurotransmitter also helps to control alertness. Too little norepinephrine is associated with depression. Too much, however, triggers agitated states. For example, amphetamines and cocaine cause hyperactive, manic states of behavior by rapidly increasing brain levels of norepinephrine (Sofuoglu, 2010).

Recall that one of the most important characteristics of the brain and nervous system is integration. In the case of neurotransmitters, they may work in teams of two or more. For example, norepinephrine works with acetylcholine to regulate states of sleep and wakefulness.

Dopamine   *Dopamine* helps to control voluntary movement and affects sleep, mood, attention, learning, and the ability to recognize opportunities for rewarding experiences in the environment (Martin-Soelch, 2009). Stimulant drugs such as cocaine and amphetamines produce excitement, alertness, elevated mood, decreased fatigue, and sometimes increased motor activity mainly by activating dopamine receptors (Eriksen, Jorgensen, & Gether, 2010).

Low levels of dopamine are associated with Parkinson disease, a degenerative neurological disorder in which a person develops jerky physical movements and a tremor and has difficulty with speech and walking (Surmeier, Guzman, & Sanchez-Padilla, 2010). This disease affects about a million people in the United States (D. H. Park & others, 2009), and actor Michael J. Fox has been diagnosed with it. Parkinson disease impairs coordinated movement to the point that just walking across a room can be a major ordeal. High levels of dopamine and elevated numbers of dopamine receptors are associated with schizophrenia (Perez-Costas, Melendez-Ferro, & Roberts, 2010), a severe psychological disorder that we will examine in Module 62.

Serotonin   *Serotonin* is involved in the regulation of sleep, mood, attention, and learning (Kranz, Kasper, & Lanzenberger, 2010). In regulating states of sleep and wakefulness, it teams with acetylcholine and norepinephrine. Lowered levels of serotonin are associated with depression (Rajkumar & Mahesh, 2010). The antidepressant drug Prozac works by slowing down the reuptake of serotonin into terminal buttons, thereby increasing brain levels of serotonin (Little, Zhang, & Cook, 2006). There are 15 known types of serotonin receptors in the brain (Hoyer, Hannon, & Martin, 2002), and each type of antidepressant drug has its effects on different receptors. Figure 6.6 shows the brain pathways for serotonin.

Endorphins   *Endorphins* are natural opiates—substances that depress nervous system activity and eliminate pain—that mainly stimulate the firing of neurons. As opiates, endorphins shield the body from pain and elevate feelings of pleasure. A long-distance runner, a woman giving birth, and a person in shock after a car wreck all have elevated levels of endorphins (Mahler & others, 2009).

As early as the fourth century B.C.E., the Greeks used wild poppies to induce euphoria. More than 2,000 years later, the magical formula behind opium's addictive action was

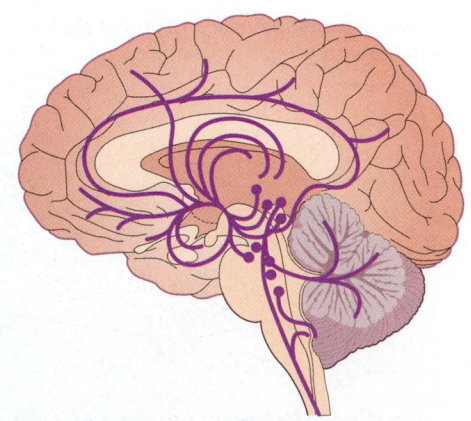

FIGURE 6.6 Serotonin Pathways
Each of the neurotransmitters in the brain has specific pathways in which it functions. Shown here are the pathways for serotonin.

finally discovered. In the early 1970s, scientists found that opium plugs into a sophisticated system of natural opiates that lie deep within the brain's pathways (Pert, 1999; Pert & Snyder, 1973). Morphine (the most important narcotic of opium) mimics the action of endorphins by stimulating receptors in the brain involved with pleasure and pain (Jiang & others, 2010).

Oxytocin *Oxytocin* is a hormone and neurotransmitter that plays an important role in the experience of love and social bonding. A powerful surge of oxytocin is released in mothers who have just given birth, and oxytocin is related to the onset of lactation (milk production) and breast feeding (Grewen, Davenport, & Light, 2010; Kamel, 2010). Oxytocin, however, is involved in more than a mother's ability to provide nourishment for her baby. It is also a factor in the experience of parents who find themselves "in love at first sight" with their newborn (Young, 2009).

Oxytocin is released as part of sexual orgasm and is thought to figure in the human experience of orgasmic pleasure and emotional attachment to romantic partners (Baskerville & others, 2009). Provocative research has related oxytocin to the way that some individuals respond to stress (Cetinel & others, 2010; Pierrehumbert & others, 2010). According to Shelley Taylor, women under stress do not experience the classic "fight or flight" response—rather, the influx of oxytocin they experience suggests that women may seek bonds with others when under stress (2011; Taylor, Saphire-Bernstein, & Seeman, 2010). Taylor refers to this response as "tend and befriend" and believes that it more accurately represents the stress response of women.

DRUGS AND NEUROTRANSMITTERS

Recall that neurotransmitters fit into the receptor sites like keys in keyholes. Other substances, such as drugs, can sometimes fit into those receptor sites as well, producing a variety of effects. Many animal venoms, such as that of the black widow spider mentioned above, act by disturbing neurotransmission. Similarly, most drugs that influence behavior do so mainly by interfering with the work of neurotransmitters (Wecker & others, 2010).

Drugs can mimic or increase the effects of a neurotransmitter, or they can block those effects. For example, the drug morphine mimics the actions of endorphins by stimulating receptors in the brain and spinal cord associated with pleasure and pain, producing feelings of pleasure. Other drugs can block a neurotransmitter's action by preventing it from getting into the receptor site. Drugs used to treat schizophrenia, for example, interfere with the activity of dopamine.

Neural Networks

● **neural networks** Networks of nerve cells that integrate sensory input and motor output.

So far, we have focused mainly on how a single neuron functions and on how a nerve impulse travels from one neuron to another. Now let's look at how large numbers of neurons work together to integrate incoming information and coordinate outgoing information.

Most information processing occurs when information moves through **neural networks**—interconnected pathways of nerve cells that integrate sensory input and motor output. For example, as you read your class notes, the input from your eyes is transmitted to your brain and then passed through many neural networks, which translate the characters on the page into neural codes for letters, words, associations, and meanings. Some of the information is stored in the neural networks, and, if you read aloud, some is passed on as messages to your lips and tongue. Neural networks can take years to develop and make up most of the brain. Working in networks allows neurons to amplify the brain's computing power (Kanamaru & Aihara, 2010). Figure 6.7 shows a simplified

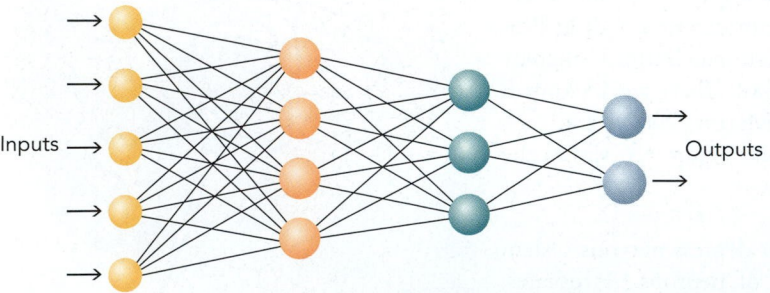

FIGURE 6.7 An Example of a Neural Network *Inputs* (information from the environment and from sensory receptors, such as the details of a person's face) become embedded in extensive connections between neurons in the brain. This embedding process leads to *outputs* such as remembering the person's face.

drawing of a neural network and gives you an idea of how the activity of one neuron is linked with that of many others.

Some neurons have short axons and communicate with other nearby neurons. Other neurons have long axons and communicate with circuits of neurons some distance away. These neural networks are not static (Wamsley & others, 2010). They can be altered through changes in the strength of synaptic connections.

Any piece of information, such as a name, might be embedded in hundreds or even thousands of connections between neurons (Larson-Prior & others, 2009). In this way, human activities such as being attentive, memorizing, and thinking are distributed over a wide range of connected neurons. The strength of these connected neurons determines how well the information is remembered (Crespo-Garcia & others, 2010). Differences in these neural networks are responsible for the differences observed in those London cab drivers discussed earlier in this module.

6·3 THE ENDOCRINE SYSTEM

The nervous system works closely with another bodily system—the endocrine system. The **endocrine system** consists of a set of glands that regulate the activities of certain organs by releasing their chemical products into the bloodstream. **Glands** are organs or tissues in the body that produce chemicals that control many of our bodily functions. The endocrine glands consist of the pituitary gland, the thyroid and parathyroid glands, the adrenal glands, the pancreas, the ovaries in women, and the testes in men (Figure 6.8). The chemical messengers produced by these glands are called **hormones.** The bloodstream carries hormones to all parts of the body, and the membrane of every cell has receptors for one or more hormones. Let's take a closer look at the function of some of the main endocrine glands.

The **pituitary gland,** a pea-sized gland just beneath the hypothalamus, controls growth and regulates other glands (Figure 6.9). The anterior (front) part of the pituitary is known as the master gland, because almost all of its hormones direct the activity of target glands elsewhere in the body. In turn, the anterior pituitary gland is controlled by the hypothalamus.

The **adrenal glands,** located at the top of each kidney, regulate moods, energy level, and the ability to cope with stress (Wirtz & others, 2009). Each adrenal gland secretes epinephrine (also called *adrenaline*) and norepinephrine (also called *noradrenaline*). Unlike most hormones, epinephrine and norepinephrine act quickly. Epinephrine helps a person get ready for an emergency by acting on smooth muscles, the heart, stomach, intestines, and sweat glands. In addition, epinephrine stimulates the reticular formation, which in turn arouses the sympathetic nervous system, and this system subsequently excites the adrenal glands to produce more epinephrine. Norepinephrine also alerts the individual to emergency situations by interacting with the pituitary and the liver. You may remember that norepinephrine functions as a neurotransmitter when it is released by neurons. In the adrenal glands, norepinephrine is released as a hormone. In both instances, norepinephrine conveys information—in the first case, to neurons; in the second case, to glands (Brooker & others, 2010). The activation of the adrenal glands has an important role to play in stress and physical health, as we will see in Psychology's Biological Foundations of Health and Wellness.

The **pancreas,** located under the stomach, is a dual-purpose gland that performs both digestive and endocrine functions. The part of the pancreas that serves endocrine functions produces a number of hormones, including

- **endocrine system** The body system consisting of a set of glands that regulate the activities of certain organs by releasing their chemical products into the bloodstream.

- **glands** Organs or tissues in the body that create chemicals that control many of our bodily functions.

- **hormones** Chemical messengers that are produced by the endocrine glands and carried by the bloodstream to all parts of the body.

- **pituitary gland** A pea-sized gland just beneath the hypothalamus that controls growth and regulates other glands.

- **adrenal glands** Glands at the top of each kidney that are responsible for regulating moods, energy level, and the ability to cope with stress.

- **pancreas** A dual-purpose gland under the stomach that performs both digestive and endocrine functions.

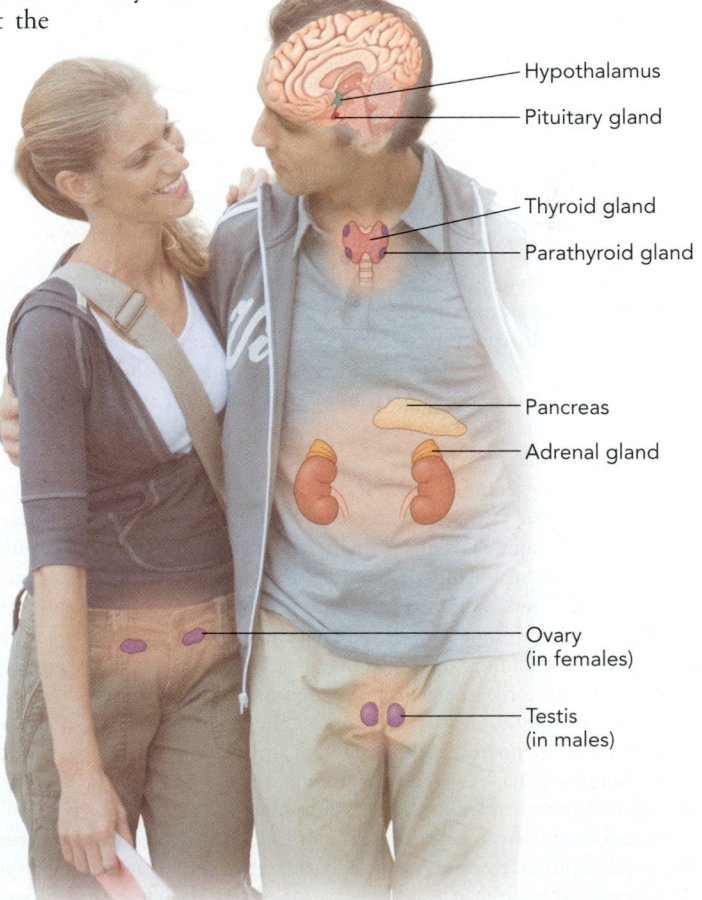

Hypothalamus
Pituitary gland
Thyroid gland
Parathyroid gland
Pancreas
Adrenal gland
Ovary (in females)
Testis (in males)

FIGURE 6.8 The Major Endocrine Glands The pituitary gland releases hormones that regulate the hormone secretions of the other glands. The pituitary gland is regulated by the hypothalamus.

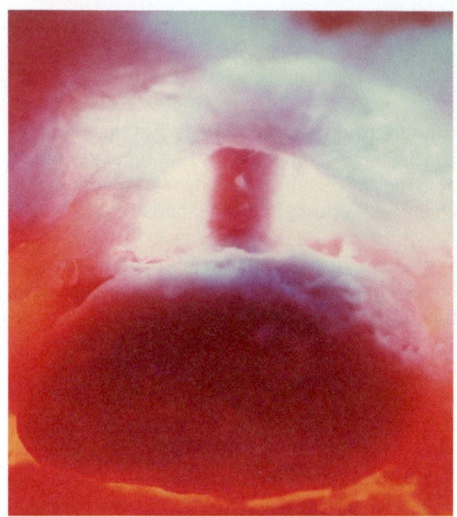

FIGURE 6.9 **The Pituitary Gland** The pituitary gland, which hangs by a short stalk from the hypothalamus, regulates the hormone production of many of the body's endocrine glands. Here it is enlarged 30 times.

● **ovaries** Sex-related endocrine glands in the uterus that produce hormones related to women's sexual development and reproduction.

● **testes** Sex-related endocrine glands in the scrotum that produce hormones related to men's sexual development and reproduction.

insulin. This part of the pancreas, called the *Islets of Langerhans,* busily turns out hormones like a little factory. Insulin is an essential hormone that controls glucose (blood sugar) levels in the body and is related to metabolism, body weight, and obesity.

The **ovaries,** located in the pelvis on either sides of the uterus in women, and **testes,** located in the scrotum in men, are the sex-related endocrine glands that produce hormones related to sexual development and reproduction. These glands and the hormones they produce play important roles in developing sexual characteristics, as we will discover in Module 38. They are also involved in other characteristics and behaviors, as we will see throughout this book.

Neuroscientists have discovered that the nervous system and endocrine system are intricately interconnected. They know that the brain's hypothalamus connects the nervous system and the endocrine system and that the two systems work together to control the body's activities (Boonen & others, 2010). Recall from earlier in the module that the autonomic nervous system regulates processes such as respiration, heart rate, and digestion. The autonomic nervous system acts on the endocrine glands to produce a number of important physiological reactions to strong emotions, such as rage and fear.

The endocrine system differs significantly from the nervous system in a variety of ways. For one thing, as you saw in Figure 6.8, the parts of the endocrine system are not all connected in the way that the parts of the nervous system are. For another, the endocrine system works more slowly than the nervous system, because hormones are transported in our blood through the circulatory system. Our hearts do a mind-boggling job of pumping blood throughout the body, but blood moves far more slowly than the neural impulses do in the nervous system's superhighway.

SUMMARY

The nervous system is the body's electrochemical communication circuitry. Four important characteristics of the brain and nervous system are complexity, integration, adaptability, and electrochemical transmission. The brain's special ability to adapt and change is called plasticity.

Decision making in the nervous system occurs in specialized pathways of nerve cells. Three of these pathways involve sensory input, motor output, and neural networks.

The nervous system is divided into two main parts: central (CNS) and peripheral (PNS). The CNS consists of the brain and spinal cord. The PNS has two major divisions: somatic and autonomic. The autonomic nervous system consists of two main divisions: sympathetic and parasympathetic. The sympathetic nervous system drives our body's response to threatening circumstances, while the parasympathetic nervous system is involved in maintaining the body, digesting food, and healing wounds.

Neurons are cells that specialize in processing information. They make up the communication network of the nervous system. The three main parts of the neuron are the cell body, dendrite (receiving part), and axon (sending part). A myelin sheath encases and insulates most axons and speeds up transmission of neural impulses.

Impulses are sent from a neuron along its axon in the form of brief electrical impulses. Resting potential is the stable, slightly negative charge of an inactive neuron. The brief wave of electrical charge that sweeps down the axon, called the action potential, is an all-or-nothing response. The synapse is the space between neurons. At the synapse, neurotransmitters are released from the sending neuron, and some of these attach to receptor sites on the receiving neuron, where they stimulate another elec-

KEY TERMS

nervous system   62

plasticity   63

afferent nerves   64

efferent nerves   64

central nervous system (CNS)   64

peripheral nervous system (PNS)   64

somatic nervous system   65

autonomic nervous system   65

sympathetic nervous system   65

parasympathetic nervous system   65

neurons   65

glial cells   65

cell body   66

dendrites   66

axon   66

myelin sheath   66

resting potential   68

action potential   68

all-or-nothing principle   68

synapses   69

neurotransmitters   70

neural networks   72

endocrine system   73

glands   73

hormones   73

pituitary gland   73

adrenal glands   73

pancreas   73

ovaries   74

testes   74

trical impulse. Neurotransmitters include acetylcholine, GABA, glutamate, norepinephrine, dopamine, serotonin, and endorphins. Neural networks are clusters of neurons that are interconnected and that develop through experience.

The endocrine glands release hormones directly into the bloodstream for distribution throughout the body. The pituitary gland is the master endocrine gland. The adrenal glands play important roles in moods, energy level, and ability to cope with stress. Other parts of the endocrine system include the pancreas, which produces insulin, and the ovaries and testes, which produce sex hormones.

TEST YOURSELF

1. Name and explain four characteristics that allow the nervous system to direct human behavior.

2. What is the difference between afferent and efferent nerves?

3. What are the two main parts of the autonomic nervous system, and what is the function of each?

4. What are neurons, and what are their three parts?

5. What is meant by the neuron's action potential? How does the all-or-nothing principle apply to it?

6. What do neurotransmitters do? Name four specific neurotransmitters and describe the role each plays.

7. What is the endocrine system's function, and what role do hormones play in it?

8. What two adrenal gland secretions prepare the body to react quickly to emergencies, and what specifically do they do?

9. Through what brain structure are the nervous and the endocrine systems connected, and what do the two systems work together to control?

APPLY YOUR KNOWLEDGE

1. Consider the four characteristics of the nervous system discussed in this module. Suppose you had to do without one of them. Which would you choose, and what would be the consequences of your decision for your behavior?

2. Do an Internet search for "nutrition" and "the brain." Examine the claims made by one or more of the websites. In light of what you have learned about the nervous system, how could nutrition affect brain function? Based on your scientific knowledge, how believable are the claims on the site? Explain.

The Brain

The extensive and intricate networks of neurons in the living brain are invisible to the naked eye. Fortunately, technology is available to help neuroscientists form pictures of the structure and organization of neurons and of the larger systems they make up without harming the organism being studied. In this module we probe the techniques that scientists use in brain research, and we consider what these tools reveal about the brain's structures and functions. We pay special attention to the cerebral cortex, the region of the brain that is most relevant to the topics we explore in this book. Finally, we look at how the brain responds to damage.

7-1 HOW RESEARCHERS STUDY THE BRAIN AND NERVOUS SYSTEM

Early knowledge of the human brain came mostly from studies of individuals who had suffered brain damage from injury or disease or who had brain surgery to relieve another condition. Modern discoveries have relied largely on technology that enables researchers to "look inside" the brain while it is at work. Let's examine some of these innovative techniques.

Brain Lesioning

Brain lesioning is an abnormal disruption in the tissue of the brain resulting from injury or disease. In a lab setting, neuroscientists produce lesions in laboratory animals to determine the effects on the animal's behavior (Pierucci & others, 2009). They create the lesions by surgically removing brain tissue, destroying tissue with a laser, or eliminating tissue by injecting it with a drug (Wolf & others, 2010). Examining the person or animal that has the lesion gives the researchers a sense of the function of the part of the brain that has been damaged. Do you know anyone who has experienced a stroke or brain-damaging head injury? These experiences create lesioned areas in the brain.

Electrical Recording

An *electroencephalograph (EEG)* records the brain's electrical activity. Electrodes placed on the scalp detect brain-wave activity, which is recorded on a chart known as an *electroencephalogram* (Figure 7.1). This device can assess brain damage, epilepsy, and other problems (Lee & others, 2010). In addition, researchers have used the electroencephalograph in studying the neuroscience of happiness, as we consider in the Intersection later in this module.

Not every recording of brain activity is made with surface electrodes that are attached to the scalp. In *single-unit recording,* which provides information about a single neuron's electrical activity, a thin probe is inserted in or near an individual neuron. The probe transmits the neuron's electrical activity to an amplifier so that researchers can "see" the activity (Noseda & others, 2010).

Brain Imaging

For years, medical practitioners have used X rays to reveal damage inside our bodies, both in the brain and in other locations. A single X ray image of the brain is hard to

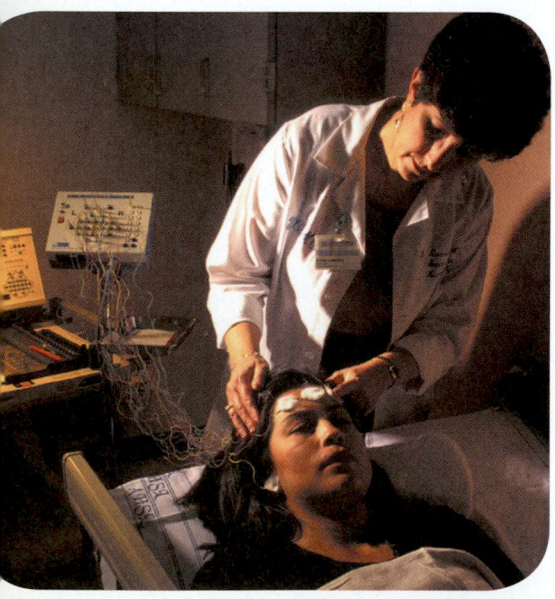

FIGURE 7.1 An EEG Recording The electroencephalograph (EEG) is widely used in sleep research. The device has led to some major breakthroughs in understanding sleep by showing how the brain's electrical activity changes during sleep.

interpret, however, because it shows a two-dimensional image of the three-dimensional interior of the brain. An improved imaging technique called *computerized axial tomography* (CAT scan or CT scan) produces a three-dimensional image obtained from X rays of the head that are assembled into a composite image by a computer. The CT scan provides valuable information about the location and extent of damage involving stroke, language disorder, or loss of memory (Kudo & others, 2010).

Another imaging method, *positron-emission tomography* (PET scan), is based on metabolic changes in the brain related to activity. PET measures the amount of glucose in various areas of the brain and sends this information to a computer for analysis. Neurons use glucose for energy, so glucose levels vary with the levels of activity throughout the brain. Tracing the amounts of glucose generates a picture of activity levels throughout the brain (Kuczynski & others, 2010).

An interesting application of the PET technique is the work of Stephen Kosslyn and colleagues (1996) on mental imagery, the brain's ability to create perceptual states in the absence of external stimuli. For instance, if you were to think of your favorite song right now, you could "hear" it in your mind's ear; or if you reflected on your mother's face, you could probably "see" it in your mind's eye. Research using PET scans has shown that often the same area of the brain—a location called Area 17—is activated when we think of seeing something as when we are actually seeing it. However, Area 17 is not always activated for all of us when we imagine a visual image. Kosslyn and his colleagues asked their participants to visualize a letter in the alphabet and then directed those individuals to answer some yes or no questions about the letter. For instance, a person might be thinking of the letter *C* and have to answer the question "Does it have curvy lines?" The answer would be yes. If the person was thinking of *F,* the answer would be no. The fascinating result of this work was that individuals who showed brain activation on the PET scan in Area 17 while engaged in the visualization task answered the questions faster than those who were not using Area 17. Even though they were doing the same task, some people used Area 17 and others did not. Although all human brains are similar in some ways, in other ways each person's brain is unique.

Another technique, *magnetic resonance imaging (MRI),* involves creating a magnetic field around a person's body and using radio waves to construct images of the person's tissues and biochemical activities. The magnetic field of the magnet used to create an MRI image is over 50,000 times more powerful than the earth's magnetic field (Parry & Matthews, 2002). MRI takes advantage of the fact that the human brain contains a great deal of water (like the rest of the body, the brain is 70 percent water). Within each water molecule there are hydrogen atoms (remember, water is H_2O). These hydrogen atoms can be thought of as tiny magnets. When these magnetlike hydrogen atoms encounter a very strong magnetic field, they align themselves with it. Neurons have more water in them than do other brain tissues, and that contrast is what provides the nuanced brain images that MRI is able to produce (Parry & Matthews, 2002).

MRI generates very clear pictures of the brain's interior, does not require injecting the brain with a substance, and (unlike X rays) does not pose a problem of radiation overexposure (Nyberg, 2004). Getting an MRI scan involves lying completely still in a large metal barrellike tunnel. MRI scans provide an excellent picture of the architecture of the brain and allow researchers to see if and how experience affects brain structure. In one MRI study, Katrin Amunts and colleagues (1997) documented a link between the number of years a person has practiced musical skills (playing the piano or violin, for example) and the size of the brain region that is responsible for controlling hand movements, demonstrating again that behavior can influence the very structure of our brains. Note that these brain changes reflect the development of neural networks.

Although MRI scans can reveal considerable information about brain *structure,* they cannot portray brain *function.* Other techniques, however, can serve as a window on the brain in action. One such method, *functional magnetic resonance imaging,* or *fMRI,*

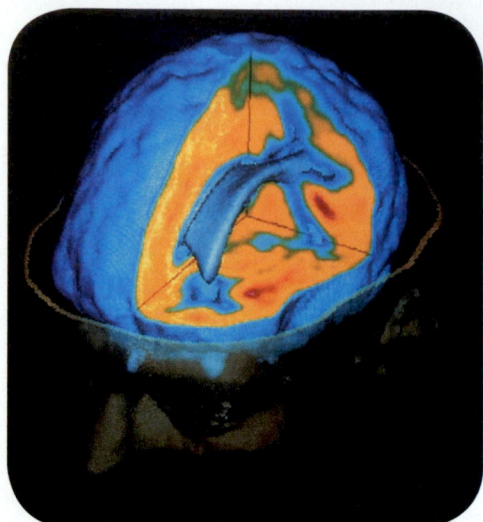

FIGURE 7.2 Functional Magnetic Resonance Imaging (fMRI) Through fMRI, scientists can literally see what areas of the brain are active during a task by monitoring oxygenated blood levels.

allows scientists literally to see what is happening in the brain while it is working (Figure 7.2). The use of fMRI in psychological studies has increased dramatically in the twenty-first century (Schweinsburg & others, 2010). The field of *cognitive neuroscience,* which involves linking cognitive processes and their underlying neural bases, has especially benefited from progress in fMRI (Harrison, Jolicoeur, & Marois, 2010; Weerda & others, 2010).

Like the PET scan, fMRI rests on the idea that mental activity is associated with changes in the brain. While PET relies on the use of glucose as fuel for thinking, fMRI exploits changes in blood oxygen that occur in association with brain activity. When part of the brain is working, oxygenated blood rushes into the area. This oxygen, however, is more than is needed. In a sense, fMRI is based on the fact that thinking is like running sprints. When you run the 100-yard dash, blood rushes to the muscles in your legs, carrying oxygen. Right after you stop, you might feel a tightness in your legs, because the oxygen has not all been used. Similarly, if an area of the brain is hard at work—for example, solving a math problem—the increased activity leads to a surplus of oxygenated blood. This "extra" oxygen allows the brain activity to be imaged.

Getting an fMRI involves reclining in the same large metal barrel as does an MRI, but in the case of fMRI, the person is actively doing something during the procedure. The individual may be listening to audio signals sent by the researcher through headphones or watching visual images on a screen mounted overhead. During these procedures, pictures of the brain are taken, both while the brain is at rest and while it is engaging in an activity such as listening to music, looking at a picture, or making a decision. By comparing the at-rest picture to the listening picture, fMRI tells us what specific brain activity is associated with the mental experience being studied.

Note that saying that fMRI tells us about the brain activity *associated* with a mental experience is a *correlational* statement. As we saw in Module 4, correlations point to the association between variables, not to the potential causal link between them. Although, for example, identifying a picture as a cat may relate to activation in a particular brain area, we do not know if recognizing the cat *caused* the brain activity (Dien, 2009).

An additional method for studying brain functioning, and one that *does* allow for causal inferences, is *transcranial magnetic stimulation (TMS)* (Lepage & Theoret, 2010). First introduced in 1985 (Barker, Jalinous, & Freeston, 1985), TMS is often combined with brain-imaging techniques to establish causal links between brain activity and behavior, to examine neuronal functioning following brain-injuring events such as accidents and strokes, and even to treat some neurological and psychological disorders.

In the TMS procedure, magnetic coils are placed over the person's head and directed at a particular brain area. TMS uses a rapidly changing magnetic field to induce brief electric current pulses in the brain, and these pulses trigger action potentials in neurons (Siebner & others, 2009). Immediately following this burst of action potentials, activity in the targeted brain area is inhibited, causing what is known as a *virtual lesion.* Completely painless, this technique, when used with brain imaging, allows scientists to examine the role of various brain regions. If a brain region is *associated* with a behavior, as demonstrated using fMRI or PET, then the temporary disruption of processing in that area should disrupt that behavior as well. So, for instance, if researchers were doing a study involving the cat recognition example described above, they might use TMS to disrupt the brain area that was associated with cat recognition and see whether the study's participants are temporarily unable to identify a picture of the feline.

7·2 HOW THE BRAIN IS ORGANIZED

As a human embryo develops inside its mother's womb, the nervous system begins forming as a long, hollow tube on the embryo's back (Nelson, 2011). At three weeks or so after conception, cells making up the tube differentiate into a mass of neurons, most of which then develop into three major regions of the brain: the hindbrain, which

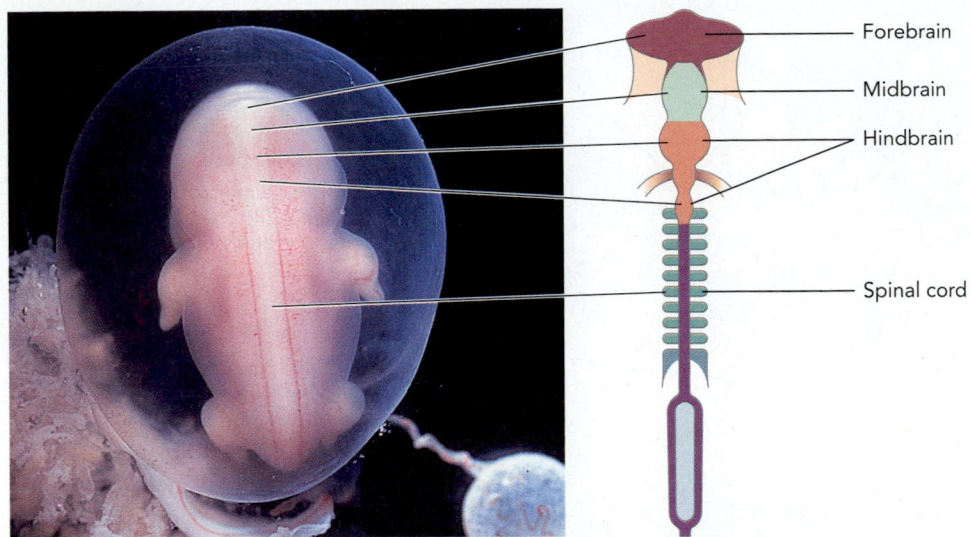

Forebrain

Midbrain

Hindbrain

Spinal cord

FIGURE 7.3 Embryological Development of the Nervous System The photograph shows the primitive tubular appearance of the nervous system at 6 weeks in the human embryo. The drawing shows the major brain regions and spinal cord as they appear early in the development of a human embryo.

is adjacent to the top part of the spinal cord; the midbrain, which rises above the hindbrain; and the forebrain, which is the uppermost region of the brain (Figure 7.3).

Hindbrain

The **hindbrain,** located at the skull's rear, is the lowest portion of the brain. The three main parts of the hindbrain are the medulla, pons, and cerebellum. Figure 7.4 locates these brain structures.

The *medulla* begins where the spinal cord enters the skull. The medulla controls many vital functions, such as breathing and heart rate. It also regulates our reflexes. The *pons* is a bridge in the hindbrain that connects the cerebellum and the brain stem. It contains several clusters of fibers involved in sleep and arousal (Thankachan, Kaur, & Shiromani, 2009).

Taken together, the medulla, pons, and much of the hindbrain (as well as the midbrain, discussed below) are called the **brain stem,** which gets its name because it looks like a stem. Embedded deep within the brain, the brain stem connects with the spinal cord at its lower end and then extends upward to encase the reticular formation in the midbrain. The most ancient part of the brain, the brain stem evolved more than 500 million years ago, when organisms needed to breathe out of water (Hagadorn & Seilacher, 2009). Clumps of cells in the brain stem determine alertness and regulate basic survival functions such as breathing, heartbeat, and blood pressure (Nicholls & Paton, 2009; Spyer & Gourine, 2009).

The *cerebellum* extends from the rear of the hindbrain. It consists of two rounded structures thought to play important roles in motor coordination (Manganotti & others, 2010). Leg and arm movements are coordinated by the cerebellum; for example, when we walk, play golf, and practice the piano, the cerebellum is hard at work. If another portion of the brain commands us to send a quick text message to a friend, it is the cerebellum that integrates the muscular activities required to do so. Damage to the cerebellum impairs the performance of coordinated movements. When this damage occurs, people's movements become awkward and jerky. Extensive damage to the cerebellum makes it impossible to stand up.

Midbrain

The **midbrain,** located between the hindbrain and forebrain, is an area in which many nerve-fiber systems ascend and descend to connect the higher and lower portions of the brain (Prescott & Humphries, 2007). In particular, the midbrain relays information

● **hindbrain** Located at the skull's rear, the lowest portion of the brain, consisting of the medulla, cerebellum, and pons.

● **brain stem** The stemlike brain area that includes much of the hindbrain (it does not include the cerebellum) and the midbrain; it connects with the spinal cord at its lower end and then extends upward to encase the reticular formation in the midbrain.

● **midbrain** Located between the hindbrain and forebrain, an area in which many nerve-fiber systems ascend and descend to connect the higher and lower portions of the brain; in particular, the midbrain relays information between the brain and the eyes and ears.

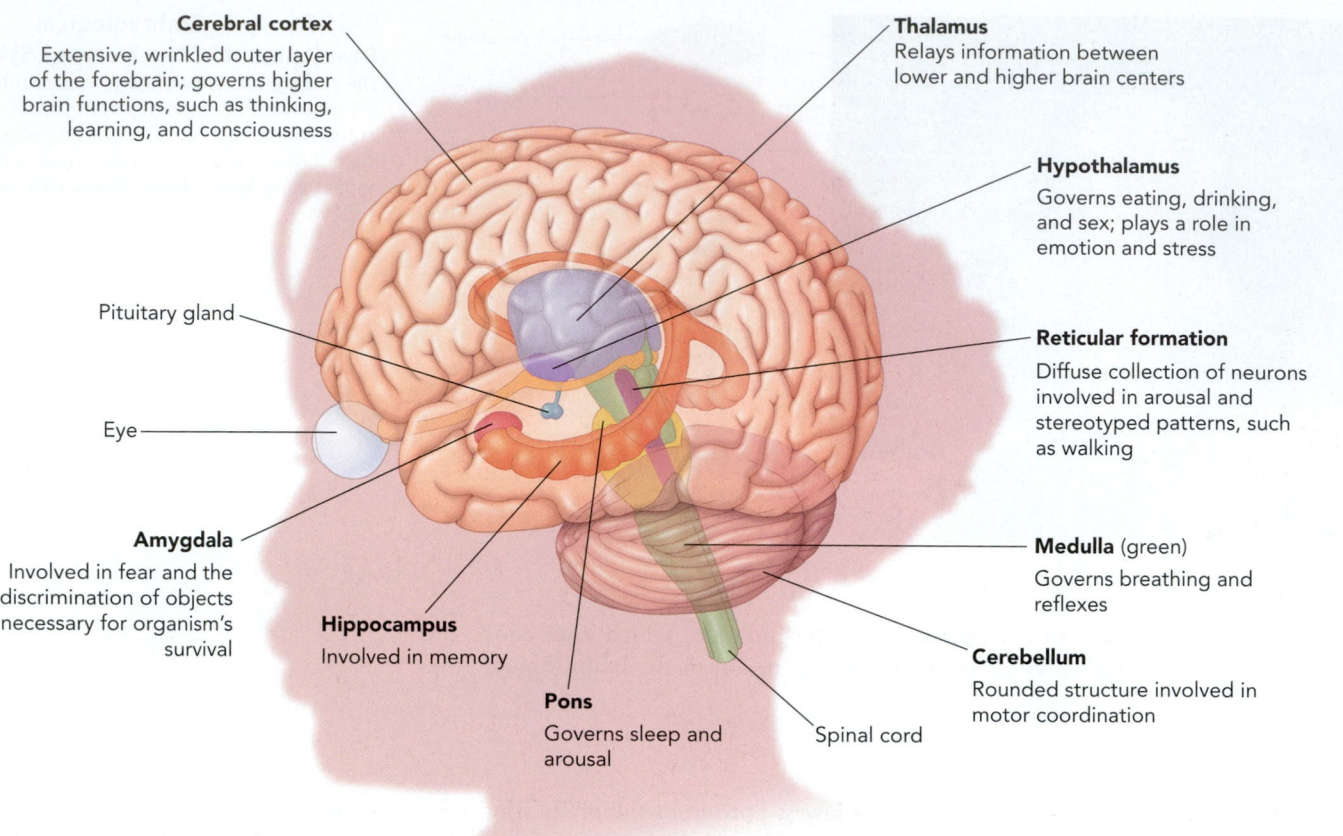

Cerebral cortex
Extensive, wrinkled outer layer of the forebrain; governs higher brain functions, such as thinking, learning, and consciousness

Pituitary gland

Eye

Amygdala
Involved in fear and the discrimination of objects necessary for organism's survival

Hippocampus
Involved in memory

Pons
Governs sleep and arousal

Spinal cord

Thalamus
Relays information between lower and higher brain centers

Hypothalamus
Governs eating, drinking, and sex; plays a role in emotion and stress

Reticular formation
Diffuse collection of neurons involved in arousal and stereotyped patterns, such as walking

Medulla (green)
Governs breathing and reflexes

Cerebellum
Rounded structure involved in motor coordination

FIGURE 7.4 **Structure and Regions in the Human Brain** To get a feel for where these structures are in your own brain, use the eye (pictured on the left of the figure) as a landmark. Note that structures such as the thalamus, hypothalamus, amygdala, pituitary gland, pons, and reticular formation reside deep within the brain.

between the brain and the eyes and ears. The ability to attend to an object visually, for example, is linked to one bundle of neurons in the midbrain.

Parkinson disease damages a section near the bottom of the midbrain called the *substantia nigra* (Grealish & others, 2010), causing deterioration in body movement, rigidity, and tremors. The substantia nigra contains a large number of dopamine-producing neurons. This part of the midbrain feeds dopamine into the *striatum*, the central input station for the basal ganglia, to which we will turn our attention in a moment.

Another important system in the midbrain is the reticular formation (see Figure 7.4). The **reticular formation** is a diffuse collection of neurons involved in stereotyped patterns of behavior such as walking, sleeping, and turning to attend to a sudden noise (Ancelet & others, 2010).

Forebrain

You try to understand what all of these terms and parts of the brain mean. You talk with friends and plan a party for this weekend. You remember that it has been six months since you went to the dentist. You are confident you will do well on the next exam in this course. All of these experiences and millions more would not be possible without the **forebrain**—the brain's largest division and its most forward part.

Before we explore the structures and function of the forebrain, though, let's stop for a moment and examine how the brain evolved. The brains of the earliest vertebrates were smaller and simpler than those of later animals. Genetic changes during the

● **reticular formation** A system in the midbrain comprising a diffuse collection of neurons involved in stereotyped patterns of behavior such as walking, sleeping, and turning to attend to a sudden noise.

● **forebrain** The brain's largest division and its most forward part.

psychological *inquiry*

The Brain in Different Species

This illustration compares the brain of a rat, a cat, a chimpanzee, and a human. In examining the figure, keep in mind that each species is adapted to differing environmental challenges.

1. In what ways is each brain well suited to the challenges faced by its particular species?

2. What structures are similar across all the species? Why do you think certain brain structures are common for these various species? What challenges do all of these species face that would account for the common features of their brains?

3. Note how much larger the cerebral cortex becomes as we go from the brain of a rat to the brain of a human. Why don't rats have a large cerebral cortex?

4. We often think of the human brain as an amazing accomplishment of nature. How might life be different for a rat or a cat with a human brain?

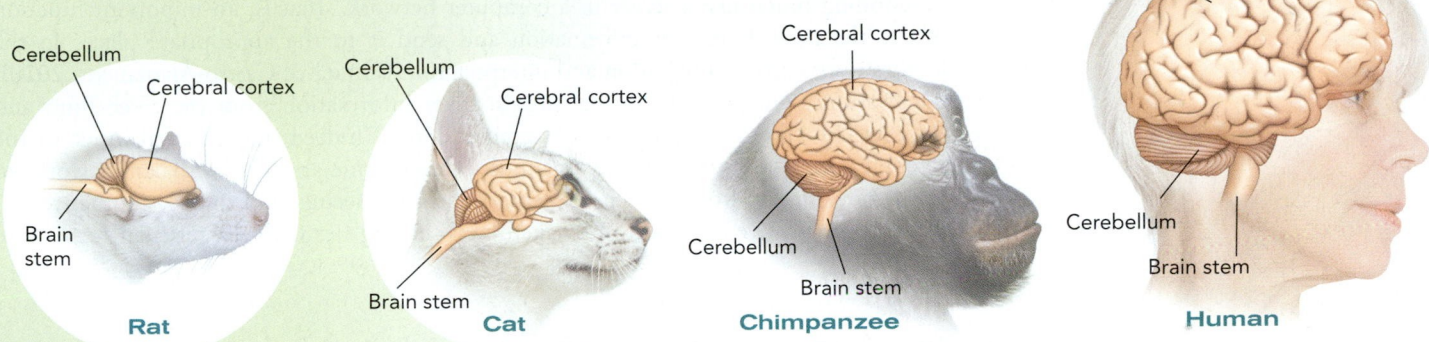

Rat   Cat   Chimpanzee   Human

evolutionary process were responsible for the development of more complex brains with additional parts and interconnections (Mader, 2011). The Psychological Inquiry compares the brain of a rat, a cat, a chimpanzee, and a human. In both the chimpanzee's brain and (especially) the human's brain, the hindbrain and midbrain structures are covered by a forebrain structure called the *cerebral cortex*. The human hindbrain and midbrain are similar to those of other animals, so it is the relative size of the forebrain that mainly differentiates the human brain from the brain of animals such as rats, cats, and chimps. The human forebrain's most important structures are the limbic system, thalamus, basal ganglia, hypothalamus, and cerebral cortex.

LIMBIC SYSTEM

The **limbic system,** a loosely connected network of structures under the cerebral cortex, is important in both memory and emotion. Its two principal structures are the amygdala and the hippocampus (see Figure 7.4).

The **amygdala** is an almond-shaped structure located inside the brain toward the base. In fact there is an amygdala (the plural is *amygdalae*) on each side of the brain. The amygdala is involved in the discrimination of objects that are necessary for the organism's survival, such as appropriate food, mates, and social rivals. Neurons in the amygdala often fire selectively at the sight of such stimuli, and lesions in the amygdala can cause animals to engage in incorrect behavior such as attempting to eat, fight with, or even mate with an object like a chair. In both humans and animals, the amygdala is active in response to unpredictable stimuli (Herry & others, 2007). In humans, damage

● **limbic system** A loosely connected network of structures under the cerebral cortex, important in both memory and emotion. Its two principal structures are the amygdala and the hippocampus.

● **amygdala** An almond-shaped structure within the base of the temporal lobe that is involved in the discrimination of objects that are necessary for the organism's survival, such as appropriate food, mates, and social rivals.

to the amygdala can result in an inability to recognize facial expressions of distress (Adolphs, 2009). The amygdalae also are involved in emotional awareness and expression through their connections with a variety of brain areas (Costa & others, 2010). Throughout this book you will encounter the amygdalae whenever we turn to discussions of intense emotions.

The **hippocampus** has a special role in memory (Bethus, Tse, & Morris, 2010). Individuals who suffer extensive hippocampal damage cannot retain any new conscious memories after the damage. It is fairly certain, though, that memories are not stored "in" the limbic system. Instead, the limbic system seems to determine what parts of the information passing through the cortex should be "printed" into durable, lasting neural traces in the cortex (Wang & Morris, 2010). The hippocampus seems to help us recall things by waking up the areas of the brain that were used when we originally encountered the information (Trinkler & others, 2009).

THALAMUS

The **thalamus** is a forebrain structure that sits at the top of the brain stem in the central core of the brain (see Figure 7.4). It serves as a very important relay station, functioning much like a server in a computer network. That is, an important function of the thalamus is to sort information and send it to the appropriate places in the forebrain for further integration and interpretation (Hirata & Castro-Alamancos, 2010). For example, one area of the thalamus receives information from the cerebellum and projects it to the motor area of the cerebral cortex. Indeed, most neural input to the cerebral cortex goes through the thalamus. Whereas one area of the thalamus works to orient information from the sense receptors (hearing, seeing, and so on), another region seems to be involved in sleep and wakefulness, having ties with the reticular formation.

BASAL GANGLIA

Above the thalamus and under the cerebral cortex lie large clusters, or *ganglia,* of neurons called basal ganglia. The **basal ganglia** work with the cerebellum and the cerebral cortex to control and coordinate voluntary movements (Coxon & others, 2010). Basal ganglia enable people to engage in habitual activities such as riding a bicycle and vacuuming a carpet. Individuals with damage to basal ganglia suffer from either unwanted movement, such as constant writhing or jerking of limbs, or too little movement, as in the slow and deliberate movements of people with Parkinson disease (Ambrosi & others, 2010).

HYPOTHALAMUS

The **hypothalamus,** a small forebrain structure just below the thalamus, monitors three rewarding activities—eating, drinking, and sex—as well as emotion, stress, and reward (see Figure 7.4 for the location of the hypothalamus). As we will see later, the hypothalamus also helps direct the endocrine system.

Perhaps the best way to describe the function of the hypothalamus is as a regulator of the body's internal state. It is sensitive to changes in the blood and neural input, and it responds by influencing the secretion of hormones and neural outputs. For example, if the temperature of circulating blood near the hypothalamus is increased by just one or two degrees, certain cells in the hypothalamus start increasing their rate of firing. As a result, a chain of events is set in motion. Increased circulation through the skin and sweat glands occurs immediately to release this heat from the body. The cooled blood circulating to the hypothalamus slows down the activity of some of the neurons there, stopping the process when the temperature is just right—37.1 degrees Celsius (98.6 degrees Fahrenheit). These temperature-sensitive neurons function like a finely tuned thermostat in maintaining the body in a balanced state.

The hypothalamus also is involved in emotional states and stress, playing an important role as an integrative location for handling stress. Much of this integration is accomplished through the hypothalamus's action on the pituitary gland, an important endocrine gland located just below it (Foley & Kirschbaum, 2010).

● **hippocampus** The structure in the limbic system that has a special role in the storage of memories.

● **thalamus** The forebrain structure that sits at the top of the brain stem in the brain's central core and serves as an important relay station.

● **basal ganglia** Large neuron clusters located above the thalamus and under the cerebral cortex that work with the cerebellum and the cerebral cortex to control and coordinate voluntary movements.

● **hypothalamus** A small forebrain structure, located just below the thalamus, that monitors three pleasurable activities—eating, drinking, and sex—as well as emotion, stress, and reward.

● **cerebral cortex** Part of the forebrain, the outer layer of the brain, responsible for the most complex mental functions, such as thinking and planning.

If certain areas of the hypothalamus are electrically stimulated, a feeling of pleasure results. In a classic experiment, James Olds and Peter Milner (1954) implanted an electrode in the hypothalamus of a rat's brain. When the rat ran to a corner of an enclosed area, a mild electric current was delivered to its hypothalamus. The researchers thought the electric current would cause the rat to avoid the corner. Much to their surprise, the rat kept returning to the corner. Olds and Milner believed they had discovered a pleasure center in the hypothalamus. Olds (1958) conducted further experiments and found that rats would press bars until they dropped over from exhaustion just to continue to receive a mild electric shock to their hypothalamus. One rat pressed a bar more than 2,000 times an hour for a period of 24 hours to receive the stimulation to its hypothalamus (Figure 7.5). Today researchers agree that the hypothalamus is involved in pleasurable feelings, but they have found that other brain areas, such as the limbic system and two other structures—the nucleus accumbens and ventral tegmental area, to be discussed in Module 15—are also important in the link between the brain and pleasure (Kobayashi, Pinto de Carvalho, & Schultz, 2010).

Certainly, the Olds studies have implications for drug addiction (Ludlow & others, 2009).

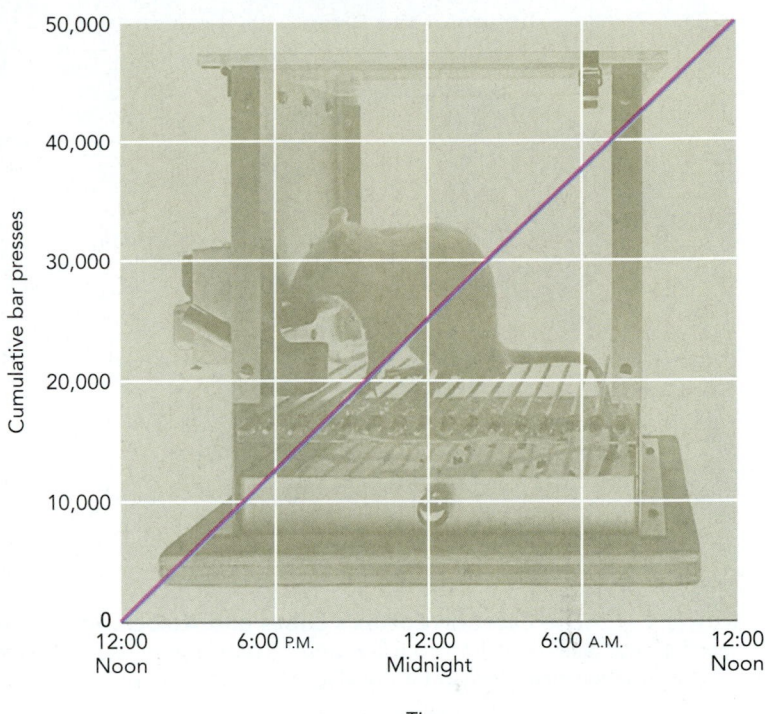

FIGURE 7.5 **Results of the Experiment on the Role of the Hypothalamus in Pleasure** The graphed results for one rat show that it pressed the bar more than 2,000 times an hour for a period of 24 hours to receive stimulation to its hypothalamus. One of the rats in Olds and Milner's experiments is shown pressing the bar.

7·3 THE CEREBRAL CORTEX

The **cerebral cortex** is part of the forebrain and is the most recently developed part of the brain in the evolutionary scheme. The word *cortex* means "bark" (as in tree bark) in Latin, and the cerebral cortex is in fact the outer layer of the brain. It is in the cerebral cortex that the most complex mental functions, such as thinking and planning, take place.

The **neocortex** (or "new bark") is the outermost part of the cerebral cortex. In humans, this area makes up 80 percent of the cortex (compared with just 30 to 40 percent in most other mammals). The size of the neocortex in mammals is strongly related to the size of the social group in which the organisms live. Some scientists theorize that this part of the human brain, which is responsible for high-level thinking, evolved so that human beings could make sense of one another (Adolphs, 2009; Chater, Reali, & Christiansen, 2009).

The neural tissue that makes up the cerebral cortex covers the lower portions of the brain like a sheet that is laid over the brain's surface. In humans the cerebral cortex is greatly convoluted with a lot of grooves and bulges, and these considerably enlarge its surface area (compared with a brain with a smooth surface). The cerebral cortex is highly connected with other parts of the brain (Salzman & Fusi, 2010). Millions of axons connect the neurons of the cerebral cortex with those located elsewhere in the brain.

Lobes

The wrinkled surface of the cerebral cortex is divided into two halves called *hemispheres* (Figure 7.6). Each hemisphere is subdivided into four regions, or *lobes*—occipital, temporal, frontal, and parietal (Figure 7.7).

The **occipital lobes,** located at the back of the head, respond to visual stimuli. Connections among various areas of the occipital lobes allow for the processing of information about such aspects of visual stimuli as their color, shape, and motion (Swisher & others, 2010). A person can have perfectly functioning eyes, but the eyes only detect and transport information. That information must be interpreted in the occipital lobes in order for the viewer to "see it." A stroke or a wound in an occipital lobe can cause blindness or, at a minimum, can wipe out a portion of the person's visual field.

● **neocortex** The outermost part of the cerebral cortex, making up 80 percent of the cortex in the human brain.

● **occipital lobes** Structures located at the back of the head that respond to visual stimuli.

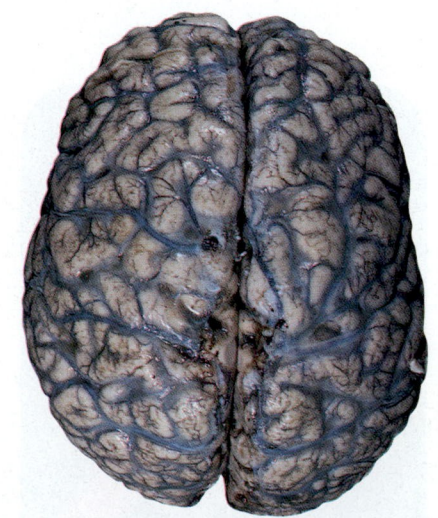

FIGURE 7.6 **The Human Brain's Hemispheres** The two halves (hemispheres) of the human brain can be seen clearly in this photograph.

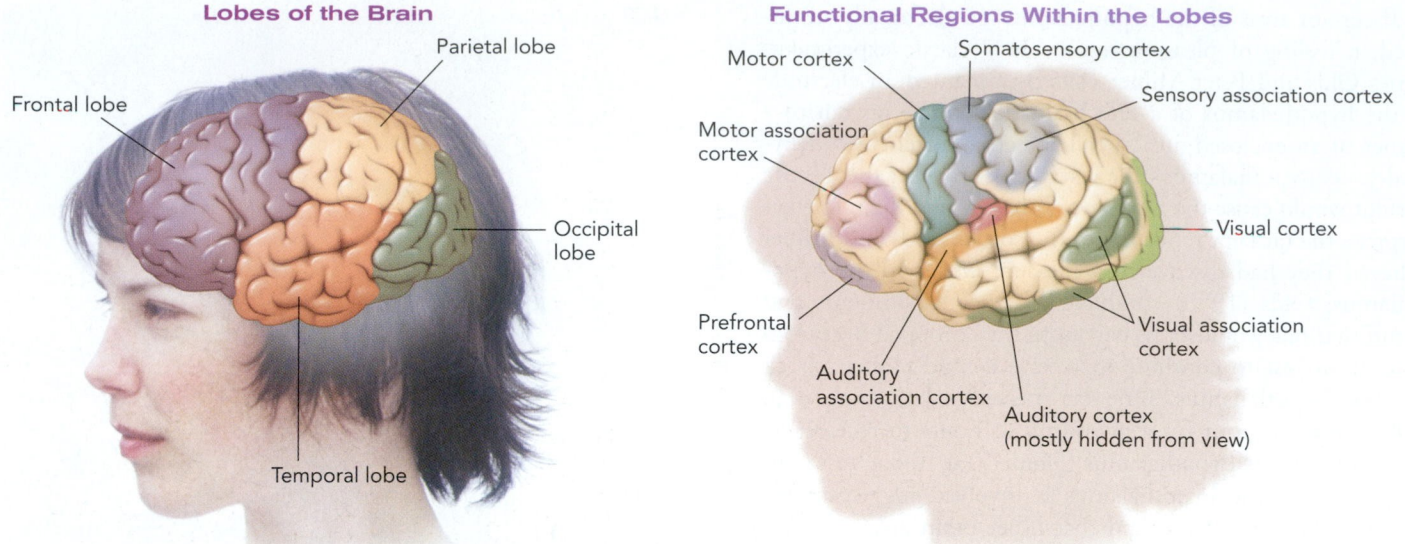

FIGURE 7.7 **The Cerebral Cortex's Lobes and Association Areas** The cerebral cortex (*left*) is roughly divided into four lobes: occipital, temporal, frontal, and parietal. The cerebral cortex (*right*) also consists of the motor cortex and somatosensory cortex. Further, the cerebral cortex includes association areas, such as the visual association cortex, auditory association cortex, and sensory association cortex.

● **temporal lobes** Structures in the cerebral cortex that are located just above the ears and are involved in hearing, language processing, and memory.

● **frontal lobes** The portion of the cerebral cortex behind the forehead, involved in personality, intelligence, and the control of voluntary muscles.

● **parietal lobes** Structures at the top and toward the rear of the head that are involved in registering spatial location, attention, and motor control.

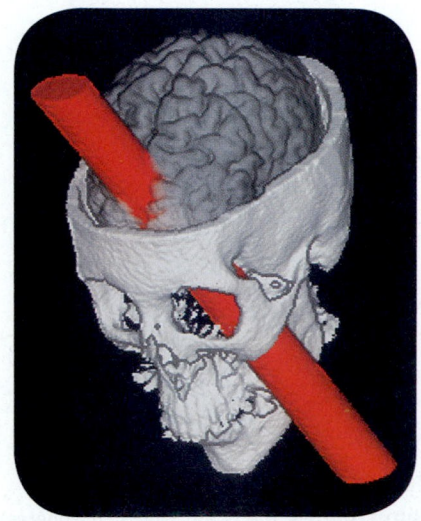

A computerized reconstruction of Phineas T. Gage's accident, based on measurements taken of his skull.

The **temporal lobes,** the part of the cerebral cortex just above the ears, are involved in hearing, language processing, and memory. The temporal lobes have a number of connections to the limbic system. For this reason, people with damage to the temporal lobes cannot file experiences into long-term memory (Lambon Ralph & others, 2010). Some researchers argue that the temporal lobes are also the location of humans' ability to process information about faces. To read further about this topic, see the Critical Controversy.

The **frontal lobes,** the portion of the cerebral cortex behind the forehead, are involved in personality, intelligence, and the control of voluntary muscles. A fascinating case study illustrates how damage to the frontal lobes can significantly alter personality. Phineas T. Gage, a 25-year-old foreman who worked for the Rutland and Burlington Railroad, was the victim of a terrible accident in 1848. Phineas and several co-workers were using blasting powder to construct a roadbed. The crew drilled holes in the rock and gravel, poured in the blasting powder, and then tamped down the powder with an iron rod. While Phineas was still tamping it down, the powder exploded, driving the iron rod up through the left side of his face and out through the top of his head. Although the wound in his skull healed in a matter of weeks, Phineas had become a different person. Previously he had been mild-mannered, hardworking, and emotionally calm, well liked by all who knew him. Afterward, he was stubborn, hot-tempered, aggressive, and unreliable. Damage to the frontal lobe area of his brain had dramatically altered Phineas's personality.

The frontal lobes of humans are especially large when compared with those of other animals. For example, the frontal cortex of rats barely exists; in cats, it occupies just 3.5 percent of the cerebral cortex; in chimpanzees, 17 percent; and in humans, approximately 30 percent.

An important part of the frontal lobes is the *prefrontal cortex,* which is at the front of the motor cortex (see Figure 7.7). The prefrontal cortex is involved in higher cognitive functions such as planning, reasoning, and self-control (de Lange, Jensen, & Dehaene, 2010). Some neuroscientists refer to the prefrontal cortex as an executive control system because of its role in monitoring and organizing thinking (Kuhn, 2009).

The **parietal lobes,** located at the top and toward the rear of the head, are involved in registering spatial location, attention, and motor control (Bisley & Goldberg, 2010; Szczepanski, Konen, & Kastner, 2010; Van der Werf & others, 2010). Thus, the parietal lobes are at work when you are judging how far you have to throw a ball to get it to someone else, when you shift your attention from one activity to another (turn your attention away from the TV to a noise outside), and when you turn the pages of this

CRITICAL CONTROVERSY

Are Human Brains Uniquely Wired to Recognize Faces?

One area of controversy in the study of neuroscience is the question of whether the human brain has a special place for processing information about faces (Dien, 2009; Hung & others, 2010). It seems obvious that faces have a unique importance to all of us and a special capacity to attract our attention. Even infants are drawn to human faces when given a choice of things to look at (Frank, Vul, & Johnson, 2009). Moreover, there is a specific disorder (*prosopagnosia*) that involves the inability to recognize faces but not other objects, and this condition would seem to suggest a specific region of brain damage (Steeves & others, 2009). If faces are special in terms of perception and memory, it makes sense that there might be a special place in the brain for processing faces.

Research by Nancy Kanwisher and colleagues has provided evidence that there is indeed a specialized area in the brain for processing faces (Kanwisher & Yovel, 2010; McKone, Crookes, & Kanwisher, 2010). This area, located in the fusiform gyrus in the right temporal lobe, is called the *fusiform face area* (FFA). The FFA is a dime-size spot just behind your right ear. Using fMRI, researchers have shown that the FFA is especially active when a person is viewing a face—a human face, a cat's face, or a cartoon face—but not cars, butterflies, or other objects (Tong & others, 2000).

The theory that humans have a brain area specialized to process the most important visual information of life—other people's faces—is appealing. It makes sense that organisms like us who live in groups and need others to survive would be especially tuned to social stimuli. However, other researchers have challenged this idea with the following argument. As human beings, we are all experts in perceiving humans. We have been doing it since birth. So, what if the FFA is in fact more involved with processing any expert knowledge, not just faces (Gauthier, Tarr, & Bub, 2010)? Maybe the FFA would be just as active when, say, an avid baseball fan is asked to identify team mascots or when a car enthusiast is asked to identify various car models.

To explore this alternative theory, Isabel Gauthier and her colleagues have conducted a number of studies (Cheung & Gauthier, 2010; Gauthier, Behrmann, & Tarr, 2004; Gauthier & Bukach, 2007; McGugin & Gauthier, 2010). In one investigation, Gauthier and her colleagues (2000) examined individuals who were experts on cars or birds. The FFAs of these experts "lit up" when the individuals were presented with the objects about which they had expertise. In a provocative study, participants were trained to recognize imaginary, faceless creatures called *greebles,* small plantlike objects made of pink clay (Tarr & Gauthier, 2000); Figure 7.8 shows some greebles used in this study). Participants quickly learned to classify the greebles according to sex and family.

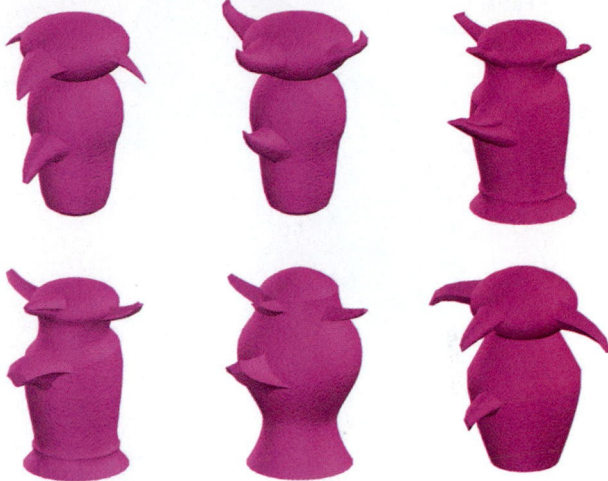

FIGURE 7.8 **Some Greebles Used in Gauthier's Study** The illustration shows sample greebles Gauthier used in her research. In individuals who had reached a level of expertise in recognizing these strange, faceless creatures, the fusiform face area became active during greeble identification.

During fMRI, the FFA was active during these judgments, suggesting that the FFA is concerned with recognition more generally rather than just with recognition of faces. These results have been countered, however, by studies showing that at the very least, the FFA is far more activated during facial recognition than during recognition of other objects (Tong & others, 2000).

The status of the FFA as a specific brain area for face recognition is at the center of a lively debate in neuroscience (McKone, Crookes, & Kanwisher, 2011; Mur & others, 2010). This area of research demonstrates the ways that, as scientists' experimental tools develop, so does their understanding of the brain. Moreover, the new questions they are asking and the way they are asking them can have a profound impact on the development of scientific knowledge (Adolphs, 2009; Dien, 2009).

WHAT DO YOU THINK?

- What are other aspects of our social worlds that you might expect the brain to be specially designed to perceive?

- How does the debate over the FFA illustrate the role of controversy in science more generally?

book. The brilliant physicist Albert Einstein said that his reasoning often was best when he imagined objects in space. It turns out that his parietal lobes were 15 percent larger than average (Witelson, Kigar, & Harvey, 1999).

A word of caution is in order about going too far in localizing function within a particular lobe. Although this discussion has attributed specific functions to a particular lobe (such as vision in the occipital lobe), considerable integration and connection occur between any two or more lobes and between lobes and other parts of the brain.

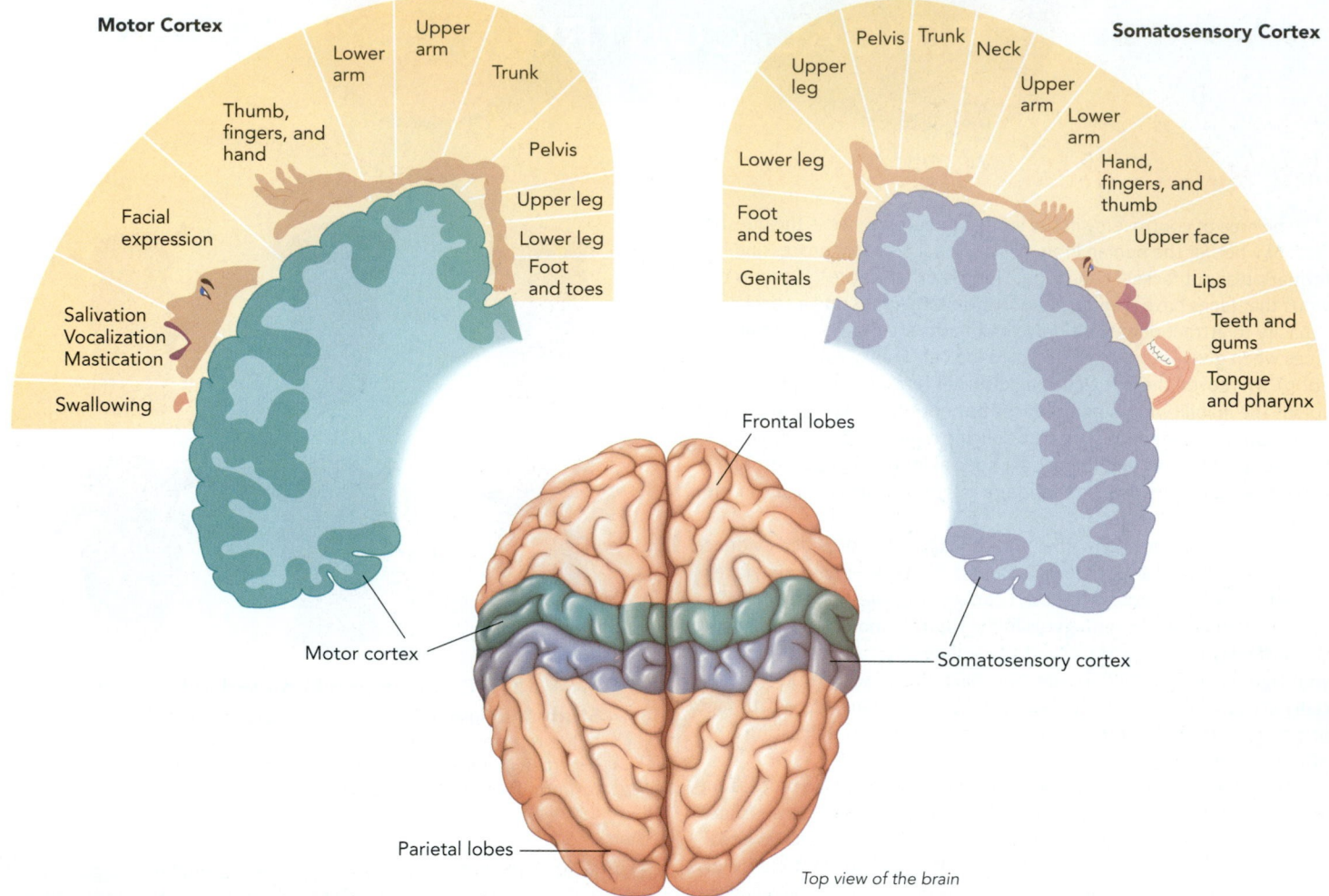

FIGURE 7.9 **Disproportionate Representation of Body Parts in the Motor and Somatosensory Areas of the Cortex** The amount of cortex allotted to a body part is not proportionate to the body part's size. Instead, the brain has more space for body parts that require precision and control. Thus, the thumb, fingers, and hand require more brain tissue than does the arm.

Somatosensory Cortex and Motor Cortex

● **somatosensory cortex** A region in the cerebral cortex that processes information about body sensations, located at the front of the parietal lobes.

● **motor cortex** A region in the cerebral cortex that processes information about voluntary movement, located just behind the frontal lobes.

Two other important regions of the cerebral cortex are the somatosensory cortex and the motor cortex (see Figure 7.7). The **somatosensory cortex** processes information about body sensations. It is located at the front of the parietal lobes. The **motor cortex,** at the rear of the frontal lobes, processes information about voluntary movement.

The map in Figure 7.9 shows which parts of the somatosensory and motor cortexes are associated with various parts of the body. It is based on research done by Wilder Penfield (1947), a neurosurgeon at the Montreal Neurological Institute. He worked with patients who had severe epilepsy, and he often performed surgery to remove portions of the epileptic patients' brains. However, he was concerned that removing a portion of the brain might impair some of the individuals' functions. Penfield's solution was to map the cortex during surgery by stimulating different cortical areas and observing the responses of the patients, who were given a local anesthetic so that they would remain awake during the operation. He found that when he stimulated certain somatosensory and motor areas of the brain, patients reported feeling different sensations, or different parts of a patient's body moved.

Penfield's approach is still used today when neurosurgeons perform certain procedures—for example, removal of a brain tumor. Keeping the patient awake allows the neurosurgeon to ask questions about what the individual is seeing, hearing, and feeling and to be sure that the parts of the brain that are being affected are not essential for consciousness, speech, and other important functions. The extreme precision of brain surgery ensures that life-saving operations do as little harm as possible to the delicate human brain.

For both somatosensory and motor areas, there is a point-to-point relation between a part of the body and a location on the cerebral cortex. In Figure 7.9, the face and hands are given proportionately more space than other body parts because the face and hands are capable of finer perceptions and movements than are other body areas and therefore need more cerebral cortex representation.

The point-to-point mapping of somatosensory fields onto the cortex's surface is the basis of our orderly and accurate perception of the world (Vidoni & others, 2010). When something touches your lip, for example, your brain knows what body part has been touched because the nerve pathways from your lip are the only pathways that project to the lip region of the somatosensory cortex.

Association Cortex

Association cortex (or *association area*) refers to the regions of the cerebral cortex that integrate sensory and motor information. (The label "association cortex" applies to cortical material that is not somatosensory or motor cortex—but it is not filler space.) Intellectual functions, such as thinking and problem solving, occur in association cortex. Embedded in the brain's lobes, association cortex makes up 75 percent of the cerebral cortex (see Figure 7.7).

Interestingly, damage to a specific part of association cortex often does not result in a specific loss of function. With the exception of language areas, which are localized, loss of function seems to depend more on the extent of damage to association cortex than on the specific site of the damage. By observing brain-damaged individuals and using a mapping technique, scientists have found that association cortex is involved in linguistic and perceptual functioning.

The largest portion of association cortex is located in the frontal lobes, directly behind the forehead. Damage to this area does not lead to somatosensory or motor loss but rather to problems in planning and problem solving, or what are called *executive functions*. Personality also may be linked to the frontal lobes. Recall the misfortune of Phineas Gage, whose personality radically changed after he experienced frontal lobe damage.

7·4 THE CEREBRAL HEMISPHERES AND SPLIT-BRAIN RESEARCH

Recall that the cerebral cortex is divided into two halves—left and right (see Figure 7.7). Do these hemispheres have different functions? A discovery by French surgeon Paul Broca provided early evidence that they do.

In 1861 Broca saw a patient who had received an injury to the left side of his brain about 30 years earlier. The patient became known as Tan because *tan* was the only word he could speak. Tan suffered from *expressive aphasia* (also called Broca's aphasia), a language disorder that involves the inability to produce language. Tan died several days after Broca evaluated him, and an autopsy revealed that the injury was to a precise area of the left hemisphere. Today we refer to this area of the brain as *Broca's area,* and we know that it plays an important role in the production of speech.

Another area of the brain's left hemisphere that has an important role in language is *Wernicke's area.* This area is named for Carl Wernicke, a German neurologist, who noticed in 1874 that individuals with injuries in the left hemisphere had difficulties in understanding language. Damage to this region causes problems in comprehending language; although an individual with an injury to Wernicke's area can produce words, he or she may not be able to understand what others are saying. Figure 7.10 shows the locations of Broca's area and Wernicke's area.

Today there continues to be considerable interest in the degree to which the brain's left hemisphere or right hemisphere is involved in various aspects of thinking, feeling,

● **association cortex** Sometimes called association areas, the region of the cerebral cortex that is the site of the highest intellectual functions, such as thinking and problem solving.

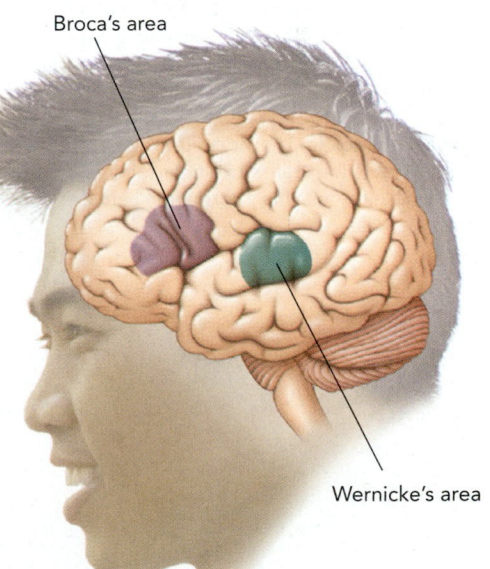

FIGURE 7.10 Broca's Area and Wernicke's Area Broca's area is located in the brain's left hemisphere and is involved in the control of speech. Individuals with damage to Broca's area have problems saying words correctly. Also shown is Wernicke's area, the portion of the left hemisphere that is involved in understanding language. Individuals with damage to this area cannot comprehend words; they hear the words but do not know what they mean.

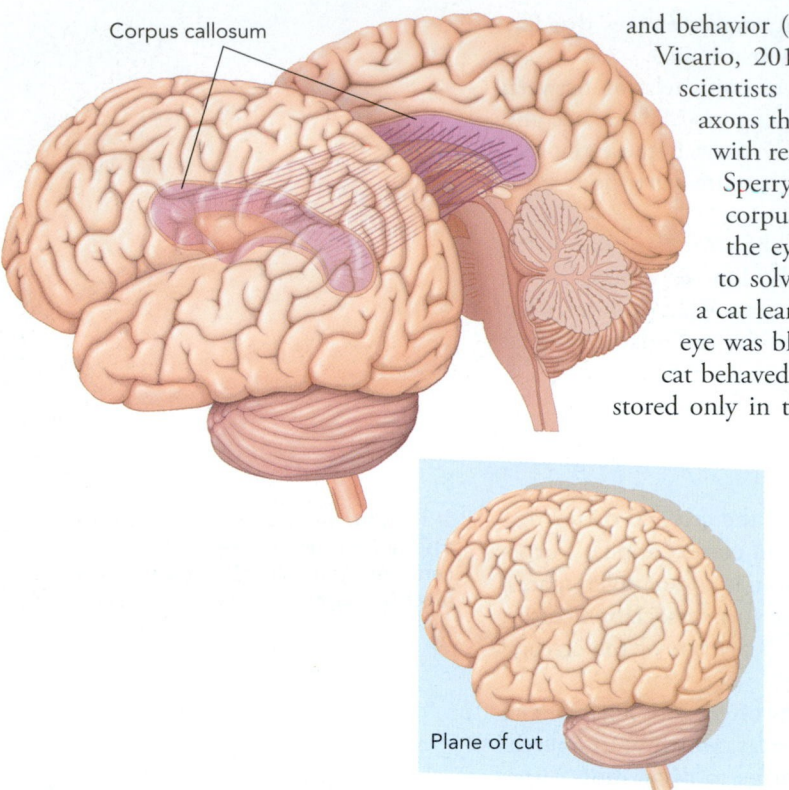

Corpus callosum

Plane of cut

FIGURE 7.11 **The Corpus Callosum**
The corpus callosum is a thick bundle of fibers (essentially axons) that connects the brain cells in one hemisphere to those in the other. In healthy brains, the two sides engage in a continuous flow of information via this neural bridge.

● **corpus callosum** The large bundle of axons that connects the brain's two hemispheres, responsible for relaying information between the two sides.

and behavior (Gazzaniga, 2010; Gazzaniga, Dorn, & Funk, 2010; Phan & Vicario, 2010; van Ettinger-Veenstra & others, 2010). For many years, scientists speculated that the **corpus callosum,** the large bundle of axons that connects the brain's two hemispheres, has something to do with relaying information between the two sides (Figure 7.11). Roger Sperry (1974) confirmed this in an experiment in which he cut the corpus callosum in cats. He also severed certain nerves leading from the eyes to the brain. After the operation, Sperry trained the cats to solve a series of visual problems with one eye blindfolded. After a cat learned the task—say, with only its left eye uncovered—its other eye was blindfolded, and the animal was tested again. The "split-brain" cat behaved as if it had never learned the task. In these cats, memory was stored only in the left hemisphere, which could no longer directly communicate with the right hemisphere.

Further evidence of the corpus callosum's function has come from studies of patients with severe, even life-threatening, forms of epilepsy. Epilepsy is caused by electrical "brainstorms" that can flash uncontrollably across the corpus callosum. In one famous case, neurosurgeons severed the corpus callosum of an epileptic patient now known as W. J. in a final attempt to reduce his unbearable seizures. Sperry (1968) examined W. J. and found that the corpus callosum functions the same in humans as in animals—cutting the corpus callosum seemed to leave the patient with "two separate minds" that learned and operated independently.

As it turns out, the right hemisphere receives information only from the left side of the body, and the left hemisphere receives information only from the right side of the body. When you hold an object in your left hand, for example, only the right hemisphere of your brain detects the object. When you hold an object in your right hand, only the left hemisphere of the brain detects it (Figure 7.12). In individuals with a normally functioning corpus callosum, both hemispheres receive this information eventually, as it travels between the hemispheres through the corpus callosum. In fact, although we might have two minds, we usually use them in tandem.

You can appreciate how well the corpus callosum rapidly integrates your experience by considering how hard it is to do two things at once (Stirling, 2002). Maybe as a child you tried to pat your head and rub your stomach at the same time. Even with two separate hands controlled by two separate hemispheres, such dual activity is hard.

In people with intact brains, hemispheric specialization of function occurs in some areas. Researchers have uncovered evidence for hemispheric differences in function by sending different information to each ear. Remember, the left hemisphere gets its information (first) from the right ear, and the right hemisphere hears what is going on (first) in the left ear. Such research has shown that the brain tends to divide its functioning into one hemisphere or the other, as we now consider.

Left Hemisphere Function

The most extensive research on the brain's two hemispheres has focused on language. Although it is a common misconception that *all* language processing occurs in the brain's left hemisphere, *much* language processing and production does come from this hemisphere (Carota & others, 2010; Harpaz, Levkovitz, & Lavidor, 2009). For example, when we are reading, the left hemisphere recognizes words and numbers and comprehends syntax (rules for forming phrases and sentences) and grammar (Dien, 2009), but the right hemisphere does not. The left hemisphere is also keenly involved when we sing the words of a song. In addition, although not generally associated with spatial perception, the left hemisphere can direct us in solving some basic spatial puzzles, such as identifying whether an object is inside or outside a box.

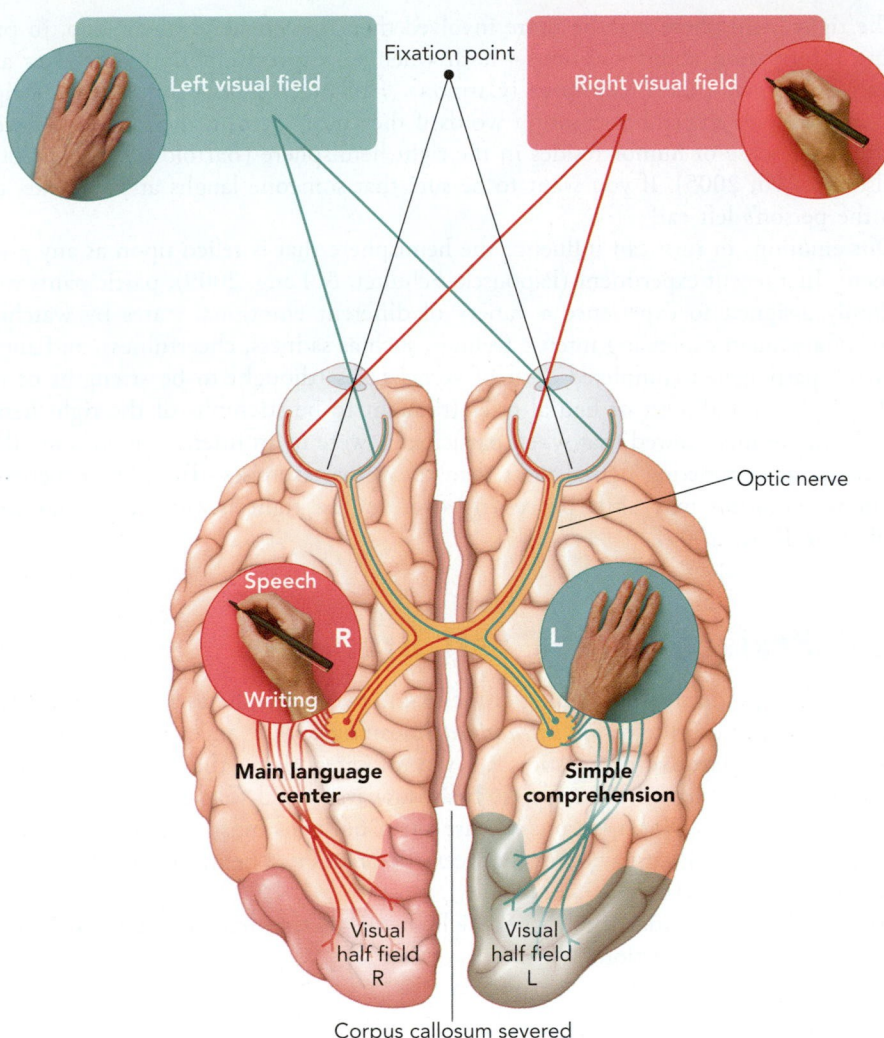

Left visual field

Fixation point

Right visual field

Optic nerve

Speech

R

Writing

L

Main language center

Simple comprehension

Visual half field R

Visual half field L

Corpus callosum severed

FIGURE 7.12 **Information Pathways from the Eyes to the Brain** Each of our eyes receives sensory input from both our left and our right field of vision. Information from the left half of our visual field goes to the brain's right hemisphere (which is responsible for simple comprehension), and information from the right half of our visual field goes to the brain's left hemisphere (the brain's main language center, which controls speech and writing). The input received in either hemisphere passes quickly to the other hemisphere across the corpus callosum. When the corpus callosum is severed, however, this transmission of information cannot occur.

Right Hemisphere Function

The right hemisphere is not as verbally oriented as the left hemisphere, but it does play a role in word recognition, especially if the words are difficult to see (Dien, 2009). The reason we know that the right hemisphere is the source of some human verbal abilities is that people with split brains can draw (with their left hand) pictures of things that are communicated to them in words that are spoken to them (in their left ear). Also, researchers have increasingly found that following damage to the left hemisphere, especially early in development, the right hemisphere can take over some language functions (Staudt, 2010). The right hemisphere moreover is adept at picking up the meaning of stories and the intonations of voices, and it excels at catching on to song melodies.

The real strength of the right hemisphere, however, appears to lie in the processing of nonverbal information such as spatial perception, visual recognition, and emotion (Kensinger & Choi, 2009). With respect to interpreting spatial information, the right hemisphere is involved in our ability to tell if something is on top of something else, how far apart two objects are, and whether two objects moving in space might crash.

As we saw in the Critical Controversy, it is the right hemisphere that is mainly at work when we process information about people's faces (Kanwisher, 2006). How do we know? One way we know is that researchers have asked people to watch images on a computer screen and to press a button with either their right or left hand if they recognize a face. Even right-handed people are faster to recognize faces with their left hand because the information goes directly from the part of the brain that recognizes faces (the right hemisphere) to the left hand (Gillihan & Farah, 2005).

The right hemisphere may be more involved than the left hemisphere, too, in processing information about emotions—both when we express emotions ourselves and when we interpret others' emotions (Carmona, Holland, & Harrison, 2009). People are more likely to remember emotion words if they hear them in the left ear. As well, much of our sense of humor resides in the right hemisphere (Bartolo & others, 2006; Coulson & Wu, 2005). If you want to be sure that someone laughs at your joke, tell it to the person's left ear!

Our emotions in turn can influence the hemisphere that is relied upon at any given moment. In a recent experiment (Papousek, Schulter, & Lang, 2009), participants were randomly assigned to experience a variety of different emotional states by watching videos of a woman expressing intense feelings, such as sadness, cheerfulness, and anger. Then the participants completed a set of verbal tasks (thought to be strengths of the left hemisphere) and a set of figural tasks (thought to be strengths of the right hemisphere). The results showed that when participants were in an intense mood state, they were better at completing figural tasks than the verbal exercises. Thus, the experience of intense emotion may shift processing over to the right hemisphere (Papousek, Schulter, & Lang, 2009).

Right-Brained Versus Left-Brained

Because differences in the functioning of the brain's two hemispheres are known to exist, people commonly use the terms *left-brained* (meaning logical and rational) and *right-brained* (meaning creative or artistic) as a way of categorizing themselves and others. Such generalizations have little scientific basis, however—and that is a good thing. We have both hemispheres for a reason: We use them both. In most complex activities in which people engage, interplay occurs between the brain's two hemispheres (Szczepanski, Konen, & Kastner, 2010).

To read about ways that the left and right hemispheres might be involved in your happiness, see the Intersection.

7·5 INTEGRATION OF FUNCTION IN THE BRAIN

How do all of the regions of the brain cooperate to produce the wondrous complexity of thought and behavior that characterizes humans? Neuroscience still does not have answers to questions such as how the brain solves a murder mystery or composes an essay. Even so, we can get a sense of integrative brain function by using a real-world scenario, such as the act of escaping from a burning building.

Imagine that you are sitting at your computer, writing an e-mail, when a fire breaks out behind you. The sound of crackling flames is relayed from your ear through the thalamus, to the auditory cortex, and on to the auditory association cortex. At each stage, the stimulus is processed to extract information, and at some stage, probably at the association cortex level, the sounds are finally matched with something like a neural memory representing sounds of fires you have heard previously. The association "fire" sets new machinery in motion. Your attention (guided in part by the reticular formation) shifts to the auditory signal being held in your association cortex and on to your auditory association cortex, and simultaneously (again guided by reticular systems) your head turns toward the noise. Now your visual association cortex reports in: "Objects matching flames are present." In other regions of the association cortex, the visual and auditory reports are synthesized ("We have things that look and sound like fire"), and neural associations representing potential actions ("flee") are activated. However, firing the neurons that code the plan to flee will not get you out of the chair. For that task, the basal ganglia must become engaged, and from there the commands will arise to set the brain stem,

Emotion and Neuroscience: Is Your Brain Happy?

Are some brains happier than others? Put your hand on your forehead. The answer to the happy brain question may be lying right there in the palm of your hand. Indeed, research using a variety of techniques to study the neuroscience of emotion suggests that there might be a pattern of brain activity associated with feeling good and that this activity takes place in the front of your brain, in the *prefrontal lobes* (van Reekum & others, 2007).

Paul Ekman, Richard Davidson, and Wallace Friesen (1990) measured EEG activity during emotional experiences provoked by film clips. Individuals in this study watched amusing film segments (such as a puppy playing with flowers and monkeys taking a bath) as well as clips likely to provoke fear or disgust (a leg amputation and a third-degree burn victim). How does the brain respond to such stimuli? The researchers found that while watching the amusing clips, people tended to exhibit more left than right prefrontal activity, as shown in EEGs. In contrast, when the participants viewed the fear-provoking films, the right prefrontal area was generally more active than the left.

Do these differences generalize to overall differences in feelings of happiness? They just might. Heather Urry and her colleagues (2004) found that individuals who have relatively more left than right prefrontal activity (what is called *prefrontal asymmetry*) tend to rate themselves higher on a number of measures of well-being, including self-acceptance, positive relations with others, purpose in life, and life satisfaction. However, the fact that a pattern of brain activation is associated with happiness does not prove that these brain processes caused happiness. Can experimental results clarify the picture?

Do you think your own brain is wired for happiness? How would you go about rewiring it?

John Allen and his colleagues have provided experimental evidence supporting the role of prefrontal asymmetry in emotional responses (Allen, Harmon-Jones, & Cavender, 2001). They used a procedure called *biofeedback* to train college women to increase right or left frontal activation. Specifically, these participants wore an electrode cap for EEG measurement and were hooked up to a computer that sounded a tone when they had effectively changed the symmetry of their brain activation in a particular direction. Half of the women were trained to increase activation of the left hemisphere; the other half, to increase activation in the right hemisphere. Seated in front of a computer screen, the participants could use trial and error, changing their thoughts or feelings, to make the tone sound. By applying their training, the participants were generally able to accomplish the goal of changing their brain activation, without any mention of emotional processes at all.

After the training, researchers found that women who were trained to activate the left more than the right side of the prefrontal brain area were less likely to frown while watching a negative clip, whereas those who were trained to activate the right side more than the left responded with less smiling to the happy clips. Among the women who were especially responsive to the biofeedback training, those who had been trained to activate the right side expressed less interest, amusement, and happiness than those who had been trained to activate the left side.

Research on the effects of mindfulness meditation on frontal activation also shows that changing the way we think can change brain processes. *Mindfulness meditation* (also called *awareness meditation*) involves maintaining a floating state of consciousness that encourages individuals to focus on whatever comes to mind—a sensation, a thought, an image—at a particular moment. Richard Davidson and colleagues have shown that mindfulness meditation training can enhance left frontal activation (Davidson, 2010; Davidson & others, 2003; Lutz & others, 2008). This technique has also been used to treat individuals who are suicidal or extremely depressed, have experienced child abuse, or have chronic pain (Kimbrough & others, 2010; Rosenzweig & others, 2010).

Bear in mind that brain structure and function depend on experience. Savoring the enjoyable moments of life—looking at the flowers in your garden, getting a phone call from a friend, hearing your favorite song—may be an opportunity to train your brain to be happy.

---

motor cortex, and cerebellum to the work of transporting you out of the room. All of this happens in mere seconds.

So, which part of your brain did you use to escape? Virtually all systems had a role. By the way, you would probably remember this event because your limbic circuitry would likely have started memory formation when the association "fire" was triggered. The next time the sounds of crackling flames reach your auditory association cortex, the associations triggered would include this most recent escape. In sum, considerable integration of function takes place in the brain (Kullman, 2010; Salzman & Fusi, 2010). All of the parts of the nervous system work together as a team to keep you safe and sound.

7·6 BRAIN DAMAGE, PLASTICITY, AND REPAIR

Recall from the discussion of the brain's important characteristics earlier in this module that plasticity is an example of the brain's remarkable adaptability. Neuroscientists have studied plasticity, especially following brain damage, and have charted the brain's ability to repair itself (Staudt, 2010). Brain damage can produce horrific effects, including paralysis, sensory loss, memory loss, and personality deterioration. When such damage occurs, can the brain recover some or all of its functions? Recovery from brain damage varies considerably, depending on the age of the individual and the extent of the damage (Anderson & Arciniegas, 2010).

The Brain's Plasticity and Capacity for Repair

The human brain shows the most plasticity in young children, before the functions of the cortical regions become entirely fixed (Nelson, 2011). For example, if the speech areas in an infant's left hemisphere are damaged, the right hemisphere assumes much of this language function. However, after age 5, damage to the left hemisphere can permanently disrupt language ability. We examine the brain's plasticity further in Modules 9–12 on sensation and perception and Modules 31–34 on human development.

A key factor in recovery is whether some or all of the neurons in an affected area are just damaged versus whether they are destroyed (Huang & Chang, 2009). If the neurons have not been destroyed, brain function often becomes restored over time. There are three ways in which repair of the damaged brain might take place:

- *Collateral sprouting,* the process by which axons of some healthy neurons adjacent to damaged cells grow new branches.
- *Substitution of function,* the process by which the damaged region's function is taken over by another area or areas of the brain.
- *Neurogenesis,* the process by which new neurons are generated.

Researchers have found that neurogenesis occurs in mammals such as mice. Recent research has revealed that exercise increases neurogenesis while social isolation decreases it (Creer & others, 2010; Leasure & Decker, 2009). It is now accepted that neurogenesis can occur in humans, but to date, the presence of new neurons has been documented only in the hippocampus, which is involved in memory, and the olfactory bulb, which is involved in the sense of smell (Hagg, 2009; Kroth & others, 2010). If researchers can discover how new neurons are generated, possibly the information can be used to fight degenerative diseases of the brain such as Alzheimer disease and Parkinson disease (Courtois & others, 2010).

Brain Tissue Implants

The brain naturally recovers some, but not all, functions that are lost following damage. Recent research has generated excitement about *brain grafts*—implants of healthy tissue into damaged brains (Grealish & others, 2010). Brain grafts have greater potential success when the brain tissue used is from the fetal stage—an early stage in prenatal development (M. Thomas & others, 2009). The reason for this advantage is that the fetal neurons are still growing and have a much higher probability of making connections with other neurons than does mature brain tissue. In a number of studies, researchers have damaged part of an adult rat's brain, waited until the animal recovered as much as possible by itself, and assessed its behavioral deficits. They then took the corresponding area of a fetal rat's brain and transplanted it into the damaged brain of the adult rat. In these studies, the rats that received the brain transplants demonstrated considerable behavioral recovery (Shetty, Rao, & Hattiangady, 2008).

Might such brain grafts be successful in humans suffering from brain damage? The research results are promising, but finding donors is a problem (Glaw & others, 2009). Although using brain tissue from aborted fetuses is a possibility, there are ethical concerns about that practice.

Perhaps one of the most heated debates in recent years has concerned the use of human embryonic stem cells in research and treatment (Daadi & others, 2010; Ideguchi & others, 2010). The human body contains more than 220 different types of cells, but **stem cells** are unique because they are primitive cells that have the capacity to develop into most types of human cells. Stem cells were first harvested from embryos by researchers at the University of Wisconsin, Madison, and Johns Hopkins University in 1998. Because of their amazing plasticity, stem cells might potentially replace damaged cells in the human body, including cells involved in spinal cord injury and brain damage (Orlacchio & others, 2010; Song & Ming, 2010).

Typically, researchers have harvested the stem cells from frozen embryos left over from *in vitro fertilization* procedures. In these procedures, a number of eggs, or *ova,* are collected from a woman's ovaries in order to be fertilized in a lab. In successful in vitro fertilization, the ova are brought together with sperm, producing human embryos. Because the procedure is difficult and delicate, doctors typically fertilize a large number of eggs in the hope that some will survive when implanted in the woman's uterus. In the typical procedure, there are leftover embryos. These embryos are in the *blastocyst* stage, which occurs five days after conception. At this stage the embryo has not yet attached to the uterus and has no brain, no central nervous system, and no mouth—it is an undifferentiated ball of cells.

Some supporters of stem cell technology (among them the late actor Christopher Reeve, 2000) emphasize that using these cells for research and treatment might relieve a great deal of human suffering. Opponents of abortion disapprove of the use of stem cells in research or treatment on the grounds that the embryos die when the stem cells are removed. (In fact, leftover embryos are likely to be destroyed in any case.) In 2009, President Barack Obama removed restrictions on stem cell research.

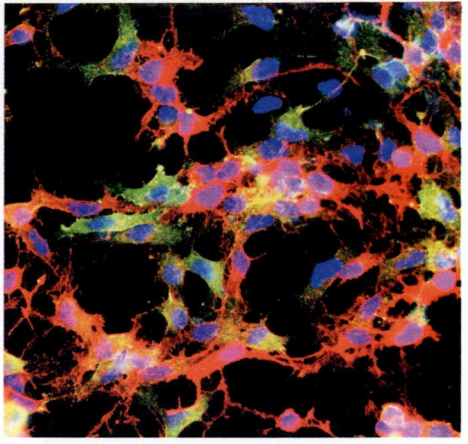

This fluorescent micrograph shows glial stem cells. Like other stem cells, these have the capacity to develop into a wide range of other cells.

● **stem cells** Unique primitive cells that have the capacity to develop into most types of human cells.

SUMMARY

The main techniques used to study the brain are brain lesioning, electrical recording, and brain imaging. These methods have revealed a great deal about the three major divisions of the brain—the hindbrain, midbrain, and forebrain.

The cerebral cortex makes up most of the outer layer of the brain, and it is here that higher mental functions such as thinking and planning take place. The wrinkled surface of the cerebral cortex is divided into hemispheres, each with four lobes: occipital, temporal, frontal, and parietal. There is considerable integration and connection among the brain's lobes.

The brain has two hemispheres. Two areas in the left hemisphere that involve specific language functions are Broca's area (speech) and Wernicke's area (language comprehension). The corpus callosum is a large bundle of fibers that connects the two hemispheres. Research suggests that the left brain is more dominant in processing verbal information (such as language) and the right brain in processing nonverbal information (such as spatial perception, visual recognition, faces, and emotion). Nonetheless, in a person whose corpus callosum is intact, both hemispheres of the cerebral cortex are involved in most complex human functioning.

The human brain has considerable plasticity, although this ability to adapt and change is greater in young children than later in development. Three ways in which a damaged brain might repair itself are collateral sprouting, substitution of function, and neurogenesis. Brain grafts are implants of healthy tissue into damaged brains. Brain grafts are more successful when fetal tissue is used. Stem cell research is a controversial new area of science that may allow for novel treatments for damaged nervous systems.

KEY TERMS

TEST YOURSELF

1. Describe three techniques that allow researchers to examine the brain while it is working.

2. What specific part of the brain is responsible for directing our most complex mental functions, such as thinking and planning, and where is it located?

3. In what ways are the brain's left and right hemispheres specialized in terms of their functioning?

4. Describe three ways in which a damaged brain may repair itself.

5. What specific discovery have researchers made about neurogenesis in human beings? For what kinds of disease might knowledge about the process lead to promising treatment?

6. What are brain grafts, and why does the use of fetal tissue in grafts often lead to successful results?

APPLY YOUR KNOWLEDGE

1. Imagine that you could make one part of your brain twice as big as it is now. Which part would it be, and how do you think your behavior would change as a result? What if you had to make another part of your brain half its current size? Which part would you choose to shrink, and what would the effects be?

2. Do you know anyone who has experienced a brain-damaging event, such as a stroke or head injury? If you feel comfortable doing so, ask the person about the experience and the life changes it may have caused. Based on your interview, which areas of the individual's brain might have been affected?

Genetics and Behavior

In addition to the brain and nervous system, other aspects of our physiology also have consequences for psychological processes. Genes, the focal point of this section, are an essential contributor to these processes (Goldsmith, 2011). As noted in the health section that follows Module 2, the influence of nature (our internal genetic endowment) and nurture (our external experience) on psychological characteristics has long fascinated psychologists. We begin by examining some basic facts about the central internal agent of our human differences: our genes.

8·1 CHROMOSOMES, GENES, AND DNA

Within the human body are literally trillions of cells. The nucleus of each human cell contains 46 **chromosomes,** threadlike structures that come in 23 pairs, with one member of each pair originating from each biological parent. Chromosomes contain the remarkable substance **deoxyribonucleic acid (DNA),** a complex molecule that carries genetic information. **Genes,** the units of hereditary information, are short chromosome segments composed of DNA. The relationship among cells, chromosomes, genes, and DNA is illustrated in Figure 8.1.

Genes hold the code for creating proteins called *amino acids* that form the bases for everything our bodies do. Specifically, genes direct and regulate the production of these proteins. Although every cell in your body contains a full complement of your genes, different genes are active in each cell. Many genes encode proteins that are unique to

● **chromosomes** In the human cell, threadlike structures that come in 23 pairs, one member of each pair originating from each parent, and that contain the remarkable substance DNA.

● **deoxyribonucleic acid (DNA)** A complex molecule in the cell's chromosomes that carries genetic information.

● **genes** The units of hereditary information, consisting of short segments of chromosomes composed of DNA.

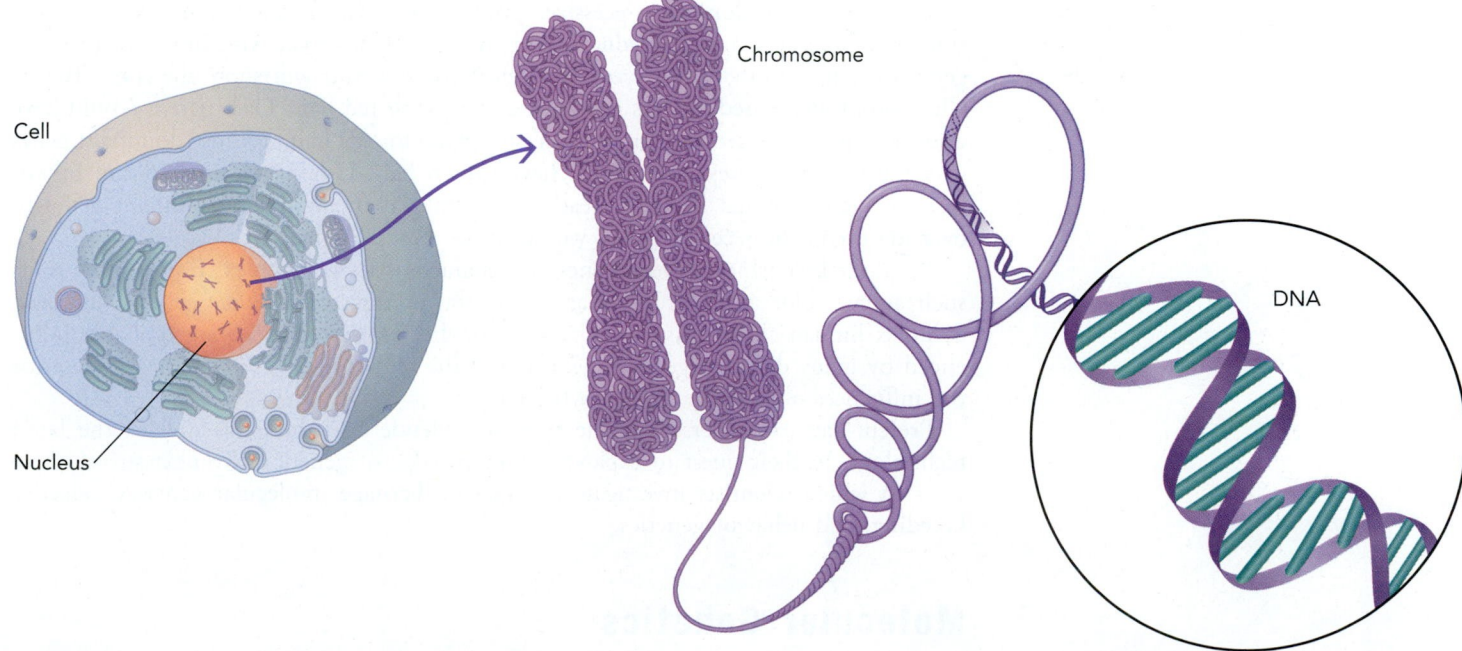

FIGURE 8.1   Cells, Chromosomes, Genes, and DNA (*Left*) The body houses trillions of cells, which are the basic structural units of life. Each cell contains a central structure, the nucleus. (*Middle*) Chromosomes and genes are located in the nucleus of the cell. Chromosomes are made up of threadlike structures composed mainly of DNA molecules. Note that inside the chromosome are the genes. (*Right*) A gene is a segment of DNA that contains the hereditary code. The structure of DNA resembles a spiral ladder.

A positive result from the Human Genome Project. Shortly after Andrew Gobea was born, his cells were genetically altered to prevent his immune system from failing.

a particular cell and give the cell its identity. Will it be a neuron or a bone cell? The activation of your genes holds the key to this question. Some genes are involved in the development of the embryo and then are turned off for the rest of life. Genes do not operate independently but work with one another and in collaboration with hormones and the environment to direct the body's function (Diamond, 2009; Diamond, Casey, & Munakata, 2011).

An international research program called the Human Genome Project (*genome* refers to an organism's complete genetic material, as discussed below) is dedicated to documenting the human genome. Human beings have approximately 20,500 genes (Ensembl Human, 2010). When these 20,500 genes from one parent combine at conception with the same number of genes from the other parent, the number of possibilities is staggering. Although scientists are still a long way from unraveling all the mysteries about the way genes work, some aspects of this process are well understood, starting with the fact that multiple genes interact to give rise to observable characteristics.

8·2 THE STUDY OF GENETICS

Historically speaking, genetics is a relatively young science. Its origins go back to the mid-nineteenth century, when an Austrian monk, Gregor Mendel, studied heredity in generations of pea plants. By cross-breeding plants with different characteristics and noting the characteristics of the offspring, Mendel discovered predictable patterns of heredity and thereby laid the foundation for modern genetics.

Mendel noticed that some genes seem to be more likely than others to show up in the physical characteristics of an organism. In some gene pairs, one gene is dominant over the other. If one gene of a pair is dominant and one is recessive, the **dominant-recessive genes principle** applies, meaning that the dominant gene overrides the recessive gene—that is, it prevents the recessive gene from expressing its instructions. The recessive gene exerts its influence only if *both* genes of a pair are recessive. If you inherit a recessive gene from only one biological parent, you may never know you carry the gene.

In the world of dominant-recessive genes, brown eyes, farsightedness, and dimples rule over blue eyes, nearsightedness, and freckles. If, however, you inherit a recessive gene for a trait from *both* of your biological parents, you will show the trait. That is why two brown-haired parents can have a child with red hair: Each parent would have dominant genes for brown hair and recessive genes for red hair. Because dominant genes override recessive genes, the parents have brown hair. However, the child can inherit recessive genes for red hair from each biological parent. With no dominant genes to override them, the recessive genes would make the child's hair red.

Yet the relationship between genes and characteristics is complex. Even simple traits such as eye color and hair color are likely the product of *multiple* genes. Moreover, complex human characteristics such as personality and intelligence are probably influenced by many different genes. Scientists use the term *polygenic inheritance* to describe the influences of multiple genes on behavior.

Present-day researchers continue to apply Mendel's methods, as well as the latest technology, in their quest to expand our knowledge of genetics. We next survey three ways in which scientists investigate our genetic heritage: molecular genetics, selective breeding, and behavior genetics.

Molecular Genetics

The field of *molecular genetics* involves the manipulation of genes using technology to determine their effect on behavior. There is currently a great deal of enthusiasm about the use of molecular genetics to discover the specific locations on genes that determine an individual's susceptibility to many diseases and other aspects of health and well-being (Clark & others, 2010; Raven & others, 2011).

● **dominant-recessive genes principle** The principle that, if one gene of a pair is dominant and one is recessive, the dominant gene overrides the recessive gene. A recessive gene exerts its influence only if both genes of a pair are recessive.

Selective Breeding

Selective breeding is a genetic method in which organisms are chosen for reproduction based on how much of a particular trait they display. Mendel developed this technique in his studies of pea plants. A more recent example involving behavior is the classic selective breeding study conducted by Robert Tryon (1940). He chose to study maze-running ability in rats. After he trained a large number of rats to run a complex maze, he then mated the rats that were the best at maze running ("maze bright") with each other and the ones that were the worst ("maze dull") with each other. He continued this process with 21 generations of rats. As Figure 8.2 shows, after several generations, the maze-bright rats significantly outperformed the maze-dull rats.

Selective breeding studies demonstrate that genes are an important influence on behavior, but that does not mean experience is unimportant. For example, in another study, maze-bright and maze-dull rats were reared in one of two environments: (1) an impoverished environment that consisted of a barren wire-mesh group cage or (2) an enriched environment that contained tunnels, ramps, visual displays, and other stimulating objects (Cooper & Zubeck, 1958). When they reached maturity, only the maze-dull rats that had been reared in an impoverished environment made more maze-learning errors than the maze-bright rats.

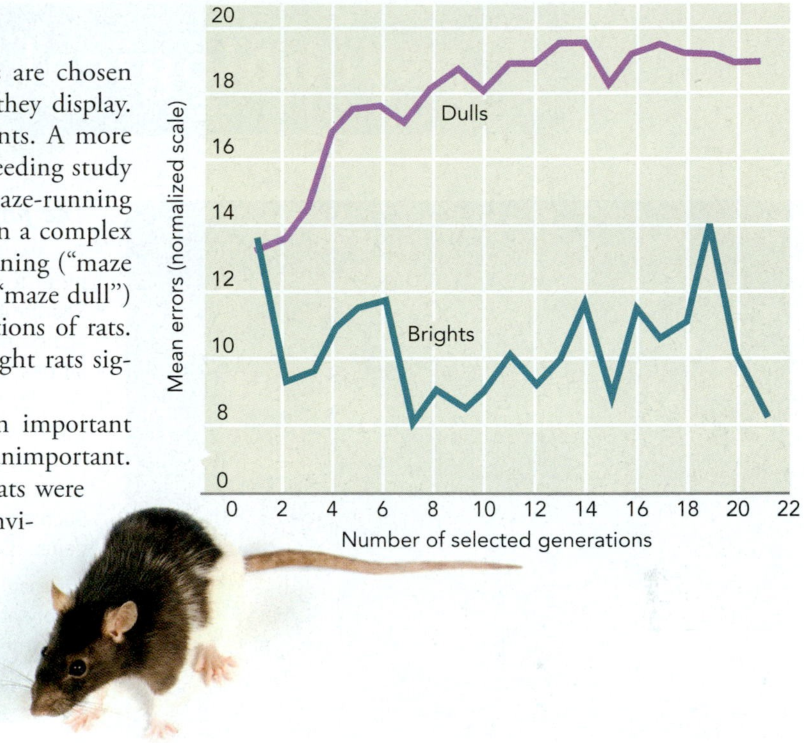

It is unethical to conduct selective breeding studies with human beings. (*Eugenics* refers to the application of selective breeding to humans; this practice was notoriously espoused by Adolf Hitler in Nazi Germany.) In humans, researchers generally examine the influence of genetics on psychological characteristics by using behavior genetics.

FIGURE 8.2 **Results of Tryon's Selective Breeding Experiment with Maze-Bright and Maze-Dull Rats** These results demonstrate genetic influences on behavior.

Behavior Genetics

Behavior genetics is the study of the degree and nature of heredity's influence on behavior. Behavior genetics is less invasive than molecular genetics and selective breeding. Using methods such as the *twin study,* behavior geneticists examine the extent to which individuals are shaped by their heredity and their environmental experiences (Plomin & others, 2009).

In the most common type of twin study, researchers compare the behavioral similarity of identical twins with the behavioral similarity of fraternal twins (Sartor & others, 2009). *Identical twins* develop from a single fertilized egg that splits into two genetically identical embryos, each of which becomes a person. *Fraternal twins* develop from separate eggs and separate sperm, and so they are genetically no more similar than non-twin siblings. They may even be of different sexes.

By comparing groups of identical and fraternal twins, behavior geneticists capitalize on the fact that identical twins are more similar genetically than are fraternal twins. In one recent study, 428 identical and fraternal twin pairs in Italy were compared with respect to their levels of self-esteem, life satisfaction, and optimism for the future (Caprara & others, 2009). The identical twins were much more similar than the fraternal twins on these measures. Furthermore, the researchers found that these various aspects of the person's well-being were similarly affected by genes but differently influenced by the environment. That means that there appeared to be a genetic tendency to have a positive attitude toward different aspects of one's life. In contrast, the environment explained how a person might have high self-esteem but lower life satisfaction (Caprara & others, 2009).

In another type of twin study, researchers evaluate identical twins who were reared in separate environments. If their behavior is similar, the assumption is that heredity

psychological *inquiry*

The Jim Twins

The Jim twins, Jim Springer (*right*) and Jim Lewis, were unaware of each other for 39 years. This pair of twins in the Minnesota Study of Twins Reared Apart was separated at 4 weeks of age and did not see each other again until they were 39 years old. As adults, the Jims had uncanny similarities. Both worked as part-time deputy sheriffs, had vacationed in Florida, had owned Chevrolets, had dogs named Toy, and had married and divorced women named Betty. Both liked math but not spelling. Both were good at mechanical drawing. Both put on 10 pounds at about the same time in life, and both started suffering headaches at 18 years of age. Such similarities seem to provide very strong evidence of the power of genes. Do they really? Think critically as you answer these questions.

1. Imagine that you did not see the photo of the two Jims and were simply asked how similar two men of the same ethnicity, age, and first name might be. In what ways might such men be similar?

2. How many dogs might be named Toy, how many women might be named Betty, and how many men own Chevrolets?

3. How common might it be for men in general to like math better than spelling, to be good at mechanical drawing, and to put on 10 pounds at some point in life?

4. Is it possible that some of the similarities between Springer and Lewis are not so surprising after all? Explain.

5. What does this exercise tell you about the power of vivid and unusual cases in the conclusions we reach?

has played an important role in shaping their behavior. This strategy is the basis for the Minnesota Study of Twins Reared Apart, directed by Thomas Bouchard and his colleagues (1996). The researchers bring identical twins who have been reared apart to Minneapolis from all over the world to study their behavior. They ask thousands of questions about their family, childhood, interests, and values. Detailed medical histories are obtained, including information about diet, smoking, and exercise habits. This approach has its critics, however, who variously argue that some of the separated twins in the Minnesota study had been together several months prior to their adoption, that some had been reunited prior to testing (in certain cases, for a number of years), that adoption agencies often put identical twins in similar homes, and that even strangers are likely to have some coincidental similarities (Joseph, 2006).

You have probably heard of instances of twins who were separated at birth and who, upon being reunited later in life, found themselves strikingly similar to each other. To think critically about such cases, consider the story of Jim Springer and Jim Lewis in the Psychological Inquiry.

8-3 GENES AND THE ENVIRONMENT

So far, we have focused a lot on genes, and you are surely getting the picture that genes are a powerful force in an organism. The role of genetics in some characteristics may seem obvious; for instance, how tall you are depends to a large degree on how tall your parents are. However, imagine a person growing up in an environment with poor nutrition, inadequate shelter, little or no medical care, and a mother who had received no prenatal care. This individual may have genes that call for the height of an NBA or a

WNBA center, but without environmental support for this genetic capacity, he or she may never reach that genetically programmed height. The relationship between an individual's genes and the actual person we see before us is not a perfect one-to-one correspondence. Even for a characteristic such as height, genes do not fully determine where a person will stand on this variable. We need to account for the role of nurture, or environmental factors, in the characteristics we see in the fully grown person.

If the environment matters for an apparently simple characteristic such as height, imagine the role it might play in a complex psychological characteristic such as being outgoing or intelligent. For such a trait, genes are, again, not directly reflected in the characteristics of the person. Indeed, genes cannot tell us exactly what a person will be like. Genes are simply related to some of the characteristics we see in a person.

To account for this gap between genes and actual observable characteristics, scientists distinguish between a genotype and a phenotype. A **genotype** is a person's genetic heritage, the actual genetic material present in every cell in the individual's body. A **phenotype** is the individual's observable characteristics. The relationship between a genotype and phenotype is not always obvious. Recall that some genetic characteristics are dominant and others are recessive. Seeing that a person has brown eyes (his or her phenotype) tells us nothing about whether the person might also have a gene for blue eyes (his or her genotype) hiding out as well. The phenotype is influenced by the genotype but also by environmental factors.

The word *phenotype* applies to both physical *and* psychological characteristics. Consider a trait such as extraversion—the tendency to be outgoing and sociable. Even if we knew the exact genetic recipe for extraversion, we still could not perfectly predict a person's level of (phenotypic) extraversion from his or her genes, because at least some of this trait comes from the person's experience. We will revisit the concepts of genotype and phenotype throughout this book.

Whether a gene is "turned on"—that is, directing cells to assemble proteins—is a matter of collaboration between hereditary and environmental factors. *Genetic expression,* a term that refers to gene activity that affects the body's cells, is influenced by the genes' environment (Gottlieb, 2007). For example, hormones that circulate in the blood make their way into the cell, where they can turn genes on and off. This flow of hormones can be affected by external environmental conditions, such as light level, day length, nutrition, and behavior. In fact, numerous studies have shown that external events outside the original cell and the person, as well as events inside the cell, can excite or inhibit gene expression (Gottlieb, 2007). One study, for instance, revealed that an increase in the concentration of stress hormones such as cortisol produced a fivefold increase in DNA damage (Flint & others, 2007). As we will see next, stress can be a powerful factor in health and wellness.

Our height depends significantly on the genes we inherit. However, even if we have genes that call for the stature of a basketball center, we may not reach that "genetically programmed" height if we lack good nutrition, adequate shelter, and medical care.

● **genotype** An individual's genetic heritage; his or her actual genetic material.

● **phenotype** An individual's observable characteristics.

SUMMARY

Chromosomes are threadlike structures that occur in 23 pairs, with one member of each pair coming from each parent. Chromosomes contain the genetic substance deoxyribonucleic acid (DNA). Genes, the units of hereditary information, are short segments of chromosomes composed of DNA. According to the dominant-recessive genes principle, if one gene of a pair is dominant and one is recessive, the dominant gene overrides the recessive gene.

KEY TERMS

chromosomes 95
deoxyribonucleic acid
  (DNA) 95
genes 95

dominant-recessive genes
  principle 96
genotype 99
phenotype 99

Two important concepts in the study of genetics are the genotype and phenotype. The genotype is an individual's actual genetic material. The phenotype is the observable characteristics of the person.

Three methods of studying heredity's influence are molecular genetics, selective breeding, and behavior genetics. Two methods used by behavior geneticists are twin studies and adoption studies.

Both genes and environment play a role in determining the phenotype of an individual. Even for characteristics in which genes play a large role (such as height and eye color), the environment also is a factor.

TEST YOURSELF

1. What is the relationship among chromosomes, genes, and DNA?

2. According to the dominant-recessive genes principle, how could two brown-haired parents have a blonde-haired child?

3. What term refers to our genetic makeup, and what term refers to the observable physical expression of that genetic makeup?

APPLY YOUR KNOWLEDGE

1. Search the Internet for information about a happiness gene. How would you evaluate research on such a gene, given what you have read so far in this book? What (if anything) would the existence of such a gene mean for your ability to find happiness in your life?

2. List five questions a behavioral geneticist might ask. Search for an answer to two of those questions. Report your findings to the class.

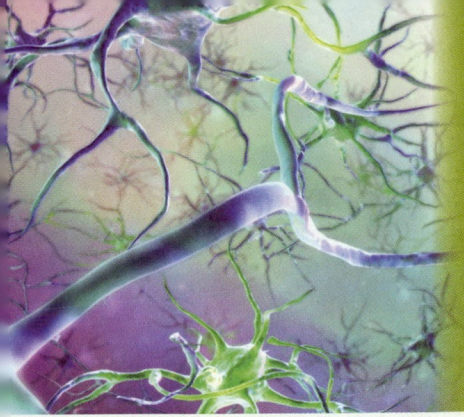

Psychology's Biological Foundations and Health and Wellness

In Modules 6–8 we explored the structure and function of various aspects of the nervous system. The components of the nervous system play an essential role in our health and wellness.

Stress is the response of individuals to **stressors,** which are the circumstances and events that threaten them and tax their coping abilities. Recall that the sympathetic nervous system jumps into action when we encounter a threat in the environment. When we experience stress, our body readies itself to handle the assault.

You certainly know what stress feels like. Imagine, for example, that you show up for class one morning, and it looks as if everyone else knows that there is a test that day. You hear others talking about how much they have studied, and you nervously ask yourself: "Test? What test?" You might start to sweat, and your heart might thump fast and hard in your chest. Sure enough, the instructor shows up with a stack of exams. You are about to be tested on material you have not even thought about, much less studied.

As we have seen, stress begins with a "fight or flight" response sparked by the sympathetic nervous system. This reaction quickly mobilizes the body's physiological resources to prepare us to deal with threats to survival. An unexpected exam is not literally a threat to your survival, but the human stress response is such that it can occur in reaction to *anything* that threatens personally important motives (Sapolsky, 2004).

Acute stress is the stress that occurs in response to an immediate perceived threat. When the stressful situation ends, so does acute stress. Acute stress is adaptive, because it allows us to do the things we need to in an emergency. Once the danger passes, the parasympathetic nervous system can calm us down and focus on body maintenance. However, we are not in a live-or-die situation most of the time when we experience stress. Indeed, we can even "stress ourselves out" just by thinking. *Chronic stress*—stress that goes on continuously—may lead to persistent autonomic nervous system arousal (Leonard & Myint, 2009). While the sympathetic nervous system is working to meet the demands of whatever is stressing us out, the parasympathetic nervous system is not getting a chance to do its job of maintenance and repair, of digesting food, and of keeping our organs in good working order. Furthermore, in chronic stress, the stress hormones adrenaline and noradrenaline, produced by the endocrine system, are constantly circulated in the body, eventually causing a breakdown of the immune system (Sapolsky, 2004). In other words, over time, chronic autonomic nervous system activity can bring about an immune system collapse (Miller, Chen, & Cole, 2009).

Chronic stress is clearly best avoided. The brain, an organ that is itself powerfully affected by chronic stress, can be our ally in helping us avoid such continuous stress. Consider that when we face a challenging situation, we can exploit the brain's abilities and interpret the experience in a way that is not so stressful. For example, maybe we can approach an upcoming audition for a play not so much as a stressor but as an opportunity to shine. Many cognitive therapists believe that changing the way people think about their life opportunities and experiences can help them live less stressfully (Rachman, 2009; Watson, 2009).

In this section, we considered how changing the way we think leads to physical changes in the brain and its operations. In light of this remarkable capacity, it is reasonable to conclude that we can use our brain's powers to change how we look at life experiences—and maybe even to deploy the brain as a defense against undergoing stress.

● **stress** The responses of individuals to environmental stressors.

● **stressors** Circumstances and events that threaten individuals and tax their coping abilities and that cause physiological changes to ready the body to handle the assault of stress.

Snapshots

"*Bridges falling down, killer pumpkin eaters, blind mice with carving knives . . . I CAN'T TAKE IT ANYMORE!*"

© Jason Love. www.CartoonStock.com.

The biological foundations of psychology are in evidence across the entire nervous system, including the brain, the intricately working neurotransmitters, the endocrine system, and our genes. These physical realities of our body work in concert to produce our behavior, thoughts, and feelings. The activities you perform every day are all signs of the success of this physical system. Your mastery of the material in this module is only one reflection of the extraordinary capabilities of this biological achievement.

SUMMARY

Stress is the body's response to changes in the environment. Stressors are the agents of those changes—that is, the circumstances and events that threaten the organism. The body's stress response is largely a function of sympathetic nervous system activation that prepares us for action in the face of a threat. The stress response involves slowing down maintenance processes (such as immune function and digestion) in favor of rapid action.

Acute stress is an adaptive response, but chronic stress can have negative consequences for our health. Although stress may be inevitable, our reaction to a stressful event is largely a function of how we think about it.

KEY TERMS

stress   101
stressors   101

TEST YOURSELF

1. Explain what stress and stressors are.

2. What part of the nervous system sets off the "fight or flight" reaction, and how does this reaction affect the body?

3. What is the difference between acute stress and chronic stress?

Sensation and Perception

Our Senses: Taking in the World

As 3-year-old Abigail Riggins sits in her car seat telling her mother "Go!" when the light turns green, she appears to be much like any other preschooler. When she goes horseback riding or ice skating, she is a typical little girl. What sets her apart is that Abigail was born with severe congenital glaucoma—a condition that left her unable to see. As a baby, she kept her eyes tightly closed in the presence of light. Fortunately, Abigail's doctors were motivated to act quickly on her condition, because they knew that Abigail needed to experience sight as early as possible if she were to be able to see later in life. The baby required surgery, they said. Abigail's parents worried because she was so young, but eventually they agreed that Abigail should have cornea transplants—at the tender age of 2. After Abigail received artificial corneas in both eyes, she became a bubbly, outgoing child.

Each year, 40,000 cornea transplants are performed in the United States. These procedures generally depend on eye banks, to which individuals can arrange to have their sight organs donated after death. Imagine all those people going through this complex surgery—and, in some cases, then seeing for the first time. For them, sight is truly a gift, one bestowed not only by nature but also by science, technology, and the generosity of others.

Vision and our other senses connect us to the world. We see a beloved friend's face, feel a comforting hand, and hear our name called. Our ability to sense and perceive the world is what allows us to reach out into life in the many ways we do every day. ●

How We Sense and Perceive the World

Sensation and perception researchers represent a broad range of specialties, including *ophthalmology*, the study of the eye's structure, function, and diseases; *audiology*, the science concerned with hearing; *neurology*, the scientific study of the nervous system; and many others. Understanding sensation and perception requires comprehending the physical properties of the objects of our perception—light, sound, texture, and so on. The psychological approach to these processes involves understanding the physical structures and functions of the sense organs, as well as the brain's conversion of information from these organs into experience.

9-1 THE PROCESSES AND PURPOSES OF SENSATION AND PERCEPTION

Our world is alive with stimuli—all the objects and events that surround us. Sensation and perception are the processes through which we detect and understand these various stimuli. We do not actually experience these stimuli directly; rather, our senses allow us to get information about aspects of our environment, and we then take that information and form a perception of the world. **Sensation** is the process of receiving stimulus energies from the external environment and transforming those energies into neural energy. Physical energy such as light, sound, and heat is detected by specialized receptor cells in the sense organs—eyes, ears, skin, nose, and tongue. When the receptor cells register a stimulus, the energy is converted to an electrochemical impulse or action potential that relays information about the stimulus through the nervous system to the brain (Xu, Kotak, & Sanes, 2010). When it reaches the brain, the information travels to the appropriate area of the cerebral cortex (Swisher & others, 2010).

The brain gives meaning to sensation through perception. **Perception** is the process of organizing and interpreting sensory information so that it has meaning. Receptor cells in our eyes record—that is, sense—a sleek silver object in the sky, but they do not "see" a jet plane. Recognizing that silver object as a plane is perception.

Bottom-Up and Top-Down Processing

Psychologists distinguish between bottom-up and top-down processing in sensation and perception. In **bottom-up processing**, sensory receptors register information about the external environment and send it up to the brain for interpretation. Bottom-up processing means taking in information and trying to make sense of it (Willenbockel & others, 2010). An illustration is the way you experience a song the first time you hear it: You listen carefully to get a "feel" for it. In contrast, **top-down processing** starts with cognitive processing in the brain; in top-down processing we begin with some sense of what is happening (the product of our experiences) and apply that framework to incoming information from the world (de Lange, Jensen, & Dehaene, 2010; Harel & others, 2010). You can experience top-down processing by "listening" to your favorite song in your head. As you "hear" the song in your mind's ear, you are engaged in a perceptual experience produced by top-down processing.

Bottom-up and top-down processing work together in sensation and perception to allow us to function accurately and efficiently (Hegarty, Canham, & Fabrikant, 2010).

* **sensation** The process of receiving stimulus energies from the external environment and transforming those energies into neural energy.

* **perception** The process of organizing and interpreting sensory information so that it has meaning.

* **bottom-up processing** The operation in sensation and perception in which sensory receptors register information about the external environment and send it up to the brain for interpretation.

* **top-down processing** The operation in sensation and perception, launched by cognitive processing at the brain's higher levels, that allows the organism to sense what is happening and to apply that framework to information from the world.

For example, by themselves our ears provide only incoming information about sound in the environment. Only when we consider both what the ears hear (bottom-up processing) and what the brain interprets (top-down processing) can we fully understand sound perception. In fact, in everyday life, the two processes of sensation and perception are essentially inseparable. For this reason, most psychologists refer to sensation and perception as a unified information-processing system (Goldstein, 2010).

Have you ever begged a friend to listen to your favorite song, only to be disappointed when he or she reacted to it with a shrug? If so, you might note that although all four ears register the same information, perception is a very subjective interpretation of that information. For further perspective on the difference between sensation and perception, check out the Psychological Inquiry feature.

The Purposes of Sensation and Perception

Why do we perceive the world? From an evolutionary perspective, the purpose of sensation and perception is adaptation that improves a species' chances for survival (Brooker, 2010; Raven & others, 2011). An organism must be able to sense and respond quickly and accurately to events in the immediate environment, such as the approach of a predator, the presence of prey, or the appearance of a potential mate. Not surprisingly, therefore, most animals—from goldfish to gorillas to humans—have eyes and ears, as well as sensitivities to touch and chemicals (smell and taste). Furthermore, a close comparison of sensory systems in animals reveals that each species is exquisitely adapted to the habitat in which it evolved (Molles, 2010). Animals that are primarily predators generally have their eyes at the front of their face so that they can perceive their prey accurately. In contrast, animals that are more likely to be someone else's lunch have their eyes on the sides of their head, giving them a wide view of their surroundings at all times.

Through sensation we take in information from the world; through perception we identify meaningful patterns in that information. Thus, sensation and perception work hand in hand when we enjoy a hug and the sweet fragrance of a flower.

psychological *inquiry*

Old Woman or Young Woman?

Study the illustration and analyze your perceptions by answering these questions.

1. What do you see? If you see an old woman, can you see a young woman as well? (Hint: The old woman's nose is the young woman's jawline.) If you see a young woman, can you see an old woman as well? (Hint: The young woman's chin is the tip of the old woman's nose.)

2. How many pictures do you sense visually in the illustration? Notice that for each of *two* possible perceptions, just *one image* is sensed.

3. What do you think determined your first response to this picture? Explain.

Most predatory animals have eyes at the front of their face; most animals that are prey have eyes on the sides of their head. Through these adaptations, predators perceive their prey accurately, and prey gain a measure of safety from their panoramic view of their environment.

9·2 SENSORY RECEPTORS AND THE BRAIN

All sensation begins with **sensory receptors,** specialized cells that detect stimulus information and transmit it to sensory (*afferent*) nerves and the brain (Ye & others, 2010). Recall from Module 6 that afferent nerves bring information to the brain from the world. Sensory receptors are the openings through which the brain and nervous system experience the world. Figure 9.1 shows the human sensory receptors for vision, hearing, touch, smell, and taste.

Figure 9.2 depicts the flow of information from the environment to the brain. Sensory receptors take in information from the environment, creating local electrical currents. The receptors trigger action potentials in sensory neurons, which carry that information to the central nervous system. Because sensory neurons (like all neurons) follow the all-or-nothing principle, described in Module 6, the intensity of the stimulus, such as that of a dim versus a bright light, cannot be communicated to the brain by changing the strength of the action potential. Instead, the receptor varies the *frequency* of action potentials sent to the brain. So, if a stimulus is very intense, like the bright sun on a hot day, the neuron will fire more frequently to let the brain know that the light is, indeed, very, very bright.

Other than frequency, the action potentials of all sensory nerves are alike. This sameness raises an intriguing question: How can an animal distinguish among sight, sound, odor, taste, and touch? The answer is that sensory receptors are selective and have different neural pathways. They are specialized to absorb a particular type of energy—light energy, sound vibrations, or chemical energy, for example—and convert it into an action potential.

Sensation involves detecting and transmitting information about different kinds of energy. The sense organs and sensory receptors fall into several main classes based on the type of energy that is detected, including

- *Photoreception:* detection of light, perceived as sight
- *Mechanoreception:* detection of pressure, vibration, and movement, perceived as touch, hearing, and equilibrium
- *Chemoreception:* detection of chemical stimuli, perceived as smell and taste

Each of these processes belongs to a particular class of receptors and brain processes. There are rare cases, however, in which the senses can become confused. The term

	Vision	Hearing	Touch	Smell	Taste
Sensory Receptor Cells	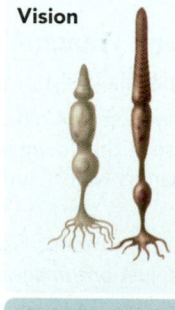	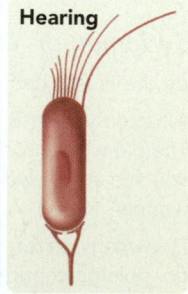			
Type of Energy Reception	Photoreception: detection of light, perceived as sight	Mechano-reception: detection of vibration, perceived as hearing	Mechano-reception: detection of pressure, perceived as touch	Chemoreception: detection of chemical stimuli, perceived as smell	Chemoreception: detection of chemical stimuli, perceived as taste
Sense Organ	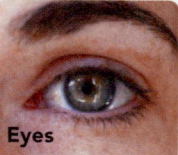 Eyes	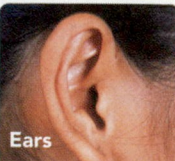 Ears	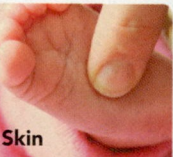 Skin	 Nose	 Tongue

FIGURE 9.1 Human Senses: Organs, Energy Stimuli, and Sensory Receptors The receptor cells for each sense are specialized to receive particular types of energy stimuli.

synaesthesia describes an experience in which one sense (say, sight) induces an experience in another sense (say, hearing) (Eagleman, 2010; Ward & others, 2010). For example, a person might "see" music or "taste" a color. One woman was able to taste sounds, so that a piece of music, to her, tasted like tuna fish (Beeli, Esslen, & Jancke, 2005). Neuroscientists are exploring the neurological bases of synaesthesia, especially in the connections among the various sensory regions of the cerebral cortex (Makioka, 2009).

Phantom limb pain is another example of confused senses. As many as 95 percent of individuals who have lost an arm or a leg report alarming and puzzling pain in the amputated limb. Although the limb that contains the sensory receptors is gone, the areas of the brain and nervous system that received information from those receptors are still there, causing confusion (Desmond & MacLachlan, 2010; Probstner & others, 2010). Amputee veterans of combat in Iraq and Afghanistan have found some relief in an unexpected place: looking in a mirror. In this treatment, individuals place a mirror in front of their existing limb and move the limb around while watching the mirror. So, if a person's left leg has been amputated, the mirror is placed so that the right leg is seen moving in the mirror where the left leg would be if it had not been amputated. This procedure seems to trick the brain into perceiving the missing limb as still there, allowing it to make sense of incoming sensation (Flor & Diers, 2009). The success of this mirror therapy demonstrates how our senses cooperate to produce experience—how the bottom-up processes (the incoming messages from the missing limb) and the top-down processes (the brain's efforts to make sense of these messages) work together.

In the brain, nearly all sensory signals go through the thalamus, the brain's relay station, described in Module 7. From the thalamus, the signals go to the sensory areas of the cerebral cortex, where they are modified and spread throughout a vast network of neurons.

Recall from Module 7 that certain areas of the cerebral cortex are specialized to handle different sensory functions. Visual information is processed mainly in the occipital lobes; hearing in the temporal lobes; and pain, touch, and temperature in the parietal lobes. Keep in mind, however, that the interactions and pathways of sensory information are complex, and the brain often must coordinate extensive information and interpret it (van Atteveldt & others, 2010).

FIGURE 9.2 Information Flow in Senses *The diagram shows a general flow of sensory information from energy stimulus to sensory receptor cell to sensory neuron to sensation and perception.*

9-3 THRESHOLDS

Any sensory system must be able to detect varying degrees of energy in the form of light, sound, chemical, or mechanical stimulation. How much of a stimulus is necessary for you to see, hear, taste, smell, or feel something? What is the lowest possible amount of stimulation that will still be detected?

● **sensory receptors** Specialized cells that detect stimulus information and transmit it to sensory (afferent) nerves and the brain.

Absolute Threshold

One way to think about the lowest limits of perception is to assume that there is an **absolute threshold,** or minimum amount of stimulus energy that a person can detect. When the energy of a stimulus falls below this absolute threshold, we cannot detect its presence; when the energy of the stimulus rises above the absolute threshold, we can detect the stimulus (Markessis & others, 2009). As an example, find a clock that ticks; put it on a table and walk far enough away that you no longer hear it. Then gradually move toward the clock. At some point, you will begin to hear it ticking. Hold your position and notice that occasionally the ticking fades, and you may have to move

● **absolute threshold** The minimum amount of stimulus energy that a person can detect.

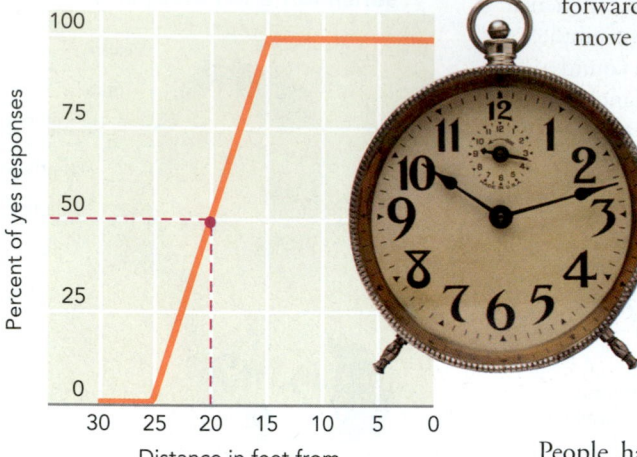

Percent of yes responses

100 · 75 · 50 · 25 · 0

30 · 25 · 20 · 15 · 10 · 5 · 0

Distance in feet from
a ticking clock

FIGURE 9.3 **Measuring Absolute Threshold** Absolute threshold is the minimum amount of energy we can detect. To measure absolute threshold, psychologists have arbitrarily decided to use the criterion of detecting the stimulus 50 percent of the time. In this graph, the person's absolute threshold for detecting the ticking clock is at a distance of 20 feet.

● **noise** Irrelevant and competing stimuli—not only sounds but also any distracting stimuli for our senses.

● **difference threshold** The degree of difference that must exist between two stimuli before the difference is detected.

● **Weber's law** The principle that two stimuli must differ by a constant minimum percentage (rather than a constant amount) to be perceived as different.

forward to reach the threshold; at other times, it may become loud, and you can move backward.

In this experiment, if you measure your absolute threshold several times, you likely will record several different distances for detecting the stimulus. For example, the first time you try it, you might hear the ticking at 25 feet from the clock. However, you probably will not hear it every time at 25 feet. Maybe you hear it only 38 percent of the time at this distance, but you hear it 50 percent of the time at 20 feet away and 65 percent of the time at 15 feet. Figure 9.3 shows one person's measured absolute threshold for detecting a clock's ticking sound. Psychologists have arbitrarily decided that absolute threshold is the point at which the individual detects the stimulus 50 percent of the time—in this case, 20 feet away. Using the same clock, another person might have a measured absolute threshold of 26 feet, and yet another, 18 feet.

People have different thresholds. Some have better hearing than others, and some have better vision. Figure 9.4 lists the approximate absolute thresholds of five senses.

Under ideal circumstances, our senses have very low absolute thresholds, so we can be remarkably good at detecting small amounts of stimulus energy. You might be surprised to learn that the human eye can see a candle flame at 30 miles on a dark, clear night. However, our environment seldom gives us ideal conditions with which to detect stimuli. If the night were cloudy, for example, you would have to be closer to see the candle flame. In addition, other lights on the horizon—car or house lights—would hinder your ability to detect the candle's flicker. **Noise** is the term given to irrelevant and competing stimuli—not just sounds but any distracting stimuli for our senses (Ikeda, Sekiguchi, & Hayashi, 2010; Otto, Bach, & Kommerell, 2010).

Difference Threshold

Psychologists also investigate the degree of *difference* that must exist between two stimuli before the difference is detected. This is the **difference threshold,** or *just noticeable difference.* An artist might detect the difference between two similar shades of color. A fashion designer might notice a difference in the texture of two fabrics. How different must the colors and textures be for someone to say, "These are different"? Like the absolute threshold, the difference threshold is the smallest difference in stimulation required to discriminate one stimulus from another 50 percent of the time.

Difference thresholds increase as a stimulus becomes stronger. That means that at very low levels of stimulation, small changes can be detected, but at very high levels, small changes are less noticeable. When music is playing softly, you may notice when your roommate increases the volume by even a small amount. If, however, he or she turns the volume up an equal amount when the music is playing very loudly, you may not notice. **Weber's law** (discovered by E. H. Weber more than 150 years ago) is the principle that two stimuli must differ by a constant proportion to be perceived as different.

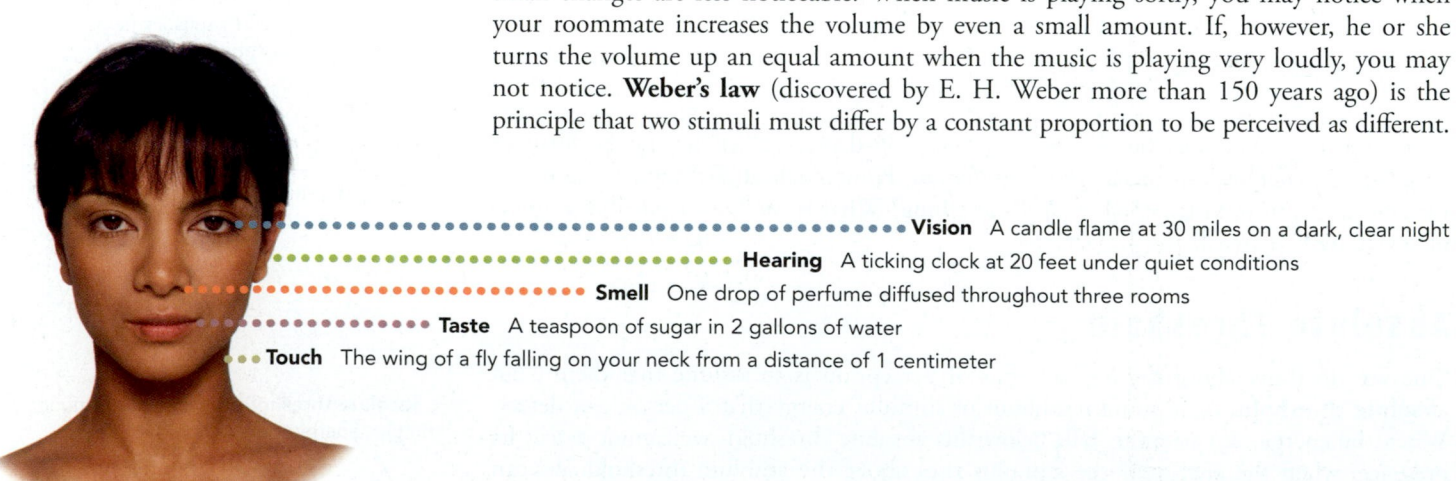

Vision A candle flame at 30 miles on a dark, clear night

Hearing A ticking clock at 20 feet under quiet conditions

Smell One drop of perfume diffused throughout three rooms

Taste A teaspoon of sugar in 2 gallons of water

Touch The wing of a fly falling on your neck from a distance of 1 centimeter

FIGURE 9.4 **Approximate Absolute Thresholds for Five Senses** These thresholds show the amazing power of our senses to detect even very slight variations in the environment.

psychological *inquiry*

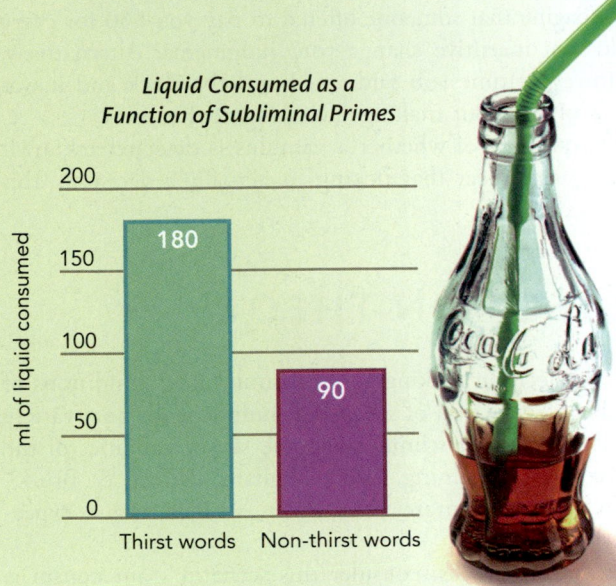

Liquid Consumed as a Function of Subliminal Primes

Subliminal Perception: Working Up a Thirst

This graph is adapted from the results of the study by Erin Strahan, Steven Spencer, and Mark Zanna (2002) described in the text. The dependent variable is represented on the vertical, or Y, axis. The columns represent the results of the study for each of the two groups—those who were exposed to "thirst words," and those who saw "non-thirst words." Answer the following questions.

1. What was the independent variable in this study? Explain.
2. Which group would be considered the experimental group? Which is the control group?
3. Why were the participants randomly assigned to conditions?

For example, we add 1 candle to 20 candles and notice a difference in the brightness of the candles; we add 1 candle to 120 candles and do not notice a difference, but we would notice the difference if we added 6 candles to 120 candles. Weber's law generally holds true (Gao & Vasconcelos, 2009; Jimenez-Sanchez & others, 2009).

Subliminal Perception

Can sensations that occur below our absolute threshold affect us without our being aware of them? **Subliminal perception** refers to the detection of information below the level of conscious awareness. In 1957, James Vicary, an advertising executive, announced that he was able to increase popcorn and soft drink sales by secretly flashing the words "EAT POPCORN" and "DRINK COKE" on a movie screen in a local theater (Weir, 1984). Vicary's claims were a hoax, but people have continued to wonder whether behavior can be influenced by stimuli that are presented so quickly that we cannot perceive them. Studies have shown that the brain responds to information that is presented below the conscious threshold, and such information can influence behavior (Dupoux, de Gardelle, & Kouider, 2008; Radel, Sarrazin, & Pelletier, 2009; Tsushima, Sasaki, & Watanabe, 2006).

In one study researchers randomly assigned participants to come to the study having not had anything to drink for at least three hours prior (Strahan, Spencer, & Zanna, 2002). The participants were shown either words related to being thirsty (such as *dry* and *thirst*) or other words of the same length not related to thirst (such as *won* and *pirate*) flashed on a computer screen for 16 milliseconds while they performed an unrelated task. None of the participants reported actually seeing the flashed words. After this subliminal exposure to thirst or non-thirst words, participants were allowed to drink a beverage. When given a chance to drink afterward, those who had seen thirst-related words drank more. The Psychological Inquiry feature explores the results of the study.

The notion that stimuli we do not consciously perceive can influence our behavior challenges the usefulness of the idea of thresholds (Rouder & Morey, 2009). If stimuli that fall below the threshold can have an impact on us, you may be wondering, what do thresholds really tell us?

● **subliminal perception** The detection of information below the level of conscious awareness.

Further, you might have noticed that the definition of absolute threshold is not very absolute. It refers to the intensity of stimulation detected *50 percent of the time*. How can something absolute change from one trial to the next? If, for example, you tried the ticking clock experiment described earlier, you might have found yourself making judgment calls. Sometimes you felt very sure you could hear the clock, but other times you were uncertain and probably took a guess. Sometimes you guessed right, and other times you were mistaken. Now, imagine that someone offered to pay you $50 for every correct answer you gave—would that incentive change your judgments? Alternatively, what if you were charged $50 for every time you said you heard the clock and it was not ticking? In fact, perception is often about making such judgment calls.

An alternative approach to the question of whether a stimulus is detected acknowledges that saying (or not saying) "Yes, I hear that ticking" is actually a decision. This approach is called signal detection theory.

9·4 SIGNAL DETECTION THEORY

- **signal detection theory** A theory of perception that focuses on decision making about stimuli in the presence of uncertainty.

Signal detection theory focuses on decision making about stimuli under conditions of uncertainty. In signal detection theory, detection of sensory stimuli depends on a variety of factors besides the physical intensity of the stimulus and the sensory abilities of the observer (Benjamin, Diaz, & Wee, 2009; Fleming, 2009; Higham, Perfect, & Bruno, 2009). These factors include individual and contextual variations, such as fatigue, expectations, and the urgency of the moment.

To grasp how signal detection theory works, consider this scenario. Your cousin is getting married in a week, and you are looking for a date for the wedding. While studying at the library, you see a potential candidate, someone with whom you have exchanged glances before. Now you face a decision: Should you proceed to ask this person out? Is the signal (that is, a good date for the wedding) present? You scan your library acquaintance for indications of availability (no wedding or engagement ring) and interest (didn't he or she smile at you as you passed by earlier?). You consider other information as well: Do you find the person attractive? Does he or she seem friendly? Based on these factors, you decide that (1) yes, you will ask the person to the wedding (because you have determined that the signal is present) or (2) no, you will keep looking (the signal is not present). These decisions might be correct or incorrect, leading to four possible outcomes (Figure 9.5):

- Hit: You ask, and he or she says yes.

- Miss: He or she would have said yes, but you do not ask.

- False alarm: You think the individual seemed interested, but your offer is politely declined—ouch.

- Correct rejection: You do not ask the person out, and he or she would have said no—whew.

Decision making in signal detection theory has two main components: information acquisition and criterion. In terms of *information acquisition,* the question applicable to our example is, what information is the person who is your potential wedding date communicating? Is the person available? Attractive? And so on. The *criterion* component of signal detection theory is the basis for making a judgment from the available information. The criterion is the decision maker's assessment of the stakes involved in each possible outcome. Is a miss (not asking out someone who would have said yes) or a false alarm (getting turned down) a worse outcome? Is getting a "hit" worth surviving some false alarms? So, in addition to relying on the characteristics of your potential wedding date, you might also be feeling desperate, because your family is always giving you a hard time about never having a date. Maybe getting a lot of rejections (false alarms) is not as bad as missing an

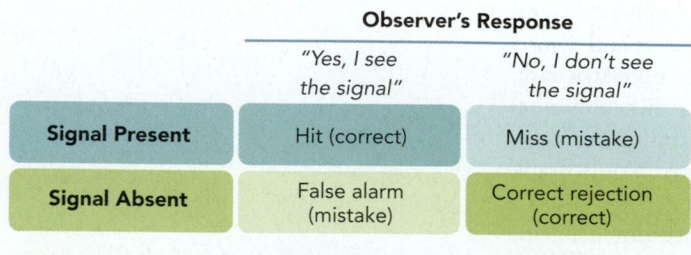

	Observer's Response	
	"Yes, I see the signal"	"No, I don't see the signal"
Signal Present	Hit (correct)	Miss (mistake)
Signal Absent	False alarm (mistake)	Correct rejection (correct)

FIGURE 9.5   Four Outcomes in Signal Detection Signal detection research helps to explain when and how perceptual judgments are correct or mistaken.

opportunity to keep them quiet. Alternatively, you may feel that rejections are just too upsetting and prefer to experience "misses" even if it means going stag to your cousin's wedding.

Let's return now to the domain of sensation and perception. Can you see how signal detection theory might provide a way to examine the processes that underlie our judgments about whether we perceive a stimulus or not? By presenting stimuli of varying intensities, as well as trials when no stimulus is presented at all, and by asking a research participant to report on his or her detection of the sound or sight of interest, a researcher can use signal detection theory to understand the results. Importantly, signal detection theory allows us to consider the mistakes a perceiver might make—and the reasons behind those errors.

9·5 PERCEIVING SENSORY STIMULI

As we just saw, perception of stimuli is influenced by more than the characteristics of the environmental stimuli themselves. Two important factors in perceiving sensory stimuli are attention and perceptual set.

Attention

Attention is the process of focusing awareness on a narrowed aspect of the environment. The world holds a lot of information to perceive. At this moment you are perceiving the letters and words that make up this sentence. Now gaze around you and fix your eyes on something other than this book. Afterward, curl up the toes on your right foot. In each of these activities, you engaged in **selective attention,** which involves focusing on a specific aspect of experience while ignoring others (Klumpp & Amir, 2009). A familiar example of selective attention is the ability to concentrate on one voice among many in a crowded airline terminal or noisy restaurant. Psychologists call this common occurrence the *cocktail party effect* (Kuyper, 1972).

Highly practiced and familiar stimuli, such as your own name and hometown, often are perceived so automatically that it is almost impossible to ignore them. The *Stroop effect*, named for John Ridley Stroop (1935), who first showed the effect, refers to the way that automatically reading a color name can make it difficult to name the color in which the word is printed (Hodgson & others, 2009; Zurron & others, 2009). To experience the Stroop effect, see Figure 9.6. Most of the time, the highly practiced and almost automatic perception of word meaning makes reading easier. However, this

● **attention** The process of focusing awareness on a narrowed aspect of the environment.

● **selective attention** The process of focusing on a specific aspect of experience while ignoring others.

As fast as you can, name each color of ink used to print each of the rectangles below.

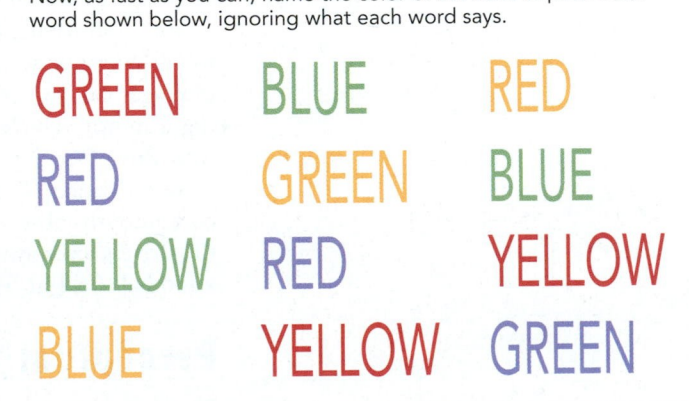

Now, as fast as you can, name the color of ink used to print each word shown below, ignoring what each word says.

GREEN BLUE RED
RED GREEN BLUE
YELLOW RED YELLOW
BLUE YELLOW GREEN

FIGURE 9.6 **The Stroop Effect** Before reading further, read the instructions above and complete the tasks. You probably had little or no difficulty naming the colors of the rectangles in the set on the left. However, you likely stumbled more when you were asked to name the color of ink used to print each word in the set on the right. This automaticity in perception is the Stroop effect.

automaticity makes it hard to ignore the meaning of the words for colors (such as *blue*) when they are printed in a different color (such as orange). Thus, the Stroop effect represents a failure of selective attention.

Attention not only is selective but also is *shiftable*. For example, you might be paying close attention to your instructor's lecture, but if the person next to you starts texting, you might look to see what is going on over there. The fact that we can attend selectively to one stimulus and shift readily to another indicates that we must be monitoring many things at once.

Certain features of stimuli draw attention to them. *Novel stimuli* (those that are new, different, or unusual) often attract our attention. *Size, color, and movement* also influence our attention; we are more likely to attend to objects that are large, vividly colored, or moving than objects that are small, dull-colored, or stationary. In addition, *emotional stimuli* can influence attention and therefore perception (Stewart & others, 2010).

In the case of emotional stimuli, here is how the process works. An emotionally laden stimulus, such as the word *torture*, captures our attention. As a result, we are often quicker and more accurate at identifying an emotional stimulus than a neutral stimulus. This advantage for emotional stimuli may come at a cost to other stimuli we experience. The term *emotion-induced blindness* refers to the fact that when we encounter an emotionally charged stimulus, we often fail to recognize a stimulus that is presented immediately after it (Arnell, Killman, & Fijavz, 2007; Bocanegra & Zeelenberg, 2009). Imagine, for example, that you are driving along a highway, and an ambulance, with sirens screaming and lights flashing, whizzes by. You might not notice the other cars around you or a road sign because you are preoccupied by the ambulance.

Sometimes, especially if our attention is otherwise occupied, we miss even very interesting stimuli. *Inattentional blindness* refers to the failure to detect unexpected events when our attention is engaged by a task (Chabris & Simons, 2010). For instance, when we are focusing intently on a task, such as finding a seat in a packed movie theater, we might not detect an unexpected stimulus such as a friend waving to us in the crowd.

Research conducted by Daniel Simons and Christopher Chabris (1999) provides a striking example of inattentional blindness. The researchers asked participants to watch a video of two teams playing basketball. The participants were instructed to closely count the number of passes thrown by each team. During the video, a small woman dressed in a gorilla suit walked through the action and was clearly visible for 5 seconds. Surprisingly, over half of the participants (who were apparently deeply engaged in the counting task) never noticed the "gorilla." When they later saw the video without having to count passes, many of the participants could not believe they had missed a gorilla in their midst (Chabris & Simons, 2010). Inattentional blindness is more likely to occur when a task is difficult (Macdonald & Lavie, 2008) and when the distracting stimulus is very different from stimuli that are relevant to the task at hand (White & Aimola Davies, 2008).

Emotion-induced blindness and inattentional blindness have important implications for driving safety. Engaging in a task such as talking on a cell phone or sending text messages can so occupy attention that little is left over for the important task of piloting a motor vehicle. Recent research revealed that individuals who text message while they drive face 23 times the risk of a crash or near-crash compared to non-distracted drivers (Blanco & others, 2009; Hanowski & others, 2009). In this research, cameras continuously observed drivers for more than 6 million miles of driving. Texting drew the drivers' eyes away from the road long enough for the vehicle to travel the length of a football field at 55 miles an hour.

Perceptual Set

Place your hand over the playing cards on the right in the illustration on the next page and look at the playing cards on the left. As quickly as you can, count how many aces of spades you see. Then place your hand over the cards on the left and count the number of aces of spades among the cards on the right.

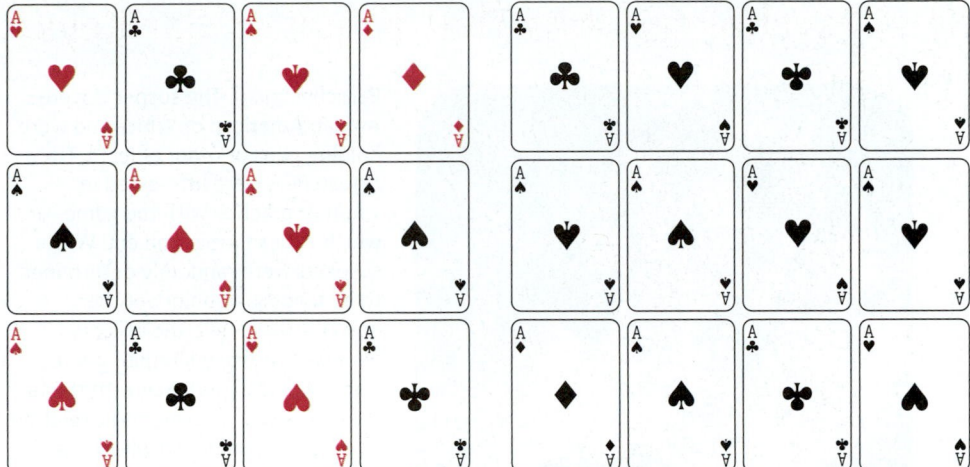

Most people report that they see two or three aces of spades in the set of cards on the left. However, if you look closely, you will see that there are five. Two of the aces of spades are black and three are red. When people look at the set of cards on the right, they are more likely to count five aces of spades. Why do we perceive the two sets of cards differently? We expect the ace of spades to be black because it is always black in a regular deck of cards. We do not expect red spades, so we skip right over the red ones: Expectations influence perceptions.

Psychologists refer to a predisposition or readiness to perceive something in a particular way as a **perceptual set.** Perceptual sets, which reflect top-down influences on perception, act as "psychological" filters in processing information about the environment (Fei-Fei & others, 2007). Interestingly, young children are more accurate than adults at the task involving the ace of spades. The reason is that they have not built up the perceptual set that the ace of spades is black. To read further about how perceptual sets can influence perceptions and subsequent actions, see the Intersection.

● **perceptual set** A predisposition or readiness to perceive something in a particular way.

9-6 SENSORY ADAPTATION

Turning out the lights in your bedroom at night, you stumble across the room to your bed, blind to the objects around you. Gradually the objects reappear and become clearer. The ability of the visual system to adjust to a darkened room is an example of **sensory adaptation**—a change in the responsiveness of the sensory system based on the average level of surrounding stimulation (Elliott & others, 2009; Preston, Kourtzi, & Welchman, 2009).

You experience sensory adaptation often in your life. For example, you adjust to the water in an initially "freezing" swimming pool. You turn on your windshield wipers while driving in the rain, and shortly you are unaware of their rhythmic sweeping back and forth. You enter a room and are at first bothered by the air conditioner's hum, but after a while you get used to it. All of these experiences represent sensory adaptation. In the example of adapting to the dark, when you turn out the lights, everything at first is black. Conversely, when you step out into the bright sunshine after spending time in a dark basement, light floods your eyes and everything appears light. These momentary blips in sensation arise because adaptation takes time.

● **sensory adaptation** A change in the responsiveness of the sensory system based on the average level of surrounding stimulation.

9-7 EXTRASENSORY PERCEPTION

Our examination of the relationship between sensation and perception may leave you wondering if there is such a thing as ESP. ESP—*extrasensory perception*—means that a person can read another person's mind or perceive future events in the absence

Perception and Social Psychology: Was That a Gun or Car Keys?

Consider the following cases:

- William J. Whitfield, 22, shot to death in a supermarket in 1997 while holding his car keys.
- Amadou Diallo, 23, killed in a flurry of gunfire outside his apartment building in 1999 while reaching for his wallet.
- Julian Alexander, a 20-year-old newlywed, killed in front of his home in 2008 while holding a wooden stick he was using to fix curtains.
- Bernard Moore, a 73-year-old grandfather shot to death on the front porch of his home as he held an energy drink bottle.

In all of these instances, the victims were Black men, shot by police officers who mistook the harmless object they were holding for a weapon. In those cases in which investigations have been completed, the police officers were cleared of wrongdoing. Juries and judges concluded that they had made terrible but honest mistakes. These and similar cases have incited critical public interest. What role did race play in these "honest" perceptual mistakes?

Social psychologist Keith Payne examined how race affects the tendency to misperceive harmless objects as handguns (Payne, 2001, 2010; Stokes & Payne, 2010). Participants were told that they would see two pictures on a computer screen. Their job was to decide, very quickly, whether the second picture was a gun or a tool. The first picture—always a picture of an African American man or a White man—cued the participants that the judgment was coming. Participants were more likely to misperceive tools as guns when the tools were shown after a picture of an African American man.

In another study, 48 police officers, Whites and African Americans, played a video game in which they had to decide whether to shoot or not shoot the suspects in the game (Plant & Peruche, 2005). The suspects were African American or White and were holding guns or other objects. The researchers were interested in whether practice with the game—in which African American and White suspects were randomly determined to be holding a gun or another object—would help the officers become less biased in their perceptions. Would experience with the fact that there was no systematic relation between ethnicity and whether a person was likely to be armed reduce the tendency to perceive harmless objects as guns? In the early trials the police officers, regardless of their own race, were more likely to mistakenly shoot an unarmed suspect when he was African American. By the experiment's end, however, this tendency had faded, and the officers treated African American and White suspects with equal levels of restraint.

In the real-world cases mentioned above, the police officers' mistakes may have been honest, but they were not inevitable. Such cases highlight the crucial role of cultural beliefs and the social world in the process of perception. Individuals in a society that does not view ethnic minority individuals as dangerous or as likely to be criminals might be less inclined to misperceive car keys, a wallet, or a bottle as a weapon—and might avoid these tragedies.

What do tragedies such as the shooting cases described in this Intersection suggest about the impact of race in U.S. society?

---

of concrete sensory input. More than half of adults in the United States believe in ESP (Moore, 2005), and many researchers have studied it (*parapsychology* is the term for the scientific study of ESP). As an example of ESP, you might recall stories about someone's "just knowing" that a friend was in trouble and later finding out that at the moment of "knowing," the friend was in a car accident. Such an experience can be fascinating, spooky, and even thrilling, but does it reflect ESP—or simply coincidence?

There are many reasons to question the existence of ESP. Think about ESP in the ways we have considered sensation and perception so far. What sort of energy transmits psychic messages? What are the sensory receptors for psychic energy? Remember that scientists evaluate evidence critically, rely on research to draw conclusions, and expect that if a conclusion is valid, it will be reproducible. From a scientific perspective, despite some 75 years of research, no evidence supports the existence of ESP (French & others, 2008; Wiseman & Watt, 2006).

Recently, Samuel Moulton and Stephen Kosslyn (2008) conducted a fascinating study to test for evidence of ESP. The researchers went directly to the source: the brain. Using fMRI, described in Module 7, they scanned the brains of individuals when they were shown (1) pictures that had been previously "sent" to them, mentally, by a partner, and (2) pictures that had not been thus sent. Moulton and Kosslyn (2008) designed the study to enhance the chances that if ESP exists, they would find it. They selected participant pairs who were related to each other biologically or emotionally (twins, sisters, mothers and sons, close friends, and romantic couples). The stimuli were emotionally evocative pictures (for example, a picture of a couple kissing). One member of each pair was given the role of "sender," and the other got the role of "receiver." The sender sat in a room alone, and the receiver was placed in the brain scanner. At the beginning of the study, senders were told to try their best to "send" the images they saw, mentally, to their partner in the next room. Then the receivers' brains were scanned as the receivers were shown two images (the one that had been sent via ESP and a control image). The receivers also tried to guess which of the two images was the one that the partner had "sent" to them. To enhance motivation, receivers received a dollar for every correct response. The results? First, receivers were no more likely than chance to guess correctly which images had been sent. Second, their brains did not differ when they were exposed to ESP stimuli versus other stimuli—a finding that provided no evidence of ESP.

© Betsy Streeter. www.CartoonStock.com.

In the absence of empirical data for the existence of ESP, why does it remain so fascinating? One possibility is that because human beings are not very good at dealing with random experiences, we sometimes make up interesting stories to account for these unusual events. However, fun stories do not necessarily reflect reality. Thinking critically about apparent experiences of ESP reveals the ways in which such perceptions are biased. Perhaps you have had an experience that seems to demonstrate ESP, such as thinking about a good friend and then having that person call you on the phone at that very moment. As a critical thinker, you might ask yourself, how many times have I had similar thoughts without my friend's actually calling me? You might note that you would probably not even remember having those thoughts before the phone rang except for the phone call that followed them. We will discuss a number of biases in human information processing in Module 28 that may help to explain the persistence of beliefs in ESP and other paranormal phenomena.

SUMMARY

Sensation is the process of receiving stimulus energies from the environment. Perception is the process of organizing and interpreting sensory information to give it meaning. Perceiving the world involves both bottom-up and top-down processing. All sensation begins with sensory receptors, specialized cells that detect and transmit information about a stimulus to sensory neurons and the brain. Sensory receptors are selective and have different neural pathways.

Psychologists have explored the limits of our abilities to detect stimuli. Absolute threshold refers to the minimum amount of energy that people can detect. The difference threshold, or just noticeable difference, is the smallest difference in stimulation required to discriminate one stimulus from another 50 percent of the time. Signal detection theory focuses on decision making about stimuli in the presence of uncertainty. In this theory, detection of sensory stimuli

KEY TERMS

sensation 106
perception 106
bottom-up processing 106
top-down processing 106
sensory receptors 109
absolute threshold 109
noise 110
difference threshold 110

Weber's law 110
subliminal perception 111
signal detection theory 112
attention 113
selective attention 113
perceptual set 115
sensory adaptation 115

depends on many factors other than the physical properties of the stimuli, and differences in these other factors may lead different people to make different decisions about identical stimuli.

Perception is influenced by attention, beliefs, and expectations. Sensory adaptation is a change in the responsiveness of the sensory system based on the average level of surrounding stimulation, essentially the ways that our senses start to ignore a particular stimulus once it is around long enough.

TEST YOURSELF

1. What are sensation and perception? How are they linked?

2. Compare and contrast top-down and bottom-up processing.

3. What is meant by the terms *absolute threshold* and *difference threshold*? What is *subliminal perception*?

APPLY YOUR KNOWLEDGE

1. Find a partner and test your absolute threshold for sugar. Have your partner set up the following sugar-and-water mixtures. Mix 2 teaspoons of sugar in 4 cups of water. Label this solution ("solution X," for example). Take 2 cups of solution X, add 2 cups of water, and give this solution a second label ("solution D," for example). Then take 2 cups of solution D, add 2 cups of water, and give this a third label ("solution Q"). Continue taking 2 cups from each successive solution until you have a total of eight solutions, making sure to keep track of which solution is which. When you are done, the concentration of the solutions should be equivalent to 1 teaspoon in each of the following amounts of water: 1 pint (2 cups), 1 quart, 1 half-gallon, 1 gallon, 2 gallons, 4 gallons, and 8 gallons. Your partner should place a sample of one of the solutions in a cup and a sample of plain water in another, identical cup. You should taste the solution in each cup and decide which one is the sugar solution. Do this with all of the solutions until you can decide what your absolute threshold is according to the text's definition. Do you think your absolute threshold would vary depending on what you had recently eaten? Why or why not?

2. Make an argument against the use of cell phones while driving that illustrates the principles of attention, selective attention, and multitasking.

The Visual System

When Michael May of Davis, California, was 3 years old, an accident left him visually impaired, with only the ability to perceive the difference between night and day. He went on to live a rich, full life, marrying and having children, founding a successful company, and becoming an expert skier. Twenty-five years passed before doctors transplanted stem cells into May's right eye, a procedure that gave him partial sight (Kurson, 2007). May can now see; his right eye is functional and allows him to detect color and negotiate the world without the use of a cane or reliance on his seeing-eye dog. His visual experience remains unusual, however, in that he sees the world as if it is an abstract painting. He can catch a ball thrown to him by his sons, but he cannot recognize his wife's face. Importantly, his brain has to work at interpreting the new information that his right eye is providing.

May's experience highlights the intimate connection between the brain and the sense organs in producing perception. Vision is a remarkable process that involves the brain's interpretation of the visual information sent from the eyes. We now explore the physical foundations of the visual system.

10-1 THE VISUAL STIMULUS AND THE EYE

When you see the beautiful colors of a fall day, what your eyes and brain are responding to is really the differences in light reflected from the various colorful leaves. Indeed, our ability to detect visual stimuli depends on the sensitivity of our eyes to differences in light.

Light

Light is a form of electromagnetic energy that can be described in terms of wavelengths. Light travels through space in waves. The *wavelength* of light is the distance from the peak of one wave to the peak of the next. Wavelengths of visible light range from about 400 to 700 nanometers (a nanometer is 1 billionth of a meter and is abbreviated nm). The wavelength of light that is reflected from a stimulus determines its *hue* or color.

Outside the range of visible light are longer radio and infrared radiation waves and shorter ultraviolet and X rays (Figure 10.1). These other forms of electromagnetic energy continually bombard us, but we do not see them.

We can also describe waves of light in terms of their height, or *amplitude,* which determines the brightness of the stimulus (Figure 10.2). Finally, the *purity* of the wavelengths—whether they are all the same or a mix of waves—determines the perceived *saturation,* or richness, of a visual stimulus. The color tree shown in Figure 10.3 can help you to understand saturation. Colors that are very pure have no white light in them. They are located on the outside of the color tree. Notice how the closer we get to the center of the color tree, the more white light has been added to the single wavelength of a particular color. In other words, the deep colors at the edge fade into pastel colors toward the center.

The Structure of the Eye

The eye, like a camera, is constructed to get the best possible picture of the world. An accurate picture is in focus, is not too dark or too light, and has good contrast between

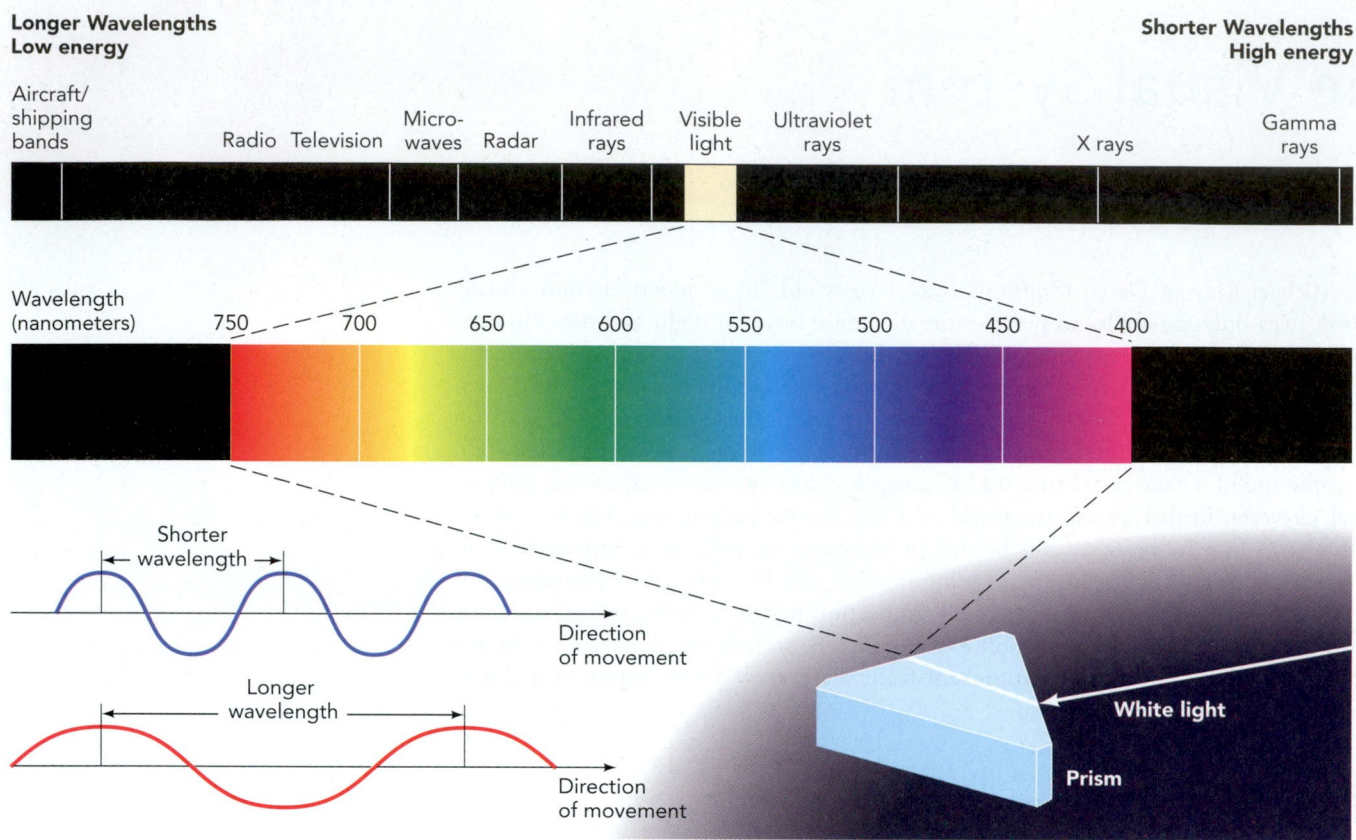

FIGURE 10.1 **The Electromagnetic Spectrum and Visible Light** (*Top*) Visible light is only a narrow band in the electromagnetic spectrum. Visible light wavelengths range from about 400 to 700 nm. X rays are much shorter; radio waves, much longer. (*Bottom*) The two graphs show how waves vary in length between successive peaks. Shorter wavelengths are higher in frequency, as reflected in blue colors; longer wavelengths are lower in frequency, as reflected in red colors.

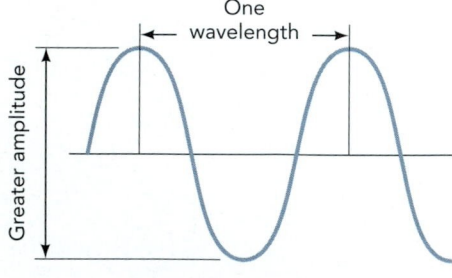

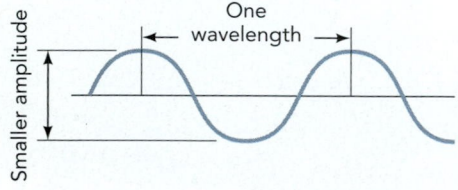

FIGURE 10.2 **Light Waves of Varying Amplitude** The top graph might suggest a spotlight on a concert stage; the bottom might represent a candlelit dinner.

the dark and light parts. Each of several structures in the eye plays an important role in this process.

If you look closely at your eyes in the mirror, you will notice three parts—the sclera, iris, and pupil (Figure 10.4). The *sclera* is the white, outer part of the eye that helps to maintain the shape of the eye and to protect it from injury. The *iris* is the colored part of the eye, which might be light blue in one individual and dark brown in another. The *pupil*, which appears black, is the opening in the center of the iris. The iris contains muscles that control the size of the pupil and, hence, the amount of light that gets into the eye. To get a good picture of the world, the eye needs to be able to adjust the amount of light that enters. In this sense, the pupil acts like the aperture of a camera, opening to let in more light when it is needed and closing to let in less light when there is too much.

Two structures bring the image into focus: the *cornea*, a clear membrane just in front of the eye, and the *lens*, a transparent and somewhat flexible, disk-shaped structure filled with a gelatin-like material. The function of both of these structures is to bend the light falling on the surface of the eye just enough to focus it at the back. The curved surface of the cornea does most of this bending, while the lens fine-tunes things. When you are looking at faraway objects, the lens has a relatively flat shape because the light reaching the eye from faraway objects is parallel, and the bending power of the cornea is sufficient to keep things in focus. However, the light reaching the eye from objects that are close is more scattered, so more bending of the light is required to achieve focus.

Without this ability of the lens to change its curvature, the eye would have a tough time focusing on close objects such as reading material. As we get older, the lens loses its flexibility and hence its ability to change from its normal flattened shape to the rounder shape needed to bring close objects into focus. That is why many people with normal vision throughout their young adult lives require reading glasses as they age.

The parts of the eye we have considered so far work together to give us the sharpest picture of the world. This effort would be useless, however, without a vehicle for recording the images the eyes take of the world—in essence, the film of the camera. Photographic film is made of a material that responds to light. At the back of the eye is the eye's "film," the multilayered **retina,** which is the light-sensitive surface that records electromagnetic energy and converts it to neural impulses for processing in the brain. The analogy between the retina and film goes only so far, however. The retina is amazingly complex and elegantly designed. It is, in fact, the primary mechanism of sight. Even after decades of intense study, the full marvel of this structure is far from understood (Takahashi & others, 2010; Tamada & others, 2010).

The human retina has approximately 126 million receptor cells. They turn the electromagnetic energy of light into a form of energy that the nervous system can process. There are two kinds of visual receptor cells: rods and cones. Rods and cones differ both in how they respond to light and in their patterns of distribution on the surface of the retina (Lewis & others, 2010). **Rods** are the receptors in the retina that are sensitive to light, but they are not very useful for color vision. Rods function well under low illumination; they are hard at work at night. Humans have about 120 million rods. **Cones** are the receptors that we use for color perception. Like rods, cones are light-sensitive. However, they require a larger amount of light to respond than the rods do, so they operate best in daylight or under high illumination. There are about 6 million cone cells in human eyes. Figure 10.5 shows what rods and cones look like.

The most important part of the retina is the *fovea*, a tiny area in the center of the retina at which vision is at its best (see Figure 10.4). The fovea contains only cones and is vital to many visual tasks. To get a sense of how well the cones in the fovea work, try reading out of the corner of your eye. The task is difficult because the fovea is not getting to "see" the page. Rods are found almost everywhere on the retina except in the fovea. Rods give us the ability to detect fainter spots of light on the peripheral retina than at the fovea. If you want to see a very faint star, you should gaze slightly away from it, to allow your rods to do their work. Figure 10.6 summarizes the characteristics of rods and cones.

Figure 10.7 shows how the rods and cones at the back of the retina convert light into electrochemical impulses. The signal is transmitted to the *bipolar cells* and then moves on to another layer of specialized cells called *ganglion cells* (Lebrun-Julien & others, 2010). The axons of the ganglion cells make up the **optic nerve,** which carries the visual information to the brain for further processing.

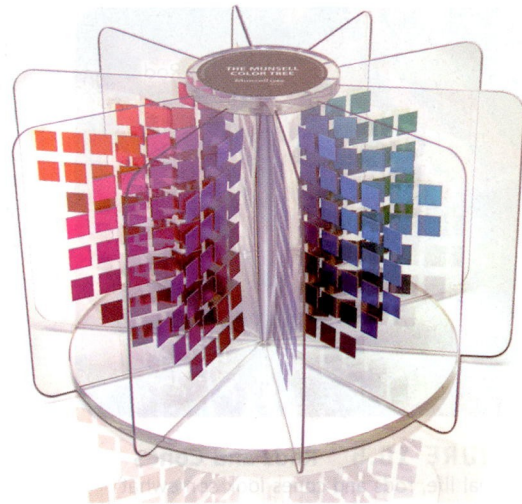

FIGURE 10.3   **A Color Tree Showing Color's Three Dimensions: Hue, Saturation, and Brightness** Hue is represented around the color tree, saturation horizontally, and brightness vertically.

● **retina** The multilayered light-sensitive surface in the eye that records electromagnetic energy and converts it to neural impulses for processing in the brain.

● **rods** The receptor cells in the retina that are sensitive to light but not very useful for color vision.

● **cones** The receptor cells in the retina that allow for color perception.

● **optic nerve** The structure at the back of the eye, made up of axons of the ganglion cells, that carries visual information to the brain for further processing.

FIGURE 10.4   **Parts of the Eye** Note that the image of the butterfly on the retina is upside down. The brain allows us to see the image right side up.

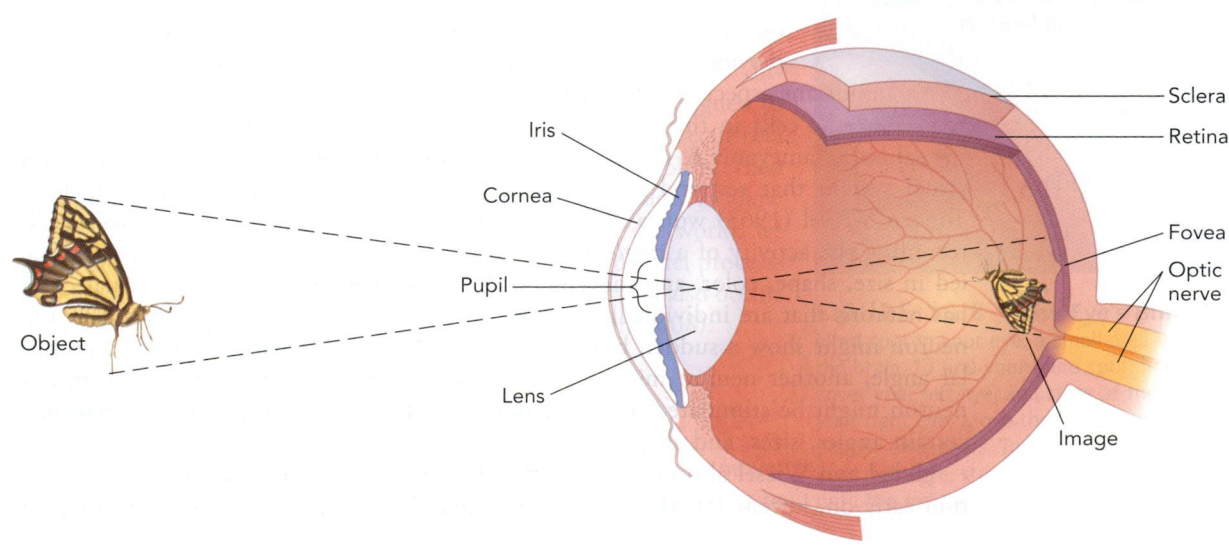

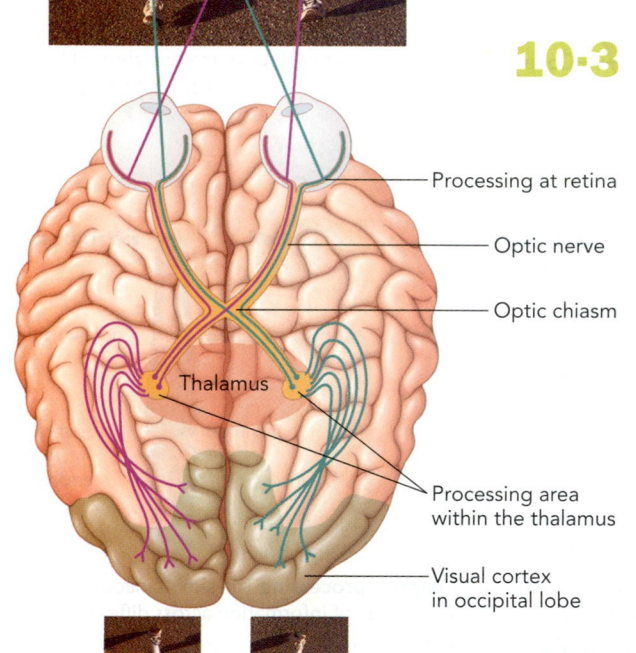

a given stimulus—for instance, a toddler running toward us. How does the brain know that these physical features, communicated by different neurons, all belong to the same object of perception? One of the most exciting topics in visual perception today is **binding,** the bringing together and integration of what is processed by different pathways or cells (Hong & Shevell, 2009; Seymour & others, 2009; Shipp & others, 2009). Binding involves the coupling of the activity of various cells and pathways. Through binding, you can integrate information about the shape of the toddler's body, his or her smile, and the child's movement into a complete image in the cerebral cortex. How binding occurs is a puzzle that fascinates neuroscientists (McMahon & Olson, 2009).

Researchers have found that all the neurons throughout pathways that are activated by a visual object pulse together at the same frequency (Engel & Singer, 2001). Within the vast network of cells in the cerebral cortex, this set of neurons appears to *bind* together all the features of the objects into a unified perception.

10·3 COLOR VISION

Imagine how dull a world without color would be. Art museums are filled with paintings that we enjoy in large part for their use of color, and flowers and sunsets would lose much of their beauty if we could not see their rich hues. The process of color perception starts in the retina, the eyes' film. Interestingly, theories about how the retina processes color were developed long before methods existed to study the anatomical and neurophysiological bases of color perception. Instead, psychologists made some extraordinarily accurate guesses about how color vision occurs in the retina by observing how people see. The two main theories proposed were the trichromatic theory and opponent-process theory. Both turned out to be correct.

The **trichromatic theory,** proposed by Thomas Young in 1802 and extended by Hermann von Helmholtz in 1852, states that color perception is produced by three types of cone receptors in the retina that are particularly sensitive to different, but overlapping, ranges of wavelengths. The theory is based on experiments showing that a person with normal vision can match any color in the spectrum by combining three other wavelengths. Young and Helmholtz reasoned that if the combination of any three wavelengths of different intensities is indistinguishable from any single pure wavelength, the visual system must base its perception of color on the relative responses of three receptor systems—cones sensitive to red, blue, and green.

The study of defective color vision, or *color blindness* (Figure 10.10), provides further support for the trichromatic theory. Complete color blindness is rare; most color-blind people, the vast majority of whom are men, can see some colors but not others. The nature of color blindness depends on which of the three kinds of cones (red, blue, or green) is inoperative (Machado, Oliveira, & Fernandes, 2009). In the most common form of color blindness, the green cone system malfunctions in some way, rendering green indistinguishable from certain combinations of blue and red.

In 1878, the German physiologist Ewald Hering observed that some colors cannot exist together, whereas others can. For example, it is easy to imagine a greenish blue but nearly impossible to imagine a reddish green. Hering also noticed that trichromatic theory could not adequately explain *afterimages,* sensations that remain after a stimulus is removed (Figure 10.11 gives you a chance to experience an afterimage). Color afterimages involve particular pairs of colors. If you look at red long enough, eventually a green afterimage will appear. If you look at yellow long enough, eventually a blue afterimage will appear.

Hering's observations led him to propose that there were not three types of color receptor cones (as proposed by trichromatic theory) but four, organized into complementary pairs: red-green and blue-yellow. Hering's view, **opponent-process theory,** states that cells in the visual system respond to red-green and blue-yellow colors; a given

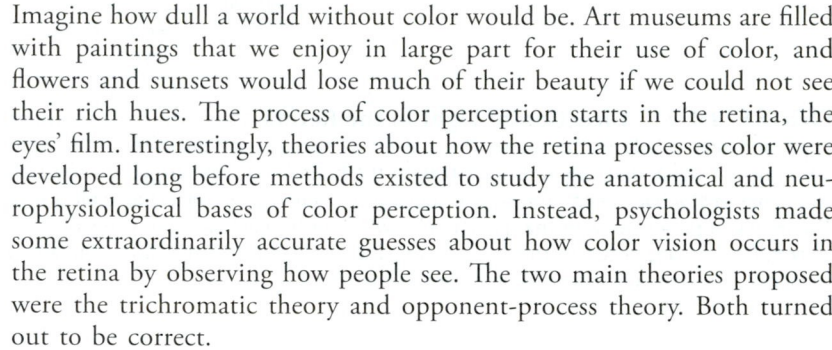

Processing at retina

Optic nerve

Optic chiasm

Thalamus

Processing area within the thalamus

Visual cortex in occipital lobe

FIGURE 10.9 **Visual Pathways to and Through the Brain** Light from each side of the visual field falls on the opposite side of each eye's retina. Visual information then travels along the optic nerve to the optic chiasm, where most of the visual information crosses over to the other side of the brain. From there visual information goes to the occipital lobe at the rear of the brain. All these crossings mean that what we see in the left side of our visual field (here, the shorter, dark-haired woman) is registered in the right side of our brain, and what we see in the right visual field (the taller, blonde woman) is registered in the left side of our brain.

cell might be excited by red and inhibited by green, whereas another cell might be excited by yellow and inhibited by blue. Hering's theory does indeed explain afterimages (Jameson & Hurvich, 1989). If you stare at red, for instance, your red-green system seems to "tire," and when you look away, it rebounds and gives you a green afterimage.

If the trichromatic theory of color perception is valid, and we do, in fact, have three kinds of cone receptors like those predicted by Young and Helmholtz, then how can the opponent-process theory also be accurate? The answer is that the red, blue, and green cones in the retina are connected to retinal ganglion cells in such a way that the three-color code is immediately translated into the opponent-process code (Figure 10.12). For example, a green cone might inhibit and a red cone might excite a particular ganglion cell. Thus, *both* the trichromatic and opponent-process theories are correct—the eye and the brain use both methods to code colors.

10-4 PERCEIVING SHAPE, DEPTH, MOTION, AND CONSTANCY

Perceiving visual stimuli means organizing and interpreting the fragments of information that the eye sends to the visual cortex. Information about the dimensions of what we are seeing is critical to this process. Among these dimensions are shape, depth, motion, and constancy.

If you have seen The Wizard of Oz, you might remember that goose bumps moment when Dorothy steps out of her house and the black-and-white of Kansas gives way to the Technicolor glory of Oz.

Shape

Think about the visible world and its shapes—buildings against the sky, boats on the horizon, the letters on this page. We see these shapes because they are marked off from the rest of what we see by *contour,* a location at which a sudden change of brightness occurs (Cavina-Pratesi & others, 2010). Now think about the letters on this page. As you look at the page, you see letters, which are shapes or figures, in a field or background—the white page. The **figure-ground relationship** is the principle by which we organize the perceptual field into stimuli that stand out (*figure*) and those that are left over (*background,* or *ground*). Generally this principle works well for us, but some figure-ground

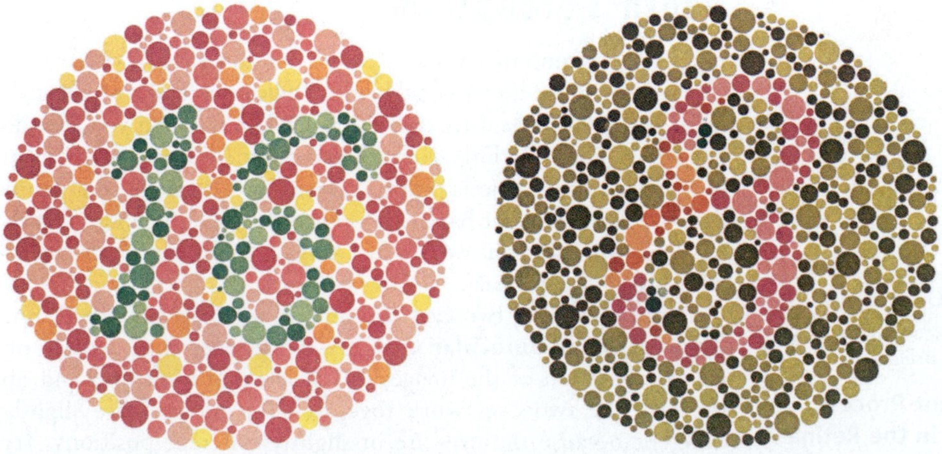

● **binding** In the sense of vision, the bringing together and integration of what is processed by different neural pathways or cells.

● **trichromatic theory** Theory stating that color perception is produced by three types of cone receptors in the retina that are particularly sensitive to different, but overlapping, ranges of wavelengths.

● **opponent-process theory** Theory stating that cells in the visual system respond to complementary pairs of red-green and blue-yellow colors; a given cell might be excited by red and inhibited by green, whereas another cell might be excited by yellow and inhibited by blue.

● **figure-ground relationship** The principle by which we organize the perceptual field into stimuli that stand out (figure) and those that are left over (ground).

FIGURE 10.10 **Examples of Stimuli Used to Test for Color Blindness** People with normal vision see the number 16 in the left circle and the number 8 in the right circle. People with red-green color blindness may see just the 16, just the 8, or neither. A complete color-blindness assessment involves the use of 15 stimuli.

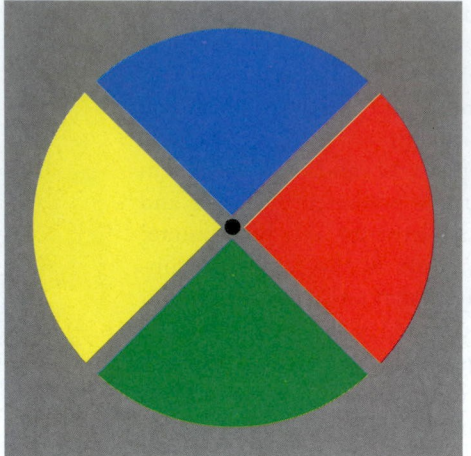

FIGURE 10.11 **Negative Afterimage—Complementary Colors** If you gaze steadily at the dot in the colored panel on the left for a few moments, then shift your gaze to the gray box on the right, you will see the original hues' complementary colors. The blue appears as yellow, the red as green, the green as red, and the yellow as blue. This pairing of colors has to do with the fact that color receptors in the eye are apparently sensitive as pairs: When one color is turned off (when you stop staring at the panel), the other color in the receptor is briefly turned on. The afterimage effect is especially noticeable with bright colors.

● **gestalt psychology** A school of thought interested in how people naturally organize their perceptions according to certain patterns.

● **depth perception** The ability to perceive objects three-dimensionally.

● **binocular cues** Depth cues that depend on the combination of the images in the left and right eyes and on the way the two eyes work together.

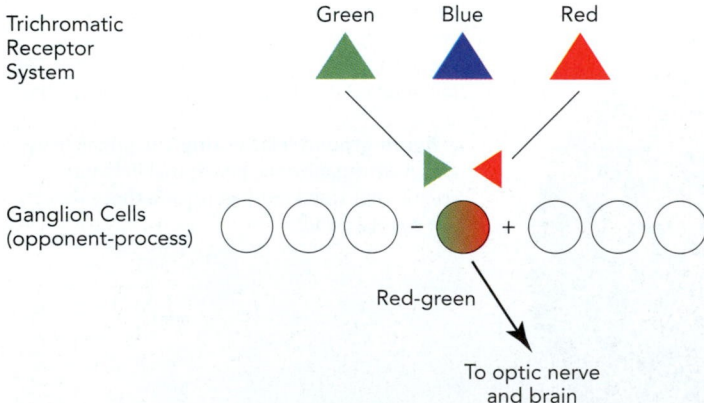

FIGURE 10.12 **Trichromatic and Opponent-Process Theories: Transmission of Color Information in the Retina** Cones responsive to green, blue, or red light form a trichromatic receptor system in the retina. As information is transmitted to the retina's ganglion cells, opponent-process cells are activated. As shown here, a retinal ganglion cell is inhibited by a green cone (−) and excited by a red cone (+), producing red-green color information.

relationships are highly ambiguous, and it may be difficult to tell what is figure and what is ground. Figure 10.13 shows a well-known ambiguous figure-ground relationship. As you look at the figure, your perception is likely to shift from seeing two faces to seeing a single goblet.

The figure-ground relationship is a gestalt principle (Figure 10.14 shows others). *Gestalt* is German for "configuration" or "form," and **gestalt psychology** is a school of thought interested in how people naturally organize their perceptions according to certain patterns. One of gestalt psychology's main principles is that the whole is different from the sum of its parts. For example, when you watch a movie, the motion you see in the film cannot be found in the film itself; if you examine the film, you see only separate frames. When you watch the film, the frames move past a light source at a rate of many per second, and you perceive a whole that is very different from the separate frames that are the film's parts. Similarly, thousands of tiny pixels make up an image (whole) on a computer screen.

Depth Perception

Images appear on our retinas in two-dimensional form, yet remarkably we see a three-dimensional world. **Depth perception** is the ability to perceive objects three-dimensionally. Look around you. You do not see your surroundings as flat. You see some objects farther away, some closer. Some objects overlap each other. The scene and objects that you are looking at have depth. How do you see depth? To perceive a world of depth, we use two kinds of information, or cues— binocular and monocular.

Because we have two eyes, we get two views of the world, one from each eye. **Binocular cues** are depth cues that depend on the combination of the images in the left and right eyes and on the way the two eyes work together. The pictures are slightly different because the eyes are in slightly different positions. Try holding your hand about 10 inches from your face. Alternately close and open your left and right eyes so that only one eye is open at a time. The image of your hand will appear to jump back and forth, because the image is in a slightly different place on the left and right retinas. The *disparity,* or difference, between the images in the two eyes is the binocular cue the brain uses to determine the depth, or distance, of an object. The combination of the two images in the brain, and the disparity between them in the eyes, give us information about the three-dimensionality of the world (Preston, Kourtzi, & Welchman, 2009). Those 3-D glasses that you wear for viewing some movies, like *Avatar,* give you a sense of depth by creating visual disparity. The coloring of the lenses presents a different image to each eye. Your eyes then compete with each other, and your brain makes sense of the conflict by creating the perception of three dimensions.

Convergence is another binocular cue to depth and distance. When we use our two eyes to look at something, they are focused on the same object. If the object is near us, our eyes converge, or move together, almost crossing. If the object is farther away, we can focus on it without pulling our eyes together. The muscle movements involved in convergence provide information about how far away or how deep something is.

In addition to using binocular cues to get an idea of objects' depth, we rely on a number of **monocular cues,** or depth cues, available from the image in one eye, either right or left. Monocular cues are powerful, and under normal circumstances they can provide a compelling impression of depth. Try closing one eye—your perception of the world still retains many of its three-dimensional qualities. Examples of monocular cues are

- *Familiar size:* This cue to the depth and distance of objects is based on what we have learned from experience about the standard sizes of objects. We know how large oranges tend to be, so we can tell something about how far away an orange is likely to be by the size of its image on the retina.

- *Height in the field of view:* All other things being equal, objects positioned higher in a picture are seen as farther away.

- *Linear perspective and relative size:* Objects that are farther away take up less space on the retina. So, things that appear smaller are perceived to be farther away. As Figure 10.15 shows, as an object recedes into the distance, parallel lines in the scene appear to converge.

- *Overlap:* We perceive an object that partially conceals or overlaps another object as closer.

- *Shading:* This cue involves changes in perception due to the position of the light and the position of the viewer. Consider an egg under a desk lamp. If you walk around the desk, you will see different shading patterns on the egg.

- *Texture gradient:* Texture becomes denser and finer the farther away it is from the viewer (Figure 10.16).

Depth perception is a remarkably complex adaptation. Individuals with only one functioning eye cannot see depth in the way that those with two eyes can. Other disorders of the eye can also lead to a lack of depth perception. Oliver Sacks (2006)

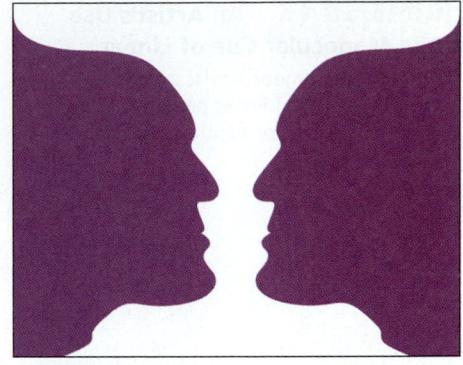

FIGURE 10.13 **Reversible Figure-Ground Pattern** Do you see the silhouette of a goblet or a pair of faces in profile?

● **convergence** A binocular cue to depth and distance in which the muscle movements in our two eyes provide information about how deep and/or far away something is.

● **monocular cues** Powerful depth cues available from the image in one eye, either the right or the left.

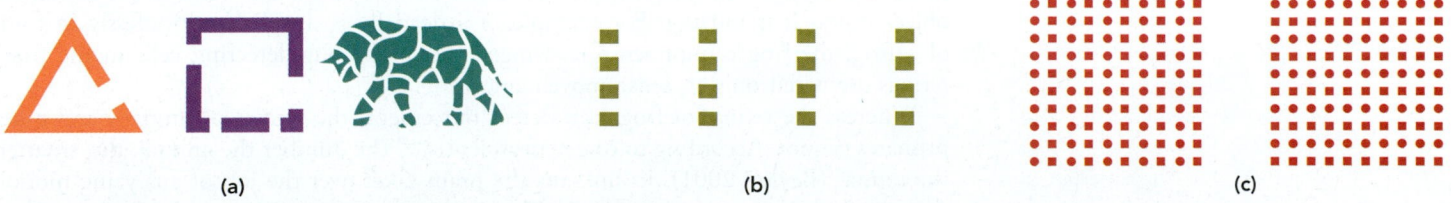

(a) (b) (c)

FIGURE 10.14 **Gestalt Principles of Closure, Proximity, and Similarity** (a) *Closure:* When we see disconnected or incomplete figures, we fill in the spaces and see them as complete figures. (b) *Proximity:* When we see objects that are near each other, they tend to be seen as a unit. You are likely to perceive the grouping as four columns of four squares, not one set of 16 squares. (c) *Similarity:* When we see objects that are similar to each other, they tend to be seen as a unit. Here, you are likely to see vertical columns of circles and squares in the left box but horizontal rows of circles and squares in the right box.

FIGURE 10.15 **An Artist's Use of the Monocular Cue of Linear Perspective** Famous landscape artist J. M. W. Turner used linear perspective to give the perception of depth in *Rain, Steam, and Speed.*

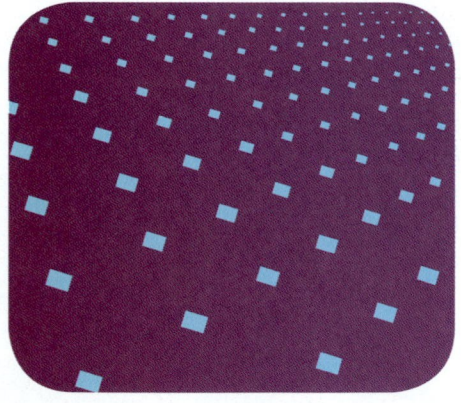

FIGURE 10.16 **Texture Gradient** The gradients of texture create an impression of depth on a flat surface.

described the case of Susan Barry, who had been born with crossed eyes. The operation to correct her eyes left her cosmetically normal, but she was unable to perceive depth throughout her life. As an adult, she became determined to see depth. With a doctor's aid, she found special glasses and undertook a process of eye muscle exercises to improve her chances of perceiving in three dimensions. It was a difficult and long process, but one day she noticed things starting to "stick out" at her—as you might experience when watching a film in 3-D. Although Barry had successfully adapted to life in a flat visual world, she had come to realize that relying on monocular cues was not the same as experiencing the rich visual world of binocular vision. She described flowers as suddenly appearing "inflated." She noted how "ordinary things looked extraordinary" as she saw the leaves of a tree, an empty chair, and her office door projecting out from the background. For the first time, she had a sense of being inside the world she was viewing.

Motion Perception

Motion perception plays an important role in the lives of many species (Boeddeker & Memmi, 2010). Indeed, for some animals, motion perception is critical for survival. Both predators and their prey depend on being able to detect motion quickly (Borst, Hag, & Reiff, 2010). Frogs and some other simple vertebrates may not even see an object unless it is moving. For example, if a dead fly is dangled motionlessly in front of a frog, the frog cannot sense its winged meal. The bug-detecting cells in the frog's retinas are wired only to sense movement.

Whereas the retinas of frogs can detect movement, the retinas of humans and other primates cannot. According to one neuroscientist, "The dumber the animal, the 'smarter' the retina" (Baylor, 2001). In humans the brain takes over the job of analyzing motion through highly specialized pathways (Raudies & Neumann, 2010).

How do humans perceive motion? First, we have neurons that are specialized to detect motion. Second, feedback from our body tells us whether we are moving or whether someone or some object is moving; for example, you move your eye muscles as you watch a ball coming toward you. Third, the environment we see is rich in cues that give us information about movement.

Psychologists are interested in both real movement and **apparent movement,** which occurs when we perceive a stationary object as moving. You can experience apparent movement at IMAX movie theaters. In watching a film of a climb of Mount Everest, you may find yourself feeling breathless as your visual field floods with startling images. In theaters without seats, viewers of these films are often warned to hold the handrail because perceived movement is so realistic that they might fall.

Perceptual Constancy

Retinal images change constantly. Yet even though the stimuli that fall on our retinas change as we move closer to or farther away from objects, or as we look at objects from different orientations and in light or dark settings, our perception of them remains stable. **Perceptual constancy** is the recognition that objects are constant and unchanging even though sensory input about them is changing.

We experience three types of perceptual constancy—size constancy, shape constancy, and color constancy—as follows:

■ *Size constancy* is the recognition that an object remains the same size even though the retinal image of the object changes (Figure 10.17). Experience is important to size perception: No matter how far away you are from your car, you know how large it is.

■ *Shape constancy* is the recognition that an object retains the same shape even though its orientation to you changes. Look around. You probably see objects of various shapes—chairs and tables, for example. If you walk around the room, you will see these objects from different sides and angles. Even though the retinal image of the object changes as you walk, you still perceive the objects as having the same shape (Figure 10.18).

■ *Color constancy* is the recognition that an object retains the same color even though different amounts of light fall on it. For example, if you are reaching for a green Granny Smith apple, it looks green to you whether you are having it for lunch, in the bright noon sun, or as an evening snack in the pale pink of sunset.

Note that perceptual constancy tells us about the crucial role of interpretation in perception: We *interpret* sensation. That is, we perceive objects as having particular characteristics regardless of the retinal image detected by our eyes. Images may flow across the retina, but experiences are made sensible through perception. The many cues we use to visually perceive the real world can lead to optical illusions when they are taken out of that real-world context, as you can experience for yourself in Figure 10.19.

FIGURE 10.17 **Size Constancy** Even though our retinal images of the hot air balloons vary, we still realize the balloons are approximately the same size. This illustrates the principle of size constancy.

● **apparent movement** The perception that a stationary object is moving.

● **perceptual constancy** The recognition that objects are constant and unchanging even though sensory input about them is changing.

FIGURE 10.18 **Shape Constancy** The various projected images from an opening door are quite different, yet you perceive a rectangular door.

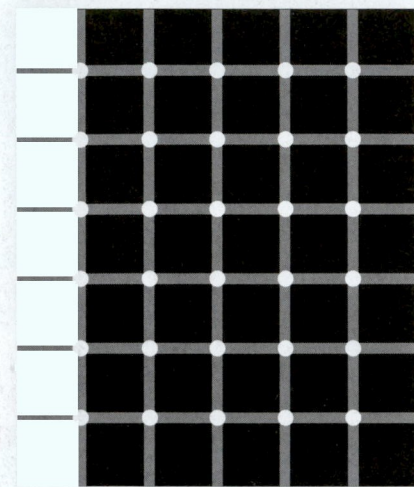

Blinking Effect Illusion
Stare at the white circles and notice the intermittent blinking effect. Your eyes make the static figure seem dynamic, attempting to fill in the white circle intersections with the black of the background.

Rotational Illusion
The two rings appear to rotate in different directions when we approach or move away from this figure while fixing our eyes on the center.

Pattern Recognition
Although the diagram contains no actual triangles, your brain "sees" two overlapping triangles. The explanation is that the notched circles and angled lines merely suggest gaps in which complete objects should be. The brain fills in the missing information.

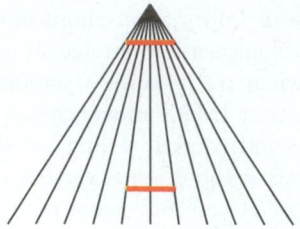

Ponzo Illusion
The top line looks much longer than the bottom, but they are the same length.

Induction Illusion
The yellow patches are identical, but they look different and seem to take on the characteristics of their surroundings when they appear against different-color backgrounds.

FIGURE 10.19 **Perceptual Illusions** These illusions show how adaptive perceptual cues can lead to errors when taken out of context. These mind-challenging images are definitely fun, but keep in mind that these illusions are based on processes that are quite adaptive in real life.

SUMMARY

Light is the stimulus that is sensed by the visual system. Light can be described in terms of wavelengths. Three characteristics of light waves determine our experience: wavelength (hue), amplitude (brightness), and purity (saturation).

In sensation, light passes through the cornea and lens to the retina, the light-sensitive surface in the back of the eye that houses light receptors called rods (which function in low illumination) and cones (which react to color). The fovea of the retina contains only cones and sharpens detail in an image. The optic nerve transmits neural impulses to the brain. There it diverges at the optic chiasm, so that what we see in the left visual field is registered in the right side of the brain and vice versa. In the occipital lobes of the cerebral cortex, the information is integrated.

The trichromatic theory of color perception holds that three types of color receptors in the retina allow us to perceive three colors (green, red, and blue). The opponent-process theory states that cells in the

KEY TERMS

retina   121
rods   121
cones   121
optic nerve   121
feature detectors   122
parallel processing   123
binding   125
trichromatic theory   125
opponent-process theory   125

figure-ground
   relationship   125
gestalt psychology   126
depth perception   126
binocular cues   126
convergence   127
monocular cues   127
apparent movement   129
perceptual constancy   129

Touring the Senses

Parts of the Eye ▪ Visual Pathways ▪ Parts of the Ear ▪ Parts of the Nose

GOALS OF THE TOUR

1 **Parts of the Eye.** Identify the structures of the human eye and describe their functions.

2 **Visual Pathways.** Identify the pathways for visual stimulation and describe the brain's role in visual information processing.

3 **Parts of the Ear.** Identify the three areas of the ear and describe the key structures of the inner ear.

4 **Parts of the Nose.** Describe how the nose (olfactory sense) processes a smell or odor.

Parts of the Eye and Visual Pathways

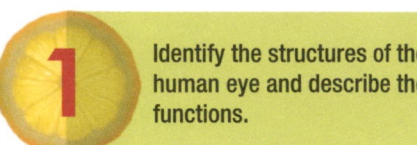

1 Identify the structures of the human eye and describe their functions.

2 Identify the pathways for visual stimulation and describe the brain's role in visual information processing.

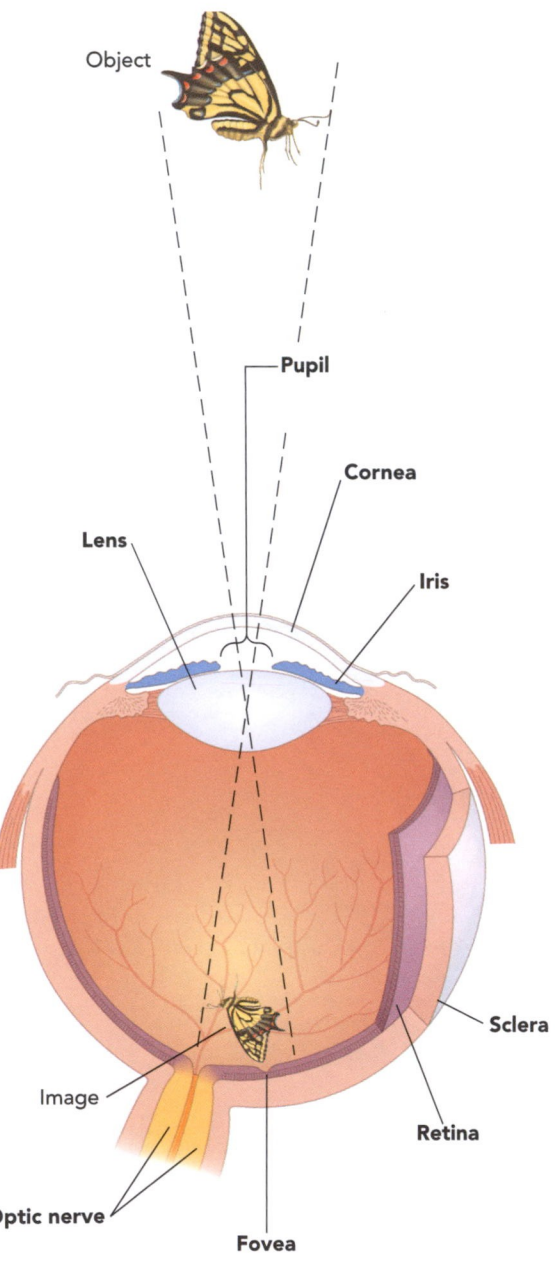

Object

Pupil

Cornea

Lens

Iris

Image

Optic nerve

Fovea

Sclera

Retina

Left visual field   Right visual field

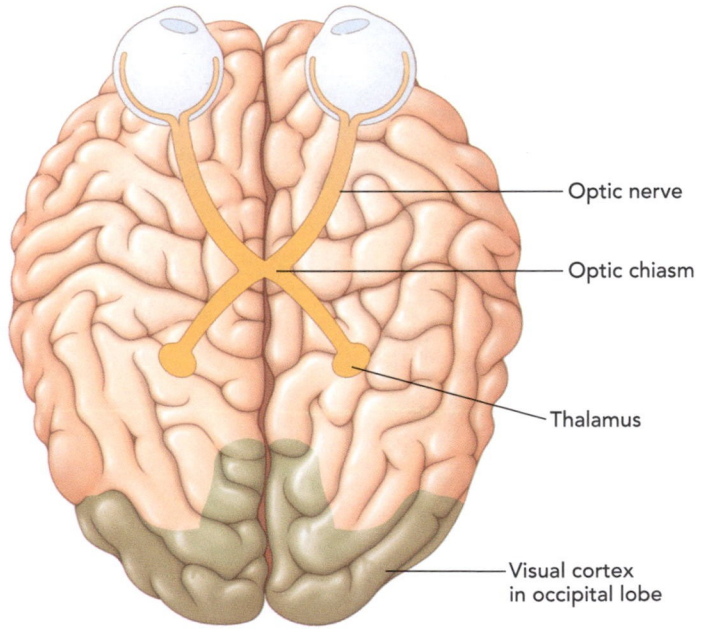

Optic nerve

Optic chiasm

Thalamus

Visual cortex in occipital lobe

Parts of the Ear and Parts of the Nose

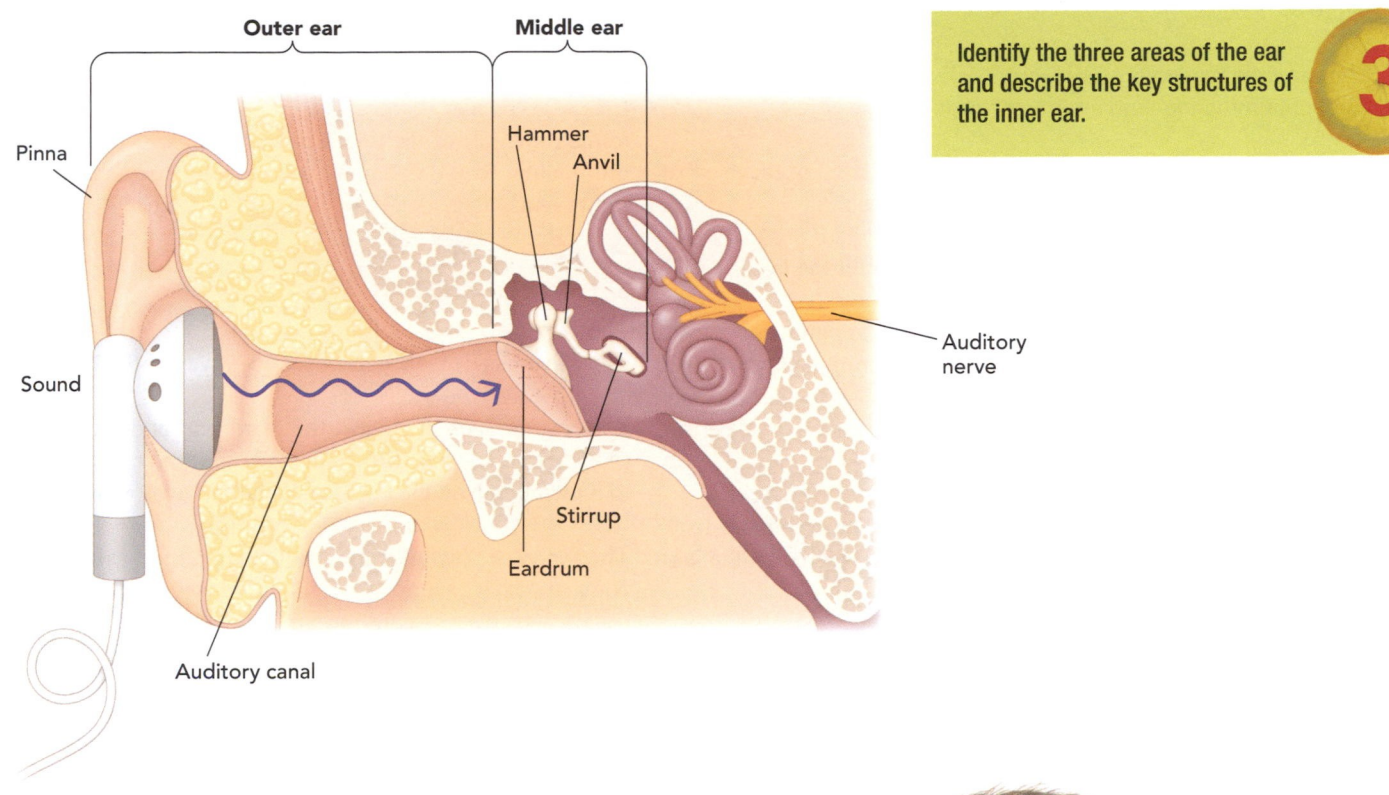

Outer ear **Middle ear**

Pinna

Sound

Hammer

Anvil

Auditory nerve

Stirrup

Eardrum

Auditory canal

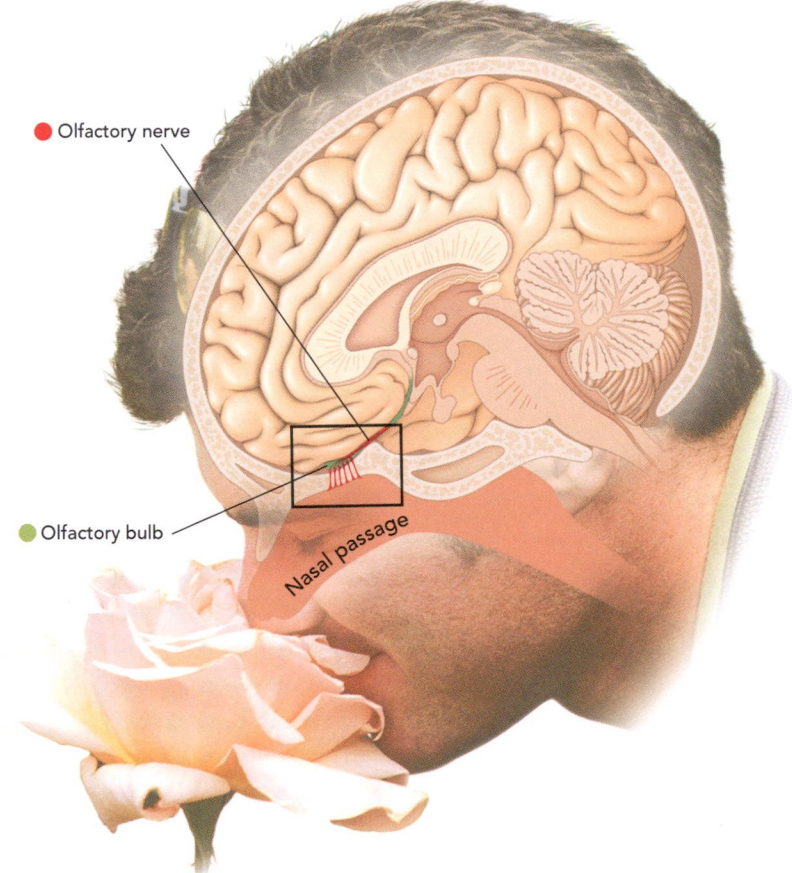

● Olfactory nerve

● Olfactory bulb

Nasal passage

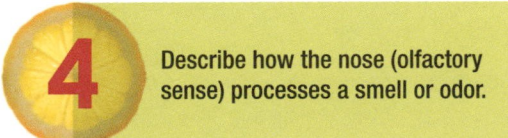

4 Describe how the nose (olfactory sense) processes a smell or odor.

1. PARTS OF THE EYE

The *sclera* is the outer membrane of the eyeball that makes up the white of the eye.

The *retina* is made up of a layer of cells in the interior of the eye that contain the *photoreceptors*, the rods and the cones.

The *cornea* is the transparent membrane in the front of the eye that protects the eye and bends light to provide focus.

The *pupil* is the opening that allows light to enter the eye.

The *iris* is the colored muscle that surrounds the pupil and adjusts the amount of light entering into the eye through the pupil. It dilates (opens) or constricts (closes) in response to the intensity (brightness) of the light. It also dilates in response to certain emotions.

The *lens* focuses the image onto the retinal layer on the back surface of the eye. As in a camera, the image projected by the lens onto the retina is reversed.

The *fovea* is the region of the retina that is directly in line with the pupil and contains mostly cones, which are involved in color perception and visual acuity (sharpness).

The *optic nerve* receives inputs from the photoreceptors and sends information to the brain.

2. VISUAL PATHWAYS

Images of objects in the right visual field are projected to the left half of the retina of each eye, which in turn sends the information first to the thalamus for initial processing and then to the visual cortex in the left hemisphere where perception takes place. Likewise, images of objects in the left visual field are projected to the right half of the retina of each eye, which in turn sends the information to the thalamus and then to the visual cortex in the right hemisphere.

3. PARTS OF THE EAR

The *outer ear* is the visible portion of the ear and the auditory canal (ear canal) that funnels sound waves to the eardrum.

The *middle ear* includes the eardrum and three tiny bones (hammer, anvil, and stirrup) that transmit the eardrum's vibrations to a membrane on the cochlea called the oval window.

The *inner ear* includes the snail-shaped tube called the *cochlea*, which translates sound waves into fluid waves, and the semicircular canals, which sense equilibrium.

4. PARTS OF THE NOSE

Airborne molecules (olfactory chemicals) enter the nasal passage and reach receptor cells located in the olfactory epithelium of the upper nasal passage. The receptors send messages to the brain's olfactory bulb and then onward to the primary smell cortex located in the temporal lobes.

visual system respond to red-green and blue-yellow colors. Both theories are probably correct—the eye and the brain use both methods to code colors.

Shape perception is the ability to distinguish objects from their background. Depth perception is the ability to perceive objects three-dimensionally and depends on binocular (two eyes) cues and monocular (one eye) cues. Motion perception by humans depends on specialized neurons, feedback from the body, and environmental cues. Perceptual constancy is the recognition that objects are stable despite changes in the way we see them.

TEST YOURSELF

1. What is light? What are some terms scientists use to describe it?

2. What are rods and cones and their functions in the eye?

3. What are the main principles of trichromatic theory? How does this theory explain color vision and color blindness?

APPLY YOUR KNOWLEDGE

1. If you found the example of inattentional blindness interesting, check out this website where you will find a video so that you can see for yourself:

   http://www.theinvisiblegorilla.com

2. Create a gestalt moment. You can use the corners of the pages of this book or a notebook. Draw a series of small, simple pictures, sketching one on the lower right-hand corner of each page. How about a stick figure—standing still, and then moving its arm, and then waving? Each successive picture should be as close to the one before it as possible but changing slightly to reflect the movement. Then, using your thumb, quickly allow the pages to flip rapidly in front of you. You have created a cartoon.

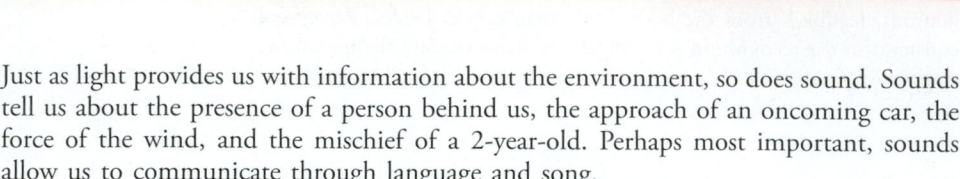

The Auditory System

Just as light provides us with information about the environment, so does sound. Sounds tell us about the presence of a person behind us, the approach of an oncoming car, the force of the wind, and the mischief of a 2-year-old. Perhaps most important, sounds allow us to communicate through language and song.

11·1 THE NATURE OF SOUND AND HOW WE EXPERIENCE IT

At a fireworks display, you may feel the loud boom of the explosion in your chest. At a concert, you might have sensed that the air around you was vibrating. Bass instruments are especially effective at creating mechanical pulsations, even causing the floor to vibrate. When the bass is played loudly, we can sense air molecules being pushed forward in waves from the speaker. How does sound generate these sensations?

Sound waves are vibrations in the air that are processed by the *auditory* (hearing) system. Remember that light waves are much like the waves in the ocean moving toward the beach. Sound waves are similar. Sound waves also vary in length. Wavelength determines the sound wave's *frequency*—that is, the number of cycles (full wavelengths) that pass through a point in a given time interval. *Pitch* is the perceptual interpretation of the frequency of a sound. We perceive high-frequency sounds as having a high pitch, and low-frequency sounds as having a low pitch. A soprano voice sounds high-pitched. A bass voice has a low pitch. As with the wavelengths of light, human sensitivity is limited to a range of sound frequencies. It is common knowledge that dogs, for example, can hear higher frequencies than humans can.

Sound waves vary not only in frequency but also, like light waves, in amplitude (see Figure 10.2). A sound wave's *amplitude,* measured in decibels (dB), is the amount of pressure the sound wave produces relative to a standard. The typical standard—0 decibels—is the weakest sound the human ear can detect. *Loudness* is the perception of the sound wave's amplitude. In general, the higher the amplitude of the sound wave, or the higher the decibel level, the louder we perceive the sound to be. In terms of amplitude, the air is pressing more forcibly against you and your ears during loud sounds and more gently during quiet sounds.

So far we have been describing a single sound wave with just one frequency. A single sound wave is similar to the single wavelength of pure colored light, discussed in the context of color matching. Most sounds, including those of speech and music, are *complex sounds,* those in which numerous frequencies of sound blend together. *Timbre* is the tone saturation, or the perceptual quality, of a sound. Timbre is responsible for the perceptual difference between a trumpet and a trombone playing the same note and for the quality differences we hear in human voices. Figure 11.1 illustrates the physical differences in sound waves that produce the different qualities of sounds.

11·2 STRUCTURES AND FUNCTIONS OF THE EAR

What happens to sound waves once they reach your ear? How do various structures of the ear transform sound waves into signals that the brain will recognize as sound? Functionally the ear is analogous to the eye. The ear serves the purpose of transmitting a high-fidelity version of sounds in the world to the brain for analysis and interpretation.

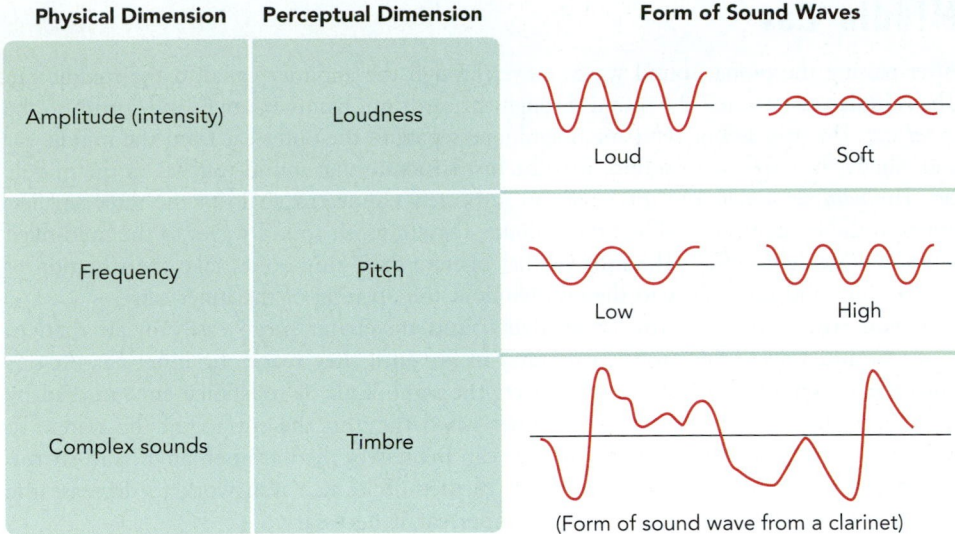

Physical Dimension	Perceptual Dimension	Form of Sound Waves	
Amplitude (intensity)	Loudness	Loud	Soft
Frequency	Pitch	Low	High
Complex sounds	Timbre	(Form of sound wave from a clarinet)	

FIGURE 11.1   Physical Difference in Sound Waves and the Qualities of Sound They Produce Here we can see how the input of sound stimuli requires our ears and brain to attend to varying characteristics of the rich sensory information that is sound.

Just as an image needs to be in focus and sufficiently bright for the brain to interpret it, a sound needs to be transmitted in a way that preserves information about its location, its frequency (which helps us distinguish the voice of a child from that of an adult), and its timbre (which allows us to identify the voice of a friend on the telephone). The ear is divided into three parts: outer ear, middle ear, and inner ear (Figure 11.2).

Outer Ear

The **outer ear** consists of the pinna and the external auditory canal. The funnel-shaped *pinna* (plural, *pinnae*) is the outer, visible part of the ear. (Elephants have very large pinnae.) The pinna collects sounds and channels them into the interior of the ear. The pinnae of many animals, such as cats, are movable and serve a more important role in sound localization than do the pinnae of humans. Cats turn their ears in the direction of a faint and interesting sound.

● **outer ear** The outermost part of the ear, consisting of the pinna and the external auditory canal.

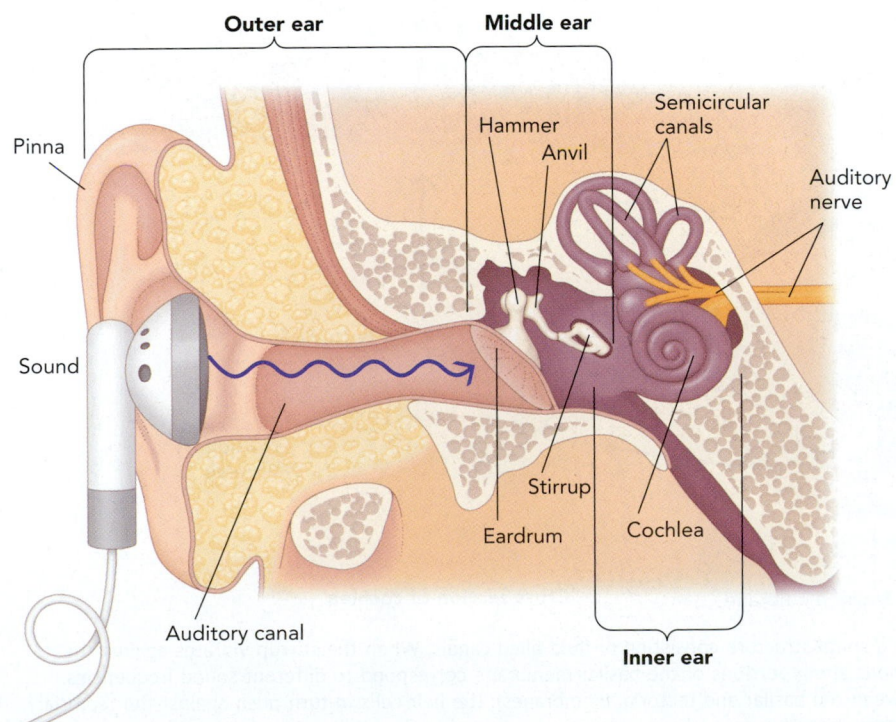

FIGURE 11.2   The Outer, Middle, and Inner Ear On entering the outer ear, sound waves travel through the auditory canal, where they generate vibrations in the eardrum. These vibrations are transferred via the hammer, anvil, and stirrup to the fluid-filled cochlea in the inner ear. There the mechanical vibrations are converted to an electrochemical signal that the brain will recognize as sound.

Middle Ear

After passing the pinna, sound waves move through the auditory canal to the middle ear. The **middle ear** channels the sound through the eardrum, hammer, anvil, and stirrup to the inner ear. The *eardrum* or tympanic membrane separates the outer ear from the middle ear and vibrates in response to sound. It is the first structure that sound touches in the middle ear. The *hammer, anvil,* and *stirrup* are an intricately connected chain of the three smallest bones in the human body. When they vibrate, they transmit sound waves to the fluid-filled inner ear (Stenfelt, 2006). The muscles that operate these tiny bones take the vibration of the eardrum and transmit it to the oval window, the opening of the inner ear.

If you are a swimmer, you know that sound travels far more easily in air than in water. Sound waves entering the ear travel in air until they reach the inner ear. At this border between air and fluid, sound meets the same kind of resistance encountered by shouts directed at an underwater swimmer when they hit the surface of the water. To compensate, the muscles of the middle ear can maneuver the hammer, anvil, and stirrup to amplify the sound waves. Importantly, these muscles can also work to decrease the intensity of sound waves, to protect the inner ear if necessary.

Inner Ear

The function of the **inner ear,** which includes the oval window, cochlea, and basilar membrane, is to convert sound waves into neural impulses and send them on to the brain (Shibata & others, 2010). The stirrup is connected to the membranous *oval window,* which transmits sound waves to the cochlea. The *cochlea* is a tubular, fluid-filled structure that is coiled up like a snail (Figure 11.3). The *basilar membrane* lines the inner wall of the cochlea and runs its entire length. It is narrow and rigid at the base of the cochlea but widens and becomes more flexible at the top. The variation in width

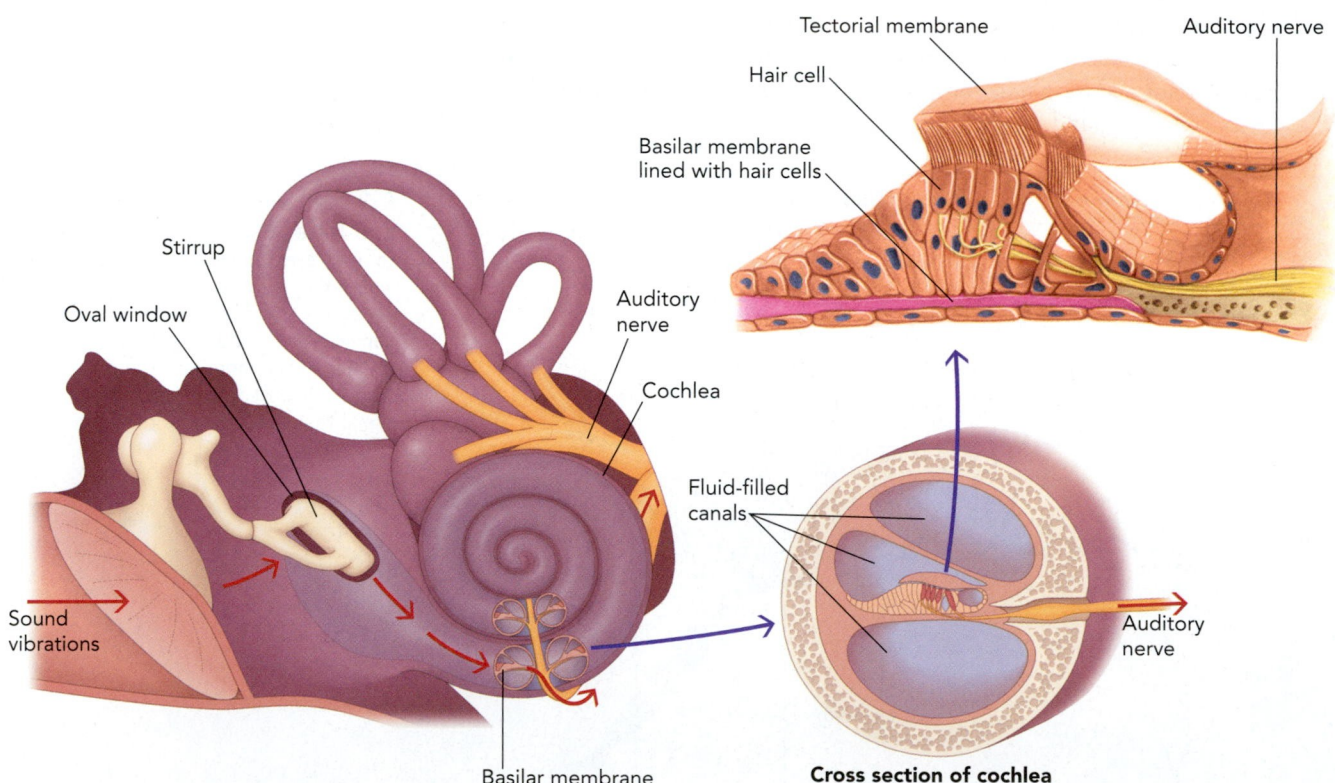

FIGURE 11.3 **The Cochlea** The cochlea is a spiral structure consisting of fluid-filled canals. When the stirrup vibrates against the oval window, the fluid in the canals vibrates. Vibrations along portions of the basilar membrane correspond to different sound frequencies. The vibrations exert pressure on the hair cells (between the basilar and tectorial membranes); the hair cells in turn push against the tectorial membrane, and this pressure bends the hairs. This sequence of events triggers an action potential in the auditory nerve.

CRITICAL CONTROVERSY

Are Cochlear Implants a "Cure" for Deafness?

Adults with hearing loss and parents of deaf children are often keenly interested in cochlear implants (Fagan & Pisoni, 2010; Hyde, Punch, & Komesaroff, 2010). For deaf adults who previously could hear and speak, implants work best if they are inserted shortly after the hearing loss. The reason? If a person is deaf for a long time, the brain adapts to this change and uses the auditory cortex for other tasks. For children especially, time is of the essence. The brain is quite sensitive and responsive to sensory processes, and a young child's brain remains somewhat "up for grabs." It can be used to process sound or other stimuli, but once it dedicates itself, change is difficult. Moreover, the language abilities of children implanted at the age of 2 tend to be superior to those who wait until the age of 4 (Niparko, 2004). Many parents are motivated to have their child receive the implant as early as possible, maximizing the chances that the child will learn to hear and speak. These parental motivations are where the controversy comes in.

Some critics say that parents who opt for a cochlear implant for their deaf daughter or son deprive the child of participation in the unique language and culture that is the child's right.

The 1990s saw an intense debate over implants, especially with respect to children. On one side were parents of deaf children, late-deafened adults, and medical professionals. On the other side were members of the deaf community. Spokespersons for the deaf stressed that life as a deaf person can be rich, rewarding, and successful. Deaf culture, they stressed, has its own language (*sign language*), opportunities, and valuable perspectives. Some argued that perhaps hearing parents simply do not want to have to learn a new language and navigate this unfamiliar world. Moreover, the use of cochlear implants in children implies that deafness is a problem that needs fixing, and in this way the procedure further undermines the many positive aspects of deaf culture.

In 2001 the National Association of the Deaf (NAD), an advocacy organization for deaf and hard-of-hearing individuals, issued a statement about the debate. The group emphasized that regardless of whether a deaf child receives an implant, he or she will live simultaneously in two worlds—the deaf world and the hearing world. The NAD also stressed the importance of realistic perceptions of the promises and limitations of cochlear implants. A cochlear implant does not provide "normal" hearing. The implant substitutes just 22 electrodes wound around the cochlea for the 16,000 delicate hairs in an intact cochlea. Hence the auditory experience of a person who has a cochlear implant is limited, and a cochlear implant does not "cure" deafness. Nonetheless, cochlear implants can allow a person to comprehend spoken language, to communicate by phone, and to hear his or her own voice.

Is there one right answer to this dilemma? Perhaps not: The NAD has recognized that the deaf community itself is diverse—and emphasizes that all individuals and all families are unique.

WHAT DO YOU THINK?
- If you were the parent of a deaf child, would you opt for the cochlear implant? Why or why not?
- What values of deaf culture might be lost if deafness were "cured"?

and flexibility allows different areas of the basilar membrane to vibrate more intensely when exposed to different sound frequencies (Wojtczak & Oxenham, 2009).

In humans and other mammals, hair cells line the basilar membrane (see Figure 11.3). These *hair cells* are the ear's sensory receptors. They are called hair cells because of the tufts of fine bristles, or *cilia,* that sprout from the top of them. The movement of the hair cells against the *tectorial membrane,* a jellylike flap above them, generates impulses that the brain interprets as sound (Parker, Brugeaud, & Edge, 2010). Hair cells are so delicate that exposure to loud noise can destroy them, leading to deafness or difficulties in hearing. Once lost, hair cells cannot regenerate.

Cochlear implants are devices that were specifically developed to replace damaged hair cells. A *cochlear implant*—a small electronic device that is surgically implanted in the ear and head—allows deaf or profoundly hard-of-hearing individuals to detect sound (Teague & others, 2010). The implant works by using electronic impulses to directly stimulate whatever working auditory nerves the recipient has in his or her cochlea (Luo, Galvin, & Fu, 2010). In the United States, approximately 41,500 adults and 25,500 children have had cochlear implants (U.S. Food and Drug Association, 2009). To read more about this technology and reactions to it, see the Critical Controversy.

11·3 THEORIES OF HEARING

One of the auditory system's mysteries is how the inner ear registers the frequency of sound—for example, how we hear a high-pitched piccolo versus the low tones of a cello. Two theories aim to explain this mystery: place theory and frequency theory.

Place theory states that each frequency produces vibrations at a particular spot on the basilar membrane. Georg von Békésy (1960) studied the effects of vibration applied at the oval window on the basilar membrane of human cadavers. Through a microscope, he saw that this stimulation produced a traveling wave on the basilar membrane. A traveling wave is like the ripples that appear in a pond when you throw in a stone. However, because the cochlea is a long tube, the ripples travel in only one direction—from the oval window at one end of the cochlea to the far tip of the cochlea. High-frequency vibrations create traveling waves that maximally displace, or move, the area of the basilar membrane closest to the oval window; low-frequency vibrations maximally displace areas of the membrane closer to the tip of the cochlea. So, the high-pitched tinkle of a little bell stimulates the narrow region of the basilar membrane at the base of the cochlea, whereas the low-pitched tones of a tuba stimulate the wide end.

Place theory adequately explains high-frequency but not low-frequency sounds. A high-frequency sound like the tinkle of a bell stimulates a precise area on the basilar membrane, just as place theory suggests. However, a low-frequency sound like that of a tuba causes a large part of the basilar membrane to be displaced, and so it is hard to identify an exact place on the membrane that is associated with low-frequency hearing. Looking only at the movement of the basilar membrane would give the impression that humans are probably not very good at hearing and discriminating between low-frequency sounds, and yet we are. Some other factors must therefore be at play in low-frequency hearing.

Frequency theory gets at these other influences by stating that the perception of a sound's frequency depends on how *often* the auditory nerve fires. Higher-frequency sounds cause the auditory nerve to fire more often than do lower-frequency sounds. One limitation of frequency theory, however, is that a single neuron has a maximum firing rate of about 1,000 times per second. Therefore, frequency theory does not apply to tones with frequencies that would require a neuron to fire more rapidly.

To deal with this limitation of frequency theory, researchers developed the **volley principle,** which states that a cluster of nerve cells can fire neural impulses in rapid succession, producing a volley of impulses. Individual neurons cannot fire faster than 1,000 times per second, but if the neurons team up and alternate their neural firing, they can attain a combined frequency above that rate. To get a sense for how the volley principle works, imagine a troop of soldiers who are all armed with guns that can fire only one round at a time and that take time to reload. If all the soldiers fire at the same time, the frequency of firing is limited and cannot go any faster than it takes to reload those guns. If, however, the soldiers are coordinated as a group and fire at different times, some of them can fire while others are reloading, leading to a greater frequency of firing. Frequency theory better explains the perception of sounds below 1,000 times per second, whereas a combination of frequency and place theory is needed for sounds above 1,000 times per second.

11·4 AUDITORY PROCESSING IN THE BRAIN

As we considered in the discussion of the visual system, once our receptors pick up energy from the environment, that energy must be transmitted to the brain for processing and interpretation. We saw that in the retina, the responses of the rod and cone receptors feed into ganglion cells and leave the eye via the optic nerve. In the auditory system, information about sound moves from the hair cells of the inner ear to the **auditory nerve,** which

● **place theory** Theory on how the inner ear registers the frequency of sound, stating that each frequency produces vibrations at a particular spot on the basilar membrane.

● **frequency theory** Theory on how the inner ear registers the frequency of sound, stating that the perception of a sound's frequency depends on how often the auditory nerve fires.

● **volley principle** Modification of frequency theory stating that a cluster of nerve cells can fire neural impulses in rapid succession, producing a volley of impulses.

● **auditory nerve** The nerve structure that receives information about sound from the hair cells of the inner ear and carries these neural impulses to the brain's auditory areas.

carries neural impulses to the brain's auditory areas. Remember that it is the movement of the hair cells that transforms the physical stimulation of sound waves into the action potential of neural impulses.

Auditory information moves up the auditory pathway via electrochemical transmission in a more complex manner than does visual information in the visual pathway. Many synapses occur in the ascending auditory pathway, with most fibers crossing over the midline between the hemispheres of the cerebral cortex, although some proceed directly to the hemisphere on the same side as the ear of reception (Landau & Barner, 2009). This means that most of the auditory information from the left ear goes to the right side of the brain, but some also goes to the left side of the brain. The auditory nerve extends from the cochlea to the brain stem, with some fibers crossing over the midline. The cortical destination of most of these fibers is the temporal lobes of the brain (beneath the temples of the head). As in the case of visual information, researchers have found that features are extracted from auditory information and transmitted along parallel pathways in the brain (Recanzone & Sutter, 2008).

11·5 LOCALIZING SOUND

When we hear the siren of a fire engine or the bark of a dog, how do we know where the sound is coming from? The basilar membrane gives us information about the frequency, pitch, and complexity of a sound, but it does not tell us where a sound is located.

Earlier in the module we saw that because our two eyes see slightly different images, we can determine how near or far away an object is. Similarly, having two ears helps us to localize a sound because each receives somewhat different stimuli from the sound source. A sound coming from the left has to travel different distances to the two ears, so if a barking dog is to your left, your left ear receives the sound sooner than your right ear. Also, your left ear will receive a slightly more intense sound than your right ear in this case. The sound reaching one ear is more intense than the sound reaching the other ear for two reasons: (1) It has traveled less distance and (2) the other ear is in what is called the *sound shadow* of the listener's head, which provides a barrier that reduces the sound's intensity (Figure 11.4).

Thus, differences in both the *timing* of the sound and the *intensity* of the sound help us to localize a sound (Salminen & others, 2010). Humans often have difficulty localizing a sound that is coming from a source that is directly in front of them because it reaches both ears simultaneously. The same is true for sounds directly above your head or directly behind you, because the disparities that provide information about localization are not present.

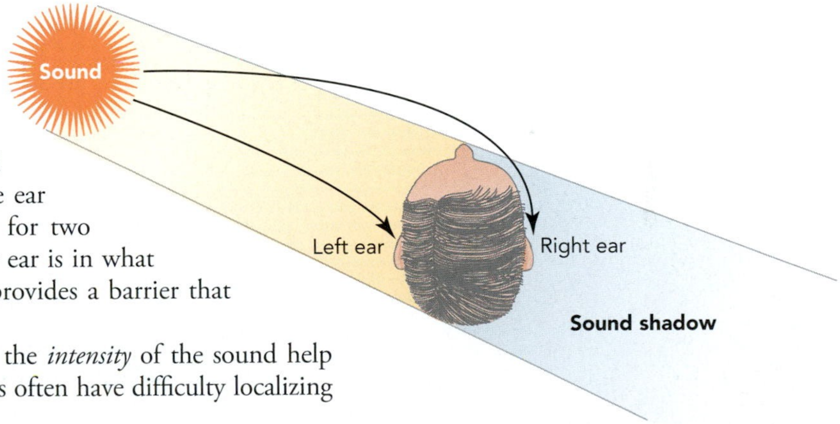

FIGURE 11.4   The Sound Shadow The sound shadow is caused by the listener's head, which forms a barrier that reduces the sound's intensity. Here the sound is to the person's left, so the sound shadow will reduce the intensity of the sound that reaches the right ear.

SUMMARY

Sounds, or sound waves, are vibrations in the air that are processed by the auditory system. These waves vary in important ways that influence what we hear. Pitch (how high or low in tone a sound is) is the perceptual interpretation of wavelength frequency. Amplitude of wavelengths, measured in decibels, is perceived as loudness. Complex sounds involve a blending of frequencies. Timbre is the tone saturation, or perceptual quality, of a sound.

KEY TERMS

outer ear   133
middle ear   134
inner ear   134
place theory   136

frequency theory   136
volley principle   136
auditory nerve   136

The outer ear consists of the pinna and external auditory canal and acts to funnel sound to the middle ear. In the middle ear, the eardrum, hammer, anvil, and stirrup vibrate in response to sound and transfer the vibrations to the inner ear. Important parts of the fluid-filled inner ear are the oval window, cochlea, and basilar membrane. The movement of hair cells between the basilar membrane and the tectorial membrane generates nerve impulses.

Place theory states that each frequency produces vibrations at a particular spot on the basilar membrane. Place theory adequately explains high-frequency sounds but not low-frequency sounds. Frequency theory holds that the perception of a sound's frequency depends on how often the auditory nerve fires. The volley principle states that a cluster of neurons can fire impulses in rapid succession, producing a volley of impulses.

Information about sound moves from the hair cells to the auditory nerve, which carries information to the brain's auditory areas. The cortical destination of most fibers is the temporal lobes of the cerebral cortex. Localizing sound involves both the timing of the sound and the intensity of the sound arriving at each ear.

TEST YOURSELF

1. When you hear the pitch of a voice or an instrument, what quality of sound are you perceiving? When you hear the loudness of music, what characteristic of sound are you perceiving?

2. When you hear any sound, what vibrates, and how are the vibrations then transferred to the inner ear?

3. What is the pinna? What role does it play in hearing?

APPLY YOUR KNOWLEDGE

1. Have you ever thought you heard your mother or someone significant call your name but then found that person looking puzzled when you responded? Based on auditory perception, how can you explain this misunderstanding?

2. How do you think the music you listen to loudly through your earbuds might affect your hearing?

The Other Senses

In addition to the visual and auditory systems, we sense through the skin senses and the chemical senses (smell and taste), and the kinesthetic and vestibular senses (systems that allow us to stay upright and to coordinate our movements).

12·1 THE SKIN SENSES

You know when a friend has a fever by putting your hand to her head; you know how to find your way to the light switch in a darkened room by groping along the wall; and you know whether a pair of shoes is too tight by the way the shoes rub different parts of your feet when you walk. Many of us think of our skin as a painter's canvas: We color it with cosmetics, dyes, and tattoos. In fact, the skin is our largest sensory system, draped over the body with receptors for touch, temperature, and pain (Hollins, 2010). These three kinds of receptors form the *cutaneous senses*.

Touch

Touch is one of the senses that we most often take for granted, yet our ability to respond to touch is astounding. What do we detect when we feel "touch"? What kind of energy does our sense of touch pick up from our external environment? In vision we detect light energy. In hearing we detect the vibrations of air or sound waves pressing against our eardrums. In touch we detect mechanical energy, or pressure against the skin. The lifting of a single hair causes pressure on the skin around the shaft of hair. This tiny bit of mechanical pressure at the base of the hair is sufficient for us to feel the touch of a pencil point. More commonly we detect the mechanical energy of the pressure of a car seat against our buttocks or of a pencil in our hand. Is this energy so different from the kind of energy we detect in vision or hearing? Sometimes the only difference is one of intensity—the sound of a rock band playing softly is an auditory stimulus, but at the high volumes that make a concert hall reverberate, this auditory stimulus is also *felt* as mechanical energy pressing against our skin.

How does information about touch travel from the skin through the nervous system? Sensory fibers arising from receptors in the skin enter the spinal cord. From there the information travels to the brain stem, where most fibers from each side of the body cross over to the opposite side of the brain. Next the information about touch moves on to the thalamus, which serves as a relay station. The thalamus then projects the map of the body's surface onto the somatosensory areas of the parietal lobes in the cerebral cortex (Hirata & Castro-Alamancos, 2010).

Just as the visual system is more sensitive to images on the fovea than to images in the peripheral retina, our sensitivity to touch is not equally good across all areas of the skin. Human toolmakers need excellent touch discrimination in their hands, but they require much less touch discrimination in other parts of the body, such as the torso and legs. The brain devotes more space to analyzing touch signals coming from the hands than from the legs. Consider the following example illustrating the hand's sensitivity. Standing in front of a vending machine, you find you need another nickel. Without looking, you are able to pull out the right coin. That is something that not even the most sophisticated robot can do. Engineers who design robots for use in surgical and other procedures have been unable to match the human hand's amazing sensitivity.

Temperature

We not only can feel the warmth of a comforting hand on our hand, we also can feel the warmth or coolness of a room. In order to maintain our body temperature, we have to be able to detect temperature. **Thermoreceptors,** sensory nerve endings under the skin, respond to changes in temperature at or near the skin and provide input to keep the body's temperature at 98.6 degrees Fahrenheit. There are two types of thermoreceptors: warm and cold. Warm thermoreceptors respond to the warming of the skin, and cold thermoreceptors respond to the cooling of the skin. When warm and cold receptors that are close to each other in the skin are stimulated simultaneously, we experience the sensation of hotness. Figure 12.1 illustrates this "hot" experience.

Pain

Pain is the sensation that warns us of damage to our bodies. When contact with the skin takes the form of a sharp pinch, our sensation of mechanical pressure changes from touch to pain. When a pot handle is so hot that it burns our hand, our sensation of temperature becomes one of pain. Intense stimulation of any one of the senses can produce pain—too much light, very loud sounds, or too many habanero peppers, for example.

Our ability to sense pain is vital for our survival as a species. In other words, this ability is adaptive. Individuals who cannot perceive pain often have serious difficulty navigating the world. They might not notice that they need to move away from a danger such as a hot burner on a stove or that they have seriously injured themselves. Pain functions as a quick-acting messenger that tells the brain's motor systems that they must act fast to eliminate or minimize damage.

Pain receptors are dispersed widely throughout the body—in the skin, in the sheath tissue surrounding muscles, in internal organs, and in the membranes around bone. Although all pain receptors are anatomically similar, they differ in the type of physical stimuli to which they most readily respond. Mechanical pain receptors respond mainly to pressure, such as when we encounter a sharp object. Heat pain receptors respond primarily to strong heat that is capable of burning the tissue in which the receptors are embedded. Other pain receptors have a mixed function, responding to both types of painful stimuli. Many pain receptors are chemically sensitive and respond to a range of pain-producing substances (Latremoliere & Woolf, 2009).

Pain receptors have a much higher threshold for firing than receptors for temperature and touch (Bloom, Nelson, & Lazerson, 2001). Pain receptors react mainly to physical stimuli that distort them or to chemical stimuli that irritate them into action. Inflamed joints or sore, torn muscles produce *prostaglandins,* which stimulate the receptors and cause the experience of pain. Drugs such as aspirin likely reduce the feeling of pain by reducing prostaglandin production.

Two different neural pathways transmit pain messages to the brain: a fast pathway and a slow pathway (Bloom, Nelson, & Lazerson, 2001). In the *fast pathway,* fibers connect directly with the thalamus and then to the motor and sensory areas of the cerebral cortex. This pathway transmits information about sharp, localized pain, as when you cut your skin. The fast pathway may serve as a warning system, providing immediate information about an injury—it takes less than a second for the information in this pathway to reach the cerebral cortex. In the *slow pathway,* pain information travels through the limbic system, a detour that delays the arrival of information at the cerebral cortex by seconds. The unpleasant, nagging pain that characterizes the slow pathway may function to remind the brain that an injury has occurred and that we need to restrict normal activity and monitor the pain (Gao & Ji, 2010; Linnman & others, 2010).

Many neuroscientists believe that the brain actually generates the experience of pain. There is evidence that turning pain signals on and off is a chemical process that probably involves *endorphins.* Recall from Module 6 that endorphins are neurotransmitters

● **thermoreceptors** Sensory nerve endings under the skin that respond to changes in temperature at or near the skin and provide input to keep the body's temperature at 98.6 degrees Fahrenheit.

● **pain** The sensation that warns us of damage to our bodies.

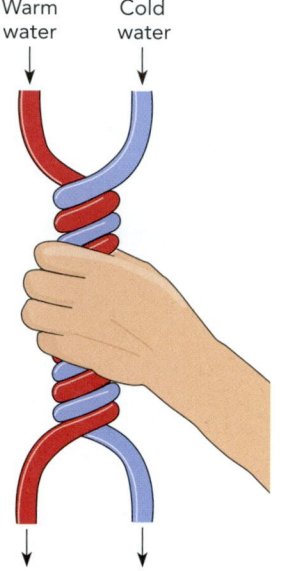

FIGURE 12.1 **A "Hot" Experience**
When two pipes, one containing cold water and the other warm water, are braided together, a person touching the pipes feels a sensation of "hot." The perceived heat coming from the pipes is so intense that the individual cannot touch them for longer than a couple of seconds.

that function as natural opiates in producing pleasure and pain (Mirilas & others, 2010; Quang & Schmidt, 2010). Endorphins are believed to be released mainly in the synapses of the slow pathway.

Perception of pain is complex and often varies from one person to the next (H. S. Smith, 2010). Some people rarely feel pain; others seem to be in great pain if they experience a minor bump or bruise. To some degree, these individual variations may be physiological. A person who experiences considerable pain even with a minor injury may have a neurotransmitter system that is deficient in endorphin production. However, perception of pain goes beyond physiology. Although it is true that all sensations are affected by factors such as motivation, expectation, and other related decision factors, the perception of pain is especially susceptible to these factors (Watson & others, 2006). A substantial research literature indicates that women experience more clinical pain, suffer more pain-related distress, and are more sensitive to experimentally induced pain than do men (Paller & others, 2009). Cultural and ethnic contexts also can greatly determine the degree to which an individual experiences pain (Dawson & List, 2009).

12·2 THE CHEMICAL SENSES

The information processed through our senses comes in many diverse forms: electromagnetic energy in vision, sound waves in hearing, and mechanical pressure and temperature in the skin senses. The two senses we now consider, smell and taste, are responsible for processing chemicals in our environment. Through smell, we detect airborne chemicals, and through taste we detect chemicals that have been dissolved in saliva. Smell and taste are frequently stimulated simultaneously. We notice the strong links between the two senses when a nasty cold with lots of nasal congestion takes the pleasure out of eating. Our favorite foods become "tasteless" without their characteristic smells. Despite this link, taste and smell are two distinct systems.

Taste

Think of your favorite food. Why do you like it? Imagine that food without its flavor. The thought of giving up a favorite taste, such as chocolate, can be depressing. Indeed, eating food we love is a major source of pleasure.

How does taste happen? To get at this question, try this. Take a drink of milk and allow it to coat your tongue. Then go to a mirror, stick out your tongue, and look carefully at its surface. You should be able to see rounded bumps above the surface. Those bumps, called **papillae,** contain taste buds, the receptors for taste. Your tongue houses about 10,000 taste buds, which are replaced about every two weeks. As we age, this replacement process is not quite as efficient, and an older individual may have just 5,000 working taste buds at any given moment. As with all of the other sensory systems we have studied, the information picked up by these taste receptors is transmitted to the brain for analysis and, when necessary, for a response (spitting something out, for example).

Traditionally, tastes were categorized as sweet, sour, bitter, and salty. However, today, most neuroscientists believe that the breakdown of taste into those four categories far underestimates the complexity of taste (Cauller, 2001). The taste fibers leading from a taste bud to the brain often respond strongly to a range of chemicals spanning *multiple* taste elements, such as salty and sour. The brain processes these somewhat ambiguous incoming signals and integrates them into a perception of taste (Bartoshuk, 2008). So, although people often categorize taste sensations along the four dimensions of sweet, bitter, salty, and sour, our tasting ability goes far beyond these.

Recently, researchers and chefs have been exploring a taste called *umami* (Maruyama & others, 2006). *Umami* is the Japanese word for "delicious" or "yummy." The taste of

● **papillae** Rounded bumps above the tongue's surface that contain the taste buds, the receptors for taste.

umami, one that Asian cooks have long recognized, is the flavor of L-glutamate. What is that taste? Umami is a savory flavor that is present in many seafoods as well as soy sauce, parmesan and mozzarella cheese, anchovies, mushrooms, and hearty meat broths.

Culture certainly influences the experience of taste. Anyone who has watched the Japanese version of *Iron Chef* or *Bizarre Foods* on television quickly notices that some people enjoy the flavor of sea urchin or raw meat, while others just do not get the appeal. In some cultures, food that is so spicy as to be practically inedible for the outsider may be viewed as quite delicious. The culture in which we live can influence the foods we are exposed to as well as our sense of what tastes good. In some cultures, very spicy food is introduced slowly into children's diets so that they can learn what is delicious at an early age.

Smell

Why do we have a sense of smell? One way to appreciate the importance of smell is to think about animals with a more sophisticated sense of smell than our own. A dog, for example, can use smell to find its way back from a long stroll, to distinguish friend from foe, and even (with practice) to detect illegal drugs concealed in a suitcase. In fact, dogs can detect odors in concentrations 100 times lower than those detectable by humans. Given the nasal feats of the average dog, we might be tempted to believe that the sense of smell has outlived its usefulness in humans.

What do humans use smell for? For one thing, humans need the sense of smell to decide what to eat. We can distinguish rotten food from fresh food and remember (all too well) which foods have made us ill in the past. The smell of a food that has previously made us sick is often by itself enough to make us feel nauseated. Second, although tracking is a function of smell that we often associate only with animals, humans are competent odor trackers. We can follow the odor of gas to a leak, the smell of smoke to a fire, and the aroma of a hot apple pie to a windowsill.

What physical equipment do we use to process odor information? Just as the eyes scan the visual field for objects of interest, the nose is an active instrument. We actively sniff when we are trying to track down the source of a fire or an unfamiliar chemical odor. The **olfactory epithelium** lining the roof of the nasal cavity contains a sheet of receptor cells for smell (Figure 12.2), so sniffing maximizes the chances of detecting an odor. The receptor cells are covered with millions of minute, hairlike antennae that project through the mucus in the top of the nasal cavity and make contact with air on its way to the throat and lungs (Bartoshuk, 2008; Rawson & Yee, 2006). Interestingly, unlike the neurons of most sensory systems, the neurons in the olfactory epithelium tend to replace themselves after injury (Vukovic & others, 2009).

● **olfactory epithelium** The lining the roof of the nasal cavity, containing a sheet of receptor cells for smell.

What is the neural pathway for information about smell? Although all other sensory pathways pass through the thalamus, the pathway for smell does not. In smell, the neural pathway first goes to the olfactory areas in the temporal lobes and then projects to various brain regions, especially the limbic system, which is involved in emotion and memory (Huart, Collet, & Rombaux, 2010). Unlike the other senses, smells take a superhighway to emotion and memory, a phenomenon we will consider in more detail in Module 23.

Smell might have a role to play in the chemistry of interpersonal attraction (Hurst, 2009). From an evolutionary perspective, the goal of

Many animals have a stronger sense of smell than humans do. Dogs have an especially powerful olfactory sense. Watson, a Labrador retriever, reliably paws his owner 45 minutes before her epileptic seizures begin, giving her time to move to a safe place. How does Watson know to do so? The best hypothesis is that the dog smells the chemical changes that precede epileptic seizures.

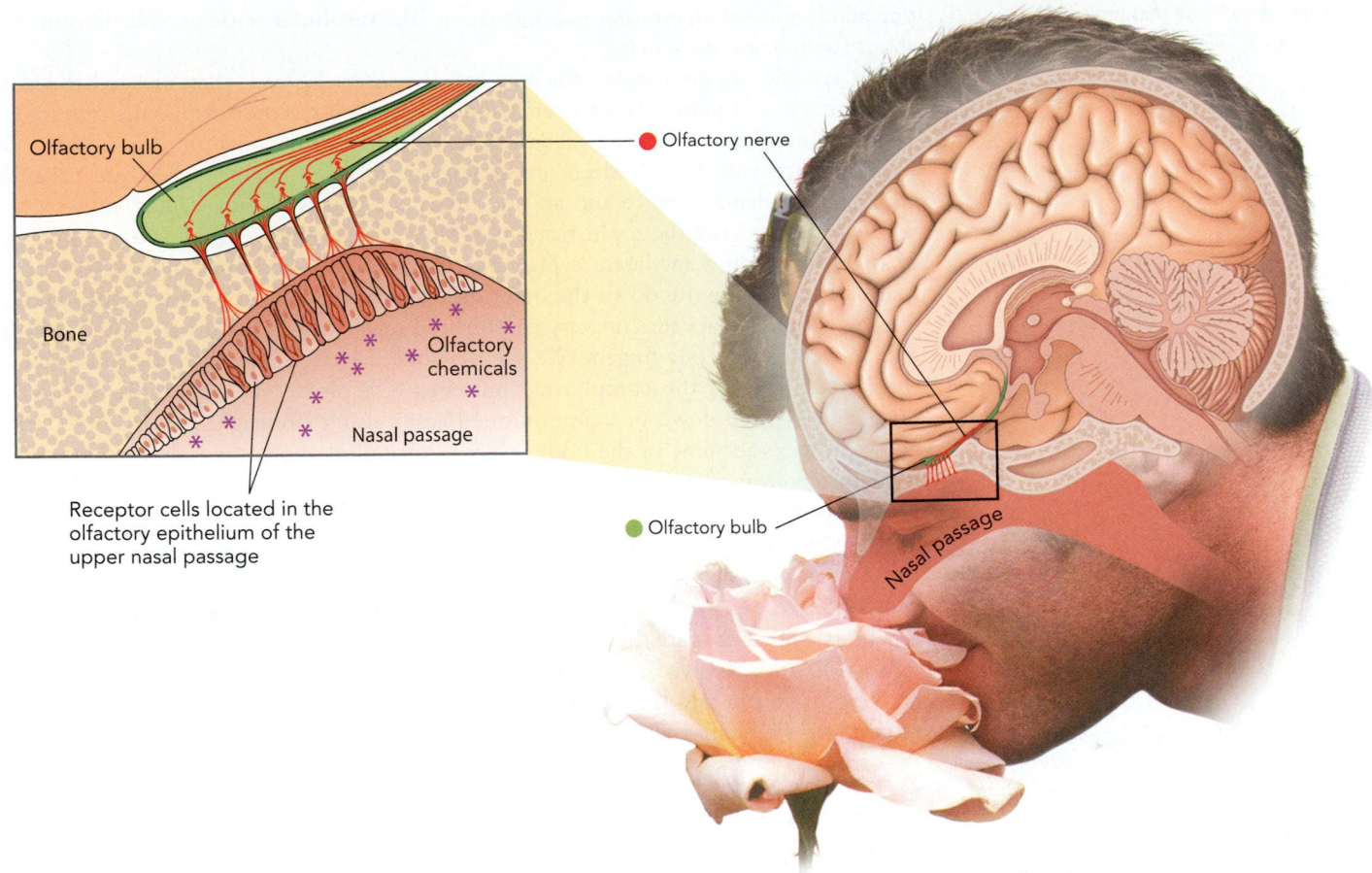

FIGURE 12.2   **The Olfactory Sense** Airborne molecules of an odor reach tiny receptor cells in the roof of the nasal cavity. The receptor cells form a mucus-covered membrane called the olfactory epithelium. Then the olfactory nerve carries information about the odor to the brain for further processing.

human mating is to find someone with whom to produce the healthiest offspring (Cosmides, 2011). Mates with differing sets of genes (known as the *major histocompatibility complex,* or *MHC*) produce healthier offspring with the broadest immune systems (Mueller, 2010). How do we find these people, short of taking a blood test? Martie Haselton (2006) has conducted studies on interpersonal attraction using the "smelly T-shirt" paradigm. In this research, men are asked to wear a T-shirt to bed every day for a week without washing it. After they have been thoroughly imbued with a male's personal scent, the T-shirts are presented to women to smell and rate for attractiveness. Women reliably rate men whose MHCs are different from their own as more attractive, on the basis of the aroma of the T-shirts. Thus, although the eyes may be the window to the soul, the nose might be the gateway to love.

12-3 THE KINESTHETIC AND VESTIBULAR SENSES

You know the difference between walking and running and between lying down and sitting up. For you to perform even the simplest act of motor coordination, such as reaching out to take a book off a shelf or getting up out of a chair, the brain must constantly receive and coordinate information from every part of the body. Your body has two kinds of senses that give you information about your movement and orientation in space, as well as help you to maintain balance. The **kinesthetic senses** provide informa-

● **kinesthetic senses** Senses that provide information about movement, posture, and orientation.

● **vestibular sense** Sense that provides information about balance and movement.

tion about movement, posture, and orientation. The **vestibular sense** provides information about balance and movement.

No specific organ contains the kinesthetic senses. Instead, they are embedded in muscle fibers and joints. As we stretch and move, these receptors signal the state of the muscle. Kinesthesia is a sense that you often do not even notice until it is gone. Try walking when your leg is "asleep" or smiling (never mind talking) when you have just come from a dentist's office and are still under the effects of Novocain.

We can appreciate the sophistication of kinesthesis when we think about it in terms of memory. Even a mediocre typist can bang out 20 words per minute—but how many of us could write down the order of the letters on a keyboard without looking? Typing is a skill that relies on very coordinated sensitivity to the orientation, position, and movements of our fingers. We say that our fingers "remember" the positions of the keys. Likewise, the complicated movements a pitcher uses to throw a baseball cannot be written down or communicated easily using language. They involve nearly every muscle and joint in the body. Most information about the kinesthetic senses is transmitted from the joints and muscles along the same pathways to the brain as information about touch.

The vestibular sense tells us whether our head (and hence usually our body) is tilted, moving, slowing down, or speeding up. It works in concert with the kinesthetic senses to coordinate our *proprioceptive feedback,* which is information about the position of our limbs and body parts in relation to other body parts. Consider the combination of sensory abilities involved in the motion of an ice hockey player skating down the ice, cradling the puck, and pushing it forward with the hockey stick. The hockey player is responding simultaneously to a multitude of sensations, including those produced by the slickness of the ice, the position of the puck, the speed and momentum of the forward progression, and the requirements of the play to turn and to track the other players on the ice.

● **semicircular canals** Three fluid-filled circular tubes in the inner ear containing the sensory receptors that detect head motion caused when we tilt or move our head and/or body.

The **semicircular canals** of the inner ear contain the sensory receptors that detect head motion caused when we tilt or move our head and/or body (Figure 12.3). These canals consist of three fluid-filled, circular tubes that lie in the three planes of the body—right-left, front-back, and up-down. We can picture these as three intersecting hula hoops. As you move your head, the fluid of the semicircular canals flows in different directions and at different speeds (depending on the force of the head movement). Our perception of head movement and position is determined by the movements of these receptor cells (Liao & others, 2010). This ingenious system of using the motion of fluid in tubes to sense head position is similar to the auditory system of the inner ear. However, the fluid movement in the cochlea results from the pressure sound exerts on the oval window, whereas the movements in the semicircular canals reflect physical movements of the head and body. Vestibular sacs in the semicircular canals contain hair cells embedded in a gelatin-like mass. Just as the hair cells in the cochlea trigger hearing impulses in the brain, the hair cells in the semicircular canals transmit information about balance and movement.

The brain pathways for the vestibular sense begin in the auditory nerve, which contains both the cochlear nerve (with information about sound) and the vestibular nerve (which has information about balance and movement). Most of the axons of the vestibular nerve connect with the medulla, although some go directly to the cerebellum. There also appear to be vestibular projections to the temporal cortex, but research has not fully charted their specific pathways.

Information from the sense of vision supplements the combination of kinesthetic and vestibular senses. This principle causes a motorist to slam on the brakes in his tiny sports car when the big truck next to him starts to move forward. When everything in our visual field appears to be moving, it is generally because *we* are moving.

FIGURE 12.3   The Semicircular Canals and Vestibular Sense The semicircular canals provide feedback to the gymnast's brain as her head and body tilt in different directions. Any angle of head rotation is registered by hair cells in one or more semicircular canals in both ears. (*Inset*) The semicircular canals.

SUMMARY

The skin senses include touch, temperature, and pain. Touch is the detection of mechanical energy, or pressure, against the skin. Touch information travels through the spinal cord, brain stem, and thalamus and on to the somatosensory areas of the parietal lobes. Thermoreceptors under the skin respond to increases and decreases in temperature. Pain is the sensation that warns us about damage to our bodies.

The chemical senses of taste and smell enable us to detect and process chemicals in the environment. Papillae are bumps on the tongue that contain taste buds, the receptors for taste. The olfactory epithelium contains a sheet of receptor cells for smell in the roof of the nose.

The kinesthetic senses provide information about movement, posture, and orientation. The vestibular sense gives us information about balance and movement. Receptors for the kinesthetic senses are embedded in muscle fibers and joints. The semicircular canals in the inner ear contain the sensory receptors that detect head motion.

KEY TERMS

thermoreceptors   140

pain   140

papillae   141

olfactory epithelium   142

kinesthetic senses   143

vestibular sense   144

semicircular canals   144

TEST YOURSELF

1. What three kinds of receptors form the cutaneous senses?
2. Describe how and why pain is adaptive.
3. What information about the body do the kinesthetic senses and the vestibular sense provide?

APPLY YOUR KNOWLEDGE

1. It has been said that we taste with our eyes first. Professional chefs give great thought to the presentation of foods. Think about your favorite food and focus not on how it tastes but on how it looks. Now think about how it smells. How do vision, smell, and taste work together to produce the experience of your favorite dish? Would your favorite beef stew be just as appetizing if it were served in a dog food bowl?

2. If you have a few minutes and a strong stomach, give your vestibular system a workout. Spin around quickly and repeatedly for a minute. You can spin in a swivel chair or standing in the center of a room (be careful of sharp edges nearby). When you stop, you will feel dizzy. Here's what is happening. The fluid in the semicircular canals moves slowly and is even slower to change direction. When we spin for a while, the fluid eventually catches up with our rate of motion and starts moving in the same direction. When we stop moving, however, the slow-moving fluid keeps on moving. It tells the hair cells in the vestibular canals (which in turn tell the brain), "We are still spinning"—and we feel as if we are.

Sensation, Perception, and Health and Wellness

Our senses are a vital connection to the world and to our experience, and we should not take them for granted. Ensuring the health of our senses means caring for our precious sensory organs—for example, by getting vision and hearing screenings and noting changes that might occur in our sensory experiences (Groenewould & others, 2010; Saito & others, 2010). Taking care of your eyes means avoiding high-fat food, not smoking, and eating a diet rich in vitamins A, E, and C, zinc, and beta carotene. This means consuming a wide variety of fruits and vegetables (including your spinach). It also means reading with appropriate lighting (three times brighter than the rest of the room light) and with your work at eye level—about 16 inches away—and wearing sunglasses that protect your eyes from UVA and UVB, the sun's damaging rays. Some of the common causes of blindness are preventable but also undetectable. A glaucoma test is especially important after the age of 60. Staying active and eating healthy are important for avoiding another cause of blindness: diabetic retinopathy.

With respect to our hearing, perhaps the most dangerous threat comes from loud noise (F. Zhao & others, 2010). Many of us enjoy listening to our favorite tunes on a portable media player. As these devices have become smaller and smaller, they have grown increasingly popular—we use them whenever we desire and wherever we are. These players use earbuds that transmit sound directly into the ear canal. How might this technology affect our hearing? A study examined the safety of iPods for the hearing of listeners. Cory Portnuff and Brian Fligor (2006) found that a typical person could safely listen to an iPod for nearly 5 hours at 70 percent volume. The researchers concluded that those who like their tunes louder should not listen as long; if you listen at 90 percent volume, for example, keep yourself plugged in for no more than 90 minutes. One important issue is the environment in which the person is listening. Participants in the study were more likely to pump up the volume if they were listening to their iPods in environments that were already noisy. Interestingly, effects on hearing did not depend on the participants' choice of music. So, whether it is Kanye West, Barry Manilow, or Mozart, sensible listening is wise.

Throughout this module we have viewed sensation and perception as our connections to the world. How about treating your senses by taking them outside? Few things engage all of our senses like being outside in a natural environment. And experiences with the natural world have been shown to improve overall physical and psychological well-being (Devlin & Arneill, 2003; Gulwadi, 2006; Ulrich, 1991). Hospital patients recover more quickly if they have a window that looks out onto trees, sky, and plants (Ulrich, 1991). Taking a walk outside is an excellent way to get exercise as well as to open up your senses to the world. While you are walking, remember to stop and smell the flowers—literally. Flowers are visually pleasant and they smell good, so they are a natural mood booster for both men and women (Haviland-Jones & others, 2005).

Our senses allow us to experience the world in all its vibrancy. Sue Berry, who achieved the ability to perceive depth only after a long, arduous effort, described her encounter with nature on a snowy day. "I felt myself within the snow fall, among the snowflakes. . . . I was overcome with a sense of joy. A snow fall can be quite beautiful—especially when you see it for the first time" (quoted in Sacks, 2006, p. 73). Recall the example of Michael May who was able to see after 25 years of blindness. One night, with his seeing-eye dog Josh at his side, he decided to go look at the sky. Lying on the grass in a field, he opened his eyes. He thought he was "seeing stars"—in the metaphorical sense. He thought that the thousands of white lights in the sky could not really be real, but they were. As he remarked in his "vision diary": "How sweet it is" (May, 2003; Stein, 2003).

SUMMARY

Senses connect us to the world. Taking care of your precious sense organs means adopting healthy practices such as eating a low-fat diet rich in vitamins and beta carotene. Caring for your eyes means wearing protective lenses when you are in the bright sun. Protecting your hearing requires avoiding dangerously loud noises. Noise at 80 decibels or higher, if heard for prolonged periods, can damage hearing. Experiences in nature have been shown to reduce stress and enhance well-being.

TEST YOURSELF

1. What are several strategies individuals can use to protect and preserve their vision?
2. What factor poses the most serious threat to hearing?
3. How do portable media players such as iPods impact hearing, and what can consumers do to reduce the potential harm from using them?

States of Consciousness

The Awesome Power of Consciousness

The daily life of Erik Ramsey would seem to be the stuff of nightmares. In 1999, at age 16, he was horribly injured in a car accident. A blood clot in his brain stem caused a stroke, leaving Erik with a rare and permanent condition called *locked-in syndrome* (Foer, 2008). Erik cannot move or speak. He can feel an itch on his face but cannot reach up and scratch it. The only muscles over which he has any control are those that allow him to move his eyes. Erik uses his eye movements to communicate, answering yes (by looking up) or no (by looking down). Asked if he ever wished he had not survived his accident, Erik looks down. For all the limitations in his life, Erik has one important thing left: his mind.

Erik also has a loving family and a team of scientists dedicated to developing a way for him to communicate. Computer–brain interfaces might eventually allow Erik to communicate with others using his ability to think. In 2004, doctors used fMRI to pinpoint the brain locations that were active when Erik imagined himself speaking. They implanted electrodes in those areas. Since then, Erik has been laboriously learning to *think* the sounds he cannot make with his voice and to do so in a way that a computer will recognize and translate them into speech. The neurosurgeons, engineers, and computer scientists who are working to develop the technology hope that Erik will be able to "say" vowels, consonants, and perhaps even words and sentences with his mind. They are devoted to this task because the person thinking and feeling inside his eerily still body remains, they believe, Erik. Such is the power of consciousness in human life—that a conscious mind, locked in a body however limited, is still a person very much worth reaching. ●

The Nature of Consciousness

Consciousness is a crucial part of human experience (H. G. Taylor & others, 2010; Wijnen & van Boxtel, 2010). Our conscious awareness represents that private inner mind where we think, feel, plan, wish, pray, imagine, and quietly relive experiences. Consider that if we did not have private thoughts and feelings, we could not tell a lie.

In the late nineteenth and early twentieth centuries, psychology pioneer William James (1950) described the mind as a **stream of consciousness,** a continuous flow of changing sensations, images, thoughts, and feelings. The content of our awareness changes from moment to moment. Information moves rapidly in and out of consciousness. Our minds can race from one topic to the next—from the person approaching us to our physical state today to the café where we will have lunch to our strategy for the test tomorrow.

During much of the twentieth century, psychologists focused less on the study of mental processes and more on the study of observable behavior. More recently, the study of consciousness has regained widespread respectability in psychology (Hansimayr & others, 2009; Nir & Tononi, 2010; Raffone & Srinivasan, 2010). Scientists from many different fields are interested in consciousness (Chica & others, 2010; Deutsch, 2010; O'Regan & others, 2010).

13-1 DEFINING CONSCIOUSNESS

We can define consciousness in terms of its two parts: awareness and arousal. **Consciousness** is an individual's awareness of external events and internal sensations under a condition of arousal. *Awareness* includes awareness of the self and thoughts about one's experiences. Consider that on an autumn afternoon, when you see a beautiful tree, vibrant with color, you are not simply perceiving the colors; you are also *aware* that you are seeing them. The term *metacognition* refers to thinking about thinking (Barkus & others, 2010; Efklides, 2009). When you think about your thoughts—for example, when you reflect on why you are so nervous before an exam—you are using your conscious awareness to examine your own thought processes. The second part of consciousness is *arousal*, the physiological state of being engaged with the environment. Thus, a sleeping person is not conscious in the same way that he or she would be while awake.

13-2 CONSCIOUSNESS AND THE BRAIN

The two aspects of consciousness, awareness and arousal, are associated with different parts of the brain (Koch, 2011). Stanilas Dehaene and his colleagues describe *awareness,* the subjective state of being conscious of what is going on, as occurring in a *global brain workspace* that involves a variety of brain areas working in parallel (Dehaene & others, 2006; Del Cul & others, 2009; Gaillard & others, 2009). These areas include the front-most part of the brain—the prefrontal cortex—as well as the *anterior cingulate* (an area

● **stream of consciousness** Term used by William James to describe the mind as a continuous flow of changing sensations, images, thoughts, and feelings.

● **consciousness** An individual's awareness of external events and internal sensations under a condition of arousal, including awareness of the self and thoughts about one's experiences.

associated with acts of will) and the association areas (Bekinschtein & others, 2009; Del Cul & others, 2009). This wide-reaching brain workspace is an assembly of neurons that are thought to work in cooperation to produce the subjective sense of consciousness.

According to the brain workspace approach to consciousness, the widespread availability of information broadcast throughout the brain is what we experience as conscious awareness (Baars, 2010; Gaillard & others, 2009). *Arousal* is a physiological state determined by the reticular activating system, a network of structures including the brain stem, medulla, and thalamus. Arousal refers to the ways that awareness is regulated: If we are in danger, we might need to be on "high alert," but if we are in a safe environment with no immediate demands, we can relax and our arousal may be quite low.

13·3 LEVELS OF AWARENESS

The flow of sensations, images, thoughts, and feelings that William James spoke of can occur at different levels of awareness. Although we might think of consciousness as either present or not, there are in fact shades of awareness, just as there are shades of perception in signal detection theory, as discussed in Module 9. Here we consider five levels of awareness: higher-level consciousness, lower-level consciousness, altered states of consciousness, subconscious awareness, and no awareness (Figure 13.1).

Higher-Level Consciousness

In **controlled processes,** the most alert states of human consciousness, individuals actively focus their efforts toward a goal (Sibbald & others, 2009). For example, watch a classmate as he struggles to master the unfamiliar buttons on his new smartphone. He does not hear you humming or notice the intriguing shadow on the wall.

● **controlled processes** The most alert states of human consciousness, during which individuals actively focus their efforts toward a goal.

Level of Awareness	Description	Examples
Higher-Level Consciousness	Involves controlled processing, in which individuals actively focus their efforts on attaining a goal; the most alert state of consciousness	Doing a math or science problem; preparing for a debate; taking an at-bat in a baseball game
Lower-Level Consciousness	Includes automatic processing that requires little attention, as well as daydreaming	Punching in a number on a cell phone; typing on a keyboard when one is an expert; gazing at a sunset
Altered States of Consciousness	Can be produced by drugs, trauma, fatigue, possibly hypnosis, and sensory deprivation	Feeling the effects of having taken alcohol or psychedelic drugs; undergoing hypnosis to quit smoking or lose weight
Subconscious Awareness	Can occur when people are awake, as well as when they are sleeping and dreaming	Sleeping and dreaming
No Awareness	Freud's belief that some unconscious thoughts are too laden with anxiety and other negative emotions for consciousness to admit them	Having unconscious thoughts; being knocked out by a blow or anesthetized

FIGURE 13.1 Levels of Awareness
Each level of awareness has its time and place in human life.

His state of focused awareness illustrates the idea of controlled processes. Controlled processes require selective attention (see Module 9), the ability to concentrate on a specific aspect of experience while ignoring others (Klumpp & Amir, 2009). Controlled processes are slower than automatic processes and are more likely to involve the prefrontal cortex (Gaillard & others, 2009). Often, after we have practiced an activity a great deal, we no longer have to think about it while doing it. It becomes automatic and faster.

Lower-Level Consciousness

Beneath the level of controlled processes are other levels of conscious awareness. Lower levels of awareness include automatic processes and daydreaming.

AUTOMATIC PROCESSES

A few weeks after acquiring his smartphone, your classmate sends a text message in the middle of a conversation with you. He does not have to concentrate on the keys and hardly seems aware of the device as he continues to talk to you while finishing his lunch. Using his phone has reached the point of automatic processing.

Automatic processes are states of consciousness that require little attention and do not interfere with other ongoing activities. Automatic processes require less conscious effort than controlled processes (Gillard & others, 2009). When we are awake, our automatic behaviors occur at a lower level of awareness than controlled processes, but they are still conscious behaviors. Your classmate pushed the right buttons, so at some level he apparently was aware of what he was doing.

DAYDREAMING

Another state of consciousness that involves a low level of conscious effort is *daydreaming*, which lies between active consciousness and dreaming while asleep. It is a little like dreaming while we are awake. Daydreams usually begin spontaneously when we are doing something that requires less than our full attention (McVay & Kane, 2010).

Mind wandering is probably the most obvious type of daydreaming. We regularly take brief side trips into our own private kingdoms of imagery and memory while reading, listening, or working. When we daydream, we drift into a world of fantasy. We perhaps imagine ourselves on a date, at a party, on television, in a faraway place, or at another time of life. Sometimes our daydreams are about everyday events such as paying the rent, going to the dentist, and meeting with somebody at school or work.

The semiautomatic flow of daydreaming can be useful. As you daydream while ironing a shirt or walking to the store, you may make plans, solve a problem, or come up with a creative idea. Daydreams can also remind us of important things ahead. Although we may think of daydreaming as goofing off or wasting time, these mental adventures keep our minds active while helping us to cope, create, and fantasize (Baars, 2010).

● **automatic processes** States of consciousness that require little attention and do not interfere with other ongoing activities.

"If you ask me, all three of us are in different states of awareness."

© Edward Frascino/The New Yorker Collection. www.cartoonbank.com.

Altered States of Consciousness

Altered states of consciousness or awareness are mental states that are noticeably different from normal awareness (Revonsuo, Kallio, & Sikka, 2009). Altered states of consciousness can range from losing one's sense of self-consciousness to hallucinating. Such states can be produced by trauma, fever, fatigue, sensory deprivation, meditation, hypnosis, and psychological disorders. Drug use can also induce altered states of consciousness (Fields, 2010), as we will consider later in this module.

Subconscious Awareness

In Module 7, we saw that a great deal of brain activity occurs beneath the level of conscious awareness. Psychologists are increasingly interested in the subconscious processing of information, which can take place while we are awake or asleep (Voss & Paller, 2009; Yamada & Decety, 2009).

WAKING SUBCONSCIOUS AWARENESS

When we are awake, processes are going on just below the surface of our awareness. For example, while we are grappling with a problem, the solution may pop into our head. Such insights can occur when a subconscious connection between ideas is so strong that it rises into awareness.

Incubation refers to the subconscious processing that leads to a solution to a problem after a break from conscious thought about the problem. Clearly, during incubation, information is being processed even if we are unaware of that processing. Interestingly, successful incubation requires that we first expend effort thinking carefully about the problem (Gonzalez-Vallejo & others, 2008).

Recall Module 10's discussion of the parallel processing of visual information. Subconscious information processing also can occur simultaneously in a distributed manner along many parallel tracks. For example, when you look at a dog running down the street, you are consciously aware of the event but not of the subconscious processing of the object's identity (a dog), its color (black), and its movement (fast). In contrast, conscious processing occurs in sequence and is slower than much subconscious processing. Note that the various levels of awareness often work together. You rely on controlled processing when memorizing material for class, but later, the answers on a test just pop into your head as a result of automatic or subconscious processing.

SUBCONSCIOUS AWARENESS DURING SLEEP AND DREAMS

When we sleep and dream, our level of awareness is lower than when we daydream, but sleep and dreams are not best regarded as the absence of consciousness (Issa & Wang, 2008). Rather, they are low levels of consciousness.

Researchers have found that when people are asleep, they remain aware of external stimuli to some degree. In sleep laboratories, when people are clearly asleep (as determined by physiological monitoring devices), they are able to respond to faint tones by pressing a handheld button (Ogilvie & Wilkinson, 1988). In one study, the presentation of pure auditory tones to sleeping individuals activated auditory processing regions of the brain, whereas participants' names activated language areas, the amygdala, and the prefrontal cortex (Stickgold, 2001). We return to the topics of sleep and dreams in the next section.

No Awareness

The term *unconscious* generally applies to someone who has been knocked out by a blow or anesthetized, or who has fallen into a deep, prolonged unconscious state (Matis & Birbilis, 2009). However, Sigmund Freud (1917) used the term *unconscious* in a very different way. **Unconscious thought,** said Freud, is a reservoir of unacceptable wishes, feelings, and thoughts that are beyond conscious awareness. In other words, Freud's interpretation viewed the unconscious as a storehouse for vile thoughts. He believed that some aspects of our experience remain unconscious for good reason, as if we are better off not knowing about them. For example, from Freud's perspective, the human mind is full of disturbing impulses such as a desire to have sex with our parents.

Although Freud's interpretation remains controversial, psychologists now widely accept the notion that unconscious processes do exist (Sampaio & Brewer, 2009; Voss

● **unconscious thought** According to Freud, a reservoir of unacceptable wishes, feelings, and thoughts that are beyond conscious awareness; Freud's interpretation viewed the unconscious as a storehouse for vile thoughts.

Consciousness and Developmental Psychology: How Do We Develop a Sense of the Minds of Others?

Imagine yourself in a conversation with a friend, describing a complex issue. While talking, you search your friend's face for signs of understanding. Does she nod? Does her brow furrow? In a sense, although you may have never thought of it this way, your observations reveal your belief in your friend's consciousness. When you pause and ask, "Do you see what I mean?" you are checking in on your friend's mind. Such interactions provide clues about how we think others think.

It might seem obvious that other people have minds of their own, but the human ability to recognize the subjective experience of another is a true developmental accomplishment. Developmental psychologists who study children's ideas about mental states use the phrase *theory of mind* to refer to individuals' understanding that they and others think, feel, perceive, and have private experiences (Bamford & Lagattuta, 2010; Gelman, 2009). Theory of mind is essential to many valuable social capacities, including empathy and sympathy (Bamford & Lagattuta, 2010; Boyd, 2008; Peterson & others, 2009). Theory of mind is also relevant to the capacity for deception (Spritz, Fergusson, & Bankoff, 2010).

To examine theory of mind, developmental psychologists use a clever procedure called the *false belief task* (Doherty, 2009). In the false belief task, a child is asked to consider a situation like the following (Wellman & Woolley, 1990). A little girl, Anna, has some chocolate that she decides to save for later. She puts it in a blue cupboard and goes outside to play. While Anna is gone, her mother moves the chocolate to the red cupboard. When Anna comes back in, where will she look for her chocolate? Three-year-olds give the wrong answer—they assume that Anna will look in the red cupboard because they know (even though Anna does not) that Anna's mother moved the chocolate to the red one.

Temple Grandin, an accomplished animal scientist who is autistic, has described in her memoir Thinking in Pictures *how she has had to memorize and practice the kinds of things that go on effortlessly in other people's heads. For example, she must commit to memory the fact that non-autistic individuals think in words, not images, and that their facial expressions reveal important information about their feelings.*

Four-year-olds answer correctly, recognizing that Anna does not know everything they do and that she will believe the chocolate is where she left it (Wellman & Woolley, 1990). Success at false belief tasks is associated with social competence (Barlow, Qualter, & Stylianou, 2010), and children who perform them well are better liked by their peers (Leslie, German, & Polizzi, 2005).

Simon Baron-Cohen (2006, 2008) has proposed that the emergence of theory of mind is so central to human functioning that evolution would not leave it up to chance. Baron-Cohen suggests that we are born with a brain mechanism that is ready to develop a theory of mind. This theory of mind mechanism (or TOMM) accounts for the fact that nearly all children over the age of 4 pass the false belief task, even children with the genetic disorder Down syndrome. Baron-Cohen believes that individuals with *autism,* a disorder that affects communication and social interaction, lack the TOMM, a situation that would explain their unique social deficits. Indeed, he has referred to autism as "mind blindness."

Of course, even with our remarkable TOMM in full working order, our intuitions about others are sometimes inaccurate. We might love someone who does not return our feelings, or we might trust a person who does not have our best interest at heart. There is perhaps no greater mystery than what is going on behind another person's eyes. What another person knows, thinks, believes, and wants—these are questions that have fascinated human beings since the beginning of our species.

> *If you could, would you want to be able to read someone's mind?*

& Paller, 2009). Recently, researchers have found that many mental processes (thoughts, emotions, and perceptions) can occur outside of awareness. Some psychologists term these processes *nonconscious* rather than *unconscious* to avoid the Freudian connotation (Finkbeiner & Palermo, 2009; Weyers & others, 2009).

For further insights on consciousness, see the Intersection, which explores children's beliefs about how the mind works and the implications of these understandings for their social functioning.

SUMMARY

Consciousness is the awareness of external events and internal sensations, including awareness of the self and thoughts about experiences. Most experts agree that consciousness is likely distributed across the brain. A global brain workspace that includes the association areas and prefrontal lobes is believed to play an important role in consciousness.

William James described the mind as a stream of consciousness. Consciousness occurs at different levels of awareness that include higher-level awareness (controlled processes and selective attention), lower-level awareness (automatic processes and daydreaming), altered states of consciousness (produced by drugs, trauma, fatigue, and other factors), subconscious awareness (waking subconscious awareness, sleep, and dreams), and no awareness (unconscious thought).

KEY TERMS

stream of consciousness   150
consciousness   150
controlled processes   151
automatic processes   152
unconscious
   thought   153

TEST YOURSELF

1. Describe (a) the brain areas that are part of the global brain workspace involved in consciousness and (b) what our experience of consciousness actually is.
2. What are controlled processes and automatic processes? In what levels of consciousness is each involved?
3. What is daydreaming, according to the text discussion?

APPLY YOUR KNOWLEDGE

1. Take 20 minutes and document your stream of consciousness. Just write whatever comes into your mind for this period. When you have finished, take a close look at what your stream of consciousness reveals. What topics came up that surprised you? Are the thoughts and feelings you wrote down reflective of your daily life? Your important goals and values? What is *not* mentioned in your stream of consciousness that is surprising to you?
2. What is an example of something you do that requires higher-level conscious processing? Now think of something you do that requires lower-level conscious processing. Do these tasks differ based on their importance to your life and their ability to satisfy your personal needs?

Sleep and Dreams

By this point in your life, you have had quite a bit of experience with sleep. You already know that sleep involves a decrease in body movement and (typically) having one's eyes closed. What is sleep, more exactly? We can define **sleep** as a natural state of rest for the body and mind that involves the reversible loss of consciousness. Surely, sleep must be important, because it comprises a third of our life, taking up more time than anything else we do. *Why* is sleep so important? Before tackling this question, let's first consider how sleep is linked to our internal biological rhythms.

14·1 BIOLOGICAL RHYTHMS AND SLEEP

Biological rhythms are periodic physiological fluctuations in the body. We are unaware of most biological rhythms, such as the rise and fall of hormones and the accelerated and decelerated cycles of brain activity, but they can influence our behavior. These rhythms are controlled by biological clocks, which include annual or seasonal cycles such as those involving the migration of birds and the hibernation of bears, as well as 24-hour cycles such as the cycling between being asleep and being awake and the cycling of temperature in the human body. Let's explore the body's 24-hour cycles.

Circadian Rhythms

Circadian rhythms are daily behavioral or physiological cycles. Daily circadian rhythms involve the sleep/wake cycle, body temperature, blood pressure, and blood sugar level

● **sleep** A natural state of rest for the body and mind that involves the reversible loss of consciousness.

● **biological rhythms** Periodic physiological fluctuations in the body, such as the rise and fall of hormones and accelerated and decelerated cycles of brain activity, that can influence behavior.

● **circadian rhythms** Daily behavioral or physiological cycles. Daily circadian rhythms involve the sleep/wake cycle, body temperature, blood pressure, and blood sugar level.

FIGURE 14.1 Suprachiasmatic Nucleus The suprachiasmatic nucleus (SCN) plays an important role in keeping our biological clock running on time. The SCN is located in the hypothalamus. It receives information from the retina about light, which is the external stimulus that synchronizes the SCN. Output from the SCN is distributed to the rest of the hypothalamus and to the reticular formation.

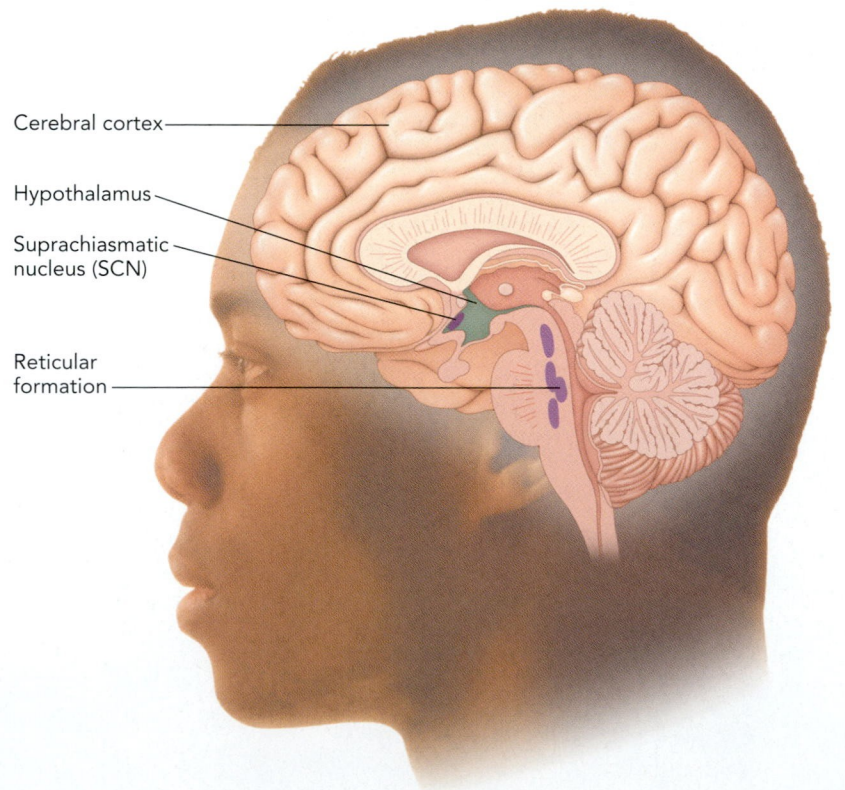

Cerebral cortex

Hypothalamus

Suprachiasmatic nucleus (SCN)

Reticular formation

(Habbal & Al-Jabri, 2009; Kujanik & Mikulecky, 2010). For example, body temperature fluctuates about three degrees Fahrenheit in a 24-hour day, peaking in the afternoon and dropping to its lowest point between 2 A.M. and 5 A.M.

Researchers have discovered that the body monitors the change from day to night by means of the **suprachiasmatic nucleus (SCN)**, a small brain structure that uses input from the retina to synchronize its own rhythm with the daily cycle of light and dark (Segall & Amir, 2010). The SCN sends information to the hypothalamus and pineal gland to regulate daily rhythms such as temperature, hunger, and the release of hormones such as melatonin. The SCN also communicates with the reticular formation to regulate daily rhythms of sleep and wakefulness (Figure 14.1). Although a number of biological clocks seem to be involved in regulating circadian rhythms, researchers have found that the SCN is the most important (Trudel & Bourque, 2010; Vimal & others, 2009).

Many individuals who are totally blind experience lifelong sleeping problems because their retinas cannot detect light. These people have a kind of permanent jet lag and periodic insomnia because their circadian rhythms often do not follow a 24-hour cycle (Waller, Bendel, & Kaplan, 2008).

Desynchronizing the Biological Clock

Biological clocks can become *desynchronized,* or thrown off their regular schedules. Among the circumstances of life that can introduce irregularities into our sleep are jet travel, changing work shifts, and insomnia. What effects might such irregularities have on circadian rhythms?

If you fly from Los Angeles to New York and then go to bed at 11 P.M. eastern time, you may have trouble falling asleep because your body is still on West Coast time. Even if you sleep for 8 hours that night, you may have a hard time waking up at 7 A.M. eastern time, because your body thinks it is 4 A.M. If you stay in New York for several days, your body will adjust to this new schedule.

The jet lag you experience when you fly from Los Angeles to New York occurs because your body time is out of phase, or synchronization, with clock time (Mahoney, 2010; Sack, 2009). Jet lag is the result of two or more body rhythms being out of sync. You usually go to bed when your body temperature begins to drop, but in your new location, you might be trying to go to sleep when it is rising. In the morning, your adrenal glands release large doses of the hormone cortisol to help you wake up. In your new geographic time zone, the glands may be releasing this chemical just as you are getting ready for bed at night.

Circadian rhythms may also become desynchronized when shift workers change their work hours (Mitchell, Gallagher, & Thomas, 2008). A number of near accidents in air travel have been associated with pilots who have not yet become synchronized to their new shifts and are not working as efficiently as usual (Kim & Lee, 2007). Shift-work problems most often affect night-shift workers who never fully adjust to sleeping in the daytime after they get off work (Culpepper, 2010). Sometimes these employees fall asleep at work, and they face an increased risk of heart disease and gastrointestinal disorders (Sadeghniiat-Haghighi & others, 2008).

Resetting the Biological Clock

If your biological clock for sleeping and waking becomes desynchronized, how can you reset it? With regard to jet lag, if you take a transoceanic flight and arrive at your destination during the day, it is a good idea to spend as much time as possible outside in the daylight. Bright light during the day, especially in the morning, increases wakefulness, whereas bright light at night delays sleep (Arendt, 2009; Goel & others, 2009).

Researchers are studying melatonin, a hormone that increases at night in humans, for its possible effects in reducing jet lag (Jackson, 2010; Sack, 2010). Recent studies have shown that a small dosage of melatonin can reduce jet lag by advancing the circadian clock—an effect that makes it useful for eastward but not westward jet lag (Arendt, 2009).

Changing to a night-shift job can desynchronize our biological clocks and affect our circadian rhythms and performance.

● **suprachiasmatic nucleus (SCN)** A small brain structure that uses input from the retina to synchronize its own rhythm with the daily cycle of light and dark; the mechanism by which the body monitors the change from day to night.

14-2 WHY DO WE NEED SLEEP?

All animals require sleep. Furthermore, the human body regulates sleep, as it does eating and drinking, and this fact suggests that sleep may be just as essential for survival. Yet why we need sleep remains a bit of a mystery (Frank, 2006).

Theories on the Need for Sleep

A variety of theories have been proposed for the need for sleep. First, from an evolutionary perspective, sleep may have developed because animals needed to protect themselves at night. The idea is that it makes sense for animals to be inactive when it is dark, because nocturnal inactivity helps them to avoid both becoming other animals' prey and injuring themselves due to poor visibility.

A second possibility is that sleep is a way to conserve energy. Spending a large chunk of any day sleeping allows animals to conserve their calories, especially when food is scarce (Siegel, 2005). For some animals, moreover, the search for food and water is easier and safer when the sun is up. When it is dark, it is adaptive for these animals to save their energy. Animals that are likely to serve as someone else's food sleep the least of all. Figure 14.2 illustrates the average amount of sleep per day of various animals.

A third explanation for the need for sleep is that sleep is restorative (Frank, 2006). Scientists have proposed that sleep restores, replenishes, and rebuilds the brain and body, which the day's waking activities can wear out. This idea fits with the feeling of being tired before we go to sleep and restored when we wake up. In support of the theory of a restorative function of sleep, many of the body's cells show increased production and reduced breakdown of proteins during deep sleep (Aton & others, 2009; Vazquez & others, 2008). Protein molecules are the building blocks needed for cell growth and for repair of damage from factors such as stress.

A final explanation for the need for sleep centers on the role of sleep in brain plasticity (Frank & Benington, 2006; Tononi & Cirelli, 2011). Recall from Module 7 that the plasticity of the brain refers to its capacity to change in response to experience. Sleep has been recognized as playing an important role in the ways that experiences influence the brain. For example, neuroscientists recently have argued that sleep enhances synaptic connections between neurons (Aton & others, 2009). Findings such as these suggest an important role for sleep in the consolidation of memories (Frank & Benington, 2006). A recent research review concluded that sleep is vital to the consolidation of memory, whether memory for specific information, for skills, or for emotional experiences (Diekelmann, Wilhelm, & Born, 2009). One possible explanation is that during sleep the cerebral cortex is free to conduct activities that strengthen memory associations, so that memories formed during recent waking hours can be integrated into long-term memory storage. Lost sleep often results in lost memories.

So, if you are thinking about studying all night for your next test, you might want to think again. Sleep can enhance your memory. In one study, participants who had studied word lists the day before performed better in a recall test for those words if they had had a good night's sleep before the test (Racsmany, Conway, & Demeter, 2010). Participants who were tested prior to sleep did not perform as well.

The Effects of Chronic Sleep Deprivation

We do our best when we sleep more than 8 hours a night (Habeck & others, 2004). Lack of sleep is stressful and has an impact on the body and the brain (Azboy & Kaygisiz, 2009). When deprived of sleep, people have trouble paying attention to tasks and solving problems (Mullington & others, 2009). Studies have shown that sleep deprivation decreases brain activity in the thalamus and the prefrontal cortex (Thomas & others, 2001) and reduces the complexity of brain activity (Jeong & others, 2001). The tired brain must compensate by using different pathways or alternative neural networks when thinking (Mander & others, 2008). Sleep deprivation can even influence

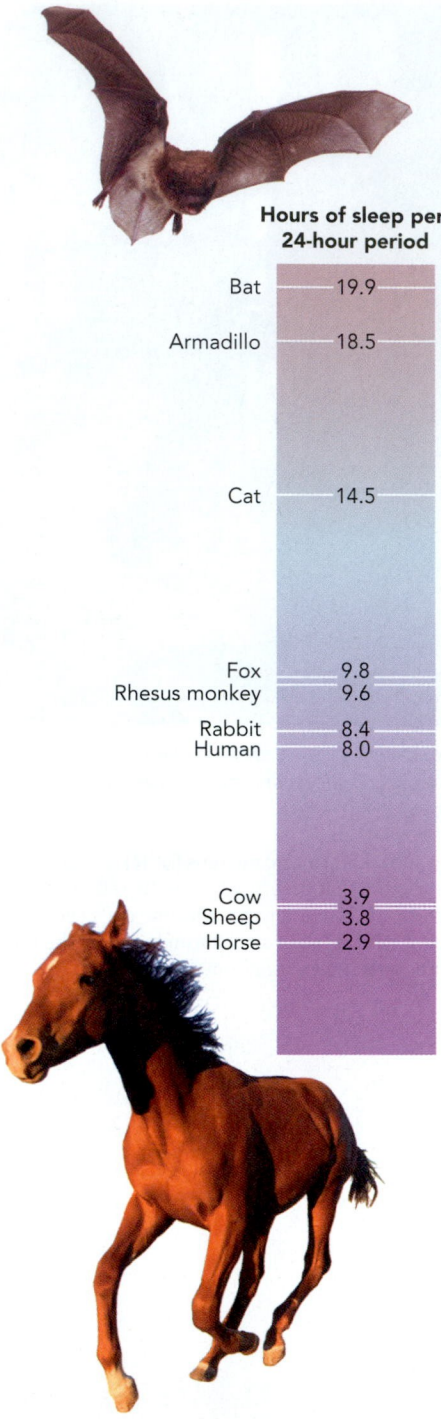

Hours of sleep per 24-hour period

Animal	Hours
Bat	19.9
Armadillo	18.5
Cat	14.5
Fox	9.8
Rhesus monkey	9.6
Rabbit	8.4
Human	8.0
Cow	3.9
Sheep	3.8
Horse	2.9

FIGURE 14.2 **From Bats to Horses: The Wide Range of Sleep in Animals** We might feel envious of bats, which sleep nearly 20 hours a day, and more than a little in awe of horses, still running on just under 3 hours of rest.

moral judgment. Following 53 hours of wakefulness, participants in a recent study had more difficulty making moral decisions and were more likely to agree with decisions that violated their personal standards (Killgore & others, 2007).

Although sleep is unquestionably the key to optimal physical and mental performance, many of us do not get sufficient sleep. The Institute of Medicine (2006) declared that sleep deprivation is an unmet health problem in the United States. Why do Americans get too little sleep? Pressures at work and school, family responsibilities, and social obligations often lead to long hours of wakefulness and irregular sleep/wake schedules (Artazcoz & others, 2009; Wiegand & others, 2010). Not having enough hours to do all that we want or need to do in a day, we cheat on our sleep. As a result we may suffer from an accumulated level of exhaustion.

14·3 STAGES OF WAKEFULNESS AND SLEEP

Have you ever awakened from sleep and been totally disoriented? Have you ever awakened in the middle of a dream and then gone right back into the dream as if it were a movie running just below the surface of your consciousness? These two experiences reflect two distinct stages in the sleep cycle.

Stages of sleep correspond to massive electrophysiological changes that occur throughout the brain as the fast, irregular, and low-amplitude electrical activity of wakefulness is replaced by the slow, regular, high-amplitude waves of deep sleep. Using the electroencephalograph (EEG) to monitor the brain's electrical activity, scientists have identified two stages of wakefulness and five stages of sleep.

Wakefulness Stages

When people are awake, their EEG patterns exhibit two types of waves: beta and alpha. *Beta waves* reflect concentration and alertness. These waves are the highest in frequency and lowest in amplitude—that is, they go up and down a great deal but do not have very high peaks or very low ebbs. They also are more *desynchronous* than other waves, meaning that they do not form a very consistent pattern. Inconsistent patterning makes sense given the extensive variation in sensory input and activities we experience when we are awake.

When we are relaxed but still awake, our brain waves slow down, increase in amplitude, and become more *synchronous,* or regular. These waves, associated with relaxation or drowsiness, are called *alpha waves.*

The five stages of sleep also are differentiated by the types of wave patterns detected with an EEG. Furthermore, the depth of sleep varies from one stage to another, as we now consider.

Sleep Stages 1 to 4

Stage 1 sleep is characterized by drowsy sleep. In this stage, the person may experience sudden muscle movements called *myoclonic jerks*. If you watch someone in your class fighting to stay awake, you might notice his or her head jerking upward. This reaction demonstrates that this first stage of sleep often involves the feeling of falling.

EEGs of individuals in stage 1 sleep are characterized by *theta waves,* which are even slower in frequency and greater in amplitude than alpha waves. The difference between being relaxed and being in stage 1 sleep is gradual. Figure 14.3 shows the EEG pattern of stage 1 sleep, along with the EEG patterns for the other four sleep stages and beta and alpha waves.

In *stage 2 sleep,* muscle activity decreases, and the person is no longer consciously aware of the environment. Theta waves continue but are interspersed with a defining characteristic of stage 2 sleep: *sleep spindles*. These

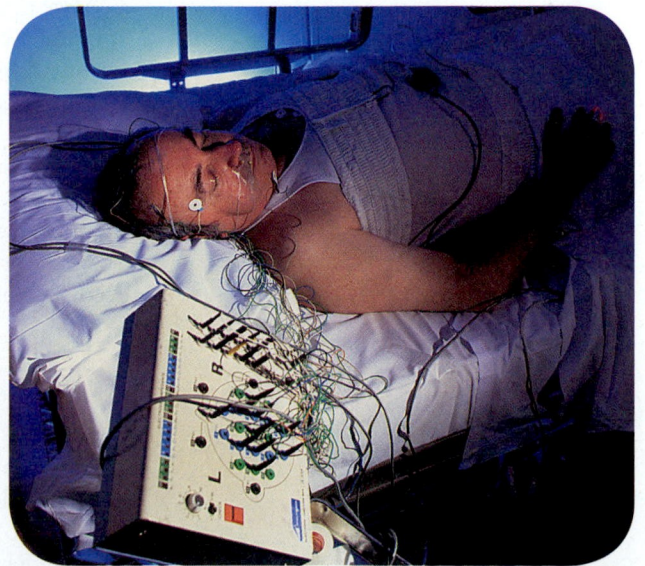

An individual being monitored by an EEG in a sleep experiment.

FIGURE 14.3 **Characteristics and Formats of EEG Recordings During Stages of Sleep** Even while you are sleeping, your brain is busy. No wonder you sometimes wake up feeling tired.

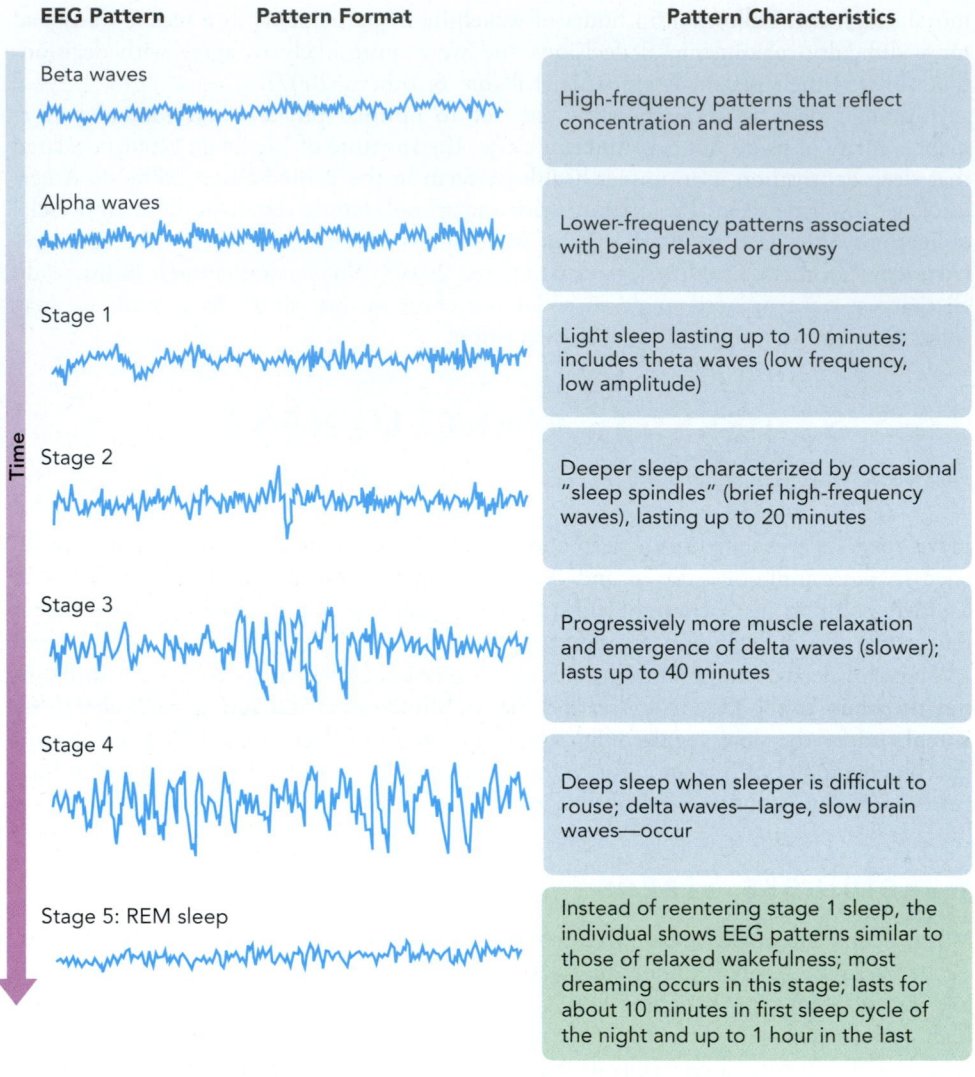

EEG Pattern	Pattern Format	Pattern Characteristics
Beta waves		High-frequency patterns that reflect concentration and alertness
Alpha waves		Lower-frequency patterns associated with being relaxed or drowsy
Stage 1		Light sleep lasting up to 10 minutes; includes theta waves (low frequency, low amplitude)
Stage 2		Deeper sleep characterized by occasional "sleep spindles" (brief high-frequency waves), lasting up to 20 minutes
Stage 3		Progressively more muscle relaxation and emergence of delta waves (slower); lasts up to 40 minutes
Stage 4		Deep sleep when sleeper is difficult to rouse; delta waves—large, slow brain waves—occur
Stage 5: REM sleep		Instead of reentering stage 1 sleep, the individual shows EEG patterns similar to those of relaxed wakefulness; most dreaming occurs in this stage; lasts for about 10 minutes in first sleep cycle of the night and up to 1 hour in the last

involve a sudden increase in wave frequency (Bastien & others, 2009). Stages 1 and 2 are both relatively light stages of sleep, and if people awaken during one of these stages, they often report not having been asleep at all.

Stage 3 and *stage 4 sleep* are characterized by *delta waves,* the slowest and highest-amplitude brain waves during sleep. These two stages are often referred to as *delta sleep.* Distinguishing between stage 3 and stage 4 is difficult, although typically stage 3 is characterized by delta waves occurring less than 50 percent of the time and stage 4 by delta waves occurring more than 50 percent of the time. Delta sleep is our deepest sleep, the time when our brain waves are least like our brain waves while we are awake. It is during delta sleep that it is the most difficult to wake sleepers. This deep, slow-wave sleep is associated with memory and learning (Yordanova, Kolev, & Verleger, 2009). This is also the stage when bed wetting (in children), sleepwalking, and sleep talking occur. When awakened during this stage, people usually are confused and disoriented.

REM Sleep

After going through stages 1 to 4, sleepers drift up through the sleep stages toward wakefulness. Instead of reentering stage 1, however, they enter stage 5, a different form of sleep called *REM (rapid eye movement) sleep* (Ravassard & others, 2009). **REM sleep** is an active stage of sleep during which dreaming occurs (Boeve, 2010). The EEG pattern for REM sleep shows fast waves similar to those of relaxed wakefulness, and the sleeper's eyeballs move up and down and from left to right (Figure 14.4).

● **REM sleep** An active stage of sleep during which dreaming occurs.

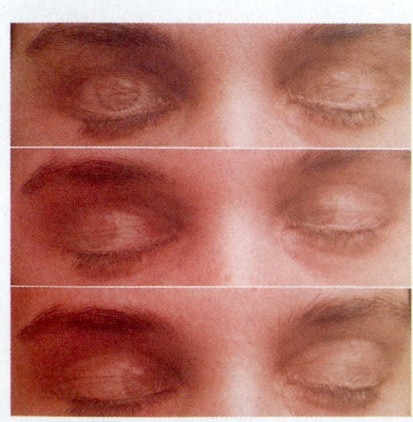

FIGURE 14.4 **REM Sleep** During REM sleep, your eyes move rapidly.

Specialists refer to sleep stages 1 to 4 as *non-REM sleep*. Non-REM sleep is character-ized by a lack of rapid eye movement and little dreaming. A person who is awakened during REM sleep is more likely to report having dreamed than when awakened at any other stage (Schredl, 2009). Even people who claim they rarely dream frequently report dreaming when they are awakened during REM sleep. The longer the period of REM sleep, the more likely the person will report dreaming. Dreams also occur during slow-wave or non-REM sleep, but the frequency of dreams in these stages is relatively low (McNamara, McLaren, & Durso, 2007), and we are less likely to remember these dreams. Reports of dreaming by individuals awakened from REM sleep are typically longer, more vivid, more physically active, more emotionally charged, and less related to waking life than reports by those awakened from non-REM sleep (Hobson, 2004). Like slow-wave sleep, REM sleep plays a role in memory (Diekelmann, Wilhelm, & Born, 2009). REM sleep is also related to creativity (Cai & others, 2009).

Sleep Cycling Through the Night

The five stages of sleep we have considered make up a normal cycle of sleep. One of these cycles lasts about 90 to 100 minutes and recurs several times during the night. The amount of deep sleep (stages 3 and 4) is much greater in the first half of a night's sleep than in the second half. Most REM sleep takes place toward the end of a night's sleep, when the REM stage becomes progressively longer. The night's first REM stage might last for only 10 minutes, but the final REM stage might continue for as long as an hour. During a normal night of sleep, individuals will spend about 60 percent of sleep in light sleep (stages 1 and 2), 20 percent in delta or deep sleep, and 20 percent in REM sleep (Webb, 2000).

Sleep Throughout the Life Span

Getting sufficient sleep is important at every stage of human life. Figure 14.5 shows how total sleep time and time spent in each type of sleep varies over the life span. Sleep may benefit physical growth and brain development in infants and children. For exam-ple, deep sleep coincides with the release of growth hormone in children. Recent

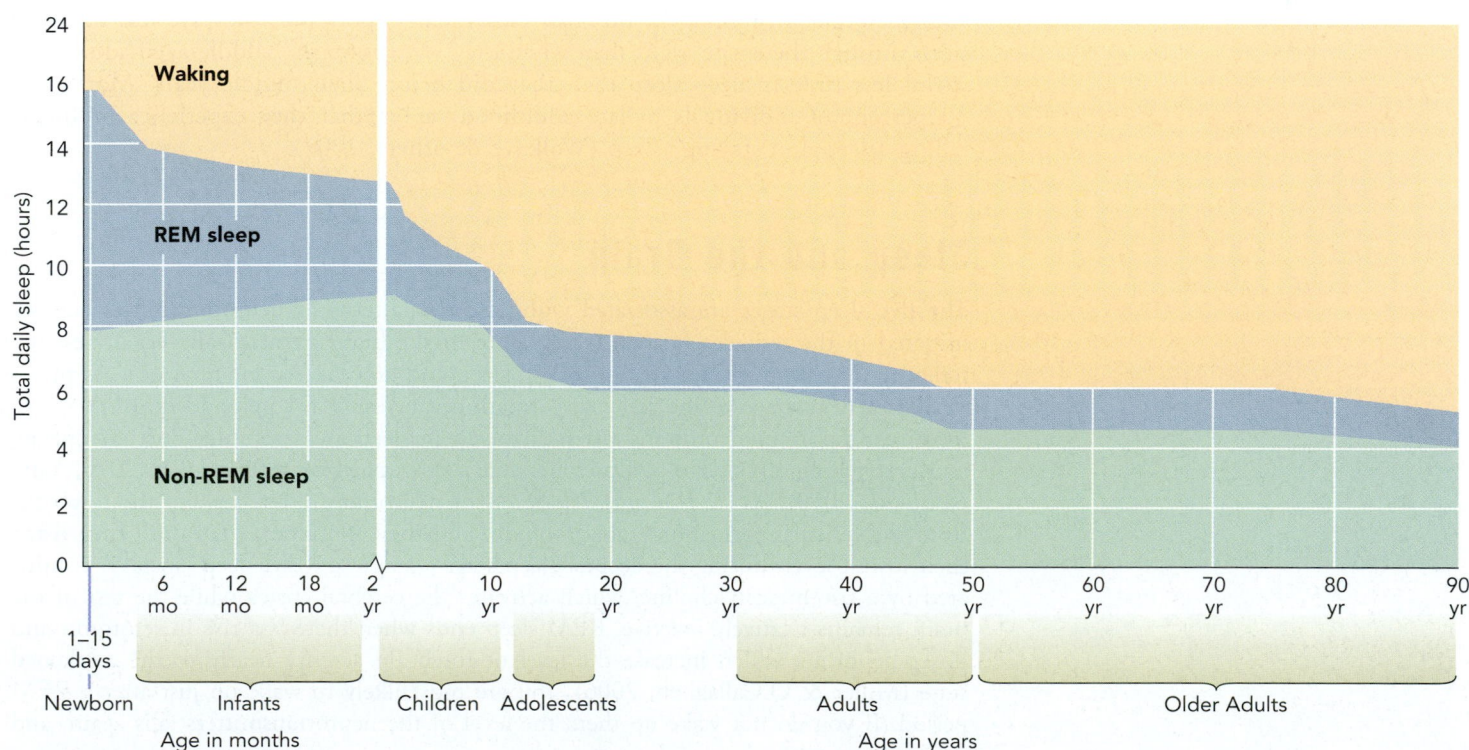

FIGURE 14.5 **Sleep Across the Human Life Span** With age, humans require less sleep.

evidence suggests that children are more likely to sleep well when they avoid caffeine, experience a regular bedtime routine, are read to before going to bed, and do not have a television in their bedroom (Mindell & others, 2009). As children age, their sleep patterns change.

Many adolescents stay up later at night and sleep longer in the morning than they did when they were children, and these changing sleep patterns may influence their academic work (Rao, Hammen, & Poland, 2009; Vallido, Jackson, & O'Brien, 2009). During adolescence, the brain, especially the cerebral cortex, is continuing to develop, and the adolescent's need for sleep may be linked to this brain development (Dahl & Spear, 2004).

Mary Carskadon and her colleagues have conducted a number of studies on adolescent sleep patterns (Carskadon, 2006; Carskadon, Mindell, & Drake, 2006; Hagenauer & others, 2009; Tarokh & Carskadon, 2008). They found that when given the opportunity, adolescents will sleep an average of 9 hours and 25 minutes a night. Most, however, get considerably less than 9 hours of sleep, especially during the week. This shortfall creates a sleep debt that adolescents often attempt to make up on the weekend.

The researchers also found that older adolescents tend to be sleepier during the day than younger adolescents. They theorized that this sleepiness was not due to academic work or social pressures. Rather, their research suggests that adolescents' biological clocks undergo a shift as they get older, delaying their period of wakefulness by about an hour. A delay in the nightly release of the sleep-inducing hormone melatonin seems to underlie this shift. Melatonin is secreted at about 9:30 P.M. in younger adolescents and approximately an hour later in older adolescents. Based on her research, Carskadon has suggested that early school starting times may cause grogginess, inattention in class, and poor performance on tests.

Sleep patterns also change as people age through the middle-adult (40s and 50s) and late-adult (60s and older) years (Goldman & others, 2008; Malhotra & Desai, 2010). Many adults in these age spans go to bed earlier at night and wake up earlier in the morning than they did in their younger years. Beginning in the 40s, individuals report that they are less likely to sleep through the entire night than when they were younger. Middle-aged adults also spend less time in deep sleep than they did before their middle years. More than 50 percent of individuals in late adulthood report that they experience problems falling asleep and staying asleep (Wolkove & others, 2007).

Sleep and the Brain

The five sleep stages are associated with distinct patterns of neurotransmitter activity initiated in the reticular formation, the core of the brain stem. In all vertebrates, the reticular formation plays a crucial role in sleep and arousal (see Figure 14.1). As previously noted, damage to the reticular formation can result in coma and death.

Three important neurotransmitters involved in sleep are serotonin, norepinephrine, and acetylcholine (Gabelle & Dauvilliers, 2010; Mitchell & Weinshenker, 2010; Yang & others, 2010). As sleep begins, the levels of neurotransmitters sent to the forebrain from the reticular formation start dropping, and they continue to fall until they reach their lowest levels during the deepest sleep stage—stage 4. REM sleep (stage 5) is initiated by a rise in acetylcholine, which activates the cerebral cortex while the rest of the brain remains relatively inactive. REM sleep ends when there is a rise in serotonin and norepinephrine, which increase the level of forebrain activity nearly to the awakened state (Miller & O'Callaghan, 2006). You are most likely to wake up just after a REM period. If you do not wake up then, the level of the neurotransmitters falls again, and you enter another sleep cycle.

To review the sleep cycles, complete the Psychological Inquiry exercise.

psychological *inquiry*

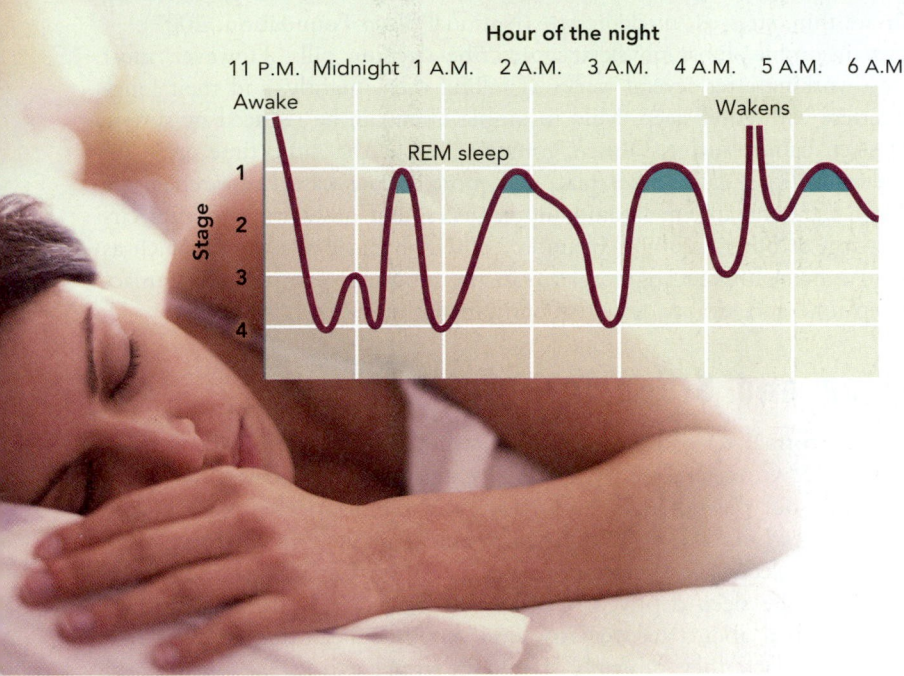

Hour of the night

11 P.M. Midnight 1 A.M. 2 A.M. 3 A.M. 4 A.M. 5 A.M. 6 A.M.

Awake

REM sleep

Wakens

Stage 1 2 3 4

Taking a Ride on the Sleep Cycles

This graph depicts a night's sleep. During nightly sleep, we go through several cycles. Depth of sleep decreases, and REM sleep (shown in light blue) increases as the night progresses. Look carefully at the graph and answer the following questions.

1. How many sleep cycles are presented?

2. What time does the sleeper wake up?

3. If you woke the sleeper up at 2 A.M., would he or she be likely to remember a dream? Explain.

4. How much time is this sleeper spending in slow-wave sleep?

5. Trace the rise and fall of the neurotransmitters acetylcholine, serotonin, and norepinephrine in the sleep cycle depicted.

6. Has the sleeper whose night's sleep is illustrated here achieved a good night's rest? Why or why not?

14·4 SLEEP AND DISEASE

Sleep plays a role in a large number of diseases and disorders (Fontana & Wohlgemuth, 2010). For example, stroke and asthma attacks are more common during the night and in the early morning, probably because of changes in hormones, heart rate, and other characteristics associated with sleep (Teodorescu & others, 2006). Sleeplessness is also associated with obesity and heart disease (Quan, Parthasarathy, & Budhiraja, 2010).

Neurons that control sleep interact closely with the immune system (Imeri & Opp, 2009). As anyone who has had the flu knows, infectious diseases make us sleepy. The probable reason is that chemicals called cytokines, produced by the body's cells while we are fighting an infection, are powerfully sleep-inducing (S. R. Patel & others, 2009). Sleep may help the body conserve energy and other resources it needs to overcome infection (Irwin & others, 2006).

Sleep problems afflict most people who have mental disorders, including those with depression (Babson & others, 2010; Rao, Hammen, & Poland, 2009). Individuals with depression often awaken in the early hours of the morning and cannot get back to sleep, and they often spend less time in delta wave or deep sleep than do non-depressed individuals.

Sleep problems are common in many other disorders as well, including Alzheimer disease, stroke, and cancer (Banthia & others, 2010; Merlino & others, 2010). In some cases, however, these problems may be due not to the disease itself but to the drugs used to treat the disease.

14·5 SLEEP DISORDERS

Many individuals suffer from undiagnosed and untreated sleep disorders that leave them feeling unmotivated and exhausted through the day (Ohayon, 2009). The major sleep disorders include insomnia, sleepwalking and sleep talking, nightmares and night terrors, narcolepsy, and sleep apnea.

Insomnia

A common sleep problem is *insomnia,* the inability to sleep. Insomnia can involve a problem in falling asleep, waking up during the night, or waking up too early. In the United States, as many as one in five adults has insomnia (Pearson, Johnson, & Nahin, 2006). Insomnia is more common among women and older adults, as well as among individuals who are thin, stressed, or depressed (National Sleep Foundation, 2007).

For short-term insomnia, most physicians prescribe sleeping pills. However, most sleeping pills stop working after several weeks of taking them nightly, and their long-term use can interfere with good sleep. Mild insomnia often can be reduced by simply practicing good sleep habits, such as always going to bed at the same time, even on weekends, and sleeping in a dark, quiet place. In more serious cases, researchers are experimenting with light therapy, melatonin supplements, and other ways to alter circadian cycles (Garzon & others, 2009; Miyamoto, 2009). Behavioral changes (such as avoiding naps and caffeine and setting an alarm in the morning) can help insomniacs increase their sleep time and awaken less frequently in the night.

Sleepwalking and Sleep Talking

Somnambulism is the formal term for sleepwalking, which occurs during the deepest stages of sleep (Harris & Grunstein, 2009). For many years, experts believed that somnambulists were acting out their dreams. However, somnambulism takes place during stages 3 and 4, usually early in the night, when a person is unlikely to be dreaming.

The specific causes of sleepwalking have not been identified, but it is more likely to occur when individuals are sleep deprived or when they have been drinking alcohol. There is nothing abnormal about sleepwalking, and despite superstition, it is safe to awaken sleepwalkers. In fact, they probably should be awakened, as they may harm themselves wandering around in the dark (Swanson, 1999).

Another quirky night behavior is sleep talking, or *somniloquy.* If you interrogate sleep talkers, can you find out what they did, for instance, last Thursday night? Probably not. Although sleep talkers will converse with you and make fairly coherent statements, they are soundly asleep. Thus, even if a sleep talker mumbles a response to your question, do not count on its accuracy.

Recently, a few cases of an even rarer sleep behavior have come to light—sleep eating. Ambien is a widely prescribed sleep medication for insomnia. Some Ambien users began to notice odd things upon waking up from a much-needed good night's sleep, such as candy wrappers strewn around the room, crumbs in the bed, and food missing from the refrigerator. One woman gained 100 pounds without changing her awake eating or exercise habits. How could this be? Dr. Mark Mahowald, the medical director of the Minnesota Regional Sleep Disorders Center in Minneapolis, has confirmed that sleep eating may be a side effect of using Ambien (CBS News, 2006).

The phenomenon of sleep eating illustrates that even when we feel fast asleep, we may be "half-awake"—and capable of putting together some unusual late-night snacks, including buttered cigarettes, salt sandwiches, and raw bacon. The maker of Ambien has noted this unusual side effect on the label of the drug. Even more alarming than sleep eating is sleep driving (Saul, 2006). Sleep experts agree that sleep driving while taking Ambien is rare and extreme but plausible.

For individuals who are battling persistent insomnia, a drug that provides a good night's rest may be worth the risk of these unusual side effects. Furthermore, no one should abruptly stop taking any medication without consulting a physician.

Nightmares and Night Terrors

A *nightmare* is a frightening dream that awakens a dreamer from REM sleep. The nightmare's content invariably involves danger—the dreamer is chased, robbed, or thrown off a cliff. Nightmares are common (Schredl, 2010); most of us have had them, especially as young children. Nightmares peak at 3 to 6 years of age and then decline, although the

Sleepwalkers Club Night Out

© Steamy Raimon. www.CartoonStock.com.

average college student experiences four to eight nightmares a year (Hartmann, 1993). Reported increases in nightmares or worsening nightmares are often associated with an increase in life stressors such as the loss of a relative or a job and conflicts with others.

A *night terror* features sudden arousal from sleep and intense fear. Night terrors are accompanied by a number of physiological reactions, such as rapid heart rate and breathing, loud screams, heavy perspiration, and movement (Mason & Pack, 2005). Night terrors, which peak at 5 to 7 years of age, are less common than nightmares, and unlike nightmares, they occur during slow-wave stage 4 (non-REM) sleep.

Narcolepsy

The disorder *narcolepsy* involves the sudden, overpowering urge to sleep. The urge is so uncontrollable that the person may fall asleep while talking or standing up. Narcoleptics immediately enter REM sleep rather than progressing through the first four sleep stages (Stores, Montgomery, & Wiggs, 2006). Individuals with narcolepsy are often very tired during the day. Narcolepsy can be triggered by extreme emotional reactions, such as surprise, laughter, excitement, or anger. The disorder appears to involve problems with the hypothalamus and amygdala (Poryazova & others, 2009). Although narcolepsy usually emerges in adulthood, signs of the problem may be evident in childhood (Nevsimalova, 2009).

Sleep Apnea

Sleep apnea is a sleep disorder in which individuals stop breathing because the windpipe fails to open or because brain processes involved in respiration fail to work properly. People with sleep apnea experience numerous brief awakenings during the night so that they can breathe better, although they usually are not aware of their awakened state. During the day, these people may feel sleepy because they were deprived of sleep at night. A common sign of sleep apnea is loud snoring, punctuated by silence (the apnea).

According to the American Sleep Apnea Association (ASAA), sleep apnea affects approximately 12 million Americans (ASAA, 2006). The disorder is most common among infants and adults over the age of 65. Sleep apnea also occurs more frequently among obese individuals, men, and individuals with large necks and recessed chins (ASAA, 2006; Scott & others, 2006).

Untreated sleep apnea can cause high blood pressure, stroke, and sexual dysfunction. In addition, the daytime sleepiness caused by sleep apnea can result in accidents, lost productivity, and relationship problems (Hartenbaum & others, 2006). Sleep apnea is commonly treated by weight-loss programs, side sleeping, propping the head on a pillow, or wearing a device (called a CPAP for *continuous positive airway pressure*) that sends pressurized air through a mask that prevents the airway from collapsing.

Sleep apnea may also be a factor in *sudden infant death syndrome (SIDS),* the sudden sleep-related death of an infant less than one year old. SIDS is typically confirmed with an autopsy that reveals no specific cause of death (Fifer & Myers, 2002; Byard & Krous, 2004). It is common for infants to have short pauses in their breathing during sleep, but for some infants frequent sleep apnea may be a sign of problems in regulating arousal (Kato & others, 2003). There is evidence that infants who die of SIDS in fact experience multiple episodes of sleep apnea in the days before the fatal event (Kahn & others, 1992). One possible explanation for SIDS is an abnormality in the brain stem areas responsible for arousal (Kinney, 2009). Such an abnormality may lead to sleep apnea, which in turn might worsen the brain stem damage, ultimately leading to death.

14·6 DREAMS

Have you ever dreamed that you left your long-term romantic partner for a former lover? If so, did you tell your partner about that dream? Probably not. However, you would have likely wondered about the dream's meaning, and if so you would not be alone. The meaning of dreams has eternally fascinated human beings. As early as 5000 B.C.E.,

Babylonians recorded and interpreted their dreams on clay tablets. Egyptians built temples in honor of Serapis, the god of dreams. Dreams are described at length in more than 70 passages in the Bible. Psychologists too have examined this intriguing topic.

Freud's Psychodynamic Approach

Sigmund Freud put great stock in dreams as a key to our unconscious minds. He believed that dreams (even nightmares) symbolize unconscious wishes and that analysis of dream symbols could uncover our hidden desires. Freud distinguished between a dream's manifest content and its latent content. **Manifest content** is the dream's surface content, which contains dream symbols that disguise the dream's true meaning; **latent content** is the dream's hidden content, its unconscious—and true—meaning. For example, if a person had a dream about riding on a train and talking with a friend, the train ride would be the dream's manifest content. Freud thought that this manifest content expresses a wish in disguised form. To get to the latent or true meaning of the dream, the person would have to analyze the dream images. In our example, the dreamer would be asked to think of all the things that come to mind when the person thinks of a train, the friend, and so forth. By following these associations to the objects in the manifest content, the latent content of the dream could be brought to light.

More recently, psychologists have approached dreams not as expressions of unconscious wishes but as mental events that come from various sources. Research has revealed a great deal about the nature of dreams. A common misconception is that dreams are typically bizarre or strange, but many studies of thousands of dreams, collected from individuals in sleep labs and sleeping at home, have shown that dreams generally are not very strange. Instead, research shows that dreams are often very similar to waking life (Domhoff, 2007; Schredl, 2009; Schwartz, 2010).

So, *why* might many of us believe that our dreams typically are very peculiar? The probable reason is that we are most likely to remember our most vividly bizarre dreams and to forget our more boring, mundane dreams. Thus, we never realize how commonplace most dreams are. Although some aspects of dreams *are* unusual, dreams often are no more bizarre than a typical fairy tale, TV show episode, or movie plot. Dreams do generally contain more negative emotion than everyday life; and certainly some unlikely characters, including dead people, sometimes show up in dreams.

There is also no evidence that dreams provide opportunities for problem solving or advice about how to handle life's difficulties. We may dream about a problem we are facing, but we typically find the solution while we are awake and thinking about the problem, not during the dream itself (Domhoff, 2007). There is also no evidence that people who remember their dreams are better adjusted psychologically than those who do not (Blagrove & Akehurst, 2000).

So, if the typical dream involves doing ordinary things, what are dreams? The most prominent theories that attempt to explain dreams are cognitive theory and activation-synthesis theory.

Cognitive Theory

The **cognitive theory of dreaming** proposes that we can understand dreaming by applying the same cognitive concepts we use in studying the waking mind. The theory rests on the idea that dreams are essentially subconscious cognitive processing. Dreaming involves information processing and memory. Indeed, thinking during dreams appears to be very similar to thinking in waking life (Schredl & Erlacher, 2008).

In the cognitive theory of dreaming, there is little or no search for the hidden, symbolic content of dreams that Freud sought (Foulkes, 1993, 1999). Instead, dreams are viewed as dramatizations of general life concerns that are similar to relaxed daydreams. Even very unusual aspects of dreams—such as odd activities, strange images, and sudden scene shifts—can be understood as metaphorically related to a person's preoccupations while awake (Domhoff, 2007).

● **manifest content** According to Freud, the surface content of a dream, containing dream symbols that disguise the dream's true meaning.

● **latent content** According to Freud, a dream's hidden content; its unconscious and true meaning.

● **cognitive theory of dreaming** Theory proposing that we can understand dreaming by applying the same cognitive concepts we use in studying the waking mind; rests on the idea that dreams are essentially subconscious cognitive processing involving information and memory.

Critics of the cognitive theory of dreaming fault the theory's lack of attention to the roles of brain structures and brain activity in dreaming. These perceived shortcomings are the main emphasis of the activation-synthesis theory of dreams.

Activation-Synthesis Theory

According to **activation-synthesis theory,** dreaming occurs when the cerebral cortex synthesizes neural signals generated from activity in the lower part of the brain. Dreams result from the brain's attempts to find logic in random brain activity that occurs during sleep (Hobson, 1999).

When we are awake and alert, our conscious experience tends to be driven by *external stimuli,* all those things we see, hear, and respond to. During sleep, according to activation-synthesis theory, conscious experience is driven predominantly by *internally generated stimuli* that have no apparent behavioral consequence. A key source of such internal stimulation is spontaneous neural activity in the brain stem (Hobson, 2000). Of course, some of the neural activity that produces dreams comes from external sensory experiences. If a fire truck with sirens blaring drives past your house, you might find yourself dreaming about an emergency. Many of us have had the experience of incorporating our alarm clock going off in an early morning dream.

Supporters of activation-synthesis theory have suggested that neural networks in other areas of the forebrain play a significant role in dreaming (Hobson, Pace-Schott, & Stickgold, 2000). Specifically, they believe that the same regions of the forebrain that are involved in certain waking behaviors also function in particular aspects of dreaming (Lu & others, 2006). As levels of neurotransmitters rise and fall during the stages of sleep, some neural networks are activated and others shut down. Random neural firing in various areas of the brain lead to dreams that are the brain's attempts to make sense of the activity. So, firing in the primary motor and sensory areas of the forebrain might be reflected in a dream of running and feeling wind on your face. From the activation-synthesis perspective, our nervous system is cycling through various activities, and our consciousness is simply along for the ride (Hobson, 2004). Dreams are merely a flashy sideshow, not the main event (Hooper & Teresi, 1993). Indeed, one activation-synthesis theorist has referred to dreams as so much "cognitive trash" (Hobson, 2002, p. 23).

Like all dream theories, activation-synthesis theory has its critics. A key criticism is that damage to the brain stem does not necessarily reduce dreaming, suggesting that this area of the brain is not the only starting point for dreaming. Furthermore, life experiences stimulate and shape dreaming more than activation-synthesis theory acknowledges (Domhoff, 2007; Malcolm-Smith & others, 2008).

● **activation-synthesis theory** Theory that dreaming occurs when the cerebral cortex synthesizes neural signals generated from activity in the lower part of the brain and that dreams result from the brain's attempts to find logic in random brain activity that occurs during sleep.

SUMMARY

The biological rhythm that regulates the daily sleep/wake cycle is the circadian rhythm. The part of the brain that keeps our biological clocks synchronized is the suprachiasmatic nucleus, a small structure in the hypothalamus that registers light. Biological clocks can become desynchronized by jet travel and work shifts; however, there are some helpful strategies for resetting the biological clock.

We need sleep for physical restoration, adaptation, growth, and memory. Research studies increasingly reveal that people do not function optimally when they are sleep-deprived.

Stages of sleep correspond to massive electrophysiological changes that occur in the brain and that can be assessed by an EEG. Humans go through four stages of non-REM sleep and one stage of REM (rapid eye movement) sleep. Most dreaming occurs during REM sleep. A sleep cycle of five stages lasts about 90 to 100 minutes and recurs several times during the night. The REM stage lasts longer toward the end of a night's sleep.

KEY TERMS

sleep   156
biological rhythms   156
circadian rhythms   156
suprachiasmatic nucleus
   (SCN)   157
REM sleep   160

manifest content   166
latent content   166
cognitive theory of
   dreaming   166
activation-synthesis
   theory   167

The sleep stages are associated with distinct patterns of neurotransmitter activity. Levels of the neurotransmitters serotonin, norepinephrine, and acetylcholine decrease as the sleep cycle progresses from stage 1 through stage 4. Stage 5, REM sleep, begins when the reticular formation raises the level of acetylcholine.

Sleep plays a role in a large number of diseases and disorders. Neurons that control sleep interact closely with the immune system, and when our body is fighting infection, our cells produce a substance that makes us sleepy. Individuals with depression often have sleep problems.

Many Americans suffer from chronic, long-term sleep disorders that can impair normal daily functioning. These include insomnia, sleepwalking and sleep talking, nightmares and night terrors, narcolepsy, and sleep apnea.

Contrary to popular belief, most dreams are not bizarre or strange. Freud thought that dreams express unconscious wishes in disguise. Cognitive theory attempts to explain dreaming in terms of the same concepts that are used in studying the waking mind. According to activation-synthesis theory, dreaming occurs when the cerebral cortex synthesizes neural signals emanating from activity in the lower part of the brain. In this view, the rising level of acetylcholine during REM sleep plays a role in neural activity in the brain stem that the cerebral cortex tries to make sense of.

TEST YOURSELF

1. Describe how the human body monitors the change from day to night.

2. What happens during each of the five stages of sleep?

3. According to researchers, what functions does sleep play in infants and children? What functions does it play in adolescents?

APPLY YOUR KNOWLEDGE

1. Keep a sleep journal for several nights. Compare your sleep patterns with those described in the text. Do you have a sleep debt? If so, which stages of sleep are you most likely missing? Does a good night's sleep affect your behavior? Keep a record of your mood and energy levels after a short night's sleep and then after you have had at least 8 hours of sleep in one night. What changes do you notice, and how do they compare with the changes predicted by research on sleep deprivation described in the module?

2. Keep a dream diary for a few days. When you wake up in the morning, immediately write down all that you can remember about your dreams. Have you had many bizarre or unusual dreams? Are there themes in your dreams that reflect the concerns of your daily life? Compare the content of your dream diary with the stream-of-consciousness document you produced for question 1, above. Are there similarities in the content of your relaxed, waking mind and your dreams?

Psychoactive Drugs

Some people seek to alter their consciousness through the use of psychoactive drugs. Illicit drug use is a global problem. According to the United Nations Office on Drugs and Crime (UNODC), more than 200 million people worldwide use illicit drugs each year (UNODC, 2008). Among those, 25 million individuals (2.7 percent of the world population) are problem drug users—individuals whose drug habit interferes with their ability to engage in work and social relationships (UNODC, 2008).

Drug use among youth is a special concern because of its relationship to problems such as unsafe sex, sexually transmitted infections, unplanned pregnancy, depression, and school-related difficulties (Eaton & others, 2008; UNODC, 2008). The consumption of drugs among U.S. secondary school students declined in the 1980s but began to increase in the early 1990s (Johnston & others, 2009). Then in the late 1990s and early 2000s, the proportion of secondary school students reporting the use of any illicit drug again declined (Johnston & others, 2009).

The United States still has the highest rate of adolescent drug use of any industrialized nation (Johnston & others, 2009). Trends in drug use by U.S. high school seniors since 1975 and by U.S. eighth- and tenth-graders since 1991 have been tracked in a national survey called *Monitoring the Future* (Johnston & others, 2009). This large-scale survey is the focus of the Psychological Inquiry feature on the next page. Let's take a look at these trends.

15·1 USES OF PSYCHOACTIVE DRUGS

Psychoactive drugs act on the nervous system to alter consciousness, modify perception, and change mood. Some people use psychoactive drugs as a way to deal with life's difficulties. Drinking, smoking, and taking drugs reduce tension, relieve boredom and fatigue, and help people to escape from the harsh realities of life. Some people use drugs because they are curious about their effects.

The use of psychoactive drugs, whether it is to cope with problems or just for fun, can carry a high price tag. These include losing track of one's responsibilities, problems in the workplace and in relationships, drug dependence, and increased risk for serious, sometimes fatal diseases (Fields, 2010; Zilney, 2011). For example, drinking alcohol may initially help people relax and forget about their worries. If, however, they turn more and more to alcohol to escape reality, they may develop a dependence that can destroy their relationships, career, and health.

Continued use of psychoactive drugs leads to **tolerance,** the need to take increasing amounts of a drug to get the same effect (Goldberg, 2010). For example, the first time someone takes 5 milligrams of the tranquilizer Valium, the person feels very relaxed. However, after taking the pill every day for six months, the individual may need to consume twice as much to achieve the same calming effect.

Continuing drug use can also result in **physical dependence,** the physiological need for a drug that causes unpleasant withdrawal symptoms such as physical pain and a craving for the drug when it is discontinued. **Psychological dependence** is the strong desire to repeat the use of a drug for emotional reasons, such as a feeling of well-being and reduction of stress. Experts on drug abuse use the term **addiction** to describe either a physical or a psychological dependence, or both, on the drug (Hales, 2011).

● **psychoactive drugs** Drugs that act on the nervous system to alter consciousness, modify perception, and change mood.

● **tolerance** The need to take increasing amounts of a drug to get the same effect.

● **physical dependence** The physiological need for a drug that causes unpleasant withdrawal symptoms such as physical pain and a craving for the drug when it is discontinued.

● **psychological dependence** The strong desire to repeat the use of a drug for emotional reasons, such as a feeling of well-being and reduction of stress.

● **addiction** Either a physical or a psychological dependence, or both, on a drug.

psychological *inquiry*

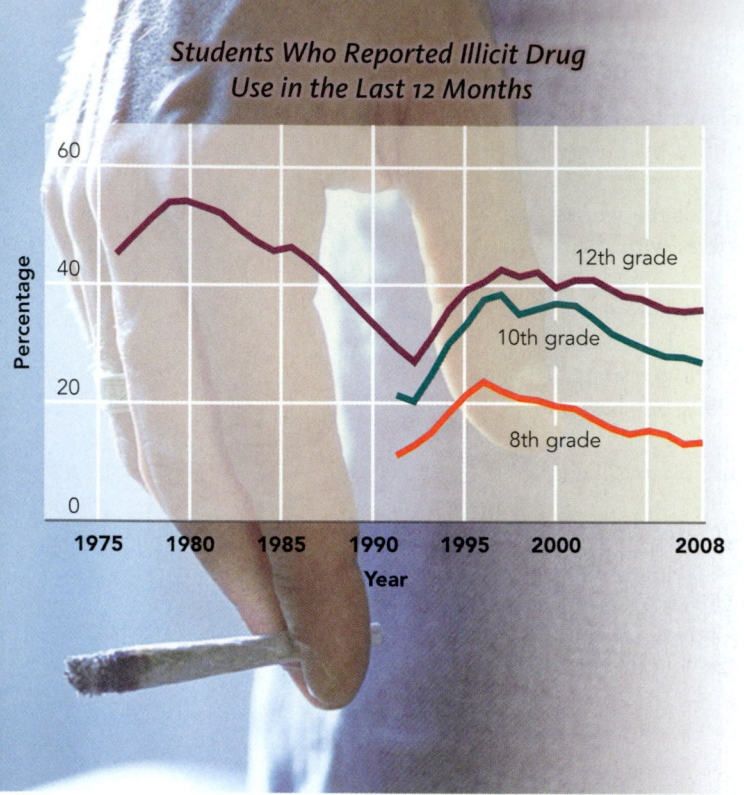

Students Who Reported Illicit Drug Use in the Last 12 Months

Drug Use by American Teenagers

This graph shows the percentage of U.S. eighth-, tenth-, and twelfth-grade students who reported having taken an illicit drug in the last 12 months from 1991 to 2008 (for eighth- and tenth-graders) and from 1975 to 2009 (for twelfth-graders) (Johnston & others, 2009). The vertical, or Y, axis shows the percentage of children and adolescents who report using illegal substances. The horizontal, or X, axis identifies the year of data collection. The most notable declines in adolescent drug use in the twenty-first century have occurred for marijuana, LSD, Ecstasy, steroids, and cigarettes. As you examine the data, answer these questions.

1. Do some research to find out about the social and cultural climate in each of the decades represented. Who was president at the time, and what historical events occurred? How does adolescent drug use reflect those times?

2. Data were not collected from eighth- and tenth-graders until 1991. Why do you think these two age groups were added?

3. After the mid-1990s, all age groups showed a similar decline in drug use. Why might this pattern have occurred in all three age groups?

4. What are the implications of using self-reports from children and adolescents to track their drug use? Do you think each age group would be similarly likely to over- or under-report their drug use? Explain.

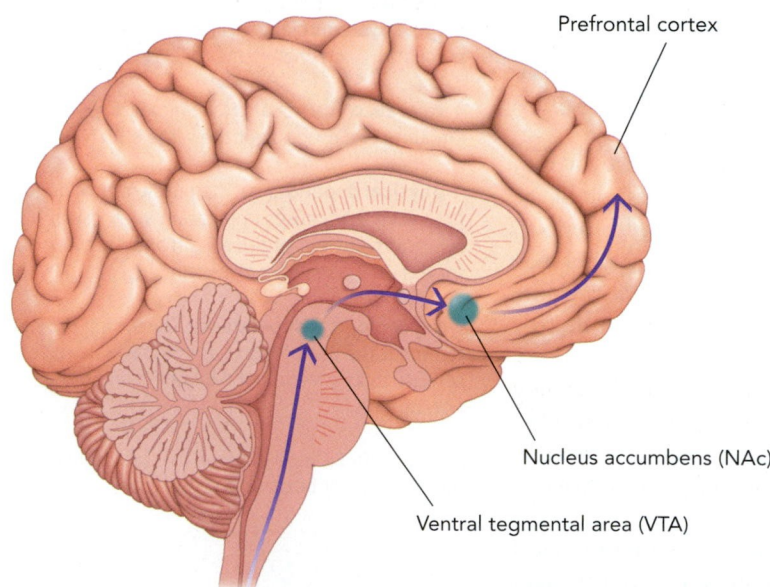

FIGURE 15.1   The Brain's Reward Pathway for Psychoactive

Drugs The ventral tegmental area (VTA) and nucleus accumbens (NAc) are important locations in the reward pathway for psychoactive drugs (Russo & others, 2010). Information travels from the VTA to the NAc and then up to the prefrontal cortex. The VTA is located in the midbrain just above the pons, and the NAc is located in the forebrain just beneath the prefrontal cortex.

How does the brain become addicted? Psychoactive drugs increase dopamine levels in the brain's reward pathways (Schmitt & Reith, 2010). This reward pathway is located in the *ventral tegmental area* (VTA) and *nucleus accumbens* (NAc) (Figure 15.1). Only the limbic and prefrontal areas of the brain are directly activated by dopamine, which comes from the VTA (Hnasko & others, 2010). Although different drugs have different mechanisms of action, each drug increases the activity of the reward pathway by increasing dopamine transmission. As we will see throughout this book, the neurotransmitter dopamine plays a vital role in the experience of rewards.

15-2 TYPES OF PSYCHOACTIVE DRUGS

Three main categories of psychoactive drugs are depressants, stimulants, and hallucinogens. All have the potential to cause health or behavior problems or both. To evaluate whether you abuse drugs, see Figure 15.2.

Depressants

Depressants are psychoactive drugs that slow down mental and physical activity. Among the most widely used depressants are alcohol, barbiturates, tranquilizers, and opiates.

ALCOHOL

Alcohol is a powerful drug. It acts on the body primarily as a depressant and slows down the brain's activities (Hales, 2011). This effect might seem surprising, as people who tend to be inhibited may begin to talk, dance, and socialize after a few drinks. However, people "loosen up" after a few drinks because the brain areas involved in inhibition and judgment slow down. As people drink more, their inhibitions decrease even further, and their judgment becomes increasingly impaired. Activities that require intellectual functioning and motor skills, such as driving, become harder to perform. Eventually the drinker falls asleep. With extreme intoxication, the person may lapse into a coma and die. Figure 15.3 illustrates alcohol's main effects on the body.

The effects of alcohol vary from person to person. Factors in this variation are body weight, the amount of alcohol consumed, individual differences in the way the body metabolizes alcohol, and the presence or absence of tolerance (Sparling & Redican, 2011). Men and women differ in terms of the intoxicating effects of alcohol. Because of differences in body fat as well as stomach enzymes, women are likely to be more strongly affected by alcohol than men.

How does alcohol affect the brain? Like other psychoactive drugs, alcohol goes to the VTA and the NAc (Hopf & others, 2010; Wanat & others, 2009). Alcohol also increases the concentration of the neurotransmitter gamma aminobutyric acid (GABA), which is widely distributed in many brain areas, including the cerebral cortex, cerebellum, hippocampus, amygdala, and nucleus accumbens (Kemppainen & others, 2010). Researchers believe that the frontal cortex holds a memory of the pleasure involved in prior alcohol use and contributes to continued drinking. Alcohol consumption also may affect the areas of the frontal cortex involved in judgment and impulse control (Nixon & McClain, 2010). It is further believed that the basal ganglia, which are involved in compulsive behaviors, may lead to a greater demand for alcohol, regardless of reason and consequences (Brink, 2001).

After caffeine, alcohol is the most widely used drug in the United States. As many as two-thirds of U.S. adults drink beer, wine, or liquor at least occasionally, and in one survey approximately 30 percent reported drinking more than five drinks at one sitting at least once in the last year (National Center for Health Statistics, 2005). The common use of alcohol is related to other serious problems, including death and injury from driving while drinking (Levinthal, 2010; National Highway Traffic Safety Administration, 2007). Research has also found a link between alcohol and violence and aggression (Gallagher & Parrott, 2010; Noel & others, 2009). More than 60 percent of homicides involve alcohol use by the offender or the victim, and 65 percent of aggressive sexual acts against women are associated with alcohol consumption by the offender.

A special concern is the high rate of alcohol use by U.S. secondary school and college students (Chassin, Hussong, & Beltran, 2009; Hoffman, 2009). In the *Monitoring the Future* survey, 43.5 percent of high school seniors surveyed reported consuming alcohol in the last 30 days in 2009 (Johnston & others, 2010). The good news: That percentage (43.5) represents a decline from 54 percent in 1991. In the most recent survey, 27.4 percent of the high school seniors surveyed had

Respond yes or no to the following items:

Yes	No	
☐	☐	I have gotten into problems because of using drugs.
☐	☐	Using alcohol or other drugs has made my college life unhappy at times.
☐	☐	Drinking alcohol or taking other drugs has been a factor in my losing a job.
☐	☐	Drinking alcohol or taking other drugs has interfered with my studying for exams.
☐	☐	Drinking alcohol or taking other drugs has jeopardized my academic performance.
☐	☐	My ambition is not as strong since I've been drinking a lot or taking drugs.
☐	☐	Drinking or taking other drugs has caused me to have difficulty sleeping.
☐	☐	I have felt remorse after drinking or taking drugs.
☐	☐	I crave a drink or other drugs at a definite time of the day.
☐	☐	I want a drink or other drug in the morning.
☐	☐	I have had a complete or partial loss of memory as a result of drinking or using other drugs.
☐	☐	Drinking or using other drugs is affecting my reputation.
☐	☐	I have been in the hospital or another institution because of my drinking or taking drugs.

College students who responded yes to items similar to these on the Rutgers Collegiate Abuse Screening Test were more likely to be substance abusers than those who answered no. If you responded yes to just 1 of the 13 items on this screening test, consider going to your college health or counseling center for further screening.

FIGURE 15.2 **Do You Abuse Drugs?** Take this short quiz to see if your use of drugs and alcohol might be a cause for concern.

● **depressants** Psychoactive drugs that slow down mental and physical activity.

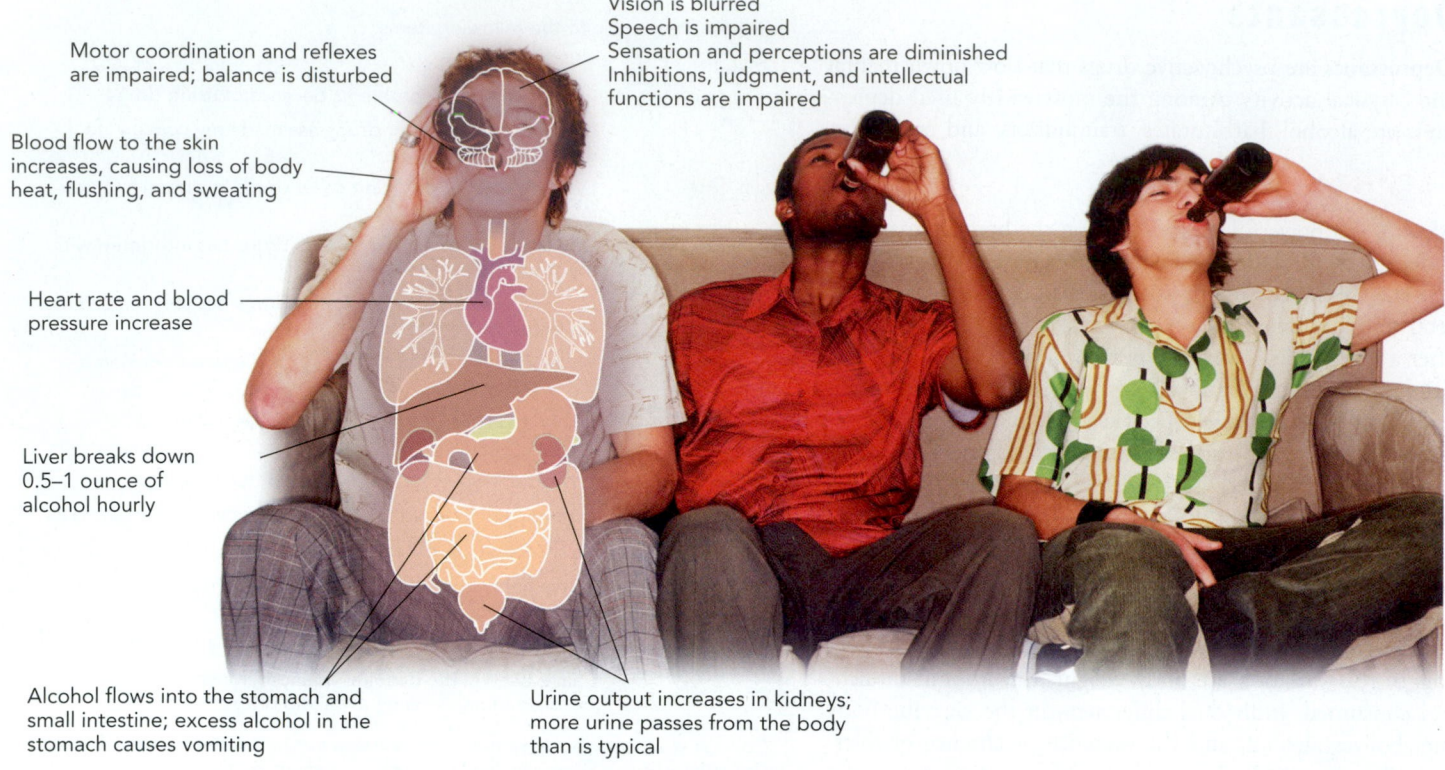

Motor coordination and reflexes
are impaired; balance is disturbed

Vision is blurred
Speech is impaired
Sensation and perceptions are diminished
Inhibitions, judgment, and intellectual
functions are impaired

Blood flow to the skin
increases, causing loss of body
heat, flushing, and sweating

Heart rate and blood
pressure increase

Liver breaks down
0.5–1 ounce of
alcohol hourly

Alcohol flows into the stomach and
small intestine; excess alcohol in the
stomach causes vomiting

Urine output increases in kidneys;
more urine passes from the body
than is typical

FIGURE 15.3   The Physiological and Behavioral Effects of Alcohol Alcohol has a powerful impact throughout the body. It affects everything from the operation of the nervous, circulatory, and digestive systems to sensation, perception, motor coordination, and intellectual functioning.

● **alcoholism** A disorder that involves long-term, repeated, uncontrolled, compulsive, and excessive use of alcoholic beverages and that impairs the drinker's health and social relationships.

engaged in binge drinking (having five or more drinks in a row) at least once during the previous month, down from 34 percent in 1997.

Binge drinking often increases during the first two years of college, and it can take its toll on students (Littlefield & Sher, 2010). In a *Monitoring the Future* survey of college students, 41 percent reported engaging in binge drinking in the last two weeks (49 percent of males, 33 percent of females) (Johnston & others, 2008). In a national survey of drinking patterns on college campuses, almost half of the binge drinkers reported problems such as missed classes, injuries, trouble with police, and unprotected sex (Wechsler & others, 2000, 2002). Binge-drinking college students were 11 times more likely to fall behind in school, 10 times more likely to drive after drinking, and twice as likely to have unprotected sex as college students who did not binge drink. Many emerging adults, however, decrease their alcohol use as they assume adult responsibilities such as a permanent job, marriage or cohabitation, and parenthood (Slutske, 2005).

Alcoholism is a disorder that involves long-term, repeated, uncontrolled, compulsive, and excessive use of alcoholic beverages and that impairs the drinker's health and social relationships. Approximately 18 million people in the United States are alcoholics (Grant & others, 2004). A longitudinal study linked early onset of drinking to later alcohol problems. Individuals who began drinking alcohol before 14 years of age were more likely to become alcohol dependent than their counterparts who began drinking alcohol at 21 years of age or older (Hingson, Heeren, & Winter, 2006).

One in nine individuals who drink continues down the path to alcoholism. Those who do are disproportionately related to alcoholics; family studies consistently find a high frequency of alcoholism in the close biological relatives of alcoholics (Edenberg & Foroud, 2006; Sintov & others, 2010). A possible explanation is that the brains of people genetically predisposed to alcoholism may be unable to produce adequate dopamine, the neurotransmitter that can make us feel pleasure (Tsuchihashi-Makay & others, 2009). For these individuals, alcohol may increase dopamine concentration and resulting pleasure to the point where it leads to addiction (Meyer, Meshul, & Phillips, 2009).

Like other psychological characteristics, though, alcoholism is not all about nature: Nurture matters too. Indeed, research shows that experience plays a role in alcoholism (Schuckit, 2009). Many alcoholics do not have close relatives who are alcoholics (Duncan & others, 2006), a finding that points to environmental influences.

What does it take to stop alcoholism? About one-third of alcoholics recover whether they are in a treatment program or not. This finding came from a long-term study of 700 individuals (Vaillant, 2003). George Vaillant followed these individuals for over 60 years, and he formulated the so-called one-third rule for alcoholism: By age 65, one-third are dead or in terrible shape; one-third are still trying to beat their addiction; and one-third are abstinent or drinking only socially. In his extensive research, Vaillant found that recovery from alcoholism was predicted by (1) having a strong negative experience with drinking, such as a serious medical emergency; (2) finding a substitute dependency, such as meditation, exercise, or overeating (which has its own adverse health effects); (3) developing new, positive relationships; and (4) joining a support group such as Alcoholics Anonymous.

BARBITURATES

Barbiturates, such as Nembutal and Seconal, are depressant drugs that decrease central nervous system activity. Physicians once widely prescribed barbiturates as sleep aids. In heavy dosages, they can lead to impaired memory and decision making. When combined with alcohol (for example, sleeping pills taken after a night of binge drinking), barbiturates can be lethal. Heavy doses of barbiturates by themselves can cause death. For this reason, barbiturates are the drug most often used in suicide attempts. Abrupt withdrawal can produce seizures. Because of the addictive potential and relative ease of toxic overdose, barbiturates have largely been replaced by tranquilizers in the treatment of insomnia.

TRANQUILIZERS

Tranquilizers, such as Valium and Xanax, are depressant drugs that reduce anxiety and induce relaxation. In small doses tranquilizers can bring on a feeling of calm; higher doses can lead to drowsiness and confusion. Tolerance for tranquilizers can develop within a few weeks of usage, and these drugs are addictive. Widely prescribed in the United States to calm anxious individuals, tranquilizers can produce withdrawal symptoms when use is stopped (Levinthal, 2010).

OPIATES

Narcotics, or **opiates,** consist of opium and its derivatives and depress the central nervous system's activity. These drugs are used as powerful painkillers. The most common opiate drugs—morphine and heroin—affect synapses in the brain that use endorphins as their neurotransmitter. When these drugs leave the brain, the affected synapses become understimulated. For several hours after taking an opiate, the person feels euphoric and pain-free and has an increased appetite for food and sex. Opiates are highly addictive, and users experience craving and painful withdrawal when the drug becomes unavailable.

Opiate addiction can also raise the risk of exposure to HIV, the virus that causes AIDS (Nath, 2010). Most heroin addicts inject the drug intravenously. When they share nonsterilized needles, one infected addict can transmit the virus to others.

Stimulants

Stimulants are psychoactive drugs that increase the central nervous system's activity. The most widely used stimulants are caffeine, nicotine, amphetamines, and cocaine.

● **barbiturates** Depressant drugs, such as Nembutal and Seconal, that decrease central nervous system activity.

● **tranquilizers** Depressant drugs, such as Valium and Xanax, that reduce anxiety and induce relaxation.

● **opiates** Opium and its derivatives; narcotic drugs that depress activity in the central nervous system and eliminate pain.

● **stimulants** Psychoactive drugs that increase the central nervous system's activity. The most widely used stimulants are caffeine, nicotine, amphetamines, and cocaine.

off the mark.com   by Mark Parisi

ATLANTIC FEATURE © 1998 MARK PARISI   offthemark.com

ANSWERING *THE QUESTION* OF HOW *THEY FLY AROUND THE WORLD* IN ONE NIGHT

Copyright by Mark Parisi. www.offthemark.com.

CAFFEINE

Often overlooked as a drug, caffeine is the world's most widely used psychoactive drug. Caffeine is a stimulant and a natural component of the plants that are the sources of coffee, tea, and cola drinks. Caffeine also is present in chocolate, in many nonprescription medications, and in energy drinks such as Red Bull. People often perceive the stimulating effects of caffeine as beneficial for boosting energy and alertness, but some experience unpleasant side effects.

Caffeinism refers to an overindulgence in caffeine. It is characterized by mood changes, anxiety, and sleep disruption. Caffeinism often develops in people who drink five or more cups of coffee (at least 500 milligrams) each day. Common symptoms are insomnia, irritability, headaches, ringing ears, dry mouth, increased blood pressure, and digestive problems (Hogan, Hornick, & Bouchoux, 2002).

Caffeine affects the brain's pleasure centers, so it is not surprising that it is difficult to kick the caffeine habit. When individuals who regularly consume caffeinated beverages remove caffeine from their diet, they typically experience headaches, lethargy, apathy, and concentration difficulties. These symptoms of withdrawal are usually mild and subside after several days.

NICOTINE

Nicotine is the main psychoactive ingredient in all forms of smoking and smokeless tobacco. Even with all the publicity given to the enormous health risks posed by tobacco, we sometimes overlook the highly addictive nature of nicotine. Nicotine stimulates the brain's reward centers by raising dopamine levels (Kovacs, Lajtha, & Sershen, 2010). Behavioral effects of nicotine include improved attention and alertness, reduced anger and anxiety, and pain relief (Levinthal, 2010). Figure 15.4 shows the main effects of nicotine on the body.

Tolerance develops for nicotine both in the long run and on a daily basis, so that cigarettes smoked later in the day have less effect than those smoked earlier. Withdrawal from nicotine often quickly produces strong, unpleasant symptoms such as irritability, craving, inability to focus, sleep disturbance, and increased appetite. Withdrawal symptoms can persist for months or longer.

Tobacco poses a much larger threat to public health than illegal drugs. According to the Centers for Disease Control and Prevention (CDC), tobacco use kills more than 400,000 people each year in the United States (CDC, 2005). That is more than the total number killed by AIDS, alcohol, motor vehicles, homicide, illegal drugs, and suicide combined. Today there are approximately 1 billion smokers globally, and estimates are that by 2030, another 1 billion young people will have started to smoke (United Nations World Youth Report, 2005). In 2008, 20.6 percent of U.S. adults said they smoked—a decline from 1998, when 24.1 percent of Americans reported that they smoked (CDC, 2009).

Cigarette smoking is decreasing among adolescents and college students. In the national *Monitoring the Future* survey by the Institute of Social Research, the percentage of U.S. adolescents who are current cigarette smokers continued to decline in 2009 (Johnston & others, 2010). Cigarette smoking peaked in 1996 and 1997 and then decreased 13 to 17 percent, depending on grade level, from 1998 to 2009 (Figure 15.5).

The drop in cigarette use by U.S. youth may have several sources, including higher cigarette prices, less tobacco advertising reaching adolescents, more antismoking advertisements, and more negative publicity about the tobacco industry than before. Increasingly, adolescents report perceiving cigarette smoking as dangerous, disapprove of it, are less accepting of being around smokers, and prefer to date nonsmokers (Johnston & others, 2010). With respect to college students and young adults, smoking has shown a smaller decline than adolescent and adult smoking (Johnston & others, 2010).

In sum, cigarette smoking appears to be generally on the decline. Most smokers recognize the serious health risks of smoking and wish they could quit. Module 67 explores the difficulty of giving up smoking and strategies for quitting.

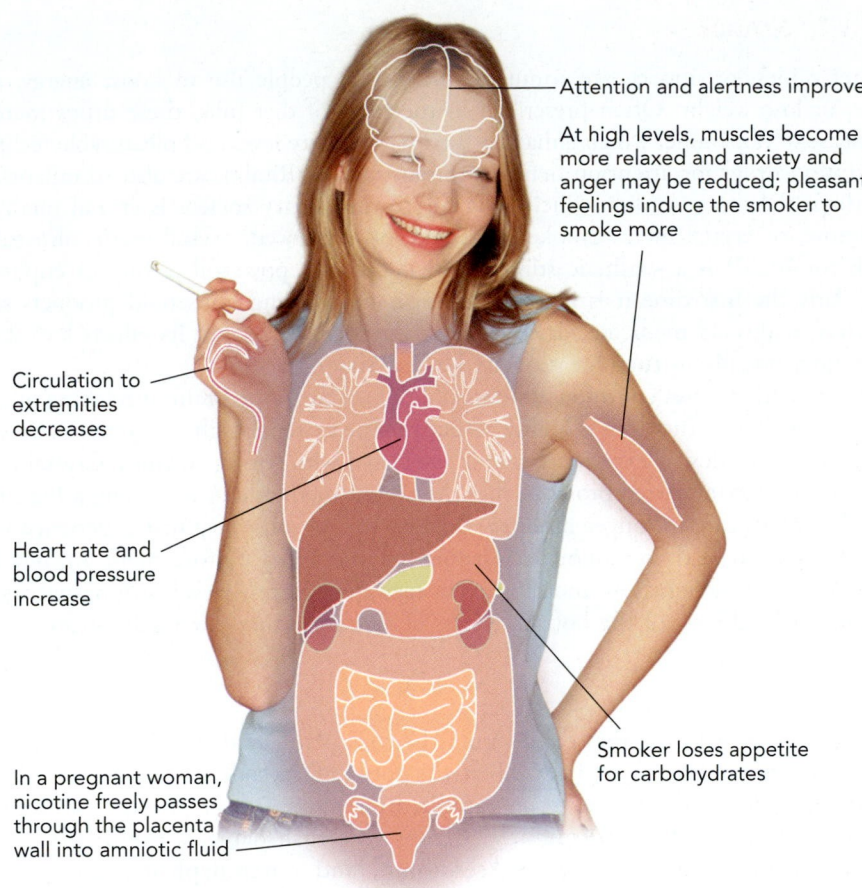

Attention and alertness improve

At high levels, muscles become more relaxed and anxiety and anger may be reduced; pleasant feelings induce the smoker to smoke more

Circulation to extremities decreases

Heart rate and blood pressure increase

Smoker loses appetite for carbohydrates

In a pregnant woman, nicotine freely passes through the placenta wall into amniotic fluid

FIGURE 15.4 **The Physiological and Behavioral Effects of Nicotine** Smoking has many physiological and behavioral effects. Highly addictive, nicotine delivers pleasant feelings that make the smoker smoke more, but tobacco consumption poses very serious health risks.

FIGURE 15.5 **Trends in Cigarette Smoking by U.S. Secondary School Students** Cigarette smoking by American high school students is on the decline.

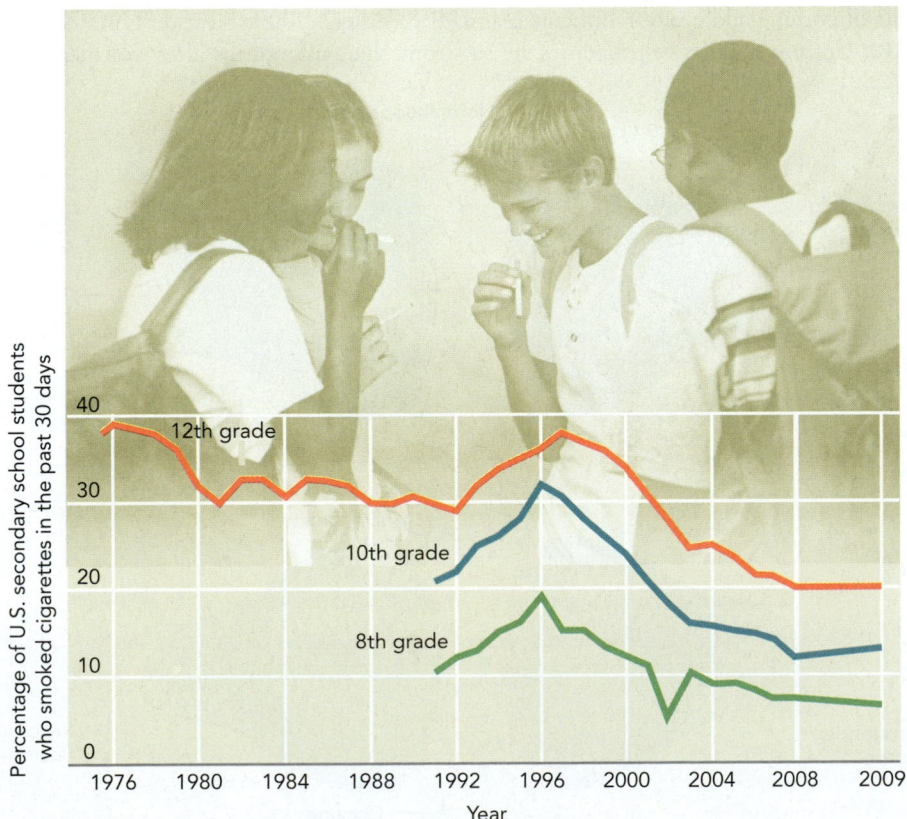

Percentage of U.S. secondary school students who smoked cigarettes in the past 30 days

40
30
20
10
0

12th grade
10th grade
8th grade

1976 1980 1984 1988 1992 1996 2000 2004 2008 2009

Year

AMPHETAMINES

Amphetamines, or uppers, are stimulant drugs that people use to boost energy, stay awake, or lose weight. Often prescribed in the form of diet pills, these drugs increase the release of dopamine, which enhances the user's activity level and pleasurable feelings. Prescription drugs for attention deficit disorder, such as Ritalin, are also stimulants.

Perhaps the most insidious illicit drug for contemporary society is crystal methamphetamine, or crystal meth. Smoked, injected, or swallowed, crystal meth (also called "crank" or "tina") is a synthetic stimulant that causes a powerful feeling of euphoria, particularly the first time it is ingested. Meth is made using household products such as battery acid, cold medicine, drain cleaner, and kitty litter, and its effects have been devastating, notably in rural areas of the United States.

Crystal meth releases enormous amounts of dopamine in the brain, producing intense feelings of pleasure. The drug is highly addictive. The extreme high of crystal meth leads to a severe "come down" experience that is associated with strong cravings. Crystal meth also damages dopamine receptors, so that the crystal meth addict is chasing a high that his or her brain can no longer produce. Because the person's very first experience with crystal meth can lead to ruinous consequences, the Drug Enforcement Agency has started a website, designed by and targeted at teenagers, http://www.justthinktwice.com, to share the hard facts of the horrific effects of this and other illicit substances.

COCAINE

Cocaine is an illegal drug that comes from the coca plant, native to Bolivia and Peru. Cocaine is either snorted or injected in the form of crystals or powder. Used this way, cocaine floods the bloodstream rapidly, producing a rush of euphoric feelings that lasts for about 15 to 30 minutes. Because the rush depletes the brain's supply of the neurotransmitters dopamine, serotonin, and norepinephrine, an agitated, depressed mood usually follows as the drug's effects decline. Figure 15.6 shows how cocaine affects dopamine levels in the brain.

Crack is a potent form of cocaine, consisting of chips of pure cocaine that are usually smoked. Scientists believe that crack is one of the most addictive substances known. Treatment of cocaine addiction is difficult (Ahmadi & others, 2009; Silva de Lima & others, 2010). Cocaine's addictive properties are so strong that, six months after treatment, more

FIGURE 15.6 **Cocaine and Neurotransmitters** Cocaine concentrates in areas of the brain that are rich in dopamine synapses such as the VTA and the nucleus accumbens (NAc). (*Top*) What happens in normal reuptake. The transmitting neuron releases dopamine, which stimulates the receiving neuron by binding to its receptor sites. After binding occurs, dopamine is carried back into the transmitting neuron for later release. (*Bottom*) What happens when cocaine is present in the synapse. Cocaine binds to the uptake pumps and prevents them from removing dopamine from the synapse. The result is that more dopamine collects in the synapse, and more dopamine receptors are activated.

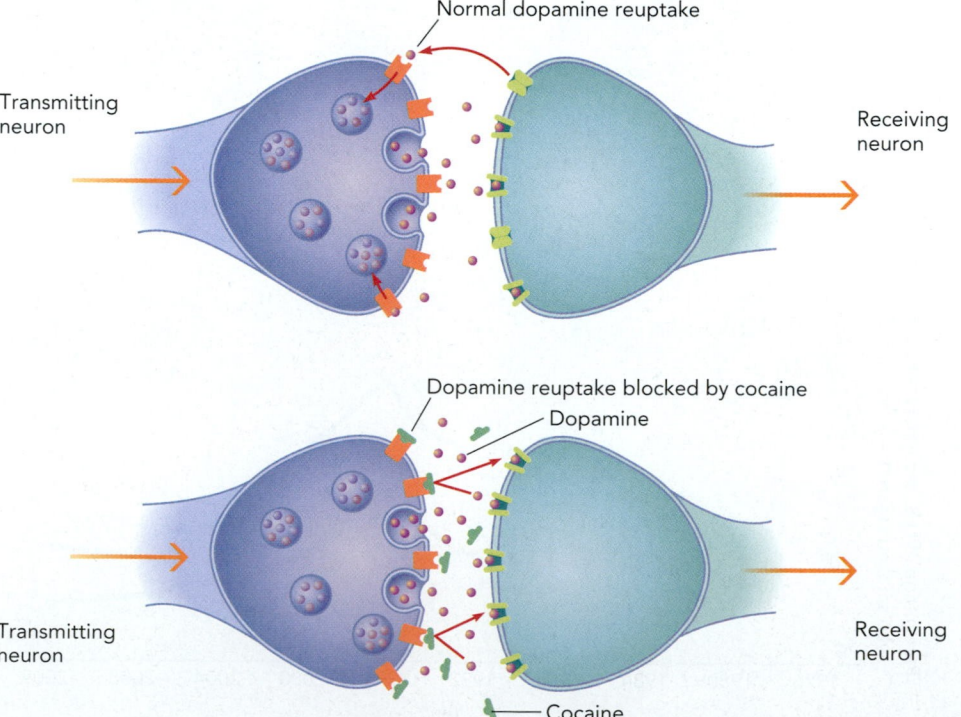

than 50 percent of abusers return to the drug, a statistic that highlights the importance of prevention.

MDMA (ECSTASY)

MDMA—called Ecstasy, X, or XTC—is an illegal synthetic drug with both stimulant and hallucinogenic properties (Degenhardt, Bruno, & Topp, 2010). People have called Ecstasy an "empathogen" because under its influence, users tend to feel warm bonds with others. MDMA produces its effects by releasing serotonin, dopamine, and norepinephrine. The effects of the drug on serotonin are particularly problematic. MDMA depletes the brain of this important neurotransmitter, producing lingering feelings of listlessness that often continue for days after use (NIDA, 2009a).

MDMA impairs memory and cognitive processing. Heavy users of Ecstasy show cognitive deficits (Gouzoulis-Mayfrank & Daumann, 2009; Sofuoglu, Sugarman, & Carroll, 2010) that persist even two years after they begin to abstain (Rogers & others, 2009). Because MDMA destroys axons that release serotonin (Riezzo & others, 2010), repeated use might lead to susceptibility to depression (Cowan, Roberts, & Joers, 2008).

Hallucinogens

Hallucinogens are psychoactive drugs that modify a person's perceptual experiences and produce visual images that are not real. Hallucinogens are also called *psychedelic* (from the Greek meaning "mind-revealing") drugs. Marijuana has a mild hallucinogenic effect; LSD, a stronger one.

● **hallucinogens** Also called psychedelics, psychoactive drugs that modify a person's perceptual experiences and produce visual images that are not real.

MARIJUANA

Marijuana is the dried leaves and flowers of the hemp plant *Cannabis sativa,* which originated in Central Asia but is now grown in most parts of the world. The plant's dried resin is known as hashish. The active ingredient in marijuana is THC (delta-9-tetrahydrocannabinol). Unlike other psychoactive drugs, THC does not affect a specific neurotransmitter. Rather, marijuana disrupts the membranes of neurons and affects the functioning of a variety of neurotransmitters and hormones.

The physical effects of marijuana include increased pulse rate and blood pressure, reddening of the eyes, coughing, and dry mouth. Marijuana smoke is more damaging to the lungs than smoke from tobacco (NIDA, 2009b). Psychological effects include a mixture of excitatory, depressive, and mildly hallucinatory characteristics that make it difficult to classify the drug. Marijuana can trigger spontaneous unrelated ideas; distorted perceptions of time and place; increased sensitivity to sounds, tastes, smells, and colors; and erratic verbal behavior. The drug can also impair attention and memory. Researchers also have found that marijuana use by pregnant women has negative outcomes for offspring, including lower intelligence (Goldschmidt & others, 2008). Long-term marijuana use can lead to addiction and difficulties in quitting (NIDA, 2009b).

Marijuana is the illegal drug most widely used by high school students. In the *Monitoring the Future* survey, 42 percent of U.S. high school seniors said they had tried marijuana in their lifetime, and 5 percent reported that they had used marijuana in the last 30 days (Johnston & others, 2010). One concern about adolescents' use of marijuana is that the drug might be a gateway to the use of other more serious illicit substances. Although there is a correlational link between using marijuana and using other illicit drugs, evidence for the gateway hypothesis for marijuana or any other illegal drug is weak (Degenhardt & others, 2010).

LSD

LSD (lysergic acid diethylamide) is a hallucinogen that even in low doses produces striking perceptual changes. Objects change their shapes and glow. Colors become kaleidoscopic and astonishing images unfold. LSD-induced images are sometimes pleasurable and sometimes grotesque. LSD can also influence a user's sense of time so that brief

Drug Classification	Medical Uses	Short-Term Effects	Overdose Effects	Health Risks	Risk of Physical/ Psychological Dependence
Depressants					
Alcohol	Pain relief	Relaxation, depressed brain activity, slowed behavior, reduced inhibitions	Disorientation, loss of consciousness, even death at high blood-alcohol levels	Accidents, brain damage, liver disease, heart disease, ulcers, birth defects	Physical: moderate Psychological: moderate
Barbiturates	Sleeping pill	Relaxation, sleep	Breathing difficulty, coma, possible death	Accidents, coma, possible death	Physical and psychological: moderate to high
Tranquilizers	Anxiety reduction	Relaxation, slowed behavior	Breathing difficulty, coma, possible death	Accidents, coma, possible death	Physical: low to moderate Psychological: moderate to high
Opiates (narcotics)	Pain relief	Euphoric feelings, drowsiness, nausea	Convulsions, coma, possible death	Accidents, infectious diseases such as AIDS	Physical: high Psychological: moderate to high
Stimulants					
Amphetamines	Weight control	Increased alertness, excitability; decreased fatigue, irritability	Extreme irritability, feelings of persecution, convulsions	Insomnia, hypertension, malnutrition, possible death	Physical: possible Psychological: moderate to high
Cocaine	Local anesthetic	Increased alertness, excitability, euphoric feelings; decreased fatigue, irritability	Extreme irritability, feelings of persecution, convulsions, cardiac arrest, possible death	Insomnia, hypertension, malnutrition, possible death	Physical: possible Psychological: moderate (oral) to very high (injected or smoked)
MDMA (Ecstasy)	None	Mild amphetamine and hallucinogenic effects; high body temperature and dehydration; sense of well-being and social connectedness	Brain damage, especially memory and thinking	Cardiovascular problems; death	Physical: possible Psychological: moderate
Caffeine	None	Alertness and sense of well-being followed by fatigue	Nervousness, anxiety, disturbed sleep	Possible cardiovascular problems	Physical: moderate Psychological: moderate
Nicotine	None	Stimulation, stress reduction, followed by fatigue, anger	Nervousness, disturbed sleep	Cancer and cardio-vascular disease	Physical: high Psychological: high
Hallucinogens					
LSD	None	Strong hallucinations, distorted time perception	Severe mental disturbance, loss of contact with reality	Accidents	Physical: none Psychological: low
Marijuana	Treatment of the eye disorder glaucoma	Euphoric feelings, relaxation, mild hallucinations, time distortion, attention and memory impairment	Fatigue, disoriented behavior	Accidents, respiratory disease	Physical: very low Psychological: moderate

FIGURE 15.7 **Categories of Psychoactive Drugs: Depressants, Stimulants, and Hallucinogens** Note that these various drugs have different effects and negative consequences.

glances at objects are experienced as deep, penetrating, and lengthy examinations, and minutes turn into hours or even days. A bad LSD trip can trigger extreme anxiety, paranoia, and suicidal or homicidal impulses.

LSD's effects on the body can include dizziness, nausea, and tremors. LSD acts primarily on the neurotransmitter serotonin in the brain, though it also can affect dopamine (Gonzalez-Maeso & Sealfon, 2009). Emotional and cognitive effects may include rapid mood swings and impaired attention and memory. The use of LSD peaked in the 1960s and 1970s, and its consumption has been decreasing in the twenty-first century (Johnston & others, 2010). Figure 15.7 summarizes the effects of LSD and a variety of other psychoactive drugs.

CRITICAL CONTROVERSY

Should Illicit Psychoactive Drugs Be Legalized for Medical Use?

Psychedelic drugs such as LSD and MDMA have mind-altering effects. Users sometimes talk about the amazing insights they have experienced under the influence of these substances. Could these effects be harnessed to promote healthier functioning in the mentally ill or to enhance well-being more generally? John Halpern, an associate director of addiction research at Harvard University's McLean Hospital, and his colleagues think so (Halpern, 2003; Halpern & Sewell, 2005; Halpern & others, 2005; Passie & others, 2008; Sewell, Halpern, & Pope, 2006). They have been advocates for research on using psychedelic drugs to treat a number of disorders. These drugs are illegal today, but they were not always so.

The effects of LSD were discovered by a Swiss chemist who accidentally ingested the substance while working in a pharmaceutical lab. He described his "trip" as both terrifying and thrilling, and his experience led others to consider whether LSD might have a use in psychological treatment. During the 1960s, more than 100 scientific articles examined the effects and potential benefits of psychedelic drugs, and over 40,000 patients were given LSD for problems such as schizophrenia, alcoholism, and depression.

The benefits of LSD were championed by the late Timothy Leary. In the 1960s, Leary, a Harvard psychologist, embarked on research dedicated to unlocking the secrets of consciousness through the use of LSD. Leary believed that LSD could free people from addiction, change the behavior of criminals, and provide entry into mystical experience. Leary ultimately fell out of favor and lost his job over his and his research associates' tendencies to sample the research stimuli (Greenfield, 2006).

Leary's controversial persona and behavior had a chilling effect on research into the potential applications of psychedelic drugs (Horgan, 2005; Sessa, 2007). By the late 1960s, LSD and other psychedelic drugs were outlawed in the United States, Canada, and Europe. Slowly, however, researchers have again begun to consider the potential benefits of these illegal substances. Although government restrictions make the research difficult, scholars are examining the legitimate uses of psychedelic drugs for a range of problems—for

Medical marijuana is now legal in 14 states, and in 2009 Attorney General Eric Holder announced an end to federal raids on medical marijuana facilities unless these facilities violated both state and federal law.

example, MDMA for anxiety and LSD for addictions (Halpern, 1996; Horgan, 2005; Krebs & others, 2009). Promising initial results are leading some to consider whether these drugs should be legalized for medical use.

The controversy over medical marijuana illustrates the conflicts that can erupt over the possibility of an illicit drug's legalization. Recently, marijuana has been considered as a potential treatment for people who suffer from a variety of diseases, including AIDS, cancer, and chronic pain. For such individuals, "medical marijuana" may promote appetite, calm anxiety, stimulate well-being, and relieve pain (P. J. Cohen, 2009; Joy, Watson, & Benson, 1999; Wilsey & others, 2008). However, when marijuana is legalized for medical purposes, does drug use rise more generally, as many fear? Researchers sought to answer this question. They examined attitudes about marijuana and marijuana use before and after the passage of Proposition 215, which legalized medical marijuana in California. The results showed that although attitudes about marijuana were more lenient after Prop 215's passage, use of the drug did not change (Khatapoush & Hallfors, 2004).

Many people ask, if marijuana can be legalized as a medical treatment, might it also be legalized to enhance everyday life? Writing as "Mr. X" in Lester Grinspoon's *Marihuana Reconsidered* (1994), the late scientist Carl Sagan described the illegality of marijuana as an impediment to "serenity, insight, sensitivity, and fellowship." Whether hallucinogenic drugs provide insight into life's great mysteries is certainly debatable; one of Timothy Leary's early participants noted that he had solved all the world's problems during an acid trip, yet the next day he could not remember how (Greenfield, 2006). The use of these drugs to help individuals struggling with serious life difficulties is certain to remain a subject of debate for years to come.

WHAT DO YOU THINK?

- Would the legalization of currently illegal psychoactive drugs for medical purposes send the wrong message about drug use? Why or why not?

- Would you support the legalization of such illicit drugs for medical purposes? Why or why not?

Given their powerful effects on consciousness, you may well wonder whether some of the illicit psychoactive drugs might have uses beyond recreation. In fact, some do have medical applications. The question is, *should* drugs such as LSD and marijuana be used for medical purposes? To read about the issue, see the Critical Controversy.

SUMMARY

Psychoactive drugs act on the nervous system to alter states of consciousness, modify perceptions, and change moods. Some people are attracted to these drugs because they seem to help them deal with difficult life situations.

Addictive drugs activate the brain's reward system by increasing dopamine concentration. The reward pathway involves the ventral tegmental area (VTA) and nucleus accumbens (NAc). The abuse of psychoactive drugs can lead to tolerance, psychological and physical dependence, and addiction—a pattern of behavior characterized by a preoccupation with using a drug and securing its supply.

Depressants slow down mental and physical activity. Among the most widely used depressants are alcohol, barbiturates, tranquilizers, and opiates.

After caffeine, alcohol is the most widely used drug in America. The high rate of alcohol abuse by high school and college students is especially alarming. Alcoholism is a disorder that involves long-term, repeated, uncontrolled, compulsive, and excessive use of alcoholic beverages that impairs the drinker's health and work and social relationships.

Stimulants increase the central nervous system's activity and include caffeine, nicotine, amphetamines, cocaine, and MDMA (Ecstasy). Hallucinogens modify a person's perceptual experiences and produce visual images that are not real. Marijuana has a mild hallucinogenic effect; LSD has a strong one.

KEY TERMS

psychoactive drugs   169
tolerance   169
physical dependence   169
psychological
    dependence   169
addiction   169
depressants   171

alcoholism   172
barbiturates   173
tranquilizers   173
opiates   173
stimulants   173
hallucinogens   177

TEST YOURSELF

1. What are psychoactive drugs, and for what reasons do people use them?

2. Describe what stimulants and depressants are, and give three examples of each.

3. What are hallucinogens? What are two common examples of hallucinogens?

APPLY YOUR KNOWLEDGE

1. Go on a caffeine hunt. Check out the ingredient lists for the beverages, painkillers, and snacks you typically consume. Which contain caffeine? Are you surprised how much caffeine you ingest regularly?

2. Identify a Hollywood celebrity who has been addicted to a psychoactive drug. Name the celebrity and his or her drug of choice. Based on your understanding of that drug, describe how the celebrity might behave while under the influence of that drug. What might be some withdrawal effects this celebrity will experience if he/she stops using the drug?

Hypnosis

Fifty-three-year-old Shelley Thomas entered a London Hospital for a 30-minute pelvic surgery. Before the operation, with her hypnotherapist guiding her, Shelley counted backward from 100 and entered a hypnotic trance. Her surgery was performed with no anesthesia (Song, 2006); rather, Shelley relied on hypnosis to harness her mind's powers to overcome pain.

You may have seen a hypnotist on TV or in a nightclub, putting a person into a trance and then perhaps making the individual act like a chicken or pretend to be a contestant on *American Idol* or enact some similarly strange behavior. When we observe someone in such a trance, we might be convinced that hypnosis involves a powerful manipulation of another person's consciousness. What is hypnosis, really? The answer to this question is itself the source of some debate.

Some psychologists think of hypnosis as an altered state of consciousness, while others believe that it is simply a product of more mundane processes such as focused attention and expectation (Lynn, Boycheva, & Barnes, 2008; Posner & Rothbart, 2010; Rossi, 2009). In fact, both views are reasonable, and we may define **hypnosis** as an altered state of consciousness or as a psychological state of altered attention and expectation in which the individual is unusually receptive to suggestions. People have used basic hypnotic techniques since the beginning of recorded history, in association with religious ceremonies, magic, and the supernatural.

© Tony Zuvela. www.CartoonStock.com.

● **hypnosis** An altered state of consciousness or a psychological state of altered attention and expectation in which the individual is unusually receptive to suggestions.

16-1 THE NATURE OF HYPNOSIS

When Shelley Thomas was in a hypnotic trance, what exactly was happening in her brain? Patterns of brain activity during the hypnotic state suggest that hypnosis produces a state of consciousness similar to other states of consciousness. For example, individuals in a hypnotic state display a predominance of alpha and beta waves, characteristic of persons in a relaxed waking state, when monitored by an EEG (Cavallaro & others, 2010; Graffin, Ray, & Lundy, 1995). In a brain-imaging study, widespread areas of the cerebral cortex—including the occipital lobes, parietal lobes, sensorimotor cortex, and prefrontal cortex—were activated when individuals were in a hypnotic state (Faymonville, Boly, & Laureys, 2006). A similar activation pattern is found in individuals in a non-hypnotic waking state who are engaging in mental imagery. How does the hypnotist lead people into this state of relaxation and imagery?

The Four Steps in Hypnosis

Hypnosis involves four steps. The hypnotist

1. Minimizes distractions and makes the person to be hypnotized comfortable.
2. Tells the person to concentrate on something specific, such as an imagined scene or the ticking of a watch.
3. Informs the person what to expect in the hypnotic state, such as relaxation or a pleasant floating sensation.
4. Suggests certain events or feelings he or she knows will occur or observes occurring, such as "Your eyes are getting tired." When the suggested effects occur,

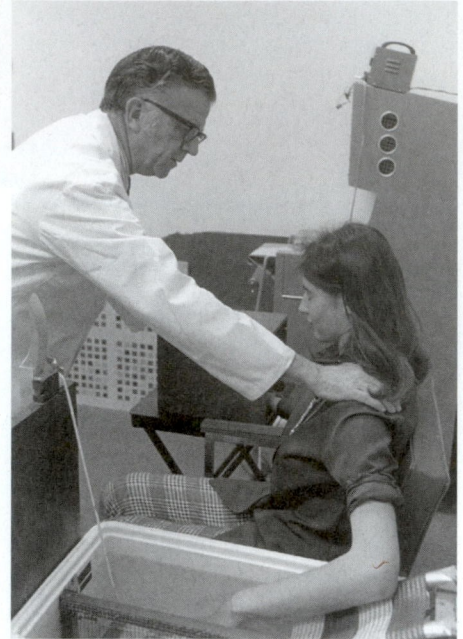

FIGURE 16.1 Divided Consciousness Ernest Hilgard tests a participant in the study in which he had individuals place one arm in ice-cold water.

● **divided consciousness view of hypnosis** Hilgard's view that hypnosis involves a splitting of consciousness into two separate components, one of which follows the hypnotist's commands and the other of which acts as a "hidden observer."

the person interprets them as being caused by the hypnotist's suggestion and accepts them as an indication that something is happening. This increase in the person's expectations that the hypnotist will make things happen in the future makes the person even more suggestible.

Individual Variations in Hypnosis

Some people are more easily hypnotized than others, and some are more strongly influenced by hypnotic suggestions. *Hypnotizability* refers to the extent to which a person's responses *are changed* by being hypnotized (Milling & others, 2010; Raz & others, 2010). There is no easy way to know if a person is hypnotizable without first trying to hypnotize the individual. If you have the capacity to immerse yourself deeply in an imaginative activity—listening to a favorite piece of music or reading a novel, for example—you might be a likely candidate (Spiegel, 2010). Still, the relationship between the ability to become completely absorbed in an experience and hypnotizability is weak (Nash, 2001).

16-2 EXPLAINING HYPNOSIS

How does hypnosis have its effects? Contemporary theorists disagree as to whether hypnosis is a divided state of consciousness or simply a learned social behavior.

A Divided State of Consciousness

Ernest Hilgard (1977, 1992), in his **divided consciousness view of hypnosis,** proposed that hypnosis involves a special divided state of consciousness, a splitting of consciousness into separate components. One component follows the hypnotist's commands, while another component acts as a "hidden observer."

Hilgard placed one hand of hypnotized individuals in a bucket of ice-cold water and told them that they would not feel pain but that a part of their mind—a hidden part that would be aware of what was going on—could signal any true pain by pressing a key with the hand that was not submerged (Figure 16.1). The individuals under hypnosis reported afterward that they had not experienced any pain; yet while their hand had been submerged in the ice-cold water, they had pressed the key with their non-submerged hand, and they had pressed it more frequently the longer their hand was in the cold water. Thus, in Hilgard's view, in hypnosis, consciousness has a hidden part that stays in contact with reality and feels pain while another part of consciousness feels no pain.

Critics of Hilgard's view suggest that the hidden observer simply demonstrates that the hypnotized person is not in an altered state of consciousness at all. From this perspective, the hidden observer is simply the person him- or herself, having been given permission to admit to the pain that he or she was always feeling (Green & others, 2005). This argument is part of the social cognitive behavior view of hypnosis.

Social Cognitive Behavior

● **social cognitive behavior view of hypnosis** Theory that hypnosis is a normal state in which the hypnotized person behaves the way he or she believes that a hypnotized person should behave.

Some experts are skeptical that hypnosis is an altered state of consciousness (Green & others, 2005; Lynn & others, 2010). In the **social cognitive behavior view of hypnosis,** hypnosis is a normal state in which the hypnotized person behaves the way he or she believes that a hypnotized person should behave. The social cognitive perspective frames the important questions about hypnosis around cognitive factors—the attitudes, expectations, and beliefs of good hypnotic participants—and around the powerful social context in which hypnosis occurs (Lynn, 2007; Spanos & Chaves, 1989). Individuals being hypnotized surrender their responsibility to the hypnotist and follow the hypnotist's suggestions; and they have expectations about what hypnosis is supposed to be like.

Experts have continued to debate whether hypnosis is indeed an altered state of consciousness (Kihlstrom, 2005) or simply a reaction to a special social situation (Green & others, 2005). Although there may be no consensus about what hypnosis is, scientists use hypnosis to explore the brain and its functions, and health professionals have begun to apply this powerful technique to a number of problems (Oakley & Halligan, 2010).

16·3 USES OF HYPNOSIS

As psychologists' interest in studying consciousness has grown, hypnosis has emerged as a useful tool (Nash & others, 2009). Some researchers employ hypnosis in a way similar to transcranial magnetic stimulation (described in Module 7), to experimentally dampen brain processes (Cox & Bryant, 2008). Combining hypnosis with brain imaging allows researchers to understand both the effects of hypnosis itself and the brain's functioning (Oakley & Halligan, 2010).

Beyond its role in basic research, hypnosis has been applied to a variety of problems. In the United States, practitioners of hypnosis use the technique to treat alcoholism, somnambulism, depression, suicidal tendencies, post-traumatic stress disorder, migraines, overeating, diabetes, and smoking (Hammond, 2010; Lynn & others, 2010; Nash & others, 2009; Shih, Yang, & Koo, 2009). Whether hypnosis actually works for these various problems remains debatable (D. Brown, 2007). Individuals in these treatment programs rarely achieve dramatic results unless they are already motivated to change. Hypnosis is most effective when combined with psychotherapy (Rossi, 2009).

A long history of research and practice has clearly demonstrated that hypnosis can reduce the experience of pain (Jensen, 2009). A fascinating study examined the pain perceptions of hypnotized individuals, with the goal of changing their pain threshold. In that study, the brains of participants were monitored while they received painful electrical shocks (rated 8 or higher on a 1 to 10 pain scale) (Schulz-Stubner & others, 2004). Those who were hypnotized to find the shocks less painful did rate them as lower in pain (giving them a 3 or less). The brain-scanning results were most interesting: The subcortical brain areas (the brain stem and midbrain) of the hypnotized patients responded the same as those of the patients who were not hypnotized, suggesting that these brain structures recognized the painful stimulation. However, the sensory cortex was not activated in the hypnotized patients, suggesting that although they sensed pain on some level, they were never conscious of it. In essence, the "ouch" signal never made it to awareness.

In summary, although the nature of hypnosis remains a mystery, evidence is increasing that hypnosis can play a role in a variety of health contexts, and it can influence the brain in fascinating ways (Nash & others, 2009). For psychologists, part of the ambiguity about the definition of hypnosis comes from the fact that it has been studied in specific social contexts, involving a hypnotist. It is also possible, however, to experience altered states of consciousness without these special circumstances, as we next consider.

SUMMARY

Hypnosis is a psychological state or possibly altered attention and awareness in which the individual is unusually receptive to suggestions. The hypnotic state is different from a sleep state, as EEG recordings confirm. Inducing hypnosis involves four basic steps, beginning with minimizing distractions and making the person feel comfortable and ending with the

KEY TERMS

hypnosis   181
divided consciousness view
    of hypnosis   182

social cognitive behavior view
    of hypnosis   182

hypnotist's suggesting certain events or feelings that he or she knows will occur or observes occurring.

There are substantial individual variations in people's susceptibility to hypnosis. Two theories have been proposed to explain hypnosis. In Hilgard's divided consciousness view, hypnosis involves a divided state of consciousness, a splitting of consciousness into separate components. One component follows the hypnotist's commands; the other acts as a hidden observer. In the social cognitive behavior view, hypnotized individuals behave the way they believe hypnotized individuals are expected to behave.

TEST YOURSELF

1. What is hypnosis?
2. What are the four steps in hypnosis?
3. Name and describe two different theories about hypnosis.

APPLY YOUR KNOWLEDGE

1. In the television show, *The Mentalist,* Patrick Jane, the CBI consultant, often uses hypnosis to solve cases. Based on your reading, how accurate do you believe the portrayal of hypnosis is in the show? Justify your answer.

2. Have you ever or would you consider being hypnotized? Why or why not? If you have been hypnotized, describe your experience to your fellow classmates and observe their reaction. What conclusions can you draw about people's perceptions of hypnosis?

Consciousness and Health and Wellness: Meditation

The altered consciousness of hypnosis can also be achieved through meditation. *Meditation* involves attaining a peaceful state of mind in which thoughts are not occupied by worry. The meditator is mindfully present to his or her thoughts and feelings but is not consumed by them. Let's look at how meditation can enhance well-being and examine further what it is.

MINDFULNESS MEDITATION

Melissa Munroe, a Canadian woman diagnosed with Hodgkin lymphoma (a cancer of the immune system), was tormented by excruciating pain (Wijesiri, 2005). Seeking ways to cope with the agony, Munroe enrolled in a meditation program. She was skeptical at first. "What I didn't realize," she said, "is that if people have ever found themselves taking a walk in the countryside or in the forest or on a nice pleasant autumn day . . . and find themselves in a contemplative state, that's a form of meditation." Munroe worked hard to use meditation to control her pain. Interestingly, the way she harnessed the power of her mind to overcome pain was by concentrating her thoughts on the pain—not by trying to avoid it.

Using *mindfulness meditation,* a technique practiced by yoga enthusiasts and Buddhist monks, Munroe focused on her pain. By doing so, she was able to isolate the pain from her emotional response to it and to her cancer diagnosis. She grew to see her physical discomfort as bearable. Munroe's success shows that contrary to what a non-meditator might think, meditation is not about avoiding one's thoughts. Indeed, the effort involved in avoidance steers the person away from the contemplative state. Munroe described her thoughts as like people striding by her on the street, walking in the other direction; she explained, "They come closer and closer, then they pass you by."

Jon Kabat-Zinn (2006, 2009) has pioneered the use of meditation techniques in medical settings. Research by Kabat-Zinn and colleagues has demonstrated the beneficial effects of mindfulness meditation for a variety of conditions, including depression, panic attacks, and anxiety (Miller, Fletcher, & Kabat-Zinn, 1995), chronic pain (Kabat-Zinn, Lipworth, & Burney, 1985), and stress and the skin condition psoriasis (Kabat-Zinn & others, 1998). Many of these effects have also been shown to be long-lasting.

As noted in Module 7, Richard Davidson and colleagues (including Jon Kabat-Zinn) studied the brain and immune system changes that might underlie the health and wellness effects of meditation (Davidson & others, 2003). They performed MRIs on the brains of individuals who were in a standard eight-week meditation training program. After the training program and as compared to a control group, those in the meditation program reported reduced anxiety and fewer negative emotions. Furthermore, brain scans revealed that these individuals showed increased activation in the left hemisphere—the "happy brain" described in Module 7. In addition, the meditators showed better immune system response to a flu vaccine (Davidson & others, 2003). These results suggest that our conscious minds may have a role to play in enhancing our psychological and physical health (Chiesa & Serretti, 2010; Goldin, Ramel, & Gross, 2009; Perlman & others, 2010; Zeidan & others, 2010).

Buddhist monks are among the many individuals who gain a higher level of consciousness through meditation.

185

THE MEDITATIVE STATE OF MIND

What actually is the meditative state of mind? As a physiological state, meditation shows qualities of sleep *and* wakefulness, yet it is distinct from both. You may have experienced a state called *hypnagogic reverie*—an overwhelming feeling of wellness right before you fall asleep, the sense that everything is going to work out. Meditation has been compared to this relaxed sense that all is well (Friedman, Myers, & Benson, 1998).

In a study of Zen meditators, researchers examined what happens when people switch from their normal waking state to a meditative state (Ritskes & others, 2003). Using fMRI, the experimenters obtained images of the brain before and after the participants entered the meditative state. They found that the switch to meditation involved initial increases in activation in the basal ganglia and prefrontal cortex (the now familiar area that is often activated during consciousness). However, and interestingly, they also found that these initial activations led to decreases in the anterior cingulate, the brain area noted earlier as associated with conscious awareness and acts of will. These results provide a picture of the physical events of the brain that are connected with the somewhat paradoxical state of meditation—controlling one's thoughts in order to let go of the need to control. Research is also beginning to explore the role of neurotransmitters in meditation (Newberg, 2010).

Regular meditation can help you to clarify your goals and purpose in life, strengthen your values, and improve your outlook.

GETTING STARTED WITH MEDITATION

Would you like to experience the meditative state? If so, you can probably reach that state by following some simple instructions:

- Find a quiet place and a comfortable chair.
- Sit upright in the chair, rest your chin comfortably on your chest, and place your arms in your lap. Close your eyes.
- Now focus on your breathing. Every time you inhale and every time you exhale, pay attention to the sensations of air flowing through your body, the feeling of your lungs filling and emptying.
- After you have focused on several breaths, begin to repeat silently to yourself a single word every time you breathe out. You can make a word up, use the word *one*, or try a word associated with an emotion you want to produce, such as *trust, love, patience,* or *happy*. Experiment with several different words to see which one works best for you.
- If you find that thoughts are intruding and you are no longer attending to your breathing, refocus on your breathing and say your chosen word each time you exhale.

After you have practiced this exercise for 10 to 15 minutes, twice a day, every day for two weeks, you will be ready for a shortened version. If you notice that you are experiencing stressful thoughts or circumstances, simply meditate, on the spot, for several minutes. If you are in public, you do not have to close your eyes; just fix your gaze on a nearby object, attend to your breathing, and say your word silently every time you exhale.

Meditation is an age-old practice. Without explicitly mentioning meditation, some religions advocate related practices such as daily prayer and peaceful introspection. Whether the practice involves praying over rosary beads, chanting before a Buddhist shrine, or taking a moment to commune with nature, a contemplative state clearly has broad appeal and conveys many benefits (Kabat-Zinn, 2009; Travis & Shear, 2010). Current research on the contemplative state suggests that there are good reasons why human beings have been harnessing its beneficial powers for thousands of years.

SUMMARY

Meditation refers to a state of quiet reflection; the practice has benefits for a wide range of psychological and physical illnesses. Meditation can also benefit the body's immune system. Research using fMRI suggests that meditation allows an individual to control his or her thoughts in order to "let go" of the need to control.

Mindfulness meditation is a powerful tool for managing life's problems. How we think about our lives and experiences plays a role in determining whether we feel stressed and worried or challenged and excited about life. Seeking times of quiet contemplation can have a positive impact on our ability to cope with life's ups and downs.

TEST YOURSELF

1. What does the meditator experience during meditation?
2. What changes in the brain and immune system did Davidson and his colleagues discover that might explain meditation's benefits for health and wellness?
3. On what body process does a meditator focus, and how is that focus maintained?

Learning

Sniffer Dogs on Call: Putting Learning to Work in Haiti

On January 12, 2010, a magnitude 7.0 earthquake rocked Haiti. One million people were left homeless, and the estimated deaths topped 200,000. In the quake's aftermath, humanitarian aid poured in. In addition to the throngs of people who rushed to help the island nation, battalions of rescue dogs were dispatched from around the world. Elite teams of humans and dogs from England, China, the United States, Peru, Mexico, Taiwan, and many other nations reported for duty.

The "sniffer" dogs in these teams rely not only on their amazing canine olfactory abilities but also on the months and years of laborious training they receive, geared toward locating survivors trapped under rubble. Indeed, rescue dogs (some of which are themselves "rescued dogs"—that is, adopted from shelters) are rigorously trained animals that have passed a set of strict criteria to earn a place on the special teams. In the United States, the Federal Emergency Management Administration (FEMA) has established strict guidelines for the training of rescue dogs (FEMA, 2003). The dogs must demonstrate mastery of a set of difficult skills, including walking off-leash with a trainer on a crowded city street, without getting distracted, and performing search-and-rescue tasks without immediate practice and without their regular trainer. They must demonstrate their abilities without food rewards (although a toy reward placed on rubble is allowed). Further, these hardworking canines must be recertified every two years to ensure that their skills remain at peak level. In the invaluable work they performed in Haiti, the dogs not only helped with rescue efforts but also raised everyone's spirits with their tirelessness and persistence.

Truly, rescue dogs are nothing less than highly skilled professionals. You might well wonder *how* the dogs are trained to perform these complex acts. It's simple—through the principles that psychologists have uncovered in studying learning, our focus in this set of modules. ●

Types of Learning

Learning anything new involves change. Once you learned the alphabet, it did not leave you; it became part of a "new you" who had been changed through the process of learning. Similarly, once you learn how to drive a car, you do not have to go through the process again at a later time. If you ever try out for the X-Games, you may break a few bones along the way, but at some point you probably will learn a trick or two through the experience, changing from a novice to an enthusiast who can at least stay on top of a skateboard.

By way of experience, too, you may have learned that you have to study to do well on a test, that there usually is an opening act at a rock concert, and that a field goal in U.S. football adds 3 points to the score. Putting these pieces together, we arrive at a definition of **learning**: a systematic, relatively permanent change in behavior that occurs through experience.

If someone were to ask you what you learned in class today, you might mention new ideas you heard about, lists you memorized, or concepts you mastered. However, how would you define learning if you could not refer to unobservable mental processes? You might follow the lead of behavioral psychologists. **Behaviorism** is a theory of learning that focuses solely on observable behaviors, discounting the importance of such mental activity as thinking, wishing, and hoping. Psychologists who examine learning from a behavioral perspective define learning as relatively stable, observable changes in behavior. The behavioral approach has emphasized general laws that guide behavior change and make sense of some of the puzzling aspects of human life (Olson & Hergenhahn, 2009).

Behaviorism maintains that the principles of learning are the same whether we are talking about animals or humans. Because of the influence of behaviorism, psychologists' understanding of learning started with studies of rats, cats, pigeons, and even raccoons. A century of research on learning in animals and in humans suggests that many of the principles generated initially in research on such animals also apply to humans (Domjan, 2010).

● **learning** A systematic, relatively permanent change in behavior that occurs through experience.

● **behaviorism** A theory of learning that focuses solely on observable behaviors, discounting the importance of such mental activity as thinking, wishing, and hoping.

● **associative learning** Learning that occurs when we make a connection, or an association, between two events.

In this module we look at two types of learning: associative learning and observational learning. **Associative learning** occurs when we make a connection, or an association, between two events. *Conditioning* is the process of learning these associations (Chance, 2009; Klein, 2009). There are two types of conditioning—classical and operant—both of which have been studied by behaviorists.

In *classical conditioning,* organisms learn the association between two stimuli. As a result of this association, organisms learn to anticipate events. For example, lightning is associated with thunder and regularly precedes it. Thus, when we see lightning, we anticipate that we will hear thunder soon afterward. In *operant conditioning,* organisms learn the association between a behavior and a consequence, such as a reward. As a result of this association, organisms learn to increase behaviors that are followed by rewards and to decrease behaviors that are followed by punishment. For example, children are likely to repeat their good manners if their parents reward them with candy after they have shown good manners. Also, if children's bad manners are followed by scolding words and harsh glances by parents, the children are less likely to repeat the bad manners. Figure 17.1 compares classical and operant conditioning.

Much of what we learn, however, is not a result of direct consequences but rather of exposure to models performing a behavior or skill (Spiegler & Guevremont, 2010). For instance, as you watch someone shoot baskets, you get a sense of how the shots are made. The learning that takes place when a person observes and imitates another's

Classical Conditioning

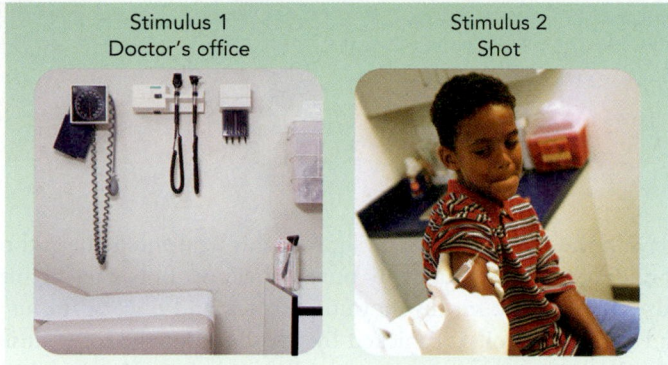

Stimulus 1
Doctor's office

Stimulus 2
Shot

Operant Conditioning

Behavior

Consequences

FIGURE 17.1 **Associative Learning: Comparing Classical and Operant Conditioning** (*Left*) In this example of classical conditioning, a child associates a doctor's office (stimulus 1) with getting a painful injection (stimulus 2). (*Right*) In this example of operant conditioning, performing well in a swimming competition (behavior) becomes associated with getting awards (consequences).

behavior is called **observational learning.** Observational learning is a common way that people learn in educational and other settings. Observational learning is different from the associative learning described by behaviorism because it relies on mental processes: The learner has to pay attention, remember, and reproduce what the model did. Observational learning is especially important to human beings. In fact, watching other people is another way in which human infants acquire skills.

Human infants differ from baby monkeys in their strong reliance on imitation (MacLeod, 2006). After watching an adult model perform a task, a baby monkey will figure out its own way to do it, but a human infant will do exactly what the model did. Imitation may be the human baby's way to solve the huge problem it faces: to learn the vast amount of cultural knowledge that is part of human life. Many of our behaviors are rather arbitrary. Why do we clap to show approval or wave "hello" or "bye-bye"? The human infant has a lot to learn and may be well served to follow the old adage, "When in Rome, do as the Romans do."

Learning applies to many areas of acquiring new behaviors, skills, and knowledge (Mayer, 2011). Our focus in this section is on the two types of associative learning—classical conditioning (Module 18) and operant conditioning (Module 19)—and on observational learning (Module 20).

● **observational learning** Learning that occurs when a person observes and imitates another's behavior.

SUMMARY

Learning is a systematic, relatively permanent change in behavior that occurs through experience. Associative learning involves learning by making a connection between two events. Observational learning is learning by watching what other people do. Conditioning is the process by which associative learning occurs. In classical conditioning, organisms learn the association between two stimuli. In operant conditioning, they learn the association between behavior and a consequence.

KEY TERMS

learning 190
behaviorism 190

associative learning 190
observational learning 191

TEST YOURSELF

1. What is associative learning?
2. What is conditioning? What two types of conditioning have behavioral psychologists studied?
3. What is observational learning? Give two examples of it.

APPLY YOUR KNOWLEDGE

1. Take a few hours out of your day and go to the nearest mall, park, or public area. Bring a notepad and pencil and take notes on people's behaviors. After you record your observations, draw some conclusions as to how these people may have learned to behave in such ways.

2. In your psychology class, identify one thing that you have learned so far. How do you know you have learned that material?

Classical Conditioning

Early one morning, Bob is in the shower. While he showers, his wife enters the bathroom and flushes the toilet. Scalding hot water suddenly bursts down on Bob, causing him to yell in pain. The next day, Bob is back for his morning shower, and once again his wife enters the bathroom and flushes the toilet. Panicked by the sound of the toilet flushing, Bob yelps in fear and jumps out of the shower stream. Bob's panic at the sound of the toilet illustrates the learning process of **classical conditioning,** in which a neutral stimulus (the sound of a toilet flushing) becomes associated with a meaningful stimulus (the pain of scalding hot water) and acquires the capacity to elicit a similar response (panic).

● **classical conditioning** Learning process in which a neutral stimulus becomes associated with a meaningful stimulus and acquires the capacity to elicit a similar response.

18·1 PAVLOV'S STUDIES

Even before beginning this course, you might have heard about Pavlov's dogs. The work of the Russian physiologist Ivan Pavlov is well known. Still, it is easy to take its true significance for granted. Importantly, Pavlov demonstrated that neutral aspects of the environment can attain the capacity to evoke responses through pairing with other stimuli and that bodily processes can be influenced by environmental cues.

In the early 1900s, Pavlov was interested in the way the body digests food. In his experiments, he routinely placed meat powder in a dog's mouth, causing the dog to salivate. By accident, Pavlov noticed that the meat powder was not the only stimulus that caused the dog to salivate. The dog salivated in response to a number of stimuli associated with the food, such as the sight of the food dish, the sight of the individual who brought the food into the room, and the sound of the door closing when the food arrived. Pavlov recognized that the dog's association of these sights and sounds with the food was an important type of learning, which came to be called *classical conditioning.*

Pavlov wanted to know *why* the dog salivated in reaction to various sights and sounds before eating the meat powder. He observed that the dog's behavior included both unlearned and learned components. The unlearned part of classical conditioning is based

Pavlov (the white-bearded gentleman in the center) is shown demonstrating the nature of classical conditioning to students at the Military Medical Academy in Russia.

on the fact that some stimuli automatically produce certain responses apart from any prior learning; in other words, they are inborn (innate). *Reflexes* are such automatic stimulus–response connections. They include salivation in response to food, nausea in response to spoiled food, shivering in response to low temperature, coughing in response to throat congestion, pupil constriction in response to light, and withdrawal in response to pain.

An **unconditioned stimulus (UCS)** is a stimulus that produces a response without prior learning; food was the UCS in Pavlov's experiments. An **unconditioned response (UCR)** is an unlearned reaction that is automatically elicited by the UCS. Unconditioned responses are involuntary; they happen in response to a stimulus without conscious effort. In Pavlov's experiment, salivating in response to food was the UCR. In the case of Bob and the flushing toilet, Bob's learning and experience did not cause him to shriek when the hot water hit his body. His cry of pain was unlearned and occurred automatically. The hot water was the UCS, and Bob's panic was the UCR.

In classical conditioning, a **conditioned stimulus (CS)** is a previously neutral stimulus that eventually elicits a conditioned response after being paired with the unconditioned stimulus. The **conditioned response (CR)** is the learned response to the conditioned stimulus that occurs after CS–UCS pairing (Pavlov, 1927). Sometimes conditioned responses are quite similar to unconditioned responses, but typically they are not as strong.

In studying a dog's response to various stimuli associated with meat powder, Pavlov rang a bell before giving meat powder to the dog. Until then, ringing the bell did not have a particular effect on the dog, except perhaps to wake the dog from a nap. The bell was a neutral stimulus. However, the dog began to associate the sound of the bell with the food and salivated when it heard the bell. The bell had become a conditioned (learned) stimulus (CS), and salivation was now a conditioned response (CR). In the case of Bob's interrupted shower, the sound of the toilet flushing was the CS, and panicking was the CR after the scalding water (UCS) and the flushing sound (CS) were paired. Figure 18.1 summarizes how classical conditioning works.

● **unconditioned stimulus (UCS)** A stimulus that produces a response without prior learning.

● **unconditioned response (UCR)** An unlearned reaction that is automatically elicited by the unconditioned stimulus.

● **conditioned stimulus (CS)** A previously neutral stimulus that eventually elicits a conditioned response after being paired with the unconditioned stimulus.

● **conditioned response (CR)** The learned response to the conditioned stimulus that occurs after conditioned stimulus–unconditioned stimulus pairing.

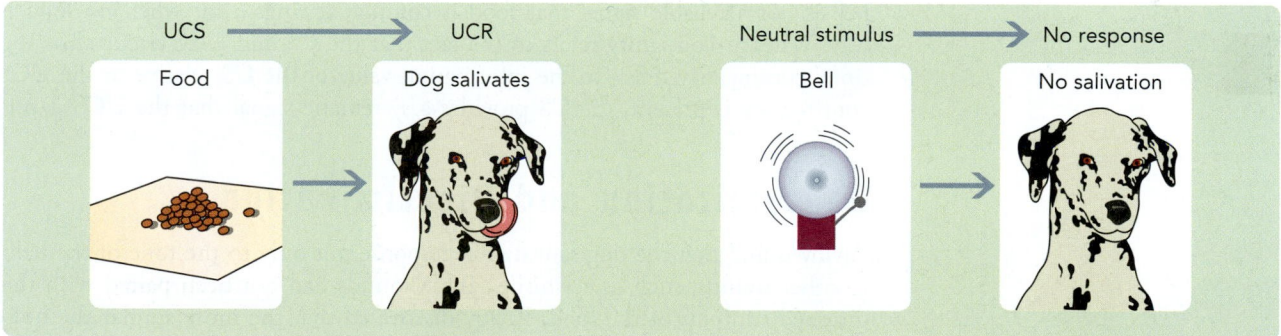

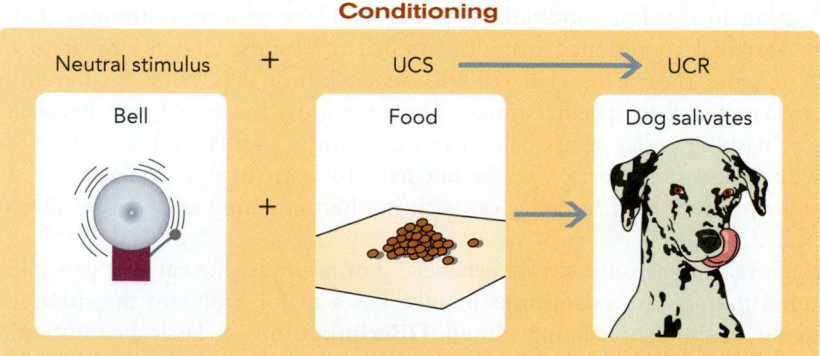

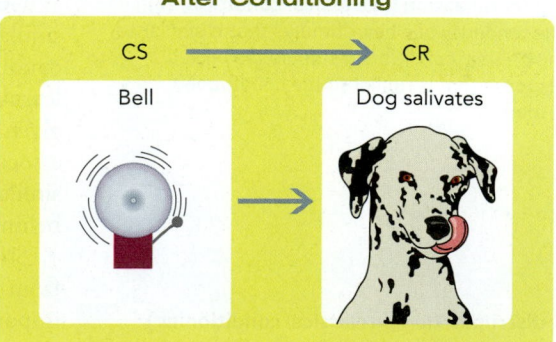

FIGURE 18.1 **Pavlov's Classical Conditioning** In one experiment, Pavlov presented a neutral stimulus (bell) just before an unconditioned stimulus (food). The neutral stimulus became a conditioned stimulus by being paired with the unconditioned stimulus. Subsequently, the conditioned stimulus (bell) by itself was able to elicit the dog's salivation.

© Harley Schwadron. www.CartoonStock.com.

● **acquisition** The initial learning of the connection between the unconditioned stimulus and the conditioned stimulus when these two stimuli are paired.

Researchers have shown that salivation can be used as a conditioned response not only in dogs and humans but also in, of all things, cockroaches (Watanabe & Mizunami, 2007). These researchers paired the smell of peppermint (the CS, which was applied to the cockroaches' antennae) with sugary water (the UCS). Cockroaches naturally salivate (the UCR) in response to sugary foods, and after repeated pairings between peppermint smell and sugary water, the cockroaches salivated in response to the smell of peppermint (the CR). When they collected and measured the cockroach saliva, the researchers found that the cockroaches had slobbered over that smell for two minutes.

Acquisition

Whether it is human beings, dogs, or cockroaches, the first part of classical conditioning is called acquisition. **Acquisition** is the initial learning of the connection between the UCS and CS when these two stimuli are paired (as with the smell of peppermint and the sugary water). During acquisition, the CS is repeatedly presented followed by the UCS. Eventually, the CS will produce a response. Note that classical conditioning is a type of learning that occurs without awareness or effort, based on the presentation of two stimuli together. For this pairing to work, however, two important factors must be present: contiguity and contingency.

Contiguity simply means that the CS and UCS are presented very close together in time—even a mere fraction of a second (Wheeler & Miller, 2008). In Pavlov's work, if the bell had rung 20 minutes before the presentation of the food, the dog probably would not have associated the bell with the food. However, pairing the CS and UCS close together in time is not all that is needed for conditioning to occur.

Contingency means that the CS must not only precede the UCS closely in time, it must also serve as a reliable indicator that the UCS is on its way (Rescorla, 1966, 1988, 2009). To get a sense of the importance of contingency, imagine that the dog in Pavlov's experiment is exposed to a ringing bell at random times all day long. Whenever the dog receives food, the delivery of the food always immediately follows a bell ring. However, in this situation, the dog will not associate the bell with the food, because the bell is not a reliable signal that food is coming: It rings a lot when no food is on the way. Whereas contiguity refers to the fact that the CS and UCS occur close together in time, contingency refers to the information value of the CS relative to the UCS. When contingency is present, the CS provides a systematic signal that the UCS is on its way.

Generalization and Discrimination

Pavlov found that the dog salivated in response not only to the tone of the bell but also to other sounds, such as a whistle. These sounds had not been paired with the unconditioned stimulus of the food. Pavlov discovered that the more similar the noise was to the original sound of the bell, the stronger the dog's salivary flow.

Generalization in classical conditioning is the tendency of a new stimulus that is similar to the original conditioned stimulus to elicit a response that is similar to the conditioned response (Pearce & Hall, 2009). Generalization has value in preventing learning from being tied to specific stimuli. Once we learn the association between a given CS (say, flashing police lights behind our car) and a particular UCS (the dread associated with being pulled over), we do not have to learn it all over again when a similar stimulus presents itself (a police car with its siren moaning as it cruises directly behind our car).

Stimulus generalization is not always beneficial. For example, the cat that generalizes from a harmless minnow to a dangerous piranha has a major problem; therefore, it is important to also discriminate among stimuli. **Discrimination** in classical conditioning is the process of learning to respond to certain stimuli and not others. To produce discrimination, Pavlov gave food to the dog only after ringing the bell and not after any other sounds. In this way, the dog learned to distinguish between the bell and other sounds.

● **generalization (in classical conditioning)** The tendency of a new stimulus that is similar to the original conditioned stimulus to elicit a response that is similar to the conditioned response.

● **discrimination (in classical conditioning)** The process of learning to respond to certain stimuli and not others.

psychological *inquiry*

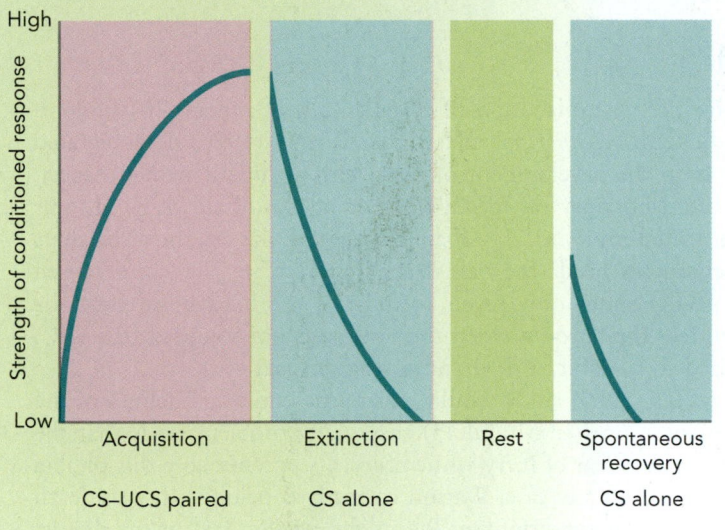

From Acquisition to Extinction (to Spontaneous Recovery)

The figure illustrates the strength of a conditioned response (CR), shown on the Y or vertical axis, across the stages from acquisition, to extinction, to a rest period, and finally to spontaneous recovery. Using the graphs, answer the following questions.

1. What happens to the unconditioned stimulus (UCS) and the conditioned stimulus (CS) during acquisition, and how does this influence the conditioned response (CR)?

2. When is the CR strongest and when is it weakest?

3. What happens to the UCS and CS during extinction, and how does this influence the CR?

4. Notice that spontaneous recovery occurs after a rest period. Why is this rest necessary?

5. In your own life, what are some CS's that are attached to CR's for you? Trace them through these steps.

Extinction and Spontaneous Recovery

After conditioning the dog to salivate at the sound of a bell, Pavlov rang the bell repeatedly in a single session and did not give the dog any food. Eventually the dog stopped salivating. This result is **extinction**, which in classical conditioning is the weakening of the conditioned response when the unconditioned stimulus is absent (Kim & others, 2010). Without continued association with the unconditioned stimulus (UCS), the conditioned stimulus (CS) loses its power to produce the conditioned response (CR).

Extinction is not always the end of a conditioned response (Urcelay, Wheeler, & Miller, 2009). The day after Pavlov extinguished the conditioned salivation to the sound of a bell, he took the dog to the laboratory and rang the bell but still did not give the dog any meat powder. The dog salivated, indicating that an extinguished response can spontaneously recur. **Spontaneous recovery** is the process in classical conditioning by which a conditioned response can recur after a time delay, without further conditioning (Rescorla, 2005; Gershman, Blei, & Niv, 2010). Consider an example of spontaneous recovery you may have experienced: You thought that you had forgotten about (extinguished) an ex-girlfriend or boyfriend, but then you found yourself in a particular context (perhaps the restaurant where you used to dine together), and you suddenly got a mental image of your ex, accompanied by an emotional reaction to him or her from the past (spontaneous recovery).

The steps in classical conditioning are reviewed in the Psychological Inquiry. The figure in the feature shows the sequence of acquisition, extinction, and spontaneous recovery. Spontaneous recovery can occur several times, but as long as the conditioned stimulus is presented alone (that is, without the unconditioned stimulus), spontaneous recovery becomes weaker and eventually ceases.

Extinction is not always the end of a conditioned response. **Renewal** refers to the recovery of the conditioned response when the organism is placed in a novel context (Gershman, Blei, & Niv, 2010). Renewal can be a powerful problem to overcome—as it is when a person leaves a drug treatment facility to return to his or her previous living situation (Stasiewicz, Brandon, & Bardizza, 2007). Indeed, drug addiction is one of the many human issues to which classical conditioning has been applied (Reichel & Bevins, 2010).

● **extinction (in classical conditioning)** The weakening of the conditioned response when the unconditioned stimulus is absent.

● **spontaneous recovery** The process in classical conditioning by which a conditioned response can recur after a time delay, without further conditioning.

● **renewal** The recovery of the conditioned response when the organism is placed in a novel context.

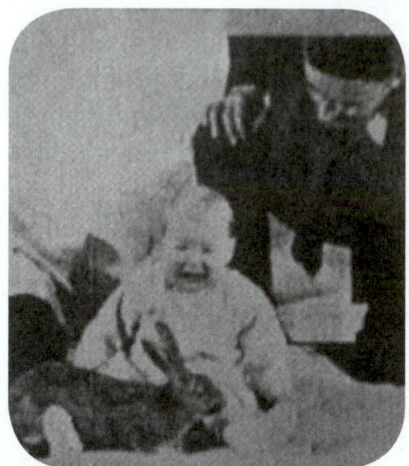

Watson and Rayner conditioned 11-month-old Albert to fear a white rat by pairing the rat with a loud noise. When little Albert was later presented with other stimuli similar to the white rat, such as the rabbit shown here with Albert, he was afraid of them too. This study illustrates stimulus generalization in classical conditioning.

18-2 CLASSICAL CONDITIONING IN HUMANS

Classical conditioning has a great deal of survival value for human beings (Powell, Symbaluk, & Honey, 2009). Here we review examples of classical conditioning at work in human life.

Explaining Fears

Classical conditioning provides an explanation of fears (Lissek & others, 2010). John B. Watson (who coined the term *behaviorism*) and Rosalie Rayner (1920) demonstrated classical conditioning's role in the development of fears with an infant named Albert. They showed Albert a white laboratory rat to see whether he was afraid of it. He was not (so the rat is a neutral stimulus or CS). As Albert played with the rat, the researchers sounded a loud noise behind his head (the bell is then the UCS). The noise caused little Albert to cry (the UCR). After only seven pairings of the loud noise with the white rat, Albert began to fear the rat even when the noise was not sounded (the CR). Albert's fear was generalized to a rabbit, a dog, and a sealskin coat.

Today, Watson and Rayner's (1920) study would violate the ethical guidelines of the American Psychological Association (see Module 5). Especially problematic is that the researchers did not reverse Albert's fear of furry white objects, so presumably this phobia remained with him into old age. In any case, Watson correctly concluded that we learn many of our fears through classical conditioning. We might develop fear of the dentist because of a painful experience, fear of driving after having been in a car crash, and fear of dogs after having been bitten by one.

If we can learn fears through classical conditioning, we also can possibly unlearn them through that process (Maier & Seligman, 2009; Ohman, 2010; Powell, Symbaluk, & Honey, 2009). In Module 65, for example, we will examine the application of classical conditioning to therapies for treating phobias.

Breaking Habits

● **counterconditioning** A classical conditioning procedure for changing the relationship between a conditioned stimulus and its conditioned response.

● **aversive conditioning** A form of treatment that consists of repeated pairings of a stimulus with a very unpleasant stimulus.

Counterconditioning is a classical conditioning procedure for changing the relationship between a conditioned stimulus and its conditioned response. Therapists have used counterconditioning to break apart the association between certain stimuli and positive feelings (Brunborg & others, 2010). **Aversive conditioning** is a form of treatment that consists of repeated pairings of a stimulus with a very unpleasant stimulus. Electric shocks and nausea-inducing substances are examples of noxious stimuli that are used in aversive conditioning (Sommer & others, 2006).

To reduce drinking, for example, every time a person drinks an alcoholic beverage, he or she also consumes a mixture that induces nausea. In classical conditioning terminology, the alcoholic beverage is the conditioned stimulus and the nausea-inducing agent is the unconditioned stimulus. Through a repeated pairing of alcohol with the nausea-inducing agent, alcohol becomes the conditioned stimulus that elicits nausea, the conditioned response. As a consequence, alcohol no longer is associated with something pleasant but rather something highly unpleasant. Antabuse, a drug treatment for alcoholism since the late 1940s, is based on this association (Ullman, 1952). When someone takes this drug, ingesting even the smallest amount of alcohol will make the person quite ill, even if the exposure to the alcohol is through mouthwash or cologne.

Classical Conditioning and the Placebo Effect

The *placebo effect* is the effect of a substance or procedure (such as taking a pill) that is used as a control to identify the actual effects of a treatment. Placebo effects are observable changes (such as a drop in pain) that cannot be explained by the effects of an actual treatment. The principles of classical conditioning can help to explain some of these effects (Price, Finniss, & Benedetti, 2008). In this case, the pill or syringe serves as a CS and the actual drug is the UCS. After the experience of pain relief following the consumption of a drug, for instance, the pill or syringe might lead to a CR of lowered pain even in the absence of actual painkiller. The strongest evidence for the role of classical conditioning on placebo effects comes from research on the immune system and the endocrine system.

Classical Conditioning and the Immune and Endocrine Systems

Even the human body's internal organ systems can be classically conditioned. The immune system is the body's natural defense against disease. Robert Ader and Nicholas Cohen have conducted a number of studies that reveal that classical conditioning can produce *immunosuppression,* a decrease in the production of antibodies, which can lower a person's ability to fight disease (Ader, 2000; Ader & Cohen, 1975, 2000).

The initial discovery of this link between classical conditioning and immunosuppression came as a surprise. In studying classical conditioning, Ader (1974) was examining how long a conditioned response would last in some laboratory rats. He paired a conditioned stimulus (saccharin solution) with an unconditioned stimulus, a drug called Cytoxan, which induces nausea. Afterward, while giving the rats saccharin-laced water without the accompanying Cytoxan, Ader watched to see how long it would take the rats to forget the association between the two.

Unexpectedly, in the second month of the study, the rats developed a disease and began to die off. In analyzing this unforeseen result, Ader looked into the properties of the nausea-inducing drug he had used. He discovered that one of its side effects was immunosuppression. It turned out that the rats had been classically conditioned to associate sweet water not only with nausea but also with the shutdown of the immune system. The sweet water apparently had become a conditioned stimulus for immunosuppression.

Researchers have found that conditioned immune responses also occur in humans (Ader, 2000; Goebel & others, 2002; Olness & Ader, 1992). For example, in one study, patients with multiple sclerosis were given a flavored drink prior to receiving a drug that suppressed the immune system. After this pairing, the flavored drink by itself lowered immune functioning, similarly to the drug (Giang & others, 1996).

Similar results have been found for the endocrine system. The endocrine system is a loosely organized set of glands that produce and circulate hormones. Research has shown that placebo pills can influence the secretion of hormones if patients had previous experiences with pills containing actual drugs that affected hormone secretion (Benedetti & others, 2003). Studies have revealed that the sympathetic nervous system (the part of the autonomic nervous systems that responds to stress) plays an important role in the learned associations between conditioned stimuli and immune and endocrine functioning (Saurer & others, 2008).

Taste Aversion Learning

Consider this scenario. Mike goes out for sushi with some friends and eats tekka maki (tuna roll), his favorite dish. He then proceeds to a jazz concert. Several hours later, he becomes very ill with stomach pains and nausea. A few weeks later, he tries to eat tekka maki again but cannot stand it. Importantly, Mike does not experience an aversion to jazz, even though he attended the jazz concert that night before getting sick. Mike's experience exemplifies *taste aversion*: a special kind of classical conditioning involving the learned association between a particular taste and nausea (Bernstein & Koh, 2007; Davis & Riley, 2010; Garcia & Koelling 1966).

Taste aversion is special because it typically requires only one pairing of a neutral stimulus (a taste) with the unconditioned response of nausea to seal that connection, often for a very long time. As we consider later, it is highly adaptive to learn taste aversion in only one trial. An animal that required multiple pairings of taste with poison would likely not survive the acquisition phase. It is notable, though, that taste aversion can occur even if the "taste" had nothing to do with getting sick—perhaps, in Mike's case, he was simply coming down with a stomach bug. Taste aversion can even occur when a person has been sickened by a completely separate event, such as being spun around in a chair (Klosterhalfen & others, 2000).

Taste aversion learning is particularly important in the context of the traditional treatment of some cancers. Radiation and the chemical treatment of cancer often produce nausea in patients, with the result that cancer patients sometimes develop strong aversions to many foods that they ingest prior to treatment (Holmes, 1993; Jacobsen & others, 1993). Consequently, they may experience a general tendency to be turned off by food, a situation that can lead to nutritional deficits (Hutton, Baracos, & Wismer, 2007).

Researchers have used classical conditioning principles to combat these taste aversions, especially in children, for whom antinausea medication is often ineffective (Skolin & others, 2006) and for whom aversions to protein-rich food is particularly problematic (Ikeda & others, 2006). Early studies demonstrated that giving children a "scapegoat" conditioned stimulus prior to chemotherapy would help contain the taste aversion to only one flavor (Broberg & Bernstein, 1987). For example, children might be given a particular flavor of Lifesaver candy or ice cream before receiving treatment. For these children, the nausea would be more strongly associated with the Lifesaver or ice cream flavor than with the foods they needed to eat for good nutrition. These results show discrimination in classical conditioning—the kids developed aversions only to the specific scapegoat flavors.

Classical Conditioning and Advertising

Classical conditioning provides the foundation for many of the commercials that we are bombarded with daily. (Appropriately, when John Watson, whom you will recall from the baby Albert study, left the field of psychology, he went on to advertising.) Think about it: Advertising involves creating an association between a product and pleasant feelings (buy that Grande Misto and be happy). TV advertisers cunningly apply classical conditioning principles to consumers by showing ads that pair something positive—such as a beautiful woman (a UCS) producing pleasant feelings (a UCR)—with a product (a CS) in hopes that you, the viewer, will experience those positive feelings toward the product (CR). Have you seen the Hardee's ad showing Padma Lakshmi in a low-cut dress (the UCS) eating a giant, messy hamburger (the CS)?

Drug Habituation

Over time, a person might develop a tolerance for a psychoactive drug and need a higher and higher dose of the substance to get the same effect. Classical conditioning helps to explain **habituation,** which refers to the decreased responsiveness to a stimulus after repeated presentations. A mind-altering drug is an unconditioned stimulus: It naturally produces a response in the person's body. This unconditioned stimulus is often paired systematically with a previously neutral stimulus (CS). For instance, the physical appearance of the drug in a pill or syringe, and the room where the person takes the drugs, are conditioned stimuli that are paired with the UCS of the drug. These repeated pairings should produce a conditioned response, and they do—but it is different from those we have considered so far.

The conditioned response to a drug can be the body's way of *preparing* for the effects of a drug (Rachlin & Green, 2009). In this case, the body braces itself for the effects of the drug with a CR that is the opposite of the UCR. For instance, if the drug (the UCS) leads to an increase in heart rate (the UCR), the CR might be a drop in heart rate. The CS serves as a warning that the drug is coming, and the conditioned response

● **habituation** Decreased responsiveness to a stimulus after repeated presentations.

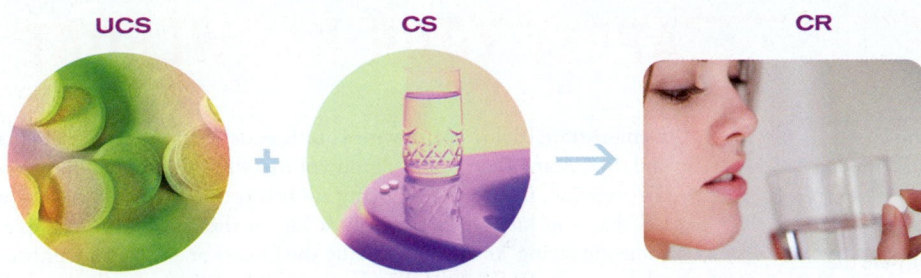

UCS

CS

CR

The psychoactive drug is an unconditioned stimulus (UCS) because it naturally produces a response in a person's body.

Appearance of the drug tablets and the room where the person takes the drug are conditioned stimuli (CS) that are paired with the drug (UCS).

The body prepares to receive the drug in the room. Repeated pairings of the UCS and CS have produced a conditioned response (CR).

FIGURE 18.2 **Drug Habituation** The figure illustrates how classical conditioning is involved in drug habituation. As a result of conditioning, the drug user will need to take more of the drug to get the same effect as the person did before the conditioning. Moreover, if the user takes the drug without the usual conditioned stimulus or stimuli—represented in the middle panel by the bathroom and the drug tablets—overdosing is likely.

in this case is the body's compensation for the drug's effects (Figure 18.2). In this situation the conditioned response works to decrease the effects of the UCS, making the drug experience less intense. Some drug users try to prevent habituation by varying the physical location of where they take the drug.

This aspect of drug use can play a role in deaths caused by drug overdoses. How might classical conditioning be involved? A user typically takes a drug in a particular setting, such as a bathroom, and acquires a conditioned response to this location (Siegel, 1988). Because of classical conditioning, as soon as the drug user walks into the bathroom, his or her body begins to prepare for and anticipate the drug dose in order to lessen the effect of the drug. However, if the user takes the drug in a location other than the usual one, such as at a rock concert, the drug's effect is greater because no conditioned responses have built up in the new setting, and therefore the body is not prepared for the drug. In cases in which heroin causes death, researchers often have found that the individuals took the drug under unusual circumstances, at a different time, or in a different place relative to the context in which they usually took the drug (Marlow, 1999). In these cases, with no CS signal, the body is unprepared for (and tragically overwhelmed by) the drug's effects.

SUMMARY

Classical conditioning occurs when a neutral stimulus becomes associated with a meaningful stimulus and comes to elicit a similar response. Pavlov discovered that an organism learns the association between an unconditioned stimulus (UCS) and a conditioned stimulus (CS). The UCS automatically produces the unconditioned response (UCR). After conditioning (CS–UCS pairing), the CS elicits the conditioned response (CR) by itself. Acquisition in classical conditioning is the initial linking of stimuli and responses, which involves a neutral stimulus being associated with the UCS so that the CS comes to elicit the CR. Two important aspects of acquisition are contiguity and contingency.

Generalization in classical conditioning is the tendency of a new stimulus that is similar to the original conditioned stimulus to elicit a response that is similar to the conditioned response. Discrimination is the process of learning to respond to certain stimuli and not to others. Extinction is the weakening of the CR in the absence of the UCS. Spontaneous recovery is the recurrence of a CR after a time delay without further conditioning. Renewal is the occurrence of the CR (even after extinction) when the CS is presented in a novel environment.

In humans, classical conditioning has been applied to eliminating fears, treating addiction, understanding taste aversion, and explaining such different experiences as pleasant emotions and drug overdose.

KEY TERMS

classical conditioning 192
unconditioned stimulus (UCS) 193
unconditioned response (UCR) 193
conditioned stimulus (CS) 193
conditioned response (CR) 193
acquisition 194
generalization (in classical conditioning) 194

discrimination (in classical conditioning) 194
extinction (in classical conditioning) 195
spontaneous recovery 195
renewal 195
counterconditioning 196
aversive conditioning 196
habituation 198

TEST YOURSELF

1. What is meant by an unconditioned stimulus (UCS) and an unconditioned response (UCR)? In Pavlov's experiments with dogs, what were the UCS and UCR?

2. What is meant by a conditioned stimulus (CS) and a conditioned response (CR)? In Pavlov's experiments with dogs, what were the CS and the CR?

3. What learning principle does the Watson and Rayner study with baby Albert illustrate?

APPLY YOUR KNOWLEDGE

1. Demonstrate Pavlov's work with your friends. First buy some lemons and slice them. Then gather a group of friends to watch something on TV together, maybe the Academy Awards or the Super Bowl. Pick a CS that you know will come up a lot on the show—for example, someone saying "thank you" during the Oscars or a soft drink or beer ad during the Super Bowl. For the first half hour, everyone has to suck on a lemon slice (the UCS) when the CS is presented. After the first half hour, take the lemons away. Have everyone report on their salivation levels (the CR) whenever the CS is presented later in the show. What happens?

2. Identify one food you do not like. Then, using what you've learned about classical conditioning, explain how you have learned to not like that food. How could you use counterconditioning to combat the effects of this taste aversion?

Operant Conditioning

Classical conditioning and operant conditioning are forms of associative learning, which involves learning that two events are connected. In classical conditioning, organisms learn the association between two stimuli (UCS and CS). Classical conditioning is a form of *respondent behavior,* behavior that occurs in automatic response to a stimulus such as a nausea-producing drug, and later to a conditioned stimulus such as sweet water that was paired with the drug.

Classical conditioning explains how neutral stimuli become associated with unlearned, *involuntary responses.* Classical conditioning is not as effective, however, in explaining *voluntary behaviors* such as a student's studying hard for a test, a gambler's playing slot machines in Las Vegas, or a dog's searching for and finding his owner's lost cell phone. Operant conditioning is usually much better than classical conditioning at explaining such voluntary behaviors.

19·1 DEFINING OPERANT CONDITIONING

Operant conditioning or *instrumental conditioning* is a form of associative learning in which the consequences of a behavior change the probability of the behavior's occurrence. American psychologist B. F. Skinner (1938) chose the term *operant* to describe the behavior of the organism. An operant behavior occurs spontaneously. According to Skinner, the consequences that follow such spontaneous behaviors determine whether the behavior will be repeated.

Imagine, for example, that you spontaneously decide to take a different route while driving to campus one day. You are more likely to repeat that route on another day if you have a pleasant experience—for instance, arriving at school faster or finding a new coffee place to try—than if you have a lousy experience such as getting stuck in traffic. In either case, the consequences of your spontaneous act influence whether that behavior happens again.

Recall that *contingency* is an important aspect of classical conditioning in which the occurrence of one stimulus can be predicted from the presence of another one. Contingency also plays a key role in operant conditioning. For example, when a rat pushes a lever (behavior) that delivers food, the delivery of food (consequence) is *contingent* on that behavior. This principle of contingency helps explain why passersby should never praise, pet, or feed a service dog while he is working (at least without asking first). Providing rewards during such times might interfere with the dog's training.

19·2 THORNDIKE'S LAW OF EFFECT

Although Skinner emerged as the primary figure in operant conditioning, the experiments of E. L. Thorndike (1898) established the power of consequences in determining voluntary behavior. At about the same time that Pavlov was conducting classical conditioning experiments with salivating dogs, Thorndike, another American psychologist, was studying cats in puzzle boxes. Thorndike put a hungry cat inside a box and placed a piece of fish outside. To escape from the box and obtain the food, the cat had to learn to open the latch inside the box. At first the cat made a number of ineffective responses. It clawed or bit at the bars and thrust its paw through the openings. Eventually the cat accidentally stepped on the lever

● **operant conditioning** Also called instrumental conditioning, a form of associative learning in which the consequences of a behavior change the probability of the behavior's occurrence.

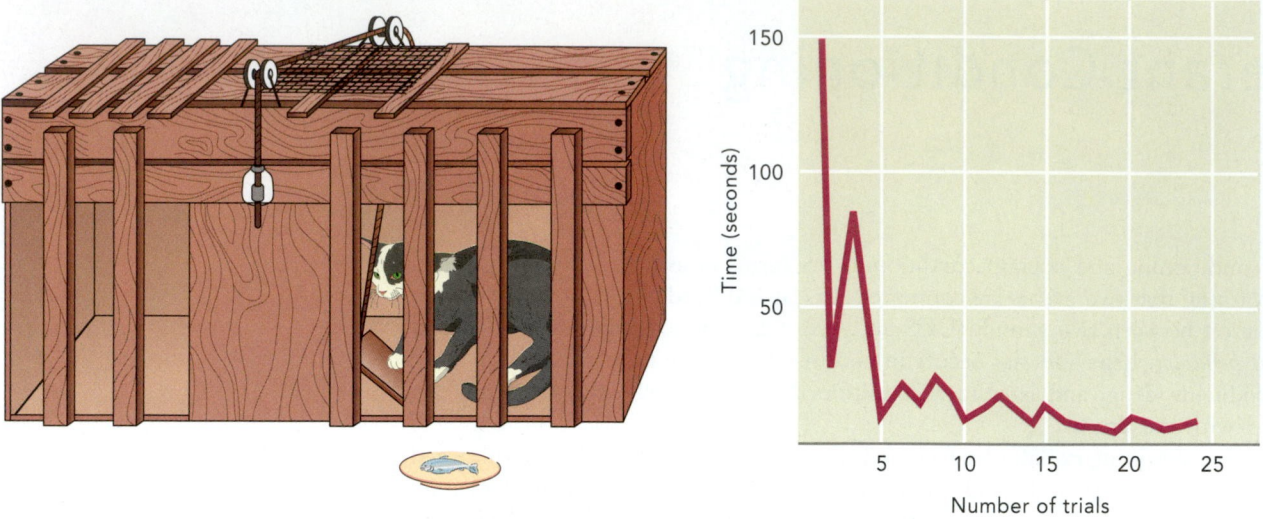

FIGURE 19.1 **Thorndike's Puzzle Box and the Law of Effect** (*Left*) A box typical of the puzzle boxes Thorndike used in his experiments with cats to study the law of effect. Stepping on the treadle released the door bolt; a weight attached to the door then pulled the door open and allowed the cat to escape. After accidentally pressing the treadle as it tried to get to the food, the cat learned to press the treadle when it wanted to escape the box. (*Right*) One cat's learning curve over 24 separate trials. Notice that the cat escaped much more quickly after about five trials. It had learned the consequences of its behavior.

● **law of effect** Thorndike's law stating that behaviors followed by positive outcomes are strengthened and that behaviors followed by negative outcomes are weakened.

that released the door bolt. When the cat returned to the box, it went through the same random activity until it stepped on the lever once more. On subsequent trials, the cat made fewer and fewer random movements until finally it immediately stepped on the lever to open the door (Figure 19.1). Thorndike's resulting **law of effect** states that behaviors followed by positive outcomes are strengthened and that behaviors followed by negative outcomes are weakened (Brown & Jenkins, 2009).

The law of effect is important because it presents the basic idea that the consequences of a behavior influence the likelihood of that behavior's recurrence. Quite simply, a behavior can be followed by something good or something bad, and the probability of a behavior's being repeated depends on these outcomes. As we now explore, Skinner's operant conditioning model expands on this basic idea.

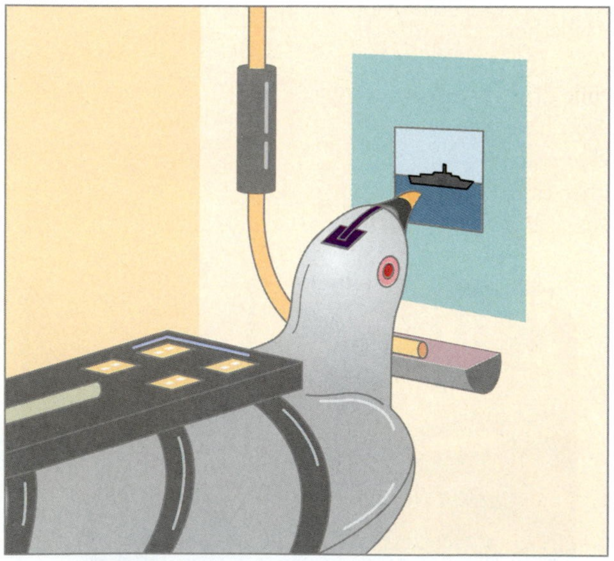

19·3 SKINNER'S APPROACH TO OPERANT CONDITIONING

Skinner believed that the mechanisms of learning are the same for all species. This conviction led him to study animals in the hope that he could discover the components of learning with organisms simpler than humans, including pigeons. During World War II, Skinner trained pigeons to pilot missiles. Naval officials would not accept pigeons piloting missiles in wartime, but Skinner congratulated himself on the degree of control he was able to exercise over the pigeons (Figure 19.2).

Skinner and other behaviorists made every effort to study organisms under precisely controlled conditions so that they could examine the connection between the operant behavior and the specific consequences in minute detail (Hernstein, 2009). One of Skinner's creations in the 1930s to control experimental conditions was the Skinner box (Figure 19.3). A device in the box delivered food pellets into a tray at random. After a rat became accustomed to the box, Skinner installed a lever and observed the rat's behavior. As the hungry rat explored the box, it occasionally pressed the lever, and a food pellet was dispensed. Soon the rat learned that the

FIGURE 19.2 **Skinner's Pigeon-Guided Missile** Skinner wanted to help the military during World War II by using pigeons' tracking behavior. He devised a system whereby a lens at the front of the missile would project an image of the target to a screen at the control station. Pigeons, with a gold electrode attached to their beak, were trained through occasional food pellet rewards to peck at the image of the target. As long as the target remained at the center of the screen, the missiles would fly straight, but pecks off-center would cause the screen to tilt. Through the connection to the missile's flight controls, the tilt would cause the missile to change course.

consequences of pressing the lever were positive: It would be fed. Skinner achieved further control by sound-proofing the box to ensure that the experimenter was the only influence on the organism. In many of the experiments, the responses were mechanically recorded, and the food (the consequence) was dispensed automatically. These precautions aimed to prevent human error.

19-4 SHAPING

We have all seen service dogs walking faithfully next to their human partners. These highly trained canines provide services to people with various disabilities. They open and close doors, help individuals dress and undress, flush toilets, and even put clothes in a washer and dryer. They have gained these skills through operant conditioning. However, just imagine the challenge of teaching even a really smart dog how to do the laundry. Your task might seem close to impossible, as it is quite unlikely that a dog would spontaneously start putting the clothes in the washing machine. You could wait a very long time for such a feat, and furthermore you could not reinforce a behavior that had not been elicited. It *is* possible, however, to train a dog or another animal to perform highly complex tasks through shaping.

Shaping refers to rewarding approximations of a desired behavior (Krueger & Dayan, 2009). For example, shaping can be used to train a rat to press a bar to obtain food. When a rat is first placed in a Skinner box, it rarely presses the bar. Thus, the experimenter may start off by giving the rat a food pellet if it is in the same half of the cage as the bar. Then the experimenter might reward the rat's behavior only when it is within 2 inches of the bar, then only when it touches the bar, and finally only when it presses the bar.

Returning to the service dog, rather than waiting for the dog spontaneously to put the clothes in the washing machine, we might reward the dog for carrying the clothes to the laundry room and for bringing them closer and closer to the washing machine. Finally, we might reward the dog only when it gets the clothes inside the washer. Indeed, trainers use this type of shaping technique extensively in teaching animals to perform tricks. A dolphin that jumps through a hoop held high above the water has been trained to perform this behavior through shaping.

Operant conditioning relies on the notion that a behavior is likely to be repeated if it is followed by a reward. What makes a reinforcer rewarding? Recent research reveals considerable interest in discovering the links between brain activity and operant conditioning (Chester & others, 2006; Fontanini & others, 2009; Rapanelli & others, 2010). To explore this topic, see the Intersection.

19-5 PRINCIPLES OF REINFORCEMENT

We noted earlier that a behavior can be followed by something pleasant or something unpleasant. *Reinforcement* refers to those nice things that follow a behavior. **Reinforcement** is the process by which a rewarding stimulus or event (a *reinforcer*) following a particular behavior increases the probability that the behavior will happen again. Pleasant or rewarding consequences of a behavior fall into two types, called *positive reinforcement* and *negative reinforcement*. Both of these types of consequences are experienced as pleasant, and both increase the frequency of a behavior.

Positive and Negative Reinforcement

In **positive reinforcement,** the frequency of a behavior increases because it is followed by the presentation of something that is good. For example, if someone you meet smiles at you after you say, "Hello, how are you?" and you keep talking, the smile has reinforced your talking. The same principle of positive reinforcement is at work when you teach a dog to "shake hands" by giving it a piece of food when it lifts its paw.

FIGURE 19.3   The Skinner Box B. F. Skinner conducting an operant conditioning study in his behavioral laboratory. The rat being studied is in a Skinner box.

Through operant conditioning, animals can learn to do amazing things—even ride a wave, like this alpaca shown with its trainer, Peruvian surfer Domingo Pianezzi.

● **shaping** Rewarding approximations of a desired behavior.

● **reinforcement** The process by which a rewarding stimulus or event (a reinforcer) following a particular behavior increases the probability that the behavior will happen again.

● **positive reinforcement** An increase in the frequency of a behavior in response to the subsequent presentation of something that is good.

Behaviorism and Cognitive Neuroscience: If It Feels Good, Is It Rewarding?

When behaviorists talk about behaviors, they rarely focus on what is going on inside the head of the organism they are studying. With remarkable innovations in the technology of brain imaging, however, researchers—even those interested in associative learning—can examine the neural underpinnings of behavior (Knight & others, 2010; Koob, 2006). In effect, researchers can look inside the "black box" of the human brain and observe how learning takes place.

A central idea behind operant conditioning is that an organism is likely to repeat a behavior when that behavior is followed by a reward. However, what is rewarding about a reward? Food is an obvious reward. Hungry rats will work hard for food. Neuroscientists have identified a part of the midbrain called the nu-

© W. B. Park. www.CartoonStock.com.

cleus accumbens (or NAc), an extension of the amygdala that plays a vital role in our learning to repeat a rewarded behavior (Schultz, 2006). In essence, a special input into the NAc tells the organism to "do it again." We can think of the brain's response as literally reinforcing the synapses in the brain that connect the stimulus and response.

Researchers have found that the neurotransmitter dopamine plays a crucial role in the reinforcement of behaviors (Darvas & Palmiter, 2010; Schlosser & others, 2009; Thomsen & others, 2009). An electrode that records dopamine cells in the brain of a monkey, for example, shows that dopamine is released not only when the monkey tastes food, but also when it sees signals in the environment suggesting that food is available (Schultz, Dayan, & Montague, 1997). By comparison, imagine that you are walking through a shopping mall. You see a "50 percent off" sign outside the shoe store. That sign might just start a dopamine explosion in your brain.

What are some of the rewarding experiences in your life that other people just don't understand? Why do you find them rewarding?

The role of dopamine in the activation of reinforcement is also demonstrated in animals that lack dopamine. Animals that have been given a drug that blocks dopamine find rewards less rewarding. They treat sugar as less sweet and fail to react to potential rewards in the environment (G. P. Smith, 1995). As researchers bring questions of basic learning principles into the neuroscience laboratory, they get ever-closer to understanding what "rewarding" really means.

● **negative reinforcement** An increase in the frequency of a behavior in response to the subsequent removal of something that is unpleasant.

In contrast, in **negative reinforcement,** the frequency of a behavior increases because it is followed by the removal of something unpleasant. For example, if your father nagged you to clean out the garage and kept nagging until you cleaned out the garage, your response (cleaning out the garage) removed the unpleasant stimulus (your dad's nagging). Taking an aspirin when you have a headache works the same way: A reduction of pain reinforces the act of taking an aspirin. Similarly, if your TV is making an irritating buzzing sound, you might give it a good smack on the side, and if the buzzing stops, you are more likely to smack the set again if the buzzing resumes. Ending the buzzing sound rewards the TV-smacking.

● **avoidance learning** An organism's learning that it can altogether avoid a negative stimulus by making a particular response.

A special kind of response to negative reinforcement is avoidance learning. **Avoidance learning** occurs when the organism learns that by making a particular response, a negative stimulus can be altogether avoided. For instance, a student who receives one bad grade might thereafter always study hard in order to avoid the negative outcome of bad grades in the future. Even when the bad grade is no longer present, the pattern of behavior sticks. Avoidance learning is very powerful in the sense that the behavior is maintained even in the absence of any aversive stimulus. For example, animals that have been trained to avoid a negative stimulus, such as an electrical shock, by jumping into a safe area may always thereafter gravitate toward the safe area, even when the shock is no longer presented.

Experience with unavoidable negative stimuli can lead to a particular deficit in avoidance learning called learned helplessness. In **learned helplessness,** the organism has learned that it has no control over negative outcomes. Learned helplessness was first identified by Martin Seligman and his colleagues (Altenor, Volpicelli, & Seligman, 1979; Hannum, Rossellini, & Seligman, 1976). Seligman and his associates found that dogs that were first exposed to inescapable shocks were later unable to learn to avoid those shocks, even when they could (Seligman & Maier, 1967). This inability to learn to escape was persistent: The dogs would suffer painful shocks hours, days, and even weeks later and never attempt to escape. Exposure to unavoidable negative circumstances may also set the stage for humans' inability to learn avoidance, such as with the experience of depression and despair (Huston, Schulz, & Topic, 2009). Learned helplessness has aided psychologists in understanding a variety of perplexing issues, such as why some victims of domestic violence fail to escape their terrible situation and why some students respond to failure at school by seeming to give up trying.

Notice that both positive and negative reinforcement involve rewarding behavior—but they do so in different ways. Positive reinforcement means following a behavior with something pleasant, and negative reinforcement means following a behavior with the removal of something unpleasant. Remember that, in this case, "positive" and "negative" have nothing to do with "good" and "bad." Rather, they refer to processes in which something is given (positive reinforcement) or something is removed (negative reinforcement). Whether it is positive or negative, reinforcement is about increasing a behavior. Figure 19.4 provides further examples to help you understand the distinction between positive and negative reinforcement.

● **learned helplessness** An organism's learning through experience with unavoidable negative stimuli that it has no control over negative outcomes.

Types of Reinforcers

Psychologists classify positive reinforcers as primary or secondary based on whether the rewarding quality of the consequence is innate or learned. A **primary reinforcer** is innately satisfying; that is, a primary reinforcer does not take any learning on the organism's part to make it pleasurable. Food, water, and sexual satisfaction are primary reinforcers. A

● **primary reinforcer** A reinforcer that is innately satisfying; one that does not take any learning on the organism's part to make it pleasurable.

Positive Reinforcement

Behavior	Rewarding Stimulus Provided	Future Behavior
You turn in homework on time.	Teacher praises your performance.	You increasingly turn in homework on time.
You wax your skis.	The skis go faster.	You wax your skis the next time you go skiing.
You randomly press a button on the dashboard of a friend's car.	Great music begins to play.	You deliberately press the button again the next time you get into the car.

Negative Reinforcement

Behavior	Unpleasant Stimulus Removed	Future Behavior
You turn in homework on time.	Teacher stops criticizing late homework.	You increasingly turn in homework on time.
You wax your skis.	People stop zooming by you on the slope.	You wax your skis the next time you go skiing.
You randomly press a button on the dashboard of a friend's car.	An annoying song shuts off.	You deliberately press the button again the next time the annoying song is on.

FIGURE 19.4   Positive and Negative Reinforcement Negative reinforcers involve taking something aversive away. Positive reinforcers mean adding something pleasant.

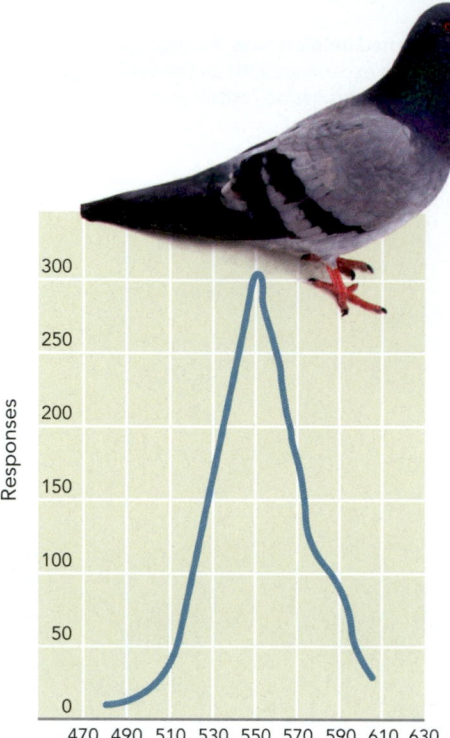

FIGURE 19.5 **Stimulus Generalization** In the experiment by Norman Guttman and Harry Kalish (1956), pigeons initially pecked a disk of a particular color (in this graph, a color with a wavelength of 550 nm) after they had been reinforced for this wavelength. Subsequently, when the pigeons were presented disks of colors with varying wavelengths, they were likelier to peck those that were similar to the original disk.

● **secondary reinforcer** A reinforcer that acquires its positive value through an organism's experience; a secondary reinforcer is a learned or conditioned reinforcer.

● **generalization (in operant conditioning)** Performing a reinforced behavior in a different situation.

● **discrimination (in operant conditioning)** Responding appropriately to stimuli that signal that a behavior will or will not be reinforced.

● **extinction (in operant conditioning)** Decreases in the frequency of a behavior when the behavior is no longer reinforced.

secondary reinforcer acquires its positive value through an organism's experience; a secondary reinforcer is a learned or conditioned reinforcer. We encounter hundreds of secondary reinforcers in our lives, such as getting an *A* on a test and a paycheck for a job. Although we might think of these as positive outcomes, they are not innately positive. We learn through experience that *A*'s and paychecks are good. Secondary reinforcers can be used in a system called a *token economy*. In a token economy behaviors are rewarded with tokens (such as poker chips or stars on a chart) that can be exchanged later for desired rewards (such as candy or money).

Generalization, Discrimination, and Extinction

Not only are generalization, discrimination, and extinction important in classical conditioning, they also are key principles in operant conditioning.

GENERALIZATION

In operant conditioning, **generalization** means performing a reinforced behavior in a different situation. For example, in one study pigeons were reinforced for pecking at a disk of a particular color (Guttman & Kalish, 1956). To assess stimulus generalization, researchers presented the pigeons with disks of varying colors. As Figure 19.5 shows, the pigeons were most likely to peck at disks closest in color to the original. When a student who gets excellent grades in a calculus class by studying the course material every night starts to study psychology and history every night as well, generalization is at work.

DISCRIMINATION

In operant conditioning, **discrimination** means responding appropriately to stimuli that signal that a behavior will or will not be reinforced (Carlsson & Swedberg, 2010). For example, you go to a restaurant that has a "University Student Discount" sign in the front window, and you enthusiastically flash your student ID with the expectation of getting the reward of a reduced-price meal. Without the sign, showing your ID might get you only a puzzled look, not cheap food.

The principle of discrimination helps to explain how a service dog "knows" when she is working. Typically, the dog wears a training harness while on duty but not at other times. Thus, when a service dog is wearing her harness, it is important to treat her like the professional that she is. Similarly, an important aspect of the training of service dogs is the need for selective disobedience. Selective disobedience means that in addition to obeying commands from its human partner, the service dog must at times override such commands if the context provides cues that obedience is not the appropriate response. So, if a guide dog is standing at the corner with her visually impaired human, and the human commands her to move forward, the dog might refuse if she sees the "Don't Walk" sign flashing. Stimuli in the environment serve as cues, informing the organism if a particular reinforcement contingency is in effect.

EXTINCTION

In operant conditioning, **extinction** occurs when a behavior is no longer reinforced and decreases in frequency (Leslie & others, 2006). If, for example, a soda machine that you frequently use starts "eating" your coins without dispensing soda, you quickly stop inserting more coins. Several weeks later, you might try to use the machine again, hoping that it has been fixed. Such behavior illustrates spontaneous recovery in operant conditioning.

Continuous Reinforcement, Partial Reinforcement, and Schedules of Reinforcement

Most of the examples of reinforcement we have considered so far involve *continuous reinforcement*, in which a behavior is reinforced every time it occurs. When continuous reinforcement takes place, organisms learn rapidly. However, when reinforcement stops, extinction takes place quickly. A variety of conditioning procedures have been developed that are particularly resistant to extinction. These involve *partial reinforcement,* in which a reinforcer follows a behavior only a portion of the time (Mitchell & others, 2010). Partial reinforcement characterizes most life experiences. For instance, a golfer does not win every tournament she enters; a chess whiz does not win every match he plays; a student does not get a pat on the back each time she solves a problem.

Schedules of reinforcement are specific patterns that determine when a behavior will be reinforced (Mitchell & others, 2010; Orduna, Garcia, & Hong, 2010). There are four main schedules of partial reinforcement: fixed ratio, variable ratio, fixed interval, and variable interval. With respect to these, *ratio schedules* involve the number of behaviors that must be performed prior to reward, and *interval schedules* refer to the amount of time that must pass before a behavior is rewarded. In a fixed schedule, the number of behaviors or the amount of time is always the same. In a variable schedule, the required number of behaviors or the amount of time that must pass changes and is unpredictable from the perspective of the learner. Let's look concretely at how each of these schedules of reinforcement influences behavior.

A *fixed-ratio schedule* reinforces a behavior after a set number of behaviors. For example, if you are playing the slot machines in Atlantic City and if the machines are on a fixed-ratio schedule, you might get $5 back every 20th time you put money in the machine. It would not take long to figure out that if you watched someone else play the machine 18 or 19 times, not get any money back, and then walk away, you should step up, insert your coin, and get back $5. The business world often uses fixed-ratio schedules to increase production. For instance, a factory might require a line worker to produce a certain number of items in order to get paid a particular amount.

Of course, if the reward schedule for a slot machine were that easy to figure out, casinos would not be so successful. What makes gambling so tantalizing is the unpredictability of wins (and losses). Slot machines are on a *variable-ratio schedule,* a timetable in which behaviors are rewarded an average number of times but on an unpredictable basis. For example, a slot machine might pay off at an average of every 20th time, but the gambler does not know when this payoff will be. The slot machine might pay off twice in a row and then not again until after 58 coins have been inserted. This averages out to a reward for every 20 behavioral acts, but *when* the reward will be given is unpredictable. Variable-ratio schedules produce high, steady rates of behavior that are more resistant to extinction than the other three schedules.

Whereas ratio schedules of reinforcement are based on the *number* of behaviors that occur, interval reinforcement schedules are determined by the *time elapsed* since the last behavior was rewarded. A *fixed-interval schedule* reinforces the first behavior after a fixed amount of time has passed. If you take a class that has four scheduled exams, you might procrastinate most of the semester and cram just before each test. Fixed-interval schedules of reinforcement are also responsible for the fact that pets seem to be able to "tell time," eagerly sidling up to their food dish at 5 P.M. in anticipation of dinner. On a fixed-interval schedule, the rate of a behavior increases rapidly as the time approaches when the behavior likely will be reinforced. For example, a government official who is running for reelection may intensify her campaign activities as Election Day draws near.

A *variable-interval schedule* is a timetable in which a behavior is reinforced after a variable amount of time has elapsed. Pop quizzes occur on a variable-interval schedule. So does fishing—you do not know if the fish will bite in the next minute, in a half hour, in an hour, or ever. Because it is difficult to predict when a reward will come, behavior is slow and consistent on a variable-interval schedule (Staddon, Chelaru, & Higa, 2002). This is why pop quizzes lead to more consistent levels of studying compared to the cramming that might be seen with scheduled tests.

To sharpen your sense of the differences between fixed- and variable-interval schedules, consider the following example. Penelope and Edith both design slot machines for their sorority's charity casino night. Penelope puts her slot machine on a variable-interval schedule of reinforcement; Edith puts hers on a fixed-interval schedule of reinforcement. On average, both machines will deliver a reward every 20 minutes. Whose slot machine is likely to make the most money for the sorority charity? Edith's machine is likely to

● **schedules of reinforcement** Specific patterns that determine when a behavior will be reinforced.

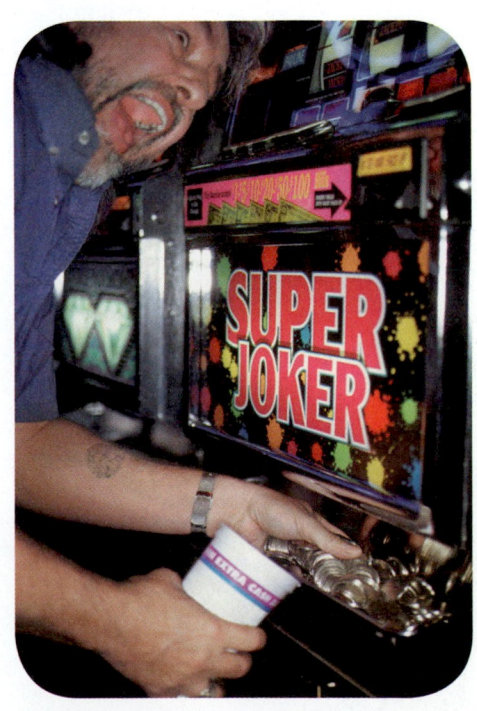

Slot machines are on a variable-ratio schedule of reinforcement.

psychological *inquiry*

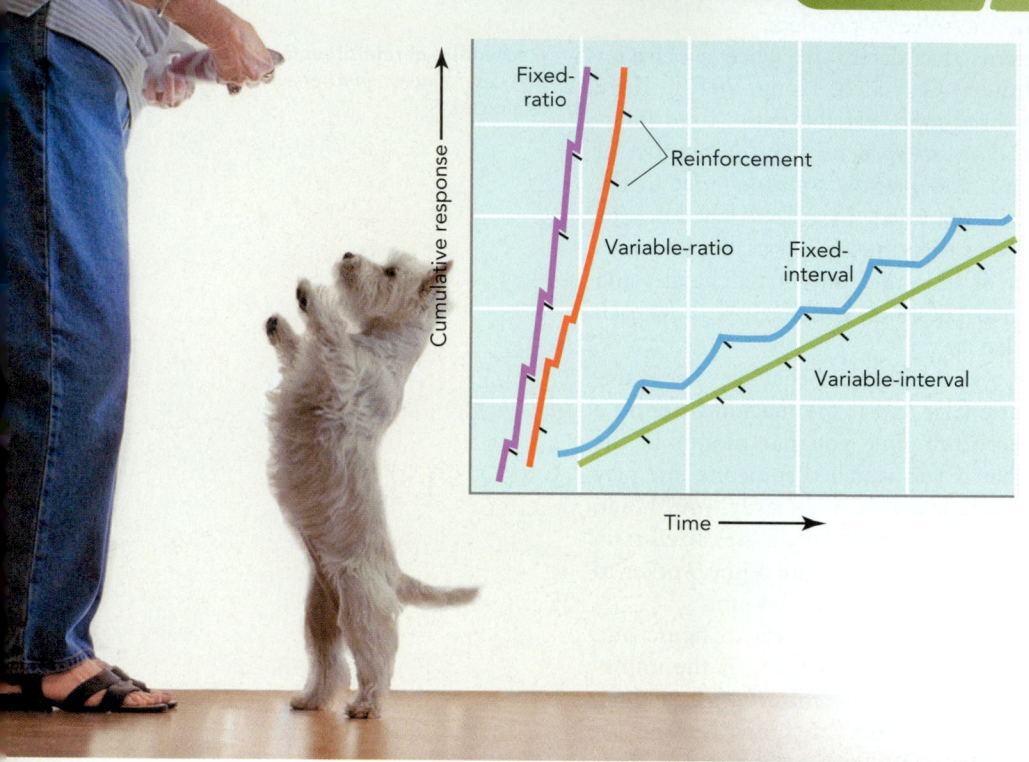

Schedules of Reinforcement and Different Patterns of Responding

This figure shows how the different schedules of reinforcement result in different rates of responding. The graph's X or horizontal axis represents time. The Y or vertical axis represents the cumulative responses. That means that as the line goes up, the total number of responses are building and building. In the figure, each hash mark indicates the delivery of reinforcement. That is, each of those little ticks indicates that a reward is being given.

Look closely at the pattern of responses over time for each schedule of reinforcement. On the fixed-ratio schedule, notice the dropoff in responding after each response; on the variable-ratio schedule, note the high, steady rate of responding. On the fixed-interval schedule, notice the immediate dropoff in responding after reinforcement and the increase in responding just before reinforcement (resulting in a scalloped curve); and on the variable-interval schedule, note the slow, steady rate of responding.

1. Which schedule of reinforcement represents the "most bang for the buck"? That is, which one is associated with the most responses for the least amount of reward?
2. Which schedule of reinforcement is most like pop quizzes?
3. Which is most like regular tests on a course syllabus?
4. Which schedule of reinforcement would be best if you have very little time for training?
5. Which schedule of reinforcement do you think is most common in your own life? Why?

lead to long lines just before the 20-minute mark, but people will be unlikely to play on it at other times. In contrast, Penelope's is more likely to entice continuous play, because the players never know when they might hit a jackpot. The magic of variable schedules of reinforcement is that the learner can never be sure exactly when the reward is coming. Let's take a closer look at the responses associated with each schedule of reinforcement in the Psychological Inquiry feature.

Punishment

We began this section by noting that behaviors can be followed by something good or something bad. So far, we have explored only the good things—reinforcers that are meant to increase behaviors. Sometimes, however, the goal is to decrease a behavior, and in such cases the behavior might be followed by something unpleasant. **Punishment** is a consequence that decreases the likelihood that a behavior will occur. For instance, a child plays with matches and gets burned when he lights one; the child consequently is less likely to play with matches in the future. As another example, a student interrupts the instructor, and the instructor scolds the student. This consequence—the teacher's verbal reprimand—makes the student less likely to interrupt in the future. In punishment, a response decreases because of its unpleasant consequences.

● **punishment** A consequence that decreases the likelihood that a behavior will occur.

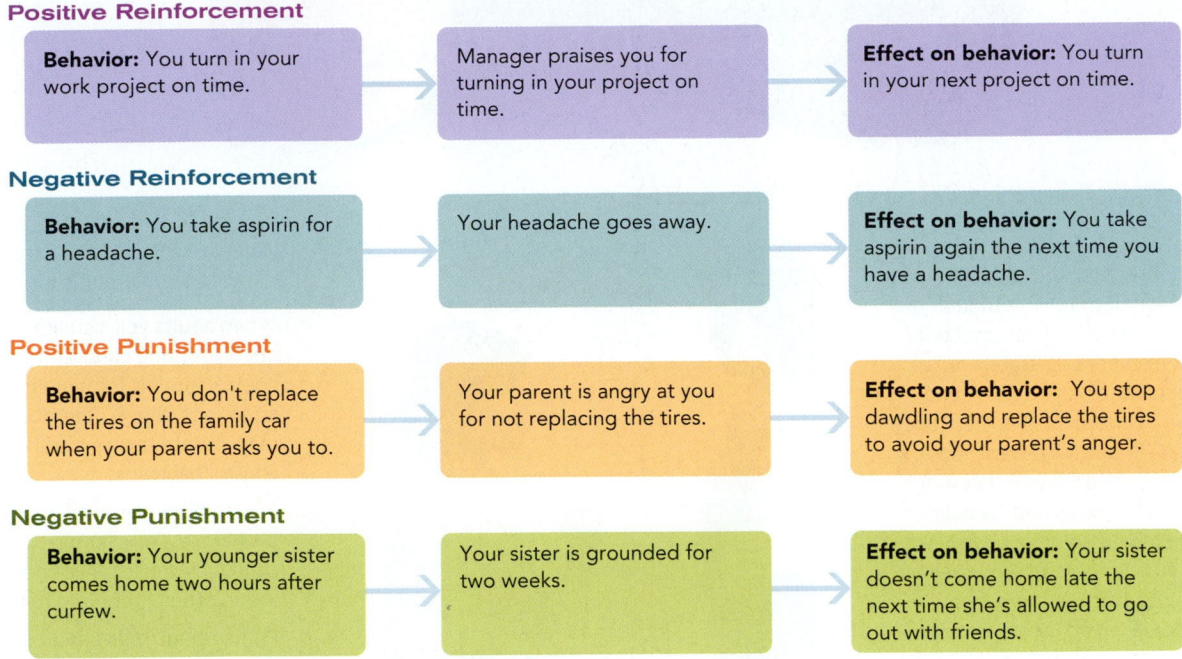

FIGURE 19.6 **Positive Reinforcement, Negative Reinforcement, Positive Punishment, and Negative Punishment** The fine distinctions here can be confusing. With respect to reinforcement, *positive* means presenting—or adding—something pleasant in order to increase a behavior's frequency, and *negative* means taking away something unpleasant in order to increase a behavior's frequency. With regard to punishment, *positive* and *negative* refer to whether the response to a behavior is adding something unpleasant (positive punishment such as being scolded) or taking away something pleasant (negative punishment such as being grounded).

Just as the positive–negative distinction applies to reinforcement, it can also apply to punishment. As was the case for reinforcement, "positive" means adding something, and "negative" means taking something away. Thus, in **positive punishment** a behavior decreases when it is followed by the presentation of an unpleasant stimulus, whereas in **negative punishment** a behavior decreases when a positive stimulus is removed. Examples of positive punishment include spanking a misbehaving child and scolding a spouse who forgot to call when she was running late at the office; the coach who makes his team run wind sprints after a lackadaisical practice is also using positive punishment. *Time-out* is a form of negative punishment in which a child is removed from a positive reinforcer, such as her toys. Getting grounded is also a form of negative punishment as it involves taking a teenager away from the fun things in his life. Figure 19.6 compares positive reinforcement, negative reinforcement, positive punishment, and negative punishment.

The use of positive punishment, especially physical punishment such as spanking children, has been a topic of some debate. To learn how psychologists view the physical punishment of children, see the Critical Controversy.

● **positive punishment** The presentation of an unpleasant stimulus following a given behavior in order to decrease the frequency of that behavior.

● **negative punishment** The removal of a positive stimulus following a given behavior in order to decrease the frequency of that behavior.

Timing, Reinforcement, and Punishment

How does the timing of reinforcement and punishment influence behavior? And does it matter whether the reinforcement is small or large?

IMMEDIATE VERSUS DELAYED REINFORCEMENT

As is the case in classical conditioning, in operant conditioning learning is more efficient when the interval between a behavior and its reinforcer is a few seconds rather than minutes or hours, especially in lower animals (Freestone & Church, 2010). If a food reward is delayed for more than 30 seconds after a rat presses a bar, it is virtually ineffective as reinforcement. Humans, however, have the ability to respond to delayed reinforcers (Holland, 1996).

CRITICAL CONTROVERSY

Will Sparing the Rod Spoil the Child?

For centuries, experts considered corporal (physical) punishment such as spanking a necessary and even desirable method of disciplining children. The use of corporal punishment is legal in every U.S. state, and an estimated 94 percent of American 3- and 4-year-olds have been spanked at least once in any given year (Straus & Stewart, 1999). A cross-cultural comparison found that individuals in the United States and Canada were among the most favorable toward corporal punishment and remembered their parents' using it (Curran & others, 2001).

Despite the widespread use of corporal punishment, there have been surprisingly few research studies on it, and those that have been conducted are correlational (Kazdin & Benjet, 2003). Recall that cause and effect cannot be determined in a correlational study. In one such study, the researchers found a link between parents' spanking and children's antisocial behavior, including cheating, telling lies, being mean to others, bullying, getting into fights, and being disobedient (Straus, Sugarman, & Giles-Sims, 1997). Moreover, culture seems to play a big role in the outcomes associated with spanking.

A research review concluded that although corporal punishment by parents is associated with children's higher levels of immediate compliance, it is also associated with aggression among children, as well as with lower levels of moral internalization and mental health (Gershoff, 2002). High and harsh levels of corporal punishment are especially detrimental to children's well-being (Alyahri & Goodman, 2008; de Zoysa, Newcombe, & Rajapakse, 2008) and may affect adolescents as well (Bender & others, 2007).

Debate is ongoing about the effects of corporal punishment on children's development (Grusec, 2009; Thompson, 2009). Some experts argue that much of the evidence for the negative effects of physical punishment is based on studies in which parents acted in an abusive manner (Baumrind, Larzelere, & Cowan, 2002). A research review of 26 studies concluded that only severe or predominant use of spanking, not mild spanking, compared unfavorably with alternative discipline practices with children (Larzelere & Kuhn, 2005). Indeed, there are few longitudinal studies of punishment and few studies that distinguish adequately between moderate and heavy use of punishment. Thus, in the view of some experts, based on the research evidence available, it is still difficult to tell whether the effects of physical punishment are harmful to children's development, although such a view might be distasteful to some individuals (Grusec, 2009). Clearly, though, when physical punishment involves abuse, it can be very harmful to children's development (Cicchetti & others, 2010).

What are some reasons for avoiding spanking or similar punishments?

- When adults yell, scream, or spank, they are presenting children with out-of-control models for handling stressful situations (Sim & Ong, 2005). Children may imitate this aggressive, out-of-control behavior.

- Punishment can instill fear, rage, or avoidance. For example, spanking the child may cause him or her to avoid being around the parent and to fear the parent.

- Punishment tells children what not to do rather than what to do. It would be preferable to give children feedback such as "Why don't you try this?"

- Punishment can be abusive. Even if parents do not so intend, they might get so carried away during the act of punishing that they become abusive (Dunlap & others, 2009).

For such reasons, Sweden passed a law in 1979 forbidding parents to punish children physically (to spank or slap them, for example). Since the law's enactment, youth rates of delinquency, alcohol abuse, rape, and suicide have dropped in Sweden (Durrant, 2008). Because this study is correlational in nature, however, we cannot assume that the anti-spanking law caused these social changes. These improvements may have occurred for other reasons, such as shifting attitudes and broadened opportunities for youth. Nonetheless, the Swedish experience suggests that the physical punishment of children may be unnecessary. Other countries with anti-spanking laws include Finland, Denmark, Norway, Austria, Cyprus, Croatia, Latvia, Germany, and Israel.

When asked why they use corporal punishment, parents often respond that their children need strong discipline to learn how to behave. Parents also sometimes reason that they were spanked by their own parents and they turned out okay, so there is nothing wrong with corporal punishment.

WHAT DO YOU THINK?

- Should the United States outlaw the physical punishment of children? Why or why not?

- Did your parents spank you when you were a child? If so, what effects do you think physical punishment had on your behavior? Might the effects on you be different depending on whether the physical punishment was severe or harsh as opposed to light or moderate?

- Might negative punishment, such as time-outs, be more effective than positive punishment, such as spanking? Explain.

Sometimes important life decisions involve whether to seek and enjoy a small, immediate reinforcer or to wait for a delayed but more highly valued reinforcer (Martin & Pear, 2007). For example, you might spend your money now on clothes, concert tickets, and the latest iPod, or you might save your money and buy a car later. You might choose to enjoy yourself now in return for immediate small reinforcers, or you might opt to study hard in return for delayed stronger reinforcers such as good grades, a scholarship to graduate school, and a better job.

IMMEDIATE VERSUS DELAYED PUNISHMENT

As with reinforcement, in most instances of research with lower animals, immediate punishment is more effective than delayed punishment in decreasing the occurrence of a behavior. However, also as with reinforcement, delayed punishment can have an effect on human behavior. Not studying at the beginning of a semester can lead to poor grades much later, and humans have the capacity to notice that this early behavior contributed to the negative outcome.

IMMEDIATE VERSUS DELAYED REINFORCEMENT *AND* PUNISHMENT

Many daily behaviors revolve around rewards and punishments, both immediate and delayed. We might put off going to the dentist to avoid a small punisher (such as the discomfort that comes with getting a cavity filled). However, this procrastination might contribute to greater pain later (such as the pain of having a tooth pulled). Sometimes life is about enduring a little pain now to avoid a lot of pain later.

How does receiving immediate small reinforcement versus delayed strong punishment affect human behavior (Martin & Pear, 2007)? One reason that obesity is such a major health problem is that eating is a behavior with immediate positive consequences—food tastes great and quickly provides a pleasurable, satisfied feeling. Although the potential delayed consequences of overeating are negative (obesity and other possible health risks), the immediate consequences are difficult to override. When the delayed consequences of behavior are punishing and the immediate consequences are reinforcing, the immediate consequences usually win, even when the immediate consequences are minor reinforcers and the delayed consequences are major punishers.

Smoking and drinking follow a similar pattern. The immediate consequences of smoking are reinforcing for most smokers—the powerful combination of positive reinforcement (enhanced attention, energy boost) and negative reinforcement (tension relief, removal of craving). The primarily long-term effects of smoking are punishing and include shortness of breath, a chronic sore throat and/or coughing, chronic obstructive pulmonary disease (COPD), heart disease, and cancer. Likewise, the immediate pleasurable consequences of drinking override the delayed consequences of a hangover or even alcoholism and liver disease.

Now think about the following situations. Why are some of us so reluctant to take up a new sport, try a new dance step, run for office on campus or in local government, or do almost anything different? One reason is that learning new skills often involves minor punishing consequences, such as initially looking and feeling stupid, not knowing what to do, and having to put up with sarcastic comments from others. In these circumstances, reinforcing consequences are often delayed. For example, it may take a long time to become a good enough golfer or a good enough dancer to enjoy these activities, but persevering through the rough patches just might be worth it.

19·6 APPLIED BEHAVIOR ANALYSIS

Some thinkers have criticized behavioral approaches for ignoring mental processes and focusing only on observable behavior. Nevertheless, these approaches do provide an optimistic perspective for individuals interested in changing their behaviors. That is, rather than concentrating on factors such as the type of person you are, behavioral

● **applied behavior analysis** Also called behavior modification, the use of operant conditioning principles to change human behavior.

approaches imply that you can modify even longstanding habits by changing the reward contingencies that maintain those habits (Watson & Tharp, 2007).

One real-world application of operant conditioning principles to promote better functioning is applied behavior analysis. **Applied behavior analysis** (also called *behavior modification*) is the use of operant conditioning principles to change human behavior. In applied behavior analysis, the rewards and punishers that exist in a particular setting are carefully analyzed and manipulated to change behaviors. Applied behavior analysis seeks to identify the rewards that might be maintaining unwanted behaviors and to enhance the rewards of more appropriate behaviors. From this perspective, we can understand all human behavior as being influenced by rewards and punishments. If we can figure out what rewards and punishers are controlling a person's behavior, we can change them—and eventually the behavior itself.

A manager who rewards his or her staff with a casual-dress day or a half day off if they meet a particular work goal is employing applied behavior analysis. So are a therapist and a client when they establish clear consequences of the client's behavior in order to reinforce more adaptive actions and discourage less adaptive ones (Chance, 2009). A teacher who notices that a troublesome student seems to enjoy the attention he receives—even when that attention is scolding—might use applied behavior analysis by changing her responses to the child's behavior, ignoring it instead (an example of negative punishment).

These examples show how attending to the consequences of behavior can be used to improve performance in settings such as the workplace and a classroom. Advocates of applied behavior analysis believe that many emotional and behavioral problems stem from inadequate or inappropriate consequences (Alberto & Troutman, 2009).

Applied behavior analysis has been effective in a wide range of situations. Practitioners have used it, for example, to train autistic individuals (Ashcroft, Argiro, & Keohane, 2010), children and adolescents with psychological problems (Miltenberger, 2008), and residents of mental health facilities (Phillips & Mudford, 2008); to instruct individuals in effective parenting (Phaneuf & McIntyre, 2007); to enhance environmentally conscious behaviors such as recycling and not littering (Geller, 2002); to get people to wear seatbelts (Streff & Geller, 1986); and to promote workplace safety (Geller, 2006). Applied behavior analysis can help people improve their self-control in many aspects of mental and physical health (Spiegler & Guevremont, 2010).

SUMMARY

Operant conditioning is a form of learning in which the consequences of behavior produce changes in the probability of the behavior's occurrence. Skinner described the behavior of the organism as operant: The behavior operates on the environment, and the environment in turn operates on the organism. Whereas classical conditioning involves respondent behavior, operant conditioning involves operant behavior. In most instances, operant conditioning is better at explaining voluntary behavior than is classical conditioning.

Thorndike's law of effect states that behaviors followed by positive outcomes are strengthened, whereas behaviors followed by negative outcomes are weakened. Skinner built on this idea to develop the notion of operant conditioning.

Shaping is the process of rewarding approximations of desired behavior in order to shorten the learning process. Principles of reinforcement include the distinction between positive reinforcement (the frequency of a behavior increases because it is followed by a rewarding stimulus) and negative reinforcement (the frequency of behavior increases because it is followed by the removal of an aversive, or unpleasant, stimulus). Positive reinforcement can be classified as primary reinforcement (using reinforcers that are innately satisfying) and secondary reinforcement (using reinforcers that acquire positive value through experience). Reinforcement can also be

KEY TERMS

operant conditioning   201
law of effect   202
shaping   203
reinforcement   203
positive reinforcement   203
negative reinforcement   204
avoidance learning   204
learned helplessness   205
primary reinforcer   205
secondary reinforcer   206
generalization (in operant conditioning)   206

discrimination (in operant conditioning)   206
extinction (in operant conditioning)   206
schedules of reinforcement   207
punishment   208
positive punishment   209
negative punishment   209
applied behavior analysis   212

continuous (a behavior is reinforced every time) or partial (a behavior is reinforced only a portion of the time). Schedules of reinforcement—fixed ratio, variable ratio, fixed interval, and variable interval—determine when a behavior will be reinforced.

Operant, or instrumental, conditioning involves generalization (giving the same response to similar stimuli), discrimination (responding to stimuli that signal that a behavior will or will not be reinforced), and extinction (a decreasing tendency to perform a previously reinforced behavior when reinforcement is stopped).

Punishment is a consequence that decreases the likelihood that a behavior will occur. In positive punishment, a behavior decreases when it is followed by an unpleasant stimulus. In negative punishment, a behavior decreases when a positive stimulus is removed from it.

Applied behavior analysis, or behavior modification, involves the application of operant conditioning principles to a variety of real-life behaviors.

TEST YOURSELF

1. What is operant conditioning?
2. Define shaping and give two examples of it.
3. What is the difference between positive reinforcement and negative reinforcement? Between positive punishment and negative punishment?

APPLY YOUR KNOWLEDGE

1. Enlist some of your classmates to play this mind game on your professor. Every time your instructor moves to the right side of the room during lecture, be more attentive, smile, and nod. Start out by shaping—every time he or she moves even a little to the right, give a smile or nod. See how far you can get the instructor to go using this simple reward. In one introductory psychology class, students got their professor to move all the way to the right wall of the classroom, where she leaned, completely clueless.

2. The next time you are alone with a friend, try your best to use shaping and the principles of operant conditioning to get the person to touch the tip of his or her nose. Can you do it?

3. Positive reinforcement and negative reinforcement can be difficult concepts to grasp. The real-world examples and accompanying practice exercises on the following website should help to clarify the distinction:
http://psych.athabascau.ca/html/prtut/reinpair.htm

Observational Learning

Would it make sense to teach a 15-year-old boy how to drive with either classical conditioning or operant conditioning procedures? Driving a car is a voluntary behavior, so classical conditioning would not apply. In terms of operant conditioning, we could ask him to try to drive down the road and then reward his positive behaviors. Not many of us would want to be on the road, though, when he makes mistakes. Albert Bandura (2007b, 2008, 2009, 2010a) believes that if all our learning was conducted in such a trial-and-error fashion, learning would be exceedingly tedious and at times hazardous. Instead, he says, many complex behaviors are the result of exposure to competent models. By observing other people, we can acquire knowledge, skills, rules, strategies, beliefs, and attitudes (Schunk, 2011). The capacity to learn by observation eliminates trial-and-error learning, and often such learning takes less time than operant conditioning.

Bandura's *observational learning*, also called *imitation* or *modeling,* is learning that occurs when a person observes and imitates behavior. Perhaps the most famous example of observational learning is the Bobo doll study (Bandura, Ross, & Ross, 1961). Bandura and his colleagues randomly assigned some children to watch an adult model aggressive behavior and other children to watch an adult behaving non-aggressively. In the experimental condition, children saw the model hit an inflated Bobo doll with a mallet, kick it in the air, punch it, and throw it, all the while hollering aggressive phrases such as "Hit him!" "Punch him in the nose!" and "Pow!" In the control condition, the model played with Tinkertoys and ignored the Bobo doll. Children who watched the aggressive model were much more likely to engage in aggressive behavior when left alone with Bobo (Bandura, Ross, & Ross, 1961).

Bandura (1986) described four main processes that are involved in observational learning: attention, retention, motor reproduction, and reinforcement. The first process that must occur is *attention.* To reproduce a model's actions, you must attend to what the model is saying or doing. You might not hear what a friend says if the stereo is blaring, and you might miss your instructor's analysis of a problem if you are admiring someone sitting in the next row. As a further example, imagine that you decide to take a class to improve your drawing skills. To succeed, you need to attend to the instructor's words and hand movements. Characteristics of the model can influence attention to the model. Warm, powerful, atypical people, for example, command more attention than do cold, weak, typical people.

Retention is the second process required for observational learning to occur. To reproduce a model's actions, you must encode the information and keep it in memory so that you can retrieve it. A simple verbal description, or a vivid image of what the model did, assists retention. In the example of taking a class to sharpen your drawing skills, you will need to remember what the instructor said and did in modeling good drawing skills.

Motor reproduction, a third element of observational learning, is the process of imitating the model's actions. People might pay attention to a model and encode what they have seen, but limitations in motor development might make it difficult for them to reproduce the model's action. Thirteen-year-olds might see a professional basketball player do a reverse two-handed dunk but be unable to reproduce the pro's play. Similarly, in your drawing class, if you lack fine motor reproduction skills, you might be unable to follow the instructor's example.

Reinforcement is a final component of observational learning. In this case, the question is whether the model's behavior is followed by a consequence. Seeing a model attain a reward for an activity increases the chances that an observer will repeat the behavior—a process called *vicarious reinforcement.* On the other hand, seeing the model punished

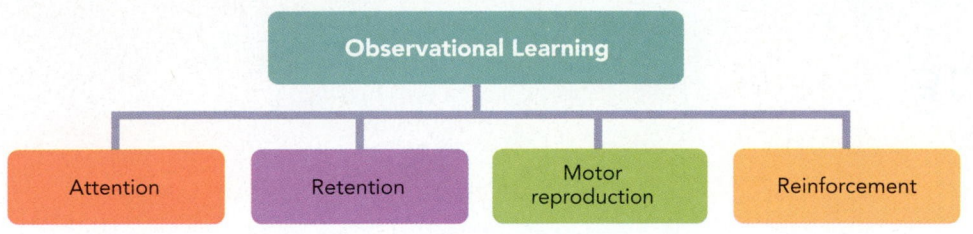

FIGURE 20.1 **Bandura's Model of Observational Learning** In terms of Bandura's model, if you are learning to ski, you need to attend to the instructor's words and demonstrations. You need to remember what the instructor did and his or her tips for avoiding disasters. You also need the motor abilities to reproduce what the instructor has shown you. Praise from the instructor after you have completed a few moves on the slopes should improve your motivation to continue skiing.

makes the observer less likely to repeat the behavior—a process called *vicarious punishment*. Unfortunately, vicarious reinforcement and vicarious punishment are often absent in, for example, media portrayals of violence and aggression.

Observational learning can be an important factor in the functioning of role models in inspiring people and changing their perceptions. Whether a model is similar to us can influence that model's effectiveness in modifying our behavior. The shortage of role models for women and minorities in science and engineering has often been suggested as a reason for the lack of women and minorities in these fields. After the election of Barack Obama as president of the United States, many commentators noted that for the first time, African American children could see concretely they might also attain the nation's highest office someday.

Figure 20.1 summarizes Bandura's model of observational learning.

SUMMARY

Observational learning occurs when a person observes and imitates someone else's behavior. Bandura identified four main processes in observational learning: attention (paying heed to what someone is saying or doing), retention (encoding that information and keeping it in memory so that you can retrieve it), motor reproduction (imitating the actions of the person being observed), and reinforcement (seeing the person attain a reward for the activity).

TEST YOURSELF

1. What are the four processes involved in observational learning?
2. What are two other names for observational learning?
3. What are vicarious reinforcement and vicarious punishment?

APPLY YOUR KNOWLEDGE

1. Imagine that you are about to begin an internship in an organization where you would like to have a permanent position someday. Use the processes of observational learning to describe your strategy for making the most of your internship.

2. Using what you know about observational learning, describe the classroom environment that would best promote student learning.

Factors in Learning

In learning about learning, we have looked at cognitive processes only as they apply in observational learning. Skinner's operant conditioning perspective and Pavlov's classical conditioning approach focus on the environment and observable behavior, not what is going on in the head of the learner. Many contemporary psychologists, including some behaviorists, recognize the importance of cognition and believe that learning involves more than environment–behavior connections (Bandura, 2007b, 2008, 2009, 2010a, 2010b; Schunk, 2011). Additionally, psychologists recognize biological, cultural, and psychological factors in learning. Take the example of Albert Einstein. Einstein had many special talents. He combined enormous creativity with keen analytic ability to develop some of the twentieth century's most important insights into the nature of matter and the universe. Genes obviously endowed Einstein with extraordinary intellectual skills that enabled him to think and reason on a very high plane, but cultural factors also contributed to his genius. Einstein received an excellent, rigorous European education, and later in the United States he experienced the freedom and support believed to be important in creative exploration. Would Einstein have been able to develop his skills fully and to make such brilliant insights if he had grown up in a less advantageous environment? It is unlikely. Clearly, both biological *and* cultural factors contribute to learning.

21·1 PURPOSIVE BEHAVIOR

E. C. Tolman (1932) emphasized the *purposiveness* of behavior—the idea that much of behavior is goal-directed. Tolman believed that it is necessary to study entire behavioral sequences in order to understand why people engage in particular actions. For example, high school students whose goal is to attend a leading college or university study hard in their classes. If we focused only on their studying, we would miss the purpose of their behavior. The students do not always study hard because they have been reinforced for studying in the past. Rather, studying is a means to intermediate goals (learning, high grades) that in turn improve their likelihood of getting into the college or university of their choice (Schunk, 2011).

We can see Tolman's legacy today in the extensive interest in the role of goal setting in human behavior (Urdan, 2010). Researchers are especially curious about how people self-regulate and self-monitor their behavior to reach a goal (Anderman & Anderman, 2010).

Expectancy Learning and Information

In studying the purposiveness of behavior, Tolman went beyond the stimuli and responses of Pavlov and Skinner to focus on cognitive mechanisms. Tolman said that when classical conditioning and operant conditioning occur, the organism acquires certain expectations. In classical conditioning, the young boy fears the rabbit because he expects it will hurt him. In operant conditioning, a woman works hard all week because she expects a paycheck on Friday. Expectancies are acquired from people's experiences with their environment. Expectancies influence a variety of human experiences. We set the goals we do because we believe that we can reach them.

Expectancies also play a role in the placebo effect, described earlier. Many painkillers have been shown to be more effective in reducing pain if patients can see the intravenous injection sites (Price, Finniss, & Benedetti, 2008). If patients can observe that they are getting a drug, they can harness their own expectations for pain reduction.

Tolman (1932) emphasized that the information value of the CS is important as a signal or an expectation that a UCS will follow. Anticipating contemporary thinking, Tolman believed that the information that the CS provides is the key to understanding classical conditioning.

One contemporary view of classical conditioning describes an organism as an information seeker, using logical and perceptual relations among events, along with preconceptions, to form a representation of the world (Rescorla, 2003, 2004, 2005, 2006a, 2006b, 2006c, 2009).

A classic experiment conducted by Leon Kamin (1968) illustrates the importance of an organism's history and the information provided by a conditioned stimulus in classical conditioning. Kamin conditioned a rat by repeatedly pairing a tone (CS) and a shock (UCS) until the tone alone produced fear (CR). Then he continued to pair the tone with the shock, but he turned on a light (a second CS) each time the tone sounded. Even though he repeatedly paired the light (CS) and the shock (UCS), the rat showed no conditioning to the light (the light by itself produced no CR). Conditioning to the light was blocked, almost as if the rat had not paid attention. The rat apparently used the tone as a signal to predict that a shock would be coming; information about the light's pairing with the shock was redundant with the information already learned about the tone's pairing with the shock. In this experiment, conditioning was governed not by the contiguity of the CS and UCS but instead by the rat's history and the information it received. Contemporary classical conditioning researchers are further exploring the role of information in an organism's learning (Beckers & others, 2006; Rescorla & Wagner, 2009; Schultz, Dayan, & Montague, 2009).

© Kes. www.CartoonStock.com.

Latent Learning

Experiments on latent learning provide other evidence to support the role of cognition in learning. **Latent learning** or *implicit learning* is unreinforced learning that is not immediately reflected in behavior. In one study, researchers put two groups of hungry rats in a maze and required them to find their way from a starting point to an end point (Tolman & Honzik, 1930). The first group found food (a reinforcer) at the end point; the second group found nothing there. In the operant conditioning view, the first group should learn the maze better than the second group, which is exactly what happened. However, when the researchers subsequently took some of the rats from the non-reinforced group and gave them food at the end point of the maze, they quickly began to run the maze as effectively as the reinforced group. The non-reinforced rats apparently had learned a great deal about the maze as they roamed around and explored it. However, their learning was *latent,* stored cognitively in their memories but not yet expressed behaviorally. When these rats were given a good reason (reinforcement with food) to run the maze speedily, they called on their latent learning to help them reach the end of the maze more quickly.

● **latent learning** Also called implicit learning, unreinforced learning that is not immediately reflected in behavior.

Outside a laboratory, latent learning is evident when you walk around a new setting to get "the lay of the land." The first time you visited your college campus, you may have wandered about without a specific destination in mind. Exploring the environment made you better prepared when the time came to find that 8 A.M. class.

21·2 INSIGHT LEARNING

Like Tolman, the German gestalt psychologist Wolfgang Köhler believed that cognitive factors play a significant role in learning. Köhler spent four months in the Canary Islands during World War I observing the behavior of apes. There he conducted two fascinating experiments—the stick problem and the box problem. Although these two experiments are basically the same, the solutions to the problems are different. In both situations, the ape discovers that it cannot reach an alluring piece of fruit, either because the fruit is too high or because it is outside of the ape's cage and beyond reach. To solve the stick problem, the ape has to insert a small stick inside a larger stick to reach the

FIGURE 21.1 **Insight Learning** Sultan, one of Köhler's brightest chimps, was faced with the problem of reaching a cluster of bananas overhead. He solved the problem by stacking boxes on top of one another to reach the bananas. Köhler called this type of problem solving "insight learning."

● **insight learning** A form of problem solving in which the organism develops a sudden insight into or understanding of a problem's solution.

fruit. To master the box problem, the ape must stack several boxes to reach the fruit (Figure 21.1).

According to Köhler (1925), solving these problems does not involve trial and error or simple connections between stimuli and responses. Rather, when the ape realizes that its customary actions are not going to help it get the fruit, it often sits for a period of time and appears to ponder how to solve the problem. Then it quickly rises, as if it has had a sudden flash of insight, piles the boxes on top of one another, and gets the fruit. **Insight learning** is a form of problem solving in which the organism develops a sudden insight into or understanding of a problem's solution.

Insight learning requires that we think "outside the box," setting aside previous expectations and assumptions. One way to enhance insight learning and creativity in human beings is through multicultural experiences (Leung & others, 2008). Correlational studies have shown that time spent living abroad is associated with higher insight learning performance among MBA students (Maddux & Galinsky, 2007). Experimental studies have also demonstrated this effect. In one study, U.S. college students were randomly assigned to view one of two slide shows—one about Chinese and U.S. culture and the other about a control topic. Those who saw the multicultural slide show scored higher on measures of creativity and insight, and these changes persisted for a week (Leung & others, 2008).

21·3 BIOLOGICAL CONSTRAINTS

Human beings cannot breathe under water, fish cannot ski, and cows cannot solve math problems. The structure of an organism's body permits certain kinds of learning and inhibits others (Chance, 2009). For example, chimpanzees cannot learn to speak human languages because they lack the necessary vocal equipment. In animals, various aspects of their physical makeup can influence what they can learn. Sometimes, species-typical behaviors (or instincts) can override even the best reinforcers, as we now consider.

Instinctive Drift

Keller and Marion Breland (1961), students of B. F. Skinner, used operant conditioning to train animals to perform at fairs and conventions and in television advertisements. They applied Skinner's techniques to teach pigs to cart large wooden nickels to a piggy bank and deposit them. They also trained raccoons to pick up a coin and drop it into a metal tray.

Although the pigs and raccoons, as well as chickens and other animals, performed most of the tasks well (raccoons became adept basketball players, for example—see Figure 21.2), some of the animals began acting strangely. Instead of picking up the large wooden nickels and carrying them to the piggy bank, the pigs dropped the nickels on the ground, shoved them with their snouts, tossed them in the air, and then repeated these actions. The raccoons began to hold on to their coins rather than dropping them into the metal tray. When two coins were introduced, the raccoons rubbed them together in a miserly fashion. Somehow these behaviors overwhelmed the strength of the reinforcement. This example of biological influences on learning illustrates **instinctive drift,** the tendency of animals to revert to instinctive behavior that interferes with learning.

Why were the pigs and the raccoons misbehaving? The pigs were rooting, an instinct that is used to uncover edible roots. The raccoons were engaging in an instinctive food-washing response. Their instinctive drift interfered with learning.

FIGURE 21.2 **Instinctive Drift** This raccoon's skill in using its hands made it an excellent basketball player, but because of instinctive drift, the raccoon had a much more difficult time dropping coins into a tray.

Preparedness

Some animals learn readily in one situation but have difficulty learning in slightly different circumstances (Garcia & Koelling, 1966, 2009). The difficulty might result not from some aspect of the learning situation but from the organism's biological predisposition (Seligman, 1970). **Preparedness** is the species-specific biological predisposition to learn in certain ways but not others.

Much of the evidence for preparedness comes from research on taste aversion (Garcia, 1989; Garcia & Koelling, 2009). Recall that taste aversion involves a single trial of learning the association between a particular taste and nausea. Rats that experience low levels of radiation after eating show a strong aversion to the food they were eating when the radiation made them ill. This aversion can last for as long as 32 days. Such long-term effects cannot be accounted for by classical conditioning, which would argue that a single pairing of the conditioned and unconditioned stimuli would not last that long (Garcia, Ervin, & Koelling, 1966). Taste aversion learning occurs in animals, including humans, that choose their food based on taste and smell. Other species are prepared to learn rapid associations between, for instance, colors of foods and illness.

Another example of preparedness comes from research on conditioning humans and monkeys to associate snakes with fear. Susan Mineka and Arne Ohman have investigated the fascinating natural power of snakes to evoke fear in many mammals (Mineka & Ohman, 2002; Ohman & Mineka, 2003). Many monkeys and humans fear snakes, and both monkeys and humans are very quick to learn the association between snakes and fear. In classical conditioning studies, when pictures of snakes (CS) are paired with electrical shocks (UCS), the snakes are likely to quickly and strongly evoke fear (the CR). Interestingly, pairing pictures of, say, flowers (CS) with electrical shocks produces much weaker associations (Mineka & Ohman, 2002; Ohman & Soares, 1998). Even more significantly, pictures of snakes can serve as conditioned stimuli for fearful responses, even when the pictures are presented so rapidly that they cannot be consciously perceived (Ohman & Mineka, 2001).

The link between snakes and fear has been demonstrated not only in classical conditioning paradigms. Monkeys that have been raised in the lab and that have never seen a snake rapidly learn to fear snakes, even entirely by observational learning. Lab monkeys that see a videotape of a monkey expressing fear toward a snake learn to be afraid of snakes faster than monkeys seeing the same fear video spliced so that the feared object is a rabbit, a flower, or a mushroom (Ohman & Mineka, 2003).

Mineka and Ohman (2002) suggest that these results demonstrate preparedness among mammals to associate snakes with fear and aversive stimuli. They suggest that

● **instinctive drift** The tendency of animals to revert to instinctive behavior that interferes with learning.

● **preparedness** The species-specific biological predisposition to learn in certain ways but not others.

On the Indonesian island of Bali, young children learn traditional dances, whereas in Norway children commonly learn to ski early in life. As cultures vary, so does the content of learning.

this association is related to the amygdala (the part of the limbic system that is related to emotion) and is difficult to modify. These researchers suggest that this preparedness for fear of snakes has emerged out of the threat that reptiles likely posed to our evolutionary ancestors.

21·4 CULTURAL INFLUENCES

Traditionally, interest in the cultural context of human learning has been limited, partly because the organisms in those contexts typically were animals. The question arises, how might culture influence human learning? Most psychologists agree that the principles of classical conditioning, operant conditioning, and observational learning are universal and are powerful learning processes in every culture. However, culture can influence the *degree* to which these learning processes are used (Goodnow, 2010). For example, Mexican American students may learn more through observational learning, while Euro-American students may be more accustomed to learn through direct instruction (Mejia-Arauz, Rogoff, & Paradise, 2005).

In addition, culture can determine the *content* of learning (Shiraev & Levy, 2010). We cannot learn about something we do not experience. The 4-year-old who grows up among the Bushmen of the Kalahari Desert is unlikely to learn about taking baths and eating with a knife and fork. Similarly, a child growing up in Chicago is unlikely to be skilled at tracking animals and finding water-bearing roots in the desert. Learning often requires practice, and certain behaviors are practiced more often in some cultures than in others. In Bali, many children are skilled dancers by the age of 6, whereas Norwegian children are much more likely to be good skiers and skaters by that age.

21·5 PSYCHOLOGICAL CONSTRAINTS

Are there psychological constraints on learning? For animals, the answer is probably no. For humans, the answer may well be yes. This section opened with the claim that fish cannot ski. The truth of this statement is clear. Biological circumstances make it impossible. If we put biological considerations aside, we might ask ourselves about times in our lives when we feel like a fish trying to ski—when we feel that we just do not have what it takes to learn a skill or master a task.

Carol Dweck (2006) uses the term *mindset* to describe the way our beliefs about ability dictate what goals we set for ourselves, what we think we *can* learn, and ultimately what we *do* learn. Individuals have one of two mindsets: a *fixed mindset,* in which they believe that their qualities are carved in stone and cannot change; or a *growth mindset,* in which they believe their qualities can change and improve through their effort. These two mindsets have implications for the meaning of failure. From a fixed mindset, failure means lack of ability. From a growth mindset, however, failure tells the person what he or she still needs to learn. Your mindset influences whether you will be optimistic or pessimistic, what your goals will be, how hard you will strive to reach those goals, and how successful you are in college and after.

Dweck (2006) studied first-year pre-med majors taking their first chemistry class in college. Students with a growth mindset got higher grades than those with a fixed mindset. Even when they did not do well on a test, the growth-mindset students bounced back on the next test. Fixed-mindset students typically read and re-read the text and class notes or tried to memorize everything verbatim. The fixed-mindset students who did poorly on tests concluded that chemistry and maybe pre-med were not for them. By contrast, growth-mindset students took charge of their motivation and learning, searching for themes and principles in the course and going over mistakes until they understood why they made them. In Dweck's analysis (2006, p. 61), "They were studying to learn, not just ace the test. And, actually, this is why they got higher grades—not because they were smarter or had a better background in science."

Dweck and her colleagues recently incorporated information about the brain's plasticity into their effort to improve students' motivation to achieve and succeed (Blackwell & Dweck, 2008; Blackwell, Trzesniewski, & Dweck, 2007; Dweck & Master, 2009). In one study, they assigned two groups of students to eight sessions of either (1) study skills instruction or (2) study skills instruction plus information about the importance of developing a growth mindset (called *incremental theory* in the research) (Blackwell, Trzesniewski, & Dweck, 2007). One of the exercises in the growth-mindset group was titled "You Can Grow Your Brain," and it emphasized that the brain is like a muscle that can change and grow as it gets exercised and develops new connections. Students were informed that the more they challenged their brain to learn, the more their brain cells would grow. Prior to the intervention, both groups had a pattern of declining math scores. Following the intervention, the group that received only the study skills instruction continued to decline, but the group that received the study skills instruction *plus* the growth-mindset emphasis reversed the downward trend and improved their math achievement.

In other work, Dweck has created a computer-based workshop, "Brainology," to teach students that their intelligence can change (Blackwell & Dweck, 2008). Students experience six modules about how the brain works and how they can make their brain improve. After the recent testing of the modules in 20 New York City schools, students strongly endorsed the value of the computer-based brain modules. One student said, "I will try harder because I know that the more you try, the more your brain knows" (Dweck & Master, 2009, p. 137).

Following are some effective strategies for developing a growth mindset (Dweck, 2006):

- *Understand that your intelligence and thinking skills are not fixed but can change.* Even if you are extremely bright, with effort you can increase your intelligence.

- *Become passionate about learning and stretch your mind in challenging situations.* It is easy to withdraw into a fixed mindset when the going gets tough. However, as you bump up against obstacles, keep growing, work harder, stay the course, and improve your strategies, you will become a more successful person.

- *Think about the growth mindsets of people you admire.* Possibly you have a hero, someone who has achieved something extraordinary. You may have thought his or her accomplishments came easy because the person is so talented. If you find out more about this person, though, you likely will discover that hard work and effort over a long period of time were responsible for his or her achievements.

- *Begin now.* If you have a fixed mindset, commit to changing now. Think about when, where, and how you will begin using your new growth mindset.

Dweck's work challenges us to consider the limits we place on our own learning. Our beliefs about ability profoundly influence what we try to learn. As any 7-year-old with a growth mindset would tell you, you never know what you can do until you try.

SUMMARY

Tolman emphasized the purposiveness of behavior. His belief was that much of behavior is goal-directed. In studying purposiveness, Tolman went beyond stimuli and responses to discuss cognitive mechanisms; he believed that expectancies, acquired through experiences with the environment, are an important cognitive mechanism in learning.

Latent learning is unreinforced learning that is not immediately reflected in behavior. Latent learning may occur when a rat or a person roams a particular location and shows knowledge of the area when that knowledge is rewarded.

Köhler developed the concept of insight learning, a form of problem solving in which the organism develops a sudden insight into or understanding of a problem's solution.

KEY TERMS

Biology restricts what an organism can learn from experience. These constraints include instinctive drift (the tendency of animals to revert to instinctive behavior that interferes with learned behavior), preparedness (the species-specific biological predisposition to learn in certain ways but not in others), and taste aversion (the biological predisposition to avoid foods that have caused sickness in the past).

Although most psychologists agree that the principles of classical conditioning, operant conditioning, and observational learning are universal, cultural customs can influence the degree to which these learning processes are used. Culture also often determines the content of learning.

In addition, what we learn is determined in part by what we believe we can learn. Dweck emphasizes that individuals benefit enormously from having a growth mindset rather than a fixed mindset.

TEST YOURSELF

1. What did Tolman mean by the purposiveness of behavior?

2. How do expectancies develop through classical and operant conditioning?

3. Define latent learning and insight learning and give an example of each.

4. What are two biological constraints on learning?

5. How does culture influence learning?

6. What is the difference between a fixed mindset and a growth mindset?

APPLY YOUR KNOWLEDGE

1. Do you consider yourself to be a life-long learner? Why or why not? What type of mindset do you need to experience the benefits of learning over a lifetime?

2. Have you ever solved a problem because of insight learning? If so, describe the experience. If you haven't ever had this experience, do some research and find someone else's example. How can insight learning impact one's ability to solve problems in daily life?

Learning and Health and Wellness

In this section, we consider specific ways that research on learning has shed light on human health and wellness. We examine in particular the factors that animal learning models have identified as playing an important role in the experience of stress—the organism's response to a threat in the environment.

WHAT CAN A RAT TELL US ABOUT STRESS?

A great deal of research in learning has relied primarily on models of animals, such as rats, to probe the principles that underlie human learning. Research on the stress response in rats provides useful insights into how we humans can deal with stress.

Predictability

One very powerful aspect of potentially stressful experiences is their predictability. For a rat, predictability might depend on getting a warning buzzer before receiving a shock. Although the rat still experiences the shock, a buzzer-preceded shock causes less stress than a shock that is received with no warning (Abbott, Schoen, & Badia, 1984). Even having *good* experiences on a predictable schedule is less stressful than having good things happen at random times. For example, a rat might do very well receiving its daily chow at specific times during the day, but if the timing is random, the rat experiences stress. Similarly, when you receive a gift on your birthday or a holiday, the experience feels good. However, if someone surprises you with a present out of the blue, you might feel some stress as you wonder, "What is this person up to?"

Also relevant is classic research by Judith Rodin and her colleagues, which demonstrated that nursing home residents showed better adjustment if they experienced a given number of visits at predictable times rather than the same number of visits at random times (Langer & Rodin, 1976).

Control

Feeling in control may be a key to avoiding feelings of stress over difficulties. Specifically, once you have experienced control over negative events, you may be "protected" from stress, even during trying times.

Returning to an animal model, suppose that a rat has been trained to avoid a shock by pressing a lever. Over time, even when the lever is no longer related to the shock, the rat presses it during the shock—and experiences less stress. We might imagine the rat thinking, "Gee, it would be really worse if I weren't pressing this lever!" Researchers have also found links between having control and experiencing stress in humans. For example, nursing home residents are more likely to thrive if they receive visits at times they personally choose. In addition, simply having a plant to take care of is associated with living longer for nursing home residents (Langer & Rodin, 1976).

A lack of control over aversive stimuli can be particularly stressful. For example, individuals exposed to uncontrollable loud blasts of noise show lowered immune system

function (Sieber & others, 1992). One result of exposure to uncontrollable negative events is *learned helplessness,* which we examined earlier. In learned helplessness, the organism has learned through experience that outcomes are not controllable. As a result, the organism stops trying to exert control.

Research has shown that, to break the lock of learned helplessness, dogs and rats have to be forcibly moved to escape an aversive shock (Seligman, Rosellini, & Kozak, 1975). From such animal studies, we can appreciate how difficult it may be for individuals who find themselves in situations in which they have little control—for example, women who are victims of domestic violence (L. E. A. Walker, 2009)—to take action. We can also appreciate the helplessness sometimes experienced by students with learning difficulties who withdraw from their coursework because they feel unable to influence outcomes in school (Gwernan-Jones & Burden, 2010).

Improvement

Imagine that you have two mice, both of which are receiving mild electrical shocks. One of them, Jerry, receives 50 shocks every hour, and the other, Chuck-E, receives 10 shocks every hour. The next day both rats are switched to 25 shocks every hour. Which one is more stressed out at the end of the second day? The answer is that even though Jerry has experienced more shocks in general, Chuck-E is more likely to show the wear and tear of stress. In Jerry's world, even with 25 shocks an hour, *things are better.* The perception of improvement, even in a situation that is objectively worse than another, is related to lowered stress (Sapolsky, 2004).

Outlets for Frustration

When things are not going well for us, it often feels good to seek out an outlet, such as going for a run or, perhaps even better, taking a kickboxing class. Likewise, for a rat, having an outlet for life's frustrations is related to lowered stress symptoms. Rats that have a wooden post to gnaw on or even a furry little friend to complain to are less stressed out in response to negative circumstances.

Although studies using rats and dogs may seem far afield of our everyday experiences, researchers' observations provide important clues for avoiding stress. When we cultivate predictable environments and take control of circumstances, stress decreases. Further, when we can see improvement, even in difficult times, stress is likely to diminish. Finally, when we have an outlet for our frustrations in life—whether it is physical exercise, writing, or art—we can relieve our stress. When it comes to stress, humans have a lot to learn from rats.

SUMMARY

Research using rats and other animals has demonstrated four important variables involved in the human stress response: predictability, perceived control, perceptions of improvement, and outlets for frustration.

TEST YOURSELF

1. Based on research involving animal models, what are four ways in which human beings can reduce stress?
2. What is the main effect of learned helplessness on an organism?
3. Why do individuals who are experiencing domestic violence often have difficulty in overcoming their troubles?

Memory

Remarkable Memories: Making Pi a Piece of Cake

On March 14, 2008, Boston College senior James Niles-Joyal won the Pi Day competition at Harvard University by reciting the first 3,141 digits of pi from memory (Wiedeman, 2008). Niles-Joyal's achievement, the product of long and laborious study, set the Harvard record but was only a fraction of the world record. The honor for that achievement is held by Akira Haraguchi, who in 2005 recited the digits of pi to the first 83,431 decimal places (BBC News, 2005). Think about memorizing a list of over 80,000 numbers.

Mnemonists are people who have astonishing memory abilities—like Niles-Joyal and Haraguchi. Psychologists have learned a good deal about memory from such exceptional individuals (Takahashi & others, 2006). However, even "ordinary" people routinely demonstrate the amazing capacity of human memory as they go about their daily life.

Imagine that you are at a restaurant with six friends. After reciting your rather complicated order to the server, you note with concern that *he is not writing anything down*. Waiting patiently through your friends' orders, you cannot help but wonder, "How can he possibly remember all this?" Surely, you will get tomatoes on your salad though you are allergic, or your pasta will be covered with cheese when you specifically requested no cheese. When the meal arrives, however, everything is exactly right. Waiters seem to commit remarkable acts of memory routinely. How do they do it?

Asked to share their secrets, a few college students who moonlight in food service explained their methods: "I always try to remember the person's face and imagine him eating the food he's ordered," "If it's something really off the wall, you'll never forget it," and "Repetition is the key." As we will see, research on memory supports these techniques surprisingly well. ●

Memory and Memory Encoding

Through memory we weave the past into the present and establish a foundation for the future. In this module, we explore the nature of memory as the first step of the memory process—encoding.

22·1 THE NATURE OF MEMORY

The stars are shining and the moon is full. A beautiful evening is coming to a close. You look at your significant other and think, "I'll never forget this night." How is it possible that in fact you never do forget it? Years from now, you might tell your children about that one special night so many years ago, even if you had not thought about it in the years since. How does one perfect night become a part of your enduring life memory?

Psychologists define **memory** as the retention of information or experience over time. Memory occurs through three important processes: encoding, storage, and retrieval. For memory to work, we have to take in information (encode the sights and sounds of that night), store it or represent it in some manner (retain it in some mental storehouse), and then retrieve it for a later purpose (recall it when someone asks, "So, how did you two end up together?"). In the three main sections that follow, we focus on these phases of memory: encoding, storage, and retrieval (Figure 22.1).

Except for the occasional annoying moment when our memory fails or the upsetting situation where someone we know experiences memory loss, we do not think about how much everything we do or say depends on the smooth operation of our memory system (Schacter & Wagner, 2011). Let's return to the restaurant server from the module introduction. He has to attend to the orders he receives—who is asking for what and how they would like it prepared. To do so, he must encode the information about each customer and each order. He might look at each customer and associate his or her face with the menu items requested. Without writing anything down, he must retain the information, at least until he gets the orders to the kitchen or onto the computer. He might rehearse the orders in his mind as he walks to the back of the restaurant. When delivering the food to the table, he must accurately retrieve the information about who ordered what. Human memory systems truly are remarkable when we consider how much information we put into our memories and how much we must retrieve to perform life's activities (Martinez, 2010).

22·2 MEMORY ENCODING

The first step in memory is **encoding,** the process by which information gets into memory storage. When you are listening to a lecture, watching a play, reading a book, or talking with a friend, you are encoding information into memory. Some information gets into memory virtually automatically, whereas encoding other information takes effort. Here we examine some of the encoding processes that require effort. These include paying attention, processing deeply, elaborating, and using mental imagery.

Attention

To begin the process of memory encoding, we have to pay attention to information (Chun, Turk-Browne, & Golomb, 2011; Flom & Bahrick, 2010). *Selective attention* involves focusing on a specific aspect of experience while ignoring others. Attention is selective because the brain's resources are limited—they cannot attend to everything. These limitations mean

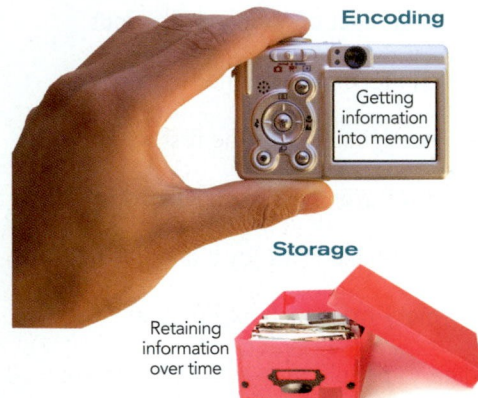

Encoding

Getting information into memory

Storage

Retaining information over time

Retrieval

Taking information out of storage

FIGURE 22.1 Processing Information in Memory As you read about the many aspects of memory in this module, think about the organization of memory in terms of these three main activities.

● **memory** The retention of information or experience over time as the result of three key processes: encoding, storage, and retrieval.

● **encoding** The first step in memory; the process by which information gets into memory storage.

that we have to attend selectively to some things in our environment and ignore others (Dixon & others, 2009; Matzel & Kolata, 2010). So, on that special night with your romantic partner, you never noticed the bus that roared by or the people whom you passed as you strolled along the street. Those aspects of that night did not make it into your enduring memory.

In addition to selective attention, psychologists have described two other ways that attention may be allocated: divided attention and sustained attention (Chun, Turk-Browne, & Golomb, 2011). **Divided attention** involves concentrating on more than one activity at the same time. If you are listening to music or the television while you are reading this module, you are engaging in divided attention. **Sustained attention** (also called *vigilance*) is the ability to maintain attention to a selected stimulus for a prolonged period of time. For example, paying close attention to your notes while studying for an exam is a good application of sustained attention.

Divided attention can be especially detrimental to encoding. *Multitasking,* which in some cases involves dividing attention not just between two activities but among three or more (Lin, 2009), may be the ultimate in divided attention. It is not unusual for high school and college students simultaneously to divide their attention among homework, instant messaging, web surfing, and looking at an iTunes playlist. Multitaskers are often very confident in their multitasking skills (Pattillo, 2010). However, a recent study revealed that heavy media multitaskers performed worse on a test of task-switching ability, apparently because of their decreased ability to filter out interference from the irrelevant task (Ophir, Nass, & Wagner, 2009). Such research indicates that trying to listen to a lecture in class while simultaneously texting or playing a game on your cell phone is likely to impede your ability to pay adequate attention to the lecture (Glenn, 2010).

● **divided attention** Concentrating on more than one activity at the same time.

● **sustained attention** Also called vigilance, the ability to maintain attention to a selected stimulus for a prolonged period of time.

Levels of Processing

Another factor that influences memory is whether we engage with information superficially or really get into it. Fergus Craik and Robert Lockhart (1972) first suggested that encoding can be influenced by levels of processing. The term **levels of processing** refers to a continuum from shallow to intermediate to deep, with deeper processing producing better memory.

Imagine that you are asked to memorize a list of words, including the word *mom.* Shallow processing includes noting the physical features of a stimulus, such as the shapes of the letters in the word *mom.* Intermediate processing involves giving the stimulus a label, as in reading the word *mom.* The deepest level of processing entails thinking about the meaning of a stimulus—for instance, thinking about the meaning of the word *mom* and about your own mother, her face, and her special qualities.

The more deeply we process, the better the memory (Howes, 2006). For example, researchers have found that if we encode something meaningful about a face and make associations with it, we are more likely to remember the face (Harris & Kay, 1995). The restaurant server who strives to remember the face of the customer and to imagine her eating the food she has ordered is using deep processing (Figure 22.2). A recent study showed that when students deeply processed information on an academic advising website, they were more likely to make good use of the information (Boatwright-Horowitz, Langley, & Gunnip, 2009). In a recent fMRI study of emotional memory formation, the brain's prefrontal cortex was involved in deep processing, and the amygdala was mainly at work in shallow processing (Ritchey, Labar, & Cabeza, 2010).

● **levels of processing** A continuum of memory processing from shallow to intermediate to deep, with deeper processing producing better memory.

Elaboration

Effective encoding of a memory depends on more than just depth of processing. Within deep processing, the more extensive the processing, the better the memory (Terry, 2009).

FIGURE 22.2 Depth of Processing

According to the levels of processing principle, deeper processing of stimuli produces more enduring memories.

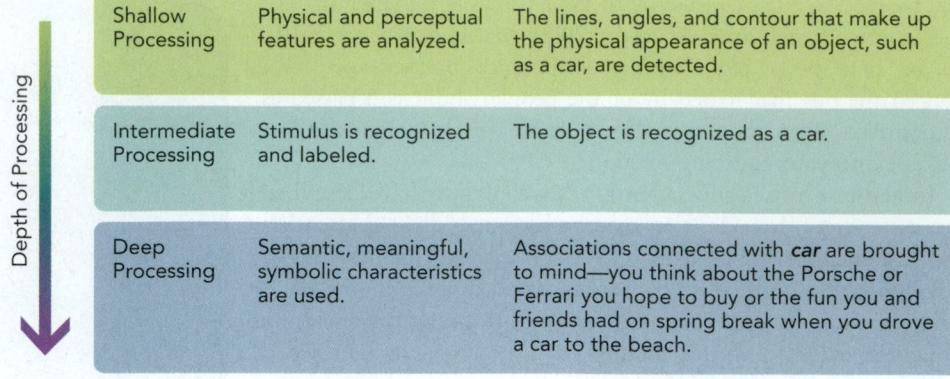

Depth of Processing			
Shallow Processing	Physical and perceptual features are analyzed.	The lines, angles, and contour that make up the physical appearance of an object, such as a car, are detected.
Intermediate Processing	Stimulus is recognized and labeled.	The object is recognized as a car.
Deep Processing	Semantic, meaningful, symbolic characteristics are used.	Associations connected with *car* are brought to mind—you think about the Porsche or Ferrari you hope to buy or the fun you and friends had on spring break when you drove a car to the beach.

● **elaboration** The formation of a number of different connections around a stimulus at a given level of memory encoding.

Elaboration refers to the formation of a number of different connections around a stimulus at any given level of memory encoding. Elaboration is like the creation of a huge spider web of links between some new information and everything one already knows, and it can occur at any level of processing. In the case of the word *mom,* a person can elaborate on *mom* even at a shallow level—for example, by thinking of the shapes of the letters and how they relate to the shapes of other letters, say, how an *m* looks like two *n*'s. At a deep level of processing, a person might focus on what a mother is or might think about various mothers he or she knows, images of mothers in art, and portrayals of mothers on television and in film. Generally speaking, the more elaborate the processing, the better memory will be. Deep, elaborate processing is a powerful way to remember.

For example, rather than trying to memorize the definition of *memory,* you would do better to weave a complex spider web around the concept of memory by coming up with a real-world example of how information enters your mind, how it is stored, and how you can retrieve it. Thinking of concrete examples of a concept is a good way to understand it. *Self-reference*—relating material to your own experience—is another effective way to elaborate on information, drawing mental links between aspects of your own life and new information (Hunt & Ellis, 2004) (Figure 22.3).

The process of elaboration is evident in the physical activity of the brain. Neuroscience research has shown a link between elaboration during encoding and brain activity (Achim & Lepage, 2005; Kirchhoff & Buckner, 2006). In one study, researchers placed individuals in magnetic resonance imaging (MRI) machines and flashed one word every two seconds on a screen inside (Wagner & others, 1998). Initially, the individuals simply noted whether the words were in uppercase or lowercase letters. As the study progressed, they were asked to determine whether each word was concrete, such as *chair* or *book,* or abstract, such as *love* or *democracy.* In this study, the participants showed more neural activity in the left frontal lobe of the brain during the concrete/abstract task than they did when they were asked merely to state whether the words were in uppercase or lowercase letters. Further, they demonstrated better memory in the concrete/abstract task. The researchers concluded that greater elaboration of information is linked with neural activity, especially in the brain's left frontal lobe, and with improved memory. Recent research also has indicated that the hippocampus is activated when individuals use elaboration during encoding (Staresina, Gray, & Davachi, 2009).

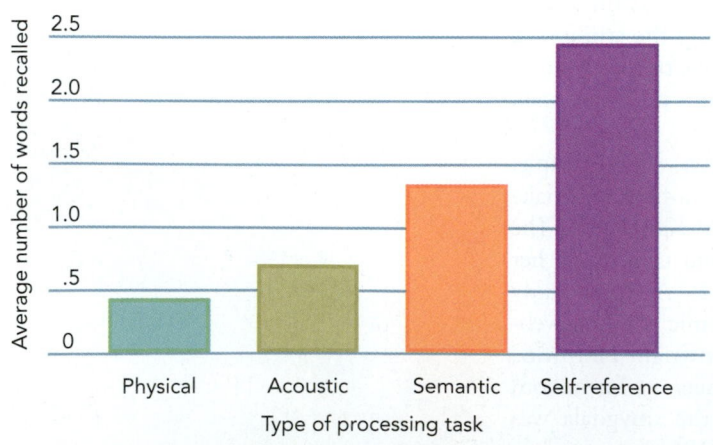

FIGURE 22.3 Memory Improves When Self-Reference Is Used

In one study, researchers asked participants to remember lists of words according to the words' physical, acoustic (sound), semantic (meaning), or self-referent characteristics. As the figure illustrates, when individuals generated self-references for the words, they remembered them better.

Imagery

One of the most powerful ways to make memories distinctive is to use mental imagery (Murray, 2007; Quinn & McConnell, 2006). Psychologist Alexander Luria (1968/1987) chronicled the life of S., whose unique visual imagination allowed him to remember an extraordinary amount of detail. Luria had become acquainted with S. in the 1920s in Russia. Luria began with some simple research to test S.'s memory. For example, he asked S. to recall a series of words or numbers, a standard method of testing memory skills. Luria concluded that S. had no apparent limits to his ability to recall. In such tests, people typically remember at most five to nine numbers. Not only could S. remember as many as 70 numbers, but he could also recall them accurately in reverse order. Moreover, S. could report the sequence flawlessly with no warning or practice even as long as 15 years after his initial exposure to the sequence. In addition, after the 15-year interval, S. could describe what Luria had been wearing and where he had been sitting when S. learned the list.

How could S. manage such tasks? As long as each number or word was spoken slowly, S. could represent it as a visual image that was meaningful to him. These images were durable—S. easily remembered the image he created for each sequence long after he learned the sequence. Imagery helped S. remember complicated lists of items and information. For example, S. once was asked to remember the following formula:

$$N \cdot \sqrt{d^2 \cdot \frac{85}{VX}} \cdot 3\sqrt{\frac{276^2 \cdot 86x}{n^2V \cdot \pi264}} \, n^2b$$
$$= sv \frac{1624}{32^2} \cdot r^2s$$

S. studied the formula for seven minutes and then reported how he memorized it. Notice in his account of this process, which follows, how he used imagery:

> Neiman (N) came out and jabbed at the ground with his cane ($\cdot$). He looked up at a tall tree, which resembled the square-root sign ($\sqrt{}$), and thought to himself: "No wonder this tree has withered and begun to expose its roots. After all, it was here when I built these two houses" (d^2). Once again he poked his cane ($\cdot$). Then he said: "The houses are old, I'll have to get rid of them; the sale will bring in far more money." He had originally invested 85,000 in them (85). . . . (Luria, 1968/1987)

S.'s complete story was four times this length, but the imagery he used must have been powerful, because S. remembered the formula perfectly 15 years later without any advance notice.

Imagery functions as a powerful encoding tool for all of us (Reed, 2010), certainly including the memory record holders shown in Figure 22.4. James Niles-Joyal, a student

Memorization of...	Record Holder	Country	Year	Record
Written numbers in 1 minute, without errors	Gunther Karsten	Germany	2007	102 numbers
Random words in 15 minutes*	Boris-Nikolai Konrad	Germany	2008	255 words
Speed to recall a single deck of 52 shuffled playing cards, without errors	Ben Pridmore	Great Britain	2007	26.28 seconds
Historic dates in 5 minutes	Johannes Mallow	Germany	2008	110.5 dates
Abstract images in 15 minutes	Gunther Karsten	Germany	2008	276 images

*Participants view random words in columns of 25 words. Scoring is tabulated by column: one point for each word. One mistake reduces the score for that column by half, and the second mistake reduces the score for that column to zero.

FIGURE 22.4 **World Champions of Memory** For memorization wizards such as these world record holders, imagery is a powerful encoding tool. Source: http:www.recordholders.org/en/list/memory.html#numbers-1min

who recited more than 3,000 digits of pi, imagined various sets of numbers of characters, emotions, and actions to aid his memory. One of the student waiters mentioned using an image of the customer eating the food to remember that individual's order.

Classic studies by Allan Paivio (1971, 1986, 2007) have documented how imagery can improve memory. Paivio argues that memory is stored in one of two ways: as a verbal code (a word or a label) or an image code. Paivio thinks that the image code, which is highly detailed and distinctive, produces better memory than the verbal code. His *dual-code hypothesis* claims that memory for pictures is better than memory for words because pictures—at least those that can be named—are stored as both image codes and verbal codes. Thus, when we use imagery to remember, we have two potential avenues by which we can retrieve information.

SUMMARY

Memory is the retention of information over time. The three processes involved in memory are encoding (getting information into storage), storage (retaining information over time), and retrieval (taking information out of storage).

Encoding requires attention, but the attention must be selective. Memory is negatively influenced by divided attention.

According to the theory of levels of processing, information is processed on a continuum from shallow (sensory or physical features are encoded) to intermediate (labels are attached to stimuli) to deep (the meanings of stimuli and their associations with other stimuli are processed). Deeper processing produces better memory. Elaboration, the extensiveness of processing at any given level of memory encoding, improves memory. Using imagery, or mental pictures, as a context for information can improve memory.

KEY TERMS

memory   228
encoding   228
divided attention   229

sustained attention   229
levels of processing   229
elaboration   230

TEST YOURSELF

1. How do psychologists define memory?
2. What three important processes play key roles in memory?
3. Which memory process is centrally involved when we recall information?
4. What four encoding processes do not happen automatically but instead require effort?
5. How does divided attention differ from selective attention?
6. Explain the process of elaboration and its importance.

APPLY YOUR KNOWLEDGE

1. Evaluate yourself on how well you multitask. What are some things you routinely do at the same time? Have you ever found yourself overdoing it and not being able to focus on any one particular task? What is the quality of work you perform when multitasking?

2. When you really want to remember something from class, what level of processing and what type of attention do you use? Describe your process.

Memory Storage

The quality of encoding does not alone determine the quality of memory. A memory also needs to be stored properly after it is encoded (Eysenck & Keane, 2010). **Storage** encompasses how information is retained over time and how it is represented in memory.

We remember some information for less than a second, some for half a minute, and some for minutes, hours, years, or even a lifetime. Richard Atkinson and Richard Shiffrin (1968) formulated an early popular theory of memory that acknowledged the varying life span of memories (Figure 23.1). The **Atkinson-Shiffrin theory** states that memory storage involves three separate systems:

- *Sensory memory:* time frames of a fraction of a second to several seconds
- *Short-term memory:* time frames up to 30 seconds
- *Long-term memory:* time frames up to a lifetime

As you read about these three memory storage systems, you will find that time frame is not the only thing that makes them different from one another. Each type of memory also operates in a distinctive way and has a special purpose.

23·1 SENSORY MEMORY

Sensory memory holds information from the world in its original sensory form for only an instant, not much longer than the brief time it is exposed to the visual, auditory, and other senses. Sensory memory is very rich and detailed, but we lose the information in it quickly unless we use certain strategies that transfer it into short-term or long-term memory.

Think about the sights and sounds you encounter as you walk to class on a typical morning. Literally thousands of stimuli come into your field of vision and hearing— cracks in the sidewalk, chirping birds, a noisy motorcycle, the blue sky, faces and voices of hundreds of people. You do not process all of these stimuli, but you do process a number of them. In general, you process many more stimuli at the sensory level than you consciously notice. Sensory memory retains this information from your senses, including a large portion of what you think you ignore. However, sensory memory does not retain the information very long.

Echoic memory (from the word *echo*) refers to auditory sensory memory, which is retained for up to several seconds. Imagine standing in an elevator with a friend who suddenly asks, "What was that song?" about the piped-in tune that just ended. If your friend asks his question quickly enough, you just might have a trace of the song left on your sensory registers.

● **storage** The retention of information over time and how this information is represented in memory.

● **Atkinson-Shiffrin theory** Theory stating that memory storage involves three separate systems: sensory memory, short-term memory, and long-term memory.

● **sensory memory** Memory system that involves holding information from the world in its original sensory form for only an instant, not much longer than the brief time it is exposed to the visual, auditory, and other senses.

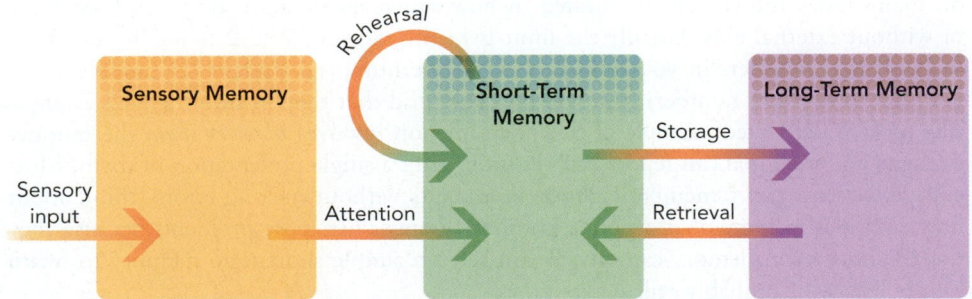

FIGURE 23.1 Atkinson and Shiffrin's Theory of Memory In this model, sensory input goes into sensory memory. Through the process of attention, information moves into short-term memory, where it remains for 30 seconds or less unless it is rehearsed. When the information goes into long-term memory storage, it can be retrieved over a lifetime.

Iconic memory (from the word *icon,* which means "image") refers to visual sensory memory, which is retained only for about 1/4 of a second (Figure 23.2). Visual sensory memory is responsible for our ability to "write" in the air using a sparkler on the Fourth of July—the residual iconic memory is what makes a moving point of light appear to be a line. The sensory memory for other senses, such as smell and touch, has received little attention in research studies.

The first scientific research on sensory memory focused on iconic memory. In George Sperling's (1960) classic study, participants viewed patterns of stimuli such as those in Figure 23.3. As you look at the letters, you have no trouble recognizing them. However, Sperling flashed the letters on a screen for very brief intervals, about 1/20 of a second. Afterward, the participants could report only four or five letters. With such a short exposure, reporting all nine letters was impossible.

Some participants in Sperling's study reported feeling that for an instant, they could see all nine letters within a briefly flashed pattern. They ran into trouble when they tried to name all the letters they had initially seen. One hypothesis to explain this experience is that all nine letters were initially processed as far as the iconic sensory memory level. This is why all nine letters were seen. However, forgetting from iconic memory occurred so rapidly that the participants did not have time to transfer all the letters to short-term memory, where they could be named.

Sperling reasoned that if all nine letters are actually processed in sensory memory, they should all be available for a brief time. To test this possibility, Sperling sounded a low, medium, or high tone just after a pattern of letters was shown. The participants were told that the tone was a signal to report only the letters from the bottom, middle, or top row. Under these conditions, the participants performed much better, and this outcome suggests a brief memory for most or all of the letters in the display.

To appreciate Sperling's discovery, glance at a page of this book for only a second. All the letters are present in your sensory memory for an instant, creating a mental image that exists in its entirety for just a moment. By giving the participants the signal, Sperling helped them to quickly scan their mental image (like the one you created by glancing at a page) so that they could find specific pieces of the information that it contained in various places. Their ability to do so demonstrates that all the material was actually there.

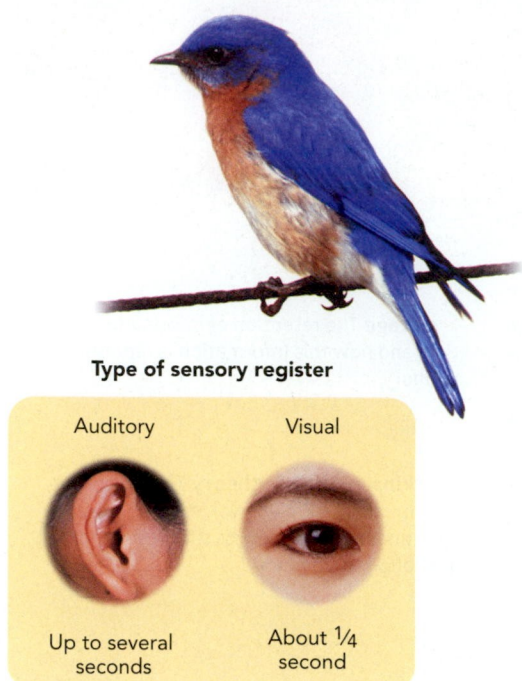

Type of sensory register

Auditory	Visual
Up to several seconds	About ¼ second

FIGURE 23.2 Auditory and Visual Sensory Memory If you hear this bird's call while walking through the woods, your auditory sensory memory holds the information for several seconds. If you see the bird, your visual sensory memory holds the information for only about ¼ of a second.

L	H	V
R	F	Z
D	T	C

FIGURE 23.3 Sperling's Sensory Memory Experiment This array of stimuli is similar to those flashed for about 1/20 of a second to the participants in Sperling's study.

● **short-term memory** Limited-capacity memory system in which information is usually retained for only as long as 30 seconds unless we use strategies to retain it longer.

23-2 SHORT-TERM MEMORY

Much information goes no further than the stage of auditory and visual sensory memory. We retain this information for only a brief instant. However, some information, especially that to which we pay attention, proceeds into short-term memory. **Short-term memory** is a limited-capacity memory system in which information is usually retained for only as long as 30 seconds unless we use strategies to retain it longer. Compared with sensory memory, short-term memory is limited in capacity, but it can store information for a longer time.

George Miller (1956) examined the limited capacity of short-term memory in the classic paper "The Magical Number Seven, Plus or Minus Two." Miller pointed out that on many tasks, individuals are limited in how much information they can keep track of without external aids. Usually the limit is in the range of 7 ± 2 items. If you think of important numbers in your life (such as phone numbers, student ID numbers, and your Social Security number), you will probably find that they fit into the 7 ± 2 range. The most widely cited example of this phenomenon involves *memory span,* the number of digits an individual can report back in order after a single presentation of them. Most college students can remember eight or nine digits without making errors (think about how easy it is to remember a phone number). Longer lists pose problems because they exceed short-term memory capacity. If you rely on simple short-term memory to retain longer lists, you probably will make errors.

Chunking and Rehearsal

Two ways to improve short-term memory are chunking and rehearsal. *Chunking* involves grouping or "packing" information that exceeds the 7 ± 2 memory span into higher-order units that can be remembered as single units. Chunking works by making large amounts of information more manageable (Gobet & Clarkson, 2004).

To get a sense of chunking, consider this list: *hot, city, book, forget, tomorrow,* and *smile*. Hold these words in memory for a moment; then write them down. If you recalled the words, you succeeded in holding 30 letters, grouped into six chunks, in memory. Now hold the following list in memory and then write it down:

O   LDH   ARO   LDAN   DYO   UNGB   EN

How did you do? Do not feel bad if you did poorly. This string of letters is very difficult to remember, even though it is arranged in chunks. The problem is that the chunks lack meaning. If you re-chunk the letters to form the meaningful words "Old Harold and Young Ben," they become much easier to remember.

Another way to improve short-term memory involves *rehearsal,* the conscious repetition of information (Theeuwes, Belopolsky, & Olivers, 2009). Information stored in short-term memory lasts half a minute or less without rehearsal. However, if rehearsal is not interrupted, information can be retained indefinitely. Rehearsal is often verbal, giving the impression of an inner voice, but it can also be visual or spatial, giving the impression of a private inner eye (Kaiser & others, 2010; Ramsoy & others, 2009).

Rehearsal works best when we must briefly remember a list of numbers or items such as entrées from a dinner menu. When we need to remember information for longer periods of time, as when we are studying for a test coming up next week or even an hour from now, other strategies usually work better. A main reason rehearsal does not work well for retaining information over the long term is that rehearsal often involves just mechanically repeating information, without imparting meaning to it. The fact that, over the long term, we remember information best when we add meaning to it demonstrates the importance of deep, elaborate processing.

Working Memory

Though useful, Atkinson and Shiffrin's theory of the three time-linked memory systems fails to capture the dynamic way short-term memory functions (Baddeley, 2008). Some key questions remain, such as how do things get in and out of memory, and where does problem solving take place?

An alternative approach to explaining short-term memory comes from British psychologist Alan Baddeley (1993, 2001, 2006, 2008, 2009, 2010). Baddeley proposed the concept of **working memory,** a three-part system that allows us to hold information temporarily as we perform cognitive tasks. Working memory is a kind of mental workbench on which the brain manipulates and assembles information to help us understand, make decisions, and solve problems. If, say, all of the information on the hard drive of your computer is like long-term memory, then working memory is comparable to what you have open and active at any given moment. Working memory has a limited capacity, and, to take the computer metaphor further, the capacity of the working memory is like RAM. Working memory is not a passive storehouse with shelves to store information until it moves to long-term memory; rather, it is an active memory system (Baddeley, Allen, & Vargh-Khadem, 2010; Karlsen & others, 2010).

Baddeley's model has three components. You can think of them as a boss (the central executive) who has two assistants (the phonological loop and visuospatial working memory) to help do the work of memory, as follows:

1. The *phonological loop* is specialized to briefly store speech-based information about the sounds of language. The phonological loop contains two separate

● **working memory** A three-part system that allows us to hold information temporarily as we perform cognitive tasks; a kind of mental workbench on which the brain manipulates and assembles information to help us understand, make decisions, and solve problems.

psychological *inquiry*

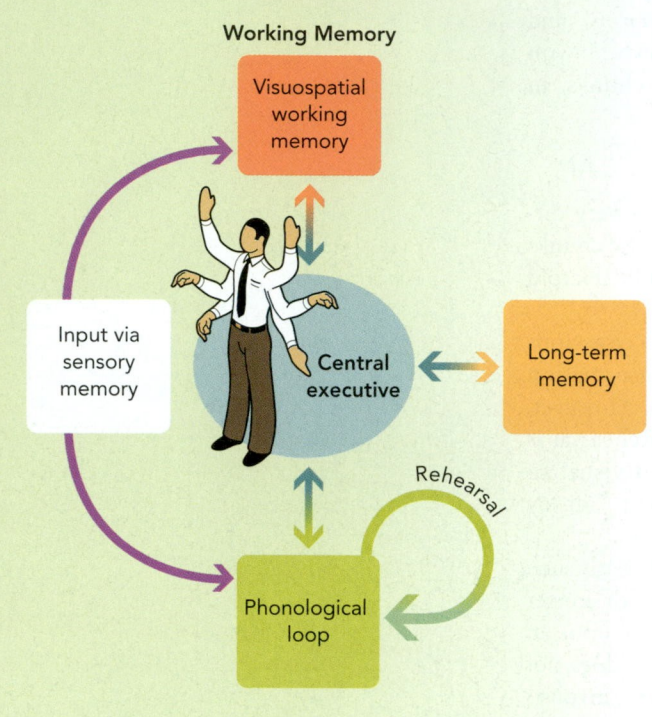

Working Memory

Visuospatial working memory

Input via sensory memory

Central executive

Long-term memory

Rehearsal

Phonological loop

The Inner Workings of Working Memory

This figure represents Baddeley's working memory model. Although the diagram might seem complicated, take a moment to answer the following questions, and it will all start to make sense.

1. What is the central executive, and why is it in the center of the figure?

2. Can you see where rehearsal takes place? Why would rehearsal fit there?

3. Notice the number of double-headed arrows in this figure. They signify that information flows in both directions. Now look for the single-headed arrows (there are three). Why does that information flow in only one direction?

4. Imagine that you have met a very attractive person whom you would like to get to know better. The individual has just given you his or her phone number. Trace that information along the steps of this figure. How does it flow, and where does it end up? When and how will you take it out and put it to use?

components: an acoustic code (the sounds we heard), which decays in a few seconds, and rehearsal, which allows us to repeat the words in the phonological store.

2. *Visuospatial working memory* stores visual and spatial information, including visual imagery. As in the case of the phonological loop, the capacity of visuospatial working memory is limited. If we try to put too many items in visuospatial working memory, we cannot represent them accurately enough to retrieve them successfully. The phonological loop and visuospatial memory function independently. We can rehearse numbers in the phonological loop while making spatial arrangements of letters in visuospatial working memory.

3. The *central executive* integrates information not only from the phonological loop and visuospatial working memory but also from long-term memory. In Baddeley's (2006, 2010) view, the central executive plays important roles in attention, planning, and organizing. The central executive acts like a supervisor who monitors which information deserves our attention and which we should ignore. It also selects which strategies to use to process information and solve problems. Like the phonological loop and visuospatial working memory, the central executive has a limited capacity. If working memory is like the files you have open on your computer, the central executive is *you*. You pull up information you need, close out other things, and so forth.

Though it is compelling, Baddeley's notion of working memory is merely a conceptual model describing processes in memory. Neuroscientists have only just begun to search for brain areas and activity that might be responsible for these processes (Beneventi & others, 2010; Budson, 2009; McGettigan & others, 2010). Still, Baddeley's working memory model is useful. Take a closer look at it in the Psychological Inquiry.

23·3 LONG-TERM MEMORY

Long-term memory is a relatively permanent type of memory that stores huge amounts of information for a long time. The capacity of long-term memory is staggering. John von Neumann, a distinguished mathematician, put the size at $2.8 \cdot 10^{20}$ (280 quintillion) bits, which in practical terms means that our storage capacity is virtually unlimited. Von Neumann assumed that we never forget anything; but even considering that we do forget things, we can hold several billion times more information than a large computer.

● **long-term memory** A relatively permanent type of memory that stores huge amounts of information for a long time.

Components of Long-Term Memory

Long-term memory is complex, as Figure 23.4 shows. At the top level, it is divided into substructures of explicit memory and implicit memory. Explicit memory can be further subdivided into episodic and semantic memory. Implicit memory includes the systems involved in procedural memory, classical conditioning, and priming.

In simple terms, explicit memory has to do with remembering who, what, where, when, and why; implicit memory has to do with remembering how. To explore the distinction, let's look at the case of a person known as H. M. Afflicted with severe epilepsy, H. M. underwent surgery in 1953 that involved removing the hippocampus and a portion of the temporal lobes of both hemispheres in his brain. H. M.'s epilepsy improved, but something devastating happened to his memory. Most dramatically, he developed an inability to form new memories that outlive working memory. H. M.'s memory time frame was only a few minutes at most, so he lived, until his death in 2007, in a perpetual present and could not remember past events (explicit memory). In contrast, his memory of *how* to do things (implicit memory) was less affected. For example, he could learn new physical tasks, even though he had no memory of how or when he learned them.

H. M.'s situation demonstrates a distinction between explicit memory, which was dramatically impaired in his case, and implicit memory, which was less influenced by his surgery. Let's explore the subsystems of explicit and implicit memory more thoroughly.

EXPLICIT MEMORY

Explicit memory (also called *declarative memory*) is the conscious recollection of information, such as specific facts and events and, at least in humans, information that can be verbally communicated (Tulving, 2000). Examples of using explicit, or declarative, memory include recounting the events in a movie you have seen and recalling the names of the people in the president's cabinet.

How long does explicit memory last? Explicit memory includes things you are learning in your classes even now. Will it stay with you? Research by Harry Bahrick has

● **explicit memory** Also called declarative memory, the conscious recollection of information, such as specific facts or events and, at least in humans, information that can be verbally communicated.

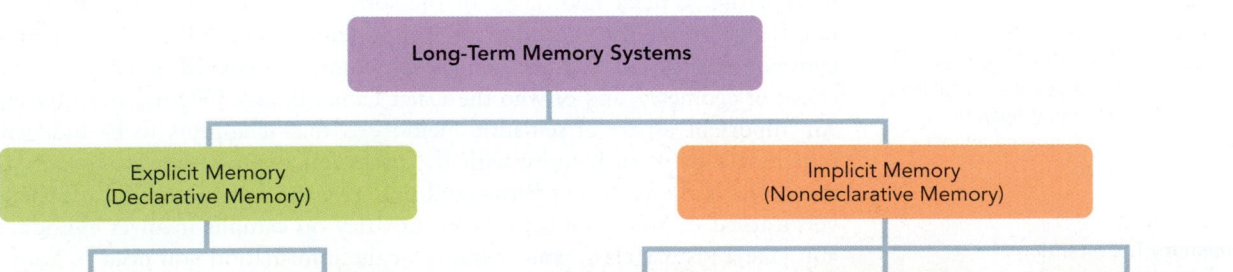

FIGURE 23.4 Systems of Long-Term Memory Long-term memory stores huge amounts of information for long periods of time, much like a computer's hard drive. The hierarchy in the figure shows the division of long-term memory at the top level into explicit memory and implicit memory. Explicit memory can be further divided into episodic and semantic memory; implicit memory includes procedural memory, priming, and classical conditioning.

Your explicit memory system is activated when you describe events in a movie you have seen.

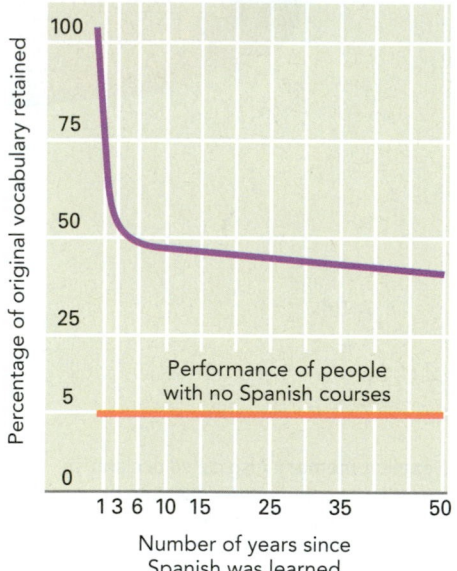

FIGURE 23.5 Memory for Spanish as a Function of Age Since Spanish Was Learned An initial steep drop over about a three-year period in remembering the vocabulary learned in Spanish classes occurred. However, there was little dropoff in memory for Spanish vocabulary from three years after taking Spanish classes to 50 years after taking them. Even 50 years after taking Spanish classes, individuals still remembered almost 50 percent of the vocabulary.

● **episodic memory** The retention of information about the where, when, and what of life's happenings—that is, how individuals remember life's episodes.

● **semantic memory** A person's knowledge about the world, including his or her areas of expertise; general knowledge, such as of things learned in school; and everyday knowledge.

examined this very question. Ohio Wesleyan University, where Bahrick is a professor of psychology, is a small (about 1,800 students) liberal arts school that boasts very loyal alumni who faithfully return to campus for reunions and other events. Bahrick (1984) took advantage of this situation to conduct an ingenious study on the retention of course material over time. He gave vocabulary tests to individuals who had taken Spanish in college as well as to a control group of college students who had not taken Spanish in college. The individuals chosen for the study had used Spanish very little since their college courses. Some individuals were tested at the end of an academic year (just after having taken the courses), but others were tested years after graduation—as many as 50 years later. When Bahrick assessed how much the participants had forgotten, he found a striking pattern (Figure 23.5): Forgetting tended to occur in the first three years after taking the classes and then leveled off, so that adults maintained considerable knowledge of Spanish vocabulary words up to 50 years later.

Bahrick (1984) assessed not only how long ago adults studied Spanish but also how well they did in Spanish during college. Those who got an *A* in their courses 50 years earlier remembered more Spanish than adults who got a *C* grade when taking Spanish only one year earlier. Thus, how well students initially learned the material was even more important than how long ago they studied it.

Bahrick calls information that is retained for such a long time "permastore" content (Bahrick, 2000, 2005; Bahrick, Hall, & Da Costa, 2008). Permastore memory represents that portion of original learning that appears destined to be with the person virtually forever, even without rehearsal. In addition to focusing on course material, Bahrick and colleagues (1974) have probed adults' memories for the faces and names of their high school classmates. Thirty-five years after graduation, the participants visually recognized 90 percent of the portraits of their high school classmates, with name recognition being almost as high. These results held even in relatively large classes (the average class size in the study was 294).

Canadian cognitive psychologist Endel Tulving (1972, 1989, 2000) has been the foremost advocate of distinguishing between two subtypes of explicit memory: episodic and semantic. **Episodic memory** is the retention of information about the where, when, and what of life's happenings—basically, how we remember life's episodes. Episodic memory is autobiographical. For example, episodic memory includes the details of where you were when your younger brother or sister was born, what happened on your first date, and what you ate for breakfast this morning.

Semantic memory is a person's knowledge about the world. It includes your areas of expertise, general knowledge of the sort you are learning in school, and everyday knowledge about the meanings of words, famous individuals, important places, and common things. For example, semantic memory is involved in a person's knowledge of chess, of geometry, and of who the Dalai Lama, Barack Obama, and Lindsey Vonn are. An important aspect of semantic memory is that it appears to be independent of an individual's personal identity with the past. You can access a fact—such as the detail that Lima is the capital of Peru—and not have the foggiest notion of when and where you learned it. Your memory of your first day on campus involves episodic memory. If you take a history class, your memory of the information you need to know to do well on the next test involves semantic memory.

The difference between episodic and semantic memory is also demonstrated in certain cases of amnesia (memory loss). A person with amnesia might forget entirely who she is—her name, family, career, and all other vital information about herself—yet still be able to talk, know what words mean, and have general knowledge about the world, such as what day it is or who currently holds the office of U.S. president (Milton & others, 2010). In such cases, episodic memory is impaired, but semantic memory is functioning.

Figure 23.6 summarizes some aspects of the episodic/semantic distinction. The differences that are listed are controversial. One criticism is that many cases of explicit, or declarative, memory are neither purely episodic nor purely semantic but fall in a gray area in between. Consider your memory for what you studied last night. You probably added knowledge to your semantic memory—that was, after all, the reason you were studying. You probably remember where you were studying, as well as about when you started and when you stopped. You probably also can remember some minor occurrences, such as a burst of loud laughter from the room next door or the coffee you spilled on the desk. Is episodic or semantic memory involved here? Tulving (1983, 2000) argues that semantic and episodic systems often work together in forming new memories. In such cases, the memory that ultimately forms might consist of an autobiographical episode *and* semantic information.

Characteristic	Episodic Memory	Semantic Memory
Units	Events, episodes	Facts, ideas, concepts
Organization	Time	Concepts
Emotion	More important	Less important
Retrieval process	Deliberate (effortful)	Automatic
Retrieval report	"I remember"	"I know"
Education	Irrelevant	Relevant
Intelligence	Irrelevant	Relevant
Legal testimony	Admissible in court	Inadmissible in court

FIGURE 23.6   Some Differences Between Episodic and Semantic Memory These characteristics have been proposed as the main ways to differentiate episodic from semantic memory.

IMPLICIT MEMORY

In addition to explicit memory, there is a type of long-term memory that is related to nonconsciously remembering skills and sensory perceptions rather than consciously remembering facts. **Implicit memory** (also called *nondeclarative memory*) is memory in which behavior is affected by prior experience without a conscious recollection of that experience. Implicit memory comes into play, for example, in the skills of playing tennis and snowboarding, as well as in the physical act of text messaging. Another example of implicit memory is the repetition in your mind of a song you heard in the supermarket, even though you did not notice the song playing. Implicit memory explains why you might find yourself knowing all the words to a song you hate. You have heard it so many times that you have memorized it without knowing it.

Three subsystems of implicit memory are procedural memory, classical conditioning, and priming. All of these subsystems refer to memories that you are not aware of but that influence behavior (Slotnick & Schacter, 2006).

Procedural memory is an implicit memory process that involves memory for skills. For example (assuming that you are an expert typist), as you type a paper, you are not conscious of where the keys are for the various letters, but your well-learned, nonconscious skill of typing allows you to hit the right keys. Similarly, once you have learned to drive a car, you remember how to go about it: You do not have to remember consciously how to drive the car as you put the key in the ignition, turn the steering wheel, depress the gas pedal, and step on the brake pedal. To grasp the distinction between explicit memory and procedural memory, imagine trying to describe to someone in words exactly how to tie a shoe—something you can do successfully in just a few seconds—without having a shoe around.

Another type of implicit memory involves *classical conditioning,* a form of learning. Classical conditioning involves the automatic learning of associations between stimuli, so that one comes to evoke the same response as the other. Classically conditioned associations such as this involve non-conscious, implicit memory (Schultz, Dayan, & Montague, 2009). So without realizing it, you might start to like the person who sits next to you in your favorite class, because she is around while you are feeling good.

A final type of implicit memory process is priming. **Priming** is the activation of information that people already have in storage to help them remember new information better and faster (Hare & others, 2009). In a common demonstration of priming, individuals study a list of words (such as *hope, walk,* and *cake*). Then they are given a standard recognition task to assess explicit memory. They must select all of the words that appeared in the list—for example, "Did you see the word *hope*? Did you see the word *form*?" Then participants perform a stem-completion task, which assesses implicit memory. In this task, they view a list of incomplete words (for example, *ho__, wa__, ca__*), called word stems, and must fill in the blanks with whatever word comes to mind. The results show that individuals more often fill in the blanks with the previously

● **implicit memory** Also called nondeclarative memory, memory in which behavior is affected by prior experience without a conscious recollection of that experience.

● **procedural memory** Memory for skills.

● **priming** The activation of information that people already have in storage to help them remember new information better and faster.

studied words than would be expected if they were filling in the blanks randomly. For example, they are more likely to complete the stem *ho__* with *hope* than with *hole*. This result occurs even when individuals do not recognize the words on the earlier recognition task. Because priming takes place even when explicit memory for previous information is not required, it is assumed to be an involuntary and non-conscious process (Soldan & others, 2009; Wiese & Schweinberger, 2010).

Priming occurs when something in the environment evokes a response in memory—such as the activation of a particular concept. Priming a term or concept makes it more available in memory (Kelly & McNamara, 2009). John Bargh and other social psychologists have demonstrated that priming can have a surprising influence on social behavior (Bargh, 2005, 2006; Bargh & Morsella, 2009; Harris, Brownell, & Bargh, 2010; McCulloch & others, 2008; P. K. Smith & Bargh, 2008). For example, in one study, college students were asked to unscramble a series of words to make a sentence (Bargh, Chen, & Burrows, 1996). For some of the participants, the items in the series included such words as *rude, aggressively, intrude,* and *bluntly.* For other students, the words included *polite, cautious,* and *sensitively.*

Upon completing the scrambled sentences, participants were to report to the experimenter, but each participant encountered the experimenter deep in conversation with another person. Who was more likely to interrupt the ongoing conversation? Among those who were primed with words connoting rudeness, 67 percent interrupted the experimenter. Among those in the "polite" condition, 84 percent of the participants waited the entire 10 minutes, never interrupting the ongoing conversation.

Priming can also spur goal-directed behavior. For example, Bargh and colleagues (2001) asked students to perform a word-search puzzle. Embedded in the puzzle were either neutral words (*shampoo, robin*) or achievement-related words (*compete, win, achieve*). Participants who were exposed to the achievement-related words did better on a later puzzle task, finding 26 words in other puzzles, while those with the neutral primes found only 21.5. Other research has shown that individuals primed with words like *professor* and *intelligent* performed better at a game of Trivial Pursuit than those primed with words like *stupid* and *hooligan* (Dijksterhuis & Van Knippenberg, 1998). These effects occur without awareness, with no participants reporting suspicion about the effects of the primes on their behavior.

How Memory Is Organized

Explaining the forms of long-term memory does not address the question of how the different types of memory are organized for storage. The word *organized* is important: Memories are not haphazardly stored but instead are carefully sorted.

Here is a demonstration. Recall the 12 months of the year as quickly as you can. How long did it take you? What was the order of your recall? Chances are, you listed them within a few seconds in chronological order (January, February, March, and so on). Now try to remember the months in alphabetical order. How long did it take you? Did you make any errors? It should be obvious that your memory for the months of the year is organized in a particular way. Indeed, one of memory's most distinctive features is its organization.

Researchers have found that if people are encouraged to organize material simply, their memories of the material improve even if they receive no warning that their memories will be tested (Mandler, 1980). Organizing information during encoding can be especially important to later memory (Polyn, Norman, & Kahana, 2009). Psychologists have developed a variety of theories of how long-term memory is organized. Let's consider two of these more closely: schemas and connectionist networks.

SCHEMAS

You and a friend have taken a long drive to a new town where neither of you has ever been before. You stop at the local diner, have a seat, and look over the menu. You have never been in this diner before, but you know exactly what is going to happen. Why? Because you have a schema for what happens in a restaurant. When we store information in memory, we often fit it into the collection of information that already exists, as you do even in a new experience with a diner. A **schema** is a pre-existing mental concept or framework that helps people to organize and interpret information. Schemas from prior encounters with the environment influence the way we handle information—how we encode it, the inferences we make about it, and how we retrieve it.

Schemas can also be at work when we recall information. Schema theory holds that long-term memory is not very exact. We seldom find precisely the memory that we want, or at least not all of what we want; hence, we have to *reconstruct* the rest. Our schemas support the reconstruction process, helping us fill in gaps between our fragmented memories.

We have schemas for lots of situations and experiences—for scenes and spatial layouts (a beach, a bathroom), as well as for common events (playing football, writing a term paper). A **script** is a schema for an event (Schank & Abelson, 1977). Scripts often have information about physical features,

Each of us has a schema for what happens in a restaurant.

people, and typical occurrences. This kind of information is helpful when people need to figure out what is happening around them. For example, if you are enjoying your after-dinner coffee in an upscale restaurant and a man in a tuxedo comes over and puts a piece of paper on the table, your script tells you that the man probably is a waiter who has just given you the check. Scripts help to organize our storage of memories about events.

CONNECTIONIST NETWORKS

Schema theory has little or nothing to say about the role of the physical brain in memory. Thus, a new theory based on brain research has generated a wave of excitement among psychologists. **Connectionism,** also called *parallel distributed processing (PDP),* is the theory that memory is stored throughout the brain in connections among neurons, several of which may work together to process a single memory (Janata, 2009; Murre, 2010).

In the connectionist view, memories are not large knowledge structures (as in schema theories). Instead, memories are more like electrical impulses, organized only to the extent that neurons, the connections among them, and their activity are organized. Any piece of knowledge—such as your dog's name—is embedded in the strengths of hundreds or thousands of connections among neurons and is not limited to a single location.

How does the connectionist process work? A neural activity involving memory, such as remembering your dog's name, is spread across a number of areas of the cerebral cortex. The locations of neural activity, called *nodes,* are interconnected. When a node reaches a critical level of activation, it can affect another node across synapses. We know that the human cerebral cortex contains millions of neurons that are richly interconnected through hundreds of millions of synapses. Because of these synaptic connections, the activity of one neuron can be influenced by many other neurons. Because of these simple reactions, the connectionist view argues that changes in the strength of synaptic connections are the fundamental bases of memory (Canals & others, 2009). From the connectionist network perspective, memories are organized sets of neurons that are routinely activated together.

Part of the appeal of the connectionist view is that it is consistent with what we know about brain function and allows psychologists to simulate human memory studies using computers (Marcus, 2001). Connectionist approaches also help to explain how priming a concept (rudeness) can influence behavior (interrupting someone). Furthermore, insights from this connectionist view support brain research undertaken to determine where memories are stored in the brain (McClelland & Rumelhart, 2009), another fascinating and complex topic.

● **schema** A preexisting mental concept or framework that helps people to organize and interpret information. Schemas from prior encounters with the environment influence the way we encode, make inferences about, and retrieve information.

● **script** A schema for an event, often containing information about physical features, people, and typical occurrences.

● **connectionism** Also called parallel distributed processing (PDP), the theory that memory is stored throughout the brain in connections among neurons, several of which may work together to process a single memory.

Indeed, so far we have examined the many ways cognitive psychologists think about how information is stored. The question remains, *where?* The puzzle of the physical location of memories has long fascinated psychologists. Although memory may seem to be a mysterious phenomenon, it, like all psychological processes, must occur in a physical place: the brain.

Where Memories Are Stored

Karl Lashley (1950) spent a lifetime looking for a location in the brain in which memories are stored. He trained rats to discover the correct pathway in a maze and then cut out various portions of the animals' brains and retested their memory of the maze pathway. Experiments with thousands of rats showed that the loss of various cortical areas did not affect rats' ability to remember the pathway, leading Lashley to conclude that memories are not stored in a specific location in the brain. Other researchers, continuing Lashley's quest, agreed that memory storage is diffuse, but they developed additional insights. Canadian psychologist Donald Hebb (1949, 1980) suggested that assemblies of cells, distributed over large areas of the cerebral cortex, work together to represent information, just as the connectionist network perspective would predict.

NEURONS AND MEMORY

Today many neuroscientists believe that memory is located in specific sets or circuits of neurons (Ardiel & Rankin, 2010; Clark & Squire, 2010). Brain researcher Larry Squire, for example, says that most memories are probably clustered in groups of about 1,000 neurons (1990, 2004, 2007). At the same time, single neurons are also at work in memory (Rutishauser & others, 2010; Squire, 2007). Researchers who measure the electrical activity of single cells have found that some respond to faces and others to eye or hair color, for example. Still, in order for you to recognize your Uncle Albert, individual neurons that provide information about hair color, size, and other characteristics must act together.

Researchers also believe that brain chemicals may be the ink with which memories are written. Remember that neurotransmitters are the chemicals that allow neurons to communicate across the synapse. These chemicals play a crucial role in forging the connections that represent memory.

Ironically, some of the answers to complex questions about the neural mechanics of memory come from studies on a very simple experimental animal—the inelegant sea slug. Eric Kandel and James Schwartz (1982) chose this large snail-without-a-shell because of the simple architecture of its nervous system, which consists of only about 10,000 neurons. (You might recall from Module 7 that the human brain has about 100 billion neurons.)

Species of sea slug similar to that studied by Kandel and Schwartz.

The sea slug is hardly a quick learner or an animal with a good memory, but it is equipped with a reliable reflex. When anything touches the gill on its back, it quickly withdraws it. First the researchers accustomed the sea slug to having its gill prodded. After a while, the animal ignored the prod and stopped withdrawing its gill. Next the researchers applied an electric shock to its tail when they touched the gill. After many rounds of the shock-accompanied prod, the sea slug violently withdrew its gill at the slightest touch. The researchers found that the sea slug remembered this message for hours or even weeks. They also determined that shocking the sea slug's gill releases the neurotransmitter serotonin at the synapses of its nervous system, and this chemical release basically provides a reminder that the gill was shocked. This "memory" informs the nerve cell to send out chemical commands to retract the gill the next time it is touched. If nature builds complexity out of simplicity, then the mechanism used by the sea slug may work in the human brain as well.

Researchers have proposed the concept of *long-term potentiation* to explain how memory functions at the neuron level. In line with connectionist theory, this concept states that if two neurons are activated at the same time, the connection between them—and

Memory and Sensation: Why Is Smell Specially Connected with Memory?

You smell a turkey roasting in the oven, and suddenly you are once again 6 years old and eagerly anticipating your family's Thanksgiving dinner. The aroma of the tamales your *abuela* (grandmother) used to make reminds you of so many Christmases past. With less pleasure, you smell the cologne of a former romantic partner and vividly recall your last argument with your ex. Of all of the senses, smell seems to bear the strongest relationship to memory, and a smell can trigger rich emotional memories. Marcel Proust described this link so powerfully in his novel *Swann's Way* that the term the *Proust effect* has come to mean the ability of smell to transport us into vivid memory.

Do you have any favorite smells? How are they related to your memories?

Why are smell and memory so closely linked? At least part of the answer is anatomical. Recall that nerves in the nose send information about smells to the primary olfactory cortex in the brain. That cortex links directly to the amygdala and hippocampus. Thus, smells have a superhighway to the brain structures involved in emotion (the amygdala) and memory consolidation (the hippocampus) (Galan & others, 2006; Herz, Schankler, & Beland, 2004). Rachel Herz (2004) found that autobiographical memories that were cued by odors (a campfire, fresh-cut grass, popcorn) were more emotional and more evocative than such memories cued by pictures or sounds. Indeed, smells can be powerful tools for memory. Herz and Gerald Cupchik found that individuals performed better on a surprise memory test if the same odor cue was present in the room during learning and recall (Herz & Cupchik, 1995; Herz, 1998). One implication of that study is that it might

be a good idea to wear the same cologne to an exam that you typically wear to class.

However, showing that smells influence memory and that the brain evidently has evolved to give smell a privileged place does not help us understand why the special status of smell is adaptive. Why would it be adaptive to give smell a special link with emotion and memory? Many other animals detect important information about their environments from smell; that is why, for instance, dogs' noses are so close to the ground (and so sensitive). Animals use smells to navigate through the world—to detect what is good (the smell of a food) and what is bad (the scent of a predator). In humans, emotions play a similar role in that they tell us how we are doing in the world in terms of what matters to us. Perhaps for humans, the special link between smells and emotions allows us quickly to learn associations between particular smells and stimuli that are good (morning coffee) or bad (spoiled milk) for us. As the holiday dinner examples above suggest, smells may have a special power in the positive emotional experience of nostalgia. The right smells alone can transport us powerfully to the good old days.

thus the memory—may be strengthened (Pujadas & others, 2010; Ruiz & others, 2010). Long-term potentiation has been demonstrated experimentally by administering a drug that increases the flow of information from one neuron to another across the synapse (Bagetta & others, 2010), raising the possibility of someday improving memory through drugs that increase neural connections (Schacter, 2001). Imagine that what you experience as a memory is really a collection of well-worn pathways in your brain.

BRAIN STRUCTURES AND MEMORY FUNCTIONS

Whereas some neuroscientists are unveiling the cellular basis of memory, others are examining its broad-scale architecture in the brain. Many different parts of the brain

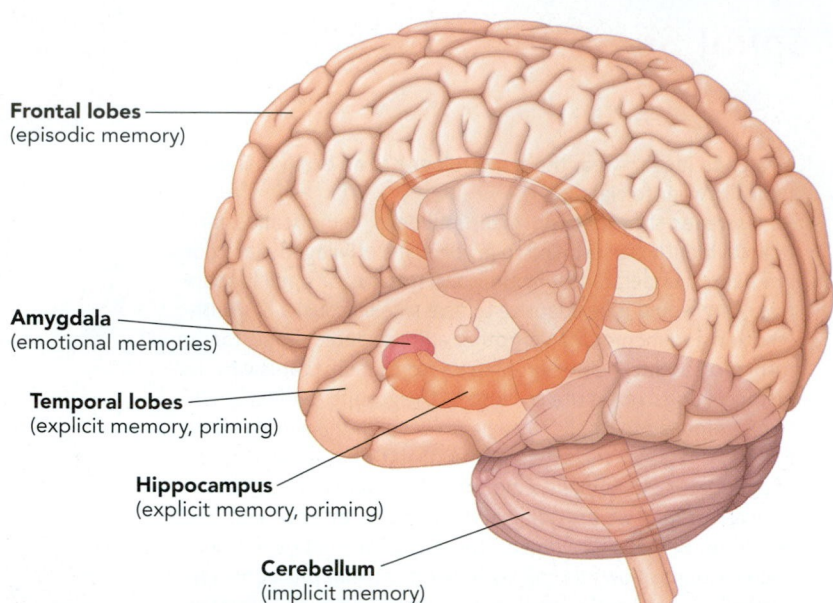

Frontal lobes
(episodic memory)

Amygdala
(emotional memories)

Temporal lobes
(explicit memory, priming)

Hippocampus
(explicit memory, priming)

Cerebellum
(implicit memory)

FIGURE 23.7 **Structures of the Brain Involved in Different Aspects of Long-Term Memory** Note that explicit memory and implicit memory appear to involve different locations in the brain.

and nervous system are involved in the rich, complex process that is memory (Schacter & Wagner, 2011; Ystad & others, 2010). Although there is no one memory center in the brain, researchers have demonstrated that specific brain structures are involved in particular aspects of memory.

Figure 23.7 shows the location of brain structures active in different types of long-term memory. Note that implicit and explicit memory appear to involve different locations in the brain.

- *Explicit memory:* Neuroscientists have found that the hippocampus, the temporal lobes in the cerebral cortex, and other areas of the limbic system play a role in explicit memory (Rose, Haider, & Buchel, 2010; Wang & Morris, 2010). In many aspects of explicit memory, information is transmitted from the hippocampus to the frontal lobes, which are involved in both retrospective (remembering things from the past) and prospective (remembering things that you need to do in the future) memory (Poppenk & others, 2010). The left frontal lobe is especially active when we encode new information into memory; the right frontal lobe is more active when we subsequently retrieve it (Babiloni & others, 2006). In addition, the amygdala, which is part of the limbic system, is involved in emotional memories (Kishioka & others, 2009).

- *Implicit memory:* The cerebellum (the structure at the back and toward the bottom of the brain) is active in the implicit memory required to perform skills (Torriero & others, 2010). Various areas of the cerebral cortex, such as the temporal lobes and hippocampus, function in priming (Gagnepain & others, 2010).

Current research is intensively studying the links between memory and neuroscience (Gamer & others, 2009; Ross, Brown, & Stern, 2009; Suzuki & others, 2009). The Intersection showcases another example of overlapping fields of psychology, this time involving memory and sensation.

SUMMARY

The Atkinson-Shiffrin theory describes memory as a three-stage process: sensory memory, short-term memory, and long-term memory.

Sensory memory holds perceptions of the world for only an instant. Visual sensory memory (iconic memory) retains information for about 1/4 of a second; auditory sensory memory (echoic memory) preserves information for several seconds.

Short-term memory is a limited-capacity memory system in which information is usually retained for as long as 30 seconds. Short-term memory's limitation is 7 ± 2 bits of information. Chunking and rehearsal can benefit short-term memory. Baddeley's concept of working memory characterizes short-term memory as active and complex. Working memory has three components: a central executive and two assistants (phonological loop and visuospatial working memory).

Long-term memory is a relatively permanent type of memory that holds huge amounts of information for a long time. Long-term memory has two main subtypes: explicit and implicit memory. Explicit memory is the conscious recollection of information, such as specific facts or events. Implicit memory affects behavior through prior experiences that are not consciously recollected. Explicit memory has two dimensions. One

KEY TERMS

storage 233
Atkinson-Shiffrin
   theory 233
sensory memory 233
short-term memory 234
working memory 235
long-term memory 237
explicit memory 237

episodic memory 238
semantic memory 238
implicit memory 239
procedural memory 239
priming 239
schema 241
script 241
connectionism 241

dimension includes episodic memory and semantic memory. The other dimension includes retrospective memory and prospective memory. Implicit memory is multidimensional too and includes systems for procedural memory, priming, and classical conditioning.

TEST YOURSELF

1. How do sensory memory and short-term memory differ in terms of their duration?
2. What two kinds of memory are at the top level of long-term memory, and how is each defined?
3. How do the schema theory of memory and the connectionist network theory of memory differ in terms of their explanation of memories?

APPLY YOUR KNOWLEDGE

1. Take the short-term memory test that appears at http://faculty.washington.edu/chudler/stm0.html. Compare your results with those of another student in class. Is there a pattern to the letters each of you remember? Explain your results.
2. Draw a diagram of how your brain stores memories. Include in your diagram the primary structures of the brain and then show which relates to each type of memory.

Memory Retrieval

Remember that unforgettable night of shining stars with your romantic partner? Let's say the evening has indeed been encoded deeply and elaborately in your memory. Through the years you have thought about the night a great deal and told your best friends about it. The story of that night has become part of the longer story of your life with your significant other. Fifty years later, your grandson asks, "How did you two end up together?" You share that story you have been saving for just such a question. What are the retrieval processes that allow you to do so?

Memory **retrieval** takes place when information that was retained in memory comes out of storage. You might think of long-term memory as a library. You retrieve information in a fashion similar to the process you use to locate and check out a book in an actual library. To retrieve something from your mental data bank, you search your store of memory to find the relevant information.

The efficiency with which you retrieve information from memory is impressive. It usually takes only a moment to search through a vast storehouse to find the information you want. When were you born? What was the name of your first date? Who developed the first psychology laboratory? You can, of course, answer all of these questions instantly. (The answer to that last one is Wilhelm Wundt.) Yet retrieval of memory is a complex and sometimes imperfect process (Benoit & others, 2009).

Before examining ways that retrieval may fall short, let's look at some basic concepts and variables that are known to affect the likelihood that information will be accurately encoded, stored, and ultimately retrieved. As we will see, retrieval depends heavily on the circumstances under which a memory was encoded and the way it was retained (Mate & Baques, 2009).

24-1 SERIAL POSITION EFFECT

The **serial position effect** is the tendency to recall the items at the beginning and end of a list more readily than those in the middle. If you are a reality TV fan, you might notice that you always seem to remember the first person to get voted off and the last few survivors. All those people in the middle, however, are a blur. The *primacy effect* refers to better recall for items at the beginning of a list; the *recency effect* refers to better recall for items at the end. Together with the relatively low recall of items from the middle of the list, this pattern makes up the *serial position effect* (Laming, 2010). You can sharpen your understanding of serial position effects by completing the exercise in the Psychological Inquiry above.

Psychologists explain these effects using principles of encoding. With respect to the primacy effect, the first few items in the list are easily remembered because they are rehearsed more or because they receive more elaborative processing than do words later in the list (Atkinson & Shiffrin, 1968; Craik & Tulving, 1975). Working memory is relatively empty when the items enter, so there is little competition for rehearsal time. Moreover, because the items get more rehearsal, they stay in working memory longer and are more likely to be encoded successfully into long-term memory. In contrast, many items from the middle of the list drop out of working memory before being encoded into long-term memory.

As for the recency effect, the last several items are remembered for different reasons. First, when these items are recalled, they might still be in working memory. Second, even if these items are not in working memory, the fact that they were just encountered makes them easier to recall. Interestingly, both primacy and recency can influence how we feel about stimuli as well. In one study, wine tasters were more likely to prefer the first wine

• retrieval The memory process that occurs when information that was retained in memory comes out of storage.

• serial position effect The tendency to recall the items at the beginning and end of a list more readily than those in the middle.

psychological *inquiry*

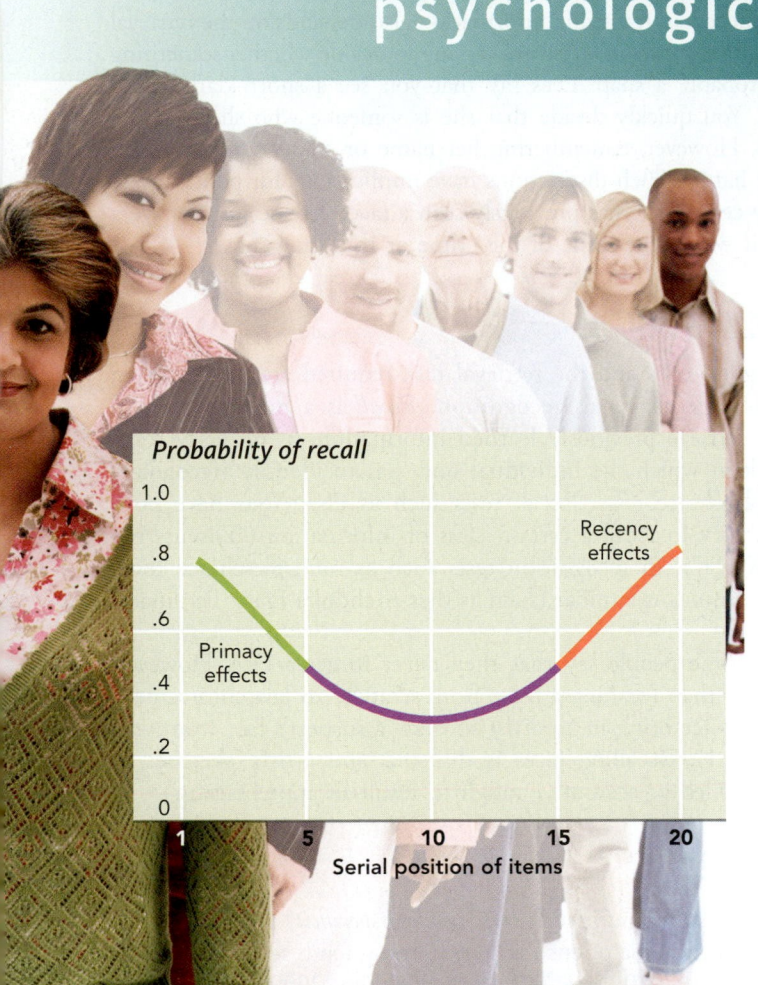

Probability of recall

Primacy effects

Recency effects

Serial position of items

The Serial Position Effect: Lost in Midstream

This figure shows typical serial position effects. The vertical or Y axis is the probability of an individual's remembering a particular item in a list. Notice the highest value on this axis is 1.0, meaning that the chance of remembering the item is 100 percent. The horizontal or X axis is the position of the items from first to last (in this case the 20th item). Examine the figure to answer the following questions:

1. What is the probability that the item presented in the 15th position will be remembered? What about the item that was presented first?

2. In this figure, which is stronger—primacy or recency? Explain.

3. When it is time for final exams, which information from your class do you think it would be best to brush up on, and why?

4. Suppose you are going for a job interview, and there are several other candidates there that day for interviews. If you want to make a memorable impression, which position in the sequence of interviews would you prefer, and why?

they sipped, an outcome demonstrating primacy (Mantonakis & others, 2009). In another study, participants felt that the best was saved for last when they evaluated paintings and *American Idol* audition tapes, an outcome demonstrating recency (Li & Epley, 2009).

24-2 RETRIEVAL CUES AND THE RETRIEVAL TASK

Two other factors are involved in retrieval: the nature of the cues that can prompt your memory and the retrieval task that you set for yourself. We consider each in turn.

If effective cues for what you are trying to remember do not seem to be available, you need to create them—a process that takes place in working memory (Carpenter & DeLosh, 2006; Rummel, 2010). For example, if you have a block about remembering a new friend's name, you might go through the alphabet, generating names that begin with each letter. If you manage to stumble across the right name, you will probably recognize it.

We can learn to generate retrieval cues. One good strategy is to use different subcategories. For example, write down the names of as many of your classmates from middle or junior high school as you can remember. When you run out of names, think about the activities you were involved in during those school years, such as math class, student

off the mark .com   by Mark Parisi

LOOK, I KNOW YOU TOLD ME YOUR NAME BUT I FORGOT TO SAVE IT...

offthemark.com   ©2006 MARK PARISI DIST. BY UFS INC.

council, lunch, drill team, and so on. Does this set of cues help you to remember more of your classmates?

Although cues help, your success in retrieving information also depends on the retrieval task you set for yourself. For instance, if you are simply trying to decide whether something seems familiar, retrieval is probably a snap. Let's say that you see a short, dark-haired woman walking toward you. You quickly decide that she is someone who shops at the same supermarket as you do. However, remembering her name or a precise detail, such as when you met her, can be harder. Such distinctions have implications for police investigations: A witness might be certain she has previously seen a face, yet she might have a hard time deciding whether it was at the scene of the crime or in a mug shot.

Recall and Recognition

The presence or absence of good cues and the retrieval task required are factors in an important memory distinction: recall versus recognition. *Recall* is a memory task in which the individual has to retrieve previously learned information, as on essay tests. *Recognition* is a memory task in which the individual only has to identify (recognize) learned items, as on multiple-choice tests. Recall tests such as essay tests have poor retrieval cues. You are told to try to recall a certain class of information ("Discuss the factors that caused World War I"). In recognition tests such as multiple-choice tests, you merely judge whether a stimulus is familiar (such as that Archduke Franz Ferdinand was assassinated in 1914).

You probably have heard some people say that they never forget a face. However, recognizing a face is far simpler than recalling a face "from scratch," as law enforcement officers know. In some cases, police bring in an artist to draw a suspect's face from witnesses' descriptions (Figure 24.1). Recalling faces is difficult, and artists' sketches of suspects are frequently not detailed or accurate enough to result in apprehension.

Encoding Specificity

Another consideration in understanding retrieval is the *encoding specificity principle,* which states that information present at the time of encoding or learning tends to be effective as a retrieval cue (Crescentini & others, 2010; Raposo, Han, & Dobbins, 2009). For example, you know your instructors when they are in the classroom setting—you see them there all the time. If, however, you run into one of them in an unexpected setting and in more casual attire, such as at the gym in workout clothes, the person's name might escape you. Your memory might fail because the cues you encoded are not available for use.

FIGURE 24.1 **Remembering Faces**
(*Left*) The FBI artist's sketch of Ted Kaczynski. Kaczynski, also known as the Unabomber, is a serial killer who conducted a sequence of mail bombings targeting universities and airlines beginning in the late 1970s. (*Right*) A photograph of Kaczynski. The FBI widely circulated the artist's sketch, which was based on bits and pieces of observations people had made of the infamous Unabomber, in the hope that someone would recognize him. Would you have been able to recognize Kaczynski from the artist's sketch? Probably not. Although most people say they are good at remembering faces, they usually are not as good as they think they are.

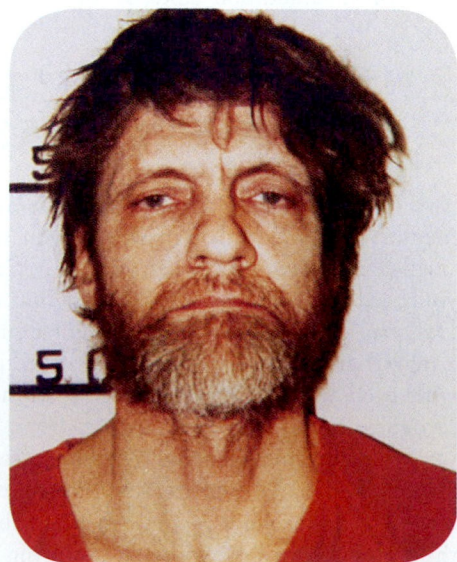

Context at Encoding and Retrieval

An important consequence of encoding specificity is that a change in context between encoding and retrieval can cause memory to fail (Schwabe, Bohringer, & Wolf, 2009). In many instances, people remember better when they attempt to recall information in the same context in which they learned it—a process referred to as *context-dependent memory*. This better recollection is believed to occur because they have encoded features of the context in which they learned the information along with the actual information. Such features can later act as retrieval cues (Bridge, Chiao, & Paller, 2010).

In one study, scuba divers learned information on land and under water (Godden & Baddeley, 1975). Later they were asked to recall the information when they were either on land or under water. The divers' recall was much better when the encoding and retrieval contexts were the same (both on land or both under water).

24-3 SPECIAL CASES OF RETRIEVAL

We began this discussion by likening memory retrieval to looking for and finding a book in the library. However, the process of retrieving information from long-term memory is not as precise as the library analogy suggests. When we search through our long-term memory storehouse, we do not always find the exact "book" we want— or we might find the book but discover that several pages are missing. We have to fill in these gaps somehow.

Our memories are affected by a number of factors, including the pattern of information we remember, schemas and scripts, the situations we associate with memories, and the personal or emotional context. Certainly, everyone has had the experience of remembering a shared situation with a particular individual, only to have him or her remind us, "Oh, that wasn't *me*!" Such moments provide convincing evidence that memory may well be best understood as "reconstructive." This subjective quality of memory certainly has implications for important day-to-day procedures such as eyewitness testimony (Greene, 1999).

While the factors that we have discussed so far relate to the retrieval of generic information, various kinds of special memory retrieval also have generated a great deal of research. These memories have special significance because of their relevance to the self, to their emotional or traumatic character, or because they show unusually high levels of apparent accuracy (Piolino & others, 2006). Researchers in cognitive psychology have debated whether these memories rely on processes that are different from those already described or are simply extreme cases of typical memory processes (Lane & Schooler, 2004; Schooler & Eich, 2000). We now turn to these special cases of memory.

Retrieval of Autobiographical Memories

Autobiographical memory, a special form of episodic memory, is a person's recollections of his or her life experiences (Fivush, 2011). An intriguing discovery about autobiographical memory is the *reminiscence bump,* the effect that adults remember more events from the second and third decades of life than from other decades (Copeland, Radvansky, & Goodwin, 2009). This reminiscence bump may occur because these are the times in our life when we have many novel experiences or because it is during our teens and 20s that we are forging a sense of identity (Berntsen & Rubin, 2002).

Autobiographical memories are complex and seem to contain unending strings of stories and snapshots, but researchers have found that they can be categorized (Roediger & Marsh, 2003). For example, based on their research, Martin Conway and David Rubin (1993) sketched a structure of autobiographical memory that has three levels (Figure 24.2). The most abstract level consists of *life time periods;* for example, you might remember something

● **autobiographical memory** A special form of episodic memory, consisting of a person's recollections of his or her life experiences.

Level	Label	Description
Level 1	Life time periods	Long segments of time measured in years and even decades
Level 2	General events	Extended composite episodes measured in days, weeks, or months
Level 3	Event-specific knowledge	Individual episodes measured in seconds, minutes, or hours.

FIGURE 24.2 The Three-Level Hierarchical Structure of Autobiographical Memory When people relate their life stories, all three levels of information are typically present and intertwined.

about your life in high school. The middle level in the hierarchy is made up of *general events,* such as a trip you took with your friends after you graduated from high school. The most concrete level in the hierarchy is composed of *event-specific knowledge;* for example, from your postgraduation trip, you might remember the exhilarating experience you had the first time you jet-skied. When people tell their life stories, all three levels of information are usually present and intertwined.

Most autobiographical memories include some reality and some myth. Personality psychologist Dan McAdams argues that autobiographical memories are less about facts and more about meanings (2001, 2006; McAdams & others, 2006). They provide a reconstructed, embellished telling of the past that connects the past to the present.

Retrieval of Emotional Memories

When we remember our life experiences, the memories are often wrapped in emotion. Emotion affects the encoding and storage of memories and thus shapes the details that are retrieved. The role that emotion plays in memory is of considerable interest to contemporary researchers and has echoes in public life.

● **flashbulb memory** The memory of emotionally significant events that people often recall with more accuracy and vivid imagery than everyday events.

Flashbulb memory is the memory of emotionally significant events that people often recall with more accuracy and vivid imagery than everyday events (Talarico, 2009). Perhaps you can remember, for example, where you were when you first heard of the terrorist attacks on the United States on September 11, 2001. An intriguing dimension of flashbulb memories is that several decades later, people often remember where they were and what was going on in their lives at the time of such an emotionally charged event. These memories seem to be part of an adaptive system that fixes in memory the details that accompany important events so that they can be interpreted at a later time.

Most people express confidence about the accuracy of their flashbulb memories. However, flashbulb memories probably are not as accurately etched in our brain as we think. One way to gauge the accuracy of flashbulb memories is to probe the consistency of the details of these memories over time. One study found that 25 percent of participants included contradictory information in their memories of the 1986 *Challenger* space shuttle disaster (Neisser & Harsch, 1992).

Still, on the whole, flashbulb memories do seem more durable and more accurate than memories of day-to-day happenings (Davidson, Cook, & Glisky, 2006). One possible explanation is that flashbulb memories are quite likely to be rehearsed in the days following the event. However, it is not just the discussion and rehearsal of information that make flashbulb memories so long-lasting. The emotions triggered by flashbulb events also figure in their durability. Although we have focused on negative news events as typical of flashbulb memories, such memories can also occur for positive events. An individual's wedding day and the birth of a child are events that may become milestones in personal history and are always remembered.

Many people have flashbulb memories of where they were and what they were doing when terrorists attacked the World Trade Center towers in New York City on September 11, 2001.

Memory for Traumatic Events

In 1890, the American psychologist and philosopher William James said that an experience can be so emotionally arousing that it almost leaves a scar on the brain. Personal traumas are candidates for such emotionally stirring experiences.

Some psychologists argue that memories of emotionally traumatic events are accurately retained, possibly forever, in considerable detail (Langer, 1991). There is good evidence that memory for traumatic events is usually more accurate than memory for ordinary events (Berntsen & Rubin, 2006; Schooler & Eich, 2000). Consider the traumatic experience of some children who were kidnapped at gunpoint on a school bus in Chowchilla, California, in 1983 and then buried underground for 16 hours before escaping. The children had the classic signs of traumatic memory: detailed and vivid recollections. However, when a child psychiatrist interviewed the children four to five years after the chilling episode, she noted striking errors and distortions in the memories of half of them (Terr, 1988).

How can a traumatic memory be so vivid and detailed yet at the same time have inaccuracies? A number of factors can be involved. Some children might have made perceptual errors while encoding information because the episode was so shocking. Others might have distorted the information and recalled the episode as being less traumatic than it was in order to reduce their anxiety about it. Other children, in discussing the terrifying event with others, might have incorporated bits and pieces of these people's recollections of what happened.

Usually, memories of real-life traumas are more accurate and longer-lasting than memories of everyday events. Where distortion often arises is in the details of the traumatic episode. Stress-related hormones likely play a role in memories that involve personal trauma. The release of stress-related hormones, signaled by the amygdala, likely accounts for some of the extraordinary durability and vividness of traumatic memories (Bucherelli & others, 2006).

Repressed Memories

A great deal of debate surrounds the question, can an individual forget, and later recover, memories of traumatic events (Colangelo, 2009; Geraerts & others, 2009; Loftus & Frenda, 2010)? *Repression* is a defense mechanism by which a person is so traumatized by an event that he or she forgets it and then forgets the act of forgetting. According to psychodynamic theory, repression's main function is to protect the individual from threatening information.

The prevalence of repression is a matter of controversy. Most studies of traumatic memory indicate that a traumatic life event such as childhood sexual abuse is very likely to be remembered. However, there is at least some evidence that childhood sexual abuse may not be remembered. Linda Williams and her colleagues have conducted a number of investigations of memories of childhood abuse (Banyard & Williams, 2007; Liang, Williams, & Siegel, 2006; L. M. Williams, 2003, 2004). One study involved 129 women for whom hospital emergency room records indicated a childhood abuse experience (L. M. Williams, 1995). Seventeen years after the abuse incident, the researchers contacted the women and asked (among other things) whether they had ever been the victim of childhood sexual abuse. Of the 129 women, most reported remembering and never having forgotten the experience. Ten percent of the participants reported having forgotten about the abuse at least for some portion of their lives.

If it does exist, repression can be considered a special case of **motivated forgetting,** which occurs when individuals forget something because it is so painful or anxiety-laden that remembering is intolerable (Fujiwara, Levine, & Anderson, 2008). This type of forgetting may be a consequence of the emotional trauma experienced by victims of rape or physical abuse, war veterans, and survivors of earthquakes, plane crashes, and other terrifying events. These emotional traumas may haunt people for many years unless they can put the details out of mind. Even when people have not experienced trauma, they may use motivated forgetting to protect themselves from memories of painful, stressful, or otherwise unpleasant circumstances.

Are so-called recovered memories authentic? See the Critical Controversy to explore this intriguing question.

● **motivated forgetting** Forgetting that occurs when something is so painful or anxiety-laden that remembering it is intolerable.

CRITICAL CONTROVERSY

Memories: Recovered, Discovered, or False?

In 1990 a jury found George Franklin guilty of the murder of an 8-year-old girl. The murder had taken place in 1969, and the primary evidence against Franklin had been his daughter's memory of the murder, which she allegedly had repressed for over 20 years and recovered during therapy (Loftus & Ketcham, 1991). Franklin spent nearly seven years in prison until his conviction was overturned on appeal when it was revealed that his daughter had recovered the memory after being hypnotized, and DNA evidence proved that he could not have been the perpetrator of a second murder that his daughter also "remembered" witnessing. There is no question that George Franklin's daughter truly believed in the reality of her memories. How could she be so wrong? Can memories that seem real to the rememberer in fact be false?

Led by the research of memory expert Elizabeth Loftus, study after study has found that it is indeed possible to create false memories (Garry & Loftus, 2009; Kaasa & Loftus, 2009; Loftus, 2009; Zhu & others, 2010). In one study, Loftus and Jacquie Pickrell (2001) persuaded people that they had met Bugs Bunny at Disneyland, even though Bugs is not a Disney character. In this study, 30 to 40 percent of participants who were simply shown a fake ad for Disneyland that included Bugs Bunny later reported remembering meeting Bugs when they had visited Disneyland. Such research has led some to question whether so-called recovered memories are ever authentic. Is there evidence that a traumatic life event might be forgotten and then recovered?

Cognitive psychologist Jonathan Schooler suggested that recovered memories are better termed *discovered memories* because, regardless of their accuracy, individuals do experience them as real (Schooler, 2002; Geraerts & others, 2009). Schooler and his colleagues (1997) investigated a number of cases of discovered memories of abuse, in which they sought independent corroboration by others. They were able to identify actual cases in which the perpetrator or some third party could verify a discovered memory. For example, Frank Fitzpatrick's memory of previously "forgotten" abuse at the hands of a Catholic priest was corroborated by witnesses who had also been abused (*Commonwealth of Massachusetts v. Porter*, 1993). The existence of such cases suggests that it is inappropriate to reject all claims by adults that they were victims of long-forgotten childhood sexual abuse.

How do psychologists consider these cases? Generally, there is consensus around a few key issues (Knapp & VandeCreek, 2000). First, all agree that child sexual abuse is an important and egregious problem that has historically been unacknowledged. Second, psychologists widely believe that most individuals who were sexually abused as children remember all or part of what happened to them and that these continuous memories are likely to be accurate. Third, there is broad agreement that it is possible for someone who was abused to forget those memories for a long time, and it is also possible to construct memories that are false but that feel very real to an individual. Finally, it is highly difficult to separate accurate from inaccurate memories, especially if methods such as hypnosis have been used in the "recovery" of memories.

WHAT DO YOU THINK?

- How should courts of law deal with "discovered" memories?

- How does our perspective on discovered memories affect our view of childhood abuse in general? If we cannot trust the testimony of adult survivors of abuse, how can we determine the frequency of childhood abuse today?

Eyewitness Testimony

By now, you should realize that memory is not a perfect reflection of reality. Understanding the distortions of memory is particularly important when people are called on to report what they saw or heard in relation to a crime. Eyewitness testimonies, like other sorts of memories, may contain errors (Laney & Loftus, 2009; Nelson & others, 2009), and faulty memory in criminal matters has especially serious consequences. When eyewitness testimony is inaccurate, the wrong person might go to jail or even be put to death, or the perpetrator of the crime might not be prosecuted. It is important to note that witnessing a crime is often traumatic for the individual, and so this type of memory typically fits in the larger category of memory for highly emotional events.

Much of the interest in eyewitness testimony focuses on distortion, bias, and inaccuracy in memory (Laney & Loftus, 2009; Steblay & Loftus, 2009). One reason for distortion is that, quite simply, memory fades with time. Furthermore, unlike a video, memory can be altered by new information (Dysart & Lindsay, 2007). In one study, researchers showed students a film of an automobile accident and then asked them how fast the white sports car was going when it passed a barn (Loftus, 1975). Although there was no barn in the film, 17 percent of the students mentioned the barn in their answer.

Bias is also a factor in faulty memory (Brigham & others, 2007). Studies have shown that people of one ethnic group are less likely to recognize individual differences among people of another ethnic group (Horry, Wright, & Tredoux, 2010). Latino eyewitnesses, for example, may have trouble distinguishing among several Asian suspects. In one experiment, a mugging was shown on a television news program (Loftus, 1993). Immediately after, a lineup of six suspects was broadcast, and viewers were asked to phone in and identify which one of the six individuals they thought had committed the robbery. Of the 2,000 callers, more than 1,800 identified the wrong person. In addition, even though the robber was a White Euro-American, one-third of the viewers identified an African American or a Latino suspect as the criminal.

Hundreds of individuals have been harmed by witnesses who have made a mistake (Loftus, 2009; Steblay & Loftus, 2009). One estimate indicates that each year approximately 7,500 people in the United States are arrested for and wrongly convicted of serious crimes (Huff, 2002). According to the Innocence Project, an organization dedicated to using DNA evidence to free wrongly convicted people, in the first 239 cases of individuals exonerated by DNA evidence, mistaken eyewitness testimony played a role 175 times (Innocence Project, 2009).

Faulty memory is not just about accusing the wrong person. For example, faulty memories were evident in descriptions of the suspects' vehicle in the sniper attacks that killed 10 people in the Washington, DC, area in 2002. Witnesses reported seeing a white truck or van fleeing several of the crime scenes. It appears that a white van may have been near one of the first shootings and that media repetition of this information contaminated the memories of witnesses to later attacks, making them more likely to remember a white truck or van. When caught, the sniper suspects were driving a blue car.

Before police even arrive at a crime scene, witnesses talk among themselves, and this dialogue can contaminate memories. This is why, during the DC sniper attacks, law enforcement officials advised any persons who might witness the next attack to write down immediately what they had seen—even on their hands if they did not have a piece of paper.

Faulty memories complicated the search for the perpetrators in the sniper attacks that killed 10 people in the Washington, DC, area in 2002. Police released photos of the type of white truck or van that witnesses said they saw fleeing some of the crime scenes (right). In the end, however, the suspects were driving a blue car when law enforcement officials apprehended them (above).

SUMMARY

The serial position effect is the tendency to recall items at the beginning and the end of a list better than the middle items. The primacy effect is the tendency to recall items at the beginning of the list better than the middle items. The recency effect is the tendency to remember the items at the end of a list better than the middle items.

Retrieval is easier when effective cues are present. Another factor in effective retrieval is the nature of the retrieval task. Simple recognition of previously remembered information in the presence of cues is generally easier than recall of the information.

According to the encoding specificity principle, information present at the time of encoding or learning tends to be effective as a retrieval cue, a process referred to as context-dependent memory.

Special cases of retrieval include autobiographical memory, emotional memory, memory for trauma, repressed memory, and eyewitness testimony. Autobiographical memory is a person's recollections of his or her life experiences. The reminiscence bump refers to the fact that most people have more autobiographical memories for the second and third decades of life. Autobiographical memory has three levels: life time periods, general events, and event-specific knowledge. Biographies of the self connect the past and the present to form our identity.

Emotional memories may be especially vivid and enduring. Particularly significant emotional memories, or flashbulb memories, capture emotionally profound events that people often recall accurately and vividly. Memory for personal trauma also is usually more accurate than memory for ordinary events, but it too is subject to distortion and inaccuracy. People tend to remember the core information about a personal trauma but might distort some of the details. Personal trauma can cause individuals to repress emotionally laden information so that it is not accessible to consciousness.

Motivated forgetting occurs when we want to forget something. It is common when a memory becomes painful or anxiety-laden, as in the case of emotional traumas such as rape and physical abuse.

Repression means forgetting a particularly troubling experience because it would be too upsetting to remember it. Eyewitness testimony may contain errors due to memory decay or bias.

KEY TERMS

retrieval   246
serial position effect   246
autobiographical memory   249
flashbulb memory   250
motivated forgetting   251

TEST YOURSELF

1. What are the primacy effect and the recency effect, and how do psychologists explain each?
2. What is the difference between recall and recognition?
3. Explain autobiographical memory and the "reminiscence bump."

APPLY YOUR KNOWLEDGE

1. Write down a memory that you feel has been especially important in making you who you are. What are some characteristics of this self-defining memory? What do you think the memory says about you? How does it relate to your current goals and aspirations? Do you think of the memory often? You might find that this part of your life story can be inspiring when things are going poorly or when you are feeling down.

2. Become a memory detective and explore the accuracy of your own memory for major events. Think about an event for which you might have a flashbulb memory. You might choose from a major event in recent history, such as the 9/11 attacks, Hurricane Katrina, or the earthquake in Haiti. Then ask yourself some easily verifiable questions about it, such as what day of the week did it happen? What time of day? What were the date and year? How many people were involved? When you have done your best to answer these questions, check your facts online. Were your memories accurate?

3. It is sometimes difficult to believe that our memories are not as accurate as we think. To test your ability to be a good eyewitness, visit one of the following websites:

   http://www.pbs.org/wgbh/pages/frontline/shows/dna/

   http://www.psychology.iastate.edu/faculty/gwells/theeyewitnesstest.html

   Did this exercise change your opinion of the accuracy of eyewitness testimony? Explain.

Forgetting

Human memory has its imperfections, as we have all experienced. It is not unusual for two people to argue about whether something did or did not happen, each supremely confident that his or her memory is accurate and the other person's is faulty. We all have had the frustrating experience of trying to remember the name of a person or a place but not quite being able to retrieve it. Missed appointments, misplaced keys, the failure to recall the name of a familiar face, and inability to recall your password for Internet access are everyday examples of forgetting. Why do we forget?

One of psychology's pioneers, Hermann Ebbinghaus (1850–1909), was the first person to conduct scientific research on forgetting. In 1885, he made up and memorized a list of 13 nonsense syllables and then assessed how many of them he could remember as time passed. (*Nonsense syllables* are meaningless combinations of letters that are unlikely to have been learned already, such as *zeq, xid, lek,* and *riy.*) Even just an hour later, Ebbinghaus could recall only a few of the nonsense syllables he had memorized. Figure 25.1 shows Ebbinghaus's learning curve for nonsense syllables. Based on his research, Ebbinghaus concluded that most forgetting takes place soon after we learn something.

If we forget so quickly, why put effort into learning something? Fortunately, researchers have demonstrated that forgetting is not as extensive as Ebbinghaus envisioned (Harris, Sutton, & Barnier, 2010; Hsieh & others, 2009). Ebbinghaus studied meaningless nonsense syllables. When we memorize more meaningful material—such as poetry, history, or the content of this text—forgetting is neither so rapid nor so extensive. Following are some of the factors that influence how well we can retrieve information from long-term memory.

Hermann Ebbinghaus (1850–1909)
Ebbinghaus was the first psychologist to conduct scientific research on forgetting.

25·1 ENCODING FAILURE

Sometimes when people say they have forgotten something, they have not really forgotten it; rather, they never encoded the information in the first place. *Encoding failure* occurs when the information was never entered into long-term memory.

As an example of encoding failure, think about what the U.S. penny looks like. In one study, researchers showed 15 versions of the penny to participants and asked them which one was correct (Nickerson & Adams, 1979). Look at the pennies in Figure 25.2 (but do not read the caption yet) and see whether you can tell which is the real penny. Most people do not do well on this task. Unless you are a coin collector, you probably have not encoded a lot of specific details about pennies. You may have encoded just enough information to distinguish them from other coins (pennies are copper-colored, dimes and nickels are silver-colored; pennies fall between the sizes of dimes and quarters).

The penny exercise illustrates that we encode and enter into long-term memory only a small portion of our life experiences. In a sense, then, encoding failures really are not cases of forgetting; they are cases of not remembering.

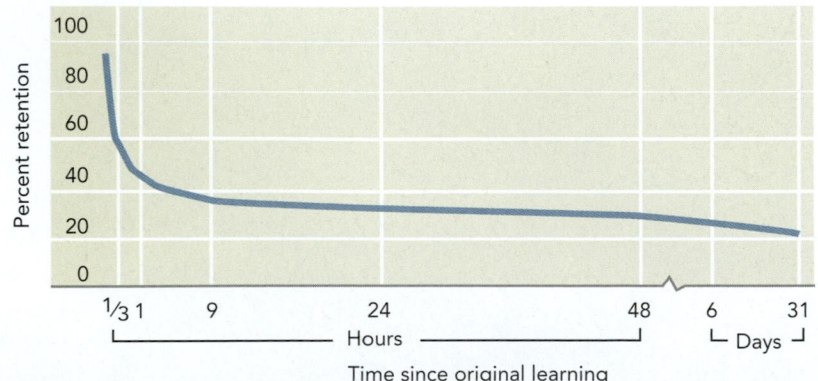

FIGURE 25.1 **Ebbinghaus's Forgetting Curve** The figure illustrates Ebbinghaus's conclusion that most forgetting occurs soon after we learn something.

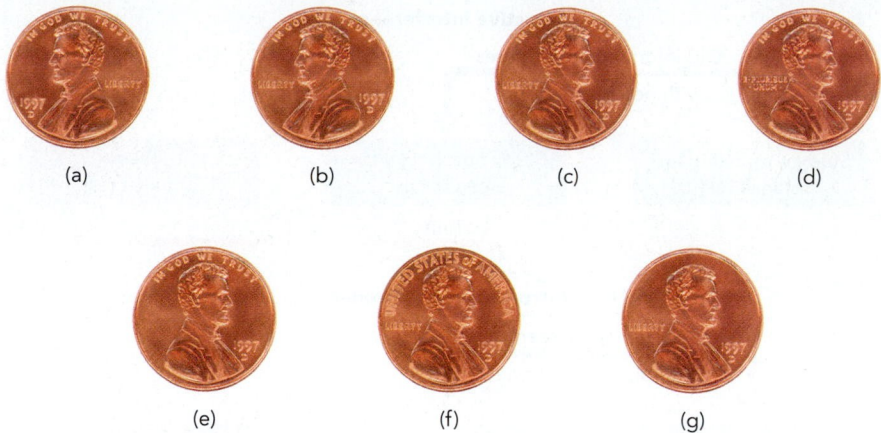

FIGURE 25.2 **Which Is a Real U.S. Penny?** In the original experiment, participants viewed 15 versions of pennies; only one version was an actual U.S. penny. This figure shows only 7 of the 15 versions, and as you likely can tell, the task is still very difficult. Why? By the way, the actual U.S. penny is (c).

25·2 RETRIEVAL FAILURE

Problems in retrieving information from memory are clearly examples of forgetting (Del Missier & Terpini, 2009; Jaeger & others, 2009). Psychologists have theorized that the causes of retrieval failure include problems with the information in storage, the effects of time, personal reasons for remembering or forgetting, and the brain's condition (Angel & others, 2010; Schneider & Logan, 2009).

Interference

Interference is one reason that people forget (Barrouillet & Camos, 2009; Schmiedek, Li, & Lindenberger, 2009). According to **interference theory,** people forget not because memories are lost from storage but because other information gets in the way of what they want to remember.

There are two kinds of interference: proactive and retroactive. **Proactive interference** occurs when material that was learned earlier disrupts the recall of material learned later (Hedden & Yoon, 2006; Yi, Driesen, & Leung, 2009). Remember that *pro* means "forward in time." For example, suppose you had a good friend 10 years ago named Prudence and that last night you met someone named Patience. You might find yourself calling your new friend Prudence because the old information (Prudence) interferes with retrieval of new information (Patience). **Retroactive interference** occurs when material learned later disrupts the retrieval of information learned earlier (Delprato, 2005). Remember that *retro* means "backward in time." Suppose you have lately become friends with Ralph. In sending a note to your old friend Raul, you might mistakenly address it to Ralph because the new information (Ralph) interferes with the old information (Raul). Figure 25.3 depicts another example of proactive and retroactive interference.

Proactive and retroactive interference might both be explained as problems with retrieval cues. The reason the name Prudence interferes with the name Patience and the name Ralph interferes with the name Raul might be that the cue you are using to remember the one name does not distinguish between the two memories. For example, if the cue you are using is "my good friend," it might evoke both names. The result might be retrieval of the wrong name or a kind of blocking in which each name interferes with the other and neither comes to mind. Retrieval cues (such as "friend" in our example) can become overloaded, and when that happens we are likely to forget or to retrieve incorrectly.

Decay

Another possible reason for forgetting is the passage of time. According to **decay theory,** when we learn something new, a neurochemical memory trace forms, but over time this trace disintegrates. Decay theory suggests that the passage of time always increases forgetting.

● **interference theory** The theory that people forget not because memories are lost from storage but because other information gets in the way of what they want to remember.

● **proactive interference** Situation in which material that was learned earlier disrupts the recall of material that was learned later.

● **retroactive interference** Situation in which material that was learned later disrupts the retrieval of information that was learned earlier.

● **decay theory** Theory stating that when we learn something new, a neurochemical memory trace forms, but over time this trace disintegrates; suggests that the passage of time always increases forgetting.

FIGURE 25.3   Proactive and Retroactive Interference *Pro* means "forward"; in proactive interference, old information has a forward influence by getting in the way of new material learned. *Retro* means "backward"; in retroactive interference, new information has a backward influence by getting in the way of material learned earlier.

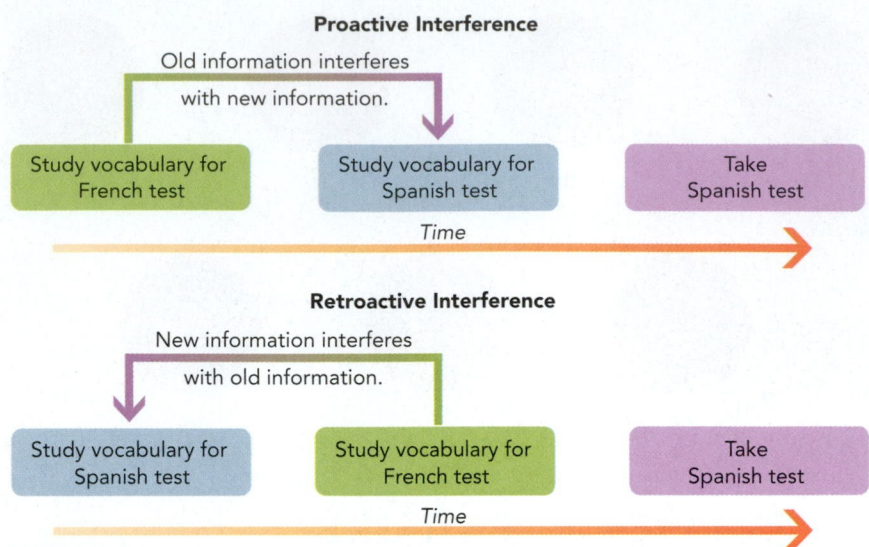

Memories often do fade with the passage of time, but decay alone cannot explain forgetting. For example, under the right retrieval conditions, we can recover memories that we seem to have forgotten (Brown & Lewandowsky, 2010). You might have forgotten the name of someone in your high school class, for instance, but when you return to the setting where you knew the person, the name pops back into your head. Similarly, you may not have thought about someone from your past for a very long time, but when the person "friends" you on Facebook, you may remember experiences you shared.

Tip-of-the-Tongue Phenomenon

● **tip-of-the-tongue (TOT) phenomenon** A type of effortful retrieval that occurs when we are confident that we know something but cannot quite pull it out of memory.

We are all familiar with the retrieval glitch called **tip-of-the-tongue (TOT) phenomenon**—a type of "effortful retrieval" that occurs when we are confident that we know something but cannot quite pull it out of memory (Hanley & Chapman, 2008). In a TOT state we usually can successfully retrieve characteristics of the word, such as the first letter and the number of syllables, but not the word itself. The TOT phenomenon arises when we can retrieve some of the desired information but not all of it (Maril, Wagner, & Schacter, 2001; Schacter, 2001).

The TOT phenomenon reveals some interesting aspects of memory. For one thing, it demonstrates that we do not store all of the information about a particular topic or experience in one way. If you have ever struggled to think of a specific word, you probably came up with various words that mean the same thing as the word you were looking for, but you still had a nagging feeling that none was quite right. Sometimes you might find the solution in an unexpected way. For example, imagine that you are doing a crossword puzzle with the clue "Colorful scarf" for a seven-letter word. You have a feeling you know this word. If you have not thought of the answer yet, say the following word aloud: *bandage*. If you were experiencing the TOT phenomenon when doing the crossword, thinking of *bandage* might have helped you come up with the correct answer, *bandana*. Although the meaning of *bandage* is unrelated to that of *bandana*, the fact that these words start with the same sounds (and therefore are linked in verbal memory) can lead you to the word *bandana* (Abrams & Rodriguez, 2005).

Prospective Memory

● **retrospective memory** Remembering information from the past.

● **prospective memory** Remembering information about doing something in the future; includes memory for intentions.

The main focus of this module has been on **retrospective memory**, which is remembering the past. **Prospective memory** involves remembering information about doing something in the future; it includes memory for intentions (Brewer & others, 2010; Rummel, 2010). Prospective memory includes both *timing*—when we have to do something—and *content*—what we have to do.

We can make a distinction between time-based and event-based prospective memory. *Time-based* prospective memory is our intention to engage in a given behavior after a specified amount of time has gone by, such as an intention to make a phone call to someone in one hour. In *event-based* prospective memory, we engage in the intended behavior when some external event or cue elicits it, as when we give a message to a roommate when we see her. The cues available in event-based prospective memory make it more effective than time-based prospective memory (McDaniel & Einstein, 2007).

Some failures in prospective memory are referred to as "absentmindedness." We are more absentminded when we become preoccupied with something else, are distracted by something, or are under a lot of time pressure (Matlin, 2001). Absentmindedness often involves a breakdown between attention and memory storage (Schacter, 2001). Fortunately, research has shown that our goals are encoded into memory along with the features of situations that would allow us to pursue them. Our memories, then, prepare us to recognize when a situation presents an opportunity to achieve those goals.

Researchers also have found that older adults perform worse on prospective memory tasks than younger adults do, but typically these findings are true only for artificial lab tasks (Bisiacchi, Tarantino, & Ciccola, 2008). In real life, older adults generally perform as well as younger adults in terms of prospective memory (Rendell & Craik, 2000). Generally, prospective memory failure (forgetting to do something) occurs when retrieval is a conscious, effortful (rather than automatic) process (Henry & others, 2004).

"This amnesia of yours . . . can you remember how long you've had it?"

© Kes. www.CartoonStock.com

Amnesia

Recall the case of H. M. in the discussion of explicit and implicit memory. In H. M.'s surgery, the part of his brain responsible for laying down new memories was damaged beyond repair. The result was **amnesia,** the loss of memory. H. M. suffered from **antero-grade amnesia,** a memory disorder that affects the retention of new information and events (*antero* indicates amnesia that moves forward in time) (Ward, 2010). What he learned before the surgery (and thus before the onset of amnesia) was not affected. For example, H. M. could identify his friends, recall their names, and even tell stories about them—*if* he had known them before the surgery. People who met H. M. after the surgery remained strangers, even if they spent thousands of hours with him. H. M.'s postsurgical experiences were rarely encoded in his long-term memory. If you are a fan of Adam Sandler, you might have seen the film *50 First Dates* in which Sandler's character falls in love with a young woman, played by Drew Barrymore, who has anterograde amnesia as the result of head injuries suffered in a car accident.

Amnesia also occurs in a form known as **retrograde amnesia,** which involves memory loss for a segment of the past but not for new events (*retro* indicates amnesia that moves back in time) (Dewar, Cowan, & Della Sala, 2010). Retrograde amnesia is much more common than anterograde amnesia and frequently occurs when the brain is assaulted by an electrical shock or a physical blow such as a head injury to a football player. In contrast to anterograde amnesia, in retrograde amnesia the forgotten information is *old*—it occurred prior to the event that caused the amnesia—and the ability to acquire new memories is not affected. Sometimes individuals have both anterograde and retrograde amnesia.

● **amnesia** The loss of memory.

● **anterograde amnesia** A memory disorder that affects the retention of new information and events.

● **retrograde amnesia** Memory loss for a segment of the past but not for new events.

SUMMARY

Encoding failure is forgetting information that was never entered into long-term memory. Retrieval failure can occur for at least three reasons.

The first reason consists of problems with storage. Interference theory stresses that we forget not because memories are lost from storage but because other information gets in the way of what we want to remember. Interference can be proactive (as occurs when material learned earlier disrupts the recall of material learned later) or retroactive (as occurs when material learned later disrupts the retrieval of information learned earlier).

KEY TERMS

interference theory   257
proactive interference   257
retroactive interference   257
decay theory   257
tip-of-the-tongue (TOT)
    phenomenon   258

retrospective memory   258
prospective memory   258
amnesia   259
anterograde amnesia   259
retrograde amnesia   259

The second reason for retrieval failure is explained by the effects of time. Decay theory states that when we learn something new, a neuro-chemical memory trace forms, but over time this chemical trail disinte-grates. Most of us are familiar with tip-of-the-tongue (TOT) phenomenon, the feeling that we know something but can't quite pull it out of memory. Also familiar are the differences between retrospective and prospective memories, and the glitches that can occur in both.

The third factor in retrieval failure relates to the brain's condition. Amnesia, a prime example, is the physiologically based loss of memory. This can be anterograde, affecting the retention of new information or events, or retrograde, affecting memories of the past but not memories of new events. Amnesia can also be a combination of both.

TEST YOURSELF

1. What is the term for the failure of information to enter long-term memory?

2. Name three factors that, according to psychologists, may be the cause of retrieval failure.

3. What is the tip-of-the-tongue (TOT) phenomenon, and what does it reveal about how we store information?

APPLY YOUR KNOWLEDGE

1. In your opinion, what theory best explains why older people tend to forget things?

2. Based on your own research and information from the health section at the end of this module, explain the difference between amnesia and dementia.

Study Tips from the Science of Memory

How can you apply your new knowledge of memory processes to improving your academic performance? No matter what model of memory you use, you can sharpen your memory by thinking deeply about the "material" of life and connecting the information to other things you know. The most well-connected node or most elaborate schema to which you can link new information is the self—what you know and think about yourself. To make something meaningful and to secure its place in memory, you must make it matter to you.

If you think about memory as a physical event in the brain, you can see that memorizing material is like training a muscle. Repeated recruitment of sets of neurons creates the connection you want available not only at exam time but throughout life as well.

26·1 ORGANIZE

Before you engage the powerful process of memory, the first step in improving your academic performance is to make sure that the information you are studying is accurate and well organized.

Tips for Organizing

- *Review your course notes routinely and catch potential errors and ambiguities early.* There is no sense in memorizing inaccurate or incomplete information.

- *Organize the material in a way that will allow you to commit it to memory effectively.* Arrange information, rework material, and give it a structure that will help you to remember it.

- *Experiment with different organizational techniques.* One approach is to use a hierarchy such as an outline. You might create analogies (such as the earlier comparison of retrieval from long-term memory to finding a book in the library) that take advantage of your preexisting schemas.

26·2 ENCODE

Once you ensure that the material to be remembered is accurate and well organized, it is time to memorize. Although some types of information are encoded automatically, academic learning usually requires considerable effort (Bruning & others, 2004).

Tips for Encoding

- *Pay attention.* Remember that staying focused on one thing is crucial. In other words, no divided attention.
- *Process information at an appropriate level.* Think about the material meaningfully and process it deeply.
- *Elaborate on the points to be remembered.* Make associations to your life and to other aspects of the material you want to remember.
- *Use imagery.* Devising images to help you remember (such as the mental picture of a computer screen to help you recall the concept of working memory) allows you to "double-encode" the information.
- *Understand that encoding is not simply something that you should do before a test.* Rather, encode early and often. During class, while reading, or in discussing issues, take advantage of opportunities to create associations to your course material.

261

26·3 REHEARSE

While learning material initially, relate it to your life and attend to examples that help you do so. After class, rehearse the course material over time to solidify it in memory.

Tips for Rehearsing

- *Rewrite, type, or retype your notes.* Some students find this exercise a good form of rehearsal.

- *Talk to people about what you have learned and how it is important to real life in order to reinforce memory.* You are more likely to remember information over the long term if you understand it and relate it to your world than if you just mechanically rehearse and memorize it. Rehearsal works well for information in short-term memory, but when you need to encode, store, and then retrieve information from long-term memory, it is much less efficient. Thus, for most information, understand it, give it meaning, elaborate on it, and personalize it.

- *Test yourself.* It is not enough to look at your notes and think, "Oh, yes, I know this." Sometimes recognition instills a false sense of knowing. If you look at a definition, and it seems so familiar that you are certain you know it, challenge yourself. What happens when you close the book and try to reconstruct the definition? Check your personal definition with the technical one in the book. How did you do?

- *While reading and studying, ask yourself questions.* Ask things such as, "What is the meaning of what I just read?" "Why is this important?" and "What is an example of the concept I just read about?" When you make a concerted effort to ask yourself questions about what you have read or about an activity in class, you expand the number of associations you make with the information you will need to retrieve later.

- *Treat your brain kindly.* If you are genuinely seeking to improve your memory performance, keep in mind that the brain is a physical organ. Perhaps the best way to promote effective memory storage is to make sure that your brain is able to function at maximum capacity. That means resting it, nourishing it by eating well, and keeping it free of mind-altering substances.

26·4 RETRIEVE

So, you have studied not just hard but deeply, elaborating on important concepts and committing lists to memory. You have slept well and eaten a nutritious breakfast, and now it is exam time. How can you best retrieve the essential information?

Tips for Retrieving

- *Use retrieval cues.* Sit in the same seat where you learned the material. Remember that the exam is full of questions about topics that you have thoughtfully encoded. Some of the questions on the test might help jog your memory for the answers to others.

- *Sit comfortably, take a deep breath, and stay calm.* Bolster your confidence by recalling that research on long-term memory has shown that material that has been committed to memory is there for a very long time—even among those who may experience a moment of panic when the test is handed out.

Memory is crucial for learning and academic success, but it also serves many other purposes. As we now consider, these include contributing to healthy functioning as we age and giving our life a sense of meaning.

SUMMARY

Effective encoding strategies when studying include paying attention and minimizing distraction, understanding the material rather than relying on rote memorization, asking yourself questions, and taking good notes. Research on memory suggests that the best way to remember course material is to relate it to many different aspects of your life.

TEST YOURSELF

1. What steps can you take to ensure that your course information is well organized?
2. Give at least three tips for encoding information and at least three tips for rehearsing information.
3. What strategies can help you retrieve essential information when taking an examination?

APPLY YOUR KNOWLEDGE

1. Students often explain their poor exam results by saying they are bad test takers. Using what you know about memory, provide a counter-argument that can help such students perform better on their exams. Share your thoughts with fellow classmates.
2. Create a mnemonic device that will help you remember one topic in this chapter. Share your strategy.

Memory and Health and Wellness

Autobiographical memory may be one of the most important aspects of human life (Fivush, 2011; N. R. Brown & others, 2009; Markowitsch, 2008). For instance, one of the many functions that autobiographical memory serves is to allow us to learn from our experiences (Pillemer, 1998). In autobiographical memory, we store the lessons we have learned from life. These memories become a resource to which we can turn when faced with life's difficulties.

Autobiographical memory also allows us to understand ourselves and provides us with a source of identity. In his studies of self-defining autobiographical memories, Jefferson Singer and his colleagues maintain that these internalized stories of personal experience serve as signs of the meaning we have created out of our life events and give our lives coherence (Baddeley & Singer, 2008; Singer & Blagov, 2004; Singer & Conway, 2008).

According to Dan McAdams (2006, 2009), autobiographical memories form the core of our personal identity. A number of studies have now shown that the stories we tell about our lives have important implications. For instance, McAdams and his colleagues have demonstrated that individuals who describe important life experiences that go from bad to better (*redemptive stories*) are more *generative*—that is, they are the kind of people who make a contribution to future generations, people who leave a legacy that will outlive them (Bauer, McAdams, & Sakaeda, 2005). These individuals are also better adjusted than those whose self-defining memories go from good to bad (*contamination stories*). Clearly, the construction and reconstruction of autobiographical memory may reveal important aspects of how individuals function, grow, and discover meaning in their lives (King & Hicks, 2006).

KEEPING MEMORY SHARP—AND PRESERVING BRAIN FUNCTION

As a process rooted in the brain, memory is also an indicator of brain functioning. Preserving memory is of vital importance as we age. A strong message from research on aging and memory is that, as for many things in life, the phrase "Use it or lose it" applies to memory.

Consider the case of Richard Wetherill, a retired lecturer and an uncommonly good chess player (Melton, 2005). Wetherill was so skilled that he was able to think eight moves ahead in a chess match. At one point, he noticed that he was having trouble playing chess—he could think only five moves ahead. He was sure that something was seriously wrong with him, despite his wife's assurances that she noticed no changes. A battery of cognitive tests revealed no abnormalities, and a brain scan was similarly reassuring. Two years later, Wetherill was dead, and the autopsy showed a brain ravaged by Alzheimer disease, a progressive, irreversible brain disorder that is characterized by gradual deterioration of memory, reasoning, language, and eventually physical functioning. Brain damage of this sort should indicate a person who was incapable of coherent thought. Wetherill's symptoms, however, had been limited to a small decline in his skill at playing chess.

Wetherill's case is surprising but also typical. Individuals who lead active intellectual lives seem to be protected against the mental decline generally associated with age. Indeed, research has shown that individuals who are educated, have high IQs, and remain mentally engaged in complex tasks tend to cope better with a variety of assaults to the brain, including Alzheimer disease, stroke, head injury, and even poisoning with

Engaging in an intellectually challenging activity such as playing chess seems to offer some protection against the mental decline associated with aging.

neurotoxins (Melton, 2005). Some research has suggested that an active mental life leads to the accumulation of a "cognitive store"—an emergency stash of mental capacity that allows individuals to avoid the negative effects of harm to the brain.

Yaakov Stern found that among a group of individuals with Alzheimer disease who appeared to be equal in terms of their outward symptoms, those who were more educated were actually suffering from much worse brain damage—yet they were functioning at a level similar to others with relatively less damage (Stern & others, 1992). Stern and his colleagues (2004) have also shown that intellectual pursuits such as playing chess and reading reduce the severity of Alzheimer symptoms. Apparently, a lifetime of mental activity and engagement produces this cognitive reserve that allows the brain to maintain its ability to recruit new neural networks that compensate for damage. These brains are better able to move to a backup plan to maintain the individual's level of functioning (Andel & others, 2005). The clear message from these studies is the importance of building up a cognitive reserve by staying mentally active throughout life. In addition to educational achievement, staying physically active also seems to play a role in maintaining a sharp mind (Kramer & Morrow, 2010; Prakash & others, 2010).

MEMORY AND THE SHAPING OF MEANINGFUL EXPERIENCES

Before we leave the science of memory, let's consider the role of memory in shaping meaningful experiences in daily life. Think of the most meaningful event of your life. Clearly, that event is one that you remember, among *all* the things you have experienced in your life. We all have certain particularly vivid autobiographical memories that stand out as indicators of meaning, such as those studied by Jefferson Singer that we reviewed above. In fact, however, everyday life is filled with potentially remarkable moments—a beautiful sunrise, a delicious meal prepared just for you, an unexpected telephone call from an old friend. Experiencing the richness of everyday life requires us to be attentive and engaged. Sometimes daily chores and problems lead us to feel that we are just going through the motions. This sort of mindless living may be a way to survive, but it is unlikely to be a way to thrive.

The processes of attention and encoding that we have explored suggest that actively engaging in life—investing ourselves in the events of the day (Cantor & Sanderson, 1999)—is the way we can be assured that our life stories are rich and nuanced. That way, when someone asks, "So, tell me about yourself," we have a story to tell.

SUMMARY

Autobiographical memories, particularly self-defining memories, provide a unique source of identity, and sharing those memories with others plays a role in social bonding.

Taking on challenging cognitive tasks throughout life can stave off the effects of age on memory and lessen the effects of Alzheimer disease.

Engaging in everyday life means living memorably. Mindfulness to life events provides a rich reservoir of experiences upon which to build a storehouse of autobiographical memories.

TEST YOURSELF

1. What crucial functions does autobiographical memory serve?

2. What did McAdams mean when he described certain individuals as "generative"?

3. What factors are involved in keeping memory sharp as we age?

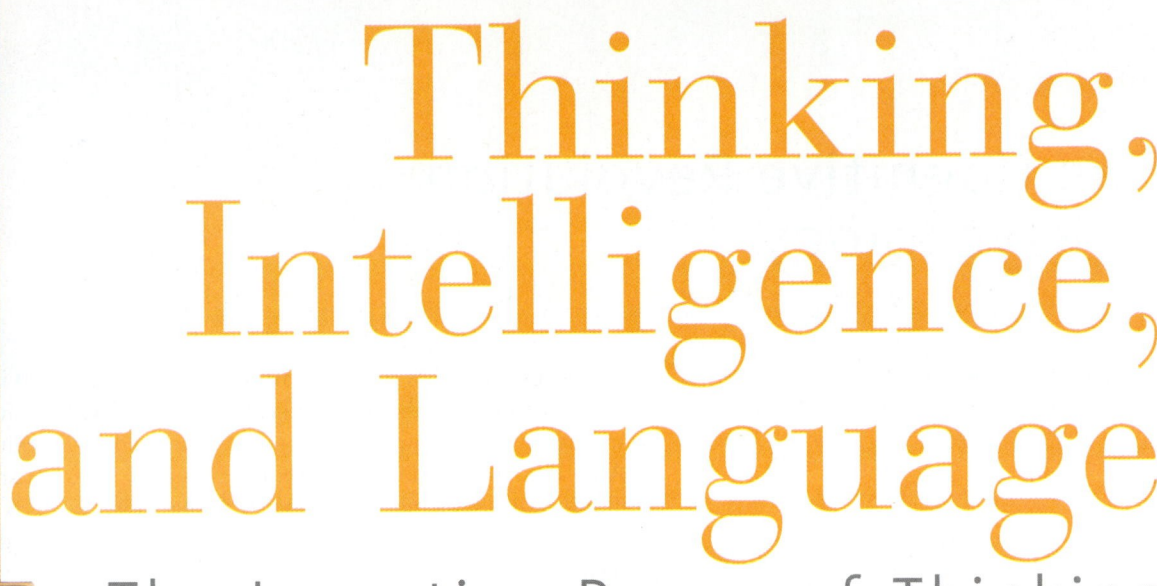

Thinking, Intelligence, and Language

The Inventive Power of Thinking

We are surrounded by evidence of people's really great ideas. From the alarm clock to the computer, human ingenuity touches us at every turn. These inventions happened because somebody noticed a problem and came up with a solution. However, the solutions to certain problems seem hopelessly out of reach. Consider that *1.1 billion* people today live without access to safe drinking water (WHO, 2010). Each year, 1.6 million individuals, many of them children, die from drinking the only water they have—water teeming with disease-causing bacteria (WHO, 2010). Because many of these people live in areas without electricity, roads, and buildings, the construction of water purification plants is impossible. Yet not everyone sees this problem as insurmountable. Recently, the Danish company Vestergaard-Frandsen came up with a simple but amazing idea to meet the challenge of providing drinkable water anywhere in the world. Packing a filter inside a simple plastic tube, the firm's engineers created the Lifestraw—a straw, producible for about $3, that filters out contaminants and allows a person to drink safely from any puddle (McNeil, 2009). Mikkel Vestergaard-Frandsen, the company's CEO, has been hailed as an audacious thinker who is dedicated to devising inventions that help the world's poorest people.

Every invention, whether simply life-enhancing or truly life-saving, started with mental processes. Inventions are physical expressions of critical thinking—of looking at the status quo, realizing that it can be improved, and devising creative solutions. ●

The Cognitive Revolution in Psychology

● **cognition** The way in which information is processed and manipulated in remembering, thinking, and knowing.

Cognitive psychologists study **cognition**—the way in which information is processed and manipulated in remembering, thinking, and knowing. Cognitive psychology is a relatively young field, scarcely more than a half-century old. We begin by tracing its history.

After the first decade of the twentieth century, behaviorism had a stranglehold on the thinking of experimental psychologists. Behaviorists such as B. F. Skinner believed that the human mind is a black box best left to philosophers, and they considered observable behavior to be psychologists' proper focus. The behaviorist perspective had little use for the mental processes occurring in that dark place between your ears.

In the 1950s, psychologists' views began to change. The advent of computers provided a new way to think about the workings of the human mind. If we could "see" what computers were doing internally, maybe we could use our observations to study human mental processes, scientists reasoned. Indeed, computer science was a key motivator in the birth of the study of human cognition. The first modern computer, developed by mathematician John von Neumann in the late 1940s, showed that machines could perform logical operations. In the 1950s, researchers speculated that some mental operations might be modeled by computers, and they believed that such modeling might shed light on how the human mind works (Marcus, 2001).

Cognitive psychologists often use the computer as an analogy to help explain the relationship between cognition and the brain (Forsythe, Bernard, & Goldsmith, 2006). They describe the physical brain as the computer's hardware, and cognition as its software. Herbert Simon (1969) was among the pioneers in comparing the human mind to computer processing systems. In this analogy, the sensory and perceptual systems provide an "input channel," similar to the way data are entered into the computer (Figure 27.1). As input (information) comes into the mind, mental processes, or operations, act on it, just as the computer's software acts on the data. The transformed input generates information that remains in memory much in the way a computer stores what it has worked on. Finally, the information is retrieved from memory and "printed out" or "displayed" (so to speak) as an observable response.

Computers provide a logical and concrete, but oversimplified, model of the mind's processing of information. Inanimate computers and human brains function quite differently in some respects. For example, most computers receive information from a human who has already coded the information and removed much of its ambiguity. In contrast, each brain cell, or neuron, can respond to ambiguous information transmitted through sensory receptors such as the eyes and ears.

Computers can do some things better than humans. For instance, computers can perform complex numerical calculations much faster and more accurately than humans could ever hope to (Forouzan, 2007). Computers can also apply and follow rules more consistently and with fewer errors than humans and can represent complex mathematical patterns better than humans.

Still, the brain's extraordinary capabilities will probably not be mimicked completely by computers at any time in the near future. Attempts to use computers to process visual information or spoken language have achieved only limited success in specific situations. The human brain also has an incredible ability to learn new rules, relationships, concepts, and patterns that it can generalize to novel situations. In comparison, computers are quite limited in their ability to learn and generalize. Although a computer can improve its ability to recognize patterns or use rules of thumb to make decisions, it does not have the means to develop new learning goals. Furthermore, the human mind is aware of itself; the computer is not. Indeed, no computer is likely to approach the richness of human consciousness (Hudson, 2009; Reder, Park, & Kieffaber, 2009).

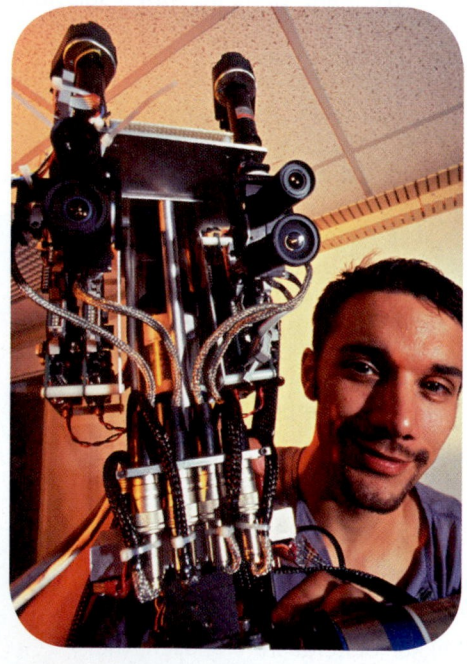

Artificial intelligence (AI) researchers are exploring frontiers that were once the context for sci-fi movie plots. Cog is a human-form robot built by the Humanoid Robotics Group at the Massachusetts Institute of Technology. The sensors and structures in Cog's AI system model human sensory and motor activity as well as perception. Cog's creators have sought to achieve humanlike functioning and interactions with people—both of which, they hope, will lead to new, humanlike learning experiences for the robot. Think about it: How might research findings from experiments such as Cog be applied to real-world situations?

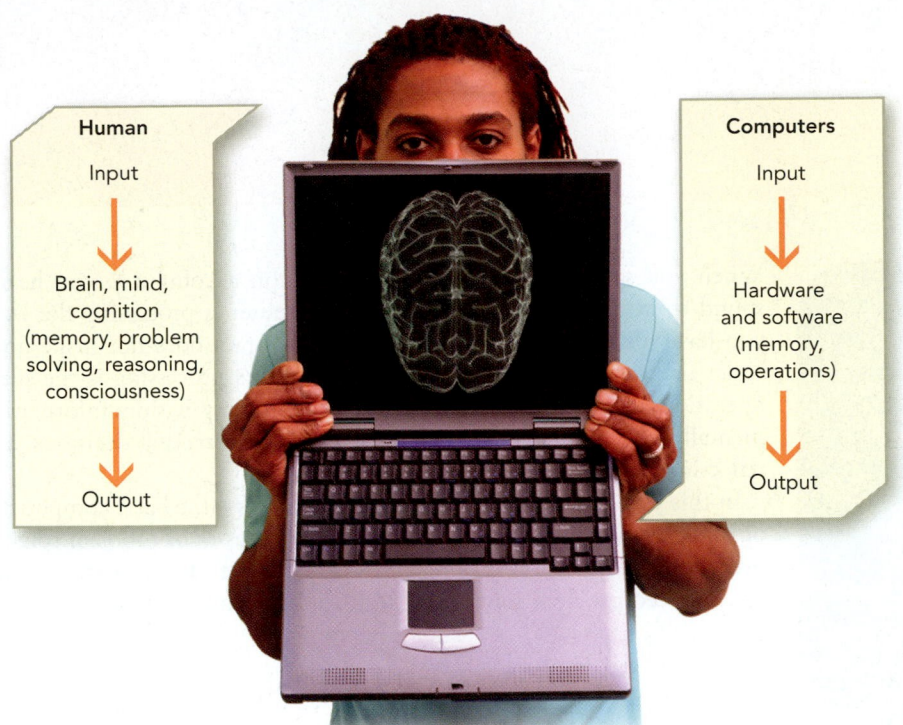

FIGURE 27.1 **Computers and Human Cognition** An analogy is commonly drawn between human cognition and the way computers work. The brain is analogous to a computer's hardware, and cognition is analogous to a computer's software.

Nonetheless, the computer's role in cognitive psychology continues to increase. An entire scientific field called **artificial intelligence (AI)** focuses on creating machines capable of performing activities that require intelligence when they are done by people. AI is especially helpful in tasks requiring speed, persistence, and a vast memory (Cassimatis, Murugesan, & Bignoli, 2009). AI systems also assist in diagnosing medical illnesses and prescribing treatment, examining equipment failures, evaluating loan applicants, and advising students about which courses to take (Lopes & Santos-Victor, 2007; Soltesz & Cohn, 2007). Computer scientists continue to develop computers that more closely approximate human thinking.

By the late 1950s the cognitive revolution was in full swing, and it peaked in the 1980s. The term *cognitive psychology* became a label for approaches that sought to explain observable behavior by investigating mental processes and structures that we cannot directly observe (Ashcraft & Radvansky, 2009; Sternberg, 2009a).

● **artificial intelligence (AI)** A scientific field that focuses on creating machines capable of performing activities that require intelligence when they are done by people.

SUMMARY

Cognition is the way in which information is processed and manipulated in remembering, thinking, and knowing. The advent of the computer in the mid-twentieth century spurred a cognitive revolution in which psychologists took on the challenge of understanding human information processing. Artificial intelligence (AI), the science of creating machines capable of performing activities that require intelligence when they are done by people, is a byproduct of the cognitive revolution.

KEY TERMS

cognition   268
artificial intelligence (AI)   269

TEST YOURSELF

1. On what did behaviorists believe that psychology should properly focus?

2. What technological development gave psychologists a new way to look at the human mind?

3. In what ways is the human mind superior to computers?

APPLY YOUR KNOWLEDGE

1. Do you think the advancement of computer technology has helped psychologists understand the cognitive processes in people? Explain.

2. List five ways in which artificial intelligence (AI) plays a part in your life or the lives of those you know. In each case, what problems or functions does it address? What, if anything, has been gained and lost by the use of AI over human intelligence in each case?

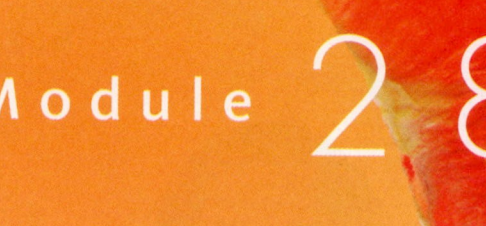

Thinking

Although it has a ducklike bill and lays eggs, the platypus is nevertheless a mammal like the tiger, because platypus females produce milk with which they feed their young. The prototypical birdlike characteristics of the platypus can lead us to think mistakenly that the platypus is a bird. Its atypical properties place the platypus on the extreme of the concept mammal.

● **thinking** The mental process of manipulating information mentally by forming concepts, solving problems, making decisions, and reflecting critically or creatively.

When you save a file you have completed on a computer, you hear a sound from inside, and you know the computer is processing the work you have just done. Unlike a computer, the brain does not make noise to let us know it is working. Rather, the brain's processing is the silent operation of thinking. **Thinking** involves manipulating information mentally by forming concepts, solving problems, making decisions, and reflecting in a critical or creative manner.

In this section we probe the nature of concepts—the basic components of thinking. We then explore the cognitive processes of problem solving, reasoning, and decision making. We also examine two capacities related to enhanced problem solving: critical thinking and creativity.

28·1 CONCEPTS

One fundamental aspect of thinking is the notion of concepts. **Concepts** are mental categories that are used to group objects, events, and characteristics. Humans have a special ability for creating categories to help us make sense of information in our world (Hemmer & Steyvers, 2009; Shea, Krug, & Tobler, 2008). We know that apples and oranges are both fruits. We know that poodles and collies are both dogs and that cockroaches and ladybugs are both insects. These items differ from one another in various ways, and yet we recognize that they belong together because we have concepts for fruits, dogs, and insects.

Concepts are important for four reasons. First, concepts allow us to generalize. If we did not have concepts, each object and event in our world would be unique and brand new to us each time we encountered it. Second, concepts allow us to associate experiences and objects. Basketball, ice hockey, and track are sports. The concept *sport* gives us a way to compare these activities. Third, concepts aid memory by making it more efficient so that we do not have to reinvent the wheel each time we come across a piece of information. Imagine having to think about how to sit in a chair every time we find ourselves in front of one. Fourth, concepts provide clues about how to react to a particular object or experience. Perhaps you have had the experience of trying an exotic new cuisine and feeling puzzled as you consider the contents of your plate. If a friend tells you reassuringly, "That's food!" you know that given the concept *food*, it is okay to dig in.

One way that psychologists explain the structure of concepts is the prototype model. The **prototype model** emphasizes that when people evaluate whether a given item reflects a certain concept, they compare the item with the most typical item(s) in that category and look for a "family resemblance" with that item's properties. Birds generally fly, sing, and build nests, so we know that robins and sparrows are both birds. We recognize exceptions to these properties, however—we know that a penguin is still a bird even though it does not fly, sing, and build a nest. The prototype model maintains that people use characteristic properties to create a representation of the average or ideal member—the prototype—for each concept. Comparing individual cases to our mental prototypes may be a good way to decide quickly whether something fits a particular category. As we will see later in this module, concepts can have particularly negative effects when they are applied to *people* rather than to objects.

28·2 PROBLEM SOLVING

Concepts tell us *what* we think about but not *why* we think (Patalano, Wengrovitz, & Sharpes, 2009). *Why* do we bother to engage in the mental effort of thinking? Consider Levi Hutchins, an ambitious young man who sought to wake up at 4 A.M. every morning. Levi had a specific goal—he wanted to beat the sun up every day. To solve this problem (and achieve his goal), he invented the alarm clock in 1787. **Problem solving** means finding an appropriate way to attain a goal when the goal is not readily available. Problem solving entails following several steps and overcoming mental obstacles.

Following the Steps in Problem Solving

Psychological research points to four steps in the problem-solving process.

1. FIND AND FRAME PROBLEMS

Recognizing a problem is the first step toward a solution (Mayer, 2000). Finding and framing problems involves asking questions in creative ways and "seeing" what others do not. The positive psychology movement began, for example, because some psychologists noticed a lack of research on human strengths (Seligman, 2000).

The ability to recognize and frame a problem is difficult to learn. Furthermore, many real-world problems are ill-defined or vague and have no clear-cut solutions (Schunk, 2011). The visionaries who developed the many inventions that influence our daily lives, such as the computer, telephone, and light bulb, all saw problems that everyone else was content to live with. Recognizing problems involves being aware of and open to experiences (two mental habits we will examine later). It also means listening carefully to that voice in your head that occasionally sighs, "There must be a better way."

2. DEVELOP GOOD PROBLEM-SOLVING STRATEGIES

Once we find a problem and clearly define it, we need to develop strategies for solving it. Among the effective strategies are subgoals, algorithms, and heuristics.

Subgoals are intermediate goals or intermediate problems that put us in a better position for reaching a final goal or solution. Imagine that you are writing a paper for a psychology class. What are some subgoaling strategies for approaching this task? One might be locating the right books and research journals on your chosen topic. At the same time that you are searching for the right publications, you will likely benefit from establishing some subgoals within your time frame for completing the project. If the paper is due in two months, you might set a subgoal of a first draft of the paper two weeks before it is due, another subgoal of completing your reading for the paper one month before it is due, and still another subgoal of starting your library research tomorrow. Notice that in establishing the subgoals for meeting the deadline, you worked backward. Working backward in establishing subgoals is a good strategy. You first create the subgoal that is closest to the final goal and then work backward to the subgoal that is closest to the beginning of the problem-solving effort.

Algorithms are strategies that guarantee a solution to a problem. Algorithms come in different forms, such as formulas, instructions, and the testing of all possible solutions (Bocker, Briesemeister, & Klau, 2009; Voyvodic, Petrella, & Friedman, 2009). We use algorithms in cooking (by following a recipe) and driving (by following directions to an address).

An algorithmic strategy might take a long time. Staring at a rack of letters during a game of Scrabble, for example, you might find yourself moving the tiles around and trying all possible combinations to make a high-scoring word. Instead of using an algorithm to solve your Scrabble problem, however, you might rely on some rules of thumb about

● **concept** A mental category that is used to group objects, events, and characteristics.

● **prototype model** A model emphasizing that when people evaluate whether a given item reflects a certain concept, they compare the item with the most typical item(s) in that category and look for a "family resemblance" with that item's properties.

● **problem solving** The mental process of finding an appropriate way to attain a goal when the goal is not readily available.

● **subgoals** Intermediate goals or intermediate problems that put us in a better position for reaching the final goal or solution.

● **algorithms** Strategies—including formulas, instructions, and the testing of all possible solutions—that guarantee a solution to a problem.

● **heuristics** Shortcut strategies or guidelines that suggest a solution to a problem but do not guarantee an answer.

words and language. **Heuristics** are such shortcut strategies or guidelines that suggest a solution to a problem but do not guarantee an answer (Cranley & others, 2009; Redondo & others, 2009). In your Scrabble game, you know that if you have a *Q*, you are going to need a *U*. If you have an *X* and a *T*, the *T* is probably not going to come right before the *X*. In this situation, heuristics allow you to be more efficient than algorithms would.

In the real world, we are more likely to solve the types of problems we face by heuristics than by algorithms. Heuristics help us to narrow down the possible solutions and quickly to find one that works.

3. EVALUATE SOLUTIONS

Once we think we have solved a problem, we will not know how effective our solution is until we find out if it works. It helps to have in mind a clear criterion for the effectiveness of the solution. For example, what will your criterion be for judging the effectiveness of your solution to the assignment of writing a psychology paper? Will you judge your solution to be effective if you simply complete the paper? If you get an *A*? If the instructor says that it is one of the best papers a student ever turned in on the topic?

4. RETHINK AND REDEFINE PROBLEMS AND SOLUTIONS OVER TIME

An important final step in problem solving is to rethink and redefine problems continually (Bereiter & Scardamalia, 1993). Good problem solvers tend to be more motivated than the average person to improve on their past performances and to make original contributions. Can we make the computer faster and more powerful? Can we make the iPod Shuffle even smaller?

An Obstacle to Problem Solving: Becoming Fixated

A key ingredient of being a good problem solver is to acknowledge that you do not know everything—that your strategies and conclusions are always open to revision. Optimal problem solving may require a certain amount of humility, or the ability to admit that you are not perfect and that there may be better ways to solve life's problems. It is easy to fall into the trap of becoming fixated on a particular strategy for solving a problem.

● **fixation** Using a prior strategy and failing to look at a problem from a fresh new perspective.

● **functional fixedness** Failing to solve a problem as a result of fixation on a thing's usual functions.

Fixation involves using a prior strategy and failing to look at a problem from a fresh new perspective. **Functional fixedness** occurs when individuals fail to solve a problem because they are fixated on a thing's usual functions. If you have ever used a shoe to hammer a nail, you have overcome functional fixedness to solve a problem.

An example of a problem that requires overcoming functional fixedness is the Maier string problem, depicted in Figure 28.1 (Maier, 1931). The problem is to figure out how to tie two strings together when you must stand in one spot and cannot reach both at the same time. It seems as though you are stuck. However, there is a pair of pliers on a table. Can you solve the problem?

The solution is to use the pliers as a weight, tying them to the end of one string (Figure 28.2). Swing this string back and forth like a pendulum and grasp the stationary string. Your past experience with pliers and your fixation on their usual function make this a difficult problem to solve. To do so, you need to find an unusual use for the pliers—in this case, as a weight to create a pendulum.

Effective problem solving often necessitates trying something new, or thinking outside the box—that is, exploring novel ways of approaching tasks and challenges and finding solutions. This way of thinking might require admitting that your past strategies were not ideal or do not readily translate to a particular situation. Students who are used to succeeding in high school by cramming for tests and relying on parental pressure to get homework done may find that in college these strategies are no longer viable ways to succeed. To explore how fixation might play a role in your own problem solving, try out the questions in the Psychological Inquiry.

FIGURE 28.1   Maier String Problem How can you tie the two strings together if you cannot reach them both at the same time?

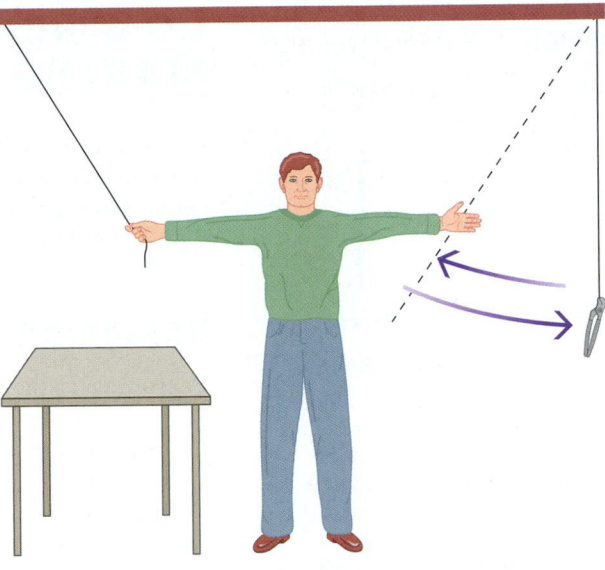

FIGURE 28.2   Solution to the Maier String Problem Use the pliers as a weight to create a pendulum motion that brings the second string closer.

psychological *inquiry*

The Candle Problem

How would you mount a candle on a wall so that it won't drip wax on a table or a floor while it is burning?

The Nine-Dot Problem

Take out a piece of paper and copy the arrangement of dots shown below. Without lifting your pencil, connect the dots using only four straight lines.

The Six-Matchstick Problem

Arrange six matchsticks of equal length to make four equilateral triangles, the sides of which are one matchstick long.

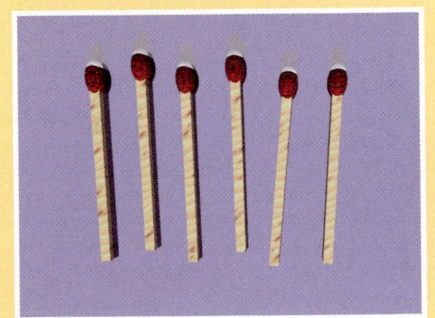

Thinking Outside the Box

The figure presents examples of how fixation impedes problem solving. The tasks shown help psychologists measure creative problem solving.

Each of the problems calls for a special kind of thinking—breaking out of your usual assumptions and looking at objects in a different way. Try your hand at solving each one and then answer the questions. (Solutions to the problems are on page 302.)

1. Which of the problems was most difficult to solve? Why?

2. Do you think these problems capture an important ability, or are they more like trick questions? Why?

3. Are these problems best solved by effortful thinking or by just going with your hunches? Explain.

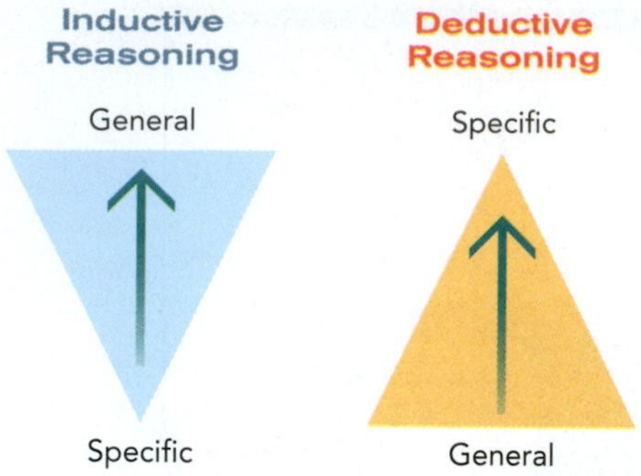

FIGURE 28.3 Inductive and Deductive Reasoning (*Left*) The upside-down pyramid represents inductive reasoning—going from specific to general. (*Right*) The right-side-up pyramid represents deductive reasoning—going from general to specific.

● **reasoning** The mental activity of transforming information to reach conclusions.

● **inductive reasoning** Reasoning from specific observations to make generalizations.

● **deductive reasoning** Reasoning from a general case that is known to be true to a specific instance.

● **decision making** The mental activity of evaluating alternatives and choosing among them.

28-3 REASONING AND DECISION MAKING

In addition to forming concepts and solving problems, thinking includes the higher-order mental processes of reasoning and decision making. These activities require rich connections among neurons and the ability to apply judgment. The end result of this type of thinking is an evaluation, a conclusion, or a decision.

Reasoning

Reasoning is the mental activity of transforming information to reach conclusions. Reasoning is involved in problem solving and decision making. It is also a skill closely tied to critical thinking (Kemp & Tenenbaum, 2009). Reasoning can be either inductive or deductive (Figure 28.3).

Inductive reasoning involves reasoning from specific observations to make generalizations (Tenenbaum, Griffiths, & Kemp, 2006). Inductive reasoning is an important way that we form beliefs about the world. For instance, having turned on your cell phone many times without having it explode, you have every reason to believe that it will not explode the next time you turn it on. From your prior experiences with the phone, you form the general belief that it is not likely to become a dangerous object.

A great deal of scientific knowledge is the product of inductive reasoning. We know, for instance, that men and women are genetically different, with women having two X chromosomes and men having an X and a Y chromosome, though no one has actually tested every single human being's chromosomes to verify this generalization. Psychological research is often inductive as well, studying a sample of participants in order to yield conclusions about the population from which the sample is drawn.

In contrast, **deductive reasoning** is reasoning from a general case that we know to be true to a specific instance (Demeure, Bonnefon, & Raufaste, 2009; Reverberi & others, 2009). Using deductive reasoning, we draw conclusions based on facts. For example, we might start with the general premise that all Texans love the Dallas Cowboys. Thus, if John is a Texan, we logically might surmise that John loves the Dallas Cowboys. Notice, however, that the logic of this deductive reasoning requires that the first statement be true; if all Texans do not love the Cowboys, John just might be a Philadelphia Eagles fan.

When psychologists and other scientists use theories to make predictions and then evaluate their predictions by making further observations, deductive reasoning is at work. When psychologists develop a hypothesis from a theory, they are using a form of deductive reasoning, because the hypothesis is a specific, logical extension of the general theory. If the theory is true, then the hypothesis will be true as well.

Decision Making

Think of all the decisions, large and small, that you have to make in life. Should you major in biology, psychology, or business? Should you go to graduate school right after college or get a job first? Should you establish yourself in a career before settling down to have a family? Do you want fries with that? **Decision making** involves evaluating alternatives and choosing among them.

Reasoning uses established rules to draw conclusions. In contrast, in decision making, such rules are not established, and we may not know the consequences of the decisions (Bongers & Dijksterhuis, 2009; Palomo & others, 2008). Some of the information might be missing, and we might not trust all of the information we have. Making decisions means weighing information and coming to some conclusion that we feel will maximize our outcome: Yes, we will be able to see the movie from this row in the theater; no, we will not run that red light to get to class on time.

Two Systems of Reasoning and Decision Making

Many psychologists similarly divide reasoning and decision making into two levels—one that is automatic (often referred to as *system 1*) and one that is controlled (often called *system 2*) (Stanovich & West, 2000). The automatic system involves processing that is rapid, heuristic, and intuitive; it entails following one's hunches or gut feelings about a particular decision or problem (Halberstadt, 2010; Kahneman & Klein, 2009). Intuitive judgment means knowing that something feels right even if the reason why is unknown (Topolinski & Strack, 2010). In contrast, the controlled system is slower, effortful, and analytical. It involves conscious reflection about an issue. This is the kind of thinking that might be required to solve a difficult math problem, for example.

Although conscious effortful thinking is invaluable for solving many problems, research has shown that intuitive processing may also have an important role to play in decision making (Dijksterhuis & Nordgren, 2006; Halberstadt, 2010; Hicks & others, 2010; Kahneman & Klein, 2009). No doubt you have had the experience of consciously grappling with a problem and spending a good deal of time trying to solve it, with no success. Then you take a break to listen to music or go running, and suddenly the solution pops into your head. Research by Ap Dijksterhuis and colleagues (2006) might ring a bell for you. In a series of laboratory studies, the experimenters presented participants with a number of pieces of information relevant to a decision, such as which apartment to pick out a variety of possibilities. After seeing the information, half of the participants were distracted while the other half had time to think consciously about the decision. The results showed that the distracted participants were more likely to pick the best option among the many choices. Similar results have been found for the accuracy of predictions about sporting events (Dijksterhuis & others, 2009; Halberstadt, 2010). Sometimes, following your gut feelings can be a good way to reach an optimal choice (Nordgren & Dijksterhuis, 2009; Topolinski & Strack, 2008).

The popular media sometimes portray intuitive hunches as sort of magical. However, these gut feelings do not emerge out of thin air. Rather, they are the product of learned associations such as those described in Module 17 (Kahneman & Klein, 2009; Unkelbach, 2007); of overlearned automatic processes like those explored in Module 13 (Halberstadt, 2010); and of implicit memory, as described in Module 23. Your gut feelings about the right answer on a test are certainly more likely to be accurate if you have put in the requisite hours of conscious effortful study.

It is also important to keep in mind that system 1 processes are as rapid as they are because they often rely on heuristics. The use of heuristics can lead to mistakes when these rules of thumb are applied inappropriately (Kahneman & Klein, 2009), as we now consider.

© Mike Baldwin. www.CartoonStock.com.

Biases and Heuristics

Another fruitful subject of decision-making research is the biases and heuristics (rules of thumb) that affect the quality of decisions. In many cases, our decision-making strategies are well adapted to deal with a variety of problems (Nisbett & Ross, 1980; Tversky & Kahneman, 1974). Heuristics, for example, are intuitive and efficient ways of solving problems and making decisions; they are often at work when we make a decision by following a gut feeling. However, heuristics and gut feelings can lead to mistakes. Here we look at a few biases and heuristic errors, summarized in Figure 28.4.

Confirmation bias is the tendency to search for and use information that supports our ideas rather than refutes them (Cook & Smallman, 2008). Our decisions can also become further biased because we tend to seek out and listen to people whose views confirm our own while we avoid those with dissenting views. It is easy to detect the confirmation bias in the way that many people think. Consider politicians. They often accept news that supports their views and dismiss contradictory evidence. Avoiding confirmation bias means applying the same rigorous analysis to both sides of an argument.

Hindsight bias is our tendency to report falsely, after the fact, that we accurately predicted an outcome. It is sometimes referred to as the "I knew it all along effect." With

● **confirmation bias** The tendency to search for and use information that supports our ideas rather than refutes them.

● **hindsight bias** The tendency to report falsely, after the fact, that we accurately predicted an outcome.

Confirmation bias

Description

Tendency to search for and use information that supports, rather than refutes, one's ideas

Example: A politician accepts news that supports his views, and dismisses evidence that runs counter to these views.

Base rate fallacy

Description

Tendency to ignore information about general principles in favor of very specific but vivid information

Example: You read a favorable expert report on a TV you are intending to buy, but you decide not to when a friend tells you about a bad experience with the model.

Hindsight bias

Description

Tendency to report falsely, after the fact, that one accurately predicted an outcome

Example: You read about the results of a particular psychological study and say, "I always knew that," though in fact you have little knowledge about the issues examined in the study.

Representative-ness heuristic

Description

Tendency to make judgments about group membership based on physical appearances or one's stereotype of a group rather than available base rate information

Example: The victim of a hold-up, you view police photos of possible perpetrators. The suspects look very similar to you, but you choose the individual whose hair and clothing look dirtiest and most disheveled.

Availability heuristic

Description

Prediction about the probability of an event based on the ease of recalling or imagining similar events

Example: A girl from an extended family in which no family member ever attended college tells her mother that she wants to be a doctor. Her mother cannot imagine her daughter in such a career and suggests that she become a home health-care aide.

FIGURE 28.4 **Decision-Making Problems: Biases and Heuristics** Biases and heuristics (rules of thumb) affect the quality of many of the decisions we make.

● **availability heuristic** A prediction about the probability of an event based on the ease of recalling or imagining similar events.

● **base rate fallacy** The tendency to ignore information about general principles in favor of very specific but vivid information.

this type of bias, people tend to view events that have happened as more predictable than they were and to represent themselves as being more accurate in their predictions than they actually were (Nestler, Blank, & von Collani, 2008). For instance, at the end of a long baseball season, fans might say they knew all along that a particular team would win the World Series. One reason for hindsight bias is that actual events are more vivid in our minds than all those things that failed to happen, an effect called the availability heuristic.

The **availability heuristic** refers to a prediction about the probability of an event based on the ease of recalling or imagining similar events (McDermott, 2009). Have you ever experienced a sudden fear of flying right after hearing about an airplane crash? Shocking events such as plane crashes stick in our minds, making it seem as if such disasters are common. The chance of dying in a plane crash in a given year, however, is tiny (1 in 400,000) compared to the chance of dying in a car accident (1 in 6,500). Because car accidents are less newsworthy, they are less likely to catch our attention and remain in our awareness. The availability heuristic can reinforce generalizations about others in daily life. Imagine that Elvedina, a Mexican American girl, tells her mother that she wants to be a doctor. Her mother, who has never seen a Latina doctor, finds it hard to conceive of her daughter's pursuing such a career and might suggest that she try nursing instead.

Also reflective of the impact of vivid cases on decision making is the **base rate fallacy,** the tendency to ignore information about general principles in favor of very specific but vivid information. Let's say that as a prospective car buyer, you read *Consumer Reports* and find that a panel of experts rates a particular vehicle exceptionally well. You might still be swayed in your purchasing decision, however, if a friend tells you about her bad experiences with that car. Similarly, imagine being told that the average exam score for a test in your psychology class was 75 percent. If you were asked to guess a random student's score, 75 percent would be a good answer—the mean tells us the central tendency of any distribution. Yet if the student provided just a little bit of information, such as how many hours he or she studied, you might give too much weight to that specific information, losing sight of the valuable base rate information you have in the class mean.

To experience another heuristic in action, consider the following example. Your psychology professor tells you she has assembled 100 men in the hallway outside your classroom. The group consists of 5 librarians and 95 members of the Hells Angels motorcycle club. She is going to randomly select one man into the room, and you can win $100 if you accurately guess whether he is a librarian or a Hells Angel. The man stands before you. He is in his 50s, with short graying hair, and he wears thick glasses, a button-down white shirt, a bow tie, neatly pressed slacks, and loafers. Is he a librarian or a Hells Angel? If you guessed librarian, you have just fallen victim to the representativeness heuristic.

The **representativeness heuristic** is the tendency to make judgments about group membership based on physical appearances or the match between a person and one's stereotype of a group rather than on available base rate information (Nilsson, Juslin, & Olsson, 2008). Essentially, a stereotype is the use of concepts to make generalizations about a group of people. We will examine stereotypes in some detail in Module 51. In the example just described, the base rate information tells you that, 95 times out of 100, the man in your class is likely to be a Hells Angel. The best approach to winning the $100 might be simply to shut your eyes and guess Hells Angel, no matter what the man looks like.

The representativeness heuristic can be particularly damaging in the context of social judgments. Consider a scenario where a particular engineering corporation seeks to hire a new chief executive officer (CEO). Lori, a top-notch candidate with an undergraduate engineering degree and an MBA from an outstanding business school, applies. If there are few women in upper management at the firm, the company's board of directors might inaccurately view Lori as "not fitting" their view of the prototypical CEO—and miss the chance to hire an exceptional candidate.

Thus, heuristics help us make decisions rapidly. To solve problems accurately and make the best decisions, however, we must sometimes override these shortcuts and think more deeply, critically, and creatively.

28·4 THINKING CRITICALLY AND CREATIVELY

Problem solving and decision making are basic cognitive processes that we use multiple times each day. Certain strategies lead to better solutions and choices than others, and some people are particularly good at these cognitive exercises. In this section we examine two skills associated with superior problem solving: critical thinking and creativity.

Critical Thinking

Critical thinking means thinking reflectively and productively and evaluating the evidence. Scientists are critical thinkers. Critical thinkers grasp the deeper meaning of ideas, question assumptions, and decide for themselves what to believe or do (Campbell, Whitehead, & Finkelstein, 2009; Vacek, 2009). Critical thinking requires maintaining a sense of humility about what we know (and what we do not know). It means being motivated to see past the obvious.

Critical thinking is vital to effective problem solving. However, few schools teach students to think critically and to develop a deep understanding of concepts (Brooks & Brooks, 2001). Instead, especially in light of pressures to maximize students' scores on standardized tests, teachers concentrate on getting students to give a single correct answer in an imitative way rather than on encouraging new ideas (Bransford & others, 2006). Further, many people are inclined to stay on the surface of problems rather than to stretch their minds. The cultivation of two mental habits is essential to critical thinking: mindfulness and open-mindedness.

Mindfulness means being alert and mentally present for one's everyday activities. The mindful person maintains an active awareness of the circumstances of his or her

● **representativeness heuristic** The tendency to make judgments about group membership based on physical appearances or the match between a person and one's stereotype of a group rather than on available base rate information.

● **mindfulness** The state of being alert and mentally present for one's everyday activities.

Emotion and Cognition: How Are You Feeling and Thinking Today?

Do you have to get into a bad mood to do well at math? Studies that link mood and thinking might lead you to think so. Researchers have examined the ways that our moods influence how we think (Clore & Palmer, 2009; Moberly & Watkins, 2009). They have shown that negative moods and positive moods are related to two different styles of problem solving and decision making (Storbeck & Clore, 2008).

Negative moods are associated with narrow, analytical thinking (Clore, Gasper, & Garvin, 2001). People who are feeling crabby are less likely to use heuristic shortcuts (Isbell, 2004) and are more likely to think problems through carefully, reaching conclusions based on logic. What about being in a good mood? Compared to people who are in a bad mood, happy individuals tend to use more heuristics, which means sometimes making errors. Do positive moods have value for thinking?

Social psychologist Alice Isen pioneered the study of the adaptive effects of positive mood on cognition. In the early 1970s, when no one else was interested in the potential benefits of positive moods, Isen began a program of research that changed the way psychologists think about the role of positive emotional experience in thinking.

In her lab, Isen found ways to make people happy—by offering cookies or money or showing funny movies—and she examined the effects of positive mood on the way people think. Isen has uncovered strong evidence for the role of positive mood in creativity, originality, and efficient thinking. In a good mood, people are likely to be more cognitively flexible and to be more creative in their concept formations and structures (Compton & others, 2004; Isen, 2007a). Positive moods are related to enhanced creative problem solving (Isen, 1984, 2007b, 2008). Positive moods allow us to be better brainstormers—to come up with more ideas in response to a task and to be more open to all of the fantastic or crazy possibilities we think of (Gasper, 2004).

In contrast to previous research showing that positive moods are related to mindlessness, Isen's work (2004) revealed that a positive mood makes people more likely to engage thoughtfully with problems and to learn from new experiences. In one study, happy doctors were more likely to make the appropriate diagnosis faster than unhappy doctors (Estrada, Isen, & Young, 1997). Happy people, compared to unhappy ones, were better able to ignore unimportant information (Isen & Means, 1983).

We face such an array of choices in today's world, from the kind of orange juice we buy to the kind of college we attend. Happy moods allow us to be more efficient at settling on a satisfying choice, while unhappy moods leave us lost in thought in the juice aisle (Dreisbach & Goschke, 2004; Schwartz & others, 2002). Both unhappy and happy moods may have a role to play in directing our thought processes.

Try using this research on mood and cognition to study for an upcoming exam or to write a creative paper for a class. What would the best mood be for each of these activities?

life. According to Ellen Langer (1997, 2000, 2005), mindfulness is a key to critical thinking. Langer distinguishes mindful behavior from *mindless* behaviors—automatic activities we perform without thought.

In a classic study, Langer found that people (as many as 90 percent) would mindlessly give up their place in line for a copy machine when someone asked, "Can I go first? I need to make copies" as compared to when the same person simply said, "Can I go first?" (just 60 percent) (Langer, Blank, & Chanowitz, 1978). For the mindless persons in the study, even a completely meaningless justification—after all, everyone in line was there to make copies—was reason enough to step aside. A mindless person engages in automatic behavior without careful thinking. In contrast, a mindful person is engaged with the environment, responding in a thoughtful way to various experiences.

Open-mindedness means being receptive to other ways of looking at things. People often do not even know that there is another side to an issue or evidence contrary to what they believe. Simple openness to other viewpoints can help to keep individuals from jumping to conclusions. As Socrates once said, knowing what it is you do not know is the first step to true wisdom.

Being mindful and maintaining an open mind may be more difficult than the alternative of going through life on automatic pilot. Critical thinking is valuable, however, because it allows us to make better predictions about the future, to evaluate situations objectively, and to effect appropriate changes. In some sense, critical thinking requires courage. When we expose ourselves to a broad range of perspectives, we risk finding out that our assumptions might be wrong. When we engage our critical minds, we may discover problems, but we are also more likely to have opportunities to make positive changes.

● **open-mindedness** The state of being receptive to other ways of looking at things.

Creative Thinking

In addition to thinking critically, coming up with the best solution to a problem may involve thinking creatively. The word *creative* can apply to an activity or a person, and creativity as a process may be open even to people who do not think of themselves as creative. When we talk about **creativity** as a characteristic of a person, we are referring to the ability to think about something in novel and unusual ways and to devise unconventional solutions to problems (Abraham & Windmann, 2007; Sternberg, 2009b; T. B. Ward, 2007).

We can look at the thinking of creative people in terms of divergent and convergent thinking. **Divergent thinking** produces many solutions to the same problem. **Convergent thinking** produces the single best solution to a problem. Creative thinkers do *both* types of thinking. Divergent thinking occurs during *brainstorming,* when a group of people openly throw out a range of possible solutions to a problem, even some that might seem crazy. Having a lot of possible solutions, however, still requires that they come up with the solution that is best. That is where convergent thinking comes in. Convergent thinking means taking all of those possibilities and finding the right one for the job. Convergent thinking is best when a problem has only one right answer.

Humans can think in many different ways, analyzing problems or following our gut, thinking divergently or convergently. To explore the role of our moods in these types of thinking, check out the Intersection.

Individuals who think creatively also show the following characteristics (Perkins, 1994).

● **creativity** The ability to think about something in novel and unusual ways and to devise unconventional solutions to problems.

● **divergent thinking** Thinking that produces many solutions to the same problem.

● **convergent thinking** Thinking that produces the single best solution to a problem.

- *Flexibility and playful thinking:* Creative thinkers are flexible and play with problems. This trait gives rise to the paradox that, although creativity takes hard work, the work goes more smoothly if it is taken lightly. In a way, humor greases the wheels of creativity (Goleman, Kaufman, & Ray, 1993). When you are joking around, you are more likely to consider any possibility and to ignore the inner censor who can condemn your ideas as off base.

- *Inner motivation:* Creative people often are motivated by the joy of creating. They tend to be less motivated by grades, money, or favorable feedback from others. Thus, creative people are inspired more internally than externally.

- *Willingness to face risk:* Creative people make more mistakes than their less imaginative counterparts because they come up with more ideas and more possibilities. They win some; they lose some. Creative thinkers know that being wrong is not a failure—it simply means that they have discovered that one possible solution does not work.

- *Objective evaluation of work:* Most creative thinkers strive to evaluate their work objectively. They may use established criteria to make judgments or rely on the judgments of respected, trusted others. In this manner, they can determine whether further creative thinking will improve their work.

SUMMARY

Concepts are mental categories used to group objects, events, and characteristics. Concepts help us to generalize; they improve our memories; and they keep us from having to learn new things with every new instance or example of a concept. The prototype model suggests that members of a concept vary in terms of their similarity to the most typical item.

Problem solving is an attempt to find a way to attain a goal when the goal is not readily available. The four steps in problem solving are to (1) find and frame the problem, (2) develop good problem-solving strategies, (3) evaluate solutions, and (4) rethink and redefine problems and solutions over time. Among effective strategies for solving problems are setting subgoals (intermediate goals that put you in a better position to reach your goal), devising algorithms (strategies that guarantee a solution), and using heuristics (shortcuts that suggest, but do not guarantee, a solution to a problem).

Reasoning is the mental activity of transforming information to reach conclusions. Inductive reasoning is reasoning from the specific to the general. Deductive reasoning is reasoning from the general to the specific. Decision making involves evaluating alternatives and making choices among them. Biases and heuristics that may lead to problematic decision making include confirmation bias, hindsight bias, the availability heuristic, and the representativeness heuristic.

Critical thinking and creativity improve problem solving. Critical thinking involves thinking productively, evaluating the evidence, being mindful, and keeping an open mind. Creativity is the ability to think in novel and unusual ways and to come up with unconventional solutions. Creative thinkers are flexible and playful, self-motivated, willing to face risk, and objective in evaluating their work.

KEY TERMS

thinking   270
concept   271
prototype model   271
problem solving   271
subgoals   271
algorithms   271
heuristics   272
fixation   272
functional fixedness   272
reasoning   274
inductive reasoning   274
deductive reasoning   274

decision making   274
confirmation bias   275
hindsight bias   275
availability heuristic   276
base rate fallacy   276
representativeness heuristic   277
mindfulness   277
open-mindedness   279
creativity   279
divergent thinking   279
convergent thinking   279

TEST YOURSELF

1. What are four reasons why concepts are important?
2. Name and explain the key steps in solving a problem.
3. Name at least two biases and two heuristics that affect the quality of our decisions, and give an example of each.

APPLY YOUR KNOWLEDGE

1. To get a sense of the roles of divergent and convergent thinking in creativity, try the following exercise. First take 10 minutes and jot down all of the uses that you can think of for a cardboard box. Don't hold back—include every possibility that comes to mind. That list represents divergent thinking. Now look the list over. Which of the possible uses are most unusual or most likely to be worthwhile? That is convergent thinking.

2. In the next week, identify one situation or problem that you need to solve. Utilize the steps in problem solving outlined in your book and decide if these steps helped or hindered you from solving your problem.

Intelligence

The word *intelligent* can apply to a behavior or a person. We might say that someone who decides to quit smoking has made an intelligent choice. When we apply the word to a person, however, defining *intelligent* can be trickier.

Cultures vary in the ways they define intelligence (Sternberg & Grigorenko, 2008; Zhang & Sternberg, 2009). Most Euro-Americans think of intelligence in terms of reasoning and thinking skills, but people in Kenya consider responsible participation in family and social life an integral part of intelligence. An intelligent person in Uganda is someone who knows what to do and follows through with appropriate action. Intelligence to the Iatmul people of Papua New Guinea involves the ability to remember the names of 10,000 to 20,000 clans. The residents of the widely dispersed Caroline Islands incorporate the talent of navigating by the stars into their definition of intelligence (Figure 29.1).

In the United States, we generally define **intelligence** as an all-purpose ability to do well on cognitive tasks, to solve problems, and to learn from experience. The idea that intelligence captures a common general ability that is reflected in performance on various cognitive tests was introduced in 1904 by Charles Spearman. Spearman noted that schoolchildren who did well in math also did well in reading, and he came up with the idea that intelligence is a general ability, which he called *g*. This view of intelligence suggests that general intelligence underlies performance in a variety of areas, whether it is mathematics, verbal ability, or abstract reasoning. Spearman's *g* essentially assumes that the intelligent person is a jack of all cognitive trades.

● **intelligence** All-purpose ability to do well on cognitive tasks, to solve problems, and to learn from experience.

29·1 MEASURING INTELLIGENCE

Psychologists measure intelligence using tests that produce a score known as the person's *intelligence quotient* (*IQ*). To understand how IQ is derived and what it means, let's first examine the criteria for a good intelligence test: validity, reliability, and standardization.

FIGURE 29.1 **Iatmul and Caroline Island Intelligence** The intelligence of the Iatmul people of Papua New Guinea involves the ability to remember the names of many clans. For the residents of the 680 Caroline Islands in the Pacific Ocean east of the Philippines, intelligence includes the ability to navigate by the stars.

Validity

Does the test measure what it purports to measure?

Reliability

Is test performance consistent?

Standardization

Are uniform procedures for administering and scoring the test used?

FIGURE 29.2 Test Construction and Evaluation Tests are a tool for measuring important abilities such as intelligence. Good tests show high reliability and validity and are standardized so that people's scores can be compared.

● **validity** The extent to which a test measures what it is intended to measure.

● **reliability** The extent to which a test yields a consistent, reproducible measure of performance.

● **standardization** The development of uniform procedures for administering and scoring a test, and the creation of norms (performance standards) for the test.

● **mental age (MA)** An individual's level of mental development relative to that of others.

● **intelligence quotient (IQ)** An individual's mental age divided by chronological age multiplied by 100.

Alfred Binet (1857–1911) Binet constructed the first intelligence test after being asked to create a measure to determine which children would benefit from instruction in France's schools.

In the realm of testing, **validity** refers to the extent to which a test measures what it is intended to measure. If a test is supposed to measure intelligence, then it should measure intelligence, not some other characteristic, such as anxiety. One of the most important indicators of validity is the degree to which it predicts an individual's performance when that performance is assessed by other measures, or criteria, of the attribute (Neukrug & Fawcett, 2010). For example, a psychologist might validate an intelligence test by asking employers of the individuals who took the test how intelligent they are at work. The employers' perceptions would be a criterion for measuring intelligence. When the scores on a measure relate to important outcomes (such as employers' evaluations), we say the test has high *criterion validity.*

Reliability is the extent to which a test yields a consistent, reproducible measure of performance. That is, a reliable test is one that produces the same score over time and repeated testing. Reliability and validity are related. If a test is valid, then it must be reliable, but a reliable test need not be valid. People can respond consistently on a test, but the test might not be measuring what it purports to measure.

Good intelligence tests are not only reliable and valid but also standardized (Salvia, Ysseldyke, & Bolt, 2010). **Standardization** involves developing uniform procedures for administering and scoring a test, as well as creating *norms,* or performance standards, for the test. Uniform testing procedures require that the testing environment be as similar as possible for all individuals. Norms are created by giving the test to a large group of individuals representative of the population for whom the test is intended. Norms tell us which scores are considered high, low, or average. Many tests of intelligence are designed for individuals from diverse groups. So that the tests are applicable to such different groups, they may have norms for individuals of different ages, socioeconomic statuses, and ethnic groups (Kaplan & Saccuzzo, 2009). Figure 29.2 summarizes the criteria for test construction and evaluation.

IQ Tests

In 1904, the French Ministry of Education asked psychologist Alfred Binet to devise a method that would determine which students did not learn effectively from regular classroom instruction. School officials wanted to reduce overcrowding by placing such students in special schools. Binet and his student Theophile Simon developed an intelligence test to meet this request. The test consisted of 30 items ranging from the ability to touch one's nose or ear on command to the ability to draw designs from memory and to define abstract concepts. To measure intelligence, Binet came up with the idea of comparing a person's mental abilities to the mental abilities that are typical for a particular age group.

Binet developed the concept of **mental age (MA),** which is an individual's level of mental development relative to that of others. Binet reasoned that a mentally retarded child would perform like a normal child of a younger age. To think about a person's level of intelligence, then, we might compare the person's mental age (MA) to his or her chronological age (CA), or age from birth. A very bright child has an MA considerably above CA; a less bright child has an MA considerably below CA.

The German psychologist William Stern devised the term **intelligence quotient (IQ)** in 1912. IQ consists of an individual's mental age divided by chronological age multiplied by 100:

$$IQ = (MA/CA) \times 100$$

If mental age is the same as chronological age, then the individual's IQ is 100 (average); if mental age is above chronological age, the IQ is more than 100 (above average); if mental age is below chronological age, the IQ is less than 100 (below average). For example, a 6-year-old child with a mental age of 8 has an IQ of 133, whereas a 6-year-old child with a mental age of 5 has an IQ of 83.

In childhood, mental age increases as the child ages, but once he or she reaches about age 16, the concept of mental age loses its meaning. That is why many experts today prefer to examine IQ scores in terms of how unusual a person's score is when compared

psychological *inquiry*

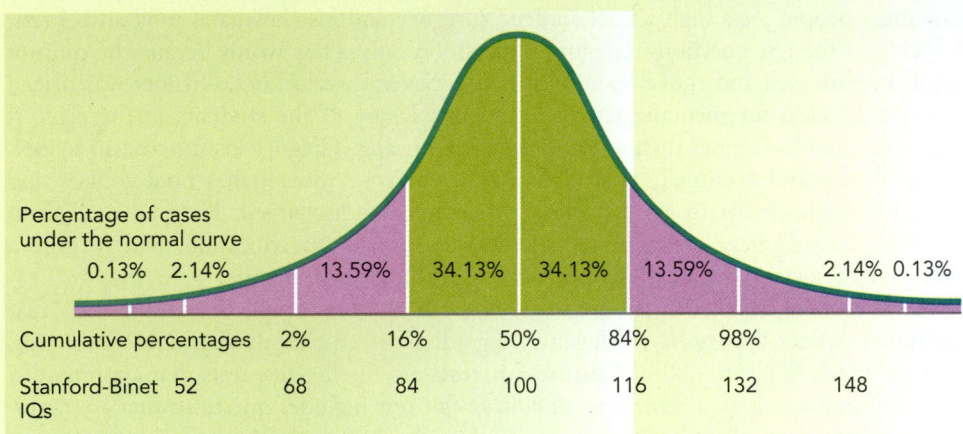

Percentage of cases
under the normal curve

| 0.13% | 2.14% | 13.59% | 34.13% | 34.13% | 13.59% | 2.14% | 0.13% |

| Cumulative percentages | 2% | 16% | 50% | 84% | 98% | |
| Stanford-Binet IQs | 52 | 68 | 84 | 100 | 116 | 132 | 148 |

The Normal Curve

This figure shows the normal curve and Stanford-Binet IQ scores. The distribution of IQ scores approximates a normal curve. Answer the following questions, keeping in mind that the area under the curve represents the number of people who obtain a given score on the test.

1. Do most of the population fall in the low, medium, or high range? How do you know?

2. If someone scored a 132 on the test, how many people scored *below* that person's score?

3. What is the mean or average on the IQ test? Where does the mean fall on the bell-shaped curve?

4. Notice that in a normal distribution, extremely high and extremely low scores are rare. What other human characteristics might follow this pattern?

to that of other adults. For this purpose, researchers and testers use standardized norms that they have identified in the many people who have been tested.

In fact, over the years, the Binet test has been given to thousands of children and adults of different ages selected at random from different parts of the United States. Administering the test to large numbers of individuals and recording the results have revealed that intelligence measured by the Binet test approximates a normal distribution. A **normal distribution** is a symmetrical, bell-shaped curve, with a majority of the scores falling in the middle of the possible range and few scores appearing toward the extremes of the range.

The Stanford-Binet (the name reflects the fact that the revisions were completed at Stanford University) continues to be one of the most widely used individual tests of intelligence (Kamphaus & Kroncke, 2004). To master the important idea of the normal distribution, complete the Psychological Inquiry.

Individuals from the age of 2 through adulthood take the current Stanford-Binet test. It includes a wide variety of items, some requiring verbal responses, others nonverbal responses. For example, items that characterize a 6-year-old's performance on the test include the verbal ability to define at least six words, such as *orange* and *envelope,* and the nonverbal ability to trace a path through a maze. Items that reflect the average adult's intelligence include defining such words as *disproportionate* and *regard,* explaining a proverb, and comparing idleness and laziness.

Cultural Bias in Testing

Many early intelligence tests were culturally biased, favoring people who were from urban rather than rural environments, of middle rather than low socioeconomic status, and White rather than African American (Provenzo, 2002). For example, a question on an early test asked what one should do if one finds a 3-year-old child in the street. The correct answer was "call the police." However, children from inner-city families who perceive the police as scary are unlikely to choose this answer. Similarly, children from rural areas might not choose this answer if there is no police force nearby. Such questions clearly do not measure the knowledge necessary to adapt to one's environment or

● **normal distribution** A symmetrical, bell-shaped curve, with a majority of the scores falling in the middle of the possible range and few scores appearing toward the extremes of the range.

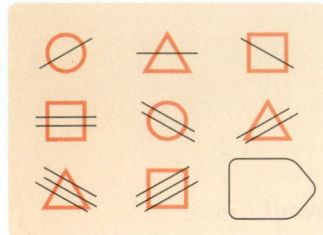

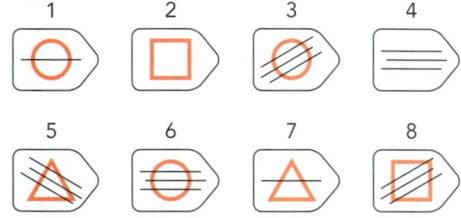

FIGURE 29.3 **Sample Item from the Raven Progressive Matrices Test** For this item, the respondent must choose which of the numbered figures would come next in the order. Can you explain why the right answer is number 6? Simulated item similar to those found in the *Raven's Progressive Matrices* (Standard, Sets A-E). Copyright © 1976, 1958, 1938 NCS Pearson, Inc. Reproduced with permission. All rights reserved. "Raven's Progressive Matrices" is a trademark, in the US and/or other countries, of Pearson Education, Inc. or its affiliate(s).

● **culture-fair tests** Intelligence tests that are intended to be culturally unbiased.

Ham. Artizans.com

● **heritability** The proportion of observable differences in a group that can be explained by differences in the genes of the group's members.

to be "intelligent" in an inner-city or a rural neighborhood (Scarr, 1984). In addition, members of minority groups may not speak English or may speak nonstandard English. Consequently, they may be at a disadvantage in trying to understand verbal questions that are framed in standard English, even if the content of the test is appropriate (Cathers-Shiffman & Thompson, 2007).

The experience of Gregory Ochoa illustrates how cultural bias in intelligence tests can affect people. As a high school student, Gregory and his classmates took an IQ test. Looking at the test questions, Gregory understood only a few words because he did not speak English well and spoke Spanish at home. Several weeks later, Gregory was placed in a special class for mentally retarded students. Many of the students in the class, it turns out, had last names such as Ramirez and Gonzales. Gregory lost interest in school, dropped out, and eventually joined the navy, where he took high school courses and earned enough credits to attend college when he was discharged. He graduated from San Jose City College as an honor student, continued his education, and became a professor of social work at the University of Washington in Seattle.

As a result of cases such as Gregory's, researchers have sought to develop tests that accurately reflect a person's intelligence, regardless of cultural background (Reynolds, Livingston, & Willson, 2006). **Culture-fair tests** are intelligence tests that are intended to be culturally unbiased. One type of culture-fair test includes questions that are familiar to people from all socioeconomic and ethnic backgrounds. A second type contains no verbal questions. Figure 29.3 shows a sample question from the Raven Progressive Matrices Test. Even though tests such as the Raven are designed to be culture-fair, people with more education still score higher than do those with less education.

Why is it so hard to create culture-fair tests? Just as the definition of intelligence may vary by culture, most tests of intelligence reflect what is important to the dominant culture. If tests have time limits, the test will be biased against groups not concerned with time. If languages differ, the same words might have different meanings for different language groups. Even pictures can produce bias, because some cultures have less experience with drawings and photographs (Anastasi & Urbina, 1996). Because of such difficulties, Robert Sternberg and his colleagues conclude that there are no culture-fair tests, only *culture-reduced tests* (Sternberg & Grigorenko, 2008; Zhang & Sternberg, 2009).

Moreover, within the same culture, different groups can have different attitudes, values, and motivation, and these variations can affect their performance on intelligence tests (Ang & van Dyne, 2009; Sternberg, 2009c). Questions about railroads, furnaces, seasons of the year, distances between cities, and so on can be biased against groups who have less experience than others with these contexts. One explanation for the effects of education on IQ test scores is that education (and other environmental factors) may influence intelligence, a possibility to which we now turn.

29-2 GENETIC AND ENVIRONMENTAL INFLUENCES ON INTELLIGENCE

There is no doubt that genes influence intelligence (Chiang & others, 2009; Friedman & others, 2008). Researchers have found unique genetic locations, called *genetic markers,* for intelligence on specific chromosomes (Craig & Plomin, 2006). Further, researchers have examined the links among genes, brain structure, and intelligence (Chiang & others, 2009). So, the question with respect to genetics and intelligence is not whether genes matter but *how much* they matter to intelligence.

In Module 8 we reviewed the concepts of genotype and phenotype. The genotype refers to an organism's genetic material. The phenotype refers to the actual characteristics the organism possesses. When we are talking about genetic influences on intelligence, we are interested in understanding how differences at the level of the genotype predict differences in the phenotype of intelligence.

Scientists often use a statistic called heritability to describe the extent to which the observable differences among people in a group (the phenotype) can be explained by the genetic differences of the group's members (the genotype). **Heritability** is the proportion of observable differences in a group that can be explained by differences in the genes of the group's members. For intelligence, that means that heritability tells us how much of the differences we observe in intelligence is attributable to differences in genes. Because heritability is a proportion, the highest degree of heritability is 100 percent. A committee of respected researchers convened by the American Psychological Association concluded that by late adolescence, the heritability of intelligence is about 75 percent, a finding that reflects a strong genetic influence (Neisser & others, 1996). Researchers have found that the heritability of intelligence increases, from as low as 22 percent in childhood to higher than 80 percent in adulthood (Bouchard, 2004; Bouchard & McGue, 2003).

Why might the influence of heredity on intelligence increase with age? Possibly, as we grow older, our interactions with the environment are shaped less by others and more by our ability to choose environments that allow the expression of genetic tendencies we have inherited (Neisser & others, 1996). For example, parents might push their child into an environment that is incompatible with the child's genetic inheritance (pressuring the child to become a doctor or an engineer, for example), but as an adult, the son or daughter might choose to follow his or her own personal interests (say, becoming a sculptor or a hardware store owner).

As you consider this discussion of genetic influences on intelligence, you might find yourself reflecting on some of the less than brilliant things your parents have done over the years and feeling a bit discouraged. If IQ is heritable, is there any hope? The heritability statistic has certainly been an important way for researchers to gauge the influence of genetics on psychological characteristics including intelligence, but we must understand this statistic for what it can and cannot tell us about intelligence or any characteristic. First and most important, heritability is a statistic that provides information about a group, not a single individual (Sesardic, 2006). This means that finding out that heritability for intelligence is 75 percent tells us nothing at all about the source of an individual person's intelligence. We cannot dissect your intelligence and determine that you got 75 percent of it from your parents and 25 percent from your schooling. Heritability has no meaning when applied to a single case. Recall that group statistics do not apply in a single given case. That is, statistics describe groups, not individuals.

Also, heritability estimates can change over time and across different groups (Turkheimer & others, 2003). If a group of individuals lives in the same advantageous setting (with good nutrition, supportive parents, great schools, stable neighborhoods, and plenty of opportunities), heritability estimates for intelligence might be quite high, as this optimal environment allows genetic characteristics to flourish to their highest potential. However, if a group of individuals lives in a highly variable environment (with some individuals experiencing rich, nurturing environments full of opportunity and others experiencing less supportive contexts), genetic characteristics may be less predictive of differences in intelligence in that group, relative to environmental factors.

Even if the heritability of a characteristic is very high, the environment still matters. Take height, for example. More than 90 percent of the variation in height is explained by genetic variation. Generally speaking, humans continue to get taller and taller, however, and this trend demonstrates that environmental factors such as nutrition have an impact. Similarly, in the case of intelligence, most researchers agree that for most people, modifications in environment can change their IQ scores considerably (F. A. Campbell, 2006; Nisbett, 2009; Ramey, Ramey, & Lanzi, 2006; Rutter, 2007). Enriching an environment can improve school achievement and develop crucial workplace skills. Children who come from impoverished socioeconomic backgrounds who are adopted into more economically advantaged families often have IQs that are higher than those of their biological parents (Sternberg, Grigorenko, & Kidd, 2005). Although genetics may influence intellectual ability, environmental factors and opportunities make a difference (Nisbett, 2009; Sternberg & Grigorenko, 2008).

Researchers are increasingly interested in manipulating the early environment of children who are at risk for impoverished intelligence (Ramey, Ramey, & Lanzi, 2006). Programs that educate parents to be more sensitive caregivers and that train them to be better teachers can make a difference in a child's intellectual development, as can support services such as high-quality child-care programs (Sameroff, 2006).

FIGURE 29.4 **The Increase in IQ Scores from 1932 to 1997** As measured by the Stanford-Binet intelligence test, American children seem to be getting smarter. Scores of a group tested in 1932 fell along a bell-shaped curve, with half below 100 and half above. Studies show that if children took that same test today, using the 1932 scale, half would score above 120. Few of them would score in the "intellectually deficient" range, and about one-fourth would rank in the "very superior" range. Such findings suggest that IQ tests may require new norms to continue to be useful.

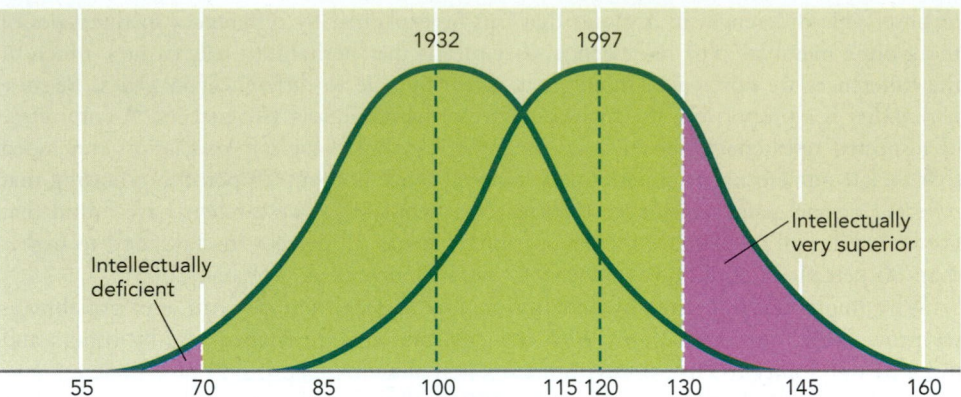

One effect of education on intelligence is evident in rapidly increasing IQ test scores around the world, a phenomenon called the *Flynn effect* (Flynn, 1999, 2006). Scores on these tests have been rising so fast that a high percentage of people regarded as having average intelligence in 1932 would be regarded as having below-average intelligence today (Figure 29.4). Because the increase has taken place in a relatively short period of time, it cannot be due to heredity but rather may be due to rising levels of education attained by a much greater percentage of the world's population or to other environmental factors, such as the explosion of information to which people are now exposed.

Environmental influences are complex (Bronfenbrenner & Morris, 2006). Growing up with all the advantages does not guarantee success. Children from wealthy families may have easy access to excellent schools, books, tutors, and travel, but they may take such opportunities for granted and not be motivated to learn and to achieve. Alternatively, poor or disadvantaged children may be highly motivated and successful. Caregivers who themselves lacked educational opportunities may instill a strong sense of the value of learning and achievement in their children.

Let's return to the idea that the word *intelligent* describes not only people but also behaviors. Mastering skills, thinking about life actively, and making life decisions thoughtfully are intelligent behaviors in which people can engage regardless of the numerical intelligence quotient on their permanent record. Intelligent behavior is always an option, no matter one's IQ score. Our beliefs about cognitive ability, specifically whether it is fixed or changeable, have important implications for the goals we set for learning new skills (Dweck, 2006). We never know what we might accomplish if we try, and no one is doomed because of a number, no matter how powerful that number may seem.

29·3 EXTREMES OF INTELLIGENCE

Intelligence, then, appears to emerge from a combination of genetic heritage and environmental factors. As we have seen, scores on IQ tests generally conform to the bell-shaped normal curve. We now examine the implications of falling on either tail of that curve.

Giftedness

There are people whose abilities and accomplishments outshine those of others—the *A*+ student, the star athlete, the natural musician. People who are **gifted** have high intelligence (an IQ of 130 or higher) and/or superior talent in a particular area. Lewis Terman (1925) conducted a study of 1,500 children whose Stanford-Binet IQs averaged 150, a score that placed them in the top 1 percent. A popular myth is that gifted children are maladjusted, but Terman found that his participants ("Termites") were not only

● **gifted** Possessing high intelligence (an IQ of 130 or higher) and/or superior talent in a particular area.

organic retardation have

h no evidence of organic
IQ between 55 and 70.
part from growing up
duals with this disability
le rewards (candy rather
ers and adults expect of
these individuals usually
cognitive skills as much.
ses as they move toward

one classification system,
according to the person's
of individuals diagnosed
ool systems still use this
erfect predictors of func-
nces between two people
luals with a similarly low
involved in the commu-
Such differences in social
behavior in their defini-
09). The American Asso-
developed an assessment
lomains:

f numbers, money,

self-esteem, and ability

personal care, occupa-
e telephone.

the amount of care the
f the person's ability to

amazing academic feats
ilding close, warm rela-
bringing smiles into an
wn syndrome moreover
ow on general cognitive
ognitive ability (or dis-
more than one concept

as a general ability or
gists have viewed intel-
escribed by Spearman
kinds of intelligence,
in ourselves and oth-
ternberg and Howard
ewpoint that there are

em later became success-
dren grow into gifted and
ically did become experts
iness; but the Termites
2006).

the information age,
tes to use their gifts
from a longitudinal
y at Johns Hopkins
Mathematically Pre-
researchers recruited
IQ estimated at 180.
es (Lubinski & others,
avid Lubinski and col-
le were doing remarkable
rate 50 times higher than
reative writing awards, cre-
, and developing commer-
mites, this group has been
2005).

both heredity and environ-
viduals recall showing signs
r to or at the beginning of
s the importance of innate
at the individuals who enjoy
rts all report strong family
). Deliberate practice is an
rts in a particular domain

lassrooms often do not meet
s, 2008; Sternberg, 2009e).
ucation of gifted adolescents
d Left Behind policy, which
doing well in school at the
, 2008; Cloud, 2008). Ellen
olescents who are not suffi-
their domain of exceptional
llege math classes at 13, and
at 15 and then attended the

gence, others are at the lower
dation) is a condition of lim-
usually below 70 on a tradi-
day life; he or she would have
tates, about 5 million people
a person to be described as
evident in childhood. We do
rain damage in a car accident,

it may be cultural and social
intellectual disability is caused
the tissues or organs of the
dation. Down syndrome, one
tra chromosome is present in

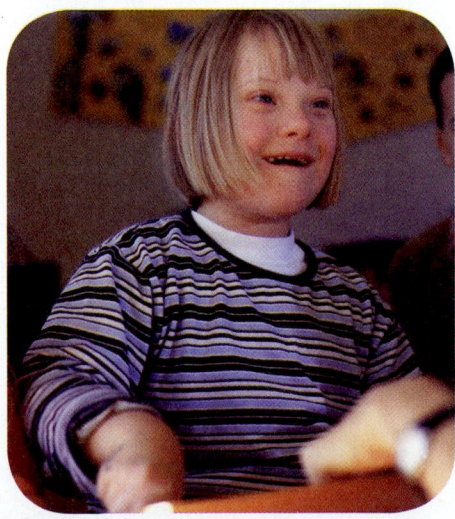

● **intellectual disability** A condition of limited mental ability in which an individual has a low IQ, usually below 70 on a traditional intelligence test, and has difficulty adapting to everyday life.

Individuals with Down syndrome may excel in sensitivity toward others. The possibility that other strengths or intelligences coexist with cognitive ability (or disability) has led some psychologists to propose the need for expanding the concept of intelligence.

the individual's genetic makeup. Most people who suffer from
an IQ between 0 and 50.

Cultural-familial intellectual disability is a mental deficit wi
brain damage. Individuals with this type of disability have ar
Psychologists suspect that such mental deficits result at least
in a below-average intellectual environment. As children, indi
can be identified in school, where they often fail, need tangi
than grades, for example), and are highly sensitive to what p
them (Vaughn, Bos, & Schumm, 2003). As adults, however,
go unnoticed, perhaps because adult settings do not tax their
It may also be that the intelligence of such individuals incre
adulthood.

There are several classifications of intellectual disability. In
disability ranges from mild, to moderate, to severe or profound
IQ (Hallahan, Kauffman, & Pullen, 2009). The large majority
with intellectual disability fall in the mild category. Most sc
system. However, these categories, based on IQ ranges, are not
tioning. Indeed, it is not unusual to find clear *functional* differe
who have the same low IQ. For example, looking at two indivi
IQ, we might find that one of them is married, employed, and
nity and the other requires constant supervision in an institution
competence have led psychologists to include deficits in adaptiv
tion of intellectual disability (Hallahan, Kauffman, & Pullen, 2(
ciation on Intellectual and Developmental Disabilities (2010) ha
that examines a person's level of adaptive behavior in three life

- *Conceptual skills:* For example, literacy and understanding
  and time.
- *Social skills:* For example, interpersonal skills, responsibility
  to follow rules and obey.
- *Practical skills:* For example, activities of daily living such a
  tional skills, health care, travel/transportation, and use of t

Assessment of capacities in these areas can be used to determin
person requires for daily living, not as a function of IQ but
negotiate life's challenges.

A person with Down syndrome may never accomplish the
of gifted individuals. However, he or she may be capable of b
tions with others, serving as an inspiration to loved ones, and
otherwise gloomy day (Van Riper, 2007). Individuals with D
might possess different kinds of intelligence, even if they are
ability. The possibility that other intelligences exist alongside
ability) has inspired some psychologists to suggest that we nee
of intelligence.

29-4 THEORIES OF MULTIPLE INTELLIGENCES

Is it more appropriate to think of an individual's intelligenc
as a number of specific abilities? Traditionally, most psycholo
ligence as a general, all-purpose problem-solving ability, as
(1904). Others have proposed that we think about differen
such as *emotional intelligence,* the ability to perceive emotio
ers accurately (Mayer, Salovey, & Caruso, 2008). Robert
Gardner have developed influential theories presenting the v
multiple intelligences.

Sternberg's and Gardner's Theories

Robert J. Sternberg (1986, 2004, 2008, 2009a, 2009b, 2009c, 2009d) developed the **triarchic theory of intelligence,** which says that intelligence comes in multiple (specifically, three) forms. These forms are

- *Analytical intelligence:* The ability to analyze, judge, evaluate, compare, and contrast.
- *Creative intelligence:* The ability to create, design, invent, originate, and imagine.
- *Practical intelligence:* The ability to use, apply, implement, and put ideas into practice.

Howard Gardner (1983, 1993, 2002) suggests there are nine types of intelligence, or "frames of mind." These are described here, with examples of the types of vocations in which they are reflected as strengths (Campbell, Campbell, & Dickinson, 2004):

- *Verbal:* The ability to think in words and use language to express meaning. Occupations: author, journalist, speaker.
- *Mathematical:* The ability to carry out mathematical operations. Occupations: scientist, engineer, accountant.
- *Spatial:* The ability to think three-dimensionally. Occupations: architect, artist, sailor.
- *Bodily-kinesthetic:* The ability to manipulate objects and to be physically adept. Occupations: surgeon, craftsperson, dancer, athlete.
- *Musical:* The ability to be sensitive to pitch, melody, rhythm, and tone. Occupations: composer, musician.
- *Interpersonal:* The ability to understand and interact effectively with others. Occupations: teacher, mental health professional.
- *Intrapersonal:* The ability to understand oneself. Occupations: theologian, psychologist.
- *Naturalist:* The ability to observe patterns in nature and understand natural and human-made systems. Occupations: farmer, botanist, ecologist, landscaper.
- *Existentialist:* The ability to grapple with the big questions of human existence, such as the meaning of life and death, with special sensitivity to issues of spirituality. Gardner has not identified an occupation for existential intelligence, but one career path would likely be philosopher.

According to Gardner, everyone has all of these intelligences to varying degrees. As a result, we prefer to learn and process information in different ways. People learn best when they can do so in a way that uses their stronger intelligences.

Evaluating Multiple-Intelligences Approaches

Sternberg's and Gardner's approaches have stimulated teachers to think broadly about what makes up children's competencies. They have motivated educators to develop programs that instruct students in multiple domains. These theories have also contributed to interest in assessing intelligence and classroom learning in innovative ways, such as by evaluating student portfolios (May, 2006; Robinson, Shore, & Enerson, 2007).

Doubts about multiple-intelligences approaches persist, however. A number of psychologists think that the proponents of multiple intelligences have taken the concept of specific intelligences too far (Reeve & Charles, 2008). Some critics argue that a research base to support the three intelligences of Sternberg or the nine intelligences of Gardner has not yet emerged. One expert on intelligence, Nathan Brody (2007), observes that people who excel at one type of intellectual task are likely to excel in others. Thus, individuals who do well at memorizing lists of digits are also likely to be good at solving verbal problems and spatial layout problems. Other critics ask, if musical skill, for example, reflects a distinct type of intelligence, why not also label the skills of outstanding chess players, prizefighters, painters, and poets as types of intelligence? In sum, controversy still characterizes whether it is more accurate to conceptualize intelligence as a general ability, specific abilities, or both (Brody, 2007; Sternberg, 2009a, 2009b, 2009c).

● **triarchic theory of intelligence** Sternberg's theory that intelligence comes in three forms: analytical, creative, and practical.

One question that remains is whether and how we can enhance our cognitive abilities. Susanne Jaeggi and colleagues found that undertaking complex cognitive tasks led to enhanced reasoning ability (Jaeggi & others, 2008). In this work, the participants engaged in a complicated memory game similar to the card game Concentration, in which all the cards are placed face down and players have to remember where each one is in order to find matches. After training for a half hour a day for several days, participants increased their scores on reasoning ability, compared to a control group who did not complete the training. The more the participants trained, the smarter they got.

One aspect of the study is particularly interesting. The researchers designed the memory game so that as participants mastered it, it became harder and harder. In short, getting smarter is not just a matter of mastering a skill and then resting on our laurels. Reasoning ability can increase, but for that to happen, we have to keep challenging ourselves to think about things in increasingly new, and sometimes difficult, ways.

Our examination of cognitive abilities has highlighted how individuals differ in the quality of their thinking and how thoughts may differ from one another. Some thoughts reflect critical thinking, creativity, or intelligence. Other thoughts are perhaps less inspired. One thing thoughts have in common is that they usually involve language. Even when we talk to ourselves, we do so with words. The central role of language in cognitive activity is the topic to which we now turn.

SUMMARY

Intelligence consists of the ability to solve problems and to adapt to and learn from everyday experiences. Traditionally, intelligence has been measured by tests designed to compare people's performance on cognitive tasks.

A good test of intelligence meets three criteria: validity, reliability, and standardization. Validity is the extent to which a test measures what it is intended to measure. Reliability is how consistently an individual performs on a test. Standardization focuses on uniform procedures for administering and scoring a test and establishing norms.

Binet developed the first intelligence test. Individuals from age 2 through adulthood take the current Stanford-Binet test. Some intelligence tests are unfair to individuals from different cultures. Culture-fair tests are intelligence tests that are intended to be culturally unbiased.

Genes are clearly involved in intelligence. The proportion of differences in intelligence that is explained by genetic variation (or heritability) is substantial. Environmental influences on intelligence have also been demonstrated. The fact that intelligence test scores have risen considerably around the world in recent decades—called the Flynn effect—supports the role of environment in intelligence.

At the extreme ends of intelligence are giftedness and intellectual disability. People who are gifted have high intelligence (IQ of 130 or higher) and/or superior talent for a particular domain. Research has shown that individuals who are gifted are likely to make important and creative contributions. Intellectual disability is a condition of limited mental ability in which the individual has a low IQ, usually below 70; has difficulty adapting to everyday life; and has an onset of these characteristics during childhood. Intellectual disability can have an organic cause or can be cultural and social in origin.

Instead of focusing on intelligence as a single, broad cognitive ability, some psychologists have broken intelligence up into a variety of life skills. Sternberg's triarchic theory states there are three main types of intelligence: analytical, creative, and practical. Gardner identifies nine types of intelligence, involving skills that are verbal, mathematical, spatial, bodily-kinesthetic, musical, interpersonal, intrapersonal, naturalist, and existential. The multiple-intelligences approaches have broadened the definition

KEY TERMS

intelligence   281

validity   282

reliability   282

standardization   282

mental age (MA)   282

intelligence quotient (IQ)   282

normal distribution   283

culture-fair tests   284

heritability   284

gifted   286

intellectual disability   287

triarchic theory of intelligence   289

of intelligence and motivated educators to develop programs that instruct students in different domains. Critics maintain that multiple-intelligences theories include factors that really are not part of intelligence, such as musical skills, and that people who are highly intelligent are likely to excel in many different areas, not just one. Critics also say that there is not enough research to support the concept of multiple intelligences.

TEST YOURSELF

1. What is Spearman's *g?*
2. With respect to testing, what do validity, reliability, and standardization mean?
3. What two terms respectively define persons at the high end and the low end of intelligence?

APPLY YOUR KNOWLEDGE

1. Ask a few friends to define the term *intelligent.* Do they mostly describe intelligent people or intelligent behaviors? Do their definitions focus on cognitive ability or other abilities?

2. Many different intelligence tests are available online, such as http://www.iqtest.com/. Give this one a try and then do a web search for intelligence tests and see if you get the same results when you take a different test. Do the websites tell you how reliable the tests are? Do they provide information on standardization or validity? If your scores on the two tests are very different, what might account for this difference?

Language

Module 30

language A form of communication—whether spoken, written, or signed—that is based on a system of symbols.

Language is a form of communication—whether spoken, written, or signed—that is based on a system of symbols. We need language to speak with others, listen to others, read, and write (Berko Gleason, 2009). In this module we first examine the fundamental characteristics of language and then trace the links between language and cognition.

30·1 THE BASIC PROPERTIES OF LANGUAGE

infinite generativity The ability of language to produce an endless number of meaningful sentences.

All human languages have **infinite generativity**, the ability to produce an endless number of meaningful sentences. This superb flexibility comes from five basic rule systems:

phonology A language's sound system.

- **Phonology:** a language's sound system. Language is made up of basic sounds, or *phonemes.* Phonological rules ensure that certain sound sequences occur (for example, *sp, ba,* or *ar*) and others do not (for example, *zx* or *qp*) (Marom & Berent, 2010; Menn & Stoel-Gammon, 2009). A good example of a phoneme in the English language is /*k*/, the sound represented by the letter *k* in the word *ski* and the letter *c* in the word *cat.* Although the /*k*/ sound is slightly different in these two words, the /*k*/ sound is described as a single phoneme in English.

morphology A language's rules for word formation.

- **Morphology:** a language's rules for word formation. Every word in the English language is made up of one or more morphemes. A morpheme is the smallest unit of language that carries meaning. Some words consist of a single morpheme—for example, *help.* Others are made up of more than one; for example, *helper* has two morphemes, *help + er.* The morpheme *-er* means "one who"—in this case, "one who helps." As you can see, not all morphemes are words; for example, *pre-, -tion,* and *-ing* are morphemes. Just as the rules that govern phonemes ensure that certain sound sequences occur, the rules that govern morphemes ensure that certain strings of sounds occur in particular sequences (Liu & McBride-Chang, 2010).

syntax A language's rules for combining words to form acceptable phrases and sentences.

- **Syntax:** a language's rules for combining words to form acceptable phrases and sentences (Lai & Bird, 2010; Tager-Flusberg & Zukowski, 2009). If someone says, "John kissed Emily" or "Emily was kissed by John," you know who did the kissing and who was kissed in each case because you share that person's understanding of sentence structure. You also understand that the sentence "You didn't stay, did you?" is a grammatical sentence but that "You didn't stay, didn't you?" is unacceptable.

semantics The meaning of words and sentences in a particular language.

- **Semantics:** the meaning of words and sentences in a particular language. Every word has a unique set of semantic features (Kemmerer & Gonzalez-Castillo, 2010; Pan & Uccelli, 2009). *Girl* and *woman,* for example, share many semantic features (for instance, both signify female human beings), but they differ semantically in regard to age. Words have semantic restrictions on how they can be used in sentences. The sentence "The bicycle talked the boy into buying a candy bar" is syntactically correct but semantically incorrect. The sentence violates our semantic knowledge that bicycles do not talk.

pragmatics The useful character of language and the ability of language to communicate even more meaning than is said.

- **Pragmatics:** the useful character of language and the ability of language to communicate even more meaning than is said (Bryant, 2009; Scott-Phillips, 2010). The pragmatic aspect of language allows us to use words to get the things we want. If you ever find yourself in a country in which you know only a little of the language, you will certainly take advantage of pragmatics. Wandering the streets of, say, Madrid, you might approach a stranger and ask, simply, "Autobus?" (the Spanish word for *bus*). You know that given your inflection and perhaps your desperate facial expression, the person will understand that you are looking for the bus stop.

With this basic understanding of language in place, we can examine the connections between language and cognition.

30·2 LANGUAGE AND COGNITION

Language is a vast system of symbols capable of expressing most thoughts; it is the vehicle for communicating most of our thoughts to one another (Allan, 2010). Although we do not always think in words, our thinking would be greatly impoverished without words.

The connection between language and thought has been of considerable interest to psychologists. Some have even argued that we cannot think without language. This proposition has produced heated controversy. Is thought dependent on language, or is language dependent on thought?

The Role of Language in Cognition

Memory is stored not only in the form of sounds and images but also in words. Language helps us think, make inferences, tackle difficult decisions, and solve problems (Horst & others, 2009). It is also a tool for representing ideas (Kovacs, 2009).

Today, most psychologists would accept these points. However, linguist Benjamin Whorf (1956) went a step further: He argued that language determines the way we think, a view that has been called the *linguistic relativity hypothesis*. Whorf and his student Edward Sapir were specialists in Native American languages, and they were fascinated by the possibility that people might perceive the world differently as the

Whorf's view is that our cultural experiences with a particular concept shape a catalog of names that can be either rich or poor. Consider how rich your mental library of names for camel might be if you had extensive experience with camels in a desert world, and how poor your mental library of names for snow might be if you lived in a tropical world of palm trees and parrots. Despite its intriguing appeal, Whorf's view likely overstates the role of language in shaping thought.

result of the different languages they speak. The Inuit people in Alaska, for instance, have a dozen or more words to describe the various textures, colors, and physical states of snow. In contrast, English has relatively few words to describe snow, and thus, according to Whorf's view, English speakers *cannot see* the different kinds of snow because they have no words for them.

Whorf's bold claim appealed to many scholars. Some even tried to apply Whorf's view to gender differences in color perception. Asked to describe the colors of two sweaters, a woman might say, "One is mauve and the other is magenta," while a man might say, "They're both pink." Whorf's view of the influence of language on perceptual ability might suggest that women are able to see more colors than men simply because they have a richer color vocabulary (Hepting & Solle, 1973). It turns out, however, that men can learn to discriminate among the various hues that women use, and this outcome suggests that Whorf's view is not quite accurate.

Indeed, critics of Whorf's ideas say that words merely reflect, rather than cause, the way we think. The Inuits' adaptability and livelihood in Alaska depend on their capacity to recognize various conditions of snow and ice. A skier or snowboarder who is not Inuit might also know numerous words for snow, far more than the average person, and a person who does not know the words for the different types of snow might still be able to perceive these differences. Interestingly, research has shown that Whorf might have been accurate for information that is presented to the left hemisphere of the brain. That is, when colors were presented in the right visual field (and therefore went to the left brain), having names for the colors enhanced perception of and discrimination among those colors (Gilbert & others, 2006).

Although research has not supported Whorf's view with regard to gender differences in vocabulary, is it true that men and women do not differ linguistically in other ways? To explore this question, see the Critical Controversy.

Although the strongest form of Whorf's hypothesis—that language determines perception—seems doubtful, research has continued to demonstrate the influence of language on how we think, even about something as fundamental as our own personalities. For example, in a series of studies, researchers interviewed bilingual individuals (that is, people who fluently speak two languages, in this case Spanish and English) (Ramirez-Esparza & others, 2006). Each person rated his or her own personality characteristics, once in Spanish and once in English. Across all studies, and regardless of whether the individuals lived in a Spanish-speaking or an English-speaking country, respondents reported themselves as more outgoing, nicer, and more responsible when responding to the survey in English.

The Role of Cognition in Language

Clearly, then, language can influence cognition. Researchers also study the possibility that cognition is an important foundation for language (Bohannon & Bonvillian, 2009). If language is a reflection of cognition in general, we would expect to find a close link between language ability and general intellectual ability. In particular, we would expect that problems in cognition are paralleled by problems in language. We would anticipate, for example, that general intellectual disability is accompanied by lowered language abilities.

It is often but not always the case that individuals with intellectual disability have a reduced language proficiency. For instance, individuals with Williams syndrome— a genetic disorder that affects about 1 in 20,000 births—tend to show extraordinary verbal, social, and musical abilities while having an extremely low IQ and difficulty with motor tasks and numbers (Marini & others, 2010). Williams syndrome demonstrates that intellectual disability is not always accompanied by poor language skills.

In summary, although thought influences language and language influences thought, there is increasing evidence that language and thought are not part of a single system. Instead, they seem to have evolved as separate but related components of the mind.

CRITICAL CONTROVERSY

Does Gender Influence Language?

Common stereotypes suggest that women are the talkative sex. The bestseller *The Female Brain* by Louann Brizendine (2006) claims that women talk three times as much as men. Brizendine suggests that women's brains are wired from birth to be extraordinarily sensitive to social information. Women, she says, have an "eight-lane superhighway" for processing emotion, whereas men have only "a single country road."

The notion that men are somehow missing out on an emotional express-way is also reflected in the *extreme male brain theory* of autism. Recall that autism is a disorder in which individuals have particular difficulty processing so-cial information. Simon Baron-Cohen has suggested that characteristics associated with autism might be considered simply extreme forms of the "male brain"—that is, one that is well suited to math and spatial reasoning but less well geared to verbal and social skills (Baron-Cohen, 2002, 2003, 2008; Baron-Cohen, Knick-meyer, & Belmonte, 2006). This controversial notion certainly shows that people seem to be prone to extreme positions and stereotypes when discussing gender differences.

Recent research challenges the idea that women are the talkers of the world. Matthias Mehl and his colleagues (Mehl & others, 2007) examined this notion in an innovative way. Nearly 400 male and fe-male college students wore a device that recorded them for a few minutes every 12½ minutes as they went about their daily routines. The device allowed the researchers to count how much each

participant spoke in the course of the day. The results of the study showed that women uttered slightly more than 16,000 words a day. And men? They spoke slightly less than 16,000 words a day. No significant difference emerged. Inter-estingly, the biggest talkers in the study (averaging 47,000 words per day) were all male. So was the quietest person in the study, speaking just 700 words per day.

The sheer number of best-selling books about gender differences high-lights our fascination with male–female contrasts. Boys, men, girls, and women live in a social world that poses different expectations and different challenges. It is easy to think of male–female differences as rooted exclusively in the biological differences of sex. A more re-alistic and balanced viewpoint might acknowl-edge that men and women are, after all, human beings and that working out our conflicts with the other sex is about negotiating common human needs rather than simply living with biologically programmed characteristics.

WHAT DO YOU THINK?

- Is research on gender differences in language ability potentially damaging to men or women? Why or why not?

- Why are gender differences so fascinating to people in general?

- Who are the biggest talkers you know? Do they have any characteristics (aside from gender) in common?

30-3 BIOLOGICAL AND ENVIRONMENTAL INFLUENCES ON LANGUAGE

Everyone who uses language in some way "knows" its rules and has the ability to create an infinite number of words and sentences. Is this knowledge the product of biology, or is language learned and influenced by experiences in the environment?

Biological Influences

Scientists believe that humans acquired language about 100,000 years ago. In evolution-ary time, then, language is a very recent human ability. However, a number of experts believe that biological evolution that occurred long before language emerged undeniably shaped humans into linguistic creatures (Chomsky, 1975). The brain, nervous system, and vocal apparatus of our predecessors changed over hundreds of thousands of years.

Noam Chomsky (b. 1928) MIT linguist Noam Chomsky was one of the early architects of the idea that children's language development cannot be explained by environmental input. In Chomsky's view, language has strong biological underpinnings, with children biologically prewired to learn language at a certain time and in a certain way.

Physically equipped to do so, *Homo sapiens* went beyond grunting and shrieking to develop abstract speech. This sophisticated language ability gave humans an enormous edge over other animals and increased their chances of survival (Pinker, 1994).

LANGUAGE UNIVERSALS

American linguist Noam Chomsky (1975) has argued that humans come into the world biologically prewired to learn language at a certain time and in a certain way. According to Chomsky and many other language experts, the strongest evidence for language's biological basis is the fact that children all over the world reach language milestones at about the same time and in about the same order, despite vast variations in the language input they receive from their environment. For example, in some cultures, such as some Samoan tribes (Schieffelin & Ochs, 1986), parents snuggle their babies but rarely talk to infants under 1 year of age, yet these infants still acquire language (Sterponi, 2010).

In Chomsky's view, children cannot possibly learn the full rules and structure of languages by only imitating what they hear. Rather, nature must provide children with a biological, prewired, universal grammar, allowing them to understand the basic rules of all languages and to apply these rules to the speech they hear. They learn language without an awareness of its underlying logic. Think about it: The terms we used above to define the characteristics of language—*phonology, morphology, semantics,* and so forth—may be new to you, but on some level you have mastered these principles. This mastery is demonstrated by your reading of this book, writing a paper for class, and talking with a friend. Like all other humans, you are engaged in the use of a rule-based language system even without knowing that you know those rules.

LANGUAGE AND THE BRAIN

There is strong evidence to back up experts who believe language has a biological foundation. Neuroscience research has shown that the brain contains particular regions that are predisposed to language use (Tremblay, Monetta, & Joanette, 2009). Accumulating evidence suggests that language processing, such as speech and grammar, mainly occurs in the brain's left hemisphere (Harpaz, Levkovitz, & Lavidor, 2009; Hornickel, Skoe, & Kraus, 2009). Recall the importance of Broca's area, which contributes to speech production, and Wernicke's area, which is involved in language comprehension (Module 7).

Using brain-imaging techniques such as PET scans, researchers have found that when an infant is about 9 months old, the hippocampus, the part of the brain that stores and indexes many kinds of memory, becomes fully functional (Bauer, 2009). This is also the time at which infants appear to be able to attach meaning to words, for instance to look at the ball if someone says "ball"—suggesting links among language, cognition, and the development of the brain.

Environmental Influences

Decades ago, behaviorists opposed Chomsky's hypothesis and argued that language represents nothing more than chains of responses acquired through reinforcement (Skinner, 1957). A baby happens to babble "ma-ma," mama rewards the baby with hugs and smiles, the baby says "mama" more and more. Bit by bit, said the behaviorists, the baby's language is built up. According to behaviorists, language is a complex learned skill, much like playing the piano or dancing.

Such a view of language development is simply not tenable, however, given the rapid way children learn language, as well as the lack of evidence that social environments carefully reinforce language skills (R. Brown, 1973). This is not to say the environment has no role in language development. Many language experts argue that a child's experiences, the particular language to be learned, and the context in which learning takes place can strongly influence language acquisition (Berko Gleason, 2009; Goldfield & Snow, 2009).

Cases of children who have lacked exposure to language provide evidence for the important role of the environment in language development. In 1970, a California social worker made a routine visit to the home of a partially blind woman who had applied for public assistance. The social worker discovered that the woman and her husband had kept their 13-year-old daughter, Genie, locked away in almost total isolation during her childhood. Genie could not speak or stand erect. She had spent every day bound naked to a child's potty seat. She could move only her hands and feet. At night, she had been placed in a kind of straightjacket and caged in a crib with wire mesh sides and a cover. Whenever Genie had made a noise, her father had beaten her. He had never communicated with her in words; he had growled and barked at her instead (Rymer, 1993).

After she was rescued from her parents, Genie spent a number of years in extensive rehabilitation programs, including speech and physical therapy (Curtiss, 1977). She eventually learned to walk, although with a jerky motion, and to use the toilet. Genie also learned to recognize many words and to speak in rudimentary sentences. Gradually, she was able to string together two-word combinations such as "big teeth," "little marble," and "two hand" and then three-word combinations such as "small two cup." As far as we know, unlike normal children, Genie did not learn to ask questions and did not develop a language system that allowed her to understand English grammar. As an adult, she speaks in short, mangled sentences such as "Father hit leg," "Big wood," and "Genie hurt."

Children who, like Genie, are abused and lack exposure to language for many years rarely speak normally. Some language experts have argued that these cases support the idea that there is a "critical period" for language development, a special time in a child's life (usually the preschool years) during which language must develop or it never will. Because these children also suffer severe emotional trauma and possible neurological deficits, however, the issue is still far from clear. Whether or not these cases suggest such a critical period, they certainly support the idea that the environment is crucial for the development of language.

Clearly, most humans do not learn language in a social vacuum. Most children are bathed in language from a very early age (Berko Gleason, 2009). The support and involvement of caregivers and teachers greatly facilitate a child's language learning (Goldfield & Snow, 2009; Pan & Uccelli, 2009). For example, one study showed that when mothers immediately smiled and touched their 8-month-old infants after they had babbled, the infants subsequently made more complex speechlike sounds than when mothers responded to their infants in a random manner (Goldstein, King, & West, 2003) (Figure 30.1).

In another study, researchers observed the language environments of children from two different backgrounds: middle-income professional families and welfare families (Hart & Risley, 1995; Risley & Hart, 2006). Then they examined the children's language development. All of the children developed normally in terms of learning to talk and acquiring the basic rules of English and a fundamental vocabulary. However, the researchers found enormous differences in the sheer amount of language to which the children were exposed and in the level of the children's language development. For example, in a typical hour, the middle-income professional parents spent almost twice as much time communicating with their children as did the welfare parents. The children from the middle-income professional families heard about 2,100 words an hour; their child counterparts in welfare families, only 600 words an hour. The researchers estimated that by 4 years of age, the average welfare-family child would have 13 million fewer words of cumulative language experience than the child in the average middle-income professional family. Amazingly, some of the 3-year-old children from middle-class professional families had a recorded vocabulary that exceeded the recorded vocabulary of some of the welfare parents.

What are some good strategies for parents in talking to their babies? Some include the following (Baron, 1992):

■ *Be an active conversational partner*. Initiate conversation with the infant. If the infant is in a daylong child-care program, ensure that he or she gets adequate language stimulation from adults.

■ *Talk as if the infant will understand what you are saying*. Adults can generate positive self-fulfilling prophecies by addressing their young children as if they will understand what is being said. The process may take four to five years, but children gradually rise to match the language model presented them.

FIGURE 30.1 **The Power of Smile and Touch** Research has shown that when mothers immediately smiled and touched their 8-month-old infants after they babbled, the infants subsequently made more complex speechlike sounds than when mothers responded randomly to their infants.

■ *Use a language style with which you feel comfortable.* Do not worry about how you sound to other adults when you talk with an infant. The mood and feeling you convey, not the content, is more important when talking with an infant. Use whatever type of baby talk with which you feel comfortable in the first years of the child's life.

Research findings about environmental influences on language learning complicate the understanding of its foundations. In the real world of language learning, children appear to be neither exclusively biologically programmed linguists nor exclusively socially driven language experts (Ratner, 1993). We have to look at how biology and environment interact when children learn language. That is, children are biologically prepared to learn language but benefit enormously from being immersed in a competent language environment from an early age (Goldfield & Snow, 2009; Pan & Uccelli, 2009).

FIGURE 30.2 Language Milestones All children are different and acquire language at varying rates, but these milestones provide a general sense of how language emerges in human life. *Note:* This list is meant not to be exhaustive but rather to highlight some of the main language milestones. Also keep in mind that there is a great deal of variation in the ages at which children can reach these milestones and still be considered within the normal range of language development.

Age	Milestones
0–6 Months	Cooing Discrimination of vowels Babbling present by 6 months
6–12 Months	Babbling expands to include sounds of spoken language Gestures used to communicate about objects First words spoken 10–13 months
12–18 Months	Understands 50+ words on average
18–24 Months	Vocabulary increases to an average of 200 words Two-word combinations
2 Years	Vocabulary rapidly increases Correct use of plurals Use of past tense Use of some prepositions
3–4 Years	Mean length of utterances increases to 3–4 morphemes in a sentence Use of "yes" and "no" questions, wh- questions Use of negatives and imperatives Increased awareness of pragmatics
5–6 Years	Vocabulary reaches an average of about 10,000 words Coordination of simple sentences
6–8 Years	Vocabulary continues to increase rapidly More skilled use of syntactical rules Conversational skills improve
9–11 Years	Word definitions include synonyms Conversational strategies continue to improve
11–14 Years	Vocabulary increases with addition of more abstract words Understanding of complex grammar forms Increased understanding of function a word plays in a sentence Understands metaphor and satire
15–20 Years	Understands adult literary works

30-4 LANGUAGE DEVELOPMENT OVER THE LIFE SPAN

Most individuals develop a clear understanding of their language's structure, as well as a large vocabulary, during childhood. Most adults in the United States have acquired a vocabulary of nearly 50,000 words. Researchers have taken a great interest in the process by which these aspects of language develop (Hollich & Huston, 2007). Their many studies have provided an understanding of the milestones of language development (Figure 30.2).

Language researchers are fascinated by babies' speech even before the little ones say their first words (Pan & Uccelli, 2009). *Babbling*—endlessly repeating sounds and syllables, such as *bababa* or *dadada*—begins at the age of about 4 to 6 months and is determined by biological readiness, not by the amount of reinforcement or the ability to hear (Menn & Stoel-Gammon, 2009). Even deaf babies babble for a time (Lenneberg, Rebelsky, & Nichols, 1965). Babbling probably allows babies to exercise their vocal cords and helps develop the ability to articulate different sounds.

Patricia Kuhl's research reveals that long before they begin to learn words, infants can sort through a number of spoken sounds in search of the ones that have meaning for their culture (Kuhl, 1993, 2000, 2007; Kuhl & Damasio, 2009). Kuhl argues that from birth to about 6 months of age, children are "universal linguists" who are capable of distinguishing each of the sounds that make up the various different human languages By about 6 months of age, they have started to specialize in the speech sounds (or phonology) of their native language (Figure 30.3).

A child's first words, uttered at the age of 10 to 13 months, name important people (*dada*), familiar animals (*kitty*), vehicles (*car*), toys (*ball*), food (*milk*), body parts (*eye*), clothes (*hat*), household items (*clock*), and greetings (*bye*). These were babies' first words a century ago, and they are babies' first words still (Bloom, 2004).

By the time children reach the age of 18 to 24 months, they usually utter two-word statements. They quickly grasp the importance of expressing concepts and the role that language plays in communicating with others (Sachs, 2009). To convey meaning in two-word statements, the child relies heavily on gesture, tone, and context. Although these two-word sentences omit many parts of speech, they are remarkably effective in conveying many messages. When a toddler demands, "Pet doggie!" parents know he means, "May I please pet the doggie?" Very young children learn that language is a good way to get what they want, suggesting that they grasp another aspect of language—its pragmatics.

Although childhood is an important time for language learning, we continue to learn language (new words, new skills) throughout life (Obler, 2009). For many years, it was claimed that if individuals did not learn a second language prior to puberty, they would never reach native-language learners' levels in the second language (Johnson & Newport, 1991). However, recent research indicates a more complex conclusion: Sensitive periods

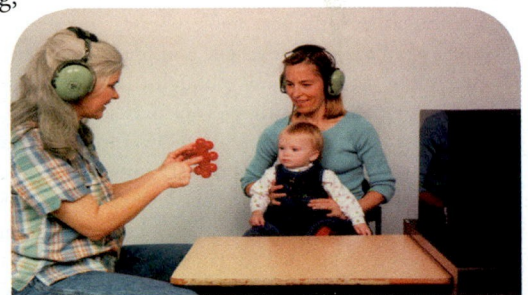

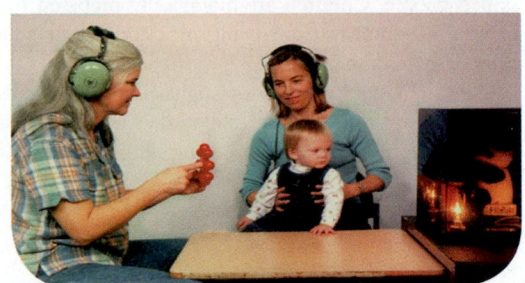

FIGURE 30.3 **From Universal Linguist to Language-Specific Listener** A baby is shown in Patricia Kuhl's research laboratory. In this research, babies listen to recorded voices that repeat syllables. When the sounds of the syllables change, the babies quickly learn to look at the bear. Using this technique, Kuhl has demonstrated that babies are universal linguists until about 6 months of age but in the next 6 months become language-specific listeners.

Around the world, young children learn to speak in two-word utterances at 18 to 24 months of age.

likely vary across different language systems (Thomas & Johnson, 2008). Thus, for late second-language learners, such as adolescents and adults, new vocabulary is easier to learn than new sounds or new grammar (Neville, 2006). For example, children's ability to pronounce words with a native-like accent in a second language typically decreases with age, with an especially sharp drop occurring after about 10 to 12 years of age.

For adults, learning a new language requires a special kind of cognitive exercise. As we have seen, a great deal of language learning in infancy and childhood involves recognizing the sounds that are part of one's native tongue. This process also entails learning to ignore sounds that are *not* important to one's first language. For instance, in Japanese, the phonemes /l/ and /r/ are not distinguished from each other, so that, for a Japanese adult, the word *lion* is not distinguishable from the name *Ryan*. Recent research suggests that mastering a new language in adulthood may involve overriding such learned habits and learning to listen to sounds that one previously ignored. Indeed, adults can learn to hear and discriminate sounds that are part of a new language, and this learning can contribute to speech fluency and language skill (Evans & Iverson, 2007). Thus, learning a new language in adulthood involves cognitively stretching ourselves away from our assumptions.

SUMMARY

Language is a form of communication that is based on a system of symbols. All human languages have common aspects, including infinite generativity and organizational rules about structure. Also, all languages have five characteristics: phonology, the sound system of a language; morphology, the rules for combining morphemes (which are meaningful strings of sounds that contain no smaller meaningful parts); syntax, the ways words are combined to form acceptable phrases and sentences; semantics, the meaning of words and sentences; and pragmatics, the uses of language.

Although language and thought influence each other, there is increasing evidence that they evolved as separate, modular, biologically prepared components of the mind. Evolution shaped humans into linguistic creatures. Chomsky said that humans are biologically prewired to learn language at a certain time and in a certain way. In addition, there is strong evidence that particular regions in the left hemisphere of the brain are predisposed to be used for language. Experience is also crucial to language development. It is important for children to interact with language-skilled people. Children are biologically prepared to learn language but benefit enormously from being in a competent language environment from early in development.

Although we often think of language, thinking, and intelligence as fixed when we are adults, research shows that we can continue to master skills and even increase intelligence by engaging in challenging mental tasks.

KEY TERMS

language   292
infinite generativity   292
phonology   292
morphology   292

syntax   292
semantics   292
pragmatics   292

TEST YOURSELF

1. What are the terms for a language's sound system, its rules for combining words to form acceptable sentences, and the meanings of its words and sentences?

2. State Whorf's linguistic relativity hypothesis and explain why some scholars have criticized it.

3. What evidence has neuroscience research provided for a biological foundation of language?

APPLY YOUR KNOWLEDGE

1. Do men and women have their own languages? Can you think of a time when you were talking with someone of the opposite gender and you just couldn't get your point across? What do you think the barriers were, and what was the end result of your conversation?

2. Find a child between the ages of 1–4 and another between the ages of 5–9. Strike up a conversation with each. What do you notice about their use of language? Who is easier to converse with and why? How is language development connected with childhood maturity?

Thinking, Problem Solving, and Health and Wellness

The way we think about life events can have a profound impact on our experience of stress. Recall that stress refers to our response to changes in the environment and that stressors are those changes. Consider the stressors in your life. They can be anything from losing irreplaceable notes from a class, to being yelled at by a friend, to failing a test, to being in a car wreck. Although everyone's body may have a similar response to stressors, not everyone perceives the same events as stressful, as we consider in this final section.

COGNITIVE APPRAISAL AND STRESS

Whether an experience "stresses us out" depends on how we think about that experience. For example, you may perceive an upcoming job interview as a threatening obligation, whereas your roommate may perceive it as a challenging opportunity. He or she might feel some anxiety but see the experience as a chance to shine. You might view a *D* on a paper as threatening; your roommate may view the same grade as an incentive to work harder. To some degree, then, what is stressful depends on how we think about events—what psychologists call cognitive appraisal (Gidron & Nyklicek, 2009; Meade & others, 2010).

Cognitive appraisal refers to a person's interpretation of a situation. This appraisal includes whether the event or situation is viewed as harmful and threatening, or challenging, and the person's determination of whether he or she has the resources to cope effectively with the events. Is moving to a new apartment stressful? It depends on how you look at it and whether you have the resources you need to handle the challenge effectively.

Coping is essentially a kind of problem solving. It involves managing taxing circumstances, expending effort to solve life's problems, and seeking to master or reduce stress. Richard Lazarus most clearly articulated the importance of cognitive appraisal to stress and coping (1993, 2000). In Lazarus's view, people appraise events in two steps: primary appraisal and secondary appraisal.

In *primary appraisal,* individuals interpret whether an event involves *harm* or loss that has already occurred, a *threat* of some future danger, or a *challenge* to be overcome. Lazarus believed that perceiving a stressor as a challenge to be overcome, rather than as a threat, is a good strategy for reducing stress. To understand Lazarus's concept of primary appraisal, consider two students, each of whom has a failing grade in a psychology class at midterm. Sam is almost frozen by the stress of the low grade and looks at the rest of the term as a threatening prospect. In contrast, Pam does not become overwhelmed by the harm already done and the threat of future failures. She looks at the low grade as a challenge that she can address and overcome.

In *secondary appraisal,* individuals evaluate their resources and determine how effectively they can be used to cope with the event. This appraisal is secondary because it both comes after primary appraisal and depends on the degree to which the event is appraised as harmful, threatening, or challenging. For example, Sam might have some helpful resources for coping with his low midterm grade, but he views the stressful circumstance as so harmful and threatening that he does not take stock of and use his resources. Pam, in contrast, evaluates the resources she can call on to improve her grade during the second half of the term. These include asking the instructor for suggestions about how to study better for the tests in the course, setting up a time management program to include more study hours, and consulting with several high-achieving classmates about their strategies. Importantly, *rethinking* our appraisals of potential stressors can influence health and wellness.

● **cognitive appraisal** Individuals' interpretation of the events in their lives as harmful, threatening, or challenging and their determination of whether they have the resources to cope effectively with the events.

● **coping** Managing taxing circumstances, expending effort to solve life's problems, and seeking to master or reduce stress.

301

The Candle Problem

The solution requires a unique perception of the function of the box in which the matches came. It can become a candleholder when tacked to the wall.

The Nine-Dot Problem

Most people have difficulty with this problem because they try to draw the lines within the boundaries of the dots. Notice that by extending the lines beyond the dots, the problem can be solved.

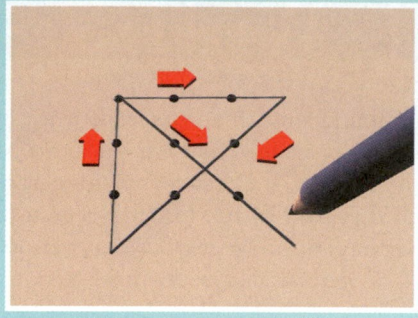

The Six-Matchstick Problem

Nothing in the instructions said that the solution had to be two-dimensional.

Solutions to problems from the Psychological Inquiry feature on page 273.

COGNITIVE REAPPRAISAL

Once an event or experience has been appraised, it need not be set in stone. Indeed, one way of dealing with potentially stressful situations is to reappraise the event actively and come up with a new way of thinking about it.

Cognitive reappraisal involves regulating our feelings about an experience by reinterpreting it or thinking about it in a different way or from a different angle (Roseman & Smith, 2009). Research has shown that reappraising an event can change not only the way people feel about it (Urry, 2010), but also the brain activity linked to the experience. For example, in one brain-imaging study, participants were shown images that were likely to produce negative feelings (McRae & others, 2010). To examine the effects of cognitive reappraisal, the researchers told participants to look at the pictures and think about them in a way that would reduce their negative feelings. Results showed that reappraising the stimuli resulted in decreased negative feelings, decreased activation in the amygdala, and increased activation in prefrontal regions.

Reappraising negative life events can involve a process called *benefit finding*. Benefit finding means looking at a stressful life event in a particular way, focusing on the good that has arisen in one's life as a result. Finding benefits in negative life events can be a way to make meaning out of those experiences (Mock & Boerner, 2010; C. L. Park, 2010). Finding benefits in negative life events has been related to better physical health (Bower, Moskowitz, & Epel, 2009) and better functioning in the context of a variety of illnesses (C. L. Park & others, 2009; C. L. Park, 2010). It may be challenging to think of negative life events as opportunities. However, the capacity to think about such events differently—to engage creatively with the notion that even objectively negative life events have helped us to become more compassionate, wiser, or better able to meet the challenges of the future—can be a powerful tool for staving off stress (King & Hicks, 2007).

● **cognitive reappraisal** Regulating one's feelings about an experience by reinterpreting that experience or thinking about it in a different way or from a different angle.

SUMMARY

The way individuals think about life events determines whether they experience them as stressful. Cognitive appraisal is individuals' interpretation of the events in their lives as either threatening (and therefore stressful) or challenging (and therefore not stressful). Coping refers to people's attempts to handle situations that they perceive as stressful. Cognitive reappraisal can be a powerfçul tool for coping with negative life events. One type of reappraisal, benefit finding, relates to enhanced psychological and physical health.

KEY TERMS

cognitive appraisal   301
coping   301

cognitive reappraisal   302

TEST YOURSELF

1. What is cognitive appraisal?

2. What is cognitive reappraisal?

3. How does benefit finding relate to physical health and to body function in a variety of illnesses?

Human Development

Welcome to the World

On any given day, about 384,000 babies are born worldwide. That translates to 16,000 babies every hour. In fact, in the time it takes you to read these few words, about 16 people have entered the world and begun their life's journey. For their parents it is a life-changing moment: a Monday or a Thursday that is not just a square on the calendar but a day they will never forget. Children are being born everywhere—in homes and hospitals, at birthing centers, and even in parking lots, as was the case for Wyatt Dean Overman, who was born in his parents' car outside a Cambridge, Minnesota, convenience store on January 12, 2010. Newborn babies are cute and fascinating, a few pounds of complete mystery. Whom does she resemble? What will her personality be like? What will she be when she grows up?

Reflect on your birthday—not the date but the actual day you were born. You cannot remember it, but you were much smaller, virtually helpless, and full of possibilities. Those possibilities have been unfolding throughout your life. Today, you are quite a bit taller and heavier (not to mention toilet trained). Some of these developments—physical growth, for instance—have "just happened." Some, such as reading and writing, you have learned through instruction and practice. Other things—such as studying psychology—have happened because you have wanted them to. Just as learning to walk was a developmental milestone, accomplishing the goals you set for yourself as an adult may also qualify as developmental changes. ●

Module 31
Exploring Human Development

● **development** The pattern of continuity and change in human capabilities that occurs throughout life, involving both growth and decline.

Development refers to the pattern of continuity and change in human capabilities that occurs throughout the course of life. Most development involves growth, although it also is concerned with decline (for example, physical abilities may decline with age). Developmental psychology is interested in how people change, physically and psychologically as they age. These changes occur on three different levels:

■ *Physical processes* involve changes in an individual's biological nature. Genes inherited from parents; the hormonal changes of puberty and menopause; and changes throughout life in the brain, height and weight, and motor skills—all of these reflect the developmental role of biological processes. Such biological growth processes are called *maturation*.

■ *Cognitive processes* involve changes in an individual's thought, intelligence, and language. Observing a colorful mobile as it swings above a crib, constructing a sentence about the future, imagining oneself as a movie star, memorizing a new telephone number—these activities reflect the role of cognitive processes in development.

■ *Socioemotional processes* involve changes in an individual's relationships with other people, in emotions, and in personality. An infant's smile in response to her mother's touch, a girl's development of assertiveness, an adolescent's joy at the senior prom, a young man's aggressiveness in sport, and an older couple's affection for each other all reflect the role of socioemotional processes.

These physical, cognitive, and socioemotional processes are intricately interwoven (Diamond, 2009; Diamond, Casey, & Munakata, 2011). Think of Hannah, an infant whose parents place a teddy bear in her crib. As an infant she might simply look at the teddy bear when her parents jiggle it in front of her. Over time, she not only can see the teddy bear but also can reach for it. She might even remember that the teddy bear exists and might cry for it when it is not with her. As a toddler, when she carries it around, she is demonstrating her physical abilities to do so, as well as her capacity to

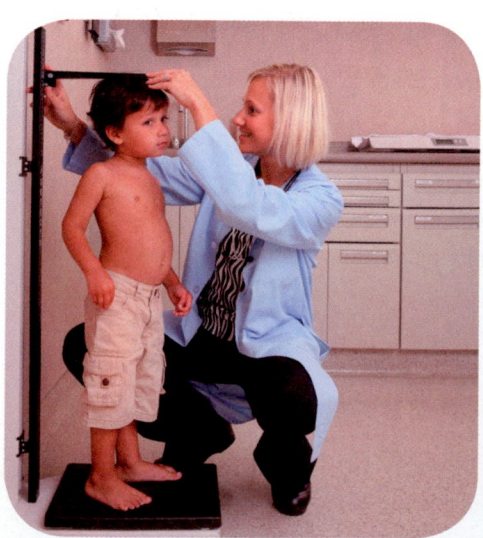

Human development is complex because it is the product of several processes. A child's growth in height and weight, a phone user's tapping out a friend's number from memory, and a young couple's joy on the occasion of their prom reflect physical, cognitive, and socioemotional processes, respectively.

use the teddy bear as a source of comfort. As an adolescent, Hannah might no longer sleep with her teddy, but she might give it a place of honor on a shelf.

As you read about development, remember that you are studying the development of an integrated human being, like Hannah, in whom body, mind, and emotion are interdependent. Researchers in developmental psychology are interested in the ways that these three processes—physical, cognitive, and socioemotional—change over the human life span. Their work centrally probes how a person's *age* relates to different aspects of his or her physical, cognitive, and socioemotional characteristics. Because age is a variable that cannot be experimentally manipulated, studies on the relationship between age and other characteristics are by definition correlational in nature. This aspect of developmental research carries important implications for research design, as we now consider.

31·1 RESEARCH METHODS IN DEVELOPMENTAL PSYCHOLOGY

Human development is about the changes that occur with age. To know what age-related differences mean, however, we must consider the kind of research presented.

In *cross-sectional studies,* a number of people of different ages are assessed at one point in time, and differences are noted. By examining how the ages of these individuals relate to the characteristics measured, researchers can find out whether younger individuals differ from older ones. Age differences, however, are not the same as developmental change.

One problem in cross-sectional studies is cohort effects. *Cohort effects* are differences between individuals that stem not necessarily from their ages but from the historical and social time period in which they were born and developed (Schaie, 2009, 2010, 2011). For instance, individuals who were born in the 1940s might be less likely to have attended college than those born in the 1990s. Differences observed between these groups might be due not to their age but rather to these differing experiences. Consider your own cohort. How might experiences that are unique to your age group lead you and your peers to be different from other generations?

In contrast to a cross-sectional study, a *longitudinal study* assesses the same participants multiple times over a lengthy period. A longitudinal study can find out not only whether age groups differ but also whether the same individuals change with respect to a particular characteristic as they age.

To get a sense of the difference between a cross-sectional and a longitudinal design, consider a large-scale cross-sectional U.S. study of approximately 28,000 individuals aged 18 to 88 indicating that happiness increased with age (Y. Yang, 2008). About 33 percent of the participants were very happy at 88 years of age, compared to only about 24 percent of those in their late teens and early 20s. From this work we *might* conclude that people become happier as they age, but this conclusion is limited by the cross-sectional nature of the design used. We simply do not know if the happy 88-year-olds were less happy when they were in their 20s. Indeed, it may be the case that these individuals were very happy even in their 20s. Perhaps the explanation is that relatively more happy people survive into their senior years. Clearly, strong statements about developmental changes in psychological characteristics require longitudinal designs. Using these and other methods, human development researchers have grappled with three big questions that are relevant to all of psychology, as we consider next.

31·2 HOW DO NATURE AND NURTURE INFLUENCE DEVELOPMENT?

Developmental psychologists seek to understand how nature and nurture influence development. **Nature** refers to a person's biological inheritance, especially his or her genes; **nurture** refers to the individual's environmental and social experiences. In Module 8 we

● **nature** An individual's biological inheritance, especially his or her genes.

● **nurture** An individual's environmental and social experiences.

considered the concept of a *genotype* (the individual's genetic heritage—his or her actual genetic material). We also examined the idea of a *phenotype* (the person's observable characteristics). The phenotype shows the contributions of both nature (genetic heritage) and nurture (environment). The genotype may be expressed in various ways, depending on both the environment and characteristics of the genotype itself. Recall, for example, that a recessive gene, though part of the genotype, will not show up in the phenotype at all if it is paired with a dominant gene.

In a long debate over the influence of nature (heredity) versus nurture (environment), some commentators have gone so far as to suggest that parenting—an environmental factor—is not especially important for children's development. To read about this debate, see the Critical Controversy.

One illustration of the role of environmental influences in genetic expression is a genetic condition called *phenylketonuria* (PKU). Caused by two recessive genes, PKU results in an inability to metabolize the amino acid phenylalanine (a major component of the artificial sweetener aspartame, which substitutes for sugar in soft drinks and many other products you might consume). Decades ago, it was thought that the genotype for PKU led to a specific phenotype—namely, irreversible brain damage, developmental disabilities, and seizures. However, scientists now know that as long as individuals with the genotype for PKU stick to a diet that is very low in phenylalanine, these phenotypic characteristics can be avoided (Grosse, 2010). Thus, environmental precautions can change the phenotype associated with this genotype.

PKU demonstrates that a person's observable and measurable characteristics (phenotype) might not reflect his or her genetic heritage (genotype) very precisely because of the particular experiences the person has had. Instead, for each genotype, a *range* of phenotypes may be expressed, depending on environmental factors. In concrete terms, an individual can inherit the genetic potential to grow very tall, but good nutrition, an environmental factor, is important for achieving that potential. The person whom we see before us emerges through an interplay of genetic and environmental experiences. In short, development is the product of nature, nurture, and the complex interaction of the two (Diamond, Casey, & Munakata, 2011).

One of the factors that must be taken into account in the development process is the developer himself or herself, as we consider next.

31·3 WHAT IS THE DEVELOPER'S ROLE IN DEVELOPMENT?

Nature and nurture have at least one thing in common. Because we cannot pick our genes or our parents, each of us would seem to be stuck with the genes and environment we got at birth. However, importantly, the developing human being also has a role to play in development (Brandstadter, 2006). Although you might think of nature and nurture as the raw ingredients of yourself as a person, the fact is that you take those ingredients and make them into the person you are.

Indeed, some psychologists believe that we can develop beyond what our genetic inheritance and our environment give us. They argue that a key aspect of development involves seeking optimal experiences in life (Armor, Massey, & Sackett, 2008). They cite examples of individuals who go beyond what life has given them to achieve extraordinary things. These individuals build and shape their own lives, authoring a unique developmental path and sometimes transforming negative characteristics into real strengths.

In our efforts to experience our lives in optimal ways, we develop *life themes* that involve activities, social relationships, and life goals (Csikszentmihalyi & Rathunde, 1998; Rathunde & Csikszentmihalyi, 2006). Some individuals are more successful at constructing optimal life experiences than others. Among the public figures who have succeeded are Martin Luther King, Jr., Mother Teresa, Nelson Mandela, Bill and Melinda Gates, and Oprah Winfrey. These individuals looked for and found meaningful life themes as they developed. Their lives were not restricted to simple biological survival

CRITICAL CONTROVERSY

Genes or Superparents: Which Matters More to Kids?

Compared to past generations, today's parents are more likely to be preoccupied with their children's lives and behaviors. Whereas decades ago parents might have worried about getting their children into the right college, today some parents obsess over enrolling their little ones in the right preschool and kindergarten. Is this obsession necessary to ensure healthy development? Some experts would give that question a definite no.

Judith Harris (1998), author of the book *The Nurture Assumption,* argues that what parents do makes no difference in children's behavior. Spank them. Hug them. Read to them. Ignore them. It will not influence how they turn out, because genes and peers are far more important than parents in children's development, Harris maintains. Similarly, developmental researcher Sandra Scarr (1992, 2000) suggests that "superparenting" is unnecessary. She asserts that the genotype is so strong that it makes most environmental experiences unimportant. Scarr suggests that the only parenting that has a negative effect on a child is parenting that is far outside the normal range—for example, chronic physical abuse. Apart from such extremes, Scarr asserts, genes are the primary determinant of developmental outcomes. So, can parents take a breather? Not necessarily.

Claims such as those of Harris and Scarr have met with a firestorm of criticism. Diana Baumrind (1993) countered that "good enough" parenting *is not* good enough, and she cited evidence that

highly demanding and highly responsive parents are more likely to have high-achieving and socially well-adjusted children. A longitudinal study by W. Andrew Collins and his colleagues (2000) supported Baumrind's claims; it showed that even with genetic influences taken into account, parenting practices made a difference in children's lives. Baumrind also expressed concern that Scarr's opinion might lead parents to give up the important responsibility of childrearing or to conclude that their efforts on behalf of their children are not worthwhile. So, in the view of those in the Baumrind and Collins camp, although a person's genetic heritage certainly has a role to play in development, we cannot cuddle our genes, be scolded by them, laugh with them, or look to them for advice. For those important aspects of experience we need parents—super or otherwise (Sandler, Wolchik, & Schoenfelder, 2011).

Despite the strong criticism of her views, Harris (2009) recently published a revised and updated edition of her earlier book, restating her claim that parents matter far less than most people think.

WHAT DO YOU THINK?

- If you have children or decide to have them in the future, how might the information in this Critical Controversy affect your approach to parenting?

- Why might today's parents be more likely than parents in the past to try to be superparents?

---

or to simply settling for their particular life situations. Many of them, in fact, faced hardships early in life and yet managed to contribute to the world in meaningful ways.

A developmental question that naturally flows from this discussion is, are early or later life experiences more important to a person's development over the life span? Let's dig into that issue.

31·4 ARE EARLY OR LATER LIFE EXPERIENCES MORE IMPORTANT IN DEVELOPMENT?

A key question in developmental psychology centers on the extent to which childhood experiences (nurture) determine aspects of later life. If early experiences provide the foundation for later development, does that mean that childhood experiences are likely to influence (and limit or damage) us for the rest of our lives? Developmental psychologists

Microsoft founder Bill Gates and his wife, Melinda, have quested after—and carved out—meaningful life experiences as they have progressed through their development.

309

debate whether early experiences or later experiences are more important (Kagan, 2010; Staudinger & Gluck, 2011; R. A. Thompson, 2010). Some believe that unless infants receive warm, nurturing caregiving in their first year or so of life, they will not develop to their full potential (Phillips & Lowenstein, 2011; Sroufe, Coffino, & Carlson, 2010). Other psychologists emphasize the power of later experience, arguing that important development occurs later on in life as well (Scheibe & Carstensen, 2010). Life-span developmentalists, who study both children and adults, in fact stress that researchers have given too little attention to adult development and aging. They argue that although early experiences contribute powerfully to development, they are not necessarily more influential than later experiences (Park & Huang, 2010; Schaie, 2010, 2011). These experts say that both early and later experiences make significant contributions to development and thus no one is doomed to be a prisoner of his or her childhood.

In approaching the question of which life-span experiences—early or later—are more important, we must look at the wide variation that can occur in individual responses to any particular life event. Consider, for example, the relationship between parental divorce and the emotional adjustment of children. According to leading researcher E. Mavis Hetherington, adjustment difficulties characterize approximately 25 percent of children and adolescents of divorced parents, compared with only 10 percent of children and adolescents of non-divorced parents (Hetherington, 2006; Hetherington & Stanley-Hagen, 2002). Note that this finding means that approximately 75 percent of children of divorced parents do *not* have adjustment problems. Among the factors that predict better adjustment for children in divorced families are harmony between the divorced partners, warm and attentive parenting, and the child's own personality characteristics (Amato, 2006; Hetherington, 2006; Ziol-Guest, 2009).

Having a supportive relationship with a parent or a competent adult outside the home can contribute to childhood resilience.

● **resilience** A person's ability to recover from or adapt to difficult times.

A key concept in understanding the role of negative early experiences in later development is resilience. **Resilience** refers to a person's ability to recover from or adapt to difficult times. Resilience means that even in the face of adversity, a person shows signs of positive functioning (Ong, Bergeman, & Boker, 2009; Vetter & others, 2010). Resilience can refer to factors that compensate for difficulties, buffering the individual from the effects of these, or to the fact that moderate difficulties may themselves help to promote development (Blum & Blum, 2009). Despite undergoing hardship time and time again, resilient children grow up to be capable adults. Researchers have found that resilient children have one or more advantages—such as strong intellectual functioning or a close, supportive relationship with a parent or other adult—that help them to overcome their disadvantages (Masten, 2007, 2009; Masten, Obradovic, & Burt, 2006). Although often studied as an aspect of childhood and adolescence (Montgomery, 2010), resilience can also characterize development in adulthood and old age (McFadden & Basting, 2010; Ryff & Singer, 2009).

SUMMARY

Development is the pattern of change in human capabilities that begins at birth and continues throughout the life span. Research on human development can be cross-sectional, which demonstrates age differences, or longitudinal, which demonstrates age-related change. To make strong conclusions about development, longitudinal data are necessary.

Both nature (biological inheritance) and nurture (environmental experience) extensively influence development. However, people are not at the mercy of either their genes or their environment when they actively construct optimal experiences. Resilience refers to the capacity of individuals to thrive during difficulties at every stage of development.

KEY TERMS

development 306
nature 307

nurture 307
resilience 310

TEST YOURSELF

1. What three broad processes of change do developmental psychologists study?

2. Why are longitudinal studies commonly used to investigate developmental questions? What are the limitations of cross-sectional studies with respect to studying such questions?

3. In what ways can the developing individual play a role in his or her own development?

APPLY YOUR KNOWLEDGE

1. Think about the tragedy of 9/11. How might resilience play a role in the development of children who witnessed that event?

2. Identify one question you have about human development and explain how a longitudinal research design could help you answer that question.

Child Development

In this section we focus on the three fundamental developmental processes—physical, cognitive, and socioemotional—of childhood. To understand childhood in all its dimensions, we must begin before it even starts, with *prenatal* ("before birth") development. Childhood continues through the elementary school years. To begin exploring child development, we first trace the ways that we grow and change physically before the life span starts, during prenatal development.

32·1 PRENATAL DEVELOPMENT

Prenatal development is a time of astonishing change, beginning with conception. *Conception* occurs when a single sperm cell from the male merges with the female's ovum (egg) to produce a *zygote,* a single cell with 23 chromosomes from the mother and 23 from the father.

The Course of Prenatal Development

Development from zygote to fetus is divided into three periods:

- *Germinal period—weeks 1 and 2:* The germinal period begins with conception. After 1 week and many cell divisions, the zygote is made up of 100 to 150 cells. By the end of 2 weeks, the mass of cells has attached to the uterine wall.

- *Embryonic period—weeks 3 through 8:* The rate of cell differentiation intensifies, support systems for the cells develop, and the beginnings of organs appear (Figure 32.1a). In the third week, the neural tube, which eventually becomes the spinal cord, starts to

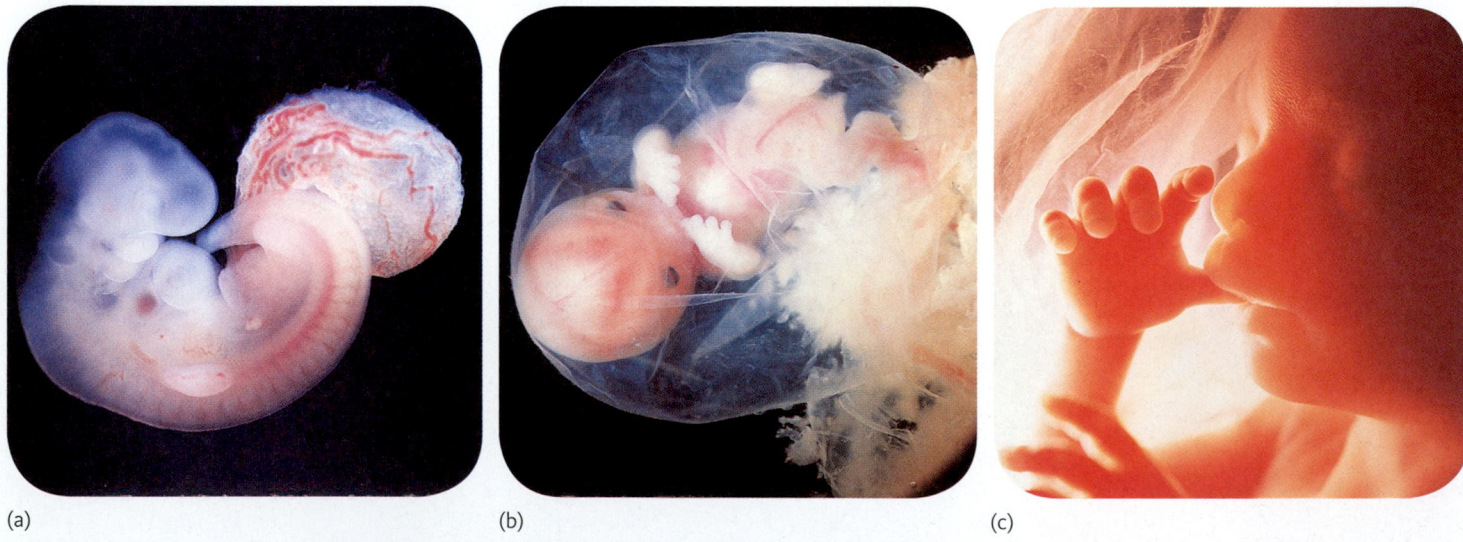

(a)   (b)   (c)

FIGURE 32.1 **From Embryo to Fetus** (*a*) At about 4 weeks, an embryo is about 0.2 inch (less than 1 centimeter) long. The head, eyes, and ears begin to show; the head and neck are half the length of the body; the shoulders will be located where the whitish arm buds are attached. (*b*) At 8 weeks, the developing individual is about 1.6 inches (4 centimeters) long and has reached the end of its embryonic phase. It has become a fetus. Everything that will be found in the fully developed human being has now begun to form. The fetal stage is a period of growth and perfection of detail. The heart has been beating for a month, and the muscles have just begun their first exercises. (*c*) At 4½ months, the fetus is just over 7 inches (about 18 centimeters) long. When the thumb comes close to the mouth, the head may turn, and the lips and tongue begin their sucking motions—a reflex for survival.

take shape. Within the first 28 days after conception, the neural tube is formed and closes, encased inside the embryo. By the end of the embryonic period, the heart begins to beat, the arms and legs become more differentiated, the face starts to form, and the intestinal tract appears (Figure 32.1b).

■ *Fetal period—months 2 through 9:* At 2 months, the fetus is the size of a kidney bean and has started to move around. At 4 months, the fetus is 5 inches long and weighs about 5 ounces (Figure 32.1c). At 6 months, the fetus has grown to a pound and a half. The last three months of pregnancy are the time when organ functioning increases and the fetus puts on considerable weight and size, adding baby fat.

Although it floats in a well-protected womb, the fetus is not immune to the larger environment surrounding the mother. Sometimes, as we will now see, normal development is disrupted by environmental insults.

Threats to the Fetus

A *teratogen* is any agent that causes a birth defect. Teratogens include chemical substances ingested by the mother (such as nicotine if the mother smokes and alcohol if she drinks) and certain illnesses (such as rubella, or German measles). Substances that are ingested by the mother can lead to serious birth defects. For example, *fetal alcohol spectrum disorders* (FASD) are a cluster of abnormalities and problems that appear in the offspring of mothers who drink alcohol heavily during pregnancy. These abnormalities include a small head, defects in the limbs and heart, and below-average intelligence (Klingenberg & others, 2010). Heavy drinking is linked to FASD, but even moderate drinking can lead to serious problems (Sayal & others, 2007). The best advice for a woman who is pregnant or thinking of becoming pregnant is to avoid alcohol.

The effects of chemical teratogens depend on the timing of exposure. The body part or organ system that is developing when the fetus encounters the teratogen is most vulnerable (Rojas & others, 2010; Torchinsky & Toder, 2010). Genetic characteristics may buffer or worsen the effects of a teratogen. Perhaps most importantly, the environment the child encounters *after birth* can influence the ultimate effects of prenatal insults.

Sexually transmitted infections (STIs) also threaten the fetus. Some STIs, such as gonorrhea, can be transferred to the baby during delivery. Others, including syphilis and the human immunodeficiency virus (HIV), the virus that causes AIDS, can also infect the fetus while it is in the womb. Besides transmission of infections to the fetus and newborns, STI exposure enhances the risk of stillbirth, as well as a number of other problems, such as eye infections and blindness (in the case of gonorrhea). Many STIs also increase the risk of preterm birth.

A *preterm infant,* one who is born prior to 37 weeks after conception, may also be at risk for developmental difficulties. Whether a preterm infant will have developmental problems is a complex issue, however. Very small preterm infants are more likely than their larger counterparts to have developmental problems (Minde & Zelkowitz, 2008). Preterm infants who grow up in poverty are more likely to have problems than are those who live in better socioeconomic conditions (Madan & others, 2006). Postnatal experience plays a crucial role in determining the ultimate effects of preterm birth. For example, research has shown that massage can improve developmental outcomes for premature infants (Field, Diego, & Hernandez-Reif, 2010).

32-2 PHYSICAL DEVELOPMENT IN CHILDHOOD

Human infants are the world's most helpless newborns. One reason for their helplessness is that they are born not quite finished. Our enormous brain sets humans apart from other animals. Getting that big brain out of the relatively small birth canal is a challenge that nature has met by sending human babies out of the womb before the brain has

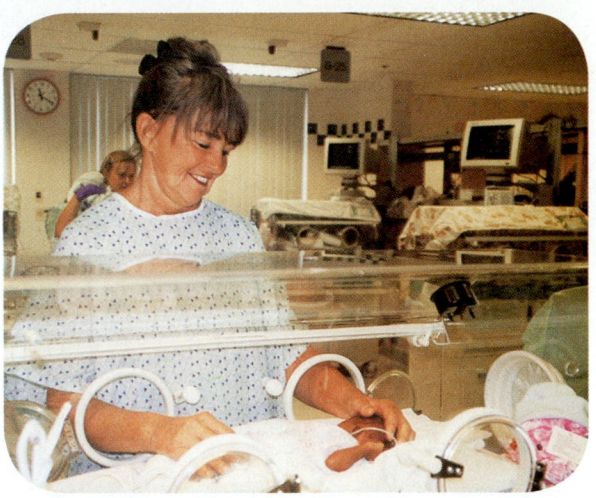

The photograph shows Tiffany Field massaging a newborn infant. Field's research has demonstrated the power of massage in improving the developmental outcome of at-risk infants. Under her direction, the Touch Research Institute in Miami, Florida, investigates the role of touch in a number of domains of health and well-being.

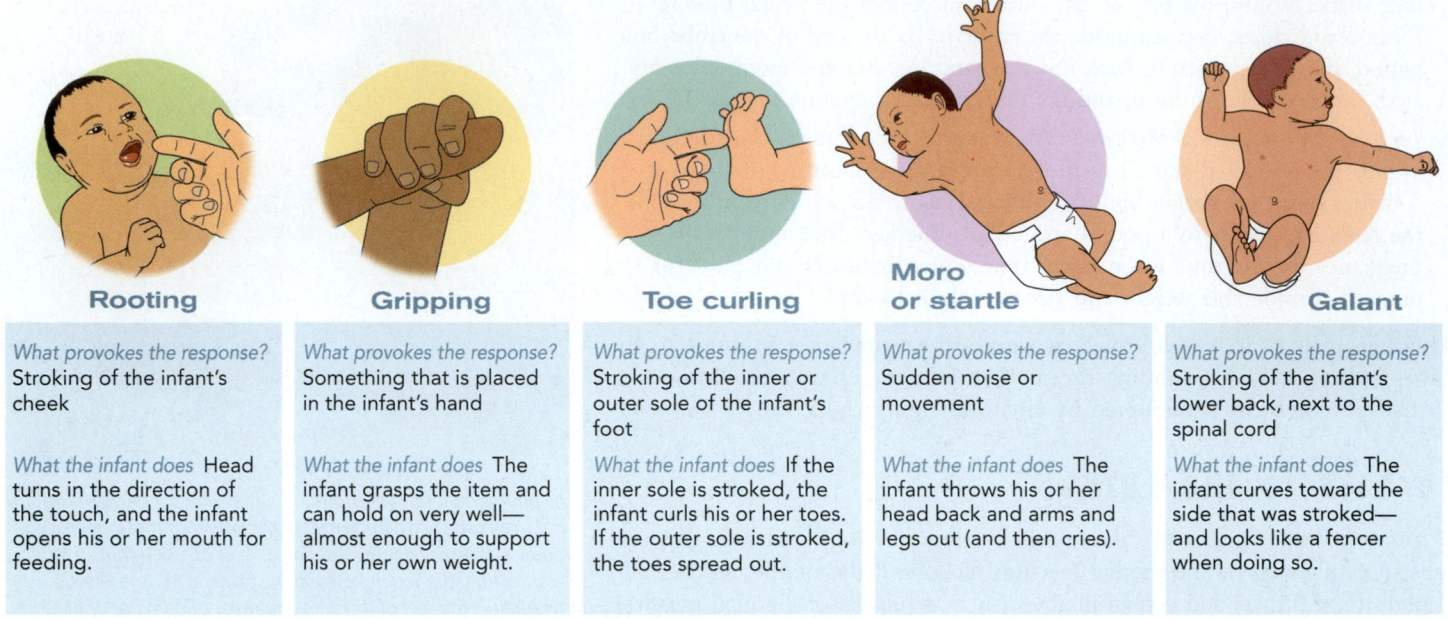

Rooting	Gripping	Toe curling	Moro or startle	Galant
What provokes the response? Stroking of the infant's cheek	*What provokes the response?* Something that is placed in the infant's hand	*What provokes the response?* Stroking of the inner or outer sole of the infant's foot	*What provokes the response?* Sudden noise or movement	*What provokes the response?* Stroking of the infant's lower back, next to the spinal cord
What the infant does Head turns in the direction of the touch, and the infant opens his or her mouth for feeding.	*What the infant does* The infant grasps the item and can hold on very well—almost enough to support his or her own weight.	*What the infant does* If the inner sole is stroked, the infant curls his or her toes. If the outer sole is stroked, the toes spread out.	*What the infant does* The infant throws his or her head back and arms and legs out (and then cries).	*What the infant does* The infant curves toward the side that was stroked—and looks like a fencer when doing so.

FIGURE 32.2   Some Infant Reflexes Infants are born with a number of reflexes to get them through life, and they are incredibly cute when they perform them. These reflexes disappear as infants mature.

fully developed. The first months and years of life allow the developing human (and his or her environment) to put the finishing touches on that important organ.

Reflexes

Newborns come into the world equipped with several genetically wired reflexes that are crucial for survival. Babies are born with the ability to suck and swallow. If they are dropped in water, they will naturally hold their breath, contract their throats to keep water out, and move their arms and legs to stay afloat at least briefly. Some reflexes persist throughout life—coughing, blinking, and yawning, for example. Others, such as automatically grasping something that touches the fingers, disappear in the months following birth as higher brain functions mature and infants develop voluntary control over many behaviors. Figure 32.2 shows some examples of reflexes.

Motor and Perceptual Skills

Relative to the rest of the body, a newborn's head is gigantic, and it flops around uncontrollably. Within 12 months, the infant becomes capable of sitting upright, standing, stooping, climbing, and often walking. During the second year, growth decelerates, but rapid gains occur in such activities as running and climbing. Researchers used to think that motor milestones—such as sitting up, crawling, and walking—unfolded as part of a genetic plan. However, psychologists now recognize that motor development is not the consequence of nature or nurture alone (Adolph, Berger, & Leo, 2010; Karasik & others, 2010).

For example, environmental experiences play a role in reaching and grasping (Needham, 2009). In one study, 3-month-old infants participated in play sessions wearing "sticky mittens"—mittens with palms that stick to the edges of toys and allow the infants to pick up the toys (Needham, Barrett, & Peterman, 2002) (Figure 32.3). Infants who participated in sessions with the mittens grasped and manipulated objects earlier in their development than a control group of infants who did not have the "mitten" experience. The experienced infants looked at the objects longer, swatted at them, and were more likely to put the objects in their mouths.

Infants are active developers, and their motor and perceptual skills develop together and mutually promote each other. Because a baby can see a new toy, she wants to reach out for it, and her motivation to do so may foster the development of her motor abilities. Babies are continually coordinating their movements with information they perceive through their senses to learn how to maintain their balance, reach for objects in space, and move across various surfaces and terrains (Adolph & others, 2009). Action in turn informs perception. For example, holding and touching an object while watching it helps infants to learn about its texture, size, and hardness. Moving from place to place in the environment teaches babies how objects and people look from different perspectives and whether surfaces will support their weight (Gibson, 2001).

Psychologists face a daunting challenge in studying infant perception. Infants cannot talk, so how can scientists learn whether they can see or hear certain things? Psychologists who study infants have no choice but to become extraordinarily clever methodologists, relying on what infants can do to understand what they know (S. P. Johnson, 2010a, 2010b; Slater & others, 2011). One thing infants can do is look. The **preferential looking** technique involves giving an infant a choice of what object to look at. If an infant shows a reliable preference for one stimulus (say, a picture of a face) over another (a scrambled picture of a face) when these are repeatedly presented in differing locations, we can infer that the infant can tell the two images apart.

Using this technique, researchers have found that as early as *7 days old*, infants are already engaged in organized perception of faces and are able to put together sights and sounds. If presented with two faces with mouths moving, infants will watch the face whose mouth matches the sounds they are hearing (Pascalls & Kelly, 2008). At 3 months, infants prefer real faces to scrambled faces, and their mother's face to a stranger's (Slater, Field, & Reif-Hernandez, 2007). These techniques have provided a great deal of information about infants' remarkable abilities, but they are also limited. Research using brain imaging suggests that infants may know more than even these clever strategies reveal.

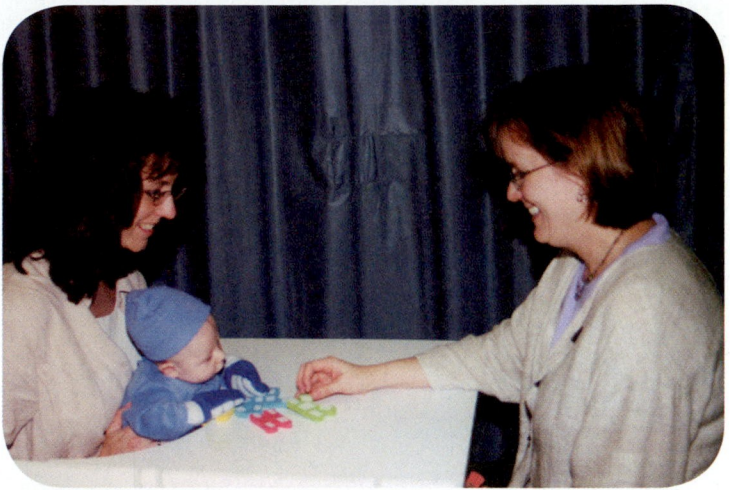

FIGURE 32.3 **Infants' Use of "Sticky Mittens" to Explore Objects** Amy Needham and her colleagues (2002) found that "sticky mittens" enhance young infants' object exploration skills.

● **preferential looking** A research technique that involves giving an infant a choice of what object to look at.

The Brain

As an infant plays, crawls, shakes a rattle, smiles, and frowns, his or her brain is changing dramatically. At birth and in early infancy, the brain's 100 billion neurons have only minimal connections. The infant brain literally is ready and waiting for the experiences that will create these connections (C. A. Nelson, 2011). During the first two years of life, the dendrites of the neurons branch out, and the neurons become far more interconnected (Figure 32.4). Myelination, the process of encasing axons with fat cells (the

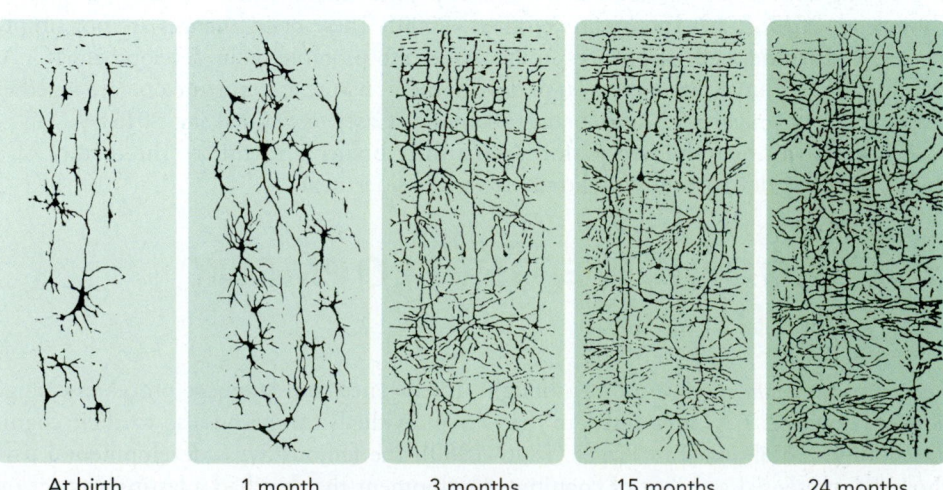

At birth   1 month   3 months   15 months   24 months

FIGURE 32.4 **Dendritic Spreading** Note the increase in connections among neurons over the course of the first two years of life. Reprinted by permission of the publisher from *The Postnatal Development of the Human Cerebral Cortex*, Volumes I–VIII, by Jesse LeRoy Conel, Cambridge, MA.: Harvard University Press, Copyright © 1939, 1941, 1947, 1951, 1955, 1959, 1963, 1967 by the President and Fellows of Harvard College. Copyright © renewed 1967, 1969, 1975, 1979, 1983, 1987, 1991.

FIGURE 32.5 Synaptic Density in the Human Brain from Infancy to Adulthood The graph shows the dramatic increase and then pruning in synaptic density in three regions of the brain: visual cortex, auditory cortex, and prefrontal cortex. Synaptic density is believed to be an important indication of the extent of connectivity between neurons.

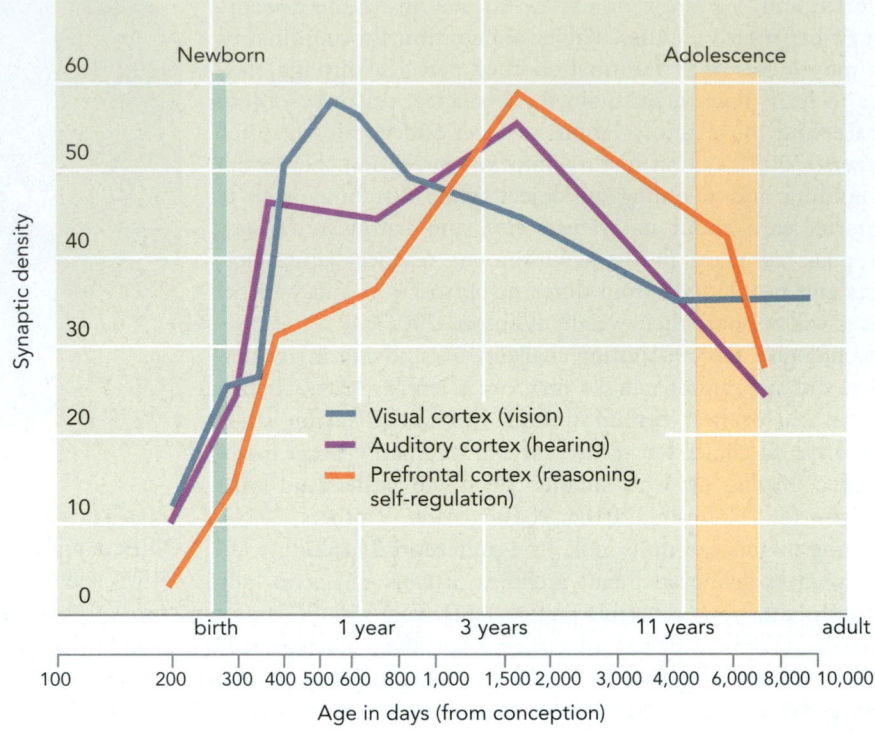

myelin sheath described in Module 6), begins prenatally and continues after birth well into adolescence and young adulthood (Tamnes & others, 2010).

During childhood, *synaptic connections* increase dramatically (C. A. Nelson, 2011). A *synapse* is a gap between neurons that is bridged by chemical neurotransmitters. Nearly twice as many synapses are available as will ever be used (Huttenlocher & Dabholkar, 1997). The connections that are made become stronger and will survive; the unused ones will be replaced by other neural pathways or disappear. In the language of neuroscience, these unused connections will be "pruned." Figure 32.5 illustrates the steep growth and later pruning of synapses during infancy in specific areas of the brain.

Brain-imaging studies demonstrate that children's brains also undergo amazing anatomical changes (Gogtay & Thompson, 2010; Paus, 2009). Repeated brain scans of the same children for up to 4 years of age show that the amount of brain material in some areas can nearly double within as little as a year, followed by a drastic loss of tissue as unneeded cells are purged and the brain continues to reorganize itself. From 3 to 6 years of age, the most rapid growth takes place in the frontal lobe areas, which are involved in planning and organizing new actions and in maintaining attention to tasks (Gogtay & Thompson, 2010; P. M. Thompson & others, 2000). These brain changes are not simply the result of nature; new experiences in the world also promote brain development (C. A. Nelson, 2011). Thus, as in other areas of development, nature and nurture operate together in the development of the child's brain (Diamond, Casey, & Munakata, 2011).

A key activity that children perform with their brains is to think. The quality of a child's thinking develops in childhood, as we consider next.

32-3 COGNITIVE DEVELOPMENT IN CHILDHOOD

Cognitive development refers to how thought, intelligence, and language processes change as people mature. *Cognition* refers to the way individuals think and also to their cognitive skills and abilities. Jean Piaget (1896–1980), the famous Swiss developmental psychologist, presented a theory of cognitive development that has had a lasting impact on our understanding of how children think. His theory traced cognitive development through childhood into adulthood.

Piaget's Theory of Cognitive Development

Piaget believed that children *actively construct* their cognitive world as they go through a series of stages. In Piaget's view, children use schemas to make sense of their experience.

A *schema* is a mental concept or framework that organizes information and provides a structure for interpreting it. Schemas are expressed as various behaviors and skills that the child can exercise in relation to objects or situations. For example, sucking is a simple early schema. More complex schemas that occur later in childhood include blowing, crawling, and hiding. In adulthood, schemas may represent more complex expectations and beliefs about the world.

Piaget (1952) described two processes responsible for how people use and adapt their schemas:

- **Assimilation** occurs when individuals incorporate new information into existing knowledge. That is, people *assimilate* the environment into a schema. Assimilation means that, faced with a new experience, the person applies old ways of doing things. For infants, this might mean applying the schema of *sucking* to whatever new thing they encounter. For an adolescent, it might mean using the skills learned while playing video games to drive a car. For an adult it might mean solving a conflict with a spouse using ways that worked in the past with friends or previous romantic partners.

- **Accommodation** occurs when individuals adjust their schemas to new information. That is, people *accommodate* their schemas to the environment. Accommodation means that rather than using one's old ways of doing things, a new experience promotes new ways of dealing with experience. Existing schemas can be changed and new schemas can be developed in response to new experiences. For example, after several months of experience, the infant who has been sticking everything in her mouth might begin to accommodate the sucking schema by being more selective with it. The adolescent who has typically gone with the flow of social pressure might develop a new way of dealing with peer pressure by standing up for his or her beliefs. For an adult, accommodation may mean rethinking old strategies for problem solving when a new challenge, such as the loss of a job or the onset of illness, presents itself.

According to Piaget, we go through four stages in understanding the world (Figure 32.6). Each stage involves a qualitatively different way of making sense of the world than the one before it.

SENSORIMOTOR STAGE

Piaget's first stage, the **sensorimotor stage,** lasts from birth to about 2 years of age. In this stage, infants construct an understanding of the world by coordinating sensory experiences (such as seeing and hearing) with motor (physical) actions—hence the term *sensorimotor.* As newborns they have little more than reflexive patterns with which to work. By the end of this stage, 2-year-olds show complex sensorimotor patterns and are beginning to use symbols or words in their thinking.

Object permanence is Piaget's term for the crucial accomplishment of understanding that objects and events continue to exist even when they cannot directly be seen, heard, or touched. Piaget believed that "out of sight" literally was "out of mind" for very young infants. Object permanence is an enormous developmental milestone. In the absence of object permanence, the world and its objects change from one moment to the next. Once the infant knows that objects still exist even if he or she cannot see them, the infant can think about future events, such as, "When will I see Mommy again?" The most common way to study object permanence was to show an infant an interesting toy and then cover the toy with a blanket. Piaget reasoned that if infants understood that the toy still existed, they would try to uncover it (Figure 32.7).

Jean Piaget (1896–1980) Piaget, the famous Swiss developmental psychologist, changed the way we think about the development of children's minds.

● **assimilation** An individual's incorporation of new information into existing knowledge.

● **accommodation** An individual's adjustment of his or her schemas to new information.

● **sensorimotor stage** Piaget's first stage of cognitive development, lasting from birth to about 2 years of age, during which infants construct an understanding of the world by coordinating sensory experiences with motor (physical) actions.

Sensorimotor Stage	**Preoperational Stage**	**Concrete Operational Stage**	**Formal Operational Stage**
The infant constructs an understanding of the world by coordinating sensory experiences with physical actions. An infant progresses from reflexive, instinctual action at birth to the beginning of symbolic thought toward the end of the stage.	The child begins to represent the world with words and images. These words and images reflect increased symbolic thinking and go beyond the connection of sensory information and physical action.	The child can now reason logically about concrete events and classify objects into different sets.	The adolescent reasons in more abstract, idealistic, and logical ways.
Birth to 2 Years of Age	**2 to 7 Years of Age**	**7 to 11 Years of Age**	**11 Years of Age Through Adulthood**

FIGURE 32.6 **Piaget's Four Stages of Cognitive Development** Jean Piaget described how human beings, through development, become ever more sophisticated thinkers about the world.

PREOPERATIONAL STAGE

● **preoperational stage** Piaget's second stage of cognitive development, lasting from about 2 to 7 years of age, during which thought is more symbolic than sensorimotor thought.

Piaget's second stage of cognitive development, the **preoperational stage,** lasts from approximately 2 to 7 years of age. Preoperational thought is more symbolic than sensorimotor thought. In preschool years, children begin to represent their world with words, images, and drawings. Thus, their thoughts begin to exceed simple connections of sensorimotor information and physical action.

The type of symbolic thinking that children are able to accomplish during this stage is limited. They still cannot perform what Piaget called *operations,* by which he meant

FIGURE 32.7 **Object Permanence** Piaget regarded object permanence as one of infancy's landmark cognitive accomplishments. According to Piaget, for this 5-month-old boy, out of sight is literally out of mind. The infant looks at the toy dog (*left*), but when his view of the toy is blocked (*right*), he does not search for it. Piaget assumed that if the child does not search for the toy, the child does not know the object still exists. We will investigate this assumption a little later in this module.

FIGURE 32.8 **Piaget's Conservation Task** The beaker test determines whether a child can think operationally—that is, can mentally reverse action and understand conservation of the substance. (*a*) Two identical beakers are presented to the child, each containing the same amount of liquid. As the child watches, the experimenter pours the liquid from B into C, which is taller and thinner than A and B. (*b*) The experimenter then asks the child whether beakers A and C have the same amount of liquid. The preoperational child says no. When asked to point to the beaker that has more liquid, the child points to the tall, thin one.

mental representations that are reversible. Preoperational children have difficulty understanding that reversing an action may restore the original conditions from which the action began.

A well-known test of whether a child can think "operationally" is to present a child with two identical beakers, A and B, filled with liquid to the same height (Figure 32.8). Next to them is a third beaker, C. Beaker C is tall and thin, whereas beakers A and B are short and wide. The liquid is poured from B into C, and the child is asked whether the amounts in A and C are the same. The 4-year-old child invariably says that the amount of liquid in the tall, thin beaker (C) is greater than that in the short, wide beaker (A). The 8-year-old child consistently says the amounts are the same. The 4-year-old child, a preoperational thinker, cannot mentally reverse the pouring action; that is, she cannot imagine the liquid going back from container C to container B. Piaget said that such a child has not grasped the concept of *conservation,* a belief in the permanence of certain attributes of objects despite superficial changes.

To sharpen your sense of how operational thinking differs from preoperational thought, consider the following example. Babysitting for two thirsty 4-year-olds, you might give them each the same amount of apple juice poured into two different cups, one tall and thin and the other short and wide. Try as you might to explain to them that the amounts are the same, they will fight over the tall, thin cup because *it looks like more.* However, in the same situation, older children—who are more sophisticated, operational thinkers—would not bat an eye, because they understand that the amounts are equal.

Children's thought in the preoperational stage is egocentric—not in the sense that they are self-centered or arrogant but because preoperational children cannot put themselves in someone else's shoes or take another person's mental state into account. Preoperational thinking is also intuitive, meaning that preoperational children make judgments based on gut feelings rather than logic. In reaching a basic level of operational understanding, children progress to the third of Piaget's cognitive stages.

CONCRETE OPERATIONAL STAGE

Piaget's **concrete operational stage** (7 to 11 years of age) involves using operations and replacing intuitive reasoning with logical reasoning in concrete situations. Children in the concrete operational stage can successfully complete the beaker task described above. They are able to imagine the operation of reversing the pouring of the liquid back into the wide beaker. Many of the concrete operations identified by Piaget are related to the properties of objects. For instance, when playing with Play-doh, the child in the concrete operational stage realizes that *the amount* of Play-doh is not changed by changing its shape.

● **concrete operational stage** Piaget's third stage of cognitive development, lasting from about 7 to 11 years of age, during which the individual uses operations and replaces intuitive reasoning with logical reasoning in concrete situations.

One important skill at this stage of reasoning is the ability to classify or divide things into different sets or subsets and to consider their interrelations. Children in the concrete operational stage might enjoy playing games that involve sorting objects into types and identifying objects that do not fit with a group. Concrete operational thought involves logical reasoning in concrete but not hypothetical contexts. According to Piaget, this kind of abstract, logical reasoning occurs in the fourth, and final, cognitive stage.

FORMAL OPERATIONAL STAGE

● **formal operational stage** Piaget's fourth stage of cognitive development, which begins at 11 to 15 years of age and continues through the adult years; it features thinking about things that are not concrete, making predictions, and using logic to come up with hypotheses about the future.

Individuals enter the **formal operational stage** of cognitive development at 11 to 15 years of age. This stage continues through the adult years. Formal operational thought is more abstract and logical than concrete operational thought. Most important, formal operational thinking includes thinking about things that are not concrete, making predictions, and using logic to come up with hypotheses about the future.

Unlike elementary schoolchildren, adolescents can conceive of hypothetical, purely abstract possibilities. This type of thinking is called *idealistic* because it involves comparing how things are to how they might be. Adolescents also think more logically. They begin to think more as a scientist thinks, devising plans to solve problems and systematically testing solutions. Piaget called this type of problem solving *hypothetical-deductive reasoning*. The phrase denotes adolescents' ability to develop hypotheses, or best hunches, about ways to solve a problem such as an algebraic equation. It also denotes their ability to systematically deduce, or come to a conclusion about, the best path for solving the problem. In contrast, before adolescence, children are more likely to solve problems by trial and error. Many of the topics we covered in Module 28 on thinking and problem solving fall into Piaget's formal operational stage.

psychological *inquiry*

Thinking Critically About Object Permanence

Let's revisit the classic object permanence task developed by Piaget. To begin with, we can consider how the methodological aspects of this task might have led Piaget to underestimate infants' abilities. Remember that from Piaget's perspective, "proving" object permanence meant that the child must search for the hidden toy, reach out, and retrieve it.

Let's assume that the child has attained the developmental milestone of object permanence. That is, the child believes that the toy exists even if he or she cannot see it. What skills must the child possess in order to enact the behaviors that Piaget thought would indicate object permanence? Answer the following questions to sharpen your understanding of this landmark developmental achievement.

1. Look at the two photos. Assuming that the child does understand that the toy still exists behind the board, what behavior must the child exhibit to indicate that understanding?

2. What motor and perceptual skills are required for the child to enact those behaviors?

3. What motivational states (or goals) are required for the child to enact them?

4. If the child does not reach out for the toy even though he or she knows it still exists, what might the failure to do so mean?

5. Why do you think it took over 50 years for psychologists to question the appropriateness of Piaget's methods? What other methods, beyond Piaget's classic object permanence task, might a researcher use to demonstrate object permanence?

In summary, over the course of Piaget's four developmental stages, a person progresses from sensorimotor cognition to abstract, idealistic, and logical thought. Piaget based his stages on careful observation of children's behavior, but there is always room to evaluate theory and research. Let's consider the current thinking about Piaget's theories of cognitive development.

Evaluating Piaget's Theory

Piaget opened up a new way of looking at how the human mind develops (P. H. Miller, 2011). We owe him for a long list of masterful concepts that have enduring power and fascination. These include the concepts of schemas, assimilation, accommodation, cognitive stages, object permanence, egocentrism, and conservation. We also owe Piaget for the currently accepted vision of children as active, constructive thinkers who play a role in their own development.

Nevertheless, just as other psychological theories have been criticized and amended, so have Piaget's. As methods have improved for assessing infants and children, researchers have found that many cognitive abilities emerge earlier in children than Piaget envisioned (Bauer, Larkina, & Deocampo, 2011; de Hevia & Spelke, 2010; Meltzoff, 2011; Quinn, 2011). Piaget's object permanence task, for example, has been criticized for not giving infants a chance to show their stuff. To get a sense of the limitations of Piaget's task, check out the Psychological Inquiry.

Renée Baillargeon (1997; Baillargeon & others, 2009, 2011) has documented that infants as young as 3 months of age know that objects continue to exist even when hidden, and that these very young infants have expectations about objects in the world. In one study (Luo & Baillargeon, 2005), researchers showed 3-month-old infants a puppet show featuring Minnie Mouse. In the center of the stage was a flat cardboard cut-out of a castle. Minnie entered stage right and proceeded toward the castle, disappearing behind it. When Minnie went behind the castle walls from one side, the infants looked for her to come out on the other side. Their behavior suggested that even though Minnie was out of sight, she was not out of mind. Not only did these 3-month-olds realize that Minnie still existed, but they also *had expectations* about where she was heading.

Just as Piaget may have *under*estimated infants, he may have *over*estimated adolescents and adults. Formal operational thought does not emerge as consistently and universally in early adolescence as Piaget envisioned (Kuhn, 2008, 2009), and many adolescents and even adults do not reason as logically as Piaget proposed.

Piaget did not think that culture and education play important roles in children's cognitive development. For Piaget, the child's active interaction with the physical world was all that was needed to go through these stages. The Russian psychologist Lev Vygotsky (1962) took a different approach, recognizing that cognitive development is very much an interpersonal process that happens in a cultural context (Gauvain & Parke, 2010). Vygotsky thought of children as apprentice thinkers who develop as they interact in dialogue with more knowledgeable others, such as parents and teachers (Daniels, 2011; Holzman, 2009). Vygotsky theorized that these expert thinkers spur cognitive development by interacting with a child in a way that is just above the level of sophistication the child has mastered. In effect, these interactions provide *scaffolding* that allows the child's cognitive abilities to be built higher and higher. Teachers and parents, then, provide a framework for thinking that is always just at a level the child can strive to attain.

Furthermore, in Vygotsky's view, the goal of cognitive development is to learn the skills that will allow the individual to be competent in his or her particular culture. Expert thinkers are not simply guiding a child into a level of cognitive sophistication but also, along the way, sharing with the child important aspects of culture, such as language and customs. For Vygotsky, a child is not simply learning to think about the world—he or she is learning to think about *his or her own world*.

32·4 SOCIOEMOTIONAL DEVELOPMENT IN CHILDHOOD

Emotionally speaking, an infant does not enter the world as a blank slate. When we observe the newborns behind the window of a hospital nursery, one thing is clear: Humans differ from one another in terms of their emotional demeanor from the very beginning of life. Some are easygoing, and some are prone to distress. Furthermore, in the earliest days of life, infants encounter a social network that will play an important role as they develop their sense of self and the world. To begin our exploration of the socioemotional aspects of development, we focus first on these early raw ingredients of emotional and social characteristics that are present very early in life—infant temperament and attachment.

Temperament

● **temperament** An individual's behavioral style and characteristic way of responding.

Temperament refers to an individual's behavioral style and characteristic way of responding. There are a number of ways to think about infant temperament. For example, psychiatrists Alexander Chess and Stella Thomas (1977, 1996) identified three basic types of temperament in children:

■ *The easy child* generally is in a positive mood, quickly establishes regular routines in infancy, and easily adapts to new experiences.
■ *The difficult child* tends to react negatively and to cry frequently, engages in irregular daily routines, and is slow to accept new experiences.
■ *The slow-to-warm-up child* has a low activity level, is somewhat negative, is inflexible, and displays a low intensity of mood.

Other researchers have suggested that we should think about infants as being high or low on different dimensions, such as *effortful control* or *self-regulation* (controlling arousal and not being easily agitated), *inhibition* (being shy and showing distress in an unfamiliar situation), and *negative affectivity* (tending to be frustrated or sad) (Kagan, 2010; Rothbart & Gartstein, 2008; Sheese & others, 2009). These emotional characteristics that a child brings into the world are thought to serve as a foundation for later personality (Evans & Rothbart, 2009). Similarly, the child's earliest social bonds might set the stage for later social relationships.

Attachment in Infancy

Just as infants require nutrition and shelter, they need warm social interaction to survive and develop. A classic study by Harry Harlow (1958) demonstrates the essential importance of warm contact. Harlow separated infant monkeys from their mothers at birth and placed them in cages in which they had access to two artificial "mothers." One of the mothers was a physically cold wire mother; the other was a warm, fuzzy cloth mother (the "contact comfort" mother). Each mother could be outfitted with a feeding mechanism. Half of the infant monkeys were fed by the wire mother; the other half, by the cloth mother. The infant monkeys nestled close to the cloth mother and spent little time on the wire one, even if it was the wire mother that gave them milk (Figure 32.9). When afraid, the infant monkeys ran to the comfy mom.

Harlow's classic work is important because it clearly demonstrates that what the researchers described as contact comfort, not feeding, is crucial to an infant's attachment to its caregiver. This work set the stage for our modern understanding of the vital role of warm physical contact between caregivers and infants. Even if an otherwise healthy child's physical needs for food and shelter are met, the child is unlikely to thrive in the absence of warmth.

● **infant attachment** The close emotional bond between an infant and its caregiver.

Infant attachment is the close emotional bond between an infant and its caregiver. British psychiatrist John Bowlby (1969, 1989) theorized that the infant and the mother

FIGURE 32.9 **Contact Time with Wire and Cloth Surrogate Mothers** Regardless of whether the infant monkeys were fed by a wire or a cloth mother, they overwhelmingly preferred to spend contact time with the cloth mother.

instinctively form an attachment. For Bowlby, the newborn comes into the world equipped to stimulate the caregiver to respond; it cries, clings, smiles, and coos. Bowlby thought that this early relationship with our primary caregiver was internalized so that it served as our schema for our sense of self and the social world. Many developmental psychologists concur that such attachment during the first year provides an important foundation for later development (Fearon & others, 2010; Sroufe, Coffino, & Carlson, 2010).

Mary Ainsworth devised a way to study differences in children's attachment, called the *strange situation* (Ainsworth, 1979; Ainsworth & others, 1978). In this procedure, caregivers leave infants alone with a stranger and then return. Children's responses to this situation are used to classify their attachment style. The term **secure attachment** means that infants use the caregiver, usually the mother, as a secure base from which to explore the environment. In the strange situation, the secure infant is upset when the mother leaves, but calms down and appears happy to see her when she returns. The securely attached infant moves freely away from the mother but also keeps tabs on her by periodically glancing at her. An insecurely attached infant, in contrast, avoids the mother or is ambivalent toward her. In the strange situation, such an infant might not even notice the mother has gone, or conversely might respond with intense distress, only to rage at the mother when she returns.

One criticism of attachment theory is that it does not adequately account for cultural variations (van IJzendoorn & Sagi-Schwartz, 2008). For example, in some cultures infants show strong attachments to many people, not just to their primary caregiver. In the African Hausa culture, both grandmothers and siblings provide a significant amount of care to infants (Harkness & Super, 1995). Another critique of attachment theory is that it may not account for temperamental differences among infants that might color the attachment relationship. In addition, caregivers and infants likely share genetic characteristics, and it might be that the attachment relationship is really a product of these shared genes (Gervai, 2009). Despite such criticisms, there is ample evidence that secure attachment is important to development (Sroufe, Coffino, & Carlson, 2010; Thompson & Newton, 2009).

Given these raw ingredients of temperament and attachment, how does a human being develop in the socioemotional domain? This question was addressed by Erik Erikson, who devised a theory of what he called *psychosocial* development. Like Piaget's theory of cognitive development, Erikson's theory has guided thinking about how human beings develop in their social and emotional capacities.

● **secure attachment** The ways that infants use their caregiver, usually their mother, as a secure base from which to explore the environment.

In the Hausa culture, siblings and grandmothers provide a significant amount of care for infants.

Trust versus mistrust	**Autonomy versus shame and doubt**	**Initiative versus guilt**	**Industry versus inferiority**
Developmental period: Infancy (Birth to 1½ years)	**Developmental period:** Toddlerhood (1½ to 3 years)	**Developmental period:** Early childhood (preschool years, ages 3–5)	**Developmental period:** Middle and late childhood (elementary school years, 6 years–puberty)
Characteristics: A sense of trust requires a feeling of physical comfort and minimal amount of fear about the future. Infants' basic needs are met by responsive, sensitive caregivers.	**Characteristics:** After gaining trust in their caregivers, infants start to discover that they have a will of their own. They assert their sense of autonomy, or independence. They realize their will. If infants are restrained too much or punished too harshly, they are likely to develop a sense of shame and doubt.	**Characteristics:** As preschool children encounter a widening social world, they are challenged more and need to develop more purposeful behavior to cope with these challenges. Children are now asked to assume more responsibility. Uncomfortable guilt feelings may arise, though, if the children are irresponsible and are made to feel too anxious.	**Characteristics:** At no other time are children more enthusiastic than at the end of early childhood's period of expansive imagination. As children move into the elementary school years, they direct their energy toward mastering knowledge and intellectual skills. The danger at this stage involves feeling incompetent and unproductive.

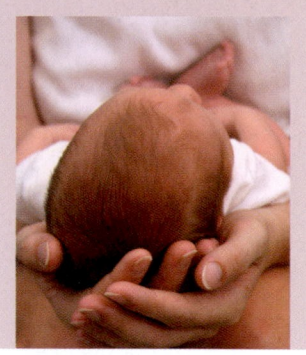   

FIGURE 32.10   Erikson's Eight Stages of Human Development Erikson changed the way psychologists think about development by tracing the process of growth over the entire life span.

Erikson's Theory of Socioemotional Development

Erik Erikson (1902–1994) proposed eight psychosocial stages of development from infancy through old age. In Erikson's (1968) view, the first four stages take place in childhood; the last four, in adolescence and adulthood (Figure 32.10). One reason why Erikson's theory is so important is that he fully expected socioemotional development to occur throughout the life span. For Erikson, movement toward greater competence and maturity was a lifelong process, marked by important developmental milestones in young and middle adulthood and into old age. Each of Erikson's stages represents the developmental task that the individual must master at a particular place in the life span.

According to Erikson, these developmental tasks are represented by two possible outcomes, such as trust versus mistrust (Erikson's first stage). If an infant's physical and emotional needs are well taken care of, he or she will experience an enduring sense of trust in others. If, on the other hand, these needs are frustrated, the individual might carry concerns about trust throughout his or her life, with bits of this unfinished business being reflected in the rest of the stages. For Erikson, each stage is a turning point with two opposing possible outcomes: one, greater personal competence; and the other, greater weakness and vulnerability. Using Erikson's stages as a guide, let's consider the various ways that human beings develop in terms of their capacities for interpersonal relationships and emotional well-being in infancy and childhood.

SOCIOEMOTIONAL DEVELOPMENT IN CHILDHOOD: FROM TRUST TO INDUSTRY

We examine Erikson's adolescence and adult stages later in this module. His four childhood stages are:

1. *Trust versus mistrust* (the first 18 months of life): Trust is built when a baby's basic needs—such as comfort, food, and warmth—are met. If infants' needs are not met by responsive, sensitive caregivers, the result is mistrust. Trust in infancy sets the stage for a lifelong expectation that the world will be a good and pleasant place to live.

Erik Erikson (1902–1994) Erikson generated one of the most important developmental theories of the twentieth century.

Identity versus identity confusion

Developmental period:
Adolescence (10–20 years)

Characteristics: Individuals are faced with finding out who they are, what they are all about, and where they are going in life. An important dimension is the exploration of alternative solutions to roles. Career exploration is important.

Intimacy versus isolation

Developmental period:
Eary adulthood (20s, 30s)

Characteristics: Individuals face the developmental task of forming intimate relationships with others. Erikson described intimacy as finding oneself yet losing oneself in another person.

Generativity versus stagnation

Developmental period:
Middle adulthood (40s, 50s)

Characteristics: A chief concern is to assist the younger generation in developing and leading useful lives.

Integrity versus despair

Developmental period:
Late adulthood (60s–)

Characteristics: Individuals look back and evaluate what they have done with their lives. The retrospective glances can be either positive (integrity) or negative (despair).

2. *Autonomy versus shame and doubt* (18 months through 3 years): Children can develop either a positive sense of independence and autonomy or negative feelings of shame and doubt. In seeking autonomy, they are likely to develop a strong sense of independence. A toddler who is experiencing toilet training is learning the beginnings of self-control. The toddler's growing independence is evident in the child's insistence that no matter how difficult the task, "I can do it myself!" Similarly common is the toddler's assertion of autonomy with a simple two-letter word: "No!"

3. *Initiative versus guilt* (3 to 5 years); During these years, children's social worlds are widening. When asked to assume more responsibility for themselves, children can develop initiative. When allowed to be irresponsible or made to feel anxious, they can develop too much guilt. The preschooler is more likely to engage in imaginative play propelled by his or her own fantasies. The child may make friends of his or her own choosing for the first time.

4. *Industry versus inferiority* (age 6 to puberty): Children can achieve industry by mastering knowledge and intellectual skills. When they do not, they can feel inferior. At the end of early childhood, children are ready to turn their energy to learning academic skills. If they do not, they can develop a sense of being incompetent and unproductive. During the beginnings of elementary school, children learn the value of what Erikson called *industry*, gaining competence in academic skills and acquiring the ability to engage in self-discipline and hard work.

From Erikson's perspective, then, children should grow toward greater levels of autonomy and self-confidence as they progress from infancy to school age and beyond. At each stage, Erikson said, either parents can facilitate the child's growth or they can thwart it by being overly protective or neglectful.

Evaluating Erikson's Theory

Like Piaget's theory, Erikson's conclusions have had their critics (Kroger, 2007). Erikson mainly practiced case study research, which some reject as the sole research foundation for his approach. Critics also argue that Erikson's attempt to capture each developmental stage with a single concept leaves out other important developmental tasks. For example, as we will see, Erikson said that the main task for young adults is to resolve a conflict between intimacy and isolation, yet another important developmental task at this life stage revolves around careers and work. Such criticisms do not tarnish Erikson's monumental contributions, however. Like Piaget, he is a giant in developmental psychology.

Parenting and Childhood Socioemotional Development

Various researchers have tried to identify styles of parenting associated with positive developmental outcomes. Diana Baumrind (1991, 1993) described four basic styles of interaction between parents and their children:

■ **Authoritarian parenting** is a strict punitive style. The authoritarian parent firmly limits and controls the child with little verbal exchange. In a difference of opinion about how to do something, for example, the authoritarian parent might say, "You do it my way or else." Children of authoritarian parents sometimes lack social skills, show poor initiative, and compare themselves with others. Importantly, culture influences the effects of authoritarian parenting. In one study (Rudy & Grusec, 2006), collectivist mothers (in this case Iranian, Indian, Egyptian, and Pakistani) described themselves as more authoritarian but did not express negative attitudes about their children, and the children did not show these more negative outcomes. For Latino families, some psychologists have suggested that authoritarian parenting may express culturally valued childrearing goals such as family, respect, and education and that this parenting style must be understood in the context of these cultural ideals (Halgunseth, Ispa, & Rudy, 2006).

■ **Authoritative parenting** encourages the child to be independent but still places limits and controls on behavior. This parenting style is more collaborative. Extensive verbal give-and-take is allowed, and parents are warm and nurturing toward the child. An authoritative father might put his arm around the child in a comforting way and say, "You know you should not have done that; let's talk about how you can handle the situation better next time." Children whose parents are authoritative tend to be socially competent, self-reliant, and socially responsible.

■ **Neglectful parenting** is distinguished by a lack of parental involvement in the child's life. Children of neglectful parents might develop a sense that other aspects of their parents' lives are more important than they are. Children whose parents are neglectful tend to be less competent socially, to handle independence poorly, and (especially) to show poor self-control.

■ **Permissive parenting** involves placing few limits on the child's behavior. A permissive parent lets the child do what he or she wants. Some parents deliberately rear their children this way because they believe that the combination of warm involvement and few limits will produce a creative, confident child. However, children with very permissive parents typically rate poorly in social competence. They often fail to learn respect for others, expect to get their own way, and have difficulty controlling their behavior. Recall that socioemotional development involves becoming increasingly adept at controlling and regulating one's emotions and behaviors (Vazsonyi & Huang, 2010). Children may require structure from their caregivers in order to acquire these skills.

Parents are crucial to child development. However, as the Intersection explores, peers play a large role in socioemotional development as well.

● **authoritarian parenting** A restrictive, punitive style in which the parent exhorts the child to follow the parent's directions and to value hard work and effort.

● **authoritative parenting** A parenting style that encourages the child to be independent but that still places limits and controls on behavior.

● **neglectful parenting** A parenting style characterized by a lack of parental involvement in the child's life.

● **permissive parenting** A parenting style characterized by the placement of few limits on the child's behavior.

Developmental Psychology and Clinical Psychology: Is "Girl Talk" Always a Good Thing?

Making friends, keeping friends, and being a friend are all tasks that face the developing human being. Friends are important to children's self-esteem, well-being, and school adjustment (Brengden & others, 2010; Erath & others, 2010; Rubin, Cheah, & Menzer, 2010). Having a friend means that there is someone to talk to when one has problems and someone to celebrate with when things go well. Thus, if a child has a lot of friends, we might think that he or she is doing pretty well. Are all friendships equally supportive, however? Research indicates that some friends might have a knack for making problems seem worse, not better.

Are some of your friends likely to co-ruminate over negative events? Why do you think co-rumination is worse for girls than boys?

Developmental psychologist Amanda Rose and her colleagues have studied how young friends' responses to their friends' problems influence the mental health of children and adolescents (Rose, 2002; Rose, Carlson, & Waller, 2007; Rose & Smith, 2009). Rose (2002) introduced the concept of *co-rumination* to describe the ways that some friends might make matters worse by giving their pals even more things to worry about

than they had originally realized. For example, if Janisa tells her friend Robin about doing poorly on a spelling test, does Robin encourage Janisa to study harder, or does she remind Janisa that not doing well now is a really bad sign because the words are only going to get harder in the future? Rumination is a way of thinking that involves worrying about a topic without finding a resolution. When we ruminate, we might dwell on all the possible horrible consequences of some negative life event or imagine everything that might go wrong in the future. Co-rumination is like that too, but it involves engaging in a conversation with someone and making a negative event that the person is going through seem even worse.

In a study of hundreds of grade-school and middle-school children, Rose (2002) found that girls were more likely than boys to engage in co-rumination, and this difference was particularly large among adolescents. Furthermore, longitudinal research has shown that co-rumination, even in the context of good friends, was associated with increased feelings of depression and anxiety, especially for girls (Rose, Carlson, & Waller, 2007). Rose and colleagues suggest that some friends represent a trade-off, especially for girls. Having close friends might be a good sign of social functioning, but when those friends are people who hurt more than help, they can negatively influence girls' well-being.

Moral Development

Another aspect of development that psychologists study is how an individual becomes not only physically able, cognitively skilled, and emotionally well but also a person of character—someone who behaves morally. This aspect of development features yet another classic theory in developmental psychology, that of Lawrence Kohlberg (1927–1987). Moral development involves changes with age in thoughts, feelings, and behaviors regarding the principles and values that guide what people should do. Much research on moral reasoning and thinking has revolved around Kohlberg's theory of moral development and reactions to it.

KOHLBERG'S THEORY

Kohlberg (1958) began his study of moral thinking by creating a series of stories and asking children, adolescents, and adults questions about the stories. One of the stories goes something like this. A man, Heinz, whose wife is dying of cancer, knows about a drug that might save her life. He approaches the pharmacist who has the drug, but the pharmacist refuses to give it to him without being paid a very high price. Heinz is unable to scrape together the money and eventually decides to steal the drug.

Lawrence Kohlberg (1927–1987)
Kohlberg created a provocative theory of moral development. In his view, "Moral development consists of a sequence of qualitative changes in the way an individual thinks."

After reading the story, each person interviewed was asked a series of questions about the moral dilemma. Should Heinz have stolen the drug? Kohlberg was less interested in the answer to this question than he was to the next one: Why? Based on the reasons people gave for their answers, Kohlberg (1986) evaluated their level of moral development. Kohlberg's stages of moral development consisted of three levels, as follows, with two stages at each level (Figure 32.11).

1. The *preconventional level* is based primarily on punishments and rewards from the external world. Moral reasoning is guided by not wanting Heinz to go to jail or concern for the druggists' profits.

2. At the *conventional level,* the individual abides by standards such as those learned from parents or society's laws. At this level the person might reason that Heinz should act in accord with expectations or his role as a good husband or reason that Heinz should follow the law no matter what.

3. At the *postconventional level,* the individual recognizes alternative moral courses, explores the options, and then develops an increasingly personal moral code. At this level, the person might reason that Heinz's wife's life is more important than a law.

Kohlberg believed that moral development advances because of the maturation of thought, the availability of opportunities for role taking, and the chance to discuss moral issues with a person who reasons at a stage just above one's own. Kohlberg studied with Piaget, and Kohlberg's approach to moral reasoning emphasized the individual's capacity to reason in a sophisticated way, as did Piaget's theory of cognitive development. As we will see, subsequent theories of moral development have focused on its social and emotional components. For Kohlberg, a sense of justice was at the heart of moral reasoning, which he believed laid the foundation for moral behavior.

EVALUATING KOHLBERG'S THEORY

Kohlberg's ideas have stimulated considerable research about how people think about moral issues (Narvaez & Lapsley, 2009; Walker & Frimer, 2011). At the same time, his theory has numerous critics. One criticism is that moral *reasoning* does not necessarily mean moral *behavior*. When people are asked about their moral reasoning, what they say might fit into Kohlberg's advanced stages, but their actual behavior might involve

LEVEL 1 **Preconventional Level** **No Internalization**	**LEVEL 2** **Conventional Level** **Intermediate Internalization**	**LEVEL 3** **Postconventional Level** **Full Internalization**
Stage 1 Heteronomous Morality *Individuals pursue their own interests but let others do the same. What is right involves equal exchange.*	**Stage 3** Mutual Interpersonal Expectations, Relationships, and Interpersonal Conformity *Individuals value trust, caring, and loyalty to others as a basis for moral judgments.*	**Stage 5** Social Contract or Utility and Individual Rights *Individuals reason that values, rights, and principles undergird or transcend the law.*
Stage 2 Individualism, Purpose, and Exchange *Children obey because adults tell them to obey. People base their moral decisions on fear of punishment.*	**Stage 4** Social System Morality *Moral judgments are based on understanding and the social order, law, justice, and duty.*	**Stage 6** Universal Ethical Principles *The person has developed moral judgments that are based on universal human rights. When faced with a dilemma between law and conscience, a personal, individualized conscience is followed.*

FIGURE 32.11 **Kohlberg's Three Levels and Six Stages of Moral Development** Kohlberg proposed that human moral development could be characterized by a sequence of age-related changes.

cheating, lying, and stealing. The cheaters, liars, and thieves might know what is right but still do what is wrong.

Another criticism is that Kohlberg's view does not adequately reflect concern for other people and social bonds (Carlo, 2006). Kohlberg's theory is called a *justice perspective* because it focuses on the rights of the individual as the key to sound moral reasoning. In contrast, the *care perspective,* which lies at the heart of Carol Gilligan's (1982) approach to moral development, views people in terms of their connectedness with others and emphasizes interpersonal communication, relationships, and concern for others. From Gilligan's perspective, this weakness in Kohlberg's approach explains why, using his measures, women generally score lower than men on moral development. Similarly, culture can influence whether a person approaches a moral dilemma from the perspective of justice or care (Gibbs, 2010). In Western cultures, where people generally tend toward an individualistic sense of self and are therefore inclined to take a justice perspective, individuals might score higher in Kohlberg's scheme than their counterparts in collectivistic Asian cultures, where people have a sense of the self as part of a larger group.

CURRENT RESEARCH ON MORAL DEVELOPMENT

Researchers interested in moral development have increasingly studied **prosocial behavior,** behavior that is intended to benefit other people (N. Eisenberg, 2010; N. Eisenberg & others, 2009). For example, researchers are probing how, when, and why children engage in everyday acts of kindness toward others (Carlo, 2006). Studies have found that supportive parenting and parental monitoring relate to increased helping and comforting of others (Dodge, Coie, & Lynam, 2006). Furthermore, research suggests that the capacities to empathize with others and engage in prosocial behavior are linked with the ability to engage in self-control more generally (N. Eisenberg, 2010).

Other recent work has focused on when a child first shows signs of possessing a conscience (Kochanska & others, 2008; R. A. Thompson, 2009b). Having a conscience means hearing that voice in our head that tells us that something is morally good or bad. Deborah Laible and Ross Thompson (2000, 2002, 2007) have examined the conversations between mothers and toddlers at times when the child did something well or got into trouble. They have found that by 3 years of age, children begin to show signs of early conscience development. This development is fostered by parent–child interactions that are clear, elaborate, and rich with emotional content and that include shared positive emotion. Childhood characteristics are important because longitudinal research shows that kind, moral children are more likely to be kind, moral adults (N. Eisenberg, 2010; Eisenberg, Fabes, & Spinrad, 2006).

How can parents successfully rear a child to be considerate of others and to understand the difference between right and wrong? Researchers have found that the following parenting strategies are most often helpful in rearing a moral child (Eisenberg & Murphy, 1995; Eisenberg & Valiente, 2002; N. Eisenberg & others, 2009):

- Being warm and supportive rather than overly punishing and rigid
- When disciplining, using reasoning the child can understand
- Providing opportunities for the child to learn about others' perspectives and feelings
- Involving children in family decision making and in thinking about moral decisions
- Modeling moral behaviors and thinking, and providing children with opportunities to engage in such behaviors and thought

Note that the last strategy includes modeling moral behaviors. That is, it calls for parents to demonstrate moral behavior to the child. However, significantly, parents are themselves still developing, even as they model this behavior for the child. Human development, then, occurs in the context of generations relating to each other, teaching each other lessons, and working in tandem.

Carol Gilligan (b. 1936) Gilligan argues that Kohlberg's approach does not give adequate attention to relationships. In Gilligan's view, "Many girls seem to fear, most of all, being alone—without friends, family, and relationships."

● **prosocial behavior** Behavior that is intended to benefit other people.

SUMMARY

Prenatal development progresses through the germinal, embryonic, and fetal periods. Particular drugs, such as alcohol and nicotine, as well as certain illnesses, can adversely affect the fetus. These environmental threats are called teratogens. Preterm birth is another potential problem, especially if the infant is very small or grows up in an adverse environment.

The infant's physical development is dramatic in the first year, and a number of motor milestones are reached in infancy. Extensive changes in the brain, including denser connections between synapses, take place in infancy and childhood.

With regard to cognitive development, in Piaget's view, children use schemas to actively construct their world, either assimilating new information into existing schemas or adjusting schemas to accommodate that information. Piaget identified four stages of cognitive development: the sensorimotor stage, the preoperational stage, the concrete operational stage, and the formal operational stage.

Socioemotional development in childhood includes consideration of Erikson's psychosocial stages as well as moral development. Erikson presented a major, eight-stage psychosocial view of life-span development; its first four stages occur in childhood. In each stage, the individual seeks to resolve a particular socioemotional conflict. Kohlberg proposed a cognitive theory of moral development with three levels (preconventional, conventional, and postconventional).

KEY TERMS

preferential looking 315
assimilation 317
accommodation 317
sensorimotor stage 317
preoperational stage 318
concrete operational stage 319
formal operational stage 320
temperament 322

infant attachment 322
secure attachment 323
authoritarian parenting 326
authoritative parenting 326
neglectful parenting 326
permissive parenting 326
prosocial behavior 329

TEST YOURSELF

1. What are teratogens? Give several examples of them.
2. According to Piaget, what two processes are responsible for how people use and adapt their schemas, and what is involved in each process?
3. What are Erikson's four childhood stages of development, and with what is each centrally concerned?

APPLY YOUR KNOWLEDGE

1. Consider the style of parenting with which you were raised. It might help to think of specific situations or moments when your parents put limits on your behavior (or did not). If you have one or more siblings, ask for their opinion, too. Do you agree with one another about your parents' style? Now give these definitions to your parents, and ask which, if any, describes them. Sometimes there are as many different views of a family as there are members of that family.

2. A major part of any child's life is playing—and when kids are playing, they are often playing with toys. Using the information on perceptual and cognitive development reviewed in this module, design a toy that you think is a perfect fit for a child of 2 months, 2 years, and 10 years old. With respect to the child's development, what features of the toy are especially good for the child of each age group?

3. Go online and Google "parenting discussion boards." Click on one or two of the many sites that come up, and see what parents are talking about. What issues seem to concern them most? Do these parents appear to have a sense of the issues addressed by developmental psychologists? Does the advice that parents share with one another seem to be based on the science of psychology?

Adolescence

Adolescence is the developmental period of transition from childhood to adulthood, beginning around 10 to 12 years of age and ending at 18 to 21 years of age. Adolescents are not all the same (Diamond & Savin-Williams, 2009). Variations in ethnicity, culture, history, gender, socioeconomic status, and lifestyle characterize their life trajectories (Galambos, Berenbaum, & McHale, 2009). Any image of adolescents should take into account the particular adolescent or group of adolescents one is considering. In this section we examine the changes that occur in adolescence in the domains of physical, cognitive, and socioemotional development.

33-1 PHYSICAL DEVELOPMENT IN ADOLESCENCE

Dramatic physical changes characterize adolescence, especially early adolescence. Among the major physical changes of adolescence are those involving puberty and the brain.

Pubertal Change

The signature physical change in adolescence is **puberty,** a period of rapid skeletal and sexual maturation that occurs mainly in early adolescence. Hormonal changes lie at the core of pubertal development. The concentrations of certain hormones increase dramatically during puberty (Susman & Dorn, 2009). *Testosterone*—an **androgen,** which is the main class of male sex hormones—is associated in boys with the development of genitals, an increase in height, and voice change. *Estradiol*—an **estrogen,** the main class of female sex hormones—is associated in girls with breast, uterine, and skeletal development. Developmental psychologists believe that hormonal changes account for at least some of the emotional ups and downs of adolescence, but hormones are not alone responsible for adolescent behavior (Graber, 2007).

Remember that physical and socioemotional development are intertwined. Nowhere is this link more apparent than in the timing of puberty. Boys who mature earlier than their peers tend to show more positive socioemotional outcomes, such as being popular with their peers and having higher self-esteem (Graber, Brooks-Gunn, & Warren, 2006). Longitudinal studies have shown that boys who matured early in adolescence were more successful and less likely to drink alcohol, smoke cigarettes, or engage in delinquent behaviors than late-maturing boys (Taga, Markey, & Friedman, 2006; van der Geest, Blokland, & Bijleveld, 2009). In contrast, girls who are early bloomers tend to be less outgoing and less popular, and they are more likely to smoke, use drugs, become sexually active, and engage less in academic pursuits (Engels, 2009; Susman & Dorn, 2009).

The Brain

Brain-imaging studies have revealed important changes in the brain during adolescence (Paus, 2009; Steinberg, 2009). These changes focus on the earlier development of the amygdala, which involves emotion, and the later development of the prefrontal

● **puberty** A period of rapid skeletal and sexual maturation that occurs mainly in early adolescence.

● **androgens** The main class of male sex hormones.

● **estrogens** The main class of female sex hormones.

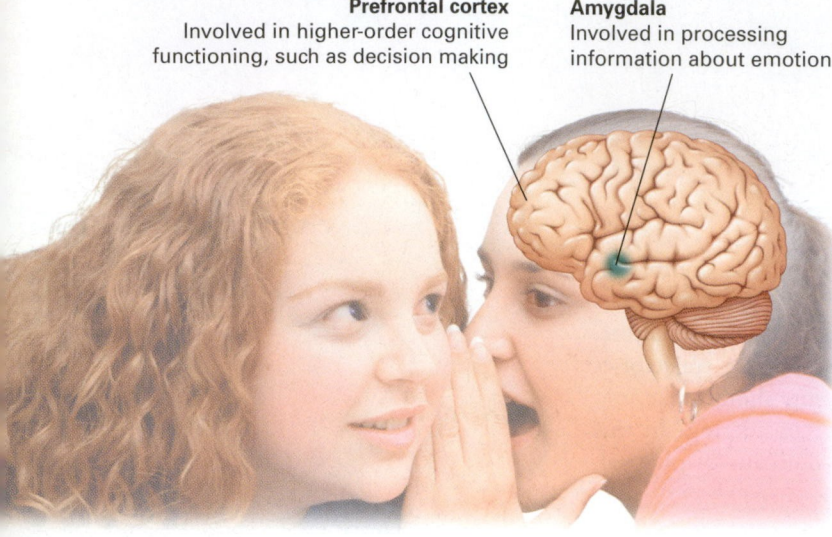

Prefrontal cortex
Involved in higher-order cognitive functioning, such as decision making

Amygdala
Involved in processing information about emotion

FIGURE 33.1 **Developmental Changes in the Adolescent's Brain** The amygdala, which is responsible for processing information about emotion, matures earlier than the prefrontal cortex, which is responsible for making decisions and other higher-order cognitive functions.

cortex, which is concerned with reasoning and decision making (Figure 33.1). These changes in the brain may help to explain why adolescents often display very strong emotions but cannot yet control these passions. It is as if the adolescent brain does not have the brakes to slow down emotions. Because of the relatively slow development of the prefrontal cortex, which continues to mature into early adulthood, adolescents may lack the cognitive skills to control their pleasure seeking effectively. This developmental disjunction may account for increased risk taking and other problems in adolescence (Steinberg, 2009).

Biological changes in the brain are linked with experiences (Lerner, Boyd, & Du, 2008). For instance, one study of adolescents found that resisting peer pressure was correlated with prefrontal cortex thickening and more brain connections (Paus & others, 2008). This correlational study cannot tell us if the brain changes promoted peer-pressure resistance or if this resistance promoted changes in the brain, but it does highlight the nature–nurture question that permeates the study of development.

33-2 COGNITIVE DEVELOPMENT IN ADOLESCENCE

● **identity versus identity confusion** Erikson's fifth psychological stage, in which adolescents face the challenges of finding out who they are, what they are all about, and where they are going in life.

As they advance into Piaget's formal operational thinking, adolescents undergo other significant cognitive changes (Byrnes, 2008; Kuhn, 2009, 2011). One characteristic of adolescent thinking, especially in early adolescence, is egocentrism. Although children are also considered egocentric, *adolescent egocentrism* has a different focus; it involves the individual's belief that others are as preoccupied with him or her as the adolescent himself or herself is and that the individual is both unique and invincible (that is, incapable of being harmed) (Elkind, 1978). Egocentric adolescents perceive others as observing them more than actually is the case—think of the eighth-grade boy who senses that everyone has noticed the small pimple on his face. However, recent research is calling into question whether adolescents believe they are invincible. In one study, 12- to 18-year-olds who were asked about their chance of dying in the next year and before age 20 greatly overestimated their chance of dying (Fischhoff & others, 2010).

off the mark.com   by Mark Parisi

RELAX, DAD! THEY'RE NOT **REAL** PIERCINGS, THEY'RE TATTOOS OF PIERCINGS...

33-3 SOCIOEMOTIONAL DEVELOPMENT IN ADOLESCENCE: THE EMERGENCE OF IDENTITY

Erikson's approach to the formation of identity during adolescence is one of his most important contributions. His ideas changed the way we think about adolescence (Kroger, Martinussen, & Marcia, 2010). Erikson (1968) viewed the key challenge of adolescence (his fifth stage) as **identity versus identity confusion.** In seeking an *identity*, adolescents face the challenges of finding out who they are, what they are all about, and where they are going in life. Adolescents are confronted with many new roles and adult statuses—from jobs and careers to friendships and romantic relationships. If they do not adequately explore their identity during this stage, they end up confused about who they are. Therefore, Erikson argues, parents should allow adolescents to explore many different roles and many paths within a particular role. Adolescents who spend this time in their lives exploring alternatives can reach some resolution of the identity crisis and emerge with a new

© Hilary B. Price.

sense of self. Those who do not successfully resolve the crisis suffer what Erikson calls *identity confusion,* which is expressed in one of two ways: the individual either withdraws, becoming isolated from peers and family, or loses himself or herself in the crowd.

Marcia's Theory of Identity Status

Building on Erikson's ideas, James Marcia (1980, 2002) proposed the concept of *identity status* to describe a person's position in the development of an identity. In Marcia's view, two dimensions of identity, exploration and commitment, are important. *Exploration* refers to a person's investigating various options for a career and for personal values. *Commitment* involves making a decision about which identity path to follow and making

psychological *inquiry*

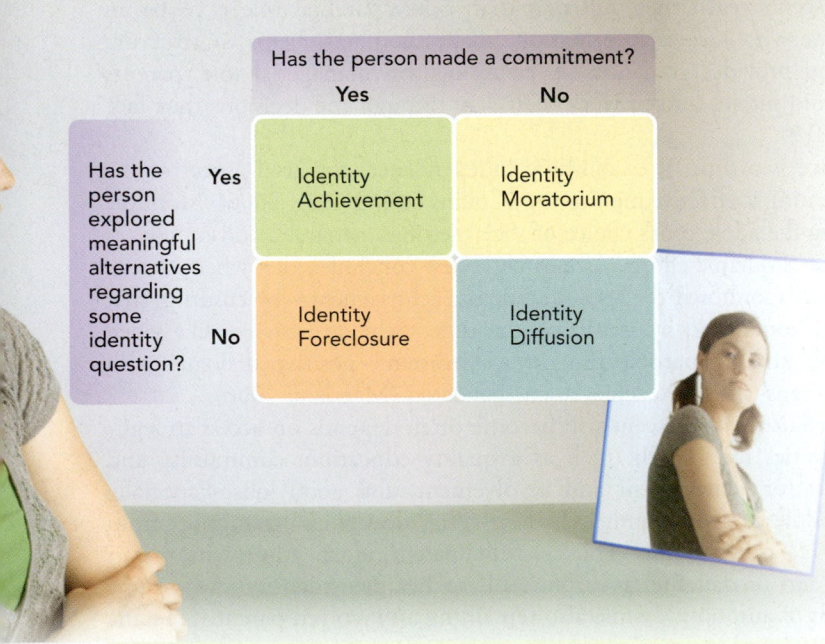

Looking at Identity Exploration

This figure summarizes Marcia's conceptualization of identity development. Notice that the different quadrants of the square represent the crossings of the two factors of commitment and exploration and that every possible combination of the two is represented. Answer the following questions.

1. Imagine a young woman who has grown up in a family of doctors. Everyone in her family expects her to follow this same course. What outcomes might be expected if she simply "goes with the flow" of her family's wishes?

2. Imagine a young woman who comes from a family in which no one ever attended college. What sorts of experiences might influence her journey to identity? How might her background influence her identity exploration?

3. Find yourself in this figure. That is, in which quadrant is your own identity located? Do you feel that you fully explored your potential identities? Why or why not?

4. Which path to identity do you think is most challenging? Why?

5. Which path to identity do you believe is most common in young people today? Why?

6. Finding one's path in life is a common theme in popular books, TV, and film. Can you identify a book or movie that depicts the combination of exploration and resolution? Why do you think this theme is so popular?

Michelle Chin, age 16, reflecting on her identity, commented, "Parents do not understand that teenagers need to find out who they are, which means a lot of experimenting, a lot of mood swings, a lot of emotions and awkwardness. Like any teenager, I am facing an identity crisis. I am still trying to figure out whether I am a Chinese American or an American with Asian eyes."

a personal investment in attaining that identity. Various combinations of exploration and commitment give rise to one of four identity statuses.

Notably, Marcia's approach focuses on identity as an active construction, an outcome of a process of thinking about and trying on different identities (Klimstra & others, 2009). To master Marcia's approach, check out the Psychological Inquiry.

Ethnic Identity

Developing an identity in adolescence can be especially challenging for individuals from ethnic minority groups (Gonzales-Backen & Umana-Taylor, 2010; Juang & Syed, 2010). As they mature cognitively, many adolescents become acutely aware of the evaluation of their ethnic group by the majority culture. In addition, an increasing number of minority adolescents face the challenge of *biculturalism*—identifying in some ways with their ethnic minority group and in other ways with the majority culture (Phinney & others, 2006).

Research has shown that for ethnic minority youth, feeling both a positive attachment to their minority group and an attachment to the larger culture is related to more positive academic and emotional outcomes (Iturbide, Raffaelli, & Carlo, 2009; Yip, Kiang, & Fuligni, 2008). Although it might seem that being a member of an ethnic minority would make life more stressful, studies have indicated that having a strong ethnic identity can buffer adolescents from the effects of discrimination (Iturbide, Raffaelli, & Carlo, 2009; Sellers & others, 2006). For both minority and majority adolescents, developing a positive identity is an important life theme (Kroger, Martinussen, & Marcia, 2010; Swanson, 2010). In addition to ethnic identity, adolescence can be a time when other aspects of one's identity come to the fore, such as sexual orientation and gender role.

Parental and Peer Roles in Identity Formation

Parents and peers can help the adolescent answer the central questions of identity, "Who am I, and who do I hope to become?" (Brown & Dietz, 2009; Rodriquez & Walden, 2010). To help adolescents reach their full potential, a key parental role is to be an effective manager—one who locates information, makes contacts, helps to structure offsprings' choices, and provides guidance. By assuming this managerial role, parents help adolescents to avoid pitfalls and to work their way through the decisions they face (Gauvain & Parke, 2010).

Although adolescence is a time of establishing independence, a crucial aspect of the managerial role of parenting is effective monitoring (Collins & Steinberg, 2006). Monitoring includes supervising the adolescent's choice of social settings, activities, and friends, as well as his or her academic efforts. A research review concluded that when African American parents monitored their sons' academic achievement—by ensuring that they completed homework; by restricting the time spent on activities like video games and TV; and by participating in a consistent, positive dialogue with teachers—their sons' academic achievement benefited (Mandara, 2006).

How competent the adolescent will become often depends on access to legitimate opportunities for growth, such as a quality education, community and societal support for achievement and involvement, and good jobs. Especially important in adolescent development is long-term, deeply caring support from adults (Lerner & others, 2009). Successfully parenting an adolescent means allowing one's son or daughter to explore his or her own identity and assume increasing levels of autonomy, while also remaining an involved parent (Smetana & others, 2009).

During adolescence, individuals spend more time with peers than they did in childhood. These peer influences can be positive or negative (Asher & McDonald, 2009). A significant aspect of positive peer relations is having one or more close friends. Adolescents can learn to be skilled and sensitive partners

The managerial role of parenting involves effective monitoring of the adolescent's friends, social activities, and academic efforts.

in intimate relationships by forging close friendships with selected peers. However, some peers and friends can negatively impact adolescents' development. Researchers have found that hanging out with delinquent peers in adolescence can be a strong predictor of substance abuse, delinquent behavior, and depression (Dishion & Piehler, 2009; Farrington, 2009).

SUMMARY

Puberty is a period of rapid skeletal and sexual maturation that occurs mainly in early adolescence. Its onset occurs about two years earlier in girls than in boys. Hormonal changes trigger pubertal development.

According to Piaget, cognitive development in adolescence is characterized by the appearance of formal operational thought, the final stage in his theory. This stage involves abstract, idealistic, and logical thought.

One of the most important aspects of socioemotional development in adolescence is identity. Erikson's fifth stage of psychosocial development is identity versus identity confusion. Marcia proposed four statuses of identity based on crisis and commitment. A special concern is the development of ethnic identity. Despite great differences among adolescents, the majority of them develop competently.

KEY TERMS

puberty   331
androgens   331
estrogens   331

identity versus identity confusion   332

TEST YOURSELF

1. What characteristics of the adolescent brain help to explain why adolescents often display strong emotions that they cannot control?

2. According to Erikson, what challenges do adolescents face in trying to establish an identity, and what happens if they do not successfully resolve this crisis?

3. In what ways do parents and peers help an adolescent develop an identity?

APPLY YOUR KNOWLEDGE

1. Think about your adolescent experiences. What were the roles or types you tried out? How did that experimentation shape who you are now?

2. How do you think Facebook, MySpace, and Twitter impacted your socioemotional development as an adolescent? Discuss this question in a small group, using what you've learned in the module.

Emerging Adulthood, Adult Development, and Aging

Development continues throughout adulthood. Developmental psychologists identify three approximate periods in adult development: early adulthood (20s and 30s), middle adulthood (40s and 50s), and late adulthood (60s until death). Each phase features distinctive physical, cognitive, and socioemotional changes.

Erikson believed that once the issues of identity are resolved, the young adult turns to the important domain of intimate relationships. However, more recently, scholars have noted that during the life stage after adolescence, many young people are putting off the commitments to marriage, family, and career that are traditionally associated with adult life. Jeffrey Arnett (2004, 2007, 2010) introduced the concept of *emerging adulthood* to describe this transitional period, which is in part an extended adolescence and in part a "trying on" of adult roles. If you are a traditional-age college student, you are at this point in the life span. We begin our survey of post-adolescent development by briefly examining this transitional life stage.

34-1 EMERGING ADULTHOOD

● **emerging adulthood** The transitional period from adolescence to adulthood, spanning approximately 18 to 25 years of age.

Emerging adulthood is the transitional period from adolescence to adulthood (Arnett, 2004, 2006, 2007). The age range for emerging adulthood is approximately 18 to 25 years of age. Experimentation and exploration characterize the emerging adult. At this point in their development, many individuals are still exploring which career path they want to follow, what they want their identity to be, and what kinds of close relationships they will have.

Jeffrey Arnett (2006, 2010) identified five main features of emerging adulthood:

■ *Identity exploration, especially in love and work:* Emerging adulthood is the time of significant changes in identity for many individuals.

■ *Instability:* Residential changes peak during emerging adulthood, a time during which there also is often instability in love, work, and education.

■ *Self-focus:* Emerging adults "are self-focused in the sense that they have little in the way of social obligations, [and] little in the way of duties and commitments to others, which leaves them with a great deal of autonomy in running their own lives" (Arnett, 2006, p. 10).

■ *A feeling of being "in between":* Many emerging adults consider themselves neither adolescents nor full-fledged adults.

■ *Access to various life possibilities and an opportunity to transform one's life:* Arnett (2006) describes two ways in which emerging adulthood is the age of possibilities: (1) Many emerging adults are optimistic about their future, and (2) for emerging adults who have experienced difficult times while growing up, emerging adulthood presents an opportunity to guide their lives in a positive direction.

Other research suggests that emerging adulthood is a time of increasing well-being (Schulenberg & Zarrett, 2006). One possible reason for this improvement is that emerging adults have more choices and more control over those choices in their daily lives. Emerging adulthood provides an opportunity for individuals who engaged in problem behavior during adolescence to get their lives together.

34-2 PHYSICAL DEVELOPMENT IN ADULTHOOD

Like other developmental periods, our bodies change during adulthood. Most of the changes that occur following adolescence involve declines in physical and perceptual abilities, as we now consider.

Physical Changes in Early Adulthood

Most adults reach their peak physical development during their 20s and are the healthiest then. Early adulthood, however, is also the time when many physical skills begin to decline. The decline in strength and speed often is noticeable in the 30s. Another realm in which physical changes occur with age is in the ability to perceive the world. Hearing loss is very common with age. In fact, starting at about age 18, hearing begins a gradual decline, though it is so slow that most people do not notice it until the age of 50 or so.

Physical Changes in Middle and Late Adulthood

By the 40s or 50s, the skin has begun to wrinkle and sag because of the loss of fat and collagen in underlying tissues. Small, localized areas of pigmentation in the skin produce age spots, especially in areas exposed to sunlight such as the hands and face (McCullough & Kelly, 2006). Hair becomes thinner and grayer due to a lower replacement rate and a decline in melanin production. Individuals lose height in middle age, and many gain weight (Page & others, 2009). The decrease in height is due to bone loss in the vertebrae. On average, body fat accounts for about 10 percent of body weight in adolescence; it makes up 20 percent or more in middle age. Once individuals hit their 40s, age-related vision changes usually become apparent, especially difficulty in seeing things up close. The sense of taste can also be affected by age, as taste buds are less likely to be replaced.

For women, entering middle age means that menopause will soon occur. Usually in the late 40s or early 50s, a woman's menstrual periods cease completely. With menopause comes a dramatic decline in the ovaries' production of estrogen. Estrogen decline produces uncomfortable symptoms in some menopausal women, such as *hot flashes* (sudden, brief flushing of the skin and a feeling of elevated body temperature), nausea, fatigue, and rapid heartbeat. Some menopausal women report depression and irritability (K. A. Matthews & others, 2007), but menopause does not produce serious psychological or physical problems for most women (Bauld & Brown, 2009; Weismiller, 2009).

For both men and women, a variety of bodily systems are likely to show the effects of wear and tear as the body becomes less and less able to repair damage and regenerate itself (Effros, 2009; Zou & others, 2009). Physical strength declines and motor speed slows, bones may become more brittle (especially for women), and nearly every bodily system may change with age. Significantly, however, even as age is associated with some inevitable decline, important aspects of successful aging are within the person's control (Martin-Joy & Vaillant, 2010). For instance, a healthy diet and regular exercise can help to prevent or slow these effects. Regular physical activity can have wide-reaching benefits not only for physical health but for cognitive functioning as well (Rolland, van Kan, & Vellas, 2010; Weis & others, 2010).

On the island of Okinawa (part of Japan), individuals live longer than anywhere else in the world, and Okinawa has the world's highest prevalence of *centenarians*— individuals who live to 100 years or beyond. Examination of Okinawans' lives provides insights into their longevity. Specific factors are diet (they eat nutritious foods such as grains, fish, and vegetables); lifestyle (they are easygoing and experience low stress); community (Okinawans look out for one another and do not isolate or ignore older adults); activity (they lead active lifestyles, and many older adults continue to work); and spirituality (they find a sense of purpose in spiritual matters) (Willcox & others,

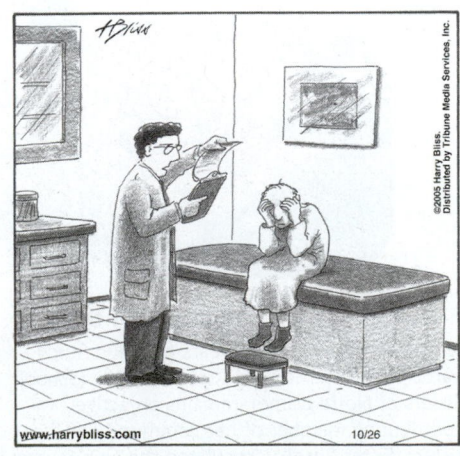

"... *All the lab work confirms it—I'm sorry Mr. Franklin ... You're old.*"

© Harry Bliss. Reprinted by permission of TMS/MCT Reprints

2008). Just as physical changes are interwoven with socioemotional processes in childhood and adolescence, so they are as human beings enter the later stages of life.

Biological Theories of Aging

Of the many proposed biological theories of aging, three especially merit attention. The first is the *cellular-clock theory,* Leonard Hayflick's (1977) view that cells can divide a maximum of about 100 times and that, as we age, our cells become less capable of dividing. Hayflick found that cells extracted from adults in their 50s to 70s had divided fewer than 100 times. The total number of cell divisions was roughly related to the individual's age. Based on the way cells divide, Hayflick places the human life span's upper limit at about 120 years.

Recently, scientists have been examining why cells lose their ability to divide (Davoli, Denchi, & de Lange, 2010; Sahin & Daphino, 2010). The answer may lie at the tips of chromosomes. Each time a cell divides, the *telomeres* protecting the ends of chromosomes shorten. After about 100 replications, the telomeres are dramatically reduced, and the cell no longer can reproduce (Shay & Wright, 2007). There is considerable interest in discovering ways to maintain high levels of the telomere-extending enzyme—telomerase—through genetic manipulation of chemical telomerase activators (Effros, 2009).

The *free-radical theory* of aging states that people age because unstable oxygen molecules known as *free radicals* are produced inside their cells. These molecules damage DNA and other cellular structures (Hepple, 2009; van Remmen & Jones, 2009). The damage done by free radicals may lead to a range of disorders, including cancer and arthritis.

Hormonal stress theory argues that aging in the body's hormonal system can lower resistance to stress and increase the likelihood of disease. As individuals age, the hormones stimulated by stress stay in the bloodstream longer than when they were younger (Brown-Borg, 2008). These prolonged, elevated levels of stress hormones are linked to increased risks for many diseases, including cardiovascular disease, cancer, and diabetes (Wolkowitz & others, 2010). Recently, the hormonal stress theory of aging has focused on the role of chronic stress in reducing immune system functioning (Bauer, Jeckel, & Luz, 2009).

Aging and the Brain

Just as the aging body has a greater capacity for renewal than previously thought, so does the aging brain (Imayoshi & others, 2009; Prakash & others, 2010). For decades, scientists believed that no new brain cells are generated past early childhood. However, researchers have recently discovered that adults can grow new brain cells throughout life (Eisch & others, 2008; Gould & others, 1999), although the evidence is limited to the hippocampus and the olfactory bulb (Arenkiel, 2010; L. Zou & others, 2010). Researchers currently are studying factors that might inhibit and promote neurogenesis, including various drugs, stress, and exercise (Gil-Mohapel & others, 2010; Marlatt, Lucassen, & van Pragg, 2010). They also are examining how grafting neural stem cells to various brain regions, such as the hippocampus, might increase neurogenesis (Farin & others, 2009; Szulwach & others, 2010).

Research from the Nun Study (described in Module 7) provides evidence for the role of experience in maintaining the brain. Recall that this study involves nearly 700 nuns in a convent in Mankato, Minnesota (Snowdon, 2003, 2007) (Figure 34.1). Although in Module 7 we surveyed the aspects of the study related to happiness, this research has also investigated brain functioning. By examining the nuns' donated brains as well as those of others, neuroscientists have documented the aging brain's remarkable ability to grow and change. Even the oldest Mankato nuns lead intellectually challenging lives, and neuroscientists believe that stimulating mental activities increase dendritic branching. Keeping the brain actively engaged in challenging activities can help to slow the effects of age.

Even in late adulthood, the brain has remarkable repair capability (Grady, 2008). Stanley Rapaport (1994) compared the brains of younger and older adults when they

FIGURE 34.1 **The Brains of the Mankato Nuns** At 90 years old, Nun Study participant Sister Rosella Kreuzer, SSND (School Sisters of Notre Dame), remains an active contributing member of her community of sisters. Sister Rosella articulated the Nun Study's mission as "That You May Have Life to the Full." (*Inset*) A neuroscientist holds a brain donated by one of the Mankato Nun Study participants.

were engaged in the same tasks. The older adults' brains literally rewired themselves to compensate for losses. If one neuron was not up to the job, neighboring neurons helped to pick up the slack. Rapaport concluded that as brains age, they can shift responsibilities for a given task from one region to another.

Changes in lateralization may provide one type of adaptation in aging adults (Angel & others, 2009; Zhu, Zacks, & Slade, 2010). *Lateralization* is the specialization of function in one hemisphere of the brain or the other. Using neuroimaging techniques, researchers have found that brain activity in the prefrontal cortex is lateralized less in older adults than in younger adults when they are engaging in mental tasks (Cabeza, 2002; Cabeza, Nyberg, & Park, 2005). For example, Figure 34.2 shows that when younger adults are given the task of recognizing words they have previously seen, they process the information primarily in the right hemisphere, whereas older adults are more likely to use both hemispheres (Madden & others, 1999). The decrease in lateralization in older adults might play a compensatory role in the aging brain. That is, using both hemispheres may help to maintain the mental abilities of older adults.

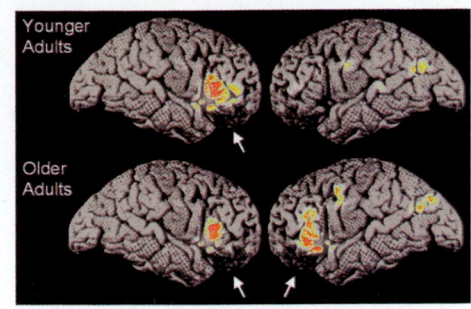

FIGURE 34.2 **The Decrease in Brain Lateralization in Older Adults** Younger adults primarily used the right prefrontal region of the brain (*top left photo*) during a memory recall task, while older adults used both the left and the right prefrontal regions (*bottom two photos*).

34-3 COGNITIVE DEVELOPMENT IN ADULTHOOD

Recall that for Piaget, each stage of cognitive development entails a way of thinking that is *qualitatively different* from the stage before. From Piaget's perspective, meaningful cognitive development ceases after the individual reaches the formal operational stage. Subsequent research has examined not qualitative differences in thinking over time, but the ebb and flow of cognitive abilities as a function of age. What kind of cognitive changes occur in adults?

Cognition in Early Adulthood

Just as physical abilities peak in early adulthood, intellectual skills are often considered to be at their peak during this time in life (Kitchener, King, & DeLuca, 2006). Some experts on cognitive development argue that the typical idealism of Piaget's formal operational stage is replaced in young adulthood by more realistic, pragmatic thinking (Labouvie-Vief, 1986). Gisela Labouvie-Vief (2006) proposed that the increasing complexity of cultures in the past century has generated a greater need for reflective, more complex thinking that takes into account the changing nature of knowledge and the kinds of challenges contemporary thinkers face. She emphasizes that key aspects of cognitive development for young adults include deciding on a particular worldview, recognizing that the worldview is subjective, and understanding that diverse worldviews should be acknowledged. In her perspective, considerable individual variation characterizes the thinking of young adults, with the highest level of thinking attained only by some.

Cognition in Middle Adulthood

What happens to cognitive skills in middle adulthood? Although some cross-sectional studies indicate that middle adulthood is a time of cognitive decline, longitudinal evidence presents a somewhat rosier picture. K. Warner Schaie is conducting an extensive longitudinal study of intellectual abilities in adulthood. Five hundred individuals initially were tested in 1956 and have been tested repeatedly over the years (Schaie, 1994, 2007, 2010, 2011). New waves of participants are added periodically. Schaie has measured a host of different cognitive abilities. As shown in Figure 34.3, the highest level of functioning for four of the six intellectual abilities occurred in middle adulthood (Schaie, 2006, 2010, 2011). Only two of the six abilities—numerical ability and perceptual speed—declined in middle age. Perceptual speed showed the earliest decline, beginning in early adulthood. Schaie found middle adulthood to be a time of peak performance for some aspects of both *crystallized intelligence* (vocabulary) and *fluid intelligence* (spatial

FIGURE 34.3 **Longitudinal Changes in Six Intellectual Abilities from Age 25 to Age 67** Some abilities show sharp declines with age. Others—such as vocabulary, reasoning, and perceptual speed—remain stable and high throughout late life.

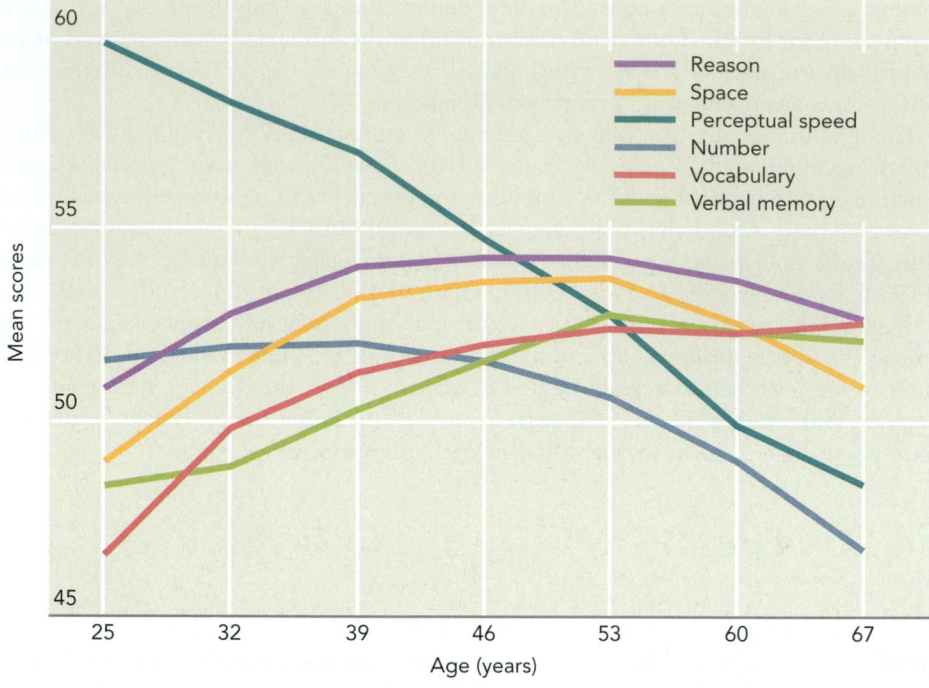

orientation and inductive reasoning). Based on the longitudinal data he has collected so far, Schaie (2006, 2007, 2010, 2011) concluded that middle adulthood, not early adulthood, is the period when many people reach their peak for a range of intellectual skills.

Cognition in Late Adulthood

Many contemporary psychologists conclude that as in middle adulthood, some dimensions of intelligence decline in late adulthood, whereas others are maintained or may even increase (Blair, 2011; Staudinger & Gluck, 2011). One of the most consistent findings is that when the speed of processing information is involved, older adults do more poorly than their younger counterparts (Figure 34.4). This decline in speed of processing is apparent in middle-aged adults and becomes more pronounced in older adults (Deary, Johnson, & Starr, 2010; Salthouse, 2009).

Older adults also tend to do more poorly than younger adults in most aspects of memory (Bialystok & Craik, 2011). In the area of memory involving knowledge of the world (for instance, the capital of Peru or the chemical formula for water), older adults usually take longer than younger adults to remember the information, but they often are able to remember it (Hoyer & Roodin, 2009). Further, in the important area of memory in which individuals manipulate and assemble information to solve problems and make decisions, decline occurs in older adults.

Some aspects of cognition might improve with age. One such area is **wisdom,** expert knowledge about the practical aspects of life (Staudinger & Gluck, 2011). Wisdom may increase with age because of the buildup of life experiences, but individual variations characterize people throughout their lives (Grossman & others, 2010). Thus, not every older person has wisdom, and some young people are wise beyond their years.

Do we all face the prospect of gradually becoming less competent intellectually? Not necessarily. Even for those aspects of cognitive aging that decline, older adults can improve their cognitive skills with training (Schaie, 2006, 2011; Willis & Schaie, 2005). Researchers have demonstrated that training older adults to use specific strategies can enhance their memory, and there is increasing evidence that physical fitness training sharpens the thinking skills of older adults (Etnier, 2009; Hillman, Erickson, & Kramer, 2008; La Rue, 2010; Park & Reuter-Lorenz, 2009). However, many experts conclude that older adults are less able to adapt than younger adults and thus are limited in how much they can improve their cognitive skills (Finch, 2009; Salthouse, 2009).

● **wisdom** Expert knowledge about the practical aspects of life.

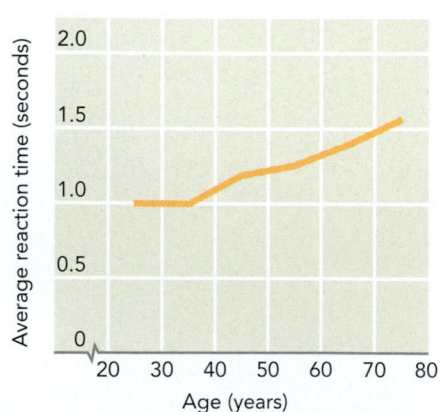

FIGURE 34.4 **The Relationship Between Age and Reaction Time** In one study, the average reaction time slowed in the 40s, and this decline accelerated in the 60s and 70s (Salthouse, 1994). The task used to assess reaction time required individuals to match numbers with symbols on a computer screen.

34-4 SOCIOEMOTIONAL DEVELOPMENT IN ADULTHOOD

In the physical and the cognitive domains, the developmental story is generally one of rapid growth during childhood, with continuing gains in adolescence, followed by steady decline with age. Does a similar pattern hold for socioemotional development? We now consider the changes that characterize adult socioemotional development, first returning to Erikson's stage theory of life-span development and then looking at what current research has to say.

Copyright by Mark Parisi, www.offthemark.com.

Socioemotional Development in Early Adulthood

According to Erikson (1968), during early adulthood, people face a developmental dilemma involving *intimacy versus isolation*. At this stage, individuals either form intimate relationships with others or become socially isolated. Erikson describes intimacy as both finding oneself and losing oneself in another person. If the young adult develops healthy friendships and an intimate relationship with a partner, intimacy will likely be achieved. One key way that a young adult achieves intimacy is through a long-term relationship with a romantic partner, often in the form of marriage.

Just as the notion of emerging adulthood would indicate, men and women have been waiting longer to marry in the last few decades. For example, in 2007, the median age for a first marriage in the United States climbed to just over 27.5 years for men and 25.6 years for women, compared to 20.8 for women and 23.2 for men in the 1970s (U.S. Bureau of the Census, 2008). This trend may be good news, because a woman's age at her first marriage is related to the ultimate survival of the marriage. As many as 59 percent of marriages in which the wife is less than 18 years old end in divorce within 15 years, compared to just 36 percent of marriages in which the woman is age 20 or older (Center for Family and Demographic Research, 2002).

What makes a marriage successful? John Gottman has been studying married couples' lives since the early 1970s (Gottman, 1994, 2006; Gottman, Gottman, & Declaire, 2006; Gottman & Silver, 1999). He interviewed couples, filmed them interacting with each other, and even took measures of their heart rate and blood pressure during their interactions. He also checked back with the couples every year to see how their marriages were faring. Gottman and his colleagues continue to follow married couples, as well as same-sex partners, to try to understand what makes relationships thrive. A significant issue, according to Gottman, is getting past the notion that love is a magical thing. From his perspective, love is a decision and a responsibility, and individuals have control over extramarital temptations (Gottman, Gottman, & Declaire, 2006).

Gottman (2006) has found these four principles at work in successful marriages:

- *Nurturing fondness and admiration:* Partners sing each other's praises. When couples put a positive spin on their talk with and about each other, the marriage tends to work.

- *Turning toward each other as friends:* Partners see each other as friends and turn toward each other for support in times of stress and difficulty.

- *Giving up some power:* Bad marriages often involve one partner who is a powermonger. Abuse of power is more common in husbands, but some wives have the problem as well.

- *Solving conflicts together:* Couples work to solve problems, regulate their emotion during times of conflict, and compromise to accommodate each other.

Socioemotional Development in Middle Adulthood

According to Erikson, following the resolution of intimacy versus isolation dilemma, the adult turns to concerns about *generativity versus stagnation* (see

"We only live once. Hop in."

Figure 32.10). *Generativity* means making a contribution to the next generation. The feeling that one has made a lasting and memorable contribution to the world is related to higher levels of psychological well-being (McAdams & others, 1997). One way in which individuals make a lasting contribution to the world is by having children and being positively involved in their development.

Research shows that engaged parenting may have benefits not only for children but also for parents. John Snarey (1993) followed fathers and their children for four decades. He found that children, especially girls, were better off if their fathers were actively engaged in their lives—especially with regard to athletic pursuits. In addition, and perhaps more importantly for fathers, those who were constructively engaged in childrearing were themselves better off in terms of marital satisfaction, life satisfaction, and even career success.

Socioemotional Development and Aging

From Erikson's perspective, the person who has entered the later years of life is engaged in looking back—evaluating his or her life and seeking meaning. Erikson called this stage of life *integrity versus despair*. Through this process of life review and reminiscence, the older adult comes to a sense of meaning or despair, Erikson theorized. The individual is also occupied with coming to terms with his or her own death, according to Erikson. If the individual had a strong sense of integrity, experiencing life as a meaningful and coherent whole, he or she faces the later years with a strong sense of meaning and low fear of death. In the absence of integrity, the older adult is filled with despair and fear.

Research on Adult Socioemotional Development

Current research on socioemotional development and aging reveals that Erikson was correct in his view that meaning is a central concern for older adults. However, he may have overlooked that this meaning derives not necessarily just from the past but also from the present. To understand the ways in which older adults maximize a sense of meaning in life, let's conclude our look at socioemotional development in adulthood by considering recent research findings about how adults' lives change socially and emotionally over time.

In terms of social relationships, older adults may become more selective about their social networks (Carstensen, 2006, 2008). This observation was first made decades ago, and it was interpreted as indicating that older adults, in preparation for death, were disengaging from social life (Cumming & Henry, 1961). Old age, according to the view of those earlier times, was characterized not as a stage of enjoying life, hobbies, and one's children and grandchildren but as a lonely period of disengagement from society and waiting to leave the earth. This older view stands in contrast to the perspectives that have emerged from various recent studies demonstrating that older adults are happier than their younger counterparts (Cornwell, Schumm, & Laumann, 2008; Mroczek, 2001; Mroczek & Kolarz, 1998; Ram & others, 2008) and that satisfaction with life increases with age, peaking at age 65 (Mroczek & Spiro, 2005).

Laura Carstensen developed *socioemotional selectivity theory* to address the narrowing of social contacts and the increase in positive emotion that occur with age (Carstensen, 2006; Charles & Carstensen, 2010). The theory states that because they recognize their limited time on earth, older adults tend to be selective in their social interactions, striving to maximize positive and meaningful experiences. Although younger adults may gain a sense of meaning in life from long-term goals and hopes for the future, older adults gain a sense of meaning by focusing on satisfying relationships and activities in the *present*. Unlike younger adults, who may be preoccupied with the future and stressing out over how they will accomplish their life goals, older adults may embrace the present moment with increasing vitality (Lachman & others, 2008). Socioemotional selectivity theory further posits that it is not old age itself that spurs people to focus on maximizing the positive meaning experienced in the present but, rather, limited time. Young adults who are asked to imagine having limited time (for instance, because they are about to go on a long trip) show the same pattern of maximizing time they spend with a narrow set of important friends and family members (Charles & Carstensen, 2010; Kurtz, 2008).

Research has found that with age, engagement in one's *present life* can be a vital source of meaning. The more active and involved older people are, the more satisfied they are and the more likely they are to stay healthy (Hendricks & Hatch, 2006). Researchers have found that older people who go to church, attend meetings, take trips, and exercise are happier than those who sit at home (George, 2006). In other words, the capacity to regulate emotions, maximizing positive experiences, appears to be a central feature of aging. Researchers have found that across diverse samples—Norwegians, Catholic nuns, African Americans, Chinese Americans, and Euro-Americans—older adults report better control of their emotions than younger adults (Carstensen & Charles, 2003).

Just as physical changes can influence socioemotional experience, socioemotional factors can influence physical health. One longitudinal study demonstrated that over time, women who avoided their problems (rather than confronting them) and who experienced low levels of positive emotion were more likely to show physical changes associated with diabetes (Tsenkova & others, 2008). Further, in one study, adults who had expressed positive attitudes about aging some 20 years previously, lived, on average, 7.5 years longer than those with more negative attitudes about aging (Levy, Slade, & Kasl, 2002). An important factor in the relationship between attitudes and longevity was a person's belief that life was full, hopeful, and worthwhile.

SUMMARY

Psychologists refer to the period between adolescence and adulthood as emerging adulthood. This period is characterized by the exploration of identity through work and relationships, instability, and self-focus.

Most adults reach their peak physical performance during their 20s and are healthiest then. Physical skills begin to decline during the 30s. The cellular-clock, free-radical, and hormonal stress theories are three important biological explanations for aging. Even in late adulthood, the brain has remarkable repair capacity and plasticity.

Piaget argued that no new cognitive changes occur in adulthood. However, some psychologists have proposed that the idealistic thinking of adolescents is replaced by the more realistic, pragmatic thinking of young adults. Longitudinal research on intelligence shows that many cognitive skills peak in middle age. Overall, older adults do not do as well on memory and other cognitive tasks and are slower to process information than younger adults. However, older adults may have greater wisdom than younger adults.

Erikson's three stages of socioemotional development in adulthood are intimacy versus isolation (early adulthood), generativity versus stagnation (middle adulthood), and integrity versus despair (late adulthood). A special concern, beginning when individuals are in their 50s, is the challenge of understanding life's meaning. Researchers have found that remaining active increases the likelihood that older adults will be happy and healthy. They also have found that older adults often reduce their general social affiliations and instead are motivated to spend more time with close friends and family members. Older adults also experience more positive emotion, are happier, and are more satisfied with their lives than younger adults.

Until recently, the positive dimensions of aging were largely ignored. Developmentalists now recognize that many adults can sustain or even improve their functioning as they age. Researchers today widely view adult development as a self-motivated process limited only by the individual's imagination.

KEY TERMS

emerging adulthood   336
wisdom   340

TEST YOURSELF

1. What are the five main features of emerging adulthood?

2. What is brain lateralization, and how might a decrease in lateralization in older adults play a role in the aging brain?

3. What do longitudinal studies indicate about intellectual abilities in middle adulthood?

APPLY YOUR KNOWLEDGE

1. Set aside 15 minutes to write a brief essay as follows. Think about your life in the future, when you are 70 or 80 years old. Imagine that everything has gone as well as it possibly could, and you have achieved your life dreams. What is your life like at this stage? What things about you are the same as they are for you now as a student of psychology? What things have changed? What is your best possible older adult self? How have aspects of your life today contributed to this happily-older-after?

2. You might have heard the statement that "40 is the new 30" or "50 is the new 40." What trend do these statements reflect? What might explain this trend? What might it mean for our understanding of adult development?

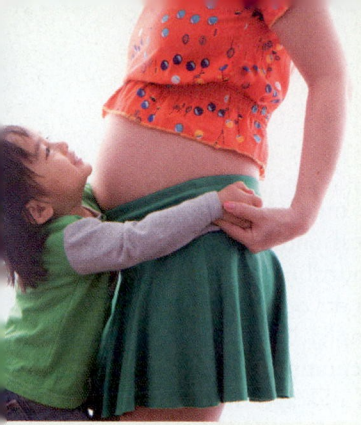

Human Development and Health and Wellness

It may be that adult development is especially important *because* it occurs in the context of some declines. Unlike childhood growth, adult growth is more likely to be a conscious process and therefore a truer mark of an individual's accomplishment (King & Hicks, 2007; Levenson & Crumpler, 1996). In this concluding section we will consider the active developer as he or she meets the challenges of adulthood. We will seek to answer the question, how do adults "grow themselves"?

COPING AND ADULT DEVELOPMENT

One way that adults develop is through coping with life's difficulties. Psychologist Carolyn Aldwin and her colleagues have suggested that stress and coping play a role in development (Aldwin, 2007; Aldwin, Levenson, & Kelly, 2009; Aldwin, Spiro, & Park, 2006; Aldwin, Yancura, & Boeninger, 2007; Boeninger & others, 2009). To understand how, consider that Piaget's ideas of assimilation and accommodation in childhood cognitive development may be applied to adult development as well (Block, 1982).

In assimilation, existing cognitive structures are used to make sense out of the current environment. Assimilation allows the person to enjoy a feeling of meaning because experiences fit into his or her preexisting schemas (King & Hicks, 2007). However, life does not always conform to our expectations. When our experience conflicts with our existing schemas, it is necessary to modify current ways of thinking. Accommodation is the process whereby existing schemas are modified or new structures are developed. Accommodation helps us to change so that we can make sense of life's previously incomprehensible events. When we encounter a negative life circumstance such as an illness or a loss, we have the opportunity to change—to develop and to mature (M. C. Davis & others, 2007). Indeed, research suggests that individuals who are faced with difficulties in life are more likely to come to a rich, complex view of themselves and the world (King & Hicks, 2007).

One of the negative events that people begin to experience in middle adulthood is death, especially the death of parents and older relatives. Also faced with less time in their own life, many individuals at this stage of life think more than before about what life is all about and what they want the rest of their life to be like. Austrian psychiatrist Victor Frankl confronted this issue personally and then shared his insights with the world. His mother, father, brother, and wife died in the concentration camps and gas chambers in Auschwitz, Poland. Frankl survived the camps and went on to write *Man's Search for Meaning* (1963/1984), in which he emphasized each person's uniqueness and the finite nature of life. Given the limited time we have to live, Frankl proposed that people actively ask themselves questions such as why they exist, what they want from life, and what their lives really mean.

LIFE THEMES AND LIFE-SPAN DEVELOPMENT

Frankl's ideas fit with the concept of a life theme. As we saw earlier, a life theme involves a person's efforts to cultivate meaningful optimal experiences (Csikszentmihalyi & Rathunde, 1998; Massimini & Delle Fave, 2000; Rathunde & Csikszentmihalyi,

Volunteering our time and talents and working with younger people can contribute to our well-being and life satisfaction as we age.

2006). Consider someone who has spent much of his or her adult life pursuing wealth and career success and who turns to more selfless pursuits in middle age. To contribute to the well-being of the next generation, the individual devotes more energy and resources to helping others—for example, by volunteering or working with young people. This reorientation can ease the individual into a positive and meaningful old age. Remaining actively engaged in life is an essential part of successful adulthood (Hillman, Erickson, & Kramer, 2008).

These motivations are demonstrated by numerous individuals who are using their successes for the betterment of the world. Among the celebrities who are exploring life themes, consider Bono, the lead singer of the rock group U2. Enriched by tremendous music sales and concert proceeds, the Grammy Award winner has spent the last few years lobbying political leaders on behalf of African nations beset with debt. More recently, he has been an advocate for DATA, a nonprofit organization dedicated to eradicating AIDS and poverty in Africa.

As children, our psychological development occurs in tandem with physical development. As we become strong and skilled enough to walk, the horizons of our world open up to new discoveries. In adulthood, we receive our developmental cues from ourselves—where do we go, once we have managed the many tasks that human beings face in childhood and adolescence? This section began by reminding you of the day of your birth, a day when you were the center of attention and a mystery waiting to unfold. From a developmental psychology perspective, today could be as important as that day. On the day you were born, you were full of possibilities—and you still are.

SUMMARY

Though often associated with childhood, psychological development can continue throughout life. Psychologists have suggested that coping with life's difficulties is one way in which adults may develop. For adults, taking an active approach to developing oneself may be an important motivator in development. Piaget's concepts of assimilation and accommodation have been applied to the process of developing through difficult times. An individual may experience meaning in life by applying his or her current understanding of the world (assimilation). In contrast, the individual may find that some experiences require a revision of that understanding (accommodation). In adulthood, people have the opportunity to pursue new goals that represent important life themes, such as leaving a legacy for the future.

TEST YOURSELF

1. How does Piaget's idea of assimilation apply to adult development?
2. How does accommodation, in Piaget's sense of the term, help adults to cope with life's difficulties?
3. What is involved when an individual pursues a life theme?

Motivation and Emotion

Climbing Unseen Mountains

In 1995, Erik Weihenmayer and his team were ascending Mount McKinley, the highest peak in North America. His wife and family arranged to fly over them in a plane. All the climbers in the team were dressed in red gear, and as they waved their ski poles madly at the plane overhead, Weihenmayer asked a friend, "Do you think they know which one is me?" His friend assured him that they probably did, because he was the only one waving in the wrong direction.

Erik Weihenmayer—an exceptional athlete, skier, and marathon runner—has been completely blind since age 13. He is also one of an elite group that has made it to the top of all the Seven Summits, including Mount Everest, which he climbed in 2001. Considering the obstacles Weihenmayer faces, we might ask why he did it. More pointedly, why did he *even imagine* doing it? For Weihenmayer, part of the motivation has been to inspire others to look beyond physical disabilities and to imagine the possibilities in every human circumstance. Although he has shattered stereotypes about what a blind person can accomplish, his tremendous efforts have also allowed him to stand on the peak of Everest as "just another climber."

When we ask "why," we are asking about motivation. The terms *motivation* and *emotion* come from the Latin word *movere,* which means "to move." Motivation and emotion are the "go" of human life, providing the steam that propels us to overcome obstacles and to accomplish the great and little things we do every day. Our emotions often define for us what we really want: We feel joy or sorrow depending on how events influence our most cherished life dreams. ●

Theories of Motivation and Approaches in Everyday Life

● **motivation** The force that moves people to behave, think, and feel the way they do.

Motivation is the force that moves people to behave, think, and feel the way they do. Motivated behavior is energized, directed, and sustained. Psychologists have proposed a variety of theories about why organisms are motivated to do what they do. Such theories include the evolutionary approach, drive reduction theory, and optimum arousal theory.

Psychologists have also investigated motivation in everyday life. Think about the wide range of human actions and achievements reported in the news, such as a man's donation of his kidney to a best friend and the appointment of a woman who grew up in poverty as the CEO of a major corporation. Such individuals' behaviors are not easily explained by motivational approaches that focus on physiological needs. Psychologists have begun to appreciate the role of the goals that people set for themselves in motivation (Mayer, 2011). To this end, we will also explore the ways that psychologists have come to understand the processes that underlie everyday human behavior.

35·1 THE EVOLUTIONARY APPROACH

In the early history of psychology, the evolutionary approach emphasized the role of instincts in motivation. *Ethology*—the study of animal behavior—also has described motivation from an evolutionary perspective.

● **instinct** An innate (unlearned) biological pattern of behavior that is assumed to be universal throughout a species.

An **instinct** is an innate (unlearned) biological pattern of behavior that is assumed to be universal throughout a species. Generally, an instinct is set in motion by a *sign stimulus*—something in the environment that turns on a fixed pattern of behavior. Instincts may explain a great deal of nonhuman animal behavior. In addition, some human behavior is instinctive. Recall, for example, the discussion of infant reflexes in Module 32. Babies do not have to learn to suck; they instinctively do it when something is placed in their mouth. So, for infants, an object touching the lips is a sign stimulus. After infancy, though, it is hard to think of specific behaviors that all human beings engage in when presented with a particular stimulus.

According to evolutionary psychologists, the motivations for sex, aggression, achievement, and other behaviors are rooted in our evolutionary past, and we can understand similarities among members of the human species through these shared evolutionary roots. Because evolutionary approaches emphasize the passing on of one's genes, these theories focus on domains of life that are especially relevant to reproduction. For example, evolutionary theorists note that in terms of romantic partners, across many cultures, men prefer younger women to older women, and women prefer men who have resources (Cosmides, 2011; Geary, 2010).

In general, however, most human behavior is far too complex to be explained on the basis of instinct. Indeed, it would hardly seem adaptive for humans to have a fixed action pattern that is invariably set in motion by a particular signal in the environment. To understand human behavior, psychologists have developed a variety of other approaches, as we now consider.

35·2 DRIVE REDUCTION THEORY

● **drive** An aroused state that occurs because of a physiological need.

Another way to think about motivation is through the constructs of drive and need. A **drive** is an aroused state that occurs because of a physiological need. You can think of a drive as a psychological itch that requires scratching. A **need** is a deprivation that

● **need** A deprivation that energizes the drive to eliminate or reduce the deprivation.

energizes the drive to eliminate or reduce the deprivation. Generally, psychologists think of needs as underlying our drives. You may have a need for water; the drive that accompanies that need is your feeling of being thirsty. Usually but not always, needs and drives are closely associated. For example, when your body needs food, your hunger drive will probably be aroused. An hour after you have eaten a hamburger, your body might still need essential nutrients (thus you need food), but your hunger drive might have subsided.

This example should reinforce the concept that drive pertains to a psychological state, whereas need involves a physiological one. Drives do not always follow from needs. For example, if you are deprived of oxygen because of a gas leak, you have a need for oxygen. You may feel lightheaded but may never realize that your condition is the result of a gas leak that is creating a need for air. That is, you might never experience the drive for oxygen that might lead you to open a window. Moreover, drives sometimes seem to come out of nowhere. Imagine having eaten a fine meal and feeling full to the point of not wanting another single bite—until the waiter wheels over the dessert cart. Suddenly you feel ready to tackle the Double Chocolate Oblivion, despite your lack of hunger.

Drive reduction theory explains that as a drive becomes stronger, we are motivated to reduce it. The goal of drive reduction is **homeostasis,** the body's tendency to maintain an equilibrium, or a steady state. Hundreds of biological states in the body must be maintained within a certain range; these include temperature, blood sugar level, potassium and sodium levels, and oxygenation. When you dive into an icy swimming pool, your body uses energy to maintain its normal temperature. When you walk out of an air-conditioned room into the heat of a summer day, your body releases excess heat by sweating. These physiological changes occur automatically to keep your body in an optimal state of functioning.

Most psychologists conclude that drive reduction theory does not provide a comprehensive framework for understanding motivation because people often behave in ways that increase rather than reduce a drive. For example, when dieting, you might choose to skip meals, but this tactic can increase your hunger drive rather than reduce it. Similarly, many other things that you might opt to do involve increasing (not decreasing) tensions—for example, taking a challenging course in school, raising a family, and working at a difficult job.

● **homeostasis** The body's tendency to maintain an equilibrium, or steady state.

● **Yerkes-Dodson law** The psychological principle stating that performance is best under conditions of moderate arousal rather than either low or high arousal.

● **overlearning** Learning to perform a task so well that it becomes automatic.

35·3 OPTIMUM AROUSAL THEORY

When psychologists talk about arousal, they are generally referring to a person's feelings of being alert and engaged. When we are very excited, our arousal levels are high. When we are bored, they are low. You have probably noticed that motivation influences arousal levels. Sometimes you can want something (for example, to do well on a test) so much that you can become overly motivated and anxious. On the other hand, you might be so unmotivated for a task (such as doing dishes) that you can hardly force yourself to complete it. Sometimes, to do well, you need to have an arousal level that is "just right" (Keeley, Zayac, & Correia, 2008).

Early in the twentieth century, two psychologists described how arousal can influence performance. According to their formulation, now known as the **Yerkes-Dodson law,** performance is best under conditions of moderate arousal rather than either low or high arousal. At the low end of arousal, you may be too lethargic to perform tasks well; at the high end, you may not be able to concentrate. To master the Yerkes-Dodson law, check out the Psychological Inquiry.

The relationship between arousal and performance is one reason that individuals in many professions are trained to overlearn important procedures. **Overlearning** means learning to perform a task so well that it becomes automatic. Recall Captain Chesley "Sully" Sullenberger, the pilot who landed the U.S. Airways plane safely in the Hudson

Performance under high-arousal conditions, such as those pilot Chesley Sullenberger faced when he had to land his damaged plane in the Hudson River, requires being trained to the point of overlearning.

psychological *inquiry*

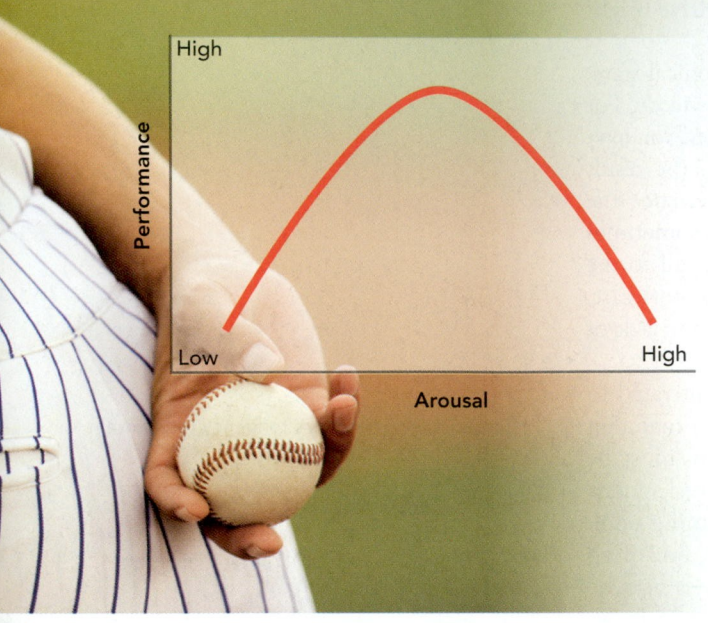

High

Performance

Low   **High**

Arousal

Obeying the (Yerkes-Dodson) Law

The graph displays the relationship between arousal (shown on the X, or horizontal, axis) and performance (shown on the Y, or vertical, axis). Note that the curve is in the form of an inverted *U*. Using the figure as a reference, answer the questions below.

1. What was your arousal level the last time you took an exam? If you were very nervous, your arousal level would be considered high. If you were excited and engaged but not too worried, it would be in the medium range. If you were feeling sluggish, your arousal level would be low.

2. How did you actually do on that test? Plot your performance on the graph. Does it fit with the Yerkes-Dodson prediction?

3. Now think about performance in sports or the arts. Imagine your favorite athlete, musician, or actor. How might that person feel when he or she is on the spot, trying to sink a winning free-throw, strike out the last batter, or impress an audience? How might arousal influence performance in those cases?

4. In many professions, individuals are forced to perform under conditions of very high arousal. These include EMTs, lifeguards, and emergency room medical professionals. (Name some others.) How might such individuals train themselves to perform even under conditions of extreme arousal?

River. For individuals who must perform at their best in a crisis, success depends on knowing what to do so well that it requires little or no thought. With this extra learning, when these individuals are under conditions of high arousal, they can rely on automatic pilot to do what needs to be done.

35·4 MASLOW'S HIERARCHY OF HUMAN NEEDS

● **hierarchy of needs** Maslow's theory that human needs must be satisfied in the following sequence: physiological needs, safety, love and belongingness, esteem, and self-actualization.

Humanistic theorist Abraham Maslow (1954, 1971) proposed a **hierarchy of needs** that must be satisfied in the following sequence: physiological needs, safety, love and belongingness, esteem, and self-actualization (Figure 35.1). The strongest needs are at the base of the hierarchy (physiological), and the weakest are at the top (self-actualization).

According to this hierarchy, people are motivated to satisfy their need for food first and to fulfill their need for safety before their need for love. If we think of our needs as calls for action, hunger and safety needs shout loudly, while the need for self-actualization beckons with a whisper. Maslow asserted that each lower need in the hierarchy comes from a deficiency—such as being hungry, afraid, or lonely—and that we can only see the higher-level needs in a person who is relatively satisfied in these most basic needs. Such an individual can then turn his or her attention to the fulfillment of a higher calling.

● **self-actualization** The motivation to develop one's full potential as a human being—the highest and most elusive of Maslow's proposed needs.

Self-actualization, the highest and most elusive of Maslow's needs, is the motivation to develop one's full potential as a human being. According to Maslow, self-actualization is possible only after the other needs in the hierarchy are met. Maslow cautions that most people stop moving up the hierarchy after they have developed a high level of esteem and thus do not become self-actualized.

The idea that human motives are hierarchically arranged is appealing; however, Maslow's ordering of the needs is debatable (Kenrick & others, 2010). Some people might seek greatness in a career to achieve self-esteem, while putting on hold their needs for love and belongingness. Certainly history is full of examples of individuals who, in the most difficult circumstances, were still able to engage in acts of kindness that seem to come from higher-level needs. Often, the poorest individuals are most likely to give generously to others.

Perhaps Maslow's greatest contribution to our understanding of motivation is that he asked the key question about motivation for modern people: How can we explain what humans do, once their bellies are full? That is, how do we explain the "why" of human behavior when survival is not the most pressing need? This is the kind of questioning that inspired *self-determination theory* (Deci & Ryan, 2002; Ryan & Deci, 2009).

35-5 SELF-DETERMINATION THEORY

Building from Maslow's humanistic perspective, Edward Deci and Richard Ryan have explored the role of motivation in optimal human functioning from a perspective that emphasizes particular kinds of needs as factors in psychological and physical well-being (Deci & Ryan, 2000; Ryan & Deci, 2009). Their **self-determination theory** asserts that there are three basic organismic needs: competence, relatedness, and autonomy. The word *organismic* here means that these psychological needs are innate and exist in every person. They are basic to human growth and functioning, just as water, soil, and sunshine are necessary for plant growth. This metaphor is especially apt, because once we plant a seed, all it requires to thrive and grow is a supportive environment. Similarly, self-determination theory holds that we all have the capacity for growth and fulfillment in us, ready to emerge if given the right context.

Importantly, from the perspective of self-determination theory, these organismic needs do not arise from deficits. Self-determination theory is not a drive reduction theory. Like Maslow, Deci and Ryan (2000) argue that these needs concern personal growth, not the filling of deficiencies. Let's examine each of these needs in depth.

The first organismic need described by self-determination theory, *competence,* is met when we feel that we are able to bring about desired outcomes (Reis & others, 2000). Competence motivation involves *self-efficacy* (the belief that you have the competence to accomplish a given goal or task) and *mastery* (the sense that you can gain skills and overcome obstacles). Competence is also related to expectancies for success. One domain in which competence needs may be met is in the realm of achievement. Some individuals are highly motivated to succeed and spend considerable effort striving to excel.

The second organismic need described by self-determination theory is *relatedness,* the need to engage in warm relations with other people. Some psychologists have proposed that the need to belong is the strongest human motivator (Baumeister & Leary, 2000). The need for relatedness is reflected in the importance of parents' nurturing children's development, the intimate moments of sharing private thoughts in friendship, the uncomfortable feelings we have when we are lonely, and the powerful attraction we have for someone else when we are in love.

The critical role of social bonds is also demonstrated in research examining the effects of being socially excluded (Hess & Pickett, 2010; K. D. Williams, 2007). When people are left out, they tend to engage in a variety of self-defeating behaviors, such as overeating and drinking to excess (Twenge, 2008). Research has shown that even when the exclusion is unintentional (for instance, when someone is ignored, though not purposely), it can lead to distress and the feeling that one's life is meaningless (K. D. Williams, 2007).

FIGURE 35.1 **Maslow's Hierarchy of Needs** Abraham Maslow developed the hierarchy of human needs to show that we have to satisfy basic physiological needs before we can satisfy other, higher needs.

● **self-determination theory** Deci and Ryan's theory asserting that all humans have three basic, innate organismic needs: competence, relatedness, and autonomy.

The third need proposed by self-determination theory is *autonomy*—the sense that we are in control of our own life. Autonomy means being independent and self-reliant, and it is a key aspect of feeling that one's behavior is self-motivated and emerging from genuine interest. Of course, many of the behaviors we engage in may feel like things we are forced to do, but a sense of autonomy is strongly related to well-being (Sheldon & others, 2005). Kennon Sheldon and colleagues (2005) have found that age relates to the experience of autonomy. For example, older Americans feel more autonomous than younger Americans when paying taxes, voting, and tipping.

Research on the role of motivation in well-being supports the idea that progress on goals that serve the three organismic needs is strongly related to well-being (Sheldon & Elliot, 1998). Further, valuing more extrinsic qualities—such as money, prestige, and physical appearance—over these organismic concerns is associated with lowered well-being, lowered self-actualization, and physical illness (Kasser & Ryan, 1996; Kasser & others, 2004).

Like any theory, self-determination theory has its controversies. One important issue is the extent to which the three needs are indeed universal. Cultures vary in how strongly they promote the needs for competence, relatedness, and autonomy. Many Western cultures—among them, the United States, Canada, and western European countries—are termed *individualistic* because they emphasize individual achievement, independence, and self-reliance. In contrast, many Eastern cultures—such as China, Japan, and Korea—are called *collectivistic* because they stress affiliation, cooperation, and interdependence (Triandis, 2000). However, cross-cultural evidence suggests that the needs emphasized by self-determination theory are likely to be valued in both Western and Eastern cultures (Sheldon & others, 2001).

Self-determination theory maintains that one of the most important aspects of healthy motivation is the sense that we do the things we do because we have freely chosen to do them. When we can choose our behaviors and feel ownership over those choices, we are likely to experience heightened fulfillment (Blumenfeld, Kempler, & Krajcik, 2006). When our behaviors follow from the needs for competence, autonomy, and relatedness, we experience intrinsic motivation. When our behavior serves needs for other values—such as prestige, money, or approval—our behavior is extrinsically motivated (Ryan & Deci, 2000, 2009). We examine this important distinction between intrinsic and extrinsic motivation next.

35·6 INTRINSIC VERSUS EXTRINSIC MOTIVATION

One way psychologists understand the "why" of our goals is by distinguishing between intrinsic and extrinsic motivation. **Intrinsic motivation** is based on internal factors such as organismic needs (competence, relatedness, and autonomy), as well as curiosity, challenge, and fun. When we are intrinsically motivated, we engage in a behavior because we enjoy it. **Extrinsic motivation** involves external incentives such as rewards and punishments. When we are extrinsically motivated, we engage in a behavior for some external payoff or to avoid an external punishment. Some students study hard because they are internally motivated to put forth considerable effort and achieve high quality in their work (intrinsic motivation). Other students study hard because they want to make good grades or avoid parental disapproval (extrinsic motivation).

Which type of motivation is related to superior performance—intrinsic or extrinsic? Do extrinsic rewards interfere with intrinsic motivation? We delve into these questions in the Critical Controversy.

Many very successful individuals are both intrinsically motivated (they have high personal standards of achievement and emphasize personal effort) and extrinsically motivated (they are strongly competitive) (Schunk, 2011). For the most part, however, psychologists believe that intrinsic motivation is the key to achievement (Blumenfeld, Kempler, & Krajcik, 2006), although elite athletes, such as members of Olympic teams, may be motivated by both intrinsic and extrinsic rewards (Ciani & Sheldon, 2010). Indeed, many of us might think of

● **intrinsic motivation** Motivation based on internal factors such as organismic needs (competence, relatedness, and autonomy), as well as curiosity, challenge, and fun.

● **extrinsic motivation** Motivation that involves external incentives such as rewards and punishments.

"Mr. Frimley, sir, can I have a word about the motivational artwork . . ."

© Clive Goddard. www.CartoonStock.com.

CRITICAL CONTROVERSY

Does Extrinsic Motivation Undermine Intrinsic Motivation?

Many psychologists believe that intrinsic motivation leads to more positive outcomes than extrinsic motivation (Blumenfeld, Kempler, & Krajcik, 2006; Patell, Cooper, & Robinson, 2008; Ryan & Deci, 2009). They argue that intrinsic motivation is more likely to produce competent behavior and mastery. Extrinsic motivation, in fact, is thought to reduce intrinsic motivation (Lepper, Greene, & Nisbett, 1973). A wide variety of social (extrinsic) events—such as deadlines, surveillance, and coercive rewards—can reduce the enjoyment (intrinsic motivation) associated with work, play, and study (Blumenfeld, Kempler, & Krajcik, 2006).

A decade ago, two reviews of studies on intrinsic and extrinsic motivation reached opposite conclusions (Cameron, Banko, & Pierce, 2001; Deci, Koestner, & Ryan, 1999). Edward Deci and his colleagues (1999) analyzed 128 studies and concluded that the main negative effect of external rewards was to restrict self-determination and interfere with intrinsic motivation. However, an analysis of 145 studies by Judy Cameron and her colleagues yielded mixed results (Cameron, Banko, & Pierce, 2001). Cameron's group found that extrinsic rewards sometimes produced the expected negative effects on intrinsic motivation but at other times had a positive effect or no effect at all. The truth, Cameron and her colleagues suggested, is that extrinsic motivation has no overall effect on intrinsic motivation.

Think back to Module 19, where we examined the role of rewards in operant conditioning. Rewarding a behavior should increase the likelihood that it will happen again, right? In fact, research on extrinsic rewards seems to indicate just the opposite: Rewarding a behavior will *reduce* the performance of that behavior, as well as the enjoyment associated with it. How can we make sense of this apparent contradiction? According to Cameron and her colleagues, a prime issue is *which behavior,* exactly, is rewarded (Cameron & Pierce, 2002; Cameron & others, 2005). When extrinsic rewards are given for the quality and creativity of a behavior, they actually enhance that behavior (Eisenberger & Aselage, 2009). Furthermore, when extrinsic rewards are provided for mastering skills, intrinsic motivation itself increases (Cameron & others, 2005).

In daily life, people often do things that are not intrinsically motivating, such as, perhaps, mowing the lawn and studying mathematics. Without external rewards, they may simply lose interest in performing those tasks. In such cases, extrinsic motivation may help foster intrinsic motivation. For example, a creative mathematics teacher might use rewards such as extra credit, math games, and verbal praise as a way to instill a lifelong love of mathematics. Similarly, if an employee is producing shoddy work, seems bored, or has a negative attitude, offering an external incentive may improve motivation. There are times, though, when external rewards can diminish intrinsic motivation. The problem with using a reward as an incentive is that individuals may perceive that the reward rather than their own motivation caused their achievement behavior.

A richer understanding of intrinsic and extrinsic motivation might allow for more accurate predictions of when extrinsic motivation will reduce, increase, or not affect intrinsic motivation. It might then be possible for employers and teachers to help employees and students develop the deep intrinsic motivation that most experts agree is indispensable to well-being.

WHAT DO YOU THINK?

- What are some instances in your own life in which your intrinsic motivation was *reduced* by external rewards? What are some instances in which your intrinsic motivation was *increased* by external rewards?

- What other factors might determine whether extrinsic motivation influences intrinsic motivation?

---

the ideal occupation as one in which we get paid (an extrinsic reward) for doing the very thing we love to do (intrinsic motivation).

35·7 SELF-REGULATION: THE SUCCESSFUL PURSUIT OF GOALS

Today many psychologists approach motivation in the way that you yourself might—by asking about goals and values and seeking to understand how these motivational forces shape behavior. Psychologists have referred to goals by various names, including *personal projects, best possible selves, life tasks,* and *personal strivings* (King, 2008). All of these terms reflect the goals a person is trying to accomplish in everyday life. Self-generated

INTERSECTION

Motivation and Cognition: How Do We Resist Temptation?

It is bound to happen. On Friday you commit to studying all weekend, and then a friend invites you to a party on Saturday night. You commit to losing those last 10 pounds, and without fail the Girl Scouts show up peddling their delicious cookies. Motivation is about committing to the pursuit of valued goals, but often it seems the world conspires against you, dangling temptation at every turn (Mischel & Ayduk, 2004). How do you stick with the program when daily life so often tries to derail you from steadfastly pursuing your goals?

One of the most important underlying problems in resisting temptation is *delay of gratification*—putting off a pleasurable experience in the interest of some larger but later reward. Successful delay of gratification is evident in the student who does not go out with friends but instead stays in and studies for an upcoming test, thinking, "There will be time to party after this test is over." Delay of gratification is challenging. Think about it—future payoffs are simply much less certain than current rewards.

Walter Mischel and his colleagues examined how children managed to delay gratification (Mischel, Cantor, & Feldman, 1996; Mischel & Moore, 1980). They placed children in a difficult situation—alone in a room with a very tempting cookie in their reach. The children were told that if they wanted to at any time, they could ring a bell and eat the cookie. Otherwise, they could wait until the experimenter returned, and then they would get two cookies. The children were then left alone to face this self-control dilemma. The researchers were interested in measuring how long the children could wait before giving in to temptation and eating the cookie.

There were a variety of responses to this unusual situation. Some children sat dead still, focused on the tempting cookie. Some smelled the cookie. Others turned away, sang songs, picked their noses, or did anything but pay attention to the cookie. How did the children who were able to resist temptation do it? Mischel and colleagues found that the kids who were able to distract themselves from the cookie by focusing on "cool thoughts" (that is, non-cookie-related things) were better able to delay gratification. In contrast, children who remained focused on the cookie and all its delightful qualities—what Mischel called "hot thoughts"—ate the cookie sooner (Metcalfe & Mischel, 1999).

What do these findings mean for self-control in your life? Imagine that you are in a long-term romantic relationship that you wish to continue, and you meet someone new to whom you are physically attracted. Should you cultivate a friendship with that person? Maybe not, if you want to avoid temptation and preserve your current relationship. Think about all the current and potential "cookies" in your life—those things that have the power to distract you from achieving your long-term plans. Mischel's research with children demonstrates that avoiding these hot issues might be a good way to see a long-term plan through to its completion.

> *What are some of the "cookies" in your life? How do you avoid being sidetracked by temptation?*

---

goals can range from trivial matters (such as letting a bad haircut grow out) to life tasks (such as becoming a good parent).

Goal approaches to motivation include the concept of self-regulation. **Self-regulation** is the process by which an organism effortfully controls behavior in order to pursue important objectives (Carver & Scheier, 2009a). A key aspect of self-regulation is getting feedback about how we are doing in our goal pursuits. Our daily mood has been proposed as a way that we may receive this feedback—that is, we feel good or bad depending on how we are doing in the areas of life we value. Note that the role of mood in self-regulation means that we cannot be happy all the time. In order to effectively pursue our goals, we have to be open to the bad news that might occasionally come our way (King, 2008).

Putting our personal goals into action is a potentially complex process that involves setting goals, planning for their implementation, and monitoring our progress.

● **self-regulation** The process by which an organism effortfully controls behavior in order to pursue important objectives.

Individuals' success improves when they set goals that are specific and moderately challenging (Bandura, 1997; Schunk, 2011). A fuzzy, nonspecific goal is "I want to be successful." A concrete, specific goal is "I want to have a 3.5 average at the end of the semester."

You can set both long-term and short-term goals. When you set long-term goals, such as "I want to be a clinical psychologist," make sure that you also create short-term goals as steps along the way, such as "I want to get an *A* on my next psychology test." Make commitments in manageable chunks. Planning how to reach a goal and monitoring progress toward the goal are critical aspects of achievement (Wigfield & others, 2006). Researchers have found that high-achieving individuals monitor their own learning and systematically evaluate their progress toward their goals more than low-achieving individuals (Schunk, 2011; Schunk, Pintrich, & Meece, 2008).

Even as we keep our nose to the grindstone in pursuing short-term goals, it is also important to have a sense of the big picture. Dedication to a long-term dream or personal mission can enhance the experience of purpose in life. *Purpose* is an intention to accomplish a goal that is meaningful to oneself and to contribute something to the world (Damon, 2008). Although short-term goals can provide a sense of accomplishment, attaching these goals to a future dream can allow individuals to experience a sense of meaning and to maintain their efforts in the face of short-term failure (Houser-Marko & Sheldon, 2008).

It can be difficult to recruit all of your willpower to pursue a goal you have consciously chosen. To learn more about the ways motivation and cognition relate to sticking with a goal, see the Intersection.

Copyright by Mark Parisi, www.offthemark.com.

SUMMARY

Motivated behavior is energized, directed, and sustained. Early evolutionary theorists considered motivation to be based on instinct—the innate biological pattern of behavior.

A drive is an aroused state that occurs because of a physiological need or deprivation. Drive reduction theory was proposed as an explanation of motivation, with the goal of drive reduction being homeostasis: the body's tendency to maintain equilibrium.

Optimum arousal theory focuses on the Yerkes-Dodson law, which states that performance is best under conditions of moderate rather than low or high arousal. Moderate arousal often serves us best, but there are times when low or high arousal is linked with better performance.

According to Maslow's hierarchy of needs, our main needs are satisfied in this sequence: physiological needs, safety, love and belongingness, esteem, and self-actualization. Maslow gave the most attention to self-actualization: the motivation to develop to one's full potential.

Self-determination theory states that intrinsic motivation occurs when individuals are engaged in the pursuit of organismic needs that are innate and universal. These needs include competence, relatedness, and autonomy. Intrinsic motivation is based on internal factors. Extrinsic motivation is based on external factors, such as rewards and punishments.

Self-regulation involves setting goals, monitoring progress, and making adjustments in behavior to attain desired outcomes. Research suggests that setting intermediate goals on the path toward a long-term goal is a good strategy.

KEY TERMS

motivation   350
instinct   350
drive   350
need   350
homeostasis   351
Yerkes-Dodson law   351
overlearning   351

hierarchy of needs   352
self-actualization   352
self-determination
    theory   353
intrinsic motivation   354
extrinsic motivation   354
self-regulation   356

TEST YOURSELF

1. What is motivation?

2. What are three theoretical approaches to motivation?

3. What is overlearning, and how can it help an individual who must perform at his or her best?

4. What is Maslow's theory of a hierarchy of needs? Explain.

5. What is self-actualization, according to Maslow, and on what does it depend?

6. How do intrinsic motivation and extrinsic motivation differ?

APPLY YOUR KNOWLEDGE

1. Ask your friends and your parents to define the word *motivation*. Compare your friends' and parents' definitions with the way psychologists define and approach motivation. What are the similarities? What are the differences? How do the definitions of your friends differ from those of your parents? Why do you think all of these variations exist?

2. To explore your own goals and sense of purpose, try the following activity. First list the top 5 or 10 goals that you are trying to accomplish in your everyday behavior. Then write your responses to the following questions that Damon used in his interviews (Damon, 2008, p. 135):

   • Do you have any long-term goals?
   • What does it mean to have a good life?
   • What does it mean to be a good person?
   • If you were looking back on your life now, how would you like to be remembered?

   Finally, consider: Are your everyday goals leading to the fulfillment of your long-term dream? How are you working in your everyday behavior to achieve your grander purposes?

Hunger, Obesity, and Eating Disorders

Part of the power of motivation in life is tied to physiological needs. We experience strong motivational forces, for example, when we are hungry or thirsty. Furthermore, the physiological state of being hungry has often been used as a path toward understanding a variety of human motivations. We might even use words about hunger in non-physiological contexts, such as when we say that someone is "craving" attention or "starving" for affection. In this section we examine the basic motivational processes underlying hunger and eating, including the related topic of eating disorders.

36·1 THE BIOLOGY OF HUNGER

You know you are hungry when your stomach growls and you feel those familiar hunger pangs. What role do such signals play in hunger?

Gastric Signals

In 1912, Walter Cannon and A. L. Washburn conducted an experiment that revealed a close association between stomach contractions and hunger (Figure 36.1). In one step of the procedure, a partially inflated balloon was passed through a tube inserted in Washburn's mouth and pushed down into his stomach. A machine that measures air pressure was connected to the balloon to monitor Washburn's stomach contractions. Every time Washburn reported hunger pangs, his stomach was also contracting. Sure enough, a growling stomach needs food. The stomach tells the brain not only how full it is but also how much nutrient is present, which is why rich food stops hunger faster than the same amount of water. The hormone cholecystokinin (CCK) helps start the digestion of food, travels to the brain through the bloodstream, and signals us to stop eating (Nefti & others, 2009). Hunger involves a lot more than an empty stomach, however.

Blood Chemistry

Three key chemical substances play a role in hunger, eating, and *satiety* (the state of feeling full): glucose, insulin, and leptin.

Glucose (blood sugar) is an important factor in hunger, probably because the brain critically depends on sugar for energy. One set of sugar receptors, located in the brain itself, triggers hunger when sugar levels fall too low. Another set of sugar receptors is in the liver, which stores excess sugar and releases it into the blood when needed. The sugar receptors in the liver signal the brain when its sugar supply falls, and this signal also can make you hungry.

The hormone *insulin* also plays a role in glucose control (Dominquez Coello & others, 2010; Oliver & others, 2009). When we eat complex carbohydrates such as bread and pasta, insulin levels go up and fall off gradually. When we consume simple sugars such as candy, insulin levels rise and then fall sharply—the

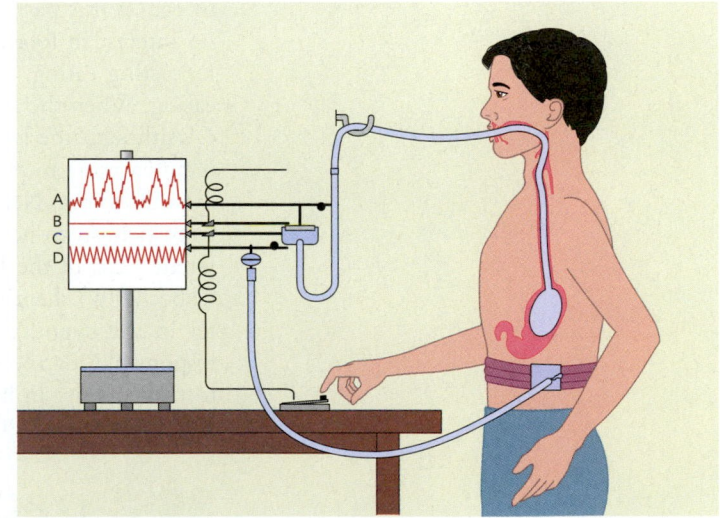

FIGURE 36.1 **Cannon and Washburn's Classic Experiment on Hunger** In this experiment, the researchers demonstrated that stomach contractions, which were detected by the stomach balloon, accompany a person's hunger feelings, which were indicated by pressing the key. Line A in the chart records increases and decreases in the volume of the balloon in the participant's stomach. Line B records the passage of time. Line C records the participant's manual signals of feelings of hunger. Line D records a reading from the belt around the participant's waist to detect movements of the abdominal wall and ensure that such movements are not the cause of changes in stomach volume.

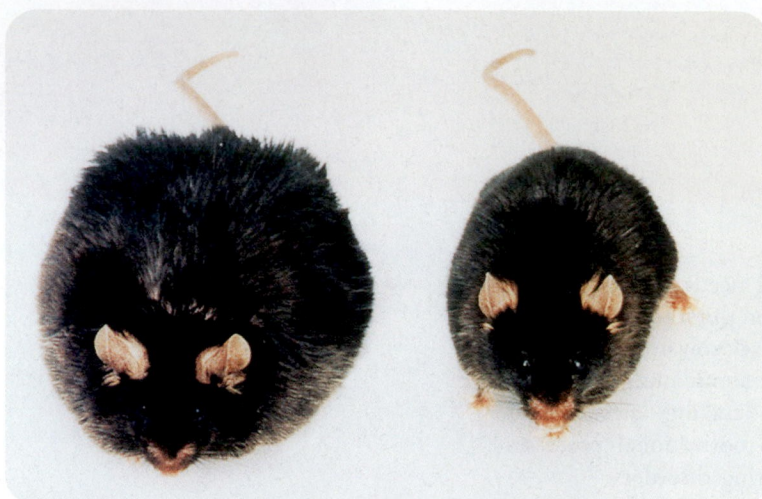

FIGURE 36.2 **Leptin and Obesity** The ob mouse on the left is untreated; the one on the right has been given injections of leptin.

all-too-familiar "sugar low" (Rodin, 1984). Blood glucose levels are affected by complex carbohydrates and simple sugars in similar ways, so we are more likely to eat within the next several hours after eating simple sugars than after eating complex carbohydrates.

Released by fat cells, the chemical substance *leptin* (from the Greek word *leptos*, meaning "thin") decreases food intake and increases energy expenditure or metabolism (Bluher & Mantzoros, 2009; Kaiyala & others, 2010). Leptin's functions were discovered in a strain of genetically obese mice, called *ob mice* (Pelleymounter & others, 1995). Because of a genetic mutation, the fat cells of ob mice cannot produce leptin. The ob mouse has a low metabolism, overeats, and gets extremely fat. Leptin appears to act as an anti-obesity hormone (Friedman, 2009; Kovalszky & others, 2010). If ob mice are given daily injections of leptin, their metabolic rate increases, and they become more active, eat less, and lose weight. Figure 36.2 shows an untreated ob mouse and an ob mouse that has received injections of leptin.

In humans, leptin concentrations have been linked with weight, body fat, and weight loss in response to dieting (Lee & Fried, 2009). Scientists continue to explore the possibility that disorders in the production and uptake of leptin may explain human obesity (Adam, 2010).

Brain Processes

The hypothalamus, a small forebrain structure, regulates important body functions, including hunger. More specifically, activity in two areas of the hypothalamus contributes to our understanding of hunger. The *lateral hypothalamus* is involved in stimulating eating. When this area is electrically stimulated in a well-fed animal, the animal begins to eat. If this part of the hypothalamus is destroyed, even a starving animal will show no interest in food. The *ventromedial hypothalamus* is involved in reducing hunger and restricting eating. When this area of an animal's brain is stimulated, the animal stops eating. When the area is destroyed, the animal eats profusely and quickly becomes obese.

Although the lateral and ventromedial hypothalamuses both influence hunger, there is much more to the brain's role in determining hunger than these on/off centers in the hypothalamus. Neurotransmitters (the chemical messengers that convey information from neuron to neuron) and neural circuits (clusters of neurons that often involve different parts of the brain) also function in hunger (Fulton, 2010; Minor, Chang, & de Cabo, 2009). Leptin influences eating by inhibiting the production of a neurotransmitter in the hypothalamus that induces eating. The neurotransmitter serotonin is partly responsible for the satiating effect of CCK, and serotonin antagonists have been used to treat obesity in humans (Garfield & Heisler, 2009; Rodgers, Holch, & Tallett, 2010; Zhang & others, 2010).

36·2 OBESITY

Given that the brain and body are so elegantly wired to regulate eating behavior, why do so many people in the United States overeat and suffer the effects of this behavior? According to the Centers for Disease Control and Prevention (CDC), 60 percent of Americans are overweight, and one-third are considered obese (dangerously overweight) (CDC, 2009a). Being obese or overweight raises one's risk for a variety of health problems, such as cardiovascular disease, diabetes, and depression (Shelton & Miller, 2010; Vega, Barlow, & Grundy, 2010). Currently, the number of people considered overweight around the world is 20 percent higher than the number suffering from hunger.

The reason so many people overeat to the point of becoming obese is a motivational puzzle, because it involves eating when one is not in need of nutrition. As is the case with much behavior, in eating, biological, cognitive, and sociocultural factors interact in diverse ways in different individuals, making it difficult to point to a specific cause (Adler & Stewart, 2009).

The Biology of Obesity

Obesity clearly has a genetic component. After the discovery of an ob gene in mice, researchers found a similar gene in humans. Some individuals do inherit a tendency to be overweight (Keller & Attie, 2010). Only 10 percent of children who do not have obese parents become obese themselves, whereas 40 percent of children who have one obese parent become obese, and 70 percent of children who have two obese parents become obese. Identical human twins have similar weights, even when they are reared apart (Maes, Neal, & Eaves, 1997).

Another factor in weight is **set point,** the weight maintained when the individual makes no effort to gain or lose weight. Set point is determined in part by the amount of stored fat in the body (Levin, 2010). Fat is stored in *adipose cells,* or fat cells. When these cells are filled, you do not get hungry. When people gain weight—because of genetic predisposition, childhood eating patterns, or adult overeating—their fat cell number increases, and they might not be able to get rid of extra ones. A normal-weight individual has 10 to 20 billion fat cells. An obese individual can have up to 100 billion fat cells (Fried, 2008). Consequently, an obese individual has to eat more to feel satisfied.

● **set point** The weight maintained when the individual makes no effort to gain or lose weight.

Psychological Factors in Hunger and Obesity

Psychologists used to think that obesity stemmed from factors such as unhappiness and external food cues. These ideas make some sense; drowning one's sorrows in chocolate or eating some cookies just because they are there seems common enough to explain overeating. However, a number of factors are more important than emotional state and external stimuli (Rodin, 1984).

Time and place affect our eating. Learned associations of food with a particular place and time are characteristic of many organisms (Fiese, Foley, & Spagnola, 2006). If it is noon, we are likely to feel hungry even if we ate a big breakfast. We also associate eating with certain places. Many people link watching television with eating and feel uncomfortable if they are not eating something while watching TV.

From an evolutionary framework, we might note that human taste preferences developed at a time when reliable food sources were scarce. Our earliest ancestors probably developed a preference for sweets and fatty foods because ripe fruit, a concentrated source of sugar (and calories), was accessible and because high-fat foods carried much-needed calories. Today many people still have a taste for such foods, but unlike our ancestors' ripe fruit (containing sugar *plus* vitamins and minerals), the soft drinks and candy bars we snack on fill us with nutrient-free calories. Furthermore, in modern life we rarely require the calorie counts that our ancestors needed to survive.

Dieting is a continuing U.S. obsession. In Module 67, we will consider ways that individuals can successfully lose weight. However, some people who focus on losing weight do so not for reasons of good health but because they have eating disorders, our next topic.

© Piero Tonin. www.CartoonStock.com.

36-3 DISORDERED EATING

Many Americans feel that life would improve greatly if they could just lose those last 5 pounds. However, for some people, concerns about weight and body image become a serious, debilitating disorder (Miller & Golden, 2010; Treasure, Claudino, & Zucker, 2010). For such individuals, the very act of eating, an activity essential for survival, becomes

an arena where a variety of complex biological, psychological, and cultural issues are played out, often with tragic consequences.

A number of famous people have coped with eating disorders, including Princess Diana, Paula Abdul, Mary-Kate Olsen, and Kelly Clarkson. Eating disorders are characterized by extreme disturbances in eating behavior—from eating very, very little to eating a great deal. In this section we examine three eating disorders—anorexia nervosa, bulimia nervosa, and binge eating disorder.

Anorexia Nervosa

Anorexia nervosa is an eating disorder that involves the relentless pursuit of thinness through starvation. Anorexia nervosa is much more common in girls and women than boys and men and affects between 0.5 and 3.7 percent of young women (NIMH, 2009). The American Psychiatric Association (2005) lists these main characteristics of anorexia nervosa:

- Weight less than 85 percent of what is considered normal for age and height and refusing to maintain weight at a healthy level.

- An intense fear of gaining weight that does not decrease with weight loss.

- A distorted body image (Costa, Vasconcelos, & Peres, 2010). Even when individuals with anorexia nervosa are extremely thin, they never think they are thin enough. They weigh themselves frequently, take their body measurements often, and gaze critically at themselves in mirrors.

- Amenorrhea (lack of menstruation) in girls who have reached puberty.

● **anorexia nervosa** Eating disorder that involves the relentless pursuit of thinness through starvation.

Over time, anorexia nervosa can lead to physical changes, such as the growth of fine hair all over the body, thinning of bones and hair, severe constipation, and low blood pressure (NIMH, 2009). Dangerous and even life-threatening complications of anorexia nervosa include damage to the heart and thyroid. Anorexia nervosa is said to have the highest mortality rate (about 5.6 percent of individuals with anorexia nervosa die within 10 years of diagnosis) of any psychological disorder (Hoek, 2006; NIMH, 2009).

Anorexia nervosa typically begins in the teenage years, often following an episode of dieting and some type of life stress (Lo Sauro & others, 2008; Sigel, 2008). Most individuals with anorexia nervosa are non-Latino White female adolescents or young adults from well-educated middle- and upper-income families. They are often high-achieving perfectionists (Forbush, Heatherton, & Keel, 2007). In addition to perfectionism, obsessive thinking about weight and compulsive exercise are related to anorexia nervosa (Finzi-Dottan & Zubery, 2009).

Bulimia Nervosa

● **bulimia nervosa** Eating disorder in which an individual (typically female) consistently follows a binge-and-purge eating pattern.

Bulimia nervosa is an eating disorder in which an individual (typically female) consistently follows a binge-and-purge eating pattern. The individual goes on an eating binge and then purges by self-induced vomiting or the use of laxatives. Most people with bulimia nervosa are preoccupied with food, have a strong fear of becoming overweight, and are depressed or anxious (Speranza & others, 2003). Because bulimia nervosa occurs within a normal weight range, the disorder is often difficult to detect (Mizes & Miller, 2000). A person with bulimia nervosa usually keeps the disorder a secret and experiences a great deal of disgust and shame.

Bulimia nervosa can lead to complications such as a chronic sore throat, kidney problems, dehydration, and gastrointestinal disorders (NIMH, 2009). The disorder is also related to dental problems, as persistent exposure to the stomach acids in vomit can wear away tooth enamel.

Bulimia nervosa typically begins in late adolescence or early adulthood (Levine, 2002). The disorder affects between 1 and 4 percent of young women (NIMH, 2008). Like those with anorexia nervosa, many young women who develop bulimia nervosa are highly perfectionistic (Forbush, Heatherton, & Keel, 2007). At the same time, they tend to have low levels of self-efficacy (Bardone-Cone & others, 2006). In other words, these are young women with very high standards but very low confidence that they can achieve their goals. Impulsivity, negative emotion, and childhood obsessive-compulsive disorder are also related to bulimia (Tchanturia & others, 2004; Vervaet, van Heeringen, & Audenaert, 2004). Bulimia nervosa is associated, too, with a high incidence of sexual and physical abuse in childhood (Lo Sauro & others, 2008).

Anorexia Nervosa and Bulimia Nervosa: Causes and Treatments

What is the etiology (cause) of anorexia nervosa and bulimia nervosa? For many years researchers thought that sociocultural factors, such as media images of very thin women and family pressures, were the central determinant of these disorders (le Grange & others, 2010). Certainly the U.S. popular media bombard their audiences with images of extremely thin women. Media images that glorify extreme thinness can influence women's body image, and emphasis on the thin ideal is related to anorexia nervosa and bulimia nervosa (Harrison & Hefner, 2006; Stice & others, 2007; Treasure, Claudino, & Zucker, 2010).

Uruguayan model Eliana Ramos posed for the camera in her native country. Tragically, the super-thin Eliana died at age 18 in February 2007, two years after this picture was taken, reportedly from health problems associated with anorexia nervosa.

However, as powerful as these media messages might be, countless females are exposed to media images of unrealistically thin women, but relatively few develop eating disorders. Many young women embark on diets, but comparatively few of them develop eating disorders. Thus, since the 1980s, researchers have moved beyond a sole focus on sociocultural factors and have increasingly probed the potential biological underpinnings of these disorders. This research has examined the interplay of social and biological factors in eating disorders.

Genes play a substantial role in both anorexia nervosa and bulimia nervosa (Calati & others, 2010; Sokol & others, 2009). In fact, genes influence many psychological characteristics (for example, perfectionism, impulsivity, obsessive-compulsive tendencies, and thinness drive) and behaviors (restrained eating, binge eating, self-induced vomiting) that are associated with anorexia nervosa and bulimia nervosa (Bulik & others, 2000; Mikolajczyk, Grzywacz, & Samochowiec, 2010; Schur, Heckbert, & Goldberg, 2010). These genes are also factors in the regulation of serotonin, and problems in regulating serotonin are related to both anorexia nervosa and bulimia nervosa (Capasso, Putrella, & Milano, 2009).

Keep in mind that even as biological factors play a role in the emergence of eating disorders, eating disorders themselves affect the body, including the brain. Most psychologists believe that while social factors and experiences may play a role in triggering dieting, the physical effects of dieting, bingeing, and purging may change the neural networks that then sustain the disordered pattern, in a kind of vicious cycle (Kaye, 2008; le Grange & others, 2010; Treasure, Claudino, & Zucker, 2010).

Although anorexia and bulimia nervosa are serious disorders, recovery is possible (Treasure, Claudino, & Zucker, 2010; van Son & others, 2010). Anorexia nervosa may require hospitalization. The first target of intervention is promoting weight gain, in extreme cases through the use of a feeding tube. A common obstacle in the treatment of anorexia nervosa is that individuals with the disorder deny that anything is wrong. They maintain their belief that thinness and restrictive dieting are correct and not a sign of mental illness (Wilson, Grilo, & Vitousek, 2007). Still, drug therapies and psychotherapy have been shown to be effective in treating anorexia nervosa, as well as bulimia nervosa (Thompson-Brenner, Boisseau, & Satir, 2010).

Binge Eating Disorder

● **binge eating disorder (BED)** Eating disorder characterized by recurrent episodes of consuming large amounts of food during which the person feels a lack of control over eating.

Binge eating disorder (BED) is characterized by recurrent episodes of consuming large amounts of food during which the person feels a lack of control over eating (NIMH, 2009; Striegel-Moore & Franko, 2008). Unlike an individual with bulimia nervosa, someone with BED does not try to purge. Most individuals with BED are overweight or obese.

Individuals with BED often eat quickly, eat a great deal when they are not hungry, and eat until they are uncomfortably full. They frequently eat alone because of embarrassment or guilt, and they experience disgust and shame after overeating. BED is the most common of all eating disorders—affecting men, women, and ethnic groups within the United States more similarly than anorexia nervosa or bulimia nervosa (Azarbad & others, 2010; Striegel-Moore & Franko, 2008). An estimated 2 to 5 percent of Americans will suffer from BED in their lifetime (NIMH, 2009).

BED is thought to characterize approximately 8 percent of individuals who are obese. Unlike obese individuals who do not suffer from BED, binge eaters are more likely to place great value on their physical appearance, weight, and body shape (Grilo, Masheb, & White, 2010). The complications of BED are those of obesity more generally, including diabetes, hypertension, and cardiovascular disease.

Unlike individuals with anorexia nervosa or bulimia nervosa, most people with binge eating disorder (BED) are overweight or obese.

Binge Eating Disorder: Causes and Treatments

Researchers are examining the role of biological and psychological factors in BED. Genes play a role (Akkermann & others, 2010), as does dopamine, the neurotransmitter related to reward pathways in the brain (C. Davis & others, 2010). The fact that binge eating often occurs after stressful events suggests that binge eaters use food as a way to regulate their emotions (Wilson, Grilo, & Vitousek, 2007). The areas of the brain and endocrine system that respond to stress are overactive in individuals with BED (Lo Sauro & others, 2008), and this overactivity leads to high levels of circulating cortisol, the hormone most associated with stress. Individuals with BED may be more likely to perceive events as stressful and then seek to manage that stress by binge eating.

Just as treatment for anorexia nervosa focuses on weight gain first, some believe that treatment for BED should focus on weight loss first (De Angelis, 2002). Others argue that individuals with BED must be treated for disordered eating per se, and insist that if the underlying psychological issues are not addressed, weight loss will not be successful or permanent (de Zwaan & others, 2005; Hay & others, 2009).

SUMMARY

Stomach signals are one factor in hunger. Glucose (blood sugar) and insulin both play an important role in hunger. Glucose is needed for the brain to function, and low levels of glucose increase hunger. Insulin can cause a rise in hunger.

Leptin, a protein secreted by fat cells, decreases food intake and increases energy expenditure. The hypothalamus plays an important role in regulating hunger. The lateral hypothalamus is involved in stimulating eating; the ventromedial hypothalamus, in restricting eating.

Obesity is a serious problem in the United States. Heredity, basal metabolism, set point, and fat cells are biological factors involved in obesity. Time and place affect eating. Our early ancestors ate fruits to satisfy nutritional needs, but today we fill up on the empty calories in sweets.

Three eating disorders are anorexia nervosa, bulimia nervosa, and binge eating disorder. Anorexia nervosa is characterized by extreme underweight

KEY TERMS

and starvation. Anorexia nervosa is related to perfectionism and obsessive-compulsive tendencies. Bulimia nervosa involves a pattern of binge eating followed by purging through self-induced vomiting or laxatives. Binge eating disorder involves binge eating without purging.

Anorexia nervosa and bulimia nervosa are much more common in women than men, but there is no gender difference in binge eating disorder. Although sociocultural factors were once thought to be primary in explaining eating disorders, more recent evidence points to the role of biological factors.

TEST YOURSELF

1. In Cannon and Washburn's classic study on hunger, what bodily associations were revealed?

2. What is leptin, and how does it function in the body?

3. What are some key ways that bulimia nervosa and binge eating disorder differ?

APPLY YOUR KNOWLEDGE

1. Choose four friends—two male and two female—and ask them the following questions: "When you are upset, do you eat? What do you eat? Do these foods bring you comfort?" Did your male and female friends answer the questions the same way? Explain your answers using what you've learned about the role food plays in emotional experiences.

2. Identify eating behaviors that are typically American. Now pick a country or culture you are not familiar with and research the role food and eating play in that culture. Compare and contrast the two eating cultures. How do your own eating behaviors compare with both of these?

Emotion

Motivation and emotion are closely linked. We can feel happy or sad depending on how events influence the likelihood of our getting the things we want in life. Sometimes our emotions take us by surprise and give us a reality check about what we really want. We might think, for example, that we have lost interest in our romantic partner until that person initiates a breakup. Suddenly, we realize how much the partner really means to us and to our happiness.

Anyone who has watched an awards show on television surely knows the link between motivation and emotion. Strolling in on the red carpet, the celebrities stress how honored they are to be nominated; but behind the Hollywood smiles is the longing to win. When the announcement is made, "And the Oscar goes to . . . ," the cameras zoom in to catch a glimpse of real emotion: the winner's face lighting up with joy and, of course, the moment of disappointment for the others.

Emotions are certainly complex. The body, the mind, and the face play key roles in emotion, although psychologists debate which of these components is most significant in emotion and how they mix to produce emotional experiences (Davidson, Scherer, & Goldsmith, 2002; Werner & Gross, 2010). For our purposes, **emotion** is feeling, or affect, that can involve physiological arousal (such as a fast heartbeat), conscious experience (thinking about being in love with someone), and behavioral expression (a smile or grimace).

● **emotion** Feeling, or affect, that can involve physiological arousal (such as a fast heartbeat), conscious experience (thinking about being in love with someone), and behavioral expression (a smile or grimace).

37-1 BIOLOGICAL FACTORS IN EMOTION

A friend whom you have been counseling about a life problem calls you to say, "We need to talk." As the time of your friend's visit approaches, you get nervous. What could be going on? You feel burdened—you have a lot of work to do, and you do not have time for a talk session. You also worry that she is angry or disappointed about something you have done. When she arrives with a gift-wrapped package and a big smile, your nerves give way to relief. She announces, "I wanted to give you this present to say thanks for all your help over the last few weeks." Your heart warms, and you feel a strong sense of your enduring bond with her. As you moved through the emotions of worry, relief, and joy, your body changed. Indeed, the body is a crucial part of our emotional experience.

Arousal

Recall that the *autonomic nervous system* (ANS) takes messages to and from the body's internal organs, monitoring such processes as breathing, heart rate, and digestion. The ANS is divided into the sympathetic and the parasympathetic nervous systems (Figure 37.1). The *sympathetic nervous system* (SNS) is involved in the body's arousal; it is responsible for a rapid reaction to a stressor, sometimes referred to as the "fight or flight" response. The SNS immediately causes an increase in blood pressure, a faster heart rate, more rapid breathing for greater oxygen intake, and more efficient blood flow to the brain and major muscle groups. All of these changes prepare us for action. At the same time, the body stops digesting food, because it is not necessary for immediate action (which could explain why just before an exam, students usually are not hungry).

The *parasympathetic nervous system* (PNS) calms the body. Whereas the sympathetic nervous system prepares the individual for fighting or running away, the parasympathetic

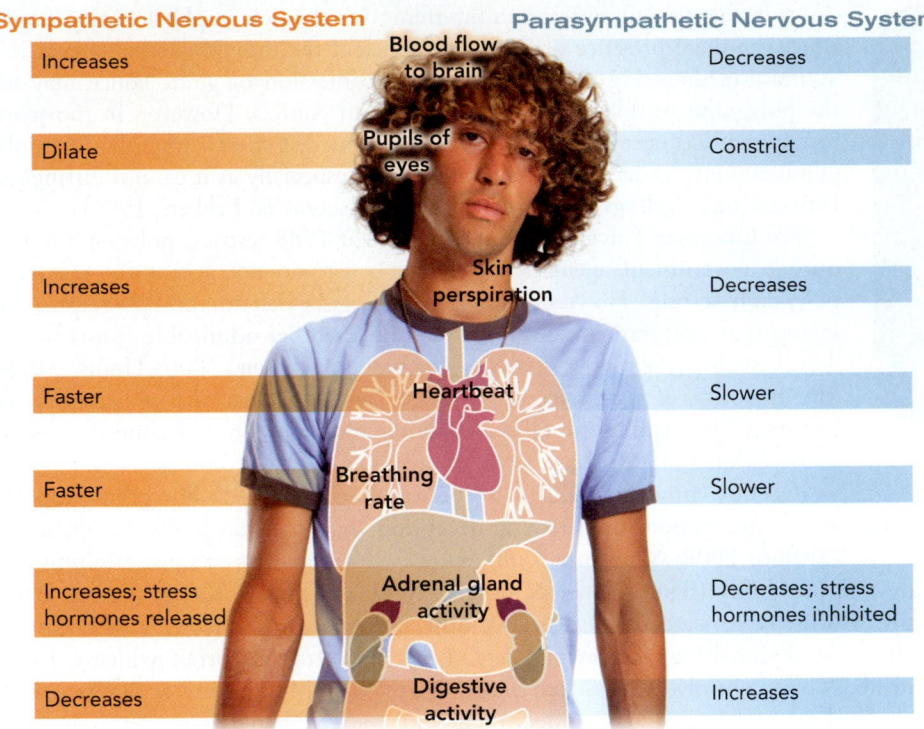

Sympathetic Nervous System		Parasympathetic Nervous System
Increases	Blood flow to brain	Decreases
Dilate	Pupils of eyes	Constrict
Increases	Skin perspiration	Decreases
Faster	Heartbeat	Slower
Faster	Breathing rate	Slower
Increases; stress hormones released	Adrenal gland activity	Decreases; stress hormones inhibited
Decreases	Digestive activity	Increases

FIGURE 37.1 **The Autonomic Nervous System and Its Role in Arousing and Calming the Body** The two parts of the autonomic nervous system work in different ways. The sympathetic nervous system arouses the body in reaction to a stressor, evoking the "fight or flight" response. In contrast, the parasympathetic nervous system calms the body, promoting relaxation and healing.

nervous system promotes relaxation and healing. When the PNS is activated, heart rate and blood pressure drop, stomach activity and food digestion increase, and breathing slows down.

The sympathetic and parasympathetic nervous systems evolved to improve the human species' likelihood for survival, but it does not take a life-threatening situation to activate them. Emotions such as anger and fear are associated with elevated SNS activity as exemplified in heightened blood pressure and heart rate. States of happiness and contentment also activate the SNS to a lesser extent.

Measuring Arousal

Because arousal includes a physiological response, researchers have been intrigued by how to measure it accurately. One aspect of emotional arousal is *skin conductance level* (SCL) response, a rise in the skin's electrical conductivity when sweat gland activity increases. A sweaty palm conducts electricity better than a dry palm, and this difference provides the basis for SCL, which produces an index of arousal that has been used in many studies of emotion.

Another measure of arousal is the **polygraph** or lie detector, a machine examiners use to try to determine whether someone is lying. The polygraph monitors changes in the body—heart rate, breathing, and SCL—thought to be influenced by emotional states. In a typical polygraph test, the examiner asks the individual a number of neutral questions and several key, less neutral questions. If the individual's heart rate, breathing, and SCL responses increase substantially when the key questions are asked, the individual is assumed to be lying. Lying also has been linked with certain emotional facial expressions (Porter & ten Brinke, 2008; Warren, Schertler, & Bull, 2009).

How accurate is the lie detector? Although it measures the degree of arousal to a series of questions, no one has found a unique physiological response to telling lies (Lykken, 1987, 2001; Seymour & others, 2000). Heart rate and breathing can increase for reasons other than lying, and this effect can make it difficult to interpret the physiological indicators of arousal.

Accurately identifying truth or deception is linked with the skill of the examiner and the skill of the individual being examined. Body movements and the presence of certain

● **polygraph** A machine, commonly called a lie detector, that monitors changes in the body, used to try to determine whether someone is lying.

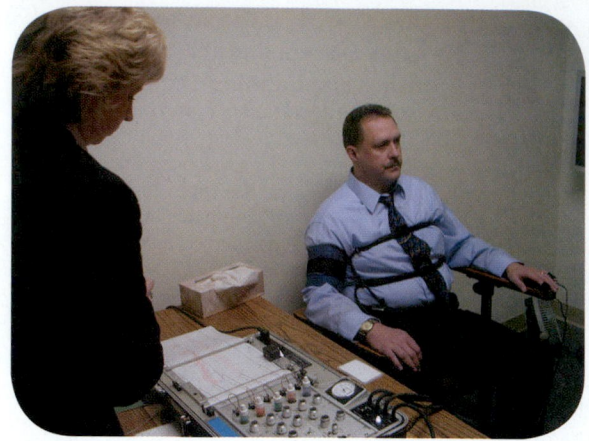

Examiners use a polygraph to tell whether someone is lying. A polygraph monitors changes in the body believed to be influenced by emotional states. Controversy has swirled about the polygraph's use because it is unreliable.

drugs in the person's system can interfere with the polygraph's accuracy. Sometimes the mere presence of the polygraph and the individual's belief that it is accurate in detecting deception trigger a confession of guilt. Police may use the polygraph in this way to get a suspect to confess. However, in too many instances it has been misused and misrepresented. Experts argue that the polygraph errs just under 50 percent of the time, especially as it cannot distinguish between such feelings as anxiety and guilt (Iacono & Lykken, 1997).

The Employee Polygraph Protection Act of 1988 restricts polygraph testing outside government agencies, and most courts do not accept the results of polygraph testing. However, some psychologists defend the polygraph's use, saying that polygraph results are as sound as other admissible forms of evidence, such as hair fiber analysis (Grubin & Madsen, 2006; Honts, 1998). The majority of psychologists, though, argue against the polygraph's use because of its inability to tell who is lying and who is not (Iacono & Lykken, 1997; Lykken, 1998; Saxe, 1998; Steinbrook, 1992).

Recently, functional magnetic brain imaging (fMRI) has been proposed as a better option for detecting deception than the polygraph (Langleben & Dattilio, 2008; Simpson, 2008). However, researchers are just beginning to study this possibility (Baumgartner & others, 2009; Fullam, McKie, & Dolan, 2009; Ganis, Morris, & Kosslyn, 2009; Kozel & others, 2009). In one recent study, the best results were obtained for changes in a region of the prefrontal cortex, which correctly identified 71 percent of the participants who were lying (Monteleone & others, 2008). As the authors of this study concluded, their findings were better than chance but well below perfection.

Theories of Emotion

Imagine that you and your date are enjoying a picnic in the country. Suddenly, a bull runs across the field toward you. Why are you afraid? Two well-known theories of emotion that involve physiological processes provide answers to this question.

Common sense tells you that you are trembling and running away from the bull because you are afraid, but William James (1950) and Carl Lange (pronounced "Long-uh") (1922) said emotion works in the opposite way. According to the **James-Lange theory,** emotion results from physiological states triggered by stimuli in the environment: Emotion occurs *after* physiological reactions. Moreover, each emotion—from anger to rapture—has a distinct set of physiological changes, evident in changes in heart rate, breathing patterns, sweating, and other responses. Essentially, the James-Lange theory proposes that after the initial perception, the experience of the emotion results from the perception of one's own physiological changes.

Let's see how the James-Lange theory would explain fear in the situation with the bull. You see the bull scratching its hoof on the ground, and you begin to run away. Your aroused body then sends sensory messages to your brain, at which point emotion is perceived. According to this theory, you do not run away because you are afraid; rather, you are afraid because you are running away. In other words, you perceive a stimulus in the environment, your body responds, and you interpret the body's reaction as emotion.

Walter Cannon (1927) objected to the assumption in the James-Lange theory that each emotional experience has its own particular set of physiological changes. He argued that different emotions could not be associated with specific physiological changes because autonomic nervous system responses are too diffuse and slow to account for rapid and differentiated emotional responses.

To understand Cannon's view, imagine the bull and the picnic once again. Seeing the bull scratching its hoof causes the thalamus of your brain to do two things simultaneously: First, it stimulates your autonomic nervous system to produce the physiological changes involved in emotion (increased heart rate, rapid breathing); second, it sends messages to your cerebral cortex, where the experience of emotion is perceived. Philip Bard (1934) supported this analysis, and so the theory became known as the

● **James-Lange theory** The theory that emotion results from physiological states triggered by stimuli in the environment.

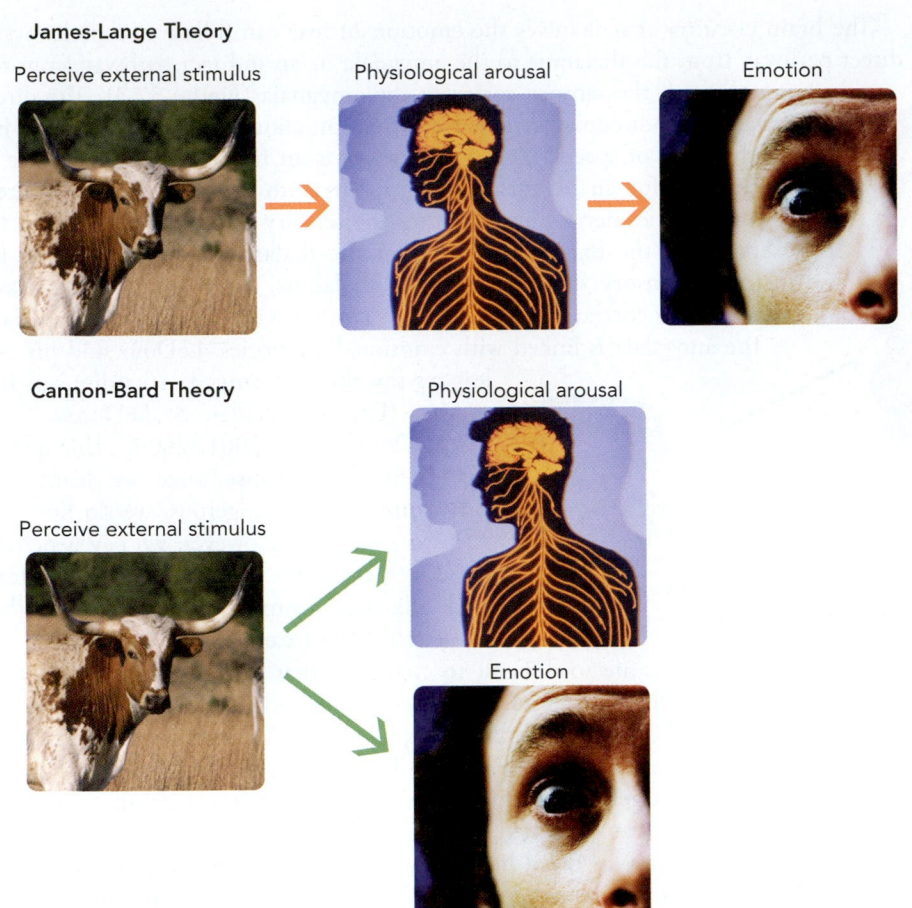

James-Lange Theory

Perceive external stimulus → Physiological arousal → Emotion

Cannon-Bard Theory

Perceive external stimulus → Physiological arousal / Emotion

FIGURE 37.2 James-Lange and Cannon-Bard Theories From the James-Lange perspective, the experience of fear is an outcome of physiological arousal. In the Cannon-Bard view, fear occurs at the same time as the physiological response.

Cannon-Bard theory—the proposition that emotion and physiological reactions occur simultaneously. In the Cannon-Bard theory, the body plays a less important role than in the James-Lange theory. Figure 37.2 shows how the James-Lange and Cannon-Bard theories differ.

The question of whether emotions involve discrete autonomic nervous system responses continues to be debated (Keltner & Ekman, 2000). Recent studies have documented some emotion-specific autonomic nervous system responses (Christie & Friedman, 2004). For example, fear, anger, and sadness are associated with increased heart rate, but disgust is not (Bryant, 2006; Hamer & others, 2007). Also, anger is linked with increased blood flow to the hands, an effect that is not triggered by fear.

● **Cannon-Bard theory** The proposition that emotion and physiological reactions occur simultaneously.

Neural Circuits and Neurotransmitters

Contemporary researchers are keenly interested in charting the neural circuitry of emotions and in discovering the role of neurotransmitters (Kindt, Soeter, & Vervliet, 2009; Pessoa, 2009). The focus of much of their work has been on the amygdala, the almond-shaped structure in the limbic system that we considered in Module 7. The amygdala houses circuits that are activated when we experience negative emotions.

Research by Joseph LeDoux and his colleagues has investigated the neural circuitry of one particular emotion: fear (Cowansage, LeDoux, & Monfils, 2010; Cunha, Monfils, & LeDoux, 2010; Debiec & others, 2010; LeDoux, 1996, 2002, 2009; Sotres-Bayon & others, 2009). The amygdala plays a central role in fear. When the amygdala determines that danger is present, it shifts into high gear, marshaling the brain's resources in an effort to protect the organism from harm. This fear system evolved to detect and respond to predators and other types of natural dangers that threaten survival or territory.

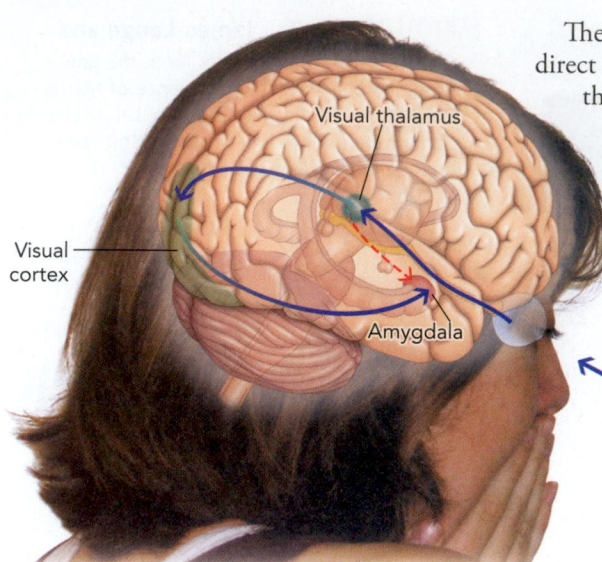

FIGURE 37.3 **Direct and Indirect Brain Pathways in the Emotion of Fear** Information about fear can follow two pathways in the brain when an individual sees a snake. The direct pathway (*broken arrow*) conveys information rapidly from the thalamus to the amygdala. The indirect pathway (*solid arrows*) transmits information more slowly from the thalamus to the sensory cortex (here, the visual cortex) and then to the amygdala.

The brain circuitry that involves the emotion of fear can follow two pathways: a direct pathway from the thalamus to the amygdala or an indirect pathway from the thalamus through the sensory cortex to the amygdala (Figure 37.3). The direct pathway does not convey detailed information about the stimulus, but it has the advantage of speed—and speed clearly is an important characteristic of information for an organism facing a threat to its survival. The indirect pathway carries nerve impulses from the sensory organs (eyes and ears, for example) to the thalamus (recall that the thalamus is a relay station for incoming sensory stimuli); from the thalamus, the nerve impulses travel to the sensory cortex, which then sends appropriate signals to the amygdala. The amygdala is linked with emotional memories. LeDoux and his colleagues say that the amygdala hardly ever forgets (Duvarci, Nader, & LeDoux, 2008; LeDoux, 2000, 2001, 2009). This quality is useful, because once we learn that something is dangerous, we do not have to relearn it. However, we pay a penalty for this ability. Many people carry fears and anxieties around with them that they would like to get rid of but cannot seem to shake.

Part of the reason fears are so difficult to change is that the amygdala is well connected to the cerebral cortex, in which thinking and decision making primarily occur (Rauch, Shin, & Phelps, 2006). The amygdala is in a much better position to influence the cerebral cortex than the other way around, because it sends more connections to the cerebral cortex than it gets back. This may explain why it is so hard to control our emotions, and why, once fear is learned, it is so hard to erase.

The amygdala is not only involved in negative emotions but also appears to participate in positive emotions (Hurleman & others, 2010; Ritchey, Labar, & Cabeza, 2010; Winecoff & others, 2010). Research reviews concluded that various regions of the limbic system, including the amygdalae, are involved in the experience of positive emotions (Burgdorf & Panksepp, 2006; Koepp & others, 2009). The neurotransmitter dopamine is especially active in the limbic system during positive emotions.

Researchers are also finding that the cerebral hemispheres may be involved in understanding emotion. Richard Davidson and his colleagues have shown that the cerebral hemispheres work differently in positive and negative emotions (Davidson, 2000, 2010a; Davidson, Shackman, & Pizzagalli, 2002; Light & others, 2009; Reuter-Lorenz & Davidson, 1981; Urry & others, 2004). Research reviewed in Module 7 suggests that people who show relatively more left than right prefrontal activation tend to be happier. Researchers are also intrigued by the roles that neurotransmitters play in the neural pathways of emotions. Endorphins and dopamine are involved in positive emotions such as happiness (Koepp & others, 2009), and norepinephrine functions in regulating arousal (Berridge & Kringelbach, 2008; Greeson & others, 2009).

37·2 COGNITIVE FACTORS IN EMOTION

Does emotion depend on the tides of the mind? Are we happy only when we think we are happy? Cognitive theories of emotion center on the premise that emotion always has a cognitive component (Frijda, 2007; Johnson-Laird, Mancini, & Gangemi, 2006). Thinking is said to be responsible for feelings of love and hate, joy and sadness. While cognitive theorists do recognize the role of the brain and body in emotion, they give cognitive processes the main credit for these responses.

The Two-Factor Theory of Emotion

● **two-factor theory of emotion** Schachter and Singer's theory that emotion is determined by two factors: physiological arousal and cognitive labeling.

In the **two-factor theory of emotion** developed by Stanley Schachter and Jerome Singer (1962), emotion is determined by two factors: physiological arousal and cognitive labeling

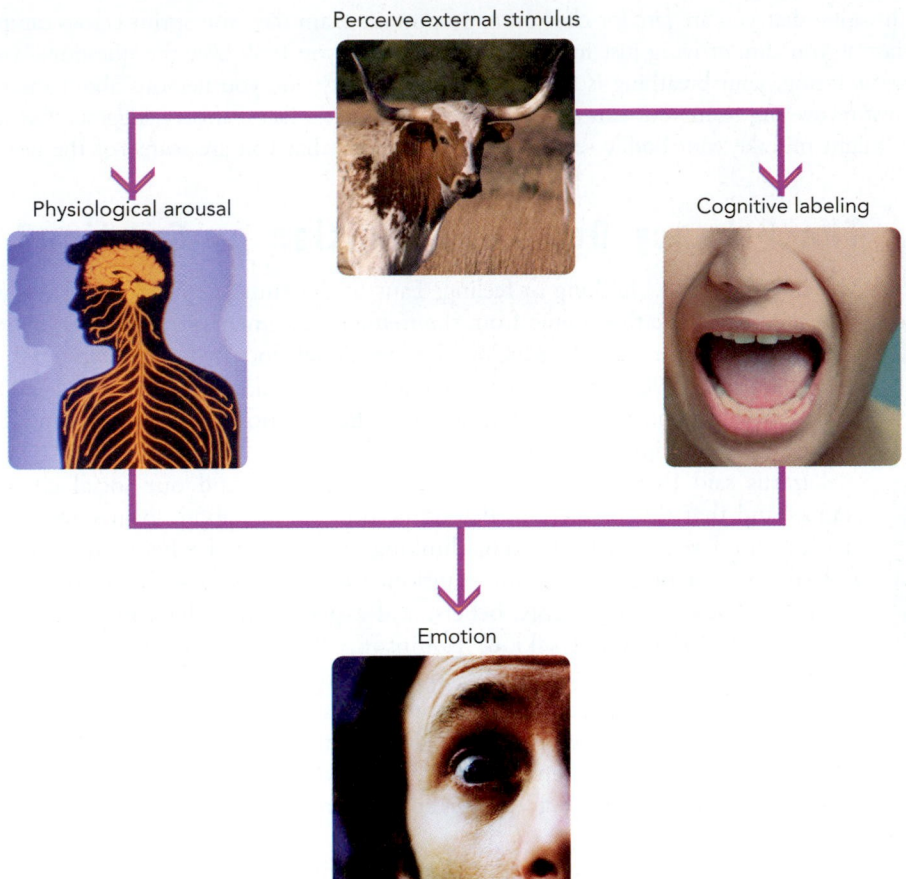

Perceive external stimulus

Physiological arousal

Cognitive labeling

Emotion

FIGURE 37.4   Schachter and Singer's Two-Factor Theory of Emotion The two-factor theory includes not only arousal but also cognitive labeling: You feel afraid of the bull because you label your physiological response "fear."

FIGURE 37.5   Capilano River Bridge Experiment: Misinterpreted Arousal Intensifies Emotional Experiences (*Top*) The precarious Capilano River Bridge in British Columbia. (*Bottom*) The experiment in progress. An attractive woman approached the men while they were crossing the bridge; she asked them to make up a story to help her with a creativity project. She also made the same request on a lower, much safer bridge. The men on the Capilano River Bridge told more sexually oriented stories, probably because they were aroused by the fear or excitement of being up so high on a swaying bridge and interpreted their arousal as sexual attraction for the female interviewer.

(Figure 37.4). Schachter and Singer argued that we look to the external world for an explanation of why we are aroused. We interpret external cues and label the emotion. For example, if you feel good after someone has made a pleasant comment to you, you might label the emotion "happy." If you feel bad after you have done something wrong, you may label the feeling "guilty."

To test their theory of emotion, Schachter and Singer (1962) injected volunteer participants with epinephrine, a drug that produces high arousal. After participants received the drug, they observed someone else behave in either a euphoric way (shooting papers at a wastebasket) or an angry way (stomping out of the room). As predicted, the euphoric and angry behavior influenced the participants' cognitive interpretation of their own arousal. When they were with a happy person, they rated themselves as happy; when they were with an angry person, they said they were angry. This effect occurred, however, only when the participants were not told about the true effects of the injection. When they were told that the drug would increase their heart rate and make them jittery, they said the reason for their own arousal was the drug, not the other person's behavior.

In general, research supports the belief that misinterpreted arousal intensifies emotional experiences (Leventhal & Tomarken, 1986). An intriguing study by Donald Dutton and Arthur Aron (1974) substantiates this conclusion. In the study, an attractive woman approached men while they were walking across the Capilano River Bridge in British Columbia. Only men without a female companion were approached. The woman asked the men to make up a brief story for a project she was doing on creativity. The Capilano River Bridge sways dangerously more than 200 feet above rapids and rocks (Figure 37.5). The female interviewer made the same request of other men crossing a much safer, lower bridge. The men on the Capilano River Bridge told more sexually oriented stories and rated the female interviewer as more attractive than did men on the lower, less frightening bridge.

Imagine that you are late for class on an important exam day. You sprint across campus as fast as you can, arriving just in time for the test. As you look over the questions, your heart is racing, your breathing is fast, and you feel sweaty. Are you nervous about the test or just recovering from your run to the classroom? The two-factor theory suggests that you just might mistake your bodily sensations as indications that you are scared of the test.

The Primacy Debate: Cognition or Emotion?

Which comes first, thinking or feeling? Fans of the vintage episodes of TV's *Star Trek* may recognize this theme from the frequent arguments between Mr. Spock, the logical Vulcan, and Dr. McCoy, the emotional doctor on the *Enterprise*. In the 1980s and 1990s, two eminent psychologists, Richard Lazarus (1922–2002) and Robert Zajonc (1923–2008), debated the question of which is central—cognition or emotion.

Lazarus said that we cognitively appraise ourselves and our social circumstances and that these appraisals determine how we feel about events and experiences. For Lazarus (1991), then, thinking is primary—he believed cognitive activity to be a precondition for emotion. Our appraisals—which are guided by values, goals, commitments, beliefs, and expectations—determine our emotions (Urry, 2010; Wilkowski & Robinson, 2010). People may feel happy because they have a deep religious commitment, angry because they did not get the raise they anticipated, or fearful because they expect to fail an exam. Zajonc (1984) disagreed with Lazarus. Emotions are primary, he said, and our thoughts are a result of them. Zajonc famously argued that "preferences need no inferences," meaning that the way we feel about something on a "gut level" requires no thought.

Vintage Star Trek *episodes explored the question, what comes first—thinking or feeling?*

Which of the two psychologists is right? *Both* are likely correct. Lazarus talked mainly about a cluster of related events that occur over a period of time, whereas Zajonc described single events or a simple preference for one stimulus over another. Lazarus was concerned with love over the course of months and years, a sense of value to the community, and plans for retirement; Zajonc spoke about a car accident, an encounter with a snake, and a preference for ice cream rather than spinach.

Some of our emotional reactions are virtually instantaneous and probably do not involve cognitive appraisal, such as shrieking upon detecting a snake (Young & Claypool, 2010). Other emotional circumstances, especially long-term feelings such as a depressed mood or anger toward a friend, are more likely to involve cognitive appraisal (Smith & Kirby, 2009). Indeed, the direct and indirect brain pathways described earlier support the idea that some of our emotional reactions do not involve deliberate thinking, whereas others do (LeDoux, 2001, 2009).

37-3 BEHAVIORAL FACTORS IN EMOTION

Remember that our definition of emotion includes not only physiological and cognitive components but also a behavioral component. The behavioral component can be verbal or nonverbal. Verbally, a person might show love for someone by professing it in words or might display anger by saying nasty things. Nonverbally, a person might smile, frown, show a fearful expression, look down, or slouch.

The most interest in the behavioral dimension of emotion has focused on the nonverbal behavior of facial expressions (Hasegawa & Unuma, 2010; Sacco & Hugenberg, 2009; Todd & others, 2010). Emotion researchers have been intrigued by people's ability to detect emotion from a person's facial expression (Sato & others, 2010; Stein & others, 2010; Yoon, Joormann, & Gotlib, 2009). In a typical research study, participants, when shown photographs like those in Figure 37.6, are usually able to identify six emotions: happiness, anger, sadness, surprise, disgust, and fear (Ekman & O'Sullivan, 1991).

FIGURE 37.6   **Recognizing Emotions in Facial Expressions** Look at the six photographs and determine the emotion reflected in each of the six faces: (*top*) happiness, anger, sadness; (*bottom*) surprise, disgust, fear.

Might our facial expressions not only reflect our emotions but also influence them? According to the **facial feedback hypothesis,** facial expressions can influence emotions as well as reflect them (Davis, Senghas, & Ochsner, 2009). In this view, facial muscles send signals to the brain that help us to recognize the emotion we are experiencing (Keillor & others, 2002). For example, we feel happier when we smile and sadder when we frown.

Support for the facial feedback hypothesis comes from an experiment by Paul Ekman and his colleagues (1983). In this study, professional actors moved their facial muscles in very precise ways, such as raising their eyebrows and pulling them together, raising their upper eyelids, and stretching their lips horizontally back to their ears (you might want to try this yourself). They were asked to hold their expression for 10 seconds, during which time the researchers measured their heart rate and body temperature. When the actors moved facial muscles in the ways described, they showed a rise in heart rate and a steady body temperature—physiological reactions that characterize fear. When they made an angry facial expression (with a penetrating stare, brows drawn together and downward, and lips pressed together or opened and pushed forward), their heart rate and body temperature both increased. The facial feedback hypothesis provides support for the James-Lange theory of emotion discussed earlier—namely, that emotional experiences can be generated by changes in and awareness of our own bodily states.

● **facial feedback hypothesis** The idea that facial expressions can influence emotions as well as reflect them.

37-4 SOCIOCULTURAL FACTORS IN EMOTION

Are the facial expressions that are associated with different emotions largely innate, or do they vary across cultures? Are there gender variations in emotion? Answering these questions requires a look at research findings on sociocultural influences in emotions.

FIGURE 37.7 **Emotional Expressions in the United States and New Guinea** (*Top*) Two women from the United States. (*Bottom*) Two men from the Fore tribe in New Guinea. Notice the similarity in their expressions of disgust and happiness. Psychologists believe that the facial expression of emotion is virtually the same in all cultures.

• **display rules** Sociocultural standards that determine when, where, and how emotions should be expressed.

In the Middle Eastern country of Yemen, male-to-male kissing is commonplace, but in the United States it is less common.

Culture and the Expression of Emotion

In *The Expression of the Emotions in Man and Animals,* Charles Darwin stated that the facial expressions of human beings are innate, not learned; are the same in all cultures around the world; and have evolved from the emotions of animals (1965). Today psychologists still believe that emotions, especially facial expressions of emotion, have strong biological ties (Gelder & others, 2006). For example, children who are blind from birth and have never observed the smile or frown on another person's face smile or frown in the same way that children with normal vision do. If emotions and facial expressions that go with them are unlearned, then they should be the same the world over. Is that in fact the case?

Extensive research has examined the universality of facial expressions and the ability of people from different cultures accurately to label the emotion that lies behind facial expressions (Sauter & others, 2010). Paul Ekman's careful observations reveal that the many faces of emotion do not differ significantly from one culture to another (Ekman, 1980, 1996, 2003). For example, Ekman and his colleague photographed people expressing emotions such as happiness, fear, surprise, disgust, and grief. When they showed the photographs to people from the United States, Chile, Japan, Brazil, and Borneo (an Indonesian island in the western Pacific), the participants recognized the emotions the faces were meant to show, across the various cultures (Ekman & Friesen, 1969).

Another study focused on the way the Fore tribe, an isolated Stone Age culture in New Guinea, matched descriptions of emotions with facial expressions (Ekman & Friesen, 1971). Before Ekman's visit, most of the Fore had never seen a Caucasian face. Ekman's team showed them photographs of faces expressing emotions such as fear, happiness, anger, and surprise. Then they read stories about people in emotional situations and asked the tribespeople to pick out the face that matched the story. The Fore were able to match the descriptions of emotions with the facial expressions in the photographs. Figure 37.7 shows the similarity of facial expressions of emotions by persons in New Guinea and the United States. More recently, one study found that East Asians and Westerners differed in their capacity to tell the difference between facial expressions of fear and surprise as well as expressions of anger and disgust (Jack & others, 2009). These differences were explained by the tendency of East Asians to focus more on the eyes (than the mouth) when judging faces.

Although facial expressions of basic emotions may be universal, display rules for emotion vary (Fischer, 2006; Matsumoto & others, 2008). **Display rules** are sociocultural standards that determine when, where, and how emotions should be expressed. For example, although happiness is a universally expressed emotion, when, where, and how people display it may vary from one culture to another (Sauter & others, 2010). The same is true for other emotions, such as fear, sadness, and anger. Members of the Utku culture in Alaska, for example, discourage anger by cultivating acceptance and by dissociating themselves from any display of anger. If an unexpected snowstorm hampers a trip, the Utku do not express frustration but accept the storm and build an igloo. The importance of display rules is especially evident when we evaluate the emotional expression of another. Does that grieving husband on a morning talk show seem appropriately distraught over his wife's murder? Or might he be a suspect?

Like facial expressions, some other nonverbal signals appear to be universal indicators of certain emotions. For example, regardless of where they live, when people are depressed, their emotional state shows not only in their sad facial expressions but also in their slow body movements, downturned heads, and slumped posture. Many nonverbal signals of emotion, though, vary from one culture to another (Mesquita, 2002). For example, male-to-male kissing is commonplace in Yemen but uncommon in the United States. The "thumbs up" sign, which in most cultures means either that everything is okay or that one wants to hitch a ride, is an insult in Greece, similar to a raised third finger in the United States—a cultural difference to keep in mind if you find yourself backpacking through Greece.

Emotional Expression in Computer Communications

"…close with 'Yours truly, Phil'—and could you sprinkle a few appropriate emoticons around?"
© Chris Wildt. www.CartoonStock.com.

Recently psychologists have become interested in examining the expression of emotion in computer-mediated communications, including e-mails, blogs, and instant messages. You have probably used emoticons in your own communications. First introduced by computer scientist Scott Fahlman in 1982 (Fahlman, 2003), emoticons are used to express a variety of feelings, from joy **:D** to sadness **:-(** to silliness **;P** to great shock and dismay **: - O.**

Emoticons allow us to compensate for the loss of information from other expressive channels, such as vocal tone and facial expression (Derks, Bos, & von Grumbkow, 2008; Lo, 2008). People use emoticons as they do other displays of emotion, such as laughter, often at the end of the statement they are trying to clarify (Provine, Spencer, & Mandell, 2007).

Just as culture influences emotional expressions, it has also influenced emoticons. For instance, East Asian emoticons are less likely to be presented sideways, so that a Japanese student might convey her level of exhaustion with **(-.-)Zzzzzz** rather than **l-)Zzzzzz.** Even with emoticons, display rules can be important. A Japanese student expressing a thumbs up **d(^_^)b** might encounter an American who thinks he is saying he has big ears.

Emoticons reveal a potentially unique aspect of computer-mediated communication. Consider that back when people often communicated by writing letters (an art that would seem to share the limitations of e-mail and texting), emoticons were not used. Looking at the letters of great writers, we do not find smileys and frownies explaining their feelings. Thus, computer-mediated communication such as instant messaging might be considered a mixture of spoken conversation and the written word (Tagliamonte & Denis, 2008). As texting and IMing have become more common, it is no wonder that humans have devised a way to inject emotional meanings into their online discourse. Emoticons certainly demonstrate how crucial emotions are to our communications.

Gender Influences

Unless you have been isolated on a mountaintop, you probably know the stereotype about gender and emotion: She is emotional; he is not. This stereotype is a powerful and pervasive image in U.S. culture (Shields, 1991).

Does science support this stereotype? Researchers have found that men and women are often more alike in the way they experience emotion than the stereotype would lead us to believe. Women and men often use the same facial expressions, adopt the same language, and describe their emotional experiences similarly when they keep diaries about their experiences. For many emotional experiences, researchers do not find gender differences—both sexes are equally likely to experience love, jealousy, anxiety in new social situations, anger when they are insulted, grief when close relationships end, and embarrassment when they make mistakes in public (Tavris & Wade, 1984).

When we go beyond stereotypes and consider some specific emotional experiences, contexts in which emotion is displayed, and certain beliefs about emotion, gender does matter in understanding emotion (Brannon, 1999; Brody, 1999; Shields, 1991). Research has shown that women are more accurate at recognizing the emotional content of faces, especially when the task is made challenging by showing the faces for a very short time (Hall & Matsumoto, 2004). Women also report themselves as experiencing emotions for a longer period than men (Birditt & Fingerman, 2003) and use more emoticons than men in their computer communications (Wolf, 2000).

It is important to keep in mind that both women and men are certainly aware of the gender-specific expectations for emotional behavior (Blakemore, Berenbaum, & Liben, 2009). Indeed, men who embrace a stereotypically masculine gender identity are more likely to report themselves as less emotional (Jakupcak & others, 2003). Gender differences in emotion are much more tied to social context than to biological sex (Brody, 1999).

37-5 CLASSIFYING EMOTIONS

There are more than 200 words for emotions in the English language, indicating the complexity and variety of emotions. Not surprisingly, psychologists have created ways to classify emotions—to summarize these many emotions along various dimensions (Izard, 2009), including their valence and arousal.

Valence

The *valence* of an emotion refers to whether it feels pleasant or unpleasant. You probably are not surprised to know that happiness, joy, pleasure, and contentment are positively valenced emotions. In contrast, sadness, anger, worry, and feeling upset are negatively valenced emotions. Research has shown that emotions tend to go together based on their valence, so that if someone is sad, he or she is also likely to be angry or worried, and if a person is happy, he is or she is also likely to be feeling confident, joyful, and content (D. Watson, 2001).

● **negative affect** Unpleasant emotions such as anger, guilt, and sadness.

● **positive affect** Pleasant emotions such as joy, happiness, and interest.

We can classify many emotional states on the basis of valence. Indeed, according to some experts in emotion (D. Watson, 2001), there are two broad dimensions of emotional experience: negative affect and positive affect. **Negative affect** refers to emotions such as anger, guilt, and sadness. **Positive affect** refers to emotions such as joy, happiness, and interest. Although it seems essential to consider the valence of emotions as a way to classify them, valence does not fully capture all that we need to know about emotional states. The joy a person experiences at the birth of a child and the mild high at finding a $5 bill are both positive states, but they clearly differ. One way in which they differ is in their level of arousal.

Arousal Level

The *arousal level* of an emotion is the degree to which the emotion is reflected in an individual's being active, engaged, or excited versus more passive, relatively disengaged, or calm. Positive and negative emotions can be high or low in arousal. Ecstasy and excitement are examples of high-arousal positive emotions, whereas contentment and tranquility are low-arousal positive emotions. Examples of high-arousal negative emotions are rage, fury, and panic, while irritation and boredom represent low-arousal negative emotions.

Valence and arousal level are independent dimensions that together describe a vast number of emotional states. Using these dimensions, psychologists have created a wheel of mood states that they call a *circumplex model of mood* (Posner, Russell, & Peterson, 2005). A circumplex is a graph that creates a circle from two independent dimensions. Using the dimensions of valence and arousal level, we can arrange emotional states in an organized fashion. To view the circumplex model and grasp its usefulness, see the Psychological Inquiry.

psychological *inquiry*

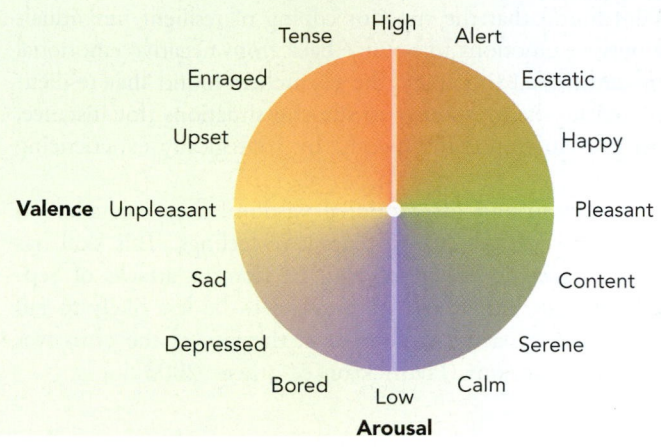

Tense — High — Alert
Enraged — Ecstatic
Upset — Happy
Valence Unpleasant — Pleasant
Sad — Content
Depressed — Serene
Bored — Calm
Low
Arousal

The Full Circle of Emotions

The figure shows a commonly used representation of human emotions, the circumplex model. Note that the circle is created by two independent dimensions: valence and arousal. Emotions that are similar are closer together, and those that differ are farther apart. Using the figure as a reference, answer the following questions.

1. Locate the emotions "upset" and "sad" on the circumplex. According to the circumplex, these two feelings differ primarily in terms of their arousal. Which is higher in arousal? Do you agree with this placement of these emotions? Explain.

2. According to the model, which emotion is the exact opposite of "serene"?

3. Where would you place the following feelings on the circle: worried, proud, angry, embarrassed?

37·6 THE ADAPTIVE FUNCTIONS OF EMOTIONS

● **broaden-and-build model** Fredrickson's model of positive emotion, stating that the function of positive emotions lies in their effects on an individual's attention and ability to build resources.

In considering the functions of emotions, it is fairly easy to come up with a good reason for us to have emotions such as fear and anger. Negative emotions carry direct and immediate adaptive benefits in situations that threaten survival. Negative emotions indicate clearly that something is wrong and that we must take action. Positive emotions do not signal a problem. So, what is the adaptive function of positive emotions?

Confronting this question, Barbara Fredrickson proposed the **broaden-and-build model** of positive emotion (Fredrickson, 1998, 2001, 2006, 2009). She argues that the function of positive emotions lies in their effects on our attention and our ability to build resources. The broaden-and-build model begins with the influence of positive emotions on cognitive processing.

Positive moods, such as contentment and humor, have been shown to broaden our attentional focus; they allow us to see the forest for the trees. As a result, when in a good mood, we may be more disposed to think outside the box—to see unusual possibilities that escaped us before. In addition, a good mood, Fredrickson says, gives us a chance to build resources—to make friends, to exercise to promote our health, to branch out in new ways. These activities allow us to build up strengths that we can use when we encounter life's difficulties (Kok, Catalino, & Fredrickson, 2008; Papousek & others, 2010). For example, joy broadens people by creating the urge to play, push the limits, and be creative. Interest broadens people by creating the motivation to explore, absorb new information and experiences, and expand the self (Csikszentmihalyi, 1990; Ryan & Deci, 2000). Positive emotions facilitate "approach" behavior, meaning that when we are feeling good, we are more likely to go after the rewards we want and to face our problems head on (Otake & others, 2006; D. Watson, 2001).

According to Fredrickson's broaden-and-build model, a good mood paves the way for building resources such as close friends and health-promoting activities.

Resilience

Resilience has been associated with the capacity to thrive during difficult times (Masten, 2006, 2009). Resilience refers to the ability to bounce back from negative experiences, to be flexible and adaptable when things are not going well. Resilient individuals might be thought of as tall trees that have the ability to bend but do not break in response to strong winds. In contrast, people who lack resilience might be characterized as more brittle—more likely to snap or break in the face of adversity (Block & Kremen, 1996).

Positive emotions might play an important role in the ability of resilient individuals to cope successfully with life's challenges. Resilient individuals are zestful, optimistic, and energetic in their approach to life (Block & Kremen, 1996). They cultivate positive emotion through the use of humor (Segerstrom, 2006). Michelle Tugade, Barbara Fredrickson, and Lisa Feldman Barrett (2004) found that the superior coping of resilient individuals came from their ability to use positive emotions to bounce back from negative emotional experiences. Using measures of cardiovascular activity, the researchers found that resilient individuals were better able to regulate their responses to stressful situations (for instance, being told they were about to give an important speech) by strategically experiencing positive emotion.

Resilient individuals seem to show a kind of emotional wisdom; they capitalize on the power of positive emotions to reverse the stress of negative feelings. This skill has been demonstrated in response to a specific stressful event: the terrorist attacks of September 11, 2001. In one study, resilient individuals were found to be less likely to fall prey to depression after 9/11, and this capacity to flourish in the face of the crisis was a result of their attention to positive emotions (Fredrickson & others, 2003).

SUMMARY

Emotion is feeling, or affect, that has three components: physiological arousal, conscious experience, and behavioral expression. The biology of emotion focuses on physiological arousal involving the autonomic nervous system and its two subsystems. Skin conductance level and the polygraph have been used to measure emotional arousal.

The James-Lange theory states that emotion results from physiological states triggered by environmental stimuli: Emotion follows physiological reactions. The Cannon-Bard theory states that emotion and physiological reactions occur simultaneously. Contemporary biological views of emotion increasingly highlight neural circuitry and neurotransmitters. LeDoux has charted the neural circuitry of fear, which focuses on the amygdala and consists of two pathways, one direct and the other indirect. It is likely that positive and negative emotions use different neural circuitry and neurotransmitters.

Schachter and Singer's two-factor theory states that emotion is the result of both physiological arousal and cognitive labeling. Lazarus believed that cognition always directs emotion, but Zajonc argued that emotion directs cognition. Both probably were right.

Research on the behavioral component of emotion focuses on facial expressions. The facial feedback hypothesis states that facial expressions can influence emotions, as well as reflect them.

Most psychologists believe that facial expressions of basic emotions are the same across cultures. However, display rules—nonverbal signals of body movement, posture, and gesture—vary across cultures. Differences in emoticons across cultures reinforce the idea that display rules depend on culture.

Emotions can be classified based on valence (pleasant or unpleasant) and arousal (high or low). Using the dimensions of valence and arousal, emotions can be arranged in a circle, or circumplex model.

Positive emotions likely play an important role in well-being by broadening our focus and allowing us to build resources. Resilience is an individual's capacity to thrive even during difficult times. Research has shown that one way resilient individuals thrive is by experiencing positive emotions.

KEY TERMS

emotion   366
polygraph   367
James-Lange theory   368
Cannon-Bard theory   369
two-factor theory
   of emotion   370

facial feedback hypothesis   373
display rules   374
negative affect   376
positive affect   376
broaden-and-build model   377

TEST YOURSELF

1. What are the key differences between the James-Lange theory and the Cannon-Bard theory of emotion?

2. What is the facial feedback hypothesis, and how has it been supported experimentally?

3. What is meant by the *valence* of an emotion and by the terms *positive affect* and *negative affect*?

APPLY YOUR KNOWLEDGE

1. Some psychologists believe that the ability to identify and regulate one's emotions is a kind of intelligence. Emotionally intelligent people are also thought to be better at reading the emotional expressions of others. Do a web search for "emotional intelligence tests" and take some online quizzes, or try the one at http://www.testcafe.com/ei/. Do you think you are emotionally intelligent? Does your performance on the test seem to reflect your actual experience? What is your opinion of the test you tried? Is there information on the site showing its validity and reliability?

2. This module reviewed the use of autonomic nervous system activity in the detection of deception. Psychologists have devised various ways to detect lying. Go online and search for information on detecting deception and lies. Is there a good way to tell if someone is being truthful? Explain.

Motivation, Emotion, and Health and Wellness: The Pursuit of Happiness

Well, you could try being happy for a while and if it doesn't work you can go back to being miserable.

Machlis. Artizans.com.

Motivation is about what people want, and a quick scan of the bestseller list or the self-help section of any bookstore would seem to indicate that one thing people want very much is to be happy—or happier. Can people get happier? Let's consider the evidence.

BIOLOGICAL FACTORS IN HAPPINESS

As we have seen, the brain is certainly at work in the experience of positive emotions. Genes also play a role. For instance, research on the heritability of well-being has tended to show that a substantial proportion of well-being differences among people can be explained by genetics. The heritability estimates for happiness range from 50 to 80 percent (Lykken, 1999). Remember that heritability is a statistic that describes characteristics of a group, that heritability estimates can vary across groups and over time, and that even highly heritable characteristics can be influenced by experience. Thus, a person is not necessarily doomed to an unhappy life, even if the person knows that he or she has particularly miserable parents.

Recall the concept of *set point* in our discussion of weight. As it happens, there may also be a happiness set point—a person's basic level of happiness when the individual is not intentionally trying to increase his or her happiness (Sheldon & Lyubomirsky, 2007). Like weight, the happiness level may fluctuate around this set point. In investigating how to increase happiness, we must consider the role of this powerful starting spot, which is likely the result of genetic factors and personal disposition.

Other factors also complicate the pursuit of happiness. As we shall see, these include getting caught up on the hedonic treadmill and making happiness itself the direct goal.

OBSTACLES IN THE PURSUIT OF HAPPINESS

The first key challenge individuals encounter in trying to increase their happiness is the hedonic (meaning "related to pleasure") treadmill (Brickman & Campbell, 1971; Fredrick & Loewenstein, 1999). The term *hedonic treadmill* captures the idea that any aspect of life that enhances one's positive feelings is likely to do so for only a short time, because individuals generally adapt rapidly to any life change that would presumably influence their happiness. Winning the lottery, moving into a dream home, or falling in love may lead to temporary gains in the experience of joy, but eventually people go back to their baseline (Schkade & Kahneman, 1998). Whether it is the switch from CDs to iTunes or from dial-up to wireless, what a person first experiences as a life-changing improvement eventually fades to a routine (but still necessary) aspect of life, all too soon to be taken for granted. How can individuals increase their happiness if such pleasure enhancers quickly lose their power? Clearly, happiness is not about shopping at the right stores, because new possessions will likely lead to only a momentary burst of pleasure, eventually giving way to the set point.

A second obstacle in the goal of enhancing happiness is that pursuing happiness for its own sake is rarely a good way to get happy or happier. When happiness is the goal, the pursuit is likely to backfire (Schooler, Ariely, & Loewenstein, 2003). Indeed, those who explicitly link the pursuit of their everyday goals to happiness fare quite poorly (McIntosh, Harlow, & Martin, 1995).

In light of this difficult path, how can we enhance our happiness without having any new capacity for joy become ho-hum? How might we achieve happiness without pursuing it in and of itself?

HAPPINESS ACTIVITIES AND GOAL STRIVING

Sonja Lyubomirsky and her colleagues have proposed a promising approach to enhancing happiness (Lyubomirsky, 2008; Sheldon & Lyubomirsky, 2007; Sin & Lyubomirsky, 2009). Lyubomirsky suggests beginning with intentional activities. For example, she notes that physical activity, kindness, and positive self-reflection all enhance positive affect (Sheldon & Lyubomirsky, 2007). Engaging in altruistic behavior—habitually helping others, especially through a wide range of acts of service—is another powerful way to enhance happiness, according to Lyubomirsky (2008).

One technique for engaging in positive self-reflection is to keep a gratitude journal. Studies by Robert Emmons and Michael McCullough (2004) have demonstrated the ways that being grateful can lead to enhanced happiness and psychological well-being. In one study, they asked individuals to keep a diary in which the participants counted their blessings every day. Those who counted their blessings were better off on various measures of well-being. Although some individuals seem to be naturally more grateful than others, experimental evidence indicates that even people who are not naturally grateful can benefit from taking a moment to count their blessings (Emmons & McCullough, 2003; McCullough, Emmons, & Tsang, 2002).

Another potentially useful approach to enhancing happiness is to commit to the pursuit of personally meaningful goals. Stop for a minute and write down the things you are typically trying to accomplish in your everyday behavior. You might identify a goal such as "to get better grades" or "to be a good friend (or partner or parent)." Such everyday goals and the pursuit of them have been shown to relate strongly to subjective well-being (Brunstein, 1993; Sheldon, 2002). Goal pursuit provides the glue that meaningfully relates a chain of life events, endowing life with beginnings, middles, and ends (King, 2008).

The scientific literature on goal investment offers a variety of ideas about the types of goals that are likely to enhance happiness. To optimize the happiness payoffs of goal pursuit, one ought to set goals that are important and personally valuable and that reflect the intrinsic needs of relatedness, competence, and autonomy (Sheldon, 2002). These goals also should be moderately challenging and should share an instrumental relationship with each other—so that the pursuit of one goal facilitates the accomplishment of another (Emmons & King, 1988).

With regard to the hedonic treadmill, goal pursuit has a tremendous advantage over many other ways of trying to enhance happiness. Goals change and are changed by life experience. As a result, goal pursuit may be less susceptible to the dreaded hedonic treadmill over time. Goals accentuate the positive but do not necessarily eliminate the negative. When we fail to reach our goals, we may experience momentary increases in unhappiness (Pomerantz, Saxon, & Oishi, 2000), which can be a very good thing. Because goals can make us happy and unhappy, they keep life emotionally interesting, and their influence on happiness does not wear off over time.

Overall, goal pursuit may lead to a happier life. Goals keep the positive possible and interesting. The conclusion to be drawn from the evidence, assuming that you want to enhance your happiness, is to strive mightily for the goals that you value. You may fail now and then, but missing the mark will only make your successes all the sweeter.

SUMMARY

Happiness is highly heritable, and there is reason to consider each person as having a happiness set point. Still, many people would like to increase their level of happiness. One obstacle to changing happiness is the hedonic treadmill: the idea that we quickly adapt to changes that might enhance happiness. Another obstacle is that pursuing happiness for its own sake often backfires.

Ways to enhance happiness include engaging in physical activity, helping others, and engaging in positive self-reflection and experiencing meaning (such as by keeping a gratitude journal). Another way to enhance happiness is to pursue personally valued goals passionately.

TEST YOURSELF

1. Explain the term *hedonic treadmill* and give some real-world examples of it.

2. According to Lyubomirsky, how can individuals cultivate positive emotion?

3. How does committing oneself to personally meaningful goals relate to well-being?

Gender, Sex, and Sexuality

Jazz Jennings: Declaring Herself Proudly

"**Is it a boy or a girl?**" That is so often our first, excited question when we hear that someone has given birth or even when we find out that she is pregnant. Although it may seem straightforward, the answer—and what it means for each newborn—can be quite complex.

Consider the young girl known to the media as Jazz Jennings. Though born with a male body, Jazz has insisted throughout her young life that she is a girl (Goldberg & Adriano, 2008). At first her parents humored their son, allowing him to play with girls' toys and to dress like a girl at home. Eventually, after observing Jazz's sadness during a dance recital when he was not permitted to wear a tutu like the "other girls," Jazz's parents decided to allow her to be herself, to dress and to act like a girl everywhere she went. Jazz entered kindergarten with long hair and wearing earrings and a dress. Although ever mindful of the difficulties she might face along the way, Jazz's parents remain committed to supporting their child wherever her gender identity takes her.

Even for individuals whose biological sex seems a perfect fit, sexuality can be complex, and the impact of sex and gender can be just as profound. Issues of gender, sex, and sexuality are everywhere around us. Why do little boys gravitate toward toy trucks, and little girls toward dolls? Why are there so few male teachers, especially for preschool and kindergarten? Should women in the military be permitted to serve in combat? Should gay men and lesbian women be permitted to marry their same-sex partners? What kind of sex education is most effective? In this module we will explore the concepts, knowledge, and psychology behind these and other provocative questions related to gender, sex, and sexuality. ●

Defining Sex and Gender

Let's begin by defining the two terms we will use throughout this module. You have no doubt heard and used the words *sex* and *gender* frequently in your life. Their technical definitions are key to understanding how scientists study these concepts.

38-1 SEX AND ITS BIOLOGICAL COMPONENTS

● **sex** The properties of a person that determine his or her classification as male or female.

● **sex chromosomes** In humans, the pair of genes that differs between the sexes and determines a person's sex as male or female.

● **gonads** Glands that produce sex hormones and generate ova (eggs) in females and sperm in males; collectively called gametes, the ova and sperm are the cells that will eventually be used in reproduction.

Sex refers to the properties of a person that determine his or her classification as male or female. One structure of our physical bodies that scientists use to classify us as male or female is chromosomes. We have seen that chromosomes are the packages of DNA that carry our genes. Human beings have 23 pairs of chromosomes, with one of each pair being provided by each of our parents. Twenty-two of these pairs are generally the same in males and females, but the 23rd pair differs across the sexes. Scientists call this differing pair of genes the **sex chromosomes** because the pair determines a person's genetic sex (male or female). In females, both sex chromosomes are similar and are called X chromosomes. Males have one X and one Y chromosome—the latter so named because it looks like an upside-down Y (Figure 38.1).

Another set of physical structures used to classify us as male or female is our gonads, a part of the endocrine system. **Gonads** are glands that produce sex hormones and generate ova (eggs) in females and sperm in males; collectively called *gametes,* the ova and sperm are the cells that will eventually be used in reproduction. In females the gonads are the *ovaries* (located on either side of the abdomen), and in males they are the *testes* (located in the *scrotum,* the pouch of skin that hangs below the penis).

Sex may also be classified by the hormones that these gonads produce. Recall that hormones are chemicals produced by the endocrine system's glands. There are no hormones that are unique to one sex, but the levels of hormones vary by sex. The levels of estrogen and progesterone are higher in women than in men, and the levels of androgens (the most common being testosterone) are higher in men than in women. In women, androgens are produced by the adrenal glands, and in men some of the androgens that are produced by

FIGURE 38.1 The Genetic Difference Between Males and Females
The chromosome structures of a male (*left*) and female (*right*). The 23rd pair is shown at bottom right. Notice that the male's Y chromosome is smaller than his X chromosome. To obtain pictures of chromosomes, a cell is removed from a person's body, usually from inside the mouth, and the chromosomes are photographed under magnification.

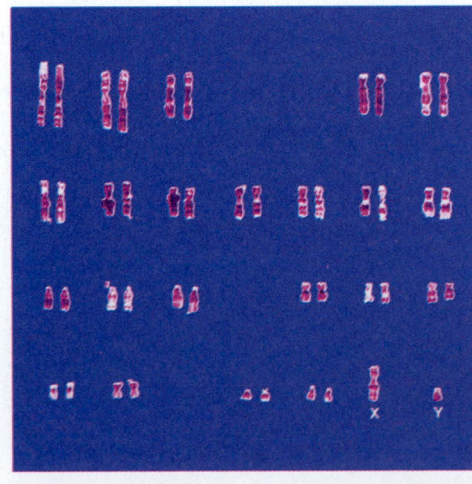

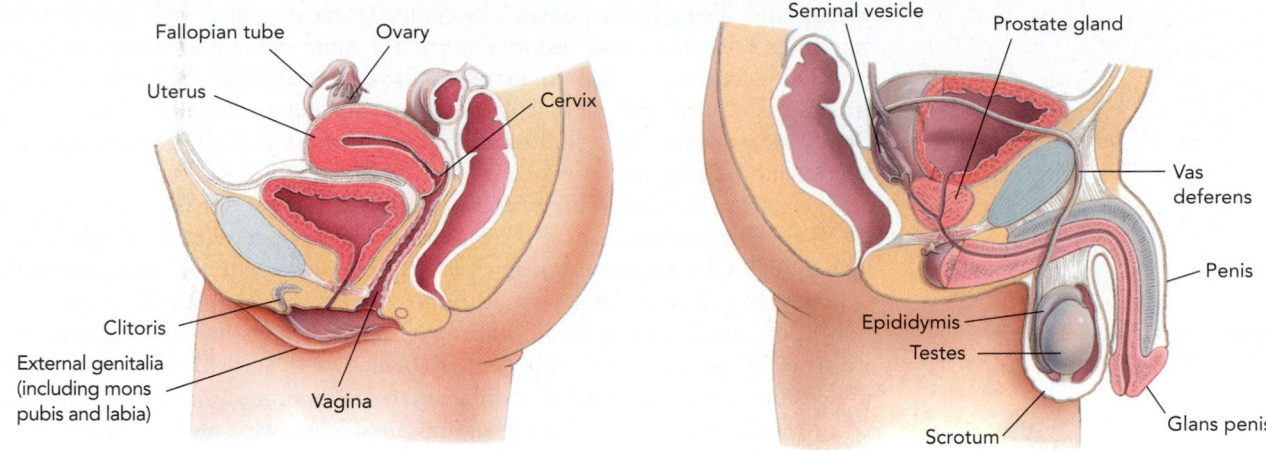

FIGURE 38.2 **Female and Male Internal Sex Organs and External Genitalia** These figures show the female (*left*) and male (*right*) internal sex organs and external genitalia.

the testes are converted into estrogens. These hormones play a role in the development of our internal reproductive structures, our external genitalia, and the secondary sex characteristics (see below) that are also used in classifying us as male or female.

Figure 38.2 shows the internal sex organs of females and males. In women, these organs allow the ovum to travel from the ovaries to the uterus, and they also play roles in sexual functioning, the menstrual cycle, and pregnancy. In men, the internal sex organs include the structures involved in the production and storage of sperm, as well as those that play a role in sexual arousal and orgasm.

The external genitalia of males and females are found between their legs, as Figure 38.2 also illustrates. The external genitalia of females, collectively called the *vulva,* include the *mons pubis* (a fleshy area just above the vagina), the *labia* (the lips surrounding the vaginal opening), and the *clitoris* (a small sensory organ at the top where the labia meet). For males, the external genitalia include the *penis* and *scrotum.*

Puberty is a period of rapid skeletal and sexual maturation that occurs mainly in early adolescence (Figure 38.3). At puberty, individuals develop **secondary sex characteristics,** traits that differ between the two sexes but are not part of the reproductive system. Breasts in females and facial hair in males are secondary sex characteristics.

To reemphasize, these many physical attributes may play a role in classifying a person as male or female. However, as we will see, physical characteristics may or may not match a person's psychological experience of himself or herself as male or female—that is, the person's gender.

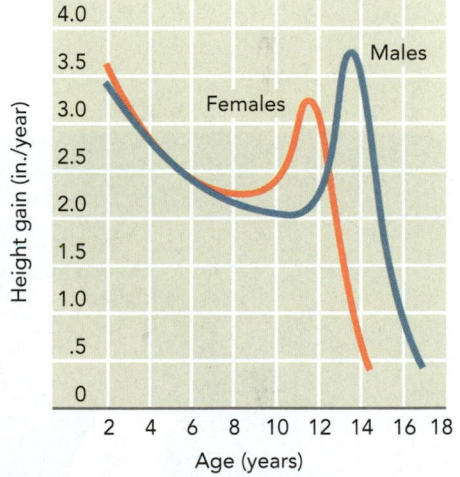

FIGURE 38.3 **Pubertal Growth Spurt** On average, the pubertal growth spurt begins and peaks about two years earlier for girls (starts at 9, peaks at 11½) than for boys (starts at 11½, peaks at 13½). From J. M. Tanner et al., in *Archives of Diseases in Childhood, 41,* 1966. Reproduced with permission from the BMJ Publishing Group.

38-2 GENDER

Gender refers to the social and psychological aspects of being female or male. Gender goes beyond biological sex to include a person's understanding of the meaning to his or her own life of being male or female. Although checking off "male" or "female" on a questionnaire may seem like a simple choice, gender is a complex variable influenced by biological factors, as well as socialization and experience.

Gender identity is an individual's sense of belonging to the male or female sex. Gender identity is multifaceted. Specifically, people differ in the extent to which they experience gender identity as central to their sense of self; in their comfort level with their own gender category; and in the degree to which they feel socially encouraged to conform to a particular gender identity (Berenbaum, 2006; Martin & Ruble, 2010).

In describing a person's gender identity, we might talk about attributes such as masculinity and femininity. Technically speaking, these words mean, respectively, "being like

● **secondary sex characteristics** Traits that differ between the two sexes but are not part of the reproductive system; they include breasts in females and facial hair in males.

● **gender** The social and psychological aspects of being female or male; gender goes beyond biological sex to include a person's understanding of the meaning to his or her own life of being male or female.

● **gender identity** An individual's multifaceted sense of belonging to the male or female sex.

a man" and "being like a woman." Psychologists have studied these gender-related characteristics using the terms *instrumentality* (for more masculine traits) and *expressiveness* (for more feminine traits) to represent broad dimensions that may or may not be strongly associated with a particular sex. Instrumental attributes include being assertive, brave, independent, and dominant. Expressive traits include being nurturing, warm, gentle, and sensitive to others.

Instrumentality and expressiveness are not systematically related to each other, so every possible combination of these characteristics is possible. We might call someone who is highly instrumental but not very expressive "masculine," and someone else who is highly expressive but not very instrumental "feminine." Individuals who are *high* on both dimensions are considered **androgynous,** meaning that they have attributes that we typically associate with both genders (Bem, 1993). Individuals who are *low* on both dimensions are referred to as undifferentiated. Importantly, although there are differences between men and women regarding these traits, with men scoring as more instrumental and women as more expressive (Fink & others, 2007; Lippa, 2008), they are not as strong as you might expect. Indeed, the degree of instrumentality or expressiveness a person feels can depend on the social context and the activity in which he or she is engaged (Leszczynski, 2009). A father playing with his toddler may feel quite expressive; a WNBA guard who is running up the basketball court on a fast break may feel quite instrumental.

● **androgynous** Having attributes that we typically associate with both genders.

Research has shown that individuals who are not strongly gender-typed according to these scales tend to have better psychological adjustment and resilience than those rated as extremely masculine or feminine (Lam & McBride-Chang, 2007). In fact, a balance between instrumentality and expressiveness relates to a variety of positive outcomes (Bruch, 2002; Danoff-Burg, Mosher, & Grant, 2006; Helgeson, 1994; Mosher & Danoff-Burg, 2008).

It is tempting to think of *sex* as the term for biologically based differences between males and females, and *gender* as the word for differences that are a product of environment or socialization. Many psychologists do in fact distinguish sex and gender in this way (Caplan & Caplan, 2005; Halpern & others, 2007). In this module we generally reserve the word *sex* to refer to biological characteristics, and we use *gender* for psychosocial attributes that are related to sex but that may or may not reflect biological differences.

Sex and gender are linked in ways that might surprise you. Let's take a close look at the processes that lead from sex to gender.

38-3 FROM GENES TO SEX TO GENDER

In the first few weeks after conception, male and female embryos look alike. Moreover, the raw materials of male and female genitals and gonads are essentially the same. The penis and clitoris take shape from the same embryonic structures. Similarly, the same embryonic structures develop into the testes (in males) and ovaries (in females), and the same is true for the scrotum and the labia. What causes the differentiation of the sexes is a particular gene on the Y chromosome, the *SRY gene,* which is activated early in the first trimester (the first three months of the pregnancy). The SRY gene causes the development of embryonic testes. These testes begin to manufacture androgens (including testosterone) that spread throughout the developing embryo, influencing the growing body and brain. Through this process,

Some successful entertainers, among them Adam Lambert and Lady Gaga, challenge common notions of gender.

Gender and Neuroscience: Are There His and Hers Brains?

Do men's and women's brains differ systematically? Research using the brain-imaging techniques we examined in Module 7 shows that male and female brains do differ from each other in significant ways.

Female brains are smaller than male brains by between 8 and 10 percent (Cahill, 2006), and this difference is not explained by the fact that women are generally smaller than men (Goldstein & others, 2001). Perhaps because of its smaller size, the female brain may use its real estate more judiciously. Compared to the male brain, a woman's brain has higher cortical volume (meaning that more of the brain is devoted to the cortex, the brain's outermost part). The female brain also has more *gray matter* (brain tissue made up of neurons that send signals), but the male brain has more *white matter* (brain tissue composed of myelinated axons that send signals rapidly to and from the gray matter). In terms of brain structures, in women, the prefrontal cortex and the hippocampus are larger, while in men the amygdalae are larger (Goldstein & others, 2001; Hamann, 2005).

Why do you think male and female brains differ?

Male and female brains differ not only in structure but in function as well (McCarthy & others, 2009). The hippocampus in women is less reactive to stress (Andreano & Cahill, 2006; Cahill, 2006) and may not be affected as strongly by chronic stress compared to the male hippocampus. Men's right amygdala is more active than the left in response to happy faces. In women the opposite pattern holds (Killgore & Yurgelun-Todd, 2001).

The hippocampus and amygdala are involved in learning, memory, and emotion. So, do sex differences in these areas translate into differences in learning, memory, and emotion? Research has begun to suggest that they might (Andreano & Cahill, 2006). For example, one study examined the release of noradrenaline (also called *norepinephrine,* a chemical that is emitted into the synapses of the brain as part of the "fight or flight" response described in Module 6) in reaction to emotionally arousing pictures and investigated the memory for those pictures in men and women (Segal & Cahill, 2009). Although there was no sex difference in memory performance, the brain processes that had occurred differed between the sexes. For women, noradrenaline release was more likely to occur in response to emotional pictures. Furthermore, in women, this release was related to better long-term memory. Men's memory was similarly accurate but was not a function of noradrenaline release.

These results suggest that when performing the same task, men and women may tap into different regions of the brain to produce identical-looking results. Sex *differences* in the brain may explain the *lack of differences* in behavior, as the brains of each sex compensate for their various differences to produce the same behavior (De Vries, 2004).

Research on the neuroscience of sex differences tells us that even when the sexes look alike behaviorally, different brain processes may be responsible for these behaviors, depending on the person's sex. A key lesson from this intriguing research is that sex matters to neuroscience—in sometimes unexpected ways. We cannot study one sex and make generalizations about the other, even when we are studying the brain (Cahill, 2006).

the XY embryo essentially turns itself into a male. Low levels of androgen in a female embryo allow for the development of the female body and brain.

Although often called the sex chromosomes, the 46th pair broadly influences human development, affecting not only sexual characteristics but other bodily systems as well (Goldstein & Reynolds, 1999; Hagerman, 2009). Given their extensive effects, might these chromosomal differences between the sexes lead to differences in the development of the brain? To explore this intriguing question, check out the Intersection.

38·4 DISORDERS OF SEXUAL DEVELOPMENT

Genes and prenatal hormones play crucial roles in the development of the genitals, and these physical structures are generally used to identify a child's sex prenatally through an ultrasound or at birth (Berenbaum, 2006; Blakemore, Berenbaum, & Liben, 2009).

● **disorders of sexual development (DSD)**
Congenital conditions in which the development of chromosomal, gonadal, or anatomical sex is atypical; formerly called intersex conditions or hermaphroditism.

Although typically the sex of a baby is straightforward, some individuals are born with external genitalia that are not clearly male or female. Prenatal hormonal exposure, chromosomal abnormalities, and environmental factors (such as exposure to radiation, chemicals, or some medications while in the womb) can affect the developing genitals. The result may be sexually ambiguous—that is, not clearly male or female—external organs such as a very small penis, an enlarged clitoris, or genitals that appear to include both a penis and vaginal labia. Formerly called *intersex conditions* (or *hermaphroditism*), these conditions now fall under the category of **disorders of sexual development (DSD)** (Hughes & others, 2006), which refers to *congenital* (that is, present at birth) conditions in which the development of chromosomal, gonadal, or anatomical sex is atypical (P. A. Lee & others, 2006). Professionals debate about how best to handle such cases.

Imagine being the parent of a child born with genitals that are not clearly male or female. How would you feel, and what would you do? Experts long believed that immediate surgery and sex assignment were crucial for both parents and children (Money, Hampson, & Hampson, 1955, 1957). Decades ago, professionals assumed that a child could not develop normally with ambiguous genitals and that gender identity was entirely determined by socialization rather than being influenced by biological factors (Berenbaum, 2006; Meyer-Bahlburg, 1998). Interestingly, these assumptions were originally supported by a case in which a child was born with *unambiguously* male genitalia.

John Money, a well-known sex researcher, believed strongly that socialization was the main determinant of gender. In the 1960s, a case presented itself that gave Money the opportunity to test this theory. In 1965 twin boys were born, and a few months after birth, one twin's penis was destroyed during circumcision. Money persuaded the boy's parents to allow him to surgically transform the injured male genitals into female genitals and to agree to treat the child as a girl. The former boy was reared as a girl and, according to Money, essentially became a girl (Money & Tucker, 1975). The "John/Joan" case became famous as an example of nurture's triumph over nature. For many years, this case was used as evidence for the amazing flexibility of gender.

Milton Diamond, a biologist and strong critic of Money's theory, decided to follow up on Money's most famous case (Diamond & Sigmundson, 1997). Diamond found that over time, "Joan" became less and less interested in being a girl and eventually refused to continue the process of feminization that Money had devised. We now know that "Joan" was really David Reimer, whose biography, *As Nature Made Him,* written by John Colapinto (2000), revealed the difficulties of his life as a boy, then a girl, then a boy, and finally a man. David struggled with traumatic gender-related life experiences and depression, eventually committing suicide in 2004.

David's story seems to indicate that biological factors powerfully guide the way from sex to gender identity. Yet this one case may not represent the full picture. Remember from Module 4 that it is difficult to make generalizations based on a single case study. However tragic, this case does not close the door on the possibility that socialization can significantly shape gender development. Indeed, there have been other cases in which genetic males have lost their penis to trauma, animal attacks, or vehicular accidents at a very young age. In such cases, doctors and parents must consider their options: to reassign the individual's sex to female and rear the child as a girl, or to rear him as a boy with eventual surgery to re-create the penis. However, regarding the latter option, male sexual anatomy is extremely complex, and such surgery is difficult. Perhaps for this reason, some parents have decided to reassign the child's sex, and a number of cases have had positive outcomes (Bradley & others, 1998; Lippa, 2005; Zucker, 1999).

What about evidence beyond vivid cases? One clear conclusion from that evidence is that the sex in which an individual is reared is the single strongest predictor of eventual gender identity (Berenbaum, 2006; Meyer-Bahlburg, 2005; Zucker, 1999). In other words, socialization is powerfully (but not perfectly) related to eventual gender identity. For example, one study showed that among genetic males born without a

NEW YORK TIMES BESTSELLER

"Riveting, cleanly written, and brilliantly researched."
—Natalie Angier, New York Times Book Review

AS NATURE MADE HIM
THE BOY WHO WAS RAISED AS A GIRL

JOHN COLAPINTO

P.S. INSIGHTS, INTERVIEWS & MORE...

Colapinto's biography documents the dramatic John/Joan case—one of the most infamous in modern medicine—in which David Reimer, who had suffered a botched circumcision as an infant, was raised as a girl until he was a teenager.

penis (due to a birth defect) and reared as females, fully 78 percent lived their adult lives as women. Of those who were reared as male, 100 percent were living as male (Meyer-Bahlburg, 2005).

After reviewing the evidence, Sheri Berenbaum (2006), an expert on sexual development, concluded that despite their distress, parents and healthcare providers might need to live with a child's unusual physical condition until the child is able to have some say in the decision. The idea that a child cannot experience healthy development with ambiguous genitals is simply an assumption that has not been systematically tested. Policies about treatment ought to be based on reproductive potential, the possibility of future sexual functioning, and a minimization of medical procedures. Further, Berenbaum stressed that all involved in the decision must realize that the child might initiate a gender change later in life. Most important, experts agree that these decisions should be made based on the child's well-being, not parental distress (Consortium on the Management of Disorders of Sexual Development, 2006).

38·5 WHEN GENETIC SEX AND GENDER CONFLICT: TRANSGENDER EXPERIENCE

This section began with the story of Jazz Jennings, the child who was born with a boy's body but is convinced that she is a girl. Among other people who feel as if they were born into the wrong sex is Chastity Bono, the daughter of pop singers Sonny and Cher; Chastity recently came out as transgendered and changed her name to Chaz. **Transgender** refers to experiencing one's psychological gender as different from one's physical sex. Transgender individuals can be biological males who identify as female, or biological females who identify as male.

How do psychologists understand transgender individuals? The American Psychiatric Association classifies individuals who feel trapped in the wrong biological sex as suffering from gender identity disorder (previously referred to as "transsexualism") (APA, 2000). **Gender identity disorder (GID)** refers to strong, persistent cross-sex identification and a continuing discomfort with, or sense of inappropriateness of, one's assigned sex. To meet the criteria for GID, the person cannot have experienced a disorder of sexual development, and the distress must be such that it interferes with daily life. Quite rare, GID occurs in an estimated 1 in 11,000–30,000 genetic males and 1 in 30,400–100,000 genetic females (APA, 2000).

The defining feature of GID is *gender dysphoria,* distress over one's born sex (Cohen-Kettenis & Pfafflin, 2010; Gijs & Brewaeys, 2007). The only empirically evaluated treatment for GID is *sex reassignment surgery,* which involves the removal of secondary sex characteristics, hormone treatments, and the surgical reconstruction of the genitals. The surgical challenges that female-to-male transgender individuals face are more complex than those for male-to-female transgender people. Studies of individuals who have undergone these procedures generally find that they express little or no regret and are satisfied with the surgery (Cohen-Kettenis & Pfafflin, 2010; Gijs & Brewaeys, 2007).

A controversial diagnosis, GID is no longer viewed as a disorder in France or Great Britain. Nonetheless, should individuals who experience themselves as one gender psychologically and another physically be considered mentally ill? Should their treatment be seen as primarily a way to alleviate suffering? Increasingly, transgender individuals have urged that society consider them as not suffering from a disorder but rather as individuals who require help in dealing with a distressing error in nature (Cohen-Kettenis & Pfafflin, 2010).

Many transgender individuals do not desire sex reassignment surgery (Cohen-Kettenis & Pfafflin, 2010). Some opt for hormone treatment

● **transgender** Experiencing one's psychological gender as different from one's physical sex, as in the cases of biological males who identify as female, and biological females who identify as male.

● **gender identity disorder (GID)** Strong, persistent cross-sex identification and a continuing discomfort with, or sense of inappropriateness of, one's assigned sex.

Chaz Bono, who has recently completed the transition from female to male, is an activist for the lesbian, gay, bisexual, and transgender communities.

only. Others prefer to think of their gender identity in an alternative, broader way: They embrace their identity as a quality that challenges the notion of sexual identity as one of two opposing categories. For such individuals, being transgender means living according to the belief that a person can experience life as a man who happens to have a vagina or as a woman who has a penis (Lev, 2007)—as an individual who occupies a different but valid gender territory (Meyer-Bahlburg, 2010; Pfafflin, 2010).

For most people, genetic sex and psychological gender are experienced as a pretty good fit. Nevertheless, we might wonder how a person who is XX or XY comes to think of him- or herself as female or male. Various theories of gender development have addressed this question.

SUMMARY

Sex refers to biological aspects of the person that are used to classify him or her as male or female. Biological features that serve in this capacity include genes, gonads, hormones, genitals, and secondary sexual characteristics. *Gender* refers to the person's psychological sense of himself or herself as male or female. Gender is sometimes described in terms of a person's level of instrumentality or expressiveness.

Disorders of sexual development are conditions in which a person's genetic, genital, or gonadal sex is atypical. In these cases, the sex in which the child was raised is the most consistent predictor of eventual gender identity.

Individuals who feel trapped in the wrong biological sex are referred to as *transgender*. Transgender individuals are sometimes considered to be suffering from gender identity disorder, which involves intense distress over one's birth sex. The only evaluated treatment for gender identity disorder is sex reassignment surgery. There is controversy about whether transgender should be considered a psychological disorder. Many transgender individuals feel that they do not have a disorder but rather occupy a different gender territory that goes beyond male versus female.

KEY TERMS

sex   386

sex chromosomes   386

gonads   386

secondary sex
   characteristics   387

gender   387

gender identity   387

androgynous   388

disorders of sexual development
   (DSD)   390

transgender   391

gender identity disorder
   (GID)   391

TEST YOURSELF

1. Explain the difference between sex and gender.
2. Discuss the causes of the differentiation of the sexes.
3. What is gender identity disorder (GID)? What is the only treatment for GID that has been evaluated by research?

APPLY YOUR KNOWLEDGE

1. Conduct web searches for "transgender experience" and "gender identity disorder." How do the sites you find differ in terms of their discussion of a person who feels trapped in the wrong sex?

2. What are some of your personal instrumental and expressive traits? How does your list fit with the statement that instrumental traits are more masculine and expressive traits are more feminine?

Theories of Gender Development

In this module we examine the major theoretical approaches to gender development. Theorists debate the relative contributions of nature and nurture to gender identity. In general, psychologists acknowledge that gender identity is complex and that to understand it we need to consider both biological and psychosocial processes (Berenbaum, 2006; Blakemore, Berenbaum, & Liben, 2009).

39-1 BIOLOGICAL APPROACHES

We have seen that a number of biological factors—including genes, gonads, and hormones—identify a person as male or female. Biological approaches to gender draw links between these aspects of the person's biological sex and his or her eventual psychological feelings of gender. Individuals who study biological factors in gender development focus on variables such as genes, prenatal hormones, and brain structures and functions, as these differ between males and females and potentially account for the experiences of ourselves in those sexes.

Biologically based research has looked at differences between the sexes in infancy, searching for clues to gender-related characteristics in the earliest days of life. One study examined 1-day-old male and female infants. The infants were shown two stimuli: a human face and a mobile made out of a picture of that face (Connellan & others, 2000). The researchers found that the baby girls spent more time looking at the human face, while the baby boys were more interested in the mobile (Connellan & others, 2000). Similarly, research on infants from 3 to 8 months of age found that males spent more time looking at typical boy toys, including trucks and machines, and females spent more time looking at typical girl toys, such as dolls (Alexander, Wilcox, & Woods, 2009). Nonhuman primates exhibit similar differences (Alexander & Hines, 2002; Hassett, Siebert, & Wallen, 2008). In humans, such differences are thought to be biologically, not socially, based because very young children have not yet had social experiences that might influence gender development.

39-2 EVOLUTIONARY PSYCHOLOGY

The evolutionary psychology approach to gender views the biological differences between the sexes through the lens of natural selection and adaptation. From this perspective, the factors that produce gender are the product of millions of years of natural selection.

Charles Darwin's theory of evolution, a species' characteristics reflect natural selection, the process by which the environment determines the adaptiveness of particular genetic characteristics. Organisms with the fittest genes are most likely to survive and reproduce. This slow process is responsible for creating the typical characteristics of any species. Applying these ideas to gender, evolutionary psychologists assert that the differences

Research on infants from 3 to 8 months of age found that males spent more time looking at boy toys, such as trucks and machines, than other toys.

This male peacock uses his beautiful plumage to attract female mates.

● **sexual selection** According to Darwin's theory of evolution, the differentiation between the male and female members of a species because of the differences between the two in competition and choice.

we see between contemporary men and women can be explained by the *selection pressures,* or environmental challenges, that confronted our distant human ancestors (Buss, 2011; Cosmides, 2011; Geary, 2010; Meston & Buss, 2009).

Sexual Selection

Differences between male and female members of the same species abound in nature. For instance, the beautiful peacock with the colorful tail and the cardinal with brilliant red feathers are both males, while the female members of those species are duller in appearance. What accounts for these sex differences within species? Darwin (1871) proposed that many sex differences that occur within species have evolved through sexual selection. **Sexual selection** means that the male and female members of a species differ from each other because of differences in competition and choice. *Competition* occurs among members of the same sex as they vie for the opportunity to mate with members of the opposite sex. Members of that opposite sex in turn exercise *choice,* selecting the lucky one (or ones) with whom they will mate. In peacocks, the males use their amazing plumage to compete with one another for females, and the female selects the prettiest male with whom to reproduce.

Who competes and who chooses? Generally, the sex that invests the most in producing offspring is the one that chooses, and the other sex is the one that competes (Andersson & Simmons, 2006; Bateman, 1948; Clutton-Brock, 2007, 2010). Applying these ideas to humans, evolutionary psychologists believe that sex differences observed in women and men are evidence that sexual selection has occurred in our species. Women are the sex that gives birth, and as such they ought to do the choosing. Men, on the other hand, show characteristics that are thought to be well suited for competing. For example, men are physically larger and stronger than women. Evolutionary psychologists explain human males' physical size as an adaptation that helps men to compete against one another for female mates.

Sexual selection is more complicated in human beings than in other species. Specifically, because human infants are so helpless, it makes sense from a survival standpoint for men to invest in their offspring—so sometimes men get to be the choosers, and women are the competitors vying for those men who are likely to invest in their children (Andersson & Simmons, 2006; Halpern & others, 2007). This aspect of sexual selection is of particular interest in humans because of the different challenges men and women face in reproducing.

Reproductive Challenges for Men and Women

Men and women share the same evolutionary goal—to reproduce—but accomplishing that objective presents different challenges to each sex. Women are the sex that experiences pregnancy and childbirth. They can reproduce only about once per year and have a limited time of fertility. Thus, women must be choosy in selecting sexual partners, putting a premium on high *quality.* Evolutionary psychologists stress that women should be picky and should seek sexual partners who have adequate resources to invest in a family.

In contrast, according to evolutionary theorists, because men are generally fertile from puberty through the rest of life, they can focus on *quantity,* reproducing as often as possible with a broad range of partners. A sticking point for this strategy, though, is that as noted above, babies are so helpless that it is adaptive for men to invest in their offspring.

Further, men have an additional problem. Because the moment when the egg is fertilized by the sperm is a mystery for the parties involved, a man cannot be certain whether the child in whom he is investing his resources is genetically *his* child. Evolutionarily speaking, for a man, the worst-case scenario is to invest his resources to ensure the survival of someone else's offspring.

How might men avoid this dreaded outcome? Evolutionary psychologists point out that across cultures, men are likely to prefer women who are younger than they are (Buss, 2011). This preference for younger women may be a way for a man to minimize the chances that his betrothed is already pregnant with someone else's offspring. Evolutionary psychologists suggest that, compared to women, men should be less selective about sexual behavior and more interested in physical appearance (which is thought to represent health and fertility), seeking partners who are young and beautiful (Buss, 2011; Geary, 2010).

The sex differences that have been discovered shortly after birth, as well as cross-cultural similarities in mate preferences, would seem strongly to support biological and evolutionary theories of gender development. However, let's stop and think beyond these theories and also look at the potential role of the *social* environment in the emergence of gender. Family and friends begin to buy pink and blue baby clothes before a child is even born. That child is introduced to a social network with strong expectations about gender-appropriate behavior. If a little boy shows a preference for playing with a truck or a ball, we might smile and conclude, "He's *all boy*." If the same child expresses interest in trying on a dress or playing with a doll, we might respond quite differently. Might not these different social responses influence the child's developing sense of self?

Furthermore, consider that the male preference for younger sexual partners may reflect social expectations or the power differences that exist between men and women in many cultures. These considerations reflect concerns that are represented in two additional views of gender development: social cognitive approaches and social role theory.

39-3 SOCIAL COGNITIVE APPROACHES

Social cognitive theories of gender development focus on how children learn about gender and how they come to occupy a particular gender identity. These approaches emphasize both the way that children internalize information about gender (Bem, 1983, 1993) and the way the environment reinforces gender-related behavior (Bussey & Bandura, 2004).

Social cognitive approaches examine how experience influences the formation of the person's sense of gender. From this perspective, gender behavior is learned through reward and punishment, observational learning, and modeling (Bandura & Bussey, 2004; Bussey & Bandura, 2004). According to Albert Bandura, modeling is an especially potent mechanism for transmitting values (Bandura, 1986; Bussey & Bandura 2004). Children gain information about gender from models of each sex. Who goes to work every day? Who does the housekeeping? When children see their parents and other adults engaging in gender-related behavior (and as they observe whether and how these behaviors are reinforced), they learn about how men and women behave.

In subtle ways, children may be rewarded for engaging in gender-conforming behavior and punished for engaging in behavior that does not fit with expectations for their sex, what is called *gender-nonconforming behavior*. Examples of gender-conforming behavior include playing with dolls (for girls) and playing with trucks (for boys). Examples of gender-nonconforming behavior are

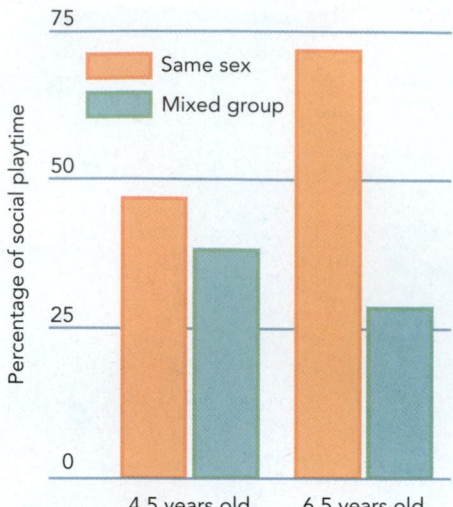

FIGURE 39.1 **Developmental Changes in Percentage of Time Spent in Same-Sex and Mixed-Group Settings** Observations of children show that they are more likely to play in same-sex than mixed-sex groups. This tendency increases between 4 and 6 years of age.

● **gender roles** Expectations for how females and males should think, act, and feel.

● **gender stereotypes** Overly general beliefs and expectations about what women and men are like.

a girl's playing with a train set and a boy's playing dress-up or house. The child's social environment responds to behaviors in various ways, coloring his or her perception of their appropriateness. A girl might learn that pretending to be a professional football player is not a way to please her parents. A boy might pick up on his mother's subtle frown when he announces that he wants to try on her high-heeled shoes.

Peers also play an important role in gender development. Especially after age 6, peer groups often segregate into boy groups and girl groups (Maccoby, 2002) (Figure 39.1). Peers are stricter than most parents in rewarding gender-conforming behavior and punishing gender-nonconforming behavior. For example, children can be punitive toward boys who engage in behaviors that are not typically boyish (Herek, 1991; Bailey & Zucker, 1995; Lippa, 2008).

Through these varied experiences, children develop a *gender schema*—a mental framework for understanding what is considered appropriate behavior for females and males in their culture (Martin & Ruble, 2010). Children learn that gender is an important organizing principle in social life, and they come to recognize that boys and girls, and men and women, are different in ways that matter. This gender schema then serves as a cognitive framework by which children interpret further experiences related to gender.

While acknowledging biological differences between males and females, social cognitive psychologists believe that social and cultural factors have a much stronger influence on eventual gender identity (Bandura & Bussey, 2004). From this perspective, differences in men's and women's career and life choices can be explained by differences in the availability of role models and beliefs about self-efficacy and personal control. Social cognitive practitioners would say, for example, that men and women differ in their career choices primarily because they have different beliefs about their ability to achieve their career goals—and about the extent to which success is in their control.

39·4 SOCIAL ROLE THEORY

Alice Eagly has proposed that to understand gender, we must recognize the larger social and cultural institutions surrounding the psychological phenomenon of gender identity (Eagly, 1987, 2010a, 2010b; Eagly & Fischer, 2009; Eagly & Sczesny, 2009; Eagly & Wood, 2010; Wood & Eagly, 2010). Eagly's approach, *social role theory*, starts off by acknowledging the very same physical differences between the sexes that were noted by evolutionary psychologists: Women are more innately and directly involved in reproduction than men, and men are larger and stronger than women. Eagly proposed that these differences resulted in a division of labor between the sexes, with women being more involved in the home and with childrearing, and men being more likely to work outside the home.

From Eagly's perspective, this division of labor can lead to the belief that the things that men and women *do* are the things that men and women *should do*. The activities and occupations we see men and women performing give rise to expectations and beliefs about what it means to be male or female, what a male or female person *ought* to do, and what we believe that person *can* do. In this way, the division of labor spawns the social construct of **gender roles,** expectations for how females and males should think, act, and feel (Leaper & Friedman, 2007). Social role theory argues that each culture creates its own sense of what is a man and what is a woman (Eagly, 2010a, 2010b; Eagly & Wood, 2010).

Gender roles are related to **gender stereotypes**—overly general beliefs and expectations about what women and men are like. Gender stereotypes might suggest that women are warm, caring, and emotional and that men are strong, dominant, and rational. These stereotypes might influence how we interpret behavior. For example, if a woman is assertive, we might view her as bossy or manly, and if a man is gentle, we might evaluate him as wimpy.

Social role theory asserts that each of us internalizes these roles and stereotypes and comes to evaluate our own behavior and life choices according to their gender typicality (Deaux & LaFrance, 1998; Eagly & Wood, 2010). For example, gender roles and gender stereotypes might influence our life goals (Diekman & Eagly, 2008; Evans & Diekman, 2009). If a particular occupation (say, an engineer, a nurse, or a kindergarten teacher) conflicts with our perceived gender role, we may view it as less desirable and less likely to bring us success. Notably, when men and women make choices that are guided by gender roles and gender stereotypes, they tend to become more and more different from each other in their behaviors, attitudes, and aspirations, with each sex engaging in more stereotypical pursuits (Eagly, Wood, & Johannesen-Schmidt, 2004). In turn, these sex-based differences, driven by gender roles and stereotypes, maintain the social structure (Eagly, 1987; Eagly & Wood, 2010).

Social role theory also takes into account the institutional structures and patterns of opportunity that perpetuate gender differences (Eagly, 1987; Eagly & Wood, 2010; Wood & Eagly, 2010). Differences between men and women in access to education and in the treatment they receive from teachers, for instance, helps to explain differences in career choices.

One prediction from social role theory is that as social structures change, gender differences should decrease—and this prediction has been borne out (Eagly & Diekman, 2003). For example, in cultures in which women have greater access to economic opportunities, education, and careers, women are much less likely to prefer men with resources as suggested by the evolutionary perspective (Eagly & Wood, 2010; Kasser & Sharma, 1999). Importantly, social role theory asserts that thinking about men and women simply in terms of their sex misses big differences among people within each group. Indeed, in Eagly's view, lumping people together according to their sex (assuming that biological sex means the same thing as gender) is essentially engaging in gender stereotyping.

39-5 EVALUATING THE THEORETICAL APPROACHES TO GENDER

Traditional gender roles and gender stereotypes often (but not always, as the photo shows) shape individuals' life goals and career choices.

In summary, scholars think about gender and its origins in a number of persuasive ways, including biological, evolutionary, social cognitive, and social role perspectives. These theories are not mutually exclusive, and a comprehensive understanding of gender might well take all of them into account.

Biology alone would not seem to offer a sufficient explanation for gender. Indeed, wide variations occur within each sex, for there are certainly girls and women who are assertive and dominant, as well as boys and men who are submissive and subordinate. Yet biological differences between the sexes are perhaps more significant than the social cognitive approach acknowledges: Just ask the parents whose daughter insists on playing with dolls instead of trucks or who witness their son turning a stuffed bunny into a weapon.

Similarities in patterns of gender differences across different cultures support evolutionary psychology approaches. However, the application of sexual selection to human behavior has been strongly criticized. Some suggest that gender differences between men and women can be better explained by social factors, among them group cooperation, than by natural selection (Roughgarden, Oishi, & Akcay, 2006).

Certainly, having role models is a vital factor in the attitudes that men and women form about their choices of life goals, as the social cognitive view suggests. Further, there is no question that social roles are also important. Indeed, it is shocking to think that although we live in a world where in some nations a woman can serve as national leader, in other countries a girl is not permitted even to go to school and a woman cannot leave home without an escort.

Biological, evolutionary, social cognitive, and social role theorists approach gender development from different levels of analysis, and each approach poses different research questions to answer (Figure 39.2). Throughout the rest of this module, we will regularly refer to these broad perspectives to see how each one applies with regard to the specific topics and issues addressed. Each of these theories, for example, has something to say about whether and how the sexes should differ from each other on various attributes, our next topic.

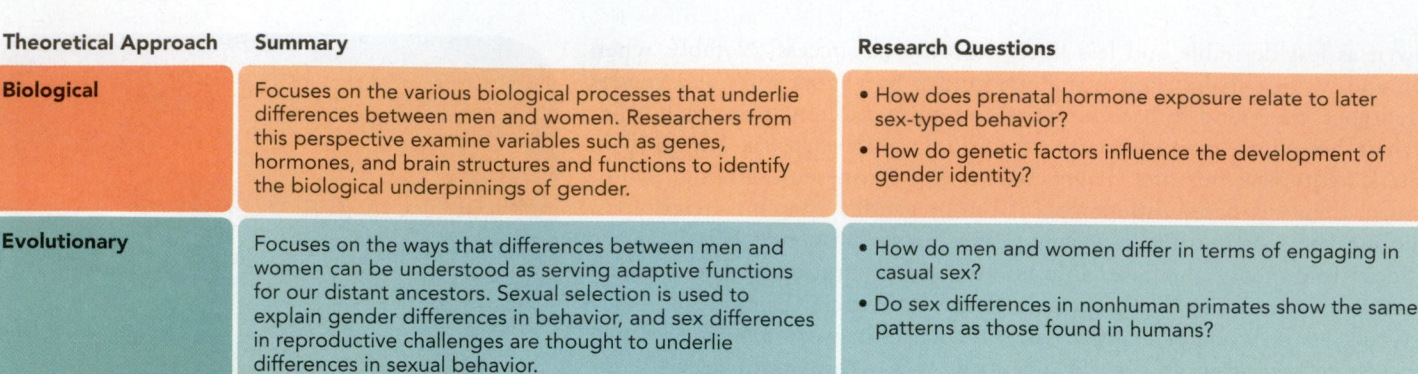

Theoretical Approach	Summary	Research Questions
Biological	Focuses on the various biological processes that underlie differences between men and women. Researchers from this perspective examine variables such as genes, hormones, and brain structures and functions to identify the biological underpinnings of gender.	• How does prenatal hormone exposure relate to later sex-typed behavior? • How do genetic factors influence the development of gender identity?
Evolutionary	Focuses on the ways that differences between men and women can be understood as serving adaptive functions for our distant ancestors. Sexual selection is used to explain gender differences in behavior, and sex differences in reproductive challenges are thought to underlie differences in sexual behavior.	• How do men and women differ in terms of engaging in casual sex? • Do sex differences in nonhuman primates show the same patterns as those found in humans?
Social Cognitive	Focuses on how processes such as learning (including modeling and rewards and punishers) and the development of cognitive schemas associated with sex lead to conceptions of male and female.	• When do children learn that a person's sex makes a difference in how he or she is treated by others? • How do peer groups react to children who behave in gender-atypical ways?
Social Role	Focuses on the ways that the division of labor between the sexes leads to expectations about what is appropriate behavior for members of each sex. The division of labor leads to the construction of gender roles and stereotypes that influence the opportunities and aspirations of men and women.	• Do women seek out different opportunities in cultures that have more egalitarian attitudes toward the sexes? • Do gender differences we see in one culture translate to another?

FIGURE 39.2 **Summary of Major Theoretical Approaches to Gender and Gender Development** Note how each approach focuses on a different aspect of human life, ranging from genetic and hormonal influences to relationships, psychological processes, and social structures.

SUMMARY

Perspectives on gender development include biological, evolutionary psychology, social cognitive, and social role theories. Biological approaches focus on the ways that genes, hormones, and brain structures relate to gender differences. Evolutionary psychology theory views gender through the lens of Darwinian natural selection and states that human beings have evolved through a process of sexual selection in which males compete for mates and females choose their male partners. Social cognitive approaches to gender emphasize how learning, modeling, and cognitive schemas influence the development of gender. Social role theory states that a division of labor between the sexes that is based on male–female physical differences can lead to the social construction of gender roles and gender stereotypes. Social role theory predicts that as social structures change, gender differences should decline.

KEY TERMS

sexual selection   394
gender roles   396

gender stereotypes   396

TEST YOURSELF

1. What are four major theoretical approaches to gender development? What is the main idea behind each?

2. Explain sexual selection, a key concept of the evolutionary psychology approach.

3. What are gender roles and gender stereotypes? What does social role theory say about them?

APPLY YOUR KNOWLEDGE

1. Ask your parents about your gender-related behavior as a child and about their views on how their parenting influenced your gender development. Do their recollections ring true with your memories? What factors do you think played a role in your gender development?

2. The evolutionary psychology approach to gender suggests that men are more likely to seek women who are younger than they are and that women are more likely to seek older men with resources. Sit down with the personal ads from a local paper and examine the ads placed by men and women. Does the ads' content support predictions about what men and women look for?

The Psychology of Gender Differences

To think about gender differences, let's start with a game we will call "Who are more _____?" For each adjective below, answer as quickly as you can with either "Men" or "Women."

Who are more...

Assertive	Rational
Emotional	Aggressive
Strong	Sexually adventurous
Creative	Reserved
Verbal	Active

Now for each of those descriptors, think of someone you know who is of the opposite sex to your answer and who is very high on the quality described. What does this game tell you about gender stereotypes? Might it suggest that even though you may have ready stereotypes for gender differences, in fact men and women vary widely with respect to a number of qualities?

In this section we will review the research on gender differences in three main areas: cognitive ability, aggression, and sexuality. As we do, keep in mind that because gender cannot be manipulated, research comparing men and women is by definition correlational, so that causal claims are not justified.

40·1 COGNITIVE DIFFERENCES

A gender difference that is a source of interest for many researchers, as well as for the public at large, is the underrepresentation of women in math and science careers. For example, in 1980, the percentage of PhDs in the physical sciences and engineering that were awarded to women in the United States was 12 percent and 4 percent, respectively. By 2001 these percentages had increased to 26 percent for the physical sciences and 17 percent for engineering (Halpern & others, 2007)—still a very large gap.

This discrepancy has been a focal point at many conferences. At just such a gathering in January 2005, Larry Summers, then president of Harvard University, sparked a major controversy. Summers commented that he believed that a key determinant of such underrepresentation of women was gender differences in innate ability in math and science—specifically, women's lack of natural cognitive ability relevant to careers in math and science. Summers's words met a firestorm of criticism. Many observers were shocked and dismayed that he would suggest such a thing, and others felt that he had been victimized by the forces of political correctness.

What do the data tell us about cognitive differences between men and women? First, the data point to no gender differences in general intellectual ability. Further, research shows that in terms of academic performance, girls tend to get better grades in school than boys, regardless of the topic (Halpern & others, 2007). Nevertheless, clearly, more boys eventually pursue careers in math and science than do girls. Why?

Many studies have examined gender differences in performance on different cognitive tasks and found that when differences emerge, they tend to be in two directions. First, girls are more likely to outperform boys on tasks of verbal ability; and second, boys are more likely to outperform girls on tasks requiring a certain type of cognitive skill—visuospatial ability (Halpern & others, 2007). For example, research has probed the verbal performance of fourth-graders in 33 different countries (Mullis & others, 2003; Ogle & others, 2003). In every country, the average performance of girls on verbal tasks was higher than the average performance of boys. In turn, research has

Research findings indicate that aptitude for science is similarly predicted by genes for both males and females. This female scientist is working on medical applications of stem cell technology.

revealed that, at least by preschool age, boys show greater accuracy in performing tasks requiring mental rotation of objects in space (S. C. Levine & others, 1999; Loring-Meier & Halpern, 1999). As children age, these differences are most likely to show up on tasks requiring the person to imagine objects moving in space—for instance, to state when two objects will crash (Liu & Huang, 1999).

What might explain these differences? Biological theorists might look to genetic or hormonal differences, although aptitude for science is similarly predicted by genes for both males and females (Haworth, Dale, & Plomin, 2009). From an evolutionary perspective, the differences are thought to be tied to females' important roles in socializing offspring and negotiating the interpersonal landscape and to ancestral males' need to traverse the landscape for food and to find their way home again (Geary, 2010). From a social cognitive and social role perspective, theorists might say that these differences reflect parents' expectations for their children. The female advantage in verbal skills and the male advantage in visuo-spatial tasks might emerge out of parents' greater expectations for their daughters to be socially engaged and for their sons to be good at stereotypically male activities such as playing video games.

The observed gender differences in verbal and visuospatial skills are relatively consistent—but they are also rather small. Janet Shibley Hyde (2005) conducted a review of major meta-analytic studies of gender differences in a wide range of characteristics. (Recall that meta-analysis is a statistical technique that allows researchers to pull together findings from a range of studies that all addressed the same questions, so that they can get a much better sense of whether differences from one study represent real differences in the world and estimate the size of those differences.) With regard to cognitive variables, Hyde found that where differences did emerge, they were quite small, with girls scoring higher on some measures of verbal ability and boys scoring higher on spatial tasks. Overall, however, Hyde found strong support for what she came to call the **gender similarities hypothesis**—the idea that men and women (and boys and girls) are much more similar than they are different (Hyde, 2005, 2006, 2007a).

Hyde's conclusion suggests that the very large gender difference in the pursuit of careers in math and science is unlikely to result from these small cognitive differences between males and females. In trying to explain the shortage of women in math and science, we might therefore think about the *multiple* factors that lead an individual to pursue a particular career. That choice is likely to be a product of many interrelated factors, including what the person feels he or she is especially good at and likes to do, the role models encountered, the social support from family and friends, and the likelihood that a particular career path will ultimately lead to the life the person envisions for himself or herself in the future (Halpern & others, 2007).

● **gender similarities hypothesis** Hyde's proposition that men and women (and boys and girls) are much more similar than they are different.

40-2 GENDER DIFFERENCES IN AGGRESSION

● **aggression** Behaviors that are intended to harm another person.

Aggression is defined as behaviors that are intended to harm another person (Crick & Grotpeter, 1995). Are men or women more aggressive? The answer depends on the particular *type* of aggression we are talking about.

● **overt aggression** Physically or verbally harming another person directly.

Overt aggression refers to physically or verbally harming another person directly. Males tend to be higher on overt aggression than females. As children, boys are more likely than girls to get in fights in which they are physically aggressive toward one another (Bukowski, Brendgen, & Vitaro, 2007). As adolescents, males are more likely to join gangs and to commit violent acts (Dodge, Coie, & Lynam, 2006). Children and adolescents who are diagnosed with **conduct disorder**—a pattern of offensive behavior that violates the basic rights of others—are three times more likely to be boys than girls (Kjelsberg, 2005). As adults, men are more likely than women to be chronically hostile and to commit violent crimes (White & Frabutt, 2006).

Women's smaller physical size may be one reason they are less likely to engage in overt aggression. In probing aggressive tendencies in girls and women, researchers have focused instead on **relational aggression,** behavior that is meant to harm the social standing of another person through activities such as gossiping and spreading rumors (Crick & Grotpeter, 1995). Relational aggression differs from overt aggression in that it requires that the aggressor have a considerable level of social and cognitive skill. To be relationally aggressive, an individual must have a strong understanding of the social environment and must be able to plant rumors that are most likely to damage the intended party. Relational aggression is more subtle than overt aggression, and the relationally aggressive individual may not seem to be aggressive to others, as the aggressive acts typically are committed secretly. Research has shown that girls are more relationally aggressive than boys (Archer, 2004; Card & others, 2008) and that this difference increases with age (Smith, Rose, & Schwartz-Mette, 2010).

Generally, both overt aggression and relational aggression are related to reduced peer acceptance (Crick & Rose, 2000). Relational aggression in girls is associated in particular with less acceptance by other girls; in contrast, relationally aggressive adolescent girls are more likely to enjoy acceptance by boys. This pattern suggests that girls who relationally aggress toward other girls may do so to improve their standing with boys (Smith, Rose, & Schwartz-Mette, 2010).

Although relational aggression may not lead to the physical injury that is often the result of overt aggression, it can be extremely painful nevertheless. In 2010, Phoebe Prince, a 15-year-old who had recently moved from Ireland to the United States with her family, became the target of unrelenting rumors and harassment from a group of popular girls at her high school after she had a brief relationship with a popular senior boy. Prince became so distraught that she hanged herself after school one day. Even after her suicide, the girls who had harassed her posted rumors about her on the Facebook page that was set up as a memorial (Cullen, 2010).

The various theoretical approaches we reviewed earlier would explain these gender differences in aggression in different ways. With regard to the overt aggression of boys and men, biological researchers might focus on the role of a hormone such as testosterone, which circulates at higher levels in men than women (van Bokhoven & others, 2006). The evolutionary psychology perspective would view the overt aggression of males as an outgrowth of ancestral male competition for females with whom to mate. Evolutionary psychologists would see the propensity for relational aggression as coming from females' need to compete for male partners with resources. From a social cognitive perspective, gender differences in styles of aggression would reflect differences in boys' and girls' socialization, with girls being taught early on that overt aggression is inappropriate (Archer, 2004). Similarly, social role theory would see these differences as emerging out of gender roles, and responses to these forms of aggression would reflect stereotypes of male and female.

Phoebe Prince's family buried her in her native Ireland because "they wanted an ocean between her and the people who hounded her to the grave" (Cullen, 2010).

● **conduct disorder** A pattern of offensive behavior that violates the basic rights of others.

● **relational aggression** Behavior that is meant to harm the social standing of another person.

40-3 GENDER DIFFERENCES IN SEXUALITY

Broadly speaking, **sexuality** refers to the ways people experience and express themselves as sexual beings. Sexuality involves activity that is associated with sexual pleasure. The evolutionary perspective on gender strongly predicts gender differences in sexual behavior—specifically, that women should be more selective, and men less selective, when it comes to

● **sexuality** The ways people experience and express themselves as sexual beings.

engaging in sex. In 1989, Russell D. Clark III and Elaine Hatfield conducted a study examining this prediction.

The researchers sent five men and five women experimenters (who were judged to range from slightly unattractive to moderately attractive) to the Florida State University campus. They were told to approach members of the opposite sex whom they found to be quite attractive. For each person they approached, the experimenters were instructed to say "I have been noticing you around campus. I find you very attractive" and then to ask one of three questions: (1) "Would you like to go out with me?" (2) "Would you like to go to my apartment with me?" or (3) "Would you like to go to bed with me?" (These data were collected in 1978 and 1982, before AIDS became a known and widespread problem.)

The Psychological Inquiry illustrates the results of the study. As you can see, men and women did not differ in terms of their answers to the "going out" question—about half of each sex said yes to this query. However, dramatic sex differences emerged for the other two questions. Nearly 70 percent of men said yes to the "apartment" question, while very few women answered in the affirmative. Finally, with regard to the "bed" question, 75 percent of the men said yes, but *none* of the women did. In fact, more men said yes to the go-to-bed question than to the go-on-a-date question. Men who said no to the request to go to bed with the female experimenters were more likely to explain themselves with a statement such as "I have a girlfriend" or "I'm married." In contrast, women who were asked if they would like to go to bed with a male experimenter were more likely to give responses such as "You've got to be kidding" and "What is wrong with you? Leave me alone" (Clark & Hatfield, 1989, p. 52).

More recently, a study conducted with college students in Germany, Italy, and the United States replicated these gender differences in students who were asked to imagine being in the study (Schutzwohl & others, 2009). Other relevant research shows that women tend to have fewer lifetime sex partners compared to men, and these differences are true regardless of whether the person is homosexual or heterosexual (Peplau & Fingerhut, 2007; Savin-Williams & Diamond, 2004). So, the data suggest that women do appear to be more selective than men when it comes to casual sex.

Men and women differ sexually in other ways as well. Men report more frequent feelings of sexual arousal, are more prone to lust, have more frequent sexual fantasies, and rate the strength of their own sex drive higher than do women (Baumeister, Catanese, & Vohs, 2001). Men also are more likely than women to masturbate, to have more permissive attitudes about casual premarital sex, and to have a more difficult time adhering to their vows of sexual fidelity when married (Oliver & Hyde, 1993; Peplau, 2003).

Compared to men, women tend to show more changes in their sexual patterns and sexual desires over their lifetime (Baumeister, 2000; Baumeister & Stillman, 2006; Diamond, 2008a). Women are more likely than men, for instance, to have had sexual experiences with same- and opposite-sex partners, even if they identify themselves strongly as heterosexual or lesbian. In one study of 9,000 twins and their siblings, participants were asked about their *potential* for same-sex sexual behavior (Santtila & others, 2008). The researchers asked the participants whether they would be able to engage in sexual activity with an attractive same-sex person whom they liked, if no one would find out about it. Nearly twice as many women (65 percent) as men (33 percent) said they would, even though more than 90 percent of these individuals had had no same-sex sexual contacts in the previous year.

In contrast, male sexuality may be more limited to particular targets of attraction. One study compared the sexual arousal of heterosexual women, lesbian women, heterosexual men, and homosexual men while they watched erotic films of various sexual acts featuring male and female actors or bonobo apes. The films included scenes of sexual activity between same- and opposite-sex human partners and between opposite-sex bonobos, and scenes of men and women masturbating alone or engaging in aerobic exercise while naked. Sexual arousal was measured physiologically by monitoring the sex organs of men and women for indicators of arousal. Both heterosexual women and lesbian women were aroused by all of the films showing sexual activity (including those featuring the bonobos). However, gay men were aroused only by the films that included men, and heterosexual men were aroused only by the films that included women (Chivers, Seto, & Blanchard, 2007).

psychological *inquiry*

Percent responding yes

- ■ Male
- ■ Female

(Bar chart y-axis values: 80, 60, 40, 20, 0)

Categories:
- Would you go on a date with me?
- Would you go to my apartment with me?
- Would you go to bed with me?

Sex and Casual Sex

The figure shows the results of the Clark and Hatfield study (1989). Recall that the experimenters approached men and women on a college campus and asked one of three questions. Review the details of the study and answer the following questions.

1. This study was an experiment. What are the independent and dependent variables?

2. Why do you think that men were more likely to say yes to the "bed" question than they were to the "date" question?

3. Recall that in this study, the experimenters were judged to range from slightly unattractive to moderately attractive and were told to approach people whom they found to be quite attractive. How might these circumstances have influenced the results?

4. Perhaps the most striking aspect of this experiment's results is the big gender difference on the "bed" question. Most men said yes, and not a single woman did. What is another question that might have produced such a stunning gender difference?

5. Imagine that you strongly favor the social role theory of gender development. How would you explain these results from that perspective?

How extensive are these gender differences in sexuality? A recent meta-analysis revealed that overall, men reported having *slightly more* sexual experience and more permissive attitudes than women for most aspects of sexuality (Petersen & Hyde, 2010). For the following factors, stronger gender differences in sexuality were found: Men engaged in more masturbation, viewed more pornography, engaged in more casual sex, and had more permissive attitudes about casual sex than did women.

How would the various theoretical approaches interpret gender differences in sexuality? From the biological perspective, differences in sexuality can be explained by genetic and hormonal differences between men and women. The evolutionary psychology approach would see these differences as supporting the role of sexual selection in human evolution. Social cognitive theories would focus on the ways that boys and girls learn about what is considered appropriate sexual behavior for each gender. Finally, social role theory would assert that these gender differences reflect the differing gender roles, stereotypes, and opportunities that cultures construct for men and women. In some cultures, for example, women cover their heads and faces when they are out in public. Their husbands are the only men who ever see them uncovered. Clearly, biological explanations are not needed to explain why these women would be very unlikely to engage in sexual activity outside of marriage.

40-4 EVALUATING THE EVIDENCE FOR GENDER DIFFERENCES

It is safe to say that in talking about gender differences, people can be prone to extremes. For instance, a bestselling book suggested that men and women are so different that they must have come from different planets, with men hailing from warlike, competitive

Mars and women from the love planet, Venus (Gray, 2004). Clearly, our survey of gender differences does not support such a radical view. Gender differences appear to be strongest in the areas of aggression and sexuality and seem to be consistent but relatively weaker in the cognitive domain. On the whole, we can state with certainty that men and women are indeed both from planet Earth.

One way in which men and women clearly differ is that men generally are sexually attracted to women, whereas women typically are sexually attracted to men. Of course, these patterns of attraction are not always the case, as human beings differ from one another in their sexual orientation, our next topic.

SUMMARY

Research indicates that girls are better at verbal tasks and boys are better at visuospatial tasks, though these differences are relatively small. In terms of aggression, males tend to be more overtly aggressive than females, but females may be more relationally aggressive than males.

Sexuality refers to the ways people experience and express themselves as sexual beings. Men are more likely to engage in casual sex and to have more lifetime sex partners compared to women. Men also report more frequent sexual arousal, are more prone to lust and sexual fantasies, and are more likely than women to masturbate. They have more permissive attitudes about casual premarital sex as well, and have a more difficult time being sexually faithful when married. Women are more likely than men to show fluidity in their sexual attractions.

KEY TERMS

gender similarities
hypothesis   400
aggression   400
overt aggression   400

conduct disorder   401
relational aggression   401
sexuality   401

TEST YOURSELF

1. What is the gender similarities hypothesis? How might even small gender differences lead to larger differences later in life?

2. How do overt aggression and relational aggression differ? Which sex is more likely to engage in each?

3. Identify at least four ways in which males and females differ in their patterns of sexual behavior, thoughts, and/or feelings.

APPLY YOUR KNOWLEDGE

1. Set aside a day and keep a gender-awareness diary. Try to notice every time you have an experience in which your gender matters to your life. From the moment you get up in the morning until you go to bed at night, if you are man, ask yourself, "Would I be doing this if I were a woman?" If you are a woman, ask yourself, "Would I be doing this if I were a man?" When you see a woman performing an activity, ask yourself, "Would this seem appropriate to me if a man were doing it?" Write down your thoughts and feelings about these activities, and reflect on the role of gender in your daily life.

2. Next time you are out with your friends, watch how males and females react to the same situation. Do they respond in the same way? If not, what could account for their differences? Do your observations support the information stated in the textbook about gender differences?

Sexual Orientation

An individual's **sexual orientation** is the direction of his or her erotic interests. Sexual orientation does not mean simply sexual behavior. A man who has sex with other men while in prison may not think of himself as homosexual, and once released from prison he may never engage in such behavior again. A woman might always find herself sexually attracted to other women but never act on those feelings. When we talk about sexual orientation, we mean a *whole range* of human experiences that interest psychologists, including not only behaviors but also desires, feelings, fantasies, and a person's sense of identity.

41·1 DEFINING SEXUAL ORIENTATION

An individual who self-identifies as **heterosexual** is generally sexually attracted to members of the opposite sex. An individual who self-identifies as **homosexual** is generally sexually attracted to members of the same sex. Today, sexual orientation is commonly viewed as a continuum from exclusive male–female relations to exclusive same-sex relations (B. M. King, 2005). Some individuals self-identify as **bisexual,** meaning that they are sexually attracted to people of both sexes.

Despite the widespread use of labels such as "homosexual," "gay," "lesbian," and "bisexual," some researchers argue that they are misleading. Instead, erotic attractions may be fluid, and references to such a construct as a fixed sexual orientation ignores the potential flexibility of human sexual attraction and behavior (Diamond, 2008a, 2009). In some cultures, engaging in same-sex sexual activity is not viewed as an indication of the person's identity (Nanda, 2008), but in Western societies, there is a strong belief that sexual orientation is a stable personal attribute. Stability of sexual orientation might also depend on the orientation. Longitudinal studies have shown very high stability for heterosexuality over time (Kinnish, Strassberg, & Turner, 2005). Non-heterosexual individuals may be more likely to shift their erotic interests, especially in adolescence (Diamond & Savin-Williams, 2011; Savin-Williams & Ream, 2007).

Related to this issue is the very definition of bisexuality. People sometimes think that bisexuality is simply a steppingstone to homosexuality, while others view it as a sexual orientation itself or as an indicator of sexual fluidity. (Comedian Woody Allen once quipped that at least bisexuality doubles your chances of finding a date on a Saturday night.) In a decade-long longitudinal study of non-heterosexual women, Lisa Diamond (2008b) found evidence for the existence of a stable bisexual identity. Among women who identified themselves as lesbian or bisexual in 1995, change was more likely to occur in the direction of lesbian women moving toward bisexuality rather than bisexual women changing to a lesbian or heterosexual orientation. Demonstrating the difference between sexual behavior and sexual orientation, Diamond's study found that although bisexual orientation was unlikely to change, sexual behavior did. Women who self-identified as bisexual were more likely, over time, to engage in exclusively homosexual or heterosexual behavior, because many of them had settled into a long-term relationship with one partner by the end of the study (Diamond, 2008b).

41·2 OCCURRENCE OF THE DIFFERENT SEXUAL ORIENTATIONS

Homosexual behavior is relatively common in nature, having been observed in 1,500 different species, including rats, nonhuman primates, giraffes, ostriches, guppies, cats, bison, dolphins, and fruit flies (Sommer & Vasey, 2006). Furthermore, long-term same-sex

● **sexual orientation** The direction of an individual's erotic interests.

● **heterosexual** Referring to a sexual orientation in which the individual is generally sexually attracted to members of the opposite sex.

● **homosexual** Referring to a sexual orientation in which the individual is generally sexually attracted to members of the same sex.

● **bisexual** Referring to a sexual orientation in which the individual is sexually attracted to people of both sexes.

partnerships occur in nonhuman species. In 2004, the *New York Times* reported the story of Roy and Silo, two male penguins who appeared to share a long-term monogamous sexual relationship at the Central Park Zoo, even raising their adopted daughter Tango (they have since broken up) (D. Smith, 2004). In humans, homosexuality is present in all cultures, regardless of whether a culture is tolerant or not. Obviously, the majority of people, regardless of culture, are heterosexual.

It is difficult to know precisely how many gays, lesbians, and bisexuals there are in the world, partly because fears of discrimination may prevent individuals from answering honestly on surveys. Estimates of the frequency of homosexuality range from 2 percent to10 percent of the population and are typically higher for men than women (Zietsch & others, 2008). With respect to the United States, a Centers for Disease Control national survey reported that the percentage of Americans who identify themselves as heterosexual was 90 percent for men and women. Approximately 4.1 percent reported themselves as homosexual or bisexual—essentially, 5 million Americans between the ages of 18 and 44 (Mosher, Chandra, & Jones, 2005).

Roy and Silo, same-sex partners who raised their adopted daughter Tango, are chinstrap penguins like these.

41-3 ORIGINS OF SEXUAL ORIENTATION: A SCIENTIFIC PUZZLE

What is the source of sexual orientation? Scientists have speculated extensively about this question (Kelly, 2006; Rahman, 2005). Charles Darwin (1862) himself commented that "we do not even in the least know the final cause of sexuality. The whole subject is hidden in darkness."

Since Darwin's time, scientists have learned something about factors that *do not* predict sexual orientation. First, being reared by a gay parent *does not* increase the chances of being gay (Golombok & Tasker, 1996; Patterson & Farr, 2010; Patterson & Wainright, 2010). In fact, the vast majority of gay individuals have heterosexual parents. Nor does a particular parenting style relate to the emergence of homosexuality (Bell, Weinberg, & Hammersmith, 1981). Further, same-sex sexual experience or experimentation in childhood does not predict eventual adult homosexuality (Bailey, 2003; Bogaert, 2000).

So, what factors might account for sexual orientation? Before we probe this intriguing question, let's pause to consider some key issues in the science behind sexual orientation.

Thinking Critically about Sexual Orientation

There is controversy over the origin of sexual orientation. Scientists approach this puzzle dispassionately and must remain open to the different potential answers the empirical data suggest. Before exploring the current evidence for various explanations of sexual orientation, it may be helpful to review five important issues for critical thinkers.

- *Unlikelihood of a single cause:* Whatever the psychological characteristic of interest, it is unlikely that a single cause can be identified, and sexual orientation is no exception. As we consider the accumulated data on this topic, keep in mind that it is very probable that *many factors work together* to foster sexual orientation and that factors that have not even been considered yet will likely emerge in the future.

- *Within-group variation:* There is a great deal of variation within any group of people who share the same sexual orientation. All heterosexual men are sexually attracted to women, but that attraction may be the only thing that any two heterosexual men have in common. Similarly, all gay men share a sexual attraction to men, but any two gay men may have little else in common.

- *Research challenges*: Comparing individuals from different sexual orientations presents research design challenges. One such challenge bears on the matter of representativeness, for in some studies the heterosexual and homosexual participants are recruited in very different ways. Gay and lesbian participants are sometimes recruited only from gay pride events, for example, and so they may not be representative of all homosexual and bisexual individuals. Similarly, small sample size can be an issue because of the difficulty involved in recruiting gay participants. Indeed, in a study reported in 2000, just 6 gay men were compared to 256 "non-gay" men (Lippa, 2000). Recall that studies using larger samples are more likely to yield results that generalize to the general population.

- *The meaning of cross-sex similarities:* In presenting research on the origins of sexual orientation, the popular media often emphasize similarities between gay men and heterosexual women and between lesbian women and heterosexual men. Keep in mind that, regardless of their sexual orientation, gay men are men, and lesbian women are women.

- *Explaining sexual orientation does not mean explaining only homosexuality:* Finally, and perhaps most importantly, keep in mind as you read this section that any good theory of sexual orientation should explain how *any of us* (gay or straight) becomes sexually oriented toward individuals *of a particular* sex. As scientists, we want to explain the sexual orientations of men and women who are attracted to men or women or both.

With these cautions in mind, let's look at the evidence concerning sexual orientation.

Genetic Influences

Researchers have examined genes as a factor in sexual orientation by using twins to estimate the heritability of sexual orientation. Recall from Module 29 that heritability is a statistic that tells us the extent to which we can explain observed differences in a given characteristic based on differences in genes. Recently, a study of nearly 4,000 twins in Sweden demonstrated that the heritability of same-sex sexual behavior was about 35 percent in men and 19 percent in women (Langstrom & others, 2010). These heritability estimates suggest that although genes play a role in sexual orientation, genes are not as strong an influence as they are for other characteristics, such as intelligence.

Of course, genes do not impact psychological characteristics as directly as they do a physical characteristic like hair color or eye color. We therefore need to consider other factors that might provide the bridge between genes and the psychological experience of sexual orientation.

Brain Differences

One way in which genes might influence sexual orientation is through their effect on brain development. Two particular types of brain differences have garnered the most attention among researchers: the thickness of the corpus callosum (the bundle of fibers that connects the two hemispheres) and the symmetry between the brain's two hemispheres. Evidence from brain-imaging studies suggests that gay men may have thicker corpus callosa than heterosexual men (Witelson & others, 2008). In terms of hemispheric symmetry, a recent brain-imaging study found that heterosexual women and gay men show a similar pattern in which the two hemispheres are alike, while heterosexual men and lesbian women display a similar pattern of having a larger right hemisphere relative to left (Savic & Lindström, 2008).

Where do these brain differences come from? Differences in the corpus callosum are thought to have a genetic basis because the corpus callosum's size is strongly heritable (Witelson & others, 2008). Differences in hemispheric symmetry are believed to emerge from prenatal hormone exposure (Savic & Lindström, 2008), another biological factor studied in the origins of sexual orientation, as we consider just below. A word of caution, however: In trying to interpret these brain characteristics, we must keep in mind that habitual patterns of *behavior* can also influence brain structure and function—and we must consider that these cross-sex similarities may therefore be explained by behavioral similarities between heterosexual women and gay men, as well as between heterosexual men and lesbian women.

Prenatal Hormones

In another approach to understanding sexual orientation, studies have examined the role of prenatal hormones. Recall that the development of male sexual characteristics is triggered by high levels of prenatal androgens. Researchers have examined whether this prenatal hormone exposure might be responsible for creating a brain that is sexually attracted to women. Because prenatal androgen levels can vary for female embryos, we can examine whether females who were exposed to prenatal androgens are more likely to be bisexual or lesbian than heterosexual. Researchers have tested this possibility in a variety of ways (Meyer-Bahlburg & others, 2008).

One strategy for examining the link between prenatal hormones and sexual orientation is to identify physical features that are associated with prenatal testosterone. These features potentially provide a window into prenatal hormonal exposure (McFadden, 2008; Rahman, 2005; Rahman, Clarke, & Morera, 2009). The idea is that once we identify the effects of prenatal testosterone on various physical features of the body, we can look at those features and see whether they differ in adults who are either gay or straight (McFadden, 2008).

The best known of these features is the ratio between the second and fourth digits on the hand (the pointer and the ring finger), called the *2D:4D ratio*. Men tend to have a ring finger that is longer than their pointer, while for women the two fingers are nearly the same length (Manning, 2002; Medland & Loehlin, 2008). Thus, women tend to have larger 2D:4D ratios than men. This ratio is influenced by prenatal testosterone (Lutchmaya & others, 2004; McFadden & others, 2005). If prenatal testosterone exposure is related to developing a brain that is attracted to females, we might expect lesbian women to show a pattern more similar to heterosexual men—that is, a smaller 2D:4D ratio. Some studies have supported such a pattern for lesbian women (Kraemer & others, 2006; McFadden & Shubel, 2002; Rahman & Wilson, 2003) or specifically for lesbian women who identify themselves as "butch," or masculine (W. M. Brown & others, 2002; James, 2005).

Social Factors

A great deal of current research on the origins of sexual orientation focuses on genetic, hormonal, and neurobiological mechanisms. What about social experience? We have seen that there is no evidence that specific parenting styles "cause" sexual orientation. Given the many different ways in which parents interact with their children and the fact that the vast majority of people are heterosexual, it seems unlikely that the emergence of heterosexuality is explained by particular parenting strategies. Furthermore, the fact that most homosexual and bisexual individuals have heterosexual parents contradicts the influence of observational learning or modeling in the development of sexual orientation.

Some scientists have attempted to explain sexual orientation as a function of early childhood experience. A particular focus has been gender-nonconforming behaviors, activities that run counter to gender stereotypes (Bem, 1996; Rieger, Linsenmeier, & Bailey, 2009; Rieger & others, 2008). Research shows that homosexual adults are more likely than heterosexual adults to remember themselves as having engaged in gender-nonconforming behaviors (Bailey & Zucker, 1995; Lippa, 2008). Moreover, some evidence suggests that in videos of their childhood activities, gay and lesbian adults pursued more gender-atypical activities as children (Rieger & others, 2008).

For boys, gender-nonconforming behavior may be related to eventual sexual development, but the picture is not clear-cut. For example, one study compared 66 extremely gender-nonconforming boys to 56 gender-conforming boys (Green, 1987). Among the nonconforming boys, 75 percent were either bisexual or homosexual at a follow-up

during adolescence or young adulthood. Among the gender-conforming boys, 96 percent were heterosexual at follow-up.

Although this study is sometimes used as evidence of the role of gender-nonconforming behavior in the development of sexual orientation (Bem, 1996), take a good look at those percentages. It may be true that gender-nonconforming boys were more likely to be homosexual or bisexual—but note that the percentage of boys in the gender-*conforming* group who eventually emerged as gay or bisexual falls within the typical percentages found in the general population. Thus, boys who are quite gender typical in their behavior can certainly turn out to be gay (or bisexual or straight).

Studies of childhood behavior and sexual orientation are correlational. One challenge of correlational research is the potential for a third variable to explain the relationship between the variables of interest. In thinking about an individual's gender-nonconforming behavior in childhood and his or her eventual sexual orientation, you might note that factors such as genes and prenatal hormone exposure might explain both of these variables (Cohen-Bendahan, van de Beek, & Berenbaum, 2005).

Consider, too, that gender-nonconforming boys may experience a very different social response than gender-nonconforming girls. In fact, many women report having been a tomboy as a child (Peplau & others, 1999). Girls who engage in boyish activities are frequently viewed as more popular by their peers, and the vast majority of tomboys turn out to be heterosexual (Peplau & others, 1999). Social responses to gender-nonconforming boys may be more negative and may play a role in eventual gender identity and sexual orientation. Parents and peers may label a gender-nonconforming boy as "homosexual," and that labeling may influence the boy's sense of self and his emerging identity (Hegarty, 2009).

An Unsolved Puzzle

Clearly, scientists have devised a number of clever ways to identify factors associated with sexual orientation. However, as we have seen, many questions remain. Although we may not still be in the "darkness" described by Darwin, it is fair to say at least that the room remains not very well lit.

Similar to many other psychological characteristics, an individual's sexual orientation most likely depends on a combination of genetic, hormonal, cognitive, and environmental factors (Langstrom & others, 2010). Most experts on sexual orientation believe that no one factor alone causes sexual orientation and that the relative weight of each factor can vary within people of the same orientation. Just as individuals can have the same sexual orientation but be different in many other respects, the underlying processes that lead to sexual orientation may differ from one person to the next. We know that whether heterosexual, homosexual, or bisexual, a person cannot be talked out of his or her sexual orientation. Indeed, Qazi Rahman, a researcher who studies the neurobiology of sexual orientation, asserted that "there is no argument anymore—if you are gay, you are born gay" (quoted in Nicholson, 2008). This work tells us that whether one is homosexual, heterosexual, or bisexual, sexual orientation is not a choice but an integral part of the functioning human being and his or her sense of self (Katz, 1995; Worthington & others, 2008).

41-4 GAY AND LESBIAN FUNCTIONING

We may not know definitively why individuals are gay or lesbian, but research has uncovered some interesting things about gay men and women. Here we briefly review selected findings as they relate to individual adjustment and well-being, gay and lesbian relationships, and gay and lesbian families.

Individual Adjustment and Well-Being

Research shows that gay and lesbian individuals are similar to their heterosexual counterparts in many ways. Researchers typically find no differences among lesbians, gays,

Lesbian women and gay men are similar to heterosexual women and heterosexual men in many respects.

bisexuals, and heterosexuals in a wide range of attitudes and behaviors, as well as in psychological adjustment (Hyde & DeLamater, 2011). Gay men and lesbian women are likely to differ from heterosexuals in terms of the gender typicality of their hobbies, activities, and occupations (Lippa, 2000). Note, however, that if gay men and women live in households that are headed by two men or two women, they will inevitably engage in gender-atypical behavior (for instance, women doing the yard work or men cooking and cleaning) simply because someone has to take care of those tasks.

One factor in the well-being of gays and lesbians is coping with prejudice and discrimination (Balsam & Mohr, 2007). Among gay and lesbian participants polled in a 2006 survey, 83 percent reported themselves as "out," including having revealed their sexual orientation to their acquaintances, family, and friends. More than half, however, reported themselves as concerned that coming out could increase their risk of being the victim of a hate crime. A third of the individuals sampled reported that they might choose not to come out primarily because of concern over rejection by family and friends or the loss of a job (Harris Interactive, 2006).

The good news for homosexual individuals is that attitudes toward gays and lesbians have become increasingly more positive in U.S. society (Kaiser Family Foundation, 2001). This increased acceptance likely stems in part from gay men's and lesbian women's greater openness with others about their lives. Individuals who know someone who is gay or lesbian are less likely to report prejudicial attitudes toward gays and lesbians (Smith, Axelton, & Saucier, 2009). In 2006, a U.S. survey found that 70 percent of the heterosexuals polled knew someone who was gay, lesbian, or bisexual—a large increase from 1984, when only 24 percent of those surveyed knew a gay or bisexual person (Harris Interactive, 2006). Younger Americans are particularly likely to support gay rights. A survey of members of Generation Next (those born between 1981 and 1988) found that 58 percent believed that homosexuality ought to be accepted, and nearly half felt that same-sex marriage should be legal (Pew Research Center, 2007).

For gays, lesbians, and bisexuals, being open about their sexual orientation not only is related to progress in changing cultural attitudes but also is a strong predictor of psychological and physical health (Savin-Williams, 2006). For gay men and lesbian women, living in accord with their sexual orientation is a matter of living authentically, and being "out" to the people around them is part of being true to themselves (King, Burton, & Geise, 2009). The more comfortable gay, lesbian, and bisexual individuals feel about coming out, the better will be scientists' chances to study them and to understand their lives.

Gay and Lesbian Relationships

Research consistently shows that gay men and lesbian women report themselves as more satisfied in their relationships compared to heterosexual couples. For example, in an 11-year longitudinal study by Lawrence Kurdek (2004), gay and lesbian couples and heterosexual married couples rated their relationships on a host of characteristics, including psychological adjustment, conflict, satisfaction, intimacy, and social support. Kurdek found that gay and lesbian couples scored higher than heterosexual marriage partners on 76 percent of the variables measured. Nevertheless, these same individuals were more likely to end their relationships than heterosexual married couples, especially heterosexual couples with children (Kurdek, 2004).

Why might gay and lesbian couples be more likely to break up than heterosexual couples? One possibility is that heterosexual couples may be more likely to stay in unsatisfying relationships out of concern for their children's welfare, and heterosexual couples are more likely than gay couples to have children.

Another possible reason for this difference is that married heterosexual couples face a legal barrier—divorce—that makes dissolving their relationships difficult. In 2000, the state of Vermont legally recognized same-sex civil unions, allowing for a test of this possibility. Kimberly Balsam and her colleagues (2008) studied three samples of couples: gay and lesbian couples who had been united in a civil union; gay and lesbian couples who had not had a civil union; and heterosexual married couples. Three years later, gay and lesbian couples who had not been joined in a civil union were more likely to have broken up—or to be on the brink of breaking up—than either gay couples who were in a civil union or heterosexual married couples. These results suggest that the legal tie of marriage is associated with relationship stability. In this study, as in Kurdek's earlier work, the gay and lesbian couples (regardless of whether they were in a civil union) reported higher relationship quality, better compatibility, and less conflict than their heterosexual counterparts.

What might explain the higher satisfaction with their relationships that gay and lesbian individuals report? One possibility is that heterosexual individuals may feel more pressure to get married and stay married, regardless of their personal choices, and they may be supported to stay in unsatisfying relationships (Green, Bettinger, & Zacks, 1996). Another factor is that having children is generally associated with lower levels of marital satisfaction, and, as mentioned above, heterosexual couples are more likely than homosexual couples to have children (Kurdek, 2004).

John Gottman and his colleagues (2003) conducted a longitudinal study of couple functioning that included video-recorded interactions over 12 years. The participants comprised gay and lesbian couples, as well as heterosexual couples. Gottman's team found that compared to heterosexual couples, gay and lesbian partners were better able to manage conflicts. They were more likely to use humor and affection in dealing with conflicts, took a more positive attitude toward negative feedback from their partners, and let conflicts go once they were resolved (Gottman & others, 2003).

It may also be the case that individuals in same-sex couples have more in common with each other because they are of the same sex (Balsam & others, 2008). In their romantic relationships, gay and lesbian couples do not have to negotiate the sorts of gender differences we reviewed earlier.

Gay and Lesbian Families

Although gay and lesbian couples may be less likely than heterosexual couples to have children, increasingly gay families do include kids. Available evidence suggests that gay and lesbian households exist in 99 percent of counties throughout the United States, and approximately one in four of these households includes children (O'Barr, 2006). Children reared by gay men and lesbian women tend to be as well adjusted as those from heterosexual households, are no more likely to be homosexual themselves, and are no less likely to be accepted by their peers (Chan, Raboy, & Patterson, 1998; Golombok & others, 2003; Patterson & Farr, 2010; Patterson & Wainright, 2010). A study comparing adolescents who had two mothers with adolescents who had opposite-sex parents revealed no differences in self-reported or peer-reported functioning. For both sets of adolescents, what mattered were their close, warm relationships with their parents (Wainwright & Patterson, 2008).

In the United States, gay marriage and gay parenting have generated strong controversy, especially in political election years. In addressing the central issues in the debate, psychologists rely on scientific evidence. Based on the research we reviewed above, the American Psychological Association issued a press release supporting gay marriage and opposing discrimination against gay men and lesbian women in matters such as parenting, adoption, and child custody (American Psychological Association, 2004).

SUMMARY

Sexual orientation refers to the direction of a person's erotic interest and includes heterosexuality, homosexuality, and bisexuality. Sexual orientation is generally measured using questionnaires. The vast majority of people are heterosexual; the number of homosexual or bisexual individuals is between 2 and 10 percent of the population.

Possible explanations for sexual orientation include genetic factors, brain differences, and prenatal hormone exposure. Genes explain a relatively small amount of the variation we see in sexual orientation. Some

KEY TERMS

sexual orientation   405
heterosexual   405

homosexual   405
bisexual   405

research indicates that gay men have thicker corpus callosa than heterosexual men. Other research suggests that lesbian women may be more similar to heterosexual men in terms of brain hemisphere asymmetry. Prenatal testosterone exposure shows some links to eventual lesbian and bisexual orientation in women. Social factors do not seem to play a large role in sexual orientation.

Gay men and lesbian women are similar to their heterosexual counterparts in many ways, but they do show higher levels of relationship satisfaction and are more likely to break up than heterosexual married couples. Gay men and lesbian women in civil unions are less likely to break up than those without such unions. Children with gay parents tend to be as well adjusted as children with heterosexual parents.

TEST YOURSELF

1. Name various factors that might influence sexual orientation.

2. What is gender-nonconforming behavior? What is the evidence for the role of gender-nonconforming behavior in the development of sexual orientation?

3. What are some factors associated with gay and lesbian well-being?

APPLY YOUR KNOWLEDGE

1. States differ in terms of their laws regarding gay and lesbian marriage, adoption rights, and employment protections. Research your own state's legal policies toward the rights of gay men and women. Summarize those rights. Does your state also have laws about the protection of transgender rights?

2. Pick one culture you want to learn about and research the topic of homosexuality within that culture. How does that culture differ from your own regarding understanding, acceptance, and development of homosexuality? Share your findings with the class.

Sexual Behaviors and Practices

Talking about sexual behaviors, practices, and attitudes can sometimes be uncomfortable or embarrassing. It can also be interesting, enlightening, and exhilarating. In this section, we take up these hot topics and explore the ways that research has addressed them.

42·1 SEXUAL BEHAVIORS

What constitutes sexual behavior—what we commonly refer to as "sex"? When President Bill Clinton was asked whether he had engaged in sex with White House intern Monica Lewinsky, he was widely ridiculed for replying that "it depends" on what sex is. Yet Clinton may have been representing a more general confusion. What counts as sex? Most people might answer that question with "vaginal intercourse," but what about other sexual behaviors, such as anal sex and oral sex? If someone has engaged in these practices, is he or she still a "virgin"? If your significant other reported to you that he or she had recently engaged in oral sex with another person, would you consider that sexual infidelity? What if he or she spent an hour sexting an attractive friend? These are the kinds of questions that come up in trying to define sexual behavior (Medley-Rath, 2007).

One possibility is to define sex as activities that are involved in reproduction and fertilization. By this interpretation, many gay men and women are virgins, as are adolescents who engage exclusively in, say, oral sex. Further, from this point of view, too, masturbation would not be a sexual behavior.

Another approach is to define sexual behavior by the arousal and sexual response that occur when the behavior is performed. Though broader, this definition still might leave out individuals who themselves might say that they are engaged in sexual behavior. For instance, if a person is unable to experience sexual arousal but performs oral sex on a partner, has that person engaged in sexual behavior? Alternatively, we might broaden the definition a great deal and define sexual behaviors to include behaviors that are specific to each individual and that are pleasurable in a particular way—one that is unusually intimate and personal.

Confusion over what counts as sex can lead to potentially risky behavior. For example, as Figure 42.1 shows, oral sex has become relatively common during the teen years (National Center for Health Statistics, 2002). For many adolescents, oral sex appears to be a recreational activity, and because many individuals under age 20 do not view the practice as sex, they believe that it is a safe alternative to intercourse (Brady & Halpern-Felsher, 2007; Brewster, Harker, & Tillman, 2008). As we will consider later, however, oral sex exposes individuals to the risk of contracting sexually transmitted infections.

42·2 SEXUAL PRACTICES

When people in the United States engage in sexual behavior, what do they do, and how often? The earliest research on this topic was conducted by Alfred Kinsey and his colleagues in 1948. Kinsey is widely recognized as the father of sexology, a pioneer who brought scientific attention to sexual behavior. Kinsey was interested in studying sex objectively without concern about guilt or shame. He collected data wherever he could find it, interviewing anyone willing to discuss the intimate details of his or her sex life.

FIGURE 42.1 **Percentage of U.S. 15- to 19-Year-Old Boys and Girls Who Report Engaging in Oral Sex** Is it really sex? This figure shows the percentage of young people under the age of 20 who report having engaged in oral sex. SOURCE: National Center for Health Statistics (2002).

psychological *inquiry*

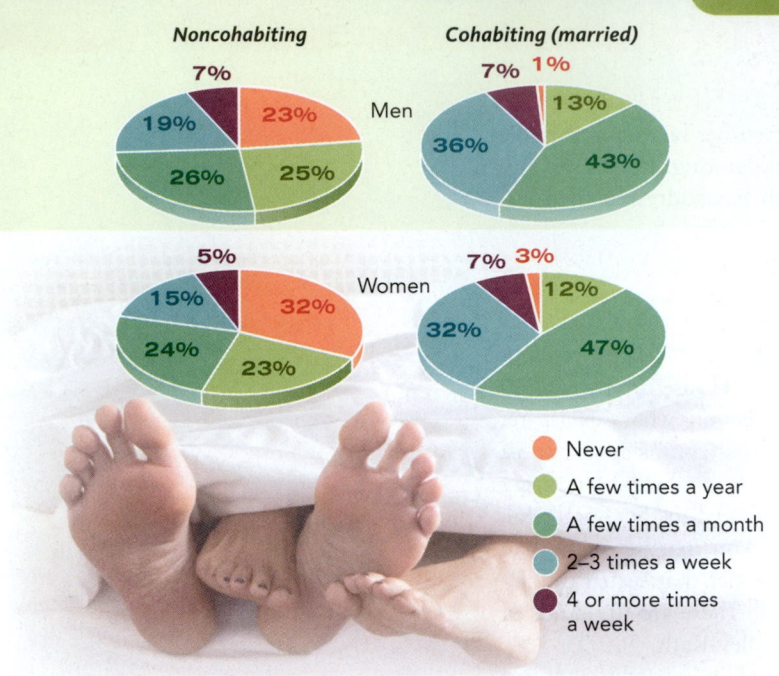

Noncohabiting

Cohabiting (married)

Men

7% 23% 19% 26% 25%

7% 1% 13% 36% 43%

Women

5% 32% 15% 24% 23%

7% 3% 12% 32% 47%

● Never

● A few times a year

● A few times a month

● 2–3 times a week

● 4 or more times a week

Sex in America

These pie charts show the responses of non-cohabiting and cohabiting (married) men and women to the question "How often have you had sex in the past year?" (Michael & others, 1994). Notice that for this type of graph, the area of the pie that is taken up by a response is proportional to the percentage of people giving that response. After studying the charts, answer these questions:

1. Overall, who reported having the most and the least sex?

2. The graphs separate those who were married from those who were not. For which gender did being married matter most in terms of frequency of sex?

3. When the respondents reported on having had sex, what behaviors do you think they included? Do you think these behaviors were the same for men and women? Explain.

4. Do you think that self-report is a good way to find out about sexual behavior? What other methods might researchers use to measure this variable?

The Kinsey Reports, published in two volumes, presented his findings for men (Kinsey, Pomeroy, & Martin, 1948) and women (Kinsey, Martin, & Pomeroy, 1953). Among the findings that shocked his readers were Kinsey's estimates of the frequency of bisexuality in men (nearly 12 percent) and women (7 percent) and his estimate that at least 50 percent of married men had been sexually unfaithful. Although acknowledged for initiating the scientific study of sexual behavior, Kinsey's work was limited by the lack of representative samples.

Not until 1994 were more accurate data obtained from a well-designed, comprehensive study of U.S. sexual patterns. Robert Michael and his colleagues (1994) interviewed nearly 3,500 randomly selected people from 18 to 50 years of age. Although 17 percent of the men and 3 percent of the women said they had had sex with at least 21 partners, the overall impression from the survey was that for most Americans, marriage and monogamy rule sexual behavior. Married couples reported having sex most often and were the most likely to have orgasms when they did. The Psychological Inquiry above shows the frequency of sex for married and non-cohabiting individuals in the year before the survey was taken. Nearly 75 percent of the married men and 85 percent of the married women indicated that they had never been unfaithful. More recent surveys have shown similar results. For instance, in 2004 ABC polled a nationally representative sample and found that individuals in committed relationships had more sex than singles, and the vast majority reported themselves as sexually faithful (ABC News, 2004).

What exactly are people doing when they say they are having sex, and how often are they doing it? In 2002, the Centers for Disease Control conducted a study of sexual behaviors in the United States (Mosher, Chandra, & Jones, 2005). The findings were that among people aged 15 to 44, 10 percent of men and 8 percent of women had never had sex, including vaginal intercourse, oral sex, and anal sex. Among adults aged 25 to 44 years, 97 percent had had vaginal intercourse, and 90 percent had had oral sex. Among men, 40 percent had had anal sex, and among women 35 percent had done so.

A recent study comprising a representative sample of nearly 3,000 Swedes examined the frequency of different sexual behaviors in the previous month (Brody & Costa, 2009). The behaviors studied were vaginal intercourse, masturbation, oral sex, and anal sex. The results showed that on average, men reported having vaginal intercourse 5 times and masturbating 4.5 times in the previous month. On average, women reported having vaginal intercourse about 5 times but masturbated less than 2 times during the previous month. For both men and women, oral sex occurred approximately 2 times and anal sex less than once (Brody & Costa, 2009).

What do gay men and lesbian women do when they "have sex"? Research is limited and generally posed in terms of risk for sexually transmitted infection. Among gay men, mutual masturbation, oral sex, and anal sex are common, although as many as a third of gay men report never having engaged in anal sex (Reisner & others, 2009). Among lesbian women, practices include genital-to-genital contact (body rubbing), mutual fondling and masturbation, penetration with the hands or other objects, and oral sex (Marrazzo, Coffey, & Bingham, 2005; Mercer & others, 2007).

42·3 THE HUMAN SEXUAL RESPONSE PATTERN

Regardless of the specific behavior, similar physical processes are involved in sexual responses. To examine the physiological processes involved in sexual activity, William Masters and Virginia Johnson (1966) carefully observed and measured the physiological responses of 382 female and 312 male volunteers as they masturbated or had vaginal intercourse. Masters and Johnson identified a **human sexual response pattern** consisting of four phases—excitement, plateau, orgasm, and resolution.

The *excitement phase* begins the process of erotic responsiveness; it lasts from several minutes to several hours, depending on the nature of the sex play involved. Engorgement of blood vessels and increased blood flow in genital areas, along with muscle tension, characterize the excitement phase. The most obvious signs of response in this phase are lubrication of the vagina and partial erection of the penis.

The second phase of the human sexual response, the *plateau phase,* is a continuation and heightening of the arousal begun in the excitement phase. The increases in breathing, pulse rate, and blood pressure that occurred during the excitement phase become more intense, penile erection and vaginal lubrication are more complete, and orgasm is closer.

The third phase of the human sexual response cycle is *orgasm.* How long does orgasm last? Some individuals sense that time is standing still when it takes place, but in fact orgasm lasts for only about 3 to 15 seconds. Orgasm involves an explosive discharge of neuromuscular tension and an intensely pleasurable feeling. With orgasm comes the release of the neurotransmitter oxytocin, which plays a role in social bonding.

Following orgasm, the individual enters the *resolution phase,* in which blood vessels return to their normal state. A sex difference in this phase is that females may be stimulated to orgasm again without delay, whereas males enter a *refractory period* during which they cannot have another orgasm.

Working around the same time as Masters and Johnson was sex therapist Helen Singer Kaplan (1974). Kaplan studied sexual response through the lens of her clinical practice, during which she talked with individuals about their sexual experiences. Kaplan's view of the sexual response differed from Masters and Johnson's in that she added a key initial stage: desire. Kaplan discovered that for many of her clients, sexual desire was sometimes lacking. Kaplan's work highlighted the very important role of motivation in sexual activity. Clearly, she argued, without the desire to have sex, the stages described by Masters and Johnson may never get started. We will return to the human sexual response and the issue of desire when we survey sexual disorders.

42·4 COGNITION AND OTHER FACTORS IN SEXUAL BEHAVIOR

Sexual behavior is influenced by a variety of factors, ranging from sensation and perception to the ways we think about sexuality (Crooks & Baur, 2011). Finding someone sexually attractive may involve seeing the person, getting to know him or her, and feeling

● **human sexual response pattern** Masters and Johnson's model of human sexual response, consisting of four phases—excitement, plateau, orgasm, and resolution.

emotionally attached. From experience, we know that our thoughts play an important role in our sexuality (Kelly, 2006). We might be sexually attracted to someone but understand that we must inhibit our sexual urges until the relationship has time to develop. We have the cognitive capacity to respect our partners and not take sexual advantage of them. We also have the cognitive resources to generate sexual images—to become sexually aroused just by thinking about something erotic.

Scripts are mental schemas for events. Sexuality is influenced by *sexual scripts,* patterns of expectancies for how people should behave sexually (Stulhofer, Busko, & Landripet, 2010). We carry these scripts with us in our memories (McCabe, Tanner, & Heiman, 2010). Typically, women and men have different sexual scripts, which contain their beliefs and expectations about sex and what it means (R. Jones, 2006; McCabe, Tanner, & Heiman, 2010). For men, sex may center more on what's going on in the genitals, with orgasm being a crucial aspect; for women, sex may be more an expression of intimacy, with orgasm an optional feature (van Lankveld, 2008).

Cognitive interpretation of sexual activity also involves our perceptions of the individual with whom we are having sex, and his or her perceptions of us (Miller, Perlman, & Brehm, 2009). Is this sexual encounter a symbol of a more enduring relationship or simply a hook-up? Amid the wash of hormones in sexual activity is the cognitive ability to control, reason about, and try to make sense of the activity.

The Influence of Culture

The influence of culture on sexuality was demonstrated dramatically in a classic analysis by John Messenger (1971) of the people living on the small island of Inis Beag off the coast of Ireland. They knew nothing about tongue kissing or hand stimulation of the penis, and they detested nudity. For both females and males, premarital sex was out of the question. Men avoided most sexual experiences because they believed that sexual intercourse reduced their energy level and was bad for their health. Under these repressive conditions, sexual intercourse occurred only at night, taking place as quickly as possible. As you might suspect, female orgasm was rare in this culture (Messenger, 1971).

In contrast, around the same time that Messenger was studying the people of Inis Beag, Donald Marshall (1971) conducted research on the Mangaian culture in the South Pacific. In Mangaia, young boys were taught about masturbation and were encouraged to engage in it as much as they liked. At age 13, the boys underwent a ritual initiating them into sexual manhood. First, their elders instructed them about sexual strategies, including how to aid their female partner in having orgasms. Two weeks later, the boy had intercourse with an experienced woman who helped him hold back from ejaculation until she experienced orgasm with him. By the end of adolescence, Mangaians had sex pretty much every day. Mangaian women reported a high frequency of orgasm.

Few cultures are as isolated and homogeneous as those of Inis Beag and Mangaia. In the United States, sexual behaviors and attitudes reflect the country's diverse multicultural population, and Americans fall somewhere in the middle of a continuum going from repressive to liberal. We are more conservative in our sexual habits than once thought but somewhat more open-minded regarding sexual orientation than a century ago.

Culture influences not only attitudes about sexual behavior but also ideas about sexual orientation. In many traditional cultures, there are accepted roles for individuals who are homosexual, lesbian, or transgender (Nanda, 2008).

Donald Marshall's work focused on the sexual practices of the people of the South Pacific island of Mangaia.

CRITICAL CONTROVERSY

Can Abstinence-Only Sex Education Be Effective?

A recent study made the headlines when it reported that an abstinence-only intervention successfully delayed sexual intercourse in youth. Let's take a look at the study to get a sense of why it worked.

John B. Jemmott III and his colleagues randomly assigned 662 African American sixth- and seventh-graders to different groups (Jemmott, Jemmott, & Fong, 2010). The groups included abstinence-only and safer-sex interventions. A third group that received information about healthy behavior (but not about sexuality) served as a control. The dependent measure was whether participants reported having sexual intercourse in the two years following the interventions.

The abstinence-only intervention was built around the principles of social cognitive theory, focusing on building self-efficacy and a sense of personal control. The facilitators in the program emphasized that sexual activity is a serious step and that it might be best to delay it for some time in the future. They did not talk about sex moralistically and never mentioned that students should wait until marriage; nor did the instructors present sexual behavior negatively. Instead, the intervention included role-play exercises and other activities that helped students build skills to resist pressures to have sex. If the topics of birth control or condoms were broached by students, the facilitators provided medically accurate information and cleared up any misconceptions students might have.

Two years later, students in the abstinence-only group were less likely to report having had sex than those in the control group. Specifically, about one-third of the abstinence-only group reported they had had sexual intercourse, compared with nearly half of the control group. The safer-sex intervention students did not differ from the controls in terms of whether they reported having sex. Importantly, those in the abstinence-only group who did have sex were no less likely to use condoms than those in the safer-sex group.

Although these results might generally seem to support the effectiveness of abstinence-only education, particular aspects of the study might raise the eyebrows of abstinence-only advocates. First, some of the middle-schoolers in the study were as young as 10 years old, certainly younger than many abstinence-only advocates might envision. Second, the information provided about contraceptives and condoms does not conform with the typical expectations for abstinence-only education. Moreover, participants were not encouraged to wait until marriage to have sex, nor were they told that sexual behavior outside of marriage is generally harmful.

There are also features of the study that limit its validity and generalizability. Note that only students in the abstinence-only group were specifically encouraged to delay sexual activity and that the dependent measure was self-report. So, these students might not have been truthful about their sexual activity. Also, because the study included only youngsters, it is not clear whether the intervention would work for older teens.

Nevertheless, this research provides the first evidence that sex education aimed at abstinence can have an influence on the sexual behavior of young people. Importantly, though, the version of abstinence-only education used in the study may be one that surprises advocates of such interventions.

WHAT DO YOU THINK?

- What kind of sex education did you have in school? Was it adequate? Explain.

- If, as a parent, you were asked to give consent for your child to participate in the study by Jemmott and others, how would the child's sex or age influence your decision?

- How might an intervention like this one be used to reduce other risky behaviors in youth?

Sex Education

One way that societies teach youth about sex and sexuality is through formal education. Although many topics associated with sex and sexuality are likely to spur controversy, most people concerned with sex education share two simple and relatively uncontroversial goals: to encourage the very young to delay sexual activity and to reduce teen pregnancy and sexually transmitted infections. Despite this consensus, there are many different opinions on *how* to achieve these goals.

One form of sex education is the *abstinence-only* approach, which has become increasingly common in the United States over the past two decades. According to federal guidelines (Family and Youth Services Bureau, 2004), abstinence-only educational programs must emphasize that any sexual behavior outside of marriage is harmful to individuals of any age. In addition, instructors can present contraceptives and condoms only in terms of their failure rates. Abstinence-only sex education promotes the notion that abstinence is the only effective way to avoid pregnancy and sexually transmitted infections (Family and Youth Services Bureau, 2004).

An alternative approach is *comprehensive* sex education; this involves providing students with comprehensive knowledge about sexual behavior, birth control, and the use of condoms in protecting against sexually transmitted infections, while encouraging them to delay sexual activity and practice abstinence.

Which approach to sex education most effectively delays sexual activity and prevents teen pregnancy? Research strongly indicates that comprehensive sex education outstrips abstinence-only programs in achieving these goals. Two recent research reviews found that abstinence-only programs do not delay the initiation of sexual intercourse and do not reduce HIV-risk behaviors (Kirby, 2008; Kirby, Laris, & Rolleir, 2007; Underhill, Montgomery, & Operario, 2007). Further, a recent study revealed that adolescents who experienced comprehensive sex education were less likely to report adolescent pregnancies than those who received abstinence-only sex education or no sex education (Kohler, Manhart, & Lafferty, 2008).

A number of leading experts on adolescent sexuality now conclude that sex education programs that emphasize contraceptive knowledge do not increase the incidence of sexual intercourse and are more likely to reduce the risk of adolescent pregnancy and sexually transmitted infections than abstinence-only programs (Constantine, 2008; M. E. Eisenberg & others, 2008; Hampton, 2008; Hyde & DeLamater, 2011). An additional key concern with abstinence-only education is that it often includes negative and even misleading information about the effectiveness of condoms, leading adolescents to be less likely to use them when they do have sex.

In many communities in the United States, educational practices have not caught up with the research findings. Indeed, inadequate knowledge about contraception, coupled with inconsistent use of effective contraceptive methods, has given Americans a dubious distinction: The United States has one of the highest rates of adolescent pregnancy and childbearing in the developed world, with as many as one-third of young women under the age of 20 becoming pregnant (Guttmacher Institute, 2010). Births to adolescent girls had fallen over the years, reaching a record low in 2004, but they took an upturn in 2006 (Guttmacher Institute, 2010), coinciding with the national trend toward abstinence-only sex education.

U.S. adolescent pregnancy rates are nearly twice those of Canada and Great Britain and at least four times the rates in France, Sweden, Germany, and Japan (Figure 42.2). Although U.S. adolescents are no more sexually active than their counterparts in countries such as France and Sweden, their adolescent pregnancy rate is much higher—perhaps because, compared to these other nations, the United States has less comprehensive sex education and less availability and use of condoms. Clearly, education and prevention are crucial to progress in reducing pregnancy among adolescents.

A recent study of a specific kind of abstinence-only sex education challenged ideas about whether abstinence-only programs can at least delay sex among younger adolescents. To read more about this study, check out the Critical Controversy on page 417.

Teen births per 1,000 women

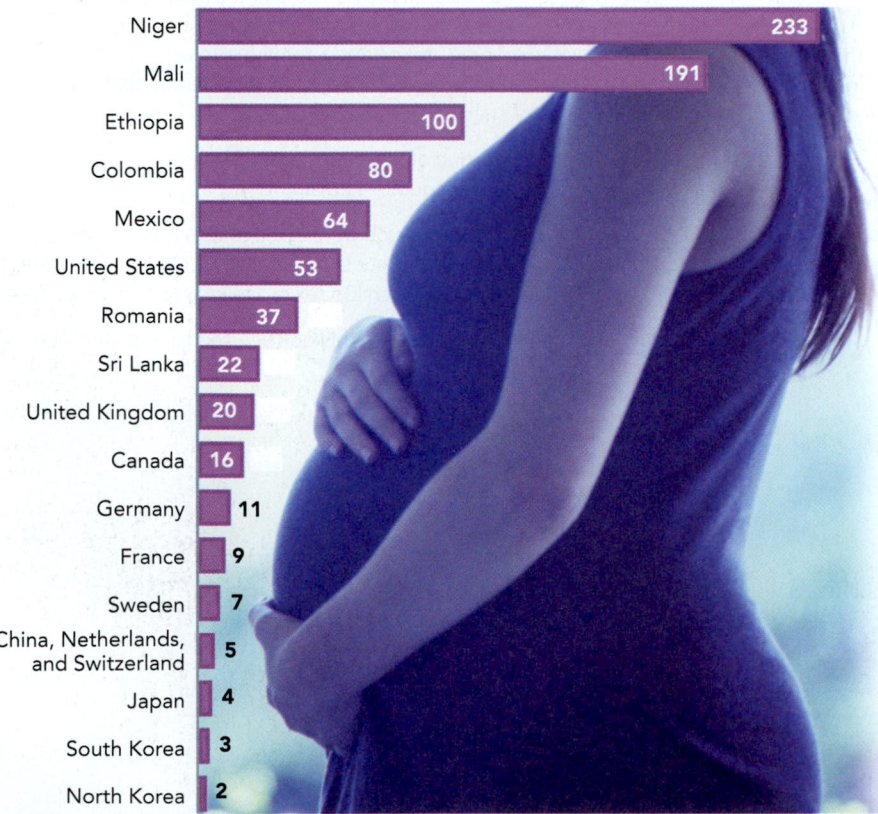

Niger	233
Mali	191
Ethiopia	100
Colombia	80
Mexico	64
United States	53
Romania	37
Sri Lanka	22
United Kingdom	20
Canada	16
Germany	11
France	9
Sweden	7
China, Netherlands, and Switzerland	5
Japan	4
South Korea	3
North Korea	2

FIGURE 42.2 **Adolescent Pregnancy Rates Across Several Countries**
Comprehensive sex education is one reason for the difference in teen pregnancy rates among countries. What other factors might be at work?

SUMMARY

Although it is difficult to study sexual behaviors and practices, research suggests that married couples have sex more often than unmarried couples and singles. Vaginal intercourse is the most common sexual practice for men and women. Both men and women report engaging in oral sex and anal sex. Regardless of the particular sexual activity, the human sexual response pattern is characterized by four stages—excitement, plateau, orgasm, and resolution.

Sexual desire is also a key element in sexual behavior. Sensation, perception, and cognition are all important components of sexual activity. Culture plays a role in sexuality as well.

Some people worry that providing adolescents with comprehensive sex education will lead to premature sexual activity. However, research strongly suggests that education is crucial to preventing unwanted pregnancy.

KEY TERMS

human sexual response
   pattern   415

TEST YOURSELF

1. What are some different ways that people define sexual behavior, or "sex"?
2. What do studies indicate about the frequency of sex among married partners and among people in committed relationships versus single people?
3. What are two kinds of sex education, and how effective is each?

APPLY YOUR KNOWLEDGE

1. What effect do media have on sexual behavior in today's society? How do video games, TV, and movies portray or distort the image of sexual behaviors in America? Give some examples.

2. Reflect on your own sexual education experience. What type of education did you receive about sex, and was this education effective? Were certain aspects of it better than others? Give examples and explain your thinking.

Sexual Variations and Disorders

If we think of sexual behavior as any behavior that involves sexual pleasure, then we can say that there are many different kinds of sexual behavior. When it comes to sexual pleasure, in fact, variation is the norm. In this section we consider some variant sexual behaviors and draw a contrast between behavior that is pleasurable but not harmful versus behavior that is potentially distressing and therefore abnormal. We also consider some common disorders of sexual response and desire.

43·1 FETISHES

People are sexually aroused by different activities. A man might be sexually stimulated by wearing women's clothing. A woman might be turned on by wearing a necktie. A **fetish** is an object or activity that arouses sexual interest and desire. Fetishes include erotic materials (such as pornographic images and films), clothing, and other physical objects (Gijs, 2008). A person with a *transvestic fetish* (who may be heterosexual or homosexual) gets sexual pleasure from wearing clothing of the opposite sex. Other fetishes include activities such as dressing up like an animal or a baby. In yet another fetish, *sadomasochism,* one person (the sadistic partner) gains sexual pleasure from dominating another person (the masochist), who in turn enjoys being dominated.

These behaviors may be unusual, but they are not generally considered abnormal. Indeed, unusual sexual practices are typically considered harmless variations as long as these three principles are not violated: The individuals are consenting adults; they do not experience personal distress; and they are not putting themselves in danger of physical harm or death as a result of their activities (Gijs, 2008). When a variation in sexual behavior violates one or more of these principles, however, it may qualify as a paraphilia, which is a psychological disorder and may be illegal.

43·2 PARAPHILIAS

The American Psychiatric Association (APA) defines **paraphilias** as sexual disorders that feature recurrent sexually arousing fantasies, urges, or behaviors involving (1) nonhuman objects, (2) the suffering or humiliation of oneself or one's partner, or (3) children or other nonconsenting persons (APA, 2000). While some paraphilias may be relatively harmless, a paraphilia is considered to require treatment if the person experiencing it feels distress or impairment in social or occupational life domains. Men are far more likely than women to suffer from paraphilias (Gijs, 2008).

Certain paraphilias, such as exhibitionism (exposing one's genitals to another person to gain sexual pleasure) and voyeurism (watching another person to experience sexual pleasure), are considered problematic even when the paraphilic individual does not suffer from personal distress, because they involve the violation of someone who is not consenting. Sexual sadism without the consent of one's partner is similarly violating. Pedophilia, which we examine below, involves sexual behavior with children; it is certainly a psychological disorder, even in the absence of personal distress, because children are not old enough to legally consent to such behavior. Figure 43.1 lists the various paraphilias that the American Psychiatric Association recognizes.

What is the etiology of paraphilias? (*Etiology* means "the causes or significant preceding conditions.") There is no one answer to this question. Each paraphilia may have its own origin. Some experts have suggested that principles of classical conditioning

● **fetish** An object or activity that arouses sexual interest and desire.

● **paraphilias** Sexual disorders that feature recurrent sexually arousing fantasies, urges, or behaviors involving nonhuman objects; the suffering or humiliation of oneself or one's partner; or children or other nonconsenting persons.

Paraphilia	Focus
Exhibitionism	Exposing one's genitals to a stranger
Fetishism	Using nonliving objects for sexual pleasure
Frotteurism	Touching and rubbing against a person who has not given consent—for instance, in a crowded subway train
Pedophilia	Sexual activity with a prepubescent child
Sexual masochism	The act of being humiliated, beaten, bound, or otherwise made to suffer
Sexual sadism	Acts in which the individual derives sexual excitement from the psychological or physical suffering of the victim
Transvestic fetishism	Cross-dressing by a male in women's clothing
Voyeurism	Observing unsuspecting individuals—usually strangers who are naked, in the process of disrobing, or engaged in sexual activity

FIGURE 43.1   Types of Paraphilias
Sexual variations are considered harmless if they (1) do not cause a person distress or physical harm and (2) do not violate another person. For some of the paraphilias in the figure, the issue is one of consent; for others, the variations may qualify as a disorder only if they cause the person distress or interfere with daily living. Notice that fetishism is included as a paraphilia if a fetish causes personal distress or interferes with daily life. Can you identify which of these principles apply to each of the other paraphilias?

can explain the emergence of some paraphilias (Gijs, 2008). Recall that in classical conditioning, a conditioned stimulus (CS) is paired with another stimulus, the unconditioned stimulus (UCS), which provokes an unconditioned response (UCR). After frequent pairings, the CS comes to evoke the response even in the absence of the UCS. Using this framework, we might say that a man with a shoe fetish might have been around shoes when he masturbated as a boy and that these experiences led to the fetish. For other paraphilias, however, it is likely that more than associative learning is involved.

43·3 PEDOPHILIA

Pedophilia is a paraphilia in which an adult or an older adolescent sexually fantasizes about or engages in sexual behavior with individuals who have not reached puberty. Pedophilia is more common in men than women, but it is not an exclusively male disorder (Seto, 2009).

The causes of this disorder are not well understood. Although it was once thought that most individuals who sexually abuse children were themselves sexually abused as children, this explanation has not held up to the evidence (U.S. General Accounting Office, 1996). Adults who sexually abuse children are more likely than other sex offenders to report themselves as having experienced sexual abuse in childhood (Jesperson, Lalumiere, & Seto, 2009), but the vast majority of individuals who have been sexually molested as children do not themselves go on to molest others.

Pedophilia is associated with low self-esteem, poor social skills, low IQ (Hall & Hall, 2007), and a history of head injuries (causing unconsciousness) in childhood (Seto, 2009). The disorder is related to a pattern of cognitive distortions, including minimizing the harm of pedophilic activities, believing that sexual impulses are uncontrollable, and thinking that sexual relationships with children are consensual (Hall & Hall, 2007). Brain-imaging studies suggest that individuals who are sexually attracted to children show a pervasive pattern of brain dysfunction, related to connections between brain regions (Cantor & others, 2008).

Given the potential damage that pedophilic behavior can inflict on its victims, identifying strategies for treatment and prevention is paramount. Therapies have targeted the learned associations between children and sexual arousal or have focused on training

● **pedophilia** A paraphilia in which an adult or an older adolescent sexually fantasizes about or engages in sexual behavior with individuals who have not reached puberty.

offenders in skills needed to recognize and avoid risky situations, such as being around children. Unfortunately, these treatments have not been effective (Marques & others, 2005; Seto, 2009).

In recent years castration (either surgically, through removal of the testes, or chemically, through drugs that reduce testosterone) has been used to treat sex offenders who victimize children. Hundreds of surgical castrations of sex offenders have been performed throughout Europe, and nine U.S. states have laws that *require* chemical or surgical castration for sex offenders who commit crimes against children as a condition of parole (Seto, 2009). It is difficult to evaluate the effectiveness of castration, however, because individuals are not randomly assigned to the treatment, and those who undergo the procedure may be particularly motivated to change their behavior (Seto, 2009). Furthermore, some critics have suggested that castration is used primarily to punish, not to treat, and as such is unethical (Spaulding, 1998; R. G. Wright, 2008).

Acknowledging the difficulties in treating pedophilia, Michael Seto (2009), an expert on the disorder, concluded that efforts should focus on prevention—both preventing pedophilia itself and implementing interventions aimed at child-victims. With respect to actually preventing pedophilia, Seto argues that, given the evidence for a neurodevelopmental basis to the problem, enhanced prenatal care and early parenting interventions might be helpful in reducing pedophilia's occurrence, in addition to having other positive benefits. With respect to preventing abuse and protecting children, Seto advocates educating children to distinguish appropriate and inappropriate touch and empowering them to share their feelings with a trusted adult if someone is making them uncomfortable.

43·4 DISORDERS OF SEXUAL DESIRE AND SEXUAL RESPONSE

Paraphilias are unusual. More common disorders of sexuality involve problems either in sexual desire or in the physical sexual response described by Masters and Johnson.

With regard to sexual desire disorders, studies suggest that up to a quarter of men and nearly half of women report sometimes being troubled with a general lack of interest in sex (Laumann & others, 2005; van Lankveld, 2008). Lack of sexual desire in both men and women can stem from low levels of androgen, stress, anxiety and depression, physical illnesses, and various drugs used to treat psychological and physical conditions (Hackett, 2008; van Lankveld, 2008). Treatments for lack of sexual desire include drug therapies, psychological therapies, and relationship counseling.

In terms of disorders related to sexual response, two common disorders in men are *erectile dysfunction,* the failure of the penis to become erect, and *premature ejaculation,* the experience of orgasm before the person wishes it. As we have seen, the male genitalia are complex, and the male sexual response involves a number of physiological reactions, from erection to ejaculation. It is not surprising that, at times, this elegant machinery does not function optimally.

Erectile dysfunction was once believed to be primarily psychological, but experts now agree that most cases involve a combination of psychological and physical factors (Heidelbaugh, 2010; Lewis, Yuan, & Wang, 2008). Erectile dysfunction may be a symptom of an underlying physical illness, such as diabetes, and is more likely to occur with age. Treatment typically involves medications, such as Viagra, that allow the individual to experience erection (Althof & others, 2010; Claes, 2010). Premature ejaculation is the most common sexual complaint among men under the age of 40 (Rowland & McMahon, 2008). Psychological, physical, and relationship factors can play a role in premature ejaculation. The problem may be treated with drugs or therapy and may also involve working together with one's sexual partner to develop greater mastery over the sexual response.

Women can also suffer from disorders of sexual response, including problems in sexual arousal as well as in the experience of orgasm. For some women, dysfunction in arousal is explained by problems in the autonomic nervous system that disrupt the engorgement of the labia and lubrication of the vagina; for other women, the subjective feeling of arousal is absent even when these physical changes occur (Meston, Seal, & Hamilton, 2008). Disorders of sexual orgasm in women involve delayed or absent orgasm during sexual activity (Meston, Seal, & Hamilton, 2008). Both of these types of disorders can be related to the experience of childhood sexual abuse, as well as to strict religious beliefs and negative sexual attitudes (van Lankveld, 2008). These disorders of sexual response may be treated with androgens or through psychotherapy. Addressing underlying physical causes can also sometimes bring relief.

The occasional occurrence of erectile dysfunction or premature ejaculation in males, and of problems with arousal and orgasm in females, is common and normal. It is when these problems cause distress for the individual or difficulties in important relationships that they are considered disorders in need of treatment.

43·5 VARIATIONS, DISORDERS, AND THE MEANING OF NORMALITY

A theme throughout this discussion has been whether variations in sexual behavior are problems that require professional help or whether they represent harmless differences that simply reflect human diversity. The difficulties people have in talking about sexuality only perpetuate anxiety, shame, and concern about sex. People are not ashamed to admit that they like certain foods and dislike others. Imagine if we treated sexual tastes in a similarly open way.

If you feel concern about your own sexual behaviors or experiences, seeking the advice of a counselor or therapist is a great way to get clarity about the issues. Sexuality can be powerful and confusing, but it is also an amazing expression of the capacity of humans to bond with others.

SUMMARY

With regard to sexual tastes and activities, variation is the norm. A fetish is an object that a person finds sexually arousing. Paraphilias are disorders in which a person experiences strong sexual interest in certain objects or activities. Paraphilias may require treatment if they violate the rights of others or put the individual at risk of physical harm.

Pedophilia is a particularly harmful paraphilia involving sexual attraction to children. Pedophilia is very difficult to treat.

More common than paraphilias are disorders of sexual desire and sexual response. Two common disorders of sexual response in men are erectile dysfunction and premature ejaculation. In women, common sexual response disorders include problems in arousal and in experiencing orgasm.

KEY TERMS

fetish   420
paraphilias   420

pedophilia   421

TEST YOURSELF

1. What three principles must not be violated for a variation in sexual behavior to be considered harmless?
2. Why is it difficult to determine the effectiveness of surgical or chemical castration as a treatment for pedophilia?
3. Give examples of sexual response disorders experienced by men, as well as examples of such disorders experienced by women.

APPLY YOUR KNOWLEDGE

1. Where do you draw the line between a sexual behavior that is just unusual and one that is disordered?
2. Search for information about the standards and practices that various social networking sites use to monitor sexual behavior online. Evaluate these guidelines. What does each define as appropriate and inappropriate? Discuss whether more or less should be done to protect the safety of members in social networking sites.

Sexuality and Health and Wellness

Many of us would agree that healthy sexual activity is an important component of the good life. Yet, for a variety of reasons, we often do not talk about this aspect of our behavior. In this concluding section, we consider two aspects of the intersection of sexuality with health and wellness—first, its implications for physical health; and second, its role in psychological well-being.

SEXUAL BEHAVIOR AND PHYSICAL HEALTH

A key consideration in any discussion of sexual health is sexually transmitted infections. A **sexually transmitted infection (STI)** is an infection that is contracted primarily through sexual activity—vaginal intercourse as well as oral and anal sex. STIs affect about one of every six adults in the United States (National Center for Health Statistics, 2005).

Types and Causes of Sexually Transmitted Infections

Some STIs are bacterial in origin, as are gonorrhea and syphilis. Others are caused by viruses, as in the case of genital herpes and HIV. STIs are a top health concern because they can have implications for a person's future fertility, risk of cancer, and life expectancy.

No single STI has had a greater impact on sexual behavior in the past decades than HIV. **Acquired immune deficiency syndrome (AIDS)** is caused by the *human immunodeficiency virus (HIV)*, a sexually transmitted infection that destroys the body's immune system. Without treatment, most people who contract HIV are vulnerable to germs that a normal immune system can destroy. Through 2007, more than 1 million Americans had been diagnosed with AIDS, and more than 560,000 Americans had died of complications from the infection (National Center for Health Statistics, 2010).

Recent improvements in drug therapies have given rise to the view that HIV is a chronic rather than terminal condition. Responses to treatment vary among individuals, and keeping up with the "cocktail" of drugs necessary to continuously fight HIV can be challenging. The treatment known as highly active antiretroviral therapy (HAART) can involve taking between 6 and 22 pills each day, although in 2006 the FDA approved the first one-pill-per-day treatment for HIV (Laurence, 2006).

Because of increased education and the development of more effective drug therapies, deaths due to

● **sexually transmitted infection (STI)** An infection that is contracted primarily through sexual activity—vaginal intercourse as well as oral and anal sex.

● **acquired immune deficiency syndrome (AIDS)** A sexually transmitted infection, caused by the human immunodeficiency virus (HIV), that destroys the body's immune system.

Along with a number of other factors, sexual activity plays a role in romantic partners' well-being.

AIDS have begun to decline in the United States (National Center for Health Statistics, 2010). There are no solid estimates for the life expectancy of someone who is HIV positive, because the existing treatments have been around for only about a decade. Even in this era of improved treatments, however, HIV remains an incurable infection that can lead to early death. Importantly, it has been estimated that as many as one-half of individuals who are HIV positive are not in treatment and that one-quarter of individuals who are HIV positive do not know that they are (National Center for Health Statistics, 2010).

Practicing Safe Sex

Anyone who is sexually active is at risk of contracting HIV and other STIs. The only 100 percent safe behavior is abstinence from sex, which most individuals do not view as an option. Sensual activities such as kissing, French kissing, cuddling, massage, and mutual masturbation (that does not involve the exchange of bodily fluids) involve no risk of an STI. Sexual activities that involve penetration, including vaginal and anal intercourse as well as oral sex, are riskier behaviors that can be made less risky with the use of proper protection.

Generally, condoms are a key tool in efforts to protect oneself from sexually trans-mitted infections. In your own sexual experience, it may be difficult to gauge the accuracy of a partner's estimates of risk and his or her status with respect to having an STI. The wisest course of action is always to protect yourself by using a latex condom. When correctly used, latex condoms help to prevent the transmission of many STIs.

Condoms are most effective in preventing gonorrhea, syphilis, chlamydia, and HIV. Research suggests that consistent condom use also significantly reduces the risk that males will transmit to their female partners the human papilloma virus (HPV), which can cause cervical cancer (Winer & others, 2006). Although condoms are less effective against the spread of herpes than against other STIs, the consistent use of condoms significantly reduces the risk of herpes infection for both men and women (Wald, Langenberg, & Krantz, 2005). In short, anyone who thinks that condom use is inconvenient or will ruin the mood might well consider this question: Which is more inconvenient—using a condom or contracting gonorrhea or AIDS?

Research has shown that programs to promote safe sex are especially effective if they include the eroticization of condom use—that is, making condoms a part of the sensual experience of foreplay (Scott-Sheldon & Johnson, 2006). Analyses of HIV prevention programs (including over 350 intervention groups and 100 control groups) by Delores Albarracin and her colleagues have produced important recommendations for the best ways to influence behavior (Albarracin, Durantini, & Earl, 2006; Albarracin & others, 2005; Durantini & others, 2006). The studies have found that fear tactics are relatively less effective and that programs emphasizing active skill building (for example, role playing the use of condoms), self-efficacy, and positive attitudes about condom use are effective with most groups. Making safe sex sexy is a great way to practice safe sex.

SEXUAL BEHAVIOR AND PSYCHOLOGICAL WELL-BEING

Researchers have been particularly interested in people's motives for having sex. Lynne Cooper and her colleagues (Cooper, Shapiro, & Powers, 1998) examined the sex motives of a sample of adolescents and young adults whom they followed longitudinally over several years. The researchers examined the reasons these individuals gave for having sex. The participants' reported motives included the following: to connect intimately with someone, to enhance their own self-esteem, to gain a partner's and peers' approval, and to avoid feeling distressed or lonely. The researchers also found that engaging in sex as a form of intimacy with another person was related to having fewer sex partners overall and to practicing less risky sex (Cooper, Shapiro, & Powers, 1998). Conversely, individuals who had sex to cope with negative feelings were less likely to have stable long-term relationships and tended to engage in more unsafe sex. Subsequent research has shown that having sex in order to be close to another person is related to enhanced well-being, but engaging in sex to avoid bad feelings is linked with decreases in well-being (Impett, Peplau, & Gable, 2005).

Research has solidly supported the role of sexual activity in well-being. In the Swedish study described earlier, frequency of vaginal intercourse was strongly related to life satisfaction for men and women (Brody & Costa, 2009). Furthermore, although the frequency of sexual behavior may decline with age, sexuality remains a significant part of human identity and relationships throughout life (DeLamater & Moorman, 2007; Lindau & Gavrilova, 2010). Importantly, partnered sexual activity is a strong predictor of satisfaction in relationships even when those activities do not include vaginal intercourse (DeLamater & Moorman, 2007; Kennedy, Haque, & Zarankow, 1997). Throughout the life span, then, sexual activities remain a source of pleasure and an avenue for the experience of intimacy with another.

SUMMARY

Sexually transmitted infections (STIs) are infections that can be spread through sexual contact, including vaginal, anal, and oral sex. When used properly and consistently, latex condoms offer excellent protection against many STIs, including AIDS.

The relationship between sexual behavior and psychological wellness depends on the reasons people have sex. Those who engage in sexual activity based on intimacy motives have fewer overall sex partners and are more likely to practice safe sex. Those who engage in sex to win a partner's approval or to cope with negative feelings tend to show decreases in well-being and to engage in more sexual risk taking. Sexuality is an important aspect of psychological well-being throughout the life span.

KEY TERMS

sexually transmitted
 infection (STI)   424

acquired immune deficiency
 syndrome (AIDS)   424

TEST YOURSELF

1. What is a sexually transmitted infection (STI)?

2. What contraceptive device is key in efforts to protect individuals from contracting STIs? Against what does it offer the most protection?

3. What motives for having sex are associated with increased well-being? With decreased well-being?

Personality

Revealing Who We *Really* Are

When you meet someone for the first time, do you ever wonder whether the person is putting on a front, maybe trying to show himself or herself in the best possible light? Increasingly, such first meetings are occurring on online social networking sites such as Facebook and MySpace. More than 700 million people worldwide have profiles on social networking sites (ComScore, 2008). How accurately do these online profiles reflect their owners?

Recently, a team of personality psychologists, led by Mitja Back, sought to address this very question, and the results might surprise you. The researchers asked 236 U.S. and 103 German college students to complete a measure of their personality characteristics. Back and colleagues then compared these reports to the information on each student's online profile (Back & others, 2010). The results? The online profiles were well matched to the students' actual characteristics. In other words, rather than presenting an idealized version of themselves, the participants had used their online profile to express their *real personality*. Indeed, Back and colleagues suggest that this is the very reason for the popularity of social networking sites: They give us a chance to share who we genuinely are.

We leave evidence of "the real us" in many of the settings we occupy in life—not just on websites but also in offices, classrooms, bedrooms, and dorm rooms (Gosling, 2008a). "Who we really are" is the topic that occupies personality psychology, our focus in this section. Personality psychologists are interested in identifying the characteristics that make each of us different from everyone else and in understanding how these characteristics relate to behavior. Personality psychology explores the psychological attributes that underlie who we really are— the unified and enduring core characteristics that account for our existence as one and the same person throughout the life span. ●

Psychodynamic Perspectives of Personality

● **personality** A pattern of enduring, distinctive thoughts, emotions, and behaviors that characterize the way an individual adapts to the world.

● **psychodynamic perspectives** Theoretical views emphasizing that personality is primarily unconscious (beyond awareness).

Personality is a pattern of enduring, distinctive thoughts, emotions, and behaviors that characterize the way an individual adapts to the world. Psychologists have approached these enduring characteristics in a variety of ways, focusing on different aspects of the person.

Psychodynamic perspectives on personality emphasize that personality is primarily unconscious (that is, beyond awareness). According to this viewpoint, those enduring patterns that make up personality are largely unavailable to our conscious awareness, and they powerfully shape our behaviors in ways that we cannot consciously comprehend. Psychodynamic theorists use the word *unconscious* differently from how other psychologists might use the term. From the psychodynamic perspective, aspects of our personality are unconscious because they *must* be; this lack of awareness is motivated. These mysterious, unconscious forces are simply too frightening to be part of our conscious awareness.

Psychodynamic theorists believe that behavior is only a surface characteristic and that to truly understand someone's personality, we have to explore the symbolic meanings of that behavior and the deep inner workings of the mind (C. Levin, 2010; Westen, Gabbard, & Soto, 2008). Psychodynamic theorists also stress the role of early childhood experience in adult personality. From this perspective, the adult is a reflection of those childhood experiences that shape our earliest conceptions of ourselves and others. These characteristics were sketched by the architect of psychoanalytic theory, Sigmund Freud.

44·1 FREUD'S PSYCHOANALYTIC THEORY

Sigmund Freud, one of the most influential thinkers of the twentieth century, was born in Freiberg, Moravia (today part of the Czech Republic), in 1856 and died in London at the age of 83. Freud spent most of his life in Vienna, but he left the city near the end of his career to escape the Holocaust.

Freud has had such a phenomenal impact that just about everyone has an opinion about him, even those who have never studied his work. If you ask others what they think of Freud, you will likely get a variety of interesting answers. Some might comment that Freud was a cocaine addict. Freud did use cocaine early in his career, but he stopped using the drug when he discovered its harmful effects. Others might claim that Freud hated women. As we will see, Freud's theory of development did include the notion that women are morally inferior to men. In truth, however, Freud was never satisfied with his approach to the psychology of women. He welcomed women interested in pursuing careers in psychoanalysis, and many of his earliest and most influential followers were women. Finally, people might declare that Freud thought everything was about sex. That claim, it turns out, is quite true, except by *sex* Freud did not mean sexual activity in the usual sense. Instead, Freud defined sex as organ pleasure. *Anything* that is pleasurable is sex, according to Freud.

For Freud, the sexual drive was the most important motivator of all human activity. As we will see, Freud thought that the human sex drive was the main determinant of personality development, and he felt that psychological disorders, dreams, and all human behavior represent the conflict between this unconscious sexual drive and the demands of civilized human society.

Sigmund Freud (1856–1939) Freud's theories have strongly influenced how people in Western cultures view themselves and their world.

Freud developed *psychoanalysis,* his approach to personality, through his work with patients suffering from hysteria. *Hysteria* refers to physical symptoms that have no physical cause. For instance, a person might be unable to see, even with perfectly healthy eyes, or unable to walk, despite having no physical injury.

In Freud's day (the Victorian era, a time marked by strict rules regarding sex), many young women suffered from physical problems that could not be explained by actual physical illness. In his practice, Freud spent long hours listening to these women talk about their symptoms. Freud came to understand that the hysterical symptoms stemmed from unconscious psychological conflicts. These conflicts centered on experiences in which the person's drive for pleasure was thwarted by the social pressures of Victorian society. Furthermore, the particular symptoms were symbolically related to these underlying conflicts. One of Freud's patients, Fraulein Elisabeth Von R., suffered from excruciating leg pains that prevented her from standing or walking. The fact that Fraulein Elisabeth could not walk was no accident. Through analysis, Freud discovered that Fraulein Elisabeth had had a number of experiences in which she wanted nothing more than to take a walk but had been prevented from doing so by her duty to her ill father.

Importantly, Freud believed that hysterical symptoms were *overdetermined*—that is, they had *many* causes in the unconscious. Eventually, Freud came to use hysterical symptoms as his metaphor for understanding dreams, slips of the tongue, and all human behavior. Everything we do, he said, has a multitude of unconscious causes.

Drawing from his work in analyzing patients (as well as himself), Freud developed his model of the human personality. He described personality as like an iceberg, existing mostly below the level of awareness, just as the massive part of an iceberg lies beneath the surface of the water. Figure 44.1 illustrates this analogy and depicts how extensive the unconscious part of our mind is, in Freud's view.

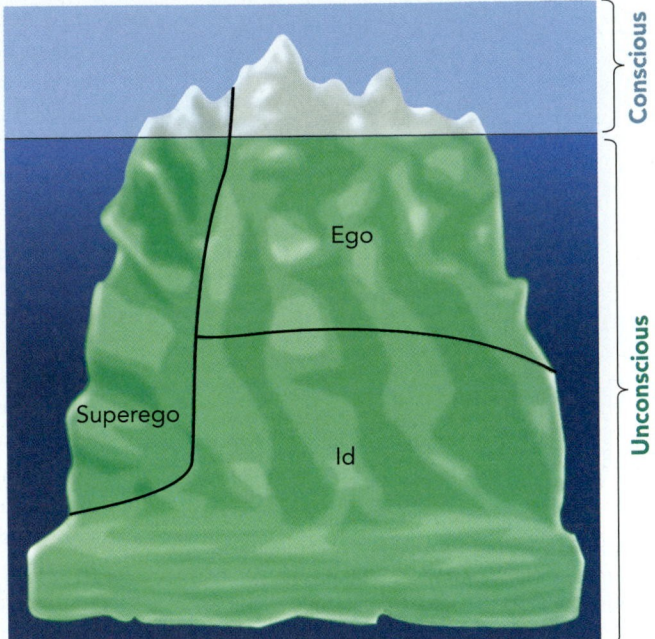

FIGURE 44.1 **The Conscious and Unconscious Mind: The Iceberg Analogy** The iceberg analogy illustrates how much of the mind is unconscious in Freud's theory. The conscious mind is the part of the iceberg above water; the unconscious mind, the part below water. Notice that the id is totally unconscious, whereas the ego and the superego can operate at either the conscious or the unconscious level.

Structures of Personality

The three parts of the iceberg in Figure 44.1 reflect the three structures of personality described by Freud. Freud (1917) called these structures the id, the ego, and the superego. You can get a better feel for these Latin labels by considering their English translations: The id is literally the "it," the ego is the "I," and the superego is the "above-I."

The **id** consists of unconscious drives and is the individual's reservoir of sexual energy. This "it" is a pool of amoral and often vile urges pressing for expression. In Freud's view, the id has no contact with reality. The id works according to the *pleasure principle,* the Freudian concept that the id always seeks pleasure.

The world would be dangerous and scary, however, if personalities were all id. As young children mature, they learn that they cannot slug other children in the face, that they have to use the toilet instead of diapers, and that they must negotiate with others to get the things they want. As children experience the constraints of reality, a new element of personality is formed—the **ego,** the Freudian structure of personality that deals with the demands of reality. Indeed, according to Freud, the ego abides by the *reality principle.* That is, it tries to bring the individual pleasure within the norms of society. The ego helps us to test reality, to see how far we can go without getting into trouble and hurting ourselves. Whereas the id is completely unconscious, the ego is partly conscious. It houses our higher mental functions—reasoning, problem solving, and decision making, for example.

The id and ego do not consider whether something is right or wrong. Rather, the **superego** is the harsh internal judge of our behavior. The superego is reflected in what we often call conscience and evaluates the morality of our behavior. Like the id, the

● **id** The part of the person that Freud called the "it," consisting of unconscious drives; the individual's reservoir of sexual energy.

● **ego** The Freudian structure of personality that deals with the demands of reality.

● **superego** The Freudian structure of personality that serves as the harsh internal judge of our behavior; what we often call conscience.

Anna Freud (1895–1982) The youngest of Freud's six children, Anna Freud not only did influential work on defense mechanisms but also pioneered in the theory and practice of child psychoanalysis.

● **defense mechanisms** Tactics the ego uses to reduce anxiety by unconsciously distorting reality.

superego does not consider reality; it considers only whether the id's impulses can be satisfied in acceptable moral terms.

The ego acts as a mediator between the conflicting demands of the id and the super-ego, as well as the real world. Your ego might say, for example, "I will have sex only in a committed relationship and always practice safe sex." Your id, however, screams, "Sex! Now!" and your superego commands, "Sex? Don't even think about it."

Defense Mechanisms

The conflicts that erupt among the demands of the id, the superego, and reality create a great deal of anxiety for the ego. The ego has strategies for dealing with this anxiety, called defense mechanisms. **Defense mechanisms** are tactics the ego uses to reduce anxiety by unconsciously distorting reality. For example, imagine that Jason's id is press-ing to express an unconscious desire to have sex with his mother. Clearly, acting on this impulse would not please the superego or society at large. If he became aware of this impulse, Jason might recoil in horror. Instead, Jason's ego might use the defense mech-anism of *displacement,* and he might develop a relationship with a girlfriend who looks and acts like his mother. Displacement means directing unacceptable impulses at a less threatening target. Through displacement, the ego allows Jason to express his id impulse in a way that will not land him in trouble. Of course, Jason's friends might chuckle at the resemblance between his mother and his girlfriend, but you can bet that Jason will never notice.

Figure 44.2 describes several defense mechanisms, many of which were introduced and developed by Freud's daughter Anna, who followed in her father's career footsteps. All these mechanisms work to reduce anxiety.

Defense Mechanism	How It Works	Example
Repression	The master defense mechanism; the ego pushes unacceptable impulses out of awareness, back into the unconscious mind.	A young girl was sexually abused by her uncle. As an adult, she can't remember anything about the traumatic experience.
Rationalization	The ego replaces a less acceptable motive with a more acceptable one.	A college student does not get into the fraternity of his choice. He tells himself that the fraternity is very exclusive and that a lot of students could not get in.
Displacement	The ego shifts feelings toward an unacceptable object to another, more acceptable object.	A woman can't take her anger out on her boss, so she goes home and takes it out on her husband.
Sublimation	The ego replaces an unacceptable impulse with a socially acceptable one.	A man with strong sexual urges becomes an artist who paints nudes.
Projection	The ego attributes personal shortcomings, problems, and faults to others.	A man who has a strong desire to have an extramarital affair accuses his wife of flirting with other men.
Reaction Formation	The ego transforms an unacceptable motive into its opposite.	A woman who fears her sexual urges becomes a religious zealot.
Denial	The ego refuses to acknowledge anxiety-producing realities.	A man won't acknowledge that he has cancer even though a team of doctors has diagnosed his cancer.
Regression	The ego seeks the security of an earlier developmental period in the face of stress.	A woman returns home to mother every time she and her husband have a big argument.

FIGURE 44.2   Defense Mechanisms Defense mechanisms reduce anxiety in various ways, in all instances by distorting reality.

Repression is the most powerful and pervasive defense mechanism. Repression pushes unacceptable id impulses back into the unconscious mind. Repression is the foundation for *all* of the psychological defense mechanisms, whose goal is to *repress* threatening impulses, that is, to push them out of awareness. Freud said, for example, that our early childhood experiences, many of which he believed were sexually laden, are too threatening for us to deal with consciously, so we reduce the anxiety of childhood conflict through repression.

Two final points about defense mechanisms are important. First, defense mechanisms are unconscious; we are not aware that we are calling on them. Second, when used in moderation or on a temporary basis, defense mechanisms are not necessarily unhealthy (Cramer, 2008a). For example, the defense mechanism of *denial* can help people cope upon first getting the news that their death is impending, and the defense mechanism of *sublimation* involves transforming unconscious impulses into activities that benefit society. Note that the defense mechanism of sublimation means that even the very best things that human beings accomplish—a beautiful work of art, an amazing act of kindness—are still explained by unconscious sexual drives and defenses.

Psychosexual Stages of Personality Development

Freud believed that human beings go through universal stages of personality development and that at each developmental stage we experience sexual pleasure in one part of the body more than in others. Each stage is named for the location of sexual pleasure at that stage. *Erogenous zones* are parts of the body that have especially strong pleasure-giving qualities at particular stages of development. Freud thought that our adult personality is determined by the way we resolve conflicts between these early sources of pleasure—the mouth, the anus, and then the genitals—and the demands of reality.

- *Oral stage (first 18 months):* The infant's pleasure centers on the mouth. Chewing, sucking, and biting are the chief sources of pleasure that reduce tension in the infant.

- *Anal stage (18 to 36 months):* During a time when most children are experiencing toilet training, the child's greatest pleasure involves the anus and urethra and their functions. Freud recognized that there is pleasure in "going" and "holding it" as well as in the experience of control over one's parents in deciding when to do either.

- *Phallic stage (3 to 6 years):* The name of Freud's third stage comes from the Latin word *phallus,* which means "penis." Pleasure focuses on the genitals as the child discovers that self-stimulation is enjoyable.

  In Freud's view, the phallic stage has a special importance in personality development because it triggers the Oedipus complex. This name comes from the Greek tragedy in which Oedipus unknowingly kills his father and marries his mother. The **Oedipus complex** is the boy's intense desire to replace his father and enjoy the affections of his mother. Eventually, the boy recognizes that his father might punish him for these incestuous wishes, specifically by cutting off the boy's penis. *Castration anxiety* refers to the boy's intense fear of being mutilated by his father. To reduce this conflict, the boy identifies with his father, adopting the male gender role. The intense castration anxiety is repressed into the unconscious and serves as the foundation for the development of the superego.

  Freud recognized that there were differences between boys and girls in the phallic stage. Because a girl does not have a penis, she cannot experience castration anxiety, Freud reasoned. Instead, she compares herself to boys and realizes that she is missing something—a penis. Without experiencing the powerful force of castration anxiety, a girl cannot develop a superego in the same sense that boys do. Given this inability, Freud concluded, women were morally inferior to men, and this inferiority explained their place as second-class citizens in Victorian society. Freud believed that girls experience "castration completed," resulting in penis envy—the intense desire to obtain a penis by eventually marrying and bearing a son.

● **Oedipus complex** According to Freud, a boy's intense desire to replace his father and enjoy the affections of his mother.

While noting that his views ran counter to the early feminist thinkers of his time, Freud stood firm that the sexes are not equal in every way. He considered women to be somewhat childlike in their development and thought it was good that fathers, and eventually husbands, should guide them through life. He asserted that the only hope for women's moral development was education.

- *Latency period (6 years to puberty):* This phase is not a developmental stage but rather a kind of psychic time-out. After the drama of the phallic stage, the child sets aside all interest in sexuality. Although we now consider these years extremely important to development, Freud felt that this was a time in which no psychosexual development occurred.

- *Genital stage (adolescence and adulthood):* The genital stage is the time of sexual reawakening, a point when the source of sexual pleasure shifts to someone outside the family. Freud believed that in adulthood the individual becomes capable of the two hallmarks of maturity: love and work. However, Freud felt that human beings are inevitably subject to intense conflict, reasoning that everyone, no matter how healthy or well adjusted, still has an id pressing for expression. Adulthood, even in the best of circumstances, still involves reliving the unconscious conflicts of childhood.

Freud argued that the individual may become stuck in any of these developmental stages if he or she is underindulged or overindulged at a given stage. For example, a parent might wean a child too early (or not early enough) or be too strict (or too lax) in toilet training. *Fixation* occurs when a particular psychosexual stage colors an individual's adult personality. For instance, an *anal retentive* person (someone who is obsessively neat and organized) is fixated at the anal stage. The construct of fixation thus explains how, according to Freud's view, childhood experiences can have an enormous impact on adult personality. Figure 44.3 illustrates possible links between adult personality characteristics and fixation at the oral, anal, and phallic stages.

44-2 PSYCHODYNAMIC CRITICS AND REVISIONISTS

Because Freud was among the first theorists to explore personality, some of his ideas have needed updating and revision over time, while others have been tossed out altogether. In particular, Freud's critics have said that his ideas about sexuality, early experience, social factors, and the unconscious mind were misguided (Adler, 1927; Erikson, 1968; Fromm, 1947; Horney, 1945; Jung, 1917; Kohut, 1977; Rapaport, 1967; Sullivan, 1953). They stress the following points:

Stage	Adult Extensions (Fixations)	Sublimations	Reaction Formations
Oral	Smoking, eating, kissing, oral hygiene, drinking, chewing gum	Seeking knowledge, humor, wit, sarcasm, being a food or wine expert	Speech purist, food faddist, prohibitionist, dislike of milk
Anal	Notable interest in one's bowel movements, love of bathroom humor, extreme messiness; or, alternatively, extreme cleanliness, stubbornness, and a strong desire for simplicity and structure	Interest in painting or sculpture, being overly giving, great interest in statistics	Extreme disgust with feces, fear of dirt, prudishness, irritability
Phallic	Heavy reliance on masturbation, flirtatiousness, expressions of virility	Interest in poetry, love of love, interest in acting, striving for success	Puritanical attitude toward sex, excessive modesty

FIGURE 44.3 **Defense Mechanisms and Freudian Stages** If a person is fixated at a psychosexual stage, the fixation can color his or her personality in many ways, including the defense mechanisms the person might use to cope with anxiety.

- Sexuality is not the pervasive force behind personality that Freud believed it to be. Furthermore, the Oedipus complex is not as universal as Freud maintained. Freud's concepts were heavily influenced by the setting in which he lived and worked—turn-of-the-century Vienna, a society that, compared with contemporary society, was sexually repressed and male-dominated.

- The first five years of life are not as powerful in shaping adult personality as Freud thought. Later experiences deserve more attention.

- The ego and conscious thought processes play a more dominant role in our personality than Freud believed; he claimed that we are forever captive to the instinctual, unconscious clutches of the id. In addition, the ego has a separate line of development from the id, so achievement, thinking, and reasoning are not always tied to sexual impulses.

- Sociocultural factors are much more important than Freud believed. In stressing the id's dominance, Freud placed more emphasis on the biological basis of personality. More contemporary psychodynamic scholars have especially emphasized the interpersonal setting of the family and the role of early social relationships in personality development (Hirsch, 2010; Leon, 2010).

A number of dissenters and revisionists to Freud's theory have been influential in the development of psychodynamic theories. Erik Erikson, whose psychosocial stages we examined in Module 32, is among these. Here we consider three other thinkers—Karen Horney, Carl Jung, and Alfred Adler—who made notable revisions to Freud's approach.

Karen Horney (1885–1952) Horney developed the first feminist criticism of Freud's theory. Horney's view emphasizes women's positive qualities and self-evaluation.

Horney's Sociocultural Approach

Karen Horney (1885–1952) rejected the classical psychoanalytic concept that anatomy is destiny and cautioned that some of Freud's most popular ideas were only hypotheses. She insisted that these hypotheses be supported with observable data before being accepted as fact. She also argued that sociocultural influences on personality development should be considered.

Consider Freud's concept of penis envy, which attributed some of the behavior of his female patients to their repressed desire to have a penis. Horney pointed out that women might envy the penis not because of these unconscious issues but because of the status that society bestows on those who have one. Further, she suggested that both sexes envy the attributes of the other, with men coveting women's reproductive capacities (Horney, 1967).

Horney also believed that the need for security, not for sex, is the prime motive in human existence. Horney reasoned that an individual whose needs for security are met should be able to develop his or her capacities to the fullest extent. She viewed psychological health as allowing the person to express talents and abilities freely and spontaneously.

● **collective unconscious** Jung's term for the impersonal, deepest layer of the unconscious mind, shared by all human beings because of their common ancestral past.

● **archetypes** Jung's term for emotionally laden ideas and images in the collective unconscious that have rich and symbolic meaning for all people.

Jung's Analytical Theory

Freud's contemporary Carl Jung (1875–1961) had a different complaint about psychoanalytic theory. Jung shared Freud's interest in the unconscious, but he believed that Freud underplayed the unconscious mind's role in personality. In fact, Jung believed that the roots of personality go back to the dawn of humanity. The **collective unconscious** is Jung's term for the impersonal, deepest layer of the unconscious mind, shared by all human beings because of their common ancestral past. In Jung's theory, the experiences of a common past have made a deep, permanent impression on the human mind.

Jung posited that the collective unconscious contains **archetypes,** emotionally laden ideas and images that have rich and symbolic meaning for all people. Jung concluded that these archetypes emerge in art, literature, religion, and dreams (Faber & Mayer, 2009; Kradin, 2009; Merchant, 2006). He used archetypes to help people understand themselves (Urban, 2008). Archetypes are essentially predispositions to respond to the environment in particular ways.

Carl Jung (1875–1961) Jung, a Swiss psychoanalytic theorist, developed the concepts of the collective unconscious and archetypes.

Jung used the terms *anima* and *animus* to identify two common archetypes. He believed each of us has a passive feminine side—the anima—and an assertive masculine side—the animus. The *persona* is another archetype; Jung thought that the persona represents the public mask that we all wear during social interactions. Jung believed that the persona is an essential archetype because it allows us always to keep some secret part of ourselves (who we really are) hidden from others.

Adler's Individual Psychology

● **individual psychology** Adler's view that people are motivated by purposes and goals and that perfection, not pleasure, is thus the key motivator in human life.

Alfred Adler (1870–1937) was one of Freud's earliest followers, although his relationship with Freud was quite brief and his approach to personality was drastically different. In Adler's **individual psychology,** people are motivated by purposes and goals—thus, perfection, not pleasure, is the key motivator in human life. Adler argued that people have the ability to take their genetic inheritance and their environmental experiences and act upon them creatively to become the person they want to be.

Adler thought that everyone strives for superiority by seeking to adapt, improve, and master the environment. Striving for superiority is our response to the uncomfortable feelings of inferiority that we experience as infants and young children when we interact with bigger, more powerful people. *Compensation* is Adler's term for the individual's attempt to overcome imagined or real inferiorities or weaknesses by developing one's own abilities. Adler believed that compensation is normal, and he said that we often make up for a weakness in one ability by excelling in a different one. For example, a person of small stature and limited physical abilities (like Adler himself) might compensate by excelling in academics.

Adler believed that birth order could influence how successfully a person could strive for superiority. He viewed firstborn children to be in a particularly vulnerable state given that they begin life as the center of attention but then are knocked off their pedestal by their siblings. Adler in fact believed that the firstborn are more likely to suffer from psychological disorders and to engage in criminal behavior. Youngest children, however, also are potentially in trouble because they are most likely to be spoiled. The healthiest birth order? According to Adler, all of us (including Adler) who are middle-born are in a particularly advantageous situation because we have our older siblings as built-in inspiration for superiority striving. Importantly, though, Adler did not believe that anyone was doomed by birth order. Rather, sensitive parents could help children at any place in the family to negotiate their needs for superiority.

44·3 EVALUATING THE PSYCHODYNAMIC PERSPECTIVES

Although psychodynamic theories have diverged from Freud's original psychoanalytic version, they share some core principles:

- Personality is determined both by current experiences and, as the original psychoanalytic theory proposed, by early life experiences.
  - Personality can be better understood by examining it developmentally—as a series of stages that unfold with the individual's physical, cognitive, and socioemotional development.
  - We mentally transform our experiences, giving them meaning that shapes our personality.
  - The mind is not all consciousness; unconscious motives lie behind some of our puzzling behavior.
  - The individual's inner world often conflicts with the outer demands of reality, creating anxiety that is not easy to resolve.

Trait Perspectives of Personality

If you are setting up a friend on a blind date, you are likely to describe the person in terms of his or her *traits,* or lasting personality characteristics. Trait perspectives on personality have been the dominant approach for the past three decades.

46-1 TRAIT THEORIES

According to **trait theories,** personality consists of broad, enduring dispositions (traits) that tend to lead to characteristic responses. In other words, we can describe people in terms of the ways they behave, such as whether they are outgoing, friendly, private, or hostile. People who have a strong tendency to behave in certain ways are referred to as "high" on the traits; those with a weak tendency to behave in these ways are "low" on the traits. Although trait theorists differ about which traits make up personality, they agree that traits are the fundamental building blocks of personality (De Pauw & Mervielde, 2010; McCrae & Sutin, 2009). The trait approach was founded by Gordon Allport (1897–1967).

Allport, sometimes referred to as the father of American personality psychology, was particularly bothered by the negative view of humanity that psychoanalysis portrayed. He rejected the notion that the unconscious was central to an understanding of personality. He further believed that to understand healthy people, we must focus on their lives in the present, not on their childhood experiences. Allport, who took a pragmatic approach to understanding the person, asserted that if you want to know something about someone, you should "just ask him" (or her).

Allport believed that personality psychology should focus on understanding healthy, well-adjusted individuals. He described such persons as showing a positive but objective sense of self and others, interest in issues beyond their own experience, a sense of humor, common sense, and a unifying philosophy of life—typically but not always provided by religious faith (Allport, 1961). Allport dedicated himself to the idea that psychology should have relevance to social issues facing modern society, and his scholarship has influenced not only personality psychology but also the psychology of religion and prejudice.

In defining personality, Allport (1961) stressed each person's uniqueness and capacity to adapt to the environment. For Allport, the unit we should use to understand personality is the trait. He defined traits as mental structures that make different situations the same for the person. For Allport, traits are structures that are inside a person that cause behavior to be similar even in different situations. For instance, if Carly is sociable, she is likely to behave in an outgoing, happy fashion whether she is at a party or in a group study session. Allport's definition implies that behavior should be consistent across different situations.

We get a sense of the down-to-earth quality of Allport's approach to personality by looking at his study of traits. In the late 1930s, Allport and his colleague H. S. Odbert (1936) sat down with two big unabridged dictionaries and pulled out all the words that could be used to describe a person—a method called the *lexical approach.*

This approach reflects the idea that if a trait is important to people in real life, it ought to be represented in the natural language people use to talk about one another. Furthermore, the more important a trait is, the more likely it is that it should be represented by a single word. Allport and Odbert started with 18,000 words and gradually pared down that list to 4,500.

As you can appreciate, 4,500 traits make for a very long questionnaire. Imagine that you are asked to rate a person, Ignacio, on some traits. You use a scale from 1 to 5,

● **trait theories** Theoretical views stressing that personality consists of broad, enduring dispositions (traits) that tend to lead to characteristic responses.

"Gerry's downloading a personality."

© Rob Murray. www.CartoonStock.com

with 1 meaning "not at all" and 5 meaning "very much." If you give Ignacio a 5 on "outgoing," what do you think you might give him on "shy"? Clearly, we may not need 4,500 traits to summarize the way we describe personality. Still, how might we whittle down these descriptors further without losing something important?

With advances in statistical methods and the advent of computers, the lexical approach became considerably less unwieldy, as researchers began to analyze the words to look for underlying structures that might account for their overlap. Specifically, a statistical procedure called *factor analysis* allowed researchers to identify which traits go together in terms of how they are rated. Factor analysis essentially tells us what items on a scale people are responding to as if they mean the same thing. For example, if Ignacio got a 5 on "outgoing," he probably would get a 5 on "talkative" and a 1 or 2 on "shy."

One important characteristic of factor analysis is that it relies on the scientist to interpret the meaning of the factors, and the researcher must make some decisions about how many factors are enough to explain the data (Goldberg & Digman, 1994). In 1963, W. T. Norman reanalyzed the Allport and Odbert traits and concluded that only five factors were needed to summarize these traits. Norman's research set the stage for the dominant approach in personality psychology today: the five-factor model (Digman, 1990).

46·2 THE FIVE-FACTOR MODEL OF PERSONALITY

Pick a friend and jot down 10 of that person's most notable personality traits. Did you perhaps list "reserved" or "a good leader"? "Responsible" or "unreliable"? "Sweet," "kind," or "friendly"? Maybe even "creative"? Researchers in personality psychology have found that there are essentially five broad personality dimensions that are represented in the natural language; these dimensions also summarize the various ways psychologists have studied traits (Costa & McCrae, 2006; Digman, 2002; Hogan, 2006; Rammstedt, Goldberg, & Borg, 2010).

● **big five factors of personality** The five broad traits that are thought to describe the main dimensions of personality: neuroticism (emotional instability), extraversion, openness to experience, agreeableness, and conscientiousness.

The **big five factors of personality**—the broad traits that are thought to describe the main dimensions of personality—are neuroticism (which refers to the tendency to worry and experience negative emotions and is sometimes identified by its opposite, emotional stability), extraversion, openness to experience, agreeableness, and conscientiousness. Although personality psychologists typically refer to the traits as N, E, O, A, and C on the basis of the order in which they emerge in a factor analysis, if you create an anagram from these first letters of the trait names, you get the word *OCEAN*.

Figure 46.1 more fully defines the big five traits. Before reading further, to find out where you stand on these traits, see the Psychological Inquiry.

Each of the big five traits has been the topic of extensive research (McCrae & Sutin, 2007; Ozer & Benet-Martinez, 2006). The following sampling of research findings on each trait sheds light on the interesting work that the five-factor model has inspired:

■ *Neuroticism* is related to feeling negative emotion more often than positive emotion in one's daily life and to experiencing more lingering negative states (Widiger, 2009).

Openness	**C**onscientiousness	**E**xtraversion	**A**greeableness	**N**euroticism (emotional instability)
• Imaginative or practical	• Organized or disorganized	• Sociable or retiring	• Softhearted or ruthless	• Calm or anxious
• Interested in variety or routine	• Careful or careless	• Fun-loving or somber	• Trusting or suspicious	• Secure or insecure
• Independent or conforming	• Disciplined or impulsive	• Energetic or reserved	• Helpful or uncooperative	• Self-satisfied or self-pitying

FIGURE 46.1 **The Big Five Factors of Personality** Each of the broad traits encompasses more narrow traits and characteristics. Use the acronym *OCEAN* to remember the big five personality factors: openness, conscientiousness, extraversion, agreeableness, and neuroticism.

psychological *inquiry*

Your Personality Traits: Who Are You?

Use the following scale to rate yourself on the trait items listed below. That is, next to each trait, write the number that best corresponds to how you rate yourself with respect to that trait.

Disagree strongly **1**	Disagree moderately **2**	Disagree a little **3**	Neither agree nor disagree **4**	Agree a little **5**	Agree moderately **6**	Agree strongly **7**

I see myself as:

1. ____ Extraverted, enthusiastic.

2. ____ Critical, quarrelsome.

3. ____ Dependable, self-disciplined.

4. ____ Anxious, easily upset.

5. ____ Open to new experiences, complex.

6. ____ Reserved, quiet.

7. ____ Sympathetic, warm.

8. ____ Disorganized, careless.

9. ____ Calm, emotionally stable.

10. ____ Conventional, uncreative.

You have just completed the Ten-Item Personality Inventory, or TIPI (Gosling, Rentfrow, & Swann, 2003), a brief measure of the big five personality traits. All of the even-numbered items are *reverse-scored,* meaning your ratings should be reversed for these. (Reverse items are included in scales to fully identify a characteristic and to make sure that respondents are actually reading the items carefully.) So, if you gave item number 2 a rating of 7, it should be a 1; a rating of 6 should be a 2, and so on. The first step in calculating your scores is to reverse your scores on these even-numbered items. Then average together your ratings for the following items for each trait, using the steps in the table below.

Trait	Items	Sum of Your Ratings	Your Score (divide the sum by 2)	Low Score	Medium Score	High Score
Emotional Stability (the opposite of neuroticism)	4, 9	____	____	3.41	4.83	6.25
Extraversion	1, 6	____	____	2.99	4.44	5.89
Openness to Experience	5, 10	____	____	4.13	5.38	6.45
Agreeableness	2, 7	____	____	4.12	5.23	6.34
Conscientiousness	3, 8	____	____	4.08	5.40	6.72

The last three columns provide information about what those scores mean. The "medium scores" reflect the mean score found in a sample of 1,813 participants. The "low scores" are that mean minus one standard deviation. The "high scores" are the mean plus one standard deviation. Now answer the following questions.

1. Do your scores reflect your sense of who you really are? Explain.

2. Why do you think the researchers included one reverse-scored item for each scale?

3. The guides for low, medium, and high scores were provided by data from a sample of college students at the University of Texas. Do you think these norms might differ at your institution? Why or why not?

4. Although this is a very short assessment, research supports the idea that it does measure these traits because scores on this short scale are highly correlated with scores on longer scales measuring the same traits (Ehrhart & others, 2009). What does it mean to say that the scores are highly correlated?

Neuroticism has been shown as well to relate to more health complaints (Carver & Connor-Smith, 2010). In a longitudinal study, individuals were tracked for nearly seven years. Neuroticism was associated with dying during the study (Fry & Debats, 2009). In general, neurotic individuals appear to suffer in silence: Acquaintances and observers have difficulty detecting how neurotic another person is (Vazire, 2010).

■ Individuals high in *extraversion* are more likely than others to engage in social activities (Emmons & Diener, 1986) and to experience gratitude (McCullough, Emmons, & Tsang, 2002) and a strong sense of meaning in life (King & others, 2006). In addition, extraverts are more forgiving (L. Thompson & others, 2005). People rate extraverts as smiling and standing energetically and as dressing stylishly (Naumann & others, 2009), and observers know an extravert when they see one (Vazire, 2010). One study found that extraverted salespeople sold more cars, especially if they were also good at picking up interpersonal cues (Blickle, Wendel, & Ferris, 2010).

■ *Openness to experience* is related to liberal values, open-mindedness, tolerance (McCrae & Sutin, 2009), and creativity (Silvia & others, 2009). Openness is also associated with superior cognitive functioning and IQ across the life span (Sharp & others, 2010). Individuals who rate themselves as open to experience are more likely to dress distinctively (Naumann & others, 2009), to pursue entrepreneurial goals (for instance, starting their own business), and to experience success in those pursuits (Zhao, Seibert, & Lumpkin, 2010). Individuals high on openness to experience are also more likely to interact with others on Internet websites and to use social media (Correa, Hinsley, & de Zuniga, 2010).

■ *Agreeableness* is related to generosity and altruism (Caprara & others, 2010), to reports of religious faith (Saroglou, 2010), and to more satisfying romantic relationships (Donnellan, Larsen-Rife, & Conger, 2005). There are also links between agreeableness and viewing other people positively (Wood, Harms, & Vazire, 2010). In online dating profiles, agreeable individuals are less likely than people who score low on this trait to lie about themselves (Hall & others, 2010).

■ *Conscientiousness* is a key factor in a variety of life domains. Researchers have found that conscientiousness is positively related to high school and college students' grade point averages (Noftle & Robins, 2007). Conscientiousness is also linked to better-quality friendships (Jensen-Campbell & Malcolm, 2007), to higher levels of religious faith (Saroglou, 2010), and to a forgiving attitude (Balliet, 2010). Conscientiousness is associated with dressing neatly, especially in the case of men (Naumann & others, 2009), and, like openness, is related to entrepreneurial success (Zhao, Seibert, & Lumpkin, 2010). Low levels of conscientiousness are associated with criminal behavior (Wiebe, 2004) and substance abuse (Walton & Roberts, 2004).

Keep in mind that because the five factors are theoretically independent of one another, a person can be any combination of them. Do you know a neurotic extravert or an agreeable introvert, for example?

Cross-Cultural Studies on the Big Five

Some research on the big five factors addresses the extent to which the factors appear in personality profiles in different cultures (Lingjaerde, Foreland, & Engvik, 2001; Miacic & Goldberg, 2007; Pukrop, Sass, & Steinmeyer, 2000). The question is, do the big five show up in the assessment of personality in cultures around the world? Some research suggests that they do: A version of the five factors appears in people in countries as diverse as Canada, Finland, Poland, China, and Japan (Paunonen & others, 1992; X. Zhou & others, 2009). Among the big five, the factors most likely to emerge across cultures and languages are extraversion, agreeableness, and conscientiousness, with neuroticism and openness to experience being more likely to emerge only in English-speaking samples (De Raad & others, 2010).

Animal Studies on the Big Five

Researchers have found evidence for at least some of the big five personality traits in animals, including domestic dogs (Gosling, 2008; Gosling, Kwan, & John, 2003) and hyenas (Gosling & John, 1999). In addition, studies have turned up evidence for general personality traits (such as overall outgoingness) in orangutans, geese, lizards, fish, cockatiels, and squid (Fox & Millam, 2010; McGhee & Travis, 2010; Sinn, Gosling, & Moltschaniwskyj, 2008; Weinstein, Capitanio, & Gosling, 2008; Wilson & Godin, 2010), though some researchers have found that squid "personality" may be more a function of environmental factors than stable individual differences (Sinn & others, 2010).

Sam Gosling, a professor at the University of Texas, is a personality psychologist who has conducted research on animal personality as well as the ways that we express our traits through websites, dorm room decoration, and other contexts.

46·3 EVALUATING THE TRAIT PERSPECTIVES

Despite strong evidence for the big five, some personality researchers say that these traits might not end up being the ultimate list of broad traits; they argue that more specific traits are better predictors of behavior (Fung & Ng, 2006; Moskowitz, 2010; Simms, 2007). One alternative, the HEXACO model, incorporates a sixth dimension, honesty/humility, to capture the moral dimensions of personality (Ashton & Kibeom, 2008). Other researchers argue that five factors is too many and that we can best understand personality as one big dimension, with extraversion, agreeableness, openness to experience, and conscientiousness at one end, and with neuroticism at the other end (Erdle & others, 2010). In this single-dimension view, high-scoring individuals might be described as being outgoing, nice, creative, reliable, and emotionally stable—in other words, having a "really good" personality.

More generally, studying people in terms of their personality traits has practical value. Identifying a person's traits allows us to know that individual better. Psychologists have learned a great deal about the connections between personality and health, ways of thinking, career success, and relations with others using traits (Fry & Debats, 2009; Leary & Hoyle, 2009a; Levenson & Aldwin, 2006; Roberts & others, 2007).

The trait approach has been faulted, however, for missing the importance of situational factors in personality and behavior (Leary & Hoyle, 2009b). For example, a person might rate herself as introverted among new people but very outgoing with family and friends. Further, some have criticized the trait perspective for painting an individual's personality with very broad strokes. They say that although traits can tell us much about someone whom we have never met, they reveal little about the nuances of an individual's personality.

SUMMARY

Trait theories emphasize that personality consists of traits—broad, enduring dispositions that lead to characteristic responses. Allport stated that traits should produce consistent behavior in different situations, and he used the lexical approach to personality traits, which involves using all the words in the natural language that could describe a person as a basis for understanding the traits of personality.

The current dominant perspective in personality psychology is the five-factor model. The big five traits include openness to experience, conscientiousness, extraversion, agreeableness, and neuroticism. Extraversion is related to enhanced well-being, and neuroticism is linked to lowered well-being.

Studying people in terms of their traits has value. However, trait approaches are criticized for focusing on broad dimensions and not attending to each person's uniqueness.

KEY TERMS

trait theories   441

big five factors of personality   442

TEST YOURSELF

1. How do trait theorists define personality?

2. What kind of work did Allport and Odbert's lexical approach involve, and what key idea about personality traits did it reflect?

3. What traits are included in the big five factors of personality? Define them.

APPLY YOUR KNOWLEDGE

1. If you are a fan of reality television, try your hand at identifying the personality characteristics of the individuals involved. Are any of the folks from *Jersey Shore* or *Real Housewives* particularly neurotic or conscientious? If you prefer fictional shows, consider your favorite characters: What are the traits these individuals express?

2. If you could add one more trait to the original Big 5 Factors of Personality, what would it be and why?

Personological and Life Story Perspectives of Personality

If two people have the same levels of the big five traits, do they essentially have the same personality? Researchers who approach personality from the personological and life story perspectives do not think so (McAdams & Olson, 2010). One of the goals of personality psychology is to understand how each of us is unique and in some ways like no other human being on earth. **Personological and life story perspectives** stress that the way to understand the uniqueness of each person is to focus on his or her life history and life story.

● **personological and life story perspectives**
Theoretical views stressing that the way to understand the person is to focus on his or her life history and life story.

47·1 MURRAY'S PERSONOLOGICAL APPROACH

Henry Murray (1893–1988) was a young biochemistry graduate student when he became interested in the psychology of personality after meeting Carl Jung and reading his work. Murray went on to become the director of the Psychological Clinic at Harvard at the same time that Gordon Allport was on the faculty there. Murray and Allport saw personality very differently. Whereas Allport was most comfortable focusing on conscious experience and traits, Murray embraced the psychodynamic notion of unconscious motivation.

Murray coined the word *personology* to refer to the study of the whole person. He believed that to understand a person, we have to know that person's history, including the physical, psychological, and sociological aspects of the person's life. Murray applied his insights into personality during World War II, when he was called upon by the Office of Strategic Services (or OSS, a precursor to the CIA) to develop a psychological profile of Adolf Hitler. That document, produced in 1943, accurately predicted that Hitler would commit suicide rather than be taken alive by the Allies. Murray's analysis of Hitler was the first "offender profile," and it has served as a model for modern criminal profiling.

The aspect of Murray's research that has had the most impact on contemporary personality psychology is his approach to motivation. Murray believed that our motives are largely unknown to us. This circumstance complicates the study of motivation: Researchers cannot simply ask people to say what it is they want. To address the issue, Murray, along with Christiana Morgan, developed the Thematic Apperception Test (TAT), to which we return later in this module (Morgan & Murray, 1935). For the TAT, a person looks at an ambiguous picture and writes or tells a story about what is going on in the scene. A variety of scoring procedures have been devised for analyzing the unconscious motives that are revealed in imaginative stories (C. P. Smith, 1992). These scoring procedures involve *content analysis,* a procedure in which a psychologist takes the person's story and codes it for different images, words, and so forth. Although Murray posited 22 different unconscious needs, three have been the focus of most current research:

Henry Murray's psychological profile of Adolf Hitler, developed in 1943 during World War II, serves as a model for criminal profiling today.

- *Need for achievement:* an enduring concern for attaining excellence and overcoming obstacles
- *Need for affiliation:* an enduring concern for establishing and maintaining interpersonal connections
- *Need for power:* an enduring concern for having impact on the social world

Research by David Winter (2005) has analyzed presidential motives in inaugural addresses such as those delivered by Richard M. Nixon (left) and John F. Kennedy (right). Winter found that certain needs revealed in these speeches corresponded to later events during these individuals' terms in office.

David Winter (2005) analyzed the motives revealed in inaugural addresses of U.S. presidents. He found that certain needs revealed in these speeches corresponded to later events during the person's presidency. For instance, presidents who scored high on need for achievement (such as Jimmy Carter) were less successful during their terms. Note that the need for achievement is about striving for personal excellence and may have little to do with playing politics, negotiating interpersonal relationships, or delegating responsibility. Presidents who scored high on need for power tended to be judged as more successful (John F. Kennedy, Ronald Reagan), and presidents whose addresses included a great deal of imagery about making positive interpersonal connections or avoiding rejection (suggesting a high need for affiliation) tended to experience scandal during their presidencies (Richard M. Nixon).

47·2 THE LIFE STORY APPROACH TO IDENTITY

Following in the Murray tradition, Dan McAdams (2001, 2006; McAdams & Olson, 2010) developed the *life story approach* to identity. His work centers on the idea that each of us has a unique life story, full of ups and downs. Our life story represents our memories of what makes us who we are. This life story is a constantly changing narrative that provides us with a sense of coherence. For McAdams, our life story is our very identity.

McAdams (1989) also introduced the concept of intimacy motivation. The *intimacy motive* is an enduring concern for warm interpersonal encounters for their own sake. Intimacy motivation is revealed in the warm, positive interpersonal imagery in the stories people tell. Intimacy motive has been shown to relate to positive outcomes. For instance, college men who were high on intimacy motivation showed heightened levels of happiness and lowered work strain some 30 years later (McAdams & Bryant, 1987). A study of the coming-out stories of gay men and lesbians demonstrated that intimacy-related imagery (for example, experiencing falling in love or warm acceptance from others) was associated with well-being and personality development (King & Smith, 2005).

Other personality psychologists have relied on narrative accounts of experiences as a means of understanding how individuals create meaning in life events (King & others, 2000). In one study, parents of children with Down syndrome wrote down the story of how they found out about their child's diagnosis. Parents whose stories ended happily scored higher on measures of happiness, life meaning, and personal growth than others. Parents who told stories about struggling to make sense of the experience tended to mature psychologically over time (King & others, 2000). By using narratives, personal documents (such as diaries), and even letters and speeches, personality psychologists search for the deeper meaning that cannot be revealed through tests that ask people directly about whether specific items capture their personality traits.

Finally, some personality psychologists take very seriously Murray's commitment to understanding the whole person, by focusing on just one case. *Psychobiography* is a means of inquiry in which the personality psychologist attempts to apply a personality theory to a single person's life (Runyon, 2007; W. T. Schultz, 2005). Erik Erikson's study of Gandhi's life, described in Module 4, is an example of a psychobiography. Psychobiographies have been written about a diverse array of figures, including Sigmund Freud, Gordon Allport, George W. Bush, Osama bin Laden, and Elvis Presley (W. T. Schultz, 2005).

47·3 EVALUATING THE PERSONOLOGICAL AND LIFE STORY PERSPECTIVES

Studying individuals through narratives and personal interviews provides an extraordinarily rich opportunity for the researcher. Imagine having the choice of reading someone's diary versus seeing that person's scores on a questionnaire measuring traits. Not many would pass up the chance to read the diary.

However, life story studies are difficult and time-consuming. Personologist Robert W. White (1992) referred to the study of narratives as exploring personality "the long way." Collecting interviews and narratives is often just the first step. Turning these personal stories into scientific data means transforming them into numbers, and that process involves extensive coding and content analysis. Further, for narrative studies to be worthwhile, they must tell us something we could not have found out in a much easier way (King, 2003). Moreover, psychobiographical inquiries are prone to the biases of the scholars who conduct them and may not serve the scientific goal of generalizability.

SUMMARY

Murray described personology as the study of the whole person. Contemporary followers of Murray study personality through narrative accounts and interviews. McAdams introduced the life story approach to identity, which views identity as a constantly changing story with a beginning, a middle, and an end. Psychobiography is a form of personological investigation that applies personality theory to one person's life.

Life story approaches to personality reveal the richness of each person's unique life story. However, this work can be very difficult to carry out.

KEY TERMS

personological and life story
   perspectives   447

TEST YOURSELF

1. What did Murray mean by *personology*, and what did he believe was essential to understanding who a person really is?

2. On what does McAdams say our identities are dependent?

3. What is the intimacy motive, and what has research revealed about it?

APPLY YOUR KNOWLEDGE

1. Spend some time thinking about your own life story. Do you think this story tells "who you really are," or does it tell about experiences you've encountered during your life?

2. Think of a famous person whose life story you would like to know. Take some time to find an autobiography or case study of this person. After doing your research, consider how you think this person ranks on need for achievement, need for affiliation, and need for power.

Social Cognitive Perspectives
of Personality

● **social cognitive perspectives** Theoretical views emphasizing conscious awareness, beliefs, expectations, and goals.

Social cognitive perspectives on personality emphasize conscious awareness, beliefs, expectations, and goals. While incorporating principles from behaviorism, social cognitive psychologists explore the person's ability to reason; to think about the past, present, and future; and to reflect on the self. They emphasize the person's individual interpretation of situations and thus focus on the uniqueness of each person by examining how behavior is tailored to the diversity of situations in which people find themselves. Social cognitive theorists are not interested in broad traits such as the big five. Rather, they investigate how more specific factors, such as beliefs, relate to behavior and performance. In this section we consider the two major social cognitive approaches, developed respectively by Albert Bandura and Walter Mischel.

Albert Bandura (b. 1925) Bandura's practical, problem-solving social cognitive approach has made a lasting mark on personality theory and therapy.

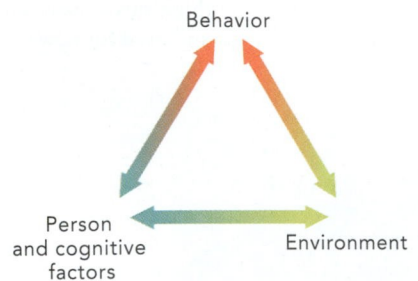

FIGURE 48.1 Bandura's Social Cognitive Theory Bandura's social cognitive theory emphasizes reciprocal influences of behavior, environment, and person/cognitive factors.

48·1 BANDURA'S SOCIAL COGNITIVE THEORY

B. F. Skinner believed that there is no such thing as "personality"; rather, he emphasized behavior and felt that internal mental states were irrelevant to psychology. Albert Bandura found Skinner's approach to be far too simplistic for understanding human functioning (1986, 2001, 2009, 2010a, 2010b). Bandura took the basic tenets of behaviorism and added a recognition of the role of mental processes in determining behavior. Whereas Skinner saw behavior as caused by the situation, Bandura pointed out that the person can cause situations, and sometimes the very definition of the situation itself depends on the person's beliefs about it. For example, is that upcoming exam an opportunity to show your stuff or a threat to your ability to achieve your goals? The test is the same either way, but a person's unique take on the test can influence a host of behaviors (studying hard, worrying, and so on).

Bandura's social cognitive theory states that behavior, environment, and person/cognitive factors are *all* important in understanding personality. Bandura coined the term *reciprocal determinism* to describe the way behavior, environment, and person/cognitive factors interact to create personality (Figure 48.1). The environment can determine a person's behavior, and the person can act to change the environment. Similarly, person/cognitive factors can both influence behavior and be influenced by behavior. From Bandura's perspective, then, behavior is a product of a variety of forces, some of which come from the situation and some of which the person brings to the situation. We now review the important processes and variables Bandura used to understand personality.

Observational Learning

Bandura believes that observational learning is a key aspect of how we learn. By observing others behave and noticing the consequences of their actions, we might come to adopt the behavior ourselves. For example, a boy might observe that his mother's hostile exchanges with people are an effective way to get what she wants. Later, when the boy is with his peers, he might adopt the same strategy. Social cognitive theorists believe that we acquire a wide range of behaviors, thoughts, and feelings by watching others' behavior and that our observations strongly shape our personality (Bandura, 2010a).

Personal Control

Social cognitive theorists emphasize that we can regulate and control our own behavior despite our changing environment (Bandura, 2008, 2009; Mischel, 2004). For example, a young executive who observes her boss behave in an overbearing and sarcastic manner toward his subordinates may find the behavior distasteful and go out of her way to encourage and support her own staff. Psychologists commonly describe a sense of behavioral control as coming from inside the person (an *internal locus of control*) or outside the person (an *external locus of control*). When we feel that we ourselves are controlling our choices and behaviors, the locus of control is internal, but when other influences are controlling them, the locus of control is external.

Consider the question of whether you will perform well on your next test. With an internal locus of control, you believe that you are in command of your choices and behaviors, and your answer will depend on what you can realistically do (for example, study hard or attend a special review session). With an external locus of control, however, you might say that you cannot predict how things will go because so many outside factors influence performance, such as whether the test is difficult, how the curve is set in the course, and whether the instructor is fair. Feeling a strong sense of personal control is vital to many aspects of performance, well-being, and physical health (Bandura, 2009; Morrison, Ponitz, & McClelland, 2010). Self-efficacy is an important aspect of the experience of control, as we next consider.

Self-Efficacy

Self-efficacy is the belief that one can master a situation and produce positive change. Bandura and others have shown that self-efficacy is related to a number of positive developments in people's lives, including solving problems and becoming more sociable (Bandura, 2001, 2009, 2010b; Schunk, 2011). Self-efficacy influences whether people even try to develop healthy habits, as well as how much effort they expend in coping with stress, how long they persist in the face of obstacles, and how much stress and pain they experience (Brister & others, 2006; Sarkar, Fisher, & Schillinger, 2006). Self-efficacy is also related to whether people initiate psychotherapy to deal with their problems and whether it succeeds (Longo, Lent, & Brown, 1992). In addition, researchers have found that self-efficacy is linked with successful job interviewing and job performance (Tay, Ang, & Van Dyne, 2006). We will return to the topics of personal control and self-efficacy at the end of this module.

● **self-efficacy** The belief that one can master a situation and produce positive change.

48·2 MISCHEL'S CONTRIBUTIONS

Like Bandura, Walter Mischel is a social cognitive psychologist who has explored how personality influences behavior. Mischel has left his mark on the field of personality in two notable ways. First, his critique of the idea of consistency in behavior ignited a flurry of controversy. Second, he has proposed the CAPS model, a new way of thinking about personality.

Mischel's Critique of Consistency

Whether we are talking about unconscious sexual conflicts, traits, or motives, all of the approaches we have considered so far maintain that these various personality characteristics are an enduring influence on behavior. This shared assumption was attacked in 1968 with the publication of Walter Mischel's *Personality and Assessment,* a book that nearly ended the psychological study of personality.

To understand Mischel's argument, recall Gordon Allport's definition of a trait as a characteristic that ought to make different situations equivalent for a given person. This quality of traits suggests that a person should behave consistently in different situations— in other words, the individual should exhibit *cross-situational consistency.* For example, an

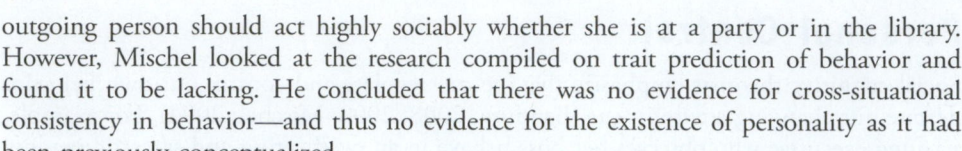

outgoing person should act highly sociably whether she is at a party or in the library. However, Mischel looked at the research compiled on trait prediction of behavior and found it to be lacking. He concluded that there was no evidence for cross-situational consistency in behavior—and thus no evidence for the existence of personality as it had been previously conceptualized.

Rather than understanding personality as consisting of broad, internal traits that make for consistent behavior across situations, Mischel said that personality often changes according to a given situation. Mischel asserted that behavior is discriminative—that is, a person looks at each situation and responds accordingly. Mischel's view is called *situationism,* the idea that personality and behavior often vary considerably from one context to another.

Personality psychologists responded to Mischel's situationist attack in a variety of ways (Donnellan, Lucas, & Fleeson, 2009; Funder, 2009; Hogan, 2009). Researchers showed that it is not a matter of *whether* personality predicts behavior but *when and how* it does so, often in combination with situational factors (Sherman, Nave, & Funder, 2010). The research findings were that

- The narrower and more limited a trait is, the more likely it will predict behavior.

- Some people are consistent on some traits, and other people are consistent on other traits.

- Personality traits exert a stronger influence on an individual's behavior when situational influences are less powerful. A very powerful situation is one that contains many clear cues about how a person is supposed to behave. For example, even a highly talkative person typically sits quietly during a class lecture. In weaker situations, however, such as during leisure time, the person may spend most of the time talking.

Moreover, individuals select the situations they are in. Consequently, even if situations determine behavior, traits play a role by influencing which situations people choose—such as going to a party or staying home to study (Sherman, Nave, & Funder, 2010).

Let's pause and reflect on what it means to be consistent. You might believe that being consistent is part of being a genuine, honest person and that tailoring behavior to different situations means being fake. On the other hand, consider that a person who never changes his or her behavior to fit a situation might be unpleasant to have around. For example, think about someone who cannot put aside his competitive drive even when playing checkers with a 4-year-old. Clearly, adaptive behavior might involve sometimes being consistent and sometimes tailoring behavior to the situation.

Over time, Mischel (2004, 2009) has developed an approach to personality that he feels is better suited to capturing the nuances of the relationship between the individual and situations in producing behavior. Imagine trying to study personality without using traits or broad motives. What would you focus on? Mischel's answer to this dilemma is his CAPS theory.

CAPS Theory

In Mischel's (2004) work on delay of gratification, children were left in a room with a tempting cookie. Mischel measured the amount of time the kids were able to delay eating the cookie, and he and his colleagues continued to study those children for many years. They found that the amount of time the children were able to delay gratification predicted their academic performance in high school and even college (Mischel, 2004). These results indicate remarkable stability in personality over time.

Mischel's revised approach to personality is concerned with just such stability (or coherence) in the pattern of behavior *over time,* not with consistency across differing situations. That is, Mischel and his colleagues have studied how behaviors in very different situations have a coherent pattern, such as a child's waiting to eat the cookie versus that same individual's (as a grown college student) deciding to stay home and study instead of going out to party.

In keeping with the social cognitive emphasis on the person's cognitive abilities and mental states, Mischel conceptualizes personality as a set of interconnected

cognitive affective processing systems (CAPS) (Mischel, 2004, 2009; Mischel & Shoda, 1999; Orom & Cervone, 2009). According to this approach, our thoughts and emotions about ourselves and the world affect our behavior and become linked in ways that matter to behavior. Personal control and self-efficacy are psychological connections that a person has made among situations, beliefs, and behaviors. Take the example of Raoul, who is excited by the challenge of a new assignment from his boss. Raoul may think about all the possible strategies to complete the project and get down to work immediately. Yet this go-getter may respond differently to other challenges, depending on who gives the assignment, what it is, or whether he feels he can do a good job.

CAPS is concerned with how personality works, not with what it is (Shoda & Mischel, 2006). From the CAPS perspective, it makes no sense to ask a person "How extraverted are you?" because the answer is always, "It depends." A person may be outgoing in one situation (on the first day of class) and not so in another (right before an exam), and that unique pattern of flexibility is what personality is all about.

Not surprisingly, CAPS theory focuses on how people behave in different situations and how they uniquely interpret situational features. From this perspective, knowing that Crystal is an extravert tells us little about how she will behave in a group discussion in her psychology class. We need to know about Crystal's beliefs and goals in the discussion. For example, does she want to impress the instructor? Is she a psychology major? We also need to know about her personal understanding of the situation itself: Is this an opportunity to shine, or is she thinking about her test for the next class? Research using the CAPS approach generally involves observing individuals behaving in a variety of contexts in order to identify the patterns of associations that exist among beliefs, emotions, and behavior for each person across different situations (Romero-Canyas & others, 2010).

● **cognitive affective processing systems (CAPS)** Mischel's theoretical model for describing that our thoughts and emotions about ourselves and the world affect our behavior and become linked in ways that matter to behavior.

48-3 EVALUATING THE SOCIAL COGNITIVE PERSPECTIVES

Social cognitive theory focuses on the interactions of individuals with their environments. The social cognitive approach has fostered a scientific climate for understanding personality that highlights the observation of behavior. Social cognitive theory emphasizes the influence of cognitive processes in explaining personality and suggests that people have the ability to control their environment.

Critics of the social cognitive perspective on personality take issue with one or more aspects of the theory. For example, they charge that

- The social cognitive approach is too concerned with change and situational influences on personality. It does not pay adequate tribute to the enduring qualities of personality.

- Social cognitive theory ignores the role biology plays in personality.

- In its attempt to incorporate both the situation and the person into its view of personality, social cognitive psychology tends to lead to very specific predictions for each person in any given situation, making generalizations impossible.

SUMMARY

Social cognitive theory states that behavior, environment, and person/cognitive factors are important in understanding personality. In Bandura's view, these factors reciprocally interact.

Two important concepts in social cognitive theory are self-efficacy and personal control. Self-efficacy is the belief that one can master a situation and produce positive outcomes. Personal control refers to individuals' beliefs about whether the outcomes of their actions depend on their own acts (internal) or on events outside of their control (external).

KEY TERMS

social cognitive
  perspectives   450
self-efficacy   451

cognitive affective processing
  systems (CAPS)   453

Mischel's controversial book *Personality and Assessment* stressed that people do not behave consistently across different situations but rather tailor their behavior to suit particular situations. Personality psychologists countered that personality does predict behavior for some people some of the time. Very specific personality characteristics predict behavior better than very general ones, and personality characteristics are more likely to predict behavior in weak versus strong situations.

Mischel developed a revised approach to personality centered on cognitive affective processing systems (CAPS). According to CAPS, personality is best understood as a person's habitual emotional and cognitive reactions to specific situations.

A particular strength of social cognitive theory is its focus on cognitive processes. However, social cognitive approaches have not given adequate attention to enduring individual differences, to biological factors, and to personality as a whole.

TEST YOURSELF

1. In what ways did Bandura react to and modify Skinner's approach to understanding human functioning?

2. What is self-efficacy, and to what kinds of positive life developments has research linked it?

3. With what is Mischel's cognitive affective processing systems (CAPS) approach centrally concerned?

APPLY YOUR KNOWLEDGE

1. Think about the people you know. Describe a person who has exhibited an external locus of control and another who has exhibited an internal locus of control in relation to their school work or other aspects of their lives.

2. What impact has observational learning had on who you are as a person? For example, have you ever told yourself that you would never do what your mother or father did but now have caught yourself behaving in exactly that way? Give an example of a behavior, thought, or feeling you have acquired via observational learning.

Biological Perspectives of Personality

The notion that physiological processes influence personality has been around since ancient times. Around 400 B.C.E., Hippocrates, the father of medicine, described human beings as having one of four basic personalities based on levels of particular bodily fluids (called *humours*). For Hippocrates, a "sanguine" personality was a happy, optimistic individual who happened to have an abundance of blood. A "choleric" person was quick-tempered with too much yellow bile. A "phlegmatic" personality referred to a placid, sluggish individual with too much phlegm (mucus), and a "melancholic" pessimist had too much black bile.

Even though Hippocrates' ideas about bodily fluids have fallen by the wayside, personality psychologists have long acknowledged that personality involves both the brain and biological processes. Psychologists' beliefs about these interacting processes in personality, though, were based on assumptions rather than on direct study. For instance, Freud's psychosexual stages bear witness to his strong belief in the connection between the mind (personality) and the body; Allport defined traits as "*neuro*psychic" structures, and personality as a "psycho*physical*" system; and Murray once declared, "No brain, no personality." More recently, advances in method and theory have led to fascinating research on the role of biological processes in personality.

49·1 PERSONALITY AND THE BRAIN

The brain is clearly important in personality as in other psychological phenomena. In the case of Phineas Gage (Module 7), an iron rod exploded up through the left side of his face and out through the top of his head in an accident. Gage miraculously survived. One of the key effects of Gage's horrific accident was that it changed his personality. He went from being gentle, kind, and reliable to being angry, hostile, and untrustworthy.

A great deal of research is currently addressing the ways in which brain activity is associated with various personality traits. For example, research has shown that an extraverted person's left prefrontal cortex is more responsive to positive stimuli and that the same area in neurotic individuals is more responsive to negative stimuli (Canli, 2008a, 2008b; Haas & others, 2007; Schmidtke & Heller, 2004). The amygdalae in extraverts are more responsive to seeing happy faces than are those in introverts (Canli & others, 2002). Two theoretical approaches to the biology of personality, by Hans Eysenck and Jeffrey Gray, have garnered the most interest.

Eysenck's Reticular Activation System Theory

British psychologist Hans Eysenck (1967) was among the first to describe the role of a particular brain system in personality. He developed an approach to extraversion/introversion based on the *reticular activation system* (RAS).

The reticular formation is located in the brain stem and plays a role in wakefulness or arousal. The RAS is the name given to the reticular formation and its connections. Eysenck posited that all of us share an optimal arousal level, a level at which we feel comfortably engaged with the world. However, Eysenck proposed, the RAS of extraverts and introverts differs with respect to the baseline level of arousal. You know that an extravert tends to be outgoing, sociable, and dominant and that an introvert is quieter and more reserved and passive. According to Eysenck, these outward differences in

FIGURE 49.1 Eysenck's Reticular Activation System Theory Eysenck viewed introversion and extraversion as characteristic behavioral patterns that aim to regulate arousal around the individual's baseline level.

behavior reflect different arousal regulation strategies (Figure 49.1). Extraverts wake up in the morning under-aroused, *below* the optimal level, whereas introverts start out *above* the optimal level.

If *you* were feeling under-engaged with life, what might you do? You might listen to loud music or hang out with friends—in other words, behave like an extravert. If, on the other hand, you were feeling over-aroused or too stimulated, what would you do? You might spend time alone, keep distractions to a minimum, maybe sit quietly and read a book—in other words, you might act like an introvert.

Thus, from Eysenck's perspective, we can understand the traits of extraversion/introversion as characteristic patterns of behavior that aim to regulate arousal around our baseline. Research has not shown that extraverts and introverts differ in terms of baseline arousal but, rather, that introverts may be more sensitive to arousing stimuli.

Gray's Reinforcement Sensitivity Theory

Building from Eysenck's work, Jeffrey Gray proposed a neuropsychology of personality, called *reinforcement sensitivity theory*, that has been the subject of much research (Gray, 1987; Gray & McNaughton, 2000). On the basis of animal learning principles, Gray posited that two neurological systems—the *behavioral activation system* (BAS) and the *behavioral inhibition system* (BIS)—could be viewed as underlying personality, as Figure 49.2 shows.

According to Gray, these systems explain differences in an organism's attention to rewards and punishers in the environment. An organism sensitive to rewards is more likely to learn associations between behaviors and rewards and therefore to show a characteristic pattern of seeking out rewarding opportunities. In contrast, an organism with a heightened sensitivity to punishers in the environment is more likely to learn associations between behaviors and negative consequences. Such an organism shows a characteristic pattern of avoiding such consequences.

In Gray's theory, the BAS is sensitive to rewards in the environment, predisposes one to feelings of positive emotion, and underlies the trait of extraversion. In contrast, the BIS is sensitive to punishments and is involved in avoidance learning; it predisposes the individual to feelings of fear and underlies the trait of neuroticism (Berkman, Lieberman, & Gable, 2009; Corr, 2008; Gray & McNaughton, 2000). Psychologists often measure the BAS and BIS in humans by using questionnaires that assess a person's attention to rewarding or punishing outcomes (Schmeichel, Harmon-Jones, & Harmon-Jones, 2010).

Gray's conceptual model of reinforcement sensitivity proposed interacting brain systems as primarily responsible for the behavioral manifestations of the BAS and BIS. Research has provided some evidence for the biological underpinnings of these systems. The amygdala, the prefrontal cortex, and the anterior cingulated cortex appear to serve together as a system for affective style (Davidson, 2005; McNaughton & Corr, 2008) and are particularly implicated in the BAS or extraversion (Pickering & Smillie, 2008).

BAS
Behavioral Approach System

Sensitive to
Environmental reward

Behavior
Seek positive consequences/rewards

Character of emotion
Positive

Personality trait
Extraversion

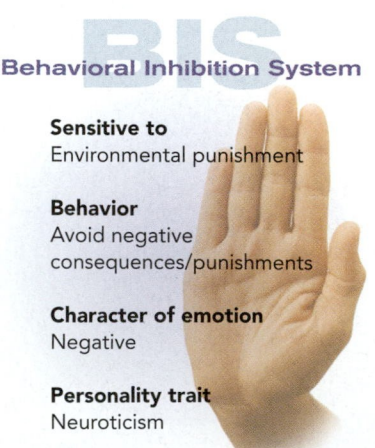

BIS
Behavioral Inhibition System

Sensitive to
Environmental punishment

Behavior
Avoid negative consequences/punishments

Character of emotion
Negative

Personality trait
Neuroticism

FIGURE 49.2 Gray's Reinforcement Sensitivity Theory Gray theorized that two neurological systems, the BAS and the BIS, explain differences in an organism's attention to environmental rewards and punishments and in this way shape personality.

The Role of Neurotransmitters

Neurotransmitters have also been implicated in personality in ways that fit Gray's model. The neurotransmitter dopamine plays a role in the experience of reward. Dopamine is a "feel good" neurotransmitter vital to learning that certain behaviors are rewarding and to sending the message to "do it again!" Research has shown that dopamine is also a factor in BAS or extraversion (Munafo & others, 2008). Studies have suggested that early encounters with warm caregivers and positive life experiences can promote the growth of dopamine-producing cells and receptors. These early experiences can make the brain especially sensitive to rewards, setting the neurochemical stage for extraversion (Depue & Collins, 1999).

Perhaps even stronger than the link between dopamine and extraversion is the relationship between the neurotransmitter serotonin and neuroticism (Brummett & others, 2008; Middeldorp & others, 2007). Neuroticism is especially related to a certain serotonin transporter gene and to the binding of serotonin in the thalamus (Gonda & others, 2009; Harro & others, 2009; Vinberg & others, 2010). Individuals who have less circulating serotonin are prone to negative mood; giving them drugs that inhibit the reuptake of serotonin tends to decrease negative mood and enhance feelings of sociability (Ksir, Hart, & Ray, 2008). Serotonin is also implicated in aggressive behavior (Neumann, Veenema, & Beiderbeck, 2010), as well as in the experience of depression (Popova & others, 2010).

Keep in mind that finding associations between brain activity or neurotransmitters and personality does not tell us about the potential causal pathways between these variables. Behavior can influence brain processes, and patterns of behavior can therefore determine brain activity. One thing that behavior cannot influence, at least not yet, is genes, another important biological factor in personality.

49-2 PERSONALITY AND BEHAVIORAL GENETICS

Behavioral genetics is the study of the inherited underpinnings of behavioral characteristics. A great deal of research in behavioral genetics has involved twin studies, and the hub of this work is, appropriately, the University of Minnesota, Twin Cities.

Twin study findings demonstrate that genetic factors explain a substantial amount of the observed differences in each of the big five traits. Remember that to conduct these studies, researchers compare identical twins, who share 100 percent of their genes, with fraternal twins, who share just 50 percent. All of the participants complete questionnaires measuring their traits. Then the researchers see if the identical twins are more similar to each other than the fraternal twins. Heritability estimates for the five factors are about 50 percent (Bouchard & Loehlin, 2001; Jang, Livesley, & Vernon, 1996; South & Krueger, 2008; Veselka & others, 2009).

Even aspects of personality that are not traits reveal some genetic influence. For example, research has shown that autobiographical memories about one's childhood and early family experiences (the kind of data that the personologist might find interesting) are influenced by genetics. Robert Krueger and his colleagues examined retrospective reports on the quality of family environments in a sample of twins who were reared apart (Krueger, Markon, & Bouchard, 2003). Participants rated their adoptive families on a variety of characteristics such as parental warmth, feelings of being wanted, and the strictness of their parents. These twins, though obviously sharing genetics, were reared by different families, so they were describing different experiences. Yet their recollections of their early family experiences were similar, and the heritability estimate for family cohesion ranged from 40 to 60 percent.

The heritability statistic describes a group, not an individual, and heritability does not mean that traits are set in stone. Understanding the

● **behavioral genetics** The study of the inherited underpinnings of behavioral characteristics.

CRITICAL CONTROVERSY

Can Personality Change?

As you talk on the phone with a friend, she tells you for what seems like the hundredth time about her boyfriend troubles. He never calls when he says he will. He always seems to have forgotten his wallet when they go out. Now she thinks he might be cheating on her *again*. As you count silently to 10, you are tempted to blurt it out: "Dump him already! He's never going to change!"

Of course, your friend might be banking on the notion that he *will* change. Can people genuinely change? The answer to this question has implications for a variety of important life domains. For example, can criminals be rehabilitated? Can addicts truly recover from addictions? Will all those self-help books ever help you to stop worrying and enjoy life? Will that lousy boyfriend turn out to be suitable husband material after all?

Whether personality can change has been a topic of controversy throughout the history of the field of personality. William James once wrote that "it is well for the world that in most of us, by the age of 30, the character has set like plaster, and will never soften again." Trait psychologists Paul Costa and Robert McCrae concluded from their own work that James was on target: They suggested that most traits are indeed "essentially fixed" by age 30, with little meaningful change occurring throughout the rest of adulthood (Costa & McCrae, 1992, 2006; McCrae & Costa, 2006). However, other research has provided evidence that meaningful personality change continues over time (Noftle & Fleeson, 2010; Roberts & Mroczek, 2008; Roberts, Wood, & Caspi, 2008).

Strong evidence that personality traits do change is provided by longitudinal studies that follow the same individuals over a long period. Brent Roberts and his colleagues analyzed 92 different longitudinal studies that included thousands of participants ranging from 12 years old to over 80 years old and that measured aspects of the big five across the life course (Edmonds & others, 2007; Roberts, Walton, & Viechtbauer, 2006; Roberts, Wood, & Caspi, 2008; Roberts & others, 2009). They found strong, consistent evidence for trait changes throughout life, even into adulthood. Social dominance (a facet of extraversion), conscientiousness, and emotional stability (the opposite of neuroticism) were found to increase especially between the ages of 20 and 40. Social vitality, another facet of extraversion, and openness to experience increased most during adolescence but then declined in old age. Agreeableness showed a steady rise over the life course. Over time, people were not just getting older—they were getting more responsible, kinder, and less worried.

Research has also shown that especially between age 17 and 24, individuals are likely to become more responsible and less distressed (Blonigen & others, 2008; Klimstra & others, 2009). In general, changes in personality traits across adulthood occur in a positive direction (Roberts & Mroczek, 2008). Over time, individuals become more confident and responsible, as well as warmer and calmer. Such positive changes equate with becoming more socially mature.

What can we conclude about stability and change in personality development during the adult years? The evidence does not support the view that personality traits become completely fixed at a certain age in adulthood (Caspi & Roberts, 2001; Noftle & Fleeson, 2010; Roberts, Wood, & Caspi, 2008). Keep in mind that, by definition, traits are considered to be stable. They might be the least likely aspect of personality to change, as compared, for example, to beliefs or goals. To find change in even these relatively stable dimensions is extraordinary and speaks to the important possibility that people can grow and change, especially in positive ways, over the life span. Researchers have discovered that other aspects of personality—such as resilience, wisdom, complexity, and insight—also increase through life experience (Helson & Soto, 2005; Helson, Soto, & Cate, 2006).

What do these findings mean for your friend and her loser boyfriend? Maybe he will shape up, but she might have to wait a very long time.

WHAT DO YOU THINK?

- In your opinion, can personality change throughout a person's life? Explain.
- Reflect on what you were like five years ago. Which aspects of your personality have changed? Which have stayed the same?
- If you have a friend who wants to be more outgoing, what would your advice be?

---

role of genetic factors in personality is enormously complex. Research on non-twin samples often suggests much lower heritability, for reasons that are not well understood (South & Krueger, 2008). Furthermore, because genes and environment are often intertwined, it is very difficult to tease apart whether, and how, genes or experience explains enduring patterns of behavior. For instance, a little girl who is genetically predisposed to disruptive behavior may often find herself in a time-out or involved in arguments with parents or teachers. When that child emerges as an adult with a "fighting spirit" or lots of "spunk," are those adult traits the product of genes, experiences, or both? Finally, most traits are probably influenced by multiple genes (P. T. Costa & others, 2010), making the task of identifying specific molecular links very challenging.

49-3 EVALUATING THE BIOLOGICAL PERSPECTIVES

Research that explores the biological aspects of personality is clearly important, and it is likely to remain a key avenue of research. This work ties the field of personality to animal learning models, advances in brain imaging, and evolutionary theory (Revelle, 2008). However, a few cautions are necessary in thinking about biological variables and their place in personality.

As we considered above, biology can be the effect, not the cause, of personality. To be sure that you grasp this idea, first recall that personality is the individual's characteristic pattern of behavior, thoughts, and feelings. Then recall from previous modules that behavior, thoughts, and feelings are physical events in the body and brain. If traits predispose individuals to particular, consistent behaviors, thoughts, and emotional responses, traits may play a role in forging particular habitually used pathways in the brain. Memory may be thought of as patterns of activation among neurons. The autobiographical memories that interest personologists, then, might be viewed as well-worn patterns of activation. To the extent that personality represents a person's characteristic pattern of thought or the accumulation of memories over the life span, personality may not only be influenced by the brain—it may also play a role in the brain's very structure and functions.

One issue that biological approaches bring to the fore is the question of whether personality is plastic—that is, whether it can change throughout a person's life. If personality is "caused" by biological processes, does that mean it is fixed? To explore this issue, see the Critical Controversy.

SUMMARY

Eysenck suggested that the brain's reticular activation system (RAS) plays a role in introversion/extraversion. He thought of these traits as the outward manifestations of arousal regulation. Gray developed a reward sensitivity theory of personality, suggesting that extraversion and neuroticism can be understood as two neurological systems that respond to rewards (the behavioral approach system, or BAS) and punishments (the behavioral inhibition system, or BIS) in the environment.

Research has found that dopamine is associated with behavioral approach (extraversion) and serotonin with behavioral avoidance (neuroticism). Behavioral genetic studies have shown that the heritability of personality traits is approximately 50 percent. Studies of biological processes in personality are valuable but can overestimate the causal role of biological factors.

KEY TERMS

behavioral genetics 457

TEST YOURSELF

1. According to Eysenck, what part of the brain influences whether a person is an introvert or an extravert?

2. How does Gray's reward sensitivity theory of personality explain extraversion and neuroticism?

3. What is behavioral genetics, and what kind of study is commonly used in research in this area?

APPLY YOUR KNOWLEDGE

1. Do you see your personality as stable, or has it changed over time? Drawing from the concepts discussed in this module, justify your answer.

2. Using Gray's or Eysenck's theory, explain the behaviors of mass murders and serial killers. Are people who commit such crimes predisposed toward this behavior?

Personality Assessment

One of the great contributions of personality psychology is its development of rigorous methods for measuring mental processes. Psychologists use a number of scientifically developed methods to evaluate personality. They assess personality for different reasons—from clinical evaluation to career counseling and job selection (J. N. Butcher, 2010; Heine & Buchtel, 2009).

50·1 SELF-REPORT TESTS

The most commonly used method of measuring personality characteristics is self-report. A **self-report test,** which is also called an *objective test* or *inventory,* directly asks people whether specific items describe their personality traits. Self-report personality tests include items such as

- I am easily embarrassed.
- I love to go to parties.
- I like to watch cartoons on TV.

Respondents choose from a limited number of answers (yes or no, true or false, agree or disagree).

One problem with self-report tests is a factor called *social desirability.* To grasp the idea of social desirability, imagine answering the item "I am lazy at times." This statement is probably true for everyone, but would you feel comfortable admitting it? When motivated by social desirability, individuals say what they think the researcher wants to hear or what they think will make them look better. One way to measure the influence of social desirability is to give individuals a questionnaire that is designed to tap into this tendency. Such a scale typically contains many universally true but threatening items ("I like to gossip at times," "I have never said anything intentionally to hurt someone's feelings"). If scores on a trait measure correlate with this measure of social desirability, we know that the test takers were probably not being straightforward with respect to the trait measure. That is, if a person answers one questionnaire in a socially desirable fashion, he or she is probably answering all the questionnaires that way.

Another way to get around social desirability issues is to design scales so that it is virtually impossible for the respondent to know what the researcher is trying to measure. One means of accomplishing this goal is to use an **empirically keyed test,** a type of self-report test that is created by first identifying two groups that are known to be different. The researcher would give these two groups a large number of questionnaire items and then see which items show the biggest differences between the groups. Those items would become part of the scale to measure the group difference. For instance, a researcher might want to develop a test that distinguishes between individuals with a history of substance abuse and those with no such history. The researcher might generate a long list of true/false items that ask about a variety of topics but do not mention substance abuse. These questions would be presented to the members of the two groups, and on the basis of the responses, the researcher can then select the items that best discriminate between the members of the differing groups (Segal & Coolidge, 2004).

Note that an empirically keyed test avoids the issue of social desirability because the items that distinguish between the two groups are not related in any obvious way to the actual purpose of the test. For instance, those without a substance abuse history might

● **self-report test** Also called an objective test or an inventory, a method of measuring personality characteristics that directly asks people whether specific items describe their personality traits.

● **empirically keyed test** A type of self-report test that presents many questionnaire items to two groups that are known to be different in some central way.

"I like the way I look, but I hate my personality."
© David Sipress/The New Yorker Collection/www.cartoonbank.com.

typically respond "true" to the item "I enjoy taking long walks," while those with a history of substance abuse might respond "false"; but this item does not mention substance use, and there is no clear reason why it should distinguish between these groups.

Indeed, an important consideration with respect to empirically keyed tests is that researchers often do *not* know why a given test item distinguishes between two groups. Imagine, for example, that an empirically keyed test of achievement motivation includes an item such as "I prefer to watch sports on TV instead of romantic movies." A researcher might find that this item does a good job of distinguishing between higher-paid versus lower-paid managers in a work setting. However, does an item such as this example measure achievement motivation or, instead, simply the respondents' gender?

MMPI

The **Minnesota Multiphasic Personality Inventory (MMPI)** is the most widely used and researched empirically keyed self-report personality test. The MMPI was initially constructed in the 1940s to assess "abnormal" personality tendencies. The most recent version of the inventory, the MMPI-2, is still widely used around the world to assess personality and predict outcomes (J. N. Butcher, 2010; Handel & others, 2010). The scale features 567 items and provides information on a variety of personality characteristics. The MMPI also includes items meant to assess whether the respondent is lying or trying to make a good impression (social desirability). Not only is the MMPI used by clinical psychologists to assess mental health (S. R. Smith & others, 2010), but it is also a tool in hiring decisions (Caillouet & others, 2010) and in forensic settings, assessing criminal risk (Bow, Flens, & Gould, 2010; Sellbom & others, 2010).

● **Minnesota Multiphasic Personality Inventory (MMPI)** The most widely used and researched empirically keyed self-report personality test.

Assessment of the Big Five Factors

Paul Costa and Robert McCrae (1992) constructed the Neuroticism Extraversion Openness Personality Inventory—Revised (or NEO-PI-R, for short), a self-report test geared to assessing the five-factor model: openness, conscientiousness, extraversion, agreeableness, and neuroticism (emotional instability). The test also evaluates six subdimensions that make up the five main factors. Other measures of the big five traits have relied on the lexical approach and offer the advantage of being available without a fee.

Unlike empirically keyed tests, measures of the big five generally contain straightforward items; for instance, the trait "talkative" might show up on an extraversion scale. These items have what psychologists call face validity. A test item has **face validity** if it seems on the surface to be testing the characteristic in question. Measures of the big five typically involve items that are obvious in terms of what they measure, but not all self-report assessments have this quality.

The MMPI and the NEO-PIR are well-established measures of personality characteristics. Yet, you may be more familiar with another assessment tool that is popular in business settings, called the Myers-Briggs Type Indicator. To learn about the way personality psychologists regard this questionnaire, see the Intersection.

It is likely that you could give a reasonably good assessment of your own levels of traits such as neuroticism and extraversion. What about the more mysterious aspects of yourself and others? If you are like most people, you think of psychological assessments as tools to find out things you do not already know about yourself. For that objective, psychologists might turn to projective tests.

● **face validity** The extent to which a test item appears to be a good fit to the characteristic it measures.

● **projective test** A personality assessment test that presents individuals with an ambiguous stimulus and asks them to describe it or tell a story about it—to project their own meaning onto the stimulus.

50·2 PROJECTIVE TESTS

A **projective test** presents individuals with an ambiguous stimulus and asks them to describe it or tell a story about it—in other words, to *project* their own meaning onto the stimulus. Projective tests are based on the assumption that the ambiguity of the stimulus allows individuals to interpret it based on their feelings, desires, needs, and attitudes. The test is especially designed to elicit the individual's unconscious feelings

© Dan Reynolds. www.CartoonStock.com.

Personality and Organizational Psychology: Hey, What's Your Type?

Personality assessment has become increasingly useful in business settings. Personality psychologists and industrial and organizational psychologists (specialists we discuss in Module 55) have investigated the ways that personality characteristics relate to success in the workplace. One of the most popular assessment tools for personnel decisions is the Myers Briggs Type Indicator (MBTI) developed in the 1940s by the mother–daughter team of Katherine Briggs and Isabel Briggs Myers (Briggs & Myers, 1998), neither of whom was trained in psychology or assessment (Saunders, 1991).

Based on a book by Carl Jung, the Myers Briggs questionnaire provides people with feedback on their personality "type" based on four dimensions:

- *Extraversion* (basing one's actions on outward conditions) versus *introversion* (being more introspective)
- *Sensing* (relying on what can be sensed about reality) versus *intuiting* (relying on gut feelings and unconscious processes)
- *Thinking* (relying on logic) versus *feeling* (relying on emotion)
- *Judgment* (using thinking and feeling) versus *perception* (using sensing and intuiting)

These MBTI dimensions are used to create categories that are labeled with letters; for example, an extraverted person who relies on sensation, thinking, and judgment would be called an ESTJ.

The MBTI has become so popular that people in some organizations introduce themselves as an INTJ or an INSP in the same way that people might exchange their astrological signs. Unfortunately, as in the case of astrology, strong evidence for the actual value of the MBTI types for personnel selection and job performance is very weak at best (Hunsley, Lee, & Wood, 2004; Pittenger, 2005). In fact, the MBTI is neither reliable (people get different scores with repeated testing) nor valid (it does not predict what it should). For example, there is no evidence that particular MBTI types are better suited to particular occupations (Bjork & Druckman, 1991; Boyle, 1995; Gardner & Martinko, 1996).

Given this lack of empirical support, why does MBTI remain popular? Some practitioners have found it to be quite useful in their own work (McCaulley, 2000), whether or not they are aware of the lack of scientific evidence for the types. The MBTI has been well marketed, and those who pay for the scale and its training may be motivated to find evidence in their own lives to support the notion that it works.

It can be fun to learn about our personalities and to be given these letter labels. When we read that an INTJ is someone who is "introspective and likely to sometimes argue a point just for the sake of argument," we might think, "They really figured me out." However, this description could be true of virtually anyone, as is the case for most astrological profiles. The tendency to see ourselves in such vague descriptions is called the *Barnum effect,* after P. T. Barnum, the famous showman. The wily Barnum—simply by dispensing vague, general descriptions that would likely be true of anyone— convinced people that he could read minds.

The popularity of the Myers Briggs letter typology attests to the power of marketing, the persistence of confirmation bias (the tendency to use information that supports our ideas rather than refutes them), and the Barnum effect. Most troubling to personality psychologists is that although other psychological measures may not be as exciting and mysterious as those four letters, they are more likely to provide reliable and valid information about job performance (Hunsley, Lee, & Wood, 2004).

If you were a manager, what personality characteristics would you look for in job candidates?

and conflicts, providing an assessment that goes deeper than the surface of personality (Bram, 2010; Hibbard & others, 2010; Husain, 2009).

Projective tests attempt to get inside the mind to discover how the test taker really feels and thinks; that is, they aim to go beyond the way the individual overtly presents himself or herself. Projective tests are theoretically aligned with the psychodynamic perspectives on personality, which give more weight to the unconscious than do other perspectives. Projective techniques also require content analysis. The examiner must code the responses for the underlying motivations revealed in the story.

Perhaps the most famous projective test is the **Rorschach inkblot test,** developed in 1921 by the Swiss psychiatrist Hermann Rorschach. The test consists of 10 cards, half in black and white and half in color, which the individual views one at a time (Figure 50.1). The person taking the Rorschach test is asked to describe what he or she sees in each of the inkblots. For example, the individual may say, "I see two fairies having a tea party" or "This is the rabbit's face from the movie *Donnie Darko*." These responses are scored based on indications of various underlying psychological characteristics (Exner, 2003; Leichtman, 2009).

The Rorschach's usefulness in research is controversial. From a scientific perspective, researchers are skeptical about the Rorschach (Feshbach & Weiner, 1996; Garb & others, 2001; Hunsley & Bailey, 2001; Weiner, 2004). The test's reliability and validity have both been criticized. If the Rorschach were reliable, two different scorers would agree on the personality characteristics of the individual being tested. If the Rorschach were valid, it would predict behavior outside of the testing situation; that is, it would predict, for example, whether an individual will attempt suicide, become severely depressed, cope successfully with stress, or get along well with others. Conclusions based on research evidence suggest that the Rorschach does not meet these criteria of reliability and validity (Lilienfeld, Wood, & Garb, 2000). Thus, many psychologists have serious reservations about the Rorschach's use in diagnosis and clinical practice.

Although still administered in clinical (Bram, 2010) and applied (Del Giudice, 2010) circles, the Rorschach is not commonly used in personality research. However, the projective method itself remains a tool for studying personality, especially in the form of the Thematic Apperception Test (TAT).

The **Thematic Apperception Test (TAT),** developed by Henry Murray and Christiana Morgan in the 1930s, is designed to elicit stories that reveal something about an individual's personality. The TAT consists of a series of pictures like the one in Figure 50.2, each on an individual card or slide. The TAT test taker is asked to tell a story about each of the pictures, including events leading up to the situation described, the characters' thoughts and feelings, and the way the situation turns out. The tester assumes that the person projects his or her own unconscious feelings and thoughts into the story (Hibbard & others, 2010).

In addition to being administered as a projective test in clinical practice, the TAT is used in research on people's need for achievement, affiliation, power, intimacy, and a variety of other needs (Brunstein & Maier, 2005; Schultheiss & Brunstein, 2005; C. P. Smith, 1992); unconscious defense mechanisms (Cramer, 2008a, 2008b; Cramer & Jones, 2007); and cognitive styles (Woike, 2008; Woike & Matic, 2004; Woike, Mcleod, & Goggin, 2003). In contrast to the Rorschach, TAT measures have shown high inter-rater reliability and validity (Woike, 2001).

50-3 OTHER ASSESSMENT METHODS

Self-report questionnaires and projective techniques are just two of the multitude of assessment methods developed and used by personality psychologists. Personality psychologists might also measure behavior directly, by observing a person either live or in a video. In addition, cognitive assessments have become more common in personality psychology, as researchers probe such topics as the relation between personality and processes of attention and memory. Many personality psychologists incorporate friend or peer ratings of individuals' traits or other characteristics. Personality psychologists also use a host of psychophysiological measures, such as heart rate and skin conductance. Increasingly, personality psychologists are incorporating brain imaging as well.

Whether personality assessments are being used by clinical psychologists, psychological researchers, or other practitioners, the choice of assessment instrument depends greatly on the researcher's theoretical perspective. Figure 50.3 summarizes which methods are associated with each of the theoretical perspectives. The figure also summarizes each approach, including its major assumptions, and gives a sample research question addressed by each. Personality psychology is a diverse field, unified by a shared interest in understanding the person you really are.

FIGURE 50.1   Type of Stimulus Used in the Rorschach Inkblot Test What do you see in this figure? Do you see two green seahorses? Or a pair of blue spiders? A psychologist who relies on the Rorschach test would examine your responses to find out who you are.

● **Rorschach inkblot test** A famous projective test that uses an individual's perception of inkblots to determine his or her personality.

● **Thematic Apperception Test (TAT)** A projective test that is designed to elicit stories that reveal something about an individual's personality.

FIGURE 50.2   Picture from the Thematic Apperception Test (TAT) What are these two women thinking and feeling? How did they come to this situation, and what will happen next? A psychologist who uses the TAT would analyze your story to find out your unconscious motives. Reprinted by permission of the publishers from *Thematic Apperception Test* by Henry A. Murray, Card 12F, Cambridge, MA: Harvard University Press. Copyright © 1943 by the President and the Fellows of Harvard College. Copyright © 1971 by Henry A. Murray.

Approach	Summary	Assumptions	Typical Methods	Sample Research Question
Psychodynamic	Personality is characterized by unconscious processes. Childhood experiences are of great importance to adult personality.	The most important aspects of personality are unconscious.	Case studies, projective techniques.	How do unconscious conflicts lead to dysfunctional behavior?
Humanistic	Personality evolves out of the person's innate, organismic motives to grow and actualize the self. These healthy tendencies can be undermined by social pressure.	Human nature is basically good. By getting in touch with who we are and what we really want, we can lead happier, healthier lives.	Questionnaires, interviews, observation.	Can situations be changed to support individuals' organismic values and enhance their well-being?
Trait	Personality is characterized by five general traits that are represented in the natural language that people use to describe themselves and others.	Traits are relatively stable over time. Traits predict behavior.	Questionnaires, observer reports.	Are the five factors universal across cultures?
Personological and Life Story	To understand personality, we must understand the whole person. We all have unique life experiences, and the stories we tell about those experiences make up our identities.	The life story provides a unique opportunity to examine the personality processes associated with behavior, development, and well-being.	Written narratives, TAT stories, autobiographical memories, interviews, and psychobiography.	How do narrative accounts of life experiences relate to happiness?
Social Cognitive	Personality is the pattern of coherence that characterizes a person's interactions with the situations he or she encounters in life. The individual's beliefs and expectations, rather than global traits, are the central variables of interest.	Behavior is best understood as changing across situations. To understand personality, we must understand what each situation means for a given person.	Multiple observations over different situations; video-recorded behaviors rated by coders; questionnaires.	When and why do individuals respond to challenging tasks with fear versus excitement?
Biological	Personality characteristics reflect underlying biological processes such as those carried out by the brain, neurotransmitters, and genes. Differences in behaviors, thoughts, and feelings depend on these processes.	Biological differences among individuals can explain differences in their personalities.	Brain imaging, twin studies, molecular genetic studies.	Do genes explain individual differences in extraversion?

FIGURE 50.3   Approaches to Personality Psychology This figure summarizes the broad approaches to personality described in this module. Many researchers in personality do not stick with just one approach but apply the various theories and methods that are most relevant to their research questions.

SUMMARY

Self-report tests assess personality by asking participants about their preferences and behaviors. One problem in self-report research is the tendency for individuals to respond in socially desirable ways. Empirically keyed tests avoid social desirability problems by using items that distinguish between groups even if we do not know why the items do so.

The most popular test for assessing the big five traits is the NEO-PIR, which uses self-report items to measure each of the traits. The Minnesota Multiphasic Personality Inventory (MMPI) is the most widely used empirically keyed personality test.

Projective tests, designed to assess unconscious aspects of personality, present individuals with an ambiguous stimulus, such as an inkblot or a picture, and ask them to tell a story about it. Projective tests are based on the assumption that individuals will project their personalities onto these

KEY TERMS

self-report test   460
empirically keyed test   460
Minnesota Multiphasic
  Personality Inventory
  (MMPI)   461

face validity   461
projective test   461
Rorschach inkblot test   463
Thematic Apperception Test
  (TAT)   463

stimuli. The Thematic Apperception Test (TAT) is a projective test that has been used in personality research. Other assessment methods include behavioral observation, reports from peers, and psychophysiological and neuropsychological measures.

TEST YOURSELF

1. What is an empirically keyed test?
2. What is a common problem with self-report tests?
3. What technique does the Thematic Apperception Test (TAT) involve?

APPLY YOUR KNOWLEDGE

1. Respond to the Rorschach presented in Figure 50.1 or the TAT image in Figure 50.2. What do you see in the image you selected? After you've formulated your thoughts, ask a friend or two to respond to the same image. How do your responses compare or contrast? What themes surface for each of you? How do your responses seem to relate to your various personalities?

2. Using what you've learned to this point about personality and psychology, consider whether a psychologist's own personality could influence the way he or she administered a projective personality test to another individual. How?

Personality and Health and Wellness

Personality comprises a set of enduring characteristics that influence behavior. As such, personality affects many behaviors that impact physical health and psychological wellness, as we consider in this concluding section.

PERSONALITY AND PHYSICAL HEALTH

We first survey personality characteristics that are linked, respectively, to health and to illness.

Conscientiousness

Conscientiousness is not the sexiest personality trait, but it might well be the most important of the big five when it comes to longevity and healthy living (Roberts & Mroczek, 2008; Roberts & others, 2009). In a longitudinal study of more than 1,200 individuals across seven decades, conscientiousness predicted a lower mortality risk from childhood through late adulthood (Martin, Friedman, & Schwartz, 2007). A variety of studies show that conscientious people tend to do all the things that they are told are good for their health, such as getting regular exercise, avoiding drinking and smoking, wearing seatbelts, and checking smoke detectors (D. B. O'Connor & others, 2009; Rush, Becker, & Curry, 2009). This capacity to follow a sensible plan may be just what it takes to do the mundane tasks required to live a long, healthy life. Indeed, research has shown that conscientious individuals are less likely to die than their counterparts who are less conscientious (Fry & Debats, 2009; Iwassa & others, 2008, 2009; Kern & Friedman, 2008; R. S. Wilson & others, 2004).

Personal Control

Another personality characteristic associated with taking the right steps toward a long, healthy life is personal control (Baumeister & Alquist, 2009; Forgas, Baumeister, & Tice, 2009). Feeling in control can reduce stress during difficult times and can lead to the development of problem-solving strategies to deal with hardship (Taylor, 2011; S. C. Thompson, 2001). An individual with a good sense of personal control might reason, "If I stop smoking now, I will not develop lung cancer" or "If I exercise regularly, I won't develop cardiovascular disease."

A sense of personal control has been linked to a lower risk for common chronic diseases such as cancer and cardiovascular disease (Sturmer, Hasselbach, & Amelang, 2006). Further, like conscientiousness, a sense of personal control might help people avoid a risky lifestyle that involves health-compromising behaviors. Consider a study of East German migrants to West Germany who found themselves unemployed (Mittag & Schwarzer, 1993). Individuals in the study often turned to heavy drinking for solace—unless, that is, they had a sense of personal control (as measured by such survey items as "When I'm in trouble, I can rely on my ability to deal with the problem effectively"). Overall, across a wide range of studies, a sense of personal control has been related to emotional well-being, successful coping with a stressful event, healthy behavior change, and good health (Little, Snyder, & Wehmeyer, 2006; Stanton, Revenson, & Tennen, 2007; Taylor, 2011; Taylor & Stanton, 2007).

Self-Efficacy

Research has shown that self-efficacy is related to success in a wide variety of positive life changes, including achieving weight loss (Annesi, 2007), exercising regularly (Lippke

& Plotnikoff, 2006), quitting smoking (Gwaltney & others, 2009), ending substance abuse (Warren, Stein, & Grella, 2007), and practicing safe sex (Abbey & others, 2007). Recent evidence suggests that self-efficacy is also strongly linked to cardiovascular functioning following heart failure and that individuals high in self-efficacy are not only less likely to suffer a second hospitalization due to heart failure but also likely to live longer (Sarkar, Ali, & Whooley, 2009).

If there is a problem to be fixed, self-efficacy—having a can-do attitude—is related to finding a solution. In one study, smokers were randomly assigned to one of three conditions. In the *self-efficacy condition,* individuals were told they had been chosen for the study because they had great potential to quit smoking (Warnecke & others, 2001). Then they participated in a 14-week program on smoking cessation. In the *treatment-alone condition,* individuals participated in the 14-week smoking cessation program but were told that they had been randomly selected for it. In the *no-treatment control condition,* individuals did not participate in the smoking cessation program. At the end of the 14 weeks, individuals in the self-efficacy condition were more likely to have quit smoking than their counterparts in the other two conditions. The Psychological Inquiry shows the results.

Optimism

A factor that is often linked to positive functioning and adjustment is optimism (Carver & Connor-Smith, 2010; Peterson & Seligman, 2003; Seligman & Pawelski, 2003; Smith & MacKenzie, 2006). Martin Seligman's (1990) theory and research view optimism as a matter of how a person explains the causes of bad events. Optimists explain the causes of bad events as external, unstable, and specific, whereas pessimists explain them as internal, stable, and global. Studies have associated explaining life events optimistically with a variety of positive outcomes (Reivich & Gillham, 2002).

Other researchers define optimism as the expectancy that good things, and not bad things, are more likely to occur in the future (Carver & Connor-Smith, 2010; Carver & Scheier, 2009; Solberg Nes, Evans, & Segerstrom, 2009; Solberg Nes & Segerstrom, 2006). This view focuses on how people pursue their goals and values. Even when faced with misfortune, optimists believe that they can attain their goals and live according to their values.

psychological *inquiry*

Percent who quit smoking

A Can-Do Attitude Means You Can Quit Smoking

The figure shows the results of the study on self-efficacy and smoking cessation (discussed in the text) in which smokers were randomly assigned to one of three conditions—self-efficacy, treatment alone, and no treatment (Warnecke & others, 2001). Notice that the Y or vertical axis shows the dependent variable, the percentage of participants who quit smoking. The X or horizontal axis shows the independent variable, the groups to which participants were assigned. Try your hand at the following questions.

1. Why were participants randomly assigned to groups?

2. If the researchers concluded that the self-efficacy manipulation caused these differences, would their conclusion be justified? Explain.

3. How might the results of this study be generalized to groups who wish to change other behaviors?

4. How would you design a correlational study that would examine the relationship between self-efficacy and smoking cessation?

Martin Seligman (b. 1942) Seligman went from pessimist to optimist and believes that others can, too. Seligman (1990) provided the details in his book *Learned Optimism*.

● **Type A behavior pattern** A cluster of characteristics—such as being excessively competitive, hard-driven, impatient, and hostile—related to the incidence of heart disease.

● **Type B behavior pattern** A cluster of characteristics—such as being relaxed and easygoing—related to good health.

● **subjective well-being** A person's assessment of his or her own level of positive affect relative to negative affect, and the individual's evaluation of his or her life in general.

Numerous studies reveal that optimists generally function more effectively and are physically and mentally healthier than pessimists (Segerstrom, 2006). In one study, people who had been classified as optimistic at age 25 were healthier at ages 45 to 60 than those who had been classified as pessimistic (Peterson, Seligman, & Vaillant, 1988). In other studies, optimism has been linked to more effective immune system functioning and better health (Segerstrom, 2003, 2005; Solberg Nes & Segerstrom, 2006).

Whereas optimism, sense of personal control, and self-efficacy can promote effective coping with stress, other personality characteristics have been shown to exacerbate stress with special significance for cardiovascular illness. In particular, people who are impatient or quick to anger or who display frequent hostility have an increased risk for cardiovascular disease (Chida & Steptoe, 2009), as we now consider.

The Type A/Type B Behavior Pattern

In the late 1950s, a secretary for two California cardiologists, Meyer Friedman and Ray Rosenman, observed that the chairs in their waiting rooms were tattered and worn, but only on the front edges. The cardiologists themselves had noticed the impatience of their cardiac patients, who often arrived exactly on time and were in a great hurry to leave. Intrigued by this consistency, they conducted a study of 3,000 healthy men between the ages of 35 and 59 over eight years to find out whether people with certain behavioral characteristics might be prone to heart problems (Friedman & Rosenman, 1974). During the eight years, one group of men had twice as many heart attacks or other forms of heart disease as the other men. Autopsies of the men who died revealed that the coronary arteries of this group were more obstructed than those of the other group.

Friedman and Rosenman described the common personality characteristics of the men who developed coronary disease as the **Type A behavior pattern.** They theorized that a cluster of characteristics—being excessively competitive, hard-driven, impatient, and hostile—is related to the incidence of heart disease. Rosenman and Friedman labeled the behavior of the healthier group, who were commonly relaxed and easygoing, the **Type B behavior pattern.**

Further research on the link between Type A behavior and coronary disease indicates that the association is not as strong as Friedman and Rosenman believed (Suls & Swain, 1998; R. B. Williams, 2001, 2002). However, researchers have found that certain components of Type A behavior are more precisely linked with coronary risk (Spielberger, 2004), especially hostility (Chida & Steptoe, 2009). People who are hostile outwardly or who turn anger inward are more likely to develop heart disease than their less angry counterparts (Eng & others, 2003; K. A. Matthews & others, 2004). Such people have been called "hot reactors" because of their intense physiological reactions to stress—racing heart, quickened breathing, and increased muscle tension. Research on hostility demonstrates that just as personality can relate to better health outcomes, some personality characteristics can be associated with health risks.

PERSONALITY AND PSYCHOLOGICAL WELL-BEING

Among the most consistent findings in personality research is the strong association between personality traits and psychological well-being. Specifically, neuroticism is strongly related to lower levels of well-being, whereas extraversion is related to higher levels (Steel, Schmidt, & Schultz, 2008; Wilt & Revelle, 2009). The links between these two traits and well-being have even been found in orangutans (Weiss, King, & Perkins, 2006). What explains these connections?

As defined by psychologists, **subjective well-being** is a person's assessment of his or her level of positive affect and negative affect, and an evaluation of his or her life in general (Diener, 2000). This definition provides a clue as to why the traits of neuroticism and extraversion are so strongly related to psychological state. Neuroticism is the tendency to worry, to feel distressed, and to experience negative emotion. Neurotic individuals experience more negative mood than others, and their moods are more changeable. David Watson, a personality and clinical psychologist who specializes in the study of mood, has suggested that negative emotion is at the very core of the trait of neuroticism (Miller, Vachon, & Lynam, 2009; Watson & Clark, 1997).

Interestingly, however, research has shown that neurotics can be happy—especially if they are also extraverted (Hotard & others, 1989). Indeed, Watson suggests that positive emotion is that core of the trait of extraversion (Watson & Naragon, 2009). Research has shown that extraverts are happier than introverts even when they are alone (Lucas, 2008). In fact, research has supported the conclusion that extraverts are happier regardless of what they are doing or with whom they are doing it (Lucas, 2007; McNiel, Lowman, & Fleeson, 2010).

If you are not very conscientious, or you are a pessimist with an external locus of control, or you are hostile, or neurotic, or an introvert—or a hostile, neurotic introvert—you may be feeling your mood deflating. If personality is stable, what good is it to find out that your personality—who you really are—might put you at risk for illness and make you miserable?

A positive way to think about these issues is to focus on the difference between traits and states (Marine & others, 2006). Recall that traits are enduring characteristics—the way you generally are. In contrast, states (such as positive or negative moods) are briefer experiences. Having a trait, such as neuroticism, that predisposes you to feelings of worry (a state) does not mean that your overall well-being must suffer. Instead, recognizing that you tend to be neurotic may be an important step in noting when your negative moods are potentially being fed by this trait and are not necessarily the result of objective events. Finding out that you have a personality style associated with higher levels of stress or lower levels of happiness does not mean that you are doomed. Rather, you can use this information to cultivate good habits and to make the most of your unique qualities.

Remember, too, that personality characteristics influence health through their relationships to behaviors and the experience of stress. Even a person very low in conscientiousness can engage in healthy behaviors. Consider that characteristics such as locus of control and self-efficacy are about your beliefs about the world, and these aspects of personality are changeable. Recall that in the Psychological Inquiry earlier in this section, self-efficacy was manipulated by simply telling people they had high potential to change. Believing in *your own* potential may be the first step to enhancing your health and wellness.

SUMMARY

Conscientiousness and personal control relate to health and longevity through their association with healthy lifestyle choices. Self-efficacy is also related to the ability to make positive changes in lifestyle. Optimism is another personality characteristic that is related to better health.

The Type A behavior pattern is a set of characteristics that may put an individual at risk for the development of heart disease. Type A behavior includes hostility, time urgency, and competitiveness. Type B behavior, in contrast, refers to a more easygoing style. The crucial aspect of Type A appears to be hostility.

Personality traits that are related to health and wellness can also be thought of as states. Thus, even if you are low on these wellness traits, you can still benefit by seeking out states that foster positive attributes.

KEY TERMS

Type A behavior pattern 468
Type B behavior pattern 468
subjective well-being 468

TEST YOURSELF

1. What are four personality characteristics that are associated with positive functioning and positive life changes?

2. How have various researchers defined optimism?

3. What is the Type A behavior pattern, and what specific aspect of it is most often linked to coronary disease?

Social Psychology

Are 180,000 Heads Better Than One?

Whether it is solving a problem, making a decision, or having influence on the world, a group of people acting together can sometimes accomplish much more than a single individual acting alone. The value of many different perspectives is illustrated in the experience of Tiffany Philippou, a 21-year-old recent college graduate from the U.K. Philippou entered a website competition in hopes of landing a summer internship at the Saatchi and Saatchi ad agency. She started with a Facebook page, called Secret London, where people could share their tips for travel to London—their favorite hotels and restaurants, along with less common travel advice. In just two weeks, Philippou had 180,000 Facebook friends who were sharing enormous amounts of information about the city. Using a technique called *crowdsourcing,* in which the web is used as a forum for brainstorming from all sides, Philippou put all those heads together and amassed a wealth of creative and interesting ideas, certainly more than any one person could have compiled. In no time, her site became more than just an entry in a competition—it became Philippou's very own startup company (Butcher, 2010).

Philippou's experience reveals that brainstorming by a (very) large group can accomplish far more than one person thinking alone. A noteworthy aspect of crowdsourcing is that it may bypass many of the issues that arise when human beings interact in person. Whether face-to-face or online, the ways that people come together—to solve problems, interact, and form bonds with one another—is the essence of social psychology. ●

Social Cognition

Social psychology is the study of how people think about, influence, and relate to other people. As you will see, social psychologists take many of the topics we have covered so far—including perception, cognition, and emotion—and examine them in a social context. Social psychologists are especially interested in the ways that social situations influence behavior.

Social cognition is the area of social psychology that explores how people select, interpret, remember, and use social information (Spaulding, 2010). Essentially, it is the way in which individuals think in social situations (Maddux, 2010; Strack & Forster, 2009).

51·1 PERSON PERCEPTION

Person perception refers to the processes by which we use social stimuli to form impressions of others (Smith & Collins, 2009). One important social cue is the face (Olivola & Todorov, 2010; Rule & others, 2010). The power of the face is demonstrated in research by Alexander Todorov and his colleagues (2005), who examined the ways that perceptions of faces can influence political elections. These researchers asked people to rate the competence of individuals from photographs of their faces. The faces were of candidates in the 2000, 2002, and 2004 U.S. House and Senate elections. Respondents' ratings accurately predicted the outcome for about *70 percent* of the elections. Those faces gave away information about the candidates that was meaningful to the perceivers, including how competent the perceivers felt each office-seeker would be (Mattes & others, 2010). Other aspects of faces can also have important implications for social perception, as we now consider.

Physical Attractiveness and Other Perceptual Cues

Physical attractiveness has been recognized as a powerful social cue (Berneburg & others, 2010). Judith Langlois and her colleagues found that even infants as young as 3 to 6 months of age showed a preference for looking at attractive faces versus unattractive faces, as rated by adults (Hoss & Langlois, 2003; Ramsey & others, 2004). Attractive individuals are generally assumed to have a variety of other positive characteristics, including being better adjusted, socially skilled, friendly, likable, extraverted, and likely to achieve superior job performance (Langlois & others, 2000). These positive expectations for physically attractive individuals have been referred to as the "beautiful is good" stereotype.

A **stereotype** is a generalization about a group's characteristics that does not consider any variations from one individual to another. Stereotypes are a natural extension of the limits on human cognitive processing and our reliance on concepts in cognitive processing (Cook, Cusack, & Dickens, 2010; Wegener, Clark, & Petty, 2006).

We simplify the task of understanding people by classifying them as members of groups or categories with which we are familiar. It takes more mental effort to consider a person's individual characteristics than it does to label him or her as a member of a particular group or category. Thus, when we categorize an individual, the categorization is often based on stereotypes.

Is there any truth to the "beautiful is good" stereotype? Research has shown that attractive people may indeed possess a number of positive characteristics (Langlois &

others, 2000). Does that mean that attractiveness is naturally related to, for example, better social skills? Not necessarily.

One way that stereotypes can influence individuals is through a phenomenon called *self-fulfilling prophecy*. In a self-fulfilling prophecy, expectations cause individuals to act in ways that serve to make the expectations come true. Robert Rosenthal and Lenore Jacobsen conducted the classic self-fulfilling prophecy study in 1968. The researchers told grade-school teachers that five students were likely to be "late bloomers"—that these students had high levels of ability that would likely shine forth over time. In reality, however, the students had been randomly selected by the researchers. Nonetheless, a year later, the researchers found that teachers' expectations for the "late bloomers" were reflected in student performance—the academic performance of these five was beyond that of other students. Self-fulfilling prophecy effects show the potential power of stereotypes and other sources of expectations on human behavior.

How might self-fulfilling prophecy effects apply when people interact with physically attractive versus unattractive individuals? Consider that attractive people may receive differential treatment from others throughout their lives. This special treatment increases the likelihood that the attractive individuals might well develop enhanced social skills and be more self-confident than others.

Another relevant question is, what makes a face attractive? *People* magazine's "50 Most Beautiful People" issue might lead you to conclude that attractiveness is about being exceptional in some physical way: Consider Julia Roberts's radiant smile or George Clooney's dreamy eyes. For some time, researchers relied on ratings to tell them who was or was not attractive. They assumed that beauty was something about which social perceivers would agree, along the lines of the editors of *People* magazine.

Researchers have examined what specifically makes a face attractive. Using computer technology that allowed them to average together digitized photographs of a large group of individuals of varying attractiveness, Langlois and her colleagues (1994) created composite faces. A large sample of college students then rated the individual faces and the composites. The results showed that individual faces were less attractive than faces that were created by averaging 8, 16, or 32 other faces. These researchers concluded that attractive faces are actually "just average." Although "averageness" is not the only predictor of attractiveness, Langlois and her colleagues suggest that being average is an essential component (along with variables such as symmetry and youthfulness) of facial attractiveness.

What makes a face attractive? Research has found that "averageness" is an essential component.

First Impressions

When we first meet someone, typically the new acquaintance quickly makes an impression. That first impression can have lasting effects (Ambady & Skowronski, 2009). Recall the primacy effect from Module 24—people's tendency to attend to and remember what they learned first (N. H. Anderson, 1965). The power of first impressions is likely due to just such an effect. How quickly do we make these initial impressions of others? In one study, judgments made after just a 100-millisecond exposure time to unfamiliar faces was sufficient for individuals to form an impression (Willis & Todorov, 2006).

Of course, once you become acquainted with someone, you have a lot more information to use to form an opinion of the person. The process by which we come to understand the causes of others' behavior and form an impression of them as individuals is called *attribution*.

51-2 ATTRIBUTION

Trying to understand why people do the things they do is a puzzle that fascinates all of us. We can observe people's behavior and listen to what they say, but to determine the underlying cause of their behavior we often have to make inferences from these observations. Making inferences means taking the information we have and coming up

Cornered by Mike Baldwin

1-1 © 2009 Mike Baldwin / Dist. by Universal Press Syndicate www.cornered.com
cornered@comic.com

"Thank God we're cute. You only get one chance to make a good first impression."

● **attribution theory** The view that people are motivated to discover the underlying causes of behavior as part of their effort to make sense of the behavior.

with a good guess about who someone is and what they are likely to do in the future (Gaunt & Trope, 2007; Krueger, 2007).

Attribution theory views people as motivated to discover the underlying causes of behavior as part of their effort to make sense of the behavior (Heider, 1958; Kelley, 1973; Weiner, 2006). Attributions vary along three dimensions (Jones, 1998):

■ *Internal/external causes:* Internal attributions include all causes inside and specific to the person, such as his or her traits and abilities. External attributions include all causes outside the person, such as social pressure, aspects of the social situation, money, the weather, and luck. Did Beth get an *A* on the test because she is smart or because the test was easy?

■ *Stable/unstable causes:* Is the cause relatively enduring and permanent, or is it temporary? Did Aaron blow up at his girlfriend because he is a hostile guy or because he was in a bad mood that day?

■ *Controllable/uncontrollable causes:* We perceive that people have power over some causes (for instance, by preparing delicious food for a picnic) but not others (rain on picnic day). So, if Henry's picnic is spoiled by a rainstorm, we would not hold that against him.

Attributional Errors and Biases

In attribution theory, the person who produces the behavior to be explained is called the *actor.* The person who offers a causal explanation of the actor's behavior is called the *observer.* Actors often explain their own behavior in terms of external causes. In contrast, observers frequently explain the actor's behavior in terms of internal causes. Susannah might explain that she honked her car horn at someone who was slow to move when the light turned green because she was in a hurry to get to the hospital to see her ill father, but the other driver might think she was rude.

● **fundamental attribution error** Observers' overestimation of the importance of internal traits and underestimation of the importance of external situations when they seek explanations of an actor's behavior.

● **false consensus effect** Observers' overestimation of the degree to which everybody else thinks or acts the way they do.

In committing the **fundamental attribution error,** observers overestimate the importance of internal traits and underestimate the importance of external situations when they seek explanations of an actor's behavior (Jones & Harris, 1967; Kressel & Uleman, 2010; Ramsey & de C. Hamilton, 2010) (Figure 51.1). For example, seeing news coverage of the prisoner abuse that occurred in the Abu Ghraib prison in Iraq, an observer might have concluded, "Those guards were cruel people." In fact, situational factors, such as orders from their superiors, may have influenced their behavior (Haney & Zimbardo, 2009).

Heuristics in Social Information Processing

Heuristics are cognitive shortcuts that allow us to make decisions rapidly. Just as heuristics are useful in general information processing, they can play a role in social information processing (Chaiken & Ledgerwood, 2007; Reimer & Rieskamp, 2007). Indeed, heuristics are helpful tools for navigating the complex social landscape, although they can lead to mistakes (Weaver & others, 2007). Stereotypes can be considered a type of heuristic in that they allow us to make quick judgments using very little information.

Observer Tends to give internal, trait explanations of actor's behavior

"She's late with her report because she can't concentrate on her own responsibilities."

Actor Tends to give external, situational explanations of own behavior

"I'm late with my report because other people keep asking me to help them with their projects."

FIGURE 51.1   The Fundamental Attribution Error In this situation, the supervisor is the observer, and the employee is the actor.

A common heuristic is the false consensus effect. Ask yourself: "How many students at your school support the death penalty?" Your answer is likely to depend on whether *you* support the death penalty. The **false consensus effect** is the overestimation of the degree to which everybody else thinks or acts the way we do. False consensus effects can be important in social interactions. Imagine, for example, that someone in a group to which you belong makes a racially insensitive remark. According to the false consensus effect, that person is likely to interpret silence on the part of others in the group as agreement.

Note that the fundamental attribution error and the false consensus effect are both related to the special significance of our own thoughts and circumstances. Both of these effects reflect the vast amount of information we have about ourselves relative to the more limited information we have about other people, and they suggest the special place of the self in social information processing.

51·3 THE SELF AS A SOCIAL OBJECT

Each of us carries around mental representations of ourselves. We can think of the self as our schema, for who we are, what we are like (and not like), and how we feel about these perceptions. The self is different from other social objects because we know so much more about ourselves than we do about others. While we are more likely to think that behavior is very important to understanding who other people really are, we are more likely to think that our private thoughts and feelings are most indicative of our true self (Johnson, Robinson, & Mitchell, 2004).

The self is special not only because we have direct access to these private experiences but also because we value ourselves. One of the most important self-related variables is *self-esteem,* the degree to which we have positive or negative feelings about ourselves (Harter, 2006). In general, research has shown that it is good to feel good about oneself (Bosson & Swann, 2009).

Individuals with high self-esteem often possess a variety of **positive illusions**—rosy views of themselves that are not necessarily rooted in reality. Constantine Sedikides and his colleagues have shown that many of us think of ourselves as above average on a number of valued characteristics, including how trustworthy and attractive we are (Gregg & Sedikides, 2010; Hepper & Sedikides, 2010; Sedikides, 2007, 2009; Sedikides, Gaertner, & Vevea, 2005; Sedikides & Gregg, 2008; Sedikides & Skowronski, 2009). Of course, the very definition of *average* indicates that not all of us can be "above average."

Shelley Taylor and her colleagues have demonstrated that having positive illusions about the self is often related to heightened well-being (Taylor, 2011; Taylor & Sherman, 2008; Taylor & others, 2003a, 2003b, 2007). Individuals who tend to have positive illusions about themselves are psychologically healthier and more likely to be judged positively by others. Self-esteem also affects our attributions about our own behavior. Individuals with high self-esteem, for instance, tend to give themselves breaks when it comes to judging their own behavior.

Self-serving bias refers to the tendency to take credit for our successes and to deny responsibility for our failures. Think about taking a psychology exam. If you do well, you are likely to take credit for that success ("I'm smart" or "I knew that stuff"); you tend to make internal attributions. If you do poorly, however, you are more likely to blame situational factors ("The test was too hard"); you tend to make external attributions.

Self-Objectification

Barbara Fredrickson and Tomi-Ann Roberts (1997) examined how another aspect of the self might relate to important outcomes. **Self-objectification** refers to the tendency to see oneself primarily as an object in others' eyes. According to these researchers, women have been socialized to think of themselves and their physical bodies as objects in the social world.

In a series of studies, Fredrickson and her colleagues asked men and women first to try on certain clothing—either a sweater or a swimsuit—and then to complete a math test. The researchers found that after trying on a swimsuit, women performed much more poorly on the math test. They surmised that trying on the swimsuit had heightened women's experience of

● **positive illusions** Positive views of the self that are not necessarily rooted in reality.

● **self-serving bias** The tendency to take credit for our successes and to deny responsibility for our failures.

● **self-objectification** The tendency to see oneself primarily as an object in the eyes of others.

psychological *inquiry*

Competence

Appearance | Personal characteristics

Adapted from Heflick & Goldenberg, 2009.

Objectifying Sarah Palin

The graph shows the results of a study in which participants first evaluated Sarah Palin (or, alternatively, Angelina Jolie) in terms of her appearance or her personal characteristics and then rated her competence. The Y axis shows the competence ratings; the X axis shows the dimension on which she was first evaluated. Answer the questions below.

1. What were the independent and dependent variables in this study?

2. Participants were randomly assigned to evaluate Sarah Palin (or Angelina Jolie) in terms of either her appearance or her personal qualities. Why was random assignment important?

3. If this study had been conducted *after* it was widely known that the Republican Party had paid for a $150,000 makeover for Palin, how do you think that might have influenced the results?

4. Objectification theory focuses primarily on appearance concerns for women. Can you think of a quality that would produce similar results for men?

self-objectification and body shame and reduced their mental resources for completing the math test (Fredrickson & others, 1998).

Subsequent studies have demonstrated that making woman aware of their status as sexual objects can induce body image concerns, shame, and restricted eating (Moradi & Huang, 2008). Chronic feelings of objectification are associated with lower self-esteem and higher levels of depression (Miner-Rubino, Twenge, & Fredrickson, 2002). Thus, research suggests that the social importance given to women's physical appearance has significant consequences for women. How might focusing on physical appearance influence *others'* perceptions of women?

Consider that in the 2008 U.S. presidential election, the media and others commented regularly on the physical appearance of Governor Sarah Palin, John McCain's vice presidential running mate. The fact that Palin had once been a beauty queen was also a common topic of discussion. Could such commentary influence perceptions of Palin's qualifications to be vice president? To address this question, in a study conducted just weeks before the election, Nathan Heflick and Jamie Goldenberg (2009) asked participants to look at pictures of either Sarah Palin or Angelina Jolie and to evaluate these women based on either their appearance or their personal characteristics. Then the participants rated the competence of the woman whose picture they had viewed. The results showed that regardless of which woman they were rating—Palin or Jolie—the participants rated her as less competent when they had first focused on evaluating her appearance. The Psychological Inquiry explores these results.

Stereotype Threat

Stereotypes not only influence our views of others but also sometimes influence the feelings and performance of individuals in stereotyped groups (Rydell & Boucher, 2010; Seacat & Mickelson, 2009). **Stereotype threat** is an individual's fast-acting, self-fulfilling fear of being judged based on a negative stereotype about his or her group. A person who experiences stereotype threat is well aware of stereotypical expectations for him or her as a member of the group. In stereotype-relevant situations, the individual experiences

● **stereotype threat** An individual's fast-acting, self-fulfilling fear of being judged based on a negative stereotype about his or her group.

anxiety about living "down" to expectations and consequently underperforms (Armenta, 2010; Schmader & others, 2009). Claude Steele and Eliot Aronson (1995, 2004) have shown that when a test is presented to African American and Euro-American students who have first simply checked a box indicating their ethnicity, the African Americans perform more poorly. In situations where ethnicity was not made salient, no differences in performance emerged.

Research has also demonstrated that stereotype threat affects performance on math tests by women compared to men, even when both groups have equally strong math training (Spencer, Steele, & Quinn, 1999). White men, too, can fall prey to stereotype threat; in a study of golf ability, Euro-American men performed more poorly than African American men when they were told the test measured "natural athletic ability" (Stone, 2002). Asian women did better on a math test if asked first for their ethnicity, but they scored more poorly if asked first about their gender (Shih & others, 2007).

Researchers have begun to identify factors that may help prevent the consequences of stereotype threat. For example, in one study, African American schoolchildren who were asked their race prior to a math test performed more poorly unless the test was presented to them as a challenge, not as a threat (Alter & others, 2010). Some research suggests that self-esteem may help buffer the effects of stereotype threat in women, especially if women are reminded of another aspect of the self (for instance, "college student") that is positively associated with math performance (Rydell & Boucher, 2010).

Social Comparison

Have you ever felt a sense of accomplishment about getting a *B* on a test, only to feel deflated when you found out that your friend in the class got an *A*? We gain self-knowledge from our own behavior, of course, but we also acquire it from others through **social comparison,** the process by which we evaluate our thoughts, feelings, behaviors, and abilities in relation to other people. Social comparison helps us to evaluate ourselves, tells us what our distinctive characteristics are, and aids us in building an identity.

More than 50 years ago, Leon Festinger (1954) proposed a theory of social comparison. According to this theory, when no objective means are available to evaluate our opinions and abilities, we compare ourselves with others. Furthermore, to get an accurate appraisal of ourselves, we are most likely to compare ourselves with others who are similar to us. Social comparison theory has been extended and modified over the years and continues to provide an important rationale for how we come to know ourselves (Dijkstra, Gibbons, & Buunk, 2010; Mussweiler, 2009).

Festinger concentrated on comparisons with those who are similar to us; other researchers have focused on downward social comparisons, that is, comparisons with those whom we consider inferior to us. Individuals under threat (from negative feedback or low self-esteem, for example) try to feel better by comparing themselves with others who are less fortunate (Wayment & O'Mara, 2008). It can be comforting to think, "Well, at least I'm not as bad off as that guy."

51·4 ATTITUDES

Attitudes are our feelings, opinions, and beliefs about people, objects, and ideas. We have attitudes about all sorts of things. Social psychologists are interested in how attitudes relate to behavior and in whether and how attitudes can change (Bohner & Dickel, 2011; Jost, Federico, & Napier, 2009).

Can Attitudes Predict Behavior?

People sometimes say one thing but do another. You might report positive attitudes about recycling on a survey but still pitch an aluminum soda can in the trash. Studies

● **social comparison** The process by which individuals evaluate their thoughts, feelings, behaviors, and abilities in relation to other people.

● **attitudes** Our feelings, opinions, and beliefs about people, objects, and ideas.

over the past half-century indicate some of the conditions under which attitudes guide actions (McGuire, 2004; Schomerus, Matschinger, & Angermeyer, 2009):

- *When the person's attitudes are strong* (Ajzen, 2001): For example, senators whose attitudes toward the president are "highly favorable" are more likely to vote for the president's policies than are senators who have only "moderately favorable" attitudes toward the chief executive.

- *When the person shows a strong awareness of his or her attitudes and when the person rehearses and practices them* (Fazio & Olsen, 2007; Fazio & others, 1982): For example, a person who has been asked to give a speech about the benefits of recycling is more likely to recycle than is an individual with the same attitude about recycling who has not put the idea into words or defined it in public.

- *When the person has a vested interest* (Sivacek & Crano, 1982): People are more likely to act on attitudes when the issue at stake is something that will affect them personally. For example, a classic study examined whether students would show up for a rally protesting a change that would raise the legal drinking age from 18 to 21 (Sivacek & Crano, 1982). Although students in general were against the change, only those in the critical age group (from 18 to 20) turned out to protest.

Can Behavior Predict Attitudes?

Just as attitudes guide behavior, ample evidence also exists that changes in behavior sometimes precede changes in attitudes. Social psychologists offer two main explanations for why behavior influences attitudes: cognitive dissonance theory and self-perception theory.

COGNITIVE DISSONANCE THEORY

● **cognitive dissonance** An individual's psychological discomfort (dissonance) caused by two inconsistent thoughts.

Cognitive dissonance, a concept developed by Festinger (1957), is an individual's psychological discomfort (*dissonance*) caused by two inconsistent thoughts. According to the theory, we feel uneasy when we notice an inconsistency between what we believe and what we do. Cognitive dissonance is at the root of that uncomfortable feeling of being a hypocrite (McConnell & Brown, 2010).

In their classic study of cognitive dissonance, Festinger and J. Merrill Carlsmith (1959) asked college students to engage in a series of very boring tasks, such as sorting spools into trays and turning wooden pegs. These participants were later asked to persuade another student (who was in fact a confederate) to participate in the study by telling him that the task was actually interesting and enjoyable. Half of the participants were randomly assigned to be paid $1 for telling this white lie, and the other half received $20. Afterward, all of the participants rated how interesting and enjoyable the task really was.

Curiously, those who were paid only $1 to tell the lie rated the task as significantly more enjoyable than those who were paid $20. Festinger and Carlsmith reasoned that those paid $20 to tell the lie could attribute their behavior to the high value of the money they received. On the other hand, those who were paid $1 experienced cognitive dissonance. The inconsistency between what they *did* (tell a lie) and what they *were paid for it* (just $1) moved these individuals to change their attitudes about the task ("I wouldn't lie for just $1. If I said I liked the task, I must have really liked it.").

We can reduce cognitive dissonance in one of two ways: change our behavior to fit our attitudes or change our attitudes to fit our behavior. In the classic study above, participants changed their attitudes about the task to match their behavior. Thus, when our attitudes and behavior are at odds, our behavior can influence our attitudes. After you have pitched that soda can, for example, you might feel guilty and relieve that guilt by deciding, "Recycling is not really that important."

Effort justification, one type of dissonance reduction, means rationalizing the amount of effort we put into something. Psychologists have used the concept of effort justification to explain an individual's strong feelings of loyalty toward a group after enduring experiences such as the initiation rites to get into Greek organizations, boot camp in the Marines, and the rigors of medical school en route to becoming a physician. From a cognitive dissonance perspective, individuals in these situations are likely to think, "If it's this tough to get into, it must be worth it." Thus, working hard to get into an organization or a profession can change our attitudes about it.

SELF-PERCEPTION THEORY

Self-perception theory is Daryl Bem's (1967) take on how behavior influences attitudes. According to self-perception theory, individuals make inferences about their attitudes by perceiving their behavior. That is, behaviors can cause attitudes, because when we are questioned about our attitudes, we think back on our behaviors for information. When asked about your attitude toward exercise, for example, you might think, "Well, I run every morning, so I must like it." From Bem's perspective, your behavior has led you to recognize something about yourself that you had not noticed before. Bem believes that we are especially likely to look to our own behavior to determine our attitudes when our attitudes are not completely clear.

Figure 51.2 compares cognitive dissonance theory and self-perception theory. Both theories have merit in explaining the connection between attitudes and behavior, and these opposing views bring to light the complexity that may exist in this connection. Both theories suggest that attitudes can be changed by behavior. Another route to attitude change is persuasion.

Working hard to get into a group inspires loyalty through cognitive dissonance.

● **self-perception theory** Bem's theory on how behaviors influence attitudes, stating that individuals make inferences about their attitudes by perceiving their behavior.

Persuasion

Persuasion involves trying to change someone's attitude—and often his or her behavior as well (Perrin & others, 2010). There are two central questions with respect to persuasion: What makes an individual decide to give up an original attitude and adopt

Festinger Cognitive Dissonance Theory

We are motivated toward consistency between attitudes and behavior and away from inconsistency.

Example: "I hate my job. I need to develop a better attitude toward it or else quit."

Bem Self-Perception Theory

We make inferences about our attitudes by perceiving and examining our behavior and the context in which it occurs, which might involve inducements to behave in certain ways.

Example: "I am spending all of my time thinking about how much I hate my job. I really must not like it."

FIGURE 51.2 Two Theories of the Connections Between Attitudes and Behavior Although we often think of attitudes as causing behavior, behavior can change attitudes, through either dissonance reduction or self-perception.

a new one, and what makes a person decide to act on an attitude that he or she has not acted on before? Teachers, lawyers, and sales representatives study techniques that will help them sway their audiences (children, juries, and buyers). Presidential candidates have arsenals of speechwriters and image consultants to help ensure that their words are persuasive. Perhaps the most skilled persuaders of all are advertisers, who draw on a full array of techniques to sell everything from cornflakes to carpets to cars. Let's review the various elements of persuasion, which were originally identified by Carl Hovland and his colleagues (Hovland, Janis, & Kelley, 1953; Janis & Hovland, 1959):

- *The communicator (source):* Suppose you are running for president of the student body. You tell your fellow students that you are going to make life at your college better. Will they believe you? Most likely, that will depend on your characteristics as a communicator. Whether the students believe you will depend in large part on your credibility—how much other students trust what you say. Trustworthiness, expertise, power, attractiveness, likability, and similarity are all credibility characteristics that help a communicator change people's attitudes or convince them to act.

- *The medium:* Another persuasion factor is the medium or technology used to get the message across. Consider the difference between watching a presidential debate on television and reading about it in the newspaper. Because it presents live images, television is generally a more powerful medium than print sources for changing attitudes.

- *The target (audience):* Age and attitude strength are two characteristics of the audience that determine whether a message will be effective. Younger people are more likely to change their attitudes than older ones. As well, it is easier to change weak attitudes than strong ones.

- *The message:* What kind of message is persuasive? Some messages involve strong logical arguments, and others focus on exciting emotions such as fear and anger in the audience. Which is more likely to work and when? The elaboration likelihood model addresses this question.

● **elaboration likelihood model** Theory identifying two ways to persuade: a central route and a peripheral route.

The **elaboration likelihood model** identifies two ways to persuade: a central route and a peripheral route (DeMarree & Petty, 2007; Petty & Brinol, 2008; Petty & Cacioppo, 1986). The central route to persuasion works by engaging someone thoughtfully with a sound, logical argument. The peripheral route involves non-message factors such as the source's credibility and attractiveness or emotional appeals. The peripheral route is effective when people are not paying close attention or do not have the time or energy to think about what the communicator is saying (Brewer, Barnes, & Sauer, 2010). As you might guess, television advertisers often use the peripheral route to persuasion on the assumption that during the commercials you are probably not paying full attention to the screen. However, the central route is more persuasive when people have the ability and the motivation to pay attention to the facts (Sparks & Areni, 2008).

SUCCESSFUL PERSUASION

Sooner or later, nearly everyone will be in a position of selling someone something. Social psychologists have studied a variety of ways in which social psychological principles influence whether a salesperson makes that sale (Cialdini, 1993).

One strategy for making a sale is called the *foot-in-the-door* technique (Freedman & Fraser, 1966). The foot-in-the-door strategy involves making a smaller request ("Would you be interested in a three-month trial subscription to a magazine?") at the beginning, saving the biggest demand ("How about a full year?") for last. The foot-in-the-door strategy relies on the notion that in agreeing to the smaller offer, the customer has created a relationship with the seller, expressing some level of trust.

Hillary Clinton called on her powers of persuasion when she ran for president in 2008, and she relies on persuasion today in her role as secretary of state.

Robert Cialdini and his colleagues introduced a different strategy, called the *door-in-the-face* technique (Cialdini & others, 1975). The door-in-the-face strategy involves making the biggest pitch at the beginning ("Would you be interested in a full-year subscription?"), which the customer probably will reject, and then making a smaller, "concessionary" demand ("Okay, then, how about a three-month trial?"). The door-in-the-face technique relies on the fact that the customer feels a sense of reciprocity and obligation: Because you let him off the hook with that big request, maybe he should be nice and take that smaller offer.

Cognitive dissonance can also be a powerful tool in sales. Sometimes the harder we work to buy something, the more we want it. After all, did you *buy* that strange lamp on eBay-—or did you *win* it?

RESISTING PERSUASION

Advertisers and salespeople work their hardest to persuade us to buy their products. How do we resist their appeals? According to William McGuire, one way to resist persuasion is through *inoculation* (McGuire, 2003; McGuire & Papageorgis, 1961). McGuire proposed that just as administering a vaccine inoculates individuals from a virus by introducing a weakened or dead version of that virus to the immune system, giving people a weak version of a persuasive message and allowing them time to argue against it can help individuals avoid persuasion.

Research has shown that such "inoculation" helps college students resist plagiarism (Compton & Pfau, 2008) as well as credit card marketing appeals (Compton & Pfau, 2004). When individuals are warned that they are going to be hit with persuasive appeals and are given arguments to help them resist these pitches, they are able to do so. Consider yourself inoculated: Credit card companies often prey on college students.

SUMMARY

The face conveys information to social perceivers, including attractiveness. Self-fulfilling prophecy means that our expectations of others can have a powerful impact on their behavior.

Attributions are our thoughts about why people behave as they do and about who or what is responsible for the outcome of events. Attribution theory views people as motivated to discover the causes of behavior as part of their effort to make sense of it. The dimensions used to make sense of the causes of human behavior include internal/external, stable/unstable, and controllable/uncontrollable.

The fundamental attribution error is observers' tendency to overestimate traits and to underestimate situations when they explain an actor's behavior. Self-serving bias means attributing our successes to internal causes and blaming our failures on external causes. Heuristics are used as shortcuts in social information processing. One such heuristic is a stereotype—a generalization about a group's characteristics that does not consider any variations among individuals in the group.

The self is our mental representation of our own characteristics. Self-esteem is important and is related to holding unrealistically positive views of ourselves. Stereotype threat is an individual's fast-acting, self-fulfilling fear of being judged based on a negative stereotype about his or her group. In order to understand ourselves better, we might engage in social comparison, evaluating ourselves by comparison with others.

Attitudes are our feelings—about people, objects, and ideas. We are better able to predict behavior on the basis of attitudes when an individual's attitudes are strong, when the person is aware of his or her attitudes and expresses them often, and when the attitudes are specifically relevant to the behavior. Sometimes changes in behavior precede changes in attitude.

KEY TERMS

social psychology   472
stereotype   472
attribution theory   474
fundamental attribution error   474
false consensus effect   474
positive illusions   475
self-serving bias   475

self-objectification   475
stereotype threat   476
social comparison   477
attitudes   477
cognitive dissonance   478
self-perception theory   479
elaboration likelihood model   480

According to cognitive dissonance theory, our strong need for cognitive consistency causes us to change our behavior to fit our attitudes or to change our attitudes to fit our behavior. Self-perception theory stresses the importance of making inferences about attitudes by observing our own behavior, especially when our attitudes are not clear.

Persuasion involves trying to change someone's attitude and often his or her behavior as well. Skilled persuaders draw on an array of techniques to accomplish their goals. But people can become resistant to persuasion via a technique called inoculation.

TEST YOURSELF

1. What do psychologists mean by a stereotype, and how do they define a stereotype threat?

2. What is involved in making a fundamental attribution error? Give an example of such an error.

3. Identify and briefly explain the four elements of persuasion.

APPLY YOUR KNOWLEDGE

1. Check out this website to see how the averaging of faces works: http://www.faceresearch.org/demos/average. Pick some faces you consider unattractive. What happens when you average them together? If you have a digital photograph of yourself and some friends, see what happens when you average those faces. Do you agree that average faces are more attractive than any single face?

2. We are often unaware of how many attributions we make about the behavior of others. To demonstrate this point to yourself, spend some time in a crowded area observing the interactions of others (or instead watch some scenes in television shows or movies). Take careful notes about the social behaviors that occur and then document your impression of why the individuals behaved as they did. What cues did you use in making your attributions about their behavior? Did your knowledge of the fundamental attribution error influence your attributions? Why or why not?

Social Behavior

Of course, we do not just think socially; we also behave in social ways. Two particular types of behavior that have interested psychologists represent the extremes of human social activity: altruism and aggression.

52·1 ALTRUISM

In 2009, Rick Hohl, a Florida man, heard about a sheriff's deputy in dire need of a kidney transplant. Hohl made an on-the-spot decision to be tested, and he eventually donated his kidney to Johnnie Briggs, a complete stranger (Farris, 2009). Asked why he did it, Hohl replied, in tears, "I'm a Christian." He added, "And I just want to make a difference."

Such a selfless act of kindness is a part of our social experience, as are the huge relief efforts that have followed disasters such as the massive earthquakes in Haiti and Chile in 2010. In everyday life, we witness and perform "random acts of kindness"—maybe adding a quarter to someone's expired parking meter or giving up our seat on a bus to someone in need. We may volunteer for the Special Olympics or serve as a literacy tutor. What all of these acts have in common is **altruism,** an unselfish interest in helping another person (N. Eisenberg & others, 2009).

In examining potentially altruistic behavior (or *prosocial behavior*), psychologists have questioned just how genuinely selfless it is. Some psychologists even argue that true altruism has never been demonstrated (Cialdini, 1991; Maner & others, 2002). True altruism means giving to another person with the ultimate goal of benefiting that person. In contrast to altruism is **egoism,** which involves giving to another person to gain self-esteem; to present oneself as powerful, competent, or caring; or to avoid censure, both from oneself and from society, for failing to live up to expectations. Egoism may also entail helping another person because we want to increase the chances that the person will return the favor someday—that is, we may be kind to another person to ensure *reciprocity.*

The principle of reciprocity encourages us to do unto others as we would have them do unto us. Reciprocity lies at the heart of the Golden Rule. Reciprocity involves an expression of trust for another person, as well as feelings of obligation and guilt. The principle of reciprocity means that we behave kindly, as kidney donor Rick Hohl did, under the assumption that someone will show us the same kindness someday.

Evolutionary Views of Altruism

Altruism has presented a puzzle for evolutionary psychologists (Leigh, 2010; Phillips, Ferguson, & Rijsdijk, 2010). How can a behavior that rewards others, and not oneself, be adaptive? Interestingly, kindness is not exclusive to humans. Ethologists studying nonhuman primates have shown that altruistic acts of kindness also occur in other species (de Waal, Leimgruber, & Greenberg, 2008). Perhaps kindness is not a mystery but an important adaptation.

Evolutionary theorists note that helping is especially likely to occur among family members, because helping a relative also means promoting the survival of the family's genes (Leigh, 2010). Evolutionary theorists believe that reciprocity in relationships with nonfamily members is essentially the mistaken application of a heuristic that made sense in human evolutionary history—to engage in selfless acts of kindness to one's own family (Nowak, Page, & Sigmund, 2000).

● **altruism** Unselfish interest in helping another person.

● **egoism** Giving to another person to ensure reciprocity; to gain self-esteem; to present oneself as powerful, competent, or caring; or to avoid censure from oneself and others for failing to live up to society's expectations.

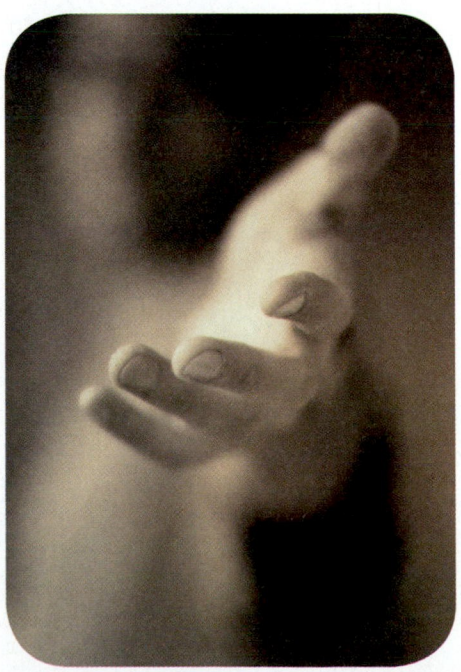

Dale Miller (1999, 2001) suggested that altruism may be an expression of true human nature. From Miller's perspective, although human beings are socialized to believe that the human species is naturally selfish, a great deal of research indicates that humans are not necessarily self-centered and do not engage in selfish acts as a natural response (Holmes, Miller, & Lerner, 2002).

Psychological Factors in Altruism

A number of psychological factors have been examined as playing a role in prosocial behavior. Here we examine mood and empathy.

MOOD AND HELPING

A distinct psychological component of altruistic behavior is mood. The research literature strongly concludes that happy people are more likely to help others than are unhappy people (Snyder & Lopez, 2007). Does it then follow that when they are in a bad mood, people are less likely to help? Not necessarily, because adults (especially) generally understand that doing good for another person can be a mood booster. Thus, when in a bad mood, they might be likely to help if they think that doing so will improve their mood. Even seeing another person act kindly can be a mood booster. The feelings we have when we see someone else do a good deed—referred to as *feelings of elevation*—also increase the chances that we will, in turn, do something kind ourselves (Schnall, Roper, & Fessler, 2010). Furthermore, sometimes those who have experienced distressing traumatic events find helping others to be an effective and meaningful way of coping (Staub & Vollhardt, 2008).

EMPATHY AND HELPING

● **empathy** A feeling of oneness with the emotional state of another person.

Another significant element of altruism is empathy (Saarni & others, 2006). **Empathy** is a person's feeling of oneness with the emotional state of another. Daniel Batson (2002, 2006; Batson & others, 2007) has spent the better part of his career searching for proof that truly altruistic behavior does exist. The key to such altruism, he believes, is the extent to which we are able to put ourselves in another person's shoes. When we are feeling empathy for someone else's plight, we are moved to action—not to make ourselves feel better but out of genuine concern for the other person. Empathy can produce altruistic behavior even toward members of rival groups and even when we believe no one will ever hear about our kind act (Fultz & others, 1986).

Sociocultural Factors in Altruism

Sociocultural research has examined the characteristics of cultures that are associated with the emergence of altruism and with the belief that everyone deserves fair treatment. A recent study comparing 15 different cultures examined two particular factors: market economies and investment in established religion (Henrich & others, 2010).

A market economy is a decentralized system featuring the free exchange of products and services between producers and consumers. Market economies, such as the U.S. economy, require individuals to extend the principle of reciprocity to strangers, because the normal flow of business requires a certain degree of trust. For example, when you order a book online, you assume a great deal on the part of the strangers who are selling you that book. You give them your credit card information, confident that they will not use it to purchase things and will not share it with someone else. Even though you have no personal knowledge of these sellers, you assume that they will not take advantage of you.

Another important factor in prosocial behavior across cultures is established religions. World religions tend to share an emphasis on the Golden Rule and on treating others fairly. A series of studies conducted with participants in places as varied as Papua New Guinea, Samburu in Kenya, and the U.S. state of Missouri demonstrated that prosocial behaviors were more common in communities characterized by market economies and by investment in established religion (Henrich & others, 2010).

In addition to these two broad cultural factors, social psychologists have examined other sociocultural variables as predictors of altruism and helping, including gender, the influence of bystanders, and the media.

ALTRUISM AND GENDER

Given the role of empathy in helping, we might think that women should be more likely to help than men. After all, stereotypes tell us that women are by nature more empathic than men. However, as in most domains, it is useful to think about gender in context (Best, 2010; N. Eisenberg & others, 2009). Researchers have found that women are more likely than men to help when the context involves nurturing, such as volunteering time to help a child with a personal problem. Men, on the other hand, are more likely to help in situations in which a perceived danger is present (for instance, picking up a hitchhiker) and in which they feel competent to help (as in assisting someone with a flat tire) (Eagly & Crowley, 1986).

THE BYSTANDER EFFECT

Nearly 50 years ago, a young woman named Kitty Genovese was brutally murdered in New York City. She was attacked at about 3 A.M. in a courtyard surrounded by apartment buildings. It took the slayer approximately 30 minutes to kill Genovese. Thirty-eight neighbors watched the gory scene from their windows and heard Genovese's screams. No one helped or called the police.

Inspired by the Genovese case, social psychologists John Darley and Bibb Latané (1968) conducted a number of studies on the **bystander effect,** the tendency of an individual who observes an emergency to help less when other people are present than when the observer is alone. Most bystander studies show that when alone, a person will help 75 percent of the time, but when another bystander is present, the figure drops to 50 percent. Apparently the difference is due to diffusion of responsibility among witnesses and the tendency to look to the behavior of others for cues about what to do. We may think that someone else will call the police or that, because no one else is helping, possibly the person does not need help.

The bystander effect is still in evidence today. In October 2009, in Richmond, California, a 15-year-old high school girl was raped and beaten by as many as 10 people outside a homecoming dance (CBS News, 2009a). During the assault, more than 20 people watched—and no one called for help.

- **bystander effect** The tendency of an individual who observes an emergency to help less when other people are present than when the observer is alone.

MEDIA INFLUENCES

Psychologists have long considered media influences to be a factor in aggressive behavior. Researchers are also investigating whether media can elicit prosocial behavior as well. Studies suggest that the answer is yes. For example, listening to music with prosocial lyrics can promote kindness (Greitemeyer, 2009), and watching television shows with positive content has been associated with prosocial behavior (Hearold, 1986).

Recently, a series of studies examined the effects of playing prosocial video games on behavior. In those studies, participants who had played a video game such as *Lemmings,* in which the player tries to save the hapless creatures from a variety of disasters, were more likely than those who had played either a neutral or a violent game to help an experimenter pick up a cup of spilled pencils (Greitemeyer & Osswald, 2010). More-over, in another study, participants who played a prosocial video game were more likely to intervene when a confederate posing as the experimenter's ex-boyfriend came in and began to harass her (Greitemeyer & Osswald, 2010). Thus, exposure to prosocial media may be an important way to spread kindness.

This discussion of altruism highlights the capacity of human beings to help one another, whether through a simple gesture like picking up pencils or a selfless act such as donating an organ. This ability to engage in kindness sits alongside other capacities, such as the capacity to cause others harm. Some evolutionary scientists have suggested that altruism, especially when it is directed at the members of one's own group, may coexist with hostile feelings and actions toward other groups (Arrow, 2007; Choi & Bowles, 2007). For example, a soldier may perform selfless, heroic acts of altruism for his or her country, but for a person on the other side of the combat, that behavior is harmful. Thus, altruism within a group may be linked to aggression.

52·2 AGGRESSION

● **aggression** Social behavior whose objective is to harm someone, either physically or verbally.

Aggression refers to social behavior whose objective is to harm someone, either physically or verbally. Aggression is an all-too-common occurrence in contemporary society. Murders in the United States take place at the rate of about 20,000 per year (U.S. Department of Justice, 2007).

Biological Influences in Aggression

There is nothing new about human aggression. The primate ancestors of human beings and the earliest humans are thought to have committed aggressive acts against others of their own kind. Researchers who approach aggression from a biological viewpoint examine the influence of evolutionary tendencies, genetics, and neurobiological factors.

EVOLUTIONARY VIEWS

Ethologists say that certain stimuli release innate aggressive responses (Lorenz, 1965; Tinbergen, 1969). For example, a male robin will attack another male bird when it sees the red patch on the other bird's breast. When the patch is removed, no attack takes place. However, in the animal kingdom, most hostile encounters do not escalate to killing or even severe harm. Much of the fighting is ritualistic and involves threat displays, for example, a cat arching its back, baring its teeth, and hissing or a chimpanzee staring, stomping the ground, and screaming.

Evolutionary theorists believe that human beings are not much different from other animals. A basic theme of their theory is the survival of the fittest (Barber, 2009; Cosmides, 2011). Thus, they conclude that early in human evolution the survivors were probably aggressive individuals.

In the animal world, aggression often is ritualistic and typically involves threat displays such as a cat's arching its back, baring its teeth, and hissing.

GENETIC BASIS

Genes are important in explaining the biological basis of aggression (Brooker & others, 2010). The selective breeding of animals provides evidence for genetic influences in aggression. After a number of breedings among only aggressive animals and among only docile animals, vicious and timid strains of animals emerge. The vicious strains attack nearly anything in sight; the timid strains rarely fight, even when attacked.

The genetic basis for aggression is more difficult to demonstrate in humans than animals and may depend on the type of aggression studied (L. A. Baker & others, 2008; Brendgen & others, 2008). Specifically, twin studies have shown that physical aggression that is proactive in nature may be more influenced by genes, but more reactive aggression and social aggression (for instance, starting rumors about someone) may be more susceptible to environmental effects. Also, genetic influences may be stronger for males than for females (L. A. Baker & others, 2008).

NEUROBIOLOGICAL FACTORS

In 1966, Charles Whitman climbed to the top of the campus tower at the University of Texas at Austin, killed 15 people below with a high-powered rifle, and then took his own life. An autopsy revealed a tumor in the limbic system of Whitman's brain, an area (including the amygdalae and hippocampus) associated with emotion. Indeed, although humans do not appear to have a specific aggression center in the brain, aggressive behavior often results when areas such as the limbic system are stimulated by electric currents (Herbert, 1988; Wood & Liossi, 2006).

The frontal lobes of the brain—the areas most involved in executive functions such as planning and self-control—have also been implicated in aggression. Research by Adriane Raine and his colleagues has examined the brains of individuals who have committed the ultimate act of violence: murder (Raine, 2008; Yang, Glen, & Raine, 2008). The results indicate that murderers may differ from others in deficits in the functioning of these areas of the brain.

Neurotransmitters—particularly, lower levels of serotonin—have been linked to aggressive behavior (Neumann, Veenema, & Beiderbeck, 2010; Rosell & others, 2010). In one study, young men whose serotonin levels were low relative to those of other men their age were far more likely to have committed a violent crime (Moffitt & others, 1998). Similarly, aggressive children have lower levels of serotonin than do children who display low rates of aggression (Blader, 2006; Nevels & others, 2010).

Hormones are another biological factor that may play a role in aggression. The hormone that is typically implicated in aggressive behavior is testosterone. Research on rats and other animals has shown that testosterone relates to aggression (Cunningham & McGinnis, 2007). However, results with humans have been less consistent (van Bokhoven & others, 2006).

A fascinating study examined how testosterone is influenced by experience and how experience and testosterone together might help explain aggression (Klinesmith, Kasser, & McAndrew, 2006). In this study, college men interacted with either a gun or a child's toy. Testosterone was measured before and after this phase of the study. Men who interacted with the gun showed higher increases in testosterone, compared to the control group. Furthermore, later in the study, the men who had interacted with the gun were more aggressive (they put more hot sauce in a cup of water they thought someone else was going to drink). The role of testosterone in this increase in aggression suggests that testosterone changes may shed light on why some people respond more aggressively to violent cues than do others (Klinesmith, Kasser, & McAndrew, 2006).

At this point it is worth noting that many of the studies of aggression that have been conducted in social psychology laboratories rely on a variety of behaviors that may be considered aggressive even if they do not involve, for example, actually punching someone in the face. In studies on aggression, participants might have an opportunity to "aggress" against another, for instance, by subjecting the individual to a blast of loud noise, dispensing a mild electrical shock, or even, as in the study described above, administering a large dose of Tabasco to swallow. Whether these operational definitions of aggression are applicable to real-life violence is a matter of much debate (Savage & Yancey, 2008).

Social psychologists sometimes ask the participants in a study to assign the amount of hot sauce a person must drink as a measure of aggression. Do you think that is a good operational definition of aggression?

Psychological Influences in Aggression

Numerous psychological factors appear to be involved in aggression. They include individuals' responses to circumstances, as well as cognitive and learning factors.

FRUSTRATING AND AVERSIVE CIRCUMSTANCES

Many years ago, John Dollard and his colleagues (1939) proposed that *frustration,* the blocking of an individual's attempts to reach a goal, triggers aggression. The *frustration-aggression hypothesis* states that frustration always leads to aggression. Soon, however, psychologists found that aggression is not the only possible response to frustration. Some individuals who experience frustration become passive, for example (N. E. Miller, 1941).

Psychologists later recognized that, besides frustration, a broad range of aversive experiences can cause aggression. They include physical pain, personal insults, crowding, and unpleasant events. Aversive circumstances also include factors in the physical environment, such as the weather. Murder, rape, and assault increase when temperatures are the highest, as well as in the hottest years and the hottest cities (Anderson & Bushman, 2002).

Aversive circumstances that might stimulate aggression include factors in the physical environment such as noise, crowding, and heat waves.

COGNITIVE DETERMINANTS

Aspects of the environment may prime us to behave aggressively (Englander, 2006). Recall that priming can involve making something salient to a person, even subliminally or without the person's awareness. Leonard Berkowitz (1993; Berkowitz & LePage, 1996) has shown how the mere presence of a weapon (such as a gun) may prime hostile thoughts and produce aggression (Anderson, Benjamin, & Bartholow, 1998). Indeed, in accordance with Berkowitz's ideas, a well-known study in 1993 found that individuals who lived in a household with a gun were 2.7 times more likely to be murdered than those dwelling in a household without a gun (Kellerman & others, 1993).

A variety of other cognitive factors determine whether an individual responds aggressively to aversive situations (Baumeister, 1999; Berkowitz, 1990; DeWall & others, 2009). For instance, if a person perceives that another's actions are unfair or intentionally hurtful, aggression is more likely to occur. Indeed, in the workplace, individuals who perceive that they have been treated unfairly are more likely to aggress, verbally and physically, against supervisors (Dupre & Barling, 2006).

OBSERVATIONAL LEARNING

Social cognitive theorists believe that individuals learn aggression through reinforcement and observational learning (Englander, 2006). Watching others engage in aggressive actions can evoke aggression, as you might recall from the classic Bobo doll study described in Module 20 (Bandura, 1986). One of the most frequent opportunities people have to observe aggression in our culture is to watch violence on television, which we consider further in the discussion below on media violence.

Sociocultural Influences in Aggression

Aggression involves not only biological and cognitive factors but also factors in the wider social world. Among the sociocultural factors in aggression are variations in economic inequity, the "culture of honor," and the extent to which people watch violence in the media.

CULTURAL VARIATIONS AND THE CULTURE OF HONOR

Aggression and violence are more common in some cultures than others (Kitayama, 2011; Kitayama & Cohen, 2007; Sorrentino & others, 2005). The U.S. homicide rate does not compare well with rates for other countries. For example, the U.S. homicide rate in 2004 was 5.5 per 100,000 (U.S. Bureau of Justice Statistics, 2006), five times the rate in Germany (BKA, 2006) and more than twice that of Canada (Canadian Statistics, 2005).

Crime rates tend to be higher in countries and communities with a considerable gap between the rich and poor (Messner, Raffalovich, & Shrock, 2002; Popp, 2006). The Gini index is a measure of income disparities between the richest and poorest citizens of a nation. The lower the number on the Gini index, the smaller the income disparity. In the United States the Gini index for 2005 was 45, compared to 30 for Germany and 31 for Canada (CIA, 2005).

Dov Cohen has examined the ways in which some cultural norms about masculine pride and family honor may foster aggressive behavior (Cohen, 2001; Vandello & Cohen, 2008; Vandello & others, 2009). In cultures of honor, a man's reputation is thought to be an essential aspect of his economic survival. Such cultures see insults to a man's honor as diminishing his reputation and view violence as a way to compensate for that loss. In these cultures, family pride might lead to so-called honor killings in which, for example, a female rape victim is slain by her male family members so that they, in turn, are not "contaminated" by the rape. In April 2009, a Jordanian man confessed to stabbing his pregnant sister with a meat cleaver because she had left her husband, and he believed she was seeing other men. He felt that he had to kill her to protect his family honor (Gavlak, 2009).

Cohen has examined how, in the United States, southerners are more likely than northerners to be aggressive when honor is at stake. In one study, Cohen and his colleagues (1996) had White men who were from either the North or the South take part in an experiment that required them to walk down a hallway. A confederate passed all the men, bumping against them and quietly calling them a derogatory name. The southerners were more likely than the northerners to think their masculine reputation was threatened, to become physiologically aroused by the insult, and to engage in actual aggressive or dominant acts. In contrast, the northerners were less likely to perceive a random insult as "fightin' words."

MEDIA VIOLENCE

Images of violence pervade the U.S. popular media: newscasts, television shows, sports broadcasts, movies, video games, and song lyrics. Evildoers kill and get killed; police and detectives violently uphold or even break society's laws; sports announcers glorify players regardless of whether their behavior is sportsmanlike or contributes to their team's success.

One reason that violence seems so alluring on TV and in the movies is that it usually is portrayed unrealistically. Viewers rarely see its lasting effects, and it is easy to get the message that aggression and violence are the norm—in fact, are the preferred mode of behavior—in the United States.

Although some critics reject the conclusion that TV violence causes aggression (Savage & Yancey, 2008), many scholars insist that TV violence can prompt aggressive or antisocial behavior in children (Anderson & Huesmann, 2007; Comstock & Scharrer, 2006; Dubow, Huesmann, & Greenwood, 2007). Of course, television violence is not the only cause of aggression in children or adults. There is no *one* cause of any social behavior. Aggression, like all other social behaviors, has multiple determinants. The link between TV violence and aggression in children is influenced by children's aggressive tendencies, by their attitudes toward violence, and by the monitoring of children's exposure to it. Perhaps the strongest predictor of aggression is witnessing aggression in one's own family (Ferguson & others, 2008).

Another type of media violence that has interested social psychologists is violent pornography. Violent pornography comprises films, videos, websites, and magazines portraying the degradation of women in a sexual context. An often asked question is, do such media foster violence toward women? Based on several meta-analyses and on research of their own, Neil Malamuth and his colleagues concluded that pornography consumption does have a small effect on male sexual aggression and is related to more

CRITICAL CONTROVERSY

Do Violent Video Games Lead to Violence?

On April 20, 1999, two teenagers, Eric Harris and Dylan Klebold, carried out a shooting rampage on their classmates and teachers at Columbine High School near Littleton, Colorado. Before killing themselves, they shot and killed 12 students and a teacher and wounded 24 others. In the wake of the slayings, the media reported that Harris and Klebold were fans of violent video games, including *Doom* and *Wolfenstein*. Some people began to wonder if the boys had been so obsessively occupied with these violent games that they could no longer distinguish between fantasy and reality. Indeed, the parents of some of the victims filed lawsuits against video game manufacturers, though with no success. Is it possible that video games promote violence?

Video games are an extremely potent medium. It has been suggested that violent video games engage children and adolescents so intensely that they experience an altered state of consciousness in which "rational thought is suspended and highly arousing aggressive scripts are increasingly likely to be learned" (Roberts, Henriksen, & Foehr, 2009, p. 328). Unlike other media, such as TV shows, video games allow the individual to play an active role in perpetrating violence.

Psychologists have examined the role of violent video games in empathy, attitudes about violence, and aggression. A recent meta-analysis concluded that children and adolescents who play violent video games extensively are more aggressive, less sensitive to real-life violence, more likely to engage in delinquent acts, and more likely to get lower grades in school than their counterparts who spend less time playing the games or do not play them at all (Anderson & others, 2010).

Social psychologist Craig Anderson has been a vocal spokesperson against media violence, especially violent video games (Anderson, 2003; Anderson & Huesmann, 2007; Bushman & Anderson, 2007; Gentile & Anderson, 2006). Critics of the work of Anderson and his colleagues have pointed out that the acts of aggression (for instance, blasting someone with loud noise) studied in the laboratory are not generalizable to real-world criminal violence (Ritter & Elsea, 2005; Savage, 2008; Savage & Yancey, 2008). Furthermore, they stress that many studies have not measured important third variables, such as family violence, in predicting both video game use and aggression (Ferguson & others, 2008; Ferguson & Kilburn, 2010).

The controversy over violent video games and aggression highlights the links among social psychology, public policy, and current events. Every technological innovation opens a new set of questions to be addressed by social psychologists.

WHAT DO YOU THINK?

- Do you or people you know play violent video games? If so, what impact, if any, do you think this activity has on your or their thoughts and feelings?
- Would you allow your child to play violent video games? Why or why not?
- What do you think policymakers should do with regard to the controversy over the effects of playing video games?

accepting attitudes about violence toward women (Hald, Malamuth, & Yuen, 2010; Malamuth, Addison, & Koss, 2000). Yet Malamuth and his colleagues caution that pornography is only one of a number of factors that may lead to sexual violence against women (Hald, Malamuth, & Yuen, 2010; Vega & Malamuth, 2007). The most problematic materials are those that depict women enjoying being the victims of male sexual violence (Hald, Malamuth, & Yuen, 2010). Such violent pornography reinforces the *rape myth*—the false belief that women desire coercive sex.

Violent video games are another form of media that might influence aggressive behavior. To read about this topic, see the Critical Controversy.

Reducing Aggression

Social cognitive theorists believe that people who act aggressively often are rewarded for their aggression and that individuals learn to be aggressive by watching others behave aggressively. Research has supported this view (Bandura, 1997). Thus, the strategies for reducing aggression that seem most promising are those designed to decrease rewards for aggression and to lessen exposure to it. Parents in particular have been targeted to help children to reduce aggression (Leaper & Friedman, 2007). Recommended parenting strategies include encouraging young children to develop empathy toward others and more closely monitoring adolescents' activities (Denham, Bassett, & Wyatt, 2007; N. Eisenberg & others, 2009).

SUMMARY

Altruism is an unselfish interest in helping someone else. Reciprocity often is involved in altruism. Individuals who are in a good mood are more helpful. Empathy is also linked to helping. The bystander effect means that individuals who observe an emergency help less when someone else is present than when they are alone.

Women are more likely to help in situations that are not dangerous and involve caregiving. Men are more likely to help in situations that involve danger or in which they feel competent.

One view of the biological basis of aggression is that early in human evolution, the most aggressive individuals were likely to be the survivors. Neurobiological factors involved in aggressive behavior include the neurotransmitter serotonin and the hormone testosterone. Psychological factors in aggression include frustrating and aversive circumstances. Sociocultural factors include cross-cultural variations, the culture of honor, and violence in the media. Males are consistently more physically aggressive than females.

KEY TERMS

altruism 483
egoism 483
empathy 484

bystander effect 485
aggression 486

TEST YOURSELF

1. What is the difference between altruism and egoism?
2. Explain the bystander effect, and give an example.
3. What have researchers found about the influence of prosocially oriented video games? What have they learned about the effects of violent video games?

APPLY YOUR KNOWLEDGE

1. Take a day and engage in altruistic behavior. Act as kindly toward others as you can, without telling anyone what you are up to. Keep track of your thoughts and feelings as you experience this day of kindness. How does it influence your feelings about altruism?

2. Reflect on your own aggressive actions. How do you explain or rationalize why you act the way you do? For one week, keep a chart that lists what happens before (antecedent) the aggressive moment, what happens during the aggressive moment (the behavior), and what results from your aggressive act (consequence).

Social Influence

Another topic of interest to social psychologists is how our behavior is influenced by other individuals and groups (Judd & Park, 2007; Monin, 2007; Perrin & others, 2010). This section explores key aspects of social influence: conformity, obedience, and group influence.

53-1 CONFORMITY AND OBEDIENCE

Research on conformity and obedience started in earnest after World War II. Psychologists sought answers to the disturbing question of how ordinary people could be influenced to commit the sort of atrocities inflicted on Jews, Gypsies, and other minorities during the Holocaust. Researchers wanted to know to what extent people would change their behavior to conform to the behavior of others.

Conformity

● **conformity** A change in a person's behavior to coincide more closely with a group standard.

Conformity is a change in a person's behavior to coincide more closely with a group standard. Conformity takes many forms and affects many aspects of people's lives, in negative and positive ways. Conformity is at work, for example, when a person comes to college and starts to drink alcohol heavily at parties, even though he or she might have never been a drinker before. Conformity is also at work when we obey the rules and regulations that allow society to run smoothly. Consider how chaotic it would be if people did not conform to social norms such as stopping at a red light, driving on the correct side of the road, and not punching others in the face. Conformity can also be a powerful way to increase group cohesion. Even something as simple as marching in step together or singing a song along with a group can lead to enhanced cooperation among group members (Wiltermuth & Heath, 2009).

ASCH'S EXPERIMENT

Put yourself in this situation: You are taken into a room where you see five other people seated along a table. A person in a white lab coat enters the room and announces that you are about to participate in an experiment on perceptual accuracy. The group is shown two cards—the first having only a single vertical line on it and the second having three vertical lines of varying length. You are told that the task is to determine which of the three lines on the second card is the same length as the line on the first card. You look at the cards and think, "What a snap. It's so obvious which is the same."

Homogeneous Originality by CIAgent

I just don't understand why you dress that way. Baggy pants and underwear showing.

I don't want to conform to a specific look. I want to show my individuality.

Yo!

Yo!

www.funnytimes.com

www.funnytimes.com

What you do not know is that the other people in the room are confederates who are working with the experimenter. On the first several trials, everyone agrees about which line matches the standard. Then on the fourth trial, each of the others picks the same incorrect line. As the last person to make a choice, you have the dilemma of responding as your eyes tell you or conforming to what the others before you said. How do you think you would answer?

Solomon Asch conducted this classic experiment on conformity in 1951 (Figure 53.1). Asch instructed the confederates to give incorrect responses on 12 of 18 trials. To his surprise, Asch (1951) found that the volunteer participants conformed to the incorrect answers 35 percent of the time. Subsequent research has supported the notion that the pressure to conform is strong (Pines & Maslach, 2002). Why do people go along with a group even when they have clear-cut information disputing the others, such as the lines in the Asch experiment? Social psychologists have addressed this question as well.

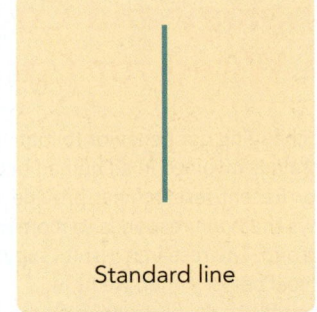
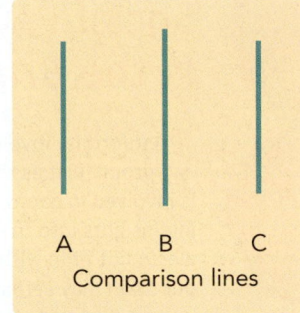

Standard line   Comparison lines

GOING ALONG TO BE RIGHT AND GOING ALONG TO BE LIKED

In general, two main factors have been identified as contributing to conformity: informational social influence and normative social influence.

Informational social influence refers to the influence other people have on us because we want to be right. The social group can provide us with information that we did not know or may help us see things in ways that had not occurred to us. As a result, we may conform because we have come to agree with the group. The tendency to conform based on informational social influence depends especially on two factors: how confident we are in our own independent judgment and how well informed we perceive the group to be. For example, in a discussion with three of your acquaintances who are IT geeks, you might just go along with their opinions about which new computer you should buy, especially if you do not know much about computers.

In contrast, **normative social influence** is the influence others have on us because we want them to like us. Whether the group is an inner-city gang or members of a profession such as medicine or law, if a particular group is important to us, we might adopt a clothing style that people in the group wear or use the same slang words, and we might assume the attitudes that characterize the group's members (Hewlin, 2009).

Conformity is a powerful social force, and on many occasions we undoubtedly feel more comfortable when we are able to go along with the crowd. You can feel the pressure of conformity for yourself if, the next time you get on an elevator with other people, you do not turn around to face the door. Why does it feel so wrong to face the back of the elevator? Recent research in social psychology and neuroscience has provided an interesting answer, as we shall see in the Intersection.

FIGURE 53.1   Asch's Conformity Experiment The figures at the top show the stimulus materials for the Asch conformity experiment on group influence. The photograph captures the puzzlement of one student after five confederates of the experimenter chose the incorrect line.

● **informational social influence** The influence other people have on us because we want to be right.

● **normative social influence** The influence others have on us because we want them to like us.

Obedience

Obedience is behavior that complies with the explicit demands of the individual in authority. We are obedient when an authority figure demands that we do something, and we do it. Note that in conformity, people change their thinking or behavior so that it will be more like that of others, while in obedience, there is an explicit demand to comply (Blass, 2007).

Obedient behavior sometimes can be distressingly cruel. One of the most infamous examples of the destructive nature of obedience is the Nazi crimes against Jews and

● **obedience** Behavior that complies with the explicit demands of the individual in authority.

Social Psychology and Cognitive Neuroscience: Is the Brain Wired for Conformity?

Conformity involves changing our behavior to match that of a group. Just as the brain is involved in all human behavior, it is involved in conformity. Recent research has provided intriguing insights into the ways the brain responds to moments when we do not fit in with a group. The research results suggest that our brain may actually "feel better" when we fit in.

In a recent study using fMRI, the brain-imaging technique described in Module 7, Vasily Klucharev and his colleagues examined what happens in the brain when people find out that their opinions conflict with those of others (Klucharev & others, 2009). Women were asked to rate a variety of female faces for attractiveness, and their brains were scanned while they received feedback about whether their ratings agreed with those of the other group members. When participants were told that their ratings differed from the group's ratings, they showed enhanced activation in the brain area typically associated with monitoring for errors. In other words, the brain responded to judgments that differed from the group judgments as if they were *mistakes*. Furthermore, when the women's ratings were different from the group's ratings, women experienced less activation in the nucleus accumbens and the ventral tegmental area, the brain's reward centers. The greater the degree to which women's brains responded to being different as an error and as

Why would humans be wired for conformity? Could the brain learn to enjoy being different?

not rewarding, the more they tended to conform when given a chance to re-rate the faces at the end of the study. Klucharev and colleagues suggest that their findings demonstrate that humans *learn* that conformity is rewarding.

In a second study, the researchers found that these effects were specific to social conformity. In that study, the women were given feedback about a *computer's* ratings of the faces. Results showed that the brain did not mind being different from a computer nearly as much as being different from a group of other humans.

others during World War II. More recent examples include the obedience of radical Muslims instructed to participate in suicide attacks against Israelis and Westerners (McCauley & Segal, 2009), as well as that of U.S. military personnel at Abu Ghraib prison in Iraq, who justified their horrendous abuse of detainees by asserting that they were "just following orders" (A. G. Miller, 2004). Millions of people throughout history have obeyed commands to commit terrible acts.

A classic series of experiments by Stanley Milgram (1965, 1974) provides insight into such obedience. Imagine that, as part of an experiment in psychology, you are asked to deliver a series of painful electric shocks to another person. You are told that the purpose of the study is to determine the effects of punishment on memory. Your role is to be the "teacher" and to punish the mistakes made by the "learner." Each time the learner makes a mistake, you are to increase the intensity of the shock.

You are introduced to the learner, a nice 50-year-old man who mumbles something about having a heart condition. He is strapped to a chair in the next room; he communicates with you through an intercom. The apparatus in front of you has 30 switches, ranging from 15 volts (slight) to 450 volts (marked as beyond dangerous, "XXX").

As the trials proceed, the learner quickly runs into trouble and is unable to give the correct answers. Should you shock him? As you increase the intensity of the shock, the learner says that he is in pain. At 150 volts, he demands to have the experiment stopped. At 180 volts, he cries out that he cannot stand it anymore. At 300 volts, he yells about his heart condition and pleads to be released. If you hesitate in shocking the learner, however, the experimenter tells you that you have no choice; the experiment must

"I don't care if you do think I'm 'dissing' you . . . I want you in the story corner NOW!"

continue. Eventually the learner stops responding altogether, and the experimenter tells you that not responding is the same as a wrong answer. At this point, the learner appears to be injured or even dead. Would you keep going?

Prior to doing the study, Milgram asked 40 psychiatrists how they thought individuals would respond to this situation. The psychiatrists predicted that most teachers would go no farther than 150 volts, that fewer than 1 in 25 would go as far as 300 volts, and that only 1 in 1,000 would deliver the full 450 volts. The psychiatrists were way off. As shown in Figure 53.2, the majority of the teachers obeyed the experimenter: Almost two-thirds delivered the full 450 volts.

By the way, the 50-year-old man was a confederate in the experiment. In Milgram's study, the learner was not being shocked at all. Of course, the teachers were unaware that the learner was only pretending to be shocked.

At very strong voltage levels, the learner quit responding. When the teacher asked the experimenter what to do, the experimenter simply replied, "You must go on. The experiment requires that you continue." Imagine that with those simple statements the experimenter was able to calmly command people to (as far as they knew) shock a man to unconsciousness and possibly death. Such is the power of obedience to authority.

In variations of the experiment, Milgram discovered that more people would disobey in certain circumstances. Specifically, disobedience was more common when participants could see others disobey, when the authority figure was not perceived to be legitimate and was not close by, and when the victim was made to seem more human.

The ethics of Milgram's studies has been a subject of controversy since he began them. The teachers in the experiment clearly felt anguish; some were very disturbed about "harming" another individual. All of the participants had been deceived by Milgram as part of the study. Even though they found out that they had not actually shocked or harmed anyone, was the anguish imposed on them ethical? Milgram's studies certainly revealed a great deal about human nature, and none of the volunteers expressed regret that they had taken part.

Under today's ethical guidelines, it is unlikely that these experiments would have been approved. Nonetheless, we are still learning from Milgram's data. A recent meta-analysis of his experiments suggested that the critical decision was at the 150-volt level, when the learner first requested that the experiment be halted. At that point, 80 percent of those who were going to stop did so (Packer, 2008). Apparently, individuals who were going to disobey were those who responded not to the later anguished cries of pain but to the learner's first request to be set free.

You might wonder whether Milgram's results would still apply in contemporary society. To examine this question, in 2006 social psychologist Jerry Burger (2009) re-created Milgram's study at Santa Clara University in California. Burger's study was very similar to Milgram's, except that in Burger's experiment the participants were never allowed to go higher than 150 volts. At 150 volts, the confederate asked to end the study, and immediately after participants decided whether to continue, the experiment was ended. Surprisingly, Burger's participants were only slightly less likely to obey than Milgram's had been. The Psychological Inquiry probes the results of Burger's study.

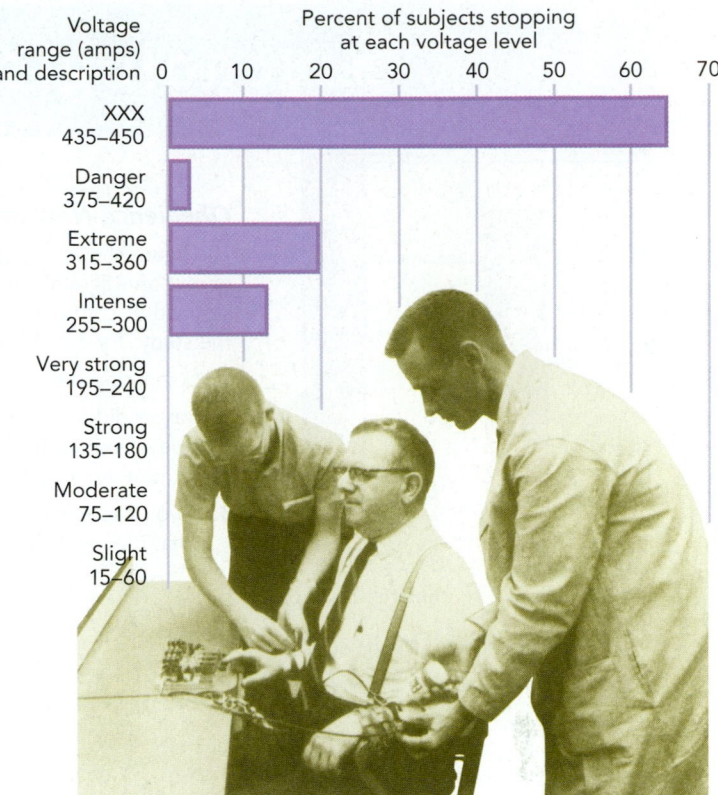

FIGURE 53.2 **Milgram Obedience Study** A 50-year-old man, the "learner," is strapped into a chair. The experimenter makes it look as if a shock generator is being connected to his body through several electrodes. The chart shows the percentage of "teachers" who stopped shocking the learner at each voltage level. Adapted from Stanley Milgram, "Behavioral Study of Obedience" in *Journal of Abnormal and Social Psychology*, 67: 371–378, 1963.

Exerting Personal Control

"If a man does not keep pace with his companions, perhaps it is because he hears a different drummer. Let him step to the music which he hears, however measured or far

psychological *inquiry*

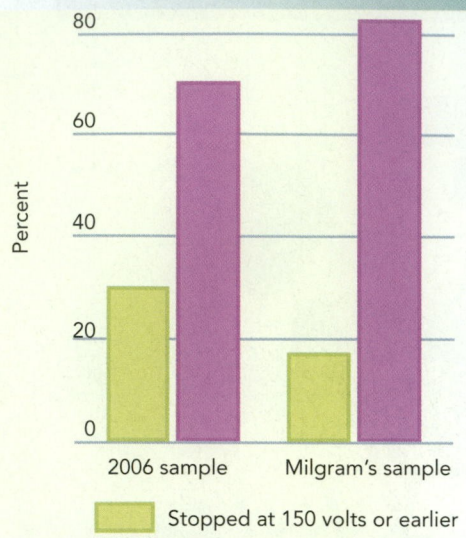

80

60

40

20

0

Percent

2006 sample   Milgram's sample

☐ Stopped at 150 volts or earlier
☐ Continued after 150 volts

Adapted from Burger, 2009.

Obedience Now and Then

The figure shows, side by side, the results of Burger's (2009) study of obedience and the results of one of Milgram's studies. The vertical or Y axis shows the percent of participants who stopped or continued shocking the learner after that individual first expressed a desire to end the study. Try out the following questions.

1. Comparing the two studies, are you surprised at the similarities? Why or why not?
2. Burger did not allow participants who had learned about Milgram's study to take part in his study. Do you think that decision was justified? Explain. How might the results have differed if these individuals had been permitted to participate?
3. If you had been a "teacher" in Burger's study—that is, involved in administering the shocks—what do you think you would have done?

These Ku Klux Klan members illustrate a variety of ways that human beings can deindividuate: turning out in a group, acting under cover of darkness, and concealing identity through special clothing.

● **deindividuation** The reduction in personal identity and erosion of the sense of personal responsibility when one is part of a group.

away." American essayist and philosopher Henry David Thoreau's words suggest that some of us resist social influence, just as Thoreau himself did. It is safe to say that as we go through life, we are both conformists and nonconformists. Sometimes we stand up and stand out, and sometimes we go with the flow.

Our relationship to the social world is reciprocal. Individuals may try to control us, but we can exert personal control over our actions and influence others in turn (Bandura, 2009; Doerr & Baumeister, 2010; Knowles, Nolan, & Riner, 2007). Although it may not be easy to resist authority, living with the knowledge that you compromised your own moral integrity may be more difficult in the long run.

53-2 GROUP INFLUENCE

On February 2, 2005, Chico State University student Matthew Carrington died following a fraternity hazing in the basement of the Chi Tau house. He and another pledge were verbally taunted and forced to do pushups in raw sewage. They were also compelled to drink gallons and gallons of water. Eventually, Carrington suffered a seizure and died of water intoxication. Among those who were convicted in his death were four fraternity brothers who had never been in trouble before. Indeed, the group's ringleader was Gabriel Maestretti, a deeply religious former altar boy, high school homecoming king, and volunteer coach. Why and how do individuals who would never perform destructive acts, if alone, perpetrate them when in a group? This is the central question that has driven research in the social psychology of group influence.

Deindividuation

One process that sheds light on the behavior of individuals in groups is **deindividuation,** which occurs when being part of a group reduces personal identity and erodes the sense of personal responsibility (Levine, Cassidy, & Jentzsch, 2010; Zimbardo, 2007). An example of the effects of deindividuation is the wild street celebrations that erupt after a team's victory in the World Series or Super Bowl.

One explanation for the effects of deindividuation is that groups give us anonymity. When we are part of a group, we may act in an uninhibited way because we believe that no one will be able to identify us. The Ku Klux Klan demonstrates a variety of ways that human beings can deindividuate: acting in groups, often under cover of darkness, and wearing white hoods to conceal identity.

Social Contagion

Have you ever noticed that a movie you watched in a crowded theater seemed funnier than it did when you watched the DVD alone at home? People laugh more when others are laughing. Babies cry when other babies are crying. The effects of others on our behavior can take the form of **social contagion,** imitative behavior involving the spread of actions, emotions, and ideas (Cohen & Prinstein, 2006; Gino, Ayal, & Ariely, 2009). Social contagion effects can be observed in such varied phenomena as social fads, the popularity of dog breeds (Herzog, 2006), the spread of unhealthy behaviors such as smoking and drinking among adolescents (Rodgers, 2007), and symptoms of eating disorders among young women (Crandall, 2004; Forman-Hoffman & Cunningham, 2008).

One way to observe social contagion is to sit in a quiet but crowded library and start coughing. You will soon notice others doing the same thing. Similarly, imagine that you are walking down the sidewalk and come upon a group of people who are all looking up. How likely is it that you can avoid the temptation of looking up to see what is so interesting to them?

● **social contagion** Imitative behavior involving the spread of actions, emotions, and ideas.

Group Performance

Are two or three heads better than one? Some studies reveal that we do better in groups; others show that we are more productive when we work alone (Mojzisch & Schulz-Hardt, 2010). We can make sense out of these contradictory findings by looking closely at the circumstances in which performance is being analyzed (Nijstad, 2009).

● **social facilitation** Improvement in an individual's performance because of the presence of others.

● **social loafing** Each person's tendency to exert less effort in a group because of reduced accountability for individual effort.

SOCIAL FACILITATION

If you have ever given a presentation in a class, you might have noticed that you did a much better job standing in front of your classmates than during any of your practice runs. **Social facilitation** occurs when an individual's performance improves because of the presence of others (Mendes, 2007). Robert Zajonc (1965) argued that the presence of other individuals arouses us. The arousal produces energy and facilitates our performance in groups. If our arousal is too high, however, we are unable to learn new or difficult tasks efficiently. Social facilitation, then, improves our performance on well-learned tasks. For new or difficult tasks, we might be best advised to work things out on our own before trying them in a group.

SOCIAL LOAFING

Another factor in group performance is the degree to which one's behavior is monitored. **Social loafing** refers to each person's tendency to exert less effort in a group because of reduced accountability for individual effort. The effect of social loafing is lowered group performance (Latané, 1981). The larger the group, the more likely it is that an individual can loaf without detection.

Social loafing commonly occurs when a group of students is assigned a class project, and it is one reason that some students intensely dislike group assignments. These same individuals will not be surprised to learn that under certain conditions, working with others can increase individual effort (D. S. Levine, 2000). For example, a person who views

The research of Norman Triplett (1898) of Indiana University, viewed by some to be the first North American sport psychologist, found that cyclists performed better when they raced in groups than when they rode by themselves, against the clock.

the group's task as important (say, a student who strongly wants an *A* on the project) and who does not expect other group members to contribute adequately is likely to work harder than usual—and perhaps to do most of the work himself or herself.

Researchers have identified ways to decrease social loafing. They include making individuals' contributions more identifiable and unique, simplifying the evaluation of these contributions, and making the group's task more attractive (Karau & Williams, 1993).

Group Decision Making

Many of the decisions we make take place in groups—juries, teams, families, clubs, school boards, and the U.S. Senate, for example (Gastil, 2009; Kerr, 2010; Mojzisch & Schulz-Hardt, 2010). What happens when people put their minds to the task of making a group decision? How do they decide whether a criminal is guilty, whether a country should attack another, whether a family should stay home or go on vacation, or whether sex education should be part of a school curriculum? Three aspects of group decision making bear special mention: risky shift and group polarization; groupthink; and majority and minority influence.

RISKY SHIFT AND GROUP POLARIZATION

Imagine that you have a friend, Lisa, who works as an accountant. All her life Lisa has longed to be a writer. In fact, she believes that she has the next great American novel in her head and that she just needs time and energy to devote to writing it. Would you advise Lisa to quit her job and go for it? What if you knew beforehand that her chances of success were 50–50? How about 60–40? How much risk would you advise Lisa to take?

In one investigation, participants were presented with fictitious dilemmas like this one and were asked how much risk the characters in the scenarios should take (Stoner, 1961). When the individuals discussed the dilemmas as a group, they were more willing to endorse riskier decisions than when they were queried alone. The so-called **risky shift** is the tendency for a group decision to be riskier than the average decision made by the individual group members (Goethals & Demorest, 1995).

However, people do not always make riskier decisions in a group than when alone. Instead, a group discussion can move individuals more strongly in the direction of the position they initially held (Moscovici, 1985). The **group polarization effect** is the solidification and further strengthening of an individual's position as a consequence of a group discussion or interaction. For example, let's say that while in a class where the students and instructor are discussing the effects of obedience on human behavior, you start out with a somewhat negative view of obedience. After hearing the full class discussion and adding your two cents, you find that your attitude toward obedience is quite a bit more negative than at first. What might explain your more extreme views at the end of the discussion? Such polarization may occur because, during the discussion, you heard new, more persuasive arguments that strengthened your original position. Group polarization might also be a product of social comparison. In the example of your classroom discussion, you might have discovered that your opinion was not as extreme as others' opinions, and you might have been influenced to take a stand at least as strong as the most extreme advocate's position.

GROUPTHINK: GETTING ALONG BUT BEING VERY WRONG

Groupthink refers to the impaired group decision making that occurs when making the right decision is less important than maintaining group harmony. Instead of engaging in an open discussion of all the available information, in groupthink, members of a group place the highest value on conformity and unanimity. Members are encouraged to "get with the program," and dissent meets with very strong disapproval.

Groupthink can result in disastrous decisions. Irving Janis (1972) introduced the concept of groupthink to explain a number of enormous decision-making errors throughout history. Such errors include the lack of U.S. preparation for the Japanese bombing of Pearl Harbor during World War II, the escalation of the Vietnam War in the 1960s, the Watergate cover-up in 1974, and the *Challenger* space shuttle disaster in 1986. After the 9/11 terrorist attacks, the possibility that groupthink interfered with the proper implementation of intelligence reared its head. Whistleblower Colleen Rowley,

● **risky shift** The tendency for a group decision to be riskier than the average decision made by the individual group members.

● **group polarization effect** The solidification and further strengthening of an individual's position as a consequence of a group discussion or interaction.

● **groupthink** The impaired group decision making that occurs when making the right decision is less important than maintaining group harmony.

an FBI special agent, revealed that the FBI power hierarchy had been unresponsive to information that might have helped prevent the attacks. More recently, many criticized former President George W. Bush and his cabinet for not listening to dissenting voices in the days leading up to the Iraq War.

Symptoms of groupthink include overestimating the power and morality of one's group, close-mindedness and lack of willingness to hear all sides of an argument, and pressure for uniformity. Groupthink can occur whenever groups value conformity over accuracy (Degnin, 2009). However, groupthink can be prevented if groups avoid isolation, allow the airing of all sides of an argument, have an impartial leader, include outside experts in the debate, and encourage members who are strongly identified with the group to speak out in dissent (Packer, 2009).

MAJORITY AND MINORITY INFLUENCE

Most groups make decisions by voting, and, even in the absence of groupthink, the majority usually wins. The majority exerts influence on group decision making through both informational influence (they have greater opportunity to share their views) and normative influence (they set group norms). Those who do not go along may be ignored or even given the boot.

Prospects might seem dim for minority opinion holders, but they *can* make a difference. Because it is outnumbered, the minority cannot win through normative pressure. Instead, it must do its work through informational pressure. If the minority presents its views consistently and confidently, then the majority is more likely to listen to the minority's perspectives. A powerful way that minority opinion holders can have influence is by winning over former majority members to their points of view.

SUMMARY

Conformity involves a change in behavior to coincide with a group standard. Factors that influence conformity include informational social influence (going along to be right) and normative social influence (going along to be liked).

Obedience is behavior that complies with the explicit demands of an authority. Milgram's classic experiment demonstrated the power of obedience.

People often change their behaviors when they are in a group. Deindividuation refers to the lack of inhibition and diffusion of responsibility that can occur in groups. Social contagion refers to imitative behaviors involving the spread of behavior, emotions, and ideas. Our performance in groups can be improved through social facilitation and lowered because of social loafing.

Risky shift refers to the tendency for a group decision to be riskier than the average decision made by the individual group members. The group polarization effect is the solidification and further strengthening of a position as a consequence of group discussion. Groupthink involves impaired decision making and avoidance of realistic appraisal to maintain harmony in the group.

KEY TERMS

conformity 492
informational social
    influence 493
normative social influence 493
obedience 493
deindividuation 496
social contagion 497

social facilitation 497
social loafing 497
risky shift 498
group polarization effect 498
groupthink 498

TEST YOURSELF

1. Compare and contrast informational social influence and normative social influence.

2. What is the difference between conformity and obedience?

3. What do the concepts of risky shift and group polarization have to say about decision making in a group context?

APPLY YOUR KNOWLEDGE

1. Compare and contrast social loafing and social facilitation. Describe a situation for each concept. Finally, describe a situation in which both concepts might be working at the same time?

2. Have you ever gone along with a group even though you didn't agree with them? What made you decide to go against your own thoughts or beliefs? How, if at all, did groupthink influence the group's decision? If you have never had the experience of being in a group that was hampered by groupthink, find an example from the news, and consider what the members might have done to improve their decision making.

Social Relations

In this module we consider social relations. We look specifically at how the groups to which we belong shape our interactions, and at the world of close relationships, including attraction and love.

54-1 INTERGROUP RELATIONS

Conflicts between groups, especially ethnic and cultural groups, are rampant around the world (Stevens & Gielen, 2007). The Islamic terrorist organization al Qaeda attacks the United States and other countries that its members perceive to be too secular and materialistic. The wronged nations retaliate. Israelis and Palestinians fight over territory in the Middle East, each claiming religious and historical rights to the disputed land. In countries across Africa, tribal chiefs try to craft a new social order favorable to their own rule. A variety of concepts introduced by social psychologists can help us understand the intensity of such cultural and ethnic conflicts and can provide insight into how to reduce their number and magnitude (Sanchez-Burks, 2007).

Group Identity: Us Versus Them

Think about the groups of which you are a member—religious and social organizations, your ethnic group, your nationality. When someone asks you to identify yourself, how often do you respond by mentioning these group memberships? And how much does it matter whether the people you associate with are members of the same groups as you?

SOCIAL IDENTITY

● **social identity** The way we define ourselves in terms of our group membership.

Social identity refers to the way we define ourselves in terms of our group membership. In contrast to personal identity, which can be highly individualized, social identity assumes some commonalities with others (Dovidio, Gaertner, & Saguy, 2009; Wenzel, 2009). A person's social identity might include identifying with a religious group, a country, a social organization, a political party, and many other groups (Carney & others, 2007; Haslam & Reicher, 2006; Vaes, Heflick, & Goldenberg, 2010). These diverse forms of social identity reflect the numerous ways people connect to groups and social categories (Abrams & Hogg, 2004; Hogg & Abrams, 2007; Postmes & Jetten, 2006). Social psychologist Kay Deaux (2001) identified five distinct types of social identity: ethnicity and religion, political affiliation, vocations and avocations, personal relationships, and stigmatized groups (Figure 54.1).

For many people, ethnic identity and religious identity are central to their social identity (Charmaraman & Grossman, 2010; King & Roeser, 2009). Ethnic identity can be a source of pride for individuals (Umana-Taylor & Guimond, 2010). In the United States, special events celebrate the rich cultural contributions of many different groups to the society. Such experiences may provide individuals with an important resource in coping with biases they may encounter in life (Crocker, Major, & Steele, 1998). Feeling connected to one's ethnic group may buffer individuals from the stressful effects of injustice (Sellers & others, 2006).

Ethnic conflict in the African country of Chad has increased in recent years. In this photograph from May 2009, a rebel soldier lies dead while Chad soldiers carry out cleanup operations in the area of Am Dam.

Ethnicity & Religion	Relationships	Vocations & Avocations	Political Affiliation	Stigmatized Identities
Jewish Asian American Southern Baptist West Indian	Parent Mother Son Widow	Artist Athlete Psychologist Military veteran	Environmentalist Feminist Republican	Overweight person Person with AIDS Homeless person Alcoholic

FIGURE 54.1   **Types of Identity** When we identify ourselves, we draw on a host of different characteristics associated with the various social groups to which we belong.

Social psychologist Henry Tajfel (1978), a Holocaust survivor, wanted to explain the extreme violence and prejudice that his religious group (Jews) experienced. Tajfel's **social identity theory** states that our social identities are a crucial part of our self-image and a valuable source of positive feelings about ourselves. To feel good about ourselves, we need to feel good about the groups to which we belong. For this reason, individuals invariably think of the group to which they belong as an *in-group,* a group that has special value in comparison with other groups, called *out-groups.* To improve our self-image, we continually compare our in-groups with out-groups (Parks, 2007). In the process, we often focus more on the differences between the two groups than on their similarities.

Research by Tajfel (1978) and many others who have used his theory shows how easy it is to lead people to think in terms of "us" and "them." In one experiment, Tajfel had participants look at a screen featuring a huge number of dots and estimate how many dots were displayed. He then assigned the participants to groups based on an arbitrary situation—whether they overestimated or underestimated the number of dots. Once assigned to one of the two groups, the participants were asked to award money to other participants. Taifel found that individuals awarded money to members of their in-group, not to participants in the out-group, even though the group assignment had been essentially arbitrary. If we favor the members of a group that was formed on such trivial bases, it is no wonder that we show intense in-group favoritism when differences are not so trivial.

ETHNOCENTRISM

The tendency to favor one's own ethnic group over other groups is called **ethnocentrism.** Ethnocentrism does not simply mean taking pride in one's group; it also involves asserting the group's superiority over other groups (Gormley & Lopez, 2010; Hall, Matz, & Wood, 2010). As such, ethnocentrism encourages in-group/out-group, we/they thinking (Brewer, 2007; Smith, Bond, & Kagitcibasi, 2006). Consequently, ethnocentrism implies that ethnic out-groups are not simply different; they are worse than one's group. Hence ethnocentrism may underlie prejudice.

Prejudice

Prejudice is an unjustified negative attitude toward an individual based on the individual's membership in a particular group. The group can be made up of people of a specific ethnicity, sex, age, religion—essentially, people who are different in some way from a prejudiced person (Brandt & Reyna, 2010; Graziano & Habashi, 2010; Jefferson & Bramlett, 2010; T. D. Nelson, 2009). Prejudice as a worldwide phenomenon can be seen in many eruptions of hatred in human history. In the Balkan Peninsula of eastern Europe, the Serbs' prejudice against Bosnians prompted the Serb policy of "ethnic cleansing." The prejudice of the Hutus against the Tutsis in Rwanda led them to go on a murderous rampage, attacking the Tutsis with machetes.

● **social identity theory** Tajfel's theory that our social identities are a crucial part of our self-image and a valuable source of positive feelings about ourselves.

● **ethnocentrism** The tendency to favor one's own ethnic group over other groups.

● **prejudice** An unjustified negative attitude toward an individual based on the individual's membership in a particular group.

Ethnic identity evokes ethnic pride. Here, Italian American soccer fans in Boston's North End rejoice at the Italian soccer team's World Cup win; Chinese American children touch the "lion" in the streets of New York City's Chinatown on the day of Chinese New Year, in hopes of receiving good luck and prosperity; and children and adults dance during a Kwanzaa celebration at Philadelphia's Canaan Baptist Church to strengthen their ties to their African heritage.

A powerful example of destructive prejudice within U.S. society is racial prejudice against African Americans. When Africans were brought to colonial America as slaves, they were considered property and treated inhumanely. In the first half of the twentieth century, most African Americans still lived in the South and remained largely segregated from White society by law; restaurants, movie theaters, and buses had separate areas for Whites and African Americans.

Despite progress in racial equality over the years, a much higher percentage of African Americans than Whites still live in impoverished neighborhoods and lack access to good schools, jobs, and healthcare, even decades after the abolition of legal segregation. Recent national events also make it clear that there is still work to be done. Following Hurricane Katrina, news reports referred to White victims as "finding" food but described African Americans who were doing the same things as "looting" (Kinney, 2005). In a revealing study, Marianne Bertrand and Sendhil Mullainathan (2004) sent out 5,000 résumés in response to 1,200 job ads placed in newspapers in Chicago and Boston. They constructed résumés so that applicants were identical in qualifications but differed in how stereotypically White or Black their names sounded. "White" names included Meredith, Emily, Brad, and Greg. "Black" names included Tamika, Lakisha, Darnell, and Kareem. The researchers found that even with identical qualifications, the applicants with "White-sounding" names were 50 percent more likely to be called for an interview.

Because racial prejudice is socially unacceptable, few people today would readily admit to racist or prejudicial views. In a CNN poll (2006), 88 percent of individuals answered no to the question "Are you racist?" It is not clear whether such results reflect a genuine change of heart or simply the recognition of this shifting social standard. Today, prejudiced individuals are more likely than before to appear unprejudiced on the surface while nevertheless holding racist views at a deeper level (Sears, 2008; Sears & Henry, 2007). Indeed, individuals may not be consciously aware of their own racial (or gender or age) biases.

To confront this problem, social psychologists examine prejudicial attitudes on two levels—explicit or overt racism and implicit or covert racism. *Explicit racism* is a person's conscious and openly shared attitude, which might be measured using a questionnaire. *Implicit racism* refers to attitudes that exist on a deeper, hidden level. Implicit attitudes must be measured with a method that does not require awareness (Trawaiter & Shapiro, 2010). For example, implicit racism is sometimes measured using the Implicit Associations Test (IAT), a computerized survey that assesses the ease with which a person can associate a Black or White person with good things (for example, flowers) or bad things (for example, misery) (Greenwald & others, 2009; Nosek & Banaji, 2007; Sriram &

Greenwald, 2009). This test is based on the idea that preexisting biases may make it easier to associate some social stimuli with positive rather than negative items.

In one study, a sample of White college students completed measures of explicit and implicit attitudes toward Black people using an implicit measure similar to the IAT (Dovidio, Kawakami, & Gaertner, 2002). The students then interacted with a Black student partner. Explicit prejudice predicted what people said to a person of a different race—that is, White students who said they were not prejudiced were unlikely to say overtly racist things. Explicit prejudice also predicted how friendly White individuals felt they had behaved toward their Black partner. However, implicit prejudice related to nonverbal aspects of the interaction, such as how close the White students sat to their partners, as well as their facial expressions.

Why do people develop prejudice? Social psychologists have explored a number of possible reasons. Competition between groups, especially when resources are scarce, can contribute to prejudice. For example, immigrants often compete with established low-income members of a society for jobs—a situation that can lead to persistent conflict between the two groups. Cultural learning is also clearly involved. Children can adopt the prejudicial attitudes of their families and friends before they even meet a person from an out-group. In addition, when people feel bad about themselves, they might bolster their self-esteem by demeaning out-group members.

A final factor that might underlie prejudice comes from the limits on our information-processing abilities. As already noted, human beings are limited in their capacity for effortful thought, but they face a complex social environment. To simplify the challenge of understanding others' behavior, people use categories or stereotypes. Stereotypes can be a powerful force in developing and maintaining prejudicial attitudes.

STEREOTYPING AND PREJUDICE

Recall that stereotypes are generalizations about a group that deny variations within the group. Researchers have found that we are less likely to detect variations among individuals who belong to "other" groups than among individuals who belong to "our" group. So, we might see the people in our in-group as varied, unique individuals while viewing the members of out-groups as "all the same" (Amodio & Mendoza, 2010). Thinking that "they all look alike" can be a particular concern in the context of eyewitness identification (Brigham, 1986). At the root of prejudice is a particular kind of stereotype: a negative generalization about a group that is applied to all members of that group (Stangor, 2009).

DISCRIMINATION

Discrimination is an unjustified negative or harmful action toward a member of a group simply because the person belongs to that group. Discrimination occurs when negative emotional reactions combine with prejudicial beliefs and are translated into behavior (Bretherton, 2007; Major & Sawyer, 2009). Many forms of discrimination are illegal in the U.S. workplace. Since the Civil Rights Act of 1964 (revised in 1991), it has been unlawful to deny someone employment on the basis of gender or ethnicity (Parker, 2006).

● **discrimination** An unjustified negative or harmful action toward a member of a group simply because the person belongs to that group.

Ways to Improve Intergroup Relations

Martin Luther King, Jr., said, "I have a dream that my four little children will one day live in a nation where they will not be judged by the color of their skin but by the content of their character." How might we attain the world that King envisioned?

One way might be for people to come to know one another better so that they can get along. However, in daily life many people interact with individuals from other ethnic groups, and this contact does not necessarily lead to tolerance or warm relations. Indeed, researchers have consistently found that contact by itself—attending the same school or working in the same company—does not necessarily improve relations among

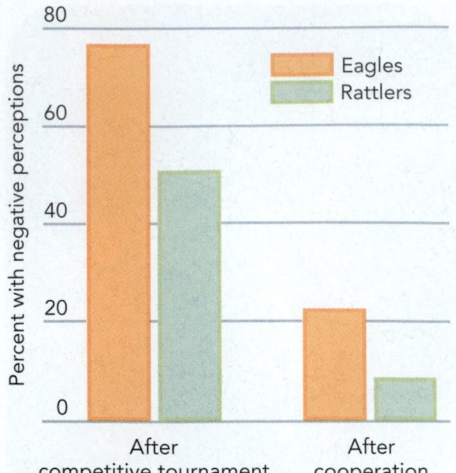

FIGURE 54.2   Attitudes Toward the Out-Group Following Competitive and Cooperative Activities In Sherif's research, hostility peaked after an athletic tournament, as reflected in the high percentage of Eagles and Rattlers who perceived the other group unfavorably following this event. However, after the groups worked together to reach a goal, their unfavorable attitudes toward each other dropped considerably.

people of different ethnic backgrounds. So, rather than focusing on contact per se, researchers have examined how *various features* of a contact situation may be optimal for reducing prejudice and promoting intergroup harmony.

Gordon Allport (1954) theorized that particular aspects of the contact between groups could help to reduce prejudice. According to Allport, intergroup contact is likely to reduce prejudice when group members

- Think that they are of equal status
- Feel that an authority figure sanctions their positive relationships
- Believe that friendship might emerge from the interaction
- Engage in cooperative tasks in which everyone has something to contribute

Research has demonstrated support for many of Allport's ideas (Pettigrew & Tropp, 2006). In particular, studies have examined the role of *task-oriented cooperation*—working together on a shared goal—in reducing tensions between groups. Two examples of the power of task-oriented cooperation are Sherif's Robbers Cave Study and Aronson's jigsaw classroom.

It may be hard to imagine in our post-*Survivor* era, but even before Jeff Probst started handing out color-coded "buffs" on the TV show *Survivor,* Muzafer Sherif and his colleagues (1961) had the idea of exploring group processes by assigning 11-year-old boys to two competitive groups (the "Rattlers" and the "Eagles") in a summer camp called Robbers Cave. Sherif, disguised as a janitor so that he could unobtrusively observe the Rattlers and the Eagles, arranged for the two groups to compete in baseball, touch football, and tug-of-war. If you have watched reality television, you have some idea how this experiment went. In short order, relations between the groups got downright ugly. Members of each group expressed negative opinions of members of the other group, and the Rattlers and Eagles became battling factions.

What would bring these clashing groups together? Sherif created tasks that required the joint efforts of both groups, such as working together to repair the camp's only water supply and pooling their money to rent a movie. When the groups were required to work cooperatively to solve problems, the Rattlers and Eagles developed more positive relationships. Figure 54.2 shows how competitive and cooperative activities changed perceptions of the out-group.

Sherif's idea was later tested in the real world in Austin, Texas, when ethnic tensions increased and violence erupted among African Americans, Mexican Americans, and Whites in desegregated schools. Social psychologist Eliot Aronson was asked to help address the problem. Aronson (1986) devised the *jigsaw classroom,* where all of the students have to pull together to get the "big picture." Let's say a class consists of 30 students, some White, some African American, and some Latino. The academic goal for all students is to learn about the life of the Indian leader Mahatma Gandhi. The class might be broken up into five study groups of six students each, with the groups being equal as possible in ethnic composition and academic achievement level. Learning about Gandhi's life becomes a class project divided into six parts, with one part given to each member of the six-person group. The components might be various books about Gandhi or information about different aspects of his life. The parts are like the pieces of a jigsaw puzzle: They have to be put together to form the complete puzzle.

U.S. classrooms have widely used the jigsaw approach (Deutsch, 2006; Deutsch, Coleman, & Marcus, 2006). This model has been associated with increased self-esteem, better academic performance, friendships among classmates, and improved interethnic perceptions (Slavin, 2006).

54-2 CLOSE RELATIONSHIPS

Along with good health and happiness, close relationships figure prominently in most people's notions of a good life. Every day we see or hear commercials lauding the ability of this or that Internet dating service to link us up with the love of our life.

U.S. consumers spent more than $490 million on Internet personals and dating services in 2005 (Online Publishers Association, 2005). Because close romantic relationships are so crucially important for most of us, it is no wonder that social psychologists should be interested in studying this fascinating aspect of human existence. Indeed, a vast literature has accumulated in social psychology, examining attraction, love, and intimacy.

Attraction

One key factor in interpersonal attraction is physical attractiveness. Research on interpersonal attraction has illuminated a variety of other factors that play a role in the dynamic of attraction.

PROXIMITY, ACQUAINTANCE, AND SIMILARITY

Even in the age of Internet dating, it is very unlikely that you are going to become attracted to someone without meeting the person. *Proximity,* or physical closeness, is a strong predictor of attraction. You are more prone to become attracted to an individual you pass in the hall every day than to someone you see rarely. One potential mechanism for the role of proximity in attraction is the mere exposure effect (Zajonc, 1968, 2001). The **mere exposure effect** is the phenomenon that the more we encounter someone or something (a person, a word, an image), the more probable it is that we will start liking the person or thing even if we do not realize we have seen it before.

We not only tend to be attracted to people whom we have seen before, but also are more likely to like someone if we are led to believe we will be meeting that person. Let's say you are sitting in a room and an experimenter tells you there are two strangers next door, one of whom you will be meeting and the other not. Research shows that you will probably begin to like the first person, in anticipation of your interaction (Insko & Wilson, 1977). In addition, if we find out that someone whom we do not know yet already likes us, it is a sure sign that we will find ourselves attracted to that person—in other words, we like those who like us. (For one thing, we know that they have excellent taste.)

In addition to proximity and the promise of acquaintanceship, similarity plays an important role in attraction (Qian, 2009). We have all heard that opposites attract, but what is true of magnets is not true of human beings, at least not typically. We like to associate with people who are similar to us (Berscheid, 2000). Our friends and lovers are much more like us than unlike us. We have similar attitudes, behavior patterns, taste in clothes, intelligence, personality, other friends, values, lifestyle, physical attractiveness, and so on.

The concept of *consensual validation* explains why people are attracted to others who are similar to them. Our own attitudes and behavior are supported when someone else's attitudes and behavior are similar to ours—their attitudes and behavior validate ours. Another reason that similarity matters is that we tend to shy away from the unknown. Similarity implies that we will enjoy doing things with another person who has similar tastes and attitudes.

Love

Some relationships never progress much beyond the attraction stage. Others deepen to friendship and perhaps even to love. Social psychologists have long puzzled over exactly what love is (Berscheid, 2006, 2010). One way to think about love is to consider the types of love that characterize different human relationships—for instance, friendships versus romantic relationships (Hendrick & Hendrick, 2009). Here we consider two types of love: romantic love and affectionate love.

Poets, playwrights, and musicians through the ages have celebrated the fiery passion of romantic love—and lamented the searing pain when it fails. Think about songs and

© Ralph Hagen. www.CartoonStock.com.

● **mere exposure effect** The phenomenon that the more we encounter someone or something, the more probable it is that we will start liking the person or thing even if we do not realize we have seen it before.

As love matures, passionate love tends to give way to affectionate love.

● **romantic love** Also called passionate love; love with strong components of sexuality and infatuation, often dominant in the early part of a love relationship.

● **affectionate love** Also called companionate love; love that occurs when individuals desire to have another person near and have a deep, caring affection for the person.

● **social exchange theory** The view of social relationships as involving an exchange of goods, the objective of which is to minimize costs and maximize benefits.

● **investment model** A model of long-term relationships that examines the ways that commitment, investment, and the availability of attractive alternative partners predict satisfaction and stability in relationships.

books that hit the top of the charts. Chances are, they are about romantic love. **Romantic love,** also called *passionate love,* is love with strong components of sexuality and infatuation, and it often predominates in the early part of a love relationship (Hendrick & Hendrick, 2006). Ellen Berscheid (1988) says that it is romantic love we mean when we say that we are "in love" with someone. It is romantic love that she believes we need to understand if we are to learn what love is all about. Berscheid judges sexual desire to be the most important ingredient of romantic love.

Love is more than just passion, however. **Affectionate love,** also called *companionate love,* is the type of love that occurs when individuals desire to have the other person near and have a deep, caring affection for the person. There is a growing belief that the early stages of love have more romantic ingredients and that as love matures, passion tends to give way to affection (Berscheid & Regan, 2005).

Models of Close Relationships

What makes long-term romantic relationships last? Two theoretical approaches to this sometimes bewildering question include social exchange theory and the investment model.

SOCIAL EXCHANGE THEORY

The social exchange approach to close relationships focuses on the costs and benefits of one's romantic partner. **Social exchange theory** is based on the notion of social relationships as involving an exchange of goods, the objective of which is to minimize costs and maximize benefits. This theory looks at human relations as an exchange of rewards between actors. From the social exchange perspective, the most important predictor of a relationship's success is *equity*—a feeling on the part of the individuals in the relationship that each is doing his or her "fair share." Essentially, social exchange theory asserts that the partners keep a mental balance sheet, tallying the plusses and minuses associated with each other—what they put in ("I paid for our last date") and what they get out ("He brought me flowers").

As relationships progress, equity may no longer apply. In fact, research shows that over time, this kind of accounting not only is less likely to explain what happens in a relationship but also becomes distasteful to the partners. Happily married couples are less likely to keep track of "what I get versus what I give," and they avoid thinking about the costs and benefits of their relationships (Buunk & Van Yperen, 1991; Clark & Chrisman, 1994). Surely we can all think of long-term relationships in which one partner remains committed even when the benefits are hard for the outsider to see—as in the case where the person's romantic partner is gravely ill for a long time.

THE INVESTMENT MODEL

Another way to think about long-term romantic relationships is to focus on the underlying factors that characterize stable, happy relationships compared to others. The **investment model** examines the ways that commitment, investment, and the availability of attractive alternative partners predict satisfaction and stability in relationships (Rusbult & Agnew, 2010; Rusbult & others, 2004).

From the investment model perspective, long-term relationships are likely to continue when both partners are committed to the relationship and both have invested a great deal; in addition, relationships are more enduring when there are few tempting alternatives for the partners. For example, college students who are committed to their romantic partners are less likely to cheat on them sexually during spring break (Drigotas, Safstrom, & Gentilia, 1999). Commitment to a relationship also predicts a willingness to sacrifice for a romantic partner. In one study, individuals were given a chance to climb up and down a short staircase, over and over, to spare their partner from having to do so. Those who were more committed to their partner worked harder to climb up and down repeatedly, in order to spare their loved one the burden (Van Lange & others, 1997). When two partners are deeply invested in a relationship, they can also bring the best out in each other, mutually helping themselves grow into their best possible selves (Rusbult, Finkel, & Kumashiro, 2009).

SUMMARY

Social identity is our definition of ourselves in terms of our group memberships. Social identity theory states that when individuals are assigned to a group, they invariably think of it as the in-group. Identifying with the group allows the person to have a positive self-image. Ethnocentrism is the tendency to favor one's own ethnic group over others.

Prejudice is an unjustified negative attitude toward an individual based on membership in a group. The underlying reasons for prejudice include competition between groups over scarce resources, a person's motivation to enhance his or her self-esteem, cognitive processes that tend to categorize and stereotype others, and cultural learning. Prejudice is also based on stereotypes. The cognitive process of stereotyping can lead to discrimination, an unjustified negative or harmful action toward a member of a group simply because he or she belongs to that group. Discrimination results when negative emotional reactions combine with prejudicial beliefs and are translated into behavior.

An effective strategy for enhancing the effects of intergroup contact is to set up task-oriented cooperation among individuals from different groups.

We tend to be attracted to people whom we see often, whom we are likely to meet, and who are similar to us. Romantic love (passionate love) includes feelings of infatuation and sexual attraction. Affectionate love (companionate love) is more akin to friendship and includes deep, caring feelings for another.

Social exchange theory states that a relationship is likely to be successful if individuals feel that they get out of the relationship what they put in. The investment model focuses on commitment, investment, and the availability of attractive alternatives in predicting relationship success.

KEY TERMS

social identity   500
social identity theory   501
ethnocentrism   501
prejudice   501
discrimination   503
mere exposure effect   505

romantic love   506
affectionate love   506
social exchange theory   506
investment model   506

TEST YOURSELF

1. What does social identity theory say about groups?

2. What is prejudice? Give two real-world examples, either historical or contemporary.

3. According to Allport, what particular aspects of the contact between groups could help to reduce prejudice?

4. Explain the concept of consensual validation.

5. What is the difference between romantic love and affectionate love, and what is another name for each?

6. What does social exchange theory say about happy romantic relationships?

APPLY YOUR KNOWLEDGE

1. Many people are surprised by the results of the IAT when they take this implicit measure. Try it out at https://implicit.harvard.edu/implicit. Do you think your results are valid? Explain.

2. Interview the happiest couple you know. Ask the partners individually about the things that they think help make their relationship work. Then examine your notes. How do the characteristics of your "ideal" couple's relationship compare with the findings of research on close relationships?

Social Psychology and Health and Wellness

The principles of social psychology have provided a strong foundation for ongoing research in the areas of health and wellness (Kok & de Vries, 2006; Taylor, 2011). In this concluding section, we glimpse some of the significant connections that researchers have uncovered among social contacts, physical health, and psychological wellness.

A long list of studies has shown that social ties are an important, if not the *most* important, variable in predicting health. For example, in a landmark study, social isolation had six times the effect on mortality rates that cigarette smoking had (House, Landis, & Umberson, 1988). In another study involving 1,234 heart attack patients, those living alone were nearly twice as likely to have a second heart attack (Case & others, 1992). Further, in a study of leukemia patients, of those who said that they had little support prior to undergoing a bone marrow transplant, only 20 percent were alive two years later, compared to 54 percent who reported that they felt strong support (Colón & others, 1991). Research shows, too, that widows die at a rate that is 3 to 13 times higher than that of married women for every known cause of death (Wortman & Boerner, 2007). Loneliness is linked with impaired physical health (Cacioppo & others, 2006; Hawkley, Preacher, & Cacioppo, 2010; Hawkley, Thisted, & Cacioppo, 2009; Munoz-Laboy, Hirsch, & Quispe-Lazaro, 2009). Chronic loneliness can lead to an early death (Cornwell & Waite, 2009; Cuijpers, 2001). Without a doubt, being connected to others is crucial to human survival.

Having many different social ties may be especially important during difficult times (Hawkley & Cacioppo, 2009; Taylor, 2011). Individuals who participate in more diverse social networks—for example, having a close relationship with a partner; interacting with family members, friends, neighbors, and fellow workers; and belonging to social and religious groups—live longer than those with a narrower range of social relationships (Vogt & others, 1992). One study investigated the effects of diverse social ties on the susceptibility to getting a common cold (S. Cohen & others, 1998). Individuals reported the extent of their participation in 12 types of social ties. Then they were given nasal drops containing a cold virus and monitored for the appearance of a cold. Individuals with more diverse social ties were less likely to get a cold than their counterparts with less diverse social networks.

Each of us has times in our life when we feel lonely, particularly when we are going through major life transitions. For example, when individuals leave the familiar world of their hometown and family to begin college, they can feel especially lonely. Indeed, experiencing loneliness at the beginning of one's college career is quite common and normal (Cutrona, 1982).

If you are lonely, there are strategies you can use to become better connected with others. You might consider joining activities, such as volunteering your time for a cause in which you believe. When interacting with others, you will improve your chances of developing enduring relationships if you are considerate, honest, trustworthy, and cooperative. If you cannot get rid of your loneliness on your own, you might want to contact the counseling services at your college.

Having completed this section's survey of social psychology, you may be surprised to learn that we have barely scratched the surface of this broad and deep field: The branch of psychology that focuses on the ways human beings relate to one another is a rich, intriguing area of study. In the next few days, think about the stories that are making the headlines and that you are talking about with your friends. Reflecting back, you might notice that social psychology would have something to say about most of these topics.

SUMMARY

Social isolation is a strong risk factor for a range of physical illnesses and even death. Loneliness relates to a number of negative health outcomes, including impaired physical health and early death. Individuals who participate in more diverse social networks live longer than those with a narrower range of social relationships. Loneliness often emerges when people make life transitions, so it is not surprising that loneliness is common among college freshmen. Strategies that can help to reduce loneliness include participating in activities with others and taking the initiative to meet new people.

TEST YOURSELF

1. What are some physical illnesses in which social isolation plays a significant role, according to researchers?
2. What kinds of social networks are especially important in times of trouble?
3. If a friend were struggling with loneliness, what strategy would you recommend for coping with it?

Industrial and Organizational Psychology

What Would You Do If You Won the Lottery?

On April 1, 2008, David Sneath found out he had won $136 million in the MegaMillions lottery. The 60-year-old Ford auto parts worker from Michigan lost no time in announcing to his boss, "I am *out* of here!" (*USA Today*, 2008).

If *you* won the lottery, would you quit your job? If you are like many people, your answer is yes. You may be surprised to learn, though, that David Sneath's decision is not typical—most lottery winners in fact do not quit working. (Arvey, Harpaz, & Liao, 2004).

Why do people work when they do not have to? The answer is that work is more than a way to earn money. It is an opportunity to use our skills and abilities and to feel successful and effective. It also provides a context in which to have meaningful relationships.

Industrial and organizational (I/O) psychology applies the science of psychology to work and the workplace. In I/O psychology, researchers are interested in a broad range of topics related to the work environment, including the selection of the right person for a particular job, and the ways people work together in groups (Zedeck, 2010). Many of these topics are also the subject of psychological research in other areas (Lord & others, 2010). I/O psychology is unique, however, in that it tests the theories of basic research in the important real-world context of work. ●

Origins of Industrial and Organizational Psychology

Industrial and organizational psychology is a relatively new idea. The notion that the principles of science should be applied to work settings has been around for less than 100 years. Contemporary I/O psychology has roots in the history of industry, as well as the twentieth century's two world wars, during which psychologists were called upon to help address the crucial military concerns of recruitment, selection, and morale. Here we review three important influences on the development of I/O psychology: scientific management, ergonomics, and the human relations approach to management.

55·1 THE ADVENT OF SCIENTIFIC MANAGEMENT

● **scientific management** The managerial philosophy that emphasizes the worker as a well-oiled machine and the determination of the most efficient methods for performing any work-related task.

The pioneers in applying scientific methods to the workplace were not psychologists but engineers (Vinchur & Koppes, 2010). They focused on **scientific management**—the managerial philosophy that emphasizes the worker as a well-oiled machine and the determination of the most efficient methods for performing any work-related task. Yet these engineers sounded like psychologists at times. Among them was Frederick Winslow Taylor, the mastermind of the idea of scientific management. Taylor (1911) suggested the following guidelines, which have continuing influence today:

- Jobs should be carefully analyzed to identify the optimal way to perform them.
- Employees should be hired according to the characteristics associated with success at a task. These characteristics should be identified by examining individuals who are already successful at a job.
- Employees should be trained at the job they will perform.
- Employees should be rewarded for productivity, to encourage high levels of performance.

Taylor's approach was influential in U.S. business, including clothing and furniture manufacturing and, most particularly, the automobile industry, where it dramatically boosted productivity and profits, especially in the years before World War I.

The advent of the assembly line perhaps best demonstrates the spirit of scientific management and its emphasis on time and motion. It may be hard to imagine, but before the twentieth century, an individual or a team of people created an entire single product. These individuals put each and every piece together from beginning to end, whether the product was a clock, a car, or a pair of shoes. Then, in 1901 came a revolution in industrial history when Ransom E. Olds invented the *assembly line,* in which each individual laborer assembled one (and only one) part of a car. Henry Ford, the founder of Ford Motor Company, added a motorized conveyor belt, so that the car being assembled automatically moved along, and workers could stay in the same place. Ford brought in Frederick Taylor to conduct *time and motion studies,* which involve examining the precise movements required to complete a task and identifying and eliminating unnecessary movements. In 1913, the first moving assembly line in history was complete, and no one could deny that it was a boon to productivity and efficiency. Indeed, by 1916, Ford Motor Company was producing twice as many automobiles as all of its competitors combined.

With the outbreak of World War I in 1914, psychologists, too, played a growing role in the application of science to the workplace. The influence of psychologists was felt first in the military, especially in the selection and training of recruits (Salas, DeRouin,

& Gade, 2007). Between the two world wars, the field that would become known as I/O psychology expanded beyond the military into a variety of settings, including private industry, as it became ever more apparent that applying scientific research to the work environment would help employers improve efficiency (Vinchur & Koppes, 2010).

55·2 ERGONOMICS: WHERE PSYCHOLOGY MEETS ENGINEERING

Today, many occupations involve the interaction of human beings with tools. Whether these tools are computers or hand-press drills, vast numbers of people earn a living by working with the help of technological advances. Understanding and enhancing the safety and efficiency of the human–machine interaction is the central focus of **ergonomics,** also called *human factors,* a field that combines engineering and psychology (Proctor & Vu, 2010). Desks, chairs, switches, buttons—all of the objects workers use every day are the product of design decisions aimed at promoting a person's efficiency on the job.

Ergonomic specialists represent a range of expertise, from perception, attention, and cognition (individuals who have good ideas about the placement of buttons on a control panel or the preferred coloring of those buttons), to learning (individuals who design training programs for the use of machines), to social and environmental psychologists (individuals who address issues such as living in a constrained environment like that of the space shuttle). Increasingly, human factors research has examined the critical role of human information processing in the interactions between people and machines (Proctor & Vu, 2010). To appreciate the role of ergonomics in daily life, see Figure 55.1, which shows how the design of something as common as the computer mouse reflects expert attention to the human–machine relationship.

Both scientific management and ergonomics share a focus on efficiency and safety. However, from the late 1920s to the present day, a third—and very different—approach has shaped thinking about the workplace. This third influence on I/O psychology—the historic Hawthorne studies—drew attention to the larger context of the workplace as a social environment, as well as to the worker as a human being with feelings, motivations, and attitudes.

55·3 THE HAWTHORNE STUDIES AND THE HUMAN RELATIONS APPROACH TO MANAGEMENT

A defining moment in I/O history occurred after the end of World War I. A series of studies was conducted at the Western Electric Hawthorne Works, a plant outside Chicago, from 1927 to 1932 under the leadership of psychologist and sociologist Elton Mayo. In what became known as the Hawthorne studies, Mayo and his colleagues were initially interested in examining how various work conditions (for example, room lighting, humidity, breaks, work hours, and management style) could influence productivity. In the first studies, they investigated the effects of room lighting on performance (Roethlisberger & Dickson, 1939). Workers were randomly assigned to one of two groups. In the control group, the lighting remained constant, but in the experimental group a variety of different lighting intensities was employed. The results were surprising. Both groups improved their performance—and they performed increasingly better over time (Roethlisberger & Dickson, 1939). Indeed, the experimental group showed declines in performance only when the lighting was so dim that the workers could hardly see.

In a later study, a group of workers was selected to work without an official supervisor, answering only to the researchers themselves. These workers received a variety of special privileges so that the researchers could see whether these changes

● **ergonomics** Also called human factors, a field that combines engineering and psychology and that focuses on understanding and enhancing the safety and efficiency of the human–machine interaction.

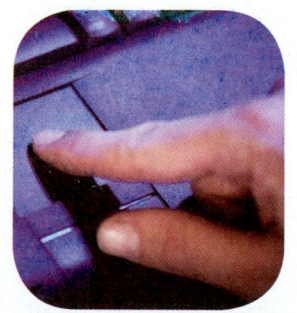

FIGURE 55.1 Building a Better Mouse The figure shows the evolution of the computer mouse from its wooden-box beginnings (*top*) to its later, sleeker forms (*middle photos*). The evolution has continued with the development of the touchpad or trackpad (*bottom*)—a built-in mouse substitute in laptop computers. The mouse and the touchpad are tools that many of us take for granted, but they are the product of design decisions that have improved their utility and efficiency.

His landmark Hawthorne studies led Elton Mayo (1880–1949) to challenge the conventional thinking that what was good for business was good for employees.

● **Hawthorne effect** The tendency of individuals to perform better simply because of being singled out and made to feel important.

● **human relations approach** A management approach emphasizing the psychological characteristics of workers and managers, stressing the importance of factors such as morale, attitudes, values, and humane treatment of workers.

influenced productivity. As it happens, any change at all did affect productivity. The results of this work led to the coining of the term **Hawthorne effect,** which refers to the tendency of individuals to perform better simply because of being singled out and made to feel important. However, later analyses of the Hawthorne data have suggested that these effects might be better understood as the results of various larger, external factors (such as the beginning of the Great Depression) that caused individuals to work harder and value their jobs more, as well as changes in factory personnel (Franke & Kaul, 1978). Others have argued that the workers at the Hawthorne plant were given feedback about their performance and that their responses to such input might be seen as reflecting operant conditioning (Chiesa & Hobbs, 2008; Parsons, 1974).

Nevertheless, the Hawthorne studies are landmark. For one thing, they persuasively demonstrated that the workplace is a social system populated by individuals who relate to one another and work in ways that are not always obvious. Moreover, the Hawthorne research showed that although individual ability may be important, workers of all levels of ability are in the social network of the workplace, and their performance is thus subject to social pressures and group norms (Sonnenfeld, 1985).

Mayo was especially critical of management's obsession with efficiency and its effect on the human side of business. He argued that when a business focuses on micro-level aspects of workers' activities and on initiatives such as creating the most efficient assembly lines, workers become alienated from both their product and their co-workers. Emphasizing the time-and-motion aspects of a job, Mayo said, takes away from both the experience of craftsmanship and the capacity of workers to identify with the products they are creating. He believed that traditional approaches to the science of work erroneously assumed that what was good for business was good for the employee. Mayo's Hawthorne studies moved researchers away from scientific management toward an emphasis on a human relations approach to management.

The **human relations approach** emphasizes the psychological characteristics of workers and managers and stresses the significance of factors such as morale, attitudes, values, and humane treatment of workers (Cameron, 2007; Dalton, Hoyle, & Watts, 2011). The human relations view focuses on the workplace as a crucially important social system. The emphasis is on positive interpersonal relations among co-workers, teamwork, leadership, job attitudes, and the social skills of managers. Human relations methods stress that fulfilling work meets other important human needs beyond purely economic considerations (Lamberton & Minor-Evans, 2010; Reece, Brandt, & Howie, 2011).

Scientific management, ergonomics, and the human relations approach have a continuing influence on I/O psychology today. Although we examine each side of industrial and organizational psychology in separate sections below, the two areas overlap a great deal, and some topics, such as motivation, are a focal point in both areas. I/O psychologists have a central interest in what "works" at work: the factors that make a job really great. Although the emphasis of the two approaches may be different, with the "I" side more concerned with maximizing efficiency, safety, and cost effectiveness, and the "O" side more targeted at the human relations processes that contribute to feelings of fulfillment, both sides seek to apply scientific methods to understanding the complex processes associated with people at work.

For insight on the workplace dimensions addressed by I/O psychology, it is useful to focus on highly successful organizations. Each year, the Great Place to Work Institute conducts a survey to identify the best workplaces in the United States, which are then announced in *Fortune* magazine. Today, the best places to work are characterized as flexible, diverse, learning-oriented, and open in communication. In 2010, SAS, a producer of statistical software used by many psychologists, was voted the number 1 best place to work in the United States. Second place went to the financial advising firm Edward Jones. Wegmans Food Market was third, and Google placed fourth (Moskowitz & Levering, 2010). Figure 55.2 provides an overview of the best places to work in the United States in the last 10 years.

Year	Employer	Location	Type	Number of Employees*	Sampling of Perks and Benefits
2010	SAS	North Carolina	Software	5,487 45% Women 16% Minorities	Unlimited sick days; child care
2009	NetApp	California	Network storage/software	5,014 24% Women 34% Minorities	Over $10,000 in adoption aid; 5 paid days for volunteering
2008	Google	California	Software/Internet services	8,134 33% Women 36% Minorities	Onsite fitness center; child care; stock options; free cappuccino
2007	Google	California	Online software/Internet services	5,063 36% Women 31% Minorities	Tuition reimbursement; onsite doctors and dentists
2006	Genentech	California	Biotechnology, pharmaceuticals	8,121 50% Women 43% Minorities	3 weeks' vacation per year
2005	Wegmans Food Markets	New York	Food/grocery	30,128 54% Women 15% Minorities	Company motto: "Employees first. Customers second."
2004	J. M. Smucker Company	Ohio	Manufacturing (jam, jelly, and other food products)	2,585 42% Women 20% Minorities	Gimmick-free management, stressing integrity
2003 and 2002	Edward Jones	Missouri	Financial services, insurance	25,278 66% Women 9% Minorities	Management rated as honest by 97% of employees; early bonuses to stockbrokers in a difficult economic year
2001	Container Store	Texas	Retail	1,473 63% Women 30% Minorities	Emphasis on open communication and employee training; salaries 50% higher than industry average

*Number of employees in the year in which the firm was named the best place to work.

FIGURE 55.2   **The Number 1 Best Places to Work in the United States, 2001–2010** These are the best places to work, according to *Fortune* magazine. Note the various locations and types of companies that are represented by these top-rated employers.

SUMMARY

Taylor introduced the notion that scientific principles should be applied to work settings. Scientific management promoted the ideas that jobs should be analyzed to determine their requirements, that people should be hired on the basis of characteristics matching these requirements, that employees should be trained, and that productivity should be rewarded.

Ergonomics, or human factors, is a field of study concerned with the relationship between human beings and the tools or machines they use in their work. Ergonomics is focused on promoting safety and efficiency.

The Hawthorne studies are a landmark series of studies conducted by Mayo and his colleagues. Although the results are controversial, the studies demonstrated the importance of acknowledging that workers are human beings operating in a social setting. This work gave rise to the human relations approach to management that stresses the importance of the psychological characteristics of workers and managers.

KEY TERMS

scientific management   512
ergonomics   513
Hawthorne effect   514
human relations approach   514

TEST YOURSELF

1. What does the managerial philosophy known as scientific management emphasize?

2. What is ergonomics, and with what aspects of the workplace is it concerned?

3. Why are the Hawthorne studies important?

APPLY YOUR KNOWLEDGE

1. Research the concept of ergonomics. Then, devise a plan using ergonomics that can enhance the use of iPhones, iPods, or iPads. Propose your ideas to the class and seek feedback on them.

2. How might your teacher use the concept of the Hawthorne Effect in the classroom? Describe one advantage of considering the Hawthorne Effect when planning for a classroom or workplace and one disadvantage.

Industrial Psychology

Industrial psychology is the older of the two sides of I/O psychology. Industrial psychology takes a company-oriented perspective and focuses on increasing efficiency and productivity through the appropriate use of a firm's personnel, or employees—its *human resources* (Bernadin, 2010; Cartwright & Cooper, 2008; Cascio, 2010). The field of industrial psychology has a four-pronged emphasis:

- *Job analysis:* Organizing and describing the tasks involved in a job.
- *Employee selection:* Matching the best person to each job.
- *Training:* Bringing new employees up to speed on the details of the position.
- *Performance appraisal:* Evaluating whether the person is doing a good job.

In this section we explore each of these dimensions of the field.

56·1 JOB ANALYSIS

Job analysis is the process of generating a description of what a job involves, including the knowledge and skills that are necessary to carry out the job's functions (Colquitt, LePine, & Wesson, 2011; J. F. Wilson, 2007). An effective job analysis includes three essential elements (Brannick & Levine, 2002). First, the analysis must follow a systematic procedure that is set up in advance. Second, it must break down the job into small units so that each aspect can be easily understood. Breaking down a job may lead to the discovery that, for example, a skill that previously was not considered important actually is. For instance, the responsibilities of a managerial position may include informing employees of termination. Social skills that might not have seemed important to the day-to-day function of the job may come to the fore in this case. Third, the analysis should lead to an employee manual that accurately characterizes the job.

A job analysis can focus on the job itself or on the characteristics of the person who is suited for the job (Mondy, 2010; Peterson & Jeanneret, 2007). A job-oriented description outlines what the job entails (say, analyzing scientific data) and what it requires (for instance, expertise with both basic computer programs and statistics software). A person-oriented job analysis involves what are sometimes called **KSAOs** (or **KSAs**). These abbreviations stand for **k**nowledge, **s**kills, **a**bilities, and **o**ther characteristics. Knowledge, of course, refers to what the person needs to know to function in the job. Skills are what the individual must be able to do. Abilities include the person's capacity to learn the job and to gain new skills. Other characteristics may also be important. For the job of professional landscaper, enjoying outside work may be an essential "other," and for a child-care worker the ability to handle frequent diaper changes and to chase energetic toddlers may be required. Patagonia, the maker of outdoor gear, prefers to hire individuals who are passionate about climbing and hiking.

● **job analysis** The process of generating a description of what a job involves, including the knowledge and skills that are necessary to carry out the job's functions.

● **KSAOs (KSAs)** Common elements in a person-oriented job analysis; an abbreviation for **k**nowledge, **s**kills, **a**bilities, and **o**ther characteristics.

Enthusiasm can be an important job qualification. Patagonia seeks to hire people who are passionate climbers and hikers.

TITLE: Actor
Portrays role in dramatic production to interpret character or present characterization to
audience: Rehearses part to learn lines and
cues as directed. Interprets serious or comic
role by speech, gesture, and body movement
to entertain or inform audience for stage, motion picture, television, radio, or other media
production. May write or adapt own material.
May dance and sing. May direct self and
others in production. May read from script or
book, utilizing minimum number of stage
properties and relying mainly on changes of
voice and inflection to hold audience's attention and be designated Dramatic Reader.

TITLE: Predatory-Animal Hunter
Hunts, traps, and kills predatory animals to
collect bounty: Hunts quarry using dogs, and
shoots animals. Traps or poisons animals
depending on environs and habits of animals
sought. Removes designated parts, such as
ears or tail from slain animals, using knife, to
present as evidence of kill for bounty. May
skin animals and treat pelts for marketing.
May train dogs for hunting. May be designated according to animal hunted as Cougar
Hunter; Coyote Hunter; Wolf Hunter.

TITLE: Personal Shopper
Selects and purchases merchandise for
department store customers, according to
mail or telephone requests. Visits wholesale
establishments or other department stores to
purchase merchandise which is out-of-stock or
which store does not carry. Records and processes mail orders and merchandise returned
for exchange. May escort customer through
store.

FIGURE 56.1 **Sample Job Descriptions** Do you aspire to a career as an actor, a predatory-animal hunter, or a personal shopper? If so, the description reproduced here from the U.S. Department of Labor's *Dictionary of Occupational Titles* will give you a distinct flavor of the job and its day-to-day responsibilities.

Creating a job analysis typically involves collecting information from a variety of informants, including job analysts, individuals who already have the job, supervisors, and trained observers (Harvey & others, 2007; Nkomo, Fottler, & McAfee, 2011). These individuals can be asked to complete a questionnaire about the importance of various skills to a job, or they might be directed to describe the essential elements of the job in an interview (Fine & Wiley, 1971).

The U.S. Department of Labor (2010) has produced an enormous database called O*NET that compiles job descriptions for thousands of occupations. The descriptions are based on authoritative ratings and interviews with experts in the various occupations, and new occupations are added frequently. A recent addition to the database is "fitness trainer." Figure 56.1 presents the descriptions given for the jobs of actor, predatory-animal hunter, and personal shopper.

Job descriptions are valuable in that they allow people to evaluate their interest in a particular occupation. Are you good at memorization? Does "removing designated parts" of an animal sound interesting to you? How about "escorting a customer through a store"? Job descriptions may be a first step for job hunters interested in finding a good match to their interests and skills.

One element missing from these descriptions is the demand for these occupations—does the world need another predatory-animal hunter? According to the Department

psychological *inquiry*

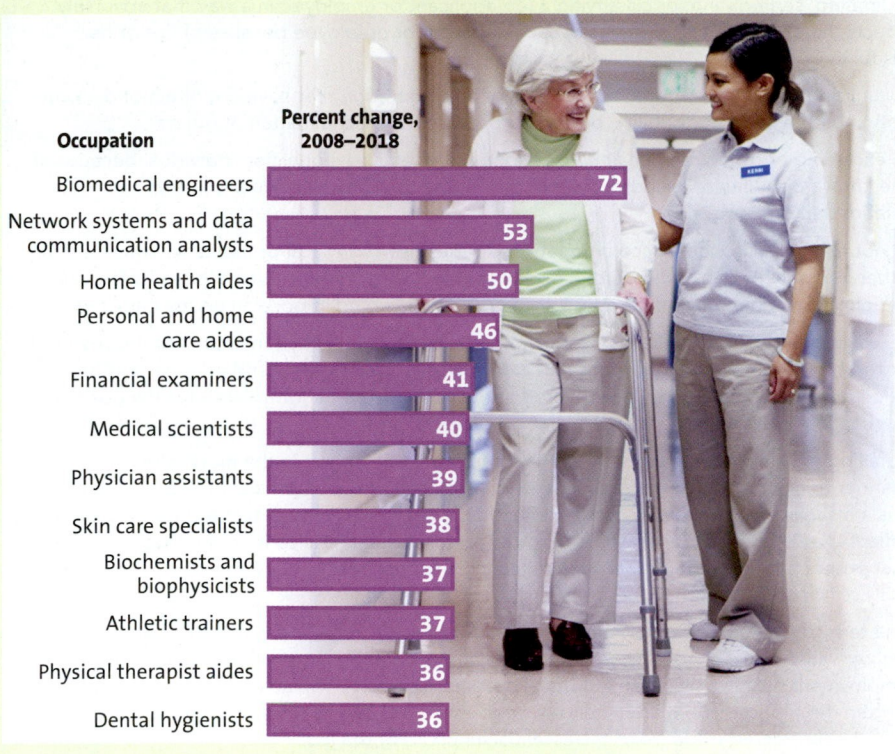

Occupation	Percent change, 2008–2018
Biomedical engineers	72
Network systems and data communication analysts	53
Home health aides	50
Personal and home care aides	46
Financial examiners	41
Medical scientists	40
Physician assistants	39
Skin care specialists	38
Biochemists and biophysicists	37
Athletic trainers	37
Physical therapist aides	36
Dental hygienists	36

The Fastest-Growing Jobs in the United States

This figure presents the projected percentage change in demand for the fastest-growing jobs in the United States. The data estimate the change from 2008 to 2018. The jobs listed have various training and/or educational requirements. To be a skin care specialist, one needs a certificate of training after high school graduation; dental hygienists are required to have an associate's degree; and a bachelor's degree is necessary to be a biomedical engineer, network systems and data communications analyst, financial examiner, or athletic trainer. A master's degree is required to be a physician assistant, and a doctorate is necessary to practice as a medical scientist. The other occupations involve on-the-job training. Answer the questions below.

1. Which of the listed occupations have the lowest projected growth?

2. Considering the training that is described above for each of these occupations, do you think the training is appropriate? Why or why not?

3. Imagine how this list might differ from similar lists compiled 20 years ago. Which careers listed above do you think are the newest arrivals? Why?

4. What do these data tell you about U.S. society today and in the coming years?

of Labor Center for Labor Statistics' *Occupational Outlook Handbook* (2010–2011), the occupations in the United States that are expected to grow fastest through 2018 are biomedical engineers, network systems and data communication analysts, and home health aides. According to projections, the number of new jobs in these occupations will increase by at least 50 percent by 2018. The Psychological Inquiry shows the relevant data and the percentage increase in other fast-growing jobs.

In addition to serving a useful function for job seekers, job analyses also establish a foundation for other aspects of personnel decision making. A thorough job analysis, for example, can provide information that directs hiring decisions and performance evaluations (Volskuijl & Evers, 2008). Quite simply, a manager cannot select the right person for the job or evaluate job performance without knowing what the job formally requires. In addition, job analyses can guide training plans and provide information to I/O researchers who are interested in examining how aspects of jobs relate to other variables, such as productivity, absenteeism, and work stress.

A final area where job analysis is important is the legal realm. The KSAOs mentioned in a job description must be clearly job relevant. Some job attributes have caused controversy in this regard—for example, should height and physical fitness be considered job-relevant characteristics for police officers? The requirement of such attributes historically has excluded some women and others of shorter stature from police duty, and many such requirements have been struck down by the courts.

Also related to legal concerns, a thorough job analysis should accurately assess the essential and nonessential functions of a job. *Essential functions* are the fundamental,

FIGURE 56.2 Excerpts from the Americans with Disabilities Act of 1990, Title I Passed in 1990, the Americans with Disabilities Act forbids discrimination in the workplace based on disability or illness.

No (employer) shall discriminate against a qualified individual with a disability because of the disability of such individual in regard to job application procedures, the hiring, advancement, or discharge of employees, employee compensation, job training, and other terms, conditions, and privileges of employment.

. . . [T]he term "discriminate" includes

1. limiting, segregating, or classifying a job applicant or employee in a way that adversely affects the opportunities or status of such applicant or employee because of (his or her) disability . . . ;

2. utilizing standards, criteria, or methods of administration that have the effect of discrimination on the basis of disability; or that perpetuate the discrimination of others . . . ;

3. excluding or otherwise denying equal jobs or benefits to a qualified individual because of the known disability of an individual with whom the qualified individual is known to have a relationship or association;

4. not making reasonable accommodations to the known physical or mental limitations of an otherwise qualified individual with a disability who is an applicant or employee, unless such (employer) can demonstrate that the accommodation would impose an undue hardship . . . ;

5. using qualification standards, employment tests or other selection criteria that screen out or tend to screen out an individual with a disability . . . unless the standard, test or other selection criteria, as used by the covered entity, is shown to be job-related for the position in question and is consistent with business necessity; and

6. failing to select and administer tests concerning employment in the most effective manner to ensure that, when such test is administered to a job applicant or employee who has a disability that impairs sensory, manual, or speaking skills, such test results accurately reflect the skills, aptitude, or whatever other factor of such applicant or employee that such test purports to measure, rather than reflecting the impaired sensory, manual, or speaking skills of (the individual). . . .

The term "qualified individual with a disability" means an individual with a disability who, with or without reasonable accommodation, can perform the essential functions of the employment position that such individual holds or desires. . . . [I]f an employer has prepared a written description before advertising or interviewing applicants for the job, this description shall be considered evidence of the essential functions of the job.

necessary tasks and duties of a job as defined by the employer, usually in writing. For example, a day-care worker must be capable of being physically active, and a data analyst must be able to utilize and apply advanced statistical techniques. *Nonessential functions* are aspects of the job that may not be necessary, although they are desirable. For example, a pizza delivery person must be able to drive and must have a valid driver's license, but driving is not essential for a kitchen worker at the pizza shop or for a health inspector who evaluates the restaurant for health standards.

The Americans with Disabilities Act (ADA) of 1990 (provisions of which are shown in Figure 56.2) made it illegal to refuse employment or a promotion to someone with a disability that prevents the person from performing only nonessential functions (Cleveland, Barnes-Farrell, & Ratz, 1997; Colella & Bruyère, 2010). The ADA defines a person with a disability as "qualified" for a position if he or she is able to perform the essential job functions—with or without reasonable accommodations. Accommodations may include changes in facilities, equipment, or policies that permit an otherwise qualified individual with disabilities to perform the essential functions of a job. An accommodation is considered reasonable—and is required—if it effectively allows the person to perform the essential job tasks while not placing an undue hardship on the employer. Although at times such regulations may seem to impose an undue burden on employers, they do promote fairness and kindness (Aguinis, 2010). Such regulations also help to diversify the workforce, bringing many unique perspectives to bear on an organization's goals (Colella & Bruyère, 2010).

Information from a job analysis increases the likelihood that individuals will feel that they have been treated fairly in hiring and promotion decisions (Mitchell, Alliger, & Morfopoulos, 1997; Truxillo & Bauer, 2010). If a job analysis is done well, it can clarify the reasons for such decisions. For example, an employee who is very shy may understand being turned down for a promotion if the job description for the new position clearly indicates that it requires an active leadership style.

As businesses increasingly have relied on teams to complete tasks, job analyses for team-oriented job functions have become necessary (Levi, 2007). Michael Brannick and Edward Levine (2002) maintained that procedures similar to those used for individuals can be adapted for team-oriented occupations. However, if a job involves teamwork, the KSAOs might change accordingly, with social abilities and communication skills coming to the fore (Morgeson, Reider, & Campion, 2005).

56-2 EMPLOYEE SELECTION

Once a position is defined, the task for hiring managers is to select the best from among the pool of recruits. That pool can be huge. Google gets a million job applicants a year—that amounts to over 2,700 a day, including weekends.

Where do qualified applicants come from? Increasingly, the answer is the Internet. Many companies now advertise positions on their own websites or use other sites geared toward recruiting, including Monster.com (Chapman & Webster, 2003); see Figure 56.3 for an example. Where employees come from makes a difference. Researchers have found that individuals who applied on the basis of referrals from insiders performed better on the job than those who came in "cold" (McManus & Ferguson, 2003). However, the Internet may be a great equalizer. Although those with connections perform best, individuals who apply through online channels turn out to be better-quality candidates than those who apply in response to a newspaper advertisement or other sources (McManus & Ferguson, 2003).

Industrial psychologists have played a significant role in developing techniques for selecting individuals and placing them in positions that match their strengths (Bernardin, 2010; Oswald & Hough, 2010). Based on a job analysis, the KSAOs necessary for a particular job should be clear. The next step is to measure the knowledge, skills, and abilities (as well as other characteristics) of the recruits in order to evaluate their appropriateness for a position. These measures include testing and interviews, as well as work samples and exercises.

FIGURE 56.3 **Job Ad on Monster.com**
Employers increasingly are finding potential job candidates through online ads.

Testing

Managers or human resource personnel may administer tests to prospective candidates to ascertain whether they are good matches for the position (Cascio & Aguinis, 2011; Oswald & Hough, 2010). Some organizations use psychological tests that assess factors such as personality traits and motivation. Other firms employ cognitive ability tests, such as intelligence tests. Recall from Module 29 that developing culture-fair tests of intelligence is difficult, and some of these assessments may be biased. Despite this controversy, research has shown that scores on these tests are related to later performance (Gregory, 2011; Ree & Carretta, 2007).

An **integrity test,** another type of examination sometimes used in personnel screening, is designed to assess whether the candidate is likely to be honest on the job. An *overt integrity test* contains items that ask the individual to give his or her attitude about lying. A sample item might be "It's okay to lie if you know you won't get caught." Alternatively, some organizations rely on measures of personality traits associated with being honest. Generally, responses of individuals on integrity tests are related to counterproductive behavior as well as job performance, although not necessarily literal lying—which is difficult to detect (Ones & Viswesvaran, 1998; Ones, Viswesvaran, & Schmidt, 1993).

● **integrity test** A type of job-screening examination that is designed to assess whether a candidate will be honest on the job.

Interviews

Perhaps the most common way that job candidates are evaluated is through an interview (Huffcutt & Culbertson, 2010). As we saw in Module 51, first impressions can be made very rapidly. This immediate first impression may predict whether a salesperson makes a sale (Ambady, Krabbenhoft, & Hogan, 2006), but it may have nothing to do with a person's ability, for example, to program a computer or to develop a new drug. For interviews to serve their purpose, they must be about more than simply whether the interviewer likes the candidate.

First impressions can be subject to gender and ethnic biases, and since the Civil Rights Act of 1964 (revised in 1991), it has been illegal in the United States to deny someone employment on the basis of gender or ethnicity (Parker, 2006). Figure 56.4 lists the provisions of the Civil Rights Act that set the standards for just personnel decisions in the United States.

A particular challenge that the interviewer faces is the job seeker's strong desire to make a good impression. Imagine interviewing for your dream job—to be a high school English teacher. During the interview, the school principal asks if you might also be able to teach history or coach the volleyball team. If you really want the job, it might not seem like a stretch to say "Yes, I might be able to do those things" (if only you had taken even a single college history class or paid better attention to last summer's Olympic Games). *Interviewer illusion* refers to interviewers' mistaken tendency to believe in their own ability to discern the truth from a job applicant (Nisbett, 1987). Of course, any objective observer might note that job candidates try to make a good impression, put their best foot forward, and refrain from revealing their failings (Tsai, Chen, & Chiu, 2005; Weiss & Feldman, 2006). This is not to say that job candidates are necessarily lying, but simply that they are, understandably, trying to get hired.

Interviewers can improve the quality of the information they obtain through interviews by asking the same specific questions of all candidates. In a **structured interview,** candidates are asked specific questions that methodically seek to obtain truly useful information for the interviewer. Rather than posing the question "Do you get along with others?" the interviewer might ask the candidate, "Can you tell me about a time when you had a conflict with someone and how you worked it out?" When conducting a structured interview, interviewers must take notes or record the interviews in order to avoid memory biases. Structured interviews have been shown to be superior to unstructured interviews in terms of being reliable and valid predictors of job performance (Blackman, 2008; Huffcutt & Culbertson, 2010).

● **structured interview** A kind of interview in which candidates are asked specific questions that methodically seek to obtain truly useful information for the interviewer.

FIGURE 56.4 **Excerpts from the Civil Rights Act of 1964, Title VII (revised, 1991)** The Civil Rights Act forbids discrimination based on race, national origin, sex, or religious affiliation.

It shall be an unlawful employment practice for an employer:

1. to fail or refuse to hire or to discharge any individual, or otherwise to discriminate against any individual with respect to his compensation, terms, conditions, or privileges of employment, because of such individual's race, color, religion, sex, or national origin;

or

2. to limit, segregate, or classify his employees or applicants for employment in any way which would deprive or tend to deprive any individual of employment opportunities or otherwise adversely affect his status as an employee, because of such individual's race, color, religion, sex, or national origin.

It shall be an unlawful employment practice for an employment agency to fail or refuse to refer for employment, or otherwise to discriminate against, any individual because of his race, color, religion, sex, or national origin, or to classify or refer for employment any individual on the basis of his race, color, religion, sex, or national origin.

It shall be an unlawful employment practice for any employer, labor organization, or joint labor-management committee controlling apprenticeship or other training or retraining, including on-the-job training programs, to discriminate against any individual because of his race, color, religion, sex, or national origin in admission to, or employment in, any program established to provide apprenticeship or other training.

MOTHER GOOSE & GRIMM © 2009 Grimmy, Inc. King Features Syndicate.

Although interviewers may sometimes be influenced by their own biases, there is no substitute for face-to-face interaction. In the selection process, Google looks for "Googleyness": the ability to work well in an organization without a strict hierarchy, in teams, and in a fast-paced and ever-changing environment. The firm seeks to hire brainy, creative, and hardworking people who work well in a context that is relatively free of structure (Moskowitz & Levering, 2007).

Work Samples and Exercises

Another technique for pinpointing the best-suited candidate for a particular job is requiring an applicant to submit work samples. For a job such as photographer, copywriter, or graphic designer, for example, the candidate typically must present samples.

An additional evaluation method devised by I/O psychologists is to require candidates to complete mock job-related tasks that allow the direct assessment of their skills. Seeing applicants handle unexpected situations or think on their feet gives potential employers a sense of the candidates' fit for the job (Ployhart & MacKenzie, 2010). These activities might include an "in-basket" exercise in which candidates must organize and prioritize a pile of potential assignments and a "leaderless group" exercise in which each prospective employee is observed in a group problem-solving task.

Applying for a job in fields such as graphic design and photography often requires showing a portfolio of work samples.

56-3 TRAINING

You got the job! Now, what was that job again? Once a new employee is hired, the challenge facing the organization (and the new recruit) is to learn all that is necessary to carry out the job effectively. Three key phases of training are orientation, formal training, and mentoring.

Orientation

Learning the ropes of a new job and workplace can be difficult for new hires (Nelson & Quick, 2011; Noe & others, 2007). To help them overcome the hurdles, most firms have a program of **orientation,** which generally involves introducing newly hired employees to the organization's goals, familiarizing them with its rules and regulations, and letting them know how to get things done. Studies suggest that orientation programs do work, especially with regard to instilling an understanding of organizational values and philosophies and socializing the new employee (Aguinis & Kraiger, 2009).

Some organizations have turned to computer-based orientation programs in order to cut expenses. One study examined the implications of using computer-based versus in-person orientation programs (Wesson & Gogus, 2005). Although both methods provided

● **orientation** A program by which an organization introduces newly hired employees to the organization's goals, familiarizes them with its rules and regulations, and lets them know how to get things done.

new employees with information, the computer-based orientation fell short on social factors. Employees who received a computer-based orientation might have learned how to work the copy machine and get a computer repaired, but they probably did not come away with a list of their new acquaintances from their orientation or a good sense of the social culture of their new workplace.

Formal Training

Training involves teaching the new employee the essential requirements to do the job well (Aguinis & Kraiger, 2009; Brown & Sitzmann, 2010). Training needs vary by occupation. The engineers who join Google probably need only an orientation and a sign pointing to the computers (and perhaps another directing them to the free cappuccino). The position of home health aide requires only basic on-the-job training. In contrast, other jobs, such the position of an airline pilot, are far more technical and require extensive training.

The foundation of any training program is to establish the goals of the training and a sense for how the trainer will know that the person is ready. An assumption of training is that whatever the employee learns in training will generalize to the real world when he or she starts work. Training in the workplace follows the same principles we examined in Module 17 with respect to learning. A key goal for training is *overlearning*, which, as described in Module 35, means learning to perform a task so well that it becomes automatic. Research shows that training is an important part of eventual job performance and mastery of the technical skills required for a job (Aguinis & Kraiger, 2009). Although fewer studies have examined the effects of training on organizational profits, the findings support the idea that sound training does positively impact the bottom line (Arthur & others, 2003).

Organizations vary with respect to the value they place on training. This difference is shown, for example, by the degree of training observed from company to company for similar jobs. Consider that trainees at the Container Store get 241 hours of training, as compared with the 7 hours of training that is the retail industry average. Moreover, although we have considered training primarily as it relates to beginning a new job, employee learning and the expansion of employee skills (what is called *employee development*) are important throughout a career, for employees and firms alike. Even individuals with a great deal of expertise can benefit from development programs (Brown & Sitzmann, 2010). These programs, sometimes called *managerial training programs,* often are developed by I/O psychologists in consultation with the organization.

Mentoring

Mentoring is a relationship between an experienced employee and a novice in which the more experienced employee—the *mentor*—serves as an advisor, a sounding board, and a source of support for the newer employee (Eby, 2010). Mentoring may benefit both the employee and the organization, as mentors guide new employees through the beginning of their career and help them achieve their goals within the organization, as well as provide a strong interpersonal bond.

Some organizations assign individuals to mentors (Raabe & Beehr, 2003). Assigned mentors may not be as effective as those that emerge naturally—and an incompetent mentor may be worse than having no mentor at all (Ragins, Cotton, & Miller, 2000). "Natural" mentoring relationships, however, may be based on common interests and other similarities and as such may be less likely to develop for women and for members of ethnic minorities in fields that are dominated by White males. In such situations, assigned mentors who are sensitive and open and who have time to devote to new protégés are all the more important. At minimum, co-workers who differ in every other way share one common bond: the organization. Indeed, as you may remember from Module 54, the lesson of the Robbers Cave study and the jigsaw classroom is that when very different people work together on shared goals and enjoy their managers' approval, prejudicial attitudes can soften.

● **training** Teaching a new employee the essential requirements to do the job well.

"This call may be monitored for training purposes or just to keep our staff amused."

© Aaron Bacall. www.CartoonStock.com.

● **mentoring** A relationship between an experienced employee—a mentor—and a novice, in which the more experienced employee serves as an advisor, a sounding board, and a source of support for the newer employee.

56·4 PERFORMANCE APPRAISAL

Industrial psychologists are also interested in **performance appraisal,** the evaluation of a person's success at meeting his or her organization's goals (Grant & Wrzesniewski, 2010). Performance appraisal is important for a variety of reasons. It allows employees to get feedback and make appropriate changes in their work habits. It also helps guide decisions about promotions and raises, as well as terminations and firings (Ivancevich & Konopaske, 2011). Within the U.S. government, for example, firing must be performance based. This requirement means that before a government employer can terminate someone, there must be documented evidence of poor performance. In Canada, this regulation applies to private businesses as well. Regular performance appraisals provide a paper trail that serves to justify decisions such as promotion and termination.

In some occupations, objective measures are available that help to gauge performance. These might include measurable factors such as the number of products a factory worker is able to make per hour, the dollar amount of sales by a sales representative, the number of on-the-job accidents per year, the number of days late to work, the number of legal cases won, and the number of surgical operations performed. Of course, not all jobs provide such measurable output (Tannenbaum, 2006). In addition, it may not be clear what a "high number" is: How high would the number have to be to be "good"? Simple counts, taken out of context, may not be informative. For example, consider a sales agent with a very challenging territory who sets a selling record even though her sales fall below the average of other sales representatives who are assigned to less difficult areas.

Finally, focusing on objective counts may miss the quality of the person's work. For these reasons, many performance evaluations, while including an assessment of objective numbers, also entail subjective ratings made by a supervisor or panel of experts. These ratings typically involve multiple items that are meant to assess different aspects of performance, such as work quality and efficiency.

Sources of Bias in Performance Ratings

As subjective judgments, performance ratings may be prone to biases and errors (Aguinis, 2009; Austin & Crespin, 2006). One error is the **halo effect,** common in performance ratings, that occurs when a rater gives a person the same rating on all of the items being evaluated, even though the individual varies across the dimensions being assessed. In making halo effect errors, the rater allows his or her general impression of the person to guide the ratings. So, for example, the supervisor might give someone a 9 on a 1-to-10 scale for all assessment items, even though the employee's work quality was a 9 but his efficiency was more like a 5.

Factors other than work quality can influence a performance evaluation. If your supervisor likes you, for example, you are more likely to get positive ratings (Ferris & others, 1994). However, it is important to consider that the main factor in your boss's affection may well be your outstanding performance (Robbins & DeNisi, 1994). The effect of rater liking on performance appraisals suggests that it is important for new workers to make an excellent first impression. Supervisors are human, and in evaluating the work of others, they are engaged in a social process. They have expectancies and look for confirming information. Winning the early respect of a supervisor may be an important part of obtaining positive performance evaluations later (Lefkowitz, 2000).

360-Degree Feedback

One way to improve the quality of the information used in a performance evaluation is to collect feedback from a variety of sources (Wildman & others, 2010). To this end, a method called 360-degree feedback has been developed (Baldwin & Padgett, 1993). In **360-degree feedback,** an employee's performance is rated by a variety of individuals, including himself or herself, a peer, a supervisor, a subordinate, and perhaps a customer

● performance appraisal The evaluation of a person's success at meeting his or her organization's goals.

● halo effect A bias, common in performance ratings, that occurs when a rater gives a person the same rating on all of the items being evaluated, even though the individual varies across the dimensions being assessed.

● 360-degree feedback A method of performance appraisal whereby an employee's performance is rated by a variety of individuals, including himself or herself, a peer, a supervisor, a subordinate, and perhaps a customer or client.

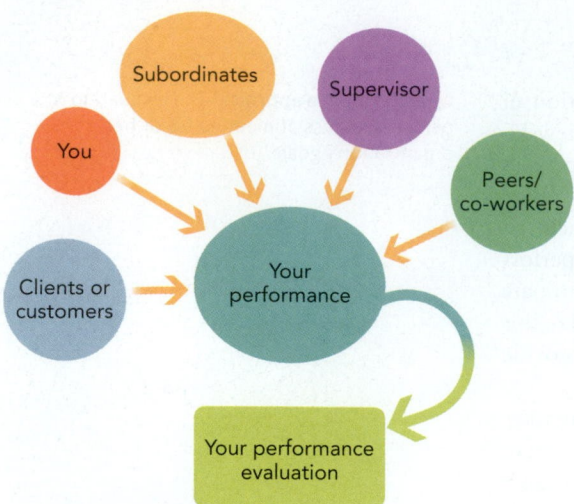

FIGURE 56.5 **360-Degree Feedback** 360-degree feedback means that everyone who is affected by your work has some input in evaluating your performance.

or client. Although there is some agreement among the different raters using the 360-degree feedback process, there is also more likely to be variability, suggesting that ratings are indeed about the person's performance and not a general impression (Brett & Atwater, 2001; Maurer, Mitchell, & Barbeite, 2002). In addition, although liking does influence ratings, these effects may average out, because not all raters are likely to be affected by liking in the same way (Wildman & others, 2010). Web-based evaluation systems have simplified the logistics of the 360-degree feedback approach and made the process much more convenient. Figure 56.5 illustrates the process of 360-degree feedback.

The Importance of Fairness

A performance appraisal can be stressful for both the evaluator(s) and the evaluated employee. Few people relish telling someone that her work has been rated poorly, and the temptation might be to send off the evaluation by e-mail. Yet talking about the evaluation face-to-face can be enormously powerful in ensuring that the employee feels that her treatment has been fair. Letting an employee self-evaluate improves work attitudes, and allowing the individual to sit down with the supervisor and openly discuss the evaluation enhances feelings of fairness in the process, even when the ratings are negative (Truxillo & Bauer, 2010).

Just as hiring decisions cannot be based on ethnicity or gender, performance evaluation systems must not discriminate. Research has suggested that in order to enhance the legal defensibility of a termination decision, a job analysis should define the dimensions that will be used in the performance appraisal; the raters should be trained; employees should have an opportunity to appeal the ratings; and the organization should meticulously document performance (Barrett & Kernan, 1987). Organizations might also offer counseling or developmental opportunities to poorly performing employees. The experience of being fired from a job can be both economically and emotionally devastating (Lucas & others, 2004), and people who feel they have been treated unfairly may take legal action. The use of multiple raters in performance evaluations is associated with greater success in defending firing decisions in the courtroom (Werner & Bolino, 1997).

Another Measure of Performance: Organizational Citizenship Behavior

● **organizational citizenship behavior (OCB)** Discretionary actions on the part of an employee that promote organizational effectiveness but are not included in the person's formal responsibilities.

One type of behavior that may find its way into a performance evaluation is **organizational citizenship behavior (OCB)**—discretionary actions on an employee's part that promote organizational effectiveness but are not included in the person's formal responsibilities (Organ, Podsakoff, & Podsakoff, 2010). OCB comprises behaviors such as coming in early, staying late, and helping a colleague with an assignment. Conscientiousness is associated with higher levels of OCB, yet even those low on conscientiousness engage in OCB when they are especially happy at their jobs (Bowling, 2010).

OCB is thought to influence organizations in two ways. First, it may directly impact productivity and economic success (MacKenzie, Podsakoff, & Ahearne, 1998). Second, OCB may have a more general influence on the social system of the workplace, making fellow employees feel more positive about their jobs (Organ, Podsakoff, & Podsakoff, 2010). As such, OCB occupies the middle ground in I/O psychology, influencing both the efficiency and profitability of business (the "I" side) and the wider social climate of the organization (the "O" side).

Taking the idea of OCB further, it is possible that the meaning of OCB cannot be fully understood outside of the wider social context of the organization. Is showing up for work early every day an example of OCB, or is it simply "kissing up" (Eastman, 1994) or playing office politics (Snell & Wong, 2007)? Did your co-worker send you that reminder e-mail or leave you that voice message at 5 A.M. to be helpful or to point out that she was at her desk working while you were still asleep?

Research by Bennett Tepper and his colleagues (2004) revealed that OCB was positively related to fellow employees' satisfaction and loyalty—but only when supervisor abusiveness was low. Abusive supervisors engage in a variety of hostile behaviors, including emotional outbursts, public criticism, sarcastic comments, and interpersonally deviant acts (Duffy, Ganster, & Pagon, 2002). In situations where employees perceived a supervisor as abusive, a person's OCB had a negative effect on the job satisfaction of co-workers, who might reasonably have wondered about the loyalty of the person who was enacting OCB. In short, the meaning of a behavior may differ depending on its organizational context. That context is the domain of organizational psychology.

SUMMARY

Job analysis involves the systematic description of the knowledge and skills necessary to carry out a job. Job evaluation is the scientific assessment of the monetary value of a particular occupation.

Some procedures involved in personnel selection include testing, interviews, work samples, and other exercises. Training individuals for their jobs is a key goal for industrial psychologists. Dimensions of training include orientation, formal training, and mentoring, as well as ongoing employee development.

Performance appraisal is an important source of feedback for employees and guides decisions about promotions, raises, and termination. One source of bias in ratings is the halo effect, in which a rater gives a candidate the same rating on all the items being evaluated even though the person varies across the dimensions being assessed. One way to avoid performance appraisal errors is 360-degree feedback, which involves rating a worker through the input of a range of individuals, including co-workers, managers, and customers. Organizational citizenship behavior may also factor into performance. This term refers to discretionary behaviors that a person engages in that are not part of the specific job description.

KEY TERMS

job analysis   517
KSAOs (KSAs)   517
integrity test   521
structured interview   522
orientation   523
training   524

mentoring   524
performance appraisal   525
halo effect   525
360-degree feedback   525
organizational citizenship
   behavior (OCB)   526

TEST YOURSELF

1. What are the four prongs that the field of industrial psychology emphasizes?
2. Name and discuss some useful functions of job analyses.
3. Identify and define the three key aspects of job training.

APPLY YOUR KNOWLEDGE

1. You might be interested in discovering your personal strengths so that you can identify the occupations that might be best for you. A variety of measures have been developed to assess vocational abilities, and you can visit your campus career center to check these out. In addition, there is a new assessment tool, developed by positive psychology scholars, that measures strengths of character such as achievement motivation, loyalty, sense of humor, capacity to love and be loved, and integrity. To determine your character strengths, visit the Values in Action website at http://www.viastrengths.org.

2. If you are interested in exploring possible careers, check out the O*NET at http://www.bls.gov/oco/. You might be surprised at some of the jobs that are out there.

Organizational Psychology and Culture

In this module we look at the "O" in I/O—organizational psychology. In doing so, we explore the topics of management styles, workers' attitudes and behavior, and leadership. Special attention is given to one aspect of the "O" side, organizational culture.

57·1 ORGANIZATIONAL PSYCHOLOGY

The main interest in organizational psychology is research and practice involving human relations (Colquitt, LePine, & Wesson, 2011; Luthans, 2011). Organizational psychology emphasizes the psychological experience of the worker. It examines how the relationships among people at work influence their job satisfaction and commitment, as well as their efficiency and productivity. Although it may seem reasonable that companies should concentrate on "the bottom line," focusing exclusively on the economic results of work may not always be the best way to do business. As the following discussion reveals, other important factors also matter, including management approaches, job satisfaction, employee commitment, the meaning of work, and leadership styles (Griffin & Moorhead, 2010; Zedeck, 2010).

Approaches to Management

Managers are in a position of power in an organization. They make decisions about personnel, direct activities, and ensure that the staff does the work correctly and on time. A manager's approach to this role can have widespread impact on organizational success as well as on employees' lives (Bateman & Snell, 2011; Mello, 2011). So it is appropriate that we examine how and why management styles matter to organizations and employees. To appreciate the importance of management styles to business, we begin by considering the historic contrast between American and Japanese automakers.

THE "JAPANESE" MANAGEMENT STYLE

In the 1980s, as the U.S. automobile industry took note of the emerging dominance of Japanese car brands in the U.S. market, Japanese management principles became all the rage. At this time, U.S. automakers also adopted the so-called Japanese principles of quality control and worker participation in organizational decision making. Interestingly, these principles are actually American principles, originally suggested by the American engineer and statistician W. Edwards Deming.

In the 1940s, Deming developed ideas about management that focused on quality; indeed, he has been called the father of the quality revolution. His philosophy of management was not well received in the United States, however, as American industry was wedded to the notions of efficiency, scientific management, and the bottom line. After World War II, Deming played a large role in the successful rebuilding of the Japanese economy, particularly the automobile industry. Deming's ideas have been recognized as directly related to Japan's eventual domination of the U.S. auto market.

Although Deming had a lot to say about management, one of his key points was that industry must embrace innovation and plan for the future, not remain narrowly focused on economic results. He compared the results-oriented management of the typical U.S. factory to driving a car with our eyes fixed on the rearview mirror (Deming, 1986). Results, he stressed, tell us about past performance—how we did. However, the question that burned in Deming's mind was, what are we going to do next? Deming called upon

So great were the contributions of American statistician W. Edwards Deming (1900–1993) in the recovery of the Japanese economy after World War II that the prime minister of Japan, on behalf of Emperor Hirohito, honored him with the Order of the Sacred Treasures, second class, in 1960.

industry to make a long-term commitment to new learning, to having an eye always trained on the future. He emphasized innovation and a managerial style that takes risks, makes decisions based on quality, and fosters strong relationships with suppliers, employees, and customers. The contrast between Frederick Taylor's approach to scientific management and Deming's innovation-oriented thinking can also be seen in other psychological approaches to management styles, as we now consider.

THEORY X AND THEORY Y

In his book *The Human Side of Enterprise,* Douglas McGregor (1960) suggested that there are two general approaches to management, which he termed Theory X and Theory Y. **Theory X managers** assume that work is innately unpleasant and that people have a strong desire to avoid it. Such managers believe that employees need direction, dislike responsibility, and must be kept in line. Theory X managers motivate performance by exerting control and threatening punishment.

In contrast, **Theory Y managers,** those with the outlook that McGregor advocates, assume that engaging in effortful behavior is natural to human beings—that even at play, people often work hard. According to the Theory Y view, control and punishment are not the only way to motivate workers. Rather, Theory Y managers recognize that people seek out responsibility and that motivation can come from allowing them to suggest creative and meaningful solutions to problems. These managers assume that people have untapped creative and intellectual potential that can benefit the organization.

The *waigawa* policy of the Japanese carmaker Honda Motors exemplifies this aspect of Theory Y management style. Under the ***waigawa* system,** when the corporation faces a difficult problem, all rank-related concerns are temporarily set aside, and anyone from any level of the organization can suggest solutions. Factory-line workers can present their ideas to the highest-level company executives. The U.S. corporation Harley-Davidson Motor Company has a similar "open door" policy.

McGregor's book is now 50 years old, but his distinctions between the two managerial styles remain a source of inspiration. This is particularly the case for practitioners in I/O psychology who seek to consult with organizations to enhance managerial effectiveness (Carson, 2005; Robinson, 2008).

STRENGTHS-BASED MANAGEMENT

Donald Clifton, a former CEO of the Gallup polling organization, emphasized the vast potential of employees. In keeping with the view of Theory Y managers, Clifton stressed that managers needed to identify and make use of their employees' strengths. In 2002, Clifton was recognized by the American Psychological Association as the founder of strengths-based psychology, and he used the findings from the emerging field of positive psychology in his work at Gallup. His **strengths-based management** stressed that maximizing an employee's existing strengths is a much easier proposition than trying to build such attributes from the ground up. By "strength" Clifton meant the consistent ability to attain a near-perfect performance on a given task (Clifton & Nelson, 1992; Hodges & Clifton, 2004). To develop worker strengths, a manager must recognize that each person has unique talents and that discovering these and putting them to use is crucial

Under the waigawa *policy in effect at Japan's Honda Motors and at the United States' Harley-Davidson Motor Company, workers from any level of the organization can present top executives with ideas for improving a system and for solving company problems.*

● **Theory X managers** Managers who assume that work is innately unpleasant and that people have a strong desire to avoid it; such managers believe that employees need direction, dislike responsibility, and must be kept in line.

● **Theory Y managers** Managers who assume that engaging in effortful behavior is natural to human beings; they recognize that people seek out responsibility and that motivation can come from allowing employees to suggest creative and meaningful solutions.

● ***waigawa* system** A management system dedicated to the idea that when the corporation faces a difficult problem, all rank-related concerns are temporarily set aside so that anyone from any level of the organization can propose a solution.

● **strengths-based management** A management style emphasizing that maximizing an employee's existing strengths is much easier than trying to build such attributes from the ground up.

Approach	Theorist	Manager's Mission	Manager's Problem-Solving Strategy	Manager's Focus When Things Are Going Well
"Japanese style"	Deming	Focus on the future, always seeking innovation and high quality. Forge strong relationships with people in every aspect of the organization.	Take risks, think about the future, and try something new.	Keep looking to the future, to potential innovation, and to risks.
Theory X	McGregor	Control employees, enforce rules, and make sure everyone is working hard. Keep the ship afloat.	Punish employees who fail.	Reward employees who succeed, and don't rock the boat.
Theory Y	McGregor	Challenge employees with responsibility; let them apply their talents, insights, and abilities.	Look to employees for input; harness their wisdom and insight to solve the problem.	Talk to employees about their insights into success and what to do next.
Strengths-based	Clifton	Identify employee strengths and match employees with jobs that will maximize these.	Reexamine the fit between employee strengths and assigned tasks.	Continue to build on employee strengths.

FIGURE 57.1 **Approaches to Management** Different approaches to management can have different consequences for employees and companies. Managers vary not only in general philosophy but also in problem-solving strategies and responses to success.

not only to an effective organization but also to the worker's sense of fulfillment (Bateman & Snell, 2011).

Focusing on employee strengths can have a powerful influence on a company's profitability. In one study of 65 organizations, only 4 were found to be taking a strengths-based approach (Clifton & Harter, 2003). Compared to the other 61, those 4 showed an increase in productivity equal to $1,000 per employee. In real money terms, that translates into about $5.4 million for the average company. The various management styles are summarized in Figure 57.1.

One reason managers are important is that they have profound influence on how people feel while at work. Someone might find her dream job ruined by a really lousy manager. Or a great manager might be able to make a boring job seem important and worthwhile. The way people feel about their occupations is another topic that has interested I/O psychologists.

Job Satisfaction

● **job satisfaction** The extent to which a person is content in his or her job.

I/O psychologists are keenly interested in people's attitudes about their jobs. **Job satisfaction** is the extent to which an individual is content in his or her job. Job satisfaction is a relatively recent term. In the past, many people simply did whatever their parents did to earn a living. However, economic conditions and social change have allowed more individuals access to education and employment, so the question has become not only whether a job puts money in the bank and food on the table but whether an individual feels fulfilled by his or her occupation. The happier that individuals are in their jobs, the more satisfied they are said to be.

The most common way to measure job satisfaction is with employee rating scales. Job satisfaction can be assessed globally, as with an item such as "How happy are you with your job, overall?" or in terms of more specific factors such as pay, work responsibilities, variety of tasks, promotional opportunities, the work itself, and co-workers. One cross-country comparative study examined job satisfaction in 24 different nations (Spector & others, 2001). Workers in Canada were the most satisfied with their jobs; workers in England, the least satisfied. U.S. respondents fell in the upper third with respect to job satisfaction.

Predictors of job satisfaction may vary for different jobs and different cultures. For example, in a study of 1,814 healthcare workers in Norway, the job satisfaction of all of the respondents was related to their feelings about the local leadership of their organizations (Krogstad & others, 2006). Differences emerged for the various occupational

"Flexible hours sounds good. Put me down for any shift you're NOT here."

groups in the study. For example, physicians' job satisfaction depended more on professional development opportunities, and nurses' job satisfaction depended more on social support at work and feedback from supervisors.

One factor that is not as strongly related to job satisfaction as might be expected is pay (Brasher & Chen, 1999). Among those who are making the minimum wage, some individuals are quite satisfied with their jobs. And among those who are earning a six-figure salary, some are dissatisfied. One study found that job satisfaction did not depend on the amount of money per se but rather on the person's perception that his or her pay was fair (Cohen-Charash & Spector, 2001).

Possibly it is the person, rather than the job, that matters most for job satisfaction. Certainly there is evidence that job satisfaction is relatively stable over time. A 50-year longitudinal study revealed that a worker's emotional disposition was linked to job satisfaction 50 years later (Staw, Bell, & Clausen, 1986). Some individuals may simply be predisposed to be satisfied. Of course, any group has its malcontents and complainers. Even in the Hawthorne studies, researchers identified individuals called "chronic kickers" who complained no matter what the researchers did (Roethlisberger, 1941). There may not be one perfect job but rather a very good but different job for each of us. Research demonstrates that the fit between the person and the job is the most important aspect of job satisfaction (Kristof-Brown & Guay, 2010; Verquer, Beehr, & Wagner, 2003).

Culture matters to job satisfaction as well. Researchers asked clerical workers in India and the United States to describe the worst things about their jobs (Narayanan, Menon, & Spector, 1999). Among the U.S. workers, lack of control was the second-greatest stressor, nominated by 25 percent of the participants. The Indian workers expressed the most stress about a lack of structure (again, about 25 percent described this issue). Interestingly, not a single American participant mentioned structure, and not a single Indian participant mentioned control. When individuals are asked "What makes a job satisfying?" the answer may very well be "It depends," and the factors might include the person, the job, and the cultural context.

I/O psychologists also have been interested in the question of whether job satisfaction relates to other aspects of work, such as absenteeism, organizational citizenship, and performance. Job satisfaction is related to lower job turnover and absenteeism (Crampton & Wagner, 1994), an increase in organizational citizenship (Organ & Ryan, 1995), and performance (Judge & others, 2001). However, whether happy workers are more productive workers has been the source of some debate, as the Critical Controversy explores.

Job satisfaction is just one of the attitudes that I/O psychologists have probed. Another fertile area of research focuses on worker commitment, as we now consider.

Employee Commitment

By the time an employee has completed training, the organization has already dedicated a great deal of resources to the person. Clearly, it is in the organization's interest to keep the employee around. Especially during times of organizational change, understanding the factors that might strengthen employee commitment is important to industry and psychologists (Amiot & others, 2006).

I/O psychologists have examined work commitment as a key determinant of work-related outcomes (Cooper-Hakim & Viswesvaran, 2005). A highly influential framework emphasizes three types of commitment—affective, continuance, and normative—that are essential to understanding an employee's level

CRITICAL CONTROVERSY

Is a Happy Worker a More Productive Worker?

Many of us have seen TV ads that show dot-com workers playing ping-pong on the job or a warehouse manager cruising around on a Segway. We hear about companies adopting policies to enhance positive feelings at work. At Google, for example, lunch is free, the dress code is jeans and sweatshirts—and pets are allowed. At the software company SAS, considered the best place to work in 2010, workers enjoy their pets, unlimited sick days, and onsite day care and summer camp for their children, as well as a 66,000-square-foot recreation center.

Sounds great, but Google and SAS are businesses that keep a close eye on the bottom line. To what extent are such policies and practices good for business? Are happy workers more productive? Research in I/O psychology has examined this question.

To begin, you might think of happiness as a consequence of work success. That is, people who do well at work probably feel happier as a result. What is most fascinating about research on the relationship between happiness and productivity is that longitudinal studies (those that follow a sample of participants over time) have demonstrated that often the happiness comes first (Lyubomirsky, King, & Diener, 2005). Even before entering the workforce, happy individuals are more likely to graduate from college and to receive an interview for a job or a callback for a second interview than their unhappy counterparts (Burger & Caldwell, 2000; Frisch & others, 2004). One study found that happiness at age 18 was related to financial independence, occupational attainment, and work autonomy at age 26 (Roberts, Caspi, & Moffitt, 2003).

Once happy individuals get a job, they are more likely to succeed than unhappy individuals. Happy employees receive relatively more favorable evaluations from supervisors and others (Wright & Staw, 1999). In one study, managers in three organizations gave higher evaluations to happy employees than to unhappy employees, based on work

quality, productivity, dependability, and creativity (Staw, Sutton, & Pelled, 1994). In two studies, job performance (as judged by supervisors) was significantly related to well-being regardless of how much people liked their jobs (Wright & Cropanzano, 2000).

A number of studies have found that happiness and positive affect are important aspects of the workplace. In one study, happy individuals performed objectively better on a task assessing managerial potential (including "leadership" and "mastery of information," as rated by objective observers) (Staw & Barsade, 1993). In other research, dormitory resident advisors were described by residents as being more effective if they were also rated highly for positive affect (DeLuga & Mason, 2000). In yet another study, service departments with happy leaders were more likely to receive high ratings from customers, and the positive affective tone of the sales force was an independent predictor of customer satisfaction (George, 1995).

One reason that happy workers are more likely to be high performers is that they are less likely to miss work, leave a job, or experience burnout (Donovan, 2000; Thoresen & others, 2003). Those who experience calmer types of positive emotions on the job, such as serenity and contentment, are less likely to want to quit and to be in conflict with other workers (Van Katwyk & others, 2000).

So, are happy workers productive workers? The research reviewed above suggests that investing in workers' overall well-being just might make great business sense (Avey & others, 2010).

WHAT DO YOU THINK?

- Are perks such as free lunches and relaxed dress codes good business or simply gimmicks? Explain.

- If you were a manager, how would you use the research discussed above?

---

of dedication to the workplace (Meyer, Becker, & Vandenberghe, 2004; Van Dick, Becker, & Meyer, 2006):

● **affective commitment** A kind of job commitment deriving from the employee's emotional attachment to the workplace.

■ **Affective commitment** refers to the person's emotional attachment to the workplace. A person with a strong affective commitment identifies closely with the goals of the organization and wants to be a part of it. Affective commitment is associated with feelings of "we-ness," of identifying with the group that is one's workplace (Johnson & Chang, 2006). The individual with strong affective commitment feels loyalty to the organization because he or she wants to. Affective commitment is thought to result in more favorable job performance because those high in affective commitment are likely to work harder (Riketta, 2002).

■ **Continuance commitment** derives from the employee's perception that leaving the organization would be too costly, both economically and socially. The person may dread the notion of relocation or the thought of the effort that a new job search would require. Such an individual might remain with an organization because of the feeling that he or she "has to." For example, a police officer may remain on the job longer than she genuinely wants because of concerns about keeping her pension or because of her deep relationship with her professional partner. Continuance commitment has been shown to be either unrelated or negatively related to job performance or citizenship behaviors (Meyer & others, 2002). In contrast to affective commitment, continuance commitment involves more of an individual sense of identity rather than a group sense (Johnson & Chang, 2006).

● **continuance commitment** A kind of job commitment deriving from the employee's perception that leaving the organization would be too costly, both economically and socially.

■ **Normative commitment** is the sense of obligation an employee feels toward the organization because of the investment the organization has made in the person's personal and professional development. If an organization has subsidized a person's education, for example, the employee might feel that she owes it to her boss to stick around. Normative commitment means being committed because one feels one "ought to."

● **normative commitment** A kind of job commitment deriving from the employee's sense of obligation to the organization for the investment it has made in the individual's personal and professional development.

Theoretically, an employee's commitment profile captures his or her level of commitment on all three dimensions at any given point in time (Meyer & Herscovitch, 2001).

The Meaning of Work

Occupations define people in fundamental ways (Hellriegel & Slocum, 2011). People identify with their work, and the work shapes many aspects of their lives. Work is an important influence on their financial standing, leisure activities, home location, friendships, and health. One of the strongest predictors of job satisfaction is feeling that one is engaged in something meaningful or significant. When asked about the meaning associated with their work, respondents nominated contributing to the economic maintenance of one's family, having a job that allowed one to have a positive impact on the organization, and work as self-expression (Wrzesniewski, Dutton, & Debebe, 2003).

Individuals' perspectives on their work and its place in their lives can have an impact on their work performance, their workplace, and their lives in general (Jones & George, 2007). I/O psychologist Amy Wrzesniewski and her colleagues (1997) studied 300 workers and found that their perceptions of their occupation had a substantial impact on important aspects of their work and well-being. Some described the occupation as a "job," one that involved no training and allowed no personal control and little freedom. These individuals tended to focus on the material benefits of work. Another group of participants identified their occupation as a "career." They saw their occupation as a steppingstone to greater advancement and accordingly focused on the attainment of better pay, promotions, and moving up the organizational ladder. A final group of participants viewed their occupation in terms of a "calling." They perceived the occupation as requiring a great deal of training and as involving personal control and freedom. For these individuals, work was not a means to financial ends but rather a valuable endeavor in and of itself. Indeed, some saw their occupation as their "mission in life." Importantly, all of these individuals were describing the same job—that of hospital maintenance worker. Other research has uncovered similar results for administrative assistants, with about equal numbers having each work orientation (Wrzesniewski, 2003).

Individuals who view their occupation as a calling are more likely to experience work as meaningful and fulfilling. They show higher levels of life satisfaction and job satisfaction. These individuals are more likely to engage in organizational citizenship behaviors, to devote more time to work, and to miss work less often (Bartel, Wrzesniewski, & Wiesenfeld, 2007; Wrzesniewski, 2003). Those with a calling orientation also derive more satisfaction from the work domain than from hobbies or leisure activities. One predictor of having a calling orientation to work is preexisting psychological well-being.

● **job crafting** The physical and cognitive changes individuals can make within the constraints of a task to make the work "their own."

You might think that those who view their work as a calling must have just gotten lucky and found the right job for themselves. Wrzesniewski (2003) argues, however, that the ability to view one's occupation as a calling is a "portable" resource that a person can take from one context to another. She uses the term **job crafting** to refer to the physical and cognitive changes individuals can make within the constraints of a task to make the work "their own." For example, one hospital maintenance worker took it upon himself to start rotating the artwork on the walls of the hospital rooms as he cleaned them. Doing so was not part of his written job description—it was his own idea for improving the quality of life for patients facing long hospital stays. Job crafting means taking advantage of the freedom one has to bring fulfillment to an occupation (Berg, Wrzesniewski, & Dutton, 2010).

I/O psychologists study the qualities of effective leaders such as Boston Celtics head coach Glenn "Doc" Rivers.

Leadership

Just about every organization has a leader. In a business it may be a CEO, on a jury it is the foreperson, and on a team it is the captain or coach. I/O psychologists are especially interested in understanding what makes an effective leader and what effect leadership characteristics have on organizations (Barling, Christie, & Hoption, 2010; Beeler, 2010).

Leaders are not necessarily the same as managers (Bateman & Snell, 2011; Bridgman, 2007). Even in informal groups at work, someone may be perceived as a leader regardless of his or her formal title. Furthermore, not all managers are effective leaders. A leader is a person who influences others, motivates them, and enables them to succeed (Barling, Christie, & Hoption, 2010; Beeler, 2010). Research has shown that what leaders do, for better or worse, matters a great deal to organizational outcomes (Hess & Cameron, 2006). Leadership may be especially crucial during an internal crisis, such as when two organizations merge or when the organization must reduce its workforce (Tikhomirov & Spangler, 2010). Two major types of leadership are transactional leadership and transformational leadership.

TRANSACTIONAL LEADERSHIP

● **transactional leader** An individual in a leadership capacity who emphasizes the exchange relationship between the worker and the leader and who applies the principle that a good job should be rewarded.

Sometimes a leader is simply "the person in charge." That is, as a leader she sees herself as responsible for running operations but not changing things. A **transactional leader** is an individual who emphasizes the exchange relationship between the worker and the leader (Bass, 1985), applying the principle "You do a good job and I will reward you." Like a Theory X manager, a transactional leader believes that people are motivated by the rewards (or punishment) they receive for their work, and such a leader gives clear and structured directions to followers. The transactional leader works within the goals of the existing organizational system ("that's how we do it around here") and may exhibit management by exception—stepping in only when a problem arises.

TRANSFORMATIONAL LEADERSHIP

● **transformational leader** An individual in a leadership capacity who is concerned not with enforcing the rules but with changing them.

While a transactional leader primarily concentrates on keeping the ship sailing, a different type of leader focuses on defining the direction of the ship. An individual with this leadership style dedicates thought to the meaning of leadership itself and to the impact she might have in improving an organization. Such a **transformational leader** is concerned not with enforcing the rules but with changing them. The transformational leader is a dynamic individual who brings charisma, passion, and, perhaps most importantly, vision to the position (Mumford, Scott, & Hunter, 2006).

Personality Psychology and Organizational Psychology: Who's in Charge?

At the beginning of a group project, as you meet with your co-workers for the first time, there is that moment of tension over the question "Who's going to be in charge?" Even if you have tried to organize a group of friends to go out to dinner, you know that someone has to take charge. What characteristics do you think are important in being an effective leader? Qualities such as intelligence, trustworthiness, responsibility, and assertiveness probably come to mind. Are these in fact the traits of good leaders? What factors best predict who shall lead? I/O psychologists and personality psychologists have examined the various ways that individuals' characteristics are related to whether they emerge as leaders.

Some aspects of leadership may be genetic, and these influences may underlie the personality traits we think of as part of a "good leader" (Ilies, Arvey, & Bouchard, 2006; Zhang, Ilies, & Arvey, 2009). Consider a longitudinal study of twins that focused on the contribution of genetics to the attainment of leadership positions (Arvey & others, 2006). In this study, 331 identical twins and 315 fraternal twins provided biographical information about

How does your personality influence your leadership skills?

all of the leadership positions they had ever occupied, including leadership in groups such as high school clubs, college organizations, professional organizations, and work groups. In comparing the overlap in leadership experience between identical and fraternal twins, the researchers found that the identical twins were more similar than the fraternal twins. The heritability for leadership positions was 30 percent. These data add to research indicating that leadership styles are influenced by genetics (Arvey & others, 2007; A. M. Johnson & others, 2004). So, perhaps leaders really are, at least to some degree, born, not made.

Of course, leadership is not the same thing as eye color—genes do not simply "turn leadership on." More likely, genes influence other psychological characteristics that in turn enhance the chances for a person's becoming a leader (Anderson & Kilduff, 2009; Avolio, Walumbwa, & Weber, 2009). Early experience can matter too. In one study, individuals whose parents were warm and supportive and who provided a structured environment were more likely to emerge as leaders (Avolio, Rotundo, & Walumbwa, 2009). In that same study, those who had engaged

in modest (but not serious) rule breaking were more likely to hold leadership positions as adults.

Personality traits relate to leadership ability in ways you might expect. In terms of the big five personality traits, high extraversion, high conscientiousness, and low neuroticism are associated with being a leader (Judge, Piccolo, & Kosalka, 2009). Members of sororities and fraternities at the University of Illinois participated in a study of personality traits and leadership (Harms, Roberts, & Woods, 2007). Each participant completed a measure of personality traits and was then rated by others in their organization for status and leadership. Extraversion and conscientiousness were both related to others' perceiving the person as having status and making a difference—in short, being a leader.

It might strike you as odd that so much research has considered the personality qualities of leaders without examining the types of group they are going to lead. However, the results of these studies seem to indicate that leadership is not the same as being the best at whatever the group does. (If you think about the captain of your favorite sports team, it is rarely the case that that person is the best player on the team.) Rather, leadership is a social process, and it likely emerges out of an individual's disposition to get noticed, to assert himself or herself, and to demonstrate responsibility. A good leader may not be the person who knows the most but rather the one whose temperamental endowments predispose him or her to flourish as the "top dog."

Four elements of transformational leadership have been described (Sivanathan & others, 2004). First, transformational leaders exert what has been referred to as *idealized influence*. This means that transformational leaders act as they do because they believe it is the right thing to do. Google's leaders, for instance, have a motto, "Don't be evil!" that has guided them in creatively implementing their idea of what a great place to work ought to be. This commitment to integrity instills trust in followers. Second, transformational leaders motivate by inspiring others to do their very best (Harms & Crede, 2010). Niro Sivanathan and his colleagues stress that transformational leaders need not have natural charm or charisma but rather a talent for bolstering employees' self-efficacy (Nielsen & Munir, 2009)—their "can-do attitude"—and for convincing others to do their best. Third, transformational leaders are devoted to intellectually stimulating their employees. They make it clear that they need input from employees because they themselves do not have all the answers. Fourth, transformational leaders provide individualized consideration to their employees, showing a sincere concern for each person's well-being (Harms & Crede, 2010; Simola, Barling, & Turner, 2010). Transformational leaders can help people do more than they believed possible. In one study, elite UK Royal Marine recruits were more likely to make it through the challenges of boot camp if they had a transformational leader (Hardy & others, 2010).

A great deal of research supports the idea that transformational leadership is associated with positive organizational outcomes in a wide variety of settings, from sports teams (Charbonneau, Barling, & Kelloway, 2001) to profit-oriented businesses (Barling, Weber, & Kelloway, 1996; Tikhomirov & Spangler, 2010) to the military (Hardy & others, 2010). The positive impact of transformational leaders (relative to transactional leaders) is based on the capacity of the leader to foster trust in the organization, to persuade employees about the meaningfulness of their work, and finally to strengthen employees' **organizational identity**—their feelings of oneness with the organization and its goals (Sivanathan & others, 2004). Of course, effective leadership may require attending both to the details of keeping the ship afloat and to the big picture (O'Shea & others, 2009).

What factors cause one to become a leader? Are leaders born or made? The Intersection addresses this intriguing question.

One notable difference between transactional and transformational leaders lies in their approach to the workplace culture. Transactional leaders *work within* the context of that culture, whereas transformational leaders seek to *define and redefine* it. Industry analysts widely consider the dynamic culture of organizations such as Google to be their biggest selling point. What does it mean to talk about organizational culture? In the next section we probe this fascinating topic.

57·2 ORGANIZATIONAL CULTURE

Creating a positive organizational culture is clearly an important aspect of great leadership. **Organizational culture** refers to an organization's shared values, beliefs, norms, and customs. How do people dress? Do they socialize? Is it okay to decorate cubicles with personal items? Can the employees talk to the CEO? These are the kinds of questions a new employee might ask, and the answers reveal the formality, warmth, and status consciousness of the workplace culture. Organizational culture describes the "flavor" of an organization—the "way we get things done around here" (Deal & Kennedy, 1982).

Even unspoken aspects of organizational culture can influence the everyday behavior of individuals within an organization (Griffin & Moorhead, 2010). Consider the phenomenon of groupthink. Groupthink is the dysfunctional side of organizational culture, and it occurs when individuals in a group squelch dissent and seek consensus above all else. A more open climate may produce greater conflict—but conflict over important matters may be a good thing. An open climate characterizes the U.S. corporation Harley-Davidson Motor Company, for example. Because many Harley-Davidson employees are themselves motorcycle enthusiasts, their ideas are welcome at any time. In Harley's open-door policy, everyone can talk to everyone else, and this free exchange is valued because the company's success relies on passion for motorcycles. J. M. Smucker's, the company that makes jams and jellies from a small factory in rural Ohio, has similarly been praised for its emphasis on face-to-face communication (Moskowitz & Levering, 2007). Such openness reveals a strong level of respect for the contributions of individuals across the organization.

● **organizational identity** Employees' feelings of oneness with the organization and its goals.

● **organizational culture** An organization's shared values, beliefs, norms, and customs.

Positive Organizational Culture

Positive organizational culture stems from a variety of factors, including active leadership, explicit policies, and less tangible aspects such as the "feel" of an organization. Creating a positive organizational culture can be as simple as giving employees constructive reinforcement for good work (Wiegand & Geller, 2004). Leaders who reward outstanding performance and acknowledge the contributions that employees make to an organization may foster achievement motivation and promote success. Similarly, a positive climate can be nurtured by leaders who incorporate fairness and safety into the cultural climate as part of a well-functioning workplace, rather than treating these concerns as hassles that must be endured (Aguinis, 2010).

Another aspect of positive organizational culture is compassion (Kanov & others, 2006). Compassion means empathizing with the suffering of another and doing something to alleviate that suffering. Does compassion have a place in the dog-eat-dog world of business? Consider the case of HomeBanc Mortgage Corp in Atlanta (Culp, 2005). A salesman in the company (who worked on commission) was diagnosed with non-Hodgkin's lymphoma, a type of cancer. To fight the disease, the man learned that he would have to be out of commission (literally and figuratively) for months. The company CEO responded with a compassionate gesture: The man would have his usual commission paid as a salary ($10,000 per month) indefinitely so that he could focus on fighting his cancer, not on worrying about making ends meet. Does such an act of compassion make business sense? In this case, the salesman returned to work earlier than expected and became a top performer. Moreover, HomeBanc Mortgage's financial returns exceeded industry expectations by $6.2 million in 2004 (Culp, 2005).

Compassion can be expressed in creative and humane corporate policies. The Container Store (the number 4 best place to work in 2007) not only pays its sales staff 50 to 100 percent above industry average, but also offers a "family friendly" shift—9 A.M. to 2 P.M.—that allows parents to drop off their children at school in the morning and pick them up in the afternoon. Similarly, Google has created a $500 take-out meal fund for employees to use as they negotiate the transition to parenthood.

Related to compassion is virtue, or moral goodness. As a vice president for HomeBanc commented, "People win just by being human." Doing the right thing can have a broad array of benefits. Employees who believe that their organization is committed to doing the right thing may be able to cope with difficult times and circumstances—even downsizing.

An increasingly popular U.S. corporate strategy to enhance profitability, **downsizing** refers to dramatically cutting the workforce, especially during difficult economic times, such as the financial crisis that began in 2007. By downsizing, companies often intend to send the message to stockholders that they are taking profit seriously. Certainly downsizing has human costs, including feelings of injustice, life disruption, and personal harm (Cameron, 2003, 2005). Does sacrificing staff members pay off for the firm? The answer is perhaps not, according to research by I/O psychologist Kim Cameron (2003). His analysis of companies that downsized revealed that less than 10 percent reported improvements in product quality, innovation, and organizational climate. In Cameron's study, a majority of firms that downsized lagged behind in stock value even three years after downsizing (Cameron, 2003). It may be that downsizing not only shows a lack of compassion but also is economically ill advised.

Cameron (2003) also examined the role of organizational virtue in response to firms' downsizing. In eight downsized companies, he found that organizational virtue was associated with the firms' better ability to weather the storm of downsizing. Specifically, organizations in which the top leaders were perceived as fostering a culture of virtuousness showed higher productivity and higher-quality output, as well as less turnover, after downsizing. Thus, virtue may help to buffer the firm against the negative effects of downsizing.

● **downsizing** A dramatic cutting of the workforce that has become a popular business strategy to enhance profitability.

"I got downsized after the king subscribed to that online joke service!"

© Harley Schwadron. www.CartoonStock.com.

Toxic Factors in the Workplace

Unfortunately, not all work settings are warm, happy environments. In some contexts, individuals engage in behaviors that demean co-workers. *Workplace incivility* refers to rude or disrespectful behaviors that reveal a lack of regard for others, such as spreading rumors, sending inflammatory e-mails, and sabotaging the work of fellow employees. Such incivility can spiral into a variety of other negative behaviors (Pearson, Andersson, & Porath, 2005). Researchers in I/O psychology have identified and studied a number of "bad behaviors" that are associated with negative workplace factors (Griffin & Lopez, 2005). Not surprisingly, incivility and workplace conflict negatively relate to job satisfaction (Barling, Dupré, & Kelloway, 2009). Here we focus on two extreme aspects of such incivility: sexual harassment and workplace aggression and violence.

SEXUAL HARASSMENT

Sexual harassment is unwelcome behavior or conduct of a sexual nature that offends, humiliates, or intimidates another person. In the workplace, sexual harassment includes unwanted sexual advances, requests for sexual favors, and other verbal or physical conduct of a sexual nature (Berdahl & Raver, 2010).

In the United States, sexual harassment is an illegal form of sexual discrimination that violates Title VII of the Civil Rights Act of 1964. The victim of sexual harassment can be a man or woman and need not be the opposite sex of the perpetrator. The victim does not necessarily have to be the person harassed; it can be anyone affected by the offensive conduct. For example, a man who works in a setting in which women are routinely demeaned may feel that the work environment is toxic. A woman who is offended by sexual comments made to other women or among men at her workplace may also be the victim of sexual harassment. The harasser can be a co-worker, supervisor, or even someone who is not an employee.

Many people meet their romantic partners at work, of course. Sexual conduct is unlawful only when it is unwelcome. Roughly 14,000 cases of sexual harassment per year have been reported to the Equal Employment Opportunity Commission (EEOC) since 2000, with 12,025 cases reported in 2006 (EEOC, 2007). Women file approximately 85 percent of the complaints.

Sexual harassment is related both to reduced job satisfaction and to heightened intentions to leave a job (Berdahl & Raver, 2010; Sims, Drasgow, & Fitzgerald, 2005). Experiences of harassment are also linked to symptoms of post-traumatic stress disorder, which we consider in Module 59 (Palmieri & Fitzgerald, 2005). Beyond its negative effects on individual workers, sexual harassment costs organizations money: Monetary benefits (not including those awarded from litigation) paid out for sexual harassment cases amount to about $50 million per year (EEOC, 2007).

Sexual harassment has two related forms: quid pro quo sexual harassment and hostile work environment sexual harassment. *Quid pro quo sexual harassment* refers to unwelcome sexual advances, requests for sexual favors, and verbal or physical conduct of a sexual nature in which submission is made either explicitly or implicitly a condition of the victim's employment. That is, the harassed individual is expected to tolerate the behavior or submit to sexual demands in order to be hired or to keep his or her job. Quid pro quo sexual harassment can also occur if rejection of the inappropriate conduct becomes the basis for employment decisions affecting the victim. For example, a woman who rejects her boss's advances may be denied a promotion or may receive a negative performance evaluation. *Hostile work environment sexual harassment* refers to unwelcome sexual behavior when this conduct has the purpose or effect of interfering with an individual's work performance or creating an intimidating or offensive work environment. Behaviors that might produce a hostile environment include sexually graphic humor, suggestive remarks, ridiculing someone's body, and touching individuals inappropriately.

Reporting sexual harassment can itself be difficult and painful (Fitzgerald, 2003). Indeed, research has shown that an individual's job satisfaction, psychological well-being, and physical health can suffer following the reporting of sexual harassment (Bergman & others, 2002). However, these negative effects are not likely to be caused by the reporting itself. Rather, they can be understood as rooted in the failure of organizations to respond effectively to sexual harassment claims. Indeed, research examining over 6,000 sexual harassment victims in the U.S. military demonstrated that an organization's tendency to minimize the negative effects of harassment, to retaliate against the victim, and to seek to remedy the situation in unsatisfactory ways is a strong predictor of distress for victims (Bergman & others, 2002). Sexual harassment is a serious problem (Jordan, Campbell, & Follingstad, 2010). No one has to tolerate inappropriate sexual conduct at work. For information on how to cope with a personal experience of sexual harassment, see Figure 57.2.

WORKPLACE AGGRESSION AND VIOLENCE

Aggression involves engaging in behavior meant to harm another person. Aggression in the workplace includes verbal abusiveness, intimidating behavior, and bullying (Barling, Dupré, & Kelloway, 2009). Such behavior can have negative effects on workers. Longitudinal research has found that individuals who have experienced mean-spirited teasing from co-workers show increases in psychological health problems (Hogh, Henriksson, & Burr, 2005). Verbal abuse from outsiders (such as customers) is more likely to occur in occupations in which individuals are expected to interact with the public regularly, and such experiences are strongly associated with emotional exhaustion (Grandey, Kern, & Frone, 2007). Nonsexual aggression shares a strong negative relationship with job satisfaction (Lapierre, Spector, & Leck, 2005).

At the extreme end of such aggression is workplace violence, which includes physical assault and even homicide (Barclay & Aquino, 2010; Barling, Dupré, & Kelloway, 2009). While sexual harassment is recognized as a form of sex-based discrimination, workplace violence falls within the realm of workplace safety. According to the Occupational Safety and Health Act, an employer is required to "furnish each of his employees employment and a place of employment which are free from recognized hazards that are causing or are likely to cause death or serious physical harm to his employees" (Occupational Safety and Health Administration, 2002).

High-profile cases of workplace violence often grab the headlines. For example, on Christmas night in 2000, Michael McDermott, a software tester for Edgewater Technology in Wakefield, Massachusetts, went to his workplace and stashed two dozen boxes of ammunition, two rifles, a shotgun, a pistol, and a bayonet. On the day after Christmas, after a morning spent at work and chatting with co-workers about video games, he strode into the human resources department and, within a few minutes, killed seven people. McDermott was convicted of seven counts of murder in 2002 (Blades, 2006).

Such acts of workplace violence are uncommon, but understanding and preventing them is a growing concern for both employers and psychologists interested in I/O psychology (Barclay & Aquino, 2010; Barling, Dupré, & Kelloway, 2009). According to the U.S. Bureau of Labor Statistics (2006), as many as half of U.S. employers with more than 1,000 employees reported at least 1 incident of workplace violence in 2005. Importantly, over 70 percent of U.S. workplaces have no formal policy addressing workplace violence.

Workplace violence may occur between co-workers, but it also includes violence perpetrated by outsiders such as customers, clients, or patients (Barling, Dupré, & Kelloway, 2009). Consider a store clerk confronted by a robber, a teacher faced with a hostile high school student in the classroom, or a nurse dealing with a physically abusive patient—all

What to Do If You Think You Are Being Sexually Harassed

1. Keep careful records. Write down times, dates, places, and names of individuals who have witnessed the behavior.

2. Build a paper trail related to the harassment. If someone has sent you offensive or troubling e-mails, letters, or phone messages, keep them. Information that is documented may be helpful in pursuing a complaint.

3. Talk to a trusted friend, counselor, or therapist who will keep the information confidential. An objective third party may have suggestions for resolving the problem. If the harassment is occurring at work, consult with the human resources department. If it is taking place at school, talk to someone at your college's counseling center.

4. Write a letter to the individual you believe is harassing you. If you feel uncomfortable talking to the harasser in person, a letter may be a good alternative. The letter should include not only a description of specific examples of the behavior and your feelings about it, but also a statement of what you would like to happen next. Keep a copy of the letter for yourself.

5. If you have concerns about your safety or have been assaulted, immediately call the police. Most students do not report sexual harassment but wish they could (AAUW, 2006). Reporting sexual harassment can be a challenge, but it is important. Sexual harassment is likely to be repeated if the perpetrator does not get feedback about the problem behavior.

FIGURE 57.2 **Coping with Sexual Harassment**
A serious problem on college campuses, sexual harassment can crop up in relations between students, students and their professors, and members of the university staff. If you feel that you are being sexually harassed, first consider that someone can sexually harass you without meaning to and that the solution can be as simple as informing the individual that his or her behavior makes you uncomfortable. If talking to the person alone is uncomfortable, take someone with you for moral support. If you feel that confronting the person might be dangerous, there are other steps you can take, as described in the figure.

are in a position in which they might become a victim of violence. Employers in these settings are expected to anticipate and take action to prevent victimization in such circumstances.

Although no organization can identify every potential problem, companies can take steps to prevent workplace violence. These include creating an open, humane environment in which employees feel they are being treated fairly. Individuals who perceive that they have been treated unfairly are more likely to aggress, verbally and physically (Barclay & Aquino, 2010; Dupré & Barling, 2006). Organizations can also strive for an open approach to resolving conflicts. In addition, commitment to solving problems head-on can defuse potentially difficult situations before they escalate to violence.

SUMMARY

The way managers approach their jobs is an important focus of research in organizational psychology. The Japanese management style—stressing innovation, future orientation, and quality—was actually developed by Deming, an American. Theory X and Theory Y management styles were introduced by McGregor. Theory X describes managers who assume that work is unpleasant to workers and who believe that a manager's main role is to keep workers in line. Theory Y managers, in contrast, assume that workers crave and value responsibility and represent important sources of creativity. Strengths-based management, developed by Clifton, asserts that the best approach to management is one that matches individuals' strengths with their jobs.

Job satisfaction is a person's attitude toward his or her occupation. Generally, job satisfaction has been shown to relate to low turnover, reduced absenteeism, and less burnout. Job satisfaction is not strongly associated with wages and may relate in important ways to the personality characteristics of the worker, as well as to the worker's culture.

Employee commitment is an individual's feeling of loyalty to his or her workplace. Three types of commitment are affective commitment (a person's emotional attachment to a job), continuance commitment (a person's perception that leaving a job would be too costly or difficult), and normative commitment (a person's feeling that he or she should stick with a job because of obligation).

Because our jobs define us in many ways, the way we think about work influences our lives more generally. Research has shown that people can perceive the same position as a job, a career, or a calling. Those who perceive their work as a calling show numerous positive benefits.

The leaders in an organization can play an important role in shaping the work experience of employees. A transactional leader is one who emphasizes the exchange relationship between the boss and employees. This leader is likely to take action only in reaction to events. A transformational leader is one who actively shapes an organization's culture and who takes a dynamic and creative approach to management.

Organizational culture refers to an organization's shared beliefs, values, customs, and norms. Positive organizational culture can be nurtured through positive reinforcement, as well as genuine concern for the safety of workers. Compassion and humane policies also promote positive organizational culture.

Factors such as sexual harassment and workplace violence represent the negative side of organizational culture. Sexual harassment is illegal and may take the form of either quid pro quo sexual harassment (the demand for sexual favors in return for employment or continued employment) or hostile workplace environment sexual harassment. Workplace violence is a growing concern for employers and I/O psychologists. Employers are obligated to create a safe environment for workers, including doing all that they can to foresee and prevent possible violence.

KEY TERMS

Theory X managers   529
Theory Y managers   529
waigawa system   529
strengths-based
    management   529
job satisfaction   530
affective commitment   532
continuance
    commitment   533

normative commitment   533
job crafting   534
transactional leader   534
transformational leader   534
organizational identity   536
organizational culture   536
downsizing   537
sexual harassment   538

TEST YOURSELF

1. With what is the field of organizational psychology primarily concerned?
2. How do Theory X and Theory Y managers differ?
3. Are leaders the same as managers? Explain.
4. What is meant by organizational culture?
5. Name some key factors in a positive organizational culture.
6. What is sexual harassment? Discuss its two related forms.

APPLY YOUR KNOWLEDGE

1. Pick up a copy of the *Wall Street Journal* and read the latest news about the corporate world. Can you detect principles of scientific management or human relations approaches in the corporations documented in the stories? What types of corporate leadership do the articles describe?

2. Pick someone you know who shows the qualities of a good leader. Interview the individual about times he or she has been in a leadership role. How did the individual manage challenges? How did the person view the people he or she led? What perspective did the person bring to the position of leader? Do you think your candidate fits the Theory X or Theory Y management profile? Is the individual a transactional or transformational leader? Explain your conclusions.

3. Ask some friends and family members to describe their jobs to you. Where do the descriptions fall with respect to the job/career/calling distinctions discussed in this module? In light of what you know about your respondents, how much do you think this distinction reflects the job itself and how much reflects the person?

I/O Psychology and Health and Wellness

Given the significant place of work in human life, it is no surprise that work impacts health and wellness (Hahn, Payne, & Lucas, 2007; Insel & Roth, 2008). Indeed, job satisfaction is strongly related to life satisfaction overall, and work can be a source of fulfillment and meaning. The importance of work in our lives is never more apparent than when individuals lose their jobs. Unemployment is related to physical problems (such as heart attack, stroke, obesity, and diabetes), psychological disorders (such as anxiety and depression), marital and family troubles, and homicide and other crimes (Gallo & others, 2006; Kilicarslan & others, 2006; Patten & others, 2006). One study revealed that immune system functioning declined with unemployment and increased with new employment (F. Cohen & others, 2007). Yet work itself can also be a source of considerable stress and conflict.

STRESS AT WORK

● **job stress** The experience of stress on the job and in the workplace setting.

Job stress refers to the experience of stress on the job (Griffin & Clarke, 2010). A key source of job stress is role conflict. **Role conflict** may occur when a person tries to meet the demands of more than one important life role, such as worker and mother (Eby, Maher, & Butts, 2010). Because work may compete with other valued activities for our time, attention, and energies, it can be difficult to resolve the demands of our various valued roles: Should I stay at work and finish this project, or head home to have dinner with my children?

● **role conflict** The kind of stress that arises when a person tries to meet the demands of more than one important life role, such as worker and mother.

Some jobs are more stressful than others. Four particular characteristics of work settings are linked with employee stress and health problems (Matthews, Bulger, & Barnes-Farrell, 2010; Moos, 1986; Wirtz & others, 2010):

■ High job demands such as having a heavy workload and time pressure
■ Inadequate opportunities to participate in decision making
■ A high level of supervisor control
■ A lack of clarity about the criteria for competent performance

● **burnout** A distressed psychological state in which a person experiences emotional exhaustion and little motivation for work.

Some individuals in the work world fall victim to **burnout,** a distressed psychological state in which a person experiences emotional exhaustion and little motivation for work. Burnout may include feelings of being overworked and underappreciated and can feature depersonalization, confusion, worry, and resentment (Ahola & others, 2006). Symptoms can be physical (exhaustion, headaches, gastrointestinal problems, suppressed immune function, sleep disturbance), behavioral (increased use of alcohol, drugs, caffeine; absenteeism; and social withdrawal), and emotional (increased cynicism and negativity, hopelessness, irritability, emotional distancing, depression, and anxiety). Burnout may result from chronic stress at work. Having support from one's co-workers, as well as a clear sense of the requirements for one's job, is related to lower levels of stress (Matthews, Bulger, & Barnes-Farrell, 2010).

MANAGING JOB STRESS

● **leisure** The pleasant times before or after work when individuals are free to pursue activities and interests of their own choosing, such as hobbies, sports, and reading.

Stress at work does not always lead to burnout, especially if individuals develop enjoyable leisure activities. Indeed, an important aspect of life, beyond being competent at and enjoying one's work, is to relax and enjoy leisure (Ahmed & others, 2005). **Leisure** refers to the

psychological *inquiry*

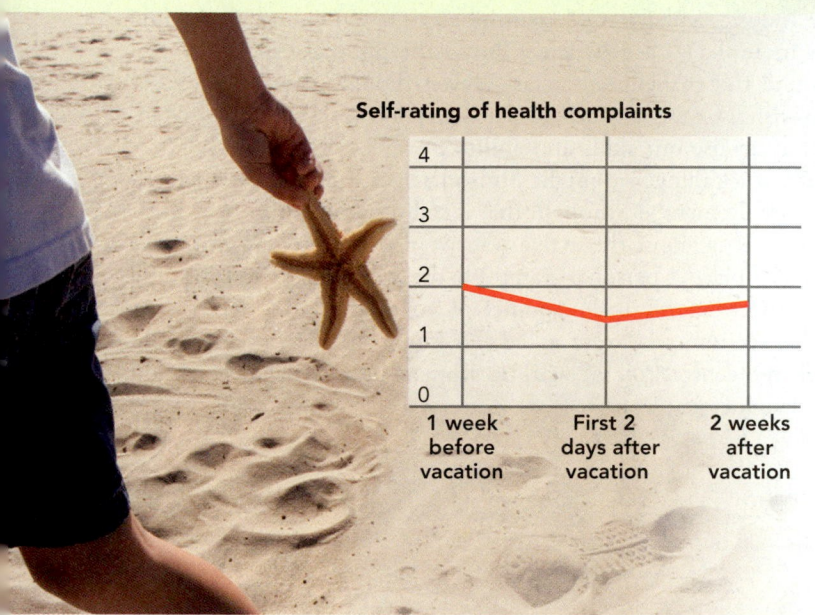

Self-rating of health complaints

[Graph with Y axis labeled 0 to 4, showing a red line starting near 2 at "1 week before vacation," dipping to about 1.3 at "First 2 days after vacation," and rising to about 1.5 at "2 weeks after vacation."]

1 week before vacation   First 2 days after vacation   2 weeks after vacation

You Need a Vacation!

This graph shows the results of a study examining employees' health complaints before and after they took a vacation. The Y axis is the self-rated score on health complaints, and the X axis represents time. Employees rated their health complaints on 12 items (for example, "Have you slept less because of worries?"). The 4-point scale ranged from 1 (not at all) to 4 (much more than normal). Consider these questions:

1. When were health complaints at their lowest and highest?

2. If the researchers had measured the employees' level of satisfaction with life, do you think the pattern would look the same? Explain.

3. Was this a correlational study or an experiment? What does your answer mean for the conclusions that can be drawn from this study?

4. In this study, participants completed self-report measures of their health. Was that a wise research decision—or not? Explain.

pleasant times before or after work when individuals are free to pursue activities and interests of their own choosing—hobbies, sports, and reading, for example. In a research study on regret, U.S. adults placed "not engaging in more leisure activities" as one of the top six regrets (Roese & Summerville, 2005). Using our leisure time to help others can be a particularly good way to recover from work-related stress (Mojza & others, 2010).

Might taking regular vacations also help individuals to combat work stress? One study found that in the days and weeks at work just after a vacation, individuals reported that they were less exhausted, had fewer health complaints, and were putting forth more efficient effort than in the week at work prior to the vacation (Fritz & Sonnentag, 2006). Check out the Psychological Inquiry for the results of that study.

Taking vacations can also be associated with living longer. In a longitudinal study, 12,338 men 35 to 57 years of age were assessed each year for 5 years on the question of whether they took vacations (Gump & Matthews, 2000). Then the researchers examined the medical and death records over nine years for men who lived for at least a year after the last vacation survey. Compared with those who never took vacations, men who went on annual vacations were 21 percent less likely to die over the nine years and 32 percent less likely to die of coronary heart disease. The same concerns that lead men to skip a vacation—such as not trusting anyone to fill in for them and fearing that they will get behind in their work and someone will replace them—tend to promote heart disease. Such apprehensions are characteristic of the Type A behavioral pattern described in the Health and Wellness portion of the Personality section.

In addition to developing enjoyable leisure activities and taking regular vacations, what else can you do to cope with work stress? Dealing with job stress in a healthy way involves taking care of your body as well as your mind (Fahey, Insel, & Roth, 2011). Physical needs must be met by eating right, exercising, and getting enough sleep (Schiff, 2011; Sparling & Redican, 2011). Because work stress, like all stress, is about our perception of experience, it makes sense to hone your coping skills and periodically to monitor your patterns of behavior and well-being (Donatelle, 2011). Have you set realistic goals at work? Are you taking work-related issues too personally? It may be

• **flow** The optimal experience of a match between one's skills and the challenge of a task.

helpful to remind yourself of the goals of Donald Clifton's strengths-based approach to management, described earlier. What are your strengths, and how can you use them to do what you do best?

We might at times think of work as a four-letter word. We might look upon the effort that work entails as something to be avoided, and we might view working hard as just that—hard. However, it is vital to keep in mind that work is an essential part of living a fulfilling life. Indeed, Mihalyi Csikszentmihalyi (1990) found that while working, we are 10 times more likely to experience **flow**—the optimal experience of a match between our skills and the challenge of a task—even though, ironically, we are also 6 times more likely to wish we were somewhere else when on the job. Work provides us an unequaled opportunity to use our skills and abilities.

When we think of work as a calling, we might find ourselves listening for that call with an open mind and heart. Remember, though, that a calling orientation to work is not just about hearing a call. It is about the active way we craft any job to our skills and abilities, finding a way to place a personal stamp on the workplace. Transforming a job into a calling is a decision that we make about our work situation.

At the beginning of this section, you were asked, "If you won the lottery, would you quit your job?" Given the central role of work in human life, perhaps we should rephrase that question: "Imagine that you won the lottery. What kind of job would you want then?"

SUMMARY

Job stress is stress experienced at the workplace. Role conflict, a key source of such stress, results from trying to meet multiple demands in a limited amount of time. Four sources of work stress include high demands, inadequate opportunity to participate in decision making, high levels of supervisor control, and unclear criteria for performance. At the extreme, work stress can lead to burnout.

One way to manage job stress is to enrich one's life while not at work. Engaging in satisfying leisure activities can promote workplace wellness. Enjoying time off can have benefits for the person when he or she is back on the job.

KEY TERMS

job stress   542
role conflict   542
burnout   542

leisure   542
flow   544

TEST YOURSELF

1. What role conflicts do you—or does someone you know well—experience?

2. Define burnout and name some physical, behavioral, and emotional symptoms of burnout.

3. What have researchers discovered about the benefits of taking a vacation?

Psychological Disorders

The Courage to Wake Up Every Morning

Bill Garrett was a freshman at Johns Hopkins University, where he had won a full four-year scholarship, when he began to hear strange voices inside his head. Those voices told him profoundly disturbing things: that he was stupid and fat, that soap and shampoo were toxic, that his father had poisoned the family dog, and that his grandmother was putting human body parts in his food. Bill withdrew into this terrifying inner world, convinced that there were conspiracies out to get him. Eventually, he was diagnosed with schizophrenia, a disorder characterized by disturbed thought. Failing in all of his classes, this previously excellent student (and track and lacrosse star) was forced to leave school and return home to struggle with his disorder.

Bill's mother realized what her son had been experiencing only when she found herself at a support group for families of individuals with schizophrenia. At one point, surrounded by 10 people all speaking to her at once, she was overwhelmed by the confusing cacophony. Afterward she told her son, "You have to be the most courageous person. You wake up every morning" (M. Park, 2009). Bill had told her that sleep was his only escape from the constant terror of those voices.

At home, Bill was faced with evidence of his previous successes. Looking at his trophies and awards, he said, "Mom, I was on top of the world. Now I'm in the gutter." His mother, however, has offered Bill a different perspective. She has encouraged him to think of his disorder not as a sign of failure but as an opportunity to use the gifts he still possesses—symbolized by those past accomplishments—to fight for the rights of individuals who, like him, find their lives turned upside-down by psychological disorders. ●

Defining and Explaining Abnormal Behavior

● abnormal behavior Behavior that is deviant, maladaptive, or personally distressful over a relatively long period of time.

What makes behavior "abnormal"? The American Psychiatric Association (2001, 2006) defines abnormal behavior in medical terms—as a mental illness that affects or is manifested in a person's brain and can affect the way the individual thinks, behaves, and interacts with others.

Three criteria help distinguish normal from abnormal behavior. **Abnormal behavior** is behavior that is *deviant, maladaptive,* or *personally distressful* over a relatively long period of time. Let's take a look at what each of the three characteristics of abnormal behavior entails:

■ Abnormal behavior is *deviant.* Abnormal behavior is certainly atypical or statistically unusual. People such as Alicia Keys, Peyton Manning, and Steven Spielberg are atypical—but we do not categorize them as abnormal. When atypical behavior deviates from what is acceptable in a culture, it often is considered abnormal. A woman who washes her hands three or four times an hour and takes seven showers a day is abnormal because her behavior deviates from what we consider acceptable.

■ Abnormal behavior is *maladaptive.* Maladaptive behavior interferes with a person's ability to function effectively in the world. A man who believes that he can endanger other people through his breathing may go to great lengths to avoid people so that he will not harm anyone. He might isolate himself from others, for what he believes is their own good. His belief separates him from society and prevents his everyday functioning; thus, his behavior is maladaptive. Behavior that presents a danger to the person or those around him or her would also be considered maladaptive (and abnormal).

■ Abnormal behavior involves *personal distress* over a long period of time. The person engaging in the behavior finds it troubling. A woman who secretly makes herself vomit after every meal may never be seen by others as deviant (because they do not know about it), but this pattern of behavior may cause her to feel intense shame, guilt, and despair. Personal distress may exist in the context of great success. Imagine a highly successful business executive who feels profound sadness because of family difficulties.

Note that the *context* of a behavior may help to determine whether the behavior is abnormal. Consider the woman who washes her hands three or four times an hour and takes repeated showers. If she works in a sterile lab with live viruses or radioactive material, her behavior might be quite adaptive rather than abnormal.

Accomplished people—such as recording artist-actor Alicia Keys, NFL superstar Peyton Manning, and award-winning film director Steven Spielberg—are atypical but not abnormal. However, when atypical behavior deviates form cultural norms, it often is considered abnormal.

Only one of the three criteria described above needs to be present for behavior to be labeled "abnormal," but typically two or all three may be present. When abnormal behavior persists, it may lead to the diagnosis of a psychological disorder.

58·1 THEORETICAL APPROACHES TO PSYCHOLOGICAL DISORDERS

What causes people to develop a psychological disorder, that is, to behave in deviant, maladaptive, and personally distressful ways? Theorists have suggested various approaches to this question.

The Biological Approach

The biological approach attributes psychological disorders to organic, internal causes. This approach primarily focuses on the brain, genetic factors, and neurotransmitter functioning as the sources of abnormality.

The biological approach is evident in the **medical model,** which describes psychological disorders as medical diseases with a biological origin. From the perspective of the medical model, abnormalities are called *mental illnesses,* the afflicted individuals are *patients,* and they are treated by *doctors.*

● **medical model** The view that psychological disorders are medical diseases with a biological origin.

The Psychological Approach

The psychological approach emphasizes the contributions of experiences, thoughts, emotions, and personality characteristics in explaining psychological disorders. Psychologists might focus, for example, on the influence of childhood experiences or of personality traits in the development and course of psychological disorders. Behavioral psychologists probe the rewards and punishers in the environment that determine abnormal behavior, whereas social cognitive psychologists focus on observational learning, cognitions, and beliefs as factors that foster or maintain abnormal behavior.

The Sociocultural Approach

The sociocultural approach emphasizes the social contexts in which a person lives, including the individual's gender, ethnicity, socioeconomic status, family relationships, and culture. For instance, individuals from low-income, minority neighborhoods have the highest rates of psychological disorders (Schwartz & Corcoran, 2010). Socioeconomic status plays a much stronger role in disorders than does ethnicity: The living conditions of poverty create stressful circumstances that can contribute to the development of a psychological disorder (E. Davis & others, 2010; Kohrt & others, 2009; South & Krueger, 2010).

The sociocultural perspective stresses the ways that cultures influence the understanding and treatment of psychological disorders. The frequency and intensity of psychological disorders vary and depend on social, economic, technological, and religious aspects of cultures (Alegria, 2011; Shiraev & Levy, 2010). Some disorders are culture-related, as indicated in Figure 58.1.

The Biopsychosocial Model

Abnormal behavior can be influenced by biological factors (such as genes), psychological factors (such as childhood experiences), and sociocultural factors (such as gender). These factors can operate alone, but they often act in combination with one another (Scheid & Brown, 2010).

To appreciate how these factors work together, let's back up for a moment. Consider that not everyone with a genetic predisposition to schizophrenia develops the disorder.

Disorder	Culture	Description/Characteristics
Amok	Malaysia, Philippines, Africa	This disorder involves sudden, uncontrolled outbursts of anger in which the person may injure or kill someone. Amok is often found in males who are emotionally withdrawn before the onset of the disorder. After the attack on someone, the individual feels exhausted and depressed and does not remember the rage and attack.
Anorexia Nervosa	Western cultures, especially the United States	This eating disorder involves a relentless pursuit of thinness through starvation and can eventually lead to death.
Windigo	Algonquin Indian hunters	This disorder involves a fear of being bewitched. The hunter becomes anxious and agitated, worrying he will be turned into a cannibal with a craving for human flesh.

FIGURE 58.1 **Some Culture-Related Disorders** Although many psychological disorders are universal, some are associated with specific cultures, as this figure illustrates.

Similarly, not everyone who experiences childhood neglect develops depression. Moreover, even women who live in cultures that strongly discriminate against them do not always develop psychological disorders. Thus, to understand the development of psychological disorders, we must consider a variety of *interacting* factors from each of the domains of experience.

Sometimes this approach is called *biopsychosocial.* From the biopsychosocial perspective, none of the factors considered is necessarily viewed as more important than another; rather, biological, psychological, and social factors are *all* significant ingredients in producing both normal and abnormal behavior. Furthermore, these ingredients may combine in unique ways, so that one depressed person might differ from another in terms of the key factors associated with the development of the disorder.

58-2 CLASSIFYING ABNORMAL BEHAVIOR

To understand, prevent, and treat abnormal behavior, psychiatrists and psychologists have devised systems classifying those behaviors into specific psychological disorders. Classifying psychological disorders provides a common basis for communicating. If one psychologist says that her client is experiencing depression, another psychologist understands that a particular pattern of abnormal behavior has led to this diagnosis. A classification system can also help clinicians make predictions about how likely it is that a particular disorder will occur, which individuals are most susceptible to it, how the disorder progresses, and what the prognosis (or outcome) for treatment is (Cuthbert & Insel, 2010; First, 2011; Nenadic, Sauer, & Gaser, 2010).

Further, a classification system may benefit the person suffering from psychological symptoms. The fact that an individual's disorder has a name can be a comfort and a signal that the person may reasonably expect relief. On the other hand, officially labeling a problem can also have serious negative implications for the person because of the potential for creating *stigma,* a mark of shame that may cause others to avoid or to act negatively toward an individual. Indeed, being diagnosed with a psychological disorder can profoundly influence a person's life, not only because of the effects of the disorder itself, but because of what the diagnosis means with respect to the person, his or her family, and the individual's larger social world.

● *DSM-IV* The *Diagnostic and Statistical Manual of Mental Disorders;* the major classification of psychological disorders in the United States.

The *DSM-IV* Classification System

In 1952, the American Psychiatric Association (APA) published the first major classification of psychological disorders in the United States, the *Diagnostic and Statistical Manual of Mental Disorders.* Its current version, the **DSM-IV** (APA, 1994), was introduced in 1994 and revised in 2000, producing the *DSM-IV-TR* (text revision) (APA, 2000). *DSM-V* is due in 2013. Throughout the development of the *DSM,* the number of diagnosable disorders has increased dramatically. The first *DSM* listed 112 disorders; the *DSM-IV-TR* includes 374.

The *DSM-IV* classifies individuals on the basis of five dimensions, or *axes,* that take into account the individual's history and highest level of functioning in the previous year. The system's creators meant to ensure that the individual is not merely assigned to a psychological disorder category but instead is characterized in terms of a number of factors. The five axes of *DSM-IV* are

Axis I: All diagnostic categories except personality disorders and mental retardation

Axis II: Personality disorders and mental retardation

Axis III: General medical conditions

Axis IV: Psychosocial and environmental problems

Axis V: Current level of functioning

Axes I and II are concerned with the classification of psychological disorders. Figure 58.2 describes the major categories of these disorders. Axes III through V may

Major Categories of Psychological Disorders	Description	
		Axis I Disorders
Disorders usually first diagnosed in infancy, childhood, or adolescence and communication disorders	Include disorders that appear before adolescence, such as attention deficit hyperactivity disorder, autism, and learning disorders (stuttering, for example).	
Anxiety disorders	Characterized by motor tension, hyperactivity, and apprehensive expectations/thoughts. Include generalized anxiety disorder, panic disorder, phobic disorder, obsessive-compulsive disorder, and post-traumatic stress disorder.	
Somatoform disorders	Occur when psychological symptoms take a physical form even though no physical causes can be found. Include hypochondriasis and conversion disorder.	
Factitious disorders	Characterized by the individual's deliberate fabrication of a medical or mental disorder, but not for external gain (such as a disability claim).	
Dissociative disorders	Involve a sudden loss of memory or change of identity. Include the disorders of dissociative amnesia, dissociative fugue, and dissociative identity disorder.	
Delirium, dementia, amnesia, and other cognitive disorders	Consist of mental disorders involving problems in consciousness and cognition, such as substance-induced delirium or dementia related to Alzheimer disease.	
Mood disorders	Disorders in which there is a primary disturbance in mood; include depressive disorders and bipolar disorder (which involves wide mood swings from deep depression to extreme euphoria and agitation).	
Schizophrenia and other psychotic disorders	Disorders characterized by distorted thoughts and perceptions, odd communication, inappropriate emotion, and other unusual behaviors.	
Substance-related disorders	Include alcohol-related disorders, cocaine-related disorders, hallucinogen-related disorders, and other drug-related disorders.	
Sexual and gender identity disorders	Consist of three main types of disorders: gender-identity disorders (person is not comfortable with identity as a female or male), paraphilias (person has a preference for unusual sexual acts to stimulate sexual arousal), and sexual dysfunctions (impairments in sexual functioning).	
Eating disorders	Include anorexia nervosa, bulimia nervosa, and binge eating disorder.	
Sleep disorders	Consist of primary sleep disorders, such as insomnia and narcolepsy (see Module 14), and sleep disorders due to a general medical condition.	
Impulse control disorders not elsewhere classified	Include kleptomania, pyromania, and compulsive gambling.	
Adjustment disorders	Characterized by distressing emotional or behavioral symptoms in response to an identifiable stressor.	
		Axis II Disorders
Intellectual disability	Low intellectual functioning and an inability to adapt to everyday life (see Module 29).	
Personality disorders	Develop when personality traits become inflexible and maladaptive. Include antisocial personality disorder and borderline personality disorder.	
Other conditions that may be a focus of clinical attention	Include relational problems (with a partner, sibling, and so on), problems related to abuse or neglect (physical abuse of a child, for example), or additional conditions (such as bereavement, academic problems, religious or spiritual problems).	

FIGURE 58.2   Main Categories of Psychological Disorders in the *DSM-IV* The *DSM-IV* provides a way for mental health professionals and researchers to communicate with one another about these well-defined psychological disorders.

CRITICAL CONTROVERSY

Are Psychological Disorders a Myth?

In a 2005 broadcast of NBC's *Today Show,* Matt Lauer interviewed Tom Cruise, who was embroiled in a heated media debate with Brooke Shields. Shields had published a book about her experience with post-partum (following childbirth) depression and her positive experience with prescription antidepressants to treat her disorder. Cruise vehemently criticized the very idea of depression and scorned the use of prescription drugs to treat psychological disorders, dubbing psychiatry "a pseudo science."

In response, the National Alliance for the Mentally Ill (NAMI), the American Psychiatric Association, and the National Mental Health Association (NMHA) issued a joint statement declaring, "While we respect the right of individuals to express their own points of view, they are not entitled to their own facts. Mental illnesses are real medical conditions that affect millions of Americans" (NAMI/APA/NMHA, 2005).

Cruise's argument was very similar to one made 50 years ago by psychiatrist Thomas Szasz (1961) in his book *The Myth of Mental Illness.* Szasz argued that psychological disorders are not illnesses and are better labeled "problems of living." Szasz said that it makes no sense to refer to a person's problems of living as "mental illness" and to treat him or her through a medical model. If a man's bizarre beliefs do nothing more than offend or frighten other people, what right do we have to label him "mentally ill" and to administer drugs to him? Szasz's arguments carry weight to this day (Cresswell, 2008; Eghigian, 2010).

The controversy over attention deficit hyperactivity disorder provides a thought-provoking example. In **attention deficit hyperactivity disorder (ADHD),** individuals show one or more of the following symptoms: inattention, hyperactivity, and impulsivity. ADHD is one of the

most common psychological disorders of childhood, and the growth in diagnosis of this disorder in recent years is staggering (Rosenberg, Westling, & McLeskey, 2011). Whereas in 1988 just 500,000 cases were diagnosed, currently *4 million* children are diagnosed with ADHD each year (Bloom & Cohen, 2007). The sheer number of ADHD diagnoses has prompted some observers to wonder whether psychiatrists, parents, and teachers are actually labeling normal childhood behavior as psychopathology (Carey, 2002). After all, the impulsivity, hyperactivity, and inattention that characterize ADHD are typical of most children, especially boys.

Non-Latino White boys are much more likely to be diagnosed with ADHD than any other group (National Center for Health Statistics, 2006). The potential overdiagnosing of ADHD is of some significance, because animal research has shown that in the absence of ADHD, exposure to stimulants such as Ritalin (a common drug treatment for ADHD) can predispose individuals to later addiction problems (Leo, 2005).

In response to the debate, the National Institute of Mental Health sponsored a conference to review the scientific evidence. The result was a "consensus statement" signed by 75 psychiatrists and psychologists, declaring that ADHD is a real psychological disorder with a biological basis in the brain, associated with a number of problems, including dropping out of school, teen pregnancy, and antisocial behavior (Barkley & 74 others, 2002). Denying that ADHD is a real disorder, the statement asserted, amounts to believing that the earth is flat.

In turn, critics of the consensus statement argued that the biological basis of ADHD is not unique to ADHD but is a pattern shared with other childhood disorders (Timimi, 2004). Furthermore, the critics argued, the use of prescription drugs removes responsibility from parents and teachers and leads society to ignore possible environmental factors in ADHD (Timimi, 2004). Finally, critics pointed out that some of those signing the consensus statement were researchers funded by the pharmaceutical companies that produce the drugs used to treat ADHD.

ADHD is not the only controversial diagnosis, nor is ADHD alone in its link to pharmaceutical companies. Drug companies commonly fund research that focuses on a disease model of psychological disorders.

Does this controversy have a resolution? Clearly, psychological disorders are "real" in the sense that they lead to objectively negative outcomes in people's lives. The controversy over ADHD is a reminder of the important role of research in clarifying and defining diagnostic categories. Nobody wants to label inappropriately, to misdiagnose, or to mistreat people who are already suffering.

Diagnoses of attention deficit hyperactivity disorder have increased sharply in recent years.

WHAT DO YOU THINK?

- When do you think it is appropriate to label someone as having a psychological disorder?
- When do you think medical treatments for psychological disorders are appropriate?
- If a teacher suggested that your child be tested for ADHD, what would you do? Why?

not be needed to diagnose a psychological disorder, but they are included so that the person's overall life situation is considered. Axis III information helps to clarify if symptoms may be rooted in physical illness. Axis IV focuses on whether the person is experiencing disruptions in various life domains, including important social relationships, his or her job, or living conditions. On Axis V, the clinician evaluates the highest level of adaptive functioning the person has attained in the preceding year in social, occupational, or school activities.

Critiques of the *DSM-IV*

A number of criticisms of the *DSM-IV* have been made (Hyman, 2010; Katschnig, 2010; Langstrom, 2010; Ronningstam, 2010). The most controversial aspect of the *DSM-IV* is that the manual classifies individuals based on their symptoms, using medical terminology in the psychiatric tradition of thinking about mental disorders in terms of disease (Oltmanns & Emery, 2010). This emphasis implies that the abnormalities have an internal cause that is relatively independent of environmental factors (Kring & others, 2007). So, even though researchers have begun to shed light on the complex interaction of genetic, neurobiological, cognitive, and environmental factors in psychological disorders, the *DSM-IV* continues to reflect the medical model (APA, 2006).

Another criticism is that the *DSM-IV* focuses strictly on pathology and problems. Critics argue that emphasizing *strengths* as well as weaknesses might help to destigmatize labels such as "schizophrenic." Indeed, professionals avoid such labels, using what is called *people-first language*. Bill Garrett, whom you met in the opening vignette, is a *person with schizophrenia,* not "a schizophrenic." Identifying a person's strengths can be an important step toward maximizing his or her ability to contribute to society (Roten, 2007).

Of course, labels such as those described by the *DSM-IV* are based on the idea that psychological disorders are real and often medically treatable. Some individuals have questioned this very assumption. To read about this controversy, see the Critical Controversy.

Before we begin our survey of the various psychological disorders, take a moment to consider this caution. It is very common for individuals who are learning about psychological disorders to recognize the symptoms and behaviors of disorders in themselves or in people around them. Keep in mind that only trained professionals can diagnose a psychological disorder.

● **attention deficit hyperactivity disorder (ADHD)** One of the most common psychological disorders of childhood, in which individuals show one or more of the following: inattention, hyperactivity, and impulsivity.

SUMMARY

Abnormal behavior is deviant, maladaptive, or personally distressful. Theoretical perspectives on the causes of psychological disorders include biological, psychological, sociocultural, and biopsychosocial approaches.

Biological approaches to disorders describe psychological disorders as diseases with origins in structural, biochemical, and genetic factors. Psychological approaches include the behavioral, social cognitive, and trait perspectives. Sociocultural approaches place emphasis on the larger social context in which a person lives, including marriage, socioeconomic status, ethnicity, gender, and culture. Biopsychosocial approaches view the interactions among biological, psychological, and social factors as significant forces in producing both normal and abnormal behavior.

The classification of disorders provides a shorthand for communication, allows clinicians to make predictions about disorders, and helps them to decide on appropriate treatment. The *Diagnostic and Statistical Manual of Mental Disorders (DSM)* is the classification system clinicians

KEY TERMS

abnormal behavior   548
medical model   549
DSM-IV   550

attention deficit hyperactivity disorder (ADHD)   553

use to diagnose psychological disorders. Some psychologists contend that the *DSM-IV* perpetuates the medical model of psychological disorders, labels everyday problems as psychological disorders, and fails to address strengths.

TEST YOURSELF

1. What three main criteria distinguish abnormal behavior from normal behavior?

2. Why is it important to have formal systems for classifying abnormal behaviors into specific psychological disorders?

3. What is the DSM-IV, and what did its authors strive to ensure with respect to individuals with psychological disorders?

APPLY YOUR KNOWLEDGE

1. Spend 15 to 20 minutes observing an area with a large number of people, such as a mall, a cafeteria, or a stadium during a game. Identify and make a list of behaviors you would classify as abnormal. How does your list of behaviors compare with the definition of *abnormal* provided above? What would change in the list if you were in a different setting, such as a church, a bar, or a library? What does this exercise tell you about the meaning of *abnormal*?

2. Although we might think of people who contend with psychological disorders as troubled and downtrodden, they (like all people) have the capacity to be astonishingly creative. Check out the website maintained by the National Art Exhibitions of the Mentally Ill (NAEMI) to experience some amazing creations of artists who suffer from mental illness. Go to http://www.naemi.org and click on "Artists." How does your exploration of this artwork influence your feelings about mental illness?

3. Go online and search for message boards where individuals with different psychological disorders share with each other. How do the discussion boards reflect what you have learned about these disorders?

Anxiety Disorders

Think about how you felt before a make-or-break exam or a big presentation—or perhaps as you noticed police lights flashing behind your speeding car. Did you feel jittery and nervous and experience tightness in your stomach? These are the feelings of normal anxiety. Anxiety is an unpleasant feeling of fear and dread.

Individuals with high levels of anxiety worry a lot, but their anxiety does not necessarily impair their ability to function. In contrast, **anxiety disorders** involve fears that are uncontrollable, disproportionate to the actual danger the person might be in, and disruptive of ordinary life (Cisler & others, 2010). They feature motor tension (jumpiness, trembling), hyperactivity (dizziness, a racing heart), and apprehensive expectations and thoughts. In this section we survey five types of anxiety disorders:

- Generalized anxiety disorder
- Panic disorder
- Phobic disorder
- Obsessive-compulsive disorder
- Post-traumatic stress disorder

● **anxiety disorders** Psychological disorders involving fears that are uncontrollable, disproportionate to the actual danger the person might be in, and disruptive of ordinary life.

59·1 GENERALIZED ANXIETY DISORDER

When you are worrying about getting a speeding ticket, you know why you are anxious; there is a specific cause. **Generalized anxiety disorder** is different from such everyday feelings of anxiety in that sufferers of this disorder experience persistent anxiety for at least six months and are unable to specify the reasons for the anxiety (Fisher, Granger, & Newman, 2010). People with generalized anxiety disorder are nervous most of the time. They may worry about their work, relationships, or health. That worry can also take a physical toll, so that individuals with generalized anxiety disorder may suffer from fatigue, muscle tension, stomach problems, and difficulty sleeping.

● **generalized anxiety disorder** Psychological disorder marked by persistent anxiety for at least six months and in which the individual is unable to specify the reasons for the anxiety.

What is the etiology of generalized anxiety disorder? (*Etiology* means the causes or significant preceding conditions.) Among the biological factors involved in generalized anxiety disorder are genetic predisposition, deficiency in the neurotransmitter GABA, sympathetic nervous system activity, and respiratory system abnormalities (Fisher, Granger, & Newman, 2010; Garner & others, 2009; Katzman, 2009).

The psychological and sociocultural factors include having harsh (or even impossible) self-standards, overly strict and critical parents, automatic negative thoughts when feeling stressed, and a history of uncontrollable traumas or stressors (such as an abusive parent).

59·2 PANIC DISORDER

Much like everyone else, you might have a specific experience that sends you into a panic. For example, you work all night on a paper, only to have your computer crash before you printed it out or saved your last changes, or you are just about

Sleep disturbance is a common problem for people with generalized anxiety disorder.

Many experts interpret Edvard Munch's painting The Scream *as an expression of the terror brought on by a panic attack.*

● **panic disorder** Anxiety disorder in which the individual experiences recurrent, sudden onsets of intense apprehension or terror, often without warning and with no specific cause.

● **phobic disorder or phobia** Anxiety disorder characterized by an irrational, overwhelming, persistent fear of a particular object or situation.

to dash across a street when you see a large truck coming right at you. Your heart races, your hands shake, and you might break into a sweat. In these situations, you know why you are experiencing feelings of panic.

In a **panic disorder,** however, a person experiences recurrent, sudden onsets of intense apprehension or terror, often without warning and with no specific cause. Panic attacks can produce severe palpitations, extreme shortness of breath, chest pains, trembling, sweating, dizziness, and a feeling of helplessness (Dammen & others, 2006). People with panic disorder fear that they will die, go crazy, or do something they cannot control. They may feel that they are having a heart attack.

Charles Darwin, the scientist who proposed the theory of evolution, suffered from intense panic disorder (Barloon & Noyes, 1997). Actor Kim Basinger and former NFL running back Earl Campbell also have dealt with this disorder.

What is the etiology of panic disorder? In terms of biological factors, individuals may have a genetic predisposition to the disorder (Battaglia & others, 2009; Maron, Hettema, & Shlik, 2010). One biological view is that individuals who experience panic disorder may have an autonomic nervous system that is predisposed to be overly active (Durand & Barlow, 2010; Hazlett-Stevens & Craske, 2009). Another biologically based possibility is that panic disorder may stem from problems involving either or both of two neurotransmitters: norepinephrine and GABA (P. L. Johnson & others, 2010).

With respect to psychological factors, one theory about panic disorder is that individuals misinterpret harmless indicators of physiological arousal (for example, a slightly raised heartbeat) as an emergency (such as a heart attack). However, this model of panic disorder remains controversial (Hazlett-Stevens & Craske, 2009).

In terms of sociocultural factors in the United States, American women are twice as likely as American men to have panic attacks (Altemus, 2006). Possible reasons for this difference include biological differences in hormones and neurotransmitters (Altemus, 2006; Fodor & Epstein, 2002). Research also suggests that women may cope with anxiety-provoking situations differently than men, and these differences may explain the gender difference in panic disorder (Schmidt & Koselka, 2000).

59-3 PHOBIC DISORDER

Many people are afraid of spiders and snakes; indeed, thinking about letting a tarantula crawl over one's face is likely to give anyone the willies. It is not uncommon to be afraid of particular objects or specific environments such as extreme heights. For most of us, these fears do not interfere with daily life. Some of us, however, have an irrational, overwhelming, persistent fear of a particular object or situation—an anxiety disorder called a **phobic disorder** or **phobia.** Whereas individuals with generalized anxiety disorder cannot pinpoint the cause of their nervous feelings, individuals with phobias can (Ollendick & others, 2010; Schienle & others, 2009).

A fear becomes a phobia when a situation is so dreaded that an individual goes to almost any length to avoid it. As with any anxiety disorder, phobias are fears that are uncontrollable, disproportionate, and disruptive. A snake phobia that keeps a citydweller from leaving his apartment is clearly disproportionate to the actual chances of encountering a snake. John Madden—former NFL coach, football commentator, and video game consultant—has a famous fear of flying that led him to take a bus to the games that he broadcast.

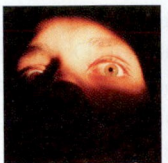 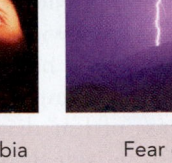   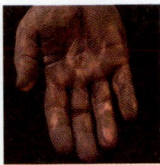  

Acrophobia	Fear of high places	Arachnophobia	Fear of spiders	Mysophobia	Fear of dirt
Aerophobia	Fear of flying	Astrapophobia	Fear of lightning	Nyctophobia	Fear of darkness
Ailurophobia	Fear of cats	Cynophobia	Fear of dogs	Ophidiophobia	Fear of nonpoisonous snakes
Algophobia	Fear of pain	Gamophobia	Fear of marriage	Thanatophobia	Fear of death
Amaxophobia	Fear of vehicles, driving	Hydrophobia	Fear of water	Xenophobia	Fear of strangers
		Melissophobia	Fear of bees		

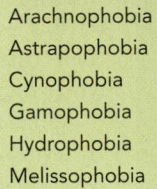

FIGURE 59.1 **Phobias** This figure features some examples of phobic disorder—an anxiety disorder characterized by irrational and overwhelming fear of a particular object or experience.

Another phobic disorder, *social phobia,* is an intense fear of being humiliated or embarrassed in social situations (Carter & Wu, 2010; Rapee, Gaston, & Abbott, 2009). Individuals with this phobia are afraid that they will say or do the wrong thing. Singers Carly Simon and Barbra Streisand have dealt with social phobia.

Phobias usually begin in childhood and come in many forms (National Institute of Mental Health, 2008). Figure 59.1 labels and describes a number of phobias.

What is the etiology of phobic disorder? Genes appear to play a role in social phobia (Reich, 2009). Researchers have proposed that there is a neural circuit for social phobia that includes the thalamus, amygdala, and cerebral cortex (Damsa, Kosel, & Moussally, 2009). Also, a number of neurotransmitters may be involved in social phobia, especially serotonin (Christensen & others, 2010).

With regard to psychological factors, some theorists consider phobias learned fears (Clark & others, 2006). According to learning researchers, perhaps the individual with the fear of falling off a building experienced a fall from a high place earlier in life and therefore associates heights with pain (a classical conditioning explanation). Alternatively, he or she may have heard about or watched others who demonstrated terror of high places (an observational learning explanation), as when a little girl develops a fear of heights after sitting next to her terrified mother and observing her clutch the handrails, white-knuckled, as the roller coaster creeps steeply uphill.

● **obsessive-compulsive disorder (OCD)** Anxiety disorder in which the individual has anxiety-provoking thoughts that will not go away and/or urges to perform repetitive, ritualistic behaviors to prevent or produce some future situation.

59-4 OBSESSIVE-COMPULSIVE DISORDER

Just before leaving on a long road trip, you find yourself checking to be sure you locked the front door. As you pull away in your car, you are stricken with the thought that you forgot to turn off the coffeemaker. Going to bed the night before an early flight, you check your alarm clock a few times to be sure it will wake you for your 8 A.M. plane. This kind of checking behavior is a normal part of worrying.

In contrast, the anxiety disorder known as **obsessive-compulsive disorder (OCD)** features anxiety-provoking thoughts that will not go away and/or urges to perform repetitive, ritualistic behaviors to prevent or produce some future situation. *Obsessions* are recurrent thoughts, and *compulsions* are recurrent behaviors. Individuals with OCD dwell on normal doubts and repeat their routines sometimes hundreds of times a day (Abramowitz, 2009). Game show host Howie Mandel has coped with OCD, and David Beckham and Leonardo DiCaprio have each described mild cases of the disorder.

"Since you have a complete record of my life, could you tell me if I remembered to turn the stove off?"

© Mike Baldwin. www.CartoonStock.com.

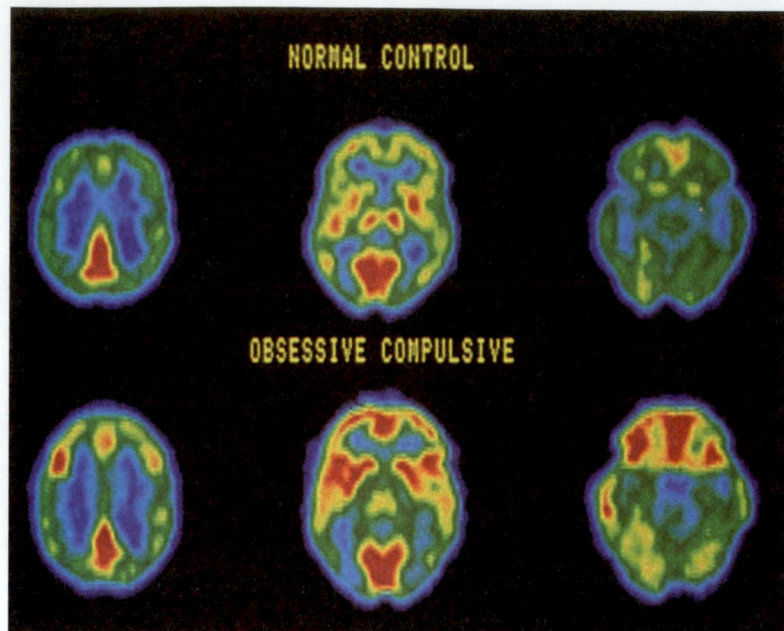

FIGURE 59.2   **PET Scans of Individuals with Obsessive-Compulsive Disorder** (*Top*) Brain images of normal individuals. (*Bottom*) Brain images of individuals with obsessive-compulsive disorder (OCD). The brain images of the individuals with OCD show more activity in the frontal cortex, basal ganglia, and thalamus than the scans of normal individuals.

The most common compulsions are excessive checking, cleansing, and counting. An individual with OCD might believe that she has to touch the doorway with her left hand whenever she enters a room and count her steps as she walks across the room. If she does not complete this ritual, she may be overcome with a sense of fear that something terrible will happen. Indeed, most individuals do not enjoy their ritualistic behavior but feel extraordinarily anxious when they do not carry it out (Victor & Bernstein, 2009).

What is the etiology of obsessive-compulsive disorder? In terms of biological factors, there seems to be a genetic component (Gelernter & Stein, 2009; Sampaio & others, 2010). Also, brain-imaging studies have suggested neurological links for OCD (Nakao & others, 2009). One interpretation of these data is that the frontal cortex or basal ganglia are so active in OCD that numerous impulses reach the thalamus, generating obsessive thoughts or compulsive actions (Figure 59.2) (Rotge & others, 2009).

Studies using fMRI have examined the brain activity of individuals with OCD before and after treatment. Following effective treatment, a number of areas in the frontal cortex show decreased activation (Freyer & others, 2010; Nakao & others, 2005). Interestingly, the amygdala, which is associated with the experience of anxiety, may be smaller in individuals with OCD compared to those who do not have the disorder (Atmaca & others, 2008). Low levels of the neurotransmitters serotonin and dopamine likely are involved in the brain pathways linked with OCD (Koo & others, 2010; Olver & others, 2009).

In terms of psychological factors, OCD sometimes occurs during a period of life stress such as that surrounding the birth of a child or a change in occupational or marital status (Uguz & others, 2007). According to the cognitive perspective, what differentiates individuals with OCD from those who do not have it is the inability to turn off negative, intrusive thoughts by ignoring or effectively dismissing them (Belloch & others, 2010; Foa & Franklin, 2011; Storch & others, 2010).

59-5 POST-TRAUMATIC STRESS DISORDER

If you have ever been in even a minor car accident, you may have had a nightmare or two about it. You might have even found yourself reliving the experience for some time. This normal recovery process takes on a particularly devastating character in post-traumatic stress disorder. **Post-traumatic stress disorder (PTSD)** is an anxiety disorder that develops through exposure to a traumatic event that has overwhelmed the person's abilities to cope (O'Donnell & others, 2010). The symptoms of PTSD vary but include

● **post-traumatic stress disorder (PTSD)** Anxiety disorder that develops through exposure to a traumatic event that has overwhelmed the person's abilities to cope.

- Flashbacks in which the individual relives the event. A flashback can make the person lose touch with reality and reenact the event for seconds, hours, or, very rarely, days. A person having a flashback—which can come in the form of images, sounds, smells, and/or feelings—usually believes that the traumatic event is happening all over again.

- Avoidance of emotional experiences and of talking about emotions with others.

- Reduced ability to feel emotions, often reported as feeling numb, resulting in an inability to experience happiness, sexual desire, or enjoyable interpersonal relationships.

- Excessive arousal, resulting in an exaggerated startle response or an inability to sleep.

- Difficulties with memory and concentration.
- Feelings of apprehension, including nervous tremors.
- Impulsive outbursts of behavior, such as aggressiveness, or sudden changes in lifestyle.

PTSD symptoms can follow a trauma immediately or after months or even years (de Roon-Cassini & others, 2010; McFarlane, 2010). Most individuals who are exposed to a traumatic event experience some of the symptoms in the days and weeks following exposure (National Center for Post-Traumatic Stress Disorder, 2006). However, not every individual exposed to the same event develops PTSD (Gil & Caspi, 2006).

Researchers have examined PTSD associated with a variety of different experiences. These experiences include combat and war-related traumas (Kennedy & others, 2010; Ling & others, 2009); sexual abuse and assault (Mouilso, Calhoun, & Gidycz, 2010); natural disasters such as hurricanes and earthquakes (Irmansyah & others, 2010); and unnatural disasters such as plane crashes and terrorist attacks (Dedert & others, 2009; B. J. Hall & others, 2010).

Clearly, one cause of PTSD is the traumatic event itself. However, because not everyone who experiences the same traumatic life event develops PTSD, other factors (aside from the event) may influence a person's vulnerability to the disorder (Markowitz & others, 2009). These factors include a history of previous traumatic events and conditions, such as abuse and psychological disorders (Walter & others, 2010), as well as genetic predispositions (Voisey & others, 2009).

Prior to deployment, troops receive stress-management training aimed at helping to prevent PTSD and other disorders that might be triggered by the high-stress conditions of war.

SUMMARY

Generalized anxiety disorder is anxiety that persists for at least 6 months with no specific reason for the anxiety. Panic disorder involves attacks marked by the sudden onset of intense terror. Biological, psychological, and sociocultural factors may contribute to the development of panic disorder.

Phobic disorders involve an irrational, overwhelming fear of a particular object, such as snakes, or a situation, such as flying. Obsessive-compulsive disorder is an anxiety disorder in which the individual has anxiety-provoking thoughts that will not go away (obsession) and/or urges to perform repetitive, ritualistic behaviors to prevent or produce some future situation (compulsion). Post-traumatic stress disorder (PTSD) is an anxiety disorder that develops through exposure to traumatic events, sexual abuse and assault, and natural and unnatural disasters. Symptoms include flashbacks, emotional avoidance, emotional numbing, and excessive arousal. A variety of experiential, psychological, and genetic factors have been shown to relate to these disorders.

KEY TERMS

anxiety disorders   555
generalized anxiety disorder   555
panic disorder   556
phobic disorder or phobia   556

obsessive-compulsive disorder (OCD)   557
post-traumatic stress disorder (PTSD)   558

TEST YOURSELF

1. What are the main characteristics of anxiety disorders?
2. Define phobic disorder (phobia) and give at least three examples of common phobias.
3. With what kinds of experiences is post-traumatic stress disorder (PTSD) associated?

APPLY YOUR KNOWLEDGE

1. Go to www.youtube.com and search for a video documenting each anxiety disorder. List your videos and their web addresses along with a critique of what makes this video an accurate or inaccurate account of the disorder. Share your video resources with the class.

2. Contact your local veteran's hospital or clinic and interview a professional who works with military veterans suffering from PTSD. Identify the common symptoms, treatment, and prognosis related to PTSD.

Mood Disorders

This painting by Vincent Van Gogh, Portrait of Dr. Gachet, *reflects the extreme melancholy that characterizes the depressive disorders.*

● **mood disorders** Psychological disorders—the main types of which are depressive disorders and bipolar disorder—in which there is a primary disturbance of mood: prolonged emotion that colors the individual's emotional state.

● **depressive disorders** Mood disorders in which the individual suffers from depression—an unrelenting lack of pleasure in life.

● **major depressive disorder (MDD)** Psychological disorder involving a significant depressive episode and depressed characteristics, such as lethargy and hopelessness, for at least two weeks.

● **dysthymic disorder (DD)** Mood disorder that is generally more chronic and has fewer symptoms than MDD; the individual is in a depressed mood for most days for at least two years as an adult or at least one year as a child or an adolescent.

560

Mood disorders are psychological disorders in which there is a primary disturbance of *mood:* prolonged emotion that colors the individual's entire emotional state. This mood disturbance can include cognitive, behavioral, and somatic (physical) symptoms, as well as interpersonal difficulties. In this module we examine the two main types of mood disorders: depressive disorders and bipolar disorder. In addition, we consider a tragic correlate of these disorders—suicide.

60-1 DEPRESSIVE DISORDERS

Everyone feels blue sometimes. A romantic breakup, the death of a loved one, or a personal failure can cast a dark cloud over life. Sometimes, however, a person might feel unhappy and not know why. **Depressive disorders** are mood disorders in which the individual suffers from *depression:* an unrelenting lack of pleasure in life. The severity of depressive disorders varies. Some individuals experience what is classified as *major depressive disorder,* whereas others are given the diagnosis of *dysthymic disorder,* a more chronic depression with fewer symptoms than major depression (Ingram, 2009; Rafanelli & others, 2010).

Depressive disorders are common, and a number of successful individuals have been diagnosed with depression. They include musicians Sheryl Crow, Eric Clapton, and Peter Gabriel; actors Drew Barrymore and Jim Carrey; and artist Pablo Picasso, photographer Diane Arbus, astronaut Buzz Aldrin (the second man to walk on the moon), and famed architect Frank Lloyd Wright.

Major depressive disorder (MDD) involves a significant depressive episode and depressed characteristics, such as lethargy and hopelessness, for at least two weeks. MDD impairs daily functioning, and it has been called the leading cause of disability in the United States (National Institute of Mental Health, 2008). Nine symptoms (at least five of which must be present during a two-week period) define a major depressive episode:

- Depressed mood most of the day
- Reduced interest or pleasure in all or most activities
- Significant weight loss or gain or significant decrease or increase in appetite
- Trouble sleeping or sleeping too much
- Psychological and physical agitation, or, in contrast, lethargy
- Fatigue or loss of energy
- Feeling worthless or guilty in an excessive or inappropriate manner
- Problems in thinking, concentrating, or making decisions
- Recurrent thoughts of death and suicide
- No history of manic episodes (periods of euphoric mood)

Dysthymic disorder (DD) is a mood disorder that is generally more chronic and has fewer symptoms than MDD. The individual is in a depressed mood for most days for at least two years as an adult or at least one year as a child or an adolescent. To be classified as having dysthymic disorder, the individual must not have experienced a major depressive episode, and the two-year period of depression must not have been broken by a normal mood lasting more than two months. Two or more of these six symptoms must be present:

- Poor appetite or overeating
- Sleep problems
- Low energy or fatigue
- Low self-esteem
- Poor concentration or difficulty making decisions
- Feelings of hopelessness

A variety of biological, psychological, and sociocultural factors have been implicated in the development of these depressive disorders.

Biological Factors

Genetic influences play a role in depression (Shyn & Hamilton, 2010; Y. Yuan & others, 2010). In addition, specific brain structures and neurotransmitters are involved in depressive disorders. For example, depressed individuals show lower levels of brain activity in a section of the prefrontal cortex that is involved in initiating behavior (Friedel & others, 2009; M. Roy & others, 2010).

Research has revealed that activity in the brain region that is associated with the perception of rewards in the environment (the ventromedial prefrontal cortex) may differ for depressed and non-depressed individuals (Tye & Janak, 2007). This discovery suggests that a depressed person's brain may not recognize opportunities for pleasurable experiences.

Depression likely involves problems in the body's regulation of a number of neurotransmitters. Recall from Module 6 that neurotransmitters are chemicals that carry impulses from neuron to neuron. In order for the brain to function smoothly, these neurotransmitters must ebb and flow, often in harmony with one another. Individuals with major depressive disorder appear to have difficulty regulating the neurotransmitter serotonin or too few receptors for serotonin and norepinephrine (Bobo & Shelton, 2010; Tourian, Jiang, & Ninan, 2010).

Psychological Factors

Psychological explanations of depression have drawn on behavioral learning theories and cognitive theories. One behavioral view of depression focuses on learned helplessness (see Module 19), an individual's acquisition of feelings of powerlessness when exposed to aversive circumstances, such as prolonged stress, over which the individual has no control. When people cannot control their stress, they eventually feel helpless and stop trying to change their situations. This helplessness spirals into a feeling of hopelessness (Becker-Weidman & others, 2009).

Cognitive explanations of depression have focused on the kinds of thoughts and beliefs that can contribute to this sense of hopelessness (Fiske, Wetherell, & Gatz, 2009; Wellen, 2010). Psychiatrist Aaron Beck (1967) proposed that negative thoughts reflect self-defeating beliefs that shape the experiences of individuals who are depressed. These habitual negative thoughts magnify and expand these individuals' negative experiences (de Graaf & others, 2010; Joorman, Teachman, & Gotlib, 2009). For example, a person who is depressed might overgeneralize about a minor occurrence—say, turning in a work assignment late—and think that he or she is worthless, or the individual might view a minor setback such as getting a *D* on a paper as the end of the world. The accumulation of cognitive distortions can lead to depression (de Graaf, Hollon, & Huibers, 2010; Gibbons & others, 2010).

The course of depression can be influenced by not only what people think but also *how* they think (Brinker & Dozois, 2009; Mathew & others, 2010). Depressed individuals may ruminate on negative experiences and negative feelings, playing them over and over again in their mind (Aldao, Nolen-Hoeksema, & Schweizer, 2010;

The incidence of depression is high among people living in poverty, as well as single women who are the heads of households.

Nolen-Hoeksema, 2011). This tendency to ruminate is associated with the development of depression as well as other psychological problems, such as binge eating and substance abuse (Aldao, Nolen-Hoeksema, & Schweizer, 2010). Combining the findings with research on the brain, we might say that individuals with depression have a brain that is wired for attention to negative information and that their habitual patterns of thought produce well-worn neurological pathways for unhappiness (De Raedt & Koster, 2010).

Another cognitive view of depression focuses on the *attributions* people make—their attempts to explain what caused something to happen (Hartley & Maclean, 2009; Wong, Kim, & Tran, 2010). Depression is thought to be related to a pessimistic attributional style. In this style, individuals regularly explain negative events as having internal causes ("It is my fault I failed the exam"), stable causes ("I'm going to fail again and again"), and global causes ("Failing this exam shows that I won't do well in any of my courses"). Pessimistic attributional style means blaming oneself for negative events and expecting the negative events to recur in the future (Abramson, Seligman, & Teasdale, 1978).

This pessimistic attributional style can be contrasted with an optimistic attributional style. Optimists make external attributions for bad things that happen ("I did badly on the test because it's hard to know what a professor wants on the first exam"). They also recognize that these causes can change ("I'll do better on the next one") and that they are specific ("It was only one test"). Optimistic attributional style has been related to lowered depression and decreased suicide risk in a variety of samples (Giltay, Zitman, & Kromhout, 2006; Hirsch & others, 2009).

Sociocultural Factors

Individuals with a low socioeconomic status (SES), especially people living in poverty, are more likely to develop depression than their higher-SES counterparts (Bryant-Davis & others, 2010). A longitudinal study of adults revealed that depression increased as standard of living and employment circumstances worsened (Lorant & others, 2007). Studies have found very high rates of depression in Native American groups, among whom poverty, hopelessness, and alcoholism are widespread (LaFromboise, Albright, & Harris, 2010; Teesson & Vogl, 2006).

In terms of gender, women are nearly twice as likely as men to be diagnosed with depression (J. Yuan & others, 2009). This gender difference occurs in many countries (Inaba & others, 2005; Nolen-Hoeksema, 2011). Incidence of depression is high as well among single women who are the heads of households and among young married women who work at unsatisfying, dead-end jobs (Whiffen & Demidenko, 2006). Minority women also are a high-risk group for depression (Diefenbach & others, 2009). The Psychological Inquiry provides a closer look at gender differences in depression.

So far, we have concentrated on depression in adults. However, there also is concern about the development of depression in children, as the Intersection explores.

60-2 BIPOLAR DISORDER

● **bipolar disorder** Mood disorder characterized by extreme mood swings that include one or more episodes of mania, an overexcited, unrealistically optimistic state.

Just as we all have our down times, there are times when things seem to be going phenomenally well. For individuals with bipolar disorder, the ups and downs of life take on an extreme and often harmful tone. **Bipolar disorder** is a mood disorder that

psychological *inquiry*

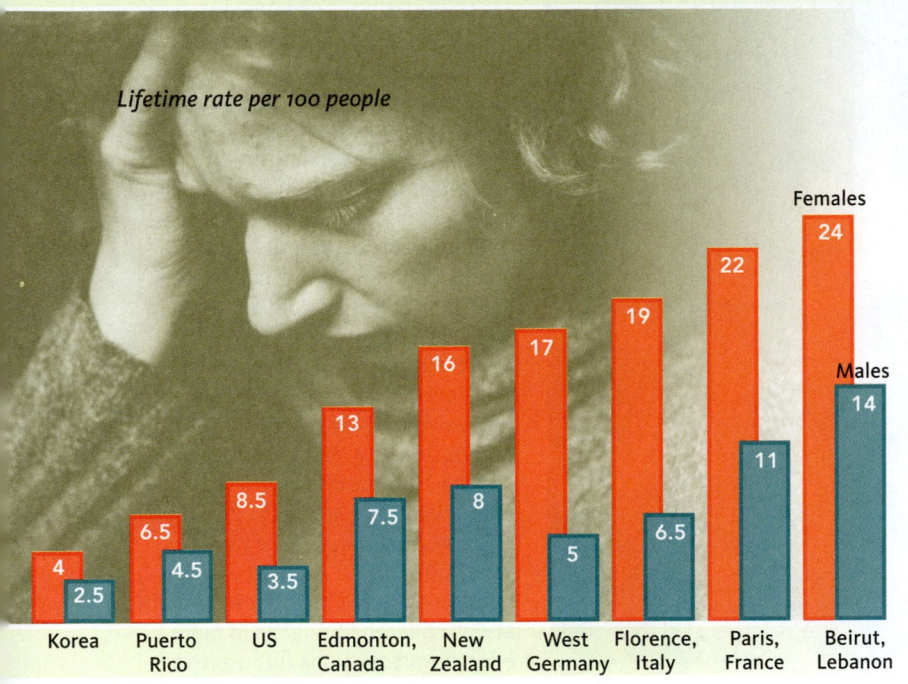

Lifetime rate per 100 people

Korea — Females 4, Males 2.5
Puerto Rico — Females 6.5, Males 4.5
US — Females 8.5, Males 3.5
Edmonton, Canada — Females 13, Males 7.5
New Zealand — Females 16, Males 8
West Germany — Females 17, Males 5
Florence, Italy — Females 19, Males 6.5
Paris, France — Females 22, Males 11
Beirut, Lebanon — Females 24, Males 14

Depression Among Women and Men Across Cultures

The graph shows the rates of depression for women and men in nine different cultures (Weissman & Olfson, 1995). The rates represent the number of diagnosed cases per 100 people.

1. Which cultures have the highest and lowest levels of depression overall? What might account for these differences?

2. Which places have the biggest gender difference in depression? What might account for these differences?

3. In order to be diagnosed with depression, a person has to seek treatment for the disorder. How might gender influence a person's willingness to seek treatment?

4. How does your answer to question 3 influence the conclusions you would draw from the data illustrated in the graph?

is characterized by extreme mood swings that include one or more episodes of *mania,* an overexcited, unrealistically optimistic state. A manic episode is like the flipside of a depressive episode (Last, 2009). The person feels euphoric and on top of the world. An individual who experiences mania has tremendous energy and might sleep very little. A manic state also features an impulsivity that can get the individual in trouble. For example, the sufferer might spend his or her life savings on a foolish business venture.

The severity of manic episodes is used to distinguish between two types of bipolar disorder. *Bipolar I disorder* refers to individuals who have extreme manic episodes during which they may experience hallucinations, that is, seeing or hearing things that are not there. We will discuss this symptom in more detail later when we examine schizophrenia. *Bipolar II disorder* refers to the milder version. In bipolar II disorder, the individual may not experience full-blown mania but rather a less extreme level of euphoria.

Most individuals with bipolar disorder experience multiple cycles of depression interspersed with mania. These people can have manic and depressive episodes four or more times a year, but they usually are separated by six months to a year. Unlike depressive disorders, which are more likely to occur in women, bipolar disorder is equally common in women and men. Bipolar disorder does not prevent a person from being successful. Academy Award–winning actor Patty Duke, famed dancer and choreographer Alvin Ailey, and actor Carrie Fisher (Princess Leia in *Star Wars*) have been diagnosed with bipolar disorder.

What factors play a role in the development of bipolar disorder? Genetic influences are stronger predictors of bipolar disorder than of depressive disorder (Craddock & Forty, 2006). An individual with an identical twin who has bipolar disorder has a more than 60 percent probability of also having the disorder, and a fraternal twin more than 10 percent (Figure 60.1). Researchers are zeroing in on the specific genetic location of bipolar disorder (Barnett & Smoller, 2009; X. Zhou & others, 2009a).

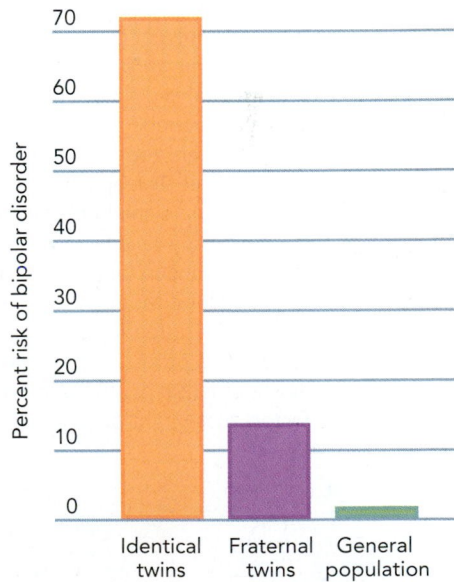

FIGURE 60.1 **Risk of Bipolar Disorder in Identical and Fraternal Twins If One Twin Has the Disorder, and in the General Population** Notice how much stronger the similarity of bipolar disorder is in identical twins, compared with fraternal twins and the general population. These statistics suggest a strong genetic role in the disorder.

Clinical Psychology and Developmental Psychology: Will New Discoveries Bring Depressed Children a Happier Future?

Imagine once again living the life of a typical 3-year-old. Your daily routine would likely revolve around eating, playing, napping, and perhaps watching cartoons. For most children in these early years, life would seem to be a time of simple happiness. For some children, however, childhood is clouded by depression. The prevalence of major depressive disorder among children ranges from 1.5 to 2.5 percent in school-age children and 15 to 20 percent in adolescents (Graber & Sontag, 2009).

Childhood depression is a significant problem (Domènech-Llaberia & others, 2009; Korczak & Goldstein, 2009). Because childhood is a time of building skills and abilities that are essential in later life, childhood depression may interfere with the normal course of development. Children who develop depression are at a higher risk of a variety of problems, including substance abuse, academic problems, increased physical illness, susceptibility to future depression, and a 30-fold increase in suicide risk (Cullen, Klimes-Dougan, & Kumra, 2009; Horowitz & Garber, 2006). How can we as a society come to better understand, treat, and prevent this debilitating childhood disorder?

Developmental psychopathology represents the merging of developmental and clinical psychology to understand, treat, and prevent childhood psychological disorders (Fontaine & others, 2009; Masten, 2009; Masten & Wright, 2009; Montgomery, 2010). Rather than applying knowledge about adult psychological disorders to children, developmental psychopathologists focus on the special developmental circumstances of children in seeking to understand what leads to negative outcomes.

Using longitudinal studies to track the relationships that exist in the unfolding of abnormal and normal behavior patterns (Ge & others, 2009; Zimmer-Gembeck & others, 2009), developmental psychopathology seeks to identify *risk factors* that might predispose a child to depression (Bureau,

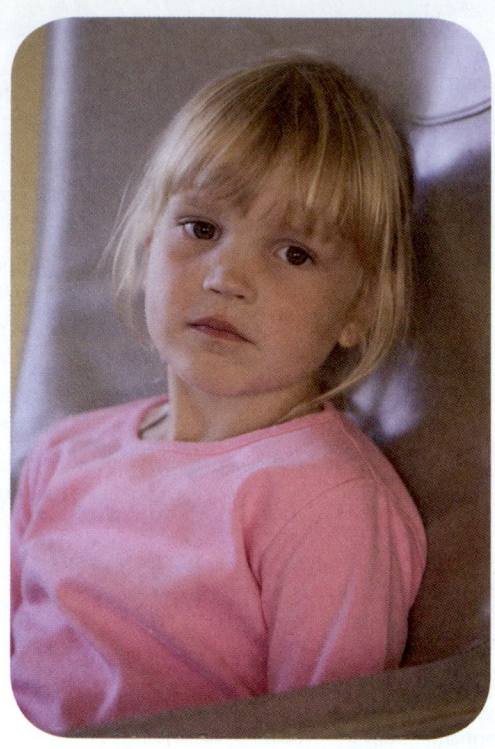

Easterbooks, & Lyons-Ruth, 2009), as well as *protective factors,* that is, aspects of a child's psychological or social experience that may provide a shield against the development of depression (Wingo & others, 2010). The identification of risk factors might suggest avenues for both prevention and treatment. For example, researchers have identified parental psychopathology as a risk factor for childhood depression: Specifically, parents who suffer from depression, an anxiety disorder, or substance abuse are more likely to have children who experience depression (Burstein & others, 2010; Shaw & others, 2009). A research review revealed that interventions aimed at youth who were at risk for depression promoted wellness in the targeted groups (Horowitz & Garber, 2006). Interventions might include training at-risk children to engage in more effective attributions for negative events or to manage their emotions in a healthier way. Protective factors might include a supportive adult who provides the child with love, encouragement, and a role model or a strong extended family that supports the child's attempts to cope with difficulties. Genetic characteristics might be both risk factors and protective factors for children (Benjet, Thompson, & Gotlib, 2010).

Childhood is a time of extraordinary development and learning. Developmental psychopathologists are taking the problems of persistently sad and disengaged children seriously and striving to understand the sources of their suffering in order to give them a more promising future (Brumariu & Kerns, 2010; Hankin, Stone, & Wright, 2010).

In what ways might you be a protective factor in the life of a child you know?

Other biological processes are also a factor. Like depression, bipolar disorder is associated with differences in brain activity. Figure 60.2 shows the metabolic activity in the cerebral cortex of an individual cycling through depressive and manic phases. Notice the decrease in metabolic activity in the brain during depression and the increase in metabolic activity during mania (Baxter & others, 1995). In addition to high levels of norepinephrine and low levels of serotonin, studies show that high levels of the neurotransmitter glutamate occur in bipolar disorder (Singh & others, 2010; Sourial-Bassillious & others, 2009). These differences between depression and bipolar disorder have led to differences in treatment.

60-3 SUICIDE

Life with a psychological disorder can be so difficult that some individuals choose to end it. Suicide is not a diagnosable disorder but is, rather, a tragic consequence of psychological disorders, most commonly depression and anxiety (Black & others, 2010; Nrugham, Holen, & Sund, 2010; Oyama & others, 2010). Individuals suffering from depression are also likely to attempt suicide more than once (da Silva Cais & others, 2009). Although it is not uncommon for individuals to contemplate suicide at some point in life and thinking about suicide is not necessarily abnormal, attempting or completing the act of suicide *is* abnormal.

According to the National Institute of Mental Health (NIMH), in 2004, 32,439 people in the United States committed suicide, and suicide was the 11th-highest cause of death (NIMH, 2008). Research indicates that for every completed suicide, 8 to 25 attempted suicides occur (NIMH, 2008). Suicide is the third-leading cause (after automobile accidents and homicides) of death today among U.S. adolescents 13 through 19 years of age (National Center for Health Statistics, 2005a). Even more shocking, suicide is the third-leading cause of death among children in the United States aged 10 to 14 (Centers for Disease Control and Prevention, 2007).

Given these grim statistics, psychologists work with individuals to reduce the frequency and intensity of suicidal impulses (Pirucello, 2010). You can do your part. Figure 60.3 provides good advice on what to do and what not to do if you encounter someone who is threatening suicide.

What might prompt an individual to end his or her own life? Biological, psychological, and sociocultural circumstances can be contributing factors.

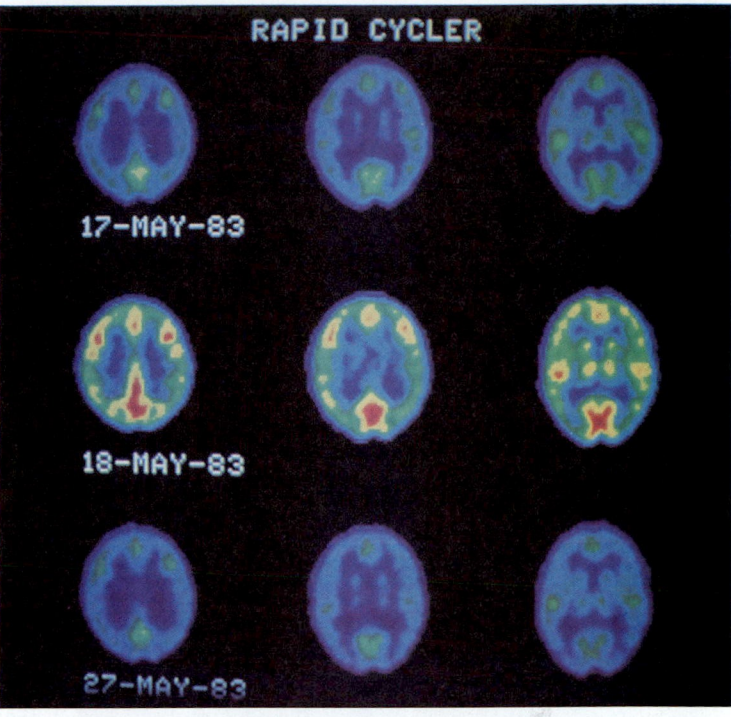

FIGURE 60.2   **Brain Metabolism in Mania and Depression**
PET scans of an individual with bipolar disorder, who is described as a rapid cycler because of how quickly severe mood changes occurred. (*Top and bottom*) The person's brain in a depressed state. (*Middle*) A manic state. The PET scans reveal how the brain's energy consumption falls in depression and rises in mania. The red areas in the middle row reflect rapid consumption of glucose.

Biological Factors

Genetic factors appear to play a role in suicide, which tends to run in families (Brezo & others, 2009; Wasserman, Wasserman, & Sokolowski, 2010). One famous family that has been plagued by suicide is the Hemingways. Five members of that family, spread across generations, committed suicide, including the writer Ernest Hemingway and his granddaughter Margaux, a model and actor. Similarly, in 2009, Nicholas Hughes—a successful marine biologist and the son of Sylvia Plath, a poet who had killed herself—tragically hanged himself. (In considering these examples, you might note that Margaux Hemingway and Nicholas Hughes had experienced the suicide of a family member—and might therefore have been more likely than most people to view ending their life as a way to cope with life's difficulties.)

A number of studies have linked suicide with low levels of the neurotransmitter serotonin (Pompili & others, 2010). Individuals who attempt suicide and who have low serotonin levels are 10 times more likely to attempt suicide again than are attempters who have high serotonin levels (Courtet & others, 2004). Poor physical health, especially when it is long-standing and chronic, is another risk factor for suicide. Ernest Hemingway had been in failing health for a number of years when he committed suicide.

Psychological Factors

Psychological factors that can contribute to suicide include mental disorders and traumas such as sexual abuse. Struggling with the stress of a psychological disorder

What to Do

1. Ask direct, straightforward questions in a calm manner. For example, "Are you thinking about hurting yourself?"

2. Be a good listener and be supportive. Emphasize that unbearable pain can be survived.

3. Take the suicide threat very seriously. Ask questions about the person's feelings, relationships, and thoughts about the type of method to be used. If a gun, pills, rope, or other means is mentioned and a specific plan has been developed, the situation is dangerous. Stay with the person until help arrives.

4. Encourage the person to get professional help and assist him or her in getting help. If the person is willing, take the person to a mental health facility or hospital.

What Not to Do

1. Don't ignore the warning signs.

2. Don't refuse to talk about suicide if the person wants to talk about it.

3. Don't react with horror, disapproval, or repulsion.

4. Don't offer false reassurances ("Everything will be all right") or make judgments ("You should be thankful for . . .").

5. Don't abandon the person after the crisis seems to have passed or after professional counseling has begun.

FIGURE 60.3 **When Someone Is Threatening Suicide** Do not ignore the warning signs if you think someone you know is considering suicide. Talk to a counselor if you are reluctant to say anything to the person yourself.

can leave a person feeling hopeless, and the disorder itself may tax the person's ability to cope with life difficulties. Indeed, approximately 90 percent of individuals who commit suicide are estimated to have a diagnosable psychological disorder (NIMH, 2008).

An immediate and highly stressful circumstance—such as the loss of a loved one or a job, flunking out of school, or an unwanted pregnancy—can lead people to threaten and/or to commit suicide (Videtic & others, 2009). In addition, substance abuse is linked with suicide more today than in the past (Britton & Conner, 2010).

In a fascinating set of studies, Thomas Joiner and his colleagues have focused on distinguishing between the suicide notes of suicide attempters and completers (Conner & others, 2007; Joiner, 2005; Joiner, Hollar, & Van Orden, 2006; Van Orden & others, 2008). They found that suicide attempters were more likely than suicide completers to feel a sense of belonging with others. Furthermore, completers were more likely to feel that their lives posed a burden on others (Selby & others, 2010; Van Orden & others, 2010).

Sociocultural Factors

Chronic economic hardship can be a factor in suicide (Ferretti & Coluccia, 2009; Rojas & Stenberg, 2010). Cultural and ethnic contexts also are related to suicide attempts. In the United States, adolescents' suicide attempts vary across ethnic groups. As Figure 60.4 illustrates, more than 20 percent of American Indian/Alaska Native (AI/AN) female adolescents reported that they had attempted suicide in the previous year, and suicide accounts for almost 20 percent of AI/AN deaths in 15- to 19-year-olds (Goldston & others, 2008). As the figure also shows, African American and non-Latino White males reported the lowest incidence of suicide attempts. A major risk factor in the high rate of suicide attempts by AI/AN adolescents is their elevated rate of alcohol abuse.

Suicide rates vary worldwide; the lowest rates occur in countries with cultural and religious norms against ending one's own life. Among the nations with the highest suicide rates are several eastern European nations—including Belarus, Bulgaria, and Russia—along with Japan and South Korea. Among the nations with the lowest rates are Haiti, Antigua and Barbuda, Egypt, and Iran (World Health Organization, 2009). Of the 104 nations ranked by the WHO, the United States ranks 40th.

There are gender differences in suicide as well (Sarma & Kola, 2010). Women are three times more likely to attempt suicide than men. Men, however, are four times more likely to complete suicide than women (Kochanek & others, 2004). Men are also more likely than women to use a firearm in a suicide attempt (Maris, 1998). The highest

Suicide tends to run in families. Five suicides occurred in different generations of the Hemingway family, including author Ernest (left) and his granddaughter Margaux (right).

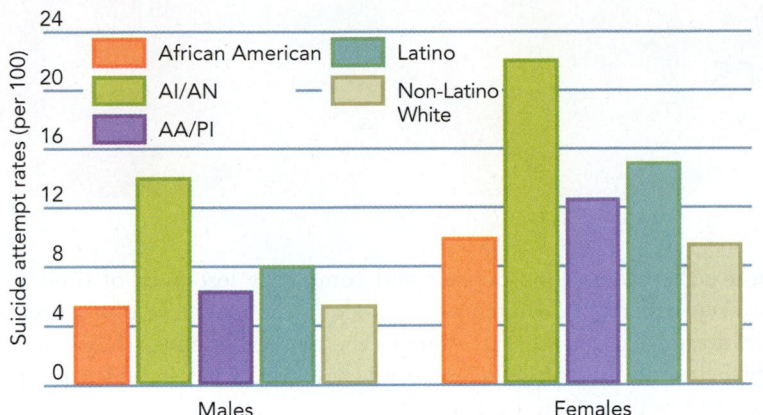

FIGURE 60.4 **Suicide Attempts by U.S. Adolescents from Different Ethnic Groups** Note that the data shown are for one-year rates of self-reported suicide attempts. AI/AN = American Indian/Alaska Native; AA/PI = Asian/American/Pacific Islander.

suicide rate is among non-Latino White men aged 85 and older (NIMH, 2008). Although women are more likely than men to be diagnosed with depression, men are more likely to commit suicide. The explanation for these patterns may be that men are less likely to seek treatment when they are suffering from depression.

SUMMARY

Two types of mood disorders are depressive disorders and bipolar disorder. The depressive disorders include major depressive disorder and dysthymic disorder. In major depressive disorder, the individual experiences a serious depressive episode and depressed characteristics such as lethargy and hopelessness. Dysthymic disorder is generally more chronic and has fewer symptoms than major depressive disorder.

Biological explanations of depressive disorders focus on heredity, neurophysiological abnormalities, and neurotransmitter deregulation. Psychological explanations include behavioral and cognitive perspectives. Sociocultural explanations emphasize socioeconomic and ethnic factors, as well as gender.

Bipolar disorder is characterized by extreme mood swings that include one or more episodes of mania (an overexcited, unrealistic, optimistic state). Individuals with bipolar I disorder have more extreme manic episodes, while those with bipolar II disorder have less extreme episodes. Most individuals with bipolar disorder go through multiple cycles of depression interspersed with mania. Genetic influences are stronger predictors of bipolar disorder than depressive disorder, and biological processes are also a factor in bipolar disorder.

Severe depression and other psychological disorders can cause individuals to want to end their lives. Theorists have proposed biological, psychological, and sociocultural explanations of suicide.

KEY TERMS

mood disorders   560
depressive disorders   560
major depressive disorder
   (MDD)   560

dysthymic disorder
   (DD)   560
bipolar disorder   562

TEST YOURSELF

1. How do major depressive disorder (MDD) and dysthymic disorder (DD) differ?

2. What are the essential characteristics of bipolar disorder?

3. Give at least two biological, two psychological, and two sociocultural factors in suicide.

APPLY YOUR KNOWLEDGE

1. Of the mood disorders, debate which disorder is the hardest to treat. Which is the easiest? Defend your answers.

2. At your college, discover what resources are available to students who are suffering from depression and/or thinking of suicide.

Dissociative Disorders

Have you ever been on a long car ride and completely lost track of time, so that you could not even remember a stretch of miles along the road? Have you been so caught up in a daydream that you were unaware of the passage of time? These are examples of normal dissociation. *Dissociation* refers to psychological states in which the person feels disconnected from immediate experience.

At the extreme of dissociation are individuals who feel a sense of disconnection *persistently*. **Dissociative disorders** are psychological disorders that involve a sudden loss of memory or change in identity. Under extreme stress or shock, the individual's conscious awareness becomes *dissociated* (separated or split) from previous memories and thoughts (Espirito-Santo & Pio-Abreu, 2009). Individuals who develop dissociative disorders may have problems putting together different aspects of consciousness, so that experiences at different levels of awareness might be felt as if they are happening to someone else (Dell & O'Neil, 2009).

Psychologists believe that dissociation is an individual's way of dealing with extreme stress (Spiegel, 2006). Through dissociation the individual mentally protects his or her conscious self from the traumatic event. Dissociative disorders often occur in individuals who also show signs of PTSD (Zucker & others, 2006). Both psychological disorders are thought to be rooted, in part, in extremely traumatic life events (Foote & others, 2006). The notion that dissociative disorders are related to problems in pulling together emotional memories is supported by findings showing lower volume in the hippocampus and amygdala in individuals with dissociative disorders (Vermetten & others, 2006). The hippocampus is especially involved in consolidating memory and organizing life experience into a coherent whole (Spiegel, 2006).

Dissociative disorders are perhaps the most controversial of all diagnostic categories, with some psychologists believing that they are often mistakenly diagnosed (Freeland & others, 1993) while others believe that they are underdiagnosed (Sar, Akyuz, & Dogan, 2007; Spiegel, 2006). Three kinds of dissociative disorders are dissociative amnesia, dissociative fugue, and dissociative identity disorder.

61·1 DISSOCIATIVE AMNESIA AND DISSOCIATIVE FUGUE

Amnesia is the inability to recall important events (Dewar & others, 2010a). Amnesia can result from a blow to the head that produces trauma in the brain. **Dissociative amnesia** is a type of amnesia characterized by extreme memory loss that stems from extensive psychological stress. A person experiencing dissociative amnesia still remembers things like how to hail a cab or use a phone. Only aspects of their own identity and autobiographical experiences are forgotten.

One case of dissociative amnesia involved a 28-year-old married woman who had given birth to her sixth child four months before (Tharoor & others, 2007). After she delivered the child, her family noticed that she did not acknowledge her newborn as her own baby and that she had neither a recollection of having given birth nor a sense of her own identity. She took care of the baby as advised by her family members but maintained a belief that, although she had been pregnant, she had not given birth. Under the influence of sodium pentathol (a narcotic sometimes referred to as "truth serum" because it renders people talkative and likely to share information), the young mother eventually described how she had not wanted to continue her sixth pregnancy,

● **dissociative disorders** Psychological disorders that involve a sudden loss of memory or change in identity due to the dissociation (separation) of the individual's conscious awareness from previous memories and thoughts.

● **dissociative amnesia** Dissociative disorder characterized by extreme memory loss that is caused by extensive psychological stress.

but her spouse, who lived in another country, had refused to consent to an abortion. She described herself as physically drained and stressed by the pregnancy. Eventually, through hypnosis and memory exercises, the woman recovered autobiographical memory for her identity as well as for the experience of having given birth.

Dissociative fugue (*fugue* means "flight") is a dissociative disorder in which the individual not only develops amnesia but also unexpectedly travels away from home and sometimes assumes a new identity. What makes dissociative fugue different from dissociative amnesia is this tendency to run away.

A recent case of dissociative fugue involved the disappearance of a middle school teacher in New York City. Twenty-three-year-old Hannah Upp disappeared while out for a run on August 28, 2008 (Marx & Didziulis, 2009). She had no wallet, no identification, no cell phone, and no money. Her family, friends, and roommates posted flyers around the city and messages on the Internet. As days went by, they became increasingly concerned that something terrible had happened. Finally, Hannah was found floating face down in the New York harbor on September 16, sunburned and dehydrated but alive. She remembered nothing of her experiences. To her, it felt like she had gone out for a run and 10 minutes later was being pulled from the harbor. To this day, she does not know what event might have led to her dissociative fugue, nor does she remember how she survived during her two-week disappearance. At one point during her fugue, Hannah was approached by someone who asked if she was the Hannah everyone was looking for, and she answered no.

61·2 DISSOCIATIVE IDENTITY DISORDER

Dissociative identity disorder (DID), formerly called *multiple personality disorder,* is the most dramatic, least common, and most controversial dissociative disorder. Individuals with this disorder have two or more distinct personalities or identities. Each identity has its own memories, behaviors, and relationships. One identity dominates at one time, another takes over at another time. Individuals sometimes report that a wall of amnesia separates their different identities (Dale & others, 2009); however, research suggests that memory does transfer across these identities, even if the person believes it does not (Kong, Allen, & Glisky, 2008). The shift between identities usually occurs under distress (Sar & others, 2007) but sometimes can also be controlled by the person (Kong, Allen, & Glisky, 2008).

● **dissociative fugue** Dissociative disorder in which the individual not only develops amnesia but also unexpectedly travels away from home and sometimes assumes a new identity.

● **dissociative identity disorder (DID)** Formerly called multiple personality disorder, a dissociative disorder in which the individual has two or more distinct personalities or identities, each with its own memories, behaviors, and relationships.

One of the most famous real-life cases of dissociative identity disorder involves the "three faces of Eve" (Thigpen & Cleckley, 1957) (Figure 61.1). Eve White was the original dominant personality. She had no knowledge of her second personality, Eve Black, although Eve Black had been alternating with Eve White for a number of years. Eve White was bland, quiet, and serious. By contrast, Eve Black was carefree, mischievous, and uninhibited. Eve Black would emerge at the most inappropriate times, leaving Eve White with hangovers, bills, and a reputation in local bars that she could not explain. During treatment, a third personality, Jane, emerged. More mature than the other two, Jane seems to have developed as a result of therapy.

More recently, former Heisman Trophy winner and legendary NFL running back Herschel Walker (2008) revealed his experience with dissociative disorder in his book *Breaking Free: My Life with Dissociative Identity Disorder.*

Research on dissociative identity disorder suggests that a high rate of extraordinarily severe sexual or physical abuse during early childhood is related to the condition (Sar, Akyuz, & Dogan, 2007). Some psychologists believe that a

FIGURE 61.1   **The Three Faces of Eve** Chris Sizemore, the subject of *The Three Faces of Eve,* is shown here with a work she painted, titled *Three Faces in One.*

child can cope with intense trauma by dissociating from the experience and developing other alternate selves as protectors. Sexual abuse has occurred in as many as 70 percent or more of dissociative identity disorder cases (Foote & others, 2006); however, the majority of individuals who have been sexually abused do not develop dissociative identity disorder. The vast majority of individuals with dissociative identity disorder are women. A genetic predisposition might also exist, as the disorder tends to run in families (Dell & Eisenhower, 1990).

Until the 1980s, only about 300 cases of dissociative identity disorder had ever been reported (Suinn, 1984). In the past 30 years, hundreds more cases have been diagnosed. Social cognitive approaches to dissociative identity disorder point out that cases have tended to increase whenever the popular media present a case, such as the film *The Three Faces of Eve,* the miniseries *Sybil,* or the Showtime drama *The United States of Tara.* From this perspective, individuals develop multiple identities through a process of social contagion. After exposure to these examples, people may be more likely to view multiple identities as a real condition.

Some experts believe, in fact, that dissociative identity disorder is a *social construction*—that it represents a category some people adopt to make sense out of their experiences (Spanos, 1996). Rather than being a single person with many conflicting feelings, wishes, and potentially awful experiences, the individual compartmentalizes different aspects of the self into independent identities. In some cases, therapists have been accused of creating alternate personalities. Encountering an individual who appears to have a fragmented sense of self, the therapist may begin to treat each fragment as its own "personality" (Spiegel, 2006).

SUMMARY

Dissociative amnesia involves memory loss caused by extensive psychological stress. Dissociative fugue also involves memory loss, but individuals with this disorder unexpectedly travel away from home or work, sometimes assume a new identity, and do not remember the old identity. In dissociative identity disorder, formerly called multiple personality disorder, two or more distinct personalities are present in the same individual; this disorder is rare.

KEY TERMS

dissociative disorders   568
dissociative amnesia   568
dissociative fugue   569

dissociative identity disorder
   (DID)   569

TEST YOURSELF

1. What are the main characteristics of dissociative disorders? What does the word *dissociative* mean in reference to them?

2. Identify the characteristics of dissociative fugue. How is it different from dissociative amnesia?

3. What explanations have experts given for the development of dissociative identity disorder (DID) in individuals?

APPLY YOUR KNOWLEDGE

1. Watch one of the following movies and identify who in the movie suffers from *Dissociative Identity Disorder:* "Primal Fear," "Secret Window," "Three Faces of Eve," or "Sybil." What makes this disorder so attractive to film makers?

2. Research the DSM-IV-TR criteria for dissociative fugue, dissociative amnesia, and dissociative identity disorder. What symptoms do these disorders share and how do they differ from each other?

Schizophrenia

Have you had the experience of watching a movie and suddenly noticing that the film bears an uncanny resemblance to your life? Have you ever listened to a radio talk show and realized that the host was saying exactly what you were just thinking? Do these moments mean something special about you, or are they coincidences? For people with schizophrenia, such experiences may take on special and personal meaning.

Schizophrenia is a severe psychological disorder that is characterized by highly disordered thought processes. These disordered thoughts are referred to as *psychotic* because they are far removed from reality. Individuals with schizophrenia may see things that are not there, hear voices inside their heads, and live in a strange world of twisted logic. They may say odd things, show inappropriate emotion, and move their bodies in peculiar ways. Often, they are socially withdrawn and isolated.

As much as schizophrenia might sound disturbing to those who have not experienced it, the ordeal of those living with it seems unimaginable. Often the experience of schizophrenia is one of extraordinary terror (NIMH, 2008). Typically diagnosed in early adulthood, the disorder can be debilitating. About one-half of the patients in psychiatric hospitals are afflicted with schizophrenia. Moreover, the suicide risk for individuals with schizophrenia is eight times that for the general population (Pompili & others, 2007).

For many people with the disorder, controlling it means using powerful medications to combat symptoms. The most common cause of relapse is that individuals stop taking their medication. They might do so because they feel better, because they do not realize that their thoughts are disordered, or because the side effects of the medications are so unpleasant. Recall Bill Garrett's story from the beginning of this module. Some medications made him drowsy and lethargic; others made him volatile. On one medication he rapidly gained 75 pounds (M. Park, 2009).

● **schizophrenia** Severe psychological disorder characterized by highly disordered thought processes, referred to as psychotic because they are so far removed from reality.

62-1 SYMPTOMS OF SCHIZOPHRENIA

Psychologists generally classify the symptoms of schizophrenia as positive symptoms, negative symptoms, and cognitive deficits (NIMH, 2008).

Positive Symptoms

The *positive symptoms* of schizophrenia are marked by a distortion or an excess of normal function. They are "positive" because they reflect something added above and beyond normal behavior. Positive symptoms of schizophrenia include hallucinations, delusions, thought disorders, and disorders of movement.

Hallucinations are sensory experiences in the absence of real stimuli. Hallucinations are usually auditory—the person might complain of hearing voices—or visual, and much less commonly they take the form of smells or tastes (Bhatia & others, 2009). Visual hallucinations involve seeing things that are not there. For example, consider the case of Moe Armstrong. At the age of 21, while serving in Vietnam as a Marine medical corpsman, Armstrong experienced a psychotic break. Dead Vietcong soldiers appeared to talk to him and beg him for help and did not seem to realize that they were dead. Armstrong, now a successful businessman and a sought-after public speaker who holds two master's degrees, relies on medication to keep such experiences at bay (Bonfatti, 2005).

● **hallucinations** Sensory experiences in the absence of real stimuli.

571

FIGURE 62.1 **Disorders of Movement in Schizophrenia** Unusual motor behaviors are positive symptoms of schizophrenia. Individuals may cease to move altogether (a state called catatonia), sometimes holding bizarre postures.

● **delusions** False, unusual, and sometimes magical beliefs that are not part of an individual's culture.

● **referential thinking** Ascribing personal meaning to completely random events.

● **catatonia** State of immobility and unresponsiveness lasting for long periods of time.

● **flat affect** The display of little or no emotion—a common negative symptom of schizophrenia.

Delusions are false, unusual, and sometimes magical beliefs that are not part of an individual's culture. A delusional person might think that he is Jesus Christ or Muhammad; another might imagine that her thoughts are being broadcast over the radio. It is crucial to distinguish delusions from cultural ideas such as the religious belief that a person can have divine visions or communicate personally with a deity. Generally, psychology and psychiatry do not treat these ideas as delusional.

For individuals with schizophrenia, delusional beliefs that might seem completely illogical to the outsider are experienced as all too real. At one point in his life, Bill Garrett was convinced that a blister on his hand was a sign of gangrene. So strong was his belief that he tried to cut off his hand with a knife, before being stopped by his family (M. Park, 2009).

Thought disorder refers to the unusual, sometimes bizarre thought processes that are characteristic positive symptoms of schizophrenia. The thoughts of persons with schizophrenia can be disorganized and confused. Often individuals with schizophrenia do not make sense when they talk or write. For example, someone with schizophrenia might say, "Well, Rocky, babe, happening, but where, when, up, top, side, over, you know, out of the way, that's it. Sign off." Such speech has no meaning for the listener. These incoherent, loose word associations are called "word salad." The individual might also make up new words (*neologisms*) (Kerns & others, 1999). In addition, a person with schizophrenia can show **referential thinking,** which means ascribing personal meaning to completely random events. For instance, the individual might believe that a traffic light has turned red *because* he or she is in a hurry.

A final type of positive symptom is *disorders of movement*. A person with schizophrenia may show unusual mannerisms, body movements, and facial expressions. The individual may repeat certain motions over and over or, in extreme cases, may become catatonic. **Catatonia** is a state of immobility and unresponsiveness that lasts for long periods of time (Figure 62.1).

Negative Symptoms

Whereas schizophrenia's positive symptoms are characterized by a distortion or an excess of normal functions, schizophrenia's *negative symptoms* reflect social withdrawal, behavioral deficits, and the loss or decrease of normal functions. One negative symptom is **flat affect,** which means the display of little or no emotion (Alvino & others, 2007). Individuals with schizophrenia also may be lacking in the ability to read the emotions of others (Chambon, Baudouin, & Franck, 2006). They may experience a lack of positive emotional experience in daily life and show a deficient ability to plan, initiate, and engage in goal-directed behavior.

Cognitive Symptoms

Cognitive symptoms of schizophrenia include difficulty sustaining attention, problems holding information in memory, and inability to interpret information and make decisions (Kerns, 2007; Sitnikova, Goff, & Kuperberg, 2009). These cognitive symptoms may be quite subtle and are often detected only through neuropsychological tests.

62·2 CAUSES OF SCHIZOPHRENIA

A great deal of research has investigated schizophrenia's causes. Here we consider the biological, psychological, and sociocultural factors involved in the disorder.

Biological Factors

Research provides strong support for biological explanations of schizophrenia. Particularly compelling is the evidence for a genetic predisposition, but structural brain abnormalities and problems with neurotransmitter regulation also are linked to this severe psychological disorder (Horn & others, 2010; Kegeles & others, 2010).

HEREDITY

Research supports the notion that schizophrenia is at least partially caused by genetic factors (Paul-Samojedny & others, 2010). As genetic similarity to a person with schizophrenia increases, so does a person's risk of developing schizophrenia (Cardno & Gottesman, 2000). Such data strongly suggest that genetic factors play a role in schizophrenia. Researchers are seeking to pinpoint the chromosomal location of genes involved in susceptibility to schizophrenia (Duan, Sanders, & Gejman, 2010; Holliday & others, 2009). The Psychological Inquiry shows the results of research examining the role of genetics in schizophrenia.

STRUCTURAL BRAIN ABNORMALITIES

Studies have found structural brain abnormalities in people with schizophrenia. Imaging techniques such as MRI scans clearly show enlarged ventricles in their brain (Acer & others, 2010; Killgore & others, 2009). Ventricles are fluid-filled spaces, and enlargement of the ventricles indicates deterioration in other brain tissue.

Individuals with schizophrenia also have a small prefrontal cortex and lower activity in this area of the brain than individuals who do not have schizophrenia (Smieskova & others, 2010). The prefrontal cortex is the region where thinking, planning, and decision making take place. Recall from Module 33 that the prefrontal cortex continues to develop throughout adolescence and into young adulthood. It may be that the emergence of symptoms of schizophrenia in young adulthood occurs because this is the time when the prefrontal cortex becomes fully functioning.

Still, differences between the brains of healthy individuals and those with schizophrenia are surprisingly small (NIMH, 2008). Microscopic studies of brain tissue after death reveal small changes in the distribution or characteristics of brain cells in persons with schizophrenia. It appears that many of these changes occurred prenatally because they are not accompanied by glial cells, which are always present when a brain injury occurs after birth (Vuillermot & others, 2010). It may be that problems in prenatal development such as prenatal infections (A. S. Brown, 2006) predispose a brain to developing schizophrenic symptoms during puberty and young adulthood (Fatemi & Folsom, 2009).

PROBLEMS IN NEUROTRANSMITTER REGULATION

An early biological explanation for schizophrenia linked excess dopamine production to schizophrenia. The link between dopamine and psychotic symptoms was first noticed when the drug L-dopa (which increases dopamine levels) was given to individuals as a treatment for Parkinson disease. In addition to relieving their Parkinson symptoms, L-dopa caused some individuals to experience disturbed thoughts (Janowsky, Addario, & Risch, 1987). Furthermore, drugs that reduce psychotic symptoms often block dopamine (van Os & Kapur, 2009). Whether it is differences in amount of dopamine, its production, or its uptake, there is good evidence that overactivation of pathways in the brain associated with dopamine plays a role in schizophrenia (D. P. Eisenberg & others, 2010; Howes & others, 2009).

Dopamine is a "feel good" neurotransmitter that helps us recognize rewarding stimuli in the environment. Dopamine is related to being outgoing and sociable. How can a neurotransmitter that is associated with good things play a crucial role in the most devastating psychological disorder?

One way to think about this puzzle is to view dopamine as a neurochemical messenger that in effect shouts out, "Hey! This is important!" whenever we encounter opportunities for reward. Imagine what it might be like to be bombarded with such messages about even the smallest details of life (Kapur, 2003; Rosier & others, 2010). The person's own thoughts might take on such dramatic proportions that they sound like someone else's voice talking inside the individual's head. Fleeting ideas, such as

psychological *inquiry*

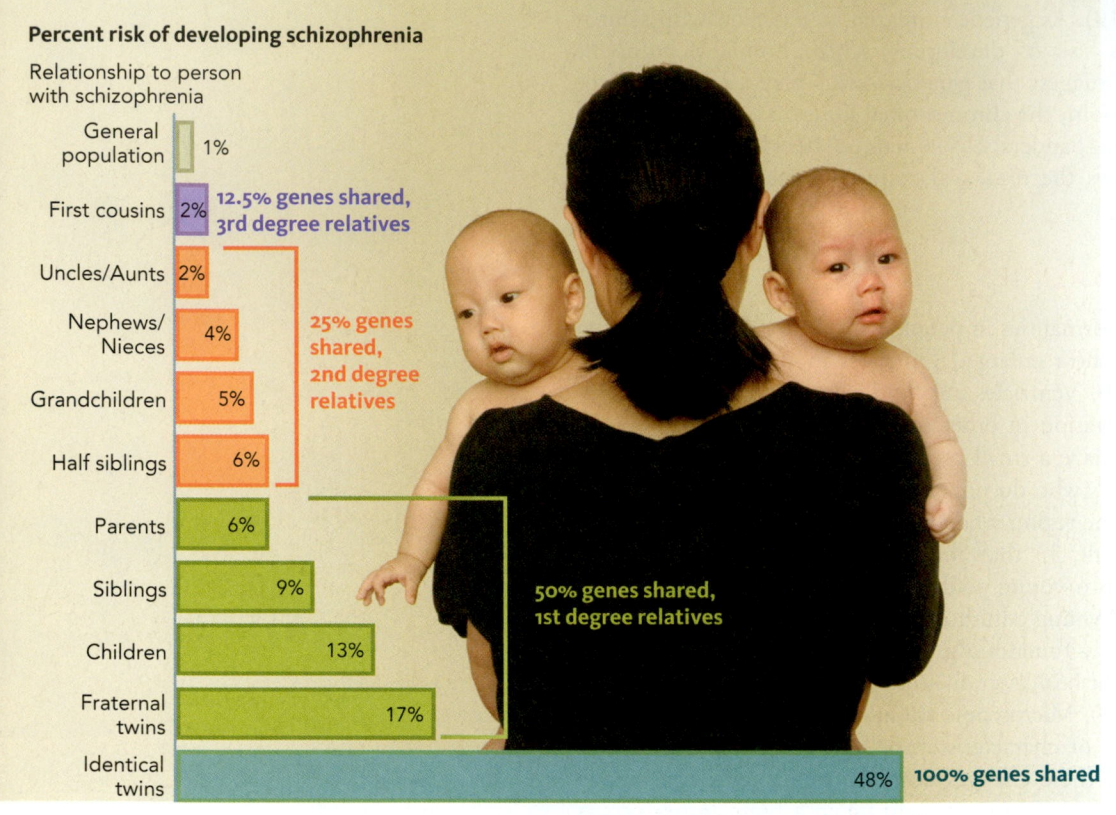

Percent risk of developing schizophrenia

Relationship to person with schizophrenia

- General population — 1%
- First cousins — 2% — **12.5% genes shared, 3rd degree relatives**
- Uncles/Aunts — 2%
- Nephews/Nieces — 4% — **25% genes shared, 2nd degree relatives**
- Grandchildren — 5%
- Half siblings — 6%
- Parents — 6%
- Siblings — 9% — **50% genes shared, 1st degree relatives**
- Children — 13%
- Fraternal twins — 17%
- Identical twins — 48% — **100% genes shared**

The Association of Genes with Schizophrenia

This figure shows that as genetic relatedness to an individual with schizophrenia increases, so does the lifetime risk of developing schizophrenia. Using the graph, answer these questions:

1. Which familial relations have the lowest and highest level of genetic overlap (shared genes)?

2. What is the difference in genetic overlap between identical twins and non-twin siblings?

3. What is the difference in risk of schizophrenia between identical twins and non-twin siblings of individuals with schizophrenia?

4. What do you think accounts for the differences in your answers to questions 2 and 3?

"It's raining today *because* I didn't bring my umbrella to work," suddenly seem not silly but true. Shitij Kapur (2003) has suggested that hallucinations, delusions, and referential thinking may be expressions of the individual's attempts to make sense of such extraordinary feelings.

A problem with the dopamine explanation of schizophrenia is that antipsychotic drugs reduce dopamine levels very quickly, but delusional beliefs take much longer to disappear. Even after dopamine levels are balanced, a person might still cling to the bizarre belief that members of a powerful conspiracy are watching his or her every move. If dopamine causes these symptoms, why do the symptoms persist even after the dopamine is under control? According to Kapur, delusions serve as explanatory schemes that have helped the person make sense of the random and chaotic experiences caused by out-of-control dopamine. Bizarre beliefs might disappear only after experience demonstrates that such schemes no longer carry their explanatory power (Kapur, 2003). That is, with time, experience, and therapy, the person might come to realize that there is, in fact, no conspiracy.

Psychological Factors

Psychologists used to explain schizophrenia as rooted in an individual's difficult childhood experiences with parents. Such explanations have mostly fallen by the wayside, but contemporary theorists do recognize that stress may contribute to the development of this disorder. The **diathesis-stress model** argues that a combination of biogenetic disposition and stress causes schizophrenia (Meehl, 1962). (The term *diathesis* means "physical vulnerability or predisposition to a particular disorder.") For instance, genetic

● **diathesis-stress model** View of schizophrenia emphasizing that a combination of biogenetic disposition and stress causes the disorder.

characteristics might produce schizophrenia only when (and if) the individual experiences extreme stress.

Sociocultural Factors

Sociocultural background is not considered a *cause* of schizophrenia, but sociocultural factors do appear to affect the *course* of the disorder. That is, sociocultural factors influence how schizophrenia progresses. Across cultures, individuals with schizophrenia in developing, nonindustrialized nations tend to have better outcomes than those in developed, industrialized nations (Jablensky, 2000). This difference may be due to the fact that in developing nations, family and friends are more accepting and supportive of individuals with schizophrenia.

In addition, in Western samples, marriage, warm supportive friends (Jablensky & others, 1992; Wiersma & others, 1998), and employment are related to better outcomes for individuals diagnosed with schizophrenia (Rosen & Garety, 2005). At the very least, this research suggests that some individuals with schizophrenia enjoy marriage, productive work, and friendships (Drake, Levine, & Laska, 2007; Fleischhaker & others, 2005; Marshall & Rathbone, 2006).

SUMMARY

Schizophrenia is a severe psychological disorder characterized by highly disordered thought processes. Positive symptoms of schizophrenia are behaviors and experiences that are present in individuals with schizophrenia but absent in healthy people; they include hallucinations and delusions. Negative symptoms of schizophrenia are behaviors and experiences that are part of healthy human life that are absent for those with this disorder; they include flat affect and an inability to plan or engage in goal-directed behavior.

Biological factors (heredity, structural brain abnormalities, and problems in neurotransmitter regulation, especially dopamine), psychological factors (diathesis-stress model), and sociocultural factors may be involved in schizophrenia. Psychological and sociocultural factors are not viewed as stand-alone causes of schizophrenia, but they are related to the course of the disorder.

KEY TERMS

schizophrenia 571
hallucinations 571
delusions 572
referential thinking 572

catatonia 572
flat affect 572
diathesis-stress model 574

TEST YOURSELF

1. What is schizophrenia?
2. What are some positive and negative symptoms of schizophrenia?
3. Give three biological explanations for schizophrenia.

APPLY YOUR KNOWLEDGE

1. If you have never met anyone with schizophrenia, check out a blog that is kept by Moe Armstrong at http://www.moearmstrong.com/Site/Welcome.html and view one of his speeches on YouTube at http://www.youtube.com/watch?v=p-_j1ZNKzsg.

2. Explain the differences between schizophrenia and dissociative identity disorder.

Personality Disorders

● **personality disorders** Chronic, maladaptive cognitive-behavioral patterns that are thoroughly integrated into an individual's personality.

● **antisocial personality disorder (ASPD)** A psychological disorder characterized by guiltlessness, law-breaking, exploitation of others, irresponsibility, and deceit.

John Wayne Gacy (top) *and Ted Bundy* (bottom) *exemplify the subgroup of people with ASPD who are also psychopathic.*

Are there aspects of your personality that you would like to change? Maybe you worry too much or fall in love too easily. Imagine that your very personality—who you really are—is the core of your life difficulties. That is what happens with **personality disorders,** which are chronic, maladaptive cognitive-behavioral patterns that are thoroughly integrated into an individual's personality. Personality disorders are relatively common. In a study of a representative U.S. sample, researchers found that 15 percent had a personality disorder (Grant & others, 2004).

The *DSM-IV* lists 10 different personality disorders. Below we survey the two that have been the object of greatest study: antisocial personality disorder and borderline personality disorder. These disorders are associated with dire consequences, including criminal activity and violence (in the case of antisocial personality disorder) and self-harm and suicide (borderline personality disorder).

63-1 ANTISOCIAL PERSONALITY DISORDER

Antisocial personality disorder (ASPD) is a psychological disorder characterized by guiltlessness, law-breaking, exploitation of others, irresponsibility, and deceit. Although they may be superficially charming, individuals with ASPD do not play by the rules, and they often lead a life of crime and violence. ASPD is far more common in men than in women and is related to criminal behavior, vandalism, substance abuse, and alcoholism (Cale & Lilienfeld, 2002).

The *DSM-IV* criteria for antisocial personality disorder include

- Failure to conform to social norms or obey the law
- Deceitfulness, lying, using aliases, or conning others for personal profit or pleasure
- Impulsivity or failure to plan ahead
- Irritability and aggressiveness, getting into physical fights or perpetrating assaults
- Reckless disregard for the safety of self or others
- Consistent irresponsibility, inconsistent work behavior, not paying bills
- Lack of remorse, showing indifference to the pain of others, or rationalizing, having hurt or mistreated another

Generally, ASPD is not diagnosed unless a person has shown persistent antisocial behavior before the age of 15.

Although ASPD is associated with criminal behavior, not all individuals with ASPD engage in crime, and not all criminals suffer from ASPD. Some individuals with ASPD can have successful careers. There are antisocial physicians, clergy members, lawyers, and just about any other occupation. Still, such individuals tend to be exploitative of others and to lack empathy. They break the rules, even if they are never caught.

What is the etiology of ASPD? Biological factors include genetic, brain, and autonomic nervous system differences. We consider these in turn.

ASPD is genetically heritable (L. F. Garcia & others, 2010). Certain genetic characteristics associated with ASPD may interact with testosterone (the hormone that is most associated with aggressive behavior) to promote antisocial behavior (Sjoberg & others, 2008). Although the experience of childhood abuse may be implicated in ASPD, there is evidence that genetic differences may distinguish abused children who go on to commit violent acts themselves from those who do not (Caspi & others, 2002; Lynam & others, 2007).

In terms of the brain, research has linked ASPD to low levels of activation in the prefrontal cortex and has related these brain differences to poor decision making and problems in learning (Yang & Raine, 2009). With regard to the autonomic nervous system, researchers have found that individuals with ASPD are less stressed than others by aversive circumstances, including punishment (Fung & others, 2005), and that they have the ability to keep their cool while engaging in deception (Verschuere & others, 2005). These findings suggest that people with ASPD might be able to fool a polygraph. The underaroused autonomic nervous system may be a key difference between adolescents who become antisocial adults and those whose behavior improves during adulthood (Raine, Venables, & Williams, 1990).

Psychopaths are one subgroup of individuals with ASPD (Weber & others, 2008). Psychopaths are remorseless predators who engage in violence to get what they want. Examples of psychopaths include serial killers John Wayne Gacy (who murdered 33 boys and young men) and Ted Bundy (who confessed to murdering at least 30 young women).

Psychopaths tend to show less prefrontal activation than normal individuals and to have structural abnormalities in the amygdala, as well as the hippocampus, the brain structure most closely associated with memory (Weber & others, 2008). Importantly, these brain differences are most pronounced in "unsuccessful psychopaths"—individuals who have been arrested for their behaviors (Y. Yang & others, 2005). In contrast, "successful psychopaths"—individuals who have engaged in antisocial behavior but have not gotten caught—are more similar to healthy controls in terms of brain structure and function (Gao & Raine, 2010).

However, in their behavior, successful psychopaths show a lack of empathy and a willingness to act immorally; they victimize other people to enrich their own lives. Successful psychopaths may even get away with murder (Y. Yang & others, 2005). Psychopaths show deficiencies in learning about fear, have difficulty processing information related to the distress of others, such as sad or fearful faces (Dolan & Fullam, 2006), and show deficits in theory of mind (Shamay-Tsoory & others, 2010).

A key challenge in treating individuals with ASPD, including psychopaths, is their ability to con even sophisticated mental health professionals. Many never seek therapy, and others end up in prison, where treatment is rarely an option.

63-2 BORDERLINE PERSONALITY DISORDER

According to the *DSM-IV*, **borderline personality disorder (BPD)** is a pervasive pattern of instability in interpersonal relationships, self-image, and emotions, and of marked impulsivity beginning by early adulthood and present in various contexts. Individuals with BPD are insecure, impulsive, and emotional (Aggen & others, 2009). BPD is related to self-harming behaviors such as cutting, which is injuring oneself with a sharp object but without suicidal intent (Chapman, 2009) and also to suicide (Soloff & others, 1994).

The *DSM-IV* specifies that BPD is indicated by the presence of five or more of the following symptoms:

- Frantic efforts to avoid being abandoned
- Unstable and intense interpersonal relationships characterized by extreme shifts between idealization and devaluation
- Markedly and persistently unstable self-image or sense of self
- Impulsivity in at least two areas that are potentially self-damaging (for example, spending, sex, substance abuse, reckless driving, and binge eating)

● **borderline personality disorder (BPD)** A psychological disorder characterized by a pervasive pattern of instability in interpersonal relationships, self-image, and emotions, and of marked impulsivity beginning by early adulthood and present in a variety of contexts.

Impulsivity of the type that can lead to self-harm can be a symptom of borderline personality disorder.

- Recurrent suicidal behavior, gestures, or threats or self-mutilating behavior
- Unstable and extreme emotional responses
- Chronic feelings of emptiness
- Inappropriate, intense anger or difficulty controlling anger
- Temporary stress-related *paranoia* (a pattern of disturbed thought featuring delusions of grandeur or persecution) or severe dissociative symptoms

BPD is far more common in women than men. Women make up 75 percent of those with the disorder (Korzekwa & others, 2008). Individuals with BPD are prone to wild mood swings and are very sensitive to how others treat them. They often feel as if they are riding a nonstop emotional rollercoaster (Selby & others, 2009), and their loved ones may have to work hard to avoid upsetting them. Individuals with BPD tend to see the world in black-and-white terms, a thinking style called *splitting*. For example, they typically view other people as either hated enemies with no positive qualities or as beloved, idealized friends who can do no wrong. To cope with their unstable emotional lives, individuals with BPD may engage in a variety of maladaptive behaviors, among them drinking alcohol and using illicit substances (Waugaman, 2005).

The potential causes of BPD are likely complex and include biological factors as well as childhood experiences (Barnow & others, 2010; Steele & Siever, 2010). The role of genes in BPD has been demonstrated in a variety of studies and across cultures, and researchers estimate the heritability of BPD to be about 40 percent (Distel & others, 2008).

Many individuals with BPD report experiences of childhood sexual abuse, as well as physical abuse and neglect (Al-Alem & Omar, 2008; Lobbestael & Arntz, 2010). It is not clear, however, whether abuse is a primary cause of the disorder (Trull & Widiger, 2003). Childhood abuse experiences may combine with genetic factors in promoting BPD, and this possibility suggests a diathesis-stress explanation for the disorder.

Cognitive factors associated with BPD include a tendency to hold a set of irrational beliefs. These include thinking that one is powerless and innately unacceptable and that other people are dangerous and hostile (Arntz, 2005). Individuals with BPD also display *hypervigilance:* the tendency to be constantly on the alert, looking for threatening information in the environment (Sieswerda & others, 2007).

As recently as within the past 20 years, experts thought that BPD was unlikely to be treatable, but newer evidence suggests that many individuals with BPD show improvement over time. As many as 50 percent of individuals with BPD improve within two years, and once improved they are not likely to relapse (Gunderson, 2008). One key aspect of improvement appears to be reductions in social stress, such as leaving an abusive romantic partner or establishing a sense of trust in a therapist (Gunderson & others, 2003).

SUMMARY

Personality disorders are chronic, maladaptive cognitive-behavioral patterns that are thoroughly integrated into an individual's personality. Two common types are antisocial personality disorder (ASPD) and borderline personality disorder (BPD).

Antisocial personality disorder is characterized by guiltlessness, law-breaking, exploitation of others, irresponsibility, and deceit. Individuals with this disorder often lead a life of crime and violence. Psychopaths—remorseless predators who engage in violence to get what they want—are a subgroup of individuals with ASPD.

KEY TERMS

personality disorders   576
antisocial personality disorder
  (ASPD)   576

borderline personality disorder
  (BPD)   577

Borderline personality disorder is a pervasive pattern of instability in interpersonal relationships, self-image, and emotions, and of marked impulsivity beginning by early adulthood and present in a variety of contexts. This disorder is related to self-harming behaviors such as cutting and suicide.

Biological factors for ASPD include genetic, brain, and autonomic nervous system differences. The potential causes of BPD are complex and include biological and cognitive factors as well as childhood experiences.

TEST YOURSELF

1. How are personality disorders defined?
2. To what sorts of behaviors is antisocial personality disorder (ASPD) related?
3. How is borderline personality disorder (BPD) defined, and what are three symptoms of this disorder, according to the *DSM-IV*?

APPLY YOUR KNOWLEDGE

1. Listen to the song *Stan* by Eminem. Using the lyrics, explain which personality disorder is best represented in this song.
2. What are the differences between someone diagnosed with major depressive disorder and someone diagnosed with borderline personality disorder?

Psychological Disorders and Health and Wellness

Putting a label on a person with a psychological disorder can make the disorder seem like something that happens only to other people (Baumann, 2007). The truth is that psychological disorders are not just about *other* people; they are about people, period. Over 26 percent of Americans aged 18 and older suffer from a diagnosable psychological disorder in a given year—an estimated 57.7 million U.S. adults (Kessler & others, 2005; NIMH, 2008). Chances are that you or someone you know will experience a psychological disorder. Figure 1 shows how common many psychological disorders are in the United States.

Psychological disorders clearly present a challenge to living a healthy, fulfilling life. For the many individuals who are diagnosed with one or more such disorders, a significant obstacle in the pursuit of that life is the fear of stigma, stereotypes, prejudice, and discrimination. To appreciate the power of the labels that are attached to individuals with psychological disorders, consider a classic and controversial study by David Rosenhan (1973). He recruited eight adults (including a stay-at-home mother, a psychology graduate student, a pediatrician, and some psychiatrists), none with a psychological disorder, to see a psychiatrist at various hospitals. These "pseudo patients" were instructed to act in a normal way except to complain about hearing voices that said things like "empty" and "thud." All eight expressed an interest in leaving the hospital and behaved cooperatively. Nevertheless, all eight were labeled with schizophrenia and kept in the hospital from 3 to 52 days. None of the mental health professionals they encountered ever questioned the diagnosis that had been given to these individuals, and all were discharged with the label "schizophrenia in remission." The label "schizophrenia" had stuck to the pseudo-patients and caused the professionals around them to interpret their quite normal behavior as abnormal. Clearly, then, once a person has been labeled with a psychological disorder, that label colors how others perceive everything else he or she does.

Labels of psychological disorder carry with them a wide array of implications for the individual. Is he or she still able to be a good friend? A good parent? A competent worker? A significant concern for individuals with psychological disorders is the negative attitudes that others might have about people struggling with mental illness (Phelan & Basow, 2007). Stigma can be a significant barrier for individuals coping with a psychological disorder, as well as for their families and loved ones (Corrigan, 2007; Hinshaw, 2007). Fear of stigma can prevent individuals from seeking treatment and from talking about their problems with family and friends. To test your own attitudes about people with psychological disorders, complete the exercise in Figure 2.

	Number of Americans in a given year (millions)	Percent of Americans
Anxiety Disorders		
General anxiety disorder	6.8	3.1%
Panic disorder	6.0	2.7%
Phobic disorder	19.2	8.7%
PTSD	7.7	3.5%
Mood Disorders		
Major depressive disorder	14.8	6.7%
Dysthymic disorder	3.3	1.5%
Bipolar disorder	5.7	2.6%
Schizophrenia	2.4	1.1%

FIGURE 1 **The 12-Month Prevalence of the Most Common Psychological Disorders** If you add up the numbers in this figure, you will see that the totals are higher than the numbers given in the text. The explanation is that people are frequently diagnosed with more than one psychological disorder. An individual who has both a depressive and an anxiety disorder would be counted in both of those categories.

CONSEQUENCES OF STIGMA

The stigma attached to psychological disorders can provoke prejudice and discrimination toward individuals who are struggling with these problems, thus adding a complication to an already difficult situation. Having a disorder and experiencing the stigma associated with it can also negatively affect the physical health of such individuals.

Prejudice and Discrimination

Labels of psychological disorders can be damaging because they may lead to negative stereotypes, which play a role in prejudice. For example, the label "schizophrenic" often has negative connotations such as "frightening" and "dangerous."

Vivid cases of extremely harmful behavior by individuals with psychological disorders can perpetuate the stereotype that people with such disorders are violent. For example, Cho Seung-Hui, a 23-year-old college student, murdered 32 students and faculty at Virginia Tech University in April 2007 before killing himself. The widely reported fact that Cho had struggled with psychological disorders throughout his life may have reinforced the notion that individuals with disorders are dangerous. In fact, however, people with psychological disorders (especially those in treatment) are no more likely to commit violent acts than the general population. Cho was no more representative of people with psychological disorders than he was representative of students at Virginia Tech.

Individuals who are diagnosed with psychological disorders are often aware of the negative stigma attached to these conditions (Brohan & others, 2010; Moses, 2010). They themselves may have previously held such negative attitudes. People with psychological disorders need help, but seeking that assistance may involve accepting a stigmatized identity (Thornicroft & others, 2009; Yen & others, 2009). They must face the prospect of sacrificing their status as mentally healthy for a new status as disordered. Even mental health professionals can fall prey to prejudicial attitudes toward those who are coping with psychological disorders (Nordt, Rossler, & Lauber, 2006).

Among the most feared aspects of stigma is discrimination. Discrimination means acting prejudicially toward a person who is a member of a stigmatized group. In the workplace, discrimination against a person with a psychological disorder is against the law. The Americans with Disabilities Act (ADA) of 1990 made it illegal to refuse employment or a promotion to someone with a psychological disorder when the person's condition does not prevent performance of the job's essentials functions (Cleveland, Barnes-Farrell, & Ratz, 1997). A person's appearance or behavior may be unusual or irritating, but as long as that individual is able to complete the duties required of a position, he or she cannot be denied employment or promotion.

Physical Health

Individuals with psychological disorders are more likely to be physically ill and two times more likely to die than their psychologically healthy counterparts (Gittelman, 2008; Kumar, 2004). They are also more likely to be obese, to smoke, to drink excessively, and to lead sedentary lives (Beard, Weisberg, & Keller, 2010; J. Y. Kim & others, 2007; Lindwall & others, 2007; Mykletun & others, 2007).

Rate the following items using a scale of 1–5, with 1 indicating that you completely *disagree* with the statement and 5 indicating that you completely *agree* with the statement.

1=completely disagree 2=slightly agree
3=moderately agree 4=strongly agree
5=completely agree

____ 1. I would rather not live next door to a person with a psychological disorder.

____ 2. A person with a psychological disorder is unfit to raise children.

____ 3. I would be afraid to be around a person with a psychological disorder.

____ 4. I would not want to live in the same neighborhood as a group home for persons with psychological disorders.

____ 5. A person with a psychological disorder cannot hold a job.

____ 6. A person with a psychological disorder is dangerous or potentially violent.

Total _____

Add up your score and divide by 6. If your score is 3 or higher, you may want to rethink your attitudes about individuals with psychological disorders.

It may be revealing to ask yourself how you would respond to these statements if the words "person with a psychological disorder" were replaced with "woman," "African American," or "gay man or lesbian." Sometimes even individuals who would not think of themselves as being prejudiced against other groups find themselves biased against the mentally ill.

FIGURE 2 **Test Your Attitudes About People with Psychological Disorders** Take the survey to discover and evaluate your own attitudes.

Although Sheila Hollingsworth struggles with schizophrenia, her story is one of success, not failure. She has refused to allow her disorder to rob her of a good life.

You might be thinking that these physical health issues are the least of their worries. If someone struggling with schizophrenia wants to smoke, why not? This type of thinking reveals the subtle way that prejudice toward those with psychological disorders can affect their lives. It sells short the capacity of psychological and psychiatric treatments to help those with psychological disorders, and, more important, it demonstrates a lack of appreciation of the fact that individuals with serious mental disorders can lead healthy, meaningful lives.

Research has shown that health-promotion programs can work well even for individuals with a severe psychological disorder (Addington & others, 1998; Chafetz & others, 2008). When we disregard the potential of physical health interventions for people with psychological disorders to make positive life changes, we reveal our own biases.

OVERCOMING STIGMA

How can we effectively combat the stigma of psychological disorders? One obstacle to changing people's attitudes toward individuals with psychological disorders is that mental illness is often invisible. That is, sometimes a person can have a disorder without those of us around him or her ever knowing. Indeed, we may be unaware of *many* courageous lives around us that are being lived within the challenging context of psychological disorders, because worries about being stigmatized keep the affected individuals from "coming out." Thus, stigma leads to a catch-22: Positive examples of individuals coping with psychological disorders are often missing from our experience because those who are doing well shun public disclosure of their disorders (Jensen & Wadkins, 2007).

A critical step toward eliminating stigma is to resist thinking of people with disorders as limited individuals whose disorder colors everything they do. Instead, it is vital to recognize their strengths—both in confronting their disorder and in carrying on despite their problems—and their achievements. By creating a positive environment for people with disorders, we encourage more of them to become confidently visible, and we empower them to be positive role models for others.

Sheila Hollingsworth—a 51-year-old divorced mother of two—is such a role model. She has a master's degree and works at the Baltic Street Mental Health Board. She is so beloved at work that everyone calls her "Sheila Love." She sings in her church choir, takes calligraphy classes, and is determined to lose 30 pounds (Bonfatti, 2005). Notably, Sheila has schizophrenia. However, she has not allowed the stigma of this disorder to rob her of a good life. She works as a peer counselor and helps others by leading groups and modeling effective treatment. It can be enormously positive for individuals coping with severe psychological disorders to have a role model, like Sheila, who is making it, one day at a time. Each of us can benefit from exposure to success stories such as Sheila's.

After reading this section, you know that many admired individuals have dealt with psychological disorders. Their diagnoses do not detract from their accomplishments. Quite the contrary, their accomplishments are all the more remarkable in the context of the challenging, courageous lives in which they have occurred.

SUMMARY

Stigma can create a significant barrier for people coping with a psychological disorder, as well as for their loved ones. Fear of being labeled can prevent individuals with a disorder from getting treatment and from talking about their problems with family and friends. In addition, the stigma attached to psychological disorders can lead to prejudice and discrimination toward individuals who are struggling with these problems. Having a disorder and experiencing the stigma associated with it can also negatively affect the physical health of such individuals.

We can help to combat stigma by acknowledging the strengths and the achievements of individuals coping with psychological disorders. By creating a positive environment for people with disorders, we encourage more of them to be open about their struggles and to thrive, with the result that they can become positive role models for others.

TEST YOURSELF

1. What did the classic study by Rosenhan reveal about the power of labels that are applied to individuals?
2. What social and physical effects can result from the stigma with which some people view psychological disorders?
3. What are some critical considerations in efforts to eliminate stigmas toward individuals with psychological disorders?

Therapies

Rebuilding Houses and Lives

On Monday, August 29, 2005, a category 5 hurricane named Katrina made violent landfall in the city of New Orleans and elsewhere along the Gulf Coast. Katrina would be the costliest—and one of the deadliest—hurricanes in U.S. history. Media coverage of the devastation in New Orleans was nonstop. Even now, years later, the rebuilding of the city is an ongoing process—and one that was recently made more complicated by the massive British Petroleum oil spill in the Gulf of Mexico in the spring of 2010.

The physical reconstruction of their city has been only one part of the recovery for the people of New Orleans. In addition, these uprooted survivors have been rebuilding their sense of hope and their very lives, with the help of teams of psychologists. Clinical psychologists from all over the United States have flocked to New Orleans many times since that day in the summer of 2005, lending an ear, teaching new skills, and dispensing therapies of all kinds to help the stricken residents manage their profound sense of loss and develop new goals toward which to strive. Just as Habitat for Humanity, a nonprofit organization dedicated to constructing decent and affordable housing, has helped the victims repair the storm's physical damage and rebuild their homes, psychologists have helped them repair the psychological damage of trauma and rebuild their lives (Borchardt, 2008).

For countless Katrina survivors, asking for help to rebuild their city was natural, but asking for psychological help was a different—and often difficult—matter. Indeed, for many of us, whatever the cause, seeking aid when we are troubled seems a mark of weakness. To the contrary, however, seeking help is a sign that we are strong enough and courageous enough to admit that we cannot go it alone. ●

Biological Therapies

● **biological therapies** Also called biomedical therapies, treatments that reduce or eliminate the symptoms of psychological disorders by altering aspects of body functioning.

Biological therapies, also called *biomedical therapies,* are treatments that reduce or eliminate the symptoms of psychological disorders by altering aspects of body functioning. Drug therapy is the most common form of biomedical therapy. Electroconvulsive therapy and psychosurgery are much less commonly used biomedical therapies.

As medical doctors, psychiatrists can prescribe drugs as part of therapy. Family doctors can also prescribe drugs for psychological disorders. In contrast, psychologists, who are not trained as medical doctors, cannot administer drugs therapeutically in most states.

64·1 DRUG THERAPY

Although people have long used medicine and herbs to alleviate symptoms of emotional distress, it was not until the twentieth century that drug treatments revolutionized mental healthcare. Psychotherapeutic drugs are used mainly in three diagnostic categories: anxiety disorders, mood disorders, and schizophrenia. In this section we explore the effectiveness of drugs for these various disorders—respectively, antianxiety drugs, antidepressant drugs, and antipsychotic drugs. As you read about these various treatments, you will note that the reasons why a particular drug works for a particular problem are not always understood. Rather, these drugs are used because they work—and research continues to explore the reasons for their effectiveness.

● **antianxiety drugs** Commonly known as tranquilizers, drugs that reduce anxiety by making the individual calmer and less excitable.

Antianxiety Drugs

Antianxiety drugs are commonly known as *tranquilizers.* These drugs reduce anxiety by making the individual calmer and less excitable. Benzodiazepines are the antianxiety drugs that generally offer the greatest relief for anxiety symptoms, though these drugs are potentially addictive. They work by binding to the receptor sites of neurotransmitters that become overactive during anxiety (Bastien, 2010; Poisnel & others, 2009). The most frequently prescribed benzodiazepines include Xanax, Valium, and Librium. A nonbenzodiazepine—buspirone, or BuSpar—is commonly used to treat generalized anxiety disorder (Mokhber & others, 2010; Pollack, 2009). Benzodiazepines are relatively fast-acting medications, taking effect within hours. In contrast, buspirone must be taken daily for two to three weeks before the patient feels benefits.

Benzodiazepines, like all drugs, have some side effects, including drowsiness, loss of coordination, fatigue, and mental slowing (Fields, 2010). These effects can be hazardous when a person is driving or operating machinery, especially when the individual first starts taking benzodiazepines. Benzodiazepines also have been linked to abnormalities in babies born to mothers who took them during pregnancy (Istaphanous & Loepke, 2009). The combination of benzodiazepines with other medications can cause problems (Vakily & others, 2009). When combined with alcohol, anesthetics, antihistamines, sedatives, muscle relaxants, and some prescription pain medications, benzodiazepines can lead to depression.

Why are antianxiety drugs so widely used? Many individuals experience stress, anxiety, or both. Family physicians or psychiatrists prescribe these drugs to improve people's ability to cope with their problems effectively. Antianxiety medications are best used only temporarily for symptomatic relief. Too often, they are overused and can become addictive (Lader, Tylee, & Donoghue, 2009; Reeves & Burke, 2010).

People have used medicinal herbs to treat emotional distress since ancient times.

Antidepressant Drugs

Antidepressant drugs regulate mood. The four main classes of antidepressant drugs are tricyclics, such as Elavil; tetracyclics such as Avanza; monoamine oxidase (MAO) inhibitors, such as Nardil; and selective serotonin reuptake inhibitors, such as Prozac. These antidepressants are all thought to help alleviate depressed mood through their effects on neurotransmitters in the brain. In different ways, they all allow the person's brain to increase or maintain its level of important neurotransmitters, especially serotonin and norepinephrine. Let's take a close look at each of these types of antidepressants.

Tricyclics, so-called because of their three-ringed molecular structure, are believed to work by increasing the level of certain neurotransmitters, especially norepinephrine and serotonin (Lopez-Munoz & Alamo, 2009; Racagni & Popoli, 2010). Low serotonin levels play a role in negative mood and aggression. The tricyclics reduce the symptoms of depression in approximately 60 to 70 percent of cases; these drugs usually take two to four weeks to improve mood. Adverse side effects may include restlessness, faintness, trembling, sleepiness, and memory difficulties.

Related to the tricyclics are *tetracyclic* antidepressants (named for their four-ringed structure). Tetracyclics are also called *noradrenergic and specific serotonergic antidepressants,* or NaSSAs. These drugs have effects on both norepinephrine and serotonin, enhancing brain levels of these neurotransmitters. According to a recent analysis, the tetracylic Remeron (mertazapine) was more effective in reducing depression than any other antidepressant drug (Cipriani & others, 2010).

MAO inhibitors are thought to work because they block the enzyme monoamine oxidase. This enzyme breaks down the neurotransmitters serotonin and norepinephrine in the brain (Hazell, 2009; Pitychoutis & others, 2010). Scientists believe that the blocking action of MAO inhibitors allows these neurotransmitters to stick around in the brain's synapses and help regulate mood. MAO inhibitors are not as widely used as the tricyclics because they are more potentially harmful to the body. However, some individuals who do not respond to the tricyclics do respond to MAO inhibitors. MAO inhibitors may be especially risky because of their potential interactions with certain fermented foods (such as cheese) and drugs, leading to high blood pressure and risk of stroke (Nishida & others, 2009).

Psychiatrists and general practitioners increasingly are prescribing a type of antidepressant drug called *selective serotonin reuptake inhibitors* (SSRIs). SSRIs target serotonin, and work mainly by interfering only with the reabsorption of serotonin in the brain (Cipriani & others, 2010; Z. Zhou & others, 2009). Figure 64.1 shows how this process works.

Three widely prescribed SSRIs are Prozac (fluoxetine), Paxil (paroxetine), and Zoloft (sertraline). The increased prescription of these drugs reflects their effectiveness in reducing the symptoms of depression with fewer side effects than other antidepressants (Amsterdam & Shults, 2010; Gentile, 2010; Ksir, Hart, & Ray, 2008). Nonetheless, they can have negative effects, including insomnia, anxiety, headache, and diarrhea (Keeton, Kolos, & Walkup, 2009). They also can impair sexual functioning and produce severe withdrawal symptoms if the individual abruptly stops taking them (Frohlich & Meston, 2005).

The number of Americans who had ever been prescribed an antidepressant doubled between 1996 and 2005, with 10 percent of Americans taking an antidepressant at some point in their life (Olfson & Marcus, 2009). Beyond their usefulness in treating mood disorders, antidepressant drugs are often effective for a number of anxiety disorders, including generalized anxiety disorder, panic disorder, obsessive-compulsive disorder, social phobia, and post-traumatic stress disorder, as well as some eating and sleep disorders (Ahmed & Thorpy, 2010; Davidson, 2009; Hollingsworth, Burgess, & Whiteford, 2010). Increasingly, antidepressants are prescribed for other common problems, among them sleeplessness

● **antidepressant drugs** Drugs that regulate mood.

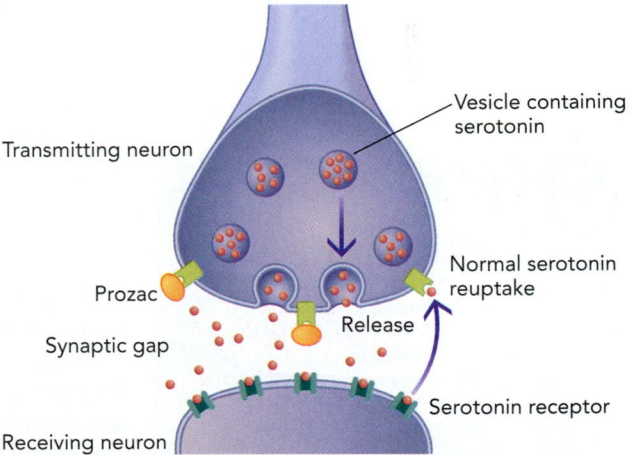

FIGURE 64.1 How the Antidepressant Prozac Works Secreted by a transmitting neuron, serotonin moves across the synaptic gap and binds to receptors in a receiving neuron. Excess serotonin in the synaptic gap is normally reabsorbed by the transmitting neuron. The antidepressant Prozac blocks this reuptake of serotonin by the transmitting neuron, however, leaving excess serotonin in the synaptic gap. The excess serotonin is transmitted to the receiving neuron and circulated through the brain. The result is a reduction of the serotonin deficit found in individuals with depression.

Labels in figure: Transmitting neuron; Vesicle containing serotonin; Prozac; Normal serotonin reuptake; Synaptic gap; Release; Serotonin receptor; Receiving neuron and chronic pain. In fact, in 2005, less than half of the individuals in the United States who had taken prescribed antidepressants were doing so for depression (Olfson & Marcus, 2009).

Lithium is widely used to treat bipolar disorder. Lithium is the lightest of the solid elements in the periodic table of elements. If you have ever used a lithium battery (or are a fan of Nirvana or Evanescence), you know that lithium has uses beyond treating psychological disorders. The amount of lithium that circulates in the bloodstream must be carefully monitored because the effective dosage is precariously close to toxic levels (Paton & others, 2010). Kidney and thyroid gland complications as well as weight gain can arise as a consequence of lithium therapy (Bauer & others, 2007). Lithium is thought to stabilize moods by influencing norepinephrine and serotonin, but the exact mechanism of its effect is largely unknown (Perlis & others, 2009; Serretti, Drago, & DeRonchi, 2009). The effectiveness of lithium of course depends on the person's staying on the medication. Some may be troubled by the association between lithium and weight gain, and others may go off the drug when they are feeling well.

The use of antidepressant drugs to treat depression in children is controversial. To read more about this issue, see the Critical Controversy.

Antipsychotic Drugs

Antipsychotic drugs are powerful drugs that diminish agitated behavior, reduce tension, decrease hallucinations, improve social behavior, and produce better sleep patterns in individuals who have a severe psychological disorder, especially schizophrenia (Uchida & Mamo, 2009; Yamin & Vaddadi, 2010). Before antipsychotic drugs were developed in the 1950s, few, if any, interventions brought relief from the torment of psychotic symptoms.

Neuroleptics are the most extensively used class of antipsychotic drugs (Garver, 2006). Numerous well-controlled investigations reveal that, when used in sufficient doses, neuroleptics reduce a variety of schizophrenic symptoms (Nasrallah & others, 2009). The most widely accepted explanation for the effectiveness of neuroleptics is their ability to block dopamine's action in the brain (Agatonovic-Kustrin, Davies, & Turner, 2009).

Neuroleptics do not cure schizophrenia. They treat only the symptoms of the disorder, not its causes. If an individual with schizophrenia stops taking the drug, the symptoms return. Neuroleptic drugs have substantially reduced the length of hospital stays for individuals with schizophrenia. However, when these individuals are able to return to the community (because the drug therapy reduces their symptoms), many have difficulty coping with the demands of society. In the absence of symptoms, many struggle to justify to themselves that they should continue to take the very medications that have reduced their symptoms—especially because neuroleptic drugs can have severe side effects (J. W. Y. Lee, 2010; Tural & Onder, 2010). Drugs that treat disturbed thought by reducing dopamine (which plays a role in positive, rewarding experiences) can also induce a lack of pleasure (Kapur, 2003).

Another potential side effect of neuroleptic drugs is *tardive dyskinesia,* a neurological disorder characterized by involuntary random movements of the facial muscles, tongue, and mouth, as well as twitching of the neck, arms, and legs (Go & others, 2009). Up to 20 percent of individuals with schizophrenia who take neuroleptics develop this disorder. As you may recall from Module 62, movement disorders are a positive symptom of schizophrenia, and tardive dyskinesia can also occur in individuals suffering from psychiatric disorders who have not taken neuroleptic drugs (Chouinard, 2006).

Newer drugs called *atypical antipsychotic medications,* introduced in the 1990s, carry a much lower risk of these side effects (Remington, 2007). The precise mechanism by which these drugs work is unknown, but they appear to influence dopamine as well as serotonin (Leucht, Kissling, & Davis, 2009; C. Lin & others, 2009). The two most widely used drugs in this group, Clozaril (clozapine) and Risperdal (risperidone), show promise for reducing schizophrenia's symptoms without the side effects of neuroleptics (Kinon & others, 2010; Smith, Weston, & Lieberman, 2009).

● **lithium** The lightest of the solid elements in the periodic table of elements, widely used to treat bipolar disorder.

● **antipsychotic drugs** Powerful drugs that diminish agitated behavior, reduce tension, decrease hallucinations, improve social behavior, and produce better sleep patterns in individuals with a severe psychological disorder, especially schizophrenia.

"Lab Rat Rehab"

© Mike Shiell. www.CartoonStock.com.

Do Antidepressants Increase Suicide Risk in Children?

In 2000, Caitlin McIntosh, a 12-year-old straight-*A* student, artist, and musician, hanged herself with her shoelaces in the girls' room of her middle school. Caitlin had been struggling with depression and had been prescribed antidepressants shortly before her suicide. Tragic cases such as Caitlin's have stirred deep concerns among parents and mental health professionals. Could the very drugs prescribed to alleviate depression be causing children to become suicidal?

In 2004, the FDA held hearings to address the concerns of parents and health professionals about the potential risk of suicide as an unexpected, tragic side effect of antidepressant treatment. Many of the stories that parents told indicated no apparent previous risk of suicide and starkly illustrated the impulsiveness of the suicides. Some of the children had made plans for family activities for the very day after their suicides. Some had left sad evidence of the apparent randomness of their acts—a half-drunk glass of soda, an unfinished letter on the computer. Such real-life case studies can be emotionally engaging and persuasive, but are they generalizable to the population as a whole? What about the scientific evidence?

During the hearings, the FDA reviewed clinical trials of antidepressant use with children, including 23 clinical trials involving 4,300 children who were randomly assigned to receive either an antidepressant or a placebo (Hammad, 2004). None of the children in the studies committed or attempted suicide. In studies that included participants' self-report ratings of their suicidal thoughts and behaviors, no differences were found between the antidepressant and placebo groups. Another variable examined was "adverse event reports"—spontaneous statements of thoughts about suicide reported by the participants or their parents. The research did show an increase in adverse event reports in the participants in the treatment group. While the placebo participants showed 2 percent of such spontaneous reports of suicidal thoughts, those taking antidepressants showed a 4 percent rate. This last finding, along with the dramatic personal cases presented by families, was the basis of the FDA's subsequent action.

In October 2004, the FDA required prescription antidepressants to carry the severest "black box" warning, describing the potential of antidepressants to be associated with suicidal thoughts and behaviors in children and adolescents (FDA, 2004). The black box warning had a chilling effect: Following the black box warning edict (and even before the box started appearing on the drug containers), prescriptions for antidepressants for children declined dramatically. Between March 2004 and June 2005, the number of prescriptions fell 20 percent compared to the same time frame the year before (Rosack, 2007). This drop in prescriptions might indicate that health professionals were being more careful about prescribing antidepressants to youth. It might also indicate that professionals were hesitant to prescribe these drugs even when they might be of real help to children with depression.

Sorting out the possible connection between antidepressants and suicide in adolescents is complex for a variety of reasons (Brent &

others, 2009; Healy, 2009; Weissman, 2009). As many as 17 percent of adolescents think about suicide in any given year, and most teen suicides do not involve antidepressants (CDC, 2004). As noted in Module 60, some 90 percent of individuals who attempt suicide are thought to suffer from a psychological disorder, with depression being the most typical factor. Would an adolescent with depression be just as likely to commit suicide with or without taking antidepressants? Studies examining the effects of antidepressants generally exclude from participation individuals who are suicidal at the outset. As a result, positive effects of these drugs on reducing suicidal thoughts and behaviors are difficult to detect. Indeed, in a large-scale population study, the number of prescriptions for Prozac was negatively related to suicide rates over time (Milane & others, 2006).

Since the FDA called for the black box warning, a number of studies have found no link between antidepressants and suicide in either adults or children (Dudley, Goldney, & Hadzi-Pavlovic, 2010; Hammond, Laughren, & Racoosin, 2006; Markowitz & Cuellar, 2007). One study revealed that Prozac and cognitive-behavior therapy were both effective in reducing depression in children and adolescents, with a drop in suicidal thoughts from 29 percent to 10 percent in the treatment groups (March & others, 2004).

Importantly, drug therapy may not be the first-choice treatment for children with depression (Jerrell, 2010). Many children and adolescents have uncomplicated depression that responds well to psychotherapy alone (Emslie, Croarkin, & Mayes, 2010; Kennard & others, 2008). Indeed, in Great Britain, guidelines allow the prescription of Prozac only in conjunction with ongoing psychotherapy (Boseley, 2006). In the United Kingdom and France, Paxil and Zoloft are not approved for pediatric use.

This controversy highlights many of the issues addressed throughout this book. How do we weigh dramatic case study evidence against less vivid scientific data that do not bear out those cases? Are special considerations required when professionals suggest the use of drug therapy in children? How can we best balance the potential benefits of drug treatment against the risks of that treatment? Throughout the debate looms the profound tragedy of suicide, and certainly professionals have been moved to change their thinking and practices with regard to treating depression in youth.

WHAT DO YOU THINK?

- Have antidepressants helped anyone you know? If so, were you aware of negative side effects? Positive side effects? What was the nature of these effects?

- What do you think of the common practice of treating depression with medication first?

- Do you think occasional bouts of depression might play a normal role in psychological development? Why or why not?

Psychological Disorder	Drug	Effectiveness	Side Effects
Everyday Anxiety and Anxiety Disorders			
Everyday anxiety	Antianxiety drugs; antidepressant drugs	Substantial improvement short term	Antianxiety drugs: less powerful the longer people take them; may be addictive Antidepressant drugs: see below under depressive disorders
Generalized anxiety disorder	Antianxiety drugs	Not very effective	Less powerful the longer people take them; may be addictive
Panic disorder	Antianxiety drugs	About half show improvement	Less powerful the longer people take them; may be addictive
Agoraphobia	Tricyclic drugs and MAO inhibitors	Majority show improvement	Tricyclics: restlessness, fainting, and trembling MAO inhibitors: toxicity
Specific phobias	Antianxiety drugs	Not very effective	Less powerful the longer people take them; may be addictive
Mood Disorders			
Depressive disorders	Tricyclic drugs, MAO inhibitors, SSRI drugs, and tetracyclic drugs	Majority show moderate improvement	Tricyclics: cardiac problems, mania, confusion, memory loss, fatigue MAO inhibitors: toxicity SSRI drugs: nausea, nervousness, insomnia, and in a few cases, suicidal thoughts Tetracyclics: drowsiness, increased appetite, weight gain
Bipolar disorder	Lithium	Large majority show substantial improvement	Toxicity
Schizophrenic Disorders			
Schizophrenia	Neuroleptics; atypical antipsychotic medications	Majority show partial improvement	Neuroleptics: irregular heartbeat, low blood pressure, uncontrolled fidgeting, tardive dyskinesia, and immobility of face Atypical antipsychotic medications: less extensive side effects than with neuroleptics, but can have a toxic effect on white blood cells

FIGURE 64.2 **Drug Therapy for Psychological Disorders** This figure summarizes the types of drugs used to treat various psychological disorders.

Strategies to increase the effectiveness of the antipsychotic drugs involve administering small dosages over time, rather than a large initial dose, and combining drug therapy with psychotherapy. Along with drug treatment, individuals with schizophrenia may need training in vocational, family, and social skills.

Figure 64.2 summarizes the drugs used to treat various psychological disorders, the disorders they target, their effectiveness, and their side effects. Notice that for some types of anxiety disorders, such as agoraphobia, MAO inhibitors (antidepressant drugs) might be used rather than antianxiety drugs.

64-2 ELECTROCONVULSIVE THERAPY

● **electroconvulsive therapy (ECT)** Also called shock therapy, a treatment, commonly used for depression, that sets off a seizure in the brain.

The goal of **electroconvulsive therapy (ECT),** commonly called *shock therapy,* is to set off a seizure in the brain, much like what happens spontaneously in some forms of epilepsy (W. A. Brown, 2007). The notion that causing someone to have a seizure might help cure a psychological disorder may seem strange, but this idea has been around for quite some time. Hippocrates, the ancient Greek father of medicine, first noticed that malaria-induced convulsions would sometimes cure individuals who were thought to be insane (Endler, 1988). Following Hippocrates, many other medical doctors noted that head traumas, seizures, and convulsions brought on by fever would sometimes lead to the apparent cure of psychological problems.

In the early twentieth century, doctors induced seizures by insulin overdose and other means and used this procedure primarily to treat schizophrenia. In 1937, Ugo Cerletti, an Italian neurologist specializing in epilepsy, developed the procedure by which seizures could be induced using electrical shock. With colleagues, he developed a fast, efficient means of causing seizures in humans, and ECT gained wide use in mental institutions (Faedda & others, 2010). Unfortunately, in earlier years, ECT was used indiscriminately, sometimes even to punish patients, as illustrated in the classic film *One Flew Over the Cuckoo's Nest*. Among the individuals who underwent ECT were Ernest Hemingway and Sylvia Plath, both of whom struggled with depression and ultimately committed suicide.

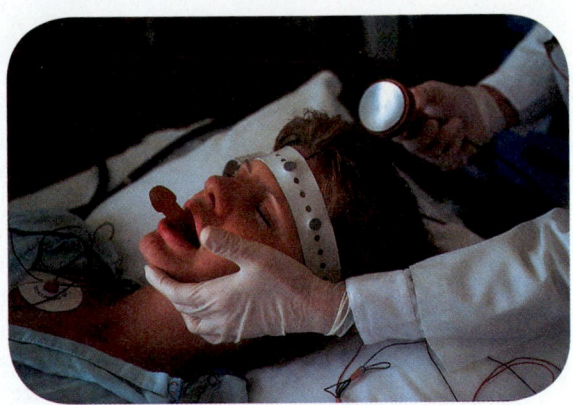

Electroconvulsive therapy (ECT), commonly called shock therapy, causes a seizure in the brain. ECT is still given to as many as 100,000 people a year, mainly to treat major depressive disorder.

Today, doctors use ECT primarily to treat severe depression (Birkenhager & others, 2010; Damm & others, 2010). As many as 100,000 individuals a year undergo ECT, primarily as treatment for major depressive disorder (Mayo Foundation, 2006). ECT has also been used in cases of severe chronic post-traumatic stress disorder (Margoob, Zaffar Ali, & Andrade, 2010). Fortunately, the contemporary use of ECT bears little resemblance to its earlier uses. Treatment involves passing a small electrical current of a second or less through two electrodes placed on the individual's head. The current excites neural tissue, stimulating a seizure that lasts for approximately a minute.

Today, ECT is given mainly to individuals who have not responded to drug therapy or psychotherapy, and its administration involves little discomfort. The patient receives anesthesia and muscle relaxants before the current is applied; this medication allows the individual to sleep through the procedure, minimizes convulsions, and reduces the risk of physical injury. Although in the past, electrical current was passed through the person's entire brain, increasingly ECT is applied only to the right side. The individual awakens shortly afterward with no conscious memory of the treatment.

How effective is ECT? One analysis of the use of ECT compared its effectiveness in treating depression with that of cognitive therapy and antidepressant drugs (Seligman, 1994). ECT was as effective as cognitive therapy or drug therapy, with about four of five individuals showing marked improvement in all three therapies. However, as with the other therapies, the relapse rate for ECT is moderate to high. What sets ECT apart from other treatments is the rapid relief it can produce in a person's mood (Merkl, Heuser, & Bajbouj, 2009; Popeo, 2009). ECT may be especially effective as a treatment for acute depression in individuals who are at great risk of suicide (Kellner & others, 2006).

ECT is controversial. Its potential side effects remain a source of debate and contradictory findings (Crowley & others, 2008; Nordenskjold, Knorring, & Engstrom, 2010). These possible effects include memory loss and other cognitive impairments and are generally more severe than drug side effects (Caverzasi & others, 2008); such problems are less likely to occur, however, when only one side of the brain is stimulated (Sienaert & others, 2010). Some individuals treated with ECT have reported prolonged and profound memory loss (Koitabashi, Oyaizu, & Ouchi, 2009). Despite these potential problems, some psychiatrists argue that for certain individuals, this invasive treatment can have life-enhancing—and even life-saving—benefits (O'Connor & others, 2009; Sherman, 2009).

More recently, rather than using electricity to set off a seizure, practitioners have begun to apply electrical stimulation in very precise locations in the brain (Sachdev & Chen, 2009). In **deep brain stimulation,** doctors surgically implant electrodes in the brain that emit signals to alter the brain's electrical circuitry (Connor, 2010). Deep brain stimulation involving the transmission of high-frequency electrical impulses to targeted areas of the brain is now being used to treat individuals with treatment-resistant depression and obsessive-compulsive disorder (Haq & others, 2010; Moreines, McClintock, & Holtzheimer, 2010). For instance, deep brain stimulation of the nucleus accumbens (part of the brain's reward pathways) has been effective in treating severe depression (Bewernick & others, 2010).

● **deep brain stimulation** A procedure for treatment-resistant depression that involves the implantation of electrodes in the brain that emit signals to alter the brain's electrical circuitry.

64-3 PSYCHOSURGERY

● **psychosurgery** A biological therapy, with irreversible effects, that involves removal or destruction of brain tissue to improve the individual's adjustment.

Psychosurgery is a biological intervention that involves the removal or destruction of brain tissue to improve the individual's adjustment. The effects of psychosurgery cannot be reversed.

In the 1930s, Portuguese physician Antonio Egas Moniz developed a surgical procedure to treat psychological disorders. In this operation, an instrument is inserted into the brain and rotated, severing fibers that connect the frontal lobe, which is important in higher thought processes, and the thalamus, which plays a key role in emotion. Moniz theorized that by severing the connections between these structures, the surgeon could alleviate the symptoms of severe mental disorders. In 1949, Moniz received the Nobel Prize for developing this procedure. Although some patients may have benefited from these lobotomies, many were left in a vegetable-like state because of the massive assaults on their brains. Moniz himself felt that the procedure should be used with extreme caution and only as a last resort.

After hearing about Moniz's procedure, American physician and neurologist Walter Freeman became the champion of *prefrontal lobotomies* (a term he coined). With his colleague James Watts, he performed the first lobotomy in the United States in 1936 (El-Hai, 2005). Freeman eventually developed his own technique, which he performed using a device similar to an ice pick, in surgeries that lasted mere minutes. Freeman was a dynamic and charismatic showman who argued strongly for the usefulness of the technique. In the 1950s and 60s, he traveled the country in a van he called the "lobotomobile," demonstrating the surgery in state-run mental institutions. In his career, Freeman performed over 3,000 lobotomies (El-Hai, 2005). Indeed, prefrontal lobotomies were conducted on tens of thousands of patients from the 1930s through the 1960s. These numbers speak not only to Freeman's persuasive charm but also to the desperation many physicians felt in treating institutionalized patients with severe psychological disorders (Lerner, 2005).

Subsequent research called the lobotomy procedure into question, with critics pointing to the considerable damage that resulted (Landis & Erlick, 1950; Mettler, 1952). Many individuals who received lobotomies suffered permanent and profound brain damage (Whitaker, 2002). Ethical concerns arose because, in many instances, giving consent for the lobotomy was a requirement for release from a mental hospital. Like ECT, lobotomies were being used as a form of punishment and control.

By the 1950s, drug therapies had emerged as alternatives to the invasive procedure of lobotomy (Juckel & others, 2009). By the late 1970s new regulations classified the procedure as experimental and established safeguards for patients. Fortunately, crude lobotomies are no longer performed, and Freeman's techniques are certainly not typical of contemporary psychosurgery. Indeed, psychosurgery today is quite precise (Heller & others, 2006; Kopell, Machado, & Rezai, 2006) and involves making just a small lesion in the amygdala or another part of the limbic system (Fountas & Smith, 2007).

Today, only several hundred patients who have severely debilitating conditions undergo psychosurgery each year. Psychosurgery may be performed for OCD, major depression, or bipolar disorders rather than for schizophrenia (Elias & Cosgrove, 2008; Shelton & others, 2010). Just as Moniz originally suggested, the procedure is now used only as a last resort—and with the utmost caution (Ruck, 2003). Psychiatrists and psychologists recognize that science should tamper with the brain only in extreme cases (Pressman, 1998).

SUMMARY

KEY TERMS

Biological approaches to therapy include drugs, electroconvulsive therapy (ECT), and psychosurgery. Psychotherapeutic drugs that treat psychological disorders fall into three main categories: antianxiety drugs, antidepressant drugs, and antipsychotic drugs.

Benzodiazepines are the most commonly used antianxiety drugs. Antidepressant drugs regulate mood; the three main classes are tricyclics,

MAO inhibitors, and SSRI drugs. Lithium is used to treat bipolar disorder. Antipsychotic drugs are administered to treat severe psychological disorders, especially schizophrenia.

Practitioners use electroconvulsive therapy to alleviate severe depression when other interventions have failed. Psychosurgery is an irreversible procedure in which brain tissue is destroyed. Though rarely used today, psychosurgery is more precise than in the days of prefrontal lobotomies.

TEST YOURSELF

1. How do antianxiety drugs work, and why do so many people take them?
2. What are SSRIs, and through what process do they have their effect?
3. Describe the procedure used in electroconvulsive therapy (ECT).

APPLY YOUR KNOWLEDGE

1. While watching television one day or reading a newspaper or magazine, document the number of advertisements you see related to drug therapy. Identify the name of the drug, what it is used for, what the potential side effects are, and how psychiatrists might prescribe this medication.

2. With the advancement of medical technology, consider the role psychosurgery could play as a treatment for people suffering from severe mental illnesses. Could it become a more commonly used treatment? Defend your position.

Psychotherapy and Its Effectiveness

● **psychotherapy** A nonmedical process that helps individuals with psychological disorders recognize and overcome their problems.

Although their ability to prescribe drugs is limited, psychologists and other mental health professionals may provide **psychotherapy,** a nonmedical process that helps individuals with psychological disorders recognize and overcome their problems. Psychotherapy may be given alone or in conjunction with biological therapy administered by psychiatrists and other medical doctors (Davidson, 2009). Indeed, in many instances, a combination of psychotherapy and medication is a desirable course of treatment (Nolen-Hoeksema, 2011). Unfortunately, even as prescriptions for medications have increased dramatically over the years, the number of people receiving psychotherapy has dropped. According to a recent study, among individuals receiving antidepressant medication, the number in therapy fell from 32 percent in 1996 to less than 20 percent in 2005 (Olfson & Marcus, 2009).

Psychotherapists employ a number of strategies to alleviate symptoms of psychological disorders: talking, interpreting, listening, rewarding, and modeling, for example (Prochaska & Norcross, 2010). Although most psychotherapy is conducted face-to-face, many contemporary therapists communicate with clients through e-mail or text messaging (Berger, Hohl, & Caspar, 2009; Wangberg, Gammon, & Spitznogle, 2007).

Another recent development is *cybertherapy,* or *e-therapy,* in which an online source provides help to people seeking therapy for psychological disorders (Klein & others, 2010; Marks & Cavanaugh, 2009; Postel, de Haan, & de Jong, 2010; Reger & Gahm, 2009). E-therapy websites are controversial among mental health professionals (Abbott, Klein, & Ciechomski, 2008). For one thing, many of these sites do not include the most basic information about the therapists' qualifications (Recupero & Rainey, 2006). In addition, because cybertherapy occurs at a distance, such sites typically exclude individuals who are having thoughts of suicide. Further, confidentiality, a crucial aspect of the therapeutic relationship, cannot always be guaranteed on a website. On the plus side, though, individuals who might be unwilling or unable to seek out face-to-face therapy may be more disposed to get help online (Postel, de Jong, & de Haan, 2005; Van Voorhees & others, 2009).

Psychotherapy is practiced by a variety of mental health professionals, including clinical psychologists, psychiatrists, counselors, and social workers. Figure 65.1 lists the main types of mental health professionals, their degrees, the years of education required, and the nature of their training. Licensing and certification are two ways in which society retains control over psychotherapy practitioners. Laws at the state level are used to license or certify such professionals. These laws vary in toughness from one state to another, but invariably they specify the training the mental health professional must have and provide for some assessment of an applicant's skill through formal examination.

Regardless of their particular occupation, psychotherapists use a variety of techniques to help alleviate suffering. This section focuses on four main approaches to psychotherapy: psychodynamic, humanistic, behavioral, and cognitive, and the effectiveness of psychotherapy.

65·1 PSYCHODYNAMIC THERAPIES

● **psychodynamic therapies** Treatments that stress the importance of the unconscious mind, extensive interpretation by the therapist, and the role of early childhood experiences in the development of an individual's problems.

The **psychodynamic therapies** stress the importance of the unconscious mind, extensive interpretation by the therapist, and the role of early childhood experiences in the development of an individual's problems. The goal of psychodynamic therapies is to help individuals recognize the maladaptive ways in which they have been coping with

Professional Type	Degree	Education Beyond Bachelor's Degree	Nature of Training
Clinical psychologist	PhD or PsyD	5–7 years	Requires both clinical and research training. Includes a 1-year internship in a psychiatric hospital or mental health facility. Some universities have developed PsyD programs, which have a stronger clinical than research emphasis. The PsyD training program takes as long as the clinical psychology PhD program and also requires the equivalent of a 1-year internship.
Psychiatrist	MD	7–9 years	Four years of medical school, plus an internship and residency in psychiatry, is required. A psychiatry residency involves supervision in therapies, including psychotherapy and biomedical therapy.
Counseling psychologist	MA, PhD, PsyD, or EdD	3–7 years	Similar to clinical psychologist but with emphasis on counseling and therapy. Some counseling psychologists specialize in vocational counseling. Some counselors complete master's degree training, others PhD or EdD training, in graduate schools of psychology or education.
School psychologist	MA, PhD, PsyD, or EdD	3–7 years	Training in graduate programs of education or psychology. Emphasis on psychological assessment and counseling practices involving students' school-related problems. Training is at the master's or doctoral level.
Social worker	MS W/DSW or PhD	2–5 years	Graduate work in a school of social work that includes specialized clinical training in mental health facilities.
Psychiatric nurse	RN, MA, or PhD	0–5 years	Graduate work in a school of nursing with special emphasis on care of mentally disturbed individuals in hospital settings and mental health facilities.
Occupational therapist	BS, MA, or PhD	0–5 years	Emphasis on occupational training with focus on physically or psychologically handicapped individuals. Stresses getting individuals back into the mainstream of work.
Pastoral counselor	None to PhD or DD (Doctor of Divinity)	0–5 years	Requires ministerial background and training in psychology. An internship in a mental health facility as a chaplain is recommended.
Counselor	MA or MEd	2 years	Graduate work in a department of psychology or department of education with specialized training in counseling techniques.

FIGURE 65.1 **Main Types of Mental Health Professionals** A wide range of professionals with varying levels of training have taken on the challenge of helping people with psychological disorders.

problems and the sources of their unconscious conflicts. Many psychodynamic approaches grew out of Freud's psychoanalytic theory of personality. Today some therapists with a psychodynamic perspective practice Freudian techniques, but others do not (Busch, Milrod, & Sandberg, 2009; Cardoso Zoppe & others, 2009).

Psychoanalysis

Psychoanalysis is Freud's therapeutic technique for analyzing an individual's unconscious thoughts. Freud believed that a person's current problems could be traced to childhood experiences, many of which involved unconscious sexual conflicts. Only through extensive questioning, probing, and analyzing was Freud able to put together the pieces of the client's personality and help the individual become aware of how these early experiences were affecting present behavior. The psychoanalyst's goal is to bring unconscious conflicts into conscious awareness, thus giving the client insight into his or her core problems and freeing the individual from unconscious influences (Dougherty, 2010).

To reach the shadowy world of the unconscious, psychoanalytic therapists use the therapeutic techniques of free association, interpretation, dream analysis, analysis of transference, and analysis of resistance. We survey each in turn.

● **psychoanalysis** Freud's therapeutic technique for analyzing an individual's unconscious thoughts.

MOTHER GOOSE & GRIMM © 2010 Grimmy, Inc. King Features Syndicate.

● **free association** A psychoanalytic technique that involves encouraging individuals to say aloud whatever comes to mind, no matter how trivial or embarrassing.

● **interpretation** A psychoanalyst's search for symbolic, hidden meanings in what the client says and does during therapy.

● **dream analysis** A psychoanalytic technique for interpreting a person's dreams.

Free association involves encouraging individuals to say aloud whatever comes to mind, no matter how trivial or embarrassing. When Freud detected a person resisting the spontaneous flow of thoughts, he probed further. He believed that the crux of the person's problem lurked below this point of resistance. Encouraging people to talk freely, Freud thought, would allow their deepest thoughts and feelings to emerge. *Catharsis* is the release of emotional tension a person experiences when reliving an emotionally charged and conflicting experience.

Interpretation plays an important role in psychoanalysis. The analyst does not take the patient's statements and behavior at face value. To understand what is causing the person's conflicts, the therapist constantly searches for symbolic, hidden meanings in what the individual says and does (Kligman, 2010). From time to time, the therapist suggests possible meanings of the person's statements and behavior.

Dream analysis is a psychoanalytic technique for interpreting a person's dreams. Psychoanalysts believe that dreams contain information about unconscious thoughts, wishes, and conflicts (Freud, 1911). From this perspective, dreams give us an outlet to express our unconscious wishes, a mental theater in which our deepest and most secret desires can be played out (Ferro, 2009; Ogden, 2010). According to Freud, every dream, even our worst nightmare, contains a hidden, disguised wish. The sheer horror we feel during a nightmare might itself disguise that unconscious wish.

Freud distinguished between the dream's manifest and latent content. *Manifest content* is the psychoanalytic term for the conscious, remembered aspects of a dream. For instance, if you wake up in the morning remembering a dream about being back in sixth grade with your teacher scolding you for not turning in your homework, that is the manifest content of the dream. *Latent content* is the unconscious, hidden aspects that are symbolized by the manifest content. In order to understand the meaning of your dream, a psychoanalyst might ask you to free-associate to each of the elements of the manifest content: What comes to your mind when you think of being in sixth grade? When you think of your teacher? According to Freud, the latent meaning of a dream is locked inside the unconscious mind of the dreamer. The goal of analysis is to unlock that secret meaning by probing into the deeper layers of the person's mind through free association about the manifest dream elements.

The psychoanalyst interprets the dream by analyzing the manifest content for disguised unconscious wishes and needs, especially those that are sexual and aggressive. Dream symbols can mean different things to different dreamers. Although countless books and websites today claim to provide guidance as to the meaning of dream symbols, Freud (1911) believed that the true meaning of any dream symbol depends on the individual dreamer.

● **transference** A client's relating to the psychoanalyst in ways that reproduce or relive important relationships in the individual's life.

Freud viewed transference as an inevitable—and essential—aspect of the analyst–patient relationship. **Transference** is the psychoanalytic term for the person's relating to the analyst in ways that reproduce or relive important relationships in the individual's life. A person might interact with an analyst as if the analyst were a parent or lover, for example. According to Freud, transference is a necessary part of the psychoanalytic relationship, as it models the way that individuals relate to important people in their lives (Meissner, 2009; Rycroft, 2010).

Resistance is the psychoanalytic term for the client's unconscious defense strategies that prevent the analyst from understanding the person's problems. Resistance occurs because it is painful for the client to bring conflicts into conscious awareness. By resisting analysis, the individual does not have to face the threatening truths that underlie his or her problems (Hoffman, 2006). Showing up late or missing sessions, arguing with the psychoanalyst, and faking free associations are examples of resistance.

● **resistance** A client's unconscious defense strategies that interfere with the psychoanalyst's understanding of the individual's problems.

Contemporary Psychodynamic Therapies

Psychodynamic therapy has changed extensively since its beginnings almost a century ago. Nonetheless, many contemporary psychodynamic therapists still probe unconscious thoughts about early childhood experiences to gain insight into their clients' current problems (Cortina, 2010; Gotthold, 2009; Messer & Abbass, 2010; Rustin, 2009). However, contemporary psychoanalysts accord more power to the conscious mind and to a person's current relationships, and they generally place less emphasis on sex (Holmes, 2010; Knoblauch, 2009). In addition, clients today rarely lie on a couch, as they did in Freud's time, or see their therapist several times a week, as was the norm in early psychodynamic therapy. Instead, they sit in a comfortable chair facing the therapist, and weekly appointments are typical.

Some contemporary psychodynamic therapists (Busch, 2007) focus on the self in social contexts, as was suggested by Heinz Kohut (1977). In Kohut's view, early social relationships with attachment figures such as one's parents are critical. As we develop, we internalize those relationships, and they serve as the basis for our sense of self. Kohut (1977) believed that the therapist's job is to replace unhealthy childhood relationships with the healthy relationship provided by the therapist. In Kohut's view, the therapist needs to interact with the client in empathic and understanding ways. Empathy and understanding are also cornerstones for humanistic therapies, our next topic.

65-2 HUMANISTIC THERAPIES

The underlying philosophy of humanistic therapies is captured by the metaphor of how an acorn, if provided with appropriate conditions, will grow in positive ways, pushing naturally toward its actualization as an oak (Schneider, 2002). In **humanistic therapies,** people are encouraged toward self-understanding and personal growth. The humanistic therapies are unique in their emphasis on the person's self-healing capacities. In contrast to psychodynamic therapies, humanistic therapies emphasize conscious rather than unconscious thoughts, the present rather than the past, and self-fulfillment rather than illness.

Client-centered therapy (also called *Rogerian therapy* or *nondirective therapy*) is a form of humanistic therapy, developed by Carl Rogers, in which the therapist provides a warm, supportive atmosphere to improve the client's self-concept and to encourage the client to gain insight into problems (Rogers, 1961, 1980). Compared with psychodynamic therapies, which emphasize analysis and interpretation by the therapist, client-centered therapy places far more emphasis on the client's self-reflection (C. E. Hill, 2000). In client-centered therapy, the goal of therapy is to help the client identify and understand his or her own genuine feelings (Hazler, 2007).

One way to achieve this goal is through active listening and **reflective speech,** a technique in which the therapist mirrors the client's own feelings back to the client. For example, as a woman is describing her grief over the traumatic loss of her husband in a drunk-driving accident, the therapist, noting her voice and facial expression, might suggest, "You sound angry" to help her identify her feelings. According to Rogers, the therapist must enter into an authentic relationship with the client, not as a physician diagnosing a disease but as one human being connecting with another. Indeed, in talking about those he was trying to help, Rogers referred to the "client," and eventually to the "person," rather than to the "patient."

● **humanistic therapies** Treatments, unique in their emphasis on people's self-healing capacities, that encourage clients to understand themselves and to grow personally.

● **client-centered therapy** Also called Rogerian therapy or nondirective therapy, a form of humanistic therapy, developed by Rogers, in which the therapist provides a warm, supportive atmosphere to improve the client's self-concept and to encourage the client to gain insight into problems.

● **reflective speech** A technique in which the therapist mirrors the client's own feelings back to the client.

"I see. So what you're saying is that you woke up this morning and your woman had done left you."

© Clive Goddard. www.CartoonStock.com.

Rogers believed that each of us is born with the potential to be fully functioning, but that we live in a world in which we are valued only if we live up to conditions of worth. That is, others value us only if we meet certain standards, and we come to apply those standards to ourselves. When we do, we become alienated from our own genuine feelings and desires.

Rogers believed that humans require three essential elements to grow: unconditional positive regard, empathy, and genuineness. These three elements are reflected in his approach to therapy. To free a person from conditions of worth, the therapist engages in unconditional positive regard, which involves creating a warm and caring environment and never disapproving of the client as a person. Rogers believed this unconditional positive regard provides a context for personal growth and self-acceptance, just as soil, water, and sunshine provide a context for the acorn to become an oak.

In addition to unconditional positive regard, Rogers emphasized the importance of empathy and genuineness. Through empathy the therapist strives to put himself or herself in the client's shoes—to feel the emotions the client is feeling. Genuineness involves letting the client know the therapist's feelings and not hiding behind a façade. For genuineness to coexist with unconditional positive regard, that regard must be a sincere expression of the therapist's true feelings. The therapist may distinguish between the person's behavior and the person himself or herself. Although the client is always acknowledged as a valuable human being, his or her behavior can be evaluated negatively: "You are a good person but your actions are not." Rogers's positive view of humanity extended to his view of therapists. He believed that by being genuine with the client, the therapist could help the client improve.

65-3 BEHAVIOR THERAPIES

Psychodynamic and humanistic approaches are called *insight therapies* because they encourage self-awareness as the key to psychological health. We now turn to therapies that take a different approach: the behavior therapies. Behavior therapists do not search for unconscious conflicts, as psychodynamic therapists do, or encourage individuals to develop accurate perceptions of their feelings and selves, as humanistic therapists do. Insight and self-awareness are not the keys to helping individuals develop more adaptive behavior patterns, the behavior therapists say. Rather, changing behavior is the key. Indeed, behavior therapies offer action-oriented strategies to help people change behavior, not underlying thoughts or emotions (Spiegler & Guevremont, 2010).

Behavior therapies use principles of learning to reduce or eliminate maladaptive behavior. Behavior therapies are based on the behavioral and social cognitive theories of learning. Behavior therapists assume that overt symptoms are the central problem and that even if clients discover why they are depressed, that does not mean the depression will cease. To alleviate depression, then, behavior therapists focus on eliminating the problematic symptoms or behaviors rather than on helping individuals gain an understanding of why they are depressed (Yamanishi & others, 2009).

Although initially based almost exclusively on the learning principles of classical and operant conditioning, behavior therapies have become more diverse in recent years. As social cognitive theory grew in popularity, behavior therapists increasingly included observational learning, cognitive factors, and self-instruction—encouraging people to change what they say to themselves—in their practice (Vassilopoulos & Watkins, 2009).

Classical Conditioning Techniques

Classical conditioning has been used in treating phobias. Recall that phobias are irrational fears that interfere with an individual's life, such as fear of heights, dogs, flying, or public speaking. Specifically for this purpose, therapists use **systematic desensitization,** a method of behavior therapy that treats anxiety by teaching the client to associate

● **behavior therapies** Treatments, based on the behavioral and social cognitive theories of learning, that use principles of learning to reduce or eliminate maladaptive behavior.

● **systematic desensitization** A method of behavior therapy that treats anxiety by teaching the client to associate deep relaxation with increasingly intense anxiety-producing situations.

deep relaxation with increasingly intense anxiety-producing situations (Wolpe, 1963). A therapist might first ask the client which aspects of the feared situation are the most and least frightening. The therapist then arranges these circumstances in order from most to least frightening. The next step is to teach the individual to relax. The client learns to recognize the presence of muscular contractions or tension in various parts of the body and then to contract and relax different muscles. Once the individual is relaxed, the therapist asks him or her to imagine the least feared stimulus in the hierarchy. Subsequently, the therapist moves up the list of items, from least to most feared, while the client remains relaxed. Eventually, the client can imagine the most fearsome circumstance without fear.

In systematic desensitization, if you are afraid of, say, spiders, the therapist might initially have you watch someone handle a spider and then ask you to engage in increasingly more feared behaviors. You might first go into the same room with a spider, next approach the spider, and then touch the spider. Eventually, you might play with the spider. Figure 65.2 shows an example of a desensitization hierarchy. Desensitization involves exposing someone to a feared situation in a real or an imagined way (Figueroa-Moseley & others, 2007).

A more intense form of exposure is *flooding*—exposing an individual to feared stimuli to an excessive degree while not allowing the person to avoid the stimuli (Berry, Rosenfield, & Smits, 2009; Wolitzky & Telch, 2009). In flooding, the patient is essentially forced to confront the frightening situation and survive. Desensitization and flooding are based on the process of extinction in classical conditioning. During extinction, the conditioned stimulus is presented without the unconditioned stimulus, leading to a decreased conditioned response.

Aversive conditioning consists of repeated pairings of an undesirable behavior with aversive stimuli to decrease the behavior's positive associations. Through aversive conditioning, people can learn to avoid such behaviors as smoking, overeating, and drinking alcohol. Electric shocks, nausea-inducing substances, and verbal insults are some of the noxious stimuli used in aversive conditioning (Sommer & others, 2006). The Psychological Inquiry illustrates conditioning principles in practice.

Operant Conditioning Techniques

The idea behind using operant conditioning as a therapy approach is that just as maladaptive behavior patterns are learned, they can be unlearned. Therapy involves conducting a careful analysis of the person's environment to determine which factors need modification. Especially important is changing the consequences of the person's behavior to ensure that healthy, adaptive replacement behaviors are followed by positive reinforcement.

Applied behavior analysis involves establishing positive reinforcement connections between behaviors and rewards so that individuals engage in appropriate behavior and extinguish inappropriate behavior. Consider, for example, a woman with obsessive-compulsive disorder (OCD) who engages in a compulsive ritual such as touching the door frame three times every time she enters a room. If she does not complete her ritual, she is overcome with anxiety that something dreadful will happen. Note that whenever she completes the ritual, nothing dreadful does happen and her anxiety is relieved. Her compulsion is a behavior that is reinforced by the relief of anxiety and the fact that nothing dreadful happens. Such a ritual, then, could be viewed as avoidance learning. An operant conditioning–based therapy would involve stopping the behavior to extinguish this avoidance. Specifically, allowing the woman to experience the lack of catastrophic consequences in the absence of the touching the door frame, as well as training her to relax, might help to eliminate the compulsive rituals. Indeed, behavior therapy has been shown to be effective in treating OCD (Bonchek, 2009; Rosa-Alcazar & others, 2008).

It may strike you as unusual that behavioral approaches do not emphasize gaining insight and self-awareness. However, for the very reason that they do not stress these goals, such treatments may be particularly useful in individuals whose cognitive abilities

1	A month before an examination
2	Two weeks before an examination
3	A week before an examination
4	Five days before an examination
5	Four days before an examination
6	Three days before an examination
7	Two days before an examination
8	One day before an examination
9	The night before an examination
10	On the way to the university on the day of an examination
11	Before the unopened doors of the examination room
12	Awaiting distribution of examination papers
13	The examination paper lies facedown before her
14	In the process of answering an examination paper

FIGURE 65.2 **A Desensitization Hierarchy Involving Test Anxiety** In this hierarchy, the individual begins with her least feared circumstance (a month before the exam) and moves through each of the circumstances until reaching her most feared circumstance (being in the process of answering the exam questions). At each step of the way, the person replaces fear with deep relaxation and successful visualization.

psychological *inquiry*

Before Aversive Conditioning

UCS $\longrightarrow$ UCR

Nausea-inducing drug $\longrightarrow$ Nausea

During Aversive Conditioning

Neutral stimulus + UCS $\longrightarrow$ UCR

Alcohol + Nausea-inducing drug $\longrightarrow$ Nausea

After Aversive Conditioning

CS $\longrightarrow$ CR

Alcohol $\longrightarrow$ Nausea

Classical Conditioning: The Backbone of Aversive Conditioning

This figure demonstrates how classical conditioning principles underlie the process of aversive conditioning. It specifically shows how classical conditioning can provide a conditional aversion to alcohol. In studying the figure, recall the abbreviations UCS (unconditioned stimulus), UCR (unconditioned response), CS (conditioned stimulus), and CR (conditioned response). Try your hand at the questions below.

1. In the example illustrated in the figure, what is the conditioned stimulus?

2. What is the likely effect of alcohol *prior to* aversion therapy? Is this effect learned (that is, a conditioned response) or not (an unconditioned response)?

3. What role, if any, does the person's motivation play in the process of conditioning?

4. Looking over the steps in aversive conditioning, how do you think classical conditioning might be applied to prevent psychological problems?

are limited, such as adults with developmental disabilities or children. Applied behavior analysis can be used, for instance, with individuals with autism who engage in self-injurious behaviors such as head banging (Vismara & Rogers, 2010).

65·4 COGNITIVE THERAPIES

● **cognitive therapies** Treatments that point to cognitions (thoughts) as the main source of psychological problems and that attempt to change the individual's feelings and behaviors by changing cognitions.

Cognitive therapies emphasize that cognitions, or thoughts, are the main source of psychological problems; these therapies attempt to change the individual's feelings and behaviors by changing cognitions. *Cognitive restructuring,* a general concept for changing a pattern of thought that is presumed to be causing maladaptive behavior or emotion, is central to cognitive therapies.

Cognitive therapies differ from psychoanalytic therapies by focusing on overt symptoms rather than on deep-seated unconscious thoughts, by providing more structure to the individual's thoughts, and by being less concerned about the origin of the problem. Compared with humanistic therapies, cognitive therapies provide a more structured framework and more analysis, and they are based on specific cognitive techniques. Cognitive therapists guide individuals in identifying their irrational and self-defeating thoughts. Then they use various techniques to get clients to challenge these thoughts and to consider different, more positive ways of thinking.

Cognitive therapies all involve these basic assumptions: Human beings have control over their feelings, and how individuals feel about something depends on how they think about it. In the next section we examine three main types of cognitive therapy: Albert Ellis's rational-emotive behavior therapy, Aaron Beck's cognitive therapy, and cognitive-behavior therapy.

Ellis's Rational-Emotive Behavior Therapy

Rational-emotive behavior therapy (REBT) was developed by Albert Ellis (1913–2007), who believed that individuals develop a psychological disorder because of irrational and self-defeating beliefs. Ellis said our emotional reactions to life events are a product of our irrational beliefs and expectations along with the central false belief that we cannot control our feelings (1962, 1996, 2000, 2002, 2005). Ellis was a very confrontational therapist who aggressively attacked these irrational beliefs.

Ellis (2000, 2002) believed that many individuals construct three basic demands, which he called "musterbating": (1) I absolutely *must* perform well and win the approval of other people; (2) other people *must* treat me kindly and fairly; and (3) my life conditions *must* not be frustrating. Once people convert their important desires into demands, they often create dysfunctional, exaggerated beliefs, such as "Because I'm not performing well, as I absolutely must, I'm an inadequate person."

The goal of REBT is to get the individual to eliminate self-defeating beliefs by rationally examining them (Sava & others, 2009). A client is shown how to dispute his or her dysfunctional beliefs—especially the absolute "musts"—and how to convert them to realistic and logical thoughts. Homework assignments provide opportunities to engage in the new self-talk and to experience the positive results of not viewing life in such a catastrophic way. For Ellis, a successful outcome means getting the client to live in reality, where life is sometimes tough and bad things happen.

Albert Ellis (1913–2007) Ellis's rational-emotive behavior therapy aims to eliminate individuals' rigid, irrational beliefs through a process of rational self-examination.

● **rational-emotive behavior therapy (REBT)** A therapy based on Ellis's assertion that individuals develop a psychological disorder because of irrational and self-defeating beliefs and whose goal is to get clients to eliminate these beliefs by rationally examining them.

Beck's Cognitive Therapy

Aaron Beck developed a somewhat different form of cognitive therapy to treat psychological problems, especially depression (Beck, 1976, 1993). He began with the basic assumption that a psychological problem such as depression results when people think illogically about themselves, their world, and the future (Beck, 2005, 2006). Similar to Ellis's method, Beck's approach derives from the idea that the goal of therapy is to help people to recognize and discard self-defeating cognitions.

In the initial phases of Beck's therapy, individuals learn to make connections between their patterns of thinking and their emotional responses. From Beck's perspective, emotions are a product of cognitions. By changing cognitions, people can change how they feel. Unfortunately, thoughts that lead to emotions can happen so rapidly that a person is not even aware of them. Thus, the first goal of therapy is to bring these automatic thoughts into awareness so that they can be changed. The therapist helps clients to identify their own automatic thoughts and to keep records of their thought content and emotional reactions.

With the therapist's assistance, clients learn to recognize logical errors in their thinking and to challenge the accuracy of these automatic thoughts. Logical errors in thinking can lead individuals to the following erroneous beliefs (Carson, Butcher, & Mineka, 1996):

■ Perceiving the world as harmful while ignoring evidence to the contrary—for example, when a young woman still feels worthless after a friend has just told her how much other people genuinely like her.

■ Overgeneralizing on the basis of limited examples—such as a man's seeing himself as worthless because one individual stopped dating him.

■ Magnifying the importance of undesirable events—such as seeing the loss of a dating partner as the end of the world.

■ Engaging in absolutist thinking—such as exaggerating the importance of someone's mildly critical comment and perceiving it as proof of total inadequacy.

Figure 65.3 describes some of the most widely used cognitive therapy techniques.

The following case study gives you a glimpse of what happens in Beck's cognitive therapy. In this dialogue, the therapist guides a depressed 26-year-old graduate student

Aaron Beck (b. 1921) Beck's method stresses that the goal of therapy should be to help people to recognize and eliminate illogical and self-defeating thinking.

Cognitive Therapy Technique	Description	Example
Challenge idiosyncratic meanings	Explore personal meaning attached to the client's words and ask the client to consider alternatives.	When a client says he will be "devastated" by his spouse leaving, ask just how he would be devastated and ways he could avoid being devastated.
Question the evidence	Systematically examine the evidence for the client's beliefs or assertions.	When a client says she can't live without her spouse, explore how she lived without the spouse before she was married.
Reattribution	Help the client distribute responsibility for events appropriately.	When a client says that his son's failure in school must be his fault, explore other possibilities, such as the quality of the school.
Examine options and alternatives	Help the client generate alternative actions to maladaptive ones.	If a client considers leaving school, explore whether tutoring or going part-time to school are good alternatives.
Decatastrophize	Help the client evaluate whether he is overestimating the nature of a situation.	If a client states that failure in a course means he or she must give up the dream of medical school, question whether this is a necessary conclusion.
Fantasize consequences	Explore fantasies of a feared situation: if unrealistic, the client may recognize this; if realistic, work on effective coping strategies.	Help a client who fantasizes "falling apart" when asking the boss for a raise to role-play the situation and develop effective skills for making the request.
Examine advantages and disadvantages	Examine advantages and disadvantages of an issue, to instill a broader perspective.	If a client says he "was just born depressed and will always be that way," explore the advantages and disadvantages of holding that perspective versus other perspectives.
Turn adversity to advantage	Explore ways that difficult situations can be transformed to opportunities.	If a client has just been laid off, explore whether this is an opportunity for her to return to school.
Guided association	Help the client see connections between different thoughts or ideas.	Draw the connections between a client's anger at his wife for going on a business trip and his fear of being alone.
Scaling	Ask the client to rate her emotions or thoughts on scales to help gain perspective.	If a client says she was overwhelmed by an emotion, ask her to rate it on a scale from 0 (not at all present) to 100 (I fell down in a faint).
Thought stopping	Provide the client with ways of stopping a cascade of negative thoughts.	Teach an anxious client to picture a stop sign or hear a bell when anxious thoughts begin to snowball.
Distraction	Help the client find benign or positive distractions to take attention away from negative thoughts or emotions temporarily.	Have a client count to 200 by 13s when he feels himself becoming anxious.
Labeling of distortions	Provide labels for specific types of distorted thinking to help the client gain more distance and perspective.	Have a client keep a record of the number of times a day she engages in all-or-nothing thinking—seeing things as all bad or all good.

FIGURE 65.3 **Cognitive Therapy Techniques** Cognitive therapists develop strategies to help change the way people think.

toward understanding the connection between how she interprets her experiences and how she feels. The goal is to help her see the inaccuracy of her interpretations:

Student: I agree with the description of me, but I guess I don't agree that the way I think makes me depressed.

Therapist: How do you understand it?

Student: I get depressed when things go wrong. Like when I fail a test.

Therapist: How can failing a test make you depressed?

Student: Well, if I fail I'll never get into law school.

Therapist: So failing the test means a lot to you. But if failing a test could drive people into clinical depression, wouldn't you expect everyone who failed the test to have depression? Did everyone who failed the test get depressed enough to require treatment?

Student: No, but it depends on how important the test was to the person.

Therapist: Right, and who decides the importance?

Student: I do.

Therapist: And so, what we have to examine is your way of viewing the test or the way that you think about the test and how it affects your chances of getting into law school. Do you agree?

Student: Right . . .

Therapist: Now what did failing mean?

Student: (*Tearful*) That I couldn't get into law school.

Therapist: And what does that mean to you?

Student: That I'm just not smart enough.

Therapist: Anything else?

Student: That I can never be happy.

Therapist: And how do these thoughts make you feel?

Student: Very unhappy.

Therapist: So it is the meaning of failing a test that makes you very unhappy. In fact, believing that you can never be happy is a powerful factor in producing unhappiness. So, you get yourself into a trap—by definition, failure to get into law school equals, "I can never be happy." (Beck & others, 1979, pp. 145–146).

The cognitive therapies of Beck and Ellis share some differences as well as similarities. Rational-emotive behavior therapy is very directive and confrontational; in contrast, Beck's cognitive therapy involves more of an open-ended dialogue between the therapist and the individual. The aim of this dialogue in Beck's approach is to get individuals to reflect on personal issues and discover their own misconceptions. Beck also encourages clients to gather information about themselves and to try out unbiased experiments that reveal the inaccuracies of their beliefs. So whereas Ellis's approach was to bring a sledgehammer down on irrational beliefs, Beck's involves a more subtle process of coaxing a client to recognize that these beliefs promote thoughts that influence feelings. Despite the differences in their approaches, a recent study showed that both Ellis's rational-emotive behavior therapy and Beck's cognitive therapy were more effective in treating depression than drug therapy (Sava & others, 2009).

Cognitive-Behavior Therapy

Cognitive-behavior therapy is a combination of cognitive therapy, with its emphasis on reducing self-defeating thoughts, and behavior therapy, with its emphasis on changing behavior. An important aspect of cognitive-behavior therapy is *self-efficacy,* Albert Bandura's concept that one can master a situation and produce positive outcomes (1997, 2001, 2009, 2010b). Bandura believes in fact that self-efficacy is the key to successful therapy. At each step of the therapy process, clients need to bolster their confidence by telling themselves messages such as "I'm going to master my problem," "I can do it," "I'm improving," and "I'm getting better." As they gain confidence and engage in adaptive behavior, the successes become intrinsically motivating. Before long, individuals persist (with considerable effort) in their attempts to solve personal problems because of the positive outcomes that were set in motion by self-efficacy.

Self-instructional methods are cognitive-behavior techniques aimed at teaching individuals to modify their own behavior (Spiegler & Guevremont, 2010). Using self-instructional techniques, cognitive-behavior therapists prompt clients to change what they say to themselves. The therapist gives the client examples of constructive statements, known as *reinforcing self-statements,* which the client can repeat in order to take positive steps to cope with stress or meet a goal. The therapist also encourages the client to practice the statements through role playing and strengthens his or her newly acquired skills through reinforcement.

● **cognitive-behavior therapy** A therapy that combines cognitive therapy and behavior therapy with the goal of developing self-efficacy.

Cognitive Therapy for Psychological Disorders

Cognitive therapy has successfully treated some anxiety disorders, mood disorders, schizophrenia, and personality disorders (Peters & others, 2010; Sava & others, 2009).

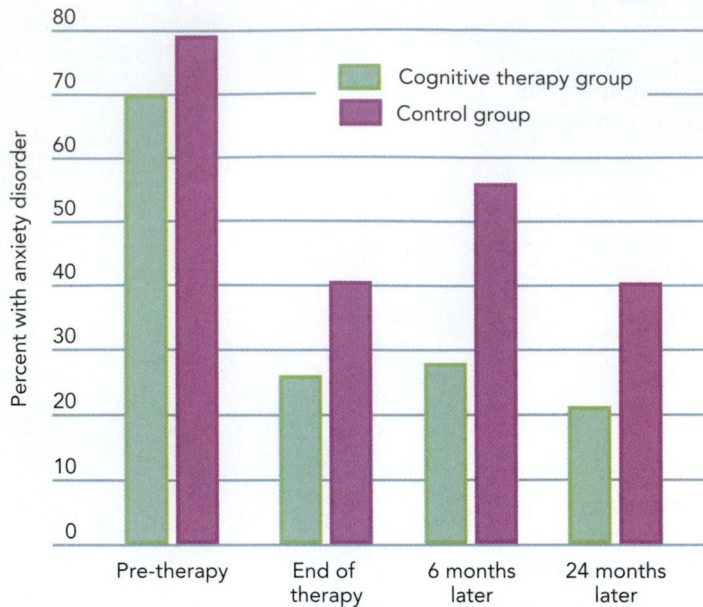

FIGURE 65.4 **Effects of Cognitive-Behavior Therapy on Children's Anxiety About School** Children and their parents participated in a 10-week cognitive-behavior therapy program. Compared with a control group, the children in the cognitive therapy program were less likely to have an anxiety disorder through 24 months after the therapy.

In many instances, cognitive therapy used together with drug therapy is an effective treatment for psychological disorders (Starcevic, 2006).

Cognitive therapy is often used to treat panic disorder, one of the anxiety disorders (Schmidt & Keough, 2003; van Apeldoorn & others, 2010). The central concept in the cognitive model of panic is that individuals catastrophically misinterpret relatively harmless physical or psychological events. In cognitive therapy, the therapist encourages individuals to test the catastrophic misinterpretations by inducing an actual panic attack. The individuals then can test the notion that they will die or go crazy, which they find out is not the case.

Cognitive therapy also shows considerable promise in the treatment of post-traumatic stress disorder, especially when therapists encourage clients to relive traumatic experiences so that they can come to grips with the threatening cognitions precipitated by those experiences (Cockram, Drummond, & Lee, 2010; Vickerman & Margolin, 2009). In addition, cognitive therapy has been successful in treating generalized anxiety disorder, certain phobias, and obsessive-compulsive disorder (Foa & Franklin, 2011; Jaurrieta & others, 2009; Roy-Byrne & others, 2010).

In one study, cognitive-behavior therapy was given to children (as well as their parents) who were highly anxious about going to school (Dadds & others, 1999). As shown in Figure 65.4, the therapy (provided over a 10-week period) was considerably more effective in reducing anxiety than no therapy at all, and the positive effects of the therapy were still present two years later.

One of the earliest applications of cognitive therapy was in the treatment of depression. A number of studies have shown that cognitive therapy can be just as successful as, or in some cases superior to, drug therapy in the treatment of depressive disorders (Sado & others, 2009; Sava & others, 2009). Some studies also have demonstrated that individuals treated with cognitive therapy are less likely to relapse into depression than individuals treated with drug therapy (Jarrett & others, 2001).

Practitioners have made considerable strides in recent years in applying cognitive therapy to the treatment of schizophrenia. Although not a substitute for drug therapy in the treatment of this disorder, cognitive therapy has been effective in reducing some schizophrenia symptoms such as belief in delusions and acting out impulsively (Christopher Frueh & others, 2009). Cognitive therapy also has proved effective in treating personality disorders (McMain & Pos, 2007). The focus is on using cognitive therapy to change individuals' core beliefs and to reduce their automatic negative thoughts.

So far, we have studied the biological therapies and psychotherapies. The four psychotherapies—psychodynamic, humanistic, behavior, and cognitive—are compared in Figure 65.5.

The cognitive approach to therapy assumes that how we think is an important part of how we feel, and that if we can change how we think about things—reinterpret events in more positive ways—we can feel better. A goal for cognitive-behavior therapy is to help us to alter our routine, automatic thinking habits (Jaurrieta & others, 2008). Remember that thinking is not only a mental event but also a physical event in the brain. How does changing our thoughts change the brain? To read about research addressing this fascinating question, see the Intersection.

65·5 THERAPY INTEGRATIONS

Having read about the major approaches to psychotherapy, you may be surprised to learn that as many as 50 percent of therapists do not identify themselves as adhering to one particular method. Rather, they refer to themselves as "integrative" or "eclectic."

	Cause of Problem	Therapy Emphasis	Nature of Therapy and Techniques
Psychodynamic Therapies	Client's problems are symptoms of deep-seated, unresolved unconscious conflicts.	Discover underlying unconscious conflicts and work with client to develop insight.	Psychoanalysis, including free association, dream analysis, resistance, and transference: therapist interprets heavily, operant conditioning.
Humanistic Therapies	Client is not functioning at an optimal level of development.	Develop awareness of inherent potential for growth.	Person-centered therapy, including unconditional positive regard, genuineness, accurate empathy, and active listening; self-appreciation emphasized.
Behavior Therapies	Client has learned maladaptive behavior patterns.	Learn adaptive behavior patterns through changes in the environment or cognitive processes.	Observation of behavior and its controlling conditions; specific advice given about what should be done; therapies based on classical conditioning, operant conditioning.
Cognitive Therapies	Client has developed inappropriate thoughts.	Change feelings and behaviors by changing cognitions.	Conversation with client designed to get him or her to change irrational and self-deflating beliefs.

FIGURE 65.5 **Therapy Comparisons** Different therapies address the same problems in very different ways. Many therapists take an eclectic approach, using the techniques that seem right for a given client and his or her problems.

Integrative therapy is a combination of techniques from different therapies based on the therapist's judgment of which particular methods will provide the greatest benefit for the client (Prochaska & Norcross, 2010). Integrative therapy is characterized by openness to various ways of applying diverse therapies. For example, a therapist might use a behavioral approach to treat an individual with panic disorder and a cognitive therapy approach to treat a client with major depressive disorder.

Because clients present a wide range of problems, it makes sense for therapists to use the best tools for each individual rather than to take a "one size fits all" approach. Sometimes a given psychological disorder is so difficult to treat that it requires the therapist to bring all of his or her tools to bear (de Groot, Verheul, & Trijsburg, 2008; Kozaric-Kovacic, 2008). For example, borderline personality disorder involves emotional instability, impulsivity, and self-injurious behaviors. This disorder responds to a form of therapy called *dialectical behavior therapy*, or DBT (Dimeff, Koerner, & Linehan, 2007; Harley & others, 2008; Neacsiu & others, 2010; Paris, 2010). Like psychodynamic approaches, DBT assumes that early childhood experiences are important to the development of borderline personality disorder. DBT includes a variety of techniques, including homework assignments, cognitive interventions, intensive individual therapy, and group sessions with others with the disorder. Group sessions focus on mindfulness training as well as emotional and interpersonal skills training.

Integrative therapy also is at work when individuals are treated with both psychotherapy and drug therapy. For example, combined cognitive therapy and drug therapy has been effective in treating anxiety and depressive disorders (Koszycki & others, 2010), eating disorders (Wilson, Grilo, & Vitousek, 2007), and schizophrenia (Rector & Beck, 2001). This integrative therapy might be conducted by a mental health team that includes a psychiatrist and a clinical psychologist. At their best, integrative therapies are effective, systematic uses of a variety of therapy approaches (Prochaska & Norcross, 2010). However, some have voiced concern that increased use of integrative therapies will result in an unsystematic, haphazard use of techniques that are no better than a narrow, dogmatic, therapeutic approach (Lazarus, Beutler, & Norcross, 1992).

Therapy integrations are conceptually compatible with the biopsychosocial model of abnormal behavior. That is, many therapists believe that abnormal behavior involves biological, psychological, and social factors. Many single-therapy approaches concentrate on one aspect of the person more than others; for example, drug therapies focus on biological factors, and cognitive therapies probe psychological factors. Therapy integrations take a broader look at individuals' problems, and such breadth is also implied in sociocultural approaches to therapy.

● **integrative therapy** A combination of techniques from different therapies based on the therapist's judgment of which particular methods will provide the greatest benefit for the client.

Clinical Psychology and Neuroscience: How Does Therapy Change the Brain?

When we change our habitual patterns of thinking, we are also making physical changes in the brain. We might be activating brain areas we have not used, and we might be establishing new physical connections in the brain. Remarkably, advances in brain-imaging technology such as functional magnetic resonance imaging (or fMRI, discussed in Module 7) have allowed researchers to examine what actually happens in the brain when, through therapy, we change the way we think (Costafreda & others, 2009; Dichter, Felder, & Smoski, 2010).

A striking example is provided by research showing that therapeutic interventions can "wake up" dormant parts of the brain. As noted in Module 62, schizophrenia is associated with low levels of activity in the prefrontal cortex, the brain area thought to be associated with high-order functions such as problem solving, judgment, and planning. In one study, a treatment called *cognitive-remediation therapy* (CRT) was administered to a group of individuals who were profoundly disabled by schizophrenia for 10 years or more (Wykes & others, 2002).

CRT is a psychological intervention that involves giving individuals practice in problem solving and information processing. The client essentially completes a variety of paper-and-pencil tasks that require skills such as cognitive flexibility, planning, and the use of working memory. Individuals with schizophrenia (who were on medication) and a control group of healthy individuals were scanned while engaging in a problem-solving task before and after those with schizophrenia completed CRT. Before CRT, the individuals with schizophrenia showed lower activation in the prefrontal cortex when solving such problems, compared with the healthy individuals. After CRT, however, participants with schizophrenia not only showed increases in activation, but they also were no longer different from the healthy participants. This result suggests that CRT had helped to normalize their brain function. This study is remarkable because it shows that a psychological intervention that focuses on engaging particular brain areas can lead to changes in the brain, even for patterns that were previously thought to be stable characteristics of a disorder.

The growing literature applying sophisticated scanning techniques to therapeutic interventions sheds light on how researchers can use knowledge about the brain to track psychological processes and to pinpoint brain changes associated with improved functioning (Pine, 2009; Reinhardt & others, 2010). Because the brain is a physical organ, we might assume that it is most sensitive to biological interventions. However, research is showing that psychological interventions also can powerfully affect the brain. In a sense, the dramatic findings are revealing how, with the help of therapy, the brain is capable of changing itself.

How does learning about these brain effects influence your view of treating disorders with therapy versus medication?

65·6 RESEARCH ON THE EFFECTIVENESS OF PSYCHOTHERAPY

Do individuals who go through therapy get better? Are some approaches more effective than others? How would we know if a therapy worked? During the past several decades, a large volume of research has addressed these questions (Kazdin, 2007).

A large body of research points to the conclusion that psychotherapy works (Beck, 2005; Butler & others, 2006; Clemens, 2010; Lambert, 2001; Luborsky & others, 2002). Researchers have carried out literally hundreds of studies examining the effects of psychotherapy. The strategy used to analyze these diverse studies is meta-analysis, in which, as we have seen, the researcher statistically combines the results of many different studies (Rosenthal & DiMatteo, 2001). A number of persuasive meta-analyses have concluded that psychotherapy does work, and works well, for many psychological disorders (Lipsey & Wilson, 1993; Wampold, 2001). In a review of studies, more than 70 percent of individuals who saw a therapist improved, whereas less than 40 percent who received a placebo and less than 20 percent who received no treatment improved (Lambert, 2001). The Psychological Inquiry summarizes these results.

psychological *inquiry*

Percent improved

(bar graph with y-axis labeled 0, 10, 20, 30, 40, 50, 60, 70, 80 and x-axis labeled Psychotherapy, Placebo, No treatment)

Does Therapy Work?

This figure provides a summary of numerous studies and reviews of research in which clients were randomly assigned to a no-treatment control group, a placebo control group, or a psychotherapy treatment (Lambert, 2001). Note that the group to which individuals were assigned is indicated on the X or horizontal axis and the percent of individuals who improved is shown on the Y or vertical axis. Use the graph to answer the following questions.

1. Which group improved most and which improved least?

2. Why might those in the "no treatment" group have improved?

3. What does the difference between the psychotherapy group and the placebo group indicate?

4. Do these results allow us to infer causal relationships between therapy and improvement? Explain.

People who are contemplating seeing a psychotherapist do not just want to know *whether* psychotherapy in general is effective but also, especially, *which form* of psychotherapy is most effective. There is no easy answer to that question. In fact, there is a term in psychotherapy describing this problem—the *Dodo bird hypothesis*—that comes from the Dodo bird in *Alice's Adventures in Wonderland*. Dodo was asked to judge the winner of a race. He proclaimed, "Everybody has won and all must have prizes." Many studies of psychotherapy lend support to the Dodo bird hypothesis—all "win" and all must have "prizes." That is, although research strongly supports the notion that therapy works, no one therapy has been shown to be significantly better than the others (Hubble & Miller, 2004; Lambert, 2001; Luborsky & others, 2002; Wampold, 2001). These results suggest that individuals considering psychotherapy should find out all they can about the various treatments and think about which might best suit their personality and problem.

Prospective clients also want to know how long it will take them to get better. In one study, people in therapy showed substantial improvement over the first six months, with diminishing returns after that (Howard & others, 1996). In another study, individuals rated their symptoms, interpersonal relations, and quality of life on a weekly basis before each treatment session (Anderson & Lambert, 2001). Figure 65.6 shows that one-third of the individuals had improved outcomes by the 10th session, 50 percent by the 20th session, and 70 percent by the 45th session. In sum, psychotherapy benefits most individuals at least through the first six months of treatment and possibly longer.

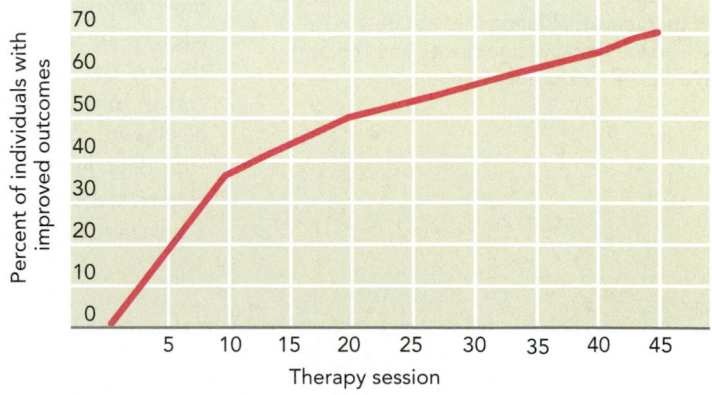

(line graph: y-axis "Percent of individuals with improved outcomes" labeled 0, 10, 20, 30, 40, 50, 60, 70; x-axis "Therapy session" labeled 5, 10, 15, 20, 25, 30, 35, 40, 45)

FIGURE 65.6 **Number of Therapy Sessions and Improvement** In one study, a large number of people undergoing therapy rated their well-being (based on symptoms, interpersonal relations, and quality of life) before each treatment session (Anderson & Lambert, 2001). The percentage of people who showed improved outcomes after each additional session of treatment indicated that about one-third of the individuals recovered by the 10th session, 50 percent by the 20th session, and 70 percent by the 45th session.

- Participates actively
- Draws on personal strengths, abilities, skills, and motivation
- Develops confidence and trust in therapist
- Becomes more hopeful and less alienated

- Participates actively
- Provides genuine support
- Monitors quality of relationship with client

FIGURE 65.7   Factors in a Successful Therapeutic Alliance This figure emphasizes the qualities and behaviors of therapists and clients that are essential to a successful therapeutic alliance and effective psychotherapy.

● **therapeutic alliance** The relationship between the therapist and client—an important element of successful psychotherapy.

65·7 COMMON THEMES IN EFFECTIVE PSYCHOTHERAPY

In this brief section, we look at some common threads in successful psychotherapy. After carefully studying the nature of psychotherapy for more than 25 years, Jerome Frank concluded that effective psychotherapies have the common elements of expectations, mastery, and emotional arousal (Frank, 1982; Frank & Frank, 1993). By inspiring expectations of help, the therapist motivates the client to continue going to therapy (Jennings & Skovholt, 1999). These expectations are powerful morale builders and symptom relievers in themselves (Arnkoff, Glass, & Shapiro, 2002). The therapist also increases the client's sense of mastery and competence (Brammer & MacDonald, 1999). For example, the client begins to feel that he or she can cope effectively with the world. Therapy also arouses the individual's emotions, an essential motivator for behavior change, according to Frank.

In addition, two specific underlying factors that have been shown to play a key role in successful therapy are the therapeutic alliance and client factors, as we now consider.

The Therapeutic Alliance

The **therapeutic alliance** is the relationship between the therapist and client. This alliance is an important element of successful psychotherapy (Prochaska & Norcross, 2010; Strupp, 1995). Effective psychotherapy depends on the client's having confidence and trust in the therapist (Knapp, 2007).

In one study, the most common ingredient in the success of different psychotherapies was the therapist's supportiveness of the client (Wallerstein, 1989). The client and therapist engage in a healing ritual that requires the active participation of both parties (Figure 65.7). As part of this ritual, the client becomes more hopeful and less alienated. It also is important for therapists to monitor the quality of the relationships with each client. Clients of therapists who did not assess the quality of the alliance were two times more likely to drop out of therapy (Hubble & Miller, 2004). Among those who completed therapy, clients of therapists who failed to assess their alliance were three to four times more likely to have a negative outcome (Hubble & Miller, 2004).

The Client as an Essential Factor

Meta-analytic studies of therapeutic outcomes have shown that one major factor in predicting effectiveness is the client. Indeed, the quality of the client's participation is the most important determinant of whether therapy is successful (Bohart & Tallman, 2010; McKay, Imel, & Wampold, 2006; Wampold, 2001). Even though individuals often seek therapy due to difficulties and problems in their life, it is their strengths, abilities, skills, and motivation that account for therapeutic success (Hubble & Miller, 2004; Wampold & Brown, 2005). A review of the extensive evidence on therapeutic efficacy concluded: "the data make abundantly clear that therapy does not make clients work, but rather clients make therapy work" (Hubble & Miller, 2004, p. 347). Therapy can be viewed as a mechanism for bringing clients' own strengths to the forefront of their life.

SUMMARY

Psychotherapy is the process that mental health professionals use to help individuals recognize, define, and overcome their disorders and improve their adjustment. In Freudian psychoanalysis, psychological disorders stem from unresolved unconscious conflicts, believed to originate in early family experiences. A therapist's interpretation of free association, dreams, transference, and resistance provides paths for understanding the client's unconscious conflicts. Although psycho-

KEY TERMS

psychotherapy   594
psychodynamic therapies   594
psychoanalysis   595
free association   596
interpretation   596
dream analysis   596

transference   596
resistance   597
humanistic therapies   597
client-centered therapy   597
reflective speech   597
behavior therapies   598

dynamic therapy has changed, many contemporary psychodynamic therapists still probe the unconscious mind for early family experiences that might provide clues to clients' current problems.

In humanistic therapies, the analyst encourages clients to understand themselves and to grow personally. Client-centered therapy, developed by Rogers, is a type of humanistic therapy that includes active listening, reflective speech, unconditional positive regard, empathy, and genuineness.

Behavior therapies use principles of learning to reduce or eliminate maladaptive behavior. They are based on the behavioral and social cognitive theories of personality. Behavior therapies seek to eliminate the symptoms or behaviors rather than to help individuals to gain insight into their problems.

The two main behavior therapy techniques based on classical conditioning are systematic desensitization and aversive conditioning. In systematic desensitization, anxiety is treated by getting the individual to associate deep relaxation with increasingly intense anxiety-producing situations. In aversive conditioning, pairings of the undesirable behavior with aversive stimuli are repeated to decrease the behavior's pleasant associations.

In operant conditioning approaches to behavior therapy, a careful analysis of the person's environment is conducted to determine which factors need modification. Applied behavior analysis is the application of operant conditioning to change human behavior. Its main goal is to replace maladaptive behaviors with adaptive ones.

Cognitive therapies emphasize that the individual's cognitions (thoughts) are the main source of abnormal behavior. Cognitive therapies attempt to change the person's feelings and behaviors by changing cognitions. Three main forms of cognitive therapy are Ellis's rational-emotive behavior therapy (REBT), Beck's cognitive therapy, and cognitive-behavior therapy.

Ellis's approach is based on the idea that individuals develop psychological disorders because of their beliefs, especially irrational beliefs. In Beck's cognitive therapy, which has been especially effective in treating depression, the therapist assists the client in learning about logical errors in thinking and then guides the client in challenging these thinking errors. Cognitive-behavior therapy combines cognitive therapy and behavior therapy techniques. Self-efficacy and self-instructional methods are used in this approach.

As many as 50 percent of practicing therapists refer to themselves as "integrative" or "eclectic." Integrative therapy uses a combination of techniques from different therapies based on the therapist's judgment of which particular techniques will provide the greatest benefit for the client.

Using meta-analysis, researchers have found that psychotherapies are successful in treating psychological disorders. The Dodo bird hypothesis states that therapy works but that no therapy is conclusively more effective than any other. People considering psychotherapy should find out all they can about the various types of treatments and think about which might best suit their personality and problem.

The therapeutic alliance and client factors are two important variables that influence therapeutic success. The key to successful therapy may lie not in a particular therapist or technique but in the client. Although an individual may be in distress when beginning treatment, his or her internal resources and strengths are brought forth by therapy, as a result of which the individual might expect a healthier, more satisfying life.

TEST YOURSELF

1. Describe what psychotherapy is, and identify four psychotherapeutic approaches.

2. What is psychoanalysis? Who developed it?

APPLY YOUR KNOWLEDGE

1. To experience Rogerian therapy firsthand, watch a video of Carl Rogers describing his approach and participating in a session with a client at http://www.viddler.com/explore/digizen/videos/14/.

3. What specific behavior therapy technique is used to treat phobias? How does it work?

4. What are three general questions that people commonly ask about psychotherapy?

5. Describe the factors in a successful therapeutic alliance.

6. According to meta-analyses, what is a major factor in predicting the outcome of psychotherapy?

2. The Beck Institute maintains a website chronicling the latest developments in cognitive therapy and including a variety of videos of Beck himself. Check out the site at http://www.beckinstituteblog.org/.

3. Behavioral and cognitive approaches may be helpful in modifying a behavior that would not be considered abnormal but that an individual might still want to change (for example, procrastinating, eating unhealthy food, or watching too much TV). Think about a behavior that you would like to do more or less frequently; then imagine that you are a behavior therapist or a cognitive therapist, and describe the kinds of recommendations you might make during a therapy session.

Sociocultural Approaches and Issues in Treatment

In the treatment of psychological disorders, biological therapies change the person's body, behavior therapies modify the person's behavior, and cognitive therapies alter the person's thinking. This module focuses on sociocultural approaches to the treatment of psychological disorders. These methods view the individual as part of a system of relationships that are influenced by various social and cultural factors (Nolen-Hoeksema, 2011).

We first review some common sociocultural approaches, including group therapy, family and couples therapy, self-help support groups, and community mental health. We then examine various cultural perspectives on therapy.

66·1 GROUP THERAPY

There is good reason to believe that individuals who share a psychological problem may benefit from observing others cope with a similar problem and that helping others cope can in turn improve individuals' feelings of competence and efficacy. The sociocultural approach known as **group therapy** brings together individuals who share a psychological disorder in sessions that are typically led by a mental health professional.

Advocates of group therapy stress that individual therapy is limited because it puts the client outside the normal context of relationships. It is these very relationships, they argue, that may hold the key to successful therapy. Many psychological problems develop in the context of interpersonal relationships—within one's family, marriage, or peer group, for example. By taking into account the context of these important groups, therapy may be more successful.

Group therapy takes many diverse forms. These include psychodynamic, humanistic, behavior, and cognitive therapy, in addition to approaches that do not reflect the major psychotherapeutic perspectives (Hornsey & others, 2009; van Ingen & Novicki, 2009). Six features make group therapy an attractive treatment format (Yalom & Leszcz, 2006):

- *Information:* Individuals receive information about their problems from either the group leader or other group members.

- *Universality:* Many individuals develop the sense that no one else has frightening and unacceptable impulses. In the group, individuals observe that others feel anguish and suffering as well.

- *Altruism:* Group members support one another with advice and sympathy and learn that they have something to offer others.

- *Experiencing a positive family group:* A therapy group often resembles a family (in family therapy, the group is a family), with the leaders representing parents and the other members of the group representing siblings. In this new family, old wounds may be healed and new, more positive family ties made.

- *Development of social skills:* Corrective feedback from peers may correct flaws in the individual's interpersonal skills. An individual may come to see that he or she is self-centered if five other group members comment on the person's self-centeredness; in individual therapy, the individual might not believe the therapist.

- *Interpersonal learning:* The group can serve as a training ground for practicing new behaviors and relationships. A hostile person may learn that he or she can get along better with others by behaving less aggressively, for example.

● **group therapy** A sociocultural approach to the treatment of psychological disorders that brings together individuals who share a particular psychological disorder in sessions that are typically led by a mental health professional.

611

66-2 FAMILY AND COUPLES THERAPY

Our relationships with family members and significant others are certainly an important part of human life. Sometimes these vital relationships can benefit from a helpful outsider. **Family therapy** is group therapy among family members. **Couples therapy** is group therapy with married or unmarried couples whose major problem lies within their relationship. These approaches stress that although one person may have some abnormal symptoms, those symptoms are a function of the family or couple relationships (Gehar, 2010; Hazell, 2009; Keitner, Ryan, & Solomon, 2009). Psychodynamic, humanistic, and behavior therapies may be used in family and couples therapy.

● **family therapy** Group therapy with family members.

● **couples therapy** Group therapy with married or unmarried couples whose major problem lies within their relationship.

Four of the most widely used family therapy techniques are

■ *Validation:* The therapist expresses an understanding and acceptance of each family member's feelings and beliefs and thus validates the person. When the therapist talks with each family member, he or she finds something positive to say.

■ *Reframing:* The therapist helps families reframe problems as family problems, not as an individual's problems. A delinquent adolescent boy's problems are reframed in terms of how each family member contributed to the situation. The mother's or father's lack of attention to the boy and marital conflict may be involved, for example.

■ *Structural change:* The family therapist tries to restructure the coalitions in a family. In a mother–son coalition, the therapist might suggest that the father take a stronger disciplinarian role to relieve the mother of some of the burden. Restructuring might be as simple as suggesting that the parents explore satisfying ways of being together. The therapist may recommend, for example, that the parents go out once a week for a quiet dinner together.

■ *Detriangulation:* In some families, one member is the scapegoat for two other members who are in conflict but pretend not to be. For example, parents of a girl with anorexia nervosa or a son who is acting out aggressively at school might insist that their marriage is fine but find themselves in subtle conflict over how to handle the child. The therapist tries to disentangle, or detriangulate, this situation by shifting attention away from the child to the conflict between the parents.

In family therapy, the assumption is that particular patterns of interaction among the family members cause the observed abnormal symptoms.

Couples therapy proceeds in much the same way as family therapy. Conflict in marriages and in relationships between unmarried individuals frequently involves poor communication. In some instances, communication has broken down entirely. The therapist tries to improve the communication between the partners (Kauffman & Silberman, 2009; Ro & Wampler, 2009). In some cases, the therapist will focus on the roles partners play: One may be strong, the other weak; one may be responsible, the other spoiled, for example. Couples therapy addresses diverse problems such as alcohol abuse, jealousy, sexual issues, delayed childbearing, infidelity, gender roles, two-career families, divorce, remarriage, and the special concerns of stepfamilies (Hernandez, Siegel, & Almeida, 2009).

© David Sipress

66·3 SELF-HELP SUPPORT GROUPS

Self-help support groups are voluntary organizations of individuals who get together on a regular basis to discuss topics of common interest. The groups are not conducted by a professional therapist but by a paraprofessional or a member of the common interest group. *Paraprofessionals* are individuals who have been taught by a professional to provide some mental health services but who do not have *formal* mental health training. Some paraprofessionals may themselves have had a disorder; for example, a chemical dependency counselor may also be a recovering addict. The group leader and members provide support to help individuals with their problems.

Self-help support groups play a key and valuable role in our nation's mental health. A survey in 2002 revealed that for mental health support alone, nearly 7,500 such groups existed in the United States, with more than 1 million members (Goldstrom & others, 2006). In addition to reaching so many people in need of help, these groups are important because they use community resources and are relatively inexpensive. They also serve people who are less likely to receive help otherwise, such as those with less education and fewer financial resources.

Self-help support groups provide members with a sympathetic audience for confession, sharing, and emotional release. The social support, role modeling, and sharing of concrete strategies for solving problems that u nfold in self-help groups add to their effectiveness. A woman who has been raped might not believe a therapist who tells her that, with time, she will put the pieces of her shattered life back together. The same message from another rape survivor—someone who has had to work through the same feelings of rage, fear, and violation—might be more believable.

Alcoholics Anonymous (AA), founded in 1935 by a reformed alcoholic and a physician, is one of the best-known self-help groups. Mental health professionals often recommend AA for their clients struggling with alcoholism (Kaskutas & others, 2009; Kelly & others, 2010; Slaymaker & Sheehan, 2008). A research review revealed that some studies show a positive effect for AA but others do not (Kaskutas, 2009).

Another self-help organization is Compeer, which matches community volunteers in supportive friendship relationships with children and adults receiving mental health treatment (McCorkle & others, 2008). In some cases, both partners in a Compeer relationship may have psychological disorders. There are myriad other self-help groups, such as lesbian and gay support groups, cocaine abuse support groups, Weight Watchers and TOPS (Take Off Pounds Sensibly), child abuse support groups, and many medical (heart disease, cancer) support groups.

For individuals who tend to cope by seeking information and affiliation with similar peers, self-help support groups can reduce stress and promote adjustment. However, as with any group therapy, there is a possibility that negative emotions will spread through the group, especially if the members face circumstances that deteriorate over time, as terminal cancer patients do. Group leaders who are sensitive to the spread of negative emotions can minimize such effects.

A multitude of online support groups has also emerged (Andersson & others, 2006; Davison, Pennebaker, & Dickerson, 2000). Many individuals feel more comfortable sharing their intimate life experiences with a group of people they cannot actually see.

"We're organizing a tantrum support group."

© Randy Glasbergen

Community mental health counselors can serve as a lifeline to many local citizens.

Although it may seem as if an online support group exists for just about every problem imaginable, that is not necessarily the case. Research has shown that an online support group is more likely to emerge for problems that are potentially stigmatizing (such as depression and AIDS) and for problems that are more likely to be suffered by women than men (such as breast cancer) (Davison, Pennebaker, & Dickerson, 2000; Thaxton, Emshoff, & Guessous, 2005; Ussher & others, 2006).

Despite their benefits, online support groups can be problematic. In the absence of guidance from a trained professional, group members may lack the expertise and knowledge to provide optimal advice. The emergence of pro-anorexia (or "pro-ana") websites, which *promote* anorexia, exemplifies the potentially negative side of the online "support" phenomenon (Harshbarger & others, 2009). Technological advances certainly have influenced therapy in some positive ways. However, they also present their own challenges—and even dangers.

66·4 COMMUNITY MENTAL HEALTH

The community mental health movement was born in the 1960s as society's attitude toward people with psychological disorders began to change. The deplorable conditions of some psychiatric facilities at the time were one catalyst for the movement. Advocates of community mental health maintained that individuals with psychological disorders ought to remain within society and with their families rather than being locked away in institutions; the troubled individuals should receive treatment in community mental health centers. This movement also reflected economic concerns, as it was thought that institutionalizing people was certainly more expensive than treating them in the community.

With the passage of the Community Mental Health Act of 1963, large numbers of individuals with psychological disorders were transferred from mental institutions to community-based facilities, a process called *deinstitutionalization.* Although at least partially motivated by a desire to treat individuals with psychological disorders more effectively and humanely, deinstitutionalization has been implicated in rising rates of homelessness. The success of community mental health services depends on the resources and commitment of the communities in which they occur.

Community mental health involves training teachers, ministers, family physicians, nurses, and others who directly interact with community members to offer lay counseling and workshops. Clients receive help in areas ranging from coping with stress to reducing their drug use to developing assertiveness (Moritsugu, Wong, & Duffy, 2010). Advocates and providers of community mental health believe that the best way to treat a psychological disorder is to prevent it from happening in the first place (Shinn & Thaden, 2010).

An explicit goal of community mental health is to help people who are disenfranchised from society, such as those living in poverty, to lead happier, more productive lives (L. Jackson & others, 2009). A key concept involved in this effort is empowerment—assisting individuals to develop the skills they need to control their own lives. Importantly, all of these programs may rely on financial support from local, state, and federal governments.

66·5 CULTURAL PERSPECTIVES

The psychotherapies discussed earlier—psychodynamic, humanistic, behavior, and cognitive—focus mainly on the individual. This focus is compatible with the needs of many people in Western cultures such as the United States, where the emphasis is on the individual rather than the group (family, community, or ethnic group). However, these psychotherapies may not be as effective with people who live in cultures that place more importance on the group—called *collectivistic cultures.* Some psychologists argue that family therapy is likely to be more effective with people in cultures that place a high value on the family, such as Latino and Asian cultures (Guo, 2005).

Ethnicity

Many ethnic minority individuals prefer discussing problems with parents, friends, and relatives rather than mental health professionals (Sue, Sue, & Sue, 2010). Might therapy progress best, then, when the therapist and the client are from the same ethnic background? Researchers have found that when there is an ethnic match between the therapist and the client and when ethnic-specific services are provided, clients are less likely to drop out of therapy early and in many cases have better treatment outcomes (Jackson & Greene, 2000). Ethnic-specific services include culturally appropriate greetings and arrangements (for example, serving tea rather than coffee to Chinese American clients), providing flexible hours for treatment, and employing a bicultural/bilingual staff (Nystul, 1999).

Nonetheless, therapy can still be effective when the therapist and client are from different ethnic backgrounds if the therapist has excellent clinical skills and is culturally sensitive (Akhtar, 2006). Culturally skilled psychotherapists have good knowledge of their clients' cultural groups, understand sociopolitical influences, and have competence in working with culturally diverse groups (Austad, 2009). Would you be comfortable sharing with a therapist who is different from you in terms of ethnic background? Gender? Religion?

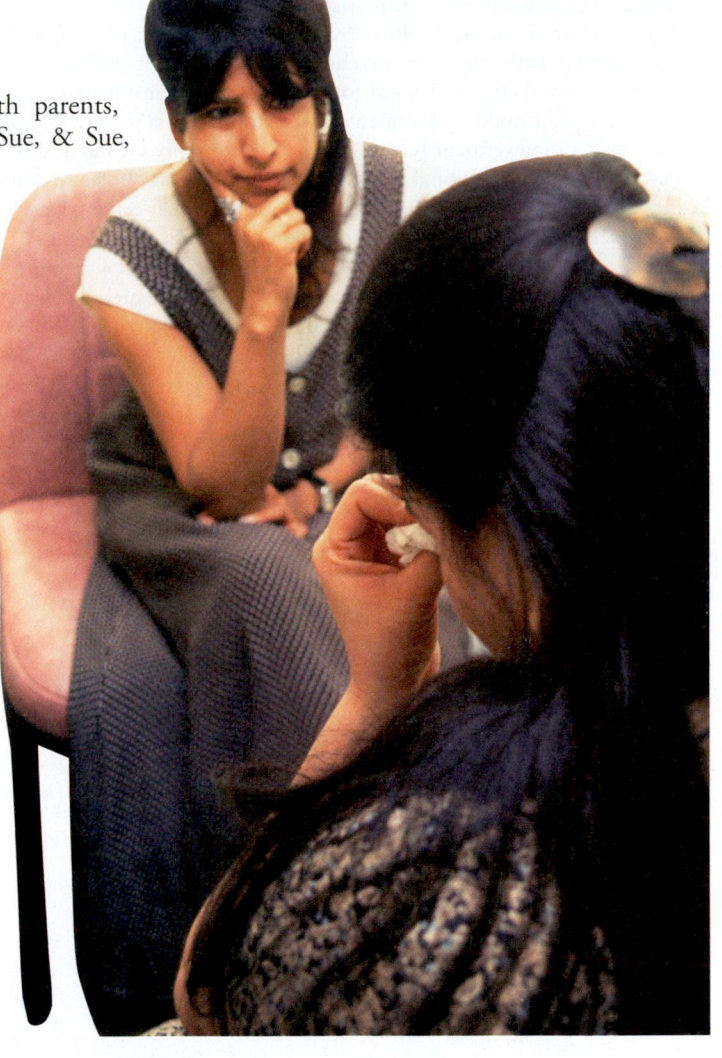

Gender

One byproduct of changing gender roles for women and men is reevaluation of the goal of psychotherapy (Gilbert & Kearney, 2006; Nolen-Hoeksema, 2011). Traditionally, therapy has focused on enhancing self-reliance and independence. However, this goal may reflect gender role expectations (as discussed in Module 39) for men more than for women. Thus, some psychologists argue that the therapeutic goal should reflect the client's life circumstances, as well as establish a balance between independence and relatedness to others (Notman & Nadelson, 2002).

Feminist therapists believe that traditional psychotherapy continues to carry considerable gender bias and has not adequately addressed the specific concerns of women. Thus, several alternative therapies have arisen that aim to help the client break free from traditional gender roles and stereotypes. In terms of improving the client's life, the goals of feminist therapists are no different from those of other therapists. However, feminist therapists maintain that the client's improvement depends in part on understanding how the nature of women's roles in U.S. society can contribute to the development of a psychological disorder. In other words, feminist therapists believe that women must become alert to the possibility of bias and discrimination in their own life in order to achieve their mental health goals (Herlihy & McCollum, 2007).

SUMMARY

Group therapies emphasize that relationships can hold the key to successful therapy. Family therapy is group therapy with family members. Four widely used family therapy techniques are validation, reframing, structural change, and detriangulation. Couples therapy is group therapy with married or unmarried couples whose major problem is within their relationship.

KEY TERMS

group therapy   611
family therapy   612

couples therapy   612

Self-help support groups are voluntary organizations of individuals who get together on a regular basis to discuss topics of common interest. They are conducted without a professional therapist.

The community mental health movement was born out of the belief that individuals suffering from psychological disorders should not be locked away from their families and communities. The deinstitutionalization that resulted from the movement caused the homeless population to rise, however. Empowerment is often a goal of community mental health.

Psychotherapies' traditional focus on the individual may be successful in individualistic Western cultures. However, individual-centered psychotherapies may not work as well in collectivistic cultures. Therapy is often more effective when there is an ethnic match between the therapist and the client, although culturally sensitive therapy can be provided by a therapist with a different background than the client's.

Psychotherapies' emphasis on independence and self-reliance may be problematic for the many women who place a strong emphasis on connectedness in relationships. To address that problem, feminist therapies have emerged.

TEST YOURSELF

1. Why might group therapy be more successful than individual therapy?
2. What are four common family therapy techniques? Briefly describe each.
3. What social and economic forces drove the community mental health movement?

APPLY YOUR KNOWLEDGE

1. For which kinds of problems would you be most likely to choose one of the sociocultural approaches to therapy? Which method would you choose? Do some research and see whether you can find a local group or therapist who would be helpful to someone with these kinds of problems. Where would you turn if an appropriate resource were not available in your area?
2. Search for information about marriage and family counselors. What type of training must a counselor go through to be certified to do marriage and family counseling? How does this training differ from that of a clinical counselor?

Therapies and Health and Wellness

Therapy is generally aimed at relieving psychological symptoms. A therapy is considered effective if it frees a person from the negative effects of psychological disorders. Does therapy have larger implications related to a person's psychological wellness and even physical health? Researchers have examined this interesting question in a variety of ways.

For example, people who learn that they have cancer are undoubtedly under stress. Might psychotherapeutic help aimed at reducing this stress improve patients' ability to cope with the disease? New research is indicating that therapy is having such a positive effect. One study revealed that group-based cognitive therapy that focused on improving prostate cancer patients' stress management skills was effective in improving their quality of life (Penedo & others, 2006). Another study found that individual cognitive-behavior therapy reduced symptom severity in cancer patients undergoing chemotherapy (Sikorskii & others, 2006).

As well, psychotherapy directed at relieving psychological disorders such as depression can have important benefits for physical health. Depression is associated with coronary heart disease, for example (Linke & others, 2009). Psychotherapy that reduces depression is likely, then, to reduce the risk of heart disease (K. W. Davidson & others, 2006). A research review also showed evidence of positive effects of psychotherapy on health behavior and physical illness, including habits and ailments such as smoking, chronic pain, chronic fatigue syndrome, and asthma (Eells, 2000).

Psychotherapy might also be a way to *prevent* psychological and physical problems. One study demonstrated the benefits of incorporating therapy into physical healthcare (Smit & others, 2006). Individuals waiting to see their primary healthcare provider received either physical health treatment as usual or that same treatment plus brief psychotherapy (a simple version of minimal contact cognitive-behavior therapy). The brief psychotherapy included a self-help manual, instructions in mood management, and six short telephone conversations with a prevention worker. The overall rate of depression was lowered significantly in the psychotherapy group, and this difference was cost effective. That is, the use of brief psychotherapy as a part of regular physical checkups was both psychologically and economically advantageous.

Finally, although typically targeted at relieving distressing symptoms, might psychotherapy enhance psychological well-being? This question is important because the absence of psychological symptoms (the goal of most psychotherapy) is not the same thing as the presence of psychological wellness. Just as an individual who is without serious physical illness is not necessarily at the height of physical health, a person who is relatively free of psychological symptoms still might not show the qualities we associate with psychological thriving. Studies have found that a lack of psychological wellness may predispose individuals to relapse or make them vulnerable to problems (Ryff & Singer, 1998; Ryff, Singer, & Love, 2004; Thunedborg, Black, & Bech, 1995). Research has demonstrated that

Psychotherapy can improve cancer patients' ability to cope with the disease.

individuals who show not only a decrease in symptoms but also an increase in well-being are less prone to relapse (Fava, 2006; Ruini & Fava, 2004).

Recently, therapists have developed a new type of treatment, aimed at enhancing well-being. **Well-being therapy (WBT)** is a short-term, problem-focused, directive therapy that encourages clients to accentuate the positive (Fava, 2006; Ruini & Fava, 2009). The first step in WBT is recognizing the positive in one's life when it happens. The initial WBT homework assignment asks clients to monitor their own happiness levels and keep track of moments of well-being. Clients are encouraged to note even small pleasures in their lives—a beautiful spring day, a relaxing chat with a friend, the great taste of morning coffee. Clients then identify thoughts and feelings that are related to the premature ending of these moments. WBT is about learning to notice and savor positive experiences and coming up with ways to promote and celebrate life's good moments. WBT is effective in enhancing well-being, and it may also allow individuals to enjoy sustained recovery from mental disorders (Fava, Ruini, & Belaise, 2007; Ruini & Fava, 2009; Ruini & others, 2006).

Life is complicated and filled with potential pitfalls. We all need help from time to time, and therapy is one way to get that help. Through therapy we can improve ourselves—physically and psychologically—to become the best person we can be. Like all human relationships, a therapeutic relationship is complex and challenging but potentially rewarding, making positive change possible for an individual through a meaningful association with another (Joseph & Linley, 2004).

SUMMARY

Psychotherapy has been shown to help individuals cope with serious physical diseases. Psychotherapy can also aid individuals by alleviating physical symptoms directly or by reducing psychological problems, such as depression, that are related to physical illness. Research has shown moreover that brief psychotherapy may be a cost-effective way to *prevent* serious psychological disorders.

Psychotherapy aims not only at reducing the presence of psychological illness but also at enhancing psychological wellness and personal growth. Individuals who gain in wellness are less likely to fall prey to recurrent psychological distress. Interventions such as well-being therapy have been designed to promote wellness itself.

KEY TERMS

well-being therapy (WBT)   618

TEST YOURSELF

1. Discuss specific research findings about whether psychotherapy can improve a person's ability to cope with the effects of a disease such as cancer.

2. For what health-related behavior and chronic ailments is psychotherapy helpful, according to a research review?

3. What is well-being therapy, and what steps does it involve on the client's part?

Health Psychology
Does It Take a Village to Lose Weight?

Troubled by the growing problem of childhood obesity, Mayor Margaret Finlay of Duarte, California, issued a challenge in February 2010 for city residents to start losing weight (Sand, 2010). Increasingly, U.S. community leaders are recognizing that the obesity epidemic requires immediate action. Their counterparts around the world share these concerns, as the problem of obesity has reached global proportions.

Some localities have formed community weight-loss clubs through churches and other organizations. In Ghent, Belgium, the city council declared their community officially vegetarian (at least one day a week) in order to reduce obesity as well as the city's environmental footprint (Mason, 2009). Advocates for change are charging that by making life too easy and far too accommodating to cars and drivers, urban designers have created an *obesogenic* (obesity-promoting) environment—a context where it is quite challenging for people to engage in healthy activities (Henderson, 2008). Countries such as the Netherlands and Denmark have adopted urban planning strategies that promote walking and biking and discourage car use. As a result, in the Netherlands, 60 percent of all journeys taken by people over age 60 are by bicycle (Henderson, 2008).

Embracing a healthy lifestyle is a choice that is made not only by individuals but sometimes by whole communities. Clearly, our physical health is influenced by our contexts, behaviors, motivations, thoughts, and feelings—in other words, by factors at the very heart of the science of psychology. ●

Health Psychology and Making Positive Life Changes

67-1 HEALTH PSYCHOLOGY AND BEHAVIORAL MEDICINE

● **health psychology** A subfield of psychology that emphasizes psychology's role in establishing and maintaining health and preventing and treating illness.

● **behavioral medicine** An interdisciplinary field that focuses on developing and integrating behavioral and biomedical knowledge to promote health and reduce illness; overlaps with health psychology.

Health psychology emphasizes psychology's role in establishing and maintaining health and preventing and treating illness. This subfield of psychology reflects the belief that lifestyle choices, behaviors, and psychological characteristics can play important roles in health (Suls, Davidson, & Kaplan, 2010; Taylor, 2011). A related discipline, **behavioral medicine,** is an interdisciplinary field that focuses on developing and integrating behavioral and biomedical knowledge to promote health and reduce illness. The concerns of health psychology and behavioral medicine overlap: Health psychology primarily focuses on behavioral, social, and cognitive influences (Brannon & Feist, 2010; Norris & others, 2009), whereas behavioral medicine centers on behavioral, social, and biomedical factors (Mann & others, 2009).

Health psychology and behavioral medicine both inform two related fields: health promotion and public health. *Health promotion* involves helping people change their lifestyle to optimize health and assisting them in achieving balance in physical, emotional, social, spiritual, and intellectual health and wellness. *Public health* is concerned with studying health and disease in large populations to guide policymakers. Public health experts identify public health concerns, set priorities, and design interventions for health promotion. An important goal of public health is to ensure that all populations have access to cost-effective healthcare and health promotion services. If you have seen a "Click It or Ticket" sign on the highway or one of thetruth.com's anti-smoking ads on TV, you have a good feel for what health promotion and public health are all about.

The Biopsychosocial Model

The interests of health psychologists and behavioral medicine researchers are broad (Baker & others, 2009; Gurung, 2010). The biopsychosocial model we examined in Module 58 in the context of psychological disorders applies to health psychology as well, because health psychology integrates biological, psychological, and social factors in health (Mihashi & others, 2009).

For example, stress is a focal point of study across the broad field of psychology. Study of the brain and behavior, for instance, acknowledges the impact of stress on the autonomic nervous system. Furthermore, an individual's state of consciousness, as well as the particular ways in which that person thinks about events, can influence the experience of stress. Stressful events also affect our emotions, which are themselves psychological and physical events. Aspects of our personalities, too, may be associated with stress and can influence our health. Finally, social contexts, relationships, and work experiences can shape both an individual's experience of stress and his or her ability to cope with it.

The "Click It or Ticket" program, publicizing seatbelt use, reflects the efforts of individuals working in the related fields of health promotion and health psychology.

The Relationship Between Mind and Body

From the biopsychosocial perspective, the many diverse aspects of the person are strongly intertwined. Our bodies and minds are deeply connected, a link introduced in Module 1.

After suffering a heart attack, one health psychologist ruefully noted that none of his colleagues in the field had thought to ask him whether heart disease was part of his family history, ignoring the obvious question that a medical doctor would ask first. Although the mind is responsible for much of what happens in the body, it is not the only factor. Even as we consider the many ways that psychological processes contribute to health and disease, we must understand that sometimes illness happens for other reasons—affecting even those who have led healthy lives.

Although it might be more exciting to think about ways the mind may influence health, it is important to appreciate that the body may influence the mind as well. That is, how we feel physically may have implications for how we think. Health psychology and behavioral medicine are concerned not only with how psychological states influence health, but also with how health and illness may influence the person's psychological experience, including cognitive abilities, stress, and coping (Holsboer & Ising, 2010; Mellon & others, 2009). For instance, one of the first symptoms experienced by someone with AIDS may be cognitive changes that are not immediately recognized as part of the disease. A person who is feeling psychologically run-down may not realize that the level of fatigue is in fact the beginning stage of an illness. In turn, being physically healthy can be a source of psychological wellness.

67·2 MAKING POSITIVE LIFE CHANGES

One of health psychology's missions is to help individuals identify and implement ways they can effectively change their behaviors for the better (Norris & others, 2009; Taylor, 2011). **Health behaviors**—practices that have an impact on physical well-being—include adopting a healthy approach to stress, exercising, eating right, brushing one's teeth, performing breast and testicular exams, not smoking, drinking in moderation (or not at all), and practicing safe sex. Before exploring what health psychologists have learned about the best ways to make healthy behavioral changes, we focus on the process of change itself.

● **health behaviors** Practices that have an impact on physical well-being, such as adopting a healthy approach to stress, exercising, eating right, brushing one's teeth, performing breast and testicular exams, not smoking, drinking in moderation (or not at all), and practicing safe sex.

Theoretical Models of Change

In many instances, changing behaviors begins by changing attitudes. Psychologists have sought to understand specifically how changing attitudes can lead to behavioral changes.

A number of theoretical models have addressed the factors that probably play a role in healthy behavior changes. For example, the **theory of reasoned action** suggests that effective change requires individuals to have specific intentions about their behaviors, as well as positive attitudes about a new behavior, and to perceive that their social group looks favorably on the new behavior as well (Ajzen & Albarracin, 2007; Ajzen & Fishbein, 1980, 2005; Fishbein & Ajzen, 2010). If you smoke and want to quit smoking, you will be more successful if you devise an explicit intention of quitting, feel good about it, and believe that your friends support you. Icek Ajzen (pronounced "I-zen") modified the theory of reasoned action to include the fact that not all of our behaviors are under our control. The **theory of planned behavior** includes the basic ideas of the theory of reasoned action but adds the person's perceptions of control over the outcome (Ajzen, 2002). As we will see later, perceiving that one has control can have important implications for a number of life domains.

● **theory of reasoned action** Theoretical model stating that effective change requires individuals to have specific intentions about their behaviors, as well as positive attitudes about a new behavior, and to perceive that their social group looks favorably on the new behavior as well.

● **theory of planned behavior** Theoretical model that includes the basic ideas of the theory of reasoned action but adds the person's perceptions of control over the outcome.

The theory of reasoned action and its extension, the theory of planned behavior, have accurately predicted whether individuals successfully engage in healthy behaviors (Ajzen & Manstead, 2007), including cancer screening (Ross & others, 2007), HIV prevention (Kalichman, 2007), prevention of smoking and marijuana use in youth (Guo & others, 2007; Lac & others, 2009), and exercise (B. H. Park & others, 2009). Other theories have stressed the importance of awareness of the health threats posed by potentially harmful behaviors such as smoking and unprotected sex (Floyd, Prentice-Dunn, &

Rogers, 2000; Fry & Prentice-Dunn, 2006). Social cognitive theories emphasize the crucial role of beliefs about one's ability to make healthy changes, as well as of the individual's knowledge and skills (Bandura, 2008, 2009, 2010b). All theoretical models of health-related behavioral changes make predictions about the type of intervention that should be most successful in producing durable change.

The Stages of Change Model

● **stages of change model** Theoretical model describing a five-step process by which individuals give up bad habits and adopt healthier lifestyles.

The **stages of change model** describes the process by which individuals give up bad habits and adopt healthier lifestyles. The model breaks down behavioral changes into five steps, recognizing that real change does not occur overnight with one monumental decision (Prochaska, DiClemente, & Norcross, 1992; Prochaska, Norcross, & DiClemente, 1994) (Figure 67.1). Rather, change occurs in progressive stages, each characterized by particular issues and challenges. Those stages are

- Precontemplation
- Contemplation
- Preparation/Determination
- Action/Willpower
- Maintenance

PRECONTEMPLATION

The *precontemplation stage* occurs when individuals are not yet genuinely thinking about changing. They may not even be aware that they have a problem behavior. Individuals who drink to excess but are not aware that their drinking is affecting their work may be in this precontemplation phase. At this stage, raising one's consciousness about the problem is crucial.

A woman who smokes may find her consciousness raised by the experience of becoming pregnant. A man who is stopped for drunk driving may be forced to take a good look at his drinking. Similarly, overweight individuals may not recognize

FIGURE 67.1 Stages of Change Model Applied to Losing Weight The stages of change model has been applied to many different health behaviors, including losing weight.

Stage	Description	Example
Precontemplation **1**	Individuals are not yet ready to think about changing and may not be aware that they have a problem that needs to be changed.	Overweight individuals are not aware that they have a weight problem.
Contemplation **2**	Individuals acknowledge that they have a problem but may not yet be ready to change.	Overweight individuals know they have a weight problem but aren't yet sure they want to commit to losing weight.
Preparation/ Determination **3**	Individuals are preparing to take action.	Overweight individuals explore options they can pursue in losing weight.
Action/Willpower **4**	Individuals commit to making a behavioral change and enact a plan.	Overweight individuals begin a diet and start an exercise program.
Maintenance **5**	Individuals are successful in continuing their behavior change over time.	Overweight individuals are able to stick with their diet and exercise regimens for 6 months.

their problem until they see photos of themselves taken at a family reunion—or until they learn that an order of a McDonald's Big Mac, large fries, and large chocolate shake amounts to over 2,000 calories, the recommended adult caloric intake for an entire day.

Consciousness-raising sometimes comes from the media. If you have seen Morgan Spurlock's documentary film *Super Size Me,* you know how harmful fast food can be to your health. Spurlock ate every meal at McDonald's for a month. By the end of filming he felt ill, had gained weight (he jumped from 185 to 210 pounds), and could not wait for the experience to end. His doctors were appalled by his increasingly fatty liver, and his (vegan) girlfriend noted the decline in his sexual energy.

It is common for people in the precontemplation phase to deny that their current pattern of behavior is a problem. The individual might defend such behaviors, claiming that "I don't drink/smoke/eat that much." Those who are overweight may discover that they do eat "that much" when they start keeping track of calories.

CONTEMPLATION

In the *contemplation stage,* people acknowledge the problem but may not be ready to commit to change. As the name of the stage suggests, at this point individuals are actively thinking about change. They might engage in a reevaluation of themselves and the place of this behavior in their life. They understandably may have mixed feelings about giving up a bad habit. For example, how will they deal with missing their friends on a smoke break? Or going out drinking? Or packing a healthy lunch instead of heading to the drive-thru? They may weigh the short-term gains of the harmful behavior against the long-term benefits of changing. As we considered in Module 19, future rewards can be difficult to pursue when immediate pleasures beckon. Sure, it would be nice to be thinner, but losing weight is going to take time, and that hot fudge sundae is right there, looking very delicious. Nevertheless, in the contemplation phase, individuals may begin to separate themselves, mentally, from the typical overeater or smoker and start to define themselves as someone who is ready to change.

PREPARATION/DETERMINATION

At the *preparation/determination stage,* people are getting ready to take action. At this point, self-belief and especially beliefs about one's ability to "see it through" are very important. A key consideration in this stage is whether individuals truly feel they are ready to change. In a study of New Year's resolutions, readiness to change predicted success at achieving those resolutions (Norcross, Mrykalo, & Blagys, 2002).

During this stage, individuals start thinking concretely about how they might take on their new challenge. For example, they explore options of the best ways to quit smoking or drinking or to start an exercise program. Some smokers might consider trying a nicotine patch or participating in a support group for people trying to quit. Individuals who are seeking to lose weight might think about joining a gym to get regular exercise or setting the alarm clock for a 6 A.M. run.

ACTION/WILLPOWER

At the *action/willpower stage,* individuals commit to making a real behavioral change and enact an effective plan. An important challenge at this stage is to find ways to support the new, healthy behavior pattern. One approach is to find reinforcements or rewards for the new behavior. Individuals who have quit smoking might focus on how much better food tastes after they have given up cigarettes. Successful dieters might treat themselves to a shopping run to buy new, smaller-size clothes. Acknowledging, enjoying, and celebrating accomplishments can motivate consistent behavior.

Another source of support for new behaviors is the individual's social network (Taylor, 2011). Friends, family, and even members of a support group can help through their encouraging words and supportive behaviors. Members of a family might all quit smoking at the same time or join the individual in physical activities or healthier eating.

"Every year it's the same thing. I resolve to lose a ton, and you say you're going to control your anger."

© Ralph Hagen. www.CartoonStock.com.

Finally, people may focus on alternative behaviors that replace the unhealthy ones. Perhaps, instead of bar hopping, they join a group dedicated to activities not associated with drinking alcohol, such as a dance club or community theater group. In other words, effective change also means avoiding tempting situations.

MAINTENANCE

In the *maintenance stage*, individuals successfully avoid temptation and consistently pursue healthy behaviors. They may become skilled at anticipating tempting situations and avoid them or actively prepare for them. If smokers seeking to kick the habit know that they always enjoy a cigarette after a big meal out with friends, they might mentally prepare themselves for that temptation before going out. Successful dieters might post a consciousness-raising photograph on the refrigerator.

At some point, people in maintenance may find that actively fighting the urge to indulge in unhealthy behaviors is no longer necessary. *Transcendence* means that they are no longer consciously engaged in maintaining their healthy lifestyle; rather, the lifestyle has become a part of who they are. They are now nonsmokers, healthy eaters, or committed runners.

RELAPSE

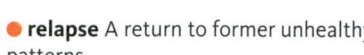

● **relapse** A return to former unhealthy patterns.

One challenge during the maintenance stage is to avoid **relapse,** a return to the former unhealthy patterns. Contrary to popular belief, relapse is a common aspect of change. That is, for most people, real change takes many attempts. Relapse can be discouraging and can lead a person to feel like a failure. However, the *majority* of people who eventually do change do not succeed on the first try. Rather, they try and fail and try again, cycling through the five stages several times before achieving a stable healthy lifestyle. Consequently, individuals who are experts in health behavior change consider relapse to be normal (Prochaska & Norcross, 2010; Prochaska, Norcross, & DiClemente, 1994).

If you have ever tried to adopt a healthier lifestyle by dieting, starting an exercise program, or quitting smoking, you might know how bad you feel when you experience relapse. One slip, however, does not mean you will never reach your goal. Rather, when a slipup occurs, you have an opportunity to learn, to think about what led to the relapse, and to devise a strategy for preventing it in the future. Successful dieters, for example, do not let one lapse ruin the week. Individuals who successfully keep weight off are those who do not get too down on themselves when they relapse (Phelan & others, 2003).

EVALUATION OF THE STAGES OF CHANGE MODEL

The stages of change model has been applied successfully to a broad range of behaviors. These include cigarette smoking (C. L. Kohler & others, 2008; Schumann & others, 2006), exercise (Lippke & Plotnikoff, 2006), safe-sex practices (Arden & Armitage, 2008; Naar-King & others, 2006), marijuana use in teenagers (Walker & others, 2006), substance abuse more broadly (DiClemente, 2006; Migneault, Adams, & Read, 2005), and weight loss (MacQueen, Brynes, & Frost, 2002).

Although the stages of change model has proved to be relevant to a variety of behaviors, the model still has its critics (Brug & others, 2004; Joseph, Breslin, & Skinner, 1999). Some have questioned whether the stages are mutually exclusive and whether individuals move from one stage to another sequentially as has been proposed (Littrell & Girvin, 2002). For example, some individuals might feel themselves to be in both action/willpower and maintenance at the same time or may move from contemplation back to precontemplation. Critics of the model also point out that it refers more to attitudes that change than to behaviors (West, 2005). The relationship between attitudes and behavior can be quite complex. Furthermore, all of the stages might be understood as promoting readiness to change rather than change itself (West, 2005).

BILL PROUD

"No, honestly, it's just diet and exercise."

© Bill Proud. www.CartoonStock.com.

Nevertheless, recent evidence suggests that the stages of change model does a good job of capturing the ways that individuals make positive life changes (Lippke & others, 2009; Schuz & others, 2009). Experts have argued that the stages of change model can be a tool for therapists who are trying to help clients institute healthy behavior patterns. Sometimes, sharing the model with individuals who are trying to change provides them with a useful language to use in understanding the change process, to reduce uncertainty, and to develop realistic expectations for the difficult journey ahead (Hodgins, 2005; Schuz & others, 2009).

SUMMARY

Health psychology is a multidimensional field that emphasizes biological, psychological, and social factors in human health. Closely aligned with health psychology is behavioral medicine, which combines medical and behavioral knowledge to reduce illness and promote health. Related fields are health promotion, which is concerned with identifying ways to foster healthy behaviors, and public health, which focuses on understanding disease at the population level and directing public policy.

Health psychology and behavioral medicine demonstrate the biopsychosocial model by examining the interaction of biological, psychological, and social variables as they relate to health and illness. Stress is an example of a biological, psychological, and social construct.

Health psychology and behavioral medicine bring the relationship of the mind and body to the forefront. These approaches examine the reciprocal relationships between the mind and body: how the body is influenced by psychological states and how mental life is influenced by physical health.

The theory of reasoned action suggests that we can make changes by devising specific intentions for behavioral change. We are more likely to follow through on our intentions if we feel good about the change and if we feel that others around us also support the change. The theory of planned behavior incorporates these factors as well as our perceptions of control over the behavior.

The stages of change model posits that personal change occurs in a series of five steps: precontemplation, contemplation, preparation/determination, action/willpower, and maintenance. Each stage has its own challenges. Relapse is a natural part of the journey toward change.

KEY TERMS

health psychology 622
behavioral medicine 622
health behaviors 623
theory of reasoned action 623

theory of planned behavior 623
stages of change model 624
relapse 626

TEST YOURSELF

1. What factors does the field of health psychology emphasize as keys to good health?

2. With what is the field of health promotion concerned?

3. Name three societal issues you might be concerned with if you worked in the field of public health.

4. How does the theory of planned behavior expand upon, or extend, the theory of reasoned action?

5. Name and briefly describe the five stages of the stages of change model.

6. What positive advice would you give to someone who experiences relapse when dieting or trying to quit smoking?

APPLY YOUR KNOWLEDGE

1. Interview someone you know who has successfully lost weight, quit smoking, or started an exercise program. Ask the person about his or her experience of each of the stages of change. Does the theory fit your friend's experience? Why or why not?

2. Select one bad habit you would like to break for one week—for example, smoking, eating sugary foods, or putting off getting aerobic exercise. Keep a journal of your progress each day in avoiding the bad habit. How easy or difficult did you find this little test in healthy life change?

Resources for Effective Life Change

Making positive changes to promote health can be very challenging. Fortunately, we all have various psychological, social, and cultural resources and tools at our disposal to help us in the journey to a healthier lifestyle. In this section we consider some of the tools that can help us achieve effective change and, ultimately, a healthier life.

68-1 MOTIVATION

Motivation refers to the "why" of behavior. Motivational tools for self-change involve changing for the right reasons. Change is most effective when you are doing it for you—because you want to. An analysis of intervention programs aimed at reducing childhood and adolescent obesity found that a strong predictor of program success (that is, weight loss in the children and adolescents) was whether the participants had been required to join the program or had done so voluntarily (Stice, Shaw, & Marti, 2006). Those who had joined voluntarily were more likely to lose weight than their counterparts who had been required to join.

Self-determination theory distinguishes between intrinsic motivation (doing something because you want to) and extrinsic motivation (doing something for external rewards). Research has shown that creating a context in which people feel more in control, more autonomous, and more competent is associated with enhanced outcomes for a broad array of health behaviors, including controlling diabetes through diet (Julien, Senecal, & Guay, 2009), quitting smoking (Gwaltney & others, 2009), and getting regular physical exercise (Hurkmans & others, 2010; Russell & Bray, 2010). Indeed, individuals are more likely to succeed in their New Year's resolutions if they approach them with a sense of both self-efficacy and autonomy—the latter meaning that they have chosen on their own to make a life change (Koestner & others, 2006).

● **implementation intentions** Specific strategies for dealing with the challenges of making a life change.

Planning and goal setting are also crucial to making effective change. Researchers have found that individuals who are able to come up with specific strategies, or **implementation intentions,** for dealing with the challenges of making a life change are more successful than others at negotiating the road to change (Armitage, 2006; Gallo & others, 2009; Tam, Bagozzi, & Spanjol, 2010). Setting short-term, achievable goals also allows individuals to experience the emotional payoff of small successes along the way to self-change (R. F. Kushner, 2007). The dieter who can take her skinny jeans out of the closet and zip them up is likely to feel a sense of accomplishment. The novice exerciser who catches a glimpse of his new biceps in the mirror gets a mood boost. These feelings of satisfaction can help to motivate continued effort toward achieving important health goals (Finch & others, 2005).

Enjoying the payoffs of our efforts to change also means that we must monitor our goal progress (Stadler, Oettingen, & Gollwitzer, 2010). As those who have watched *The Biggest Loser* will attest,

Children and adolescents who voluntarily join a weight-loss program are more likely to shed pounds than those who are required to join.

Health Psychology and Motivation: Why Do We Do the Things We Shouldn't Do?

Motivation can be a powerful force for positive life change. What about behaviors that are not so positive, however, such as drinking too much, smoking, and having unsafe sex? Are these behaviors motivated as well? Health psychologists recognize that probing the motives that guide even unhealthy behavior is important for understanding, changing, and preventing these behaviors.

Some health psychologists have been especially interested in analyzing why individuals consume alcohol. Lynne Cooper and her colleagues have identified three motivations for drinking (Cooper, 1994; Cooper & others, 1992):

- *Social motives* include drinking alcohol because it is what your friends do or because you want to be sociable.
- *Coping motives* center on drinking alcohol to help you relax, to deal with stress, or to forget your worries.
- *Enhancement motives* include drinking because it is fun, because you like how it feels, or because it is exciting.

What motives might underlie unhealthy behaviors in your own life?

Research has shown that young adults most commonly drink for social reasons, with enhancement motives coming in a distant second (Kuntsche & others, 2006). Like enhancement motives, coping motives are not as common in young adults. Although all three motives for drinking are related to higher levels of drinking frequency (with enhancement motives being especially linked to drinking for men—Cooper & others, 1992), the motives that drive drinking can have implications for whether the behavior is harmful or harmless. Drinking to cope with life's negative events is typically associated with negative outcomes, such as social and work problems or potential substance abuse.

Research has related drinking motives to difficulties an individual might experience in reducing alcohol consumption. Individuals who drink because of coping or enhancement motives—that is, for internal reasons—are more likely to experience preoccupation with drinking when they try to limit their alcohol consumption (Stewart & Chambers, 2000).

Researchers conclude that motivation is a factor even in behaviors that might seem obviously self-defeating, such as smoking and unsafe sex (Cooper, 2010; Cooper & others, 2006, 2008; Gynther & others, 1999). Although this Intersection has focused primarily on young adults, examining the motives that drive unhealthy behavior patterns can be useful for anyone, at any age or life stage.

Viewing maladaptive behavior from a motivational perspective helps us not only to understand the "why" behind those behaviors but also to think about how we might meet our needs for social interaction, coping, and enhancement without alcohol (or cigarettes or unsafe sex). If you recognize that you drink—and occasionally drink too much—because of a desire for positive social interactions, you might think about ways to enjoy your social network without putting your health at risk.

---

stepping on a scale can be a scary prospect for someone who is trying to lose weight. However, it is important to get feedback on progress in the pursuit of any goal. If an individual finds out that she is falling short, she can try to identify areas that need work. If on the other hand she discovers that she is doing well, it is a potent motivator for future progress.

As we have seen, motivation is instrumental to engaging in healthier behaviors. For further insight into its influence on health, see the Intersection.

68·2 SOCIAL RELATIONSHIPS

One way that social connections make a difference in our lives is through social support. **Social support** is information and feedback from others indicating that one is loved and cared for, esteemed and valued, and included in a network of communication and

● **social support** Information and feedback from others indicating that one is loved and cared for, esteemed and valued, and included in a network of communication and mutual obligation.

Experiencing the emotional payoff of small successes is important in achieving long-term goals. Being able to zip up skinny jeans, for example, gives a dieter a sense of accomplishment.

mutual obligation. Social support has three types of benefits: tangible assistance, information, and emotional support (Taylor, 2011):

- *Tangible assistance:* Family and friends can provide goods and services in stressful circumstances. For example, gifts of food are often given after a death in the family occurs, so that bereaved family members will not have to cook at a time when their energy and motivation are low.

- *Information:* Individuals who provide support can also recommend specific actions and plans to help the person under stress cope more successfully. Friends may notice that a co-worker is overloaded with work and suggest ways for him or her to manage time or to delegate tasks more effectively.

- *Emotional support:* In stressful situations, individuals often suffer emotionally and may develop depression, anxiety, and loss of self-esteem. Friends and family can reassure the person under stress that he or she is valuable and loved. Knowing that others care allows a person to manage stress with greater assurance.

One way that people gain support during difficult times is through *social sharing*—turning to others who act as a sounding board or a willing ear. Individuals who are striving to make healthy life changes might join a group of others who are also struggling with the same issue. Such social sharing can also occur in online support groups.

Getting support from others is important, but *giving* support can have benefits, too. A study of 423 older adult couples who were followed for five years revealed how helping others benefits physical health (S. L. Brown & others, 2003). At the beginning of the study, the couples were asked about the extent to which they had given or received emotional or practical help in the past year. Five years later, those who said they had helped others were half as likely to have died. One possible reason for this finding is that helping others may reduce the output of stress hormones, an effect that improves cardiovascular health and strengthens the immune system (Cacioppo, Berntson, & Aue, 2010; Decety & Cacioppo, 2011; Hawkley & others, 2010; Norman & others, 2010).

68·3 RELIGIOUS FAITH

Religious faith is strongly related to the maintenance of a healthy lifestyle and to good health (Sapp, 2010; Waddell & Jacobs-Lawson, 2010). Many religions frown on excess and promote moderation. Indeed, weekly religious attendance relates to a host of healthy

Both getting and giving support can benefit individuals.

psychological *inquiry*

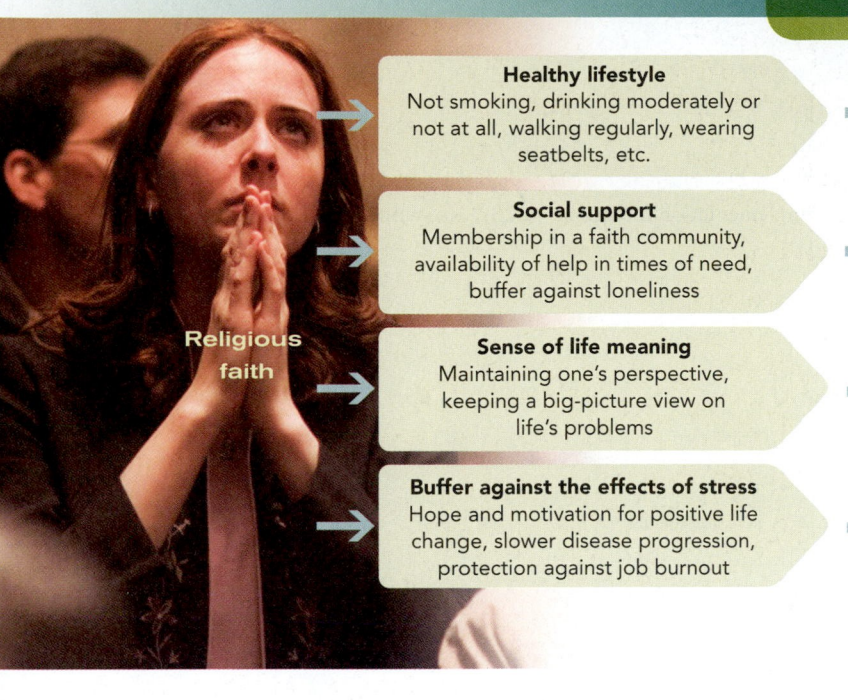

Religious faith

Healthy lifestyle
Not smoking, drinking moderately or not at all, walking regularly, wearing seatbelts, etc.

Social support
Membership in a faith community, availability of help in times of need, buffer against loneliness

Sense of life meaning
Maintaining one's perspective, keeping a big-picture view on life's problems

Buffer against the effects of stress
Hope and motivation for positive life change, slower disease progression, protection against job burnout

Better health

Longer life

Praying for Good Health

This figure presents a model of the relationship between religious faith and health and longevity. Notice that the placement of the boxes and arrows suggests that religious faith has its influence on health through four intervening variables. Answer the questions below:

1. Of the four factors included in this model, which do you think is most important? Why?

2. Give another variable that ought to be added to this model. Where would it be placed?

3. According to this model, religious faith "comes first," and the other four variables are consequences of religious involvement. Do you think this schema is accurate, or would you change the placement of any of the variables? Explain.

4. How might this model be applied to individuals who are not religious at all?

behaviors, including not smoking, taking vitamins, walking regularly, wearing seatbelts, exercising strenuously, sleeping soundly, and drinking moderately or not at all (T. D. Hill & others, 2006). A number of studies have definitively linked religious participation to a longer and healthier life (Campbell, Yoon, & Johnstone, 2010; Hummer & others, 2004; Krause, 2006; McCullough & Willoughby, 2009; McCullough & others, 2000). For example, a recent study revealed that religious affiliation, frequent attendance at religious services, and religious strength and comfort were linked to reduced risk of premature death from any cause (Schnall & others, 2010). The Psychological Inquiry breaks down the various factors that might play a role in the association between religious faith and health.

Religious participation may also benefit health through its relation to social support (George, 2009; Taylor, 2011). Belonging to a faith community may give people access to a warm group of others who are available during times of need. This community is "there" to provide transportation to the doctor, to check in with the individual during hard times, and simply to stand next to the individual during a worship service, as a fellow member of the community. The social connections promoted by religious activity can forestall anxiety and depression and can help to prevent isolation and loneliness (Rosmarin, Krumrei, & Andersson, 2009; Ross & others, 2009a).

Religious faith, and spirituality more generally, may also be important factors in good health because they provide a sense of life meaning and a buffer against the effects of stressful events (Emmons, 2005; C. Park, 2009). Religious thoughts can play a role in maintaining hope and stimulating motivation for positive life changes. For example, studies have shown that some individuals with AIDS who lived much longer than expected had used religion as a coping strategy—specific benefits came from participating in religious activities such as praying and attending church services (Ironson & others, 2001)—and that an increase in spirituality after testing positive for HIV is associated with slower disease progression over four years (Ironson, Stuetzle, & Fletcher, 2006). Faith may also help individuals to avoid burnout at work (Murray-Swank & others, 2006) and to negotiate life's difficulties without feeling overwhelmed (Mascaro

& Rosen, 2006). Belief in the enduring meaningfulness of one's life can help one keep perspective and see life's hassles in the context of the big picture (C. Park, 2009).

In summary, making positive life changes can be complex and challenging. Fortunately, though, we have powerful resources and tools to help us attain a healthier life.

SUMMARY

Motivation is an important part of sustaining behavioral change. Change is more effective when the person does it for intrinsic reasons (because he or she really wants to) rather than extrinsic reasons (to gain rewards). Implementation intentions are the specific ways individuals plan to institute changes successfully.

Social relationships are strongly related to health and survival. Social support refers to the aid provided by others to a person in need. Support can take the form of tangible assistance, information, or emotional support. Social support has been found to have strong relations to functioning and coping with stress.

Religious faith is associated with enhanced health. One reason for this association is that religions often frown on excess and promote healthy behavior. Religious participation also allows individuals to benefit from a social group. Finally, religion provides a meaning system on which to rely in times of difficulty.

KEY TERMS

implementation intentions   628   social support   629

TEST YOURSELF

1. Name three tools or resources on which we can draw in trying to make positive life changes.

2. Discuss the importance of motivation in efforts at self-change.

3. Identify and describe three types of benefits provided by social support.

APPLY YOUR KNOWLEDGE

1. Have you tried to change something in your life because someone else wanted you to? What was the end result of your attempt to change? How did extrinsic versus intrinsic motivation affect your ability or willingness to change?

2. Name five resources or tools you have that can help you live a more positive and healthier lifestyle.

Toward a Healthier Mind (and Body): Controlling Stress

Complete the following sentence: "I wish I could stop_____." If you could change one thing about your behavior, what would you choose? Would the change perhaps have to do with feeling stressed out much of the time? Maybe you wish you could quit worrying so much or stop facing every daily challenge with tension. Let's look at the problems that can arise when you feel chronically stressed and the ways you can better manage your stress.

69·1 STRESS AND ITS STAGES

Stress is an individual's response to environmental *stressors,* the circumstances and events that threaten the person and tax his or her coping abilities. We often think of negative life events as stressful, but positive occasions—such as graduating from college, getting married, and starting a new job—can also produce stress if these events present significant changes. Hans Selye (1974, 1983), the founder of stress research, focused on the physical response to stressors, especially the wear and tear on the body due to the demands placed on it. After observing patients with different problems—the death of someone close, loss of income, arrest for embezzlement—Selye concluded that any number of environmental events or stimuli would produce the same stress symptoms: loss of appetite, muscular weakness, and decreased interest in the world.

General adaptation syndrome (GAS) is Selye's term for the common effects on the body when stressful demands are placed on it (Figure 69.1). The GAS consists of three stages: alarm, resistance, and exhaustion. Selye's model is especially useful in helping us understand the link between stress and health.

The body's first reaction to a stressor, in the *alarm stage,* is a temporary state of shock during which resistance to illness and stress falls below normal limits. In trying to cope with the initial effects of stress, the body quickly releases hormones that, in a short time, adversely affect the functioning of the immune system, our body's network of natural defenses. During this time the individual is prone to infections from illness and injury.

In the *resistance stage* of Selye's general adaptation syndrome, a number of glands throughout the body manufacture different hormones that protect the individual in many ways. Endocrine and sympathetic nervous system activity are not as high as in the alarm stage, although they still are elevated. During the resistance stage, the body's immune system can fight off infection with remarkable efficiency. Similarly, hormones that reduce the inflammation normally associated with injury circulate at high levels.

If the body's all-out effort to combat stress fails and the stress persists, the individual moves into the *exhaustion stage.* At this point, the wear and tear on the body takes its toll—the person might collapse in a state of exhaustion, and vulnerability to disease increases. Serious, possibly irreversible damage to the body, such as a heart attack, or even death may occur.

The body system that plays the greatest role in Selye's GAS is called the **hypothalamic-pituitary-adrenal axis (HPA axis).** The HPA axis is a complex set of interactions among the hypothalamus (part of the brain's limbic system), the pituitary gland (the master gland of the endocrine system), and the adrenal glands (endocrine system glands that are located on top of each kidney).

● **general adaptation syndrome (GAS)** Selye's term for the common effects of stressful demands on the body, consisting of three stages: alarm, resistance, and exhaustion.

● **hypothalamic-pituitary-adrenal axis (HPA axis)** The complex set of interactions among the hypothalamus, the pituitary gland, and the adrenal glands that regulates various body processes and controls reactions to stressful events.

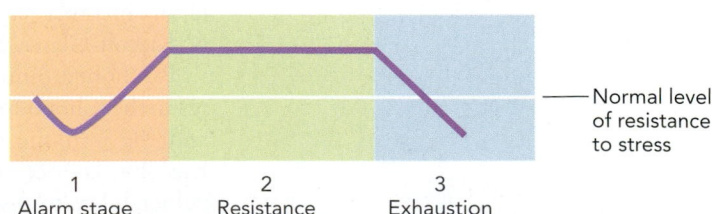

FIGURE 69.1   Selye's General Adaptation Syndrome The general adaptation syndrome (GAS) describes an individual's response to stress in terms of three stages: (1) alarm, in which the body mobilizes its resources; (2) resistance, in which the body strives mightily to endure the stressor; and (3) exhaustion, in which resistance becomes depleted.

The HPA axis regulates various body processes, including digestion, immune system responses, emotion, and energy expenditure. The axis also controls reactions to stressful events, and these responses will be our focus here.

When the brain detects a threat in the environment, it signals the hypothalamus to release corticotropin-releasing hormone (CRH). In turn, CRH stimulates the pituitary gland to produce another hormone that causes the adrenal glands to release cortisol. Cortisol is itself the "stress hormone" that directs cells to make sugar, fat, and protein available so the body can take quick action. Cortisol also suppresses the immune system.

The body responds differently to acute stress and chronic stress. Acute stress can sometimes be adaptive, and in acute stress cortisol plays an important role in helping us to take the necessary action to avoid dire consequences. Typically, once the body has dealt with a given stressor, our cortisol level returns to normal. However, under chronic stress, the HPA axis can remain activated over the long haul.

The activity of the HPA axis varies from one person to the next. These differences may be explained by genes as well as by particular stressful experiences (Hatzinger & others, 2010). Research with rats has shown that prenatal stress can influence the development of the HPA axis (Kjaer & others, 2010; Murray & others, 2010). When the HPA is chronically active, various systems in the body suffer, as we now consider.

69-2 STRESS AND THE IMMUNE SYSTEM

Chronic stress can have serious implications for the body, in particular for the immune system. Interest in links between the immune system and stress spawned a new field of scientific inquiry, **psychoneuroimmunology,** which explores connections among psychological factors (such as attitudes and emotions), the nervous system, and the immune system (Kiecolt-Glaser, 2009, 2010; Leonard & Myint, 2009).

The immune system and the central nervous system are similar in their modes of receiving, recognizing, and integrating signals from the external environment (Sternberg & Gold, 1996). The central nervous system and the immune system both possess "sensory" elements, which receive information from the environment and other parts of the body, and "motor" elements, which carry out an appropriate response. Both systems also rely on chemical mediators for communication. CRH, the hormone discussed above, is shared by the central nervous system and the immune system, uniting the stress and immune responses.

A variety of research supports the idea that stress can profoundly influence the immune system (Bob & others, 2009; Grippo & Johnson, 2009; Ho & others, 2010). Acute stressors (sudden, stressful, one-time life events or stimuli) can produce immunological changes. For example, in relatively healthy HIV-infected individuals, as well as in individuals with cancer, acute stressors are associated with poorer immune system functioning (Pant & Ramaswamy, 2009). In addition to acute stressors, chronic stressors (long-lasting agents of stress) are associated with an increasing downturn in immune system responsiveness. This effect has been documented in a number of circumstances, including worries about living next to a damaged nuclear reactor, failures in close relationships (divorce, separation, and marital distress), and burdensome caregiving for a family member with progressive illness (Glaser & Kiecolt-Glaser, 2005; Gouin, Hantsoo, & Kiecolt-Glaser, 2009; Graham, Christian, & Kiecolt-Glaser, 2006).

Psychoneuroimmunology is a relatively young field. As it continues to develop, researchers hope to determine the precise links among psychological factors, the brain, and the immune system (Bauer, Jeckel, & Luz, 2009; Campbell & Edwards, 2009; Kiecolt-Glaser & others, 2010). Preliminary hypotheses about the interaction that causes vulnerability to disease include the following:

- Stressful experiences lower the efficiency of immune systems, making individuals more susceptible to disease.

- Stress directly promotes disease-producing processes.

- Stressful experiences may cause the activation of dormant viruses that diminish the individual's ability to cope with disease.

● **psychoneuroimmunology** A new field of scientific inquiry that explores connections among psychological factors (such as attitudes and emotions), the nervous system, and the immune system.

These hypotheses may lead to clues for more successful treatments for some of the most challenging diseases to conquer—cancer and AIDS among them (Armaiz-Pena & others, 2009; Bormann & others, 2008).

Sheldon Cohen and his colleagues have conducted a number of studies on the effects of stress, emotion, and social support on immunity and susceptibility to infectious disease (Cohen, Doyle, & Skoner, 1999; Cohen & Janicki-Deverts, 2009; Cohen & Lemay, 2007; Cohen & others, 2009; Doyle & others, 2010; Janicki-Deverts, Cohen, & Doyle, 2010). Cohen and his colleagues (1998) found that adults who faced interpersonal or work-related stress for at least one month were more likely than their less-stressed counterparts to catch a cold after exposure to viruses. In the study, 276 adults were exposed to viruses and then quarantined for five days. The longer people had experienced major stress, the more likely they were to catch a cold. Individuals who reported high stress for the preceding two years tripled their risk of catching a cold (Figure 69.2). Those who experienced work-related stress for a month or longer were nearly five times more likely to develop colds than individuals without chronic stress. Those who experienced interpersonal stress for a month or more were twice as likely to catch a cold. Cohen concluded that stress-triggered changes in the immune system and hormones might create greater vulnerability to infection. The findings suggest that when we know we are under stress, we need to take better care of ourselves than usual, although often we do just the opposite (Cohen & Janicki-Deverts, 2009; Cohen & others, 2009; Doyle & others, 2010).

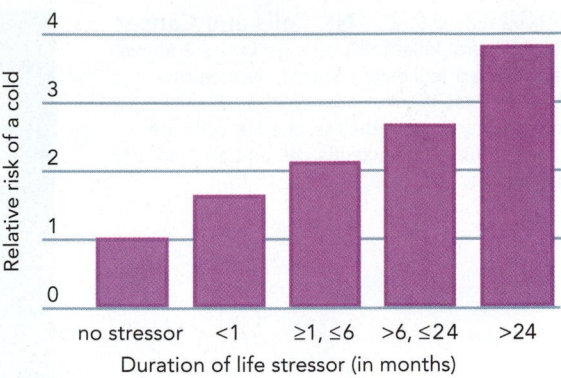

FIGURE 69.2 **Stress and the Risk of Developing a Cold** In a study by Cohen and others (1998), the longer individuals had a life stressor, the more likely they were to develop a cold. The four-point scale is based on the odds (0 = lower; 4 = higher) of getting a cold.

69·3 STRESS AND CARDIOVASCULAR DISEASE

There is also reason to believe that stress can increase an individual's risk for cardiovascular disease (Kibler, 2009; Williams & Davidson, 2009). Chronic emotional stress is associated with high blood pressure, heart disease, and early death (Schulz, 2007). Apparently, the surge in adrenaline caused by severe emotional stress causes the blood to clot more rapidly, and blood clotting is a major factor in heart attacks (Strike & others, 2006). Emotional stress also can contribute to cardiovascular disease in other ways. Individuals who have had major life changes (such as the loss of a spouse or another close relative and the loss of a job) have a higher incidence of cardiovascular disease and early death (Nakao, 2010; Taylor, 2011). A longitudinal study of involuntary job loss among workers 50 years and older over a 10-year period revealed that displaced workers have a twofold increase in the risk of developing a stroke (Gallo & others, 2006). Consider the behavior pattern of those who are Type A. Individuals who are Type A tend to be very reactive to stressful circumstances and to become hostile when frustrated.

The body's internal reactions to stress are not the only risk. People in a chronically stressed condition are more likely to take up smoking, start overeating, and avoid exercising. All of these stress-related behaviors are linked with the development of cardiovascular disease (Kodama & others, 2009; Patel & others, 2009).

69·4 STRESS AND CANCER

Given the association of stress with poor health behaviors such as smoking, it is not surprising that stress has also been related to cancer risk (Hamer, Chida, & Molloy, 2009). Stress sets in motion biological changes involving the autonomic, endocrine, and immune systems. If the immune system is not compromised, it appears to help provide resistance to cancer and slow its progress. Researchers have found, however, that the physiological effects of stress inhibit a number of cellular immune responses (Anderson, Golden-Kreutz, & DiLillo, 2001). Cancer patients show diminished natural killer

FIGURE 69.3 **NK Cells and Cancer**
Two natural killer (NK) cells (*yellow*) are shown attacking a leukemia cell (*red*). Notice the blisters that the leukemia cell has developed to defend itself. Nonetheless, the NK cells are surrounding the leukemia cell and are about to destroy it.

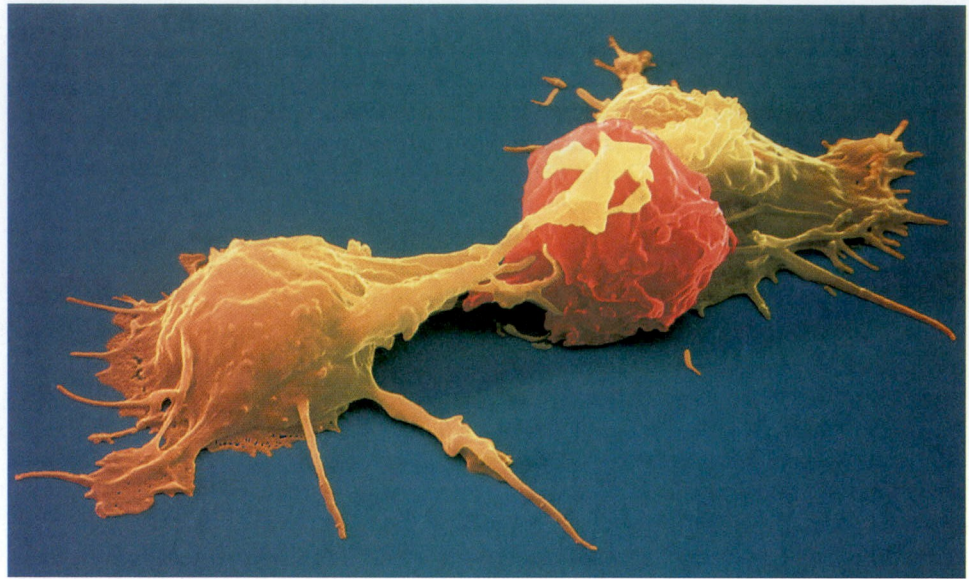

(NK)-cell activity in the blood (Bagnara & others, 2009) (Figure 69.3). Low NK-cell activity is linked with the development of further malignancies, and the length of survival for the cancer patient is related to NK-cell activity (Cho & Campana, 2009).

Thus, stress is clearly a factor not only in immune system functioning and cardiovascular health but also in the risk for cancer. In light of these links, understanding the psychological processes by which individuals can effectively handle stressful circumstances is a crucial topic in health psychology (Faul & others, 2009).

69·5 COPING WITH STRESS

What stresses you out? Stressors can be anything from losing irreplaceable notes from a class, to being yelled at by a friend, to failing a test, to being in a car wreck.

Although everyone's body may have a similar response to stressors, not everyone perceives the same events as stressful. Indeed, whether or not an experience stresses us out depends on how we think about that experience. *Cognitive appraisal* refers to an individual's interpretation of an experience either as harmful and threatening or as challenging, and the person's determination of whether he or she has the resources to cope effectively with the event. Coping means managing taxing circumstances, expending effort to solve life's problems, and seeking to master or reduce stress.

Types of Coping

Research has identified two types of coping. **Problem-focused coping** is the cognitive strategy of squarely facing one's troubles and trying to solve them. For example, if you are having trouble with a class, you might go to the campus study skills center and sign up for a program to learn how to study more effectively. In taking this step, you have faced your problem and attempted to do something about it. Problem-focused coping might involve coming up with goals and implementation intentions, the problem-solving steps we examined earlier in this module. A recent meta-analysis revealed that problem-focused coping was linked to a lower level of psychopathology in such areas as anxiety, depression, eating disorders, and substance use disorders (Aldao, Nolen-Hoeksema, & Schweizer, 2010).

Emotion-focused coping involves responding to the stress that you are feeling—trying to manage your emotional reaction—rather than confronting the problem itself. In emotion-focused coping, you might avoid the source of your stress, rationalize

● **problem-focused coping** The coping strategy of squarely facing one's troubles and trying to solve them.

● **emotion-focused coping** The coping strategy that involves responding to the stress that one is feeling—trying to manage one's emotional reaction—rather than focusing on the problem itself.

what has happened to you, deny the problem is occurring, laugh it off, or call on your religious faith for support. If you use emotion-focused coping, you might avoid going to a class that is a problem for you. You might say the class does not matter, deny that you are having difficulty with it, joke about it with your friends, or pray that you will do better.

Although problem-focused coping is generally associated with better outcomes, in some circumstances emotion-focused coping can help a person deal with life's problems. Denial is one of the main protective psychological mechanisms for navigating the flood of feelings that occurs when the reality of death or dying becomes too great. For example, one study found that following the death of a loved one, bereaved individuals who directed their attention away from their negative feelings had fewer health problems and were rated as better adjusted by their friends, compared to bereaved individuals who did not use this coping strategy (Coifman & others, 2007). Denial can be used to avoid the destructive impact of shock by postponing the time when a person has to deal with stress. In other circumstances, however, emotion-focused coping can be problematic. Denying that your ex does not love you anymore keeps you from getting on with life. Yet emotion-focused coping may be useful in situations in which there is no solution to a problem, such as long-term grieving over the loss of a loved one. In such cases, the emotion itself might be the stressor.

Many individuals successfully use both problem-focused and emotion-focused coping when adjusting to a stressful circumstance. For example, in one study individuals said they used both problem-focused and emotion-focused coping strategies in 98 percent of the stressful encounters they face (Folkman & Lazarus, 1980). Over the long term, though, problem-focused coping rather than emotion-focused coping usually works best (Nagase & others, 2009).

Strategies for Successful Coping

Successful coping can improve even the most stressful situations. Several specific factors are associated with effective coping, including a sense of personal control, a healthy immune system, personal resources, and positive emotions.

When one is experiencing stressful life events, multiple coping strategies often work better than a single strategy, as is true with any problem-solving challenge (Folkman & Moskowitz, 2004). People who have experienced a stressful life event or a cluster of difficulties (such as a parent's death, a divorce, and a significant loss of income) might actively embrace problem solving and consistently take advantage of opportunities for positive experiences, even in the context of the bad times they are going through. Positive emotion can give them a sense of the big picture, help them devise a variety of possible solutions, and allow them to make creative connections.

Optimism can play a strong role in effective coping. Recall from the Health and Wellness section following Module 50 that optimism is the expectancy that good things are likely to occur in the future (Carver & Scheier, 2009; Solberg Nes, Evans, & Segerstrom, 2009). Having an optimistic view of what lies ahead tends to help people engage constructively with potentially threatening information (Aspinwall, 1998; Aspinwall & Brunhart, 1996; Aspinwall, Leaf, & Leachman, 2009; Aspinwall & Tedeschi, 2010a, 2010b). Lisa Aspinwall views optimism as a resource that allows individuals to address their problems. Optimists are more likely than others to seek out genetic testing in order to learn about their risk for disease (Aspinwall, Leaf, & Leachman, 2009). Furthermore, optimists face life's challenges from a place of strength, so, for instance, when an optimist finds out that tanning, a favorite pastime, is related to an elevated risk of skin cancer, the information is important but not overwhelming. In contrast, pessimists are already living in a bleak world and prefer not to hear more bad news.

Another personal quality that appears to promote thriving during difficult times is hardiness. **Hardiness** is characterized by a sense of commitment rather than alienation, and of control rather than powerlessness; a hardy individual sees problems as challenges

● **hardiness** A personal quality characterized by a sense of commitment rather than alienation, and of control rather than powerlessness; a hardy person sees problems as challenges rather than threats.

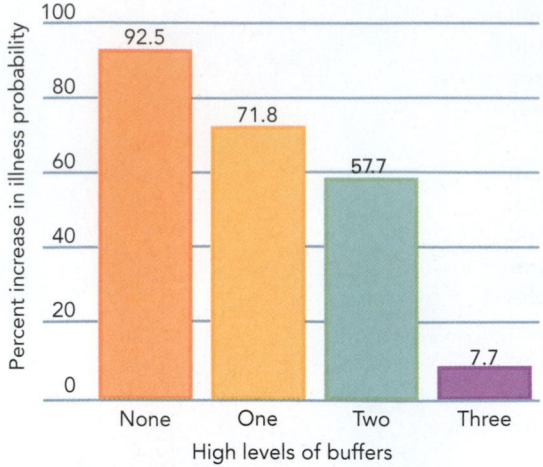

FIGURE 69.4 **Illness in High-Stress Business Executives** In one study of high-stress business executives (all of whom were selected for this analysis because they were above the stress mean for the entire year of the study), a low level of all three buffers (hardiness, exercise, and social support) involved a high probability of at least one serious illness in that year. High levels of one, two, and all three buffers decreased the likelihood of at least one serious illness occurring in the year of the study.

● **stress management program** A regimen that teaches individuals how to appraise stressful events, how to develop skills for coping with stress, and how to put these skills into use in everyday life.

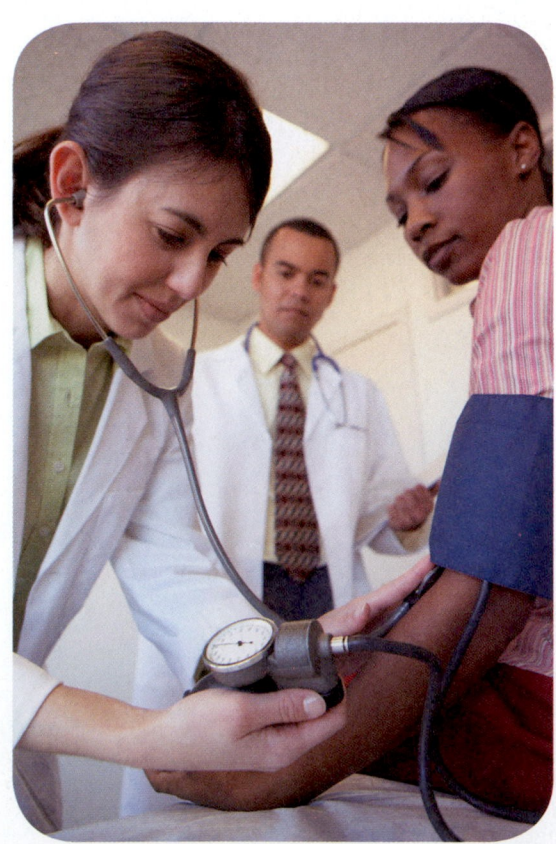

rather than threats (Maddi & others, 2006). Hardiness is exemplified by the basketball player whose team is down by two points with seconds remaining on the clock when he shouts, "Coach! Give me the ball!"

The links among hardiness, stress, and illness were the focus of the Chicago Stress Project, which studied male business managers 32 to 65 years of age over a five-year period (Kobasa, Maddi, & Kahn, 1982; Maddi, 1998). During the five years, most of the managers experienced stressful events such as divorce, job transfers, the death of a close friend, inferior performance evaluations at work, and reporting to an unpleasant boss. In one aspect of the study, managers who developed an illness, ranging from the flu to a heart attack, were compared with those who did not (Kobasa, Maddi, & Kahn, 1982). Those who did not were more likely to have hardy personalities. Another aspect of the study investigated whether hardiness, along with exercise and social support, provided a buffer against stress and reduced illness in executives' lives (Kobasa & others, 1986). When all three factors were present in an executive's life, the level of illness dropped dramatically (Figure 69.4).

Other researchers also have found support for the role of hardiness in illness and health (Heckman & Clay, 2005). The results of this research on hardiness suggest the power of multiple factors, rather than any single factor, in cushioning individuals against stress and maintaining their health (Maddi, 1998, 2008; Maddi & others, 2006).

69-6 STRESS MANAGEMENT PROGRAMS

Nearly every day we are reminded that stress is bad for our health. "Avoid stress" may be a good prescription, but life is full of potentially stressful experiences. Sometimes just checking e-mail or answering a cell phone can be an invitation for stress. Sometimes, too, trying to manage stress on our own can be overwhelming. Thus, it makes sense to explore options for breaking the stress habit.

Because many people have difficulty in regulating stress, psychologists have developed various techniques that people can learn to apply themselves (Marshall, Walizer, & Vernalis, 2009; Willert, Thulstrup, & Hertz, 2009). **Stress management programs** teach individuals how to appraise stressful events, develop coping skills, and put these skills into use in everyday life. Effective stress management programs are generally based on the principles of cognitive-behavior therapy (Mercer, 2009), as described in Module 65. Some stress management programs are broad in scope, teaching a range of techniques to handle stress; others teach a specific technique, such as relaxation or assertiveness training (Fahey, Insel, & Roth, 2011).

Stress management programs are often taught through workshops, which are becoming more common in the workplace (Taylor, 2011). Aware of the costs in lost productivity due to stress-related disorders, many organizations have become increasingly motivated to help their workers identify and cope with the stressful circumstances in their lives. Colleges and universities similarly run stress management programs for students. If you are finding the experience of college extremely stressful and having difficulty coping with the pressures, you might consider enrolling in a stress management program at your school or in your community.

Do stress management programs work? In one study, researchers randomly assigned men and women with hypertension (blood pressure greater than 140/90) to one of three groups (Linden, Lenz, & Con, 2001). One group received 10 hours of individual stress management training; a second group was placed in a wait-list control group and eventually received stress management training; and a third group (a control group) received no such training. The two groups that received the stress management training showed significantly reduced blood pressure. The control group experienced no reduction in blood pressure. Also, the reduced blood pressure in the first two groups was linked to a reported decrease in psychological stress and improved ability to cope with anger.

Coping effectively with stress is essential for physical and mental health (Lim, Bogossian, & Ahern, 2010; Nagase & others, 2009). Still, there is a lot more we can do to promote our health. Healthful living—establishing healthy habits and evaluating and changing behaviors that interfere with good health—helps us avoid the damaging effects of stress (Frosch & others, 2009; Kodama & others, 2009). Just as the biopsychosocial perspective predicts, healthy changes in one area of life can have benefits that overflow to others.

SUMMARY

Stress is the response of individuals when life circumstances threaten them and tax their ability to cope. Selye characterized the stress response with his concept of a general adaptation syndrome (GAS), which has three stages: alarm, resistance, and exhaustion.

The hypothalamic-pituitary-adrenal axis (HPA axis) comprises the interactions among the hypothalamus, pituitary gland, and adrenal glands. This axis plays an important role in human responses to stress. Chronic stress takes a toll on the body's natural disease-fighting abilities. Stress is also related to cardiovascular disease and cancer.

Kicking the stress habit means remembering that stress is a product of how we think about life events. Coping may be divided into the categories of problem-focused coping and emotion-focused coping. Overall, problem-focused coping is more adaptive than emotion-focused coping. Hardiness is associated with thriving during stressful times.

KEY TERMS

general adaptation syndrome (GAS)   633
hypothalamic-pituitary-adrenal axis (HPA axis)   633
psychoneuroimmunology   634

problem-focused coping   636
emotion-focused coping   636
hardiness   637
stress management program   638

TEST YOURSELF

1. What is Selye's term for the pattern of common effects on the body when demands are placed on it?

2. How does the HPA axis function in regulating stress? How is the body affected when the HPA axis is chronically active?

3. What personality characteristic applies to an individual who faces difficulties with a sense of commitment and control, and who perceives problems as challenges rather than threats?

APPLY YOUR KNOWLEDGE

1. Take one day and become a stress detective. Every time a friend mentions how stressed out he or she is feeling, ask your friend to describe the source of the stress. What is the stressful event? How is the person appraising the event? How might he or she appraise the situation in ways that would help decrease stress?

2. Search the web on the topic of stress management or coping with stress. Visit three or four sites and critically evaluate the suggestions made on the sites. How are they similar to the suggestions given in the text? How much information is available to evaluate the claims on the sites? Based on your critical evaluation, is the advice something you would follow or not? Explain.

Toward a Healthier Body (and Mind): Behaving As If Your Life Depends upon It

There's no escaping it: Getting stress under control is crucial for a healthy mind and body. Where health and wellness are concerned, it is also important to make wise behavioral choices when it comes to physical activity, diet and nutrition, and smoking.

70-1 BECOMING PHYSICALLY ACTIVE

Imagine that there was a time when, to change a TV channel, people had to get up and walk a few feet to turn a knob. Consider the time when people physically had to go to the library and hunt through card catalogs and shelves to find information rather than going online and Googling. As our daily tasks have become increasingly easy, we have become less active, and inactivity is a serious health problem (Carnethon & others, 2010; Puterman & others, 2010).

Any activity that expends physical energy can be part of a healthy lifestyle. It can be as simple as taking the stairs instead of an elevator, walking or biking to class instead of driving, going ice skating instead of to a movie, or getting up and dancing instead of sitting at the bar. One study of older adults revealed that the more they expended energy in daily activities, the longer they were likely to live (Manini & others, 2006).

In addition to being related to life expectancy, physical activity corresponds with a host of other positive outcomes, including a lower probability of developing cardiovascular disease (Lewis & others, 2010; Sui & others, 2009), diabetes (Colagiuri, 2010), weight loss in overweight individuals (Ades, Savage, & Harvey-Berino, 2010), improved cognitive functioning (Erickson & Kramer, 2009; Klusmann & others, 2010), positive coping with stress (Collins & others, 2009), and increased self-esteem (Hallal & others, 2006). Physical exercise has also been shown to reduce levels of anxiety (Rethorst, Wipfli, & Landers, 2009) and depression (Ryan, 2008).

Even a real pig can benefit from exercise; Figure 70.1 shows a hog getting a workout. In this study, a group of hogs was trained to run approximately 100 miles a week (Bloor & White, 1983). After training, the researchers narrowed the arteries that supplied blood to the hogs' hearts. Compared to a control group of untrained hogs, the jogging hogs developed extensive alternative pathways that provided a blood supply to their hearts. These results suggest that being physically active is like investing energy in a wellness bank account: Activity enhances physical well-being and gives us the ability to face life's potential stressors energetically.

Exercise is one special type of physical activity. **Exercise** formally refers to structured activities whose goal is to improve health. Although exercise designed to strengthen muscles and bones or to improve flexibility is important to fitness, many health experts stress the benefits of **aerobic exercise,** which is sustained activity—jogging, swimming, or cycling, for example—that stimulates heart and lung functioning.

In one study, exercise literally meant the difference between life and death for middle-aged and older adults (Blair & others, 1989). More than 10,000 men and women were divided into categories of low fitness, medium fitness, and high fitness. Then they were studied over eight years. Sedentary participants (low fitness) were more than twice as likely to die during the study's eight-year time span than those who were moderately fit, and more than three times as likely to die as those who were highly fit. The positive effects of physical fitness occurred for both men and women. The Psycho-

● **exercise** Structured activities whose goal is to improve health.

● **aerobic exercise** Sustained activity—jogging, swimming, or cycling, for example—that stimulates heart and lung functioning.

FIGURE 70.1 The Jogging Hog Experiment Jogging hogs reveal the dramatic effects of exercise on health. In one investigation, a group of hogs was trained to run approximately 100 miles per week (Bloor & White, 1983). Then the researchers narrowed the arteries that supplied blood to the heart. The hearts of the jogging hogs developed extensive alternate pathways for blood supply, and 42 percent of the threatened heart tissue was salvaged, compared with only 17 percent in a control group of non-jogging hogs.

psychological *inquiry*

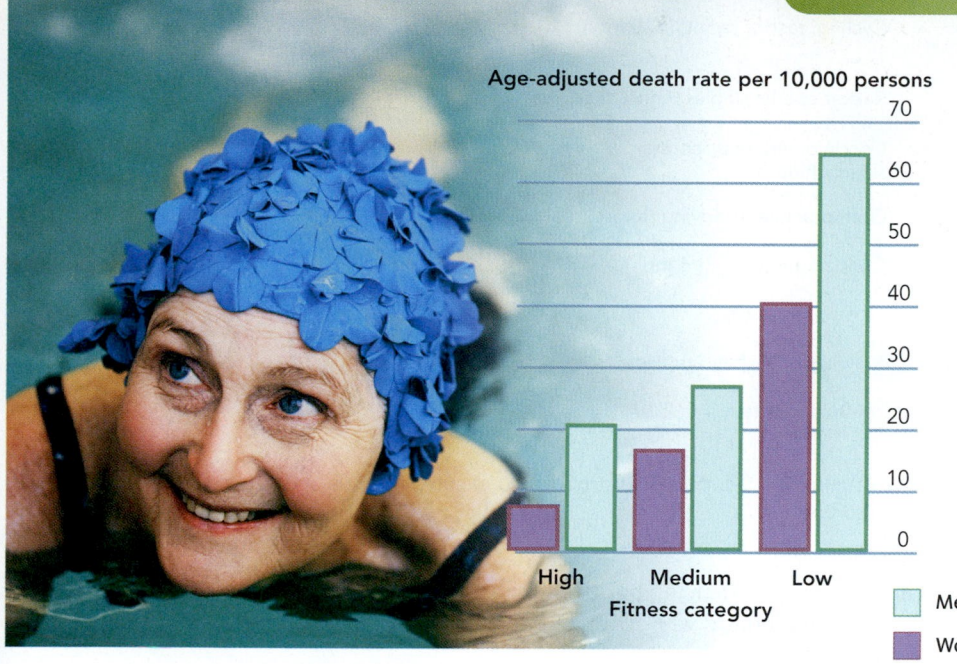

Age-adjusted death rate per 10,000 persons

Fitness category

High   Medium   Low

Men

Women

Physical Activity: A Matter of Life and Death

This graph shows the results of an 8-year-long longitudinal study of over 10,000 men and women (Blair & others, 1989). The X or horizontal axis shows the fitness level of participants, and the Y or vertical axis shows the death rates within those groups. Note that results are separated for men and women. Using the figure, answer the questions below.

1. Which groups had the highest and lowest death rates?

2. Comparing the results for men and women separately, what role does gender play in mortality? What might explain this difference?

3. Because this is a correlational study, the results cannot be assumed to show that a low fitness level causes mortality. What third variables might explain the relationship between activity level and mortality?

logical Inquiry examines the study's results. Furthermore, a recent study revealed that adults aged 60 and over who were in the lowest fifth in terms of physical fitness as determined by a treadmill test were four times more likely to die over a 12-year period than their counterparts who were in the top fifth of physical fitness (Sui & others, 2007). This study also showed that older adults who were overweight but physically fit had a lower mortality risk over the 12 years than their normal-weight counterparts who were low in fitness. In addition, a recent study of more than 11,000 women found that low cardiorespiratory fitness was a significant factor for all causes of early mortality (Farrell & others, 2010).

One reason that exercise plays a role in how long people live may involve telomeres. Recall from Module 34 that telomeres protect the tips of chromosomes and become significantly shorter as individuals age; that shortening is theorized to be a main reason for aging (Davoli, Denchi, & de Lange, 2010; Sahin & DePinho, 2010). A recent study revealed that vigorous physical activity protected individuals who were experiencing high stress by reducing telomere shortening (Puterman & others, 2010).

Health experts recommend that adults engage in at least 30 minutes of moderate physical activity on most, preferably all, days of the week and that children exercise for 60 minutes. Most advise that you should try to raise your heart rate to at least 60 percent of your maximum rate. However, only about one-fifth of adults are active at these recommended levels of physical activity. Figure 70.2 lists examples of the physical activities that qualify as moderate (and, for comparison, vigorous) activities.

Research suggests that both moderate and intense activities may produce important physical and psychological gains (Aihara & others, 2010; Paschalis & others, 2010). Some people enjoy intense exercise; others prefer moderate exercise. The enjoyment derived from exercise, added to its aerobic benefits, makes exercise one of life's most important activities.

One hint for becoming more physically active is not to limit yourself to only a few options. There are many activities that require physical exertion. Choose one that you genuinely like. Important factors in sticking to an exercise plan include self-efficacy,

Moderate	Vigorous
Walking briskly (3–4 mph)	Walking briskly uphill or with a load
Swimming, moderate effort	Swimming, fast treading crawl
Cycling for pleasure or transportation (≤10 mph)	Cycling, fast or racing (>10 mph)
Racket sports, table tennis	Racket sports, singles tennis, racketball
Conditioning exercise, general calisthenics	Conditioning exercise, stair ergometer, ski machine
Golf, pulling cart or carrying clubs	Golf, practice at driving range
Canoeing, leisurely (2.0–3.9 mph)	Canoeing, rapidly (≥4 mph)
Home care, general cleaning	Moving furniture
Mowing lawn, power mower	Mowing lawn, hand mower
Home repair, painting	Fix-up projects

FIGURE 70.2 **Moderate and Vigorous Physical Activities** At minimum, adults should strive for 30 minutes of moderate activity each day. That activity can become even more beneficial if we "pump it up" to vigorous.

making active choices, and experiencing positive reinforcement and social support (Cress & others, 2005). Finding a buddy who is interested in working out with you might be a powerful motivator.

One often-welcome payoff for increasing physical activity is weight loss. Researchers have found that the most effective component of weight-loss programs is regular exercise (Duncan, 2010; Nagashima & others, 2010). Another way to combat weight problems is through changes in diet, our next topic.

70·2 EATING RIGHT

The biggest health risk facing modern North Americans is being overweight or obese (Flegal & others, 2010). "Overweight" and "obese" are labels for ranges of weight that are greater than what experts consider healthy for an individual's height (Ogden & Carroll, 2010). In recent years, the percentage of individuals who are overweight or obese has been increasing at an alarming rate. As Figure 70.3 indicates, the prevalence of being overweight or obese in the United States changed little from 1960 to 1980 (Ogden & Carroll, 2010). However, the percentage of overweight and obese adults in the United States increased from less than 50 percent in 1960 to almost 70 percent in 2008. At this rate, it has been estimated that by 2030, the percentage of overweight or obese Americans could reach as high as *86 percent* (Beydoun & Wang, 2009).

Exercising regularly is one great way to lose weight (Fahey, Insel, & Roth, 2011). Making healthy dietary choices is another (Ross & others, 2009b). Eating right means eating sensible, nutritious foods that maximize health and wellness. Despite the growing variety of choices Americans can make in the grocery store, many of us are unhealthy eaters. We take in too much sugar and not enough foods high in vitamins, minerals, and fiber, such as fruits, vegetables, and grains. We eat too much fast food and too few well-balanced meals—choices that increase our fat and cholesterol intake, both of which are implicated in long-term health problems (Schiff, 2011).

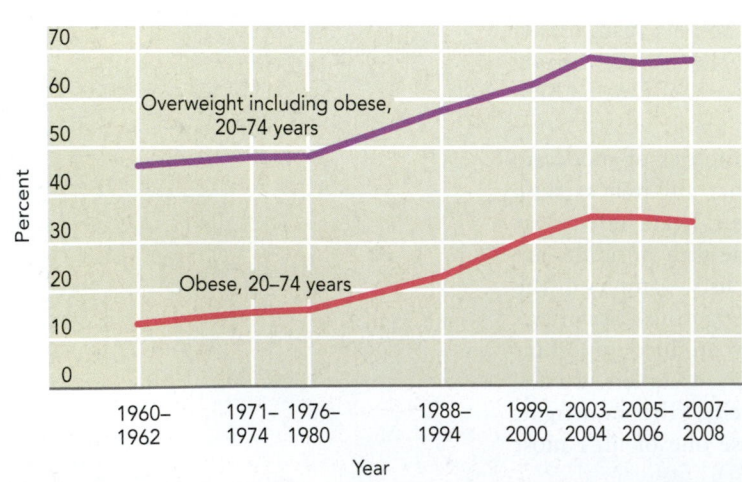

FIGURE 70.3 **Changes in the Percentage of U.S. Adults 20 to 74 Years of Age Classified as Overweight or Obese, 1960–2008** Obesity and overweight continue to be major public health concerns in the United States.

Healthy eating does not mean trying out every fad diet that comes along but rather incorporating tasty, healthy foods into meals and snacks. Healthy eating is not something that people should do just to lose weight—it is about committing to lifelong healthy food habits. Several health goals can be accomplished through a sound nutritional plan. Not only does a well-balanced diet provide more energy, but it also can lower blood pressure and lessen the risk for cancer and tooth decay (Levitan, Wolk, & Mittleman, 2009; Wardlaw & Smith, 2011).

Losing weight and opting for healthier foods can be difficult, especially when one is just starting out. Many weight-loss fads promise weight loss with no effort, no hunger, and no real change in one's food consumption. These promises are unrealistic. Making genuine, enduring changes in eating behavior is hard work. This reality does not mean adopting a pessimistic attitude. Rather, positive expectations and self-efficacy are important because the task at hand is a challenging one.

The National Weight Control Registry is an ongoing study of people who have lost at least 40 pounds and kept it off for at least two years. Research on these successful dieters gives us important tips on how people who keep the weight off achieve this goal (Raynor & others, 2005).

Successful dieters also show consistency in what they eat, sticking to the same regimen even on the weekends and during the holiday season (Gorin & others, 2004). A study of approximately 2,000 U.S. adults found that exercising 30 minutes a day, planning meals, and weighing themselves daily were the main strategies of successful dieters (Kruger, Blanck, & Gillespie, 2006) (Figure 70.4).

The truth is that keeping weight off is an ongoing process. Moreover, the longer a dieter keeps the weight off, the less likely he or she is to gain it back (McGuire & others, 1999). The goal is difficult, but accomplishing it is a testament to the power of belief in oneself.

We have considered how exercise and nutrition can help individuals live healthily. In the Critical Controversy, we explore a question related to fitness, nutrition, and health—whether a person can be fat *and* fit.

70-3 QUITTING SMOKING

Another health-related goal is giving up smoking. Evidence from a number of studies underscores the dangers of smoking and being around smokers (American Cancer Society, 2010). For example, smoking is linked to 30 percent of cancer deaths, 21 percent of heart disease deaths, and 82 percent of chronic pulmonary disease deaths. Secondhand smoke is implicated in as many as 9,000 lung cancer deaths a year. Children of smokers are at special risk for respiratory and middle-ear diseases (Butz & others, 2010; Goodwin & Cowles, 2008).

Fewer people smoke today than in the past, and almost half of the living adults who ever smoked have quit. In 2008, 20.6 percent of all adults in the United States smoked, with men being more likely to smoke (23.1 percent) than women (18.3 percent) (National Center for Health Statistics, 2009). Although these numbers represent a substantial decline from 40 years ago, when 50 percent of men smoked, many individuals still smoke.

Quitting smoking has enormous health benefits. Figure 70.5 shows that when individuals quit smoking, their risk of fatal lung cancer declines over time. It is

FIGURE 70.4 **Comparison of Strategies in Successful and Unsuccessful Dieters** Losing weight—and keeping it off—can be challenging, but reaching these goals is not impossible. Success in dieting depends on engaging in physical activity, planning meals, and monitoring progress.

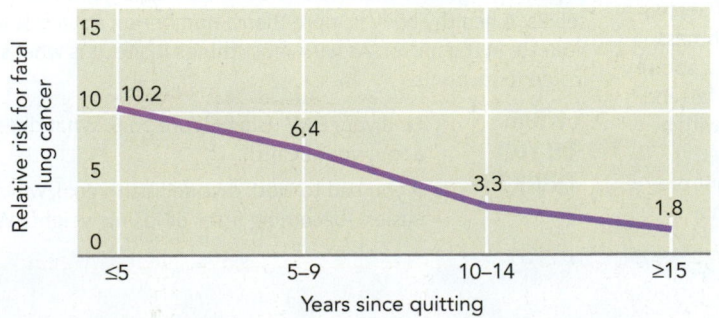

FIGURE 70.5 **Fatal Lung Cancer and Years Since Quitting Smoking** One study compared more than 43,000 former male smokers with almost 60,000 males who had never smoked (Enstrom, 1999). For comparison purposes, a zero level was assigned as the risk for fatal lung cancer for men who had never smoked. Over time, the relative risk for smokers who had quit declined, but even after 15 years it was still above that of nonsmokers.

CRITICAL CONTROVERSY

Can You Be Fat and Fit?

What does a healthy body look like? During your spinning class, you notice that your instructor is overweight. Is she really healthy? Later, while watching your favorite baseball team, you check out the dugout. How many of the players are truly thin? Even Babe Ruth, perhaps the greatest baseball player of all time, was a rotund guy, known for his hearty appetite. One day at Coney Island, Ruth ate four steaks and eight hot dogs and drank eight sodas. The workout favored by "the Bambino" was generally limited to running the bases after hitting one of his many home runs.

Body weight is certainly an important factor in physical health. On the basis of longitudinal studies on large numbers of people, researchers have estimated that individuals who are obese at age 40 will live six to seven years less than their thin counterparts, and individuals who are overweight at 40 lose three years of life on average (Peeters & others, 2003).

How do we know if someone is overweight or obese? One of the most commonly used measures is the *body mass index* (BMI), which quantifies the relationship between a person's weight and his or her height (National Heart, Lung, and Blood Institute, 2009).

Figure 70.6 features a chart for determining BMI. Generally, body mass index gauges a person's weight in relation to his or her height. Measures of BMI may overestimate body fat in athletic individuals because muscle weighs more than fat. According to the Centers for Disease Control and Prevention (2009b), a healthy BMI for an adult ranges between 18.5 and 24. Overweight refers to a BMI that is greater than or equal to 25, and obese is greater than or equal to 30. (Babe Ruth's BMI? A solidly overweight 28.)

Another important factor in physical health and the risk for serious illness is fitness. *Cardiorespiratory fitness* (CRF) refers to the ability of the body's circulatory and respiratory systems to supply fuel during sustained physical activity. CRF, usually measured with a treadmill test, is increased by engaging in aerobic exercise regularly (Kodama & others, 2009).

One study that compared BMI and CRF challenged the notion that BMI is an important risk factor for disease (Lee, Blair, & Jackson, 1999). The researchers measured leanness, obesity, and CRF in nearly 22,000 men 30 to 83 years of age. The men were followed over eight years. During that time, 428 died. The researchers were interested in the contributions of weight and cardiorespiratory fitness to risk for death. Controlling for age, smoking, alcohol consumption, and parental history of heart disease, unfit lean men had double the risk of mortality of fit lean men, from all causes. Unfit lean men also had a higher risk of dying than *fit obese* men. Regardless of body size, unfit men were more likely to die than fit men.

Although the idea that one can be fat and still fit has popular appeal, the scientific community has been skeptical about its validity. A wide range of studies have examined whether being fit can compensate for being fat. Although research has supported the importance of CRF (Gerson & Braun, 2006), studies have not found support for the idea that fitness can compensate for being overweight (Duncan, 2010; Hu & others, 2004). Being fit does not protect a person from the health risks of being fat, and being thin does not protect the person from the risks associated with being unfit (Church & others, 2005; Sullivan & others, 2005).

The conclusion is that fitness and fatness are two independent predictors of health risk, and both have an impact on longevity. Can a

Weight (pounds)

Height	120	130	140	150	160	170	180	190	200	210	220	230	240	250
4'6"	29	31	34	36	39	41	43	46	48	51	53	56	58	60
4'8"	27	29	31	34	36	38	40	43	45	47	49	52	54	56
4'10"	25	27	29	31	34	36	38	40	42	44	46	48	50	52
5'0"	23	25	27	29	31	33	35	37	39	41	43	45	47	49
5'2"	22	24	26	27	29	31	33	35	37	38	40	42	44	46
5'4"	21	22	24	26	28	29	31	33	34	36	38	40	41	43
5'6"	19	21	23	24	26	27	29	31	32	34	36	37	39	40
5'8"	18	20	21	23	24	26	27	29	30	32	34	35	37	38
5'10"	17	19	20	22	23	24	26	27	29	30	32	33	35	36
6'0"	16	18	19	20	22	23	24	26	27	28	30	31	33	34
6'2"	15	17	18	19	21	22	23	24	26	27	28	30	31	32
6'4"	15	16	17	18	20	21	22	23	24	26	27	28	29	30
6'6"	14	15	16	17	19	20	21	22	23	24	25	27	28	29
6'8"	13	14	15	17	18	19	20	21	22	23	24	25	26	28

Underweight ■ Healthy weight ■ Overweight ■ Obese

FIGURE 70.6 **Determining Your Body Mass Index** Body mass index is a measure of weight in relation to height. Anyone with a BMI of 25 or more is considered overweight, and people who have a body mass index of 30 or more (a BMI of 30 is roughly 30 pounds over a healthy weight) are considered obese. BMI has some limitations: It can overestimate body fat in people who are very muscular, and it can underestimate body fat in people who have lost muscle mass, such as the elderly.

person be both fat and fit? Yes, but fat and fit people are not as healthy as lean and fit people. Similarly, fat and fit people may be healthier than lean sedentary individuals. Essentially, research has shown that there are two avenues to pursue for optimal health: being physically active *and* maintaining a reasonable weight.

This controversy has highlighted the common tendency to equate a healthy body with a thin one. However, lean individuals who are inactive, smoke, drink to excess, or otherwise fail to take care of their bodies are not healthier than individuals who carry a few extra pounds but engage in vigorous exercise and otherwise take good care of themselves. A healthy body is more than a number on a scale or a slim silhouette in the mirror. As with most things in life, it is what's on the inside that counts.

WHAT DO YOU THINK?

● Find your BMI using Figure 70.6. What does it tell you about your health?

● If you had to work on one health goal, which would be easier—becoming fitter or losing weight? Why?

difficult to imagine that there is a person living today who is not aware that smoking causes cancer, and there is little doubt that most smokers would like to quit. However, their addiction to nicotine makes quitting a challenge. Nicotine, the active drug in cigarettes, is a stimulant that increases the smoker's energy and alertness, a pleasurable and reinforcing experience. In addition, nicotine stimulates neurotransmitters that have a calming or pain-reducing effect (Johnstone & others, 2006; Plaza-Zabala & others, 2010).

Research confirms that giving up smoking can be difficult, especially in the early days of quitting (Pilnick & Coleman, 2010). There are various ways to quit smoking (Fant & others, 2009; McRobbie & others 2010; Tong & others, 2010). Common methods include:

■ *Going cold turkey:* Some individuals succeed by simply stopping smoking without making any major changes in their lifestyle. They decide they are going to quit, and they do. Lighter smokers usually have more success with this approach than heavier smokers.

■ *Using a substitute source of nicotine:* Nicotine gum, the nicotine patch, the nicotine inhaler, and nicotine spray work on the principle of supplying small amounts of nicotine to diminish the intensity of withdrawal (Frishman & others, 2006). *Nicotine gum,* available without a prescription, delivers nicotine orally when an individual gets the urge to smoke. The *nicotine patch* is a nonprescription adhesive pad that releases a steady dose of nicotine to the individual. The dose is gradually reduced over an 8- to 12-week period. *Nicotine spray* delivers a half-milligram squirt of nicotine to each nostril. The usual dosage is one to two administrations per hour and then as needed to reduce cravings. The spray is typically used for three to six months. Success rates for nicotine substitutes are encouraging. All of these nicotine replacement therapies have been shown to enhance the chances of quitting and remaining smoke-free.

■ *Seeking therapeutic help:* Some smokers get professional help to kick the habit. Therapies for quitting include prescribing medication such as antidepressants and teaching behaviorally based therapeutic techniques. Bupropion SR, an antidepressant sold as Zyban, helps smokers control their cravings while they ease off nicotine. Zyban works at the neurotransmitter level in the brain by inhibiting the uptake of dopamine, serotonin, and norepinephrine. Smokers using Zyban to quit have had a 21 percent average success rate after 12 months of taking the antidepressant (Paluck & others, 2006), which is similar to results for individuals using nicotine replacement. More recently, varenicline (trade name Chantix) has been approved to help smokers quit. This drug partially blocks nicotine receptors, reducing cravings and also decreasing the pleasurable sensations of smoking.

"I told you smoking was bad for you."

© Adey Bryant. www.CartoonStock.com.

Varenicline, especially when combined with counseling/psychotherapy, is more effective for smoking cessation than buproprion SR (Garrison & Dugan, 2009; Nides, 2008). For example, a recent study that combined varenicline with cognitive-behavior therapy resulted in a 58 percent smoking cessation rate after12 weeks (Ramon & Bruguera, 2009). One concern about the use of varenicline is an increase in suicide attempts by users of the drug. A recent study indicated this concern may pertain only to individuals with a history of suicide attempts before taking the drug and/or those experiencing a highly stressful event while taking the drug (Kasliwal, Wilton, & Shakir, 2009).

No one method is foolproof for quitting smoking (Fant & others, 2009). Often a combination of these approaches is the best strategy. Furthermore, quitting for good typically requires more than one try, as the stages of change model would suggest.

SUMMARY

Exercise has many positive psychological and physical benefits. Tips for increasing one's activity level include starting small by making changes in one's routine to incorporate physical activity (such as walking instead of driving to school); trying a variety of activities to find something one likes; finding an exercise partner; and swapping exercise for sedentary activities such as TV viewing. Keeping track of progress helps the individual to monitor his or her goal progress.

Overweight and obesity pose the greatest health risks to Americans today. They can be largely avoided by eating right, which means selecting nutritious foods and maintaining healthy eating habits for a lifetime, not just while on a diet. A combination of healthy eating and exercise is the best way to achieve weight loss.

Despite widespread knowledge that smoking causes cancer, some people still smoke. Methods of quitting include going cold turkey, using a substitute source of nicotine, and seeking therapy. While difficult at first, quitting smoking can be achieved, though quitting for good usually takes more than one try. Usually a combination of methods is the best strategy for quitting.

KEY TERMS

exercise   640

aerobic exercise   640

TEST YOURSELF

1. Identify and discuss three benefits of regular physical activity (in particular, exercise).

2. What is the biggest health risk facing Americans today?

3. Describe the best approach to quitting smoking.

APPLY YOUR KNOWLEDGE

1. One method that has helped to decrease unhealthy behaviors, such as smoking, is to make them more expensive. Some local governments have suggested imposing taxes on unhealthy foods, such as sugary soft drinks. Would such a tax be useful? Would you be in favor of such a tax, or opposed? Why?

2. For one week, chart what you eat each day. Then create a plan to decrease one unhealthy item from the list of foods or beverages that you consume. Explain your reasons for choosing that particular food or beverage.

Psychology and Your Good Life

In this section, we have examined how the mental and physical aspects of your existence intertwine and influence each other in dynamic ways. The field of health psychology serves to illustrate how all of the various areas of psychology converge to reveal that interplay.

As a human being, you are both a physical entity and a system of mental processes that are themselves reflected in that most complex of physical organs, the human brain. At every moment, both body and mind are present and affecting each other. Caring for your brain and mind—the resources that make it possible for you to read this book, study for tests, listen to lectures, fall in love, share with friends, help others, and make a difference in the world—is worthy of being a life mission.

Many pages ago, we defined psychology as the scientific study of behavior and mental processes, broadly meaning the things we do, think, and feel. Reflect for a moment on the psychological dimensions of vision, which we explored in Module 10. When we studied the human visual system, we examined the processes by which those amazing sense organs, our eyes, detect color, light, dark, shape, and depth. We probed the ways that the brain takes that information and turns it into perception—how a pattern of colors, shapes, and light comes to be perceived as a flower, a fall day, a sunset. Visual systems, we discovered, are generally the same from one person to the next. Thus, you can memorize the different parts of the human eye and know that your understanding is true for just about all the human eyes you will encounter in life.

However, even something as deceptively simple as perceiving a sunset through the sense of vision becomes amazingly complex when we put it in the context of a human life. Is that sunset the first you see while on your honeymoon, or right after a painful romantic breakup, or on the eve of the first day of your life as a new parent? Placing even the most ordinary moment in the context of a human life renders it remarkably complex and undeniably fascinating.

This fascination is one of the primary motivations for the science of psychology itself. From time immemorial, individuals have pondered the mysteries of human behavior, thought, and emotion. Why do we do the things we do? How do we think and feel? In this book, we have explored the broad range of topics that have interested psychologists throughout the history of this young science.

Coming to the close of this introduction to psychology allows you to look back but also ahead. It allows you to take stock of what psychology has come to mean to you now, as well as to consider what it might mean to you in the future. Whether or not you continue coursework in psychology, this book has highlighted opportunities for your future exploration about yourself and your world. In each of the real-life examples of human experience we have considered in the text—moments of heroism, weakness, joy, pain, and more—psychology has had a lesson to share with respect to the person that is *you*. Making the most of what you have learned about psychology means making the most of yourself and your life.

An everyday experience such as taking in and perceiving a sunset (or a painting of a sunset) becomes complex when we put it in the context of our life.

© Joseph Farris. www.CartoonStock.com.

SUMMARY

More than any other science, psychology is about *you*—understanding how you work. This book has aimed to show the relevance of psychology to your health and wellness and to help you appreciate the many, and deep, connections between this comparatively new science and your everyday life.

GLOSSARY

A

abnormal behavior Behavior that is deviant, maladaptive, or personally distressful over a relatively long period of time.

absolute threshold The minimum amount of stimulus energy that a person can detect.

accommodation An individual's adjustment of his or her schemas to new information.

acquired immune deficiency syndrome (AIDS) A sexually transmitted infection, caused by the human immunodeficiency virus (HIV), that destroys the body's immune system.

acquisition The initial learning of the connection between the unconditioned stimulus and the conditioned stimulus when these two stimuli are paired.

action potential The brief wave of positive electrical charge that sweeps down the axon.

activation-synthesis theory Theory that dreaming occurs when the cerebral cortex synthesizes neural signals generated from activity in the lower part of the brain and that dreams result from the brain's attempts to find logic in random brain activity that occurs during sleep.

addiction Either a physical or a psychological dependence, or both, on a drug.

adrenal glands Glands at the top of each kidney that are responsible for regulating moods, energy level, and the ability to cope with stress.

aerobic exercise Sustained activity—jogging, swimming, or cycling, for example—that stimulates heart and lung functioning.

affectionate love Also called companionate love; love that occurs when individuals desire to have another person near and have a deep, caring affection for the person.

affective commitment A kind of job commitment deriving from the employee's emotional attachment to the workplace.

afferent nerves Also called sensory nerves; nerves that carry information about the external environment *to* the brain and spinal cord via sensory receptors.

aggression Behaviors that are intended to harm another person.

alcoholism A disorder that involves long-term, repeated, uncontrolled, compulsive, and excessive use of alcoholic beverages and that impairs the drinker's health and social relationships.

algorithms Strategies—including formulas, instructions, and the testing of all possible solutions—that guarantee a solution to a problem.

all-or-nothing principle The principle that once the electrical impulse reaches a certain level of intensity (its threshold), it fires and moves all the way down the axon without losing any intensity.

altruism Unselfish interest in helping another person.

amnesia The loss of memory.

amygdala An almond-shaped structure within the base of the temporal lobe that is involved in the discrimination of objects that are necessary for the organism's survival, such as appropriate food, mates, and social rivals.

androgens The main class of male sex hormones.

androgynous Having attributes that we typically associate with both genders.

anorexia nervosa Eating disorder that involves the relentless pursuit of thinness through starvation.

anterograde amnesia A memory disorder that affects the retention of new information and events.

antianxiety drugs Commonly known as tranquilizers, drugs that reduce anxiety by making individuals calmer and less excitable.

antidepressant drugs Drugs that regulate mood.

antipsychotic drugs Powerful drugs that diminish agitated behavior, reduce tension, decrease hallucinations, improve social behavior, and produce better sleep patterns in individuals with a severe psychological disorder, especially schizophrenia.

antisocial personality disorder (ASPD) A psychological disorder characterized by guiltlessness, law-breaking, exploitation of others, irresponsibility, and deceit.

anxiety disorders Psychological disorders involving fears that are uncontrollable, disproportionate to the actual danger the person might be in, and disruptive of ordinary life.

apparent movement The perception that a stationary object is moving.

applied behavior analysis Also called behavior modification, the use of operant conditioning principles to change human behavior.

archetypes Jung's term for emotionally laden ideas and images in the collective unconscious that have rich and symbolic meaning for all people.

artificial intelligence (AI) A scientific field that focuses on creating machines capable of performing activities that require intelligence when they are done by people.

assimilation An individual's incorporation of new information into existing knowledge.

association cortex Sometimes called association areas, the region of the cerebral cortex that is the site of the highest intellectual functions, such as thinking and problem solving.

associative learning Learning that occurs when we make a connection, or an association, between two events.

Atkinson-Shiffrin theory Theory stating that memory storage involves three separate systems: sensory memory, short-term memory, and long-term memory.

attention The process of focusing awareness on a narrowed aspect of the environment.

attention deficit hyperactivity disorder (ADHD) One of the most common psychological disorders of childhood, in which individuals show one or more of the following: inattention, hyperactivity, and impulsivity.

attitudes Our feelings, opinions, and beliefs about people, objects, and ideas.

attribution theory The view that people are motivated to discover the underlying causes of behavior as part of their effort to make sense of the behavior.

auditory nerve The nerve structure that receives information about sound from the hair cells of the inner ear and carries these neural impulses to the brain's auditory areas.

authoritarian parenting A restrictive, punitive style in which the parent exhorts the child to follow the parent's directions and to value hard work and effort.

authoritative parenting A parenting style that encourages the child to be independent but that still places limits and controls on behavior.

autobiographical memory A special form of episodic memory, consisting of a person's recollections of his or her life experiences.

automatic processes States of consciousness that require little attention and do not interfere with other ongoing activities.

autonomic nervous system The body system that takes messages to and from the body's internal organs, monitoring such processes as breathing, heart rate, and digestion.

availability heuristic A prediction about the probability of an event based on the ease of recalling or imagining similar events.

aversive conditioning A form of treatment that consists of repeated pairings of a stimulus with a very unpleasant stimulus.

avoidance learning An organism's learning that it can altogether avoid a negative stimulus by making a particular response.

axon The part of the neuron that carries information away from the cell body toward other cells.

B

barbiturates Depressant drugs, such as Nembutal and Seconal, that decrease central nervous system activity.

basal ganglia Large neuron clusters located above the thalamus and under the cerebral cortex that work with the cerebellum and the cerebral cortex to control and coordinate voluntary movements.

base rate fallacy The tendency to ignore information about general principles in favor of very specific but vivid information.

behavior Everything we do that can be directly observed.

behavioral approach An approach to psychology emphasizing the scientific study of observable behavioral responses and their environmental determinants.

behavioral genetics The study of the inherited underpinnings of behavioral characteristics.

behavioral medicine An interdisciplinary field that focuses on developing and integrating behavioral and biomedical knowledge to promote health and reduce illness; overlaps with health psychology.

behaviorism A theory of learning that focuses solely on observable behaviors, discounting the importance of such mental activity as thinking, wishing, and hoping.

behavior therapies Treatments, based on the behavioral and social cognitive theories of learning, that use principles of learning to reduce or eliminate maladaptive behavior.

big five factors of personality The five broad traits that are thought to describe the main dimensions of personality: neuroticism (emotional instability), extraversion, openness to experience, agreeableness, and conscientiousness.

binding In the sense of vision, the bringing together and integration of what is processed by different neural pathways or cells.

binge eating disorder (BED) Eating disorder characterized by recurrent episodes of consuming large amounts of food during which the person feels a lack of control over eating.

binocular cues Depth cues that depend on the combination of the images in the left and right eyes and on the way the two eyes work together.

biological approach An approach to psychology focusing on the body, especially the brain and nervous system.

biological rhythms Periodic physiological fluctuations in the body, such as the rise and fall of hormones and accelerated and decelerated cycles of brain activity, that can influence our behavior.

biological therapies Also called biomedical therapies, treatments that reduce or eliminate the symptoms of psychological disorders by altering aspects of body functioning.

bipolar disorder Mood disorder characterized by extreme mood swings that include one or more episodes of mania, an overexcited, unrealistically optimistic state.

bisexual Referring to a sexual orientation in which the individual is sexually attracted to people of both sexes.

borderline personality disorder (BPD) A psychological disorder characterized by a pervasive pattern of instability in interpersonal relationships, self-image, and emotions, and of marked impulsivity beginning by early adulthood and present in a variety of contexts.

bottom-up processing The operation in sensation and perception in which sensory receptors register information about the external environment and send it up to the brain for interpretation.

brain stem The stemlike brain area that includes much of the hindbrain (it does not include the cerebellum) and the midbrain; it connects with the spinal cord at its lower end and then extends upward to encase the reticular formation in the midbrain.

broaden-and-build model Fredrickson's model of positive emotion, stating that the function of positive emotions lies in their effects on an individual's attention and ability to build resources.

bulimia nervosa Eating disorder in which an individual (typically female) consistently follows a binge-and-purge eating pattern.

burnout A distressed psychological state in which a person experiences emotional exhaustion and little motivation for work.

bystander effect The tendency of an individual who observes an emergency to help less when other people are present than when the observer is alone.

C

Cannon-Bard theory The proposition that emotion and physiological reactions occur simultaneously.

case study or case history An in-depth look at a single individual.

catatonia State of immobility and unresponsiveness lasting for long periods of time.

cell body The part of the neuron that contains the nucleus, which directs the manufacture of substances that the neuron needs for growth and maintenance.

central nervous system (CNS) The brain and spinal cord.

cerebral cortex Part of the forebrain, the outer layer of the brain, responsible for the most complex mental functions, such as thinking and planning.

chromosomes In the human cell, threadlike structures that come in 23 pairs, one member of each pair originating from each parent, and that contain the remarkable substance DNA.

circadian rhythms Daily behavioral or physiological cycles. Daily circadian rhythms involve the sleep/wake cycle, body temperature, blood pressure, and blood sugar level.

classical conditioning Learning process in which a neutral stimulus becomes associated with a meaningful stimulus and acquires the capacity to elicit a similar response.

client-centered therapy Also called Rogerian therapy or nondirective therapy, a form of humanistic therapy, developed by Rogers, in which the therapist provides a warm, supportive atmosphere to improve the client's self-concept and to encourage the client to gain insight into problems.

cognition The way in which information is processed and manipulated in remembering, thinking, and knowing.

cognitive affective processing systems (CAPS) Mischel's theoretical model for describing that our thoughts and emotions about ourselves and the world affect our behavior and become linked in ways that matter to behavior.

cognitive appraisal Individuals' interpretation of the events in their lives as harmful, threatening, or challenging and their determination of whether they have the resources to cope effectively with the events.

cognitive approach An approach to psychology emphasizing the mental processes involved in knowing: how we direct our attention, perceive, remember, think, and solve problems.

cognitive-behavior therapy A therapy that combines cognitive therapy and behavior therapy with the goal of developing self-efficacy.

cognitive dissonance An individual's psychological discomfort (dissonance) caused by two inconsistent thoughts.

cognitive reappraisal Regulating one's feelings about an experience by reinterpreting that experience or thinking about it in a different way or from a different angle.

cognitive theory of dreaming Theory proposing that we can understand dreaming by applying the same cognitive concepts we use in studying the waking mind; rests on the idea that dreams are essentially subconscious cognitive processing involving information and memory.

cognitive therapies Treatments that point to cognitions (thoughts) as the main source of psychological problems and that attempt to change the individual's feelings and behaviors by changing cognitions.

collective unconscious Jung's term for the impersonal, deepest layer of the unconscious mind, shared by all human beings because of their common ancestral past.

concept A mental category that is used to group objects, events, and characteristics.

concrete operational stage Piaget's third stage of cognitive development, lasting from about 7 to 11 years of age, during which the individual uses operations and replaces intuitive reasoning with logical reasoning in concrete situations.

conditioned response (CR) The learned response to the conditioned stimulus that occurs after conditioned stimulus–unconditioned stimulus pairing.

conditioned stimulus (CS) A previously neutral stimulus that eventually elicits a conditioned response after being paired with the unconditioned stimulus.

conditions of worth The standards that the individual must live up to in order to receive positive regard from others.

conduct disorder A pattern of offensive behavior that violates the basic rights of others.

cones The receptor cells in the retina that allow for color perception.

confederate A person who is given a role to play in a study so that the social context can be manipulated.

confirmation bias The tendency to search for and use information that supports our ideas rather than refutes them.

conformity A change in a person's behavior to coincide more closely with a group standard.

connectionism Also called parallel distributed processing (PDP), the theory that memory is stored throughout the brain in connections among neurons, several of which may work together to process a single memory.

consciousness An individual's awareness of external events and internal sensations under a condition of arousal, including awareness of the self and thoughts about one's experiences.

continuance commitment A kind of job commitment deriving from the employee's perception that leaving the organization would be too costly, both economically and socially.

control group The participants in an experiment who are as much like the experimental group as possible and who are treated in every way like the experimental group except for a manipulated factor, the independent variable.

controlled processes The most alert states of human consciousness, during which individuals actively focus their efforts toward a goal.

convergence A binocular cue to depth and distance in which the muscle movements in our two eyes provide information about how deep and/or far away something is.

convergent thinking Thinking that produces the single best solution to a problem.

coping Managing taxing circumstances, expending effort to solve life's problems, and seeking to master or reduce stress.

corpus callosum The large bundle of axons that connects the brain's two hemispheres, responsible for relaying information between the two sides.

correlational research Research that examines the relationships between variables, whose purpose is to examine whether and how two variables change together.

counterconditioning A classical conditioning procedure for changing the relationship between a conditioned stimulus and its conditioned response.

couples therapy Group therapy with married or unmarried couples whose major problem lies within their relationship.

creativity The ability to think about something in novel and unusual ways and to devise unconventional solutions to problems.

critical thinking The process of reflecting deeply and actively, asking questions, and evaluating the evidence.

culture-fair tests Intelligence tests that are intended to be culturally unbiased.

D

decay theory Theory stating that when we learn something new, a neurochemical memory trace forms, but over time this trace disintegrates; suggests that the passage of time always increases forgetting.

decision making The mental activity of evaluating alternatives and choosing among them.

deductive reasoning Reasoning from a general case that is known to be true to a specific instance.

deep brain stimulation A procedure for treatment-resistant depression that involves the implantation of electrodes in the brain that emit signals to alter the brain's electrical circuitry.

defense mechanisms Tactics the ego uses to reduce anxiety by unconsciously distorting reality.

deindividuation The reduction in personal identity and erosion of the sense of personal responsibility when one is part of a group.

delusions False, unusual, and sometimes magical beliefs that are not part of an individual's culture.

demand characteristics Any aspects of a study that communicate to the participants how the experimenter wants them to behave.

dendrites Treelike fibers projecting from a neuron, which receive information and orient it toward the neuron's cell body.

deoxyribonucleic acid (DNA) A complex molecule in the cell's chromosomes that carries genetic information.

dependent variable The outcome; the factor that can change in an experiment in response to changes in the independent variable.

depressants Psychoactive drugs that slow down mental and physical activity.

depressive disorders Mood disorders in which the individual suffers from depression—an unrelenting lack of pleasure in life.

depth perception The ability to perceive objects three-dimensionally.

descriptive research Research that determines the basic dimensions of a phenomenon, defining what it is, how often it occurs, and so on.

descriptive statistics Mathematical procedures that are used to describe and summarize sets of data in a meaningful way.

development The pattern of continuity and change in human capabilities that occurs throughout life, involving both growth and decline.

diathesis-stress model View of schizophrenia emphasizing that a combination of biogenetic disposition and stress causes the disorder.

difference threshold The degree of difference that must exist between two stimuli before the difference is detected.

discrimination An unjustified negative or harmful action toward a member of a group simply because the person belongs to that group.

discrimination (in classical conditioning) The process of learning to respond to certain stimuli and not others.

discrimination (in operant conditioning) Responding appropriately to stimuli that signal that a behavior will or will not be reinforced.

disorders of sexual development (DSD) Congenital conditions in which the development of chromosomal, gonadal, or anatomical sex is atypical; formerly called *intersex conditions* (or *hermaphroditism*).

display rules Sociocultural standards that determine when, where, and how emotions should be expressed.

dissociative amnesia Dissociative disorder characterized by extreme memory loss that is caused by extensive psychological stress.

dissociative disorders Psychological disorders that involve a sudden loss of memory or change in identity due to the dissociation (separation) of the individual's conscious awareness from previous memories and thoughts.

dissociative fugue Dissociative disorder in which the individual not only develops amnesia but also unexpectedly travels away from home and sometimes assumes a new identity.

dissociative identity disorder (DID) Formerly called multiple personality disorder, a dissociative disorder in which the individual has two or more distinct personalities or identities, each with its own memories, behaviors, and relationships.

divergent thinking Thinking that produces many solutions to the same problem.

divided attention Concentrating on more than one activity at the same time.

divided consciousness view of hypnosis Hilgard's view that hypnosis involves a splitting of consciousness into two separate components, one of which follows the hypnotist's commands and the other of which acts as a "hidden observer."

dominant-recessive genes principle The principle that, if one gene of a pair is dominant and one is recessive, the dominant gene overrides the recessive gene. A recessive gene exerts its influence only if both genes of a pair are recessive.

double-blind experiment An experimental design in which neither the experimenter nor the participants are aware of which participants are in the experimental group and which are in the control group until the results are calculated.

downsizing A dramatic cutting of the workforce that is an increasingly popular business strategy to enhance profitability.

dream analysis A psychoanalytic technique for interpreting a person's dreams.

drive An aroused state that occurs because of a physiological need.

DSM-IV The *Diagnostic and Statistical Manual of Mental Disorders;* the major classification of psychological disorders in the United States.

dysthymic disorder (DD) Mood disorder that is generally more chronic and has fewer symptoms than MDD; the individual is in a depressed mood for most days for at least two years as an adult or at least one year as a child or an adolescent.

E

efferent nerves Also called motor nerves; nerves that carry information *out of* the brain and spinal cord to other areas of the body.

ego The Freudian structure of personality that deals with the demands of reality.

egoism Giving to another person to ensure reciprocity; to gain self-esteem; to present oneself as powerful, competent, or caring; or to avoid censure from self and others for failing to live up to society's expectations.

elaboration The formation of a number of different connections around a stimulus at a given level of memory encoding.

elaboration likelihood model Theory identifying two ways to persuade: a central route and a peripheral route.

electroconvulsive therapy (ECT) Also called shock therapy, a treatment, commonly used for depression, that sets off a seizure in the brain.

emerging adulthood The transitional period from adolescence to adulthood, spanning approximately 18 to 25 years of age.

emotion Feeling, or affect, that can involve physiological arousal (such as a fast heartbeat), conscious experience (thinking about being in love with someone), and behavioral expression (a smile or grimace).

emotion-focused coping The coping strategy that involves responding to the stress that one is feeling—trying to manage one's emotional reaction—rather than focusing on the problem itself.

empathy A feeling of oneness with the emotional state of another person.

empirically keyed test A type of self-report test that presents many questionnaire items to two groups that are known to be different in some central way.

empirical method Gaining knowledge through the observation of events, the collection of data, and logical reasoning.

encoding The first step in memory; the process by which information gets into memory storage.

endocrine system The body system consisting of a set of glands that regulate the activities of certain organs by releasing their chemical products into the bloodstream.

episodic memory The retention of information about the where, when, and what of life's happenings—that is, how individuals remember life's episodes.

ergonomics Also called human factors, a field that combines engineering and psychology and that focuses on understanding and enhancing the safety and efficiency of the human–machine interaction.

estrogens The main class of female sex hormones.

ethnocentrism The tendency to favor one's own ethnic group over other groups.

evolutionary approach An approach to psychology centered on evolutionary ideas such as adaptation, reproduction, and natural selection as the basis for explaining specific human behaviors.

exercise Structured activities whose goal is to improve health.

experiment A carefully regulated procedure in which the researcher manipulates one or more variables that are believed to influence some other variable.

experimental group The participants in an experiment who receive the drug or other treatment under study—that is, those who are exposed to the change that the independent variable represents.

experimenter bias Occurs when the experimenter's expectations influence the outcome of the research.

explicit memory Also called declarative memory, the conscious recollection of information, such as specific facts or events and, at least in humans, information that can be verbally communicated.

external validity The degree to which an experimental design actually reflects the real-world issues it is supposed to address.

extinction (in classical conditioning) The weakening of the conditioned response when the unconditioned stimulus is absent.

extinction (in operant conditioning) Decreases in the frequency of a behavior when the behavior is no longer reinforced.

extrinsic motivation Motivation that involves external incentives such as rewards and punishments.

F

face validity The extent to which a test item appears to be a good fit to the characteristic it measures.

facial feedback hypothesis The idea that facial expressions can influence emotions as well as reflect them.

false consensus effect Observers' overestimation of the degree to which everybody else thinks or acts the way they do.

family therapy Group therapy with family members.

feature detectors Neurons in the brain's visual system that respond to particular features of a stimulus.

fetish An object or activity that arouses sexual interest and desire.

figure-ground relationship The principle by which we organize the perceptual field into stimuli that stand out (figure) and those that are left over (ground).

fixation Using a prior strategy and failing to look at a problem from a fresh new perspective.

flashbulb memory The memory of emotionally significant events that people often recall with more accuracy and vivid imagery than everyday events.

flat affect The display of little or no emotion—a common negative symptom of schizophrenia.

flow The optimal experience of a match between one's skills and the challenge of a task.

forebrain The brain's largest division and its most forward part.

formal operational stage Piaget's fourth stage of cognitive development, which begins at 11 to 15 years of age and continues through the adult years; it features thinking about things that are not concrete, making predictions, and using logic to come up with hypotheses about the future.

free association A psychoanalytic technique that involves encouraging individuals to say aloud whatever comes to mind, no matter how trivial or embarrassing.

frequency theory Theory on how the inner ear registers the frequency of sound, stating that the perception of a sound's frequency depends on how often the auditory nerve fires.

frontal lobes The portion of the cerebral cortex behind the forehead, involved in personality, intelligence, and the control of voluntary muscles.

functional fixedness Failing to solve a problem as a result of fixation on a thing's usual functions.

functionalism James's approach to mental processes, emphasizing the functions and purposes of the mind and behavior in the individual's adaptation to the environment.

fundamental attribution error Observers' overestimation of the importance of internal traits and underestimation of the importance of external situations when they seek explanations of an actor's behavior.

G

gender The social and psychological aspects of being female or male; gender goes beyond biological sex to include a person's understanding of the meaning to his or her own life of being male or female.

gender identity An individual's multifaceted sense of belonging to the male or female sex.

gender identity disorder (GID) Strong, persistent cross-sex identification and a continuing discomfort with, or sense of inappropriateness of, one's assigned sex.

gender roles Expectations for how females and males should think, act, and feel.

gender similarities hypothesis Hyde's proposition that men and women (and boys and girls) are much more similar than they are different.

gender stereotypes Overly general beliefs and expectations about what women and men are like.

general adaptation syndrome (GAS) Selye's term for the common effects of stressful demands on the body, consisting of three stages: alarm, resistance, and exhaustion.

generalization (in classical conditioning) The tendency of a new stimulus that is similar to the original conditioned stimulus to elicit a response that is similar to the conditioned response.

generalization (in operant conditioning) Performing a reinforced behavior in a different situation.

generalized anxiety disorder Psychological disorder marked by persistent anxiety for at least six months and in which the individual is unable to specify the reasons for the anxiety.

genes The units of hereditary information, consisting of short segments of chromosomes composed of DNA.

genotype An individual's genetic heritage; his or her actual genetic material.

gestalt psychology A school of thought interested in how people naturally organize their perceptions according to certain patterns.

gifted Possessing high intelligence (an IQ of 130 or higher) and/or superior talent in a particular area.

glands Organs or tissues in the body that create chemicals that control many of our bodily functions.

glial cells Also called glia; the second of two types of cells in the nervous system; glial cells provide support, nutritional benefits, and other functions and keep neurons running smoothly.

gonads Glands that produce sex hormones and generate ova (eggs) in females and sperm in males; collectively called gametes, the ova and sperm are the cells that will eventually be used in reproduction.

group polarization effect The solidification and further strengthening of an individual's position as a consequence of a group discussion or interaction.

group therapy A sociocultural approach to the treatment of psychological disorders that brings together individuals who share a particular psychological disorder in sessions that are typically led by a mental health professional.

groupthink The impaired group decision making that occurs when making the right decision is less important than maintaining group harmony.

H

habituation Decreased responsiveness to a stimulus after repeated presentations.

hallucinations Sensory experiences that occur in the absence of real stimuli.

hallucinogens Also called psychedelics, psychoactive drugs that modify a person's perceptual experiences and produce visual images that are not real.

halo effect A bias, common in performance ratings, that occurs when a rater gives a person the same rating on all of the items being evaluated, even though the individual varies across the dimensions being assessed.

hardiness A personal quality characterized by a sense of commitment rather than alienation, and of control rather than powerlessness; a hardy person sees problems as challenges rather than threats.

Hawthorne effect The tendency of individuals to perform better simply because of being singled out and made to feel important.

health behaviors Practices that have an impact on physical well-being, such as adopting a healthy approach to stress, exercising, eating right, brushing one's teeth, performing breast and testicular exams, not smoking, drinking in moderation (or not at all), and practicing safe sex.

health psychology A subfield of psychology that emphasizes psychology's role in establishing and maintaining health and preventing and treating illness.

heritability The proportion of observable differences in a group that can be explained by differences in the genes of the group's members.

heterosexual Referring to a sexual orientation in which the individual is generally sexually attracted to members of the opposite sex.

heuristics Shortcut strategies or guidelines that suggest a solution to a problem but do not guarantee an answer.

hierarchy of needs Maslow's theory that human needs must be satisfied in the following sequence: physiological needs, safety, love and belongingness, esteem, and self-actualization.

hindbrain Located at the skull's rear, the lowest portion of the brain, consisting of the medulla, cerebellum, and pons.

hindsight bias The tendency to report falsely, after the fact, that we accurately predicted an outcome.

hippocampus The structure in the limbic system that has a special role in the storage of memories.

homeostasis The body's tendency to maintain an equilibrium, or steady state.

homosexual Referring to a sexual orientation in which the individual is generally sexually attracted to members of the same sex.

hormones Chemical messengers that are produced by the endocrine glands and carried by the bloodstream to all parts of the body.

humanistic approach An approach to psychology emphasizing a person's positive qualities, the capacity for positive growth, and the freedom to choose any destiny.

humanistic perspectives Theoretical views stressing a person's capacity for personal growth and positive human qualities.

humanistic therapies Treatments, unique in their emphasis on people's self-healing capacities, that encourage clients to understand themselves and to grow personally.

human relations approach A management approach emphasizing the psychological characteristics of workers and managers, stressing the importance of factors such as morale, attitudes, values, and humane treatment of workers.

human sexual response pattern Masters and Johnson's model of human sexual response, consisting of four phases—excitement, plateau, orgasm, and resolution.

hypnosis An altered state of consciousness or a psychological state of altered attention and expectation in which the individual is unusually receptive to suggestions.

hypothalamic-pituitary-adrenal axis (HPA axis) The complex set of interactions among the hypothalamus, the pituitary gland, and the adrenal glands that regulates various body processes and controls reactions to stressful events.

hypothalamus A small forebrain structure, located just below the thalamus, that monitors three pleasurable activities—eating, drinking, and sex—as well as emotion, stress, and reward.

hypothesis An educated guess that derives logically from a theory; a prediction that can be tested.

I

id The part of the person that Freud called the "it," consisting of unconscious drives; the individual's reservoir of sexual energy.

identity versus identity confusion Erikson's fifth psychological stage, in which adolescents face the challenges of finding out who they are, what they are all about, and where they are going in life.

implementation intentions Specific strategies for dealing with the challenges of making a life change.

implicit memory Also called nondeclarative memory, memory in which behavior is affected by prior experience without a conscious recollection of that experience.

independent variable A manipulated experimental factor; the variable that the experimenter changes to see what its effects are.

individual psychology Adler's view that people are motivated by purposes and goals and that perfection, not pleasure, is thus the key motivator in human life.

inductive reasoning Reasoning from specific observations to make generalizations.

infant attachment The close emotional bond between an infant and its caregiver.

inferential statistics Mathematical methods that are used to indicate whether results for a sample are likely to generalize to a population.

infinite generativity The ability of language to produce an endless number of meaningful sentences.

informational social influence The influence other people have on us because we want to be right.

inner ear The part of the ear that includes the oval window, cochlea, and basilar membrane and whose function is to convert sound waves into neural impulses and send them to the brain.

insight learning A form of problem solving in which the organism develops a sudden insight into or understanding of a problem's solution.

instinct An innate (unlearned) biological pattern of behavior that is assumed to be universal throughout a species.

instinctive drift The tendency of animals to revert to instinctive behavior that interferes with learning.

integrative therapy A combination of techniques from different therapies based on the therapist's judgment of which particular methods will provide the greatest benefit for the client.

integrity test A type of job-screening examination that is designed to assess whether a candidate will be honest on the job.

intellectual disability A condition of limited mental ability in which an individual has a low IQ, usually below 70 on a traditional intelligence test, and has difficulty adapting to everyday life.

intelligence All-purpose ability to do well on cognitive tasks, to solve problems, and to learn from experience.

intelligence quotient (IQ) An individual's mental age divided by chronological age multiplied by 100.

interference theory The theory that people forget not because memories are lost from storage but because other information gets in the way of what they want to remember.

internal validity The degree to which changes in the dependent variable are due to the manipulation of the independent variable.

interpretation A psychoanalyst's search for symbolic, hidden meanings in what the client says and does during therapy.

intrinsic motivation Motivation based on internal factors such as organismic needs (competence, relatedness, and autonomy), as well as curiosity, challenge, and fun.

investment model A model of long-term relationships that examines the ways that commitment, investment, and the availability of attractive alternative partners predict satisfaction and stability in relationships.

J

James-Lange theory The theory that emotion results from physiological states triggered by stimuli in the environment.

job analysis The process of generating a description of what a job involves, including the knowledge and skills that are necessary to carry out the job's functions.

job crafting The physical and cognitive changes individuals can make within the constraints of a task to make the work "their own."

job satisfaction The extent to which a person is content in his or her job.

job stress The experience of stress on the job and in the workplace setting.

K

kinesthetic senses Senses that provide information about movement, posture, and orientation.

KSAOs (KSAs) Common elements in a person-oriented job analysis; an abbreviation for knowledge, skills, abilities, and other characteristics.

L

language A form of communication—whether spoken, written, or signed—that is based on a system of symbols.

latent content According to Freud, a dream's hidden content; its unconscious and true meaning.

latent learning Also called implicit learning, unreinforced learning that is not immediately reflected in behavior.

law of effect Thorndike's law stating that behaviors followed by positive outcomes are strengthened and that behaviors followed by negative outcomes are weakened.

learned helplessness An organism's learning through experience with unavoidable negative stimuli that it has no control over negative outcomes.

learning A systematic, relatively permanent change in behavior that occurs through experience.

leisure The pleasant times before or after work when individuals are free to pursue activities and interests of their own choosing, such as hobbies, sports, and reading.

levels of processing A continuum of memory processing from shallow to intermediate to deep, with deeper processing producing better memory.

limbic system A loosely connected network of structures under the cerebral cortex, important in both memory and emotion. Its two principal structures are the amygdala and the hippocampus.

lithium The lightest of the solid elements in the periodic table of elements, widely used to treat bipolar disorder.

longitudinal design A special kind of systematic observation, used by correlational researchers, that involves obtaining measures of the variables of interest in multiple waves over time.

long-term memory A relatively permanent type of memory that stores huge amounts of information for a long time.

M

major depressive disorder (MDD) Psychological disorder involving a significant depressive episode and depressed characteristics, such as lethargy and hopelessness, for at least two weeks.

manifest content According to Freud, the surface content of a dream, containing dream symbols that disguise the dream's true meaning.

mean A measure of central tendency that is the average for a sample.

median A measure of central tendency that is the middle score in a sample.

medical model The view that psychological disorders are medical diseases with a biological origin.

memory The retention of information or experience over time as the result of three key processes: encoding, storage, and retrieval.

mental age (MA) An individual's level of mental development relative to that of others.

mental processes The thoughts, feelings, and motives that each of us experiences privately but that cannot be observed directly.

mentoring A relationship between an experienced employee—a mentor—and a novice, in which the more experienced employee serves as an advisor, a sounding board, and a source of support for the newer employee.

mere exposure effect The phenomenon that the more we encounter someone or something, the more probable it is that we will start liking the person or thing even if we do not realize we have seen it before.

meta-analysis A method that allows researchers to combine the results of several different studies on a similar topic in order to establish the strength of an effect.

midbrain Located between the hindbrain and forebrain, an area in which many nerve-fiber systems ascend and descend to connect the higher and lower portions of the brain; in particular, the midbrain relays information between the brain and the eyes and ears.

middle ear The part of the ear that channels sound through the eardrum, hammer, anvil, and stirrup to the inner ear.

mindfulness The state of being alert and mentally present for one's everyday activities.

Minnesota Multiphasic Personality Inventory (MMPI) The most widely used and researched empirically keyed self-report personality test.

mode A measure of central tendency that is the most common score in a sample.

monocular cues Powerful depth cues available from the image in one eye, either the right or the left.

mood disorders Psychological disorders—the main types of which are depressive disorders and bipolar disorder—in which there is a primary disturbance of mood: prolonged emotion that colors the individual's entire emotional state.

morphology A language's rules for word formation.

motivated forgetting Forgetting that occurs when something is so painful or anxiety-laden that remembering it is intolerable.

motivation The force that moves people to behave, think, and feel the way they do.

motor cortex A region in the cerebral cortex that processes information about voluntary movement, located just behind the frontal lobes.

myelin sheath A layer of fat cells that encases and insulates most axons.

N

naturalistic observation The observation of behavior in a real-world setting.

natural selection Darwin's principle of an evolutionary process in which organisms that are best adapted to their environment will survive and produce offspring.

nature An individual's biological inheritance, especially his or her genes.

need A deprivation that energizes the drive to eliminate or reduce the deprivation.

negative affect Unpleasant emotions such as anger, guilt, and sadness.

negative punishment The removal of a positive stimulus following a given behavior in order to decrease the frequency of that behavior.

negative reinforcement An increase in the frequency of a behavior in response to the subsequent removal of something that is unpleasant.

neglectful parenting A parenting style characterized by a lack of parental involvement in the child's life.

neocortex The outermost part of the cerebral cortex, making up 80 percent of the cortex in the human brain.

nervous system The body's electrochemical communication circuitry.

neural networks Networks of nerve cells that integrate sensory input and motor output.

neurons One of two types of cells in the nervous system; neurons are the nerve cells that handle the information-processing function.

neuroscience The scientific study of the structure, function, development, genetics, and biochemistry of the nervous system, emphasizing that the brain and nervous system are central to understanding behavior, thought, and emotion.

neurotransmitters Chemical substances that are stored in very tiny sacs within the terminal buttons and involved in transmitting information across a synaptic gap to the next neuron.

noise Irrelevant and competing stimuli—not only sounds but also any distracting stimuli for our senses.

normal distribution A symmetrical, bell-shaped curve, with a majority of the scores falling in the middle of the possible range and few scores appearing toward the extremes of the range.

normative commitment A kind of job commitment deriving from the employee's sense of obligation to the organization for the investment it has made in the individual's personal and professional development.

normative social influence The influence others have on us because we want them to like us.

nurture An individual's environmental and social experiences.

O

obedience Behavior that complies with the explicit demands of the individual in authority.

observational learning Learning that occurs when a person observes and imitates another's behavior.

obsessive-compulsive disorder (OCD) Anxiety disorder in which the individual has anxiety-provoking thoughts that will not go away and/ or urges to perform repetitive, ritualistic behaviors to prevent or produce some future situation.

occipital lobes Structures located at the back of the head that respond to visual stimuli.

Oedipus complex According to Freud, a boy's intense desire to replace his father and enjoy the affections of his mother.

olfactory epithelium The lining of the roof of the nasal cavity, containing a sheet of receptor cells for smell.

open-mindedness The state of being receptive to other ways of looking at things.

operant conditioning Also called instrumental conditioning, a form of associative learning in which the consequences of a behavior change the probability of the behavior's occurrence.

operational definition A definition that provides an objective description of how a variable is going to be measured and observed in a particular study.

opiates Opium and its derivatives; narcotic drugs that depress activity in the central nervous system and eliminate pain.

opponent-process theory Theory stating that cells in the visual system respond to complementary pairs of red-green and blue-yellow colors; a given cell might be excited by red and inhibited by green, whereas another cell might be excited by yellow and inhibited by blue.

optic nerve The structure at the back of the eye, made up of axons of the ganglion cells, that carries visual information to the brain for further processing.

organizational citizenship behavior (OCB) Discretionary actions on the part of an employee that promote organizational effectiveness but are not included in the person's formal responsibilities.

organizational culture An organization's shared values, beliefs, norms, and customs.

organizational identity Employees' feelings of oneness with the organization and its goals.

orientation A program by which an organization introduces newly hired employees to the organization's goals, familiarizes them with its rules and regulations, and lets them know how to get things done.

outer ear The outermost part of the ear, consisting of the pinna and the external auditory canal.

ovaries Sex-related endocrine glands in the uterus that produce hormones related to women's sexual development and reproduction.

overlearning Learning to perform a task so well that it becomes automatic.

overt aggression Physically or verbally harming another person directly.

P

pain The sensation that warns us of damage to our bodies.

pancreas A dual-purpose gland under the stomach that performs both digestive and endocrine functions.

panic disorder Anxiety disorder in which the individual experiences recurrent, sudden onsets of intense apprehension or terror, often without warning and with no specific cause.

papillae Rounded bumps above the tongue's surface that contain the taste buds, the receptors for taste.

parallel processing The simultaneous distribution of information across different neural pathways.

paraphilias Sexual disorders that feature recurrent sexually arousing fantasies, urges, or behaviors involving nonhuman objects; the suffering or humiliation of oneself or one's partner; or children or other nonconsenting persons.

parasympathetic nervous system The part of the autonomic nervous system that calms the body.

parietal lobes Structures at the top and toward the rear of the head that are involved in registering spatial location, attention, and motor control.

pedophilia A paraphilia in which an adult or an older adolescent sexually fantasizes about or engages in sexual behavior with individuals who have not reached puberty.

perception The process of organizing and interpreting sensory information so that it has meaning.

perceptual constancy The recognition that objects are constant and unchanging even though sensory input about them is changing.

perceptual set A predisposition or readiness to perceive something in a particular way.

performance appraisal The evaluation of a person's success at meeting his or her organization's goals.

peripheral nervous system (PNS) The network of nerves that connects the brain and spinal cord to other parts of the body.

permissive parenting A parenting style characterized by the placement of few limits on the child's behavior.

personality A pattern of enduring, distinctive thoughts, emotions, and behaviors that characterize the way an individual adapts to the world.

personality disorders Chronic, maladaptive cognitive-behavioral patterns that are thoroughly integrated into an individual's personality.

personological and life story perspectives Theoretical views stressing that the way to understand the person is to focus on his or her life history and life story.

phenotype An individual's observable characteristics.

phobic disorder or phobia Anxiety disorder characterized by an irrational, overwhelming, persistent fear of a particular object or situation.

phonology A language's sound system.

physical dependence The physiological need for a drug that causes unpleasant withdrawal symptoms such as physical pain and a craving for the drug when it is discontinued.

pituitary gland A pea-sized gland just beneath the hypothalamus that controls growth and regulates other glands.

placebo In a drug study, a harmless substance that has no physiological effect, given to participants in a control group so that they are treated identically to the experimental group except for the active agent.

placebo effect Occurs when participants' expectations, rather than the experimental treatment, produce an outcome.

place theory Theory on how the inner ear registers the frequency of sound, stating that each frequency produces vibrations at a particular spot on the basilar membrane.

plasticity The brain's special capacity for change.

polygraph A machine, commonly called a lie detector, that monitors changes in the body, used to try to determine whether someone is lying.

population The entire group about which the investigator wants to draw conclusions.

positive affect Pleasant emotions such as joy, happiness, and interest.

positive illusions Positive views of the self that are not necessarily rooted in reality.

positive psychology A branch of psychology that emphasizes human strengths.

positive punishment The presentation of an unpleasant stimulus following a given behavior in order to decrease the frequency of that behavior.

positive reinforcement An increase in the frequency of a behavior in response to the subsequent presentation of something that is good.

post-traumatic stress disorder (PTSD) Anxiety disorder that develops through exposure to a traumatic event that has overwhelmed the person's abilities to cope.

pragmatics The useful character of language and the ability of language to communicate even more meaning than is said.

preferential looking A research technique that involves giving an infant a choice of what object to look at.

prejudice An unjustified negative attitude toward an individual based on the individual's membership in a particular group.

preoperational stage Piaget's second stage of cognitive development, lasting from about 2 to 7 years of age, during which thought is more symbolic than sensorimotor thought.

preparedness The species-specific biological predisposition to learn in certain ways but not others.

primary reinforcer A reinforcer that is innately satisfying; one that does not take any learning on the organism's part to make it pleasurable.

priming The activation of information that people already have in storage to help them remember new information better and faster.

proactive interference Situation in which material that was learned earlier disrupts the recall of material that was learned later.

problem-focused coping The coping strategy of squarely facing one's troubles and trying to solve them.

problem solving The mental process of finding an appropriate way to attain a goal when the goal is not readily available.

procedural memory Memory for skills.

projective test A personality assessment test that presents individuals with an ambiguous stimulus and asks them to describe it or tell a story about it—to project their own meaning onto the stimulus.

prosocial behavior Behavior that is intended to benefit other people.

prospective memory Remembering information about doing something in the future; includes memory for intentions.

prototype model A model emphasizing that when people evaluate whether a given item reflects a certain concept, they compare the item with the most typical item(s) in that category and look for a "family resemblance" with that item's properties.

psychoactive drugs Drugs that act on the nervous system to alter consciousness, modify perception, and change mood.

psychoanalysis Freud's therapeutic technique for analyzing an individual's unconscious thoughts.

psychodynamic approach An approach to psychology emphasizing unconscious thought, the conflict between biological drives (such as the drive for sex) and society's demands, and early childhood family experiences.

psychodynamic perspectives Theoretical views emphasizing that personality is primarily unconscious (beyond awareness).

psychodynamic therapies Treatments that stress the importance of the unconscious mind, extensive interpretation by the therapist, and the role of early childhood experiences in the development of an individual's problems.

psychological dependence The strong desire to repeat the use of a drug for emotional reasons, such as a feeling of well-being and reduction of stress.

psychology The scientific study of behavior and mental processes.

psychoneuroimmunology A new field of scientific inquiry that explores connections among psychological factors (such as attitudes and emotions), the nervous system, and the immune system.

psychopathology The scientific study of psychological disorders and the development of diagnostic categories and treatments for those disorders.

psychosurgery A biological therapy, with irreversible effects, that involves removal or destruction of brain tissue to improve the individual's adjustment.

psychotherapy A nonmedical process that helps individuals with psychological disorders recognize and overcome their problems.

puberty A period of rapid skeletal and sexual maturation that occurs mainly in early adolescence.

punishment A consequence that decreases the likelihood that a behavior will occur.

R

random assignment Researchers' assignment of participants to groups by chance, to reduce the likelihood that an experiment's results will be due to preexisting differences between groups.

random sample A sample that gives every member of the population an equal chance of being selected.

range A measure of dispersion that is the difference between the highest and lowest scores.

rational-emotive behavior therapy (REBT) A therapy based on Ellis's assertion that individuals develop a psychological disorder because of irrational and self-defeating beliefs and whose goal is to get clients to eliminate these beliefs by rationally examining them.

reasoning The mental activity of transforming information to reach conclusions.

referential thinking Ascribing personal meaning to completely random events.

reflective speech A technique in which the therapist mirrors the client's own feelings back to the client.

reinforcement The process by which a rewarding stimulus or event (a reinforcer) following a particular behavior increases the probability that the behavior will happen again.

relapse A return to former unhealthy patterns.

relational aggression Behavior that is meant to harm the social standing of another person.

reliability The extent to which a test yields a consistent, reproducible measure of performance.

REM sleep An active stage of sleep during which dreaming occurs.

renewal The recovery of the conditioned response when the organism is placed in a novel context.

representativeness heuristic The tendency to make judgments about group membership based on physical appearances or the match between a person and one's stereotype of a group rather than on available base rate information.

research participant bias Occurs when the behavior of research participants during the experiment is influenced by how they think they are supposed to behave or their expectations about what is happening to them.

resilience A person's ability to recover from or adapt to difficult times.

resistance A client's unconscious defense strategies that interfere with the psychoanalyst's understanding of the individual's problems.

resting potential In an inactive neuron, the voltage between the inside and outside of the axon wall.

reticular formation A system in the midbrain comprising a diffuse collection of neurons involved in stereotyped patterns of behavior such as walking, sleeping, and turning to attend to a sudden noise.

retina The multilayered light-sensitive surface in the eye that records electromagnetic energy and converts it to neural impulses for processing in the brain.

retrieval The memory process that occurs when information that was retained in memory comes out of storage.

retroactive interference Situation in which material that was learned later disrupts the retrieval of information that was learned earlier.

retrograde amnesia Memory loss for a segment of the past but not for new events.

retrospective memory Remembering information from the past.

risky shift The tendency for a group decision to be riskier than the average decision made by the individual group members.

rods The receptor cells in the retina that are sensitive to light but not very useful for color vision.

role conflict The kind of stress that arises when a person tries to meet the demands of more than one important life role, such as worker and mother.

romantic love Also called passionate love; love with strong components of sexuality and infatuation, often dominant in the early part of a love relationship.

Rorschach inkblot test A famous projective test that uses an individual's perception of inkblots to determine his or her personality.

S

sample The subset of the population chosen by the investigator for study.

schedules of reinforcement Specific patterns that determine when a behavior will be reinforced.

schema A preexisting mental concept or framework that helps people to organize and interpret information. Schemas from prior encounters with the environment influence the way we encode, make inferences about, and retrieve information.

schizophrenia Severe psychological disorder characterized by highly disordered thought processes, referred to as psychotic because they are so far removed from reality.

science The use of systematic methods to observe the natural world, including human behavior, and to draw conclusions.

scientific management The managerial philosophy that emphasizes the worker as a well-oiled machine and the determination of the most efficient methods for performing any work-related task.

script A schema for an event, often containing information about physical features, people, and typical occurrences.

secondary reinforcer A reinforcer that acquires its positive value through an organism's experience; a secondary reinforcer is a learned or conditioned reinforcer.

secondary sex characteristics Traits that differ between the two sexes but are not part of the reproductive system; they include breasts in females and facial hair in males.

secure attachment The ways that infants use their caregiver, usually their mother, as a secure base from which to explore the environment.

selective attention The process of focusing on a specific aspect of experience while ignoring others.

self-actualization The motivation to develop one's full potential as a human being—the highest and most elusive of Maslow's proposed needs.

self-determination theory Deci and Ryan's theory asserting that all humans have three basic, innate organismic needs: competence, relatedness, and autonomy.

self-efficacy The belief that one can master a situation and produce positive change.

self-objectification The tendency to see oneself primarily as an object in the eyes of others.

self-perception theory Bem's theory on how behaviors influence attitudes, stating that individuals make inferences about their attitudes by perceiving their behavior.

self-regulation The process by which an organism effortfully controls behavior in order to pursue important objectives.

self-report test Also called an objective test or an inventory, a method of measuring personality characteristics that directly asks people whether specific items describe their personality traits.

self-serving bias The tendency to take credit for our successes and to deny responsibility for our failures.

semantic memory A person's knowledge about the world, including his or her areas of expertise; general knowledge, such as of things learned in school; and everyday knowledge.

semantics The meaning of words and sentences in a particular language.

semicircular canals Three fluid-filled circular tubes in the inner ear containing the sensory receptors that detect head motion caused when we tilt or move our head and/or body.

sensation The process of receiving stimulus energies from the external environment and transforming those energies into neural energy.

sensorimotor stage Piaget's first stage of cognitive development, lasting from birth to about 2 years of age, during which infants construct an understanding of the world by coordinating sensory experiences with motor (physical) actions.

sensory adaptation A change in the responsiveness of the sensory system based on the average level of surrounding stimulation.

sensory memory Memory system that involves holding information from the world in its original sensory form for only an instant, not much longer than the brief time it is exposed to the visual, auditory, and other senses.

sensory receptors Specialized cells that detect stimulus information and transmit it to sensory (afferent) nerves and the brain.

serial position effect The tendency to recall the items at the beginning and end of a list more readily than those in the middle.

set point The weight maintained when the individual makes no effort to gain or lose weight.

sex The properties of a person that determine his or her classification as male or female.

sex chromosomes In humans, the pair of genes that differs between the sexes and determines a person's sex as male or female.

sexual harassment Unwelcome behavior or conduct of a sexual nature that offends, humiliates, or intimidates another person.

sexuality The ways people experience and express themselves as sexual beings.

sexually transmitted infection (STI) An infection that is contracted primarily through sexual activity—vaginal intercourse as well as oral and anal sex.

sexual orientation The direction of an individual's erotic interests.

sexual selection According to Darwin's theory of evolution, the differentiation between the male and female members of a species because of the differences between the two in competition and choice.

shaping Rewarding approximations of a desired behavior.

short-term memory Limited-capacity memory system in which information is usually retained for only as long as 30 seconds unless we use strategies to retain it longer.

signal detection theory A theory of perception that focuses on decision making about stimuli in the presence of uncertainty.

sleep A natural state of rest for the body and mind that involves the reversible loss of consciousness.

social cognitive behavior view of hypnosis Theory that hypnosis is a normal state in which the hypnotized person behaves the way he or she believes that a hypnotized person should behave.

social cognitive perspectives Theoretical views emphasizing conscious awareness, beliefs, expectations, and goals.

social comparison The process by which individuals evaluate their thoughts, feelings, behaviors, and abilities in relation to those of other people.

social contagion Imitative behavior involving the spread of actions, emotions, and ideas.

social exchange theory The view of social relationships as involving an exchange of goods, the objective of which is to minimize costs and maximize benefits.

social facilitation Improvement in an individual's performance because of the presence of others.

social identity The way we define ourselves in terms of our group membership.

social identity theory Tajfel's theory that our social identities are a crucial part of our self-image and a valuable source of positive feelings about ourselves.

social loafing Each person's tendency to exert less effort in a group because of reduced accountability for individual effort.

social psychology The study of how people think about, influence, and relate to other people.

social support Information and feedback from others indicating that one is loved and cared for, esteemed and valued, and included in a network of communication and mutual obligation.

sociocultural approach An approach to psychology that examines the ways in which social and cultural environments influence behavior.

somatic nervous system The body system consisting of the sensory nerves, whose function is to convey information from the skin and muscles to the CNS about conditions such as pain and temperature, and the motor nerves, whose function is to tell muscles what to do.

somatosensory cortex A region in the cerebral cortex that processes information about body sensations, located at the front of the parietal lobes.

spontaneous recovery The process in classical conditioning by which a conditioned response can recur after a time delay, without further conditioning.

stages of change model Theoretical model describing a five-step process by which individuals give up bad habits and adopt healthier lifestyles.

standard deviation A measure of dispersion that tells us how much scores in a sample differ from the mean of the sample.

standardization The development of uniform procedures for administering and scoring a test, and the creation of norms (performance standards) for the test.

stem cells Unique primitive cells that have the capacity to develop into most types of human cells.

stereotype A generalization about a group's characteristics that does not consider any variations from one individual to another.

stereotype threat An individual's fast-acting, self-fulfilling fear of being judged based on a negative stereotype about his or her group.

stimulants Psychoactive drugs that increase the central nervous system's activity. The most widely used stimulants are caffeine, nicotine, amphetamines, and cocaine.

storage The retention of information over time and how this information is represented in memory.

stream of consciousness Term used by William James to describe the mind as a continuous flow of changing sensations, images, thoughts, and feelings.

strengths-based management A management style emphasizing that maximizing an employee's existing strengths is much easier than trying to build such attributes from the ground up.

stress The responses of individuals to environmental stressors.

stress management program A regimen that teaches individuals how to appraise stressful events, how to develop skills for coping with stress, and how to put these skills into use in everyday life.

stressors Circumstances and events that threaten individuals and tax their coping abilities and that cause physiological changes to ready the body to handle the assault of stress.

structuralism Wundt's approach to discovering the basic elements, or structures, of mental processes; so called because of its focus on identifying the structures of the human mind.

structured interview A kind of interview in which candidates are asked specific questions that methodically seek to obtain truly useful information for the interviewer.

subgoals Intermediate goals or intermediate problems that put us in a better position for reaching the final goal or solution.

subjective well-being A person's assessment of his or her own level of positive affect relative to negative affect, and the individual's evaluation of his or her life in general.

subliminal perception The detection of information below the level of conscious awareness.

superego The Freudian structure of personality that serves as the harsh internal judge of our behavior; what we often call conscience.

suprachiasmatic nucleus (SCN) A small brain structure that uses input from the retina to synchronize its own rhythm with the daily cycle of light and dark; the mechanism by which the body monitors the change from day to night.

sustained attention Also called vigilance, the ability to maintain attention to a selected stimulus for a prolonged period of time.

sympathetic nervous system The part of the autonomic nervous system that arouses the body.

synapses Tiny spaces between neurons; the gaps between neurons are referred to as synaptic gaps.

syntax A language's rules for combining words to form acceptable phrases and sentences.

systematic desensitization A method of behavior therapy that treats anxiety by teaching the client to associate deep relaxation with increasingly intense anxiety-producing situations.

T

temperament An individual's behavioral style and characteristic way of responding.

temporal lobes Structures in the cerebral cortex that are located just above the ears and are involved in hearing, language processing, and memory.

testes Sex-related endocrine glands in the scrotum that produce hormones related to men's sexual development and reproduction.

thalamus The forebrain structure that sits at the top of the brain stem in the brain's central core and serves as an important relay station.

Thematic Apperception Test (TAT) A projective test that is designed to elicit stories that reveal something about an individual's personality.

theory A broad idea or set of closely related ideas that attempts to explain observations and to make predictions about future observations.

theory of planned behavior Theoretical model that includes the basic ideas of the theory of reasoned action but adds the person's perceptions of control over the outcome.

theory of reasoned action Theoretical model stating that effective change requires individuals to have specific intentions about their behaviors, as well as positive attitudes about a new behavior, and to perceive that their social group looks positively on the new behavior as well.

Theory X managers Managers who assume that work is innately unpleasant and that people have a strong desire to avoid it; such managers believe that employees need direction, dislike responsibility, and must be kept in line.

Theory Y managers Managers who assume that engaging in effortful behavior is natural to human beings; they recognize that people seek out responsibility and that motivation can come from allowing employees to suggest creative and meaningful solutions.

therapeutic alliance The relationship between the therapist and client—an important element of successful psychotherapy.

thermoreceptors Sensory nerve endings under the skin that respond to changes in temperature at or near the skin and provide input to keep the body's temperature at 98.6 degrees Fahrenheit.

thinking The mental process of manipulating information mentally by forming concepts, solving problems, making decisions, and reflecting critically or creatively.

third variable problem The circumstance where a variable that has not been measured accounts for the relationship between two other variables. Third variables are also known as confounds.

360-degree feedback A method of performance appraisal whereby an employee's performance is rated by a variety of individuals, including himself or herself, a peer, a supervisor, a subordinate, and perhaps a customer or client.

tip-of-the-tongue (TOT) phenomenon A type of effortful retrieval that occurs when we are confident that we know something but cannot quite pull it out of memory.

tolerance The need to take increasing amounts of a drug to get the same effect.

top-down processing The operation in sensation and perception, launched by cognitive processing at the brain's higher levels, that allows the organism to sense what is happening and to apply that framework to information from the world.

training Teaching a new employee the essential requirements to do the job well.

trait theories Theoretical views stressing that personality consists of broad, enduring dispositions (traits) that tend to lead to characteristic responses.

tranquilizers Depressant drugs, such as Valium and Xanax, that reduce anxiety and induce relaxation.

transactional leader An individual in a leadership capacity who emphasizes the exchange relationship between the worker and the leader and who applies the principle that a good job should be rewarded.

transference A client's relating to the psycho-analyst in ways that reproduce or relive important relationships in the individual's life.

transformational leader An individual in a leadership capacity who is concerned not with enforcing the rules but with changing them.

transgender Experiencing one's psychological gender as different from one's physical sex, as in the cases of biological males who identify as female, and biological females who identify as male.

triarchic theory of intelligence Sternberg's theory that intelligence comes in three forms: analytical, creative, and practical.

trichromatic theory Theory stating that color perception is produced by three types of cone receptors in the retina that are particularly sensitive to different, but overlapping, ranges of wavelengths.

two-factor theory of emotion Schachter and Singer's theory that emotion is determined by two factors: physiological arousal and cognitive labeling.

Type A behavior pattern A cluster of characteristics—such as being excessively competitive, hard-driven, impatient, and hostile—related to the incidence of heart disease.

Type B behavior pattern A cluster of characteristics—such as being relaxed and easygoing—related to good health.

U

unconditional positive regard Rogers's construct referring to the individual's need to be accepted, valued, and treated positively regardless of his or her behavior.

unconditioned response (UCR) An unlearned reaction that is automatically elicited by the unconditioned stimulus.

unconditioned stimulus (UCS) A stimulus that produces a response without prior learning.

unconscious thought According to Freud, a reservoir of unacceptable wishes, feelings, and thoughts that are beyond conscious awareness; Freud's interpretation viewed the unconscious as a storehouse for vile thoughts.

V

validity The extent to which a test measures what it is intended to measure.

variable Anything that can change.

vestibular sense Sense that provides information about balance and movement.

volley principle Modification of frequency theory stating that a cluster of nerve cells can fire neural impulses in rapid succession, producing a volley of impulses.

W

***waigawa* system** A management system dedicated to the idea that when the corporation faces a difficult problem, all rank-related concerns are temporarily set aside so that anyone from any level of the organization can propose a solution.

Weber's law The principle that two stimuli must differ by a constant minimum percentage (rather than a constant amount) to be perceived as different.

well-being therapy (WBT) A short-term, problem-focused, directive therapy that encourages clients to accentuate the positive.

wisdom Expert knowledge about the practical aspects of life.

working memory A three-part system that allows us to hold information temporarily as we perform cognitive tasks; a kind of mental workbench on which the brain manipulates and assembles information to help us understand, make decisions, and solve problems.

Y

Yerkes-Dodson law The psychological principle stating that performance is best under conditions of moderate arousal rather than either low or high arousal.

REFERENCES

A

Abbott, B. B., Schoen, L. S, & Badia, P. (1984). Predictable and unpredictable shock: Behavioral measures of aversion and physiological measures of stress. *Psychological Bulletin, 96,* 45–71.

Abbott, J. M., Klein, B., & Ciechomski, L. (2008). Best practices in online therapy. *Journal of Technology in Human Services, 26,* 360–375.

ABC News. (2004, October 21). Poll: American sex survey. http://abcnews.go.com/Primetime/PollVault/story?id=156921&page=1

Abraham, A., & Windmann, S. (2007). Creative cognition: The diverse operations and the prospect of applying a cognitive neuroscience perspective. *Methods, 42,* 38–48.

Abramowitz, J. S. (2009). *Getting over OCD.* New York: Guilford.

Abrams, D., & Hogg, M. A. (2004). Metatheory: Lessons from social identity research. In A. W. Kruglanski & E. T. Higgins (Eds.), *Theory construction in social-personality psychology.* Mahwah, NJ: Erlbaum.

Abrams, L., & Rodriguez, E. L. (2005). Syntactic class influences phonological priming of tip-of-the-tongue resolution. *Psychonomic Bulletin & Review, 12* (6), 1018–1023.

Abramson, L. Y., Seligman, M. E. P., & Teasdale, J. (1978). Learned helplessness in humans: Critique and reformulation. *Journal of Abnormal Psychology, 87,* 49–74.

Acer, N., & others. (2010). Comparison of two volumetric techniques for estimating volume of intracerebral ventricles using magnetic resonance imaging: A stereological study. *Anatomical Science International.* (in press)

Achim, A. M., & Lepage, M. (2005). Neural correlates of memory for items and for associations: An event-related functional magnetic resonance imaging study. *Journal of Cognitive Neuroscience, 17,* 652–667.

Adam, C. L. (2010). Leptin: Primary central site of action? *Endocrinology, 151,* 1975–1979.

Addington, J., el-Guebaly, N., Campbell, W., Hodgkins, D. C., & Addington, D. (1998). Smoking cessation treatment for patients with schizophrenia. *American Journal of Psychiatry, 155,* 974–976.

Ader, R. (1974). Letter to the editor: Behaviorally conditioned immunosuppression. *Psychosomatic Medicine, 36,* 183–184.

Ader, R. (2000). On the development of psycho-neuroimmunology. *European Journal of Pharmacology, 405,* 167–176.

Ader, R., & Cohen, N. (1975). Behaviorally conditioned immunosuppression. *Psychosomatic Medicine, 37,* 333–340.

Ader, R., & Cohen, N. (2000). Conditioning and immunity. In R. Ader, D. L. Felton, & N. Cohen (Eds.), *Psychoneuroimmunology* (3rd ed.). San Diego: Academic.

Ades, P. A., Savage, P. D., & Harvey-Berino, J. (2010). The treatment of obesity in cardiac rehabilitation. *Journal of Cardiopulmonary Rehabilitation and Prevention.* (in press)

Adlard, P. A., Parncutt, J. M., Finkeelstein, D. I., & Bush, A. L. (2010). Cognitive loss in zinc transporter-3 knock-out mice: A phenocopy for the synaptic and memory deficits of Alzheimer's disease. *Journal of Neuroscience, 30,* 1631–1636.

Adler, A. (1927). *The theory and practice of individual psychology.* Fort Worth, TX: Harcourt Brace.

Adler, N. E., & Stewart, J. (2009). Reducing obesity: Motivating action while not blaming the victim. *Milbank Quarterly, 87,* 49–70.

Adolph, K. E., Berger, S. E., & Leo, A. (2010). Developmental continuity? Crawling, cruising, and walking. *Developmental Science.* (in press)

Adolph, K. E., Eppler, M. A., & Joh, A. S. (2010). Infants' perception of affordances of slopes under low and high friction conditions. *Journal of Experimental Psychology: Human Perception and Performance.* (in press)

Adolphs, R. (2009). The social brain: Neural basis of social knowledge. *Annual Review of Psychology* (vol. 60). Palo Alto, CA: Annual Reviews.

Agatonovic-Kustrin, S., Davies, P., & Turner, J. V. (2009). Structure-activity relationships for serotonin transporter and dopamine receptor selectivity. *Medicinal Chemistry, 5,* 271–278.

Aggen, S. H., Neale, M. C., Roysamb, E., Reichborn-Kjennerud, T., & Kendler, K. S. (2009). A psychometric evaluation of the DSM-IV borderline personality disorder criteria: Age and sex moderation of criterion functioning. *Psychological Medicine, 39,* 1967–1978.

Aguinis, H. (2009). *Performance management* (2nd ed.). Upper Saddle River, NJ: Prentice-Hall.

Aguinis, H. (2010). Organizational responsibility: Doing good and doing well. In S. Zedeck (Ed.), *APA handbook of industrial and organizational psychology.* Washington, DC: APA. (in press)

Aguinis, H., & Kraiger, K. (2009). Benefits of training and development for individuals and teams, organizations, and society. *Annual Review of Psychology* (vol. 60). Palo Alto, CA: Annual Reviews.

Ahmadi, J., Kampman, K. M., Oslin, D. M., Pettinati, H. M., Dackis, C., & Sparkman, T. (2009). Predictors of treatment outcome in outpatient cocaine and alcohol dependency treatment. *American Journal of Addiction, 18,* 81–86.

Ahmed, I., & Thorpy, M. (2010). Clinical features, diagnosis, and treatment of narcolepsy. *Clinics in Chest Medicine, 31,* 371–381.

Ahmed, N. U., Smith, G. L., Flores, A. M., Pamies, R. J., Mason, H. R., Woods, K. F., & Stain, S. C. (2005). Racial/ethnic disparity and predictors of leisure-time activity among U.S. men. *Ethnicity and Disease, 15,* 40–52.

Ahola, K., Honkonen, T., Kivimaki, M., Virtanen, M., Isometsa, E., Aromaa, A., & Lonnqvist, J. (2006). Contribution of burnout to the association between job strain and depression: The Health 2000 Study. *Journal of Occupational and Environmental Medicine, 48,* 1023–1030.

Aihara, Y., Minai, J., Aoyama, A., & Shiman-ouchi, S. (2010). Depressive symptoms and past lifestyle among Japanese elderly people. *Community Mental Health Journal.* (in press)

Ainsworth, M. D. S. (1979). Infant–mother attachment. *American Psychologist, 34,* 932–937.

Ainsworth, M. S., Blehar, M. C., Waters, E., & Wall, S. (1978). *Patterns of attachment: A psychological study of the strange situation.* Oxford, U.K.: Erlbaum.

Ajzen, I. (2001). Nature and operation of attitudes. *Annual Review of Psychology* (vol. 52). Palo Alto, CA: Annual Reviews.

Ajzen, I. (2002). Perceived behavioral control, self-efficacy, locus of control, and the theory of planned behavior. *Journal of Applied Social Psychology, 32,* 665–683.

Ajzen, I., & Albarracin, D. (2007). Predicting and changing behavior: A reasoned action approach. In I. Ajzen, D. Albarracin, & R. Hornik (Eds.), *Prediction and change in health behavior.* Mahwah, NJ: Erlbaum.

Ajzen, I., & Fishbein, M. (1980). *Understanding attitudes and predicting social behavior.* Englewood Cliffs, NJ: Prentice-Hall.

Ajzen, I., & Fishbein, M. (2005). The influence of attitudes on behavior. In D. Albarracin, B. T. Johnson, & M. P. Zanna (Eds.), *The handbook of attitudes* (pp. 173–221). Mahwah, NJ: Erlbaum.

Ajzen, I., & Manstead, A. S. R. (2007). Changing health-related behaviours: An approach based on the theory of planned behaviour. In M. Hewstone, H. Schut, J. de Wit, K. van den Bos, & M. S. Stroebe (Eds.), *The scope of social psychology: Theory and applications* (pp. 43–63). New York: Psychology Press.

Akhtar, S. (2006). Technical challenges faced by the immigrant psychoanalyst. *Psychoanalytic Quarterly, 75,* 21–43.

Akkermann, K., Nordquist, N., Oreland, L., & Harro, J. (2010). Serotonin transporter gene promoter polymorphism affects the severity of binge eating in general population. *Progress in Neuro-Psychopharmacology and Biological Psychiatry, 34,* 111–114.

Al-Alem, L., & Omar, H. A. (2008). Borderline personality: An overview of history, diagnosis, and treatment in adolescents. *International Journal of Adolescent Medicine, 20,* 395–404.

Albarracin, D., Durantini, M. R., & Earl, A. (2006). Empirical and theoretical conclusions of an analysis of outcomes of HIV-prevention interventions. *Current Directions in Psychological Science, 15,* 73–78.

Albarracin, D., Gillette, J. C., Earl, A. N., Glasman, L. R., Durantini, M. R., & Ho, M. (2005). A test of major assumptions about behavior change: A comprehensive look at the effects of passive and active HIV-prevention interventions since the beginning of the epidemic. *Psychological Bulletin, 131,* 856–897.

Alberto, P. A., & Troutman, A. C. (2009). *Applied behavior analysis for teachers* (8th ed.). Upper Saddle River, NJ: Prentice-Hall.

Aldao, A., Nolen-Hoeksema, S., & Schweizer, S. (2010). Emotion-regulation strategies across psychopathology: A meta-analytic review. *Clinical Psychology Review, 30,* 217–237.

Aldwin, C. M., Levenson, M. R., & Kelly, L. L. (2009). Lifespan developmental perspectives on stress-related growth. In C. L. Park, S. Lechner, A. Stanton, & M. Antoni (Eds.), *Positive life changes in the context of medical illness.* Washington, DC: APA Press.

Aldwin, C. M., Spiro, A., & Park, C. L. (2006). Health, behavior, and optimal aging. In J. E. Birren & K. W. Schaie (Eds.), *Handbook of the psychology of aging* (6th ed.). San Diego: Academic.

Aldwin, C. M., Yancura, L. A., & Boeninger, D. K. (2007). In C. M. Aldwin, C. L. Park, & A. Spiro (Eds.), *Handbook of health and aging.* New York: Guilford.

Alegria, M. (2011). Epidemiology of mental disorders in Latino and Asian populations. *Annual Review of Clinical Psychology* (vol. 7). Palo Alto, CA: Annual Reviews.

Alexander, G. M., & Hines, M. (2002). Sex differences in response to children's toys in nonhuman primates (*Cercopithecus aethiops sabaeus*). *Evolution and Human Behavior, 23,* 467–479.

Alexander, G. M., Wilcox, T., & Woods, R. (2009). Sex differences in infants' visual interest in toys. *Archives of Sexual Behavior, 38,* 427–433.

Allan, K. (2010). Vantage theory and linguistic relativity. *Language Sciences, 32,* 158–169.

Allen, J. J. B., Harmon-Jones, E., & Cavender, J. H. (2001). Manipulation of frontal EEG asymmetry through biofeedback alters self-reported emotional responses and facial EMG. *Psychophysiology, 38,* 685–693.

Allport, G. W. (1954). *The nature of prejudice.* Cambridge, MA: Perseus.

Allport, G. W. (1961). *Pattern and growth in personality.* New York: Holt, Rinehart & Winston.

Allport, G. W., & Odbert, H. (1936). *Trait-names: A psycho-lexical study. No. 211.* Princeton, NJ: Psychological Review Monographs.

Altemus, M. (2006). Sex differences in depression and anxiety disorders: Potential biological determinants. *Hormones and Behavior, 50,* 534–538.

Altenor, A., Volpicelli, J. R., & Seligman, M. E. P. (1979). Debilitated shock escape is produced by both short- and long-duration inescapable shock: Learned helplessness vs. learned inactivity. *Bulletin of the Psychonomic Society, 14,* 337–339.

Alter, A. L., Aronson, J., Darley, J. M., Rodriguez, C., & Ruble, D. N. (2010). Rising to the threat: Reducing stereotype threat by reframing the threat as a challenge. *Journal of Experimental Social Psychology, 46,* 166–171.

Althof, S. E., & others. (2010). Impact of tadalafil once daily in men with erectile dysfunction—including a report of the partner's evaluation. *Urology.* (in press)

Alvino, C., Kohlber, C., Barrett, F., Gur, R. E., Gur, R. C., & Verma, R. (2007). Computerized measurement of facial expression of emotions in schizophrenia. *Journal of Neuroscience Methods, 163,* 350–361.

Alyahri, A., & Goodman, R. (2008). Harsh corporal punishment of Yemeni children: Occurrence, type, and associations. *Child Abuse and Neglect, 32,* 766–773.

Amato, P. R. (2006). Marital discord, divorce, and children's well-being: Results from a 20-year longitudinal study of two generations. In A. Clarke-Stewart & J. Dunn (Eds.), *Families count.* New York: Cambridge University Press.

Ambady, N., Krabbenhoft, M. A., & Hogan, D. (2006). The 30-sec sale: Using thin-slice judgments to evaluate sales effectiveness. *Journal of Consumer Psychology, 16,* 4–13.

Ambady, N., & Skowronski, J. J. (Eds.). (2009). *First impressions.* New York: Guilford.

Ambrosi, G., Armentero, M. T., Levandis, G., Bramanti, P., Nappi, G., & Blandini, F. (2010). Effects of early and delayed treatment with an mGluR5 antagonist on motor impairment, nigrostriatal damage and neuorinflammation in a rodent model of Parkinson disease. *Brain Research Bulletin.* (in press)

American Association of University Women (AAUW). (2006). *Drawing the line: Sexual harassment on campus (2006).* Washington, DC: Author.

American Association on Intellectual and Developmental Disabilities. (2010). Diagnostic Adaptive Behavior Scale. http://www.aamr.org/content_106.cfm?navID=23 (accessed April 2, 2010)

American Cancer Society. (2010). *Guide to quitting smoking.* Washington, DC: Author.

American Psychiatric Association (APA). (1994). *Diagnostic and statistical manual of mental disorders* (4th ed.). Washington, DC: Author.

American Psychiatric Association (APA). (2000). *Diagnostic and statistical manual of mental disorders* (4th ed., text revision). Washington, DC: Author.

American Psychiatric Association (APA). (2001). *Mental illness.* Washington, DC: Author.

American Psychiatric Association (APA). (2005). *Let's talk about eating disorders.* Arlington, VA: Author.

American Psychiatric Association (APA). (2006). *American Psychiatric Association practice guidelines for the treatment of psychiatric disorders.* Washington, DC: Author.

American Psychological Association. (2004, July 28). *APA supports legalization of same-sex civil marriages and opposes discrimination against lesbian and gay parents: Denying same-sex couples legal access to civil marriage is discriminatory and can adversely affect the psychological, physical, social, and economic well-being of gay and lesbian individuals.* Washington, DC: Author.

American Sleep Apnea Association (ASAA). (2006). *Get the facts about sleep apnea.* Washington, DC: Author.

Amiot, C. E., Terry, D. J., Jimmieson, N. L., & Callan, V. J. (2006). A longitudinal investigation of coping processes during a merger: Implications for job satisfaction and organizational identification. *Journal of Management, 32,* 552–574.

Amodio, D. M., & Mendoza, S. A. (2010). Implicit outgroup bias: Cognitive, affective, and motivational underpinnings. In B. Gawronski & B. K. Payne (Eds.), *Handbook of implicit social cognition.* New York: Guilford.

Amsterdam, J. D., & Shults, J. (2010). Efficacy and safety of long-term fluoxetine versus lithium monotherapy of bipolar II disorder: A randomized, double-blind, placebo-substitution study. *American Journal of Psychiatry.* (in press)

Amunts, K., Schlaug, G., Jancke, L., Steinmetz, H., Schleicher, A., Dabringhaus, A., & Zilles, K. (1997). Motor cortex and hand motor skills: Structural compliance in the human brain. *Human Brain Mapping, 5* (3), 206–215.

Anastasi, A., & Urbina, S. (1996). *Psychological testing* (7th ed.). Upper Saddle River, NJ: Prentice-Hall.

Ancelet, C., Pedersen, N. P., Fuller, P. M., & Lu, J. (2010). Brainstem circuitry regulation phasic activation and trigeminal motoneurons during REM sleep. *PLoS One, 5,* e8788.

Andel, R., Crowe, M., Pedersen, N. L., Mortimer, J., Crimmins, E., Johansson, B., & Gatz, M. (2005). Complexity of work and risk of Alzheimer's disease: A population-based study of Swedish twins. *Journals of Gerontology: Series B: Psychological Sciences and Social Sciences, 60B,* 251–258.

Anderman, E. M., & Anderman, L. H. (2010). *Classroom motivation.* Upper Saddle River, NJ: Merrill.

Anderson, B. A., Golden-Kreutz, D. M., & DiLillo, V. (2001). Cancer. In A. Baum, T. A.

Revenson, & J. E. Singer (Eds.), *Handbook of health psychology*. Mahwah, NJ: Erlbaum.

Anderson, C. A. (2003). Video games and aggressive behavior. In D. Ravitch and J. P. Viteritti (Eds.), *Kid stuff: Marketing sex and violence to America's children* (pp. 143–167). Baltimore: Johns Hopkins University Press.

Anderson, C. A., & Arciniegas, D. B. (2010). Cognitive sequelae of hypoxic-ischemic brain injury: A review. *NeuroRehabilitation, 26,* 47–63.

Anderson, C. A., Benjamin, A. J., Jr., & Bartholow, B. D. (1998). Does the gun pull the trigger? Automatic priming effects of weapon pictures and weapon names. *Psychological Science, 9,* 308–314.

Anderson, C. A., & Bushman, B. J. (2002). Human aggression. *Annual Review of Psychology* (vol. 53). Palo Alto, CA: Annual Reviews.

Anderson, C. A., & Huesmann, L. R. (2007). Human aggression. In M. A. Hogg & J. Cooper (Eds.), *The Sage handbook of social psychology* (concise 2nd ed.). Thousand Oaks, CA: Sage.

Anderson, C. A., & Kilduff, G. J. (2009). Why do dominant personalities attain influence in face-to-face groups? The competence-signaling effects of trait dominance. *Journal of Personality and Social Psychology, 96,* 491–503.

Anderson, C. A., Shibuya, A., Ihori, N., Swing, E. L., Bushman, B. J., Sakamoto, A., Rothstein, H. R., & Saleem, M. (2010). Violent video game effects on aggression, empathy, and prosocial behavior in Eastern and Western countries: A meta-analytic review. *Psychological Bulletin, 136,* 151–173.

Anderson, E. M., & Lambert, M. J. (2001). A survival analysis of clinically significant change in outpatient psychotherapy. *Journal of Clinical Psychology, 57,* 875–888.

Anderson, N. H. (1965). Primacy effects in personality impression formation using a generalized order effect paradigm. *Journal of Personality and Social Psychology, 2,* 1–9.

Andersson, M., & Simmons, L. W. (2006). Sexual selection and mate choice. *Trends in Ecology and Evolution, 21,* 296–302.

Andreano, J. M., & Cahill, L. (2006). Glucocorticoid release and memory consolidation in men and women. *Psychological Science, 17,* 466–470.

Ang, S., & van Dyne, L. (Eds.). (2009). *Handbook on cultural intelligence.* New York: M. E. Sharpe.

Angel, L., Fay, S., Bourazzaouli, B., Granjon, L., & Isingrini, M. (2009). Neural correlates of cued recall in younger and older adults: An event-related potential study. *NeuroReport, 20,* 75–79.

Angel, L., & others. (2010). The amount of retrieval support modulates age effects on episodic memory: Evidence from event-related potentials. *Brain Research.* (in press)

Annesi, J. J. (2007). Relations of changes in exercise self-efficacy, physical self-concept, and body satisfaction with weight changes in obese white and African American women initiating a physical activity program. *Ethnicity and Disease, 17,* 19–22.

Aquino, K., & Thau, S. (2009). Workplace victimization: Aggression from the target's perspective. *Annual Review of Psychology* (vol. 60), Palo Alto, CA: Annual Reviews.

Archer, J. (2004). Sex differences in aggression in real-world settings: A meta-analytic review. *Review of General Psychology, 8,* 291–322.

Arden, M., & Armitage, C. J. (2008). Predicting and explaining transtheoretical model stage transitions in relation to condom-carrying behaviour. *British Journal of Health Psychology, 13,* 719–735.

Ardiel, E. L., & Rankin, C. H. (2010). An elegant mind: Learning and memory in *Caenorhabditis elegans. Learning and Memory, 17,* 191–201.

Arendt, J. (2009). Managing jet lag: Some of the problems and possible new solutions. *Sleep Medicine Reviews, 13,* 247–248.

Arenkiel, B. R. (2010). Adult neurogenesis supports short-term olfactory memory. *Journal of Neurophysiology.* (in press)

Armaiz-Pena, G. N., Lutgendorf, S. K., Cole, S. W., & Sood, A. K. (2009). Neuroendocrine modulation of cancer progression. *Brain, Behavior, and Immunity, 23,* 10–15.

Armenta, B. E. (2010). Stereotype boost and stereotype threat effects: The moderating role of ethnic identification. *Cultural Diversity and Ethnic Minority Psychology.* (in press)

Armitage, C. J. (2006). Evidence that implementation intentions promote transitions between the stages of change. *Journal of Consulting and Clinical Psychology, 74,* 141–151.

Armor, D. A., Massey, C., & Sackett, A. M. (2008). Prescribed optimism. *Psychological Science, 19,* 329–331.

Arnell, K. M., Killman, K. V., & Fijavz, D. (2007). Blinded by emotion: Target misses follow attention capture by arousing distractors in RSVP. *Emotion, 7,* 465–477.

Arnett, J. J. (2004). *Emerging adulthood.* New York: Oxford University Press.

Arnett, J. J. (2006). Emerging adulthood: Understanding the new way of coming of age. In J. J. Arnett & J. L. Tanner (Eds.), *Emerging adults in America.* Washington, DC: American Psychological Association.

Arnett, J. J. (2007). Socialization in emerging adulthood. In J. E. Grusec & P. D. Hastings (Eds.), *Handbook of socialization.* New York: Oxford University Press.

Arnett, J. J. (2010). Oh, grow up! Generational grumbling and the new life stage of emerging adulthood. *Perspectives on Psychological Science.* (in press)

Arnkoff, D. B., Glass, C. R., & Shapiro, S. J. (2002). Expectations and preferences. In J. C. Norcross (Ed.), *Psychotherapy relationships that work.* New York: Oxford University Press.

Arntz, A. (2005). Cognition and emotion in borderline personality disorder. *Journal of Behavior Therapy and Experimental Psychiatry, 36,* 167–172.

Aron, A., Aron, E. N., & Coups, E. (2011). *Statistics for the behavioral and social sciences* (5th ed.). Upper Saddle River, NJ: Prentice-Hall.

Aronson, E. (1986, August). *Teaching students things they think they already know all about: The case of prejudice and desegregation.* Paper presented at the meeting of the American Psychological Association, Washington, DC.

Arrow, H. (2007). The sharp end of altruism. *Science, 318,* 581–582.

Artazcoz, L., Cortes, I., Escriba-Aguir, V., Cascant, L., & Villegas, R. (2009). Understanding the relationship of long working hours with health status and health-related behaviors. *Journal of Epidemiology and Community Health, 63,* 521–527.

Arthur, W. J., Bennett, W. J., Edens, P., & Bell, S. T. (2003). Effectiveness of training in organizations: A meta-analysis of design and evaluation features. *Journal of Applied Psychology, 88,* 234–245.

Arvey, R. D., Harpaz, I., & Liao, H. (2004). Work centrality and post-award work behavior of lottery winners. *Journal of Psychology: Interdisciplinary and Applied, 138,* 404–420.

Arvey, R. D., Rotundo, M., Johnson, W., Zhang, Z., & McGue, M. (2006). The determinants of leadership role occupancy: Genetic and personality factors. *Leadership Quarterly, 17* (1), 1–20.

Arvey, R. D., Zhang, Z., Avolio, B. J., & Krueger, R. F. (2007). Developmental and genetic determinants of leadership role occupancy among women. *Journal of Applied Psychology, 92* (3), 693–706.

Asch, S. E. (1951). Effects of group pressure on the modification and distortion of judgments. In H. S. Guetzkow (Ed.), *Groups, leadership, and men.* Pittsburgh: Carnegie University Press.

Ash, M., & Sturm, T. (Eds.). (2007). *Psychology's territories.* Mahwah, NJ: Erlbaum.

Ashcraft, M. H., & Radvansky, G. (2009). *Cognition* (5th ed.). Upper Saddle River, NJ: Prentice-Hall.

Ashcroft, W., Argiro, S., & Keohane, J. (2010). *Success strategies for teaching kids with autism.* Waco, TX: Prufrock Press.

Asher, S. R., & McDonald, K. L. (2009). Friendship in childhood and adolescence. In B. McGraw, P. L. Peterson, & E. Baker (Eds.), *International encyclopedia of education* (3rd ed.). Amsterdam: Elsevier.

Ashton, M. C., & Kibeom, L. (2008). The HEXACO model of personality structure and the importance of the H factor. *Social and Personality Psychology Compass, 2,* 1952–1962.

Aspinwall, L. G. (1998). Rethinking the role of positive affect in self-regulation. *Motivation and Emotion, 22,* 1–32.

Aspinwall, L. G., & Brunhart, S. M. (1996). Distinguishing optimism from denial: Optimistic beliefs predict attention to health threats. *Personality and Social Psychology Bulletin, 22,* 993–1003.

Aspinwall, L. G., Leaf, S. L., & Leachman, S. A. (2009). Meaning and agency in the context of genetic testing for familial cancer. To appear in P. T. P. Wong (Ed.), *The human quest for meaning* (2nd ed.). Hillsdale, NJ: Erlbaum.

Aspinwall, L. G., & Tedeschi, R. G. (2010a). The value of positive psychology for health psychology: Progress and pitfalls in examining the relation of positive phenomena to health. *Annals of Behavioral Medicine, 39*, 4–15.

Aspinwall, L. G., & Tedeschi, R. G. (2010b). Of babies and bathwater: A reply to Coyne and Tennen's views on positive psychology and health. *Annals of Behavioral Medicine, 39*, 27–34.

Associated Press. (2007). College students think they're so special. www.msnbc.msn.com/id/17349066/ (accessed October 5, 2007)

Assor, A., Roth, G., & Deci, E. L. (2004). The emotional costs of parents' conditional regard: A self-determination theory analysis. *Journal of Personality, 72*, 47–88.

Atkinson, R. C., & Shiffrin, R. M. (1968). Human memory: A proposed system and its control processes. In K. W. Spence & J. T. Spence (Eds.), *The psychology of learning and motivation* (vol. 2). San Diego: Academic.

Atmaca, M., Yildirim, H., Ozdemir, H. N., Ozler, S., Kara, B., Ozler, Z., Kanmaz, E., Mermi, O., & Tezcan, E. (2008). Hippocampus and amygdalar volumes in patients with refractory obsessive-compulsive disorder. *Progress in Neuro-Psychopharmacology & Biological Psychiatry, 32*, 1283–1286.

Aton, S. J., Seibt, J., Dumoulin, M., Steinmetz, N., Coleman, T., Naidoo, N., & Frank, M. G. (2009). Mechanisms of sleep-dependent consolidation of cortical plasticity. *Neuron, 61*, 454–466.

Austad, C. S. (2009). *Counseling and psychotherapy today.* New York: McGraw-Hill.

Austin, J. T., & Crespin, T. R. (2006). Problems of criteria in industrial and organizational psychology. In W. Bennett, C. E. Lance, & D. J. Woehr (Eds.), *Performance measurement.* Mahwah, NJ: Erlbaum.

Avey, J. B., Luthans, F., Smith, R. M., & Palmer, N. F. (2010). Impact of positive psychological capital on employee well-being over time. *Journal of Occupational Health Psychology, 15*, 17–28.

Avolio, B. J., Rotundo, M., & Walumbwa, F. O. (2009). Early life experiences as determinants of leadership role occupancy: The importance of parental influence and rule breaking behavior. *Leadership Quarterly, 20*, 329–342.

Avolio, B. J., Walumbwa, F. O., & Weber, T. J. (2009). Leadership: Current theories, research, and future directions. *Annual Review of Psychology* (vol. 60). Palo Alto, CA: Annual Reviews.

Azarbad, L., Corsica, J., Hall, B., & Hood, M. (2010). Psychosocial correlates of binge eating in Hispanic, African American, and Caucasian women presenting for bariatric surgery. *Eating Behaviors, 11*, 79–84.

Azboy, O., & Kaygisiz, Z. (2009). Effects of sleep deprivation on cardiorespiratory functions of the runners and volleyball players during rest and exercise. *Acta Physiologica Hungarica, 96*, 29–36.

Azevedo, F. A., & others. (2009). Equal numbers of neuronal and nonneuronal cells make the human brain an isometrically scaled-up primate brain. *Journal of Comparative Neurology, 513*, 532–541.

B

Baars, B. J. (2010). Spontaneous repetitive thoughts can be adaptive: Postscript on "mind wandering." *Psychological Bulletin, 136*, 208–210.

Babiloni, C., Vecchio, F., Cappa, S., Pasqualetti, P., Rossi, S., Miniussi, C., & Rossini, P. M. (2006). Functional frontoparietal connectivity during encoding and retrieval processes follows HERA model: A high resolution study. *Brain Research Bulletin, 68*, 203–212.

Babson, K. A., Trainor, C. D., Feldner, M. T., & Blumenthal, H. (2010). A test of the effects of acute sleep deprivation on general and specific self-reported anxiety and depressive symptoms: An experimental extension. *Journal of Behavior Therapy and Experimental Psychiatry.* (in press)

Back, M. D., Stopfer, J. M., Vazire, S., Gaddis, S., Schmukle, S. C., Egloff, B., & Gosling, S. D. (2010). Facebook profiles reflect actual personality, not self idealization. *Psychological Science, 21*, 372–374.

Baddeley, A. D. (2001). *Is working memory still working?* Paper presented at the meeting of the American Psychological Association, San Francisco.

Baddeley, A. D. (2006). Working memory: An overview. In S. Pickering (Ed.), *Working memory and education.* San Diego: Academic.

Baddeley, A. D. (2008). What's new in working memory? *Psychological Review, 13*, 2–5.

Baddeley, A. D. (2009). Baddeley, A. *Current Biology, 19*, R1019–R1020.

Baddeley, A. D. (2010). Working memory. *Current Biology, 20*, R136–R140.

Baddeley, A. D., Allen, R., & Vargh-Khadem, F. (2010). Is the hippocampus necessary for visual and verbal binding in working memory? *Neuropsychologia, 48*, 1089–1095.

Baddeley, J. L., & Pennebaker, J. W. (2009). Expressive writing. In W. T. O'Donohue & J. E. Fisher (Eds.), *General principles and empirically supported techniques of cognitive behavior therapy* (pp. 295–299). Hoboken, NJ: Wiley.

Baddeley, J. L., & Singer, J. A. (2008). Telling losses: Personality correlates and functions of bereavement narratives. *Journal of Research in Personality, 42*, 421–438.

Bagetta, V., Ghiglieri, V., Sgobio, C., Calabresi, P., & Picconi, B. (2010). Synaptic dysfunction in Parkinson's disease. *Biochemical Society Transactions, 38*, 493–497.

Bagnara, D., & others. (2009). Adoptive immunotherapy mediated by ex vivo expanded natural killer T cells against CD1d-expressing lymphoid neoplasms. *Haematologica, 94* (7), 967–974.

Bahrick, H. P. (1984). Semantic memory content in permastore: Fifty years of memory for Spanish learned in school. *Journal of Experimental Psychology: General, 113*, 1–29.

Bahrick, H. P. (2000). Long-term maintenance of knowledge. In E. Tulving & F. I. M. Craik (Eds.), *The Oxford handbook of memory* (pp. 347–362). New York: Oxford University Press.

Bahrick, H. P. (2005). The long-term neglect of long-term memory: Reasons and remedies. In A. F. Healey (Ed.), *Experimental cognitive psychology and its applications.* (pp. 89–100). Washington, DC: American Psychological Association.

Bahrick, H. P., Bahrick, P. O., & Wittlinger, R. P. (1974). Long-term memory: Those unforgettable high-school days. *Psychology Today, 8*, 50–56.

Bahrick, H. P., Hall, L. K., & Da Costa, L. A. (2008). Fifty years of memory of college grades: Accuracy and distortions. *Emotion, 8*, 13–22.

Bailey, J. M. (2003). Biological perspectives on sexual orientation. In L. D. Garnets & D. C. Kimmel (Eds.), *Psychological perspectives on lesbian, gay, and bisexual experiences* (2nd ed., pp. 50–85). New York: Columbia University Press.

Bailey, J. M., & Zucker, K. J. (1995). Childhood sex-typed behavior and sexual orientation: A conceptual and quantitative review. *Developmental Psychology, 31*, 43–55.

Baillargeon, R., Li, J., Gertner, Y., & Wu, D. (2011). How do infants reason about physical events? In U. Goswami (Ed.), *Wiley-Blackwell handbook of childhood cognitive development* (2nd ed.). New York: Wiley Blackwell.

Baillargeon, R., Wu, D., Yan, S., Li, J., & Luo, Y. (2009). Young infants' expectations about self-propelled objects. In B. Hood & L. Santos (Eds.), *The origins of object knowledge.* New York: Oxford University Press.

Baker, C. K., Norris, F. H., Jones, E. C., & Murphy, A. D. (2009). Childhood trauma and adult physical health in Mexico. *Journal of Behavioral Medicine, 32*, 255–269.

Baker, L. A., Raine, A., Liu, J., & Jacobson, K. C. (2008). Differential genetic and environmental influences on reactive and proactive aggression in children. *Journal of Abnormal Child Psychology, 36*, 1265–1278.

Baldwin, T. T., & Padgett, M. Y. (1993). Management development: A review and commentary. In C. L. Cooper & I. T. Robertson (Eds.), *International review of industrial and organizational psychology* (pp. 35–38). Chichester, U.K.: Wiley.

Balliet, D. (2010). Conscientiousness and forgivingness: A meta-analysis. *Personality and Individual Differences, 48*, 259–263.

Balsam, K. F., Beauchaine, T. P., Rothblum, E. D., & Solomon, S. E. (2008). Three-year follow-up of same-sex couple who had civil unions in Vermont, same-sex couples not in civil unions, and heterosexual married couples. *Developmental Psychology, 44*, 102–116.

Balsam, K. F., & Mohr, J. J. (2007). Adaptation to sexual orientation stigma: A comparison of bisexual and lesbian/gay adults. *Journal of Counseling Psychology, 54*, 306–319.

Bamford, C., & Lagattuta, K. H. (2010). A new look at children's understanding of mind and emotion: The case of prayer. *Developmental Psychology, 46,* 78–92.

Bandura, A. (1986). *Social foundations of thought and action.* Englewood Cliffs, NJ: Prentice-Hall.

Bandura, A. (1997). *Self-efficacy.* New York: Freeman.

Bandura, A. (2001). Social cognitive theory. *Annual Review of Psychology* (vol. 52). Palo Alto, CA: Annual Reviews.

Bandura, A. (2007a). Self-efficacy in health functioning. In S. Ayers & others (Eds.), *Cambridge handbook of psychology, health, and medicine.* New York: Cambridge University Press.

Bandura, A. (2007b). Social cognitive theory. In W. Donsbach (Ed.), *International handbook of communication.* Thousand Oaks, CA: Sage.

Bandura, A. (2008). Reconstrual of "free will" from the agentic perspective of social cognitive theory. In J. Baer, J. C. Kaufman, & R. F. Baumeister (Eds.), *Are we free? Psychology and free will.* Oxford, U.K.: Oxford University Press.

Bandura, A. (2009). Social and policy impact of social cognitive theory. In M. Mark, S. Donaldson, & B. Campbell (Eds.), *Social psychology and program/policy evaluation.* New York: Guilford.

Bandura, A. (2010a). Vicarious learning. In D. Matsumoto (Ed.), *Cambridge dictionary of psychology.* New York: Cambridge University Press. (in press)

Bandura, A. (2010b). Self-efficacy. In D. Matsumoto (Ed.), *Cambridge dictionary of psychology.* New York: Cambridge University Press. (in press)

Bandura, A., & Bussey, K. (2004). On broadening the cognitive, motivational, and sociostructural scope of theorizing about gender development and functioning: Comment on Martin, Ruble, and Szkrybalo (2002). *Psychological Bulletin, 130,* 690–701.

Bandura, A., Ross, D., & Ross, S. A. (1961). Transmission of aggression through imitation of aggressive models. *Journal of Abnormal and Social Psychology, 63,* 575–582.

Banks, J. A. (Ed.). (2010). *Routledge international handbook of multicultural education.* New York: Routledge.

Banthia, R., Malcarne, V. L., Ko, C. M., Varni, J. W., & Sadler, G. R. (2009). Fatigued breast cancer survivors: The role of sleep quality, depressed mood, stage, and age. *Psychology & Health, 24,* 965–980.

Banyard, V. L., & Williams, L. M. (2007). Women's voices on recovery: A multi-method study of the complexity of recovery from child sexual abuse. *Child Abuse and Neglect, 31,* 275–290.

Barber, N. (2009). Evolutionary social science: A new approach to violent crime. *Aggression and Violent Behavior, 13,* 237–250.

Barclay, L. J., & Aquino, K. (2010). Workplace aggression and violence. In S. Zedeck (Ed.), *APA handbook of industrial and organizational psychology.* Washington, DC: APA. (in press)

Bard, P. (1934). Emotion. In C. Murchison (Ed.), *Handbook of general psychology.* Worcester, MA: Clark University Press.

Bardone-Cone, A. M., Abramson, L. Y., Vohs, K. D., Heatherton, T. F., & Joiner, T. E., Jr. (2006). Predicting bulimic symptoms: An interactive model of self-efficacy, perfectionism, and perceived weight status. *Behaviour Research and Therapy, 44,* 27–42.

Bargh, J. A. (2005). Bypassing the will: Towards demystifying the nonconscious control of social behavior. In R. Hassin, J. Uleman, & J. Bargh (Eds.), *The new unconscious.* New York: Oxford University Press.

Bargh, J. A. (2006). Agenda 2006: What have we been priming all these years? On the development, mechanism, and ecology of nonconscious social behavior. *European Journal of Social Psychology, 36,* 147–168.

Bargh, J. A., Chen, M., & Burrows, L. (1996). The automaticity of social behavior: Direct effects of trait concept and stereotype activation on action. *Journal of Personality and Social Psychology, 71,* 230–244.

Bargh, J. A., Gollwitzer, P. M., Lee-Chai, A., Barndollar, K., & Trotschel, R. (2001). The automated will: Nonconscious activation and pursuit of behavioral goals. *Journal of Personality and Social Psychology, 81,* 1014–1027.

Bargh, J. A., & Morsella, E. (2009). Unconscious behavioral guidance systems. In C. Agnew & others (Eds.), *Then a miracle occurs: Focusing on behavior and social psychological theory and research.* New York: Oxford University Press.

Barker, A. T., Jalinous, R., & Freeston, I. L. (1985). Non-invasive magnetic stimulation of human motor cortex. *Lancet, 1,* 1106–1107.

Barkley, R., & 74 others. (2002). International consensus statement on ADHD. *Clinical Child and Family Psychology, 5,* 89–111.

Barkus, E. & others. (2010). Distress and metacognition in psychosis prone individuals: Comparing high schizotypy to the at-risk mental state. *Journal of Nervous and Mental Disease, 198,* 99–104.

Barling, J., Christie, A., & Hoption, C. (2010). Leadership. In S. Zedeck (Ed.), *APA handbook of industrial and organizational psychology.* Washington, DC: APA. (in press)

Barling, J., Dupré, K., & Kelloway, E. K. (2009). Predicting workplace violence and aggression, *Annual Review of Psychology* (vol. 60). Palo Alto, CA: Annual Reviews.

Barling, J., Weber, T., & Kelloway E. K. (1996). Effects of transformational leadership training on attitudinal and financial outcomes: A field experiment. *Journal of Applied Psychology, 81,* 827–832.

Barloon, T., & Noyes, R., Jr. (1997). Charles Darwin and panic disorder. *Journal of the American Medical Association, 277,* 138–141.

Barlow, A., Qualter, P., & Stylianou, M. (2010). Relationships between Machiavellianism, emotional intelligence, and theory of mind in children. *Personality and Individual Differences, 48,* 78–82.

Barnett, J. H., & Smoller, J. W. (2009). The genetics of bipolar disorder. *Neuroscience, 164* (1), 331–343.

Barnow, S., & others. (2010). Borderline personality disorder and psychosis: A review. *Current Psychiatry Reports, 12,* 186–195.

Baron, N. (1992). *Growing up with language.* Reading, MA: Addison-Wesley.

Baron-Cohen, S. (2002). The extreme male brain theory of autism. *Trends in Cognitive Science, 6,* 248–254.

Baron-Cohen, S. (2003). *The essential difference: Men, women, and the exreme male brain.* New York: Basic.

Baron-Cohen, S. (2006). The hyper-systemizing, assortative mating theory of autism. *Progress in Neuro-Psychopharmacology & Biological Psychiatry, 30,* 865–872.

Baron-Cohen, S. (2008). Autism, hypersystemizing, and the truth. *Quarterly Journal of Experimental Psychology, 61,* 64–75.

Baron-Cohen, S., Knickmeyer, R. C., & Belmonte, M. K. (2006). Sex differences in the brain: Implications for explaining autism. *Science, 311,* 952.

Barrett, G. V., & Kernan, M. G. (1987). Performance appraisal and terminations: A review of court decisions since Brito v. Zia with implications for personnel practices. *Personnel Psychology, 40,* 489–503.

Barrouillet, P., & Camos, V. (2009). Interference: Unique source of forgetting in working memory. *Trends in Cognitive Science, 13,* 145–146.

Bartel, C. A., Blader, S., & Wrzesniewski, A. (Eds.). (2007). *Identity and the modern organization.* Mahwah, NJ: Erlbaum.

Bartolo, A., Benuzzi, F., Nocetti, L., Baraldi, P., & Nichelli, P. (2006). Humor comprehension and appreciation: An fMRI study. *Journal of Cognitive Neuroscience, 18,* 1789–1798.

Bartoshuk, L. (2008). Chemical senses: Taste and smell. *Annual Review of Psychology* (vol. 59). Palo Alto, CA: Annual Reviews.

Baskerville, T. A., Allard, J., Wayman, C., & Douglas, A. J. (2009). Dopamine-oxytocin interactions in penile erection. *European Journal of Neuroscience, 30,* 2151–2164.

Bass, B. M. (1985). *Leadership and performance beyond expectations.* New York: Free Press.

Bastien, C. H., St-Jean, G., Turcotte, I., Morin, C. M., Lavallee, M., & Carrier, J. (2009). Sleep spindles in chronic psychophysiological insomnia. *Journal of Psychosomatic Research, 66,* 59–65.

Bastien, D. L. (2010). Pharmacological treatment of combat-induced PTSD: A literature review. *British Journal of Nursing, 19,* 318–321.

Bateman, A. J. (1948). Intra-sexual selection in *Drosophila. Heredity, 2,* 349–358.

Bateman, T. S., & Snell, S. A. (2011). *Management* (9th ed.). New York: McGraw-Hill.

Batson, C. D. (2002). Addressing the altruism question experimentally. In S. G. Post, L. G. Underwood, J. P. Schloss, & W. B. Hurlbut (Eds.), *Altruism and altruistic love.* New York: Oxford University Press.

Batson, C. D. (2006). "Not all self-interest after all": Economics of empathy-induced altruism. In D. DeCremer, M. Zeelenberg, & J. K. Murnigham (Eds.), *Social psychology and economics* (pp. 281–299). Mahwah, NJ: Erlbaum.

Batson, C. D., Duncan, B. D., Ackerman, P., Buckley, T., Birch, K., Cialdini, R. B., Schaller, M., Houlihan, D., Arps, K., Fultz, J., & Beaman, A. L. (2007). Issue 17: Does true altruism exist? In J. A. Nier (Ed.), *Taking sides: Clashing views in social psychology* (2nd ed., pp. 348–371). New York: McGraw-Hill.

Battaglia, M., Pesenti-Gritti, P., Medland, S. E., Ogilari, A., Tambs, K., & Spatola, C. A. (2009). A genetically informed study of the association between childhood separation anxiety, sensitivity to CO(2), panic disorder, and the effect of childhood parental loss. *Archives of General Psychiatry, 66,* 64–71.

Bauer, J. J., McAdams, D. P., & Sakaeda, A. R. (2005). The crystallization of desire and the crystallization of discontent in narratives of life-changing decisions. *Journal of Personality, 73,* 1181–1213.

Bauer, M., & others. (2007). Using ultrasonography to determine thyroid size and prevalence of goiter in lithium-treated patients with affective disorders. *Journal of Affective Disorders, 104* (1–3), 45–51.

Bauer, M. E., Jeckel, C. M., & Luz, C. (2009). The role of stress factors during aging of the immune system. *Annals of the New York Academy of Sciences, 1153,* 139–152.

Bauer, P. J., Larkina, M., & Deocampo, J. (2011). Early memory development. In U. Goswami (Ed.), *Wiley-Blackwell handbook of childhood cognitive development* (2nd ed.). New York: Wiley Blackwell.

Bauld, R., & Brown, R. F. (2009). Stress, psychological stress, psychosocial factors, menopause symptoms, and physical health in women. *Maturitas, 62,* 160–165.

Baumann, A. E. (2007). Stigmatization, social distance and exclusion because of mental illness: The individual with mental illness as a "stranger." *International Review of Psychiatry, 19,* 131–135.

Baumeister, R. F. (1999). *Evil: Inside human violence and cruelty.* New York: Freeman.

Baumeister, R. F. (2000). Gender differences in erotic plasticity: The female sex drive as socially flexible and responsive. *Psychological Bulletin, 126* (3), 347–374.

Baumeister, R. F., & Alquist, J. L. (2009). Self-regulation as limited resource: Strength model of control and depletion. In J. P. Forgas, R. F. Baumeister, & D. M. Tice (Eds.), *Psychology of self-regulation.* New York: Psychology Press.

Baumeister, R. F., Bushman, B. J., & Campbell, W. K. (2000). Self-esteem, narcissism, and aggression: Does violence result from low self-esteem or from threatened egotism? *Current Directions in Psychological Science, 9,* 26–29.

Baumeister, R. F., & Butz, D. A. (2005). Roots of hate, violence, and evil. In R. J. Sternberg

(Ed.), *The psychology of hate* (pp. 87–102). Washington, DC: American Psychological Association.

Baumeister, R. F., Campbell, J. D., Krueger, J. I., Vohs, K. D., DuBois, D. L., & Tevendale, H. D. (2007). Issue 5: Applying social psychology: Are self-esteem programs misguided? In J. A. Nier (Ed.), *Taking sides: Clashing views in social psychology* (2nd ed., pp. 92–115). New York: McGraw-Hill.

Baumeister, R. F., Catanese, K. R., & Vohs, K. D. (2001). Is there a gender difference in strength of sex drive? *Personality and Social Psychology Review, 5,* 242–273.

Baumeister, R. F., & Leary, M. R. (2000). The need to belong: Desire for interpersonal attachments as a fundamental human motivation. In E. T. Higgins & A. W. Kruglanski (Eds.), *Motivational science: Social and personality perspectives* (pp. 24–49). New York: Psychology Press.

Baumeister, R. F., & Stillman, T. (2006). Erotic plasticity: Nature, culture, gender, and sexuality. In R. D. McAnulty & M. M. Burnette (Eds.), *Sex and sexuality: Sexuality today: Trends and controversies* (vol. 1, pp. 343– 359, 377). Westport, CT: Praeger/Greenwood.

Baumgartner, T., Fischbacher, U., Feierabend, A., Lutz, K., & Fehr, E. (2009). The neural circuitry of a broken promise. *Neuron, 64,* 756–770.

Baumrind, D. (1991). Parenting styles and adolescent development. In J. Brooks-Gunn, R. Lerner, & A. C. Petersen (Eds.), *The encyclopedia of adolescence* (vol. 2). New York: Garland.

Baumrind, D. (1993). The average expectable environment is not good enough: A response to Scarr. *Child Development, 64,* 1299–1307.

Baumrind, D., Larzelere, R. E., & Cowan, P. A. (2002). Ordinary physical punishment: Is it harmful? Comment on Gershoff (2002). *Psychological Bulletin, 128,* 590–595.

Baxter, L. R., Jr., Phelps, M. E., Mazziotta, J. C., Schwartz, J. M., Gerner, R. H., Selin, C. E., & Sumida, R. M. (1995). Cerebral metabolic rates for glucose in mood disorders: Studies with positron emission tomography and fluorodeoxyglucose F 18. *Archives of General Psychiatry, 42,* 441–447.

Baylor, D. (2001). *Seeing, hearing, and smelling the world* [Commentary]. http://www.hhmi.org/senses (accessed October 2001)

BBC News. (2005, July 5). Japanese breaks *pi* record. http://news.bbc. co.uk/2/hi/asia-pacific/4644103.stm (accessed October 10, 2006)

Beard, C., Weisberg, R. B., & Keller, M. B. (2010). Health-related quality of life across the anxiety disorders: Findings from a sample of primary care patients. *Journal of Anxiety Disorders.* (in press)

Beck, A. (1967). *Depression.* New York: Harper & Row.

Beck, A. T. (1976). *Cognitive therapies and the emotional disorders.* New York: International Universities Press.

Beck, A. T. (1993). Cognitive therapy: Past, present, and future. *Journal of Consulting and Clinical Psychology, 61,* 194–198.

Beck, A. T. (2005). The current state of cognitive therapy: A 40-year retrospective. *Archives of General Psychiatry, 62,* 953–959.

Beck, A. T. (2006). How an anomalous finding led to a new system of psychotherapy. *Nature Medicine, 12,* 1139–1141.

Beck, A. T., Rush, A. J., Shaw, B. F., & Emery, G. (1979). *Cognitive therapy of depression.* New York: Guilford.

Beckers, T., Miller, R. R., De Houwer, J., & Urushihara, K. (2006). Reasoning rats: Forward blocking in Pavlovian animal conditioning is sensitive to constraints of causal inference. *Journal of Experimental Psychology: General, 135,* 92–102.

Becker-Weidman, E. G., Reinecke, M. A., Jacobs, R. H., Martinovich, Z., Silva, S. G., & March, J. S. (2009). Predictors of hopelessness among clinically depressed youth. *Behavioral and Cognitive Psychotherapy, 37* (3), 267–291.

Beeler, C. K. (2010). Leader traits, skills and behaviors. In M. D. Mumford (Ed.), *Leadership 101* (pp. 87–116). New York: Springer.

Beeli, G., Esslen, M., & Jancke, L. (2005). Synaesthesia: When coloured sounds taste sweet. *Nature, 434,* 38.

Beeson, M., Davison, I., Vostanis, P., & Windwo, S. (2006). Parenting programs for behavioral problems: Where do tertiary units fit in a comprehensive service? *Clinical Child Psychology and Psychiatry, 11,* 335–348.

Beidas, R. S., & Kendall, P. C. (2010). Training therapists in evidence-based practice: A critical review of studies from a systems-contextual perspective. *Clinical Psychology: Science and Practice, 17,* 1–30.

Bekinschtein, T. A., Dehaene, S., Rohaut, B., Tadel, F., Cohen, L., & Naccache, L. (2009). Neural signature of the conscious processing of auditory regularities. *Proceedings of the National Academy of Sciences USA, 106,* 1672–1677.

Bell, A. P., Weinberg, M. S., & Hammersmith, S. K. (1981). *Sexual preference: Its development in men and women.* Bloomington: Indiana University Press.

Belloch, A., Cabedo, E., Carrio, C., & Larsson, C. (2010). Cognitive therapy for autogenous and reactive obsessions: Clinical and cognitive outcomes at post-treatment and 1-year follow-up. *Journal of Anxiety Disorders.* (in press)

Bem, D. (1967). Self-perception: An alternative explanation of cognitive dissonance phenomena. *Psychological Review, 74,* 183–200.

Bem, D. J. (1996). The exotic becomes erotic: A developmental theory of sexual orientation. *Psychological Review, 103,* 320–335.

Bem, S. L. (1983). Gender schema theory and its implications for child development: Raising gender-aschematic children in a gender-schematic society. *Signs, 8,* 598–616.

Bem, S. L. (1993). *The lenses of gender: Transforming the debate on sexual inequality.* New Haven, CT: Yale University Press.

Bender, H. L., Allen, J. P., McElhaney, K. B., Antonishak, J., Moore, C. M., Kello, H. O.,

& Davis, S. M. (2007). Use of harsh physical discipline and developmental outcomes in adolescence. *Development and Psychopathology, 19,* 227–242.

Benedetti, F., and others. (2003). Conscious expectation and unconscious conditioning in analgesic; motor and hormonal placebo/nocebo responses. *Journal of Neuroscience, 23,* 4315–4323.

Beneventi, H., Tonnessen, F. E., Ersland, L., & Hugdahl, K. (2010). Executive working memory processes in dyslexia: Behavioral and fMRI evidence. *Scandinavian Journal of Psychology.* (in press)

Benjamin, A. S., Diaz, M., & Wee, S. (2009). Signal detection with criterion noise: Applications to recognition memory. *Psychological Review, 116,* 84–115.

Benjet, C., Thompson, R. J., & Gotlib, I. H. (2010). 5-HTTLPR moderates the effect of relational peer victimization on depressive symptoms in adolescent girls. *Journal of Child Psychology and Psychiatry, 51,* 173–179.

Benoit, R. G., Werkle-Bergner, M., Mecklinger, A., & Kray, J. (2009). Adapting to changing memory retrieval demands: Evidence from event-related potentials. *Brain and Cognition, 70,* 123–135.

Benoit-Bird, K. J., & Au, W. W. (2009). Phonation behavior of cooperatively foraging spinner dolphins. *Journal of the Acoustical Society of America, 125,* 539–546.

Berdahl, J. L., & Raver, J. L. (2010). Sexual harassment. In S. Zedeck (Ed.), *APA handbook of industrial and organizational psychology.* Washington, DC: APA. (in press)

Berenbaum, S. A. (2006). Psychological outcome in children with disorders of sex development: Implications for treatment and understanding typical development. *Annual Review of Sex Research, 17,* 1–38.

Berg, J. M., Wrzesniewski, A., & Dutton, J. E. (2010). Perceiving and responding to challenges in job crafting at different ranks: When proactivity requires adaptivity. *Journal of Organizational Behavior, 31,* 158–186.

Berger, T., Hohl, E., & Caspar, F. (2009). Internet-based treatment for social phobia. *Journal of Clinical Psychology, 65* (10), 1021–1035.

Bergman, M. E., Langhout, R. D., Palmieri, P. A., Cortina, L. M., & Fitzgerald, L. F. (2002). The (un)reasonableness of reporting: Antecedents and consequences of reporting sexual harassment. *Journal of Applied Psychology, 87,* 230–242.

Berkman, E. T., Lieberman, M. D., & Gable, S. L. (2009). BIS, BAS, and response conflict: Testing predictions of the revised reinforcement sensitivity theory. *Personality and Individual Differences, 46,* 586–591.

Berko Gleason, J. (2009). The development of language: An overview. In J. Berko Gleason & N. Ratner (Eds.), *The development of language* (7th ed.). Boston: Allyn & Bacon.

Berkowitz, L. (1990). On the formation and regulation of anger and aggression: A cognitive neoassociationistic analysis. *American Psychologist, 45,* 494–503.

Berkowitz, L. (1993). *Aggression.* New York: McGraw-Hill.

Berkowitz, L., & LePage, A. (1996). Weapons as aggression-eliciting stimuli. In S. Fein & S. Spencer (Eds.), *Readings in social psychology: The art and science of research* (pp. 67–73). Boston: Houghton Mifflin.

Bernadin, H. J. (2010). *Human resource management* (5th ed.). New York: McGraw-Hill.

Berneburg, M., Dietz, K., Niederle, C., & Goz, G. (2010). Changes in esthetic standards since 1940. *American Journal of Orthodontics and Dentofacial Orthopedics, 137,* e1–e9.

Bernstein, I. L., & Koh, M. T. (2007). Molecular signaling during taste aversion learning. *Chemical Senses, 32* (1), 99–103.

Berntsen, D., & Rubin, D. C. (2002). Emotionally charged autobiographical memories across the life span: The recall of happy, sad, traumatic, and involuntary memories. *Psychology and Aging, 17,* 636–652.

Berntsen, D., & Rubin, D. C. (2006). Flashbulb memories and posttraumatic stress reactions across the life span: Age-related effects of the German occupation of Denmark during World War II. *Psychology of Aging, 21,* 127–139.

Berridge, K. C., & Kringelbach, M. L. (2008). Affective neuroscience of pleasure: Reward in humans and animals. *Psychopharmacology, 199,* 457–480.

Berry, A. C., Rosenfield, D., & Smits, J. A. (2009). Extinction retention predicts improvement in social anxiety symptoms following exposure therapy. *Depression and Anxiety, 26,* 22–27.

Berscheid, E. (1988). Some comments on love's anatomy. Or, whatever happened to an old-fashioned lust? In R. J. Sternberg & M. L. Barnes (Eds.), *Anatomy of love.* New Haven, CT: Yale University Press.

Berscheid, E. (2000). Attraction. In A. Kazdin (Ed.), *Encyclopedia of psychology.* Washington, DC, & New York: American Psychological Association and Oxford University Press.

Berscheid, E. (2006). Searching for the meaning of "love." In R. J. Sternberg & K. Weis (Eds.), *The new psychology of love* (pp. 171–183). New Haven, CT: Yale University Press.

Berscheid, E. (2010). Love in the fourth dimension. *Annual Review of Psychology* (vol. 61). Palo Alto, CA: Annual Reviews.

Berscheid, E., & Regan, P. C. (2005). *The psychology of interpersonal relationships.* New York: Prentice-Hall.

Bertrand, M., & Mullainathan, S. (2004). Are Emily and Greg more employable than Lakisha and Jamal? A field experiment on labor market discrimination. *American Economic Review, 94,* 991–1013.

Best, D. L. (2010). Gender. In M. H. Bornstein (Ed.), *Handbook of cultural developmental science.* New York: Psychology Press.

Bethus, I., Tse, D., & Morris, R. G. (2010). Dopamine and memory: Modulation of the persistence of memory for novel hippocampal NMDA receptor-dependent paired associates. *Journal of Neuroscience, 30,* 1610–1618.

Bewernick, B. H., Hurlemann, R., Matusch, A., Kayser, S., Grubert, C., Hadrysiewicz, B.,

Axmacher, N., Lemke, M., Cooper-Mahkorn, D., Cohen, M. X., Brockmann, H., Lenartz, D., Sturm, V., & Schlaepfer, T. E. (2010). Nucleus accumbens deep brain stimulation decreases ratings of depression and anxiety in treatment-resistant depression. *Biological Psychiatry, 67,* 110–116.

Beydoun, M. A., & Wang, Y. (2009). Gender-ethnic disparity in BMI and waist circumference distribution shifts in U.S. adults. *Obesity, 17,* 169–176.

Bhatia, T., Garg, K., Pogue-Geile, M., Nimaonkar, V. L., & Deshpande, S. N. (2009). Executive functions and cognitive deficits in schizophrenia: Comparisons between probands, parents, and controls in India. *Journal of Postgraduate Medicine, 55,* 3–7.

Bialystok, E., & Craik, F. I. M. (2011). Structure and process in life-span cognitive development. In R. M. Lerner & W. F. Overton (Eds.), *Handbook of life-span development* (vol. 1). New York: Wiley.

Birditt, K. S., & Fingerman, K. L. (2003). Age and gender differences in adults' descriptions of emotional reactions to interpersonal problems. *Journals of Gerontology: Series B: Psychological Sciences and Social Sciences, 58B,* 237–245.

Birkenhager, T. K., & others. (2010). Influence of age on the efficacy of electroconvulsive therapy in major depression: A retrospective study. *Journal of Affective Disorders.* (in press)

Bisiacchi, P. S., Tarantino, V., & Ciccola, A. (2008). Aging and prospective memory: The role of working memory and monitoring processes. *Aging: Clinical and Experimental Research, 20,* 569–577.

Bisley, J., & Goldberg, M. E. (2010). Attention, intention, and priority in the parietal lobe. *Annual Review of Neuroscience* (vol. 33). Palo Alto, CA: Annual Reviews.

Biswas-Diener, R., Kashdan, T., & King, L. A. (2009). Two traditions of happiness research, not two distinct types of happiness. *Journal of Positive Psychology, 4,* 208–211.

Biswas-Diener, R., Vitterso, J., & Diener, E. (2005). Most people are pretty happy, but there is cultural variation: The Inughuit, the Amish, and the Maasai. *Journal of Happiness Studies, 6,* 205–226.

Bjork, R. S., & Druckman, D. (1991). *In the mind's eye: Enhancing human performance.* Washington, DC: National Academy Books.

Black, D. W., Gunter, T., Loveless, P., Allen, J., & Sieleni, B. (2010). Antisocial personality disorder in incarcerated offenders: Psychiatric comorbidity and quality of life. *Annals of Clinical Psychiatry, 22,* 113–120.

Blackman, M. (2008). The effective interview. In S. Cartwright & C. L. Cooper (Eds.), *The Oxford handbook of personnel psychology* (pp. 194–214). New York: Oxford University Press.

Blackwell, L. S., & Dweck, C. S. (2008). *The motivational impact of a computer-based program that teaches how the brain changes with learning.* Unpublished manuscript, Department of Psychology, Stanford University.

Blackwell, L. S., Trzesniewski, K. H., & Dweck, C. S. (2007). Implicit theories of intelligence predict achievement across an adolescent transition: A longitudinal study and an intervention. *Child Development, 78,* 246–263.

Blader, J. C. (2006). Pharmacotherapy and postdischarge outcomes of child inpatients admitted for aggressive behavior. *Journal of Clinical Psychopharmacology, 26,* 419–425.

Blades, H. B. (2006). Killer coworker: The case of Michael McDermott, the Christmas killer. *Forensic Examiner, 156,* 49–52.

Blagrove, M., & Akehurst, L. (2000). Personality and dream recall frequency: Further negative findings. *Dreaming, 10,* 139–148.

Blair, C. (2011). Fluid cognitive abilities and general intelligence: A life-span neuroscience perspective. In R. M. Lerner & W. F. Overton (Eds.), *Handbook of life-span development* (vol. 1). New York: Wiley.

Blair, S. N., Kohl, H. W., Paffenbarger, R. S., Clark, D. G., Cooper, K. H., & Gibbons, L. W. (1989). Physical fitness and all-cause mortality: A prospective study of healthy men and women. *Journal of the American Medical Association, 262,* 2395–2401.

Blakemore, J. E. O., Berenbaum, S. E., & Liben, L. S. (2009). *Gender development.* New York: Psychology Press.

Blanco, M., & others. (2009). *Investigating critical incidents, driver restart period, sleep quantity, and crash countermeasures in commercial operations using naturalistic data collection: A final report* (Contract No. DTFH61-01-00049, Task Order #23). Washington, DC: Federal Motor Carrier Safety Administration.

Blass, T. (2007). Unsupported allegations about a link between Milgram and the CIA: Tortured reasoning in *A Question of Torture. Journal of the History of the Behavioral Sciences, 43,* 199–203.

Blickle, G., Wendel, S., & Ferris, G. R. (2010). Political skill as moderator of personality—Job performance relationships in socioanalytic theory: Test of the getting ahead motive in automobile sales. *Journal of Vocational Behavior, 76,* 326–335.

Block, J. (1982). Assimilation, accommodation, and the dynamics of personality development. *Child Development, 53,* 281–295.

Block, J., & Kremen, A. M. (1996). IQ and ego-resiliency: Conceptual and empirical connections and separateness. *Journal of Personality and Social Psychology, 70,* 349–361.

Blonigen, D. M., Carlson, M. D., Hicks, B. M., Krueger, R. F., & Iacono, W. G. (2008). Stability and change in personality traits from late adolescence to early adulthood: A longitudinal twin study. *Journal of Personality, 76,* 229–266.

Bloom, B. (1985). *Developing talent in young people.* New York: Ballantine.

Bloom, B., & Cohen, R. A. (2007). Summary health statistics for U.S. children: National Health Interview Survey, 2006. National Center for Health Statistics. *Vital Health Statistics, 10* (234).

Bloom, F., Nelson, C. A., & Lazerson, A. (2001). *Brain, mind, and behavior* (3rd ed.). New York: Worth.

Bloom, P. (2004). Myths of word learning. In D. G. Hall & S. R. Waxman (Eds.), *Weaving a lexicon* (pp. 205–224). Cambridge, MA: MIT Press.

Bloor, C., & White, F. (1983). Unpublished manuscript. LaJolla, CA: University of California, San Diego.

Bluher, S., & Mantzoros, C. S. (2009). Leptin in humans: Lessons from translational research. *American Journal of Clinical Nutrition, 89,* 991S–997S.

Blum, L. M., & Blum, R. W. (2009). Resilience in adolescence. In R. A. Crosby (Ed.), *Adolescent health: Understanding and preventing risk behaviors* (pp. 51–76). San Francisco: Jossey-Bass.

Blumenfeld, P. C., Kempler, T. M., & Krajcik, J. S. (2006). Motivation and cognitive engagement in learning environments. In R. K. Sawyer (Ed.), *The Cambridge handbook of learning sciences.* New York: Cambridge University Press.

Boatright-Horowitz, S. L., Langley, M., & Gunnip, M. (2009). Depth-of-processing effects as college students use academic advising web sites. *CyberPsychology & Behavior, 12,* 331–335.

Bob, P., & others. (2009). Depression, traumatic stress, and interleukin-6. *Journal of Affective Disorders, 120,* 231–234.

Bobo, W. V., & Shelton, R. C. (2010). Efficacy, safety, and tolerability of Symbyax for acute-phase management of treatment-resistant depression. *Expert Review of Neurotherapeutics, 10,* 651–670.

Bocanegra, B. R., & Zeelenberg, R. (2009). Dissociating emotion-induced blindness and hypervision. *Emotion, 9,* 865–873.

Bocker, S., Briesemeister, S., & Klau, G. W. (2009). On optimal comparability editing with applications to molecular diagnostics. *BMC Bioinformatics, 10, Suppl. 1,* S61.

Boeddeker, N., & Memmi, J. M. (2010). Visual gaze control during peering flight manoeuvres in honeybees. *Proceedings. Biological Sciences.* (in press)

Boekaerts, M. (2010). Goal-directed behavior in the classroom. In K. Wentzel & A. Wigfield (Eds.), *Handbook of motivation at school.* New York: Routledge.

Boeninger, D. K., Shiraishi, R. W., Aldwin, C. M., & Spiro, A. (2009). Why do older men report lower stress ratings? Findings from the Normative Aging Study. *International Journal of Aging and Human Development, 2,* 149–170.

Boeve, B. F. (2010). REM sleep disorder: Updated review of the core features, the REM sleep disorder-neurodegenerative disease association, evolving concepts, controversies, and future directions. *Annals of the New York Academy of Sciences, 1184,* 15–54.

Bogaert, A. F. (2000). Birth order and sexual orientation in a national probability sample. *Journal of Sex Research, 37,* 361–368.

Bohannon, J. N., & Bonvillian, J. D. (2009). Theoretical approaches to language acquisition. In J. Berko Gleason & N. Ratner (Eds.), *The development of language* (7th ed.). Boston: Allyn & Bacon.

Bohart, A. C., & Tallman, K. (2010). Clients: The neglected common factor in psychotherapy. In B. L. Duncan, S. D. Miller, B. E. Wampold, & M. A. Hubble (Eds.), *The heart and soul of change: Delivering what works in therapy* (2nd ed., pp. 83–111). Washington, DC: American Psychological Association.

Bohner, G., & Dickel, N. (2011). Attitudes and attitude change. *Annual Review of Psychology* (vol. 62). Palo Alto, CA: Annual Reviews.

Bonchek, A. (2009). What's broken with cognitive behavior therapy treatment of obsessive-compulsive disorder and how to fix it. *American Journal of Psychotherapy, 63,* 69–86.

Bonfatti, J. F. (2005). Hope holds the key: Finding inspiration. *Schizophrenia Digest* (Summer), 31–34. www.schizophreniadigest.com

Bongers, K. C. A., & Dijksterhuis, A. (2009). Consciousness as a trouble shooting device? The role of consciousness in goal pursuit. In E. Morsella, J. A. Bargh, & P. Gollwitzer (Eds.), *The Oxford handbook of human action.* New York: Oxford University Press.

Bono, G., & McCullough, M. E. (2006). Positive responses to benefit and harm. Bringing forgiveness and gratitude into cognitive psychotherapy. *Journal of Cognitive Psychotherapy, 20,* 147–158.

Bono, G., McCullough, M. E., & Root, L. M. (2008). Forgiveness, feeling connected to others, and well-being: Two longitudinal studies. *Personality and Social Psychology Bulletin, 34,* 182–195.

Boonen, K., & others. (2010). Identification and relative quantification of neuropeptides from the endocrine tissues. *Methods in Molecular Biology, 615,* 191–206.

Borchardt, J. (2008, May 16). MU volunteers reach trauma victims worldwide. *Columbia Missourian.* http://www.Columbiamissourian.com/stories/2008/06/16/mu-volunteers-reach-trauma-victims-worldwide.htm (accessed April 15, 2009)

Bormann, J. E., Aschbacher, K., Wetherell, J. L., Roesch, S., & Redwine, L. (2008). Effects of faith/assurance on cortisol levels are enhanced by a spiritual mantram intervention in adults with HIV: A randomized trial. *Journal of Psychosomatic Research, 66,* 161–171.

Borst, A., Haag, J., & Reiff, D. F. (2010). Fly motion vision. *Annual Review of Neuroscience* (vol. 33). Palo Alto, CA: Annual Reviews.

Boseley, S. (2006, June 12). Tough curbs on Prozac prescribed for children. *The Guardian.*

Bosson, J. K., & Swann, W. B. (2009). Self-esteem. In M. R. Leary & R. H. Hoyle (Eds.), *Handbook of individual differences in social behavior* (pp. 527–546). New York: Guilford.

Bouchard, T. J. (2004). Genetic influences on human psychological traits. *Current Directions in Psychological Science, 13,* 148–151.

Bouchard, T. J., Jr., & Loehlin, J. C. (2001). Genes, evolution, and personality. *Behavior Genetics, 31,* 243–273.

Bouchard, T. J., Jr., & McGue, M. (2003). Genetic and environmental influences on human psychological differences. *Journal of Neurobiology, 54,* 4–45.

Bouchard, T. J., Lykken, D. T., Tellegen, A., & McGue, M. (1996). Genes, drives, environment, and experience. In D. Lubinski & C. Benbow (Eds.), *Psychometrics and social issues concerning intellectual talent.* Baltimore: Johns Hopkins University Press.

Bow, J. N., Flens, J. R., & Gould, J. W. (2010). MMPI-2 and MCMI-III in forensic evaluations: A survey of psychologists. *Journal of Forensic Psychology Practice, 10,* 37–52.

Bower, J. E., Moskowitz, J. T., & Epel, E. (2009). Is benefit finding good for your health? Pathways linking positive life changes after stress and physical health outcomes. *Current Directions in Psychological Science, 18,* 337–341.

Bowlby, J. (1969). *Attachment and loss* (vol. 1). London: Hogarth Press.

Bowlby, J. (1989). *Secure and insecure attachment.* New York: Basic.

Bowling, N. A. (2010). Effects of job satisfaction and conscientiousness on extra-role behaviors. *Journal of Business and Psychology, 25,* 119–130.

Boyd, J. H. (2008). Have we found the holy grail? Theory of mind as a unifying concept. *Journal of Religion and Health, 47,* 366–385.

Boyle, G. J. (1995). Myers-Briggs Type Indicator (MBTI): Some psychometric limitations. *Australian Psychologist, 30,* 71–74.

Bradley, S. J., Oliver, G. D., Chernick, A. B., & Zucker, K. J. (1998). Experiments of nurture: Ablatio penis at 2 months, sex reassignment at 7 months, and a psychosexual follow-up in young adulthood. *Pediatrics, 102,* e9.

Brady, S. S., & Halpern-Felsher, B. L. (2007). Adolescents' reported consequences of having oral sex versus vaginal sex. *Pediatrics, 119,* 229–236.

Bram, A. D. (2010). The relevance of the Rorschach and patient-examiner relationship in treatment planning and outcome assessment. *Journal of Personality Assessment, 92,* 91–115.

Brammer, L. M., & MacDonald, G. (1999). *The helping relationship* (7th ed.). Boston: Allyn & Bacon.

Brandstadter, J. (2006). Action perspectives in human development. In W. Damon & R. Lerner (Eds.), *Handbook of child psychology* (6th ed.). New York: Wiley.

Brandt, M. J., & Reyna, C. (2010). The role of prejudice and the need for closure in religious fundamentalism. *Personality and Social Psychology Bulletin.* (in press)

Brannick, M. T., & Levine, E. L. (2002). *Job analysis: Methods, research, and applications.* Thousand Oaks, CA: Sage.

Brannon, L. (1999). *Gender: Psychological perspectives* (2nd ed.). Boston: Allyn & Bacon.

Brannon, L., & Feist, P. (2010). *Health psychology* (7th ed.). Boston: Cengage.

Bransford, J., & others. (2006). Learning theories and education: Toward a decade of synergy. In P. A. Alexander & P. H. Winne (Eds.), *Handbook of educational psychology* (2nd ed.). Mahwah, NJ: Erlbaum.

Brasher, E. E., & Chen, P. Y. (1999). Evaluation of success criteria in job search: A process

perspective. *Journal of Occupational and Organizational Psychology, 72,* 57–70.

Breland, K., & Breland, M. (1961). The misbehavior of organisms. *American Psychologist, 16,* 681–684.

Brendgen, M., Boivin, M., Vitaro, F., Bukowski, W. M., Dionne, G., Tremblay, R. E., & Perusse, D. (2008). Linkages between children's and their friends' social and physical aggression: Evidence for a gene-environment interaction? *Child Development, 79,* 13–29.

Brendgen, M., Lamarche, V., Wanner, B., & Vitaro, F. (2010). Links between friendship relations and early adolescents' trajectories of depressed mood. *Developmental Psychology, 46,* 491–501.

Brent, D. A., & others. (2009). Predictors of spontaneous and systematically assessed suicidal adverse events in the treatment of SSRI-resistant depression in adolescents (TORDIA) study. *American Journal of Psychiatry, 166,* 418–426.

Brett, J. G., & Atwater, L. E. (2001). 360-degree feedback: Accuracy, reactions, and perceptions of usefulness. *Journal of Applied Psychology, 86,* 930–942.

Brettell, C. B., & Sargent, C. F. (2009). *Gender in cross-cultural perspective.* Upper Saddle River, NJ: Prentice-Hall.

Brewer, G. A., Knight, J. B., Marsh, R. L., & Unsworth, N. (2010). Individual differences in event-based prospective memory: Evidence for multiple processes supporting cue detection. *Memory and Cognition, 38,* 304–311.

Brewer, M. B. (2007). The social psychology of intergroup relations: Social categorization, ingroup bias, and outgroup prejudice. In A. W. Kruglanski & E. Tory Higgins (Eds.), *Social psychology: Handbook of basic principles* (2nd ed.). New York: Guilford.

Brewer, N., Barnes, J., & Sauer, J. (2010). The effects of peripheral message cues on clinicians' judgments about clients' psychological status. *British Journal of Clinical Psychology.* (in press)

Brewster, K. L., & Harker Tillman, K. (2008). Who's doing it? Patterns and predictors of youths' oral sexual experiences. *Journal of Adolescent Health, 42,* 73–80.

Brezo, J., & others. (2009). Differences and similarities In the serotonergic diathesis for suicide attempts and mood disorders: A 22-year longitudinal gene-environment study. *Molecular Psychiatry.* doi: 10.1038/mp.2009.19.

Brickman, P., & Campbell, D. T. (1971). Hedonic relativism and planning the good society. In M. H. Appley (Ed.), *Adaptation-level theory* (pp. 287–302). New York: Academic.

Bridge, D. J., Chiao, J. Y., & Paller, K. A. (2010). Emotional context at learning systematically biases memory for facial information. *Memory and Cognition, 38,* 125–133.

Bridgman, T. (2007). Review of the three faces of leadership: Manager, artist, priest. *Personnel Review, 36,* 494–496.

Briggs, K. C., & Myers, I. B. (1998). *Myers-Briggs Types Indicator.* Palo Alto, CA: Consulting Psychologists Press.

Brigham, J. C. (1986). Race and eyewitness identifications. In S. Worschel & W. G. Austin (Eds.), *Psychology of intergroup relations.* Chicago: Nelson-Hall.

Brigham, J. C., Bennett, L. B., Meissner, C. A., & Mitchell, T. L. (2007). The influence of race on eyewitness memory. In R. C. L. Lindsay, D. F. Ross, J. D. Read, & M. P. Toglia (Eds.), *The handbook of eyewitness memory: Vol II.* Mahwah, NJ: Erlbaum.

Brink, S. (2001, May 7). Your brain on alcohol. *U.S. News & World Report, 130* (18), 50–57.

Brinker, J. K., & Dozois, D. J. (2009). Ruminative thought style and depressed mood. *Journal of Clinical Psychology, 65,* 1–19.

Brister, H., Turner, J. A., Aaron, L. A., & Manci, L. (2006). Self-efficacy is associated with pain, functioning, and coping in patients with chronic temporomandibular disorder pain. *Journal of Orofacial Pain, 20,* 115–124.

Britton, P. C., & Conner, K. R. (2010). Suicide attempts within 12 months of treatment for substance use disorders. *Suicide and Life-Threatening Behavior, 40,* 14–21.

Brizendine, L. (2006). *The female brain.* New York: Random House.

Broberg, D. J., & Bernstein, I. L. (1987). Candy as a scapegoat in the prevention of food aversions in children receiving chemotherapy. *Cancer, 60,* 2344–2347.

Brody, L. R. (1999). *Gender, emotion and the family.* Cambridge, MA: Harvard University Press.

Brody, N. (2007). Does education influence intelligence? In P. C. Kyllonen, R. D. Roberts, & L. Stankov (Eds.), *Extending intelligence.* Mahwah, NJ: Erlbaum.

Brody, S., & Costa, R. M. (2009). Satisfaction (sexual, life, relationship, and mental health) is associated directly with penile-vaginal intercourse, but inversely with other sexual behavior frequencies. *Journal of Sexual Medicine, 6,* 1947–1954.

Brohan, E., Eglie, R., Sartorius, N., & Thornicroft, G., for the GAMIAN-Europe Study Group. (2010). Self-stigma, empowerment, and perceived discrimination among people with schizophrenia in 14 European countries: The GAMIAN-Europe study. *Schizophrenia Research.* (in press)

Bronfenbrenner, U., & Morris, P. A. (2006). The bioecological model of human development. In W. Damon & R. Lerner (Eds.), *Handbook of child psychology* (6th ed.). New York: Wiley.

Brooker, R. J., Widmaier, E. P., Graham, L. E., & Stiling, P. D. (2010). *Biology* (2nd ed.). New York: McGraw-Hill.

Brooks, J. G., & Brooks, M. G. (2001). *In search of understanding: The case for the constructivist classroom.* Upper Saddle River, NJ: Prentice-Hall.

Brown, A. S. (2006). Prenatal infection as a risk factor for schizophrenia. *Schizophrenia Bulletin, 32,* 200–202.

Brown, B. B., & Dietz, E. L. (2009). Informal peer groups in middle childhood and adolescence. In K. H. Rubin, W. M. Bukowski, &

B. Laursen (Eds.), *Handbook of peer interactions, relationships, and groups.* New York: Guilford.

Brown, D. (2007). Evidence-based hypnotherapy for asthma: A critical review. *International Journal of Clinical and Experimental Hypnosis, 55,* 220–249.

Brown, G. D. A., & Lewandowsky, S. (2010). Forgetting in memory models: Arguments against trace theory and consolidation failure. In S. D. Sala (Ed.), *Forgetting.* New York: Psychology Press.

Brown, K. G., & Sitzmann, T. (2010). Training and employee development for improved performance In S. Zedeck (Ed.), *APA handbook of industrial and organizational psychology.* Washington, DC: APA. (in press)

Brown, P. L., & Jenkins, H. M. (2009). On the law of effect. In D. Shanks (Ed.), *Psychology of learning.* Thousand Oaks, CA: Sage.

Brown, R. (1973). *A first language: The early stages.* Cambridge, MA: Harvard University Press.

Brown, S. L., Nesse, R. N., Vinokur, A. D., & Smith, D. M. (2003). Providing social support may be more beneficial than receiving it: Results from a prospective study of mortality. *Psychological Science, 14,* 320–327.

Brown, W. A. (2007). Treatment response in melancholia. *Acta Psychiatrica Scandinavica, 433,* 125–129.

Brown, W. M., Finn, C. J., Cooke, B. M., & Breedlove, S. M. (2002). Differences in finger length ratios between self-defined "butch" and "femme" lesbians, *Archives of Sexual Behavior, 31,* 123–127.

Brown-Borg, H. M. (2008). Hormonal regulation of longevity in mammals. *Aging Research Reviews, 6,* 28–45.

Bruch, M. A. (2002). The relevance of mitigated and unmitigated agency and communion for depression vulnerabilities and dysphoria. *Journal of Counseling Psychology, 49,* 449–459.

Brug, J., Conner, M., Harré, N., Kremers, S., McKellar, S., & Whitelaw, S. (2004). The transtheoretical model and stages of change: A critique. Observations by five commentators on the paper by Adams, J. and White, M. (2004) Why don't stage-based activity promotion interventions work? *Health Education Research, 20,* 244–258.

Brumariu, L. E., & Kerns, K. A. (2010). Parent-child attachment and internalizing symptoms in adolescence: A review of empirical findings and future directions. *Development and Psychopathology, 22,* 177–203.

Brummett, B. H., Boyle, S. H., Kuhn, C. M., Siegler, I. C., & Williams, R. B. (2008). Associations among central nervous system serotonergic function and neuroticism are moderated by gender. *Biological Psychology, 78,* 200–203.

Brunborg, G. S., & others. (2010). The relationship between aversive conditioning and risk-avoidance in gambling. *Journal of Gambling Studies.* (in press)

Bruning, R. H., Schraw, G. J., Norby, M. M., & Ronning, R. R. (2004). *Cognitive psychology and instruction* (4th ed.). Upper Saddle River, NJ: Prentice-Hall.

Brunstein, J. (1993). Personal goals and subjective well-being: A longitudinal study. *Journal of Personality and Social Psychology, 65,* 1061–1070.

Brunstein, J., & Maier, G. W. (2005). Implicit and self-attributed motives to achieve: Two separate but interacting needs. *Journal of Personality and Social Psychology, 89,* 205–222.

Bryant, J. B. (2009). Language in social contexts: Communication competence in the preschool years. In J. Berko Gleason & N. Ratner (Eds.), *The development of language* (7th ed.). Boston: Allyn & Bacon.

Bryant, R. A. (2006). Longitudinal psychophysiological studies of heart rate: Mediating effects and implications for treatment. *Annals of the New York Academy of Science, 1071,* 19–26.

Bryant-Davis, T., Ullman, S. E., Tsong, Y., Tillman, S., & Smith, K. (2010). Struggling to survive: Sexual assault, poverty, and mental health outcomes of African American women. *American Journal of Orthopsychiatry, 80,* 61–70.

Bucherelli, C., Baldi, E., Mariottini, C., Passani, M. B., & Blandina, P. (2006). Aversive memory reactivation engages in the amygdala only some neurotransmitters involved in consolidation. *Learning and Memory, 13,* 426–430.

Budson, A. E. (2009). Understanding memory dysfunction. *Neurologist, 15,* 71–79.

Bukowski, W. M., Brendgen, M., & Vitaro, F. (2007). Peers and socialization: Effects on externalizing and internalizing problems. In J. E. Grusec & P. D. Hastings (Eds.), *Handbook of socialization: Theory and research* (pp. 355–381). New York: Guilford.

Bulik, C. M., & others. (2000). Twin studies of eating disorders: A review. *International Journal of Eating Disorders, 27,* 1–20.

Bureau, J.-F., Easterbrooks, M. A., & Lyons-Ruth, K. (2009). Maternal depressive symptoms in infancy: Unique contribution to children's depressive symptoms in childhood and adolescence? *Development and Psychopathology, 21,* 519–537.

Burgdorf, J., & Panksepp, J. (2006). The neurobiology of positive emotions. *Neuroscience and Biobehavioral Reviews, 30,* 173–187.

Burger, J. (2009). Replicating Milgram: Would people still obey today? *American Psychologist, 64,* 1–11.

Burger, J. M., & Caldwell, D. F. (2000). Personality, social activities, job-search behavior and interview success: Distinguishing between PANAS trait positive affect and NEO extraversion. *Motivation and Emotion, 24,* 51–62.

Burstein, M., Ginsburg, G. S., Petras, H., & Ialongo, N. (2010). Parent psychopathology and youth internalizing symptoms in an urban community sample: A latent growth model analysis. *Child Psychiatry and Human Development, 41,* 61–87.

Burton, C. M., & King, L. A. (2004). The health benefits of writing about peak experiences. *Journal of Research in Personality, 38,* 150–163.

Burton, C. M., & King, L. A. (2008). The effects of (very) brief writing on health: The 2-minute miracle. *British Journal of Health Psychology, 13,* 9–14.

Burton, C. M., & King, L. A. (2009). The benefits of writing about positive experiences: Applying the broaden and build model. *Psychology and Health, 24,* 867–879.

Busch, F. (2007). "I noticed": The emergence of self-observation in relationship to pathological attractor sites. *International Journal of Psychoanalysis, 88,* 423–441.

Busch, F. N., Milrod, B. L., & Sandberg, L. S. (2009). A study demonstrating efficacy of a psychoanalytic psychotherapy for panic disorder: Implications for psychoanalytic research, theory, and practice. *Journal of the American Psychoanalytic Association, 57,* 131–148.

Bushman, B. J., & Anderson, C. A. (2007). Measuring the strength of the effect of violent media on aggression. *American Psychologist, 62,* 253–254.

Bushman, B. J., & Baumeister, R. F. (2002). Does self-love or self-hate lead to violence? *Journal of Research in Personality, 36,* 543–545.

Buss, D. M. (2011). *Evolutionary psychology* (4th ed.). Boston: Allyn & Bacon.

Bussey, K., & Bandura, A. (2004). Social cognitive theory of gender development and functioning. In A. H. Eagly, A. Beall, & R. Sternberg (Eds.), *The psychology of gender* (2nd ed., pp. 92–119). New York: Guilford.

Butcher, J. N. (2010). Personality assessment from the nineteenth century to the early twenty-first century: Past achievements and contemporary challenges. *Annual Review of Psychology* (vol. 61). Palo Alto, CA: Annual Reviews.

Butcher, M. (2010, February 10). Startup to launch after secret London facebook group amasses 180,000 members. *Techcrunch.com.* http://eu.techcrunch.com/2010/02/07/startup-to-launch-after-secret-london-facebook-group-amasses-180000/ (accessed February 15, 2010)

Butler, A. C., Chapman, J. E., Forman, E. M., & Beck, A. T. (2006). The empirical status of cognitive-behavioral therapy: A review of meta-analyses. *Clinical Psychology Review, 26,* 17–31.

Butz, A. M., & others. (2010). Household smoking behavior: Effects on indoor air quality and health of urban children with asthma. *Maternal and Child Health Journal.* (in press)

Buunk, B. P., & Van Yperen, N. W. (1991). Referential comparisons, relational comparisons, and exchange orientation: Their relation to marital satisfaction. *Personality and Social Psychology Bulletin, 17,* 709–717.

Byard, R. W., & Krous, H. F. (2004). Research and sudden infant death syndrome: Definitions, diagnostic difficulties and discrepancies. *Journal of Paediatrics and Child Health, 40,* 419–421.

Byrnes, J. P. (2008). Piaget's cognitive developmental theory. In M. M. Haith & J. B. Benson (Eds.), *Encyclopedia of infant and early childhood development.* Oxford, U.K.: Elsevier.

C

Cabanac, M., Cabanac, A. J., & Parent, A. (2009). The emergence of consciousness in phylogeny. *Behavioral Brain Research, 198,* 267–272.

Cabeza, R. (2002). Hemispheric asymmetry reduction in older adults: The HAROLD model. *Psychology and Aging, 17,* 85–100.

Cabeza, R., Nyberg, L., & Park, D. (Eds.). (2005). *Cognitive neuroscience of aging.* New York: Oxford University Press.

Cacioppo, J. T., Bernsten, G. G., & Aue, T. (2010). Social psychophysiology. In I. Wiener & E. Craighead (Eds.), *Corsini encyclopedia of psychology* (4th ed.). New York: Wiley.

Cacioppo, J. T., Hughes, M. E., Waite, L. J., Hawkley, L. C., & Thisted, R. A. (2006). Loneliness as a specific risk factor for depressive symptoms: Cross-sectional and longitudinal analyses. *Psychology and Aging, 21,* 140–151.

Cahill, L. (2006). Why sex matters for neuroscience. *Nature Reviews Neuroscience, 7,* 477–484.

Cai, D. J., & others (2009). REM, not incubation, improves creativity by priming associative networks. *PNAS, 106,* 10130–10134.

Caillouet, B. A., Boccaccini, M. T., Varela, J. G., Davis, R. D., & Rostow, C. D. (2010). Predictive validity of the MMPI-2 PSY-5 scales and facets for law enforcement officer employment outcomes. *Criminal Justice and Behavior, 37,* 217–238.

Cain, D. J. (2001). Defining characteristics, history, and evolution of humanistic psychotherapies. In D. J. Cain & J. Seeman (Eds.), *Humanistic psychotherapies.* Washington, DC: American Psychological Association.

Calati, R., De Ronchi, D., Bellini, M., & Serretti, A. (2010). The 5-HTTLPR polymorphism and eating disorders: A meta-analysis. *International Journal of Eating Disorders.* (in press)

Cale, E. M., & Lilienfeld, S. O. (2002). Sex differences in psychopathy and antisocial personality disorder: A review and integration. *Clinical Psychology Review, 22,* 1179–1207.

Calkins, S. D., & Bell, M. A. (Eds.). (2010). *Child development at the intersection of emotion and cognition.* Washington, DC: American Psychological Association.

Cameron, J., Banko, K. M., & Pierce, W. D. (2001). Pervasive negative effects of rewards on intrinsic motivation: The myth continues. *Behavior Analyst, 24,* 1–44.

Cameron, J., & Pierce, W. D. (2002). *Rewards and intrinsic motivation: Resolving the controversy.* Westport, CT: Bergin & Garvey.

Cameron, J., Pierce, W. D., Banko, K. M., & Gear, A. (2005). Achievement-based rewards and intrinsic motivation: A test of cognitive mediators. *Journal of Educational Psychology, 97,* 641–655.

Cameron, K. S. (2003). Organizational virtuousness and performance. In K. S. Cameron, J. E. Dutton, & R. E. Quinn (Eds.), *Positive organizational scholarship: Foundations of a new discipline* (pp. 48–65). San Francisco: Berrett-Koehler.

Cameron, K. S. (2005). Organizational downsizing. In N. Nicholson, P. G. Audia, & M. M. Pilluta (Eds.), *The Blackwell encyclopedia of management.* Malden, MA: Blackwell.

Cameron, K. S. (2007). Positive organizational change. In S. Clegg & B. James (Eds.), *International encyclopedia of organizational studies.* Thousand Oaks, CA: Sage.

Campbell, C. M., & Edwards, R. R. (2009). Mind-body interactions in pain: The neurophysiology of anxious and catastrophic pain-related thoughts. *Translational Research, 153,* 97–101.

Campbell, F. A. (2006). The malleability of the cognitive development of children of low income African-American families. In P. C. Kyllonen, R. D. Roberts, & L. Stankov (Eds.), *Extending intelligence.* Mahwah, NJ: Erlbaum.

Campbell, J. D., Yoon, D. P., & Johnstone, B. (2010). Determining relationships between physical health and spiritual experience, religious practice, and congregational support in a heterogeneous sample. *Journal of Religion and Health, 49,* 3–17.

Campbell, J. M., & Brown, E. A. (2010). *Cambridge handbook of forensic psychology.* Cambridge, U.K.: Cambridge University Press.

Campbell, L., Campbell, B., & Dickinson, D. (2004). *Teaching and learning through multiple intelligences.* Boston: Allyn & Bacon.

Campbell, W. K., Bonacci, A. M., Shelton, J., Exline, J. J., & Bushman, B. J. (2004). Psychological entitlement: Interpersonal consequences and validation of a self-report measure. *Journal of Personality Assessment, 83,* 29–45.

Canadian Statistics. (2005). Crime in Canada. http://www.statcan.ca/Daily/English/050721/d050721a.htm|title=Crime in Canada (accessed June 13, 2007)

Canals, S., Beyerlein, M., Merkle, H., & Logothetis, N. K. (2009). Functional MRI evidence for LTP-induced neural network reorganization. *Current Biology, 19,* 398–403.

Canino, G., & others. (2004). The DSM-IV rates of child and adolescent disorders in Puerto Rico. *Archives of General Psychiatry, 61,* 85–93.

Canli, T. (2008a). Toward a neurogenetic theory of neuroticism. In D. W. Pfaff & B. L. Kieffer (Eds.), *Molecular and biophysical mechanisms of arousal, alertness, and attention* (pp. 153–174). Malden, MA: Blackwell.

Canli, T. (2008b). Toward a "molecular psychology" of personality. In O. P. John, R. W. Robins, & L. A. Pervin (Eds.), *Handbook of personality theory and research* (3rd ed., pp. 311–327). New York: Guilford.

Canli, T., Sivers, H., Whitfield, S. L., Gotlib, I. H., & Gabrieli, J. D. E. (2002). Amygdala response to happy faces as a function of extraversion. *Science, 296,* 2191.

Cannon, W. B. (1927). The James-Lange theory of emotions: A critical examination and an alternative theory. *American Journal of Psychology, 39,* 106–124.

Cannon, W. B., & Washburn, A. L. (1912). An explanation of hunger, *American Journal of Physiology, 29,* 441–454.

Cantor, J. M., Kabani, N., Christensen, B. K., Zipursky, R. B., Barbaree, H. E., Dickey, R., Klassen, P. E., Mikulis, D. J., Kuban, M. E., Blak, T., Richards, B. A., Hanratty, M. K., & Blanchard, R. (2008). Cerebral white matter deficiencies in pedophilic men. *Journal of Psychiatric Research, 42,* 167–183.

Cantor, N., & Sanderson, C. A. (1999). Life task participation and well-being: The importance of taking part in daily life. In D. Kahneman, E. Diener, & N. Schwarz (Eds.), *Well-being: The foundations of hedonic psychology* (pp. 230–243). New York: Russell Sage Foundation.

Capasso, A., Putrella, C., & Milano, W. (2009). Recent clinical aspects of eating disorders. *Reviews on Recent Clinical Trials, 4,* 63–69.

Caplan, J. B., & Caplan, P. J. (2005). The perseverative search for sex differences in mathematics ability. In A. M. Gallagher & J. C. Kaufman (Eds.), *Gender differences in mathematics* (pp. 25–47). Cambridge, U.K.: Cambridge University Press.

Caprara, G. V., Alessandri, G., Di Giunta, L., Panerai, L., & Eisenberg, N. (2010). The contribution of agreeableness and self-efficacy beliefs to prosociality. *European Journal of Personality, 24,* 36–55.

Caprara, G. V., Fagnani, C., Alessandri, G., Steca, P., Gigantesco, A., Sforza, L., Cavalli, L., & Stazi, M. A., (2009). Human optimal functioning: The genetics of positive orientation towards self, life, and the future. *Behavior Genetics, 39,* 277–284.

Card, N. A., Stucky, B. D., Sawalani, G. M., & Little, T. D. (2008). Direct and indirect aggression during childhood and adolescence: A meta-analytic review of gender differences, intercorrelations, and relations to maladjustment. *Child Development, 79,* 1185–1229.

Cardno, A. G., & Gottesman, I. I. (2000). Twin studies of schizophrenia: From bow-and-arrow concordances to Star Wars Mx and functional genomics. *American Journal of Medical Genetics, 97,* 12–17.

Cardoso Zoppe, E. H., Schoueri, P., Castro, M., & Neto, F. L. (2009). Teaching psychodynamics to psychiatric residents through psychiatric outpatient interviews. *Academic Psychiatry, 33,* 51–55.

Carey, B. (2009, August 9). After injury, fighting to regain a sense of self. *New York Times.* http://www.nytimes.com/2009/08/09/health/research/09brain.html

Carey, W. B. (2002). Is ADHD a valid disorder? In P. Jensen & J. Cooper (Eds.), *Attention deficit hyperactivity disorder: State of the science, best practices.* Kingston, NJ: Civic Research Institute.

Carlo, G. (2006). Care-based and altruistically-based morality. In M. Killen & J. Smetana (Eds.), *Handbook of moral development.* Mahwah, NJ: Erlbaum.

Carlsson, M. A., & Swedberg, M. D. (2010). A behavioural operant discrimination model for assessment and pharmacological manipulation of visual function in rats. *Brain Research, 1321,* 78–87.

Carmona, J. E., Holland, A. K., & Harrison, D. W. (2009). Extending the functional cerebral theory of emotion to the vestibular modality: A systematic and integrative approach. *Psychological Bulletin, 135,* 286–302.

Carnethon, M. R., & others. (2010). Joint associations of physical activity and aerobic fitness on the development of incident hypertension: Coronary artery risk development in young adults. *Hypertension.* (in press)

Carney, D. R., Nosek, B. A., Greenwald, A. G., & Banaji, M. R. (2007). Implicit Association Test (IAT). In R. Baumeister & K. Vohs (Eds.), *Encyclopedia of social psychology.* Thousand Oaks, CA: Sage.

Carota, F., Posada, A., Harquel, S., Delpuech, C., Bertrand, O., & Sirigu, A. (2010). Neural dynamics of intention to speak. *Cerebral Cortex.* (in press)

Carpenter, S. K., & DeLosh, E. L. (2006). Impoverished cue support enhances subsequent retention: Support for the elaborative retrieval explanation of the testing effect. *Memory and Cognition, 34,* 268–276.

Carskadon, M. A. (2006, March). *Too little, too late: Sleep bioregulatory processes across adolescence.* Paper presented at the meeting of the Society for Research on Adolescence, San Francisco.

Carskadon, M. A., Mindell, J., & Drake, C. (2006, September). *Contemporary sleep patterns in the USA: Results of the 2006 National Sleep Foundation Poll.* Paper presented at the European Sleep Research Society, Innsbruck, Austria.

Carson, C. M. (2005). A historical view of Douglas McGregor's Theory Y. *Management Decision, 43,* 450–460.

Carson, R. C., Butcher, J. N., & Mineka, S. (1996). *Abnormal psychology and life* (10th ed.). New York: HarperCollins.

Carstensen, L. L. (2006). The influence of a sense of time on human development. *Science, 312,* 1913–1915.

Carstensen, L. L. (2008, May). *Long life in the twenty-first century.* Paper presented at the meeting of the Association of Psychological Science, Chicago.

Carstensen, L. L., & Charles, S. T. (2003). Human aging: Why is even good news taken as bad? In L. A. Aspinall & U. M. Staudinger (Eds.), *A psychology of human strengths.* Washington, DC: American Psychological Association.

Carter, S. A., & Wu, K. D. (2010). Symptoms of specific and generalized social phobia: An examination of discriminant validity and structural relations with mood and anxiety symptoms. *Behavior Therapy, 41,* 254–265.

Cartwright, S., & Cooper, C. L. (Eds.). (2008). *The Oxford handbook of personnel psychology.* New York: Oxford University Press.

Carver, C. S., & Connor-Smith, J. (2010). Personality and coping. *Annual Review of Psychology* (vol. 61). Palo Alto, CA: Annual Reviews.

Carver, C. S., & Scheier, M. F. (2009). Optimism. In M. R. Levy & R. H. Hoyle (Eds.), *Handbook of individual differences in social behavior* (pp. 330–342). New York: Guilford.

Carver, C. S., & Scheier, M. F. (2009a). Action, affect, multitasking, and layers of control. In J. P. Forgas, R. F. Baumeister, & D. M. Tice (Eds.), *Psychology of self-regulation: Cognitive, affective, and motivational processes* (pp. 109–126). New York: Psychology Press.

Cascio, W. (2010). *Managing human resources* (8th ed.). New York: McGraw-Hill.

Cascio, W. F., & Aguinis, H. (2011). *Applied psychology in human resource management* (7th ed.). Upper Saddle River, NJ: Prentice-Hall.

Case, R. B., Moss, A. J., Case, N., McDermott, M., & Eberly, S. (1992). Living alone after myocardial infarction. Impact on prognosis. *Journal of the American Medical Association, 267,* 515–519.

Caspi, A., McClay, J., Moffitt, T. E., Mill, J., Martin, J., Craig, I. W., Taylor, A., & Poulton, R. (2002). Role of genotype in the cycle of violence in maltreated children. *Science, 297,* 851–854.

Caspi, A., & Roberts, B. W. (2001). Personality development across the life course: The argument for change and continuity. *Psychological Inquiry, 12,* 49–66.

Cassimatis, N. L., Murugesan, A., & Bignoli, P. G. (2009). Reasoning as simulation. *Cognitive Processing, 10,* 343–353.

Cathers-Schiffman, T. A., & Thompson, M. S. (2007). Assessment of English- and Spanish-speaking students with the WISC-III and Leiter-R. *Journal of Psychoeducational Assessment, 25,* 41–52.

Cattaneo, L., & Rizzolatti, G. (2009). The mirror neuron system. *Archives of Neurology, 66,* 557–560.

Cauller, L. (2001, May). Review of *Santrock, Psychology* (7th ed.). New York: McGraw-Hill.

Cavallaro, F. I., & others. (2010). Hypnotizability-related EEG alpha and theta activities during visual and somesthetic imageries. *Neuoroscience Letters, 470,* 13–18.

Caverzasi, E., & others. (2008). Complications in major depressive disorder therapy: A review of magnetic resonance spectroscopy studies. *Functional Neurology, 23,* 129–132.

Cavina-Pratesi, C., Kentridge, R. W., Heywood, C. A., & Milner, A. D. (2010). Separate channels for processing form, texture, and color: Evidence from fMRI adaptation and visual object agnosia. *Cerebral Cortex.* (in press)

CBS News. (2006, March 15). Ambien may prompt sleep eating. http://www.cbsnews.com/stories/2006/03/15/earlyshow/health/health_news/main1404632.shtml (accessed December 15, 2006)

CBS News. (2009). Sullenberger recalls moment engines died. http://www.cbsnews.com/stories/2009/01/30/60minutes/main4764852.shtml (accessed February 3, 2010)

CBS News. (2009a, December 2). Richmond High gang rape: Six plead not guilty to raping teen while others watched. http://www.cbsnews.com/8301-504083_162-5697504083.html (accessed December 15, 2009)

Centers for Disease Control and Prevention (CDC), National Center for Injury Prevention and Control. (2004). *Web-based injury statistics query and reporting system* (WISQARS). http://www.cdc.gov/ncipc/wisqars/default.Htm (accessed June 21, 2004)

Centers for Disease Control and Prevention (CDC). (2005). National Youth Risk Behavior Survey: 1991–2005. U.S. Department of Health and Human Services, Centers for Disease Control and Prevention.

Centers for Disease Control and Prevention (CDC). (2007, September 7). Suicide trends among youths and young adults aged 10–24 Years—United States, 1990–2004. *Morbidity and Mortality Weekly Report, 56,* 905–908.

Centers for Disease Control and Prevention (CDC). (2009a). *Obesity: Halting the epidemic by making health easier.* Atlanta: Author.

Centers for Disease Control and Prevention (CDC). (2009b). *Defining obesity and overweight.* Atlanta: Author.

Centers for Disease Control and Prevention (CDC). (2009c). *HIV/AIDS.* Atlanta: Author.

Centers for Disease Control and Prevention (CDC). (2009, November 13). Cigarette smoking among adults and trends in smoking cessation—United States, 2008. *Morbidity and Mortality Weekly Report, 58,* 1227–1232.

Cetinel, S., & others. (2010). Oxytocin treatment alleviates stress-activated colitis by a receptor-dependent mechanism. *Regulatory Peptides, 160,* 146–152.

Chabris, C., & Simons, D. (2010). *The invisible gorilla, and other ways our intuitions deceive us.* New York: Crown.

Chafetz, L., White, M., Collins-Bride, G., Cooper, B. A., & Nickens, J. (2008). Clinical trial of wellness training: Health promotion for severely mentally ill adults. *Journal of Nervous and Mental Disease, 196,* 475–483.

Chaiken, S., & Ledgerwood, A. (2007). Heuristic processing. In R. Baumeister & K. D. Vohs (Eds.), *Encyclopedia of social psychology.* Thousand Oaks, CA: Sage.

Chakraborty, S., Kaushik, D. K., Gupta, M., & Basu, A. (2010). Inflammasome signaling at the heart of central nervous system pathology. *Journal of Neuroscience Research.* (in press)

Chambon, V., Baudouin, J., & Franck, N. (2006). The role of configural information in facial emotion recognition in schizophrenia. *Neuropsychologia, 44,* 2437–2444.

Chan, R. W., Raboy, B., & Patterson, C. J. (1998). Psychosocial adjustment among children conceived via donor insemination by lesbian and heterosexual mothers. *Child Development, 69,* 326–332.

Chance, P. (2009). *Learning and behavior* (6th ed.). Belmont, CA: Cengage.

Chapman, A. L. (2009). Borderline personality disorder. In D. McKay, J. S. Abramowitz, & S. Taylor (Eds.), *Cognitive-behavioral therapy for refractory cases: Turning failure into success* (pp. 347–367). Washington, DC: American Psychological Association.

Chapman, D. S., & Webster, J. (2003). The use of technologies in the recruiting, screening, and selection processes for job candidates. *International Journal of Selection and Assessment, 11,* 113–120.

Charbonneau, D., Barling, J., & Kelloway, E. K. (2001). Transformational leadership behaviors, upward trust, and satisfaction in self-managed work teams. *Organizational Development Journal, 17,* 13–28.

Charles, S. T., & Carstensen, L. L. (2010). Social and emotional aging. *Annual Review of Psychology* (vol. 61). Palo Alto, CA: Annual Reviews.

Charmaraman, L., & Grossman, J. M. (2010). Importance of race and ethnicity: An exploration of Asian, Black, Latino, and multiracial ethnic identity. *Cultural Diversity and Ethnic Minority Psychology, 16,* 144–151.

Chassin, L., Hussong, A., & Beltran, I. (2009). Adolescent substance use. In R. M. Lerner & L. Steinberg (Eds.), *Handbook of adolescent psychology* (3rd ed.). New York: Wiley.

Chater, N., Reali, F., & Christiansen, M. H. (2009). Restrictions on biological adaptation in language evolution. *Proceedings of the National Academy of Sciences, 106,* 1015–1020.

Cheng, P. W., & Holyoak, K. J. (2011). Learning and inference with causal models. *Annual Review of Psychology* (vol. 62). Palo Alto, CA: Annual Reviews.

Chess, S., & Thomas, A. (1977). Temperamental individuality from childhood to adolescence. *Journal of Child Psychiatry, 16,* 218–226.

Chess, S., & Thomas, A. (1996). *Temperament: Theory and practice.* Philadelphia: Brunner/Mazel.

Cheung, O. S., & Gauthier, I. (2010). Selective interference on the holistic processing of faces in working memory. *Journal of Experimental Psychology: Human Perception and Performance.* (in press)

Chiang, M., Barysheva, M., Shattuck, D. W., Lee, A. D., Madsen, S. K., Avedissian, C., Klunder, A. D., Toga, A. W., McMahon, K. L., de Zubicaray, G. I., Wright, M. J., Srivastava, A., Balov, N., & Thompson, P. M. (2009). Genetics of brain fiber architecture and intellectual performance. *Journal of Neuroscience, 29,* 2212–2224.

Chiang, M. C., & others. (2009). Genetics of brain fiber architecture and intellectual performance. *Journal of Neuroscience, 29,* 2214–2224.

Chica, A. B., & others. (2010). Exogenous attention can capture perceptual consciousness: ERP and behavioral evidence. *NeuroImage.* (in press)

Chida, Y., & Steptoe, A. (2009). The association of anger and hostility with future coronary heart disease: A meta-analytic review of prospective evidence. *Journal of the American College of Cardiology, 53,* 936–946.

Chiesa, A., & Serretti, A. (2010). A systematic review of neurobiological and clinical features of mindfulness meditations. *Psychological Medicine.* (in press)

Chiesa, M., & Hobbs, S. (2008). Making sense of social research: How useful is the Hawthorne effect? *European Journal of Social Psychology, 38,* 67–74.

Chivers, M. L., Seto, M. C., & Blanchard, R. (2007). Gender and sexual orientation differences in sexual response to sexual activities versus gender of actors in sexual films. *Journal of Personality and Social Psychology, 93,* 1108–1121.

Cho, D., & Campana, D. (2009). Expansion and activation of natural killer cells for cancer immunotherapy. *Korean Journal of Laboratory Medicine, 29,* 89–96.

Choi, J. K., & Bowles, S. (2007). The co-evolution of parochial altruism and war. *Science, 318,* 636–640.

Chomsky, N. (1975). *Reflections on language.* New York: Pantheon.

Chouinard, G. (2006). Interrelations between psychiatric symptoms and drug-induced movement disorder. *Journal of Psychiatry and Neuroscience, 31,* 177–180.

Christensen, H., & others. (2010). Protocol for a randomized trial investigating the effectiveness of an online e-health application compared to attention placebo or sertraline in the treatment of generalized anxiety disorder. *Trials.* (in press)

Christensen, L. B. (2007). *Experimental methodology* (10th ed.). Boston: Allyn & Bacon.

Christensen, L. B., Johnson, R. B., & Turner, L. (2011). *Research design, methods, and analysis* (11th ed.). Upper Saddle River, NJ: Prentice-Hall.

Christie, I. C., & Friedman, B. H. (2004). Autonomic specificity of discrete emotion and dimensions of affective space: A multivariate approach. *International Journal of Psychophysiology, 51,* 143–153.

Christopher Frueh, B., Grubaugh, A. L., Cusack, K. J., Kimble, M. O., Elhai, J. D., & Knapp, R. G. (2009). Exposure-based cognitive-behavioral treatment of PTSD in adults with schizophrenia or schizoaffective disorder: A pilot study. *Journal of Anxiety Disorders, 23,* 665–675.

Chun, M. M., Turk-Browne, N., & Golomb, J. (2011). Toward a taxonomy of attention. *Annual Review of Psychology* (vol. 62). Palo Alto, CA: Annual Reviews.

Church, T. S., LaMonte, M. J., Barlow, C. E., & Blair, S. N. (2005). Cardiorespiratory fitness and body mass index as predictors of cardiovascular disease mortality among men with diabetes. *Archives of Internal Medicine, 165,* 2114–2120.

CIA. (2005). *CIA world fact book.* https://www.cia.gov/library/publications/the-world-factbook/index.html

Cialdini, R. B. (1991). Altruism or egoism? That is (still) the question. *Psychological Inquiry, 2,* 124–126.

Cialdini, R. B. (1993). *Influence: Science and practice.* New York: HarperCollins.

Cialdini, R. B., Vincent, J. E., Lewis, S. K., Catalan, J., Wheeler, D., & Darby, B. L. (1975). Reciprocal concessions procedure for inducing compliance: The door-in-the-face technique. *Journal of Personality and Social Psychology, 31,* 206–215.

Ciani, K. D., Middleton, M. J., Summers, J. J., & Sheldon, K. M. (2010). Buffering against performance classroom goal structures: The importance of autonomy support and classroom community. *Contemporary Educational Psychology, 35,* 88–99.

Ciani, K. D., & Sheldon, K. M. (2010). Evaluating the mastery-avoidance goal construct: A study of elite college baseball players. *Psychology of Sport and Exercise, 11,* 127–132.

Cicchetti, D., Rogosch, F. A., Gunnar, M. R., & Toth, S. L. (2010). The differential impacts of early physical and sexual abuse and internalizing problems on daytime cortisol rhythm in school-aged children. *Child Development, 81,* 252–269.

Cipriani, A., La Ferla, T., Furukawa, T. A., Signoretti, A., Nakagawa, A., Churchill, R., McGuire, H., & Barbui, C. (2010). Sertraline versus other antidepressive agents for depression. *Cochrane Database of Systematic Reviews, 4:* CD006117. doi: 10.1002/14651858.CD006117.pub4

Cisler, J. M., Olatunji, B. O., Feldner, M. T., & Forsyth, J. P. (2010). Emotion regulation and the anxiety disorders: An integrative review. *Journal of Psychopathology and Behavioral Assessment, 32,* 68–82.

Claes, H. I. (2010). Understanding the effects of sildenafil on erection maintenance and erection hardness. *Journal of Sexual Medicine.* (in press)

Clark, B. (2008). *Growing up gifted* (7th ed.). Upper Saddle River, NJ: Prentice-Hall.

Clark, D. M., Ehlers, A., Hackmann, A., McManus, F., Fennell, M., Grey, N., Waddington, L., & Wild, J. (2006). Cognitive therapy versus exposure and applied relaxation in social phobia: A randomized controlled trial. *Journal of Consulting and Clinical Psychology, 74,* 568–578.

Clark, M. J., & others (2010). U87MG decoded: The genomic sequence of a cytogenetically aberrant human cancer cell line. *PLoS Genetics, 6,* e1000832.

Clark, M. S., & Chrisman, K. (1994). Resource allocation in intimate relationships: Trying to make sense of a confusing literature. In M. J. Lerner & G. Mikula (Eds.), *Entitlement and the affectional bond: Justice in close relationships* (pp. 65–88). New York: Plenum.

Clark, R. D., & Hatfield, E. (1989). Gender differences in receptivity to sexual offers. *Journal of Psychology and Human Sexuality, 2,* 39–55.

Clark, R. E., & Squire, L. R. (2010). An animal model of recognition memory and medial temporal lobe amnesia: History and current issues. *Neuropsychologia.* (in press)

Cleeremans, A., & Sarrazin, J. C. (2007). Time, action, and consciousness. *Human Movement Science, 26,* 180–202.

Clemens, N. A. (2010). Evidence base for psychotherapy: Two perspectives. *Journal of Psychiatric Practice, 16,* 183–186.

Cleveland, J. N., Barnes-Farrell, J. L., & Ratz, J. M. (1997). Accommodation in the workplace. *Human Resource Management Review, 7,* 77–107.

Clifton, D. O., & Harter, J. K. (2003). Strengths investment. In K. S. Cameron, J. E. Dutton, & R. E. Quinn (Eds.), *Positive organizational scholarship* (pp. 111–121). San Francisco: Berrett & Koehler.

Clifton, D. O., & Nelson, P. (1992). *Soar with your strengths.* New York: Delacourt.

Clore, G. L., Gasper, K., & Garvin, E. (2001). Affect as information. In J. P. Forgas (Ed.), *Handbook of affect and social cognition* (pp. 121–144). Mahwah, NJ: Erlbaum.

Clore, G. L., & Palmer, J. (2009). Affective guidance of intelligent agents: How emotion controls cognition. *Cognitive Systems Research, 10,* 21–30.

Cloud, J. (2008, August 27). Failing our geniuses. *Time,* 40–47.

Clutton-Brock, T. H. (2007). Sexual selection in males and females. *Science, 318,* 1882–1885.

Clutton-Brock, T. H. (2010) We do not need a sexual selection 2.0—nor a theory of genial selection. *Animal Behaviour.* (in press)

CNN Poll. (2006, December 12). Most Americans see lingering racism—in others. http://www.cnn.com/2006/US/12/12/racism.poll/index.html (accessed June 13, 2007)

Coch, D., Fischer, K. W., & Dawson, G. (Eds.). (2007). *Human behavior, learning, and the developing brain.* New York: Guilford.

Cockram, D. M., Drummond, P. D., & Lee, C. W. (2010). Role and treatment of early maladaptive schemas in Vietnam veterans with PTSD. *Clinical Psychology and Psychotherapy, 17,* 165–182.

Cohen, D. (2001). Cultural variation: Considerations and implications. *Psychological Bulletin, 127,* 451–471.

Cohen, D., Nisbett, R. E., Bowdle, B. F., & Schwarz, N. (1996). Insult, aggression, and the southern culture of honor: An "experimental ethnography." *Journal of Personality and Social Psychology, 70,* 945–960.

Cohen, F., & others. (2007). Immune system declines with unemployment and recovers after stress termination. *Psychosomatic Medicine, 69,* 225–234.

Cohen, G. L., & Prinstein, M. J. (2006). Peer contagion of aggression and health risk behavior among adolescent males: An experimental investigation of effects on public conduct and private attitudes. *Child Development, 77,* 967–983.

Cohen, P. J. (2009). Medical marijuana: The conflict between scientific evidence and political ideology. Part one of two. *Journal of Pain & Palliative Care Pharmacotherapy, 23,* 4–25.

Cohen, S., Alper, C. M., Doyle, W. J., Treanor, J. J., & Turner, R. B. (2006). Positive emotional style predicts resistance to illness after experimental exposure to rhinovirus or influenza a virus. *Psychosomatic Medicine, 68,* 809–815.

Cohen, S., Doyle, W. J., & Skoner, D. P. (1999). Psychological stress, cytokine production, and severity of upper respiratory illness. *Psychosomatic Medicine, 61,* 175–180.

Cohen, S., Doyle, W. J., Alper, C. M., Janicki-Deverts, D., & Turner, R. B. (2009). Sleep habits and susceptibility to the common cold. *Archives of Internal Medicine, 169,* 62–67.

Cohen, S., Frank, E., Doyle, W., Skoner, D. P., Rabin, B. S., & Gwaltney, J. M. (1998). Types of stressors that increase susceptibility to the common cold in healthy adults. *Health Psychology, 17,* 214–223.

Cohen, S., & Janicki-Deverts, D. (2009). Can we improve our physical health by altering our social networks? *Perspectives on Psychological Science, 4* (4), 375–378.

Cohen, S., & Lemay, E. (2007). Why would social networks be linked to affect and health practices? *Health Psychology, 27,* 410–417.

Cohen-Bendahan, C. C. C., van de Beek, C., & Berenbaum, S. (2005). Prenatal sex hormone effects on child and adult sex-typed behavior: Methods and findings. *Neuroscience & Biobehavioral Reviews, 29,* 353–384.

Cohen-Charash, Y., & Spector, P. E. (2001). The role of justice in organizations: A meta-analysis. *Organizational Behavior and Human Decision Processes, 86,* 278–321.

Cohen-Kettenis, P. T., & Pfafflin, F. (2010). The DSM diagnostic criteria for gender identity disorder in adolescents and adults. *Archives of Sexual Behavior, 39* (2), 499–513.

Coifman, K. G., Bonanno, G. A., Ray, R. D., & Gross, J. J. (2007). Does repressing coping promote resilience? Affective-autonomic response discrepancy during bereavement. *Journal of Personality and Social Psychology, 92,* 745–758.

Colagiuri, S. (2010). Disabesity: Therapeutic options. *Diabetes and Obesity Medicine, 12,* 463–473.

Colangelo, J. J. (2009). The recovered memory controversy: A representative case study. *Journal of Child Sexual Abuse, 18,* 103–121.

Colapinto, J. (2000). *As nature made him.* New York: Harper Academic.

Colella, A. J., & Bruyère, S. M. (2010). Disability and employment: New directions for industrial and organizational psychology. In S. Zedeck (Ed.), *APA handbook of industrial and organizational psychology.* Washington, DC: APA. (in press)

Collins, A., Hill, L. E., Chandramohan, Y., Witcomb, D., Droste, S. K., & Reul, J. M. (2009). Exercise improves cognitive responses to stress through enhancement of epigenetic mechanisms and gene expression in the dentate gyrus. *PLoS One, 4,* e4330.

Collins, W. A., Maccoby, E. E., Steinberg, L., Hetherington, E. M., & Bornstein, M. H. (2000). Contemporary research on parenting: The case for nature and nurture. *American Psychologist, 55,* 218–232.

Collins, W. A., & Steinberg, L. (2006). Adolescent development in interpersonal context. In W. Damon & R. Lerner (Eds.), *Handbook of child psychology* (6th ed.). New York: Wiley.

Colón, E. A., Callies, A. L., Popkin, M. K., & McGlave, P. B. (1991). Depressed mood and other variables related to bone marrow transplantation survival in acute leukemia. *Psychosomatics, 32,* 420–425.

Colquitt, J. A., LePine, J. A., & Wesson, M. J. (2011). *Organizational behavior* (2nd ed.). New York: McGraw-Hill.

***Commonwealth of Massachusetts vs. Porter* 31285–330.** (1993, Massachusetts).

Compton, J. A., & Pfau, M. (2004). Use of inoculation to foster resistance to credit card marketing targeting college students. *Journal of Applied Communication Research, 32,* 343–364.

Compton, J. A., & Pfau, M. (2008). Inoculating against pro-plagiarism justifications: Rational and affective strategies. *Journal of Applied Communication Research, 36,* 98–119.

Compton, R. J., Wirtz, D., Pajoumand, G., Claus, E., & Heller, W. (2004). Association between positive affect and attentional shifting. *Cognitive Therapy and Research, 28,* 733–744.

ComScore. (2008). *Social networking explodes worldwide as sites increase their focus on cultural relevance.* http://www.comscore.com/press/release/.asp?/press=2396 (accessed April 15, 2010)

Connellan, J., Baron-Cohen, S., Wheelwright, S., Batki, A., & Ahluwalia, J. (2000). Sex differences in human neonatal social perception. *Infant Behavior & Development, 23,* 113–118.

Connor, D. F. (2010). Electroconvulsive therapy, transcranial magnetic stimulation, and deep brain stimulation. In M. K. Dulcan (Ed.), *Dulcan's textbook of child and adolescent psychiatry* (pp. 795–804). Arlington, VA: American Psychiatric Publishing.

Consortium on the Management of Disorders of Sexual Development. (2006). *Clinical guidelines for the management of disorders of sexual development.* Rohnert, CA: Intersex Society of North America.

Constantine, N. A. (2008). Converging evidence leaves policy behind: Sex education in the United States. *Journal of Adolescent Health, 42,* 324–326.

Conway, M., & Rubin, D. (1993). The structure of autobiographical memory. In A. F. Collins, S. E. Gathercole, M. A. Conway, & P. E. Morris (Eds.), *Theories of memory.* Hillsdale, NJ: Erlbaum.

Cook, M. B., & Smallman, H. S. (2008). Human factors of the confirmation bias in intelligence analysis: Decision support from graphical evidence landscapes. *Human Factors, 50,* 745–754.

Cook, R. J., Cusack, S., & Dickens, B. M. (2010). Unethical female stereotyping in reproductive health. *International Journal of Gynecology and Obstetrics.* (in press)

Cooper, M., & others. (2010). Randomized controlled trial of school-based humanistic counseling for emotional distress in young people: Feasibility study and preliminary indications of efficacy. *Child and Adolescent Psychiatry and Mental Health.* (in press)

Cooper, M. L. (1994). Motivations for alcohol use among adolescents: Development and validation of a four-factor model. *Psychological Assessment, 6,* 117–128.

Cooper, M. L. (2010). Toward a person × situation model of sexual risk-taking behaviors: Illuminating the conditional effects of traits across sexual situations and relationship contexts. *Journal of Personality and Social Psychology, 98,* 319–341.

Cooper, M. L., Pioli, M., Levitt, A., Talley, A. E., Micheas, L., & Collins, N. L. (2006). Attachment styles, sex motives, and sexual behavior: Evidence for gender-specific expressions of attachment dynamics. In M. Mikulincer & G. S. Goodman (Eds.),

Dynamics of romantic love: Attachment, care-giving, and sex (pp. 243–274). New York: Guilford.

Cooper, M. L., Russell, M., Skinner, J. B., & Windle, M. (1992). Development and validation of a three-dimensional measure of drinking motives. *Psychological Assessment, 4,* 123–132.

Cooper M. L., Shapiro, C. M., & Powers, A. M. (1998). Motivations for sex and risky sexual behavior among adolescents and young adults: A functional perspective. *Journal of Personality and Social Psychology, 75,* 1528–1558.

Cooper, M. L., Talley, A., Sheldon, M. S., Levitt, A., & Barber, L. (2008). A dyadic perspective on approach and avoidance motives for sex. In A. J. Elliot (Ed.), *Handbook of approach and avoidance motivation.* New York: Psychology Press.

Cooper, R. M., & Zubek, J. P. (1958). Effects of enriched and restricted early environments on the learning ability of bright and dull rats. *Canadian Journal of Psychology, 12,* 159–164.

Cooper-Hakim, A., & Viswesvaran, C. (2005). The construct of work commitment: Testing an integrative framework. *Psychological Bulletin, 131,* 241–259.

Copeland, D. E., Radvansky, G. A., & Goodwin, K. A. (2009). A novel study: Forgetting curves and the reminiscence bump. *Memory, 17,* 323–336.

Cornell, J. L., & Halpern-Felsher, B. L. (2006). Adolescents tell us why teens have oral sex. *Journal of Adolescent Health, 38,* 299–301.

Cornwell, B., Schumm, L. P., & Laumann, E. O. (2008). The social connectedness of older adults. *American Sociological Review, 73,* 185–203.

Cornwell, E. Y., & Waite, L. J. (2009). Social disconnectedness, perceived isolation, and health among older adults. *Journal of Health and Social Behavior, 50,* 31–48.

Corr, P. J. (2008). Reinforcement sensitivity theory (RST): Introduction. In P. J. Corr (Ed.), *The reinforcement sensitivity theory of personality* (pp. 1–43). New York: Cambridge University Press.

Correa, T., Hinsley, A. W., & de Zuniga, H. G. (2010). Who interacts on the web?: The intersection of users' personality and social media use. *Computers in Human Behavior, 26,* 247–253.

Corrigan, P. W. (2007). How clinical diagnosis might exacerbate the stigma of mental illness. *Social Work, 52,* 31–39.

Cortina, M. (2010). The future of psychodynamic psychotherapy. *Psychiatry, 73,* 43–56.

Cosmides, L. (2011). Evolutionary psychology. *Annual Review of Psychology* (vol. 62). Palo Alto, CA: Annual Reviews.

Costa, L. C., Vasconcelos, F. A., & Peres, K. G. (2010). Influence of biological, social, and psychological factors on abnormal eating attitudes among female university students in Brazil. *Journal of Health, Population, and Nutrition, 28,* 173–181.

Costa, P. T., & McCrae, R. R. (1992). *Revised NEO personality inventory.* Odessa, FL: Psychological Assessment Resources.

Costa, P. T., Terraciano, A., McCrae, R. R., Scally, M., & Abecasis, G. (2010). An alternative to the search for single polymorphisms: Toward molecular personality scales for the five-factor model. *Journal of Personality and Social Psychology.* (in press)

Costa, V. D., Lang, P. J., Sabatinelli, D., Versace, F., & Bradley, M. M. (2010). Emotional imagery: Assessing pleasure and arousal in the brain's reward circuitry. *Human Brain Mapping.* (in press)

Costafreda, S. G., Khanna, A., Mourao-Miranda, J., & Fu, C. H. (2009). Neural correlates of sad faces predict clinical remission to cognitive behavioral therapy in depression. *NeuroReport, 20,* 637–641.

Coulson, S., & Wu, Y. C. (2005). Right hemisphere activation of joke-related information: An event-related brain potential study. *Journal of Cognitive Neuroscience, 17,* 494–506.

Courtet, P., & others. (2004). Serotonin transporter gene may be involved in short-term risk of subsequent suicide attempts. *Biological Psychiatry, 55,* 46–51.

Courtois, E. T., & others. (2010). In vitro and in vivo enhanced generation of human A9 dopamine neurons from neural stem cells by Bcl-XL. *Journal of Biological Chemistry.* (in press)

Cowan, R. L., Roberts, D. M., & Joers, J. M. (2008). Neuroimaging in human MDMA (Ecstasy) users. *Annals of the New York Academy of Sciences, 1139,* 291–298.

Cowansage, K. K., LeDoux, J. E., & Monfils, M. H. (2010). Brain-deprived neurotrophic factor: A dynamic gatekeeper of neural plasticity. *Current Molecular Pharmacology, 3,* 12–29.

Cox, R. E., & Bryant, R. A. (2008) Advances in hypnosis research: Methods, designs, and contributions of intrinsic and instrumental hypnosis. In M. R. Nash & A. J. Barnier (Eds.), *The Oxford handbook of hypnosis: Research theory and practice* (pp. 311–336). New York: Oxford University Press.

Coxon, J. P., Goble, D. J., Van Impe, A., De Vos, J., Wenderoth, N., & Swinnen, S. P. (2010). Reduced basal ganglia function when elderly switch between coordinated movement patterns. *Cerebral Cortex.* (in press)

Craddock, N., & Forty, L. (2006). Genetics of affective (mood) disorders. *European Journal of Human Genetics, 14,* 660–668.

Craig, I., & Plomin, R. (2006). Quantitative trait loci for IQ and other complex traits: Single-nucleotide polymorphism genotyping using pooled DNA and microarrays. *Genes, Brain, and Behavior, 5,* 32–37.

Craik, F. I. M., & Lockhart, R. S. (1972). Levels of processing: A framework for memory research. *Journal of Verbal Learning and Verbal Behavior, 11,* 671–684.

Craik, F. I. M., & Tulving, E. (1975). Depth of processing and retention of words in episodic memory. *Journal of Experimental Psychology: General, 104,* 268–294.

Cramer, P. (2008). Longitudinal study of defense mechanisms: Late childhood to late adolescence. *Journal of Personality, 75,* 1–23.

Cramer, P. (2008a). Seven pillars of defense mechanism theory. *Social and Personality Psychology Compass, 2,* 1963–1981.

Cramer, P. (2009). An increase in early adolescent undercontrol is associated with the use of denial. *Journal of Personality Assessment, 91,* 331–339.

Cramer, P., & Jones, C. J. (2007). Defense mechanisms predict differential lifespan change in self-control and self-acceptance. *Journal of Research in Personality, 41,* 841–855.

Crampton, S. M., & Wagner, J. A., III. (1994). Percept-percept inflation in microorganizational research: An investigation of prevalence and effect. *Journal of Applied Psychology, 79,* 67–76.

Crandall, C. S. (2004). Social contagion of binge eating. In R. M. Kowalski & M. R. Leary (Eds.), *The interface of social and clinical psychology: Key readings* (pp. 99–115). New York: Psychology Press.

Cranley, L., Doran, D. M., Tourangeau, A. E., Kushniruk, A., & Nagle, L. (2009). Nurses' uncertainty in decision-making: A literature review. *Worldviews in Evidence-Based Nursing, 6,* 3–15.

Creer, D. J., Romberg, C., Saksida, L. M., van Praag, H., & Bussey, T. J. (2010). Running enhances spatial pattern separation in mice. *Proceedings of the National Academy of Sciences USA, 107,* 2367–2372.

Crescentini, C., Shallice, T., Del Missier, F., & Macaluso, E. (2010). Neural correlates of episodic retrieval: An fMRI study of the part-list cueing effect. *NeuroImage, 50,* 678–692.

Crespo-Garcia, M., Cantero, J. L., Pomyalov, A., Boccaletti, S., & Atienza, M. (2010). Functional neural networks underlying semantic encoding of associative memories. *NeuroImage.* (in press)

Cress, M. E., Buchner, D. M., Prohaska, T., Rimmer, J., Brown, M., Macera, C., DiPietro, L., & Chodzko-Zajko, W. (2005). Best practices for physical activity programs and behavior counseling in older adult populations. *Journal of Aging and Physical Activity, 13,* 61–74.

Cresswell, M. (2008). Szasz and his interlocutors: Reconsidering Thomas Szasz's "Myth of Mental Illness" thesis. *Journal for the Theory of Social Behaviour, 38,* 23–44.

Crick, N. R., & Grotpeter, J. K. (1995). Relational aggression, gender, and social-psychological adjustment. *Child Development, 66,* 710–722.

Crick, N. R., & Rose, A. J. (2000). Toward a gender-balanced approach to the study of social-emotional development: A look at relational aggression. In P. H. Miller & E. Kofsky Scholnick (Eds.), *Toward a feminist developmental psychology* (pp. 153–168). Florence, KY: Taylor & Frances/Routledge.

Crooks, R. L., & Baur, K. (2011). *Our sexuality* (11th ed.). Boston: Cengage.

Crowley, K., Pickle, J., Dale, R., & Fattal, O. (2008). A critical examination of bifrontal electroconvulsive therapy: Clinical efficacy, cognitive side effects, and directions for future research. *Journal of ECT, 24,* 268–271.

Csikszentmihalyi, M. (1990). *Flow: The psychology of optimal experience.* New York: Harper Perennial.

Csikszentmihalyi, M., & Rathunde, K. (1998). The development of the person: An experiential perspective on the ontogenesis of psychological complexity. In W. Damon (Ed.), *Handbook of child psychology* (5th ed., vol. 1). New York: Wiley.

Cuijpers, P. (2001). Mortality and depressive symptoms in inhabitants of residential homes. *International Journal of Geriatric Psychiatry, 16,* 131–138.

Cullen, K. (2010, January 14). The untouchable mean girls. *Boston Globe.* http://www.boston.com/news/local/massachusetts/articles/2010/01/24/the_untouchable_mean_girls/ (accessed May 16, 2010)

Cullen, K., Klimes-Dougan, B., & Kumra, S. (2009). Pediatric depression: Issues and treatment recommendations. *Minnesota Medicine, 92,* 45–48.

Culp, M. C. (2005, December 25). The business case for compassion. *San Bernardino Sun.* http://www.sbsun.com/workwise/ci_3829431 (accessed June 15, 2006)

Culpepper, L. (2010). The social and economic burden of shift-work disorder. *Journal of Family Practice, 59, Suppl. 1,* S3–S11.

Cumming, E., & Henry, W. E. (1961). *Growing older: The process of disengagement.* New York: Basic.

Cunha, C., Monfils, M. H., & LeDoux, J. E. (2010). GABA(C) receptors in the lateral amygdala: A possible novel target for the treatment of fear and anxiety disorders? *Frontiers in Behavioral Neuroscience.* (in press)

Cunningham, R. L., & McGinnis, M. Y. (2007). Factors influencing aggression toward females by male rats exposed to anabolic androgenic steroids during puberty. *Hormones and Behavior, 51,* 135–141.

Curran, K., DuCette, J., Eisenstein, J., & Hyman, I. A. (2001, August). *Statistical analysis of the cross-cultural data: The third year.* Paper presented at the meeting of the American Psychological Association, San Francisco.

Curtiss, S. (1977). *Genie.* New York: Academic.

Cuthbert, B., & Insel, T. (2010). Classification issues in women's mental health: Clinical utility and etiological mechanisms. *Archives of Women's Mental Health, 13,* 57–59.

Cutrona, C. E. (1982). Transition to college: Loneliness and the process of social adjustment. In L. A. Peplau & D. Perlman (Eds.), *Loneliness.* New York: Wiley.

D

Daadi, M. M., & others (2010). Human neural stem cell grafts modify microglial response and enhance axon sprouting in neonatal hypoxic-ischemic brain injury. *Stroke.* (in press)

Dadds, M. R., Holland, D. E., Barrett, P. M., & Spence, S. H. (1999). Early intervention and prevention of anxiety disorders in children:

Results at 2-year follow-up. *Journal of Consulting & Clinical Psychology, 67,* 145–150.

Dahl, R., & Spear, L. P. (Eds.). (2004). Adolescent brain development: Vulnerabilities and opportunities. *Annals of the New York Academy of Sciences, 1021.*

Dale, K. Y., Berg, R., Elden, A., Odegard, A., & Holte, A. (2009). Testing the diagnosis of dissociative identity disorder through measures of dissociation, absorption, hypnotizability, and PTSD: A Norwegian pilot study. *Journal of Trauma and Dissociation, 10,* 102–112.

Dalton, M., Hoyle, D. G., & Watts, M. W. (2011). *Human relations* (4th ed.). Boston: Cengage.

Damm, J., & others. (2010). Influence of age on effectiveness and tolerability of electroconvulsive therapy. *Journal of ECT.* (in press)

Damon, W. (2008). *The path to purpose: Helping our children find their calling in life.* New York: Free Press.

Damsa, C., Kosel, M., & Moussally, J. (2009). Current status of brain imaging in anxiety disorders. *Current Opinion in Psychiatry, 22,* 96–110.

Daniels, H. (2011). Vygotsky and psychology. In U. Goswami (Ed.), *Wiley-Blackwell handbook of childhood cognitive development* (2nd ed.). New York: Wiley Blackwell.

Danner, D. D., Snowdon, D. A., & Friesen, W. V. (2001). Positive emotions in early life and longevity: Findings from the Nun Study. *Journal of Personality and Social Psychology, 80,* 804–813.

Danoff-Burg, S., Mosher, C. E., & Grant, C. A. (2006). Relations of agentic and communal personality traits to health behavior and substance use among college students. *Personality and Individual Differences, 40,* 353–363.

Darley, J. M., & Latané, B. (1968). Bystander intervention in emergencies: Diffusion of responsibility. *Journal of Personality and Social Psychology, 8,* 377–383.

Darvas, M., & Palmiter, R. D. (2010). Restricting dopaminergic signaling to either dorsolateral or medial striatum facilitates cognition. *Journal of Neuroscience, 30,* 1158–1165.

Darwin, C. (1862). *On the various contrivances by which British and foreign orchids are fertilised by insects, and on the good effects of intercrossing.* London: John Murray.

Darwin, C. (1871). *The descent of man and selection in relation to sex.* London: John Murray.

Darwin, C. (1965). *The expression of the emotions in man and animals.* Chicago: University of Chicago Press. (original work published 1872)

Darwin, C. (1979). *On the origin of species.* New York: Avenal Books. (original work published 1859)

da Silva Cais, C. F., Stefanello, S., Fabrício Mauro, M. L., Vaz Scavini de Freitas, G., & Botega, N. J. (2009). Factors associated with repeated suicide attempts: Preliminary results of the WHO Multisite Intervention Study on Suicidal Behavior (SUPRE-MISS) from Campinas, Brazil. *Crisis: The Journal of Crisis Intervention and Suicide Prevention, 30,* 73–78.

Davidson, J. R. (2009). First-line pharmacotherapy approaches for generalized anxiety disorder. *Journal of Clinical Psychiatry, 70, Suppl. 2,* S25–S31.

Davidson, K. W., & others. (2006). Assessment and treatment of depression in patients with cardiovascular disease: National Heart, Lung, and Blood Institute Working Group Report. *Psychosomatic Medicine, 68,* 645–650.

Davidson, P. S., Cook, S. P., & Glisky, E. L. (2006). Flashbulb memories for September 11th can be preserved in older adults. *Neuropsychology, Development, and Cognition B, 13,* 196–206.

Davidson, R. J. (2000). Affective style, psychopathology, and resilience: Brain mechanisms and plasticity. *American Psychologist, 55,* 196–214.

Davidson, R. J. (2005). Neural substrates of affective style and value. In Y. Christen (Series Ed.) & J.-P. Changeux, A. R. Damasio, W. Singer, & Y. Christen (Vol. Eds.), *Research and perspectives in neurosciences: Neurobiology of human values* (pp. 67–90). Germany: Springer-Verlag.

Davidson, R. J. (2010). Empirical explorations of mindfulness: Conceptual and methodological conundrums. *Emotion.* (in press)

Davidson, R. J. (2010a, April 22). *Change your brain by transforming your mind.* Paper presented at the Wisconsin Symposium on Emotion, University of Wisconsin, Madison.

Davidson, R. J., Kabat-Zinn, J., Schumacher, J., Rosenkranz, M. M., Daniel, S., Saki, F., Urbanowski, F., Harrington, A., Bonus, K., & Sheridan, J. F. (2003). Alterations in brain and immune function produced by mindfulness meditation. *Psychosomatic Medicine, 65* (4), 564–570.

Davidson, R. J., Scherer, K. R., & Goldsmith, H. H. (Eds.). (2002). *Handbook of affective sciences.* New York: Oxford University Press.

Davidson, R. J., Shackman, A., & Pizzagalli, D. (2002). The functional neuroanatomy of emotion and affective style. In R. J. Davidson, K. R. Scherer, & H. H. Goldsmith (Eds.), *Handbook of affective sciences.* New York: Oxford University Press.

Davis, C., Patte, K., Curtis, C., & Reid, C. (2010). Immediate pleasures and future consequences: A neuropsychological study of binge eating and obesity. *Appetite, 54,* 208–213.

Davis, C. M., & Riley, A. L. (2010). Conditioned taste aversion learning: Implications for animal models of drug abuse. *Annals of the New York Academy of Sciences, 1187,* 247–275.

Davis, E., Sawyer, M. G., Lo, S. K., Priest, N., & Wake, M. (2010). Socioeconomic risk factors for mental health problems in 4–5-year old children: Australian population study. *Academic Pediatrics, 10,* 41–47.

Davis, J. I., Senghas, A., & Ochsner, K. N. (2009). How does facial feedback modulate emotional experience? *Journal of Research in Personality, 43,* 822–829.

Davis, M. C., Zautra, A. J., Johnson, L. M., Murray, K. E., & Okvat, H. A. (2007). Psychosocial stress, emotion regulation, and resilience among older adults. In C. M. Aldwin,

C. L. Park, & A. Spiro (Eds.), *Handbook of health and aging.* New York: Guilford.

Davison, K. P., Pennebaker, J. W., & Dickerson, S. S. (2000). Who talks? The social psychology of illness support groups. *American Psychologist, 55,* 205–217.

Davoli, T., Denchi, E. L., & de Lange, T. (2010). Persistent telomere damage induces bypass of mitosis and teraploidy. *Cell, 141,* 81–83.

Dawson, A., & List, T. (2009). Comparison of pain thresholds and pain tolerance levels between Middle Easterners and Swedes and between genders. *Journal of Oral Rehabilitation, 36,* 271–278.

Deal, T. E., & Kennedy, A. A. (1982). *Corporate cultures: The rites and rituals of corporate life.* New York: Penguin.

De Angelis, T. (2002). Binge-eating disorder: What's the best treatment? *Monitor on Psychology, 33.* http://www.apa.org/monitor/mar02/binge.html

Deary, I. J., Johnson, W., & Starr, J. M. (2010). Are processing speed tasks biomarkers of aging? *Psychology and Aging, 25,* 219–228.

Deaux, K. (2001). Social identity. In J. Worell (Ed.), *Encyclopedia of gender and women.* San Diego: Academic.

Deaux, K., & LaFrance, M. (1998). Gender. In D. T. Gilbert, S. T. Fiske, & G. Lindzey (Eds.), *The handbook of social psychology* (vols. 1 and 2, 4th ed., pp. 788–827). New York: McGraw-Hill.

Debiec, J., Diaz-Mataix, L., Bush, D. E., Doyere, V., & LeDoux, J. E. (2010). The amygdala encodes specific sensory features of an aversive reinforcer. *Nature Neuroscience, 13,* 536–537.

Decety, J., & Cacioppo, J. T. (2011). *Handbook of social neuroscience.* New York: Oxford University Press.

Deci, E., Koestner, R., & Ryan, R. (1999). The undermining effect is a reality after all—Extrinsic rewards, task interest, and self-determination: Repy to Eisenberger, Pierce, and Cameron (1999) and Lepper, Henderlong, and Gingras (1999). *Psychological Bulletin, 125,* 692–700.

Deci, E. L., & Ryan, R. M. (2000). The "what" and "why" of goal pursuits: Human needs and the self-determination of behavior. *Psychological Inquiry, 4,* 227–268.

Deci, E. L., & Ryan, R. M. (Eds.). (2002). *Handbook of self-determination research.* Rochester, NY: University of Rochester Press.

Dedert, E. A., & others. (2009). Association of trauma exposure with psychiatric morbidity in military veterans who have served since September 11, 2001. *Journal of Psychiatric Research, 43,* 830–836.

Degenhardt, L., Bruno, R., & Topp, L. (2010). Is ecstasy a drug of dependence? *Drug and Alcohol Dependence, 107,* 1–10.

Degenhardt, L., & others. (2010). Evaluating the drug use "gateway" theory using cross-national data: Consistency and associations of the order of initiation of drug use among participants in the WHO World Mental Health Surveys. *Drug and Alcohol Dependence, 108,* 84–97.

Degnin, F. D. (2009). Difficult patients, overmedication, and groupthink. *Journal of Clinical Ethics, 20,* 64–74.

de Graaf, L. E., Hollon, S. D., & Huibers, J. J. (2010). Predicting outcome in computerized cognitive behavior therapy for depression in primary care: A randomized trial. *Journal of Consulting and Clinical Psychology, 78,* 184–189.

de Graaf, L. E., Huibers, J. J., Cuijpers, P., & Arntz, A. (2010). Minor and major depression in the general population: Does dysfunctional thinking play a role? *Comprehensive Psychiatry, 51,* 266–274.

de Groot, E. R., Verheul, R., & Trijsburg, R. W. (2008). An integrative perspective on psychotherapeutic treatments for borderline personality disorder. *Journal of Personality Disorders, 22,* 332–352.

Dehaene, S., Changeux, J., Naccache, L., Sackur, J., & Sergent, C. (2006). Conscious, preconscious, and subliminal processing: A testable taxonomy. *Trends in Cognitive Sciences, 10,* 204–211.

de Hevia, M. D., & Spelke, E. S. (2010). Number-space mapping in human infants. *Psychological Science.* (in press)

DeLamater, J., & Moorman, S. M. (2007). Sexual behavior in later life. *Journal of Aging and Health, 19,* 921–945.

de Lange, F. P., Jensen, O., & Dehaene, S. (2010). Accumulation of evidence during sequential decision making: The importance of top-down factors. *Journal of Neuroscience, 30,* 731–738.

Del Cul, A., Dehaene, S., Reyes, P., Bravo, E., & Slachevsky, A. (2009). Causal role of prefrontal cortex in the threshold for access to consciousness. *Brain, 132,* 2531–2540.

Del Giudice, M. J. (2010). What might this be? Rediscovering the Rorschach as a tool for personnel selection in organizations. *Journal of Personality Assessment, 92,* 78–89.

Dell, P. F., & Eisenhower, J. W. (1990). Adolescent multiple personality disorder: A preliminary study of eleven cases. *Journal of the American Academy of Child & Adolescent Psychiatry, 29,* 359–366.

Dell, P. F., & O'Neil, J. A. (Eds.). (2009). *Dissociation and the dissociative disorders: DSM-V and beyond.* New York: Routledge/Taylor & Francis.

Del Missier, F., & Terpini, C. (2009). Part-set cueing in option generation. *Memory and Cognition, 37,* 265–276.

Delprato, D. J. (2005). Retroactive interference as a function of degree of interpolated study without overt retrieval practice. *Psychonomic Bulletin and Review, 12,* 345–349.

DeLuga, R. J., & Mason, S. (2000). Relationship of resident assistant conscientiousness, extraversion, and positive affect with rated performance. *Journal of Research in Personality, 34,* 225–235.

DeMarree, K. G., & Petty, R. E. (2007). The elaboration likelihood model of persuasion. In R. F. Baumeister & K. D. Vohs (Eds.), *Encyclopedia of social psychology.* Thousand Oaks, CA: Sage.

Demeure, V., Bonnefon, J. F., & Raufaste, E. (2009). Politeness and conditioned reasoning: Interpersonal cues to the indirect suppression of

deductive inferences. *Journal of Experimental Psychology: Learning, Memory, and Cognition, 35,* 260–266.

Deming, W. E. (1986). *Out of the crisis.* Cambridge, MA: MIT Press.

Denham, S. A., Bassett, H. H., & Wyatt, T. (2007). The socialization of emotional competence. In J. E. Grusec & P. D. Hastings (Eds.), *Handbook of socialization.* New York: Guilford.

Dennis, A. (2005). Osama bin Laden: The sum of all fears. In W. T. Schultz (Ed.), *Handbook of psychobiography* (pp. 311–322). Oxford, U.K.: Oxford University Press.

De Pauw, S. S., & Mervielde, I. (2010). Temperament, personality, and developmental psychopathology: A review on the conceptual dimensions underlying childhood traits. *Child Psychiatry and Human Development, 41,* 313–329.

Depue, R. A., & Collins, P. F. (1999). Neurobiology of the structure of personality: Dopamine, facilitation of incentive motivation, and extraversion. *Behavioural and Brain Sciences, 22,* 491–569.

De Raad, B., Barelds, D. P. H., Levert, E., Ostendorf, F., Mlacic, B., Di Blas, L., Hrebickova, M., Perugini, M., Church, A. T., & Katigbak, M. S. (2010). Only three factors of personality description are fully replicable across languages: A comparison of 14 trait taxonomies. *Journal of Personality and Social Psychology, 98,* 160–173.

De Raedt, R., & Koster, E. H. W. (2010). Understanding vulnerability for depression from a cognitive neuroscience perspective: A reappraisal of attentional factors and a new conceptual framework. *Cognitive, Affective & Behavioral Neuroscience, 10,* 50–70.

Derks, D., Bos, A. E. R., & von Grumbkow, J. (2008). Emoticons in computer-mediated communication: Social motives and social context. *CyberPsychology & Behavior, 11,* 99–101.

de Roon-Cassini, T. A., Mancini, A. D., Rusch, M. D., & Bonanno, G. A. (2010). Psychopathology and resilience following traumatic injury: A latent growth mixture model analysis. *Rehabilitation Psychology, 55,* 1–11.

Desmond, D. M., & MacLachlan, M. (2010). Prevalence and characteristics of phantom limb pain and residual limb pain in the long term after upper limb amputation. *International Journal of Rehabilitation Research.* (in press)

Deutsch, M. (2006). Cooperation and competition. In M. Deutsch, P. T. Coleman, & E. C. Marcus (Eds.), *Handbook of conflict resolution.* San Francisco: Jossey-Bass.

Deutsch, M., Coleman, P. T., & Marcus, E. C. (Eds.). (2006). *Handbook of conflict resolution* (2nd ed.). San Francisco: Jossey-Bass.

Deutsch, S. (2010). Consciousness platform: The greatest mystery of all time. *IEEE Engineering in Medicine and Biology Magazine, 29,* 60–62.

Devlin, S., & Arneill, A. B. (2003). Health care environments and patient outcomes: A review of the literature. *Environment and Behavior, 35,* 665–694.

De Vries, G. J. (2004). Sex differences in adult and developing brains: Compensation, compensation, compensation. *Endocrinology, 145,* 1063–1068.

de Waal, F. B. M., Leimgruber, K., & Greenberg, A. R. (2008). Giving is self-rewarding for monkeys. *PNAS Proceedings of the National Academy of Sciences USA, 105,* 13685–13689.

DeWall, C. N., Twenge, J. M., Gitter, S. A., & Baumeister, R. F. (2009). It's the thought that counts: The role of hostile cognition in shaping aggressive responses to social exclusion. *Journal of Personality and Social Psychology, 96,* 45–59.

Dewar, M., Cowan, N., & Della Sala, S. (2010). Forgetting due to retroactive interference in amnesia findings and implications. In S. D. Sala (Ed.), *Forgetting.* New York: Psychology Press.

Dewar, M., Della Sala, S., Beschin, N., & Cowan, N. (2010a). Profound retroactive interference in anterograde amnesia: What interferes? *Neuropsychology.* (in press)

de Zoysa, P., Newcombe, P. A., & Rajapakse, L. (2008). Consequences of parental corporal punishment on 12-year-old children in the Colombo district. *Ceylon Medical Journal, 53,* 7–9.

de Zwaan, M., Mitchell, J. E., Crosby, R. D., Mussell, M. P., Raymond, N. C., Specker, S. M., & Seim, H. C. (2005). Short-term cognitive behavioral treatment does not improve outcome of a comprehensive very-low-calorie diet program in obese women with binge eating disorder. *Behavior Therapy, 36,* 89–99.

Diamond, A. (2009). The interplay of biology and the environment broadly defined. *Developmental Psychology, 45,* 1–8.

Diamond, A. (2009a). All or none hypothesis: A global-default mode that characterizes the brain and mind. *Developmental Psychology, 45,* 130–138.

Diamond, A., Casey, B. J., & Munakata, Y. (2011). *Developmental cognitive neuroscience.* New York: Oxford University Press.

Diamond, L. M. (2008a). *Sexual fluidity: Understanding women's love and desire.* Cambridge, MA: Harvard University Press.

Diamond, L. M. (2008b). Female bisexuality from adolescence to adulthood: Results from a 10-year longitudinal study. *Developmental Psychology, 44,* 5–14.

Diamond, L. M. (2009). Emotion in relationships. In H. R. Reis & S. Sprecher (Eds.), *Encyclopedia of human relationships.* Thousand Oaks, CA: Sage.

Diamond, L. M., & Savin-Williams, R. C. (2009). Adolescent sexuality. In R. M. Lerner & L. Steinberg (Eds.), *Handbook of adolescent psychology* (3rd ed.). New York: Wiley.

Diamond, L. M., & Savin-Williams, R. C. (2011). Same-sex activity in adolescence: Multiple meanings and implications. In L. Morrow & R. F. Fassinger (Eds.), *Sex in the margins.* Washington, DC: American Psychological Association. (in press)

Diamond, M., & Sigmundson, H. K. (1997). Sex reassignment at birth. *Archives of Pediatric and Adolescent Medicine, 151,* 298–304.

Dichter, G. S., Felder, J. N., & Smoski, M. J. (2010). The effects of brief behavioral activation therapy for depression on cognitive control in affective contexts: An f MRI investigation. *Journal of Affective Disorders.* (in press)

DiClemente, C. C. (2006). Natural change and the troublesome use of substances: A life-course perspective. In W. R. Miller & K. M. Carroll (Eds.), *Rethinking substance abuse: What the science shows, and what we should do about it* (pp. 81–96). New York: Guilford.

Diefenbach, G. J., Disch, W. B., Robinson, J. T., Baez, E., & Coman, E. (2009). Anxious depression among Puerto Rican and African American older adults. *Aging and Mental Health, 13,* 118–126.

Diekelmann, S., Wilhelm, I., & Born, J. (2009). The whats and whens of sleep-dependent memory consolidation. *Sleep Medicine Reviews, 13,* 309–321.

Diekman, A. B., & Eagly, A. H. (2008). Of women, men, and motivation: A role congruity account. In J. Y. Shah & W. L. Gardner (Eds.), *Handbook of motivational science* (pp. 434–447). New York: Guilford.

Dien, J. (2009). A tale of two recognition systems: Implications of the fusiform face area and the visual work face area for lateralized object recognition models. *Neuropsychologia, 47,* 1–16.

Diener, E. (1999). Introduction to the special section on the structure of emotion. *Journal of Personality and Social Psychology, 76,* 803–804.

Diener, E. (2000). Subjective well-being: The science of happiness and a proposal for a national index. *American Psychologist, 55,* 34–43.

Diener, E., & Diener, C. (1996). Most people are happy. *Psychological Science, 7,* 181–185.

Diener, E., Emmons, R. A., Larsen, R. J., & Griffin, S. (1985). The Satisfaction with Life Scale. *Journal of Personality Assessment, 49,* 71–75.

Digman, J. M. (1990). Personality structure: Emergence of the five-factor model. *Annual Review of Psychology* (vol. 41). Palo Alto, CA: Annual Reviews.

Digman, J. M. (2002). Historical antecedents of the five-factor model. In P. T. Costa & T. A. Widiger (Eds.), *Personality disorders and the five-factor model of personality* (2nd ed., pp. 17–22). Washington, DC: American Psychological Association.

Dijksterhuis, A., Bos, M. W., Van der Leij, A., & Van Baaren, R. B. (2009). Predicting soccer matches after unconscious and conscious thought as a function of expertise. *Psychological Science, 20,* 1381–1387.

Dijksterhuis, A., & Nordgren, L. F. (2006). A theory of unconscious thought. *Perspectives on Psychological Science, 1,* 95–109.

Dijksterhuis, A., & Van Knippenberg, A. (1998). The relation between perception and behavior or how to win a game of Trivial Pursuit. *Journal of Personality and Social Psychology, 74,* 865–877.

Dijkstra, P., Gibbons, F., & Buunk, A. P. (2010). Social comparison theory. In *Social psychological foundations of clinical psychology.* New York: Guilford. (in press)

Dimeff, L. A., Koerner, K., & Linehan, M. M. (2007). *Dialectical behavior therapy in clinical practice: Applications across disorders and settings.* New York: Guilford.

Dishion, T. J., & Piehler, T. F. (2009). Deviant by design: Peer contagion in development, interventions, and schools. In K. H. Rubin, W. M. Bukowski, & B. Laursen (Eds.), *Handbook of peer interactions, relationships, and groups.* New York: Guilford.

Distel, M. A., Trull, T. J., Derom, C. A., Thiery, E. W., Grimmer, M. A., Martin, N. G., Willemsen, G., & Boomsma, D. I. (2008). Heritability of borderline personality disorder features is similar across three countries. *Psychological Medicine, 38,* 1219–1229.

Dixon, M. L., Ruppel, J., Pratt, J., & De Rosa, E. (2009). Learning to ignore: Acquisition of sustained attentional suppression. *Psychonomic Bulletin and Review, 16,* 418–423.

Dodge, K. A., Coie, J. D., & Lynam, D. (2006). Aggression and antisocial behavior in youth. In W. Damon & R. Lerner (Eds.), *Handbook of child psychology* (6th ed.). New York: Wiley.

Doerr, C. E., & Baumeister, R. F. (2010). Self-regulatory strength and adjustment: Implications of the limited resource model of self-regulation. In J. E. Maddux & J. P. Tagney (Eds.), *Social psychological foundations of clinical psychology.* New York: Guilford.

Doherty, M. J. (2009). *Theory of mind: How children understand others' thoughts and feelings.* New York: Psychology Press.

Dolan, M., & Fullam, R. (2006). Face affect recognition deficits in personality disordered offenders: Associate with psychopathy. *Psychological Medicine, 36,* 1563–1569.

Dollard, J., Doob, L. W., Miller, N. E., Mowrer, O. H., & Sears, R. R. (1939). *Frustration and aggression.* New Haven, CT: Yale University Press.

Domènech-Llaberia, E., Vinas, F., Pla, E., Jane, M. C., Mitjavila, M., Corbella, T., & Canals, J. (2009). Prevalence of major depression in school children. *European Child and Adolescent Psychiatry, 18* (10), 597–604.

Domhoff, G. W. (2007). Realistic simulation and bizarreness in dream content: Past findings and suggestions for future research. In D. Barrett & P. McNamara (Eds.), *The new science of dreaming: Content, recall, and personality correlates* (vol. 2, pp. 1–27). Westport, CT: Praeger.

Dominquez Coello, S., & others. (2010). Association between glycemic index, glycemic load, and fructose with insulin resistance: The CDC of the Canary Islands study. *European Journal of Nutrition.* (in press)

Domjan, M. (2010). *The principles of learning and behavior* (6th ed.). Boston: Cengage.

Donatelle, R. J. (2011). *Health* (9th ed.). Upper Saddle River, NJ: Pearson.

Donnellan, M. B., Larsen-Rife, D., & Conger, R. D. (2005). Personality, family history, and competence in early adult romantic relationships. *Journal of Personality and Social Psychology, 88,* 562–576.

Donnellan, M. B., Lucas, R. E., & Fleeson, W. (2009). Introduction to personality and assessment at age 40: Reflections on the legacy of the person-situation debate and the future of person-situation integration. *Journal of Research in Personality, 43,* 117–119.

Donnellan, M. B., Trzesniewski, K., & Robins, R. (2009). An emerging epidemic of narcissism or much ado about nothing? *Journal of Research in Personality.*

Donnellan, M. B., Trzesniewski, K., Robins, R. W., Moffitt, T. E., & Caspi, A. (2005). Low self-esteem is related to aggression, anti-social behavior, and delinquency. *Psychological Science, 16,* 328–335.

Donovan, M. A. (2000). Cognitive, affective, and satisfaction variables as predictors of organizational behaviors: A structural equation modeling examination of alternative models. *Dissertation Abstracts International, 60* (9-B), 4943 (UMI No. AAI9944835).

Dougherty, S. (2010). Computing the unconscious. *Psychoanalytic Quarterly, 79,* 171–201.

Dovidio, J. F., Gaertner, S. L., & Saguy, T. (2009). Commonality and the complexity of "we": Social attitudes and social change. *Personality and Social Psychology Review, 13,* 3–20.

Dovidio, J. F., Kawakami, K., & Gaertner, S. L. (2002). Implicit and explicit prejudice and interracial interaction. *Journal of Personality and Social Psychology, 82,* 62–68.

Doyle, W. J., & others. (2010). The interleukin 6-174C/C genotype predicts greater rhinovirus illness. *Journal of Infectious Diseases, 201,* 199–206.

Drake, C., Levine, R., & Laska, E. A. (2007). Identifying prognostic factors that predict recovery in the presence of loss to follow-up. In K. Hopper, G. Harrison, A. Janca, & N. Sartorius (Eds.), *Recovery from schizophrenia: An international perspective: A report from the WHO Collaborative Project, the international study of schizophrenia* (pp. 69–72). New York: Oxford University Press.

Dreisbach, G., & Goschke, T. (2004). How positive affect modulates cognitive control: Reduced perseveration at the cost of increased distractibility. *Journal of Experimental Psychology: Learning, Memory, and Cognition, 30,* 343–353.

Dricot, L., Sorger, B., Schiltz, C., Goebel, R., & Rossion, B. (2008). Evidence for individual face discrimination in non-face selective areas of the visual cortex in acquired prosopagnosia. *Behavioral Neuroscience, 19,* 75–79.

Drigotas, S. M., Safstrom, C. A., & Gentilia, T. (1999). An investment model prediction of dating infidelity. *Journal of Personality and Social Psychology, 77,* 509–524.

Duan, J., Sanders, A. R., & Gejman, P. V. (2010). Genome-wide approaches to schizophrenia. *Brain Research Bulletin.* (in press)

Dubový, P., Klusáková, I., Svízenská, I., & Brázda, V. (2010). Spatio-temporal changes of SDF1 and its CXCR4 receptor in the dorsal root ganglia following unilateral sciatic nerve injury as a model of neuropathic pain. *Histochemistry and Cell Biology, 133,* 323–337.

Dubow, E. F., Huesmann, L. R., & Greenwood, D. (2007). Media and youth socialization: Underlying processes and moderators of effects. In J. E. Grusec & P. D. Hastings (Eds.), *Handbook of socialization* (pp. 404–430). New York: Guilford.

Dudley, M., Goldney, R., & Hadzi-Pavlovic, D. (2010). Are adolescents dying by suicide taking SSRI antidepressants? A review of observational studies. *Australasian Psychiatry, 18,* 242–245.

Duffy, M. K., Ganster, D. C., & Pagon, M. (2002). Social undermining and social support in the workplace., *Academy of Management Journal, 45,* 331–351.

Duncan, A. E., Scherrer, J., Fu, Q., Bucholz, K. K., Heath, A. C., True, W. R., Haber, J. R., Howell, D., & Jacob, T. (2006). Exposure to paternal alcoholism does not predict development of alcohol-use disorders in offspring: Evidence from an offspring-of-twins study. *Journal of Studies on Alcohol, 67,* 649–656.

Duncan, G. E. (2010). The "fit but fat" concept revisited: Population-based estimates using NHANES. *International Journal of Behavioral Nutrition and Physical Activity.* (in press)

Dunlap, E., Golub, A., Johnson, B. D., & Benoit, E. (2009). Normalization of violence: Experiences of childhood abuse by inner-city crack users. *Journal of Ethnicity in Substance Abuse, 8,* 15–34.

Dunn, E. W., Aknin, L. B., & Norton, M. I. (2008). Spending money on others promotes happiness. *Science, 319,* 1687–1688.

Dupoux, E., de Gardelle, V., & Kouider, S. (2008). Subliminal speech perception and auditory streaming. *Cognition, 109,* 267–273.

Dupré, K. E., & Barling, J. (2006). Predicting and preventing supervisory workplace aggression. *Journal of Occupational Health Psychology, 11,* 13–26.

Durand, V. M., & Barlow, D. H. (2010). *Essentials of abnormal psychology* (5th ed.). Boston: Cengage.

Durantini, M. R., Albarracin, D., Mitchell, A. L., Earl, A. N., & Gillette, J. C. (2006). Conceptualizing the influence of social agents of behavior change: A meta-analysis of the effectiveness of HIV-prevention interventionists for different groups. *Psychological Bulletin, 132,* 212–248.

Durrant, J. E. (2008). Physical punishment, culture, and rights: Current issues for professionals. *Developmental and Behavioral Pediatrics, 29,* 55–66.

Dutton, D., & Aron, A. (1974). Some evidence for heightened sexual attraction under conditions of high anxiety. *Journal of Personality and Social Psychology, 30,* 510–517.

Duvarci, S., Nader, K., & LeDoux, J. E. (2008). De novo mRNA synthesis is required for both consolidation and reconsolidation of fear memories in the amygdala. *Learning and Memory, 15,* 747–755.

Dweck, C. S. (2006). *Mindset.* New York: Random House.

Dweck, C. S., & Master, A. (2009). Self-theories and motivation: Students' beliefs about intelligence. In K. R. Wentzel & A. Wigfield (Eds.), *Handbook of motivation at school.* New York: Routledge.

Dysart, J. E., & Lindsay, R. C. L. (2007). The effects of delay on eyewitness identification witness accuracy: Should we be concerned? In R. C. L. Lindsay, D. F. Ross, J. D. Read, & M. P. Toglia (Eds.), *The handbook of eyewitness memory: Vol. II.* Mahwah, NJ: Erlbaum.

E

Eagleman, D. M. (2010). Synaesthesia. *British Medical Journal, 340,* 4616.

Eagly, A. H. (1987). *Sex differences in social behavior: A social-role interpretation.* Hillsdale, NJ: Erlbaum.

Eagly, A. H. (2010a). Gender roles. In J. Levine & M. Hogg (Eds.), *Encyclopedia of group processes and intergroup relations.* Thousand Oaks, CA: Sage. (in press)

Eagly, A. H. (2010b). The his and hers of prosocial behavior: An examination of the social psychology of gender. *American Psychologist.* (in press)

Eagly, A. H., & Crowley, M. (1986). Gender and helping behavior: A meta-analytic review of the social psychological literature. *Psychological Bulletin, 100,* 283–308.

Eagly, A. H., & Diekman, A. B. (2003). The malleability of sex differences in response to changing social roles. In L. G. Aspinwall & U. M. Staudinger (Eds.), *A psychology of human strengths: Fundamental questions and future directions for a positive psychology* (pp. 103–115). Washington, DC: American Psychological Association.

Eagly, A. H., & Fischer, A. (2009). Gender inequities in power in organizations. In B. van Krippenberg & D. Tjosvold (Eds.), *Power and interdependence in organizations.* New York: Cambridge University Press.

Eagly, A. H., & Sczesny, S. (2009). Stereotypes about women, men, and leaders: Have times changed? In M. Barreto, M. K. Ryan, & M. T. Schmitt (Eds.), *The glass ceiling in the 21st century.* Washington, DC: APA Books.

Eagly, A. H., & Wood, W. (2010). Gender roles in a biosocial world. In P. van Lange, A. Kruglanski, & E. T. Higgins (Eds.), *Handbook of theories in social psychology.* Thousand Oaks, CA: Sage. (in press)

Eagly, A. H., Wood, W., & Johannesen-Schmidt, M. C. (2004). Social role theory of sex differences and similarities: Implications for the partner preferences of women and men. In A. H. Eagly, A. Beall, & R. S. Sternberg (Eds.). *The psychology of gender* (2nd ed., pp. 269–295). New York: Guilford.

Eastman, K. K. (1994). In the eyes of the beholder: An attributional approach to ingratiation and organizational citizenship behavior. *Academy of Management Journal, 37,* 1379–1391.

Eaton, D. K., & others. (2008). Youth risk behavior surveillance—United States, 2007. *Morbidity and Mortality Weekly Reports, 57,* 1–131.

Eby, L. T. (2010). Mentoring. In S. Zedeck (Ed.), *APA handbook of industrial and organizational psychology.* Washington, DC: APA. (in press)

Eby, L. T., Maher, C. P., & Butts, M. M. (2010). The intersection of work and family life: The role of affect. *Annual Review of Psychology* (vol. 61). Palo Alto, CA: Annual Reviews.

Edmonds, G. W., Jackson, J. J., Fayard, J. V., & Roberts, B. W. (2007). Is character fate or is there hope to change my personality yet? *Social and Personality Psychology Compass, 2,* 399–413.

Eells, T. D. (2000). Can therapy affect physical health? *Journal of Psychotherapy Practice and Research, 9,* 100–104.

Effros, R. B. (2009). Kleemeier Award Lecture 2008—The canary in the coal mine: Telomeres and human healthspan. *Journals of Gerontology: Biological Sciences and Medical Sciences, 64,* 511–515.

Efklides, A. (2009). The role of metacognitive experiences in the learning process. *Psicothema, 21,* 76–82.

Eghigian, G. (Ed.). (2010). *From madness to mental health: Psychiatric disorder and its treatment in Western civilization.* New Brunswick, NJ: Rutgers University Press.

Ehrhart, M. G., Ehrhart, K. H., Roesch, S. C., Chung-Herrera, B. G., Nadler, K., & Bradshaw, K. (2009). Testing the latent factor structure and construct validity of the Ten-Item Personality Inventory. *Personality and Individual Differences, 47,* 900–905.

Eisenberg, D. P., Sarpal, D., Kohn, P. D., Meyer-Lindenberg, A., Wint, D., Kolachana, B., Apud, J., Weinberger, D. R., & Berman, K. F. (2010). Catechol-o-methyltransferase valine(158)methionine genotype and resting regional cerebral blood flow in medication-free patients with schizophrenia. *Biological Psychiatry, 67,* 287–290.

Eisenberg, M. E., & others. (2008). Support for comprehensive sexuality education: Perspectives from parents of school-age youth. *Journal of Adolescent Health, 42,* 352–359.

Eisenberg, N. (2010). Empathy-related responding: Links with self-regulation, moral judgment, and moral behavior. In M. Mikulincer & P. R. Shaver (Eds.), *Prosocial motives, emotions, and behavior: The better angels of our nature* (pp. 129–148). Washington, DC: American Psychological Association.

Eisenberg, N., Fabes, R. A., & Spinrad, T. L. (2006). Prosocial development. In W. Damon & R. Lerner (Eds.), *Handbook of child psychology* (2nd ed.). New York: Wiley.

Eisenberg, N., Morris, A. S., McDaniel, B., & Spinrad, T. L. (2009). Moral cognitions and prosocial responding. In R. M. Lerner & L. Steinberg (Eds.), *Handbook of adolescent psychology* (3rd ed.). New York: Wiley.

Eisenberg, N., & Murphy, B. (1995). Parenting and children's moral development. In M. H. Bornstein (Ed.), *Children and parenting* (vol. 4). Hillsdale, NJ: Erlbaum.

Eisenberg, N., & Valiente, C. (2002). Parenting and children's prosocial and moral development. In M. H. Bornstein (Ed.), *Handbook of parenting* (2nd ed.). Mahwah, NJ: Erlbaum.

Eisenberger, R., & Aselage, J. (2009). Incremental effects of reward on experienced performance pressure: Positive outcomes for intrinsic interest and creativity. *Journal of Organizational Behavior, 30,* 95–117.

Ekman, P. (1980). *The face of man.* New York: Garland.

Ekman, P. (1996). Lying and deception. In N. L. Stein, C. Brainerd, P. A. Ornstein, & B. Tversky (Eds.), *Memory for everyday emotional events.* Mahwah, NJ: Erlbaum.

Ekman, P. (2003). Emotions inside out: 130 years after Darwin's "The expression of emotions in man and animal." *Annals of the New York Academy of Sciences, 1000,* 1–6.

Ekman, P., Davidson, R. J., & Friesen, W. V. (1990). The Duchenne smile: Emotional expression and brain physiology: II. *Journal of Personality and Social Psychology, 58,* 342–353.

Ekman, P., Davidson, R. J., Ricard, M., & Wallace, B. A. (2005). Buddhist and psychological perspectives on emotions and well-being. *Current Directions in Psychological Science, 14,* 59–63.

Ekman, P., & Friesen, W. V. (1969). The repertoire of nonverbal behavior: Categories, origins, usage, and coding. *Semiotica, 1,* 49–98.

Ekman, P., & Friesen, W. V. (1971). Constants across cultures in the face and emotion. *Journal of Personality and Social Psychology, 17,* 124–129.

Ekman, P., Levenson, R. W., & Friesen, W. V. (1983). Autonomic nervous system activity distinguishes among emotions. *Science, 223,* 1208–1210.

Ekman, P., & O'Sullivan, M. (1991). Facial expressions: Methods, means, and moues. In R. S. Feldman & B. Rime (Eds.), *Fundamentals of nonverbal behavior.* Cambridge, U.K.: Cambridge University Press.

El-Hai, J. (2005). *The lobotomist: A maverick medical genius and his tragic quest to rid the world of mental illness.* Hoboken, NJ: Wiley.

Elias, W. J., & Cosgrove, G. R. (2008). Psychosurgery. *Neurosurgery Focus, 25,* E1.

Elkind, D. (1978). Understanding the young adolescent. *Adolescence, 13,* 127–134.

Elliott, T., Kuang, X., Shadbolt, N. R., & Zauner, K. P. (2009). Adaptation in multisensory neurons: Impact of cross-modal enhancement. *Network, 20,* 1–31.

Ellis, A. (1962). *Reason and emotion in psychotherapy.* New York: Lyle Stuart.

Ellis, A. (1996). A rational-emotive behavior therapist's perspective on Ruth. In G. Corey (Ed.), *Case approach to counseling and psychotherapy.* Pacific Grove, CA: Brooks/Cole.

Ellis, A. (2000). Rational emotive behavior therapy. In A. Kazdin (Ed.), *Encyclopedia of psychology.* Washington, DC, & New York: American Psychological Association and Oxford University Press.

Ellis, A. (2002). Rational emotive behavior therapy. In M. Hersen & W. H. Sledge (Eds.), *Encyclopedia of psychotherapy.* San Diego: Academic.

Ellis, A. (2005). Why I (really) became a therapist. *Journal of Clinical Psychology, 61,* 945–948.

Emmons, R. A. (2005). Striving for the sacred: Personal goals, life meaning, and religion. *Journal of Social Issues, 61,* 731–745.

Emmons, R. A., & Diener, E. (1986). Situation selection as a moderator of response consistency and stability. *Journal of Personality and Social Psychology, 51,* 1013–1019.

Emmons, R. A., & King, L. A. (1988). Conflict among personal strivings: Immediate and long-term implications for psychological and physical well-being. *Journal of Personality and Social Psychology, 48,* 1040–1048.

Emmons, R. A., & McCullough, M. E. (2003). Counting blessings versus burdens: An experimental investigation of gratitude and subjective well-being in daily life. *Journal of Personality and Social Psychology, 84,* 377–389.

Emmons, R. A., & McCullough, M. E. (Eds.). (2004). *The psychology of gratitude.* New York: Oxford University Press.

Emslie, G. J., Croarkin, P., & Mayes, T. L. (2010). Antidepressants. In M. K. Dulcan, (Ed.), *Dulcan's textbook of child and adolescent psychiatry* (pp. 701–723). Arlington, VA: American Psychiatric Publishing.

Endler, N. S. (1988). The origins of electroconvulsive therapy (ECT). *Convulsive Therapy, 4,* 5–23.

Eng, P. M., Fitzmaurice, G., Kubzansky, L. D., Rimm, E. B., & Kawachi, I. (2003). Anger expression and risk of stroke and coronary heart disease among male health professionals. *Psychosomatic Medicine, 65,* 100–110.

Engel, A. K., & Singer, W. (2001). Temporal binding and the neural correlates of sensory awareness. *Trends in Cognitive Science, 5,* 16–25.

Engels, R. C. M. E. (2009). Early pubertal maturation and drug use: Underlying mechanisms. *Addiction, 104,* 67–68.

Englander, E. K. (2006). *Understanding violence* (3rd ed.). Mahwah, NJ: Erlbaum.

Ensembl Human. (2010). *Explore the human genome.* www.ensemblhuman.org (accessed February 5, 2010)

Enstrom, J. E. (1999). Smoking cessation and mortality trends among two United States populations. *Journal of Clinical Epidemiology, 52,* 813–825.

Equal Employment Opportunity Commission (EEOC). (2007). *Sexual harassment charges EEOC & FEPAs combined FY 1997–2006.* Washington, DC: Author. http://eeoc.gov/stats/harass/html

Erath, S. A., Flanaggan, K. S., Bierman, K. L., & Tu, K. M. (2010). Friendships moderate psychosocial maladjustment in socially anxious early adolescents. *Journal of Applied Developmental Psychology, 31,* 15–26.

Erber, R., & Erber, M. (2011). *Intimate relationships* (2nd ed.). Upper Saddle River, NJ: Prentice-Hall.

Erdle, S., Irwing, P., Rushton, J. P., & Park, J. (2010). The general factor of personality and its relation to self-esteem in 628,640 internet respondents. *Personality and Individual Differences, 48,* 343–346.

Erickson, K. I., & Kramer, A. F. (2009). Aerobic exercise effects on cognitive and neural plasticity in older adults. *British Journal of Sports Medicine, 43,* 22–24.

Eriksen, J., Jorgensen, T. N., & Gether, U. (2010). Regulation of the dopamine transporter function by protein-protein interactions: New discoveries and methodological challenges. *Journal of Neurochemistry.* (in press)

Erikson, E. H. (1968). *Identity: Youth and crisis.* New York: Norton.

Erikson, E. H. (1969). *Gandhi's truth.* New York: Norton.

Erol, A. (2010). Are paradoxical cell cycle activities in neurons and glia related to the metabolic theory of Alzheimer disease? *Journal of Alzheimer's Disease, 19,* 129–135.

Espirito-Santo, H., & Pio-Abreu, J. L. (2009). Psychiatric symptoms and dissociation in conversion, somatization, and dissociative disorders. *Australian and New Zealand Journal of Psychiatry, 43,* 270–276.

Estrada, C., Isen, A. M., & Young, M. J. (1997). Positive affect influences creative problem solving and reported source of practice satisfaction in physicians. *Motivation and Emotion, 18,* 285–299.

Etaugh, C. A., & Bridges, J. S. (2010). *Women's lives* (2nd ed.). Upper Saddle River, NJ: Prentice-Hall.

Etnier, J. (2009). Chronic exercise and cognition in older adults. In T. McMorris, P. Tomporowski, & M. Audiffren (Eds.), *Exercise and cognitive function* (pp. 227–247). New York: Wiley-Blackwell.

Evans, C., & Diekman, A. B. (2009). On motivated role selection: Gender beliefs, distant goals, and career interest. *Psychology of Women Quarterly, 33,* 235–249.

Evans, D. E., & Rothbart, M. K. (2009). A two-factor model of temperament. *Personality and Individual Differences, 47,* 565–570.

Exner, J. E., Jr. (2003). *The Rorschach: A comprehensive system* (4th ed.). Hoboken, NJ: Wiley.

Eysenck, H. J. (1967). *The biological basis of personality.* Springfield, IL: Thomas.

Eysenck, M. W., & Keane, M. (2010). *Cognitive psychology.* New York: Psychology Press.

F

Faber, M. A., & Mayer, J. D. (2009). Resonance to archetypes in media: There's some accounting for taste. *Journal of Research in Personality, 43,* 307–322.

Faedda, G. L., Becker, I., Baroni, A., Tondo, L., Aspland, E., & Koukopoulos, A. (2010). The origins of electroconvulsive therapy: Prof. Bini's first report on ECT. *Journal of Affective Disorders, 120,* 12–15.

Fagan, M. K., & Pisoni, D. B. (2010). Hearing experience and receptive vocabulary development in deaf children with cochlear implants. *Journal of Deaf Studies and Deaf Education.* (in press)

Fahey, T. D., Insel, P. M., & Roth, W. T. (2011). *Fit and well* (9th ed.). New York: McGraw-Hill.

Fahlman, S. E. (2003). *Smiley lore.* http://www.cs.cmu.edu/~sef/sefSmiley.htm (accessed April 29, 2009)

Falk, C. F., Heine, S. J., Yuki, M., & Takemura, K. (2009). Why do Westerners self-enhance more than East Asians? *European Journal of Personality, 23,* 183–203.

Family and Youth Services Bureau. (2004). *Fact sheet: Section 510 state abstinence education program.* Bethesda, MD: U.S. Department of Health and Human Services.

Fant, R. V., Buchhalter, A. R., Buchman, A. C., & Heningfield, J. E. (2009). Pharmacotherapy for tobacco dependence. *Handbook of Experimental Pharmacology, 192,* 487–510.

Farin, A., Liu, C. Y., Langmoen, I. A., & Apuzzo, M. L. (2009). The biological restoration of central nervous system architecture and function: Part 2—emergence of the realization of adult neurogenesis. *Neurosurgery, 64,* 581–600.

Farrell, S. W., Fitzgerald, S. J., McAuley, P., & Barlow, C. E. (2010). Cardiorespiratory fitness, adiposity, and all-cause mortality in women. *Medicine and Science in Sports and Exercise.* (in press)

Farris, M. (2009, November 2). *Man donates kidney to complete stranger.* http://www.wwltv.com/home/wwl110209cbstranger-68784452.html (accessed April 10, 2010)

Fatemi, S. H., & Folsom, T. D. (2009). The neurodevelopmental hypothesis of schizophrenia, revisited. *Schizophrenia Bulletin, 35,* 528–548.

Faul, L. A., Jim, H. S., Williams, C., Loftus, L., & Jacobsen, P. B. (2009). Relationship of stress management skill to psychological distress and quality of life in adults with cancer. *Psychooncology, 19* (1), 102–109.

Fava, G. A. (2006). The intellectual crisis in psychiatric research. *Psychotherapy and Psychosomatics, 75,* 202–208.

Fava, G. A., Ruini, C., & Belaise, C. (2007). The concept of recovery in depression. *Psychological Medicine, 37,* 307–317.

Faymonville, M. E., Boly, M., & Laureys, S. (2006). Functional neuroanatomy of the hypnotic state. *Journal of Physiology, Paris, 99,* 463–469.

Fazio, R. H., Chen, J., McDonel, E. C., & Sherman, S. J. (1982). Attitude accessibility, attitude-behavior consistency, and the strength of the object-evaluation association. *Journal of Experimental Social Psychology, 18,* 339–357.

Fazio, R. H., & Olsen, A. (2007). Attitudes. In M. A. Hogg & J. Cooper (Eds.), *The Sage handbook of social psychology* (concise 2nd ed.). Thousand Oaks, CA: Sage.

Fearon, R. P., & others. (2010). The significance of insecure attachment and disorganization in the development of children's externalizing behavior: A meta-analytic study. *Child Development, 81,* 435–456.

Federal Emergency Management Agency (FEMA). (2003, July 10). *Disaster search canine readiness evaluation process.* Washington, DC: Author.

Fehm, H. L., Kern, W., & Peters, A. (2006). The selfish brain: Competition for energy resources. *Progress in Brain Research, 153,* 129–140.

Fei-Fei, L., Iyer, A., Koch, C., & Perona, P. (2007). What do we perceive in a glance at a real-world scene? *Journal of Vision, 7,* 10.

Feldman, D. (2009). Synaptic mechanisms for plasticity in neocortex. *Annual Review of Neuroscience* (vol. 32). Palo Alto, CA: Annual Reviews.

Ferguson, C. J., & Kilburn, J. (2010). Much ado about nothing: The misestimation and overinterpretation of violent video game effects in Eastern and Western nations: Comment on Anderson et al. (2010). *Psychological Bulletin, 136,* 174–178.

Ferguson, C. J., Rueda, S. M., Cruz, A. M., Ferguson, D. E., Fritz, S., & Smith, S. M. (2008). Violent video games and aggression: Causal relationship or byproduct of family violence and intrinsic violence motivation? *Criminal Justice and Behavior, 35,* 311–332.

Ferrari, P. F., Paukner, A., Ruggiero, A., Darcey, L., Unbehagen, S., & Suomi, S. J. (2009). Interindividual differences in neonatal imitation and the development of action chains in rhesus macaques. *Child Development, 80,* 1057–1068.

Ferretti, F., & Coluccia, A. (2009). Socio-economic factors and suicide rates in European Union countries. *Legal Medicine, 11, Suppl. 1,* S92–S94.

Ferris, G. R., Judge, T. A., Rowland, K. M., & Fitzgibbons, D. E. (1994). Subordinate influence and the performance evaluation process: Test of a model. *Organizational and Human Decision Processes, 58,* 101–135.

Ferro, A. (2009). Transformations in dreaming and characters in the psychoanalytic field. *International Journal of Psychoanalysis, 90,* 209–230.

Feshbach, S., & Weiner, B. (1996). *Personality* (4th ed.). Lexington, MA: Heath.

Festinger, L. (1954). A theory of social comparison processes. *Human Relations, 7,* 117–140.

Festinger, L. (1957). *A theory of cognitive dissonance.* Evanston, IL: Row Peterson.

Festinger, L., & Carlsmith, J. M. (1959). Cognitive consequences of forced compliance. *Journal of Abnormal and Social Psychology, 58,* 203–211.

Field, T. M., Diego, M., & Hernandez-Reif, M. (2010). Preterm infant massage therapy research: A review. *Infant Behavior and Development.* (in press)

Fields, R. (2010). *Drugs in perspective* (7th ed.). New York: McGraw-Hill.

Fiese, B. H., Foley, K. P., & Spagnola, M. (2006). Routine and ritual elements in family mealtimes: Contexts for child well-being and family identity. *New Directions in Child and Adolescent Development, 111,* 67–89.

Fifer, W. P., & Myers, M. M. (2002) Sudden fetal and infant deaths: Shared observations and distinctive features. *Seminar in Perinatology, 26,* 89–96.

Figueroa-Moseley, C., Jean-Pierre, P., Roscoe, J. A., Ryan, J. L., Kohli, S., Palesh, O. G., Ryan, E. P., & Finch, C. E. (2009). The neurobiology of middle-age has arrived. *Neurobiology and Aging, 30,* 515–520.

Finch, E. A., Linde, J. A., Jeffery, R. W., Rothman, A. J., King, C. M., & Levy, R. L. (2005). The effects of outcome expectations and satisfaction on weight loss and maintenance:

Correlational and experimental analyses—a randomized trial. *Health Psychology, 24* (6), 608–616.

Fine, S. A., & Wiley, W. W. (1971). *An introduction to functional job analysis.* Kalamazoo, MI: W. E. Upjohn Institute.

Fink, B., Brewer, G., Fehl, K., & Neave, N. (2007). Instrumentality and lifetime number of sexual partners. *Personality and Individual Differences, 43,* 747–756.

Finkbeiner, M., & Palermo, R. (2009). The role of spatial attention in nonconscious processing: A comparison of face and nonface stimuli. *Psychological Science, 20,* 42–51.

Finzi-Dottan, R., & Zubery, E. (2009). The role of depression and anxiety in impulsive and obsessive-compulsive behaviors among anorexic and bulimic patients. *Eating Disorders, 17,* 162–182.

First, M. B. (2011). The clinical utility of psychiatric diagnoses. *Annual Review of Clinical Psychology* (vol. 7). Palo Alto, CA: Annual Reviews.

Fischer, J., Spotswood, N., & Whitney, D. (2010). The emergence of perceived position in the visual system. *Journal of Cognitive Neuroscience.* (in press)

Fischhoff, B., Bruine de Bruin, W., Parker, A. M., Millstein, S. G., & Halpern-Felsher, B. L. (2010). Adolescents' perceived risk of dying. *Journal of Adolescent Health, 46,* 265–269.

Fishbein, M., & Ajzen, I. (2010). *Predicting and changing behavior.* New York: Psychology Press.

Fisher, A. J., Granger, D. A., & Newman, M. G. (2010). Sympathetic arousal moderates self-reported physiological arousal symptoms at baseline and physiological flexibility in response to a stressor in generalized anxiety disorder. *Biological Psychology, 83,* 191–200.

Fiske, A., Wetherell, J. L., & Gatz, M. (2009). Depression in older adults. *Annual Review of Clinical Psychology, 5,* 363–389.

Fitzgerald, L. F. (2003). Sexual harassment and social justice: Reflections on the distance yet to go. *American Psychologist, 58,* 915–924.

Fivush, R. (2011). The development of autobiographical memory. *Annual Review of Psychology* (vol. 62). Palo Alto, CA: Annual Reviews.

Flegal, K. M., Carroll, M. G., Ogden, C. L., & Curin, L. R. (2010). Prevalence and trends in obesity among U.S. adults, 1999–2008. *Journal of the American Medical Association, 303,* 235–241.

Fleischhaker, S., Schulz, E., Tepper, K., Martin, M., Hennighausen, K., & Remschmidt, H. (2005). Long-term course of adolescent schizophrenia. *Schizophrenia Bulletin, 31,* 769–780.

Fleming, S. M. (2009). Shaping what we see: Pinning down the influence of value on perceptual judgements. *Frontiers in Human Neuroscience, 3,* ArtID 9.

Flom, R., & Bahrick, L. E. (2010). The effects of intersensory redundancy on attention and memory: Infants' long-term memory for orientation in audiovisual events. *Developmental Psychology, 46,* 428–436.

Flor, H., & Diers, M. (2009). Sensorimotor training and cortical reorganization. *NeuroRehabilitation, 25,* 19–27.

Floyd, D. L., Prentice-Dunn, S., & Rogers, R. W. (2000). A meta-analysis of research on protection motivation theory. *Journal of Applied Social Psychology, 30,* 407–429.

Flynn, J. R. (1999). Searching for justice: The discovery of IQ gains over time. *American Psychologist, 54,* 5–20.

Flynn, J. R. (2006). The history of the American mind in the 20th century: A scenario to explain gains over time and a case for the irrelevance of g. In P. C. Kyllonen, R. D. Roberts, & L. Stankov (Eds.), *Extending intelligence.* Mahwah, NJ: Erlbaum.

Foa, E. B., & Franklin, M. E. (2011). Obsessive compulsive disorder. *Annual Review of Clinical Psychology* (vol. 7). Palo Alto, CA: Annual Reviews.

Fodor, I., & Epstein, J. (2002). Agoraphobia, panic disorder, and gender. In J. Worell (Ed.), *Encyclopedia of women and gender.* San Diego: Academic.

Foer, J. (2008). The unspeakable odyssey of the motionless boy. *Esquire.* http://www.esquire.com/features/unspeakable-odyssey-motionless-boy-1008

Foley, P., & Kirschbaum, C. (2010). Human hypothalamic-pituitary-adrenal axis responses to acute psychosocial stress in laboratory settings. *Neuroscience and Biobehavioral Reviews.* (in press)

Folkman, S., & Lazarus, R. S. (1980). An analysis of coping in a middle-aged community sample. *Journal of Health and Social Behavior, 21,* 219–239.

Folkman, S., & Moskowitz, J. T. (2004). Coping: Pitfalls and promises. *Annual Review of Psychology* (vol. 54). Palo Alto, CA: Annual Reviews.

Fontaine, R. G., Yang, C., Burks, V. S., Dodge, K. A., Price, J. M., Pettit, G. S., & Bates, J. E. (2009). Loneliness as a partial mediator of the relation between low social preference in childhood and anxious/depressed symptoms in adolescence. *Development and Psychopathology, 21,* 479–491.

Fontana, M. A., & Wohlgemuth, S. D. (2010). The surgical treatment of metabolic disease and morbid obesity. *Gastroenterology Clinics of North America, 39,* 125–133.

Fontanini, A., Grossman, S. E., Figueroa, J. A., & Katz, D. B. (2009). Distinct subtypes of basolateral amygdala taste neurons reflect palatability and reward. *Journal of Neuroscience, 29,* 2486–2495.

Foote, B., Smolin, Y., Kaplan, M., Legatt, M. E., & Lipschitz, D. (2006). Prevalence of dissociative disorders in psychiatric outpatients. *American Journal of Psychiatry, 163,* 566–568.

Forbey, J. D., & Ben-Porath, Y. S. (2007). Computerized adaptive personality testing: A review and illustration with the MMPI-2 computerized adaptive version. *Psychological Assessment, 19,* 14–24.

Forbush, K., Heatherton, T. F., & Keel, P. K. (2007). Relationships between perfectionism and specific disordered eating behaviors. *International Journal of Eating Disorders, 40,* 37–41.

Forgas, J. P., Baumeister, R. F., & Tice, D. M. (2009). The psychology of self-regulation: An introduction. In J. P. Forgas, R. F. Baumeister, & D. M. Tice (Eds.), *Psychology of self-regulation.* New York: Psychology Press.

Forgas, J. P., Dunn, E., & Granland, S. (2008). Are you being served . . . ? An unobtrusive experiment of affective influences on helping in a department store. *European Journal of Social Psychology, 38,* 333–342.

Forman-Hoffman, V. L., & Cunningham, C. L. (2008). Geographical clustering of eating disordered behaviors in U.S. high school students. *International Journal of Eating Disorders, 41,* 209–214.

Forouzan, B. A. (2007). *Data communication networking* (4th ed.). New York: McGraw-Hill.

Forrest, L. (2010). Linking international psychology, professional competence, and leadership: Counseling psychologists as learning partners. *The Counseling Psychologist, 38,* 96–120.

Forsythe, C., Bernard, M. L., & Goldsmith, T. E. (Eds.). (2006). *Cognitive systems.* Mahwah, NJ: Erlbaum.

Foulkes, D. (1993). Cognitive dream theory. In M. A. Carskadon (Ed.), *Encyclopedia of sleep and dreams.* New York: Macmillan.

Foulkes, D. (1999). *Children's dreaming and the development of consciousness.* Cambridge, MA: Harvard University Press.

Fountas, K. N., & Smith, J. R. (2007). Historical evolution of stereotactic amygdalotomy for the management of severe aggression. *Journal of Neurosurgery, 106,* 710–713.

Fox, R., & Millam, J. R. (2010). The use of ratings and direct behavioural observation to measure temperament traits in cockatiels (*nymphicus hollandicus*). *Ethology, 116,* 59–75.

Frank, J. D. (1982). Therapeutic components shared by all psychotherapies. In J. H. Harvey & M. M. Parks (Eds.), *Psychotherapy research and behavior change.* Washington, DC: American Psychological Association.

Frank, J. D., & Frank, J. B. (1993). *Persuasion and healing: A comparative study of psychotherapy.* Baltimore: Johns Hopkins University Press.

Frank, M. C., Vul, E., & Johnson, S. P. (2009). Development of infants' attention to faces during the first year. *Cognition, 110,* 160–170.

Frank, M. G. (2006). The mystery of sleep function: Current perspectives and future directions. *Reviews in the Neurosciences, 17,* 375–392.

Frank, M. G., & Benington J. H. (2006). The role of sleep in memory consolidation and brain plasticity: Dream or reality? *Neuroscientist, 12,* 477–488.

Franke, R. H., & Kaul, J. D. (1978). The Hawthorn experiments: First statistical interpretation. *American Sociological Review, 43,* 623–643.

Frankl, V. E. (1963/1984). *Man's search for meaning* (3rd ed.). New York: First Washington Square Press. (original work published 1946)

Frattaroli, J. (2006). Experimental disclosure and its moderators: A meta-analysis. *Psychological Bulletin, 132,* 823–865.

Fredrick, S., & Loewenstein, G. (1999). Hedonic adaptation. In D. Kahneman, E. Diener, & N. Schwarz (Eds.), *Well-being: The foundations of hedonic psychology* (pp. 302–329). New York: Russell Sage Foundation.

Fredrickson, B. L. (1998). What good are positive emotions? *Review of General Psychology, 2,* 300–319.

Fredrickson, B. L. (2001). The role of positive emotions in positive psychology. *American Psychologist, 56,* 218–226.

Fredrickson, B. L. (2006). Unpacking positive emotions: Investigating the seeds of human flourishing. *Journal of Positive Psychology, 1,* 57–60.

Fredrickson, B. L. (2009). *Positivity.* New York: Crown.

Fredrickson, B. L., & Roberts, T. (1997). Objectification theory: Toward understanding women's lived experiences and mental health risks. *Psychology of Women Quarterly, 21,* 173–206.

Fredrickson, B. L., Roberts, T., Noll, S. M., Quinn, D. M., & Twenge, J. M. (1998). That swimsuit becomes you: Sex differences in self-objectification, restrained eating, and math performance. *Journal of Personality and Social Psychology, 75,* 269–284.

Fredrickson, B. L., Tugade, M. M., Waugh, C. E., & Larkin, G. R. (2003). What good are positive emotions in crisis? A prospective study of resilience and emotions following the terrorist attacks on the United States on September 11th, 2001. *Journal of Personality and Social Psychology, 84,* 365–376.

Freedman, J. L., & Fraser, S. C. (1966). Compliance without pressure: The foot-in-the-door technique. *Journal of Personality and Social Psychology, 4,* 195–202.

Freeland, A., Manchanda, R., Chiu, S., Sharma, V., & Merskey, H. (1993). Four cases of supposed multiple personality disorder: Evidence of unjustified diagnoses. *Canadian Journal of Psychiatry, 38,* 245–247.

Freeman, S., & Herron, J. C. (2007). *Evolutionary analysis* (4th ed.). Upper Saddle River, NJ: Prentice-Hall.

Freestone, D. M., & Church, R. M. (2010). The importance of the reinforcer as a time marker. *Behavioral Processes.* (in press)

French, C. C., Santomauro, J., Hamilton, V., Fox, R., & Thalbourne, M. A. (2008). Psychological aspects of alien contact experience. *Cortex, 44,* 1387–1395.

Freud, S. (1911). *The interpretation of dreams* (3rd ed.). A. A. Brill (Trans). New York: Macmillan. (original work published 1899)

Freud, S. (1917). *A general introduction to psychoanalysis.* New York: Washington Square Press.

Freud, S. (1953). The interpretation of dreams. In J. Strachey (Ed.), *The standard edition of the complete psychological works of Sigmund Freud.* New York: Washington Square Press. (original work published 1900)

Freud, S. (1996). Number 23091. In R. Andrews, M. Seidel, & M. Biggs (Eds.), *Columbia world of quotations.* New York: Columbia University Press. (original work published 1918)

Freyer, T., & others. (2010). Frontostriatal activation in patients with obsessive-compulsive disorder before and after cognitive behavioral therapy. *Psychological Medicine.* (in press)

Fried, S. (2008, October 9). Commentary in "Think fat just hangs around, does nothing." *USA Today,* 6D.

Friedel, E., & others. (2009). 5-HTT genotype effect on prefrontal-amygdala coupling differs between major depression and controls. *Psychopharmacology, 205* (2), 261–271.

Friedman, J. M. (2009). Leptin at 14 y of age: An ongoing story. *American Journal of Clinical Nutrition, 89,* 973S–979S.

Friedman, M., & Rosenman, R. (1974). *Type A behavior and your heart.* New York: Knopf.

Friedman, N. P., Miyake, A., Young, S. E., DeFries, J. C., Corley, R. P., & Hewitt, J. K. (2008). Individual differences in executive functions are almost entirely genetic in origin. *Journal of Experimental Psychology: General, 137* (2), 201–225.

Friedman, R., Myers, P., & Benson, H. (1998). Meditation and the relaxation response. In H. S. Friedman (Ed.), *Encyclopedia of mental health* (vol. 2). San Diego: Academic.

Frijda, N. H. (2007). *The laws of emotion.* Mahwah, NJ: Erlbaum.

Frisch, M. B., & others. (2004). Predictive and treatment validity of life satisfaction and the Quality of Life Inventory. *Assessment, 10,* 1–13.

Frishman, W. H., Mitta, W., Kupersmith, A., & Ky, T. (2006). Nicotine and non-nicotine smoking cessation pharmacotherapies. *Cardiology in Review, 14,* 57–73.

Fritz, C., & Sonnentag, S. (2006). Recovery, well-being, and performance-related outcomes: The role of work overload and vacation experiences. *Journal of Applied Psychology, 91,* 936–945.

Frohlich, P., & Meston, C. M. (2005). Fluoxetine-induced changes in tactile sensation and sexual functioning among clinically depressed women. *Journal of Sex & Marital Therapy, 31* (2), 113–128.

Fromm, E. (1947). *Man for himself.* New York: Holt, Rinehart & Winston.

Frosch, Z. A., Dierker, L. C., Rose, J. S., & Waldinger, R. J. (2009). Smoking trajectories, health, and mortality across the adult lifespan. *Addictive Behaviors, 34* (8), 701–704.

Fry, P. S., & Debats, D. L. (2009). Perfectionism and the five-factor personality traits as predictors of mortality in older adults. *Journal of Health Psychology, 14,* 513–524.

Fry, R. B., & Prentice-Dunn, S. (2006). Effects of a psychosocial intervention on breast self-examination attitudes and behaviors. *Health Education Research, 21,* 287–295.

Fryberg, S. A., & Markus, H. R. (2003). On being American Indian: Current and possible selves. *Self and Identity, 2,* 325–344.

Fujiwara, E., Levine, B., & Anderson, A. K. (2008). Intact implicit and reduced explicit memory for negative self-related information in repressive coping. *Cognitive, Affective, and Behavioral Neuroscience, 8,* 254–263.

Fullam, R. S., McKie, S., & Dolan, M. C. (2009). Psychopathic traits and deception: Functional magnetic resonance imaging study. *British Journal of Psychiatry, 194,* 229–235.

Fulton, S. (2010). Appetite and reward. *Frontiers in Neuroendocrinology, 31,* 85–103.

Fultz, J., Batson, C. D., Fortenbach, V. A., McCarthy, P. M., & Varney, L. L. (1986). Social evaluation and the empathy-altruism hypothesis. *Journal of Personality and Social Psychology, 50,* 761–769.

Funder, D. C. (2009). Persons, behaviors, and situations: An agenda for personality psychology in the postwar era. *Journal of Research in Personality, 43,* 120–126.

Fung, H. H., & Ng, S. K. (2006). Age differences in the sixth personality factor: Age difference in interpersonal relatedness among Canadians and Hong Kong Chinese. *Psychology and Aging, 21,* 810–814.

Fung, M. T., Raine, A., Loeber, R., Lynam, D. R., Steinhauer, S. R., Venables, P. H., & Stouthamer-Loeber, M. (2005). Reduced electrodermal activity in psychopathy-prone adolescents. *Journal of Abnormal Psychology, 114,* 187–196.

G

Gabelle, A., & Dauvilliers, Y. (2010). Editorial: Sleep and dementia. *Journal of Nutrition, Health, and Aging, 14,* 201–202.

Gagnepain, P., Henson, R., Chetelat, G., Desgranges, B., Lebreton, K., & Eustache, F. (2010). Is neocortical–hippocampal connectivity a better predictor of subsequent recollection than local increases in hippocampal activity? New insights on the role of priming. *Journal of Cognitive Neuroscience.* (in press)

Gaillard, R., Dehaene., S., Adam, C., Clémenceau, S., Hasboun, D., Baulac, M., Cohen, L., & Naccache, L. (2009). Converging intracranial markers of conscious access. *PLoS Biology, 7,* e1000061.

Galambos, N. L., Berenbaum, S. A., & McHale, S. M. (2009). Gender development in adolescence. In R. M. Lerner & L. Steinberg (Eds.), *Handbook of adolescent psychology* (3rd ed.). New York: Wiley.

Galan, R. F., Weidert, M., Menzel, R., Herz, A. V., & Galizia, C. G. (2006). Sensory memory for odors is encoded in spontaneous correlated activity between olfactory glomeruli. *Neural Computation, 18,* 10–25.

Gallagher, K. E., & Parrott, D. J. (2010). Influence of heavy episodic drinking on the relation between men's locus of control and aggression toward intimate partners. *Journal of Studies on Alcohol and Drugs, 71,* 299–306.

Gallo, I. S., Keil, A., McCulloch, K. C., Rockstroh, B., & Gollwitzer, P. M. (2009). Strategic automation of emotion regulation. *Journal of Personality and Social Psychology, 96,* 11–31.

Gallo, W. T., Bradley, E. H., Dubin, J. A., Jones, R. N., Falba, T. A., Teng, H. M., & Kasi, S. V. (2006). The persistence of depressive symptoms in older workers who experience involuntary job loss: Results from the health and retirement survey. *Journals of Gerontology B: Psychological Sciences and Social Sciences, 61,* S221–S228. doi: 10.1093/scan/nsp005

Ganis, G., Morris, R. R., & Kosslyn, S. M. (2009). Neural processes underlying self- and other-related lies: An individual difference approach using MRI. *Social Neuroscience, 4,* 539–553.

Gao, D., & Vasconcelos, N. (2009). Decision-theoretic saliency: Computational principles, biological plausibility, and implications for neurophysiology. *Neural Computation, 21,* 239–271.

Gao, Y., & Raine, A. (2010). Successful and unsuccessful psychopaths: A neurobiological model. *Behavioral Sciences and Law, 28,* 194–210.

Gao, Y. J., & Ji, R. R. (2010). Chemokines, neuronal-glial interactions, and central processing of neuropathic pain. *Pharmacology & Therapeutics.* (in press)

Garb, H. N., Wood, J. M., Nezworski, M. T., Grove, W. M., & Stejskal, W. J. (2001). Toward a resolution of the Rorschach controversy. *Psychological Assessment, 13,* 433–448.

Garbett, K. A., & others. (2010). Novel animal models for studying complex brain disorders: BAC-driven *miRNA*-mediated *in vivo* silencing of gene expression. *Molecular Psychiatry.* (in press)

Garcia, B. G., Neely, M. D., & Deutsch, A. Y. (2010). Cortical regulation of striatal medium spiny neuron dendritic remodeling in Parkinsonism: Modulation of glutamate release reverses dopamine depletion-induced dendritic spine loss. *Cerebral Cortex.* (in press)

Garcia, J. (1989). Food for Tolman: Cognition and cathexis in concert. In T. Archer & L. Nilsson (Eds.), *Aversion, avoidance, and anxiety.* Mahwah, NJ: Erlbaum.

Garcia, J., Ervin, F. E., & Koelling, R. A. (1966). Learning with prolonged delay of reinforcement. *Psychonomic Science, 5,* 121–122.

Garcia, J., & Koelling, R. A. (1966). Relation of cue to consequence in avoidance learning. *Psychonomic Science, 4,* 123–124.

Garcia, J., & Koelling, R. A. (2009). Specific hungers and poison avoidance as adaptive specializations of learning. In D. Shanks (Ed.), *Psychology of learning.* Thousand Oaks, CA: Sage.

Garcia, L. F., Aluja, A., Fibla, J., Cuevas, L., & Garcia, O. (2010). Incremental effect for antisocial personality disorder genetic risk combining 5-HTTLPR and 5-HTTVNTR polymorphisms *Psychiatry Research, 177,* 161–166.

Gardner, H. (1983). *Frames of mind.* New York: Basic.

Gardner, H. (1993). *Multiple intelligences.* New York: Basic.

Gardner, H. (2002). The pursuit of excellence through education. In M. Ferrari (Ed.), *Learning from extraordinary minds.* Mahwah, NJ: Erlbaum.

Gardner, W. L., & Martinko, M. J. (1996). Using the Myers-Briggs Type Indicator to study managers: A literature review and research agenda. *Journal of Management, 22,* 45–83.

Garfield, A. S., & Heisler, L. K. (2009). Pharmacological targeting of the serotonergic system for the treatment of obesity. *Journal of Physiology, 587,* 49–60.

Garner, M., Mohler, H., Stein, D. J., Mueggler, T., & Baldwin, D. S. (2009). Research in anxiety disorders: From the bench to the bedside. *European Neuropsychopharmacology, 19,* 381–390.

Garrison, G. D., & Dugan, S. E. (2009). Varenicline: A first-line treatment for smoking cessation. *Clinical Therapeutics, 31,* 463–491.

Garry, M., & Loftus, E. F. (2009). Repressed memory. In D. Clark (Ed.), *Encyclopedia of law and society* (pp. 555–556). Thousand Oaks, CA: Sage.

Garver, D. L. (2006). Evolution of antipsychotic intervention in the schizophrenic psychosis. *Current Drug Targets, 7,* 1205–1215.

Garzon, C., Guerrero, J. M., Aramburu, O., & Guzman, T. (2009). Effect of melatonin administration on sleep, behavioral disorders, and hypnotic drug discontinuation in the elderly: A randomized, double-blind, placebo-controlled study. *Aging: Clinical and Experimental Research, 21,* 38–42.

Gasper, K. (2004). Permission to seek freely? The effect of happy and sad moods on generating old and new ideas. *Creativity Research Journal, 16* (2–3), 215–229.

Gastil, J. W. (2009). *The group in society.* Thousand Oaks, CA: Sage.

Gaunt, R., & Trope, Y. (2007). Attribution and person perception. In M. A. Hogg & J. Cooper (Eds.), *The Sage handbook of social psychology* (concise 2nd ed.). Thousand Oaks, CA: Sage.

Gauthier, I., Behrmann, M., & Tarr, M. J. (2004). Are greebles like faces? Using the neuropsychological exception to test the rule. *Neuropsychologia, 42,* 1961–1970.

Gauthier, I., & Bukach, C. (2007). Should we reject the expertise hypothesis? *Cognition, 103,* 322–330.

Gauthier, I., Skudlarski, P., Gore, J. C., & Anderson, A. W. (2000). Expertise for cars and birds recruits brain areas involved in face recognition. *Nature Neuroscience, 3,* 191–197.

Gauthier, I., Tarr, M. J., & Bub, D. (Eds.). (2010). *Perceptual expertise: Bridging brain and behavior.* New York: Oxford University Press.

Gauvain, M., & Parke, R. D. (2010). Socialization. In M. H. Bornstein (Ed.), *Handbook of cultural developmental science.* New York: Psychology Press.

Gavlak, D. (2009, April 12). Jordan honor killing: Man confesses to brutally stabbing to death pregnant sister. http://www.huffingtonpost.com/2009/04/12/jordan-honor-killing-man-_n_185977.html (accessed May 29, 2009)

Gazzaniga, M. S. (Ed.). (2010). *The cognitive neurosciences* (4th ed.). New York: Cambridge University Press.

Gazzaniga, M. S., Dorn, K. W., & Funk, C. M. (2010). Looking towards the future: Perspectives on examining the architecture and function of the human brain as a complex system. In M. S. Gazzaniga (Ed.), *The cognitive*

neurosciences (4th ed.). New York: Cambridge University Press.

Ge, X., Natsuaki, M. N., Neiderhiser, J. M., & Reiss, D. (2009). The longitudinal effects of stressful life events on adolescent depression are buffered by parent-child closeness. *Development and Psychopathology, 21,* 621–635.

Geary, D. C. (2010). *Male, female: The evolution of human sex differences* (2nd ed.). Washington, DC: American Psychological Association.

Gehar, D. R. (2010). *Mastering competencies in family therapy.* Boston: Cengage.

Gelder, B. D., Meeren, H. K., Righart, R., Stock, J. V., van de Riet, W. A., & Tamietto, M. (2006). Beyond the face: Exploring rapid influences of context on face processing. *Progress in Brain Research, 155PB,* 37–48.

Gelernter, J., & Stein, M. B. (2009). Heritability and genetics of anxiety disorders. In M. M. Antony &. M. B. Stein (Eds.), *Oxford handbook of anxiety and related disorders* (pp. 87–96). New York: Oxford University Press.

Geller, E. S. (2002). The challenge of increasing proenvironmental behavior. In R. B. Bechtel & A. Churchman (Eds.), *Handbook of environmental psychology* (pp. 525–540). Hoboken, NJ: Wiley.

Geller, E. S. (2006). Occupational injury prevention and applied behavior analysis. In A. C. Gielen, D. A. Sleet, & R. J. DiClemente (Eds.), *Injury and violence prevention: Behavioral science theories, methods, and applications* (pp. 297–322). San Francisco: Jossey-Bass.

Gelman, S. A. (2009). Learning from others: Children's constructions of concepts. *Annual Review of Psychology* (vol. 60). Palo Alto, CA: Annual Reviews.

Gentile, D. A., & Anderson, C. A. (2006). Violent video games: Effects on youth and public policy implications. In N. Dowd, D. G. Singer, & R. F. Wilson (Eds.), *Handbook of children, culture, and violence* (pp. 225–246). Thousand Oaks, CA: Sage.

Gentile, S. (2010). Antidepressant use in children and adolescents diagnosed with major depressive disorder: What can we learn from published data? *Reviews on Recent Clinical Trials, 5,* 63–75.

George, J. M. (1995). Leader positive mood and group performance: The case of customer service. *Journal of Applied Social Psychology, 25,* 778–795.

George, L. K. (2006). Perceived quality of life. In R. H. Binstock & L. K. George (Eds.), *Handbook of aging and the social sciences* (6th ed.). San Diego: Academic.

George, L. K. (2009). Religiousness and spirituality, later life. In D. Carr (Ed.), *Encyclopedia of the life course and human adjustment.* Boston: Gale Cengage.

Geraerts, E., Lindsay, D. S., Merckelbach, H., Jelicic, M., Raymaekers, L., Arnold, M. M., & Schooler, J. W. (2009). Cognitive mechanisms underlying recovered-memory experiences of childhood sexual abuse. *Psychological Science, 20,* 92–98.

Gershman, S. J., Blei, D. M., & Niv, Y. (2010). Context, learning, and extinction. *Psychological Review, 117,* 197–209.

Gershoff, E. T. (2002). Corporal punishment by parents and associated child behaviors and experiences: A meta-analysis and theoretical review. *Psychological Bulletin, 128,* 539–579.

Gerson, L. S., & Braun, B. (2006). Effect of high cardiorespiratory fitness and high body fat on insulin resistance. *Medicine and Science in Sports and Exercise, 38,* 1709–1715.

Gervai, J. (2009). Environmental and genetic influences on early attachment. *Child and Adolescent Psychiatry and Mental Health, 3,* ArtID 25.

Giang, D. W., and others. (1996). Conditioning of cyclophosphamide-induced leukopenia in humans. *Journal of Neuropsychiatry and Clinical Neuroscience, 8,* 194–201.

Gibbons, C. J., & others. (2010). The clinical effectiveness of cognitive behavior therapy in an outpatient clinic. *Journal of Affective Disorders.* (in press)

Gibbons, R. D., Hedeker, D., & DuToit, S. (2010). Advances in analysis of longitudinal data. *Annual Review of Clinical Psychology* (vol. 6). Palo Alto, CA: Annual Reviews.

Gibbs, J. C. (2010). *Moral development and reality: Beyond the theories of Kohlberg and Hoffman* (2nd ed.). Boston: Allyn & Bacon.

Gibson, E. J. (2001). *Perceiving the affordances.* Mahwah, NJ: Erlbaum.

Gidron, Y., & Nyklicek, I. (2009). Experimentally testing Taylor's stress, coping, and adaptation framework. *Anxiety, Stress, and Coping, 22,* 1477–2205.

Giedd, J. N. (2008). The teen brain: Insights from neuroimaging. *Journal of Adolescent Medicine, 42,* 335–343.

Gifford, R. (2009). Environmental psychology: Manifold visions, unity of purpose. *Journal of Environmental Psychology, 29,* 387–389.

Gigerenzer, G. (2011). Heuristic decision making in individuals and organizations. *Annual Review of Psychology* (vol. 62). Palo Alto, CA: Annual Reviews.

Gijs, L. (2008). Paraphilia and paraphilia-related disorders: An introduction. In D. L. Rowland & L. Incrocci (Eds.), *Handbook of sexual and gender identity disorders* (pp. 491–528). Hoboken, NJ: Wiley.

Gijs, L., & Brewaeys, A. (2007). Surgical treatment of gender dysphoria in adults and adolescents: Recent developments, effectiveness, and challenges. *Annual Review of Sex Research, 18,* 178–224.

Gilbert, A. L., Regier, T., Kay, P., & Ivry, R. B. (2006). Whorf hypothesis is supported in the right visual field but not the left. *Proceedings of the National Academy of Sciences USA, 103* (2), 489–494.

Gilbert, L. A., & Kearney, L. K. (2006). The psychotherapeutic relationship as a positive and powerful resource for girls and women. In J. Worell & C. D. Goodheart (Eds.), *Handbook of girls' and women's psychological health: Gender and well-being across the lifespan.* New York: Oxford University Press.

Gillard, E., Van Dooren, W., Schaeken, W., & Verschaffel, L. (2009). Proportional reasoning as a heuristic-based processs. *Experimental Psychology, 56,* 92–99.

Gilligan, C. (1982). *In a different voice.* Cambridge, MA: Harvard University Press.

Gillihan, S. J., & Farah, M. J. (2005). Is self special? A critical review of evidence from experimental psychology and cognitive neuroscience. *Psychological Bulletin, 131,* 76–97.

Gil-Mohapel, J., Simpson, J. M., Titerness, A. K., & Christie, B. R. (2010). Characterization of the neurogenesis quiet zone in the rodent brain: Effects on age and exercise. *European Journal of Neuroscience, 31,* 797–807.

Giltay, E. J., Zitman, F. G., & Kromhout, D. (2006). Dispositional optimism and the risk of depressive symptoms during 15 years of follow-up: The Zutphen Elderly Study. *Journal of Affective Disorders, 91,* 45–52.

Gino, F., Ayal, S., & Ariely, D. (2009). Contagion and differentiation in unethical behavior: The effect of one bad apple on the barrel. *Psychological Science, 20,* 393–398.

Gittelman, M. (2008). Editor's introduction: Why are the mentally ill dying? *International Journal of Mental Health, 37,* 3–12.

Glaser, R., & Kiecolt-Glaser, J. K. (2005). Stress-induced immune dysfunction: Implications for health. *Nature Reviews: Immunology, 5,* 243–251.

Glaw, X. M., Garrick, T. M., Terwee, P. J., Patching, J. R., Blake, H., & Harper, C. (2009). Brain donation: Who and why? *Cell and Tissue Banking, 10* (3), 241–246.

Glenn, D. (2010, February 5). Divided attention. *Chronicle of Higher Education, 56,* B5–B8.

Go, C. L., Raosales, R. L., Caraos, R. J., & Fernandez, H. H. (2009). The current prevalence and factors associated with tardive dyskinesia among Filipino schizophrenic patients. *Parkinsonism and Related Disorders, 15* (9), 655–659.

Gobet, F., & Clarkson, G. (2004). Chunks in expert memory: Evidence for the magical number four . . . or is it two? *Memory, 12,* 732–747.

Godden, D. R., & Baddeley, A. D. (1975). Context-dependent memory in two natural environments: On land and under water. *British Journal of Psychology, 66,* 325–331.

Goebel, M. U., Trebst, A. E., Steiner, J., Xie, Y. F., Exton, M. S., and others. (2002). Behavioral conditioning of immunosuppression is possible in humans. *Federation of American Societies for Experimental Biology Journal, 16,* 1869–1873.

Goel, N., & others. (2009). Circadian rhythm profiles in women with night eating syndrome. *Journal of Biological Rhythms, 24,* 85–94.

Goethals, G. R., & Demorest, A. P. (1995). The risky shift is a sure bet. In M. E. Ware & D. E. Johnson (Eds.), *Demonstrations and activities in teaching of psychology* (vol. 3). Mahwah, NJ: Erlbaum.

Gogtay, N., & Thompson, P. M. (2010). Mapping gray matter development: Implications for typical development and vulnerability to psychopathology. *Brain and Cognition, 72,* 6–15.

Goldberg, A., & Adriano, J. (2008, June 27). "I'm a girl"—Understanding transgender children: Parents of transgender 6 year old support her choice. ABC News. http://abcnews.go.com/2020/story?id=5261464&page=1 (accessed January 10, 2010)

Goldberg, L. R., & Digman, J. M. (1994). Revealing structure in the data: Principles of exploratory factor analysis. In S. Strack & M. Lorr (Eds.), *Differentiating normal and abnormal personality* (pp. 216–242). New York: Springer.

Goldberg, R. (2010). *Drugs across the spectrum* (6th ed.). Boston: Cengage.

Goldfield, B. A., & Snow, C. E. (2009). Individual differences: Implications for the study of language acquisition. In J. Berko Gleason & N. Ratner (Eds.), *The development of language* (7th ed.). Boston: Allyn & Bacon.

Goldin, P., Ramel, W., & Gross, J. (2009). Mindfulness meditation training and self-referential processing in social anxiety disorder: Behavioral and neural effects. *Journal of Cognitive Psychotherapy, 23,* 242–257.

Goldman, S. E., & others. (2008). Sleep problems associated with daytime fatigue in community-dwelling older individuals. *Journals of Gerontology A: Biological Sciences and Medical Sciences, 63,* 1069–1075.

Goldschmidt, L., Richardson, G. A., Willford, J., & Day, N. L. (2008). Prenatal marijuana exposure and intelligence test performance at age 6. *Journal of the American Academy of Child and Adolescent Psychiatry, 47,* 254–263.

Goldsmith, H. H. (2011). Human development: Biological and genetic processes in development. *Annual Review of Psychology* (vol. 62). Palo Alto, CA: Annual Reviews.

Goldstein, E. B. (2010). *Sensation and perception* (8th ed.). Boston: Cengage.

Goldstein, J. M., Seidman, L. J., Horton, N. J., Makris, N., Kennedy, D. N., Caviness, C., Faraone, S. V. & Tsuang, M. T. (2001). Normal sexual dimorphism of the adult human brain assessed by *in vivo* magnetic resonance imaging. *Cerebral Cortex, 11,* 490–497.

Goldstein, R., & Reynolds, C. R. (Eds.). (1999). *Handbook of neurodevelopmental and genetic disorders in children.* New York: Guilford.

Goldston, D. B., Molock, S. D., Whibeck, L. B., Murakami, J. L., Zayas, L. H., & Hall, G. C. (2008). Cultural considerations in adolescent suicide prevention and psychosocial treatment. *American Psychologist, 63,* 14–31.

Goldstrom, I. D., Campbell, J., Rogers, J. A., Lambert, D. B., Blacklow, B., Henderson, M. J., & Manderscheid, R. W. (2006). National estimates for mental health mutual support groups, self-help organizations, and consumer-operated services. *Administration and Policy in Mental Health, 33,* 92–103.

Goleman, D., Kaufman, P., & Ray, M. (1993). *The creative mind.* New York: Plume.

Golombok, S., Perry, B., Burston, A., Murray, C., Mooney-Somers, J., Stevens, M., & Golding, J. (2003). Children with lesbian parents: A community study. *Developmental Psychology, 39,* 20–33.

Golombok, S., & Tasker, F. (1996). Do parents influence the sexual orientation of their children? Findings from a longitudinal study of lesbian families. *Developmental Psychology, 32,* 3–11.

Gonda, X., & others. (2009). Association of the s allele of the 5-HTTLPR with neuroticism-related traits and temperaments in a psychiatrically healthy population. *European Archives of Psychiatry and Clinical Neuroscience, 259,* 106–113.

Gonzales-Backen, M. A., & Umana-Taylor, A. J. (2010). Examining the role of physical appearance in Latino adolescents' ethnic identity. *Journal of Adolescence.* (in press)

Gonzalez-Maeso, J., & Sealfon, S. C. (2009). Psychedelics and schizophrenia. *Trends in Neuroscience, 32,* 225–232.

Gonzalez-Vallejo, C., Lassiter, G. D., Bellezza, F. S., & Lindberg, M. J. (2008). "Save angels perhaps": A critical examination of unconscious thought theory and the deliberation-without-attention effect. *Review of General Psychology, 12,* 282–296.

Goodnow, J. J. (2010). Culture. In M. H. Bornstein (Ed.), *Handbook of cultural developmental science.* New York: Psychology Press.

Goodwin, R. D., & Cowles, R. A. (2008). Household smoking and childhood asthma in the United States: A state-level analysis. *Journal of Asthma, 45,* 607–610.

Gorin, A., Phelan, S., Wing, R. R., & Hill, J. O. (2004). Promoting long-term weight control: Does dieting consistency matter? *International Journal of Obesity Related Metabolic Disorder, 28,* 278–281.

Gormley, B., & Lopez, F. G. (2010). Authoritarian and homophobic attitudes: Gender and adult attachment style differences. *Journal of Homosexuality, 57,* 525–538.

Gosling, S. D. (2008). Personality in nonhuman animals. *Social and Personality Psychology Compass, 2,* 985–1001.

Gosling, S. D. (2008a). *Snoop: What your stuff says about you.* New York: Basic.

Gosling, S. D., & John, O. P. (1999). Personality dimensions in nonhuman animals: A cross-species review. *Current Directions in Psychological Science, 8,* 69–75.

Gosling, S. D., Kwan, V. S. Y., & John, O. (2003). A dog's got personality: A cross-species comparison of personality judgments in dogs and humans. *Journal of Personality and Social Psychology, 85,* 1161–1169.

Gosling, S. D., Rentfrow, P. J., & Swann, W. B. (2003). A very brief measure of the Big-Five personality domains. *Journal of Research in Personality, 37,* 504–528.

Gotthold, J. J. (2009). Peeling the onion: Understanding layers of treatment. *Annals of the New York Academy of Sciences, 1159,* 301–312.

Gottlieb, G. (2007). Probabilistic epigenesis. *Developmental Science, 10,* 1–11.

Gottman, J. M. (1994). *What predicts divorce?* Mahwah, NJ: Erlbaum.

Gottman, J. M. (2006, April 29). Secrets of long term love. *New Scientist, 2549,* 40.

Gottman, J. M., Gottman, J. S., & Declaire, J. (2006). *10 lessons to transform your marriage: America's love lab experts share their strategies for strengthening your relationship.* New York: Random House.

Gottman, J. M., Levenson, R. W., Swanson, C., Swanson, K., Tyson, R., & Yoshimoto, D. (2003). Observing gay, lesbian and heterosexual couples' relationships: Mathematical modeling of conflict interaction. *Journal of Homosexuality, 45,* 65–91.

Gouin, J. P., Hantsoo, L., & Kiecolt-Glaser, J. K. (2008). Immune dysregulation and chronic stress among older adults: A review. *Neuro-immunomodulation, 15,* 251–259.

Gould, E., Reeves, A. J., Graziano, M. S., & Gross, C. G. (1999). Neurogenesis in the neocortex of adult primates. *Science, 286* (1), 548–552.

Gouzoulis-Mayfrank, E., & Daumann, J. (2009). Neurotoxicity of drugs of abuse—the case of methylenedioxyamphetamines (MDMA, ecstasy), and amphetamines. *Dialogues in Clinical Neuroscience, 11,* 305–317.

Graber, J. A. (2007). Pubertal and neuroendocrine development and risk for depressive disorders. In N. B. Allen & L. Sheeber (Eds.), *Adolescent emotional development and the emergence of depressive disorders.* New York: Cambridge University Press.

Graber, J. A., Brooks-Gunn, J., & Warren, M. P. (2006). Pubertal effects on adjustment in girls: Moving from demonstrating effects to identifying pathways. *Journal of Youth and Adolescence, 35,* 391–401.

Graber, J. A., & Sontag, L. M. (2009). Internalizing problems during adolescence. In R. M. Lerner & L. Steinberg (Eds.), *Handbook of adolescent psychology* (3rd ed.). New York: Wiley.

Grady, C. L. (2008). Cognitive neuroscience of aging. *Annals of the New York Academy of Sciences, 1124,* 127–144.

Graffin, N. F., Ray, W. J., & Lundy, R. (1995). EEG concomitants of hypnosis and hypnotic susceptibility. *Journal of Abnormal Psychology, 104,* 123–131.

Graham, J. E., Christian, L. M., & Kiecolt-Glaser, J. K. (2006). Stress, age, and immune function: Toward a lifespan approach. *Journal of Behavioral Medicine, 29,* 389–400.

Grandey, A. A., Kern, J. H., & Frone, M. R. (2007). Verbal abuse from outsiders versus insiders: Comparing frequency, impact on emotional exhaustion, and the role of emotional labor. *Journal of Occupational Health Psychology, 12,* 63–79.

Grandin, T. (1995/2006). *Thinking in pictures: My life with autism* (expanded ed.). New York: Random House.

Grant, A. M., & Wrzesniewski, A. (2010). I won't let you down . . . or will I? Core self-evaluations, other orientation, anticipated guilt, and gratitude, and job performance. *Journal of Applied Psychology, 95,* 108–121.

Grant, B. F., Stinson, F. S., Dawson, D. A., Chou, P., Dufour, M. C., Compton, W., Pickering, R. P., & Kaplan, K. (2004). Prevalence and co-occurrence of substance use disorders and independent mood and anxiety disorders: Results from the national epidemiologic survey on alcohol and related conditions. *Archives of General Psychiatry, 61,* 807–816.

Gravetter, F. J. (2009). *Research methods for the behavioral sciences* (3rd ed.). Belmont, CA: Wadsworth.

Gray, J. (2004). *Men are from Mars, Women are from Venus.* New York: HarperCollins.

Gray, J. A. (1987). *The psychology of fear and stress.* Cambridge, U.K.: Cambridge University Press.

Gray, J. A., & McNaughton, N. (2000). *The neuropsychology of anxiety: An enquiry into the functions of the septo-hippocampal system.* Oxford, U.K.: Oxford University Press.

Graziano, A. M., & Raulin, M. L. (2010). *Research methods* (7th ed.). Boston: Allyn & Bacon.

Graziano, W. G., & Habashi, M. M. (2010). Motivational processes underlying both prejudice and helping. *Personality and Social Psychology Review.* (in press)

Grealish, S., Johnsson, M. E., Li, M., Kirik, D., Bjorklund, A., & Thompson, L. H. (2010). The A9 dopamine neuron component in grafts of ventral mesencephalon is an important determinant for recovery of motor function in a rat model of Parkinson's disease. *Brain.* (in press)

Green, J. P., Page, R. A., Handley, G. W., & Rasekhy, R. (2005). The "hidden observer" and ideomotor responding: A real–simulator comparison. *Contemporary Hypnosis, 22,* 123–137.

Green, R. (1987). *The "sissy boy syndrome" and the development of homosexuality.* New Haven, CT: Yale University Press.

Green, R. J., Bettinger, M., & Zacks, E. (1996). Are lesbian couples fused and gay male couples disengaged? Questioning gender straitjackets. In J. Laird & R. J. Green (Eds.), *Lesbian and gays in couples and families: A handbook for therapists* (pp. 185–230). New York: Jossey-Bass.

Greene, R. L. (1999). Applied memory research: How far from bankruptcy? *Contemporary Psychology, 44,* 29–31.

Greenfield, P. M. (2009). Linking social change and developmental change: Shifting pathways of human development. *Developmental Psychology, 43,* 401–418.

Greenfield, R. (2006). *Timothy Leary: A biography.* New York: Harcourt.

Greenwald, A. G., Poehlman, T. A., Uhlmann, E., & Banaji, M. R. (2009). Understanding and using the Implicit Association Test: III. Meta-analysis of predictive validity. *Journal of Personality and Social Psychology, 97,* 17–41.

Greeson, J. M., Lewis, J. G., Achanzar, K., Zimmerman, E., Young, K. H., & Suarez, E. C. (2009). Stress-induced changes in the expression of monocytic beta-2-integrins: The impact of arousal of negative affect and adrenergic responses to the Anger Recall interview. *Brain, Behavior, and Immunity, 23,* 251–256.

Gregg, A. P., & Sedikides, C. (2010). Narcissistic fragility: Rethinking its link to explicit and implicit self-esteem. *Self and Identity, 9,* 142–146.

Gregory, R. J. (2011). *Psychological testing* (6th ed.). Upper Saddle River, NJ: Pearson.

Greitemeyer, T. (2009). Effects of songs with prosocial lyrics on prosocial thoughts, affect, and behavior. *Journal of Experimental Social Psychology, 45,* 186–190.

Greitemeyer, T., & Osswald, S. (2010). Effects of prosocial video games on prosocial behavior. *Journal of Personality and Social Psychology, 98,* 211–221.

Grewen, K. M., Davenport, R. E., & Light, K. C. (2010). An investigation of plasma and salivary oxytocin responses in breast- and formula-feeding mothers of infants. *Psychophysiology.* (in press)

Griffin, M. A., & Clarke, S. (2010). Stress and well-being at work. In S. Zedeck (Ed.), *APA handbook of industrial and organizational psychology.* Washington, DC: APA. (in press)

Griffin, R. W., & Lopez, Y. P. (2005). "Bad behavior" in organizations: A review and typology for future research. *Journal of Management, 31,* 988–1005.

Griffin, R. W., & Moorhead, G. (2010). *Organizational behavior* (9th ed.). Boston: Cengage.

Grigorenko, E., & Takanishi, R. (2010). *Immigration, diversity, and education.* New York: Routledge.

Grigorenko, E. L., Jarvin, L., Tan, M., & Sternberg, R. J. (2008). Something new in the garden: Assessing creativity in academic domains. *Psychology Science Quarterly, 50,* 295–307.

Grilo, C. M., Masheb, R. M., & White, M. A. (2010). Significance of overvaluation of shape/weight in binge-eating disorder: Comparative study with overweight and bulimia nervosa. *Obesity, 18,* 499–504.

Grinspoon, L. (1994). *Marihuana reconsidered.* Cambridge, MA: Harvard University Press.

Grippo, A. J., & Johnson, A. K. (2009). Stress, depression, and cardiovascular dysregulation: A review of neurobiological mechanisms and the integration of research from preclinical disease models. *Stress, 12,* 1–21.

Groenewould, J. H., & others. (2010). Rotterdam Amblyopia Screening Effectiveness Study: Detection and causes of amblyopia in a large birth cohort. *Investigative Ophthalmology & Visual Science.* (in press)

Gronlund, N. E. (2006). *Assessment of student achievement* (8th ed.). Boston: Allyn & Bacon.

Grosse, S. D. (2010). Late-treated phenylketonuria and partial reversibility of intellectual impairment. *Child Development, 81,* 200–211.

Grossi, E., Buscema, M. P., Snowdon, D., & Antuono, P. (2007). Neuropathological findings processed by artificial neural networks (ANNs) can perfectly distinguish Alzheimer's patients from controls in the Nun Study. *BMC Neurology, 7,* 15.

Grossman, I., Na, J., Varnum, M. E. W., Park, D. C., Kitayama, S., & Nisbett, R. E. (2010). Reasoning about social conflicts improves into old age. *Proceedings of the National Academy of Science.* (in press)

Grubin, D., & Madsen, L. (2006). Accuracy and utility of post-conviction polygraph testing of sex offenders. *British Journal of Psychiatry, 188,* 479–483.

Grusec, J. E. (2009). Unpublished review of J. W. Santrock's *Child Development* (13th ed.). New York: McGraw-Hill.

Grusec, J. E. (2011). Human development: Development in the family. *Annual Review of Psychology* (vol. 62). Palo Alto, CA: Annual Reviews.

Guérard, K., Tremblay, S., & Saint-Aubin, J. (2009). The processing of spatial information in short-term memory: Insights from eye-tracking the path length effect. *Acta Psychologica.* (in press)

Guerrini, I., Thomson, A. D., & Gurling, H. M. (2009). Molecular genetics of alcohol-related brain damage. *Alcohol and Alcoholism, 44,* 166–170.

Gueta, R., Barlam, D., Shneck, R. Z., & Rousso, I. (2006). Measurement of the mechanical properties of isolated tectorial membrane using atomic force microscopy. *Proceedings of the National Academy of Sciences USA, 103,* 14790–14795.

Gulwadi, B. (2006). Seeking restorative experiences: Elementary school teachers' choices for places that enable coping with stress. *Environment and Behavior, 38,* 503–520.

Gump, B., & Matthews, K. (2000, March). Are vacations good for your health? The 9-year mortality experience after the multiple risk factor intervention trial. *Psychosomatic Medicine, 62,* 608–612.

Gunderson, J. (2008). Borderline personality disorder: An overview. *Social Work in Mental Health, 6,* 5–12.

Gunderson, J. G., Bender, D., Sanislow, C., Yen, S., Rettew, J. B., Dolan-Sewell, R., Dyck, I., Morey, L. C., McGlashan, T. H., Shea, M. T., & Skodol, A. E. (2003). Plausibility and possible determinants of sudden "remissions" in borderline patients. *Psychiatry: Interpersonal and Biological Processes, 66,* 111–119.

Guo, Q., Johnson, C. A., Unger, J. B., Lee, L., Xie, B., Chou, C. P., Palmer, P. H., Sun, P., Gallaher, P., & Pentz, M. (2007). Utility of theory of reasoned action and theory of planned behavior for predicting Chinese adolescent smoking. *Addictive Behaviors, 32,* 1066–1081.

Guo, Y. (2005). Filial therapy for children's behavioral and emotional problems in mainland China. *Journal of Child and Adolescent Psychiatric Nursing, 18,* 171–180.

Gurung, R. A. R. (2010). *Health psychology* (2nd ed.). Boston: Cengage.

Guttmacher Institute. (2010, January). *Facts on American teens' sexual and reproductive health.* Washington, DC: Author.

Guttman, N., & Kalish, H. I. (1956). Discriminability and stimulus generalization. *Journal of Experimental Psychology, 51,* 79–88.

Gwaltney, C. J., Metrik, J., Kahler, C. W., & Shiffman, S. (2009). Self-efficacy and smoking cessation: A meta-analysis. *Psychology of Addictive Behaviors, 23,* 56–66.

Gwernan-Jones, R., & Burden, R. L. (2010). Are they just lazy? Student teachers' attitudes about dyslexia. *Dyslexia: An International Journal of Research and Practice, 16,* 66–86.

Gynther, L. M., Hewitt, J. K., Heath, A. C., & Eaves, L. J. (1999). Phenotypic and genetic factors in motives for smoking. *Behavior Genetics, 29,* 291–302.

H

Haas, B. W., Omura, K., Constable, R. T., & Canli, T. (2007). Emotional conflict and neuroticism: Personality-dependent activation in the amygdala and subgenual anterior cingulate. *Behavioral Neuroscience, 121,* 249–256.

Habbal, O. A., & Al-Jabri, A. A. (2009). Circadian rhythm and the immune system: A review. *International Reviews of Immunology, 28,* 93–108.

Habeck, C., Rakitin, B. C., Moeller, J., Scarmeas, N., Zarahn, E., Brown, T., & Stern, Y. (2004). An event-related fMRI study of the neuro-behavioral impact of sleep deprivation on performance of a delayed-match-to-sample task. *Brain Research, 18,* 306–321.

Hackett, G. I. (2008). Disorders of male sexual desire. In D. L. Rowland & L. Incrocci (Eds.), *Handbook of sexual and gender identity disorders* (pp. 5–29). Hoboken, NJ: Wiley.

Hagadorn, J. A., & Seilacher. A. (2009). Hermit arthropods 500 million years ago? *Geology, 37,* 295–298.

Hagenauer, M. H., Perryman, J. L., Lee, T. M., & Carskadon, M. A. (2009). Adolescent changes in homeostatic and circadian regulation of sleep. *Developmental Neuroscience, 31,* 276–284.

Hagerman, R. J. (2009). Fragile X syndrome and associated disorders in adulthood. *CONTINUUM: Lifelong Learning in Neurology, 15,* 32–49.

Hagg, T. (2009). From neurotransmitters to neurotrophic factors to neurogenesis. *Neuroscientist, 15,* 20–27.

Hagner, M. (2007). Mind reading, brain mirror, neuroimaging: Insight into the brain or the mind? In M. Ash & T. Sturm (Eds.), *Psychology's territories.* Mahwah, NJ: Erlbaum.

Hahn, D. B., Payne, W. A., & Lucas, E. B. (2007). *Focus on health* (8th ed.). New York: McGraw-Hill.

Halberstadt, J. (2010). Dumb but lucky: Fortuitous affect cues and their disruption by analytic thought. *Social and Personality Psychology Compass, 4,* 64–76.

Hald, G. M., Malamuth, N. M., & Yuen, C. (2010). Pornography and attitudes supporting violence against women: Revisiting the relationship in nonexperimental studies. *Aggressive Behavior, 36,* 14–20.

Hales, D. (2011). *An invitation to health* (14th ed.). Boston: Cengage.

Halgunseth, L. C., Ispa, J. M., & Rudy, D. (2006). Parental control in Latino families: An integrated review of the literature. *Child Development, 77,* 1282–1297.

Hall, B. J., & others. (2010). Exploring the association between posttraumatic growth and PTSD: A national study of Jews and Arabs following the 2006 Israeli-Hezbollah war. *Journal of Nervous and Mental Disease, 198,* 180–186.

Hall, D. L., Matz, D. C., & Wood, W. (2010). Why don't we practice what we preach? A meta-analytic review of racism. *Personality and Social Psychology Review, 14,* 126–139.

Hall, J. A., & Matsumoto, D. (2004). Gender differences in judgments of multiple emotions from facial expressions. *Emotion, 14,* 201–206.

Hall, J. A., Park, N., Song, H., & Cody, M. J. (2010). Strategic misrepresentation in online dating: The effects of gender, self-monitoring, and personality traits. *Journal of Social and Personal Relationships, 27,* 117–135.

Hall, R. C. W., & Hall, R. C. W. (2007). A profile of pedophilia: Definition, characteristics of offenders, recidivism, treatment outcomes, and forensic issues. *Mayo Clinic Proceedings, 82,* 457–471.

Hallal, P. C., Victora, C. G., Azevedo, M. R., & Wells, J. C. (2006). Adolescent physical activity and health: A systematic review. *Sports Medicine, 36,* 1019–1030.

Halpern, D. S., Benbow, C. P., Geary, D. C., Gur, R. C., Hyde, J. S., & Gernsbacher, M. A. (2007). The science of sex differences in science and mathematics. *Psychological Science in the Public Interest, 8,* 1–51.

Halpern, J. H. (2003). Hallucinogens: An update. *Current Psychiatry Reports, 5,* 347–354.

Halpern, J. H., & Sewell, R. A. (2005). Hallucinogenic botanicals of America: A growing need for focused drug education and research. *Life Sciences, 78,* 519–526.

Halpern, J. H., Sherwood, A. R., Hudson, J. I., Yurgelun-Todd, D., & Pope, H. G. (2005). Psychological and cognitive effects of long-term peyote use among Native Americans. *Biological Psychiatry, 58,* 624–631.

Hamann, S. (2005). Sex differences in the responses of the human amygdala. *Neuroscientist, 11,* 288–293.

Hamer, M., Chida, Y., & Molloy, G. J. (2009). Psychological distress and cancer mortality. *Journal of Psychosomatic Research, 66,* 255–258.

Hamer, M., Tanaka, G., Okamura, H., Tsuda, A., & Steptoe, A. (2007). The effects of depressive symptoms on cardiovascular and catecholamine responses to the induction of depressive mood. *Biological Psychology, 74,* 20–25.

Hammad, T. A. (2004, September 13). *Results of the analysis of suicidality in pediatric trials of newer antidepressants.* Presentation at the U.S. Food and Drug Administration, Psychopharmacologic Drugs Advisory Committee and the Pediatric Advisory Committee. www.fda.gov/ohrms/dockets/ac/04/slides/2004-4065S1 08 FDA-Hammad files/frame.htm (accessed July 26, 2006)

Hammond, D. C. (2010). Hypnosis in the treatment of anxiety- and stress-related disorders. *Expert Review of Neurotherapeutics, 10,* 263–273.

Hammond, T. A., Laughren, T., & Racoosin, J. (2006). Suicidality in pediatric patients treated with antidepressant drugs. *Archives of General Psychiatry, 63,* 332–339.

Hampton, J. (2008). Abstinence-only programs under fire. *Journal of the American Medical Association, 17,* 2013–2015.

Handel, R. W., Ben-Porath, Y. S., Tellegen, A., & Archer, R. P. (2010). Psychometric functioning of the MMPI-2-RF VRIN-r and TRIN-r scales with varying degrees of randomness, acquiescence, and counter-acquiescence. *Psychological Assessment, 22,* 87–95.

Haney, C., & Zimbardo, P. G. (2009). Persistent dispositionalism in interactionist clothing: Fundamental attribution error in explaining prison abuse. *Personality and Social Psychology Bulletin, 35,* 807–814.

Hankin, B. L., Stone, L., & Wright, P. A. (2010). Corumination, interpersonal stress generation, and internalizing symptoms: Accumulating effects and transactional influences in a multiwave study of adolescents. *Development and Psychopathology, 22,* 217–235.

Hanley, J. R., & Chapman, E. (2008). Partial knowledge in a tip-of-the-tongue state about two- and three-word proper names. *Psychonomic Bulletin and Review, 15,* 156–160.

Hannum, R. D., Rosellini, R. A., & Seligman, M. E. P. (1976). Learned helplessness in the rat: Retention and immunization. *Developmental Psychology, 12,* 449–454.

Hanowski, R. J., Olson, R. L., Hickman, J. S., & Bocanegra, J. (2009, September). *Driver distraction in commercial vehicle operations.* Paper presented at the First International Conference on Driver Distraction and Inattention, Gothenburg, Sweden.

Hansimayr, S., Leipold, P., Pastotter, B., & Baumi, K. H. (2009). Anticipatory signatures of voluntary memory suppression. *Journal of Neuroscience, 29,* 2742–2747.

Haq, I. U., Foote, K. D., Goodman, W. G., Wu, S. S., Sudhyadhom, A., Ricciuti, N., Siddiqui, M. S., Bowers, D., Jacobson, C. E., Ward, H., & Okun, M. S. (2010). Smile and laughter induction and intraoperative predictors of response to deep brain stimulation for obsessive-compulsive disorder. *NeuroImage.* (in press)

Hardy, L., Arthur, C. A., Jones, G., Shariff, A., Munnoch, K., Isaacs, I., & Allsopp, A. J. (2010). The relationship between transformational leadership behaviors, psychological, and training outcomes in elite military recruits. *Leadership Quarterly, 21,* 20–32.

Hare, M., Jones, M., Thomson, C., Kelly, S., & McRae, K. (2009). Activating event knowledge. *Cognition, 11,* 151–167.

Harel, A., Gilaie-Dotan, S., Mlach, R., & Bentin, S. (2010). Top-down engagement modulates the neural expressions of visual expertise. *Cerebral Cortex.* (in press)

Harker, L. A., & Keltner, D. (2001). Expressions of positive emotion in women's college yearbook pictures and their relationship to personality and life outcomes across adulthood. *Journal of Personality and Social Psychology, 80,* 112–124.

Harkness, S., & Super, C. M. (1995). Culture and parenting. In M. H. Bornstein (Ed.), *Children and parenting* (vol. 2). Hillsdale, NJ: Erlbaum.

Harley, R., Sprich, S., Safren, S., Jacobo, M., & Fava, M. (2008). Adaptation of dialectical behavior therapy skills training group for treatment-resistant depression. *Journal of Nervous and Mental Disease, 196,* 136–143.

Harlow, H. F. (1958). The nature of love. *American Psychologist, 13,* 673–685.

Harms, P., Roberts, B. W., & Woods, D. D. (2007). Who shall lead? An integrative personality approach to the study of the antecedents of status in informal social organizations. *Journal of Research in Personality, 41,* 689–699.

Harms, P. D., & Crede, M. (2010). Emotional intelligence and transformational and transactional leadership: A meta-analysis. *Journal of Leadership and Organizational Studies, 17,* 5–17.

Harpaz, Y., Levkovitz, Y., & Lavidor, M. (2009). Lexical ambiguity resolution in Wernicke's area and its right homologue. *Cortex, 45,* 1097–1103.

Harris, C. B., Sutton, J., & Barnier, A. J. (2010). Autobiographical forgetting. In S. D. Sala (Ed.), *Forgetting.* New York: Psychology Press.

Harris, D. M., & Kay, J. (1995). I recognize your face but I can't remember your name: Is it because names are unique? *British Journal of Psychology, 86,* 345–358.

Harris, J. L., Brownell, K. D., & Bargh, J. A. (2010). The food marketing defense model: Integrating psychological research to protect youth and inform public policy. *Social Issues and Policy Review.* (in press)

Harris, J. R. (1998). *The nurture assumption: Why children turn out the way they do.* New York: Free Press.

Harris, J. R. (2009). *The nurture assumption* (rev. and updated edition). New York: Free Press.

Harris, M., & Grunstein, R. R. (2009). Treatments for somnambulism in adults: Assessing the evidence. *Sleep Medicine Reviews, 13,* 295–297.

Harris Interactive. (2006, October 10). *7 in 10 report knowing someone who is gay.* http://www.harrisinteractive.com/news/allnewsbydate.asp?NewsID=1099 (accessed April 2010)

Harrison, A., Jolicoeur, P., & Marois, R. (2010). "What" and "where" in the intraparietal sulcus: An fMRI study of object identity and location in visual short-term memory. *Cerebral Cortex.* (in press)

Harro, J., Merenakk, L., Nordquist, N., Konstabel, K., Comasco, E., & Oreland, L. (2009). Personality and the serotonin transporter gene: Associations in a longitudinal population-based study. *Biological Psychology, 81,* 9–13.

Harshbarger, J. L., Ahlers-Schmidt, C. R., Mayans, L., Mayans, D., & Hawkins, J. H. (2009). Pro-anorexia websites: What a clinician should know. *International Journal of Eating Disorders, 42,* 367–370.

Hart, B., & Risley, T. R. (1995). *Meaningful differences in the everyday experience of young Americans.* Baltimore: Paul H. Brookes.

Hartenbaum, N., & others. (2006). Sleep apnea and commercial motor vehicle operators. *Chest, 130,* 902–905.

Harter, S. (2006). The development of self-esteem. In M. H. Kernis (Ed.), *Self-esteem issues and* answers: A sourcebook of current perspectives (pp. 144–150). New York: Psychology Press.

Hartley, S. L., & Maclean, W. E. (2009). Depression in adults with mild intellectual disability: Role of stress, attributions, and coping. *American Journal on Intellectual and Developmental Disabilities, 114,* 147–160.

Hartmann, E. (1993). Nightmares. In M. A. Carskadon (Ed.), *Encyclopedia of sleep and dreams.* New York: Macmillan.

Hartmann, P., & Apaolaza-Ibanez, V. (2010). Beyond savanna: An evolutionary and environmental psychology approach to behavioral effects of nature scenery in green advertising. *Journal of Environmental Psychology, 30,* 119–128.

Harvey, J. L., Anderson, L. E., Baranowski, L. E., & Morath, R. (2007). Job analysis: Gathering job specific information. In D. L. Whetzel & G. R. Wheaton (Eds.), *Applied measurement.* Mahwah, NJ: Erlbaum.

Hasegawa, H., & Unuma, H. (2010). Facial features in perceived intensity of schematic facial expressions. *Perceptual and Motor Skills, 110,* 129–149.

Haselton, M. G. (2006, April 29). How to pick a perfect mate. *New Scientist, 2549,* 36.

Haslam, S. A., & Reicher, S. D. (2006). Debating the psychology of tyranny: Fundamental issues of theory, perspective and science. *British Journal of Social Psychology, 45,* 55–63.

Hassett, J. M., Siebert, E. R., & Wallen, K. (2008). Sex differences in rhesus monkey toy preferences parallel those of children. *Hormones and Behavior, 54,* 359–364.

Hatzinger, M., Brand, S., Perren, S., Stadelmann, S., von Wyl, A., von Klitzing, K., & Holsboer-Trachsler, E. (2010). Sleep actigraphy pattern and behavioral/emotional difficulties in kindergarten children: Association with hypothalamic-pituitary-adrenocortical (HPA) activity. *Journal of Psychiatric Research, 44,* 253–261.

Haviland-Jones, J., Rosario, H. H., Wilson, P., & McGuire, T. R. (2005). An environmental approach to positive emotion: Flowers. *Evolutionary Psychology, 3,* 104–132.

Hawkley, L. C., & Cacioppo, J. T. (2009). Loneliness. In M. R. Leary & R. H. Hoyle (Eds.), *Handbook of individual differences in social behavior* (pp. 227–240). New York: Guilford.

Hawkley, L. C., Preacher, K. J., & Cacioppo, J. T. (2010). Loneliness impairs daytime functioning but not sleep duration. *Health Psychology, 29,* 124–129.

Hawkley, L. C., Thisted, R. A., & Cacioppo, J. T. (2009). Loneliness predicts reduced physical activity: Cross-sectional and longitudinal analyses. *Health Psychology, 28,* 354–363.

Hawkley, L. C., Thisted, R. A., Masi, C. M., & Cacioppo, J. T. (2010). Loneliness predicts increased blood pressure: Five-year cross-lagged analyses in middle-aged and older adults. *Psychology and Aging, 25,* 132–141.

Haworth, C. M., Dale, P. S., & Plomin, R. (2009). The etiology of science performance: Decreasing heritability and increasing importance of shared

environment from 9 to 12 years of age. *Child Development, 80,* 662–673.

Hay, P. P., Bacaltchuk, J., Stefano, S., & Kashyap, P. (2009). Psychological treatments for bulimia nervosa and binging. *Cochrane Database of Systematic Reviews, 4,* CD000562.

Hayflick, L. (1977). The cellular basis for biological aging. In C. E. Finch & L. Hayflick (Eds.), *Handbook of the biology of aging.* New York: Van Nostrand.

Hazell, P. (2009). Depression in children and adolescents. *Clinical Evidence, 15,* 398–414.

Hazler, R. J. (2007). Person-centered therapy. In D. Capuzzi & D. Gross (Eds.), *Counseling and psychotherapy* (4th ed.). Upper Saddle River, NJ: Prentice-Hall.

Hazlett-Stevens, H., & Craske, M. G. (2009). Breathing retraining and diaphragmatic breathing techniques. In W. T. O'Donohue & J. E. Fisher (Eds.), *General principles and empirically supported techniques of cognitive behavior therapy* (pp. 167–172). Hoboken, NJ: Wiley.

Healy, D. (2009). Are selective serotonin reuptake inhibitors a risk factor for adolescent suicide? *Canadian Journal of Psychiatry, 54,* 69–71.

Hearold, S. (1986). A synthesis of 1043 effects of television on social behavior. In G. Comstock (Ed.), *Public communication of behavior* (pp. 65–133). San Diego: Academic.

Hebb, D. O. (1980). *Essay on mind.* Mahwah, NJ: Erlbaum.

Heckman, C. J., & Clay, D. L. (2005). Hardiness, history of abuse, and women's health. *Journal of Health Psychology, 10,* 767–777.

Hedden, T., & Yoon, C. (2006). Individual differences in executive processing predict susceptibility to interference in verbal working memory. *Neuropsychology, 20,* 511–528.

Heflick, N. A., & Goldenberg, J. L. (2009). Objectifying Sarah Palin: Evidence that objectification causes women to be perceived as less competent and less fully human. *Journal of Experimental Social Psychology, 45,* 598–601.

Hegarty, M., Canham, M. S., & Fabrikant, S. I. (2010). Thinking about the weather: How salience and knowledge affect performance in the graphic interference task. *Journal of Experimental Psychology: Learning, Memory, and Cognition, 36,* 37–53.

Hegarty, P. (2009). Toward an LGBT-informed paradigm for children who break gender norms: A comment on Drummond, et al., (2008) and Rieger et al., (2008). *Developmental Psychology, 45,* 895–900.

Heidelbaugh, J. J. (2010). Management of erectile dysfunction. *American Family Physician, 81,* 305–312.

Heider, F. (1958). *The psychology of interpersonal relations.* Hoboken, NJ: Wiley.

Heiman, G. W. (2011). *Basic statistics for the behavioral sciences* (6th ed.). Boston: Cengage.

Heine, S. J. (2005). Constructing good selves in Japan and North America. In R. M. Sorrentino, D. Cohen, J. M. Olson, & M. P. Zanna (Eds.), *Cultural and social behavior: The Ontario symposium* (vol. 10, pp. 95–116). Mahwah, NJ: Erlbaum.

Heine, S. J., & Buchtel, E. E. (2009). Personality: The universal and the culturally specific. *Annual Review of Psychology* (vol. 60). Palo Alto, CA: Annual Reviews.

Heine, S. J., & Hamamura, T. (2007). In search of East Asian self-enhancement. *Personality and Social Psychology Review, 11,* 1–24.

Heine, S. J., Lehman, D. R., Markus, H. R., & Kitayama, S. (1999). Is there a universal need for positive self-regard? *Psychological Review, 106,* 766–794.

Heine, S. J., & Raineri, A. (2009). Self-improving motivations and collectivism: The case of Chileans. *Journal of Cross-Cultural Psychology, 40,* 158–163.

Helgeson, V. S. (1994). Relation of agency and communion to well-being: Evidence and potential explanations. *Psychological Bulletin, 116,* 412–428.

Heller, A. C., Amar, A. P., Liu, C. Y., & Apuzzo, M. L. (2006). Surgery of the mind and mood: A mosaic of issues in time and evolution. *Neurosurgery, 59,* 720–733.

Hellriegel, D., & Slocum, J. W. (2011). *Organizational behavior* (13th ed.). Boston: Cengage.

Helson, R., & Soto, C. J. (2005). Up and down in middle age: Monotonic and nonmonotonic changes in roles, status, and personality. *Journal of Personality and Social Psychology, 89,* 194–204.

Helson, R., Soto, C. J., & Cate, R. A. (2006). From young adulthood through the middle ages. In D. K. Mroczek & T. D. Little (Eds.), *Handbook of personality development.* Mahwah, NJ: Erlbaum.

Hemmer, P., & Steyvers, M. (2009). Integrating episodic memories and prior knowledge at multiple levels of abstraction. *Psychonomic Bulletin and Review, 16,* 80–87.

Henderson, M. (2008, February 18). Welcome to the town that will make you lose weight. *Times Online.* http://www.timesonline.co.uk/tol/news/uk/health/article3386817.ece

Hendrick, C., & Hendrick, S. S. (2006). Styles of romantic love. In R. J. Sternberg & K. Weis (Eds.), *The new psychology of love* (pp. 149–170). New Haven, CT: Yale University Press.

Hendrick, C., & Hendrick, S. S. (2009). Love. In S. Lopez & C. R. Snyder (Eds.), *Oxford handbook of positive psychology* (2nd ed., pp. 447–454). New York: Oxford University Press.

Hendricks, J., & Hatch, L. R. (2006). Lifestyle and aging. In R. H. Binstock & L. K. George (Eds.), *Handbook of aging and the social sciences* (6th ed.). San Diego: Academic.

Henrich, J., Ensminger, J., McElreath, R., Barr, A., Barrett, C., Bolyanatz, A., Cardenas, J. C., Gurven, M., Gwako, E., Henrich, N., Lesorogoi, C., Marlowe, F., Tracer, D., & Ziker, J. (2010). Markets, religion, community size, and the evolution of fairness and punishment. *Science, 327,* 1480–1484.

Hepper, E. G., & Sedikides, C. (2010). Self-enhancing feedback. In R. Sutton, M. Hornsey, & K. Douglas (Eds.), *Feedback: The handbook of praise, criticism, and advice.* Bern, Switzerland: Peter Lang. (in press)

Hepple, R. T. (2009). Why eating less keeps mitochondria working in aged skeletal muscle. *Exercise and Sport Sciences Reviews, 37,* 23–38.

Hepting, U., & Solle, R. (1973). Sex-specific differences in color coding. *Archiv fur Psychologie, 125* (2–3), 184–202.

Herbert, J. (1988). The physiology of aggression. In J. Groebel & R. Hinde (Eds.), *Aggression and war: The biological and social bases.* New York: Cambridge University Press.

Herek, G. M. (1991). Stigma, prejudice, and violence against lesbians and gay men. In J. Gonsiorek & J. Weinrich (Eds.), *Homosexuality: Research implications for public policy* (pp. 60–80). Newbury Park, CA: Sage.

Hering, E. (1878). *Zur Lehre vom Lichtsinne* (illustration, 2nd ed.). Wien: C. Gerold's Sohn.

Herlihy, B., & McCollum, V. (2007). Feminist theory. In D. Capuzzi & D. Gross (Eds.), *Counseling and psychotherapy* (4th ed.). Upper Saddle River, NJ: Prentice-Hall.

Hernandez, P., Siegel, A., & Almeida, R. (2009). The cultural context model: How does it facilitate couples' therapeutic change? *Journal of Marital and Family Therapy, 35,* 97–110.

Hernstein, R. J. (2009). Selection by consequences. In D. Shanks (Ed.), *Psychology of learning.* Thousand Oaks, CA: Sage.

Herry, C., Bach, D. R., Esposito, F., Di Salle, F., Perrig, W. J., Scheffler, K., Luthi, A., & Seifritz, E. (2007). Processing of temporal unpredictability in human and animal amygdala. *Journal of Neuroscience, 27,* 5958–5966.

Hersen, M., & A. M. Gross, A. M. (Eds.). (2008). *Handbook of clinical psychology, vol 2: Children and adolescents.* Hoboken, NJ: Wiley.

Herz, R. S. (1998). Are odors the best cues to memory? A cross-modal comparison of associative memory stimuli. *Annals of the New York Academy of Sciences, 855,* 670–674.

Herz, R. S. (2004). A naturalistic analysis of autobiographical memories triggered by olfactory, visual, and auditory stimuli. *Chemical Senses, 29,* 217–224.

Herz, R. S., & Cupchik, G. C. (1995). The emotional distinctiveness of odor-evoked memories. *Chemical Senses, 20,* 517–528.

Herz, R. S., Schankler, C., & Beland, S. (2004). Olfaction, emotion and associative learning: Effects on motivated behavior. *Motivation and Emotion, 28,* 363–383.

Herzog, H. (2006). Forty-two thousand and one Dalmatians: Fads, social contagion, and dog breed popularity. *Society & Animals, 14,* 383–397.

Hess, E., & Cameron, K. S. (2006). *Developing management skills* (6th ed.). Upper Saddle River, NJ: Prentice-Hall.

Hess, Y. D., & Pickett, C. L. (2010). Social rejection and self- versus other-awareness. *Journal of Experimental Social Psychology, 46,* 453–456.

Hetherington, E. M. (2006). The influence of conflict, marital problem solving, and parenting on children's adjustment in nondivorced, divorced, and remarried families. In A. Clarke-Stewart &

J. Dunn (Eds.), *Families count.* New York: Cambridge University Press.

Hetherington, E. M., & Stanley-Hagan, M. (2002). Parenting in divorced and remarried families. In M. Bornstein (Ed.), *Handbook of parenting* (2nd ed.). Mahwah, NJ: Erlbaum.

Hewlin, P. F. (2009). Wearing the cloak: Antecedents and consequences of creating facades of conformity. *Journal of Applied Psychology, 94,* 727–741.

Hibbard, S., Porcerelli, J., Kamoo, R., Schwartz, M., & Abell, S. (2010). Defense and object relational maturity on thematic apperception test scales indicate levels of personality organization. *Journal of Personality Assessment, 92,* 241–253.

Hickok, G. (2010). The role of mirror neurons in speech and language processing. *Brain and Language, 112,* 1–2.

Hicks, J. A, Cicero, D. C., Trent, J., Burton, C. M., & King, L. A. (2010). Positive affect, intuition, and the feeling of meaning. *Journal of Personality and Social Psychology.* (in press)

Higham, P. A., Perfect, T. J., & Bruno, D. (2009). Investigating strength and frequency effects in recognition memory using type-2 signal detection theory. *Experimental Psychology: Learning, Memory, and Cognition, 35,* 57–80.

Hilgard, E. R. (1977). *Divided consciousness: Multiple controls in human thought and action.* New York: Wiley.

Hilgard, E. R. (1992). Dissociation and theories of hypnosis. In E. Fromm & M. R. Nash (Eds.), *Contemporary hypnosis research.* New York: Guilford.

Hill, C. E. (2000). Client-centered therapy. In A. Kazdin (Ed.), *Encyclopedia of psychology.* Washington, DC, & New York: American Psychological Association and Oxford University Press.

Hill, T. D., Burdette, A. M., Ellison, C. G., & Musick, M. A. (2006). Religious attendance and the health behaviors of Texas adults. *Preventive Medicine: An International Journal Devoted to Practice and Theory, 42,* 309–312.

Hillman, C. H., Erickson, K. I., & Kramer. A. F. (2008). Be smart, exercise your heart: Exercise effects on the brain and cognition. *Nature Reviews: Neuroscience, 9,* 58–65.

Hingson, R. W., Heeren, T., & Winter, M. R. (2006). Age at drinking onset and alcohol dependence: Age of onset, duration, and severity. *Archives of Pediatric and Adolescent Medicine, 160,* 739–746.

Hinshaw, S. P. (2007). *The mark of shame: Stigma of mental illness and an agenda for change.* New York: Oxford University Press.

Hirata, A., & Castro-Alamancos, M. A. (2010). Neocortex network activation and deactivation states controlled by the thalamus. *Journal of Neurophysiology.* (in press)

Hirsch, I. (2010). Discussion: On some contributions of the interpersonal tradition to contemporary psychoanalytic praxis. *American Journal of Psychoanalysis, 70,* 86–93.

Hirsch, J. K., Wolford, K., Lalonde, S. M., Brunk, L., & Parker-Morris, A. (2009). Optimistic explanatory style as a moderator

between negative life events and suicide ideation. *Crisis, 30,* 48–53.

Hnasko, T. S., & others. (2010). Vesicular glutamate transport promotes dopamine storage and glutamate corelease in vivo. *Neuron, 65,* 643–656.

Ho, R. C., Neo, L. F., Chua, A. N., Cheak, A. A., & Mak, A. (2010). Research on psychoneuroimmunology: Does stress influence immunity and cause coronary artery disease? *Annals of the Academy of Medicine, Singapore, 39,* 191–196.

Hobson, J. A. (1999). Dreams. In R. Conlan (Ed.), *States of mind.* New York: Wiley.

Hobson, J. A. (2000). Dreams: Physiology. In A. Kazdin (Ed.), *Encyclopedia of psychology.* Washington, DC, and New York: American Psychological Association and Oxford University Press.

Hobson, J. A. (2002). *Dreaming.* New York: Oxford University Press.

Hobson, J. A. (2004). Freud returns? Like a bad dream. *Scientific American, 290,* 89.

Hobson, J. A., Pace-Schott, E. F., & Stickgold, R. (2000). Dreaming and the brain. *Behavior and Brain Sciences, 23,* 793–842.

Hodges, T. D., & Clifton, D. O. (2004). Strengths-based development in practice. In A. Linley & S. Joseph (Eds.), *Positive psychology in practice* (pp. 256–268). Hoboken, NJ: Wiley.

Hodgins, D. C. (2005). Weighing the pros and cons of changing change models: A comment on West (2005). *Addiction, 100,* 1042–1043.

Hodgson, T. L., Parris, B. A., Gregory, N. J., & Jarvis, T. (2009). The saccadic Stroop effect: Evidence for involuntary programming of eye movements by linguistic cues. *Vision Research, 49,* 569–574.

Hoek, H. W. (2006). Incidence, prevalence and mortality of anorexia nervosa and other eating disorders. *Current Opinion in Psychiatry, 19,* 389–394.

Hoffman, I. Z. (2006). The myths of free association and the potentials of the analytic relationship. *International Journal of Psychoanalysis, 87,* 43–61.

Hoffman, J. P. (2009). Drug use, adolescent. In D. Carr (Ed.), *Encyclopedia of the life course and human development.* Boston: Cengage.

Hogan, E. H., Hornick, B. A., & Bouchoux, A. (2002). Focus on communications: Communicating the message: Clarifying the controversies about caffeine. *Nutrition Today, 37,* 28–35.

Hogan, R. (2006). *Personality and the fate of organizations.* Mahwah, NJ: Erlbaum.

Hogan, R. (2009). Much ado about nothing. *Journal of Research in Personality, 43,* 249.

Hogg, M. A., & Abrams, D. (2007). Intergroup behavior and social identity. In M. A. Hogg & J. Cooper (Eds.), *The Sage handbook of social psychology* (concise 2nd ed.). Thousand Oaks, CA: Sage.

Hogh, A., Henriksson, M. E., & Burr, H. (2005). A 5-year follow-up study of aggression at work and psychological health. *International Journal of Behavioral Medicine, 12,* 256–265.

Holland, P. C. (1996). The effects of intertrial and feature-target intervals on operant serial feature-positive discrimination learning. *Animal Learning & Behavior, 24,* 411–428.

Hollich, G. J., & Huston, D. M. (2007). Language development: From speech to first words. In A. Slater & M. Lewis (Eds.), *Introduction to infant development* (2nd ed.). New York: Oxford University Press.

Holliday, E. G., & others. (2009). Strong evidence for a novel schizophrenia risk locus on chromosome 1p31.1 in homogeneous pedigrees from Tamil Nadu, India. *American Journal of Psychiatry, 166,* 206–215.

Hollingsworth, S. A., Burgess, P. M., & Whiteford, H. A. (2010). Affective and anxiety disorders: Prevalence, treatment, and antidepressant medication use. *Australian and New Zealand Journal of Psychiatry, 44,* 513–519.

Hollins, M. (2010). The somesthetic senses. *Annual Review of Psychology* (vol. 61). Palo Alto, CA: Annual Reviews.

Holmes, J. (2010). Charles Rycroft's contribution to contemporary psychoanalytic psychotherapy. *American Journal of Psychoanalysis, 70,* 180–192.

Holmes, J. G., Miller, D. T., & Lerner, M. J. (2002). Committing altruism under the cloak of self-interest: The exchange fiction. *Journal of Experimental Social Psychology, 38* (2), 144–151.

Holmes, S. (1993). Food avoidance in patients undergoing cancer chemotherapy. *Support Care Cancer, 1* (6), 326–330.

Holsboer, F., & Ising, M. (2010). Stress hormone regulation: Biological role and translation into therapy. *Annual Review of Psychology* (vol. 61). Palo Alto, CA: Annual Reviews.

Holzman, L. (2009). *Vygotsky at work and play.* Oxford, U.K.: Routledge.

Hong, S. W., & Shevell, S. K. (2009). Color-binding errors during rivalrous suppression of form. *Psychological Science, 20,* 1084–1091.

Honts, C. (1998, June). Commentary. *APA Monitor, 30.*

Hooper, J., & Teresi, D. (1993). *The 3-pound universe.* New York: Tarcher/Putnam.

Hopf, F. W., & others. (2010). Reduced nucleus accumbens SK channel activity enhances alcohol seeking abstinence. *Neuron, 65,* 682–694.

Horgan, J. (2005, February 26). Psychedelic medicine: Mind bending, health giving. *New Scientist, 2488,* 36.

Horn, H., & others. (2010). Gray matter volume differences specific to formal thought disorder in schizophrenia. *Psychiatry Research.* (in press)

Horney, K. (1945). *Our inner conflicts.* New York: Norton.

Horney, K. (1967). *Feminine psychology (collected essays, 1922–1937).* New York: Norton.

Hornickel, J., Skoe, E., & Kraus, N. (2009). Subcortical laterality of speech encoding. *Audiology and Neuro-Otology, 14,* 198–207.

Hornsey, M. J., Dwyer, L., Oei, T. P., & Dingle, G. A. (2009). Group processes and outcomes in group psychotherapy: Is it time to let go of "cohesiveness"? *International Journal of Group Psychotherapy, 59,* 267–278.

Horowitz, J. L., & Garber, J. (2006). The prevention of depressive symptoms in children and adolescents: A meta-analytic review. *Journal*

of Consulting and Clinical Psychology, 74 (3), 401–415.

Horry, R., Wright, D. B., & Tredoux, C. G. (2010). Recognition and context memory for faces from own and other ethnic groups: A remember-know investigation. *Memory and Cognition, 38,* 134–141.

Horst, J. S., Ellis, A. E., Samuelson, L. K., Trejo, E., Worzalla, S. L., Peltan, J. R., & Oakes, L. M. (2009). Toddlers can adaptively change how they categorize: Same objects, same session, two different categorical distinctions. *Developmental Science, 12,* 96–105.

Hoss, R. A., & Langlois, J. H. (2003). Infants prefer attractive faces. In O. Pascalis & A. Slater (Eds.), *The development of face processing in infancy and early childhood: Current perspectives* (pp. 27–38). Hauppauge, NY: Nova Science.

Hotard, S. R., McFatter, R. M., McWhirter, R. M., & Stegall, M. E. (1989). Interactive effects of extraversion, neuroticism, and social relationships on subjective well-being. *Journal of Personality and Social Psychology, 57,* 321–331.

House, J. S., Landis, K. R., & Umberson, D. (1988). Social relationships and health. *Science, 241,* 540–545.

Houser-Marko, L., & Sheldon, K. M. (2008). Eyes on the prize or nose to the grindstone? The effects of level of goal evaluation on mood and motivation. *Personality and Social Psychology Bulletin, 34,* 1556–1569.

Hovland, C. I., Janis, I. L., & Kelley, H. H. (1953). *Communication and persuasion.* New Haven, CT: Yale University Press.

Howard, K. I., Moras, K., Brill, P. L., Martinovich, Z., & Lutz, W. (1996). Evaluation of psychotherapy: Efficacy, effectiveness, and patient progress. *American Psychologist, 51,* 1059–1064.

Howe, M. J. A., Davidson, J. W., Moore, D. G., & Sloboda, J. A. (1995). Are there early childhood signs of musical ability? *Psychology of Music, 23,* 162–176.

Howell, D. C. (2010). *Fundamental statistics for the behavioral sciences* (7th ed.). Belmont, CA: Wadsworth.

Howes, M. B. (2006). *Human memory.* Thousand Oaks, CA: Sage.

Howes, O. D., & others. (2009). Elevated striatal dopamine function linked to prodromal signs of schizophrenia. *Archives of General Psychiatry, 66,* 13–20.

Hoyer, D., Hannon, J. P., & Martin, G. R. (2002). Molecular, pharmacological, and functional diversity of 5-HT receptors. *Pharmacology, Biochemistry, and Behavior, 71,* 533–554.

Hoyer, W. J., & Roodin, P. A. (2009). *Adult development and aging* (6th ed.). New York: McGraw-Hill.

Hoyle, R. H. (2009). *Handbook of personality and social regulation.* Malden, MA: Blackwell.

Hsieh, L. T., Hung, D. L., Tzeng, O. J., Lee, J. R., & Cheng, S. K. (2009). An event-related potential investigation of the processing of remember/forget cues and item encoding in item-method directed forgetting. *Brain Research, 1250,* 190–201.

Hu, F. B., Willett, W. C., Li, T., Stampfer, M. J., Colditz, G. A., & Manson, J. E. (2004). Adiposity as compared with physical activity in predicting mortality among women. *New England Journal of Medicine, 351,* 2694–2703.

Huang, C. C., & Chang, Y. C. (2009). The long-term effects of febrile seizures on the hippocampal neuronal plasticity—clinical and experimental evidence. *Brain and Development, 31,* 383–387.

Huang, X., Lei, Z., Li, X. P., & El-Mallakh, R. S. (2009). Response of sodium pump to ouabain challenge in human glioblastoma cells in culture. *World Journal of Biological Psychiatry, 10,* 884–892.

Huart, C., Collet, S., & Rombaux, P. (2009). Chemosensory pathways: From periphery to cortex. *B-ENT, 5, Suppl. 13,* S3–S9.

Hubble, M. A., & Miller, S. D. (2004). The client: Psychotherapy's missing link for promoting a positive psychology. In A. Linley & S. Joseph (Eds.), *Positive psychology in practice* (pp. 335–353). Hoboken, NJ: Wiley.

Hubel, D. H., & Wiesel, T. N. (1963). Receptive fields of cells in striate cortex of very young, visually inexperienced kittens. *Journal of Neurophysiology, 26,* 994–1002.

Hudson, A. J. (2009). Consciousness: Physiological dependence on rapid memory access. *Frontiers in Biology, 14,* 2779–2800.

Huff, C. R. (2002). What can we learn from other nations about the problem of wrongful conviction? *Judicature, 86,* 91–97.

Huffcutt, A. L., & Culbertson, S. S. (2010). Interviews. In S. Zedeck (Ed.), *APA handbook of industrial and organizational psychology.* Washington, DC: APA. (in press)

Hughes, I. A., Houk, C., Ahmed, F., Lee, P. A., & LWPES-ESPE Consensus Group. (2006). Consensus statement on management of intersex disorders. *Archives of Disease in Childhood, 91,* 554–563.

Hummer, R. A., Ellison, C. G., Rogers, R. G., Moulton, B. C., & Romero, R. R. (2004). Religious involvement and adult mortality in the United States: Review and perspective. *Southern Medical Journal, 97,* 1223–1230.

Hung, Y., Smith, M. L., Bayle, D. J., Mills, T., Cheyne, D., & Taylor, M. J. (2010). Unattended emotional faces elicit early lateralized amygdala-frontal and fusiform activations. *NeuroImage.* (in press)

Hunsley, J., & Bailey, J. M. (2001). Whither the Rorschach? An analysis of the evidence. *Psychological Assessment, 13,* 472–485.

Hunsley, J., Lee, C. M., & Wood, J. M. (2004). Controversial and questionable assessment techniques. In S. O. Lilienfeld, J. M. Lohr, & S. J. Lynn (Eds.), *Science and pseudoscience in clinical psychology* (pp. 39–76). New York: Guilford.

Hunt, R. R., & Ellis, H. C. (2004). *Fundamentals of cognitive psychology* (7th ed.). New York: McGraw-Hill.

Hurkmans, E. J., & others. (2010). Motivation as a determinant of physical activity in patients with rheumatoid arthritis. *Arthritis Care Research, 62,* 371–377.

Hurleman, R., & others. (2010). Oxytocin enhances amygdala-dependent, socially reinforced learning and empathy in humans. *Journal of Neuroscience, 30,* 4999–5007.

Hurst, J. L. (2009). Female recognition and assessment of males through scent. *Behavioural Brain Research, 200,* 295–303.

Husain, O. (2009). Paul Lerner and the heart of assessment: A tale of three relations. *Journal of Personality Assessment, 91,* 30–34.

Huston, J. P., Schulz, D., & Topic, B. (2009). Toward an animal model of extinction-induced despair: Focus on aging and physiological indices. *Journal of Neural Transmission, 116,* 1029–1036.

Huttenlocher, P. R., & Dabholkar, A. S. (1997). Regional differences in synaptogenesis in human cerebral cortex. *Journal of Comparative Neurology, 37* (2), 167–178.

Hutton, J. L., Baracos, V. E., & Wismer, W. V. (2007). Chemosensory dysfunction is a primary factor in the evolution of declining nutritional status and quality of life in patients with advanced cancer. *Journal of Pain Symptom Management, 33* (2), 156–165.

Hyde, J. S. (2005). The gender similarities hypothesis. *American Psychologist, 60,* 581–592.

Hyde, J. S. (2006). Gender similarities in mathematics and science. *Science, 314,* 599–600.

Hyde, J. S. (2007). New directions in the study of gender similarities and differences. *Current Directions in Psychological Science, 16,* 259–263.

Hyde, J. S., & DeLamater, J. D. (2011). *Understanding human sexuality* (11th ed.). New York: McGraw-Hill.

Hyde, M., Punch, R., & Komesaroff, L. (2010). Coming to a decision about cochlear implantation: Parents making choices for their deaf children. *Journal of Deaf Studies and Deaf Education.* (in press)

Hyman, S. (2001, October 23). *Basic and clinical neuroscience in the post-genomic era.* Paper presented at the centennial symposium on the Celebration of Excellence in Neuroscience, the Rockefeller University, New York City.

Hyman, S. E. (2010). The diagnosis of mental disorders: The problem of reification. *Annual Review of Clinical Psychology* (vol. 6). Palo Alto, CA: Annual Reviews.

I

Iacono, W. G., & Lykken, D. T. (1997). The validity of the lie detector: Two surveys of scientific opinion. *Journal of Applied Psychology, 82,* 426–433.

Ideguchi, M., Palmer, T. D., Recht, L. D., & Weimann, J. M. (2010). Murine embryonic stem cell–derived pyramidal neurons integrate into the cerebral cortex and appropriate project axons to subcortical targets. *Journal of Neuroscience, 30,* 894–904.

Ikeda, B. E., Collins, C. E., Alvaro, F., Marshall, G., & Garg, M. L. (2006). Well-being and nutrition-related side effects in children undergoing chemotherapy. *Nutrition and Dietetics, 63,* 227–239.

Ikeda, K., Sekiguchi, T., & Hayashi, A. (2010). Concentrated pitch discrimination modulates auditory brainstem responses during contralateral noise exposure. *NeuroReport.* (in press)

Ilies, R., Arvey, R. D., & Bouchard T. J., Jr. (2006). Darwinism, behavioral genetics, and organizational behavior: A review and agenda for future research. *Journal of Organizational Behavior, 27* (2), 121–141.

Imayoshi, I., Sakamoto, M., Ohtsuka, T., & Kageyama, R. (2009). Continuous neurogenesis in the adult brain. *Development, Growth, and Differentiation, 51,* 379–386.

Imeri, L., & Opp, M. R. (2009). How (and why) the immune system makes us sleep. *Nature Reviews: Neuroscience, 10,* 199–210.

Impett, E. A., Peplau, L. A., & Gable, S. L. (2005). Approach and avoidance sexual motives: Implications for personal and interpersonal well-being. *Personal Relationships, 12,* 465–482.

Inaba, A., Thoits, P. A., Ueno, K., Gove, W. R., Evenson, R. J., & Sloan, M. (2005). Depression in the United States and Japan: Gender, marital status, and SES patterns. *Social Science & Medicine, 61,* 2280–2292.

Ingram, R. E. (Ed.). (2009). *The international encyclopedia of depression.* New York: Springer.

Innocence Project. (2009). *Eyewitness misidentification.* http://www.innocenceproject.org/understand/Eyewitness-Misidentification.php (accessed February 18, 2010)

Insel, P. M., & Roth, W. T. (2008). *Core concepts in health* (10th ed.). New York: McGraw-Hill.

Insko, C. A., & Wilson, M. (1977). Interpersonal attraction as a function of social interaction. *Journal of Personality and Social Psychology, 35,* 903–911.

Institute of Medicine. (2006, April). *Sleep disorders and sleep deprivation: An unmet public health problem.* Washington, DC: National Academies.

Irmansyah, I., Dharmono, S., Maramis, A., & Minas, H. (2010). Determinants of psychological morbidity in survivors of the earthquake and tsunami in Aceh and Nias. *International Journal of Mental Health Systems.* (in press)

Ironson, G., Solomon, G., Balbin, E., O'Cleirigh, C., George, A., Schneiderman, N., & Woods, T. (2001, March). *Religious behavior, religious coping, and compassionate view of others is associated with long-term survival with AIDS.* Paper presented at the meeting of the American Psychosomatic Society, Monterey, CA.

Ironson, G., Stuetzle, R., & Fletcher, M. A. (2006). An increase in religiousness/spirituality occurs after HIV diagnosis and predicts slower disease progression over 4 years in people with HIV. *Journal of General Internal Medicine, 21,* S62–S68.

Irwin, M. R., Wang, M., Campomayor, C. O., Coliado-Hidalgo, A., & Cole, S. (2006). Sleep deprivation and activation of morning levels of cellular and genomic markers of inflammation. *Archives of Internal Medicine, 166,* 1756–1762.

Isbell, L. M. (2004). Not all people are lazy or stupid: Evidence of systematic processing in happy moods. *Journal of Experimental Social Psychology, 40,* 341–349.

Isen, A. M. (2004). Some perspectives on positive feelings and emotions: Positive affect facilitates thinking and problem solving. In A. S. R. Manstead, N. Frijda, & A. Fischer (Eds.), *Feelings and emotions: The Amsterdam symposium* (pp. 263–281). New York: Cambridge University Press.

Isen, A. M. (2007a). Positive affect, cognitive flexibility, and self-control. In Y. Shoda, D. Cervone, & G. Downey (Eds.), *Persons in context.* New York: Guilford.

Isen, A. M. (2007b). Positive affect. In R. Baumeister & K. Vohs (Eds.), *Encyclopedia of social psychology.* Thousand Oaks, CA: Sage.

Isen, A. M. (2008). Some ways in which positive affect influences problem solving and decision making. In M. Lewis, J. Haviland-Jones, & L. F. Barrett (Eds.), *Handbook of emotions* (3rd ed.). New York: Guilford.

Isen, A. M., & Means, B. (1983). The influence of positive affect on decision-making strategy. *Social Cognition, 2,* 18–31.

Issa, E. B., & Wang, X. (2008). Sensory responses during sleep in primary and secondary auditory cortex. *Journal of Neuroscience, 28,* 14467–14480.

Istaphanous, G. K., & Loepke, A. W. (2009). General anesthetics and the developing brain. *Current Opinion in Anesthesiology, 22,* 368–373.

Iturbide, M. I., Raffaelli, M., & Carlo, G. (2009). Protective effects of ethnic identity on Mexican American college students' psychological well-being. *Hispanic Journal of Behavioral Sciences, 31,* 536–552.

Ivancevich, J. M., & Konopaske, R. (2011). *Organizational behavior and management* (9th ed.). New York: McGraw-Hill.

Iwassa, H., Masul, Y., Gondo, Y., Inagaki, H., Kawaal, C., & Suzuki, T. (2008). Personality and all-cause mortality among older adults dwelling in a Japanese community: A five-year population-based prospective study. *American Journal of Geriatric Psychiatry, 16,* 399–405.

Iwassa, H., & others. (2009). Personality and participation in mass health checkups among Japanese community-dwelling elderly. *Journal of Psychosomatic Research, 66,* 155–159.

Izard, C. E. (2009). Emotion theory and research: Highlights, unanswered questions, and emerging issues. *Annual Review of Psychology* (vol. 60). Palo Alto, CA: Annual Reviews.

J

Jablensky, E. (2000). Epidemiology of schizophrenia: The global burden of disease and disability. *European Archives of Psychiatry and Clinical Neuroscience, 250,* 274–285.

Jablensky, E., & others. (1992). Schizophrenia: Manifestations, incidence and course in different cultures: A World Health Organization 10-country study. *Psychological Medicine, Monograph Suppl. 20,* 1–97.

Jack, R. E., Blais, C., Scheepers, C., Schyns, P. G., & Caldara, R. (2009). Cultural confusions show that facial expressions are not universal. *Current Biology, 19,* 1543–1548.

Jackson, G. (2010). Come fly with me: Jet lag and melatonin. *International Journal of Clinical Practice, 64,* 135.

Jackson, L., Langille, L., Lyons, R., Hughes, J., Martin, D., & Winstanley, V. (2009). Does moving from a high-poverty to lower-poverty neighborhood improve mental health? A realist view of "Moving to Opportunity." *Health and Place, 15* (4), 961–970.

Jackson, L. C., & Greene, B. (2000). *Psychotherapy with African-American women.* New York: Guilford.

Jacobsen, P. B., Bovbjerg, D. H., Schwartz, M. D., Andrykowski, M. A., Futterman, A. D., Gilewski, T., Norton, L., & Redd, W. H. (1993). Formation of food aversions in cancer patients receiving repeated infusions of chemotherapy. *Behavior Reseach Therapy, 31* (8), 739–748.

Jaeger, A., Johnson, J. D., Corona, M., & Rugg, M. D. (2009). ERP correlates of the incidental retrieval of emotional information: Effects of study-test delay. *Brain Research, 1269,* 105–113.

Jaeggi, S. M., Buschkuehl, M., Jonides, J., & Perrig, W. J. (2008). Improving fluid intelligence with training on working memory. *Proceedings of the National Academy of Sciences USA, 105* (19), 6829–6833.

Jakupcak, M., Salters, K., Gratz, K. L., & Roemer, L. (2003). Masculinity and emotionality: An investigation of men's primary and secondary emotional responding. *Sex Roles, 49,* 111–120.

James, W. (1950). *Principles of psychology.* New York: Dover. (original work published 1890)

James, W. H. (2005). Biological and psychosocial determinants of male and female human sexual orientation. *Journal of Biosocial Science, 37,* 555–567.

Jameson, D., & Hurvich, L. M. (1989). Essay concerning color constancy. *Annual Review of Psychology* (vol. 40). Palo Alto, CA: Annual Reviews.

Janata, P. (2009). The neural architecture of music-evoked autobiographical memories. *Cerebral Cortex, 19,* 2579–2594.

Jang, K. L., Livesley, W. J., & Vernon, P. A. (1996). Heritability of the big five personality dimensions and their facets: A twin study. *Journal of Personality, 64,* 577–591.

Janicki-Deverts, D., Cohen, S., & Doyle, W. J. (2010). Cynical hostility and stimulated Th1 and Th2 cytokine production. *Brain, Behavior, and Immunity, 24,* 58–63.

Janis, I. (1972). *Victims of groupthink: A psychological study of foreign-policy decisions and fiascos.* Boston: Houghton Mifflin.

Janis, I. L., & Hovland, C. I. (1959). An overview of persuasability research. In C. I. Hovland & I. L. Janis (Eds.), *Personality and persuasability* (pp. 1–26). New Haven, CT: Yale University Press.

Janowsky, D. S., Addario, D., & Risch, S. C. (1987). *Psychopharmacology case studies* (2nd ed.). New York: Guilford.

Jarrett, R. B., Kraft, D., Doyle, J., Foster, B. M., Eaves, G. G., & Silver, P. C. (2001). Prevent-

ing recurrent depression using cognitive therapy with and without a continuation phase: A randomized clinical trial. *Archives of General Psychiatry, 58,* 381–388.

Jaurrieta, N., & others. (2008). Individual versus group cognitive behavioral treatment for obsessive-compulsive disorder: Follow-up. *Psychiatry and Clinical Neuroscience, 62,* 697–704.

Jefferson, S. D., & Bramlett, F. (2010). The moderating roles of gender and anti-gay prejudice in explaining stigma by association in male dyads. *Journal of Homosexuality, 57,* 401–414.

Jemmott, J. B., III, Jemmott, L. S., & Fong, G. T. (2010). Efficacy of a theory-based abstinence-only intervention over 24 months: A randomized controlled trial with young adolescents. *Archives of Pediatrics and Adolescent Medicine, 164,* 52–159.

Jennings, L., & Skovholt, T. M. (1999). The cognitive, emotional, and relational characteristics of master therapists. *Journal of Counseling Psychology, 46,* 3–11.

Jensen, L. W., & Wadkins, T. A. (2007). Mental health success stories: Finding paths to recovery. *Issues in Mental Health Nursing, 28,* 325–340.

Jensen, M. P. (2009). The neurophysiology of pain perception and hypnotic analgesia: Implications for clinical practice. *American Journal of Clinical Hypnosis, 51,* 123–148.

Jensen-Campbell, L. A., & Malcolm, K. T. (2007). The importance of conscientiousness in adolescent interpersonal relationships. *Personality and Social Psychology Bulletin, 33,* 368–383.

Jeong, J., Kim, D. J., Kim, S. Y., Chae, J. H., Go, H. J., & Kim, K. S. (2001). Effect of total sleep deprivation on the dimensional complexity of the waking EEG. *Sleep, 15,* 197–202.

Jerrell, J. M. (2010). Neuroendocrine-related adverse events associated with antidepressant treatment in children and adolescents. *CNS Neuroscience & Therapeutics, 16,* 83–90.

Jespersen, A. E., Lalumiere, M. L., & Seto, M. C. (2009). Sexual abuse history among adult sex offenders and non–sex offenders: Meta-analysis. *Child Abuse and Neglect, 33,* 179–192.

Jiang, Y. H., & others. (2010). Clinical efficacy of acupuncture on the morphine-related side effects in patients undergoing spinal-epidural anesthesia and analgesia. *Chinese Journal of Integrative Medicine, 16,* 71–74.

Jimenez-Sanchez, A. R., & others. (2009). Morphological background detection and enhancement of images with poor lighting. *IEEE Transactions on Image Processing, 18,* 613–623.

Job, R. F. S. (1987). The effect of mood on helping behavior. *Journal of Social Psychology, 127,* 323–328.

Johnson, A. M., Vernon, P. A., Harris, J. A., & Jang, K. L. (2004). Behavior genetic investigation of the relationship between leadership and personality. *Twin Research, 7* (1), 27–32.

Johnson, G. B. (2008). *The living world* (5th ed.). New York: McGraw-Hill.

Johnson, J. S., & Newport, E. L. (1991). Critical period effects on universal properties of

language: The status of subjacency in the acquisition of a second language. *Cognition, 39,* 215–258.

Johnson, J. T., Robinson, M., & Mitchell, E. B. (2004). Inferences about the authentic self: When do actions say more than mental states? *Journal of Personality and Social Psychology, 87,* 615–630.

Johnson, P. L., & others. (2010). A key role for orexin in panic anxiety. *Nature Medicine, 16,* 111–115.

Johnson, R. E., & Chang, C. (2006). "I" is to continuance as "we" is to affective: The relevance of the self-concept for organizational commitment. *Journal of Organizational Behavior, 27* (5), 549–570.

Johnson, S. P. (2010a). Perceptual completion in infancy. In S. P. Johnson (Ed.), *Neoconstructionism: The new science of cognitive development.* New York: Oxford University Press. (in press)

Johnson, S. P. (2010b). A constructivist view of object perception in infancy. In L. M. Oakes, C. H. Cashon, M. Cassola, & D. H. Rakison (Eds.), *Early perceptual and cognitive development.* New York: Oxford University Press. (in press)

Johnson-Laird, P. N., Mancini, F., & Gangemi, A. (2006). A hyper-emotion theory of psychological illnesses. *Psychological Review, 113,* 822–841.

Johnston, L. D., O'Malley, P. M., Bachman, J. G., & Schulenberg, J. E. (2008). *Monitoring the Future national survey results on drug use, 1975–2007.* Bethesda, MD: National Institute on Drug Abuse.

Johnston, L. D., O'Malley, P. M., Bachman, J. G., & Schulenberg, J. E. (2009). *Monitoring the Future national results on adolescent drug use: Overview of key findings, 2008.* Bethesda, MD: National Institute on Drug Abuse.

Johnston, L. D., O'Malley, P. M., Bachman, J. G., & Schulenberg, J. E. (2010). *Monitoring the Future national survey results on drug use, 1975–2009.* Bethesda, MD: National Institute on Drug Abuse. (in press)

Johnstone, E., Benowitz, N., Cargill, A., Jacob, R., Hinks, L., Day, I., Murphy, M., & Walton, R. (2006). Determinants of the rate of nicotine metabolism and the effects on smoking behavior. *Clinical Pharmacology and Therapeutics, 80,* 319–330.

Joiner, T. E., Jr. (2005). *Why people die by suicide.* Cambridge, MA: Harvard University Press.

Joiner, T. E., Jr., Hollar, D., & Van Orden, K. (2006). On Buckeyes, Gators, Super Bowl Sunday, and the miracle on ice: "Pulling together" is associated with lower suicide rates. *Journal of Social & Clinical Psychology, 25,* 179–195.

Jones, E. E. (1998). Major developments in five decades of social psychology. In D. T. Gilbert, S. T. Fiske, & G. Lindzey (Eds.), *Handbook of social psychology* (4th ed., vol. 1). New York: McGraw-Hill.

Jones, E. E., & Harris, V. A. (1967). The attribution of attitudes. *Journal of Experimental Social Psychology, 3,* 1–24.

Jones, G. R., & George, J. M. (2007). *Essentials of contemporary management* (2nd ed.). New York: McGraw-Hill.

Joorman, J., Teachman, B. A., & Gotlib, I. H. (2009). Sadder and less accurate? False memory for negative material in depression. *Journal of Abnormal Psychology, 118,* 412–417.

Jordan, C. E., Campbell, R., & Follingstad, D. (2010). Violence and women's mental health: The impact of physical, sexual, and psychological aggression. *Annual Review of Clinical Psychology* (vol. 6). Palo Alto, CA: Annual Reviews.

Joseph, J. (2006). *The missing gene.* New York: Algora.

Joseph, J., Breslin, C., & Skinner, H. (1999). Critical perspectives on the transtheoretical model and stages of change. In J. A. Tucker, D. M. Donovan, & G. A. Marlatt (Eds.), *Changing addictive behavior: Bridging clinical and public health strategies* (pp. 160–190). New York: Guilford.

Joseph, S., & Linley, P. A. (2004). Positive therapy: A positive psychological approach to therapeutic practice. In P. A. Linley & S. Joseph (Eds.), *Positive psychology in practice* (pp. 354–368). Hoboken, NJ: Wiley.

Jost, J. T., Federico, C. M., & Napier, J. L. (2009). Attitude structure. *Annual Review of Psychology* (vol. 60). Palo Alto, CA: Annual Reviews.

Joy, J. E., Watson, S. J., & Benson, J. A. (Eds.). (1999). *Institute of medicine. Marijuana and medicine: Assessing the science base.* Washington, DC: National Academy Press.

Juang, L., & Syed, M. (2010). Family cultural socialization practices and ethnic identity in college-going emerging adults. *Journal of Adolescence.* (in press)

Juckel, G., Uhl, I., Padberg, F., Brune, M., & Winter, C. (2009). Psychosurgery and deep brain stimulation as ultima ratio treatment for refractory depression. *European Archives of Psychiatry and Clinical Neuroscience, 259,* 1–7.

Judge, T. A., Piccolo, R. F., & Kosalka, T. (2009). The bright and dark sides of leader traits: A review and theoretical extension of the leader trait paradigm. *Leadership Quarterly, 20,* 855–875.

Judge, T. A., Thorson, C. J., Bono, J. E., & Patton, G. K. (2001). The job satisfaction–job performance relationship: A qualitative and quantitative review. *Psychological Bulletin, 127,* 376–407.

Julien, E., Senecal, C., & Guay, F. (2009). Longitudinal relations among perceived autonomy support from health care practitioners, motivation, coping strategies and dietary compliance in a sample of adults with type 2 diabetes. *Journal of Health Psychology, 14,* 457–470.

Jung, C. (1917). *Analytic psychology.* New York: Moffat, Yard.

K

Kaasa, S. O., & Loftus, E. F. (2009). False memories. In F. T. L. Leong (Ed.), *Encyclopedia of counseling.* Thousand Oaks, CA: Sage.

Kabat-Zinn, J. (2006). *Coming to our senses: Healing ourselves and the world through mindfulness.* New York: Hyperion.

Kabat-Zinn, J. (2009, March 18). This analog life; Reconnecting with what is important in an always uncertain world. Presentation at the 7th Annual Conference at the Center for Mindful Meditation, Worcester, MA.

Kabat-Zinn, J., Lipworth, L., & Burney, R. (1985). The clinical use of mindfulness meditation for the self-regulation of chronic pain. *Journal of Behavioral Medicine, 8,* 163–190.

Kabat-Zinn, J., Wheeler, E., Light, T., Skillings, A., Scharf, M. J., Cropley, T. G., Hosmer, D., & Bernhard, J. D. (1998). Influence of a mindfulness meditation–based stress reduction intervention on rates of skin clearing in patients with moderate to severe psoriasis undergoing phototherapy (UVB) and photochemotherapy (PUVA). *Psychosomatic Medicine, 60,* 625–632.

Kagan, J. (2010). Emotions and temperament. In M. H. Bornstein (Ed.), *Handbook of cultural developmental science.* New York: Psychology Press.

Kahn, A., & others. (1992) Sleep and cardiorespiratory characteristics of infant victim of sudden death: A prospective case-control study. *Sleep, 15,* 287–292.

Kahneman, D., & Klein, G. (2009). Conditions for intuitive experience: A failure to disagree. *American Psychologist, 64,* 515–526.

Kaiser Family Foundation. (2001). *Inside-OUT: A report on the experiences of lesbians, gays, and bisexuals in America and the public's views on issues and policies related to sexual orientation.* Menlo Park, CA: Henry J. Kaiser Family Foundation.

Kaiser, S., & others. (2010). Maintenance of real objects and their verbal designations in working memory. *Neuroscience Letters, 469,* 65–69.

Kaiyala, K. J., & others. (2010). Identification of body fat mass as a major determinant of metabolic rate in mice. *Diabetes.* (in press)

Kalichman, S. C. (2007). The theory of reasoned action and advances in HIV/AIDS prevention. In I. Ajzen, D. Albarracin, & R. Hornik (Eds.), *Prediction and change of health behavior.* Mahwah, NJ: Erlbaum.

Kamel, R. M. (2010). The onset of human parturition. *Archives of Gynecology and Obstetrics.* (in press)

Kameyama, K., Sohya, K., Ebina, T., Fukuda, A., Yanagawa, Y., & Tsumoto, T. (2010). Difference in binocularity and ocular dominance plasticity between GABAergic and excitatory cortical neurons. *Journal of Neuroscience, 30,* 1551–1559.

Kamin, L. J. (1968). Attention-like processes in classical conditioning. In M. R. Jones (Ed.), *Miami symposium on the prediction of behavior: Aversive stimuli.* Coral Gables, FL: University of Miami Press.

Kamphaus, R. W., & Kroncke, A. P. (2004). "Back to the future" of the Stanford-Binet Intelligence Scales. In M. Hersen (Ed.), *Comprehensive handbook of psychological assessment* (vol. 1). New York: Wiley.

Kanamaru, T., & Aihara, K. (2010). Roles of inhibitory neurons in rewiring-induced synchronization in pulse-coupled neural networks. *Neural Computation.* (in press)

Kandel, E. R., & Schwartz, J. H. (1982). Molecular biology of learning: Modulation of transmitter release. *Science, 218,* 433–443.

Kanov, J. M., Maitlis, S., Worline, M. C., Dutton, J. E., Frost, P. J., & Lilius, J. M. (2006). Compassion in organizational life. In J. V. Gallos (Ed.), *Organization development: A Jossey-Bass reader* (pp. 793–812). San Francisco: Jossey-Bass.

Kantowitz, B. H., Roediger, H. L., & Elmes, D. G. (2009). *Experimental psychology* (9th ed.). Belmont, CA: Wadsworth.

Kanwisher, N. (2006). Neuroscience: What's in a face? *Science, 311,* 617–618.

Kanwisher, N., & Yovel, G. (2010). Cortical specialization for face perception in humans. In J. T. Cacioppo & G. G. Berentson (Eds.), *Handbook of neuroscience for the behavioral sciences.* New York: Wiley. (in press)

Kaplan, H. S. (1974). *The new sex therapy: Active treatment of sexual dysfunctions.* New York: Routledge.

Kapur, S. (2003). Psychosis as a state of aberrant salience: A framework linking biology, phenomenology, and pharmacology. *American Journal of Psychiatry, 160,* 13–23.

Karasik, L. B., Adolph, K. E., Tamis-LeMonda, C. S., & Bornstein, M. H. (2010). WEIRD walking: Cross-cultural differences in motor development. *Behavior and Brain Sciences.* (in press)

Karau, S. J., & Williams, K. D. (1993). Social loafing: A meta-analytic review and theoretical integration. *Journal of Personality and Social Psychology, 65,* 681–706.

Karlsen, P. J., Allen, R. J., Baddeley, A. D., & Hitch, G. J. (2010). Binding across space and time in visual working memory. *Memory and Cognition, 33,* 292–303.

Karnes, F. A., & Stephens, K. R. (2008). *Achieving excellence: Educating the gifted and the talented.* Upper Saddle River, NJ: Prentice-Hall.

Kaskutas, L. A. (2009). Alcoholics Anonymous effectivness: Faith meets science. *Journal of Addictive Diseases, 28,* 145–157.

Kaskutas, L. A., Subbaraman, M. S., Witbordt, J., & Zemore, S. E. (2009). Effectiveness of making Alcoholics Anonymous easier: A group format 12-step facilitation approach. *Journal of Substance Abuse Treatment, 37* (3), 228–239.

Kasliwal, R., Wilton, L. V., & Shakir, S. A. (2009). Safety and drug utilization profile of varenicline as used in general practice in England: Interim results from a prescription-event monitoring study. *Drug Safety, 32,* 499–507.

Kasser, T., & Ryan, R. M. (1993). A dark side of the American dream: Correlates of financial success as a central life aspiration. *Journal of Personality and Social Psychology, 65,* 410–422.

Kasser, T., & Ryan, R. M. (1996). Further examining the American dream: Differential correlates of intrinsic and extrinsic goals. *Personality and Social Psychology Bulletin, 22,* 280–287.

Kasser, T., Ryan, R. M., Couchman, C. E., & Sheldon, K. M. (2004). Materialistic values: Their causes and consequences. In T. Kasser & A. D. Kanner (Eds.), *Psychology and consumer culture: The struggle for a good life in a materialistic world* (pp. 11–28). Washington, DC: American Psychological Association.

Kasser, T., & Sharma, Y. S. (1999). Reproductive freedom, educational equality, and females' preference for resource-acquisition characteristics in mates. *Psychological Science, 10,* 374–377.

Kato, I., & others. (2003). Incomplete arousal processes in infants who were victims of sudden death. *American Journal of Respiratory Critical Care Medicine, 168,* 1298–1303.

Katschnig, H. (2010). Are psychiatrists an endangered species? Observations on internal and external challenges to the profession. *World Psychiatry, 9,* 21–28.

Katz, J. N. (1995). *The invention of heterosexuality.* New York: Dutton.

Katzman, M. A. (2009). Current considerations in the treatment of generalized anxiety disorder. *CNS Drugs, 23,* 103–120.

Kauffman, C., & Silberman, J. (2009). Finding and fostering the positive in relationships: Positive interventions in couples therapy. *Journal of Clinical Psychology, 65,* 520–531.

Kaye, W. (2008). Neurobiology of anorexia and bulimia nervosa. *Physiology & Behavior, 94,* 121–135.

Kazdin, A. E. (2007). Mediators and mechanisms of change in psychotherapy change. *Annual Review of Clinical Psychology* (vol. 3). Palo Alto, CA: Annual Reviews.

Kazdin, A. E., & Benjet, C. (2003). Spanking children: Evidence and issues. *Current Directions in Psychological Science, 12,* 99–103.

Keeley, J., Zayac, R., & Correia, C. (2008). Curvilinear relationships between statistics anxiety and performance among undergraduate students: Evidence for optimal anxiety. *Statistics Education Research Journal, 7,* 4–15.

Keen, R. (2011). Prefatory. *Annual Review of Psychology* (vol. 62). Palo Alto, CA: Annual Reviews.

Keeton, C. P., Kolos, A. C., & Walkup, J. T. (2009). Pediatric generalized anxiety disorder: Epidemiology, diagnosis, and management. *Pediatric Drugs, 11,* 171–183.

Kegeles, L. S., & others. (2010). Increased synaptic dopamine function in associative regions of the striatum in schizophrenia. *Archives of General Psychiatry, 67,* 231–239.

Keillor, J. M., Barrett, A. M., Crucian, G. P., Kortenkamp, S., & Heilman, K. M. (2002). Emotional experience and perception in the absence of facial feedback. *Journal of the International Neuropsychological Society, 8,* 130–135.

Keitner, G. I., Ryan, C. E., & Solomon, D. A. (2009). Family focused therapy shortens recovery time from depression but not mania in adolescents with bipolar disorder. *Evidence Based Mental Health, 12,* 48.

Keller, M. P., & Attie, A. D. (2010). Physiological insights gained from gene expression analysis in obesity and diabetes. *Annual Review of Nutrition* (vol. 30). Palo Alto, CA: Annual Reviews.

Kellerman, A. L., & others. (1993). Gun ownership as a risk factor for homicide in the home. *New England Journal of Medicine, 329,* 1084–1091.

Kelley, H. H. (1973). The processes of causal attribution. *American Psychologist, 28,* 107–128.

Kellner, C. H., Knapp, R. G., Petrides, G., Rummans, T. A., Husain, M. M., Rasmussen, K., Mueller, M., & Kelly, G. F. (2006). *Sexuality today* (8th ed.). New York: McGraw-Hill.

Kelly, J. F., Dow, S. J., Yeterian, J. D., & Kahler, C. W. (2010). Can 12-step group participation strengthen and extend the benefits of adolescent addiction treatment? A prospective analysis. *Drug and Alcohol Dependence.* (in press)

Kelly, J. W., & McNamara, T. P. (2009). Facilitated pointing to remembered objects: Evidence for egocentric retrieval or for spatial priming. *Psychonomic Bulletin and Review, 16,* 295–300.

Kelsch, W., Sim, S., & Lois, C. E. (2010). Watching synaptogenesis in the human brain. *Annual Review of Neuroscience* (vol. 33). Palo Alto, CA: Annual Reviews.

Keltner, D., & Ekman, P. (2000). Emotion: An overview. In A. Kazdin (Ed.), *Encyclopedia of psychology.* Washington, DC, and New York: American Psychological Association and Oxford University Press.

Kemmerer, D., & Gonzalez-Castillo, J. (2010). The two-level theory of verb meaning: An approach to integrating the semantics of action with the mirror neuron system. *Brain and Language, 112,* 54–76.

Kemp, C., & Tenenbaum, J. B. (2009). Structured statistical models of inductive reasoning. *Psychological Review, 116,* 20–58.

Kemppainen, H., Raivio, N., Nurmi, H., & Kiianmaa, K. (2010). GABA and glutamate overflow in the VTA and ventral pallidum of alcohol-preferring AA and alcohol-avoiding ANA rats after ethanol. *Alcohol and Alcoholism, 45,* 111–118.

Kennard, B. D., & others. (2008). Cognitive-behavioral therapy to prevent relapse in pediatric responders to pharmacotherapy for major depressive disorder. *Journal of the American Academy of Child and Adolescent Psychiatry, 47,* 1395–1404.

Kennedy, G. J., Haque, M., & Zarankow, B. (1997). Human sexuality in late life. *International Journal of Mental Health, 26,* 35–46.

Kennedy, J. E., & others. (2010). Posttraumatic stress symptoms in OIF/OEF service members with blast-related and non-blast-related mild TBI. *NeuroRehabilitation, 26,* 223–231.

Kenrick, D. T., Griskevicius, V., Neuberg, S. L., & Schaller, M. (2010). Renovating the pyramid of needs: Contemporary extensions built upon ancient foundations. *Perspectives on Psychological Science, 5,* 292–314.

Kensinger, E. A., & Choi, E. S. (2009). When side matters: Hemispheric processing and the visual specificty of emotional memories. *Journal of Experimental Psychology: Learning, Memory, and Cognition, 35,* 247–253.

Kern, M. L., & Friedman, H. S. (2008). Do conscientious individuals live longer? A quantitative review. *Health Psychology, 27,* 505–512.

Kerns, J. G., Berenbaum, H., Barch, D. M., Banich, M. T., & Stolar, N. (1999). Word production in schizophrenia and its relationship to positive symptoms. *Psychiatry Research, 87,* 29–37.

Kerr, N. L. (2010). Explorations in juror emotion and juror judgment. In B. H. Bornstein & R. L. Wiener (Eds.), *Emotion and the law: Psychological perspectives* (pp. 97–132). New York: Springer.

Kessler, R. C., Chiu, W. T., Demler, O., & Walters, E. E. (2005). Prevalence, severity, and comorbidity of twelve-month DSM-IV disorders in the National Comorbidity Survey Replication (NCS-R). *Archives of General Psychiatry, 62,* 617–627.

Khatapoush, S., & Hallfors, D. (2004). "Sending the wrong message": Did medical marijuana legalization in California change attitudes about and use of marijuana? *Journal of Drug Issues, 34,* 751–770.

Kibler, J. L. (2009). Posttraumatic stress and cardiovascular disease risk. *Journal of Trauma and Dissociation, 10,* 135–150.

Kiecolt-Glaser, J. K. (2009). Psychoneuroimmunology: Psychology's gateway to the biomedical future. *Perspectives on Psychological Science, 4,* 367–369.

Kiecolt-Glaser, J. K. (2010). Stress, food, and inflammation: Psychoneuroimmunology and nutrition at the cutting edge. *Psychosomatic Medicine, 72,* 365–372.

Kiecolt-Glaser, J. K., & others. (2010). Stress, inflammation, and yoga practice. *Psychosomatic Medicine, 72,* 113–121.

Kiess, H. O., & Green, B. A. (2010). *Statistical concepts for the behavioral sciences* (4th ed.). Boston: Allyn & Bacon.

Kihlstrom, J. (2005). Is hypnosis an altered state of consciousness or what?: Comment. *Contemporary Hypnosis, 22,* 34–38.

Kilicarslan, A., Isildak, M., Guven, G. S., Oz, S. G., Tannover, M. D., Duman, A. E., Saracbasi, O., & Sozen, T. (2006). Demographic, socio-economic, and educational aspects of obesity in an adult population. *Journal of the National Medical Association, 98,* 1313–1317.

Killgore, W., & Yurgelun-Todd, D. (2001). Sex differences in amygdala activation during the perception of facial affect. *NeuroReport, 12,* 2543–2547.

Killgore, W. D., Rosso, I. M., Gruber, S. A., & Yurgelun-Todd, D. A. (2009). Amygdala volume and verbal memory performance in schizophrenia and bipolar disorder. *Cognitive and Behavioral Neurology, 22,* 28–37.

Killgore, W. D. S., Killgore, D. B., Day, L. M., Li, C., Kamimori, G. H., & Balkin, T. J. (2007). The effects of 53 hours of sleep deprivation on moral judgment. *SLEEP, 30,* 345–352.

Kim, J. N., & Lee, B. M. (2007). Risk factors, health risks, and risk management for aircraft personnel and frequent flyers. *Journal of Toxicology and Environmental Health B: Critical Reviews, 10,* 223–234.

Kim, J. Y., Oh, D. J., Yoon, T. Y., Choi, J. M., & Choe, B. K. (2007). The impacts of obesity on psychological well-being: A cross-sectional study about depressive mood and quality of life. *Journal of Preventive Medicine and Public Health, 40,* 191–195.

Kim, S. C., Jo, Y. S., Kim, I. H., Kim, H., & Choi, J. S. (2010). Lack of medial prefrontal cortex activation underlies the immediate extinction deficit. *Journal of Neuroscience, 30,* 832–837.

Kimbrough, E., Magyari, T., Langenberg, P., Chesney, M., & Berman, B. (2010). Mindfulness intervention with child abuse survivors. *Journal of Clinical Psychology, 66,* 17–33.

Kindt, M., Soeter, M., & Vervliet, B. (2009). Beyond extinction: Erasing human fear responses and preventing the return of fear. *Nature Neuroscience, 12,* 256–258.

King, B. M. (2005). *Human sexuality today* (5th ed.). Upper Saddle River, NJ: Prentice-Hall.

King, L. A. (2001). The health benefits of writing about life goals. *Personality and Social Psychology Bulletin, 27,* 798–807.

King, L. A. (2002). Gain without pain: Expressive writing and self regulation. In S. J. Lepore & J. Smyth (Eds.), *The writing cure.* Washington, DC: American Psychological Association.

King, L. A. (2003). Measures and meanings: The use of qualitative data in social and personality psychology. In C. Sansone, C. Morf, & A. Panter (Eds.), *Handbook of methods in social psychology* (pp. 173–194). New York: Sage.

King, L. A. (2008). Personal goals and life dreams: Positive psychology and motivation in daily life. In W. Gardner & J. Shah (Eds.), *Handbook of motivation science* (pp. 518–532). New York: Guilford.

King, L. A., Burton, C. M., & Geise, A. (2009). The good (gay) life: The search for signs of maturity in the narratives of gay adults. In P. Hammack & B. J. Kohler (Eds.), *The story of sexual identity: Narrative, social change, and the development of sexual orientation* (pp. 375–396). New York: Oxford University Press.

King, L. A., & Hicks, J. A. (2007). Whatever happened to "what might have been"? Regret, happiness, and maturity. *American Psychologist, 62,* 625–636.

King, L. A., & Hicks, J. A. (2010). Positive affect and meaning in life: The intersection of hedonism and eudaimonia. In P. T. Wong, P. T. Wong, & P. S. Fry (Eds.), *The human quest for meaning* (2nd ed.). New York: Oxford University Press. (in press)

King, L. A., Hicks, J. A., Krull, J., & Del Gaiso, A. K. (2006). Positive affect and the experience of meaning in life. *Journal of Personality and Social Psychology, 90,* 179–196.

King, L. A., & Miner, K. N. (2000). Writing about the perceived benefits of traumatic life events: Implications for physical health. *Personality and Social Psychology Bulletin, 26,* 220–230.

King, L. A., Scollon, C. K., Ramsey, C. M., & Williams, T. (2000). Stories of life transition: Happy endings, subjective well-being, and ego development in parents of children with Down syndrome. *Journal of Research in Personality, 34,* 509–536.

King, L. A., & Smith, S. N. (2005). Happy, mature, and gay: Intimacy, power, and difficult times in coming out stories. *Journal of Research in Personality, 39,* 278–298.

King, P. E., & Roeser, R. W. (2009). Religion and spirituality in adolescent development. In R. W. Lerner & L. Steinberg (Eds.), *Handbook of adolescent psychology* (3rd ed.). New York: Wiley.

Kinney, A. (2005, September 1). Looting or finding? *Salon.com.* http://dir.salon.com/story/news/feature/2005/09/01/photo_controversy/index.html (accessed March 21, 2009)

Kinney, H. (2009). Neuropathology provides new insight in the pathogenesis of the sudden infant death syndrome. *Acta Neuropathologica, 117,* 247–255.

Kinnish, K. K., Strassberg, D. S., & Turner, C. M. (2005). Sex differences in the flexibility of sexual orientation: A multidimensional retrospective assessment. *Archives of Sexual Behavior, 35,* 173–183.

Kinon, B. J., Chen, L., Ascher-Svanum, H., Stauffer, V. L., Kollack-Walker, S., Zhou, W., Kapur, S., Kane, J. M., & Naber, D. (2010). Challenging the assumption that improvement in functional outcomes is delayed relative to improvement in symptoms in the treatment of schizophrenia. *Schizophrenia Research.* (in press)

Kinsey, A. C., Martin, C. E., & Pomeroy, W. B. (1953). *Sexual behavior in the human female.* Philadelphia: Saunders.

Kinsey, A. C., Pomeroy, W. B., & Martin, C. E. (1948). *Sexual behavior in the human male.* Philadelphia: Saunders.

Kirby, D. B. (2008). The impact of abstinence and comprehensive sex and STD/HIV education programs on adolescent sexual behavior. *Sexuality Research & Social Policy, 5,* 18–27.

Kirby, D. B., Laris, B. A., & Rolleri, L. A. (2007). Sex and HIV education programs: Their impact on sexual behavior of young people throughout the world. *Journal of Adolescent Health, 40,* 206–217.

Kirchhoff, B. A., & Buckner, R. L. (2006). Functional-anatomic correlates of individual differences in memory. *Neuron, 51,* 263–274.

Kishioka, A., & others. (2009). A novel form of memory for auditory fear conditioning at a low-intensity unconditioned stimulus. *PLoS One, 4,* e4157.

Kitayama, S. (2011). Psychology and culture: Cross-country or regional comparisons. *Annual Review of Psychology* (vol. 62). Palo Alto, CA: Annual Reviews.

Kitayama, S., & Cohen, D. (Eds.). (2007). *Handbook of cultural psychology.* New York: Guilford.

Kitchener, K. S., King, P. M., & DeLuca, S. (2006). The development of reflective judgment in adulthood. In C. Hoare (Ed.), *Handbook of adult development and learning.* New York: Oxford University Press.

Kjaer, S. L., Wegener, G., Rosenberg, R., Lund, S. P., & Hougaard, K. S. (2010). Prenatal and adult stress interplay—Behavioral implications. *Brain Research, 1320,* 106–113.

Kjelsberg, E. (2005). Conduct disordered adolescents hospitalised 1963–1990. Secular trends in criminal activity. *European Journal of Child and Adolescent Psychiatry, 14,* 191–199.

Klein, B., & others. (2010). A therapist-assisted cognitive behavior therapy internet intervention for posttraumatic stress disorder: Pre-, post-, and 3-month follow-up results from an open trial. *Journal of Anxiety Disorders, 24,* 635–644.

Klein, S. B. (2009). *Learning.* Thousand Oaks, CA: Sage.

Kligman, D. H. (2010). The logic of psychoanalytic interpretation. *Psychoanalytic Quarterly, 79,* 491–522.

Klimstra, T. A., Hale, W. W., Raaijmakers, Q. A., Branje, S. J., & Meeus, W. H. (2009). Maturation of personality in adolescence. *Journal of Personality and Social Psychology, 96,* 898–912.

Klinesmith, J., Kasser, T., & McAndrew, F. T. (2006). Guns, testosterone, and aggression: An experimental test of a mediational hypothesis. *Psychological Science, 17,* 568–571.

Klingenberg, C. P., & others. (2010). Prenatal alcohol exposure alters the pattern of facial asymmetry. *Alcohol.* (in press)

Klosterhalfen, S., Rüttgers, A., Krumrey, E., Otto, B., Stockhorst, U., Riepl, R. L., Probst, T., & Enck, P. (2000). Pavlovian conditioning of taste aversion using a motion sickness paradigm. *Psychosomatic Medicine, 62,* 671–677.

Klucharev, V., Hytonen, K., Rijpkema, M., Smidts, A., & Fernandez, G. (2009). Reinforcement learning signal predicts social conformity. *Neuron, 61,* 140–151.

Klumpp, H., & Amir, N. (2009). Examination of vigilance and disengagement of threat in social anxiety with a probe detection task. *Anxiety, Stress, and Coping, 2,* 1–13.

Klusmann, V., & others. (2010)). Complex mental and physical activity in older women and cognitive performance: A 6-month randomized controlled trial. *Journals of Gerontology A: Biological Sciences and Medical Sciences, 65,* 680–688.

Knapp, H. (2007). *Therapeutic communication.* Thousand Oaks, CA: Sage.

Knapp, S., & VandeCreek, L. (2000). Recovered memories of childhood abuse: Is there an underlying consensus? *Professional Psychology: Research and Practice, 31,* 365–371.

Knight, D. C., Waters, N. S., King, M. K., & Bandettini, P. A. (2010). Learning-related diminution of unconditioned SCR and fMRI signal responses. *NeuroImage, 49,* 843–848.

Knoblauch, S. H. (2009). From self psychology to selves in relationships: A radical process of micro and macro expansion in conceptual experience. *Annals of the New York Academy of Sciences, 1159,* 262–278.

Knowles, E. S., Nolan, J., & Riner, D. D. (2007). Resistance to persuasion. In R. Baumeister & K. Vohs (Eds.), *Encyclopedia of social psychology.* Newbury Park, CA: Sage.

Kobasa, S., Maddi, S., & Kahn, S. (1982). Hardiness and health: A prospective study. *Journal of Personality and Social Psychology, 42,* 168–177.

Kobasa, S. C., Maddi, S. R., Puccetti, M. C., & Zola, M. (1986). Relative effectiveness of hardiness, exercise, and social support as resources against illness. *Journal of Psychosomatic Research, 29,* 525–533.

Kobayashi, S., Pinto de Carvalho, O., & Schultz, W. (2010). Adaptation of reward sensitivity in orbitofrontal neurons. *Journal of Neuroscience, 30,* 534–544.

Koch, C. (2011). Neuroscience of consciousness. *Annual Review of Psychology* (vol. 62). Palo Alto, CA: Annual Reviews.

Kochanek, K. D., Murphy, S. L. Anderson, R. N, & Scott, C. (2004, October 12). Deaths: Final data for 2002. *National Vital Statistics Reports, 53* (5). Washington, DC: U.S. Department of Health and Human Services.

Kochanska, G., Aksan, N., Prisco, T. R., & Adams, E. E. (2008). Mother-child and father-child mutually responsive orientation in the first two years and children's outcomes at preschool age: Mechanisms of influence. *Child Development, 79,* 30–44.

Kodama, S., & others. (2009). Cardiorespiratory fitness as a quantitative predictor of all-cause mortality and cardiovascular events in healthy men and women: A meta-analysis. *Journal of the American Medical Association, 301,* 2024–2035.

Koepp, M. J., Hammers, A., Lawrence, A. D., Asselin, M. C., Grasby, P. M., & Bench, C. J. (2009). Evidence for endogenous opioid release in the amygdale during positive emotion. *NeuroImage, 44,* 252–256.

Koestner, R., Horberg, E. J., Gaudreau, P., Powers, T., Di Dio, P., Bryan, C., Jochum, R., & Salter, N. (2006). Bolstering implementation plans for the long haul: The benefits of simultaneously boosting self-concordance or self-efficacy. *Personality and Social Psychology Bulletin, 32,* 1547–1558.

Kohlberg, L. (1958). *The development on modes of moral thinking and choice in the years 10 to 16.* Unpublished doctoral dissertation, University of Chicago.

Kohlberg, L. (1986). A current statement on some theoretical issues. In S. Modgil & C. Modgil (Eds.), *Lawrence Kohlberg.* Philadelphia: Falmer.

Kohler, C. L., Schoenberger, Y., Tseng, T., & Ross, L. (2008). Correlates of transitions in stage of change for quitting among adolescent smokers. *Addictive Behaviors, 33,* 1615–1618.

Kohler, P. K., Manhart, L. E., & Lafferty, W. E. (2008). Abstinence-only and comprehensive sex education and the initiation of sexual activity and teen pregnancy. *Journal of Adolescent Health, 42,* 344–351.

Köhler, W. (1925). *The mentality of apes.* New York: Harcourt Brace Jovanovich.

Kohrt, B. A., & others. (2009). Culture in psychiatric epidemiology: Using ethnography and multiple mediator models to assess the relationship of caste with depression and anxiety in Nepal. *Annals of Human Biology, 36,* 261–280.

Kohut, H. (1977). *Restoration of the self.* New York: International Universities Press.

Koitabashi, T., Oyaizu, T., & Ouchi, T. (2009). Low bispectral index values following electroconvulsive therapy associated with memory impairment. *Journal of Anesthesiology, 23,* 182–187.

Kok, B. E., Catalino, L. I., & Fredrickson, B. L. (2008). The broadening, building, buffering effects of positive emotion. In S. J. Lopez (Ed.), *Positive psychology: Exploring the best of people* (vol. 3). Westport, CT: Greenwood.

Kok, G., & de Vries, N. K. (2006). Social psychology and health promotion. In P. A. M. Van Lange (Ed.), *Bridging social psychology.* Mahwah, NJ: Erlbaum.

Kong, L. L., Allen, J. J. B., & Glisky, E. L. (2008). Interidentity memory transfer in dissociative identity disorder. *Journal of Abnormal Psychology, 117,* 686–692.

Konrath, S., Bushman, B. J., & Campbell, W. K. (2006). Attenuating the link between threatened egotism and aggression. *Psychological Science, 17,* 995–1001.

Koo, M. S., Kim, E. J., Roh, D., & Kim, C. H. (2010). Role of dopamine in the pathophysiology and treatment of obsessive-compulsive disorder. *Expert Review of Neurotherapeutics, 10,* 275–290.

Koob, G. F. (2006). The neurobiology of addiction: A neuroadaptational view. *Addiction, 101, Suppl. 1,* S23–S30.

Kopell, B. H., Machado, A. G., & Rezai, A. R. (2006). Not your father's lobotomy: Psychiatric surgery revisited. *Clinical Neurosurgery, 52,* 315–330.

Korczak, D. J., & Goldstein, B. I. (2009). Childhood onset major depressive disorder: Course of illness and psychiatric comorbidity in a community sample. *Journal of Pediatrics, 155,* 118–123.

Korzekwa, M. I., Dell, P. F., Links, P. S., Thabane, L., & Webb, S. P. (2008). Estimating the prevalence of borderline personality disorder in psychiatric outpatients using a two-phase procedure. *Comprehensive Psychiatry, 49* (4), 380–386.

Kosslyn, S. M., Thompson, W. L., Kim, I. J., Rauch, S. L., & Alpert, N. M. (1996). Individual differences in cerebral blood flow in Area 17 predict the time to evaluate visualized letters. *Journal of Cognitive Neuroscience, 8,* 78–82.

Koszycki, D., Taljaard, M., Segal, Z., & Bradwein, J. (2010). A randomized trial of sertraline, self-administered cognitive behavior therapy, and their combination for panic disorder. *Psychological Medicine.* (in press)

Kovacs, A. M. (2009). Early bilingualism enhances mechanisms of false-belief reasoning. *Developmental Science, 12,* 48–54.

Kovacs, K., Lajtha, A., & Sershen, H. (2010). Effect of nicotine and cocaine on neurofilaments and receptors in whole brain tissue and synaptoneurosome preparations. *Brain Research Bulletin.* (in press)

Kovalszky, I., & others. (2010). Leptin-based glycopeptide induces weight loss and simultaneously restores fertility in animal models. *Diabetes, Obesity, and Metabolism, 12,* 393–402.

Kozaric-Kovacic, D. (2008). Integrative psychotherapy. *Psychiatria Danubina, 20,* 352–363.

Kozel, F. A., & others. (2009). Functional MRI detection of deception after commiting a mock sabotage crime. *Journal of Forensic Science, 54,* 220–231.

Kraemer, B., Noll, T., Delsignore, A., Milos, G., Schnyder, U., & Hepp, U. (2006). Finger length ratio (2D:4D) and dimensions of sexual orientation. *Neuropsychobiology, 53,* 210–214.

Kramer, A. F., & Morrow, D. (2010). Cognitive training and expertise. In D. Park & N. Schwartz (Eds.), *Cognitive aging: A primer.* New York: Psychology Press. (in press)

Kranz, G. S., Kasper, S., & Lanzenberger, R. (2010). Reward and the serotonergic system. *Neuroscience.* (in press)

Krause, N. (2006). Religion and health in late life. In J. E. Birren & K. W. Schaie (Eds.), *Handbook of the psychology of aging* (6th ed.). San Diego: Academic.

Krebs, T. S., Johansen, P. Ø., Jerome, L., & Halpern, J. H. (2009). Importance of psychiatric confounding in non-randomized studies of heavy ecstasy users. *Psychological Medicine, 39,* 876–878.

Kressel, L. M., & Uleman, J. S. (2010). Personality traits function as causal concepts. *Journal of Experimental Social Psychology, 46,* 213–216.

Kring, A. M., Davison, G. C., Neale, J. M., & Johnson, S. L. (2007). *Abnormal psychology* (10th ed.). New York: Wiley.

Kristof-Brown, A., & Guay, R. P. (2010). Person–environment fit. In S. Zedeck (Ed.), *APA handbook of industrial and organizational psychology.* Washington, DC: APA. (in press)

Kroger, J., Martinussen, M., & Marcia, J. E. (2010). Identity change in adolescence and young adulthood: A meta-analysis. *Journal of Adolescence.* (in press)

Krogstad, U., Hofoss, D., Veenstra, M., & Hjortdahl, P. (2006). Predictors of job satisfaction among doctors, nurses and auxiliaries in Norwegian hospitals: Relevance for micro unit culture. *Human Resources for Health, 4,* 3.

Kroth, R., & others. (2010). Murine features of neurogenesis in the human hippocampus across the lifespan from 0 to 100 years. *PLoS One, 5,* e8809.

Krueger, J. I. (2007). From social projection to social behaviour. *European Review of Social Psychology, 18,* 1–35.

Krueger, K. A., & Dayan, P. (2009). Flexible shaping: How learning in small steps helps. *Cognition, 110,* 380–394.

Krueger, R. F., Markon, K. E., & Bouchard, T. J. (2003). The extended genotype: The heritability of personality accounts for the heritability of recalled family environments in twins reared apart. *Journal of Personality, 71,* 809–833.

Kruger, J., Blanck, H. M., & Gillespie, C. (2006). Dietary and physical activity behaviors among adults successful at weight loss maintenance. *International Journal of Behavioral Nutrition and Physical Activity, 3,* 17.

Ksir, C. J., Hart, C. L., & Ray, O. S. (2008). *Drugs, society, and human behavior* (12th ed.). New York: McGraw-Hill.

Kuan, T. S. (2009). Current studies on myofascial pain syndrome. *Current Pain and Headache Reports, 13,* 365–369.

Kuczynski, B., & others. (2010). White matter integrity and cortical metabolic associations in aging and dementia. *Alzheimer's and Dementia, 6,* 54–62.

Kudo, K., & others. (2010). Differences in CT perfusion maps generated by different commercial software: Quantitative analysis by using identical source data of acute stroke patients. *Radiology, 254,* 200–209.

Kuhl, P. K. (2000). A new view of language acquisition. *Proceedings of the National Academy of Sciences USA, 97,* 11850–11857.

Kuhl, P. K. (2007). Is speech learning "gated" by the social brain? *Developmental Science, 10,* 110–120.

Kuhl, P. K., & Damasio, A. (2009). In E. R. Kandel & others (Eds.), *Principles of neural science* (5th ed.). New York: McGraw-Hill.

Kuhn, D. (2008). Formal operations from a twenty-first-century perspective. *Human Development, 51,* 48–55.

Kuhn, D. (2009). Adolescent thinking. In R. M. Lerner & L. Steinberg (Eds.), *Handbook of adolescent psychology* (3rd ed.). New York: Wiley.

Kuhn, D. (2011). What is scientific thinking and how does it develop? In U. Goswami (Ed.), *Wiley-Blackwell handbook of childhood cognitive development* (2nd ed.). New York: Wiley Blackwell.

Kujanik, S., & Mikulecky, M. (2010). Circadian and ultradian extrasystole rhythms in healthy individuals at elevated versus lowland altitudes. *International Journal of Biometeorology.* (in press)

Kullmann, D. M. (2010). The neurological channelpathies. *Annual Review of Neuroscience* (vol. 33). Palo Alto, CA: Annual Reviews.

Kumar, C. T. S. (2004). Physical illness and schizophrenia. *British Journal of Psychiatry, 184,* 541.

Kuntsche, E., Knibbe, R., Gmel, G., & Engels, R. (2006). Who drinks and why? A review of socio-demographic, personality, and contextual issues behind the drinking motives in young people. *Addictive Behaviors, 31,* 1844–1857.

Kurdek, L. (1992). Relationship quality in gay and lesbian cohabiting couples: A prospective longitudinal test of the contextual and interdependence models. *Journal of Social and Personal Relationships, 9,* 125–142.

Kurdek, L. (2004). Are gay and lesbian cohabiting couples *really* different from heterosexual married couples? *Journal of Marriage and Family, 66,* 880–900.

Kurson, R. (2007). *Crashing through: A true story of risk, adventure, and the man who dared to see.* New York: Random House.

Kurtz, J. (2008). Looking to the future to appreciate the present. *Psychological Science, 19,* 1238–1241.

Kushner, M. G. (2007). The use of cognitive-behavioral therapy in the University of Minnesota's outpatient psychiatry clinic. *Minnesota Medicine, 90,* 31–33.

Kushner, R. F. (2007). Obesity management. *Gastroenterology Clinics of North America, 36,* 191–210.

Kuyper, P. (1972). The cocktail party effect. *Audiology, 11,* 277–282.

L

Labouvie-Vief, G. (1986, August). *Modes of knowing and life-span cognition.* Paper presented at the meeting of the American Psychological Association, Washington, DC.

Labouvie-Vief, G. (2006). Emerging structures of adult thought. In J. J. Arnett & J. L. Tanner (Eds.), *Emerging adults in America* (pp. 60–84). Washington, DC: American Psychological Association.

Lac, A., Alvaro, E. M., Crano, W. D., & Siegel, J. T. (2009). Pathways from parental knowledge and warmth to adolescent marijuana use: An extension to the theory of planned behavior. *Prevention Science, 10,* 22–32.

Lachman, M. E., Rocke, C., Rosnick, C., & Ryff, C. D. (2008). Realism and illusion in Americans' temporal views of their life satisfaction: Age differences in reconstructing the past and anticipating the future. *Psychological Science, 19,* 89–897.

Lader, M., Tylee, A., & Donoghue, J. (2009). Withdrawing benzodiazepines in primary care. *CNS Drugs, 23,* 19–34.

LaFromboise, T. D., Albright, K., & Harris, A. (2010). Patterns of hopelessness among American Indian adolescents: Relationships by levels of acculturation and residence. *Cultural Diversity and Ethnic Minority Psychology, 16,* 68–76.

Lai, C., & Bird, S. (2010). Querying linguistic trees. *Journal of Logic, Language and Information, 19,* 53–73.

Laible, D. J., & Thompson, R. A. (2000). Mother–child discourse, attachment security, shared positive affect, and early conscience development. *Child Development, 71,* 1424–1440.

Laible, D. J., & Thompson, R. A. (2002). Mother–child conflict in the toddler years: Lessons in emotion, morality, and relationships. *Child Development, 73,* 1187–1203.

Laible, D. J., & Thompson, R. A. (2007). Early socialization: A relationship perspective. In J. E. Grusec & P. D. Hastings (Eds.), *Handbook of socialization.* New York: Guilford.

Lam, C. B., & McBride-Chang, C. A. (2007). Resilience in young adulthood: The moderating influences of gender-related personality traits and coping flexibility. *Sex Roles, 56,* 159–172.

Lambert, M. J. (2001). The effectiveness of psychotherapy: What a century of research tells us about the effects of treatment. *Psychotherapeutically speaking—Updates from the Division of Psychotherapy* (29). Washington, DC: American Psychological Association.

Lamberton, L., & Minor-Evans, L. (2010). *Human relations* (4th ed.). New York: McGraw-Hill.

Lambon Ralph, M. A., Sage, K., Jones, R. W., & Mayberry, E. J. (2010). Coherent concepts are computed in the anterior temporal lobes. *Proceedings of the National Academy of Sciences USA.* (in press)

Laming, D. (2010). Serial position curves in free recall. *Psychological Review, 117,* 93–133.

Landau, M. E., & Barner, K. C. (2009). Vestibulocochlear nerve. *Seminars in Neurology, 29,* 66–73.

Landis, C., & Erlick, D. (1950). An analysis of the Porteus Maze Test as affected by psychosurgery. *American Journal of Psychology, 63,* 557–566.

Lane, S. M., & Schooler, J. W. (2004). Skimming the surface: Verbal overshadowing of analogical retrieval. *Psychological Science, 15,* 715–719.

Laney, C., & Loftus, E. F. (2009). Eyewitness memory. In R. N. Kocsis (Ed.), *Applied criminal psychology.* Springfield, IL: Thomas.

Lange, C. G. (1922). *The emotions.* Baltimore: Williams & Wilkins.

Langer, E., Blank, A., & Chanowitz, B. (1978). The mindlessness of ostensibly thoughtful action: The role of "placebic" information in interpersonal interaction. *Journal of Personality and Social Psychology, 36* (6), 635–642.

Langer, E. J. (1997). *The power of mindful learning.* Reading, MA: Addison-Wesley.

Langer, E. J. (2000). Mindful learning. *Current Directions in Psychological Science, 9,* 220–223.

Langer, E. J. (2005). *On becoming an artist.* New York: Ballantine.

Langer, E. J., & Rodin, J. (1976). The effects of choice and enhanced personal responsibility for the aged: A field experiment in an institutional setting. *Journal of Personality and Social Psychology, 34,* 191–198.

Langer, J. J. (1991). *Holocaust testimonies: The ruins of memory.* New Haven, CT: Yale University Press.

Langleben, D. D., & Dattilio, F. M. (2008). Commentary: The future of forensic functional brain imaging. *Journal of the American Academy of Psychiatry and the Law, 36,* 502–504.

Langlois, J. H., Kalakanis, L., Rubenstein, A. J., Larson, A., Hallam, M., & Smoot, M. (2000). Maxims or myths of beauty? A meta-analytic and theoretical review. *Psychological Bulletin, 126,* 390–423.

Langlois, J. H., Roggman, L. A., & Musselman, L. (1994). What is average and what is not average about attractive faces? *Psychological Science, 5,* 214–220.

Langston, W. (2011). *Research methods: Laboratory manual for psychology* (3rd ed.). Boston: Cengage.

Langstrom, N. (2010). The DSM diagnostic criteria for exhibitionism, voyeurism, and frotteurism. *Archives of Sexual Behavior, 39,* 317–324.

Langstrom, N., Rahman, Q., Carlstrom, E., & Lichtenstein, P. (2010). Genetic and environmental effects on same-sex sexual behaviour: A population study of twins in Sweden. *Archives of Sexual Behavior, 39,* 75–80.

Lapierre, L. M., Spector, P. E., & Leck, J. D. (2005). Sexual versus non-sexual workplace aggression and victims' overall job satisfaction: A meta-analysis. *Journal of Occupational Health Psychology, 10,* 155–169.

Larson-Prior, L. J., Zempel, J. M., Nolan, T. S., Prior, F. W., Snyder, A. Z., & Rachlie, M. E. (2009). Cortical network functional connectivity in the descent to sleep. *Proceedings of the National Academy of Sciences USA, 106,* 4489–4494.

La Rue, A. (2010). Healthy brain aging: Role of cognitive reserve, cognitive stimulation, and cognitive exercises. *Clinics in Geriatric Medicine, 26,* 99–111.

Larzerele, R. E., & Kuhn, B. R. (2005). Comparing child outcomes of physical punishment and alternative discipline practices: A meta-analysis. *Clinical Child and Family Psychology Review, 8,* 1–37.

Lashley, K. (1950). In search of the engram. In *Symposium of the Society for Experimental Biology* (vol. 4). New York: Cambridge University Press.

Last, C. G. (2009). *When someone you love is bipolar.* New York: Guilford.

Latané, B. (1981). The psychology of social impact. *American Psychologist, 36,* 343–356.

Latrémolière, A., & Woolf, C. J. (2009). Central sensitization: A generator of pain hypersensitivity by central neural plasticity. *Journal of Pain, 10,* 895–926.

Laumann, E. O., Nicolosi, A., Glasser, D. B., Paik, A., & Gingell, C. (2005). Sexual problems among men and women aged 40–80 yrs: Prevalence and correlates identified in the global study of sexual attitudes and behaviours. *International Journal of Impotence Research, 17,* 39–57.

Laurence, J. (2006). Editorial: Treating HIV with one pill per day. *AIDS Patient Care and STD, 20,* 610–603.

Lawler-Row, K. A., Karremans, J. C., Scott, C., Edlis-Matityahou, M., & Edwards, L. (2008). Forgiveness, physiological reactivity, and health: The role of anger. *International Journal of Psychophysiology, 68,* 51–58.

Lazarus, A. A., Beutler, L. E., & Norcross, J. C. (1992). The future of technical eclecticism. *Psychotherapy, 29,* 11–20.

Lazarus, R. S. (1991). On the primacy of cognition. *American Psychologist, 39,* 124–129.

Lazarus, R. S. (1993). Coping theory and research: Past, present, and future. *Psychosomatic Medicine, 55,* 234–247.

Lazarus, R. S. (2000). Toward better research on stress and coping. *American Psychologist, 55,* 665–673.

Lazarus, R. S. (2003). Does the positive psychology movement have legs? *Psychological Inquiry, 14,* 93–109.

Leaper, C., & Friedman, C. K. (2007). The socialization of gender. In J. E. Grusec & P. D. Hastings (Eds.), *Handbook of socialization.* New York: Guilford.

Leary, M. R. (2008). *Introduction to behavioral research methods* (5th ed.). Boston: Allyn & Bacon.

Leary, M. R., & Hoyle, R. H. (Eds.). (2009a). *Handbook of individual differences in social behavior* New York: Guilford.

Leary, M. R., & Hoyle, R. H. (Eds.). (2009b). Situations, dispositions, and the study of social behavior. In M. R. Leary & R. H. Hoyle (Eds.), *Handbook of individual differences in social behavior* (pp. 3–11). New York: Guilford.

Leasure, J. L., & Decker, L. (2009). Social isolation prevents exercise-induced proliferation of hippocampal progenitor cells in female rats. *Hippocampus, 19,* 907–912.

Le Bel, R. M., Pineda, J. A., & Sharma, A. (2009). Motor-auditory-visual integration: The role of the human mirror neuron system in communication and communication disorders. *Journal of Communication Disorders, 42,* 299–304.

Lebrun-Julien, F., & others. (2010). ProNGF induces TNF (alpha)-dependent death of retinal ganglion cells through a p75NTR non-cell-autonomous signaling pathway. *Proceedings of the National Academy of Sciences USA.* (in press)

LeDoux, J. E. (1996). *The emotional brain: The mysterious underpinnings of emotional life.* New York: Simon & Schuster.

LeDoux, J. E. (2000). Emotion circuits in the brain. *Annual Review of Neuroscience, 23,* 155–184.

LeDoux, J. E. (2001). *Emotion, memory, and the brain.* http://www.cns.nyu.edu/home/ledoux.html (accessed October 15, 2001)

LeDoux, J. E. (2002). *The synaptic self.* New York: Viking.

LeDoux, J. E. (2008). Amygdala. *Scholarpedia, 3,* 2698.

LeDoux, J. E. (2009). Emotional coloration of consciousness: How feelings come about. In L. W. Weiskrantz & M. Davis (Eds.), *Frontiers of consciousness.* New York: Oxford University Press.

Lee, C. D., Blair, S. N., & Jackson, A. S. (1999). Cardiorespiratory fitness, body composition, and all-cause and cardiovascular disease mortality in men. *American Journal of Clinical Nutrition, 69,* 373–380.

Lee, J. W., & others. (2010). Evaluation of postoperative sharp waveforms through EEG and magnetoencephalography. *Journal of Clinical Neurophysiology, 27,* 7–11.

Lee, J. W. Y. (2010). Neuroleptic-induced catatonia: Clinical presentation, response to benzodiazepines, and relationship to neuroleptic malignant syndrome. *Journal of Clinical Psychopharmacology, 30,* 3–10.

Lee, M.-J., & Fried, S. K. (2009). Integration of hormonal and nutrient signals that regulate leptin synthesis and secretion. *American Journal of Physiology, Endocrinology, and Metabolism.* doi:10.1152/ajpendo.90927.2008

Lee, P. A., Houk, C. P., Ahmed, S. F., & Hughes, I. A. (2006). Consensus statement on management of intersex disorders. *Pediatrics, 118,* e488–e500.

Leedy, P. D., & Ormrod, J. E. (2010). *Practical research* (9th ed.). Upper Saddle River, NJ: Prentice-Hall.

Lefkowitz, J. (2000). The role of interpersonal affective regard in supervisory performance ratings: A literature review and proposed causal model. *Journal of Occupational and Organizational Psychology, 73,* 67–85.

Legaree, T. A., Turner, J., & Lollis, S. (2007). Forgiveness and therapy: A critical review of conceptualizations, practices, and values in the literature. *Journal of Marital and Family Therapy, 33,* 192–213.

le Grange, D., Lock, J., Loeb, K., & Nicholls, D. (2010). Academy for Eating Disorders position paper: The role of the family in eating disorders. *International Journal of Eating Disorders, 43,* 1–5.

Leibel, R. L. (2008). Molecular physiology of weight regulation in mice and humans. *International Journal of Obesity, 32, Suppl. 7,* S98–S108.

Leichtman, M. (2009). Concepts of development and the Rorschach: The contributions of Paul Lerner and John Exner in historical context. *Journal of Personality Assessment, 91,* 24–29.

Leigh, E. G. (2010). The group selection controversy. *Journal of Evolutionary Biology, 23,* 6–19.

Leo, J. L. (2005). Editorial: Methylphenidate-induced neuropathology in the developing rat brain: Implications for humans. *Ethical Human Psychology and Psychiatry, 7,* 107–110.

Leon, I. G. (2010). Understanding and treating infertility: Psychoanalytic considerations. *Journal of the American Academy of Psychoanalysis and Dynamic Psychiatry, 38,* 47–75.

Leonard, B. E., & Myint, A. (2009). The psychoneuroimmunology of stress. *Human Psychopharmacology, 24,* 165–175.

Lepage, J. F., & Theoret, H. (2010). Brain connectivity: Finding a cause. *Current Biology, 20,* R66–R67.

Lepper, M., Greene, D., & Nisbett, R. E. (1973). Undermining children's intrinsic interest with extrinsic rewards. *Journal of Personality and Social Psychology, 28,* 129–137.

Lepore, S. J., & Smyth, J. (Eds.). (2002). *The writing cure.* Washington, DC: American Psychological Association.

Lerner, B. H. (2005). Last-ditch medical therapy—revisiting lobotomy. *New England Journal of Medicine, 353,* 119–121.

Lerner, J. V., Phelps, E., Forman, Y. E., & Bowers, E. (2009). Positive youth development. In R. M. Lerner & L. Steinberg (Eds.), *Handbook of adolescent psychology* (3rd ed.). New York: Wiley.

Lerner, R. D., Boyd, M., & Du, D. (2008). Adolescent development. In I. B. Weiner & C. B. Craighead (Eds.), *Encyclopedia of psychology* (4th ed.). New York: Wiley.

Leslie, A. M., German, T. P., & Polizzi, P. (2005). Belief-desire reasoning as a process of selection. *Cognitive Psychology, 50,* 45–85.

Leslie, J. C., Shaw, D., Gregg, G., McCormick, N., Reynolds, D. S., & Dawson, G. R. (2006). Effects of reinforcement schedule on facilitation of operant extinction by chlordiazepoxide. *Journal of the Experimental Analysis of Behavior, 84,* 327–338.

Leszczynski, J. P. (2009). A state conceptualization: Are individuals' masculine and feminine personality traits situationally influenced? *Personality and Individual Differences, 47,* 157–162.

Leucht, S., Kissling, W., & Davis, J. M. (2009). Second-generation antipsychotics for schizophrenia: Can we resolve the conflict? *Psychological Medicine, 39,* 1591–1602.

Leung, A. K., Maddux, W. W., Galinsky, A. D., & Chiu, C. (2008). Multicultural experience enhances creativity. *American Psychologist, 63,* 169–181.

Lev, A. I. (2007). Transgender communities: Developing identity through connection. In K. J. Bieschke, R. M. Perez, & K. A. DeBord, (Eds.), *Handbook of counseling and psychotherapy with lesbian, gay, bisexual, and transgender clients* (2nd ed., pp. 147–175). Washington, DC: American Psychological Association.

Levenson, M. R., & Aldwin, C. M. (2006). Change in personality processes and health outcomes. In D. K. Mroczek & T. D. Little (Eds.), *Handbook of personality development* (pp. 423–444). Mahwah, NJ: Erlbaum.

Leventhal, H., & Tomarken, A. J. (1986). Emotion: Today's problems. *Annual Review of Psychology* (vol. 37). Palo Alto, CA: Annual Reviews.

Levi, D. (2007). *Group dynamics for teams* (2nd ed.). Thousand Oaks, CA: Sage.

Levin, B. E. (2010). Developmental gene × environment interactions affecting systems regulating homeostasis and obesity. *Frontiers in Neuroscience.* (in press)

Levin, C. (2010). The mind as a complex internal object: Inner estrangement. *Psychoanalytic Quarterly, 79,* 95–27.

Levin, J., & Fox, J. A. (2011). *Elementary statistics for social research* (3rd ed.). Upper Saddle River, NJ: Prentice-Hall.

Levine, D. S. (2000). *Introduction to neural and cognitive modeling* (2nd ed.). Mahwah, NJ: Erlbaum.

Levine, M., Cassidy, C., & Jentzsch I. (2010). The implicit identity effect: Identity primes, group size, and helping. *British Journal of Social Psychology.* (in press)

Levine, R. L. (2002). Endocrine aspects of eating disorders in adolescents. *Adolescent Medicine, 13,* 129–144.

Levine, S. C., Huttenlocher, J., Taylor, A., & Langrock, A. (1999). Early sex differences in spatial skill. *Developmental Psychology, 35,* 940–949.

Levinthal, C. F. (2010). *Drugs, behavior, and modern society* (6th ed.). Upper Saddle River, NJ: Prentice-Hall.

Levitan, E. B., Wolk, A., & Mittleman, M. A. (2009). Consistency with the DASH diet and the incidence of heart failure. *Archives of Internal Medicine, 169,* 851–857.

Levy, B. R., Slade, M. D., & Kasl, S. V. (2002). Increased longevity by positive self-perceptions of aging. *Journal of Personality and Social Psychology, 83,* 261–270.

Lewis, A., Williams, P., Lawrence, O., Wong, R. O., & Brockerhoff, S. E. (2010). Wild-type cone photoreceptors persist despite neighboring mutant cone degeneration. *Journal of Neuroscience, 30,* 382–389.

Lewis, G. D., & others. (2010). Metabolic signatures of exercise in human plasma. *Science Translation Medicine.* (in press)

Lewis, R. W., Yuan, J., & Wang, R. (2008). Male sexual arousal disorder. In D. L. Rowland & L. Incrocci (Eds.), *Handbook of sexual and gender identity disorders* (pp. 32–67). Hoboken, NJ: Wiley.

Li, Y., & Epley, N. (2009). When the best appears to be saved for last: Serial position effects on choice. *Journal of Behavioral Decision Making, 22,* 378–389.

Liang, B., Williams, L. M., & Siegel, J. A. (2006). Relational outcomes of childhood sexual trauma in female survivors: A longitudinal study. *Journal of Interpersonal Violence, 21,* 42–57.

Liao, K., Walker, M. F., Joshi, A. C., Reschke, M., Strupp, M., Wagner, J., & Leigh, R. J. (2010). The linear vestibulo-ocular reflex, locomotion and falls in neurological disorders. *Restorative Neurology and Neuroscience, 28,* 91–103.

Light, S. N., Goldsmith, H. H., Coan, J. A., Frye, C., & Davidson, R. J. (2009). Dynamic variation in pleasure in children predicts non-linear change in lateral frontal activity. *Developmental Psychology, 45,* 525–533.

Lilienfeld, S. O., Wood, J. M., & Garb, H. N. (2000, November). The scientific status of projective techniques. *Psychological Science in the Public Interest, 1* (2).

Lim, J., Bogossian, F., & Ahern, K. (2010). Stress and coping in Australian nurses: A systematic review. *International Nursing Review, 57,* 22–31.

Lin, L. (2009). Breadth-biased versus focused cognitive control in media multitasking behaviors. *Proceedings of the National Academy of Sciences USA, 106,* 15521–15522.

Lin, Y.-C., & Koleske, A. J. (2010). Mechanisms of synapse and dendrite maintenance and their disruption in psychiatric and neurogenerative disorders. *Annual Review of Neuroscience* (vol. 33). Palo Alto, CA: Annual Reviews.

Lindau, S. T., & Gavrilova, N. (2010). Sex, health, and years of sexually active life gained due to good health: Evidence from two U.S. population based cross sectional surveys of aging. *British Medical Journal.* (in press)

Linden, W., Lenz, J. W., & Con, A. H. (2001). Individualized stress management for primary hypertension: A randomized trial. *Archives of Internal Medicine, 161,* 1071–1080.

Lindvall, O., & Kokaia, Z. (2010). Stem cells in neurodegenerative disorders—time for clinical translation? *Journal of Clinical Investigation, 120,* 29–40.

Lindwall, M., Rennemark, M., Halling, A., Berglund, J., & Hassmen, P. (2007). Depression and exercise in elderly men and women: Findings from the Swedish national study on aging and care. *Journal of Aging and Physical Activity, 15,* 41–55.

Ling, G., Bandak, F., Armonda, R., Grant, G., & Ecklund, J. (2009). Explosive blast neurotrauma. *Journal of Neurotrauma, 26,* 815–825.

Lingjaerde, O., Foreland, A. R., & Engvik, H. (2001). Personality structure in patients with winter depression, assessed in a depression-free state according to the five-factor model of personality. *Journal of Affective Disorders, 62,* 165–174.

Linke, S. E., & others. (2009). Depressive symptom dimensions and cardiovascular prognosis among women with suspected myocardial ischemia: A report from the National Heart, Lung, and Blood Institute-sponsored women's Ischemia Syndrome Foundation. *Archives of General Psychiatry, 66,* 499–507.

Linnman, C., Appel, L., Furark, T., Soderlund, A., Gordh, T., Langstrom, B., & Fredrikson, M. (2010). Ventromedial prefrontal neurokinin 1 receptor availability is reduced in chronic pain. *Pain.* (in press)

Lippa, R. (2000). Gender-related traits in gay men, lesbian women and heterosexual men and women: The virtual identity of homosexual-heterosexual diagnosticity and gender diagnosticity. *Journal of Personality, 68,* 899–926.

Lippa, R. (2003). Handedness, sexual orientation, and gender-related personality traits in men and women. *Archives of Sexual Behavior, 32,* 103–114.

Lippa, R. A. (2005). *Gender: Nature and nurture* (2nd ed.). Mahwah, NJ: Erlbaum.

Lippa, R. (2008). The relation between childhood gender nonconformity and adult masculinity-femininity and anxiety in heterosexual and homosexual men and women. *Sex Roles, 59,* 684–693.

Lippke, S., & Plotnikoff, R. C. (2006). Stages of change in physical exercise: A test of stage discrimination and nonlinearity. *American Journal of Health Behavior, 30,* 290–301.

Lippke, S., Ziegelmann, J. P., Schwarzer, R., & Velicer, W. F. (2009). Validity of stage assessment in the adoption and maintenance of physical activity and fruit and vegetable consumption. *Health Psychology, 28,* 183–193.

Lipsey, M. W., & Wilson, D. B. (1993). The efficacy of psychological, educational, and behavioral treatment: Confirmation from meta-analysis. *American Psychologist, 48,* 1181–1209.

Lissek, S., & others. (2010). Overgeneralization of conditioned fear as a pathogenic marker of panic disorder. *American Journal of Psychiatry, 167,* 47–55.

Little, K. Y., Zhang, L., & Cook, E. (2006). Fluoxetine-induced alterations in human platelet serotonin transporter expression: Serotonin transporter polymorphism effects. *Psychiatry and Neuroscience, 31,* 333–339.

Little, T. D., Snyder, C. R., & Wehmeyer, M. (2006). The agentic self: On the nature and origins of personal agency across the life span. In D. K. Mroczek & T. D. Little (Eds.), *Handbook of personality development.* Mahwah, NJ: Erlbaum.

Littlefield, A. K., & Sher, K. J. (2010). Alcohol use disorders in young adulthood. In J. E. Grant (Ed.), *Young adult mental health* (pp. 292–310). New York: Oxford University Press.

Littrell, J. H., & Girvin, H. (2002). Stages of change: A critique. *Behavior Modification, 26,* 223–273.

Liu, C. C., Doong, J. L., Hsu, W. S., Huang, W. S., & Jeng, M. C. (2009). Evidence from the selective attention mechanism and dual-task interference. *Applied Ergonomics, 40,* 341–347.

Liu, P. D., & McBride-Chang, C. (2010). What is morphological awareness? Tapping lexical compounding awareness in Chinese third graders. *Journal of Educational Psychology, 102,* 62–73.

Liu, R., & Huang, X. (1999). A study on time-perceptual cues in visual information. *Acta Psychologic Sinica, 31,* 15–20.

Lo, S. (2008). The nonverbal communication functions of emotions in computer-mediated communication. *CyberPsychology & Behavior, 11,* 595–597.

Lobbestael, J., & Arntz, A. (2010). Emotional, cognitive, and physiological correlates of abuse-related stress in borderline and antisocial personality disorder. *Behavior Research and Therapy, 48,* 116–124.

Loftus, E. F. (1975). Spreading activation within semantic categories. *Journal of Experimental Psychology, 104,* 234–240.

Loftus, E. F. (1993). Psychologists in the eyewitness world. *American Psychologist, 48,* 550–552.

Loftus, E. F. (2009). Crimes of memory: False memories and social justice. In M. A. Gernsbacher, L. Hough, R. Pew, & J. Pomerantz (Eds.), *Psychology in the real world.* New York: Worth.

Loftus, E. F., & Frenda, S. J. (2010). Bad theories can harm victims. *Science, 327,* 1329–1330.

Loftus, E. F., & Ketcham, K. (1991). *Witness for the defense: The accused, the eyewitness, and the expert who puts memory on trial.* New York: St. Martin's Press.

Loftus, E. F., & Pickrell, J. E. (2001, June). *Creating false memories.* Paper presented at the meeting of the American Psychological Society, Toronto.

Longo, D. A., Lent, R. W., & Brown, S. D. (1992). Social cognitive variables in the prediction of client motivation and attribution. *Journal of Counseling Psychology, 39,* 447–452.

Lopes, M., & Santos-Victor, J. (2007). A developmental roadmap for learning by imitation in robots. *IEEE Transactions on Systems, Man, and Cybernetics B, 37,* 308–321.

Lopez-Munoz, F., & Alamo, C. (2009). Mono-aminergic neurotransmission: The history of the discovery of antidepressants from 1950s until today. *Current Pharmaceutical Design, 15,* 1563–1586.

Lorant, V., Croux, C., Weich, S., Deliege, D., Mackenbach, J., & Ansseau, M. (2007). Depression and socioeconomic risk factors: 7-year longitudinal population study. *British Journal of Psychiatry, 190,* 293–298.

Lord, R. G., Diefendorff, J. M., Schmidt, A. M., & Hall, R. J. (2010). Self-regulation at work. *Annual Review of Psychology* (vol. 61). Palo Alto, CA: Annual Reviews.

Lorenz, K. Z. (1965). *Evolution and the modification of behavior.* Chicago: University of Chicago Press.

Loring-Meier, S., & Halpern, D. F. (1999). Sex differences in visual-spatial working memory: Components of cognitive processing. *Psychonomic Bulletin & Review, 6,* 464–471.

Lo Sauro, C., Ravaldi, C., Cabras, P. L., Faravelli, C., & Ricca, V. (2008). Stress, hypothalamic-pituitary-adrenal axis, and eating disorders. *Neuropsychobiology, 57,* 95–115.

Lovinger, D. M. (2010). Neurotransmitter roles in synaptic modulation, plasticity, and learning in the dorsal striatum. *Neuropharmacology.* (in press)

Low, C. A., Stanton, A., & Danoff-Burg, S. (2006). Expressive disclosure and benefit finding among breast cancer patients: Mechanisms for positive health effects. *Health Psychology, 25,* 181–189.

Lu, J., Sherman, D., Devor, M., & Saper, C. B. (2006). A putative flip-flop switch for control of REM sleep. *Nature, 441,* 589–594.

Lubinski, D., Benbow, C. P., Webb, R. M., & Bleske-Rechek, A. (2006). Tracking exceptional human capital over two decades. *Psychological Science, 17,* 194–199.

Lubinski, D., Webb, R. M., Morelock, M. J., & Benbow, C. P. (2001). Top 1 in 10,000: A 10-year follow-up of the profoundly gifted. *Journal of Applied Psychology, 86,* 718–729.

Luborsky, L., Rosenthal, R., Diguer, L., Andrusyna, T. P., Berman, J. S., Levitt, J. T., Seligman, D. A., & Krause, E. D. (2002). The dodo bird verdict is alive and well—mostly. *Clinical Psychology: Science and Practice, 9,* 2–12.

Lucas, R. E. (2007). Extraversion. In R. Baumeister & K. Vohs (Eds.), *The encyclopedia of social psychology.* Thousand Oaks, CA: Sage.

Lucas, R. E. (2008). Personality and subjective well-being. In M. Eid & R. J. Larsen (Eds.), *The science of subjective well-being* (pp. 171–194). New York: Psychology Press.

Lucas, R. E., Clark, A. E., Yannis, G., & Diener, E. (2004). Unemployment alters the setpoint for life satisfaction. *Psychological Science, 15,* 8–13.

Ludlow, K. H., & others. (2009). Acute and chronic ethanol modulate dopamine d2-subtype receptor responses in ventral tegmental area GABA neurons. *Alcoholism: Clinical and Experimental Research, 33,* 804–811.

Luo, X., Galvin, J. J., & Fu, Q. J. (2010). Effects of stimulus duration on amplitude modulation processing with cochlear implants. *Journal of Acoustical Society of America, 127,* EL23.

Luo, Y., & Baillargeon, R. (2005). Can a self-propelled box have a goal? Psychological reasoning in 5-month-old infants. *Psychological Science, 16,* 601–608.

Luria, A. R. (1968/1987). *The mind of a mnemonist.* L. Solotaroff (Trans.). Cambridge, MA: Harvard University Press.

Lutchmaya, S., Baron-Cohen, S., Raggatt, P., Knickmeyer, R., & Manning, J. T. (2004). 2nd to 4th digit ratios, fetal testosterone and estradiol. *Early Human Development, 77,* 23–28.

Luthans, F. (2011). *Organizational behavior* (12th ed.). New York: McGraw-Hill.

Lykken, D. (1999). *Happiness: What studies on twins show us about nature, nurture, and the happiness set-point.* New York: Golden Books.

Lykken, D. T. (1987). The probity of the polygraph. In S. M. Kassin & L. S. Wrightsman (Eds.), *The psychology of evidence and trial procedures.* Newbury Park, CA: Sage.

Lykken, D. T. (1998). *A tremor in the blood: Uses and abuses of the lie detector* (2nd ed.). New York: Plenum Press.

Lykken, D. T. (2001). Lie detection. In W. E. Craighead & C. B. Nemeroff (Eds.), *The Corsini encyclopedia of psychology and behavioral science* (3rd ed.). New York: Wiley.

Lynam, D. R., Caspi, A., Moffitt, T. E., Loeber, R., & Stouthamer-Loeber, M. (2007). Longitudinal evidence that psychopathy scores in early adolescence predict adult psychopathy. *Journal of Abnormal Psychology, 116,* 155–165.

Lynn, S. J. (2007). Hypnosis reconsidered. *American Journal of Clinical Hypnosis, 49,* 195–197.

Lynn, S. J., Boycheva, E., & Barnes, S. (2008). To assess or not assess hypnotic susceptibility? That is the question. *American Journal of Clinical Hypnosis, 51,* 161–165.

Lynn, S. J., Green, J. P., Accaradi, M., & Cleere, C. (2010). Hypnosis and smoking cessation: The state of the science. *American Journal of Clinical Hypnosis, 52,* 177–181.

Lyubomirsky, S. (2008). *The how of happiness: A scientific approach to getting the life you want.* New York: Penguin.

Lyubomirsky, S., King, L. A., & Diener, E. (2005). The benefits of frequent positive affect: Does happiness lead to success? *Psychological Bulletin, 131,* 803–855.

M

Maccoby, E. E. (2002). Gender and group processes. *Current Directions in Psychological Science, 11,* 54–58.

Macdonald, J. S. P., & Lavie, N. (2008). Load induced blindness. *Journal of Experimental Psychology: Human Perception and Performance, 34,* 1078–1091.

Machado, G. M., Oliveira, M. M., & Fernandes, L. A. (2009). A physiologically-based model for simulation of color vision deficiency. *IEEE Transactions on Visualization and Computer Graphics, 15,* 1291–1298.

MacKenzie, S. B., Podsakoff, P. M., & Ahearne, M. (1998). Some possible antecedents and consequences of in-role and extra-role sales-person performance. *Journal of Marketing, 62,* 87–98.

MacLeod, M. (2006, April 1). Mindless imitation teaches us how to be human. *New Scientist, 2545,* 42.

MacQueen, C. E., Brynes, A. E., & Frost, G. S. (2002). Treating obesity: A follow-up study. Can the stages of change model be used as a postal screening tool? *Journal of Human Nutrition and Dietetics, 15* (1), 3–7.

Madan, A., Palaniappan, L., Urizar, G., Wang, Y., Formann, S. P., & Gould, J. B. (2006). Sociocultural factors that affect pregnancy outcomes in two dissimilar immigrant groups in the United States. *Journal of Pediatrics, 148,* 341–346.

Maddi, S. (1998). Hardiness. In H. S. Friedman (Ed.), *Encyclopedia of mental health* (vol. 3). San Diego: Academic.

Maddi, S. R. (2008). The courage and strategies of hardiness as helpful in growing despite major, disruptive stresses. *American Psychologist, 63,* 563–564.

Maddi, S. R., Harvey, R. H., Khoshaba, D. M., Lu, J. L., Persico, M., & Brow, M. (2006). The personality construct of hardiness, III: Relationships with repression, innovativeness, authoritarianism, and performance. *Journal of Personality, 74,* 575–597.

Maddux, J. E. (2010). Social cognitive theories and clinical interventions: Basic processes. In J. E. Maddux & J. P. Tagney (Eds.), *Social psychological foundations of clinical psychology.* New York: Guilford.

Maddux, W. W., & Galinsky, A. D. (2007, September). *Cultural borders and mental barriers: Living in and adapting to foreign countries facilitates creativity.* Working Paper No. 2007/51/B. Fountainbleau, France: INSEAD.

Mader, S. S. (2010). *Biology* (10th ed.). New York: McGraw-Hill.

Mader, S. S. (2011). *Inquiry into life* (13th ed.). New York: McGraw-Hill.

Maes, H. H. M., Neal, M. C., & Eaves, L. J. (1997). Genetic and environmental factors in relative body weight and human adiposity. *Behavior Genetics, 27,* 325–351.

Maggio, N., & Segal, M. (2009). Differential corticosteroid modulation of inhibitory synaptic currents in the dorsal and ventral hippocampus. *Journal of Neuroscience, 29,* 2857–2866.

Maguire, E. A., Gadian, G. D., Johnsrude, I. S., Good, C. D., Ashburner, J., Frackowiak, R. S. J., & Frith, C. D. (2000). Navigation-related structural change in the hippocampi of taxi drivers. *Proceedings of the National Academy of Sciences USA, 97,* 4398–4403.

Mahler, D. A., Murray, J. A., Waterman, L. A., Ward, J., Kraemer, W. J., Zhang, X., & Baird, J. C. (2009). Endogenous opioids modify dyspnoea during treadmill exercise in patients with COPD. *European Respiratory Journal, 33,* 771–777.

Mahoney, M. M. (2010). Shift work, jet lag, and female reproduction. *International Journal of Endocrinology.* (in press)

Maier, N. R. F. (1931). Reasoning in humans. *Journal of Comparative Psychology, 12,* 181–194.

Maier, S. F., & Seligman, M. E. P. (2009). Fears, phobias, and preparedness: Toward an evolved module of fear and fear learning. In D. Shanks (Ed.), *Psychology of learning.* Thousand Oaks, CA: Sage.

Major, B., & Sawyer, P. J. (2009). Attributions to discrimination: Antecedents and consequences. In T. D. Nelson (Ed.), *Handbook of prejudice, stereotyping, and discrimination.* New York: Psychology Press.

Makioka, S. (2009). A self-organizing learning account of number-form synaesthesia. *Cognition, 112,* 397–414.

Malamuth, N. M., Addison, T., & Koss, M. (2000). Pornography and sexual aggression: Are there reliable effects and can we understand them? *Annual Review of Sex Research, 11,* 26–91.

Malcolm-Smith, S., Solms, M., Turnbull, O., & Tredoux, C. (2008). Threat in dreams: An adaptation? *Consciousness and cognition, 17,* 1281–1291.

Malhotra, R. K., & Desai, A. K. (2010). Healthy brain aging: what has sleep got to do with it? *Clinics in Geriatric Medicine, 26,* 46–56.

Mandara, J. (2006). The impact of family functioning on African American males' academic achievement: A review and clarification of the empirical literature. *Teachers College Record, 108,* 206–233.

Mander, B. A., & others. (2008). Sleep deprivation alters functioning within the neural network underlying the covert orienting of attention. *Brain Research, 1217,* 148–156.

Mandler, G. (1980). Recognizing: The judgment of previous occurrence. *Psychological Review, 87,* 252–271.

Maner, J. K., Luce, C. L., Neuberg, S. L., Cialdini, R. B., Brown, S., & Sagarin, B. J. (2002). The effects of perspective taking on motivations for helping: Still no evidence for altruism. *Personality and Social Psychology Bulletin, 28,* 1601–1610.

Manganotti, P., & others. (2010). Changes in cerebral activity after decreased upper-limb hypertonus: An EMG-fMRI study. *Magnetic Resonance Imaging.* (in press)

Manini, T. M., & others. (2006). Daily activity energy expenditure and mortality among older adults. *Journal of the American Medical Association, 296,* 216–218.

Mann, D. M., Ponieman, D., Leventahl, H., & Halm, E. A. (2009). Predictors of adherence to diabetes medications: The role of disease and medication beliefs. *Journal of Behavioral Medicine, 32,* 278–284.

Manning, J. T. (2002). *Digit ratio: A pointer to fertility, behavior and health.* New Brunswick, NJ: Rutgers University Press.

Mantonakis, A., Rodero, P., Lesschaeve, I., & Hastie, R. (2009). Order in choice: Effects of serial position on preferences. *Psychological Science, 20,* 1309–1312.

March, J., Silva, S., Petrycki, S., Curry, J., Wells, K., Fairbank, J., Burns, B., Domino, M., McNulty, S., Vitiello, B., & Severe, J. (2004). Fluoxetine, cognitive-behavioral therapy, and their combination for adolescents with depression: Treatment for Adolescents with Depression Study (TADS) randomized controlled trial. *Journal of the American Medical Association, 292,* 807–820.

Marcia, J. E. (1980). Ego identity development. In J. Adelson (Ed.), *Handbook of adolescent psychology.* New York: Wiley.

Marcia, J. E. (2002). Identity and psychosocial development in adulthood. *Identity, 2,* 7–28.

Marcus, G. F. (2001). *The algebraic mind.* Cambridge, MA: MIT Books.

Marder, S. R., Davis, J. M., & Chouinard, G. (1997). The effects of risperidone on the five dimensions of schizophrenia derived by factor analysis: Combined results of the North American trials. *Journal of Clinical Psychiatry, 58,* 538–546.

Margoob, M. A., Zaffar Ali, Z., & Andrade, C. (2010). Efficacy of ECT in chronic, severe, antidepressant- and CBT-refractory PTSD: An open, prospective study. *Brain Stimulation, 3,* 28–35.

Margrett, J. A., Allaire, J. C., Johnson, T. L., Daugherty, K. E., & Weatherbee, S. R. (2010). Everyday problem solving. In J. C. Cavanaugh, C. K. Cavanaugh, J. Berry, & R. West, (Eds.), *Aging in America, vol 1: Psychological aspects.* (pp. 80–101). Santa Barbara, CA: Praeger/ABC-CLIO.

Maril, A., Wagner, A. D., & Schacter, D. L. (2001). On the tip of the tongue: An event-related fMRI study of semantic retrieval failure and cognitive conflict. *Neuron, 31,* 653–660.

Marine, A., Rutosalainen, J., Serra, C., & Verbeek, J. (2006). Preventing occupational stress in healthcare workers. *Cochrane Database System Review, 18* (4), CD002892.

Marini, A., Martelli, S., Gagliardi, C., Fabbro, F., & Borgatti, R. (2010). Narrative language in Williams syndrome and its neuropsychological correlates. *Journal of Neurolinguistics, 23,* 97–111.

Maris, R. W. (1998). Suicide. In H. S. Friedman (Ed.), *Encyclopedia of mental health* (vol. 3). San Diego: Academic.

Markessis, E., & others. (2009). Effect of presentation level on diagnosis of dead regions using the threshold equalizing noise test. *International Journal of Audiology, 48,* 55–62.

Markowitsch, H. J. (2008). Autobiographical memory: A biocultural relais between subject and environment. *European Archives of Psychiatry and Clinical Neuroscience, 258,* Suppl. 5, S98–S103.

Markowitz, J. C., Milrod, B., Bleiberg, K., & Marshall, R. D. (2009). Interpersonal factors in understanding and treating posttraumatic stress disorder. *Journal of Psychiatric Practice, 15,* 133–140.

Markowitz, S., & Cuellar, A. (2007). Antidepressants and youth: Healing or harmful? *Social Science Medicine, 64,* 2138–2151.

Marks, I., & Cavanaugh, K. (2009). Computer-aided psychological treatments. *Annual Review of Clinical Psychology, 5,* 121–141.

Marlatt, M. W., Lucassen, P. J., & van Pragg, H. (2010). Comparison of neurogenic effects of fluoxetine, duloxetine and running in mice. *Brain Research.* (in press)

Marlow, A. (1999). *How to stop time: Heroin from A to Z.* New York: Basic.

Marom, M., & Berent, I. (2010). Phonological constraints on the assembly of skeletal structure in reading. *Journal of Psycholinguistic Research, 39,* 67–88.

Maron, E., Hettema, J. M., & Shlik, J. (2010). Advances in molecular genetics of panic disorder. *Molecular Psychiatry.* (in press)

Marques, J. K., Wiederanders, M., Day, D. M., Nelson, C., & van Ommeren A. (2005). Effects of a relapse prevention program on sexual recidivism: Final results from California's Sex Offender Treatment Evaluation Project (SOTEP). *Sex Abuse, 17,* 79–107.

Marrazzo, J. M., Coffey, P., & Bingham, A. (2005). Sexual practices, risk perception, and knowledge of bacterial vaginosis among lesbian and bisexual women. *Perspectives on Sexual and Reproductive Health, 37,* 6–12.

Marshall, D. A., Walizer, E. M., & Vernalis, M. N. (2009). Achievement of heart health characteristics through participation in an intensive lifestyle change program (Coronary

Artery Disease Reversal Study). *Journal of Cardiopulmonary Rehabilitation and Prevention, 29,* 84–94.

Marshall, D. S. (1971). Sexual behavior in Mangaia. In D. S. Marshall & R. C. Suggs (Eds.), *Human sexual behavior: Variations in the ethnographic spectrum* (pp. 103–162). New York: Basic.

Marshall, M., & Rathbone, J. (2006). Early intervention for psychosis. *Cochrane Database of Systematic Reviews, 4,* CD004718.

Martin, C. L., & Ruble, D. N. (2010). Patterns of gender development. *Annual Review of Psychology* (vol. 61). Palo Alto, CA: Annual Reviews.

Martin, G. L., & Pear, J. (2007). *Behavior modification* (8th ed.). Upper Saddle River, NJ: Prentice-Hall.

Martin, L. R., Friedman, H. S., & Schwartz, J. E. (2007). Personality and mortality risk across the lifespan: The importance of conscientiousness as biopsychosocial attribute. *Health Psychology, 26,* 428–436.

Martinez, M. E. (2010). *Learning and cognition.* Upper Saddle River, NJ: Merrill.

Martin-Joy, J., & Vaillant, G. E. (2010). Recognizing and promoting resilience. In C. A. Depp & D. V. Jeste (Eds.), *Successful cognitive and emotional aging* (pp. 363–381). Arlington, VA: American Psychiatric Publishing.

Maruyama, Y., Pereira, M., Margolskee, R. F., Chaudhari, N., & Roper, S. D. (2006). Umami responses in mouse taste cells indicate more than one receptor. *Journal of Neuroscience, 26,* 2227–2234.

Marx, R. F., & Didziulis, V. (2009, March 1). A life, interrupted. *New York Times.*

Mascaro, N., & Rosen, D. H. (2006). The role of existential meaning as a buffer against stress. *Journal of Humanistic Psychology, 46,* 168–190.

Maslow, A. H. (1954). *Motivation and personality.* New York: Harper & Row.

Maslow, A. H. (1971). *The farther reaches of human nature.* New York: Viking.

Mason, C. (2009, May 12). Belgian city plans "veggie" days. BBC. http://news.bbc.co.uk/2/hi/europe/8046970.stm

Mason, T. B., & Pack, A. I. (2005). Sleep terrors in childhood. *Journal of Pediatrics, 147,* 388–392.

Massimini, F., & Delle Fave, A. (2000). Individual development in bio-cultural perspective. *American Psychologist, 55,* 24–33.

Masten, A. S. (2006). Developmental psychopathology: Pathways to the future. *International Journal of Behavioral Development, 31,* 46–53.

Masten, A. S. (2007). Resilience in developing systems: Progress and promise as the fourth wave rises. *Development and Psychopathology, 19,* 921–930.

Masten, A. S. (2009). Ordinary magic: Lessons from research on human development. *Education Canada, 49,* 28–32.

Masten, A. S., Obradovic, J., & Burt, K. B. (2006). Resilience in emerging adulthood. In J. J. Arnett & J. L. Tanner (Eds.), *Emerging adults in America.* Washington, DC: American Psychological Association.

Masten, A. S., & Wright, M. O'D. (2009). Resilience over the lifespan: Developmental perspectives on resistance, recovery, and transformation. In J. W. Reich, A. J. Zautra, & J. S. Hall (Eds.), *Handbook of adult resilience.* New York: Guilford.

Masters, W. H., & Johnson, V. E. (1966). *Human sexual response.* Boston: Little, Brown.

Mate, J., & Baques, J. (2009). Visual similarity at encoding and retrieval in an item recognition task. *Quarterly Journal of Experimental Psychology, 18,* 1–8.

Mathew, K. L., Whitford, H. S., Kenny, M. A., & Denson, L. A. (2010). The long-term effects of mindfulness-based cognitive therapy as a relapse prevention treatment for major depressive disorder. *Behavioral and Cognitive Psychotherapy.* (in press)

Matis, G., & Birbilis, T. (2009). The Glasgow Coma Scale—A brief review. Past, present, future. *Acta Neurologica Belgica, 108,* 75–89.

Matlin, M. W. (2001). *Cognition* (5th ed.). Fort Worth, TX: Harcourt Brace.

Matsumoto, D., & others. (2008) Mapping expressive differences around the world: The relationship between emotional display rules and individualism versus collectivism. *Journal of Cross-Cultural Psychology, 39,* 55–74.

Mattes, K., Spezio, M., Kim, H., Todorov, A., Adolphs, R., & Alvarez, R. M. (2010). Predicting election outcomes from positive and negative trait assessments of candidate images. *Political Psychology, 31,* 41–58.

Matthews, K., & Gallo, L. C. (2011). Psychological perspectives on the association of socioeconomic status and physical health. *Annual Review of Psychology* (vol. 62). Palo Alto, CA: Annual Reviews.

Matthews, K. A., Gump, B. B., Harris, K. F., Haney, T. L., & Barefoot, J. C. (2004). Hostile behaviors predict cardiovascular mortality among men enrolled in the multiple risk factor intervention trial. *Circulation, 109,* 66–70.

Matthews, K. A., Schott, L. L., Bromberger, J., Cyranowski, J., Everson-Rose, S. A., & Sowers, M. F. (2007). Associations between depressive symptoms and inflammatory/hemostatic markers in women during the menopausal transition. *Psychosomatic Medicine, 69,* 124–130.

Matthews, R. A., Bulger, C. A., & Barnes-Farrell, J. L. (2010). Work social supports, role stressors, and work–family conflict: The moderating effect of age. *Journal of Vocational Behavior, 76,* 78–90.

Matzel, L. D., & Kolata, S. (2010). Selective attention, working memory, and animal intelligence. *Neuroscience and Biobehavioral Reviews, 34,* 23–30.

Maurer, T. J., Mitchell, D. R. D., & Barbeite, F. G. (2002). Predictors of attitudes toward a 360-degree feedback system and involvement in post-feedback management development activity. *Journal of Occupational and Organizational Psychology, 75,* 87–107.

May, F. B. (2006). *Teaching reading creatively* (7th ed.). Upper Saddle River, NJ: Prentice-Hall.

May, M. (2003). *Vision diary.* http://www.guardian.co.uk/g2/story/0,3604,1029268,00.html (accessed October 11, 2006)

Mayer, J. D., Salovey, P., & Caruso, D. R. (2008). Emotional intelligence: New ability or eclectic traits? *American Psychologist, 63,* 503–517.

Mayer, R. (2000). Problem solving. In M. A. Runco & S. Pritzker (Eds.), *Encyclopedia of psychology.* San Diego: Academic.

Mayer, R. E. (2011). *Applying the science of learning.* Boston: Allyn & Bacon.

Mayo Foundation. (2006). *Electroconvulsive therapy (ECT):* Treating severe depression and mental illness. Rochester, MN: Author. http://www.mayo-clinic.com/health/electroconvulsive-therapy/MH00022

McAdams, D. P. (1989). *Intimacy: The need to be close.* New York: Doubleday.

McAdams, D. P. (2001). The psychology of life stories. *Review of General Psychology, 5,* 100–122.

McAdams, D. P. (2006). *The redemptive self: Stories Americans live by.* NewYork: Oxford University Press.

McAdams, D. P. (2009). *The person* (5th ed.). New York: Wiley.

McAdams, D. P., Bauer, J. J., Sakaeda, A. R., Anyidoho, N. A., Machado, M. A., Magrino-Failla, K., White, K. W., & Pals, J. L. (2006). Continuity and change in life story: A longitudinal study of autobiographical memories in emerging adulthood. *Journal of Personality, 74,* 1371–1400.

McAdams, D. P., & Bryant, F. B. (1987). Intimacy motivation and subjective mental health in a nationwide sample. *Journal of Personality, 55,* 395–413.

McAdams, D. P., & Olson, B. D. (2010). Personality development: Continuity and change over the lifespan. *Annual Review of Psychology* (vol. 61). Palo Alto, CA: Annual Reviews.

McBurney, D. H., & White, T. L. (2010). *Research methods* (8th ed.). Boston: Cengage.

McCabe, J., Tanner, A., & Heiman, J. R. (2010). The impact of gender expectations on meanings of sex and sexuality: Results from a cognitive interview study. *Sex Roles, 62,* 252–263.

McCarthy, M. M., Auger, A. P., Bale, T. L., De Vries, G. J., Dunn, G. A., Forger, N. G., Murray, E. K., Nugent, B. M., Schwarz, J. M., & Wilson, M. E. (2009). The epigenetics of sex differences in the brain. *Journal of Neuroscience, 29,* 12815–12823.

McCauley, C., & Segal, M. E. (2009). Social psychology of terrorist groups. In J. Victoroff & A. W. Kruglanski (Eds.), *Psychology of terrorism: Classic and contemporary insights* (pp. 331–346). New York: Psychology Press.

McCaulley, M. H. (2000). Myers-Briggs Type Indicator: A bridge between counseling and consulting. *Consulting Psychology Journal: Practice and Research, 52,* 117–132.

McClelland, J. L., & Rumelhart, D. E. (2009). Why there are complementary learning systems in the hippocampus and neocortex: Insights from the successes and failures of connectionist models of learning and memory. In D. Shanks (Ed.), *Psychology of learning.* Thousand Oaks, CA: Sage.

McConnell, A. R., & Brown, C. M. (2010). Dissonance averted: Self-concept organization moderates the effect of hypocrisy on attitude change. *Journal of Experimental Social Psychology, 46,* 361–366.

McCorkle, B. H., Rogers, E. S., Dunn, E. C., Lyass, A., & Wan, Y. M. (2008). Increasing social support for individuals with serious mental illness: Evaluating the compeer model of intentional friendship. *Community Mental Health Journal, 44,* 359–366.

McCrae, R. R., & Costa, P. T. (2006). Cross-cultural perspectives on adult personality trait development. In D. K. Mroczek & T. D. Little (Eds.), *Handbook of personality development.* Mahwah, NJ: Erlbaum.

McCrae, R. R., & Sutin, A. R. (2007). New frontiers for the five factor model: A preview of the literature. *Social and Personality Psychology Compass, 1,* 423–440.

McCrae, R. R., & Sutin, A. R. (2009). Openness to experience. In M. R. Leary & R. H. Hoyle (Eds.), *Handbook of individual differences in social behavior* (pp. 257–273). New York: Guilford.

McCulloch, K. C., Ferguson, M. J., Kawada, C. C. K., & Bargh, J. A. (2008). Taking a closer look: On the operation of nonconscious impression formation. *Journal of Experimental Social Psychology, 44,* 614–623.

McCullough, J. L., & Kelly, K. M. (2006). Prevention and treatment of skin aging. *Annals of the New York Academy of Sciences, 1067,* 323–331.

McCullough, M. E., Bono, G., & Root, L. M. (2007). Rumination, emotion, and forgiveness: Three longitudinal studies. *Journal of Personality and Social Psychology, 92,* 490–505.

McCullough, M. E., Emmons, R. A., & Tsang, J. (2002). The grateful disposition: A conceptual and empirical topography. *Journal of Personality and Social Psychology, 82,* 112–127.

McCullough, M. E., Hoyt, W. T., Larson, D. B., Koenig, H. G., & Thoresen, C. (2000). Religious involvement and mortality: A meta-analytic review. *Health Psychology, 19,* 211–222.

McCullough, M. E., & Willoughby, B. L. (2009). Religion, self-regulation, and self-control: Associations, explanations, and implications. *Psychological Bulletin, 135,* 69–93.

McDaniel, M. A., & Einstein, G. O. (2007). *Prospective memory: An overview and synthesis of an emerging field.* Thousand Oaks, CA: Sage.

McDermott, R. (2009). Medical decision making: Lessons from psychology. *Urologic Oncology, 26,* 665–668.

McDonald, M. A., Hildebrand, J. A., Wiggins, S. M., Johnston, D. W., & Polovina, J. J. (2009). An acoustic survey of beaked whales at Cross Seamount near Hawaii. *Journal of the Acoustical Society of America, 125,* 624–627.

McDonald, S. D., & others. (2010). Preterm birth and low birth weight among in vitro fertilization twins: A systematic review and meta-analyses. *European Journal of Obstetrics, Gynecology, and Reproductive Biology, 148,* 105–113.

McFadden, D. (2008) What do sex, twins, spotted hyenas, ADHD, and sexual orientation have in

common? *Perspectives on Psychological Science, 3,* 309–323.

McFadden, D., Loehlin, J. C., Breedlove, S. M., Lippa, R. A., Manning, J. T., & Rahman, Q. (2005). A reanalysis of five studies on sexual orientation and the relative length of the 2nd and 4th fingers (the 2D:4D ratio). *Archives of Sexual Behavior, 34,* 341–356.

McFadden, D., & Shubel, E. (2002). Relative lengths of fingers and toes in human males and females. *Hormones and Behavior, 42,* 492–500.

McFadden, S. H., & Basting, A. D. (2010). Healthy aging persons and their brains: Promoting resilience through creative engagement. *Clinics in Geriatric Medicine, 26,* 149–161.

McFarlane, A. C. (2010). The long-term costs of traumatic stress: Intertwined physical and psychological consequences. *World Psychiatry, 9,* 3–10.

McGettigan, C., & others. (2010). Neural correlates of sublexical processing in phonological working memory. *Journal of Cognitive Neuroscience.* (in press)

McGhee, K. E., & Travis, J. (2010). Repeatable behavioural type and stable dominance rank in the bluefin killifish. *Animal Behaviour, 79,* 497–507.

McGregor, D. M. (1960). *The human side of enterprise.* New York: McGraw-Hill.

McGugin, R. W., & Gauthier, I. (2010). Perceptual expertise with objects predicts another hallmark of face perception. *Journal of Vision.* (in press)

McGuire, M. T., Wing, R. R, Klem, M. L., Lang, W., & Hill, J. O. (1999). What predicts weight regain in a group of successful weight losers? *Journal of Consulting and Clinical Psychology, 67,* 177–185.

McGuire, W. J. (2003). Doing psychology my way. In R. J. Sternberg (Ed.), *Psychologists defying the crowd: Stories of those who battled the establishment and won* (pp. 119–137). Washington, DC: American Psychological Association.

McGuire, W. J. (2004). The morphing of attitude-change into social-cognition. In G. V. Bodenhausen & A. J. Lambert (Eds.), *Foundations of social cognition.* Mahwah, NJ: Erlbaum.

McGuire, W. J., & Papageorgis, D. (1961). The relative efficacy of various types of prior belief-defense in producing immunity against persuasion. *Public Opinion Quarterly, 26,* 24–34.

McIntosh, W. D., Harlow, T. F., & Martin, L. L. (1995). Linkers and non-linkers: Goal beliefs as a moderator of the effects of everyday hassles on rumination, depression, and physical complaints. *Journal of Applied Social Psychology, 25,* 1231–1244.

McKay, K. M., Imel, Z. E., & Wampold, B. E. (2006). Psychiatrist effects in the psychopharmacological treatment of depression. *Journal of Affective Disorders, 92,* 287–290.

McKone, E., Crookes, K., & Kanwisher, N. (2010). The cognitive and neural development of face recognition in humans. In M. Gazzaniga (Ed.), *The cognitive neurosciences* (4th ed.). New York: Cambridge University Press.

McMahon, D. B., & Olson, C. R. (2009). Linearly additive shape and color signals in monkey inferotemporal cortex. *Journal of Neurophysiology, 101,* 1867–1875.

McMain, S., & Pos, A. E. (2007). Advances in psychotherapy of personality disorders: A research update. *Current Psychiatry Reports, 9,* 46–52.

McManus, M. A., & Ferguson, M. W. (2003). Biodata, personality, and demographic differences of recruits from three sources. *International Journal of Selection and Assessment, 11,* 175–183.

McMillan, J. H. (2008). *Educational research* (5th ed.). Boston: Allyn & Bacon.

McMillan, J. H., & Wergin, J. F. (2010). *Understanding and evaluating educational research* (4th ed.). Upper Saddle River, NJ: Merrill.

McMillan, K. A., Enns, M. W., Asmundson, G. J., & Sareen, J. (2010). The association between income and distress, mental disorders, and suicidal ideation and attempts: Findings from the collaborative psychiatric epidemiology surveys. *Journal of Clinical Psychology.* (in press)

McNamara, P., McLaren, D., & Durso, K. (2007). Representation of the self in REM and NREM dreams. *Dreaming, 17,* 113–126.

McNaughton, N., & Corr, P. J. (2008). The neuropsychology of fear and anxiety: A foundation for reinforcement sensitivity theory. In P. J. Corr (Ed.), *The reinforcement sensitivity theory of personality* (pp. 44–94). New York: Cambridge University Press.

McNeil, D. G. (2009, February 2). A company prospers by saving poor people's lives. *New York Times,* D4.

McNiel, J. M., Lowman, J. C., & Fleeson, W. (2010). The effect of state extraversion on four types of affect. *European Journal of Personality, 24,* 18–35.

McRae, K., Hughes, B., Chopra, S., Gabrieli, J. D. E., Gross, J. J., & Ochsner, K. N. (2010). The neural bases of distraction and reappraisal. *Journal of Cognitive Neuroscience, 22,* 248–262.

McRobbie, H., & others. (2010). A randomized trial of the effects of two novel nicotine replacement therapies on tobacco withdrawal symptoms and user satisfaction. *Addiction.* (in press)

McVay, J. C., & Kane, M. J. (2010). Does mind wandering reflect executive function or executive failure? Comment on Smallwood and Schooler (2006) and Watkins (2008). *Psychological Bulletin, 136,* 188–197.

Meade, C. S., Wang, J., Lin, X., Wu, H., & Poppen, P. J. (2010). Stress and coping in HIV-positive former plasma/blood donors in China: A test of cognitive appraisal theory. *AIDS Behavior, 14,* 328–338.

Medland, S. E., & Loehlin, J. C. (2008). Multivariate genetic analyses of the 2D:4D ratio: Examining the effects of hand and measurement technique in data from 757 twin families. *Twin Research and Human Genetics, 11,* 335–341.

Medley-Rath, S. R. (2007). "Am I still a virgin?": What counts as sex in 20 years of *Seventeen*.

Sexuality & Culture: An Interdisciplinary Quarterly, 11, 24–38.

Medvec, V. H., Madey, S. F., & Gilovich, T. (1995). When less is more: Counterfactual thinking and satisfaction among Olympic medalists. *Journal of Personality and Social Psychology, 69,* 603–610.

Meehl, P. (1962). Schizotonia, schizotypy, schizophrenia. *American Psychologist, 17,* 827–838.

Mehl, M. R., Vazire, S., Ramirez-Esparza, N., Slatcher, R. B., & Pennebaker, J. W. (2007). Are women really more talkative than men? *Science, 317,* 82.

Meissner, W. W. (2009). Religion in the psychoanalytic relationship—some aspects of transference and countertransference. *Journal of the American Academy of Psychoanalysis and Dynamic Psychiatry, 37,* 123–136.

Mejia-Arauz, R., Rogoff, B., & Paradise, R. (2005). Cultural variation in children's observation during a demonstration. *International Journal of Behavioral Development, 29,* 282–291.

Mello, J. A. (2011). *Strategic human resource management* (3rd ed.). Boston: Cengage.

Mellon, S., & others. (2009). Predictors of decision making in families at risk for inherited breast/ovarian cancer. *Health Psychology, 28,* 38–47.

Melton, L. (2005, December 17). How brain power can help you cheat old age. *New Scientist, 2530,* 32.

Meltzoff, A. N. (2011). Social cognition and the origins of imitation, empathy, and theory of mind. In U. Goswami (Ed.), *Wiley-Blackwell handbook of childhood cognitive development* (2nd ed.). New York: Wiley Blackwell.

Mendes, W. B. (2007). Social facilitation. In R. Baumeister & K. Vohs (Eds.), *Encyclopedia of social psychology.* Thousand Oaks, CA: Sage.

Menn, L., & Stoel-Gammon, C. (2009). Phonological development: Learning sounds and sound patterns. In J. Berko Gleason & N. Ratner (Eds.), *The development of language* (7th ed.). Boston: Allyn & Bacon.

Mercer, C. H., Bailey, J. V., Johnson, A. M., Erens, B., Wellings, K., Fenton, K. A., & Copas, A. J. (2007). Women who report having sex with women: British national probability data on prevalence, sexual behaviors, and health outcomes. *American Journal of Public Health, 97,* 1126–1133.

Mercer, V. E. (2009). Stress management intervention. In W. T. O'Donohue & J. E. Fisher (Eds.), *General principles and empirically supported techniques of cognitive behavior therapy* (pp. 631–639). Hoboken, NJ: Wiley.

Merkl, A., Heuser, I., & Bajbouj, M. (2009). Antidepressant electroconvulsive therapy: Mechanism of action, recent advances, and limitations. *Experimental Neurology, 219* (1), 20–26.

Merlino, G., & others. (2010). Daytime sleepiness is associated with dementia and cognitive decline in older Italian adults: A population-based study. *Sleep Medicine.* (in press)

Mesquita, B. (2002). Emotions as dynamic cultural phenomena. In R. J. Davidson, K. R. Scherer, &

H. H. Goldsmith (Eds.), *Handbook of affective sciences.* New York: Oxford University Press.

Messenger, J. C. (1971). Sex and repression in an Irish folk community. In D. S. Marshall & R. C. Suggs (Eds.), *Human sexual behavior.* New York: Basic.

Messer, S. B., & Abbass, A. A. (2010). Evidence-based psychodynamic therapy with personality disorders. In J. J. Magnavita (Ed.), *Evidence-based treatment of personality dysfunction: Principles, methods, and processes* (pp. 79–111). Washington, DC: American Psychological Association.

Messner, S. F., Raffalovich, L. E., & Shrock, P. (2002). Reassessing the cross-national relationship between income inequality and homicide rates: Implications of data quality control in the measurement of income distribution. *Journal of Quantitative Criminology, 18,* 377–395.

Meston, C. M., & Buss, D. M. (2009). *Why women have sex: Understanding sexual motivations from adventure to revenge (and everything in between).* New York: Holt.

Meston, C. M., Seal, B. N., & Hamilton, L. D. (2008). Problems with arousal and orgasm in women. In D. L. Rowland & L. Incrocci (Eds.), *Handbook of sexual and gender identity disorders* (pp. 188–219). Hoboken, NJ: Wiley.

Metcalfe, J., & Mischel, W. (1999). A hot/cool system analysis of delay of gratification: Dynamics of will power. *Psychological Review, 106,* 3–19.

Mettler, F. A. (Ed.). (1952). *Psychosurgical problems.* Oxford: Blakiston.

Meyer, J. P., Becker, T. E., & Vandenberghe, C. (2004). Employee commitment and motivation: A conceptual analysis and integrative model. *Journal of Applied Psychology, 89,* 991–1007.

Meyer, J. P., & Herscovitch, L. (2001). Commitment in the workplace: Toward a general model. *Human Resource Management Review, 11,* 299–326.

Meyer, J. P., Stanley, D. J., Herscovitch, L., & Topolnytsky, L. (2002). Affective, continuance, and normative commitment to the organization: A meta-analysis of antecedents, correlates, and consequences. *Journal of Vocational Behavior, 61,* 20–52.

Meyer, P. J., Meshul, C. K., & Phillips, T. J. (2009). Ethanol- and cocaine-induced locomotion are genetically related to increases in accumbal dopamine. *Genes, Brain, and Behavior, 8,* 346–355.

Meyer-Bahlburg, H. F. L. (1998). Gender assignment in intersexuality. *Journal of Psychology and Human Sexuality, 10,* 1–21.

Meyer-Bahlburg, H. F. L. (2005). Gender identity outcome in female-raised 46, XY persons with penile agenesis, cloacal exstrophy of the bladder, or penile ablation. *Archives of Sexual Behavior, 34,* 423–438.

Meyer-Bahlburg, H. F. L. (2010). From mental disorder to iatrogenic hypogonadism: Dilemmas in conceptualizing gender identity variants as psychiatric conditions. *Archives of Sexual Behavior, 39,* 461–476.

Meyer-Bahlburg, H. F. L, Dolezal, C., Baker, S. W., & New, M. I. (2008). Sexual orientation in women with classical or non-classical congenital

adrenal hyperplasia as a function of degree of prenatal androgen excess. *Archives of Sexual Behavior, 37,* 85–99.

Miacic, B., & Goldberg, L. R. (2007). An analysis of a cross-cultural personality inventory: The IPIP big five factors markers in Croatia. *Journal of Personality Assessment, 88,* 168–177.

Michael, R. T., Gagnon, J. H., Laumann, E. O., & Kolata, G. (1994). *Sex in America.* Boston: Little, Brown.

Middeldorp, C. M., de Geus, E. J. C., Beem, A. L., Lakenberg, N., Hottenga, J., Slagboom, P. E., & Boomsma, D. I. (2007). Family based association analyses between the serotonin transporter gene polymorphism (5-HTTLPR) and neuroticism, anxiety and depression. *Behavior Genetics, 37,* 294–301.

Migneault, J. P., Adams, T. B., & Read, J. P. (2005). Application of the transtheoretical model to substance abuse: Historical development and future directions. *Drug and Alcohol Review, 24,* 437–448.

Mihashi, M., & others. (2009). Predictive factors of psychological disorder development during recovery following SARS outbreak. *Health Psychology, 28,* 91–100.

Mikolajczyk, E., Grzywacz, A., & Samochowlec, J. (2010). The association of catechol-O-methyltransferace genotype with the phenotype of women with eating disorders. *Brain Research, 1307,* 142–148.

Milane, M. S., Suchard, M. A., Wong, M., & Licinio, J. (2006). Modeling of the temporal patterns of fluoxetine prescriptions and suicide rates in the United States. *PloS Medicine, 3,* e190. doi:10.1371/jo.

Milgram, S. (1965). Some conditions of obedience and disobedience to authority. *Human Relations, 18,* 56–76.

Milgram, S. (1974). *Obedience to authority.* New York: Harper & Row.

Miller, A. G. (2004). What can the Milgram obedience experiments tell us about the Holocaust? Generalizing from the social psychology laboratory. In A. G. Miller (Ed.), *The social psychology of good and evil* (pp. 193–239). New York: Guilford.

Miller, C. A., & Golden, N. H. (2010). An introduction to eating disorders: Clinical presentation, epidemiology, and prognosis. *Nutrition in Clinical Practice, 25,* 110–115.

Miller, D. J., Vachon, D. D., & Lynam, D. R. (2009). Neuroticism, negative affect, and negative affect instability: Establishing convergent and discriminant validity using ecological momentary assessment. *Personality and Individual Differences, 47,* 873–877.

Miller, D. T. (1999). The norm of self-interest. *American Psychologist, 54* (12), 1053–1060.

Miller, D. T. (2001). The norm of self-interest. In J. Dienhart, D. Moberg, & R. Duska (Eds.), *The next phase of business ethics: Integrating psychology and ethics* (pp. 193–210). New York: Elsevier Science/JAI Press.

Miller, G., Chen, E., & Cole, S. W. (2009). Health psychology: Developing biologically plausible models linking the social world and physical health. *Annual Review of Psychology* (vol. 60). Palo Alto, CA: Annual Reviews.

Miller, G. A. (1956). The magical number seven, plus or minus two: Some limits on our capacity for information processing. *Psychological Review, 48,* 337–442.

Miller, J. J., Fletcher, K., & Kabat-Zinn, J. (1995). Three-year follow-up and clinical implications of a mindfulness meditation–based stress reduction intervention in the treatment of anxiety disorders. *General Hospital Psychiatry, 17,* 192–200.

Miller, N. E. (1941). The frustration-aggression hypothesis. *Psychological Review, 48,* 337–442.

Miller, N. E. (1985). The value of behavioral research on animals. *American Psychologist, 40,* 432–440.

Miller, P. H. (2011). Piaget's theory: Past, present, and future. In U. Goswami (Ed.), *Wiley-Blackwell handbook of childhood cognitive development* (2nd ed.). New York: Wiley Blackwell.

Miller, R., Perlman, D., & Brehm, S. S. (2009). *Intimate relationships* (5th ed.). New York: McGraw-Hill.

Milling, L. S., Coursen, E. L., Shores, J. S., & Waszkiewicz, J. A. (2010). The predictive utility of hypnotizability: The change in suggestibility produced by hypnosis. *Journal of Consulting and Clinical Psychology, 78,* 126–130.

Miltenberger, R. G. (2008). Behavior modification. In M. Hersen & A. M. Gross (Eds.), *Handbook of clinical psychology, vol. 2: Children and adolescents* (pp. 626–652). Hoboken, NJ: Wiley.

Milton, F., & others. (2010). Remote memory deficits in transient epileptic amnesia. *Brain.* (in press)

Minde, K., & Zelkowitz, P. (2008). Premature babies. In M. M. Haith & J. B. Benson (Eds.), *Encyclopedia of infant and early childhood development.* Oxford, U.K.: Elsevier.

Mindell, J. A., Meltzer, L. J., Carskadon, M. A., & Chervin, R. D. (2009). Developmental aspects of sleep hygiene: Findings from the 2004 National Sleep in America Poll. *Sleep Medicine, 10,* 771–779.

Mineka, S., & Ohman, A. (2002). Phobias and preparedness: The selective, automatic, and encapsulated nature of fear. *Biological Psychiatry, 52,* 927–937.

Miner-Rubino, K., Twenge, J. M., & Fredrickson, B. L. (2002). Trait self-objectification in women: Affective and personality correlates. *Journal of Research in Personality, 36,* 147–172.

Mirilas, P., & others. (2010). Serum beta-endorphin response to stress before and after operation under fentanyl anesthesia in neonates, infants, and preschool children. *European Journal of Pediatric Surgery.* (in press)

Mischel, W. (1968). *Personality and assessment.* New York: Wiley.

Mischel, W. (2004). Toward an integrative science of the person. *Annual Review of Psychology* (vol. 55). Palo Alto, CA: Annual Reviews.

Mischel, W. (2009). From *Personality and Assessment* (1968) to personality science, 2009. *Journal of Research in Personality, 43,* 282–290.

Mischel, W., & Ayduk, O. (2004). Willpower in a cognitive-affective processing system: The dynamics of delay of gratification. In R. F. Baumeister & K. D. Vohs (Eds.), *Handbook of self-regulation: Research, theory, and applications* (pp. 99–129). New York: Guilford.

Mischel, W., Cantor, N., & Feldman, S. (1996). Principles of self-regulation: The nature of will power and self-control. In E. T. Higgins & A. W. Kruglanski (Eds.), *Social psychology: Handbook of basic principles.* New York: Guilford.

Mischel, W., & Moore, B. S. (1980). The role of ideation in voluntary delay for symbolically presented rewards. *Cognitive Therapy and Research, 4,* 211–221.

Mischel, W., & Shoda, Y. (1999). Integrating dispositions and processing dynamics within a unified theory of personality: The cognitive-affective personality system. In L. A. Pervin & O. P. John (Eds.), *Handbook of personality: Theory and research* (2nd ed., pp. 197–218). New York: Guilford.

Mitchell, C. J., & others. (2010). Do reaction times in the Perruchet effect reflect variations in the strength of the associative link? *Journal of Experimental Psychology: Learning, Memory, and Cognition, 36,* 567–572.

Mitchell, D. L., Gallagher, T. V., & Thomas, R. E. (2008). The human factors of implementing shift work in logging operations. *Journal of Agricultural Safety and Health, 14,* 391–404.

Mitchell, H. A., & Weinshenker, D. (2010). Good night and good luck: Norepinephrine in sleep pharmacology. *Biochemical Pharmacology, 79,* 801–809.

Mitchell, K. E., Alliger, G. M., & Morfopoulos, R. (1997). Toward an ADA-appropriate job analysis. *Human Resource Management Review, 7,* 5–26.

Mittag, W., & Schwarzer, R. (1993). Interaction of employment status and self-efficacy on alcohol consumption: A two-wave study on stressful life transitions. *Psychology and Health, 8,* 77–87.

Miyamoto, M. (2009). Pharmacology of ramelteon, a selective MT1/MT2 receptor agonist: A novel therapeutic drug for sleep disorders. *CNS Neuroscience and Therapeutics, 15,* 32–51.

Mizes, J. S., & Miller, K. J. (2000). Eating disorders. In M. Hersen & R. T. Ammerman (Eds.), *Advanced abnormal child psychology* (2nd ed.). Mahwah, NJ: Erlbaum.

Moberly, N. J., & Watkins, E. R. (2009). Negative affect and ruminative self-focus during everyday goal pursuit. *Cognition and Emotion,* 1–15.

Mock, S., & Boerner, K. (2010). Sense making and benefit finding among patients with amyotrophic lateral sclerosis and their primary caregivers. *Journal of Health Psychology, 15,* 115–121.

Moffitt, T. E., Brammer, G. L., Caspi, A., Fawcet, J. P., Raleigh, M., Yuwiler, A., & Silva, P. A. (1998). Whole blood serotonin relates to violence in an epidemiological study. *Biological Psychiatry, 43,* 446–457.

Mojza, E. J., Lorenz, C., Sonnentag, S., & Binnewies, C. (2010). Daily recovery experiences: The role of volunteer work during leisure time. *Journal of Occupational Health Psychology, 15,* 60–74.

Mojzisch, A., & Schulz-Hardt, S. (2010). Knowing others' preferences degrades the quality of group decisions. *Journal of Personality and Social Psychology, 98,* 794–808.

Mokhber, N., & others. (2010). Randomized, single-blind, trial of sertraline and buspirone for treatment of elderly patients with generalized anxiety disorder. *Psychiatry and Clinical Neurosciences, 64,* 128–134.

Molles, M. C. (2010). *Ecology* (5th ed.). New York: McGraw-Hill.

Mondy, R. W. (2010). *Human resource management* (11th Ed.). Upper Saddle River, NJ: Prentice-Hall.

Money, J. (1986). *Lovemaps: Clinical concepts of sexual/erotic health and pathology, paraphilia, and gender transposition in childhood, adolescence, and maturity.* New York: Irvington.

Money, J., Hampson, J. G., & Hampson, J. L. (1955). Hermaphroditism: Recommendations concerning assignment of sex, change of sex, and psychological management. *Bulletin of Johns Hopkins Hospital, 97,* 284–300.

Money, J., Hampson, J. G., & Hampson, J. L. (1957). Imprinting and the establishment of gender role. *Archives of Neurology and Psychiatry, 77,* 333–336.

Money, J., & Tucker P. (1975). *Sexual signatures: On being a man or woman.* Boston: Little, Brown.

Monteleone, G. T., Phan, K. L., Nusbaum, H. C., Fitzgerald, D., Irick, J. S., Fienberg, S. E., & Cacioppo, J. T. (2009). Detection of deception using fMRI: Better than chance, but well below perfection. *Social Neuroscience, 4,* 528–538.

Montgomery, E. (2010). Trauma and resilience in young refugees: A 9-year follow-up study. *Developmental Psychology, 22,* 477–489.

Moore, D. W. (2005, June 16). Three in four Americans believe in paranormal (press release). Washington, DC: Gallup News Service.

Moos, R. H. (1986). Work as a human context. In M. S. Pallack & R. Perloff (Eds.), *Psychology and work.* Washington, DC: American Psychological Association.

Moradi, B., & Huang, Y. (2008). Objectification theory and psychology of women: A decade of advances and future directions. *Psychology of Women Quarterly, 32,* 377–398.

Moreines, J. L., McClintock, S. M., & Holtzheimer, P. E. (2010). Neuropsychologic effects of neuromodulation techniques for treatment-resistant depression: A review. *Brain Stimulation.* (in press)

Morgan, C. D., & Murray, H. A. (1935). A method of investigating fantasies: The Thematic Apperception Test. *Archives of Neurology and Psychiatry, 34,* 289–306.

Morgeson, F. P., Reider, M. H., & Campion, M. A. (2005). Selecting individuals in team settings: The importance of social skills, personality characteristics, and teamwork knowledge. *Personnel Psychology, 58,* 583–611.

Moritsugu, J., Wong, F. Y., & Duffy, K. G. (2010). *Community psychology* (4th ed.). Boston: Allyn & Bacon.

Morrison, F. J., Ponitz, C. C., & McClelland, M. M. (2010). Self-regulation and academic achievement in the transition to school. In S. D. Calkins & M. A. Bell (Eds.), *Child development at the intersection of emotion and cognition.* Washington, DC: American Psychological Association.

Mortimer, J. A., Snowdon, D. A., & Markesbery, W. R. (2009). The effect of APOE-epsilon4 on dementia is mediated by Alzheimer neuropathology. *Alzheimer Disease and Associated Disorders, 23,* 152–157.

Moscovici, S. (1985). Social influence and conformity. In G. Lindzey & E. Aronson (Eds.), *Handbook of social psychology* (3rd ed., vol. 2). New York: Random House.

Moses, T. (2010). Being treated differently: Stigma experiences with family, peers, and school staff among adolescents with mental health disorders. *Social Science Medicine, 70,* 985–993.

Mosher, C. E., & Danoff-Burg, S. (2008). Agentic and communal personality traits: Relations to disordered eating behavior, body shape concern, and depressive symptoms. *Eating Behaviors, 9,* 497–500.

Mosher, W. D., Chandra, A., & Jones, J. (2005). Sexual behavior and selected health measures: Men and women 15–44 years of age, United States, 2002. *Advance data from vital and health statistics, no. 362.* Hyattsville, MD: National Center for Health Statistics.

Moskowitz, D. S. (2010). Quarrelsomeness in daily life. *Journal of Personality. 78,* 39–66.

Moskowitz, M., & Levering, R. (2007). 2007 "100 Best Companies to Work For" in America. http://www.greatplacetowork.com/best/100best2007.php

Moskowitz, M., & Levering, R. (2010). 2010 "100 Best Companies to Work For" in America. http://www.greatplacetowork.com/what_we_do/lists-us-bestusa-2010.htm

Mouilso, E. R., Calhoun, K. S., & Gidycz, C. A. (2010). Effects of participation in a sexual assault risk reduction program on psychological distress following revictimization. *Journal of Interpersonal Violence.* (in press)

Moulton, S. T., & Kosslyn, S. M. (2008). Using neuroimaging to resolve the psi debate. *Journal of Cognitive Neuroscience, 20,* 182–192.

Mroczek, D. K. (2001). Age and emotion in adulthood. *Current Directions in Psychological Science, 10,* 87–90.

Mroczek, D. K., & Kolarz, C. M. (1998). The effect of age on positive and negative affect: A developmental perspective on happiness. *Journal of Personality and Social Psychology, 75,* 1333–1349.

Mroczek, D. K., & Spiro, A. (2005). Change in life satisfaction during adulthood: Findings from the Veterans Affairs Normative Aging Study. *Journal of Personality and Social Psychology, 88,* 189–202.

Mueller, D. L. (2010). Mechanisms maintaining peripheral tolerance. *Nature Immunology, 11,* 21–27.

Mullington, J. M., Haack, M., Toth, M., Serrador, J. M., & Meier-Ewert, H. K. (2009). Cardiovascular, inflammatory, and metabolic consequences of sleep deprivation. *Progress in Cardiovascular Diseases, 51,* 294–302.

Mullis, I. V. S., Marting, M. O., Gonzales, E. J., & Kennedy, A. M. (2003). *PIRLS 2001 International Report: IEA's study of reading literacy achievement in primary schools.* Chestnut Hill, MA: Boston College. timss.bc.edu/pirls2001html (accessed April 15, 2010)

Mumford, M. D., Scott, G., & Hunter, S. T. (2006). Theory—charismatic, ideological, and pragmatic leaders: How do they lead, why do they lead, and who do they lead? In M. D. Mumford (Ed.), *Pathways to outstanding leadership.* Mahwah, NJ: Erlbaum.

Munafo, M. R., Yalcin, B., Willis-Owen, S. A., & Flint, J. (2008). Association of the dopamine D4 receptor (DRD4) gene and approach-related personality traits: Meta-analysis and new data. *Biological Psychiatry, 63,* 197–206.

Munoz-Laboy, M., Hirsch, J. S., & Quispe-Lazaro, A. (2009). Loneliness as a sexual risk for male Mexican migrant workers. *American Journal of Public Health, 99,* 802–810.

Mur, M., Ruff, D. A., Bodurka, J., Bandettini, P. A., & Kriegeskorte, N. (2010). Face-identity change activation outside the face system: "Release from adaptation" may not always indicate neuronal selectivity. *Cerebral Cortex.* (in press)

Murray, E. A. (2007). Visual memory. *Annual Review of Neuroscience* (vol. 29). Palo Alto, CA: Annual Reviews.

Murray, L., Halligan, S. L., Goodyer, I., & Herbert, J. (2010). Disturbances in early parenting of depressed mothers and cortisol secretion in offspring: A preliminary study. *Journal of Affective Disorders, 122,* 218–223.

Murray-Swank, A. B., Lucksted, A., Medoff, D. R., Yang, Y., Wohlheiter, K., & Dixon, L. B. (2006). Religiosity, psychosocial adjustment, and subjective burden of persons who care for those with mental illness. *Psychiatric Services, 57,* 361–365.

Murre, J. M. J. (2010). Connectionist models of forgetting. In S. D. Sala (Ed.), *Forgetting.* New York: Psychology Press.

Mussweiler, T. (2009). Social comparison. In F. Strack & J. Forster (Eds.), *Social cognition: The basis of human interaction.* New York: Psychology Press.

Mykletun, A., Bjerkeset, O., Dewey, M., Prince, M., Overland, S., & Stewart, R. (2007). Anxiety, depression, and cause-specific mortality: The Hunt Study. *Psychosomatic Medicine, 69,* 323–331.

N

Naar-King, S., Wright, K., Parsons, J. T., Frey, M., Templin, T., & Ondersma, S. (2006). Transtheoretical model and condom use in HIV-positive youths. *Health Psychology, 25,* 648–652.

Nagase, Y., & others. (2009). Coping strategies and their correlates with depression in the Japanese general population. *Psychiatry Research, 168,* 57–66.

Nagashima, J., & others. (2010). Three-month exercise and weight loss program improves heart rate recovery in obese persons along with cardiopulmonary function. *Journal of Cardiology.* (in press)

Nakao, M. (2010). Work-related stress and psychosomatic medicine. *Biopsychosocial Medicine.* (in press)

Nakao, T., & others. (2009). Working memory dysfunction in obsessive-compulsive disorder: A neuropsychological and functional MRI study. *Journal of Psychiatric Research, 43,* 784–791.

Nanda, S. (2008). Cross-cultural issues. In D. L. Rowland & L. Incrocci (Eds.), *Handbook of sexual and gender identity disorders* (pp. 457–485). Hoboken, NJ: Wiley.

Narayanan, L., Menon, S., & Spector, P. E. (1999). A cross-cultural comparison of job stressors and reactions among employees holding comparable jobs in two countries. *International Journal of Stress Management, 6,* 197–212.

Nardi, P. M. (2006). *Doing survey research* (2nd ed.). Boston: Allyn & Bacon.

Narvaez, D., & Lapsley, D. (2009). *Moral personality, identity, and character: An interdisciplinary future.* New York: Cambridge University Press.

Nash, M. R., Perez, N., Tasso, A., & Levy, J. J. (2009). Clinical research on the utility of hypnosis in the prevention, diagnosis, and treatment of medical and psychiatric disorders. *International Journal of Clinical and Experimental Hypnosis, 57,* 443–450.

Nasrallah, H. A., & others. (2009). Proceedings and data from the Schizophrenia Summit: A critical appraisal to improve management of schizophrenia. *Journal of Clinical Psychiatry, 70,* Suppl. 1, 4–46.

Nassi, J. J., & Callaway, E. M. (2009). Parallel processing strategies of the primate visual system *Nature Review Neuroscience, 10,* 360–372.

Nath, A. (2010). Human immunodeficiency virus-associated neurocognitive disorder: Pathophysiology in relation to drug addiction. *Annals of the New York Academy of Sciences, 1187,* 122–128.

National Alliance for the Mentally Ill, American Psychiatric Association, National Mental Health Association (NAMI/APA, NMHA). (2005, June 24). *Joint statement in response to Tom Cruise's* Today Show *interview.* Author.

National Center for Health Statistics. (2002). *Sexual behavior and selected health measures: Men and women 15–44 years of age, United States, 2002.* Atlanta: Centers for Disease Control and Prevention.

National Center for Health Statistics. (2005). *Early release of selected estimates from Jan–Mar 2005 National Health Interview Survey.* Washington, DC: Author.

National Center for Health Statistics. (2005a). *Death statistics.* Atlanta: Centers for Disease Control and Prevention.

National Center for Health Statistics. (2006). *Vital and health statistics.* Atlanta: Centers for Disease Control and Prevention.

National Center for Health Statistics. (2006a). *Health United States, 2006.* Atlanta: Centers for Disease Control and Prevention.

National Center for Health Statistics. (2009). Cigarette smoking among adults and trends in smoking cessation—United States, 2008. Atlanta: Centers for Disease Control and Prevention.

National Center for Health Statistics. (2010). *HIV/AIDS in the United States.* Atlanta: Centers for Disease Control and Prevention.

National Center for Post-Traumatic Stress Disorder (PTSD). (2006). *Facts about PTSD.* www.ncptsd.va.gov (accessed November 25, 2006)

National Heart, Lung, and Blood Institute. (2009). BMI calculator. http://www.nhlbisupport.com/bmi/

National Highway Traffic Safety Administration (NHTSA). (2007, December). *Traffic safety facts: Crash stats.* Washington, DC: NHTSA's Center for Statistics and Analysis.

National Institute on Drug Abuse (NIDA). (2009a). *Research report series—MDMA (Ecstasy) abuse.* Bethesda, M.D: Author.

National Institute on Drug Abuse (NIDA). (2009b). *NIDA infofacts: Marijuana.* Bethesda, MD: Author.

National Institute of Mental Health (NIMH). (2008). *The numbers count: Mental disorders in America.* Bethesda, MD: U.S. Department of Health and Human Services. http://www.nimh.nih.gov/health/publications/the-numbers-count-mental-disorders-in-america/index.shtml

National Institute of Mental Health (NIMH). (2009). *Eating disorders.* Bethesda, MD: Author.

National Sleep Foundation. (2007, March 6). *Stressed-out American women have no time for sleep.* Washington, DC: Author.

Naumann, L. P., Vazire, S., Rentfrow, P. J., & Gosling, S. D. (2009). Personality judgments based on physical appearance. *Personality and Social Psychology Bulletin, 35,* 1661–1671.

Neacsiu, A. D., Rizvi, S. L., Vitaliano, P. P., Lynch, T. R., & Linehan, M. M. (2010). The dialectical behavior therapy ways of coping checklist: Developmental and psychometric properties. *Journal of Clinical Psychology, 66,* 563–582.

Needham, A. (2009). Learning in infants' object perception, object-directed action, and tool use. In A. Woodward & A. Needham (Eds.), *Learning and the infant mind.* New York: Oxford University Press.

Needham, A., Barrett, T., & Peterman, K. (2002). A pick-me-up for infants' exploratory skills: Early simulated experiences reaching for objects using "sticky mittens" enhances young infants' object exploration skills. *Infant Behavior and Development, 25,* 279–295.

Nefti, W., Chaumontet, C., Fromentin, G., Tomé, D., & Darcel, N. (2009). A high fat diet attenuates the central response to within-meal satiation signals and modifies the receptor expression of vagal afferents in mice. *American Journal of Physiology: Regulatory, Integrative, and Comparative Physiology, 296,* R1681–R1686.

Neisser, U., Boodoo, G., Bouchard, T. J., Boykin, A. W., Brody, N., Ceci, S. J.,

Halpern, D. F., Loehlin, J. C., Perloff, R., Sternberg, R. J., & Urbina, S. (1996). Intelligence: Knowns & unknowns. *American Psychologist, 51,* 77–101.

Neisser, U., & Harsch, N. (1992). Phantom flashbulbs: False recollections of hearing the news about *Challenger.* In E. Winograd & U. Neisser (Eds.), *Affect and accuracy in recall: Studies of "flashbulb" memories* (pp. 9–31). New York: Cambridge University Press.

Nelson, C. A. (2011). Brain development and behavior. In A. M. Rudolph, C. Rudolph, L. First, G. Lister, & A. A. Gershon (Eds.), *Rudolph's pediatrics* (22nd ed.). New York: McGraw-Hill.

Nelson, D. L., & Quick, J. C. (2011). *ORGB 2* (2nd ed.). Boston: Cengage.

Nelson, K. J., Bowman-Fowler, N., Berkowitz, S. R., & Loftus, E. F. (2009). Eyewitness testimony. In C. Edwards (Ed.), *Encyclopedia of forensic science.* New York: Wiley.

Nelson, T. D. (Ed.). (2009). *Handbook of prejudice, stereotyping, and discrimination.* New York: Psychology Press.

Nenadic, I., Sauer, H., & Gaser, C. (2010). Distinct pattern of brain structural deficits in subsyndromes of schizophrenia delineated by psychopathology. *NeuroImage, 49,* 1153–1160.

Neukrug, E. S., & Fawcett, R. C. (2010). *Essentials of testing and assessment* (2nd ed.). Boston: Cengage.

Neumann, I. D., Veenema, A. H., & Beiderbeck, D. I. (2010). Aggression and anxiety: Social context and neurobiological links. *Frontiers in Behavioral Neuroscience.* (in press)

Nevels, R. M., Dehon, E. E., Alexander, K., & Gontkovsky, S. T. (2010). Psychopharmacology of aggression in children and adolescents with primary neuropsychiatric disorders: A review of current and potentially promising treatment options. *Experimental and Clinical Psychopharmacology, 18,* 184–201.

Neville, H. J. (2006). Different profiles of plasticity within human cognition. In Y. Munakata & M. H. Johnson (Eds.), *Attention and performance.* Oxford, U.K.: Oxford University Press.

Nevsimalova, S. (2009). Narcolepsy in childhood. *Sleep Medicine Reviews, 13,* 169–180.

Newberg, A. B. (2010). The neurobiology of meditation. In D. A. Monti & B. D. Beitman (Eds.), *Integrative psychiatry* (pp. 339–358). New York: Oxford University Press.

Nicholls, J. G., & Paton, J. F. R. (2009). Brainstem: Neural networks vital for life. *Philosophical Transactions of the Royal Society B: Biological Sciences, 364,* 2447–2451.

Nicholson, C. (2008). In the news: Scanning sexuality. *Nature Reviews Neuroscience. 9,* 582.

Nickerson, R. S., & Adams, M. J. (1979). Long-term memory for a common object. *Cognitive Psychology, 11,* 287–307.

Nides, M. (2008). Update on pharmacological options for smoking cessation treatment. *American Journal of Medicine, 121, Suppl. 4,* S20–S31.

Nielsen, K., & Munir, F. (2009). How do transformational leaders influence followers'

affective well-being? Exploring the mediating role of self-efficacy. *Work & Stress, 23,* 31–329.

Nijstad, B. (2009). *Group performance.* New York: Psychology Press.

Nilsson, H., Juslin, P., & Olsson, H. (2008). Exemplars in the mist: The cognitive substrate of the representativeness heuristic. *Scandinavian Journal of Psychology, 49,* 201–212.

Niparko, J. K. (2004). Speech, language, and reading skills after early cochlear implantation. *Journal of the American Medical Association, 291,* 2378–2380.

Nir, Y., & Tononi, G. (2010). Dreaming and the brain: From phenomenology to neurophysiology. *Trends in Cognitive Science, 14,* 88–100.

Nisbett, R. E. (1987). Lay trait theory: Its nature, origins, and utility. In N. E. Grunberg, R. E. Nisbett, J. Rodin, & J. E. Singer (Eds.), *A distinctive approach to psychological research: The influence of Stanley Schachter.* Hillsdale, NJ: Erlbaum.

Nisbett, R. E. (2009). *Intelligence and how to get it: Why schools and cultures count.* New York: Norton.

Nisbett, R. E., & Ross, L. (1980). *Human inference.* Upper Saddle River, NJ: Prentice-Hall.

Nishida, A., Miyaoka, T., Inagaki, T., & Horiguchi, J. (2009). New approaches to antidepressant drug design: Cytokine-regulated pathways. *Current Pharmaceutical Design, 15,* 1683–1687.

Niswender, C. M., & Conn, P. J. (2010). Metabotropic glutamate receptors: Physiology, pharmacology, and disease. *Annual Review of Toxicology and Pharmacology, 50,* 295–322.

Nixon, K., & McClain, J. A. (2010). Adolescence as a critical window for developing an alcohol use disorder: Current findings in neuroscience. *Current Opinion in Psychiatry.* (in press)

Nkomo, S. M., Fottler, M. D., & McAfee, R. B. (2011). *Human resource management applications.* (7th Ed.). Boston: Cengage.

Noe, R. A., Hollenbeck, J. R., Gerhart, B., & Wright, P. M. (2007). *Fundamentals of human resource management* (2nd ed.). New York: McGraw-Hill.

Noel, N. E., Maisto, S. A., Johnson, J. D., & Jackson, L. A. (2009). The effects of alcohol and cue salience on young men's acceptance of sexual aggression. *Addictive Behaviors, 34,* 386–394.

Noftle, E. E., & Fleeson, W. (2010). Age differences in big five behavior averages and variabilities across the adult life span: Moving beyond retrospective, global summary accounts of personality. *Psychology and Aging, 25,* 95–107.

Noftle, E. E., & Robins, R. W. (2007). Personality predictors of academic outcomes: Big five correlates of GPA and SAT scores. *Journal of Personality and Social Psychology, 93,* 116–130.

Nolen-Hoeksema, S. (2011). *Abnormal psychology* (5th ed.). New York: McGraw-Hill. (in press)

Norcross, J. C., Mrykalo, M. S., & Blagys, M. D. (2002). Auld lang syne: Success predictors, change processes, and self-reported outcomes of New Year's resolvers and nonresolvers. *Journal of Clinical Psychology, 58,* 397–405.

Nordenskjold, A., Knorring, L. V., & Engstrom, I. (2010). Rehospitalization rate after continued electroconvulsive therapy: A retrospective chart review of patients with severe depression. *Nordic Journal of Psychiatry.* (in press)

Nordgren, L. F., & Dijksterhuis, A. P. (2009). The devil is in the deliberation: Thinking too much reduces preference consistency. *Journal of Consumer Research, 36,* 39–46.

Nordt, C., Rossler, W., & Lauber, C. (2006). Attitudes of mental health professionals toward people with schizophrenia and major depression. *Schizophrenia Bulletin, 32,* 709–714.

Norman, G. J., Devries, A. C., Cacioppo, J. T., & Bernsten, G. G. (2010). Multilevel analyses of stress. In J. Contrada & A. Baum (Eds.), *Handbook of stress science.* Springer.

Norman, W. T. (1963). Toward an adequate taxonomy of personality attributes. *Journal of Abnormal and Social Psychology, 66,* 574–583.

Norris, J., & others. (2009). Cognitive mediation of alcohol's effects on women's in-the-moment sexual decision making. *Health Psychology, 28,* 20–28.

Noseda, R., & others. (2010). A neural mechanism for exacerbation of headache by light. *Nature Neuroscience, 13,* 239–245.

Nosek, B. A., & Banaji, M. R. (2007). Implicit attitude. In P. Wilken, T. Bayne, & A. Cleeremans (Eds.), *Oxford companion to consciousness.* Oxford, U.K.: Oxford University Press.

Notman, M. T., & Nadelson, C. C. (2002). Women's issues. In M. Hersen & W. H. Sledge (Eds.), *Encyclopedia of psychotherapy.* San Diego: Academic.

Nowak, M. A., Page, K. M., & Sigmund, K. (2000). Fairness versus reason in the ultimatum game. *Science, 289,* 1773–1775.

Nrugham, L., Holen, A., & Sund, A. M. (2010). Associations between attempted suicide, life events, depressive symptoms, and resilience in adolescents and young adults. *Journal of Nervous and Mental Disease, 198,* 131–136.

Nystul, M. S. (1999). *Introduction to counseling.* Boston: Allyn & Bacon.

O

Oakley, D. A., & Halligan, P. W. (2010). Using hypnosis to gain insights into healthy and pathological cognitive functioning. *Consciousness and Cognition.* (in press)

O'Barr, W. M. (2006). Multiculturalism in the marketplace: Targeting Latinas, African American women, and gay consumers. *Advertising and Society Review, 7* (4). http://muse.jhu.edu/journals/advertising_and_society_review/

Obler, L. K. (2009). Development in the adult years. In J. Berko Gleason & N. Ratner (Eds.), *The development of language* (7th ed.). Boston: Allyn & Bacon.

Occupational Safety and Health Administration (OSHA). (2002). *Fact sheet.* http://www.osha.gov/OshDoc/data_General_Facts/factsheet-workplace-violence.pdf. Washington, DC: Author.

O'Connor, D. B., Conner, M., Jones, F., McMillan, B., & Ferguson, E. (2009). Exploring the benefits of conscientiousness: An investigation of the role of daily stressors and health behaviors. *Annals of Behavioral Medicine, 37,* 184–196.

O'Donnell, M. L., Creamer, M., McFarlane, A. C., Silove, D., & Bryant, R. A. (2010). Should A2 be a diagnostic requirement for posttraumatic stress disorder in DSM-V? *Psychiatry Research, 176,* 257–260.

Ogden, C. L., & Carroll, M. D. (June 2010). *Prevalence of Overweight, Obesity, and Extreme Obesity Among Adults: United States, Trends 1976–1980 Through 2007–2008.* Hyattsville, MD: National Center for Health Statistics.

Ogden, T. H. (2010). On three forms of thinking: Magical thinking, dream thinking, and transformative thinking. *Psychoanalytic Quarterly, 79,* 317–347.

Ogilvie, R. D., & Wilkinson, R. T. (1988). Behavioral versus EEG-based monitoring of all-night sleep/wake patterns. *Sleep, 11* (2), 139–155.

Ogle, L., Sen, A., Pahlke, E., Jocelyn, L., Kostberg, D., Roey, S., & Williams, T. (2003). *International comparisons in fourth grade reading literacy: Finding from the Progress in International Literacy Study (PIRLS) of 2001.* (NCES 2003-073). Washington, DC: U.S. Government Printing Office.

Ohayon, M. M. (2009). Difficulty in resuming or inability to resume sleep and the links to daytime impairment: Definition, prevalence, and comorbidity. *Journal of Psychiatric Research, 43,* 934–940.

Ohman, A. (2010). Post-traumatic fear memories: Analysing a case study of a sexual assault. In L. Backman & L. Nyberg (Eds.), *Memory, aging, and the brain: A Festschrift in honour of Lars-Goran Nilsson* (pp. 211–228). New York: Psychology Press.

Ohman, A., & Mineka, S. (2001). Fears, phobias, and preparedness: Toward an evolved module of fear and fear learning. *Psychological Review, 108,* 483–522.

Ohman, A., & Mineka, S. (2003). The malicious serpent: Snakes as a prototypical stimulus for an evolved module of fear. *Current Directions in Psychological Science, 12,* 5–9.

Ohman, A., & Soares, J. J. P. (1998). Emotional conditioning to masked stimuli: Expectancies for aversive outcomes following nonrecognized fear-relevant stimuli. *Journal of Experimental Psychology, 127,* 69–82.

Olds, J. M. (1958). Self-stimulation experiments and differential reward systems. In H. H. Jasper, L. D. Proctor, R. S. Knighton, W. C. Noshay, & R. T. Costello (Eds.), *Reticular formation of the brain.* Boston: Little, Brown.

Olds, J. M., & Milner, P. M. (1954). Positive reinforcement produced by electrical stimulation of the septal area and other areas of the rat brain. *Journal of Comparative and Physiological Psychology, 47,* 419–427.

Olfson, M., & Marcus, S. C. (2009). National patterns in antidepressant medication treatment. *Archives of General Psychiatry, 66,* 848–856.

Oliver, M. B., & Hyde, J. S. (1993). Gender differences in sexuality: A meta-analysis. *Psychological Bulletin, 114,* 29–51.

Oliver, N. S., Toumazou, C., Cass, A. E., & Johnston, D. G. (2009). Glucose sensors: A review of current and emerging technology. *Diabetic Medicine, 26,* 197–2010.

Olivola, C. Y., & Todorov, A. (2010). Fooled by first impressions? Reexamining the diagnostic value of appearance-based inferences. *Journal of Experimental Social Psychology, 46,* 315–324.

Ollendick, T. H., Raishevich, N., Davis, T. E., Sirbu, C., & Ost, L. G. (2010). Specific phobia in youth: Phenomenology and psychological characteristics. *Behavior Therapy, 41,* 133–141.

Olness, K., & Ader, R. (1992). Conditioning as an adjunct in the pharmacotherapy of lupus erythematosus. *Journal of Developmental and Behavioral Pediatrics, 13,* 124–125.

Olson, M., & Hergenhahn, B. R. (2009). *Introduction to theories of learning* (8th ed.). Upper Saddle River, NJ: Prentice-Hall.

Oltmanns, T. F., & Emery, R. E. (2010). *Abnormal psychology* (6th ed.). Boston: Allyn & Bacon.

Olver, J. S., & others. (2009). Dopamine D1 receptor binding in the striatum of patients with obsessive-compulsive disorder. *Journal of Affective Disorders, 114,* 321–326.

Ones, D. S., & Viswesvaran, C. (1998). Gender, age, and race differences in overt integrity tests: Results across four large-scale job applicant datasets. *Journal of Applied Psychology, 83,* 35–42.

Ones, D. S., & Viswesvaran, C., & Schmidt, F. L. (1993). Comprehensive meta-analysis of integrity test validities: Finding and implications for personnel selection and theories of job performance. *Journal of Applied Psychology, 78,* 679–703.

Ong, A. D., Bergeman, C. S., & Boker, S. M. (2009). Resilience comes of age: Defining features in later adulthood. *Journal of Personality, 77,* 1777–1804.

Online Publishers Association. (2005, October). *Online paid content U.S. market spending report.* New York: Online Publishers Association and Comscore Networks.

Ophir, E., Nass, C., & Wagner, A. D. (2009). Cognitive control in media multitaskers. *Proceedings of the National Academy of Sciences USA, 106,* 15583–15587.

Orduna, V., Garcia, A., & Hong, E. (2010). Choice behavior in spontaneously hypertensive rats: Variable vs. fixed schedules of reinforcement. *Behavioural Processes.* (in press)

O'Regan, D., Wong, K., Bouras, I., Foot, C., & Wigmore, T. (2010). Falling in and out of consciousness: Catatonia in a postoperative patient. *Journal of Research in Social Medicine, 103,* 107–108.

Organ, D. W., Podsakoff, P. M., & Podsakoff, N. P. (2010). Expanding the criterion domain to include organizational citizenship behavior: Implications for employee selection. In S. Zedeck (Ed.), *APA handbook of industrial and organizational psychology.* Washington, DC: APA. (in press)

Organ, D. W., & Ryan, K. (1995). A meta-analytic review of attitudinal and dispositional predictors of organizational citizenship behavior. *Personnel Psychology, 48,* 775–802.

Orlacchio, A., Bernardi, G., Orlacchio, A., & Martino, S. (2010). Stem cells: An overview of the current status of therapies for central and peripheral nervous system diseases. *Current Medicinal Chemistry.* (in press)

Orom, H., & Cervone, D. (2009). Personality dynamics, meaning, and idiosyncrasy: Identifying cross-situational coherence by assessing personality architecture. *Journal of Research in Personality, 43,* 228–240.

O'Shea, P. G., Foti, R. J., Haunenstein, N. M. A., & Bycio, P. (2009). Are the best leaders both transformational and transactional? A pattern-oriented analysis. *Leadership, 5,* 237–259.

Ostir, G. V., Markides, K. S., Black, S. A., & Goodwin, J. S. (2000). Emotional well-being predicts subsequent functional independence and survival. *Journal of the American Geriatrics Society, 48,* 473–478.

Oswald, F. L., & Hough, L. M. (2010). Personality and its assessment in organizations: Theoretical and empirical developments. In S. Zedeck (Ed.), *APA handbook of industrial and organizational psychology.* Washington, DC: APA. (in press)

Otake, K., Shimai, S., Tanaka-Matsumi, J., Otsui, K., & Fredrickson, B. L. (2006). Happy people becoming happier through kindness: A counting kindnesses intervention. *Journal of Happiness Studies, 7,* 361–375.

Otto, J. M., Bach, M., & Kommerell, G. (2010). Advantage of binocularity in the presence of external visual voice. *Graefe's Archive for Clinical and Experimental Ophthalmology.* (in press)

Oyama, H., & others. (2010). A community-based survey and screening for depression in the elderly. *Crisis, 31,* 100–108.

Ozer, D. J., & Benet-Martinez, V. (2006). Personality and the prediction of consequential outcomes. *Annual Review of Psychology* (vol. 57). Palo Alto, CA: Annual Reviews.

P

Packer, D. J. (2008). Identifying systematic disobedience in Milgram's obedience experiments: A meta-analytic review. *Perspectives on Psychological Science, 3,* 301–304.

Packer, D. J. (2009). Avoiding groupthink: Whereas weakly identified members stay silent, strongly identified members dissent about collective matters. *Psychological Science, 20,* 546–548.

Page, J. H., Rexrode, K. M., Hu, F., Albert, C. M., Chae, C. U., & Manson, J. E. (2009). Waist-height ratio as a predictor of coronary heart disease among women. *Epidemiology, 20,* 361–366.

Page, S. (2009, December 29). Americans most admire Obama, Clinton, Palin. *USA Today.* http://www.usatoday.com/news/washington/2009-12-29-admire-gallup-poll_N.htm (accessed February 3, 2010)

Paivio, A. (1971). *Imagery and verbal processes.* New York: Holt, Rinehart & Winston.

Paivio, A. (1986). *Mental representations: A dual coding approach.* New York: Oxford University Press.

Paivio, A. (2007). *Mind and its evolution: A dual coding theoretical approach.* Mahwah, NJ: Erlbaum.

Paller, C. J., Campbell, C. M., Edwards, R. R., & Dobs, A. S. (2009). Sex-based differences in pain perception and treatment. *Pain Medicine, 10,* 289–299.

Palmieri, P. A., & Fitzgerald, L. F. (2005). Confirmatory factor analysis of posttraumatic stress symptoms in sexually harassed women. *Journal of Traumatic Stress, 18,* 657–666.

Palomo, T., Beninger, R. J., Kostrzewa, R. M., & Archer, T. (2008). Focusing on symptoms rather than diagnoses in brain dysfunction: Conscious and nonconscious expression in impulsiveness and decision-making. *Neurotoxicity Research, 14,* 1–20.

Paluck, E. C., McCormack, J. P., Ensom, M. H. H., Levine, M., Soon, J. A., & Fielding, D. W. (2006). Outcomes of bupropion therapy for smoking cessation during routine clinical use. *Annals of Pharmacotherapy, 40,* 185–190.

Pan, B. A., & Uccelli, P. (2009). Semantic development. In J. Berko Gleason & N. Ratner (Eds.), *The development of language* (7th ed.). Boston: Allyn & Bacon.

Pant, S., & Ramaswamy, B. (2009). Association of major stressors with elevated risk of breast cancer incidence or relapse. *Drugs Today, 45,* 115–126.

Pantazopoulos, H., Woo, T. U., Lim, M. P., Lange, N., & Berretta, S. (2010). Extracellular matrix-glial abnormalities in the amygdale and entorhinal cortex of subjects diagnosed with schizophrenia. *Archives of General Psychiatry, 67,* 155–166.

Papousek, I., Nauschnegg, K., Paechter, M., Lackner, H. K., Goswami, N., & Schulter, G. (2010). Trait and state positive affect and cardiovascular recovery from experimental academic stress. *Biological Psychology, 83,* 108–115.

Papousek, I., Schulter, G., & Lang, B. (2009). Effects of emotionally contagious films on changes in hemisphere-specific cognitive performance. *Emotion, 9,* 510–519.

Paris, J. (2010). Effectiveness of different therapeutic approaches in the treatment of borderline personality disorder. *Current Psychiatric Reports, 12,* 56–80.

Park, B. H., Lee, M. S., Hong, J. Y., Bas, S. H., Kim, E. Y., Kim, K. K., & Kim, D. K. (2009). The stages of physical activity and exercise behavior: An integrated approach to the theory of planned behavior. *Asia-Pacific Journal of Mental Health, 21,* 71–83.

Park, C. (2009). Meaning making in cancer survivorship. In P. T. P. Wong (Ed.), *Handbook of meaning* (2nd ed.). Thousand Oaks, CA: Sage.

Park, C. L. (2010). Making sense of the meaning literature: An integrative review of meaning making and its effects on adjustment to stressful life events. *Psychological Bulletin, 136,* 257–301.

Park, C. L., Lechner, S. C., Antoni, M. H., & Stanton, A. L. (Eds.). (2009). *Medical illness and positive life change: Can crisis lead to personal transformation?* Washington, DC: American Psychological Association.

Park, D. C., & Huang, C. M. (2010). Culture wires the brain: A cognitive neuroscience perspective. *Perspectives on Psychological Science.* (in press)

Park, D. C., & Reuter-Lorenz, P. (2009). The adaptive brain: Aging and neurocognitive scaffolding. *Annual Review of Psychology* (vol. 60). Palo Alto, CA: Annual Reviews.

Park, D. H., Eve, D. J., Borlongan, C. V., Klasko, S. K., Cruz, L. E., & Sanberg, P. R. (2009). From the basics to application of cell therapy, a steppingstone to the conquest of neurodegeneration: A meeting report. *Medical Science Monitor, 15,* RA23–31.

Park, M. (2009, April 4). Teen tries to quiet the voices caused by schizophrenia. *CNN.com.* http://www.cnn.com/2009/HEALTH/04/24/schizophrenia.soloist.brain/index.html (accessed April 14, 2009)

Parker, M., Brugeaud, A., & Edge, A. S. (2010). Primary culture and plasmid electroporation of the murine organ of corti. *Journal of Visualized Experiments.* (in press)

Parker, P. S. (2006). *Race, gender, and leadership.* Mahwah, NJ: Erlbaum.

Parks, M. R. (2007). *Personal relationships and personal networks.* Mahwah, NJ: Erlbaum.

Parry, A., & Matthews, P. M. (2002). Functional magnetic resonance imaging: A window into the brain. *Interdisciplinary Science Reviews, 27,* 50–60.

Parsons, H. M. (1974). What happened at Hawthorne? *Science, 183,* 922–932.

Pascalls, O., & Kelly, D. J. (2008). Face processing. In M. M. Haith & J. B. Benson (Eds.), *Encyclopedia of infant and early childhood development.* Oxford, U.K.: Elsevier.

Paschalis, V., & others. (2010). A weekly bout of eccentric exercise is sufficient to induce health-promoting effects. *Medicine and Science in Sports and Exercise.* (in press)

Passie, T., Halpern, J. H., Stichtenoth, D. O., Emrich, H. M., & Hintzen, A. (2008). The pharmacology of lysergic acid diethylamide: A review. *CNS Neuroscience and Therapeutics, 14,* 295–314.

Patalano, A. L., Wengrovitz, S. M., & Sharpes, K. M. (2009). The influence of category coherence on inference about cross-classified entities. *Memory and Cognition, 37,* 21–38.

Patel, A. R., Hui, H., J. T., Pandian, N. G., & Karas, R. H. (2009). Modestly overweight women have vascular endothelial dysfunction. *Clinical Cardiology, 32,* 269–273.

Patel, S. R., Zhu, X., Storfer-Isser, A., Mehra, A., Jenny, N. S., Tracy, R., & Redline, S. (2009). Sleep duration and biomarkers of inflammation. *Sleep, 32,* 200–204.

Patell, E. A., Cooper, H., & Robinson, J. C. (2008). The effects of choice on intrinsic motivation and related outcomes: A meta-analysis of research findings. *Psychological Bulletin, 134,* 270–300.

Paton, C., & others. (2010). Lithium in bipolar and other affective disorders: Prescribing practice in the UK. *Journal of Psychopharmacology.* (in press)

Patten, S. B., Wang, J. L., Williams, J. V., Currie, S., Beck, C. A., Maxwell, C. A., &

el-Guebaly, N. (2006). Descriptive epidemiology of major depression in Canada. *Canadian Journal of Psychology, 51,* 84–90.

Patterson, C. J., & Farr, R. H. (2010). Children of gay and lesbian parents: Reflections on the research-policy interface. In H. R. Schaffer & K. Durkin (Eds.), *Blackwell handbook of developmental psychology in action.* London: Blackwell. (in press)

Patterson, C. J., & Wainright, J. L. (2010). Adolescents with same-sex parents: Findings from the National Longitudinal Study of Adolescent Health. In D. Brodzinsky, A. Pertman, & D. Kunz (Eds.), *Lesbian and gay adoption: A new American reality.* New York: Oxford University Press. (in press)

Pattillo, R. (2010). Are students as good at multitasking as they think? *Nurse Educator, 35,* 24.

Paul-Samojedny, M., & others. (2010). Functional polymorphism in the interleukin-6 and interleukin-10 genes in patients with paranoid schizophrenia—a case control study. *Journal of Molecular Neuroscience.* (in press)

Paunonen, S., Jackson, D., Trzebinski, J., & Forserling, F. (1992). Personality structures across cultures: A multimethod evaluation. *Journal of Personality and Social Psychology, 62,* 447–456.

Paus, T. (2009). Brain development. In R. M. Lerner & L. Steinberg (Ed.), *Handbook of adolescent psychology* (3rd ed.). New York: Wiley.

Paus, T., Toro, R., Leonard, G., Lerner, J. V., Lerner, R. M., Perron, M., Pike, G. B., Richer, L., Steinberg, L., Veillete, S., & Pausova, Z. (2008). Morphological properties of the action-observation cortical network in adolescents with low and high resistance to peer influence. *Social Neuroscience, 3,* 303–316.

Pavlov, I. P. (1927). *Conditioned reflexes.* G. V. Anrep (Trans.). New York: Dover.

Pavot, W., & Diener, E. (2008). The Satisfaction with Life Scale and the emerging construct of life satisfaction. *Journal of Positive Psychology, 3,* 137–152.

Payne, B. K. (2001). Prejudice and perception: The role of automatic and controlled processes in misperceiving a weapon. *Journal of Personality and Social Psychology, 81,* 181–192.

Payne, B. K. (2010). Divided minds, divided morals: How implicit social cognition underpins and undermines our sense of social justice. In B. Gawronski & B. K. Payne (Eds.), *Handbook of implicit social cognition.* New York: Guilford.

Pearce, J. M., & Hall, G. (2009). A model for stimulus generalization in Pavlovian conditioning. In D. Shanks (Ed.), *Psychology of learning.* Thousand Oaks, CA: Sage.

Pearson, C. M., Andersson, L. M., & Porath, C. L. (2005). Workplace incivility. In S. Fox & P. E. Spector (Eds.), *Counterproductive work behavior: Investigations of actors and targets* (pp. 177–200). Washington, DC: American Psychological Association.

Pearson, N. J., Johnson, L. L., & Nahin, R. L. (2006). Insomnia, trouble sleeping, and complementary and alternative medicine: Analysis of the 2002 National Health Interview Survey data. *Archives of Internal Medicine, 166,* 1775–1782.

Peeters, A., & Barendregt, J. J., Willekens, F., Mackenbach, J. P., Al Mamun, A., & Bonneux, L. (2003). Obesity in adulthood and its consequences for life expectancy: A Life-Table analysis. *Annals of Internal Medicine, 138,* 24–32.

Pelleymounter, M. A., & others. (1995). Effects of the obese gene product on body weight regulation in ob/ob mice. *Science, 269,* 540–543.

Penedo, F. J., Molton, I., Dahn, J. R., Shen, B. J., Kinsigner, D., Traeger, L., Siegel, S., Schneiderman, N., & Antoni, M. (2006). A randomized clinical trial of group-based cognitive-behavioral stress management in localized prostate cancer: Development of stress management skills improves quality of life and benefit finding. *Annals of Behavioral Medicine, 31,* 261–270.

Penfield, W. (1947). Some observations in the cerebral cortex of man. *Proceedings of the Royal Society, 134,* 349.

Pennebaker, J. W. (1997a). *Opening up: The healing power of expressing emotions* (rev. ed.). New York: Guilford.

Pennebaker, J. W. (1997b). Writing about emotional experiences as a therapeutic experience. *Psychological Science, 8,* 162–166.

Pennebaker, J. W. (2004). *Writing to heal: A guided journal for recovering from trauma emotional upheaval.* Oakland, CA: New Harbinger Press.

Pennebaker, J. W., & Chung, C. K. (2007). Expressive writing, emotional upheavals, and health. In H. S. Friedman & R. C. Silver (Eds.), *Foundations of health psychology* (pp. 263–284). New York: Oxford University Press.

Pennebaker, J. W., & Graybeal, A. (2001). Patterns of natural language use: Disclosure, personality, and social integration. *Current Directions in Psychological Science, 32,* 90–93.

Pennebaker, J. W., & O'Heeron, R. C. (1984). Confiding in others and illness rate among spouses of suicide and accidental-death victims. *Journal of Abnormal Psychology, 93,* 473–476.

Penner, J., Rupsingh, R., Smith, M., Wells, J. L., Borrie, M. J., & Bartha, R. (2010). Increased glutamate in the hippocampus after galantamine treatment for Alzheimer disease. *Progress in Neuro-Psychopharmacology and Biological Psychiatry, 34,* 104–110.

Peplau, L. A. (2001). Rethinking women's sexual orientation: An interdisciplinary, relationship-focused approach. *Personal Relationships, 8,* 1–19.

Peplau, L. A. (2003). Human sexuality: How do men and women differ? *Current Directions in Psychological Science, 12,* 37–40.

Peplau, L. A., & Fingerhut, A. W. (2007). The close relationships of lesbians and gay men. *Annual Review of Psychology* (vol. 58). Palo Alto, CA: Annual Reviews.

Peplau, L. A., Spalding, L. R., Conley, T. D., & Veniegas, R. C. (1999). The development of sexual orientation in women. *Annual Review of Sex Research, 10,* 70–99.

Perez-Costas, E., Melendez-Ferro, M., & Roberts, R. C. (2010). Basal ganglia pathology in schizophrenia: Dopamine connections and anomalies. *Journal of Neurochemistry.* (in press)

Perkins, D. (1994, September). Creativity by design. *Educational Leadership,* 18–25.

Perlis, R. H., & others. (2009). A genomewide association study of response to lithium for prevention of recurrence in bipolar disorder. *American Journal of Psychiatry, 166,* 718–725.

Perlman, D. M., Salomons, T. V., Davidson, R. J., & Lutz, A. (2010). Differential effects of pain intensity and unpleasantness of two meditation practices. *Emotion, 10,* 65–71.

Perrin, P. B., Heesacker, M., Pendley, C., & Smith, M. B. (2010). Social influence processes and persuasion in psychotherapy and counseling. In J. E. Maddux & J. P. Tagney (Eds.), *Social psychological foundations of clinical psychology.* New York: Guilford.

Pert, C. B. (1999). *Molecules of emotion.* New York: Simon & Schuster.

Pert, C. B., & Snyder, S. H. (1973). Opiate receptor: Demonstration in a nervous tissue. *Science, 179,* 1011.

Pessoa, L. (2009). How do emotion and motivation direct executive control? *Trends in Cognitive Science, 13,* 160–166.

Peters, E., & others. (2010). A randomized controlled trial of cognitive behavior therapy for psychosis in a routine clinical service. *Acta Psychiatrica Scandinavica.* (in press)

Petersen, J. L., & Hyde, J. S. (2010). A meta-analytic review of research on gender differences in sexuality, 1973–2007. *Psychological Bulletin, 136,* 21–38.

Peterson, C., Seligman, M. E. P., & Vaillant, G. E. (1988). Pessimistic explanatory style is a risk factor for physical illness: A thirty-five year longitudinal study. *Journal of Personality and Social Psychology, 55,* 23–27.

Peterson, C. C., Garnett, M., Kelly, A., & Attwood, T. (2009). Everyday social and conversation applications of theory-of-mind understanding by children with autism-spectrum disorders or typical development. *European Child and Adolescent Psychology, 18,* 105–115.

Peterson, N. G., & Jeanneret, P. R. (2007). Job analysis: An overview and description of deductive methods. In D. L. Whetzel & G. R. Wheaton (Eds.), *Applied measurement.* Mahwah, NJ: Erlbaum.

Pettigrew, T. F., & Tropp, L. R. (2006). A meta-analytic test of intergroup contact theory. *Journal of Personality and Social Psychology, 90,* 751–783.

Petty, R. E., & Brinol, P. (2008). Persuasion: From single to multiple to metacognitive processes. *Perspectives on Psychological Science, 3,* 137–147.

Petty, R. E., & Cacioppo, J. T. (1986). The elaboration likelihood of persuasion. In L. Berkowitz (Ed.), *Advances in experimental social psychology* (vol. 19). New York: Academic.

Pew Research Center. (2007, January 9). *A portrait of "Generation Next": How young people view their lives, futures and politics.* Washington, DC: Author.

Pfafflin, F. (2010). Understanding transgendered phenomena. In S. B. Levine, C. B. Risen, & S. E. Althof (Eds.), *Handbook of clinical sexuality for mental health professionals* (2nd ed., pp. 425–447). New York: Routledge/Taylor & Francis.

Phan, M. L., & Vicario, D. S. (2010). Hemispheric differences in processing of vocalizations depend on early experience. *Proceedings of the National Academy of Sciences USA, 107,* 2301–2306.

Phaneuf, L., & McIntyre, L. L. (2007). Effects of individualized video feedback combined with group parent training on inappropriate maternal behavior. *Journal of Applied Behavior Analysis, 40* (4), 737–741.

Phelan, J. E., & Basow, S. A. (2007). College students' attitudes toward mental illness: An examination of the stigma process. *Journal of Applied Social Psychology, 37,* 2877–2902.

Phelan, S., Hill, J. O., Lang, W., Dibello, J. R., & Wing, R. R. (2003). Recovery from relapse among successful weight maintainers. *American Journal of Clinical Nutrition, 78,* 1079–1084.

Phillips, D. A., & Lowenstein, A. (2011). Early care, education, and child development. *Annual Review of Psychology* (vol. 62). Palo Alto, CA: Annual Reviews.

Phillips, K. J., & Mudford, O. C. (2008). Functional analysis skills training for residential caregivers. *Behavioral Interventions, 23* (1), 1–12.

Phillips, T., Ferguson, E., & Rijsdijk, F. (2010). A link between altruism and sexual selection: Genetic influence on altruistic behavior and mate preference towards it. *British Journal of Psychology.* (in press)

Phinney, J. S., Berry, J. W., Berry, D. L., & Vedder, S. P. (2006). Understanding immigrant youth: Conclusions and implications. In J. W. Berry, J. S. Phinney, D. L. Sam, & S. P. Vedder (Eds.), *Immigrant youth in cultural transmission.* Mahwah, NJ: Erlbaum.

Piaget, J. (1952). *The origins of intelligence in children.* New York: Oxford University Press.

Pickering, A. D., & Smillie, L. D. (2008). The behavioral activation system: Challenges and opportunities. In P. J. Corr (Ed.), *The reinforcement sensitivity theory of personality* (pp. 120–154). New York: Cambridge University Press.

Pierrehumbert, B., Torrisi, R., Laufer, D., Halfon, O., Ansermet, F., & Beck Popovic, M. (2010). Oxytocin response to an experimental psychosocial challenge in adults exposed to traumatic experiences during childhood or adolescence. *Neuroscience, 166,* 168–177.

Pierucci, M., Di Matteo, V., Benigno, A., Crescimanno, G., Esposito, E., & Di Giovanni, G. (2009). The unilateral nigral lesion induces dramatic bilateral modification on a rat brain monoamine neurochemistry. *Annals of the New York Academy of Sciences, 1155,* 316–323.

Pillemer, D. B. (1998). *Momentous events: Vivid memories.* Cambridge, MA: Harvard University Press.

Pilnick, A., & Coleman, T. (2010). "Do your best for me": The difficulties of finding a clinically

effective endpoint in smoking cessation consultations in primary care. *Health, 14,* 57–74.

Pine, D. S. (2009). A social neuroscience approach to adolescent depression. In M. de Haan & M. R. Gunnar (Eds.), *Handbook of developmental social neuroscience.* New York: Guilford.

Pinel, J. P. J. (2009). *Biopsychology* (7th ed.). Upper Saddle River, NJ: Prentice-Hall.

Pinel, P., & Dehaene, S. (2010). Beyond hemispheric dominance: Brain regions underlying the joint lateralization of language and arithmetic to the left hemisphere. *Journal of Cognitive Neuroscience, 22* (1), 48–66.

Pines, A. M., & Maslach, C. (2002). *Experiencing social psychology* (4th ed.). New York: McGraw-Hill.

Pinker, S. (2007). The mystery of consciousness. *Time, 169,* 58–62.

Piolino, P., Desgranges, B., Clarys, D., Guillery-Girard, B., Taconnat, L., Isingrini, M., & Eustache, F. (2006). Autobiographical memory, autonoetic consciousness, and self-perspective in aging. *Psychology and Aging, 21,* 510–525.

Pirucello, L. M. (2010). Preventing adolescent suicide. *Journal of Psychosocial Nursing and Mental Health Services.* (in press)

Pittenger, D. J. (2005). Cautionary comments regarding the Myers-Briggs Type Indicator. *Consulting Psychology Journal: Practice and Research, 57,* 210–221.

Pitychoutis, P. M., Zisaki, A., Dallas, C., & Papadopoulou-Daifoti, Z. (2010). Pharmacogenic insights into depression and antidepressant response: Does sex matter? *Current Pharmaceutical Design.* (in press)

Plant, E. A., & Peruche, B. M. (2005). The consequences of race for police officers' responses to criminal suspects. *Psychological Science, 16,* 180–183.

Plaza-Zabala, A., Martin-Garcia, E., de Lecea, L., Maldonado, R., & Berrendero, F. (2010). Hypcretins regulate the anxiogenic-like effects of nicotine and induce reinstatement of nicotine-seeking behavior. *Journal of Neuroscience, 30,* 2300–2310.

Plomin, R., DeFries, J. C., McClearn, G. E., & McGuffin, P. (2009). *Biological psychology and neuroscience* (5th ed.). New York: Worth.

Ploog, B. O., & Williams, B. A. (2010). Serial discrimination reversal learning in pigeons as a function of intertrial interval and delay of reinforcement. *Learning & Behavior, 38,* 96–102.

Ployhart, R. E., & MacKenzie, W. I. (2010). Situational judgment tests: A critical review and agenda for the future. In S. Zedeck (Ed.), *APA handbook of industrial and organizational psychology.* Washington, DC: APA. (in press)

Poisnel, G., Dhilly, M., Boisselier, R. L., Barre, L., & Debruyne, D. (2009). Comparison of five benzodiazepine-receptor agonists on buprenorphine-induced mu-opioid receptor regulation. *Journal of Pharmacological Sciences, 110,* 36–46.

Pollack, M. H. (2009). Refractory generalized anxiety disorder. *Journal of Clinical Psychiatry, 70,* Suppl. 2, S32–S38.

Polyn, S. M., Norman, K. A., & Kahana, M. J. (2009). Task context and organization in free recall. *Neuropsychologia, 47,* 2158–2163.

Pomerantz, E. M., Saxon, J. L., & Oishi, S. (2000). The psychological trade-offs of goal investment. *Journal of Personality and Social Psychology, 79,* 617–630.

Pompili, M., & others. (2007). Suicide risk in schizophrenia: Learning from the past to change the future. *Annals of General Psychiatry, 6,* 10.

Pompili, M., & others. (2010). The hypothalamic-pituitary-adrenal axis and serotonin abnormalities: A selective overview for the implications of suicide prevention. *European Archives of Psychiatry and Clinical Neuroscience.* (in press)

Popeo, D. M. (2009). Electroconvulsive therapy for depressive episodes: A brief review. *Geriatrics, 64,* 9–12.

Popova, N. K., Naumenko, V. S., Cybko, A. S., & Bazovkina, D. V. (2010). Receptor-genes cross-talk: Effect of chronic 5-HT1A agonist 8-OH-DPAT treatment on the expression of key genes in brain serotonin system and on behavior. *Neuroscience.* (in press)

Popp, A. (2006, November). *Inequality and segregation as correlates of urban crime rates.* Paper presented at the annual meeting of the American Society of Criminology (ASC), Los Angeles.

Poppenk, J., Moscovitch, M., McIntosh, A. R., Ozcelik, E., & Craik, F. L. (2010). Encoding the future: Successful processing of intentions engages predictive brain networks. *NeuroImage, 49,* 905–913.

Porter, S., & ten Brinke, L. (2008). Reading between the lies: Identifying concealed and falsified emotions in universal facial expressions. *Psychological Science, 19,* 508–514.

Portnuff, C. D. F., & Fligor, B. J. (2006, October). *Output levels of portable music players.* Presented at the American Auditory Society Conference, Cincinnati.

Poryazova, R., Schnepf, B., Werth, E., Khatami, R., Dydak, U., Meier, D., Boesiger, P., & Bassetti, C. L. (2009). Evidence for metabolic hypothalamo-amygdala dysfunction in narcolepsy. *Sleep: Journal of Sleep and Sleep Disorders Research, 32,* 607–613.

Posner, J., Russell, J., & Peterson, B. S. (2005). The circumplex model of affect: An integrative approach to affective neuroscience, cognitive development, and psychopathology. *Developmental Psychopathology, 17,* 715–734.

Posner, M. I., & Rothbart, M. K. (2010). Brain states and hypnosis research. *Consciousness and Cognition.* (in press)

Postel, M. G., de Haan, H. A., & de Jong, C. A. (2010). Evaluation of an e-therapy program for problem drinkers: A pilot study. *Substance Use and Misuse.* (in press)

Postel, M. G., de Jong, C. A. J., & de Haan, H. A. (2005). Does e-therapy for problem drinking reach hidden populations? *American Journal of Psychiatry, 162,* 2393.

Powell, R. A., Symbaluk, D. G., & Honey, P. L. (2009). *Introduction to learning and behavior* (3rd ed.). Belmont, CA: Cengage.

Prakash, R. S., Snook, T., Motl, R. W., & Kramer, A. F. (2010). Aerobic fitness is associated with gray matter volume and white matter integrity in multiple sclerosis. *Brain Research.* (in press)

Prescott, T. J., & Humphries, M. D. (2007). Who dominates the dark basements of the brain? *Behavioral and Brain Sciences, 30,* 104–105.

Pressman, J. (1998). *Last resort, Psychosurgery and the limits of medicine.* New York: Cambridge University Press.

Preston, T. J., Kourtzi, Z., & Welchman, A. E. (2009). Adaptive estimation of three-dimensional structure in the human brain. *Journal of Neuroscience, 29,* 1688–1699.

Price, D. D., Finniss, D. G., & Benedetti, F. (2008). A comprehensive review of the placebo effect. *Annual Review of Psychology* (vol. 59). Palo Alto: Annual Reviews.

Probstner, D., Thuler, L. C., Ishikawa, N. M., & Alvarenga, R. M. (2010). Phantom limb phenomena in cancer amputees. *Pain Practice.* (in press)

Prochaska, J. O., DiClemente, C. C., & Norcross, J. C. (1992). In search of how people change: Applications to addictive behaviors. *American Psychologist, 47,* 1102–1114.

Prochaska, J. O., & Norcross, J. C. (2010). *Systems of psychotherapy* (7th ed.). Pacific Grove, CA: Brooks/Cole.

Prochaska, J. O., Norcross, J. C., & DiClemente, C. C. (1994). *Changing for good: A revolutionary six-stage program for overcoming bad habits and moving your life positively forward.* New York: Avon Books.

Proctor, R. W., & Vu, K. (2010). Cumulative knowledge and progress in human factors. *Annual Review of Psychology* (vol. 61). Palo Alto, CA: Annual Reviews.

Pronk, T. M., Karremans, J. C., Overbeek, G., Vermulst, A. A., & Wigboldus, D. H. J. (2010). What it takes to forgive: When and why executive functioning facilitates forgiveness. *Journal of Personality and Social Psychology, 98,* 119–131.

Provenzo, E. F. (2002). *Teaching, learning, and schooling in American culture: A critical perspective.* Boston: Allyn & Bacon.

Provine, R. R., Spencer, R. J., & Mandell, D. L. (2007). Emotional expression online: Emoticons punctuate website text messages. *Journal of Language and Social Psychology, 26,* 299–307.

Pujadas, L., & others. (2010). Reelin regulates postnatal neurogenesis and enhances spin hypertrophy and long-term potentiating. *Journal of Neuroscience, 30,* 4636–4649.

Pukrop, R., Sass, H., & Steinmeyer, E. M. (2000). Circumplex models for the similarity relationships between higher-order factors of personality and personality disorders: An empirical analysis. *Contemporary Psychiatry, 41,* 438–445.

Puterman, E., Lin, J., Blackburn, E., O'Donovan, A., Adler, N., & Epel, E. (2010). The power of exercise: Buffering the effect of chronic stress on telomere length. *PLoS One, 5,* e10837.

Q

Qian, Z. (2009). Mate selection. In D. Carr (Ed.), *Encyclopedia of the life course and human development.* Boston: Gale Cengage.

Quan, S. F., Parthasarathy, S., & Budhiraja, R. (2010). Healthy sleep education—a salve for obesity. *Journal of Clinical Sleep Medicine, 6,* 18–19.

Quang, P. N., & Schmidt, B. L. (2010). Endothelin-A receptor antagonism attenuates carcinoma-induced pain through opioids in mice. *Journal of Pain.* (in press)

Quinn, J. G., & McConnell, J. (2006). The interval for interference in conscious visual imagery. *Memory, 14,* 241–252.

Quinn, P. C. (2011). Born to categorize. In U. Goswami (Ed.), *Wiley-Blackwell handbook of childhood cognitive development* (2nd ed.). New York: Wiley Blackwell.

R

Raabe, B., & Beehr, T. A. (2003). Formal mentoring versus supervisor and co-worker relationships: Differences in perceptions and impact. *Journal of Organizational Behavior, 24,* 271–293.

Racagni, G., & Popoli, M. (2010). The pharmacological properties of antidepressants. *International Clinical Psychopharmacology, 25,* 117–131.

Rachlin, H., & Green, L. (2009). The neural basis of drug craving: An incentive-sensitization theory of addiction. In D. Shanks (Ed.), *Psychology of learning.* Thousand Oaks, CA: Sage.

Rachman, S. (2009). Psychological treatment of anxiety: The evolution of behavior therapy and cognitive-behavior therapy. *Annual Review of Clinical Psychology* (vol. 5). Palo Alto, CA: Annual Reviews.

Racsmany, M., Conway, M. A., & Demeter, G. (2010). Consolidation of episodic memory during sleep: Long-term effects of retrieval practice. *Psychological Science, 21,* 80–85.

Radel, R., Sarrazin, P., & Pelletier, L. (2009). Evidence of subliminally primed motivational orientations: The effects of unconscious motivational processes on the performance of a new motor task. *Journal of Sport and Exercise Psychology, 31,* 657–674.

Rafanelli, C., Milaneschi, Y., Roncuzzi, R., & Pancaldi, L. G. (2010). Dysthymia before myocardial infarction as a cardiac risk factor at 2.5-year follow-up. *Psychosomatics, 51,* 8–13.

Raffone, A., & Srinivasan, N. (2010). The exploration of meditation in the neuroscience of attention and consciousness. *Cognitive Processes.* (in press)

Ragins, B. R., Cotton, J. L., & Miller, J. S. (2000). Marginal mentoring: The effects of type of mentor, quality of relationship, and program design on work and career attitudes. *Academy of Management Journal, 43,* 1177–1194.

Rahman, Q. (2005). The neurodevelopment of human sexual orientation. *Neuroscience & Biobehavioral Reviews, 29,* 1057–1066.

Rahman, Q., Clarke, K., & Morera, T. (2009). Hair whorl direction and sexual orientation in human males. *Behavioral Neuroscience, 123,* 252–256.

Rahman, Q., & Wilson, G. D. (2003). Sexual orientation and the 2nd to 4th finger length ratio: Evidence for organising effects of sex hormones or developmental instability? *Psychoneuroendocrinology, 28,* 288–303.

Raine, A. (2008). From genes to brain to antisocial behavior. *Current Directions in Psychological Science, 17,* 323–328.

Raine, A., Venables, P. H., & Williams, M. (1990). Relationships between N1, P300 and CNV recorded at age 15 and criminal behavior at age 24. *Psychophysiology, 27,* 567–575.

Rajkumar, R., & Mahesh, R. (2010). The auspicious role of the 5-HT3 receptor in depression: A probably neuronal target? *Journal of Psychopharmacology.* (in press)

Ram, N., Morelli, S., Lindberg, C., & Carstensen, L. L. (2008). From static to dynamic: The ongoing dialectic about human development. In K. W. Schaie & R. P. Abeles (Eds.), *Social structures and aging individuals.* Mahwah, NJ: Erlbaum.

Ramey, C. T., Ramey, S. L., & Lanzi, R. G. (2006). Children's health and education. In W. Damon & R. Lerner (Eds.), *Handbook of child psychology* (6th ed.). New York: Wiley.

Ramirez-Esparza, N., Gosling, S. D., Benet-Martinez, V., Potter, J. P., & Pennebaker, J. W. (2006). Do bilinguals have two personalities? A special case of cultural frame switching. *Journal of Research in Personality, 40,* 99–120.

Rammstedt, B., Goldberg, L. R., & Borg, I. (2010). The measurement equivalence of Big Five factor markers for persons with different levels of education. *Journal of Research in Personality, 44,* 53–61.

Ramon, J. M., & Bruguera, E. (2009). Real world study to evaluate the effectiveness of varenicline and cognitive-behavioral interventions for smoking cessation. *International Journal of Environmental Research and Public Health, 6,* 1530–1538.

Ramsey, J. L., Langlois, J. H., Hoss, R. A., Rubenstein, A. J., & Griffin, A. M. (2004). Origins of a stereotype: Categorization of facial attractiveness by 6-month-old infants. *Developmental Science, 7* (2), 201–211.

Ramsey, R., & de C. Hamilton, A. F. (2010). Understanding actors and object-goals in the human brain. *NeuroImage, 50,* 1142–1147.

Ramsoy, T. Z., Liptrot, M. G., Skimminge, A., Lund, T. E., Sidaros, K., Christensen, M. S., Baare, W., Paulson, O. B., & Jernigan, T. L. (2009). Regional activation of the human medial temporal lobe during intentional encoding of objects and positions. *NeuroImage, 47,* 1863–1872.

Rao, U., Hammen, C. L., & Poland, R. E. (2009). Risk markers for depression in adolescents: Sleep and HPA measures. *Neuropsychopharmacology, 34,* 1936–1945.

Rapanelli, M., Lew, S. E., Frick, L. R., & Zanutto, B. S. (2010). Plasticity in the rate prefrontal cortex: Linking gene expression and an operant learning with a computational theory. *PLoS One, 5,* e8656.

Rapaport, D. (1967). On the psychoanalytic theory of thinking. In M. M. Gill (Ed.), *The collected papers of David Rapaport.* New York: Basic.

Rapaport, S. (1994, November 28). Interview. *U.S. News and World Report,* 94.

Rapee, R. M., Gaston, J. E., & Abbott, M. J. (2009). Testing the efficacy of theoretically derived improvements in the treatment of social phobia. *Journal of Consulting and Clinical Psychology, 77,* 317–327.

Raposo, A., Han, S., & Dobbins, I. G. (2009). Ventrolateral prefrontal cortex and self-initiated semantic elaboration during memory retrieval. *Neuropsychologia, 47,* 2261–2271.

Rathunde, K., & Csikszentmihalyi, M. (2006). The developing person: An experiential perspective. In W. Damon & R. Lerner (Eds.), *Handbook of child psychology* (6th ed.). New York: Wiley.

Ratner, N. B. (1993). Learning to speak. *Science, 262,* 260.

Rauch, S. L., Shin, L. M., & Phelps, E. A. (2006). Neurocircuitry models of posttraumatic stress disorder and extinction: Human neuro-imaging research—past, present, and future. *Biological Psychiatry, 60,* 376–382.

Raudies, F., & Neumann, H. (2010). A neural model of the temporal dynamics of figure-ground segregation in motion perception. *Neural Networks, 23,* 160–176.

Ravassard, P., & others. (2009). Paradoxical (REM) sleep deprivation causes a large and rapidly reversible decrease in long-term potentiation, synaptic transmission, glutamate receptor protein levels, and ERK/MAPK activation in the dorsal hippocampus. *Sleep, 32,* 227–240.

Raven, P. H., Johnson, G. B., Mason, K. A., Losos, J. B., & Singer, S. S. (2011). *Biology* (9th ed.). New York: McGraw-Hill.

Rawson, N. E., & Yee, K. K. (2006). Transduction and coding. *Advances in Otorhinolaryngology, 63,* 23–43.

Ray, W. J. (2009). *Methods toward a science of behavior and experience* (9th ed.). Belmont, CA: Wadsworth.

Raynor, H. A., Jeffrey, R. W., Phelan, S., Hill, J. O., & Wing, R. R. (2005). Amount of food groups variety consumed in the diet and long term weight loss maintenance. *Obesity Research, 13,* 883–890.

Raz, A., Schwiezer, H. R., Zhu, H., & Bowles, E. N. (2010). Hypnotic dreams as a lens into hypnotic dynamics. *International Journal of Clinical and Experimental Hypnosis, 58,* 69–81.

Rector, N. A., & Beck, A. T. (2001). Cognitive behavioral therapy for schizophrenia: An empirical review. *Journal of Nervous and Mental Disorders, 189,* 278–287.

Recupero, P. R., & Rainey, S. E. (2006). Characteristics of E-therapy, web sites. *Journal of Clinical Psychiatry, 67,* 1435–1440.

Reder, L. M., Park, H., & Kieffaber, P. D. (2009). Memory systems do not divide on consciousness: Reinterpreting memory in terms of activation and binding. *Psychological Bulletin, 135,* 23–49.

Redondo, J. L., Fernandez, J., Garcia, I., & Ortigosa, P. M. (2009). Solving the multiple competitive facilities location and design problem on the plane. *Evolutionary Computation, 17,* 21–53.

Ree, M. J., & Carretta, T. R. (2007). Tests of cognitive ability. In D. L. Whetzel & G. R. Wheaton (Eds.), *Applied measurement.* Mahwah, NJ: Erlbaum.

Reece, B. L., Brandt, R., & Howie, K. T. (2011). *Effective human relations* (11th ed.). Boston: Cengage.

Reed, S. K. (2010). *Thinking visually.* New York: Psychology Press.

Reeve, C. (2000, May 1). Use the body's repair kit. *Time, 155,* 18.

Reeve, C. L., & Charles, J. E. (2008). Survey of opinions on the primacy of g and social consequences of ability testing: A comparison of expert and non-expert views. *Intelligence, 36,* 681–688.

Reeves, R. R., & Burke, R. S. (2010). Carisoprodol: Abuse potential and withdrawal syndrome. *Current Drug Abuse Reviews, 3,* 33–38.

Reger, M. A., & Gahm, G. A. (2009). A meta-analysis of the effects of internet- and computer-based cognitive-behavioral treatments for anxiety. *Journal of Clinical Psychology, 65,* 53–75.

Reich, J. (2009). Avoidant personality disorder and its relationship to social phobia. *Current Psychiatry Reports, 11,* 89–93.

Reichel, C. M., & Bevins, R. A. (2010). Competition between novelty and cocaine conditioned reward is sensitive to drug dose and retention interval. *Behavioral Neuroscience, 124,* 141–151.

Reimer, T., & Rieskamp, J. (2007). Fast and frugal heuristics. In R. F. Baumeister & K. D. Vohs (Eds.), *Encyclopedia of social psychology.* Thousand Oaks, CA: Sage.

Reinhardt, I., & others. (2010). Neural correlates of aversive conditioning: Development of a functional imaging paradigm for the investigation of anxiety disorders. *European Archives of Psychiatry and Clinical Neuroscience.* (in press)

Reis, H. T., Sheldon, K. M., Gable, S. L., Roscoe, J., & Ryan, R. M. (2000). Daily well-being: The role of autonomy, competence, and relatedness. *Personality and Social Psychology Bulletin, 26,* 419–435.

Reisner, S. L., Mimiaga, M. J., Skeer, M., & Mayer, K. H. (2009). Beyond anal sex: Sexual practices associated with HIV risk reduction among men who have sex with men in Boston, Massachusetts. *AIDS Patient Care and STDs, 23,* 545–550.

Reivich, K., & Gillham, J. (2003). Learned optimism: The measurement of explanatory style. In S. J. Lopez & C. R. Snyder (Eds.), *Positive psychological assessment: A handbook of models and measures* (pp. 57–74). Washington, DC: American Psychological Association.

Remington, G. (2007). Tardive dyskinesia: Eliminated, forgotten or overshadowed? *Current Opinion in Psychiatry, 20,* 131–137.

Rendell, P. G., & Craik, F. I. M. (2000). Virtual week and actual week: Age-related differences in prospective memory. *Applied Cognitive Psychology, 14,* S43–S62.

Rescorla, R. A. (1966). Predictability and number of pairings in Pavlovian fear conditioning. *Psychonomic Science, 4,* 383–384.

Rescorla, R. A. (1988). Pavlovian conditioning: It's not what you think it is. *American Psychologist, 43,* 151–160.

Rescorla, R. A. (2003). Contemporary study of Pavlovian conditioning. *Spanish Journal of Psychology, 6,* 185–195.

Rescorla, R. A. (2004). Spontaneous recovery varies inversely with the training-extinction interval. *Learning and Behavior, 32,* 401–408.

Rescorla, R. A. (2005). Spontaneous recovery of excitation but not inhibition. *Journal of Experimental Psychology: Animal Behavior Processes, 31,* 277–288.

Rescorla, R. A. (2006a). Stimulus generalization of excitation and inhibition. *Quarterly Journal of Experimental Psychology, 59,* 53–67.

Rescorla, R. A. (2006b). Spontaneous recovery from overexpectation. *Learning and Behavior, 34,* 13–20.

Rescorla, R. A. (2006c). Deepened extinction from compound stimulus presentation. *Journal of Experimental Psychology: Animal Behavior Processes, 32*(2), 135–144.

Rescorla, R. A. (2009). A theory of Pavlovian conditioning: Variations in the effectiveness of reinforcement and nonreinforcement. In D. Shanks (Ed.), *Psychology of learning.* Thousand Oaks, CA: Sage.

Rescorla, R. A., & Wagner, A. R. (2009). A theory of attention: Variations in the associability of stimuli with reinforcement. In D. Shanks (Ed.), *Psychology of learning.* Thousand Oaks, CA: Sage.

Rethorst, C. D., Wipfli, B. M., & Landers, D. M. (2009). The antidepressive effects of exercise: A meta-analysis of randomized trials. *Sports Medicine, 39,* 491–511.

Reuter-Lorenz, P., & Davidson, R. J. (1981). Differential contributions of the two cerebral hemispheres to the perception of happy and sad faces. *Neuropsychologia, 19,* 609–613.

Revelle, W. (2008). The contribution of reinforcement sensitivity theory to personality theory. In P. J. Corr (Ed.), *The reinforcement sensitivity theory of personality* (pp. 508–527). New York: Cambridge University Press.

Reverberi, C., Shallice, T., D'Agostini, S., Skrap, M., & Bonatti, L. L. (2009). Cortical bases of elementary deductive reasoning, inference, memory, and metadeduction. *Neuropsychologia, 47,* 1107–1116.

Revonsuo, A., Kallio, S., & Sikka, P. (2009). What is an altered state of consciousness? *Philosophical Psychology, 22,* 187–204.

Reynolds, C. R., Livingston, R., & Willson, V. (2006). *Measurement and assessment in education.* Boston: Allyn & Bacon.

Rhoades, G. K., Stanley, S. M., & Markham, H. J. (2009). The pre-engagement cohabitation effect: A replication and extension of previous findings. *Journal of Family Psychology, 23,* 107–111.

Rieger, G., Linsenmeier, J. A. W., & Bailey, J. M. (2009). Childhood gender nonconformity remains a robust and neutral correlate of sexual orientation: Reply to Hegary (2009). *Developmental Psychology, 45,* 901–903.

Rieger, G., Linsenmeier, J. A. W., Gygax, L., & Bailey, J. M. (2008). Sexual orientation and childhood gender nonconformity: Evidence from home videos. *Developmental Psychology, 44,* 46–58.

Riezzo, I., Cerretani, D., Fiore, C., Bello, S., Centini, F., D'Errico, S., Fiaschi, A. I., Giorgi, G., Neri, M., Pomara, C., Turillazzi, E., & Fineschi, V. (2010). Enzymatic-nonenzymatic cellular antioxidant defense systems response and immunohistochemical detection of MDMA, VMAT2, HSP70, and apoptosis as biomarkers for MDMA (ecstasy) neurotoxicity. *Journal of Neuroscience Research, 88,* 905–916.

Riketta, M. (2002). Attitudinal organizational commitment and job performance: A meta-analysis. *Journal of Organizational Behavior, 23,* 257–266.

Rilling, J. K., & Sanfey, A. (2011). The neuroscience of decision making. *Annual Review of Psychology* (vol. 62). Palo Alto, CA: Annual Reviews.

Risley, T. R., & Hart, B. (2006). Promoting early language development. In N. F. Watt, C. Ayoub, R. H. Bradley, J. E. Puma, & W. A. LeBoeuf (Eds.), *The crisis in youth mental health: Critical issues and effective programs, vol. 4: Early intervention programs and policies* (pp. 83–88). Westport, CT: Praeger.

Ritchey, M., Labar, K. S., & Cabeza, R. (2010). Level of processing modulates the neural correlates of emotional memory formation. *Journal of Cognitive Neuroscience.* (in press)

Ritskes, R., Ritskes-Hoitinga, M., Stodkilde-Jorgensen, H., Baerentsen, K., & Hartman, T. (2003). MRI scanning during Zen meditation: The picture of enlightenment? *Constructivism in the Human Sciences, 8* (1), 85–90.

Ritter, D., & Elsea, M. (2005). Hot sauce, toy guns, and graffiti: A critical account of current laboratory aggression paradigms. *Aggressive Behavior, 31,* 407–419.

Ro, H. S., & Wampler, R. S. (2009). What's wrong with these people? Clinicians' views of clinical couples. *Journal of Marital and Family Therapy, 35,* 3–17.

Robbins, T. L., & DeNisi, A. S. (1994). A closer look at interpersonal affect as a distinct influence on cognitive processing in performance evaluations. *Journal of Applied Psychology, 79,* 341–353.

Roberts, B. W., Caspi, A., & Moffitt, T. E. (2003). Work experiences and personality development in young adulthood. *Journal of Personality and Social Psychology, 84,* 582–593.

Roberts, B. W., Jackson, J. J., Fayard, J. V., Edmonds, G., & Meints, J. O. (2009). Conscientiousness. In M. Leary & R. Hoyle (Eds.), *Handbook of individual differences in social behavior* (pp. 369–381). New York: Guilford.

Roberts, B. W., Kuncel, N., Shiner, R. N., Caspi, A., & Goldberg, L. (2007). The power of personality: A comparative analysis of the predictive validity of personality traits, SES,

and IQ. *Perspectives on Psychological Science, 2,* 313–345.

Roberts, B. W., & Mroczek, D. (2008). Personality trait change in adulthood. *Current Directions in Psychological Science, 17,* 31–35.

Roberts, B. W., Walton, K. E., & Viechtbauer, W. (2006). Patterns of mean level change in personality traits across the life course: A meta-analysis of longitudinal studies. *Psychological Bulletin, 132,* 1–25.

Roberts, B. W., Wood, D., & Caspi, A. (2008). Personality development. In O. P. John, R. W., Robins, & L. A. Pervin (Eds.), *Handbook of personality: Theory and research* (3rd ed.). New York: Guilford.

Roberts, D. F., Henriksen, L., & Foehr, U. G. (2009). Adolescence, adolescents, and the media. In R. M. Lerner & L. Steinberg (Eds.), *Handbook of adolescent psychology* (3rd ed.). New York: Wiley.

Robinson, A., Shore, B. M., & Enersen, D. L. (2007). Best practices in gifted education: An evidence-based guide. Waco, TX: Prufrock Press.

Robinson, A. J. (2008). McGregor's Theory X-Theory Y model. In J. Gordon (Ed.), *The Pfeiffer book of successful leadership development tools: The most enduring, effective, and valuable training activities for developing leaders* (pp. 63–66). San Francisco: Pfeiffer/Wiley.

Rodgers, J. L. (2007). The shape of things to come: Diagnosing social contagion from adolescent smoking and drinking curves. In T. D. Little, J. A. Bovaird, & N. A. Card (Eds.), *Modeling contextual effects in longitudinal studies* (pp. 343–362). Mahwah, NJ: Erlbaum.

Rodgers, R. J., Holch, P., & Tallett, A. J. (2010). Behavioral satiety sequence (BSS): Separating wheat from chaff in the behavioral pharmacology of appetite. *Pharmacology, Biochemistry, and Behavior.* (in press)

Rodin, J. (1984, December). Interview: A sense of control. *Psychology Today,* 38–45.

Rodriquez, M. L., & Walden, N. J. (2010). Socializing relationships. In D. P. Swanson, M. C. Edwards, & M. B. Spencer (Eds.), *Adolescence: Development in a global era.* San Diego: Academic.

Roediger, H. L., & Marsh, E. J. (2003). Episodic and autobiographical memory. In I. B. Weiner (Ed.), *Handbook of psychology* (vol. 4). New York: Wiley.

Roese, N. J., & Summerville, A. (2005). What we regret most . . . and why. *Personality and Social Psychology Bulletin, 31,* 1273–1285.

Roethlisberger, F. J. (1941). *Management and morale.* Cambridge, MA: Harvard University Press.

Roethlisberger, F. J., & Dickson, W. J. (1939). *Management and the worker.* Cambridge, MA: Harvard University Press.

Rogers, C. R. (1961). *On becoming a person.* Boston: Houghton Mifflin.

Rogers, C. R. (1980). *A way of being.* Boston: Houghton Mifflin.

Rogers, G., & others. (2009). The harmful health effects of recreational Ecstasy: A systematic review of observational evidence. *Health Technology Assessment, 13,* 1–315.

Rojas, A., Khoo, A., Tejedo, J. R., Bedoya, F. J., Soria, B., & Martin, F. (2010). Islet cell development. *Advances in Experimental Medicine and Biology, 654,* 59–75.

Rojas, Y., & Stenberg, S. A. (2010). Early life circumstances and male suicide—a 30-year follow-up of a Stockholm cohort born in 1953. *Social Science Medicine, 70,* 420–427.

Rolland, Y., van Kan, G. A., & Vellas, B. (2010). Healthy brain aging: Role of exercise and physical activity. *Clinics in Geriatric Medicine, 26,* 75–87.

Romero-Canyas, R., Downey, G., Berenson, K., Ayduk, O., & Kang, N. J. (2010). Rejection sensitivity and the rejection-hostility link in romantic relationships. *Journal of Personality, 78,* 119–148.

Ronningstam, E. (2010). Narcissistic personality disorder: A current review. *Current Psychiatry Reports, 12,* 68–75.

Rosa-Alcazar, A. I., Sanchez-Meca, J., Gomez-Conesa, A., & Marin-Martinez, F. (2008). Psychological treatment of obsessive-compulsive disorder: A meta-analysis. *Clinical Psychology Review, 28,* 1310–1325.

Rosack, J. (2007). Impact of FDA warning questioned in suicide rise. *Psychiatric News, 5,* 1.

Rose, A. J. (2002). Co-rumination in the friendships of girls and boys. *Child Development, 73,* 1830–1843.

Rose, A. J., Carlson, W., & Waller, E. M. (2007). Prospective associations of co-rumination with friendship and emotional adjustment: Considering the socioemotional trade-offs of co-rumination. *Developmental Psychology, 43,* 1019–1031.

Rose, A. J., & Smith, R. L. (2009). Sex differences in peer relationships. In K. H. Rubin, W. M. Bukowski, & B. Laursen (Eds.), *Handbook of peer interactions, relationships, and groups.* New York: Guilford.

Rose, M., Haider, H., & Buchel, C. (2010). The emergence of explicit memory during learning. *Cerebral Cortex.* (in press)

Rosell, D. R., & others. (2010). Increased serotonin 2A receptor availability in the orbitofrontal cortex of physically aggressive personality disordered patients. *Biological Psychiatry.* (in press)

Roseman, I. J., & Smith, C. A. (2009). Appraisal theory: Overview, assumptions, varieties, controversies. In K. R. Scherer, A. Schorr, T. Johnstone (Eds.), *Appraisal processes in emotion: Theory, methods, research* (pp. 3–19). Oxford, U.K.: Oxford University Press.

Rosen, K., & Garety, P. (2005). Predicting recovery from schizophrenia: A retrospective comparison of characteristics at onset of people with single and multiple episodes. *Schizophrenia Bulletin, 31,* 735–750.

Rosenberg, M. S., Westling, D. L., & McLeskey, J. (2011). *Special education for today's teachers* (2nd ed.). Upper Saddle River, NJ: Merrill.

Rosenhan, D. L. (1973). On being sane in insane places. *Science, 179,* 250–258.

Rosenthal, R. (1966). *Experimenter effects in behavioral research.* New York: Appleton-Century-Crofts.

Rosenthal, R., & DiMatteo, M. R. (2001). Meta-analysis: Recent developments in quantitative methods for literature reviews. *Annual Review of Psychology* (vol. 52). Palo Alto, CA: Annual Reviews.

Rosenthal, R., & Jacobsen, L. (1968). *Pygmalion in the classroom.* Fort Worth, TX: Harcourt Brace.

Rosenzweig, S., Greenson, J. M., Reibel, D. K., Green, J. S., Jasser, S. A., & Beasley, D. (2010). Mindfulness-based stress reduction for chronic pain conditions: Variations in treatment outcomes and role of home meditation practice. *Journal of Psychosomatic Research, 68,* 29–36.

Rosier, J. P., Stephan, K. E., den Ouden, H. E. M., Friston, K. J., & Joyce, E. M. (2010). Adaptive and aberrant reward prediction signals in the human brain. *Neuro-Image, 50,* 657–664.

Rosmarin, D. H., Krumrei, E. J., & Andersson, G. (2009). Religion as a predictor of psychological distress in two religious communities. *Cognitive Behavior Therapy, 38,* 54–64.

Rosnow, R. L., & Rosenthal, R. (2008). *Beginning behavioral research* (6th ed.). Upper Saddle River, NJ: Prentice-Hall.

Ross, K., Handel, P. J., Clark, E. M., & Vander Wal, J. S. (2009a). The relationship between religion and religious coping: Religious coping as a moderator between coping and adjustment. *Journal of Religion and Health.*

Ross, K. M., Milsom, V. A., Debraganza, N., Gibbons, L. M., Murawski, M. E., & Perri, M. G. (2009b). The contributions of weight loss and increased physical fitness to improvements in health-related quality of life. *Eating Behaviors, 10,* 84–88.

Ross, L., Kohler, C. L., Grimley, D. M., & Anderson-Lewis, C. (2007). The theory of reasoned action and intention to seek cancer information. *American Journal of Health Behavior, 31,* 123–134.

Ross, R. S., Brown, T. I., & Stern, C. E. (2009). The retrieval of learned sequences engages the hippocampus: Evidence from fMRI. *Hippocampus, 19,* 790–799.

Rossi, E. L. (2009). The psychosocial genomics of therapeutic hypnosis, psychotherapy, and rehabilitation. *American Journal of Clinical Hypnosis, 51,* 281–298.

Rotella, R. J. (2010). *Case studies in sport psychology.* Sudbury, MA: Jones & Bartlett.

Roten, R. G. (2007). DSM-IV and the taxonomy of roles: How can the taxonomy of roles complement the DSM-IV to create a more holistic diagnostic tool? *The Arts in Psychotherapy, 34,* 53–68.

Rotge, J. Y., & others. (2009). Inverse relationship between thalamic and orbitofrontal volumes in obsessive-compulsive disorder. *Progress in Neuro-Psychopharmacology & Biological Psychiatry, 33,* 682–686.

Rothbart, M. K., & Gartstein, M. A. (2008). Temperament. In M. M. Haith & J. B. Benson (Eds.), *Encyclopedia of infant and early childhood development.* London: Elsevier.

Rouder, J. N., & Morey, R. D. (2009). The nature of psychological thresholds. *Psychological Review, 116,* 655–660.

Roughgarden, J., Oishi, M., & Akcay, E. (2006). Reproductive social behavior: Cooperative games to replace sexual selection. *Science, 311,* 965–968.

Rowland, D. L., & McMahon, C. G. (2008). Premature ejaculation. In D. L. Rowland & L. Incrocci (Eds.), *Handbook of sexual and gender identity disorders* (pp. 68–97). Hoboken, NJ: Wiley.

Roy, M., & others. (2010). Medial frontal cortex activity during memory encoding of pictures and its relation to symptomatic improvement after citalopram treatment in patients with major depression. *Journal of Psychiatry and Neuroscience, 35,* 152–162.

Roy-Byrne, P., & others. (2010). Delivery of evidence-based treatment for multiple anxiety disorders in primary care: A randomized controlled trial. *Journal of the American Medical Association, 303,* 1921–1928.

Rubin, K. H., Cheah, C., & Menzer, M. M. (2010). Peers. In M. H. Bornstein (Ed.), *Handbook of cultural developmental science.* New York: Psychology Press.

Rubin, Z., & Mitchell, C. (1976). Couples research as couples counseling: Some unintended effects of studying close relationships. *American Psychologist, 31,* 17–25.

Ruck, C. (2003). Psychosurgery. *Journal of Neurosurgery, 99,* 1113–1114.

Rudy, D., & Grusec, J. E. (2006). Authoritarian parenting in individualist and collectivist groups: Associations with maternal emotion and cognition and children's self-esteem. *Journal of Family Psychology, 20,* 68–78.

Ruini, C., Belaise, C., Brombin, C., Caffo, E., & Fava, G. A. (2006). Well-being therapy in school settings: A pilot study. *Psychotherapy and Psychosomatics, 75,* 331–336.

Ruini, C., & Fava, G. A. (2004). Clinical applications of well-being therapy. In A. Linley & S. Joseph (Eds.), *Positive psychology in practice* (pp. 371–387). Hoboken, NJ: Wiley.

Ruini, C., & Fava, G. A. (2009). Well-being therapy for generalized anxiety disorder. *Journal of Clinical Psychology, 65,* 510–519.

Ruiz, A., Campanac, E., Scott, R. S., Rusakov, D. A., & Kullman, D. M. (2010). Presynaptic GABA (A) receptors enhance transmission and LTP induction at hippocampal mossy fiber synapses. *Nature Neuroscience, 13,* 431–438.

Rule, N. O., Ambady, N., Adams, R. B., Ozono, H., Nakashima, S., Yoshikawa, S., & Watabe, M. (2010). Polling the face: Prediction and consensus across cultures. *Journal of Personality and Social Psychology, 98,* 1–15.

Rummel, J. (2010). Psychological distance to a prospective memory cue influences the probability of fulfilling a delayed intention. *Memory.* (in press)

Runyon, W. M. (2007). *Psychology and historical interpretation.* New York: Oxford University Press.

Rusbult, C. E., & Agnew, C. R. (2010). Prosocial motivation and behavior in close relationships. In M. Mikulincer & P. R. Shaver (Eds.), *Prosocial motives, emotions, and behavior: The better angels of our nature* (pp. 327–345).

Washington, DC: American Psychological Association.

Rusbult, C. E., Finkel, E. J., & Kumashiro, M. (2009). The Michelangelo phenomenon. *Current Directions in Psychological Science, 18,* 305–309.

Rusbult, C. E., Kumashiro, M., Coolsen, M. K., & Kirchner, J. L. (2004). Interdependence, closeness, and relationships. In D. J. Mashek & A. P. Aaron (Eds.), *Handbook of closeness and intimacy* (pp. 137–161). Mahwah, NJ: Erlbaum.

Rush, C. C., Becker, S. J., & Curry, J. F. (2009). Personality factors and styles among college students who binge eat and drink. *Psychology of Addictive Behaviors, 23,* 140–145.

Russell, K. L, & Bray, S. R. (2010). Promoting self-determined motivation for exercise in cardiac rehabilitation: The role of autonomy support. *Rehabilitation Psychology, 55,* 74–80.

Russo, S. J., & others. (2010). The addicted synapse: Mechanisms of synaptic and structural plasticity in nucleus accumbens. *Trends in Neuroscience.* (in press)

Rustin, J. (2009). The interface of self psychology, infant research, and neuroscience in clinical practice. *Annals of the New York Academy of Sciences, 1159,* 204–217.

Rutishauser, U., Ross, I. B., Mamelak, A. N., & Schuman, E. M. (2010). Human memory strength is predicted by theta-frequency phase-locking of single neurons. *Nature.* (in press)

Rutter, M. (2007). Gene-environment interplay and developmental psychopathology. In A. S. Masten (Ed.), *Multilevel dynamics in developmental psychology.* Mahwah, NJ: Erlbaum.

Ryan, M. P. (2008). The antidepressant effects of physical activity: Mediating self-esteem and self-efficacy mechanisms. *Psychology and Health, 23,* 279–307.

Ryan, R. M., & Deci, E. L. (2000). Self-determination theory and the facilitation of intrinsic motivation, social development, and well-being. *American Psychologist, 55,* 68–78.

Ryan, R. M., & Deci, E. L. (2009). Promoting self-determined school engagement, motivation, learning, and well-being. In K. R. Wentzel & A. Wigfield (Eds.), *Handbook of research on schools, schooling, and human development.* New York: Routledge.

Rycroft, C. (2010). Why analysts need their patients' transferences. *American Journal of Psychoanalysis, 70,* 112–118.

Rydell, R. J., & Boucher, K. L. (2010). Capitalizing on multiple social identities to prevent stereotype threat: The moderating role of self-esteem. *Personality and Social Psychology Bulletin, 36,* 239–250.

Ryff, C. D., & Singer, B. (1998). Contours of positive human health. *Psychological Inquiry, 9,* 1–28.

Ryff, C. D., & Singer, B. H. (2009). Understanding healthy aging: Key components and their integration. In V. L. Bengtson, D. Gans, N. Pulney, & M. Silverstein, (Eds.), *Handbook of theories of aging* (2nd ed., pp. 117–144). New York: Springer.

Ryff, C. D., Singer, B. H., & Love, G. D. (2004). Positive health: Connecting well-being with biology. *Philosophical Transactions of the Royal Society of London, 359,* 1383–1394.

Rymer, R. (1993). *Genie.* New York: HarperCollins.

S

Saad, L. (2008, December 26). Obama, Hillary Clinton share "Most Admired" billing. Gallup Press Release. http://www.gallup.com/poll/113572/Obama-Hillary-Clinton-Share-Most-Admired-Billing.aspx (accessed January 19, 2009)

Saarni, C., Campos, J. J., Camras, L. A., & Witherington, D. (2006). Emotional development: Action, communication, and understanding. In W. Damon & R. Lerner (Eds.), *Handbook of child psychology* (6th ed.). New York: Wiley.

Sacco, D. F., & Hugenberg, K. (2009). The look of anger and fear: Facial maturity modulates recognition of fearful and angry expressions. *Emotion, 9,* 39–49.

Sachdev, P. S., & Chen, X. (2009). Neurosurgical treatment of mood disorders: Traditional psychosurgery and the advent of deep brain stimulation. *Current Opinion in Psychiatry, 22,* 25–31.

Sachs, J. (2009). Communication development in infancy. In J. Berko Gleason & N. Ratner (Eds.), *The development of language* (7th ed.). Boston: Allyn & Bacon.

Sack, R. L. (2009). The pathology of jet lag. *Travel Medicine and Infectious Disease, 7,* 102–110.

Sack, R. L. (2010). Clinical practice. Jet lag. *New England Journal of Medicine, 362,* 440–447.

Sacks, O. (2006, June 19). Stereo Sue. *New Yorker,* 64–73.

Sadeghniiat-Haghighi, K., Aminian, O., Pouryaghoub, G., & Yazdi, Z. (2008). Efficacy and hypnotic effects of melatonin in shift-work nurses: Double-blind, placebo-controlled crossover trial. *Journal of Circadian Rhythms, 6,* 10.

Sado, M., Knapp, M., Yamauchi, K., Fujisawa, D., So, M., Nakagawa, A., Kikuchi, T., & Ono, Y. (2009). Cost-effectiveness of combination therapy versus antidepressant therapy for management of depression in Japan. *Australian and New Zealand Journal of Psychiatry, 43,* 539–547.

Safren, S. A., & others. (2009). A randomized controlled trial of cognitive behavioral therapy for adherence and depression (CBT-AD) in HIV-infected individuals. *Health Psychology, 28,* 1–10.

Sahin, E., & DePinho, R. A. (2010). Linking functional decline of telomeres, mitochondria, and stem cells during aging. *Nature, 464,* 520–528.

Saito, H., & others. (2010). Hearing handicap predicts the development of depressive symptoms after 3 years in older community-dwelling Japanese. *Journal of the American Geriatrics Society, 58,* 93–97.

Salas, E., DeRouin, R. E. & Gade, P. A. (2007). The military's contribution to our science and practice: People, places, and findings. In L. L. Koppes (Ed.), *Historical perspectives in industrial and organizational psychology.* Mahwah, NJ: Erlbaum.

Salkind, J. J. (Ed.). (2009). *Encyclopedia of educational psychology.* Thousand Oaks, CA: Sage.

Salminen, N. H., Tiitinen, H., Yrttiaho, S., & May, P. J. (2010). The neural code for interaural time difference in human auditory cortex. *Journal of Acoustical Society of America, 127,* EL60.

Salthouse, T. A. (1994). The nature of the influence of speed on adult age differences in cognition. *Developmental Psychology, 30,* 240–259.

Salthouse, T. A. (2009). When does age-related cognitive decline begin? *Neurobiology of Aging, 30,* 507–514.

Salvia, J., Ysseldyke, J. E., & Bolt, S. (2010). *Assessment* (11th ed.). Boston: Cengage.

Salzman, C. D., & Fusi, S. (2010). Emotion, cognition, and mental state representation in amygdala and cerebral cortex. *Annual Review of Neuroscience* (vol. 33). Palo Alto, CA: Annual Reviews.

Sameroff, A. (2006). Identifying risk and protective factors for healthy child development. In A. Clarke-Stewart & J. Dunn (Eds.), *Families count.* New York: Oxford University Press.

Sampaio, A. S., & others. (2010). Association between polymorphisms in GRIK2 gene and obsessive-compulsive disorder: A family-based study. *CNS Neuroscience and Therapeutics.* (in press)

Sampaio, C., & Brewer, W. F. (2009). The role of unconscious memory errors in judgments of confidence for sentence recognition. *Memory and Cognition, 37,* 158–163.

Sanchez-Burks, J. (2007). Cultural differences. In R. Baumeister & K. Vohs (Eds.), *Encyclopedia of social psychology.* Thousand Oaks, CA: Sage.

Sand, S. (2010, February 7). Small town mayor issues big weight loss challenge. *Digital Journal.* http://www.digitaljournal.com/article/287210

Sandler, I., Wolchik, S., & Schoenfelder, E. (2011). Evidence-based family-focused prevention programs for children. *Annual Review of Psychology* (vol. 62). Palo Alto, CA: Annual Reviews.

Santtila, P., Sandnabba, N. K., Harlaar, N., Varjonen, M., Alanko, K., & von der Pahlen, B. (2008). Potential for homosexual response is prevalent and genetic. *Biological Psychology, 77,* 102–105.

Sapolsky, R. M. (2004). *Why zebras don't get ulcers* (3rd ed.). New York: Henry Holt.

Sapp, S. (2010). What have religion and spirituality to do with religion? Three approaches. *Gerontologist.* (in press)

Sar, V., Akyuz, G., & Dogan, O. (2007). Prevalence of dissociative disorders among women in the general population. *Psychiatry Research, 149,* 169–176.

Sar, V., Koyuncu, A., Ozturk, E., Yargic, L. I., Kundakci, T., Yazici, A., Kuskonmaz, E., & Aksut, D. (2007). Dissociative disorders in the psychiatric emergency ward. *General Hospital Psychiatry, 29,* 45–50.

Sarkar, U., Ali, S., & Whooley, M. A. (2009). Self-efficacy as a marker of cardiac function and predictor of heart failure hospitalization and mortality in patients with stable coronary heart disease: Findings from the Heart and Soul Study. *Health Psychology, 28,* 166–173.

Sarkar, U., Fisher, L., & Schillinger, D. (2006). Is self-efficacy associated with diabetes self-management across race/ethnicity and health literacy? *Diabetes Care, 29,* 323–329.

Sarma, K., & Kola, S. (2010). Firearms, hanging, and drowning suicides in the Republic of Ireland. *Crisis, 31,* 69–75.

Saroglou, V. (2010). Religiousness as a cultural adaptation of basic traits: A five-factor model perspective. *Personality and Social Psychology Review, 14,* 108–125.

Sartor, C. E., Agrawal, A., Lynskey, M. T., Bucholz, K. K., Madden, P. A., & Heath, A. C. (2009). Common genetic influences on the timing of first use for alcohol, cigarettes, and cannabis in young African-American women. *Drug and Alcohol Dependence, 102,* 49–55.

Sato, W., Kochiyama, T., Unono, S., & Yoshikawa, S. (2010). Amygdala integrates emotional expression and gaze direction in response to dynamic facial expressions. *NeuroImage, 50,* 1658–1665.

Saul, S. (2006, March 8). Some sleeping pill users range far beyond bed. *New York Times.*

Saunders, F. W. (1991). *Katherine and Isabel: Mother's light, daughter's journey.* Palo Alto, CA: Consulting Psychologists Press.

Saurer, T. B., Ijames, S. G., Carrigan, K. A., & Lysle, D. T. (2008). Neuroimmune mechanisms of opioid-mediated conditioned immunomodulation. *Brain, Behavior, and Immunity, 22,* 89–97.

Sauter, D. A., Eisner, F., Ekman, P., & Scott, S. K. (2010). Cross-cultural recognition of basic emotions through nonverbal emotional vocalizations. *Proceedings of the National Academy of Sciences USA, 107,* 2408–2412.

Sava, F. A., Yates, B. T., Lupu, V., Szentagotal, A., & David, D. (2009). Cost-effectiveness and cost-utility of cognitive therapy, rational emotive behavioral therapy, and fluoxetine (Prozac) in treating depression: A randomized clinical trial. *Journal of Clinical Psychology, 65,* 36–52.

Savage, J. (2008). The role of exposure to media violence in the etiology of violent behavior: A criminologist weighs in. *American Behavioral Scientist, 51,* 1123–1136.

Savage, J., & Yancey, C. (2008). The effects of media violence exposure on criminal aggression: A meta-analysis. *Criminal Justice and Behavior, 35,* 772–791.

Savic, I., & Lindström, P. (2008). PET and MRI show differences in cerebral asymmetry and functional connectivity between homo- and heterosexual subjects. *Proceedings of the National Academy of Sciences, 105,* 9403–9408.

Savin-Williams, R. (2006). *The new gay teenager.* Cambridge, MA: Harvard University Press.

Savin-Williams, R. C., & Ream, G. L. (2007). Prevalence and stability of sexual orientation components during adolescence and young adulthood. *Archives of Sexual Behavior, 36,* 385–394.

Savitz, J. B., & Ramesar R. S. (2004). Genetic variants implicated in personality: A review of the more promising candidates. *American Journal of Medical Genetics Part B, Neuropsychiatric Genetics, 131B,* 20–32.

Saxe, L. (1998, June). Commentary. *APA Monitor,* 30.

Sayal, K., Heron, J., Golding, J., & Emond, A. (2007). Prenatal alcohol exposure and gender differences in childhood mental health problems: A longitudinal population-based study. *Pediatrics, 119,* e426–e434.

Scarr, S. (1984, May). Interview. *Psychology Today,* 59–63.

Scarr, S. (1992). Keep our eyes on the prize: Family and child care policy in the United States, as it should be. In A. Booth (Ed.), *Child care in the 1990s: Trends and consequences* (pp. 215–222). Hillsdale, NJ: Erlbaum.

Scarr, S. (2000). Toward voluntary parenthood. *Journal of Personality, 68,* 615–623.

Schacter, D. L., & Wagner, A. D. (2011). Learning and memory. In E. R. Kandel, J. R. Schwartz, & T. M. Jessell (Eds.), *Principles of neural science* (5th ed.). New York: McGraw-Hill.

Schachter, S., & Singer, J. E. (1962). Cognitive, social, and physiological determinants of emotional state. *Psychological Review, 69,* 379–399.

Schaie, K. W. (1994). The life course of adult intellectual abilities. *American Psychologist, 49,* 304–313.

Schaie, K. W. (2006). Intelligence. In R. Schultz (Ed.), *Encyclopedia of aging* (4th ed.). New York: Springer.

Schaie, K. W. (2007). Generational differences: The age-cohort period model. In J. E. Birren & K. W. Schaie (Eds.), *Encyclopedia of gerontology.* Oxford, U.K.: Elsevier.

Schaie, K. W. (2009). "When does age-related cognitive decline begin?" Salthouse again reifies the "cross-sectional fallacy." *Neurobiology of Aging, 30,* 528–529.

Schaie, K. W. (2010). Adult intellectual abilities. *Corsini encyclopedia of psychology.* New York: Wiley.

Schaie, K. W. (2011). *Developmental influences on adult intellectual development.* New York: Oxford University Press. (in press)

Schank, R., & Abelson, R. (1977). *Scripts, plans, goals, and understanding.* Mahwah, NJ: Erlbaum.

Scheer, F. A., Hilton, M. F., Mantzoros, C. S., & Shea, S. A. (2009). Adverse metabolic and cardiovascular consequences of circadian misalignment. *Proceedings of the National Academy of Sciences USA, 106,* 4453–4458.

Scheibe, S., & Carstensen, L. L. (2010). Emotional aging: Recent findings and future trends. *Journals of Gerontology B: Psychological Sciences and Social Sciences, 65B,* 135–144.

Scheid, T. L., & Brown, T. N. (Eds.). (2010). *A handbook for the study of mental health: Social contexts, theories, and systems* (2nd ed.). New York: Cambridge University Press.

Schieffelin, B., & Ochs, E. (Eds.). (1986). *Language socialization across cultures.* Cambridge, U.K.: Cambridge University Press.

Schienle, A., Schaefer, A., Stark, R., & Vaiti, D. (2009). Long-term effects of cognitive behavior therapy on brain activation in spider phobia. *Psychiatry Research, 172,* 99–102.

Schiff, W. J. (2011). *Nutrition for healthy living* (2nd ed.). New York: McGraw-Hill.

Schiffman, J., & Walker, E. (1998). Schizophrenia. In H. S. Friedman (Ed.), *Encyclopedia of mental health* (vol. 2). San Diego: Academic.

Schira, M. M., Tyler, C. W., Spehar, B., & Breakspear, M. (2010). Modeling magnification and anisotropy in the primate foveal confluence. *PLoS Computational Biology, 6,* e1000651.

Schkade, D. A., & Kahneman, D. (1998). Does living in California make people happy? A focusing illusion in judgments of life satisfaction. *Psychological Science, 9,* 340–346.

Schlosser, R. G., Nenadic, I., Wagner, G., Zysset, S., Koch, K., & Sauer, H. (2009). Dopaminergic modulation of brain systems subserving decision making under uncertainty: A study with fMRI and methylphenidate challenge. *Synapse, 63,* 429–442.

Schmader, T., Forbes, C. E., Zhang, S., & Berry Mendes, W. (2009). A metacognitive perspective on the cognitive deficits experiences in intellectually threatening environments. *Personality and Social Psychology Bulletin, 35,* 584–596.

Schmeichel, B. J., Harmon-Jones, C., & Harmon-Jones, E. (2010). Exercising self-control increases approach motivation. *Journal of Personality and Social Psychology.* (in press)

Schmidt, N. B., & Keough, M. E. (2010). Treatment of panic. *Annual Review of Clinical Psychology* (vol. 6). Palo Alto, CA: Annual Reviews.

Schmidt, N. B., & Koselka, M. (2000). Gender differences in patients with panic disorder: Evaluating cognitive mediation of phobic avoidance. *Cognitive Therapy and Research, 24,* 533–550.

Schmidtke, J. I., & Heller, W. (2004). Personality, affect, and EEG: Predicting patterns of regional brain activity related to extraversion and neuroticism. *Personality and Individual Differences, 36,* 717–732.

Schmiedek, F., Li, S. C., & Lindenberger, U. (2009). Interference and facilitation in spatial working memory: Age-associated differences in lure effects in the n-back paradigm. *Psychology and Aging, 24,* 203–210.

Schmitt, K. C., & Reith, M. E. (2010). Regulation of the dopamine transporter: Aspects relevant to psychostimulant drugs of abuse. *Annals of the New York Academy of Sciences, 1187,* 316–340.

Schnall, E., & others. (2010). The relationship between religion and cardiovascular outcomes and all-cause mortality in the women's health initiative observational study. *Psychology and Health, 25,* 249–263.

Schnall, S., Roper, J., & Fessler, D. M. (2010). Elevation leads to altruistic behavior. *Psychological Science, 21,* 315–320.

Schneider, D. W., & Logan, G. D. (2009). Selecting a response in task switching: Testing a model of compound cue retrieval. *Journal of Experimental Psychology: Learning, Memory, and Cognition, 35,* 122–136.

Schneider, K. J. (2002). Humanistic psychotherapy. In M. Hersen & W. H. Sledge (Eds.), *Encyclopedia of psychotherapy.* San Diego: Academic.

Schneider, K. J. (2009). Editor's commentary. *Journal of Humanistic Psychology, 49,* 6–8.

Schomerus, G., Matschinger, H., & Angermeyer, M. C. (2009). Attitudes that determine willingness to seek psychiatric help for depression: A representative population survey applying the theory of planned behavior. *Psychological Medicine, 39,* 1855–1865.

Schooler, J. W. (2002). Re-representing consciousness: Dissociations between experience and meta-consciousness. *Trends in Cognitive Sciences, 6,* 339–344.

Schooler, J. W., Ambadar, Z., & Bendiksen, M. (1997). A cognitive corroborative case study approach for investigating discovered memories of sexual abuse. In J. D. Read & D. S. Lindsay (Eds.), *Recollections of trauma: Scientific evidence and clinical practice* (pp. 379–387). New York: Plenum Press.

Schooler, J. W., Ariely, D., & Loewenstein, G. (2003). The explicit pursuit and assessment of happiness can be self-defeating. In I. Brocas & J. Carrillo (Eds.), *The psychology of economic decisions.* Oxford, U.K.: Oxford University Press.

Schooler, J. W., & Eich, E. (2000). Memory for emotional events. In E. Tulving & F. I. M. Craik (Eds.), *The Oxford handbook of memory* (pp. 379–392). New York: Oxford University Press.

Schredl, M. (2009). Dreams in patients with sleep disorders. *Sleep Medicine Reviews, 13,* 215–221.

Schredl, M. (2010). Nightmare frequency and nightmare topics in a representative German sample. *European Archives of Psychiatry and Clinical Neuroscience.* (in press)

Schredl, M., & Erlacher, D. (2008). Relation between waking sport activities, reading, and dream content in sport students and psychology students. *Journal of Psychology, 142,* 267–275.

Schuckit, M. A. (2009). Alcohol-use disorders. *Lancet, 373,* 492–501.

Schulenberg, J. E., & Zarrett, N. R. (2006). Mental health in emerging adulthood: Continuities and discontinuities in course, content, and meaning. In J. J. Arnett & J. Tanner (Eds.), *Advances in emerging adulthood.* Washington, DC: American Psychological Association.

Schultheiss, O. C., & Brunstein, J. C. (2005). An implicit motive perspective on competence.

In A. J. Elliot & C. S. Dweck (Eds.), *Handbook of competence and motivation* (pp. 31–51). New York: Guilford.

Schultz, W. (2006). Behavioral theories and the neurophysiology of reward. *Annual Review of Psychology* (vol. 57). Palo Alto, CA: Annual Reviews.

Schultz, W., Dayan, P., & Montague, P. R. (1997). A neural substrate of prediction and reward. *Science, 275,* 1593–1599.

Schultz, W., Dayan, P., & Montague, P. R. (2009). Context, time, and memory retrieval in the interference paradigms of Pavlovian conditioning. In D. Shanks (Ed.), *Psychology of learning.* Thousand Oaks, CA: Sage.

Schultz, W. T. (Ed.). (2005). *The handbook of psychobiography.* New York: Oxford University Press.

Schulz, R. (2007). Cardiovascular health study. In K. S. Markides (Ed.), *Encyclopedia of health and aging.* Thousand Oaks, CA: Sage.

Schulz-Stubner, S., Krings, T., Meister, I. G., Rex, S., Thron, A., & Rossaint, R. (2004). Clinical hypnosis modulates functional magnetic resonance imaging signal intensities and pain perception in a thermal stimulation paradigm. *Regional Anesthesia and Pain Medicine, 29,* 549–556.

Schumann, A., John, U., Rumpf, H., Hapke, U., & Meyer, C. (2006). Changes in the "stages of change" as outcome measures of a smoking cessation intervention: A randomized controlled trial. *Preventive Medicine: An International Journal Devoted to Practice and Theory, 43,* 101–106.

Schunk, D. H. (2011). *Learning theories* (6th ed.). Boston: Allyn & Bacon. (in press)

Schunk, D. H., Pintrich, P. R., & Meece, J. L. (2008). *Motivation in education* (3rd ed.). Upper Saddle River, NJ: Prentice-Hall.

Schupak, C., & Rosenthal, J. (2009). Excessive daydreaming: A case history and discussion of mind wandering and high fantasy proneness. *Consciousness and Cognition, 18,* 290–292.

Schur, E. A., Heckbert, S. R., & Goldberg, J. H. (2010). The association of restrained eating with weight change over time in a community-based sample of twins. *Obesity.* (in press)

Schütz-Bosbach, S., Tausche, P., & Weiss, C. (2009). Roughness perception during the rubber band illusion. *Brain and Cognition, 70* (1), 136–144.

Schutzwohl, A., Fuchs, A., McKibbin, W. F., & Shackelford, T. K. (2009). How willing are you to accept sexual requests from slightly unattractive to exceptionally attractive imagined requestors? *Human Nature, 20,* 282–293.

Schuz, B., Sniehotta, F. F., Mallach, N., Wiedemann, A. U., & Schwarzer, R. (2009). Predicting transitions from preintentional, intentional, and actional stages of change. *Health Education Research, 24,* 64–75.

Schwabe, L., Bohringer, A., & Wolf, O. T. (2009). Stress disrupts context-dependent memory. *Learning and Memory, 16,* 110–113.

Schwartz, B., Ward, A. H., Monterosso, J., Lyubomirsky, S., White, K., & Lehman, D. (2002). Maximizing versus satisficing: Happiness is a matter of choice. *Journal of Personality and Social Psychology, 83,* 1178–1197.

Schwartz, S. (2010). Life goes on in dreams. *Sleep, 33,* 15–16.

Schwartz, S., & Corcoran, C. (2010). Biological theories of psychiatric disorders: A sociological approach. In T. L. Scheid & T. N. Brown (Eds.), *A handbook for the study of mental health: Social contexts, theories, and systems* (2nd ed., pp. 64–88). New York: Cambridge University Press.

Schweinsburg, A. D., McQueeny, T., Nagle, B. J., Eyler, L. T., & Tapert, S. F. (2010). A preliminary study of functional magnetic resonance imaging response during verbal encoding among adolescent binge drinkers. *Alcohol, 44,* 111–117.

Scott, S. K., Rabito, F. A., Price, P. D., Butler, N. N., Schwartzbaum, J. A., Jackson, B. M., Love, R. L., & Harris, R. E. (2006). Comorbidity among the morbidly obese: A comparative study of 2002 U.S. hospital patient surcharges. *Surgery for Obesity and Related Disorders, 2,* 105–111.

Scott-Phillips, T. C. (2010). Animal communication: Insights from linguistic pragmatics. *Animal Behaviour, 79,* e1–e4.

Scott-Sheldon, L. A. J., & Johnson, B. T. (2006). Eroticizing creates safer sex: A research synthesis. *Journal of Primary Prevention, 27,* 619–640.

Seacat, J. D., & Mickelson, K. D. (2009). Stereotype threat and the exercise/dietary health intentions of overweight women. *Journal of Health Psychology, 14,* 556–567.

Sears, D. O. (2008). The American color line 50 years after *Brown v. Board:* Many "peoples of color" or Black exceptionalism? In G. Adams, M. Biernat, N. R. Branscombe, C. S. Crandall, & L. S. Wrightsman (Eds.), *Commemorating Brown: The social psychology of racism and discrimination.* Washington, DC: American Psychological Association.

Sears, D. O., & Henry, P. J. (2007). Symbolic racism. In R. Baumeister & K. Vohs (Eds.), *Encyclopedia of social psychology.* Newbury Park, CA: Sage.

Sedikides, C. (2007). Self-enhancement and self-protection: Powerful, pancultural, and functional. *Hellenic Journal of Psychology, 4,* 1–13.

Sedikides, C. (2009). On self-protection and self-enhancement regulation: The role of self-improvement and social norms. In J. P. Forgas, R. F. Baumeister, & D. Tice (Eds.), *The psychology of self-regulation.* New York: Psychology Press.

Sedikides, C., Gaertner, L., & Vevea, J. L. (2005). Pancultural self-enhancement reloaded: A meta-analytic reply to Heine (2005). *Journal of Personality and Social Psychology, 89,* 539–551.

Sedikides, C., & Gregg, A. P. (2008). Self-enhancement: Food for thought. *Perspectives on Psychological Science, 3,* 102–116.

Sedikides, C., & Skowronski, J. J. (2009). Social cognition and self-cognition: Two sides of the same evolutionary coin? *European Journal of Social Psychology, 39,* 1245–1249.

Segal, D. L., & Coolidge, F. L. (2004). Objective assessment of personality and psychopathology. In M. Hersen (Ed.), *Comprehensive handbook of psychological assessment* (vol. 2). New York: Wiley.

Segal, S. K., & Cahill, L. (2009). Endogenous noradrenergic activation and memory for emotional material in men and women. *Psychoneuroendocrinology, 34,* 1263–1271.

Segall, L. A., & Amir, S. (2010). Glucocorticoid regulation of clock gene expression in the mammalian limbic forebrain. *Journal of Molecular Neuroscience.* (in press)

Segerstrom, S. C. (2003). Individual differences, immunity, and cancer: Lessons from personality psychology. *Brain, Behavior and Immunity, 17, Suppl. 1,* S92–S97.

Segerstrom, S. C. (2005). Optimism and immunity: Do positive thoughts always lead to positive effects? *Brain, Behavior and Immunity, 19,* 195–200.

Segerstrom, S. C. (2006). *Breaking Murphy's law: How optimists get what they want from life and pessimists can too.* New York: Guilford.

Selby, E. A., Anestis, M. D., Bender, T. W., & Joiner, T. E. (2009). An exploration of the emotional cascade model of borderline personality disorder. *Journal of Abnormal Psychology, 118,* 375–387.

Selby, E. A., & others. (2010). Overcoming the fear of lethal injury: Evaluating suicide in the military through the lens of the interpersonal-psychological theory of suicide. *Clinical Psychology Review, 30,* 298–307.

Seligman, M. E. P. (1970). On the generality of the laws of learning. *Psychological Review, 77,* 406–418.

Seligman, M. E. P. (1990). *Learned optimism.* New York: Knopf.

Seligman, M. E. P. (1994). *What you can change and what you can't.* New York: Knopf.

Seligman, M. E. P. (2000). Positive psychology. In J. E. Gillham (Ed.), *The science of optimism and hope: Research essays in honor of Martin E. P. Seligman* (pp. 415–429). West Conshohocken, PA: Templeton Foundation Press.

Seligman, M. E. P., & Csikszentmihalyi, M. (2000). Positive psychology: An introduction. *American Psychologist, 55,* 5–14.

Seligman, M. E. P., & Maier, S. F. (1967). Failure to escape traumatic shock. *Journal of Experimental Psychology, 74,* 1–9.

Seligman, M. E. P., & Pawelski, J. O. (2003). Positive psychology: FAQs. *Psychological Inquiry, 14,* 159–163.

Seligman, M. E. P., Rosellini, R. A., & Kozak, M. J. (1975). Learned helplessness in the rat: Time course, immunization, and reversibility. *Journal of Comparative and Physiological Psychology, 88,* 542–547.

Sellbom, M., Toomey, J. A., Wygant, D. B., Kucharski, L. T., & Duncan, S. (2010). Utility of the MMPI-2-RF (restructured form) validity scales in detecting malingering in a criminal forensic setting: A known-groups design. *Psychological Assessment, 22,* 22–31.

Sellers, R. M., Copeland-Linder, N., Martin, P. P., & Lewis, R. L. (2006). Racial identity matters: The relationship between racial discrimination and psychological functioning in African American adolescents. *Journal of Research on Adolescence, 16,* 187–216.

Selye, H. (1974). *Stress without distress.* Philadelphia: Saunders.

Selye, H. (1983). The stress concept: Past, present, and future. In C. I. Cooper (Ed.), *Stress research.* New York: Wiley.

Serretti, A., Drago, A., & DeRonchi, D. (2009). Lithium pharmacogenetics. *Current Medicinal Chemistry, 16,* 1917–1948.

"Sertraline versus other antidepressive agents for depression." *Cochrane Database of Systematic Reviews, 4,* CD006117.

Sesardic, N. (2006). *Making sense of heritability.* New York: Cambridge University Press.

Sessa, B. (2007). Is there a case for MDMA-assisted psychotherapy in the UK? *Journal of Psychopharmacology, 21,* 220–224.

Seto, M. C. (2009). Pedophilia. *Annual Review of Clinical Psychology, 5,* 391–407.

Sewell, R. A., Halpern, J. H., & Pope, H. G. (2006). Response of cluster headache to psilocybin and LSD. *Neurology, 66,* 1920–1922.

Seymour, K., Clifford, C. W., Logothetis, N. K., & Bartels, A. (2009). The coding of color, motion, and their conjunction in the human visual cortex. *Current Biology, 19,* 177–183.

Seymour, T. L., Seifert, C. M., Shafto, M. G., & Mosmann, A. L. (2000). Using response time measures to assess "guilty knowledge." *Journal of Applied Psychology, 85,* 30–37.

Shamay-Tsoory, S. G., Harari, H., Aharon-Peretz, J., & Levkovitz, Y. (2010). The role of the orbitofrontal cortex in affective theory of mind deficits in criminal offenders with psychopathic tendencies. *Cortex, 46,* 668–677.

Shanks, D. R. (2010). Learning: From association to cognition. *Annual Review of Psychology* (vol. 61). Palo Alto, CA: Annual Reviews.

Sharp, E. S., Reynolds, C. A., Pedersen, N. L., & Gatz, M. (2010). Cognitive engagement and cognitive aging: Is openness protective? *Psychology and Aging, 25,* 60–73.

Shaver, P., & Mikulincer, M. (2011). Recent advances in the study of close relationships. *Annual Review of Psychology* (vol. 62). Palo Alto, CA: Annual Reviews.

Shaw, D. S., Connell, A., Dishion, T. J., Wilson, M. N., & Gardner, F. (2009). Improvements in maternal depression as a mediator of intervention effects on early childhood problem behavior. *Development and Psychopathology, 21,* 417–439.

Shay, J. W., & Wright, W. E. (2007). Hallmarks of telomere aging research. *Journal of Pathology, 211,* 114–123.

Shea, N., Krug, K., & Tobler, P. N. (2008). Conceptual representations in goal-directed decision making. *Cognitive, Affective, and Behavioral Neuroscience, 8,* 418–428.

Sheese, B. E., Voleker, P., Posner, M. I., & Rothbart, M. K. (2009). Genetic variation influences on early development of reactive emotions and their regulation. *Cognitive Neuropsychiatry, 14,* 4–5.

Sheldon, K. M. (2002). The self-concordance model of healthy goal-striving: When personal goals correctly represent the person. In E. L. Deci & R. M. Ryan (Eds.), *Handbook of self-determination research* (pp. 65–86). Rochester, NY: University of Rochester Press.

Sheldon, K. M., & Elliot, A. J. (1998). Not all personal goals are personal: Comparing autonomous and controlled reasons for goals as predictors of effort and attainment. *Personality and Social Psychology Bulletin, 24,* 546–557.

Sheldon, K. M., Elliot, A. J., Kim, Y., & Kasser, T. (2001). What is satisfying about satisfying events? Testing 10 candidate psychological needs. *Journal of Personality and Social Psychology, 80,* 325–339.

Sheldon, K. M., & Gunz, A. (2009). Psychological needs as basic motives, not just experiential requirements. *Journal of Personality, 77,* 1467–1492.

Sheldon, K. M., Kasser, T., Houser-Marko, L., Jones, T., & Turban, D. (2005). Doing one's duty: Chronological age, felt autonomy, and subjective well-being. *European Journal of Personality, 19,* 97–115.

Sheldon, K. M., & Lyubomirsky, S. (2007). Is it possible to become happier? (And if so, how?). *Social and Personality Psychology Compass, 1,* 129–145.

Shelton, R. C., & Miller, A. H. (2010). Eating ourselves to death and despair: The contribution of adiposity and inflammation to depression. *Progress in Neurobiology.* (in press)

Shelton, R. C., Osuntokun, O., Heinloth, A. N., & Corya, S. A. (2010). Therapeutic options for treatment-resistant depression. *CNS Drugs, 24,* 131–161.

Shen, K., & Scheiffele, P. (2010). Genetics and cell biology of synapse recognition and formation. *Annual Review of Neuroscience* (vol. 33). Palo Alto, CA: Annual Reviews.

Sherif, M., Harvey, O. J., White, B. J., Hood, W. R., & Sherif, C. W. (1961). *Intergroup cooperation and competition: The Robbers Cave experiment.* Norman: University of Oklahoma Press.

Sherman, A. C., Plante, T. G., Simonton, U. L., & Anaissie, E. J. (2009). Prospective study of religious coping among patients undergoing autologous stem cell transplantation. *Journal of Behavioral Science, 32,* 118–128.

Sherman, F. T. (2009). Life-saving treatment for depression in the elderly: Always think of electroconvulsive therapy (ECT). *Geriatrics, 64,* 8, 12.

Sherman, R. A., Nave, C., & Funder, D. C. (2010). Situational similarity and personality predict behavioral consistency. *Journal of Personality and Social Psychology,* (in press)

Shibata, S. B., & others. (2010). Transgenic BDNF induces nerve fiber regrowth into the auditory epithelium in deaf cochlee. *Experimental Neurology.* (in press)

Shields, S. A. (1991). Gender in the psychology of emotion. In K. T. Strongman (Ed.), *International Review of Studies of Emotion* (vol. 1). New York: Wiley.

Shier, D. N., Butler, J. L., & Lewis, R. (2010). *Hole's human anatomy and physiology* (12th ed.). New York: McGraw-Hill.

Shih, M., Bonam, C., Sanchez, D., & Peck, C. (2007). The social construction of race: Biracial identity and vulnerability to stereotypes. *Cultural Diversity & Ethnic Minority Psychology, 13,* 125–133.

Shih, M., Yang, Y.-H., & Koo, M. (2009). A meta-analysis of hypnosis in the treatment of depressive symptoms: A brief communication. *International Journal of Clinical and Experimental Hypnosis, 57,* 431–432.

Shinn, M., & Thaden, E. (2010). *Current directions in community psychology.* Boston: Allyn & Bacon.

Shipp, S., Adams, D. L, Moutoussis, K., & Zeki, S. (2009). Feature binding in the feedback layers of area V2. *Cerebral Cortex, 19,* 2230–2239.

Shiraev, E., & Levy, D. (2010). *Cross-cultural psychology* (4th ed.). Boston: Allyn & Bacon.

Shoda, Y., & Mischel, W. (2006). Applying meta-theory to achieve generalisability and precision in personality science: Comment. *Applied Psychology: An International Review, 55,* 439–452.

Shyn, S. I., & Hamilton, S. P. (2010). The genetics of major depression: Moving beyond the monoamine hypothesis. *Psychiatric Clinics of North America, 33,* 125–140.

Sieber, W. J., Rodin, J., Larson, L., Ortega, S., & Cummings, N. (1992). Modulation of human natural killer cell activity by exposure to uncontrollable stress. *Brain, Behavior, and Immunity, 6,* 141–156.

Siebner, H. R., Hartwigsen, G., Kassuba, T., & Rothwell, J. C. (2009). How does transcranial magnetic stimulation modify neuronal activity in the brain? Implications for studies of cognition. *Cortex, 45,* 1035–1042.

Siegel, J. M. (2005). Clues to the functions of mammalian sleep. *Nature, 437,* 1264–1271.

Siegel, S. (1988). State dependent learning and morphine tolerance. *Behavioral Neuroscience, 102,* 228–232.

Sienaert, P., Vansteelandt, K., Demyttenaere, K., & Peuskens, J. (2010). Randomized comparison of ultra-brief bifrontal and unilateral electroconvulsive therapy for major depression: Cognitive side-effects. *Journal of Affective Disorders, 122,* 60–67.

Sieswerda, S., Arntz, A., Mertens, I., & Vertommen, S. (2007). Hypervigilance in patients with borderline personality disorder: Specificity, automaticity, and predictors. *Behaviour Research and Therapy, 45,* 1011–1024.

Sigel, E. (2008). Eating disorders. *Adolescence Medicine: State of the Art Reviews, 19,* 547–572.

Sigurdsson, T., Doyere, V., Cain, C. K., & LeDoux, J. E. (2007). Long-term potentiation in the amygdale: A cellular mechanism of learning and memory. *Neuropharmacology, 52,* 215–227.

Sikorskii, A., Given, C., Given, B., Jeon, S., & McCorkle, R. (2006). Testing the effects of treatment complications on a cognitive-behavioral intervention for reducing symptom severity. *Journal of Pain and Symptom Management, 32,* 129–139.

Silva de Lima, M., Farrell, M., Lima Reisser, A. A., & Soares, B. (2010). WITHDRAWN: Antidepressants for cocaine dependence.

Cocharine Database of Systematic Reviews, CD002950.

Silvia, P. J., Nusbaum, E. C., Berg, C., Martin, C., & O'Connor, A. (2009). Openness to experience, plasticity, and creativity: Exploring lower-order, high-order, and interactive effects. *Journal of Research in Personality, 43,* 1087–1090.

Sim, T. N., & Ong, L. P. (2005). Parent punishment and child aggression in a Singapore Chinese preschool sample. *Journal of Marriage and the Family, 67,* 85–99.

Simms, L. J. (2007). The big seven model of personality and its relevance to personality pathology. *Journal of Personality, 75,* 65–94.

Simola, S. K., Barling, J., & Turner, N. (2010). Transformational leadership and leader moral orientation: Contrasting an ethic of justice and an ethic of care. *Leadership Quarterly, 21,* 179–188.

Simon, H. A. (1969). *The sciences of the artificial.* Cambridge, MA: MIT Press.

Simons, D. J., & Chabris, C. F. (1999). Gorillas in our midst: Sustained inattentional blindness for dynamic events. *Perception, 28* (9), 1059–1074.

Simpson, J. R. (2008). Functional fMRI lie detection: Too good to be true? *Journal of the American Academy of Psychiatry and Law, 36,* 491–498.

Sims, C. S., Drasgow, F., & Fitzgerald, L. F. (2005). The effects of sexual harassment on turnover in the military: Time-dependent modeling. *Journal of Applied Psychology, 90,* 1141–1152.

Sin, N. L., & Lyubomirsky, S. (2009). Enhancing well-being and alleviating depressive symptoms with positive psychology interventions: A practice-friendly meta-analysis. *Journal of Clinical Psychology, 65,* 467–487.

Singer, J. A., & Conway, M. A. (2008). Should we forget about forgetting? *Memory Studies, 1,* 279–285.

Singh, M., & others. (2010). Brain glutamatergic characteristics of pediatric offspring of parents with bipolar disorder. *Psychiatry Research.* (in press)

Sinn, D. L., Gosling, S. D., & Moltschaniwskyj, N. A. (2008). Development of shy/bold behaviour in squid: Context-specific phenotypes associated with developmental plasticity. *Animal Behaviour, 75,* 433–442.

Sinn, D. L., Moltschaniwskyj, N. A., Wapstra, E., & Dall, S. R. X. (2010). Are behavioral syndromes invariant? Spatiotemporal variation in shy/bold behavior in squid. *Behavioral Ecology and Sociobiology, 64,* 693–702.

Sintov, N. D., & others. (2010). Empirically defined subtypes of alcohol dependence in an Irish family sample. *Drug and Alcohol Dependence, 107,* 230–236.

Sitnikova, T., Goff, D., & Kuperberg, G. R. (2009). Neurocognitive abnormalities during comprehension of real-world goal-directed behaviors in schizophrenia. *Journal of Abnormal Psychology, 118,* 256–277.

Sivacek, J., & Crano, W. D. (1982). Vested interest as a moderator of attitude-behavior consistency. *Journal of Personality and Social Psychology, 43* (2), 210–221.

Sivanathan, N., Arnold, K. A., Turner, N., & Barling, J. (2004). Leading well: Transformational leadership and well-being. In P. A. Linley & S. Joseph (Eds.), *Positive psychology in practice* (pp. 241–255). Hoboken, NJ: Wiley.

Skinner, B. F. (1938). *The behavior of organisms: An experimental analysis.* New York: Appleton-Century-Crofts.

Skinner, B. F. (1957). *Verbal behavior.* New York: Appleton-Century-Crofts.

Skinner, E. I., & Fernandes, M. A. (2009). Illusory recollection in older adults and younger adults under divided attention. *Psychology and Aging, 24,* 211–216.

Skolin I., Wahlin, Y. B., Broman, D. A., Koivisto Hursti, U., Vikström, L. M., & Hernell, O. (2006). Altered food intake and taste perception in children with cancer after start of chemotherapy: Perspectives of children, parents and nurses. *Supportive Care in Cancer, 14,* 369–378.

Slater, A., Field, T., & Hernandez-Reif, M. (2007). The development of the senses. In A. Slater & M. Lewis (Eds.), *Introduction to infant development* (2nd ed.). New York: Oxford University Press.

Slater, A. M., Riddell, P., Quinn, P. C., Pacalis, O., Lee, K., & Kelly, D. J. (2011). Visual perception. In U. Goswami (Ed.), *Wiley-Blackwell handbook of childhood cognitive development* (2nd ed.). New York: Wiley Blackwell.

Slavin, R. E. (2006). Translating research into widespread practice: The case of success for all. In M. A. Constas & R. J. Sternberg (Eds.), *Translating theory and research into educational practice: Developments in content domains, large-scale reform, and intellectual capacity* (pp. 113–126). Mahwah, NJ: Erlbaum.

Slaymaker, V. J., & Sheehan, T. (2008). The impact of AA on professional treatment. *Recent Developments in Alcoholism, 18,* 59–70.

Slotnick, S. D., & Schacter, D. L. (2006). The nature of memory related activity in early visual areas. *Neuropsychologia, 44,* 2874–2886.

Slutske, W. S. (2005). Alcohol use disorders among US college students and their non-college-attending peers. *Archives of General Psychiatry, 62,* 321–327.

Smetana, J. G., Tasopoulos-Chan, M., Gettman, D. C., Villalobos, M., Campione-Barr, N., & Metzger, A. (2009). Adolescents' and parents' evaluations of helping versus fulfilling personal desires in family situations. *Child Development, 80,* 280–294.

Smieskova, R., & others. (2010). Neuroimaging predictors of transition to psychosis—A systematic review and meta-analysis. *Neuroscience and Biobehavioral Reviews.* (in press)

Smit, F., Willemse, G., Koopmanschap, M., Onrust, S., Cuijpers, P., & Beekman, A. (2006). Cost-effectiveness of preventing depression in primary care patients: Randomized trial. *British Journal of Psychiatry, 188,* 330–336.

Smith, B. (2007). *The psychology of sex and gender.* Belmont, CA: Wadsworth.

Smith, C. A., & Kirby, L. D. (2009). Putting appraisal in context: Toward a relational model of appraisal and emotion. *Cognition and Emotion, 23,* 1352–1372.

Smith, C. P. (Ed.). (1992). *Thematic content analysis for motivation and personality research.* New York: Cambridge University Press.

Smith, D. (2004, February 7). Love that dare not squeak its name. *New York Times.* http://www.nytimes.com/2004/02/07/arts/07GAY.html

Smith, G. P. (1995). Dopamine and food reward. *Progress in Psychobiology and Physiological Psychology, 16,* 83–144.

Smith, H. S. (2010). The role of genomic oxidative-reductive balance as predictor of complex regional pain syndrome development: A novel theory. *Pain Physician, 13,* 79–90.

Smith, M. B. (2001). Humanistic psychology. In W. E. Craighead & C. B. Nemeroff (Eds.), *The Corsini encyclopedia of psychology and behavioral science* (3rd ed.). New York: Wiley.

Smith, P. B., Bond, M. H., & Kagitcibasi, C. (2006). *Understanding social psychology across cultures: Living and working in a changing world.* Thousand Oaks, CA: Sage.

Smith, P. K., & Bargh, J. A. (2008). Nonconscious effects of power on basic approach and avoidance tendencies. *Social Cognition, 26,* 1–24.

Smith, R. A., & Davis, S. F. (2010). *Psychologist as detective* (5th ed.). Boston: Cengage.

Smith, R. L., Rose, R. J., & Schwartz-Mette, R. A. (2010). Relational and overt aggression in childhood and adolescence: Clarifying mean-level gender differences and associations with peer acceptance. *Social Development, 19,* 243–269.

Smith, S. J., Axelton, A. M., & Saucier, D. A. (2009). The effects of contact on sexual prejudice: A meta-analysis. *Sex Roles, 61,* 178–191.

Smith, S. R., Gorske, T. T., Wiggins, C., & Little, J. A. (2010). Personality assessment use by clinical neuropsychologists. *International Journal of Testing, 10,* 6–20.

Smith, T. E., Weston, C. A., & Lieberman, J. A. (2009, April 16). Schizophrenia (maintenance treatment). *Clinical Evidence,* PMID: 19445748.

Smith, T. W., & MacKenzie, J. (2006). Personality and risk of physical illness. *Annual Review of Clinical Psychology* (vol. 2). Palo Alto, CA: Annual Reviews.

Smyth, J. (1998). Written emotional expression: Effect sizes, outcome types, and moderating variables. *Journal of Consulting and Clinical Psychology, 66,* 174–184.

Snarey, J. R. (1993). *How fathers care for the next generation: A four-decade study.* Cambridge, MA: Harvard University Press.

Snell, R. S., & Wong, Y. L. (2007). Differentiating good soldiers from good actors. *Journal of Management Studies.* doi:10.1111/j.1467-6486.2007.00699.x

Snowdon, D. A. (2003). Healthy aging and dementia: Findings from the Nun study. *Annals of Internal Medicine, 139,* 450–454.

Snowdon, D. A. (2007, April). *Aging with grace: findings from the nun study.* Paper presented at the 22nd annual Alzheimer's regional conference, Seattle.

Snyder, C. R., & Lopez, S. J. (Eds.). (2007). *Positive psychology: The scientific and practical explorations of human strengths.* Thousand Oaks, CA: Sage.

Snyder, C. R., & Lopez, S. (2009). *The Oxford handbook of positive psychology* (2nd ed.). New York: Oxford University Press.

Sofuoglu, M. (2010). Cognitive enhancement as a pharmacotherapy target for stimulant addiction. *Addiction, 105,* 38–48.

Sofuoglu, M., Sugarman, D. E., & Carroll, K. M. (2010). Cognitive function as an emerging treatment target for marijuana addiction. *Experimental and Clinical Psychopharmacology, 18,* 109–119.

Sokol, M. S., Carroll, A. K., Heebink, D. M., Hoffman-Riken, K. M., Goudge, C. S., & Ebers, D. D. (2009). Anorexia nervosa in identical triplets. *CNS Spectrums, 14,* 156–162.

Solberg Nes, L., Evans, D. R., & Segerstrom, S. C. (2009). Optimism and college retention: Mediation by motivation, performance, and adjustment. *Journal of Applied Social Psychology, 39,* 1887–1912.

Solberg Nes, L., & Segerstrom, S. C. (2006). Dispositional optimism and coping: A meta-analytic review. *Personality and Social Psychology Review, 10,* 235–251.

Soldan, A., Hilton, H. J., Cooper, L. A., & Stern, Y. (2009). Priming of familiar and unfamiliar visual objects over delays in young and older adults. *Psychology and Aging, 24,* 93–104.

Soloff, P. H., & others. (1994). Self-mutilation and suicidal behavior in borderline personality disorder. *Journal of Personality Disorders, 8,* 257–267.

Soltesz, E. G., & Cohn, L. H. (2007). Minimally invasive valve surgery. *Cardiology Review, 15,* 109–115.

Sommer, M., Hajak, G., Dohnel, K., Schwerdtner, J., Meinhardt, J., & Muller, J. L. (2006). Integration of emotion and cognition in patients with psychopathy. *Progress in Brain Research, 156C,* 457–466.

Sommer, V., & Vasey, P. L. (Eds.). (2006). *Homosexual behaviour in animals: An evolutionary perspective.* New York: Cambridge University Press.

Song, H., & Ming, G.-L. (2010). Application of neurons from stem cells for neurological diseases. *Annual Review of Neuroscience* (vol. 33). Palo Alto, CA: Annual Reviews.

Song, S. (2006, March 27). Mind over medicine. *Time, 167,* 13.

Sonnenfeld, J. A. (1985). Shedding light on the Hawthorne studies. *Journal of Occupational Behavior, 6,* 111–130.

Sorrentino, R., Cohen, D., Olson, J. M., & Zanna, M. P. (2005). *Cultural and social behavior: The Ontario symposium* (vol. 10). Mahwah, NJ: Erlbaum.

Sotres-Bayon, F., Diaz-Mataix, L., Bush, D. E., & LeDoux, J. E. (2009). Dissociable roles for the ventromedial prefrontal cortex and amygdale in fear extinction: NR2B contribution. *Cerebral Cortex, 19,* 472–482.

Sourial-Bassillious, N., Rydelius, P. A., Aperia, A., & Aizman, O. (2009). Glutamate-mediated calcium signaling: A potential target for lithium action. *Neuroscience, 161* (4), 1126–1134.

South, S. C., & Krueger, R. F. (2008). An interactionist on genetic and environmental contributions to personality. *Social and Personality Psychology Compass, 2,* 929–948.

South, S. C., & Krueger, R. F. (2010). Genetic and environmental influences on internalizing psychopathology vary as a function of economic status. *Psychological Medicine.* (in press)

Spanos, N. P. (1996). *Multiple identities and false memories: A sociocognitive perspective.* Washington, DC: American Psychological Association.

Spanos, N. P., & Chaves, J. F. (Eds.). (1989). *Hypnosis: The cognitive-behavior perspective.* Buffalo, NY: Prometheus.

Sparks, J. R., & Areni, C. S. (2008). Style versus substance: Multiple roles of language power in persuasion. *Journal of Applied Social Psychology, 38,* 37–60.

Sparling, P., & Redican, K. (2011). *MP iHealth.* New York: McGraw-Hill.

Spaulding, L. H. (1998). Florida's 1997 chemical castration law: A return to the Dark Ages. *Florida State University Law Review, 117,* 125–135.

Spaulding, S. (2010). Embodied cognition and mindreading. *Mind & Language, 25,* 119–140.

Spearman, C. (1904). "General intelligence" objectively determined and measured. *American Journal of Psychology, 15,* 201–293.

Spector, P. E., & others. (2001). Do national levels of individualism and internal locus of control relate to well-being? An ecological level international study. *Journal of Organizational Behavior, 22,* 815–832.

Spellman, B. A. (2005). Could reality shows become reality experiments? *APS Observer, 18,* 34–35.

Spencer, S. J., Steele, C. M., & Quinn, D. M. (1999). Stereotype threat and women's math performance. *Journal of Experimental Social Psychology, 35,* 4–28.

Speranza, M., Corcos, M., Atger, F., Paterniti, S., & Jeammet, P. (2003). Binge eating behaviours, depression and weight control strategies. *Eating and Weight Disorders, 8,* 201–206.

Sperling, G. (1960). The information available in brief presentations. *Psychological Monographs, 74* (11).

Sperry, R. W. (1968). Hemisphere deconnection and unity in conscious awareness. *American Psychologist, 23,* 723–733.

Sperry, R. W. (1974). Lateral specialization in surgically separated hemispheres. In F. O. Schmitt & F. G. Worden (Eds.), *The neurosciences: Third study program.* Cambridge, MA: MIT Press.

Spiegel, D. (2006). Editorial: Recognizing traumatic dissociation. *American Journal of Psychiatry, 163,* 566–568.

Spiegel, D. (2010). Hypnosis testing. In A. F. Barabasz, K. Olness, R. Boland, & S. Kahn (Eds.), *Medical hypnosis primer: Clinical and research evidence* (pp. 11–18). New York: Routledge/Taylor & Francis.

Spiegler, M. D., & Guevremont, D. C. (2010). *Contemporary behavior therapy* (5th ed.). Boston: Cengage.

Spielberger, C. D. (2004, August). *Type A behavior, anger-hostility, and heart disease.* Paper presented at the 28th International Congress of Psychology, Beijing, China.

Spritz, B. L., Fergusson, A. S., & Bankoff, S. M. (2010). False beliefs and the development of deception. In E. H. Sandberg & B. L. Spritz (Eds.), *A clinician's guide to normal cognitive development in childhood* (pp. 101–120). New York: Routledge/Taylor & Francis.

Spyer, K. M., & Gourine, A. V. (2009). Chemosensory pathways in the brainstem controlling cardiorespiratory activity, *Philosophical Transactions of the Royal Society B: Biological Sciences 364,* 2603–2610.

Squire, L. R. (1990, June). *Memory and brain systems.* Paper presented at the meeting of the American Psychological Society, Dallas.

Squire, L. R. (2004). Memory systems of the brain: A brief history and current perspective. *Neurobiology of Learning and Memory, 82,* 171–177.

Squire, L. R. (2007). Memory systems as a biological concept. In H. L. Roediger, Y. Dudai, & S. Fitzpatrick (Eds.), *Science of memory: Concepts.* New York: Oxford University Press.

Sriram, N., & Greenwald, A. G. (2009). The Brief Implicit Association Test. *Experimental Psychology, 56,* 283–204

Sroufe, L. A., Coffino, B., & Carlson, E. A. (2010). Conceptualizing the role of early experience: Lessons from the Minnesota Longitudinal Study. *Developmental Review, 30,* 36–51.

Staddon, J. E., Chelaru, I. M., & Higa, J. J. (2002). A tune-trace theory of interval-timing dynamics. *Journal of the Experimental Analysis of Behavior, 77,* 105–124.

Stadler, G., Oettingen, G., & Gollwitzer, P. M. (2010). Intervention effects of information and self-regulation on eating fruits and vegetables over two years. *Health Psychology, 29,* 274–283.

Stake, R. E. (2010). *Qualitative research.* New York: Guilford.

Stangor, C. (2009). The study of stereotyping, prejudice, and discrimination within social psychology: A quick history of theory and research. In T. D. Nelson (Ed.), *Handbook of prejudice, stereotyping, and discrimination.* New York: Psychology Press.

Stangor, C. (2011). *Research methods for the behavioral sciences* (4th ed.). Boston: Cengage.

Stanovich, K. E. (2010). *How to think straight about psychology* (9th ed.). Upper Saddle River, NJ: Prentice-Hall.

Stanovich, K. E., & West, R. F. (2000). Individual differences in reasoning: Implications for the rationality debate. *Behavioral and Brain Sciences, 23,* 645–665.

Stanton, A. L., Revenson, T. A., & Tennen, H. (2007). Health psychology: Psychological adjustment to chronic disease. *Annual Review of Psychology* (vol. 58). Palo Alto, CA: Annual Reviews.

Starcevic, V. (2006). Anxiety states: A review of conceptual and treatment issues. *Current Opinions in Psychiatry, 19,* 79–83.

Staresina, B. P., Gray, J. C., & Davachi, L. (2010). Event congruency enhances episodic memory encoding through semantic elaboration and relational binding. *Cerebral Cortex, 19,* 1198–1207.

Stasiewicz, P. R., Brandon, T. H., & Bradizza, C. M. (2007). Effects of extinction context and retrieval cues on renewal of alcohol-cue reactivity among alcohol-dependent outpatients. *Psychology of Addictive Behaviors, 21* (2), 244–248.

Staub, E., & Vollhardt, J. (2008). Altruism born of suffering: The roots of caring and helping after victimization and other trauma. *American Journal of Orthopsychiatry, 78,* 267–280.

Staudinger, U. M., & Gluck, J. (2011). Psychological wisdom research. *Annual Review of Psychology* (vol. 62). Palo Alto, CA: Annual Reviews.

Staudt, M. (2010). Brain plasticity following early life brain injury: Insights from neuuroimaging. *Seminars in Perinatology, 34,* 87–92.

Staw, B. M., & Barsade, S. G. (1993). Affect and managerial performance: A test of the sadder-but-wiser vs. happier-and-smarter hypothesis. *Administrative Science Quarterly, 38,* 304–331.

Staw, B. M., Bell, N. E. & Clausen, J. A. (1986). The dispositional approach to job attitudes: A lifetime longitudinal test. *Administrative Science Quarterly, 31,* 56–77.

Staw, B. M., Sutton, R. I., & Pelled, L. H. (1994). Employee positive emotion and favorable outcomes at the workplace. *Organization Science, 5,* 51–71.

Steblay, N., & Loftus, E. (2009). Eyewitness memory and the legal system. In E. Shafir (Ed.), *The behavioral foundations of policy.* Princeton, NJ: Princeton University Press and the Russell Sage Foundation.

Steel, P., Schmidt, J., & Schultz, J. (2008). Refining the relationship between personality and subjective well-being. *Psychological Bulletin, 134,* 138–161.

Steele, C. M., & Aronson, J. (1995). Stereotype threat and the intellectual test performance of African-Americans. *Journal of Personality and Social Psychology, 69,* 797–811.

Steele, C. M., & Aronson, J. A. (2004). Stereotype threat does not live by Steele and Aronson (1995) alone. *American Psychologist, 59,* 47–48.

Steele, H., & Siever, L. (2010). An attachment perspective on borderline personality disorder: Advances in gene-environment considerations. *Current Psychiatry Reports, 12,* 61–67.

Steeves, J., Dricot, L., Goltz, H. C., Sorger, B., Peters, J., Milner, A. D., Goodale, M. A., Goebel, R., & Rossion, B. (2009). Abnormal face identity coding in the middle fusiform gyrus of two brain-damaged prosopagnosic patients. *Neuropsychologia, 47,* 2584–2592.

Steger, M. F., & Frazier, P. (2005). Meaning in life: One link in the chain from religion to

well-being. *Journal of Counseling Psychology, 52,* 574–582.

Stein, R. (2003). *Blinded by the light.* http://www.theage.com.au/articles/2003/09/01/1062403448264.html (accessed October 11, 2006)

Stein, T., Peelen, M. V., Funk, J., & Seidi, K. N. (2010). The fearful-face advantage is modulated by task demands: Evidence from the attentional blink. *Emotion, 10,* 136–140.

Steinberg, L. (2009). Adolescent development and juvenile justice. *Annual Review of Clinical Psychology* (vol. 5). Palo Alto, CA: Annual Reviews.

Steinbrook, R. (1992). The polygraph test: A flawed diagnostic method. *New England Journal of Medicine, 327,* 122–123.

Stenfelt, S. (2006). Middle ear ossicles motion at hearing thresholds with air conduction and bone conduction stimulation. *Journal of the Acoustical Society of America, 119,* 2848–2858.

Stern, Y., Alexander, G. E., Prohovnik, I., & Mayeux, R. (1992). Inverse relationship between education and parietotemporal perfusion deficit in Alzheimer's disease. *Annals of Neurology, 32,* 371–375.

Stern, Y., Scarmeas, N., & Habeck, C. (2004). Imaging cognitive reserve. *International Journal of Psychology, 39,* 18–26.

Sternberg, E. M., & Gold, P. W. (1996). The mind–body interaction in disease. *Mysteries of the mind.* New York: Scientific American.

Sternberg, R. J. (1986). *Intelligence applied.* Fort Worth, TX: Harcourt Brace.

Sternberg, R. J. (Ed.). (2004). *Definitions and conceptions of giftedness.* Thousand Oaks, CA: Corwin.

Sternberg, R. J. (2007a). *G, g's, or Jeez:* Which is the best model for developing abilities, competencies, and expertise? In P. C. Kyllonen, R. D. Roberts, & L. Stankov (Eds.), *Extending intelligence.* Mahwah, NJ: Erlbaum.

Sternberg, R. J. (2007b). Developing successful intelligence in all children: A potential solution to underachievement in ethnic minority children. In M. C. Wang & R. D. Taylor (Eds.), *Closing the achievement gap.* Philadelphia: Laboratory for Student Success at Temple University.

Sternberg, R. J. (2008). The triarchic theory of human intelligence. In N. Salkind (Ed.), *Encyclopedia of educational psychology.* Thousand Oaks, CA: Sage.

Sternberg, R. J. (2009a). *Cognitive psychology* (5th ed.). Belmont, CA: Wadsworth.

Sternberg, R. J. (2009b). Teaching for creativity. In R. A. Beghetto & J. C. Kaufman (Eds.), *Nurturing creativity in the classroom.* New York: Cambridge University Press.

Sternberg, R. J. (2009c). Successful intelligence as a framework for understanding cultural adaption. In S. Ang & L. van Dyne (Eds.), *Handbook on cultural intelligence.* New York: M. E. Sharpe.

Sternberg, R. J. (2009d). The triarchic theory of intelligence. In B. Kerr (Ed.), *Encyclopedia of giftedness, creativity, and talent.* Thousand Oaks, CA: Sage.

Sternberg, R. J. (2009e). Wisdom, intelligence, creativity, synthesized: A model of giftedness. In T. Balchin, B. Hymer, & D. Matthews (Eds.), *International companion to gifted education.* London: RoutledgeFalmer.

Sternberg, R. J. (2009f). Wisdom. In S. J. Lopez (Ed.), *Encyclopedia of positive psychology.* Amsterdam: Springer.

Sternberg, R. J. (2011). Human intelligence. In V. S. Ramachandran (Ed.), *Encyclopedia of human behavior* (2nd ed.). New York: Elsevier.

Sternberg, R. J., & Grigorenko, E. L. (2008). Ability testing across cultures. In L. Suzuki (Ed.), *Handbook of multicultural assessment* (3rd ed., pp. 335–359). New York: Jossey-Bass.

Sternberg, R. J., Grigorenko, E. L., & Kidd, K. K. (2005). Intelligence, race, and genetics. *American Psychologist, 60,* 46–59.

Sternberg, R. J., Roediger, H., & Halpern, D. (Eds.). (2007). *Critical thinking in psychology.* New York: Cambridge University Press.

Sterponi, L. (2010). Learning communicative competence. In D. F. Lancy, J. Bock, & S. Gaskins (Eds.), *The anthropology of learning in childhood* (pp. 235–259). Walnut Creek, CA: AltaMira.

Stevens, M. J., & Gielen, U. P. (Eds.). (2007). Toward a global psychology: Theory, research, intervention, and pedagogy. Mahwah, NJ: Erlbaum.

Stewart, J. L., Silton, R. L., Sass, S. M., Fisher, J. E., Edggar, J. C., Heller, W., & Miller, G. A. (2010). Attentional bias to negative emotion as a function of approach and withdrawal anger styles: An ERP investigation. *International Journal of Psychophysiology.* (in press)

Stewart, S. H., & Chambers, L. (2000). Relationships between drinking motives and drinking restraint. *Addictive Behaviors, 25,* 269–274.

Stice, E., Shaw, H., & Marti, C. N. (2006). A meta-analytic review of obesity prevention programs for children and adolescents: The skinny on interventions that work. *Psychological Bulletin, 132,* 667–691.

Stickgold, R. (2001). Watching the sleeping brain watch us: Sensory processing during sleep. *Trends in Neuroscience, 24,* 307–309.

Stirling, J. D. (2002). *Introducing neuropsychology.* East Sussex, U.K.: Psychology Press.

Stokes, M. B., & Payne, B. K. (2010). Mental control and visual illusions: Errors of action and construal in race-based weapon misidentification. In R. B. Adams, N. Ambady, K. Nakayama, & S. Shimojo (Eds.), *The science of social vision.* New York: Oxford University Press.

Stone, J. (2002). Battling doubt by avoiding practice: The effects of stereotype threat on self-handicapping in white athletes. *Personality and Social Psychology Bulletin, 28,* 1667–1678.

Stoner, J. (1961). *A comparison of individual and group decisions, including risk.* Unpublished master's thesis, School of Industrial Management, MIT.

Storbeck, J., & Clore, G. L. (2008). The affective regulation of cognitive priming. *Emotion, 8,* 208–215.

Storch, E. A., & others. (2010). Does cognitive-behavior therapy response among adults with obsessive-compulsive disorder differ as a function of certain comorbidities? *Journal of Anxiety Disorders.* (in press)

Stores, G., Montgomery, P., & Wiggs, L. (2006). The psychosocial problems of children with narcolepsy and those with excessive daytime sleepiness of unknown origin. *Pediatrics, 118,* e1116–e1123.

Strack, F., & Forster, J. (2009). Social cognition: An introduction. In F. Strack & J. Forster (Eds.), *Social cognition: The basis of human interaction.* New York: Psychology Press.

Strahan, E., Spencer, S. J., & Zanna, M. P. (2002). Subliminal priming and persuasion: Striking while the iron is hot. *Journal of Experimental Social Psychology, 38,* 556–568.

Straus, M. A., & Stewart, J. H. (1999). Corporal punishment by American parents: National data on prevalence, chronicity, severity, and duration in relation to child and family characteristics. *Clinical Child and Family Psychology Review, 2,* 55–70.

Straus, M. A., Sugarman, D. B., & Giles-Sims, J. (1997). Spanking by parents and subsequent antisocial behavior of children. *Archives of Pediatric and Adolescent Medicine, 151,* 761–767.

Streff, F. M., & Geller, E. S. (1986). Strategies for motivating safety belt use: The application of applied behavior analysis. *Health Education Research, 1* (1), 47–59.

Strick, M., Dijksterhuis, A., & van Baaren, R. B. (2010). Unconscious-thought effects take place off-line, not on-line. *Psychological Science, 21,* 484–488.

Striegel-Moore, R. H., & Franko, D. L. (2008). Should binge eating disorder be included in the DSM-V? A critical review of the state of the evidence. *Annual Review of Clinical Psychology, 4,* 305–324.

Strike, P. C., Magid, K., Whitehead, D. L., Brydon, L., Bhattacharyya, M. R., & Steptoe, A. (2006). Pathophysiological processes underlying emotional triggering of acute cardiac events. *Proceedings of the National Academy of Sciences USA, 103,* 4322–4327.

Stroop, J. R. (1935). Studies of interference in serial verbal reactions. *Journal of Experimental Psychology, 28,* 643–662.

Strupp, H. H. (1995). The psychotherapist's skills revised. *Clinical Psychology: Science and Practice, 2,* 70–74.

Stulhofer, A., Busko, V., & Landripet, I. (2010). Pornography, sexual socialization, and satisfaction among young men. *Archives of Sexual Behavior, 39,* 168–178.

Sturmer, T., Hasselbach, P., & Amelang, M. (2006). Personality, lifestyle, and risk of cardiovascular disease and cancer: Follow-up of population-based cohort. *British Medical Journal, 332,* 1359.

Sue, D., Sue, D. W., & Sue, S. (2010). *Understanding abnormal behavior* (9th ed.). Boston: Cengage.

Sui, X., Laditka, J. N., Church, T. S., Hardin, J. W., Chase, N., Davis, K., & Blair, S. N. (2009). Prospective study of cardiovascular fitness and depressive symptoms in women and men. *Journal of Psychiatric Research, 43,* 546–552.

Sui, X., LaMonte, M. J., Laditka, J. N., Hardin, J. W., Chase, N., Hooker, S. P., & Blair, S. N. (2007). Cardiorespiratory fitness and adiposity as mortality predictors in older adults. *Journal of the American Medical Association, 298,* 2507–2516.

Suinn, R. M. (1984). *Fundamentals of abnormal psychology.* Chicago: Nelson-Hall.

Sullivan, H. S. (1953). *The interpersonal theory of psychiatry.* New York: Norton.

Sullivan, P. W., Morrato, E. H., Ghushchyan, V., Wyatt, H. R., & Hill, J. O. (2005). Obesity, inactivity, and the prevalence of diabetes and diabetes-related cardiovascular comorbidities in the U.S., 2000–2002. *Diabetes Care, 28,* 1599–1603.

Suls, J., & Swain, A. (1998). Type A–Type B personalities. In H. S. Friedman (Ed.), *Encyclopedia of mental health* (vol. 3). San Diego: Academic.

Suls, J. M., Davidson, K. W., & Kaplan, R. M. (Eds.). (2010). *Handbook of health psychology and behavioral medicine.* New York: Guilford.

Surmeier, D. J., Guzman, J. N., & Sanchez-Padilla, J. (2010). Calcium, cellular aging, and selective neuronal vulnerability in Parkinson's disease. *Cell Calcium.* (in press)

Susman, E. J., & Dorn, L. D. (2009). Puberty: Its role in development. In R. M. Lerner & L. Steinberg (Eds.), *Handbook of adolescent psychology* (3rd ed.). New York: Wiley.

Suzuki, C., Tsukiura, T., Mochiizuki-Kawai, H., Shigemune, Y., & Iijima, T. (2009). Prefrontal and medial temporal contributions to episodic memory-based reasoning. *Neuroscience Research, 63,* 177–183.

Swanson, D. P. (2010). Adolescent psychosocial processes: Identity, stress, and competence. In D. P. Swanson, M. C. Edwards, & M. B. Spencer (Eds.), *Adolescence: Development in a global era.* San Diego: Academic.

Swanson, D. P., Edwards, M. C., & Spencer, M. B. (Eds.). (2010). *Adolescence: Development during a global era.* Burlington, MA: Academic.

Swanson, J. (Ed.). (1999). *Sleep disorders sourcebook.* New York: Omnigraphics.

Swisher, J. D., Gatenby, J. C., Gore, J. C., Wolfe, B. A., Moon, C. H., Kim, S. G., & Tong, F. (2010). Multiscale pattern analysis of orientation-selective activity in the primary visual cortex. *Journal of Neuroscience, 30,* 325–330.

Szasz, T. S. (1961). *The myth of mental illness: Foundations of a theory of personal conduct.* New York: Hoeber-Harper.

Szczepanski, S. M., Konen, C. S., & Kastner, S. (2010). Mechanisms of spatial attention control in frontal and parietal cortex. *Journal of Neuroscience, 30,* 148–160.

Szulwach, K. E., & others. (2010). Cross talk between microRNA and epigenetic regulation in adult neurogenesis. *Journal of Cell Biology, 189,* 127–141.

Taga, K. A., Markey, C. N., & Friedman, H. S. (2006). A longitudinal investigation of associations between boys' pubertal timing and adult behavioral health and well-being. *Journal of Youth and Adolescence, 35,* 380–390.

Tager-Flusberg, H., & Zukowski, A. (2009). Putting words together; Morphology and syntax in the preschool years. In J. Berko Gleason & N. Ratner (Eds.), *The development of language* (7th ed.). Boston: Allyn & Bacon.

Tagliamonte, S. A., & Denis, D. (2008). Linguistic ruin? LOL! Instant messaging and teen language. *American Speech, 83,* 3–34.

Tajfel, H. (1978). The achievement of group differentiation. In H. Tajfel (Ed.), *Differentiation between social groups.* London: Academic.

Takahashi, A., Nagaoka, T., Ishiko, S., Kameyama, D., & Yoshida, A. (2010). Foveal anatomic changes in a progressing stage 1 macular hole documented by spectral-domain optical coherence tomography. *Ophthalmology, 117,* 806–810.

Takahashi, M., Shimizu, H., Saito, S., & Tomoyori, H. (2006). One percent ability and ninety-nine percent perspiration: A study of a Japanese memorist. *Journal of Experimental Psychology: Learning, Memory, and Cognition, 32,* 1195–1200.

Takeuchi, T., & De Valois, K. K. (2009). Visual motion mechanisms under low retinal illuminance revealed by motion-reversal. *Vision Research, 49,* 801–809.

Talarico, J. M. (2009). Freshman flashbulbs: Memories of unique and first-time events in starting college. *Memory, 17,* 256–265.

Tam, L., Bagozzi, R. P., & Spanjol, J. (2010). When planning isn't enough: The self-regulatory effect of implementation intentions on changing snacking habits. *Health Psychology, 29,* 284–292.

Tamada, K., Machida, S., Oikawa, T., Miyamoto, H., Nishimura, T., & Kurosaka, D. (2010). Correlation between photopic negative response of focal electroretinograms and local loss of retinal neurons in glaucoma. *Current Eye Research, 35,* 155–164.

Tamis-LeMonda, C., & McFadden, K. E. (2010). The United States of America. In M. H. Bornstein (Ed.), *Handbook of cultural developmental science.* New York: Psychology Press.

Tamminga, C. A. (2006). The neurobiology of cognition in schizophrenia. *Journal of Clinical Psychology, 67,* e11.

Tamnes, C. K., Ostby, Y., Fjell, A. M., Westlye, L. T., Due-Tønnessen, P., & Walhovd, K. W. (2010). Brain maturation in adolescence and young adulthood: Regional age-related changes in cortical thickness and white matter volume and microstructure. *Cerebral Cortex, 20,* 534–548.

Tannenbaum, S. I. (2006). Applied measurement: Practical issues and challenges. In W. Bennett, C. E. Lance, & D. J. Woehr (Eds.), *Performance measurement.* Mahwah, NJ: Erlbaum.

Tarokh, L., & Carskadon, M. A. (2008). In L. R. Squire (Ed.), *New Encyclopedia of Neuroscience.* London: Elsevier.

Tarr, M. J., & Gauthier, I. (2000). FFA: A flexible fusiform area for subordinate-level visual processing automatized by expertise. *Nature Neuroscience, 3,* 764–769.

Tarter, R. E., Vanyukov, M., Kirisci, L., Reynolds, M., & Clark, D. B. (2006). Predictors of marijuana use in adolescents before and after illicit drug use: Examination of the gateway hypothesis. *American Journal of Psychiatry, 163,* 2134–2140.

Tavris, C., & Wade, C. (1984). *The longest war: Sex differences in perspective* (2nd ed.). Fort Worth, TX: Harcourt Brace.

Tay, C., Ang, S., & Van Dyne, L. (2006). Personality, biographical characteristics, and job interview success: A longitudinal study of the mediating effects of self-efficacy and the moderating effects of internal locus of causality. *Journal of Applied Psychology, 91,* 446–454.

Taylor, F. W. (1911). *Scientific management.* New York: Harper & Row.

Taylor, H. G., & others (2010). Post-concussive symptoms in children with mild traumatic brain injury. *Neuropsychology, 24,* 148–159.

Taylor, S. E. (2011). *Health psychology* (8th ed.). New York: McGraw-Hill.

Taylor, S. E., Brown, J. D., Colvin, C. R., Block, J., & Funder, D. C. (2007). Issue 6: Do positive illusions lead to healthy behavior? In J. A. Nier (Ed.), *Taking sides: Clashing views in social psychology* (2nd ed., pp. 116–137). New York: McGraw-Hill.

Taylor, S. E., Lerner, J. S., Sherman, D. K., Sage, R. M., & McDowell, N. K. (2003a). Are self-enhancing cognitions associated with healthy or unhealthy biological profiles? *Journal of Personality and Social Psychology, 85,* 605–615.

Taylor, S. E., Lerner, J. S., Sherman, D. K., Sage, R. M., & McDowell, N. K. (2003b). Portrait of the self-enhancer: Well adjusted and well liked or maladjusted and friendless? *Journal of Personality and Social Psychology, 84,* 165–176.

Taylor, S. E., Saphire-Bernstein, S., & Seeman, T. E. (2010). Are plasma oxytocin in women and plasma vasopressin in men biomarkers of distressed pair bond relationships? *Psychological Science, 21,* 3–7.

Taylor, S. E., & Sherman, D. K. (2008). Self-enhancement and self-affirmation: The consequences of positive self-thoughts for motivation and health. In W. Gardner & J. Shah (Eds.), *Handbook of motivation science.* New York: Guilford.

Teague, H. F., Rouch, P. A., Woodard, J. S., Hatch, D. R., Zdanski, C. J., Buss, E., & Buchman, C. A. (2010). Cochlear implantation in children with auditory neuropathy spectrum disorder. *Ear and Hearing.* (in press)

Teesson, M., & Vogl, L. (2006). Major depressive disorder is common among Native Americans, women, the middle aged, the poor, the widowed, separated, or divorced people. *Evidence-Based Mental Health, 9,* 59.

Tellegen, A., Ben-Porath, Y. S., & Sellbom, M. (2009). Construct validity of the MMPI-2 restructured clinical (RC) scales: Reply to Rouse, Green, Butcher, Nichols, and Williams. *Journal of Personality Assessment, 91,* 211–221.

Tenenbaum, J. B., Griffiths, T. L., & Kemp, C. (2006). Theory-based Bayesian models of inductive learning and reasoning. *Trends in Cognitive Science, 10,* 309–318.

Teodorescu, M., & others. (2006). Correlates of daytime sleepiness in patients with asthma. *Sleep Medicine, 7,* 607–613.

Tepper, B. J., Duffy, M. K., Hoobler, J., & Ensley, M. D. (2004). Moderators of the relationships between coworkers' organizational citizenship behavior and fellow employees' attitudes. *Journal of Applied Psychology, 89,* 455–465.

Terman, L. (1925). *Genetic studies of genius. Vol. 1: Mental and physical traits of a thousand gifted children.* Stanford, CA: Stanford University Press.

Terr, L. C. (1988). What happens to early memories of trauma? *Journal of the American Academy of Child and Adolescent Psychiatry, 27,* 96–104.

Terry, S. (2009). *Learning and memory* (4th ed.). Upper Saddle River, NJ: Prentice-Hall.

Tharoor, H., Dinesh, N., Chauhan, A., Mathew, A., & Sharma, P. S. V. N. (2007). Dissociative amnesia related to pregnancy. *German Journal of Psychiatry, 10,* 119–121.

Thaxton, L., Emshoff, J. G., & Guessous, O. (2005). Prostate cancer support groups: A literature review. *Journal of Psychosocial Oncology, 23* (1), 25–40.

Theeuwes, J., Belopolsky, A., & Olivers, C. N. (2009). Interactions between working memory, attention, and eye movements. *Acta Psychologica, 132,* 106–114.

Thigpen, C. H., & Cleckley, H. M. (1957). *Three faces of Eve.* New York: McGraw-Hill.

Thomas, M., Sing, H., Belenky, G., Holcomb, H., Mayberg, H., Dannals, R., Wagner, H., Thorne, D., Popp, K., Rowland, L., Welsh, A., Balwinksi, S., & Redmond, D. (2001). Neural basis of alertness and cognitive performance impairments during sleepiness: I. Effects of 24 hours of sleep deprivation on waking human regional brain activity. *Journal of Sleep Research, 9,* 335–352.

Thomas, M., Tyers, P., Lazic, S. E., Barker, R. A., Beazley, L., & Ziman, M. (2009). Graft outcomes influences by co-expression of Pax7 in graft and host tissue. *Journal of Anatomy, 214,* 396–405.

Thomas, M. S. C., & Johnson, M. H. (2008). New advances in understanding sensitive periods in brain development. *Current Directions in Psychological Science, 17,* 1–5.

Thompson, L., & others. (2005). Dispositional forgiveness of self, others, and situations. *Journal of Personality, 73,* 313–359.

Thompson, P. M., Giedd, J. N., MacDonald, D., Evans, A. C., & Toga, A. W. (2000). Growth patterns in the developing brain by using continuum sensor maps. *Nature, 404,* 190–193.

Thompson, R. A. (2009). Unpublished review of J. W. Santrock's *Life-Span Development* (13th ed.). New York: McGraw-Hill.

Thompson, R. A. (2009b). Early foundations: Conscience and the development of moral character. In D. Narvaez & D. Lapsley (Eds.), *Moral self, identity, and character.* New York: Cambridge University Press.

Thompson, R. A. (2010). Feeling and understanding through the prism of relationships. In S. D. Calkins & M. A. Bell (Eds.), *Child development at the intersection of emotion and cognition* (pp. 79–95). Washington, DC: American Psychological Association.

Thompson, R. A., & Newton, E. (2009). Infant-caregiver communicaton. In H. T. Reis & S. Sprecher (Eds.), *Encyclopedia of human relationships.* Thousand Oaks, CA: Sage.

Thompson, S. C. (2001). The role of personal control in adaptive functioning. In C. R. Snyder & S. J. Lopez (Eds.), *Handbook of positive psychology.* New York: Oxford University Press.

Thompson-Brenner, H., Boisseau, C. L., & Satir, D. A. (2010). Adolescent eating disorders: Treatment and response in a naturalistic study. *Journal of Clinical Psychology, 66,* 277–301.

Thomsen, D. K. (2009). There is more to life stories than memory. *Memory, 17,* 1–13.

Thomsen, M., Hall, F. S., Uhl, G. R., & Caine, S. B. (2009). Dramatically decreased cocaine self-administration in dopamine but not serotonin transporter knock-out mice. *Journal of Neuroscience, 29,* 1087–1092.

Thoresen, C. J., Kaplan, S. A., Barsky, A. P., Warren, C. R., & de Chermont, K. (2003). The affective underpinnings of job perceptions and attitudes: A meta-analytic review and integration. *Psychological Bulletin, 129,* 914–945.

Thorndike, E. L. (1898). *Animal intelligence: An experimental study of the associative processes in animals* (Psychological Review, monograph supplements, no. 8). New York: Macmillan.

Thornicroft, G., Brohan, E., Rose, D., Sartorius, N., Lees, M., & the INDIGO Study Group. (2009). Global pattern of experienced and anticipated discrimination against people with schizophrenia: A cross-sectional survey. *Lancet, 373,* 408–415.

Thunedborg, K., Black, C. H., & Bech, P. (1995). Beyond the Hamilton depression scores in long-term treatment of manic-melancholic patients: Prediction of recurrence of depression by quality of life measurements. *Psychotherapy and Psychosomatics, 64,* 131–140.

Tikhomirov, A. A., & Spangler, W. D. (2010). Neo-charismatic leadership and the fate of mergers and acquisitions: An institutional model of CEO leadership. *Journal of Leadership and Organizational Studies, 17,* 44–60.

Timimi, S. (2004). A critique of the international consensus statement on ADHD. *Clinical Child and Family Psychology Review, 7* (1), 59–63.

Tinbergen, N. (1969). *The study of instinct.* New York: Oxford University Press.

Todorov, A., Mandisodza, A. N., Goren, A., & Hall, C. C. (2005). Inferences of competence from faces predict election outcomes. *Science, 308* (5728), 1623–1626.

Todd, R. M., Evans, J. W., Morris, D., Lewis, M. D., & Taylor, M. J. (2010). The changing face of emotion: Age-related patterns of amygdala activation to salient faces. *Social Cognitive and Affective Neuroscience.* (in press)

Tolman, E. C. (1932). *Purposive behavior in animals and man.* New York: Appleton-Century-Crofts.

Tolman, E. C., & Honzik, C. H. (1930). Degrees of hunger, reward and non-reward, and maze performance in rats. *University of California Publications in Psychology, 4,* 21–256.

Tong, E. K., Strouse, R., Hall, J., Kovac, M., & Schroeder, S. A. (2010). National survey of U.S. health professionals' smoking prevalence, cessation practices, and beliefs. *Nicotine and Tobacco Research.* (in press)

Tong, F., Nakayama, K., Moscovitch, M., Weinrib, O., & Kanwisher, N. (2000). Response properties of the human fusiform face area. *Cognitive Neuropsychology, 17,* 257–279.

Tononi, G., & Cirelli, C. (2011). Sleep and synaptic plasticity. *Annual Review of Psychology* (vol. 62). Palo Alto, CA: Annual Reviews.

Topolinski, S., & Strack, F. (2008). Where there's a will—there's no intuition: The unintentional basis of semantic coherence judgments. *Journal of Memory and Language, 58,* 1032–1048.

Topolinski, S., & Strack, F. (2010). Scanning the "fringe of consciousness": What is felt and what is not felt in intuition about semantic coherence. *Consciousness and Cognition.* (in press)

Torchinsky, A., & Toder, V. (2010). Mechanisms of the embryo's response to embryopathic stressors: A focus on p53. *Journal of Reproductive Immunology.* (in press)

Torriero, S., & others. (2010). Changes in cerebello–motor connectivity during procedural learning by actual execution and observation. *Journal of Cognitive Neuroscience.* (in press)

Tourian, K. A., Jiang, Q., & Ninan, P. T. (2010). Analysis of the effect of desvenlafaxine on anxiety symptoms associated with major depressive disorder: Pooled data from 9 short-term, double-blind, placebo controlled trials. *CNS Spectrums, 15,* 187–93.

Travis, F., & Shear, J. (2010). Focused attention, open monitoring, and automatic self-transcending: Categories to organize meditations from Vedic, Buddhist, and Chinese traditions. *Consciousness and Cognition.* (in press)

Trawaiter, S., & Shapiro, J. R. (2010). Racial bias and stereotyping: Interpersonal processes. In B. Gawronski & B. K. Payne (Eds.), *Handbook of implicit cognition.* New York: Guilford.

Treasure, J., Claudino, A. M., & Zucker, N. (2010). Eating disorders. *Lancet, 375,* 583–593.

Tremblay, T., Monetta, L., & Joanette, Y. (2009). Complexity and hemispheric abilities: Evidence for a differential impact on semantics and phonology. *Brain and Language, 108,* 67–72.

Triandis, H. C. (2000). Cross-cultural psychology: History of the field. In A. Kazdin (Ed.), *Encyclopedia of psychology.* Washington, DC, & New York: American Psychological Association and Oxford University Press.

Triandis, H. C. (2007). Culture and psychology: A history of the study of their relationship. In S. Kitayama & D. Cohen (Eds.), *Handbook of cultural psychology* (pp. 59–76). New York: Guilford.

Trickett, E. J. (2009). Multilevel community-based culturally situated interventions and community impact: An ecological perspective. *American Journal of Community Psychology, 43,* 257–266.

Trinkler, I., King, J. A., Doeller, C. F., Rugg, M. D., & Burgess, N. (2009). Neural bases of autobiographical support for episodic recollection of faces. *Hippocampus, 19,* 718–730.

Triplett, N. (1898). The dynamogenic factors in pacemaking and competition. *American Journal of Psychology, 9,* 507–533.

Tropp, L. R., & Wright, S. C. (2003). Evaluations and perceptions of self, ingroup, and outgroup: Comparisons between Mexican-American and European-American children. *Self and Identity, 2,* 203–221.

Trudel, E., & Bourque, C. W. (2010). Central clock excites vasopressin neurons by waking osmosensory afferents during late sleep. *Nature Neuroscience.* (in press)

Trull, T. J., & Widiger, T. A. (2003). Personality disorders. In I. B. Weiner (Ed.), *Handbook of Psychology* (vol. 8). New York: Wiley.

Truxillo, D. M., & Bauer, T. N. (2010). Applicant reactions to organizations and selection systems. In S. Zedeck (Ed.), *APA handbook of industrial and organizational psychology.* Washington, DC: APA. (in press)

Tryon, R. C. (1940). Genetic differences in maze-learning ability in rats. In *39th Yearbook, National Society for the Study of Education.* Chicago: University of Chicago Press.

Trzesniewski, K. H., & Donnellan, M. B. (2009). Reevaluating the evidence for increasingly positive self-views among high school students: More evidence for consistency across generations (1976–2006). *Psychological Science, 20,* 920–922.

Trzesniewski, K. H., & Donnellan, M. B. (2010). Rethinking "Generation Me": A study of cohort effects from 1976–2006. *Perspectives on Psychological Science, 5,* 58–75.

Trzesniewski, K. H., Donnellan, M. B., Moffitt, T. E., Robins, R. W., Poulton, R., & Caspi, A. (2006). Low self-esteem during adolescence predicts poor health, criminal behavior, and limited economic prospects during adulthood. *Developmental Psychology, 42,* 381–390.

Trzesniewski, K. H., Donnellan, M. B., & Robins, R. W. (2008). Do today's young people really think they are so extraordinary? An examination of secular trends in narcissism and self-enhancement. *Psychological Science, 19,* 181–188.

Tsai, W., Chen, C., & Chiu, S. (2005). Exploring boundaries of the effects of applicant impression management tactics in job interviews. *Journal of Management, 31,* 108–125.

Tsenkova, V. K., Dienberg Love, G., Singer, B. H., & Ryff, C. D. (2008). Coping and positive affect predict longitudinal change in glycosylated hemoglobin. *Health Psychology, 27, Suppl. 2,* S163–S171.

Tsushima, Y., Sasaki, Y., & Watanabe, T. (2006). Greater disruption due to failure of inhibitory control on an ambiguous distractor. *Science, 314,* 1786–1788.

Tugade, M. M., Fredrickson, B. L., & Feldman Barrett, L. (2004). Psychological resilience and positive emotional granularity: Examining the benefits of positive emotions on coping and health. *Journal of Personality, 72,* 1161–1190.

Tulving, E. (1972). Episodic and semantic memory. In E. Tulving & W. Donaldson (Eds.), *Origins of memory.* San Diego: Academic.

Tulving, E. (1983). *Elements of episodic memory.* New York: Oxford University Press.

Tulving, E. (1989). Remembering and knowing the past. *American Scientist, 77,* 361–367.

Tulving, E. (2000). Concepts of memory. In E. Tulving & F. I. M. Craik (Eds.), *The Oxford handbook of memory.* New York: Oxford University Press.

Tural, U., & Onder, E. (2010). Clinical and pharmacologic risk factors for neuroleptic malignant syndrome and their association with death. *Psychiatry and Clinical Neurosciences, 64,* 79–87.

Turkheimer, E., Haley, A., Waldron, M., D'Onofrio, B., & Gottesman, I. I. (2003). Socioeconomic status modifies heritability of IQ in young children. *Psychological Science, 14,* 623–628.

Turrigiano, G. (2010). Synaptic homeostasis. *Annual Review of Neuroscience* (vol. 33). Palo Alto, CA: Annual Reviews.

Tversky, A., & Kahneman, J. (1974). Judgment under uncertainty: Heuristics and biases. *Science, 185,* 1124–1131.

Twenge, J. M. (2006). *Generation Me: Why today's young Americans are more confident, assertive, entitled—and more miserable than ever before.* New York: Free Press.

Twenge, J. M. (2008). Social exclusion, motivation, and self-defeating behavior: Why breakups lead to drunkenness and ice cream. In J. Y Shah & W. L. Gardner (Eds.), *Handbook of motivation science* (pp. 508–517). New York: Guilford.

Twenge, J. M., & Campbell, S. M. (2010). Generation Me and the changing world of work. In A. P. Linley, S. Harrington, & N. Garcea (Eds.), *Oxford handbook of positive psychology and work* (pp. 25–35). New York: Oxford University Press.

Twenge, J. M., & Campbell, W. K. (2008). Increases in positive self-views among high school students: Birth cohort changes in anticipated performance, self-satisfaction, self-liking, and self-competence. *Psychological Science, 19,* 1082–1086.

Twenge, J. M., & Campbell, W. K. (2009). *The narcissism epidemic: Living in the age of enlightenment.* New York: Free Press

Twenge, J. M., & Foster, J. D. (2008). Mapping the scale of the narcissism epidemic: Increases in narcissism 2002–2007 within ethnic groups. *Journal of Research in Personality, 42,* 1619–1622.

Tye, K. M., & Janak, P. H. (2007). Amygdala neurons differentially encode motivation and reinforcement. *Journal of Neuroscience, 27,* 3937–3945.

U

Uchida, H., & Mamo, D. C. (2009). Dosing of antipsychotics across the life-spectrum. *Progress in Neuro-Psychopharmacology and Biological Psychiatry, 33* (6), 917–920.

Uguz, F., Akman, C., Kaya, N., & Cilli, A. S. (2007). Postpartum-onset obsessive-compulsive disorder: Incidence, clinical features, and related factors. *Journal of Clinical Psychiatry, 68,* 132–138.

Ullman, A. D. (1952). Review of "Antabuse" in the treatment of alcoholism. *Psychological Bulletin, 49,* 557–558.

Ulrich, R. S. (1991). Stress recovery during exposure to natural and urban environments. *Journal of Environmental Psychology, 11,* 201–230.

Umana-Taylor, A. J., & Guimond, A. B. (2010). A longitudinal examination of parenting behaviors and perceived discrimination predicting Latino adolescents' ethnic identity. *Developmental Psychology, 46,* 636–650.

Underhill, K., Montgomery, P., & Operario, D. (2007). Sexual abstinence programs to prevent HIV infection in high-income countries. *British Medical Journal, 335,* 248.

United Nations Office on Drugs and Crime (UNODC). (2008). *World drug report.* Vienna: United Nations.

United Nations World Youth Report. (2005). *World youth report 2005: Young people today and in 2015.* Geneva, Switzerland: United Nations.

Unkelbach, C. (2007). Reversing the truth effect: Learning the interpretation of processing fluency in judgments of truth. *Journal of Experimental Psychology: Learning, Memory, and Cognition, 33,* 219–230.

Urban, E. (2008). The "self" in analytical psychology: The function of the "central archetype" within Fordham's model. *Journal of Analytical Psychology, 53,* 329–350.

Urcelay, G. P., Wheeler, D. S., & Miller, R. R. (2009). Spacing extinction trials alleviates renewal and spontaneous recovery. *Learning and Behavior, 37,* 60–73.

Urdan, T. (2010). Classroom goal structures, motivation, and learning. In J. L. Meece & J. S. Eccles (Eds.), *Handbook of schools, schooling, and human development.* New York: Routledge.

Urry, H. L. (2010). Seeing, thinking, and feeling: Emotion-regulating effects of gaze-directed cognitive reappraisal. *Emotion, 10,* 125–135.

Urry, H. L., Nitschke, J. B., Dolski, I., Jackson, D. C., Dalton, K. M., Mueller, C. J., Rosenkranz, M. A., Ryff, C. D., Singer, B. H., & Davidson, R. J. (2004). Making a life worth living: Neural correlates of well-being. *Psychological Science, 15,* 367–372.

USA Today. (2008, April 4). *Jackpot winner to boss: I'm outta here!* http://www.usatoday.com/news/nation/2008-04-04-jackpot-winner_N.htm (accessed April 10, 2010)

U.S. Bureau of Labor Statistics. (2006, October 27). *Survey of workplace violence prevention, 2005.* http://www.bls.gov/iif/oshwc/osnr0026.pdf. Washington, DC: Author. (accessed June 13, 2007)

U.S. Census Bureau. (2008). *People.* Washington, DC: U.S. Department of Labor.

U.S. Department of Justice. (2007). *Homicide trends in the U.S.* http://www.ojp.usdoj.gov/bjs/homicide/tables/totalstab.htm (accessed May 29, 2009)

U.S. Department of Labor. (2010–2011). *Occupational outlook handbook.* Washington, DC: Bureau of Labor Statistics.

U.S. Department of Labor. (2010). *O*NET database.* http://www.bls.gov/oco/

U.S. Food and Drug Administration. (2004, October 15). *FDA launches a multi-pronged strategy to strengthen safeguards for children treated with antidepressant medications.* News release. Washington, DC: Author.

U.S. Food and Drug Administration. (2009). *Office of Device Evaluation annual report, fiscal year 2008.* Washington, DC: Center for Devices and Radiological Health.

U.S. General Accounting Office. (1996, September). *Cycle of sexual abuse: Research inconclusive about whether child victims become adult abusers.* Report to the Chairman, Subcommittee on the Judiciary, House of Representatives.

Ussher, J., Kirsten, L., Butow, P., & Sandoval, M. (2006). What do cancer support groups provide which other supportive relationships do not? The experience of peer support groups for people with cancer. *Social Science & Medicine, 62,* 2565–2576.

Uusi-Oukari, M., & Korpi, E. R. (2010). Regulation of GABAA receptor subunit expression by pharmacological agents. *Pharmacological Reviews.* (in press)

V

Vacek, J. E. (2009). Using a conceptual approach with a concept map of psychosis as an exemplar to promote critical thinking. *Journal of Nursing Education, 48,* 49–53.

Vaes, J., Heflick, N. A., & Goldenberg, J. L. (2010). "We are people": Ingroup humanization as an existential defense. *Journal of Personality and Social Psychology, 98,* 750–760.

Vaillant, G. (2003). A 60-year follow-up of alcoholic men. *Addiction, 98,* 1043–1051.

Vakily, M., Lee, R. D., Wu, J., Gunawardhana, L., & Mulford, D. (2009). Drug interaction studies with dexiansoprazole modified release (TAK-390MR), a proton pump inhibitor with a dual delayed-release formulation. *Clinical Drug Investigation, 29,* 35–50.

Vallido, T., Jackson, D., & O'Brien, L. (2009). Mad, sad, and hormonal: The gendered nature of adolescent sleep disturbance. *Journal of Child Health Care, 13,* 7–18.

van Apeldoorn, F. J., & others. (2010). A randomized trial of cognitive-behavioral therapy or selective serotonin reuptake inhibitor or both combined for panic disorder with or without agoraphobia: treatment results through 1-year follow-up. *Journal of Clinical Psychology, 71,* 574–586.

van Atteveldt, N. M, Blau, V. C, Blomert, L., & Goebel, R. (2010). fMR-adaptation indicates selectivity to audiovisual content congruency in distributed clusters in human superior temporal cortex. *BMC Neuroscience, 11,* 11.

van Bokhoven, I., van Goozen, S. H. M., van Engeland, H., Schaal, B., Arseneault, L., Seguin, J. R., Assaad, J., Nagin, D. S., Vitaro, F., & Tremblay, R. E. (2006). Salivary testosterone and aggression, delinquency, and social dominance in a population-based longitudinal study of adolescent males. *Hormones and Behavior, 50,* 118–125.

Vandello, J. A., & Cohen, D. (2008). Culture, gender, and men's intimate partner violence. *Social and Personality Psychology Compass, 2,* 652–667.

Vandello, J. A., Cohen, D., Grandon, R., & Franiuk, R. (2009). Stand by your man: Indirect prescriptions for honorable violence and feminine loyalty in Canada, Chile, and the United States. *Journal of Cross-Cultural Psychology, 40,* 81–104.

van der Geest, V., Blokland, A., & Bijleveld, C. (2009). Delinquent development in a sample of high-risk youth: Shape, content, and predictors of delinquent trajectories from age 12 to 32. *Journal of Research in Crime and Delinquency, 46,* 111–143.

Van der Werf, J., Jensen, O., Fries, P., & Medendorp, W. P. (2010). Neuronal synchronization in human posterior parietal cortex during reach planning. *Journal of Neuroscience, 30,* 1402–1412.

Van Dick, R., Becker, T. E., & Meyer, J. P. (2006). Commitment and identification: Forms, foci, and future. *Journal of Organizational Behavior, 27,* 545–548.

van Driel, M. A., & Brunner, H. G. (2006). Bioinformatics methods for identifying candidate disease genes. *Human Genomics. 2,* 429–432.

van Ettinger-Veenspheric, H. M., & others. (2010). Right-hemispheric brain activation correlates to language performance. *NeuroImage, 49,* 3481–3488.

van IJzendoorn, M. H., & Sagi-Schwartz, A. (2008). Cross-cultural patterns of attachment: Universal and contextual dimensions. In J. Cassidy & P. R. Shaver (Eds.), *Handbook of attachment.* New York: Guilford.

van Ingen, D. J., & Novicki, D. J. (2009). An effectiveness study of group therapy for anxiety disorders. *International Journal of Group Psychotherapy, 59,* 243–251.

Van Katwyk, P. T., Fox, S., Spector, P. E., & Kelloway, E. K. (2000). Using the job-related affective well-being scale (JAWS) to investigate affective responses to work stressors. *Journal of Occupational Health Psychology, 52,* 219–230.

Van Lange, P. A. M., Rusbult, C. E., Drigotas, S. M., & Arriaga, X. B. (1997). Willingness to sacrifice in close relationships. *Journal of Personality and Social Psychology, 72,* 1373–1395.

van Lankveld, J. (2008). Problems with sexual interest and desire in women. In D. L. Rowland & L. Incrocci (Eds.), *Handbook of sexual and gender identity disorders* (pp. 154–185). Hoboken, NJ: Wiley.

Van Orden, K. A., Whitte, T. K., Gordon, K. H., Bender, T. W., & Joiner, T. E. (2008). Suicidal desire and the capability of suicide: Tests of the interpersonal-psychological theory of suicidal behavior among adults. *Journal of Consulting and Clinical Psychology, 76,* 72–83.

Van Orden, K. A., & others. (2010). The interpersonal theory of suicide. *Psychological Review, 117,* 575–600.

van Os, J., & Kapur, S. (2009). Schizophrenia. *Lancet, 374,* 635–645.

van Remmen, H., & Jones, D. P. (2009). Current thoughts on the role of mitochondria and free radicals in the biology of aging. *Journals of Gerontology A: Biological Sciences and Medical Sciences, 64,* 171–174.

Van Riper, M. (2007). Families of children with Down syndrome: Responding to "a change in plans" with resilience. *Journal of Pediatric Nursing, 22,* 116–128.

van Son, G. E., van Hoeken, D., van Furth, E. F., Donker, G. A., & Hoek, H. W. (2010). Course and outcome of eating disorders in a primary care–based cohort. *International Journal of Eating Disorders, 43,* 130–138.

Van Voorhees, B. W., & others. (2009). Randomized clinical trial of an Internet-based depression prevention program for adolescents (Project CATCH-IT) in primary care: 12-week outcomes. *Journal of Developmental and Behavioral Pediatrics, 30,* 23–37.

Vassilopoulos, S. P., & Watkins, E. R. (2009). Adaptive and maladaptive self-focus: A pilot extension study with individuals high and low in fear of negative evaluation. *Behavior Therapy, 40,* 181–189.

Vaughn, S., Bos, C. S., & Schumm, J. S. (2003). *Teaching exceptional, diverse, and at-risk students in the general education classroom* (3rd ed.). Boston: Allyn & Bacon.

Vazire, S. (2010). Who knows what about a person? The self-other knowledge asymmetry (SOKA) model. *Journal of Personality and Social Psychology, 98,* 281–300.

Vazsonyi, A. T., & Huang, L. (2010). Where self-control comes from: On the development of self-control and its relationship to deviance over time. *Developmental Psychology, 46,* 245–257.

Vega, G. L., Barlow, C. E., & Grundy, S. M. (2010). Prevalence of the metabolic syndrome as influenced by the measure of obesity employed. *American Journal of Cardiology, 105,* 1306–1302.

Vega, V., & Malamuth, N. M. (2007). Predicting sexual aggression: The role of pornography in the context of general and specific risk factors. *Aggressive Behavior, 33,* 104–117.

Vermetten, E., Schmahl, C., Lindner, S., Loewenstein, R. J., & Bremner, J. D. (2006). Hippocampal and amygdalar volumes in dissociative identity disorder. *American Journal of Psychiatry, 163,* 630–636.

Verquer, M. L., Beehr, T. A., & Wagner, S. H. (2003). A meta-analysis of relations between person–organization fit and work attitudes. *Journal of Vocational Behavior, 63,* 473–489.

Verschuere, B., Crombez, G., De Clercq, A., & Koster, E. H. W. (2005). Psychopathic traits and autonomic responding to concealed information in a prison sample. *Psychophysiology, 42,* 239–245.

Vervaet, M., van Heeringen, C., & Audenaert, K. (2004). Personality-related characteristics in restricting versus binging and purging eating disordered patients. *Comprehensive Psychiatry, 45,* 37–43.

Veselka, L., Schermer, J. A., Petrides, K. V., & Verson, P. A. (2009). Evidence for a heritable general factor of personality in two studies. *Twin Research and Human Genetics, 12,* 254–260.

Vetter, S., & others. (2010). Impact of resilience enhancing programs on youth surviving the Belsan school siege. *Child and Adolescent Psychiatry and Mental Health.* (in press)

Vickerman, K. A., & Margolin, G. (2009). Rape treatment outcome research: Empirical findings and state of the literature. *Clinical Psychology Review, 29* (5), 431–448.

Victor, A. M., & Bernstein, G. A. (2009). Anxiety disorders and posttraumatic stress disorder update. *Psychiatric Clinics of North America, 32,* 57–69.

Videtic, A., Zupanic, T., Pregelj, P., Balazic, J., Tomori, M., & Komel, R. (2009). Suicide, stress, and serotonin receptor 1A promotor polymorphism -1019>G in Slovenian suicide victims. *European Archives of Psychiatry and Clinical Neuroscience, 259,* 234–238.

Vidoni, E. D., Acerraa, N. E., Dao, E., Meehan, S. K., & Boyd, L. A. (2010). Role of the primary somatosensory cortex in motor learning: An rTMS study. *Neurobiology of Learning and Memory.* (in press)

Vimal, R. L., & others. (2009). Activation of the suprachiasmatic nuclei and primary visual cortex depends upon time of day. *European Journal of Neuroscience, 29,* 399–410.

Vinberg, M., Mellerup, E., Andersen, P. K., Bennike, B., & Kessing, L. V. (2010). Variations in 5-HTTLPR: Relation to familiar risk of affective disorder, life events, neuroticism, and cortisol. *Progress in Neuro-Psychopharmacology & Biological Psychiatry, 34,* 86–91.

Vinchur, A. J., & Koppes, L. L. (2010). A historical survey of research and practice in industrial and organizational psychology. In S. Zedeck (Ed.), *APA handbook of industrial and organizational psychology.* Washington, DC: APA. (in press)

Vismara, L. A., & Rogers, S. J. (2010). Behavioral treatments in autism spectrum disorder: What do we know? *Annual Review of Clinical Psychology, 6,* 447–468.

Vogt, T. M., Mullooly, J. P., Ernst, D., Pople, C. R., & Hollis, J. F. (1992). Social networks as predictors of ischemic heart disease, cancer, stroke, and hypertension. *Journal of Clinical Epidemiology, 45,* 659–666.

Volskuijl, O. F., & Evers, A. (2008). Job analysis and competency modeling. In S. Cartwright & C. L. Cooper (Eds.), *The Oxford handbook of personnel psychology* (pp. 138–162). New York: Oxford University Press.

von Békésy, G. (1960). Vibratory patterns of the basilar membrane. In E. G. Wever (Ed.), *Experiments in hearing.* New York: McGraw-Hill.

von Helmholtz, H. (1852). On the theory of compound colors. *Philosophical Magazine, 4,* 519–534.

Voshaar, R. C., & others. (2006). Predictors of long-term benzodiazepine abstinence in participants of a randomized controlled benzodiazepine withdrawal program. *Canadian Journal of Psychiatry, 51,* 445–452.

Voss, J. L., & Paller, K. A. (2009). An electrophysiological signature of unconscious recognition memory. *Nature Neuroscience, 13,* 349–355.

Voyvodic, J. T., Petrella, J. R., & Friedman, A. H. (2009). fMRI activation mapping as a percentage of local excitation: Consistent presurgical motor maps without threshold adjustment. *Journal of Magnetic Resonance Imaging, 29,* 751–759.

Vuillermot, S., Weber, L., Feldon, J., & Meyer, U. (2010). A longitudinal examination of the neurodevelopmental impact of prenatal immune activation in mice reveals primary defects in dopaminergic development relevant to schizophrenia. *Journal of Neuroscience, 30,* 1270–1287.

Vukovic, J., & others. (2009). Lack of fibulin-3 alters regenerative tissue responses in the primary olfactory pathway. *Matrix Biology, 28,* 406–415.

Vygotsky, L. S. (1962). *Thought and language.* Cambridge, MA: MIT Press.

W

Waddell, E. L., & Jacobs-Lawson, J. M. (2010). Predicting positive well-being in older men and women. *International Journal of Aging and Human Development, 70,* 181–197.

Wagner, A. D., Schacter, D. L., Rotte, M., Koutstaal, B., Maril, A., Dale, A. M., Rosen, B. R., & Buckner, R. L. (1998). Building memories: Remembering and forgetting of verbal experiences as predicted by brain activity. *Science, 281,* 1185–1187.

Wai, J., Lubinski, D., & Benbow, C. P. (2005). Creativity and occupational accomplishments among intellectually precocious youths: An age 13 to age 33 longitudinal study. *Journal of Educational Psychology, 97,* 484–492.

Wainwright, J. L., & Patterson, C. J. (2008). Peer relations among adolescents with female same-sex parents. *Developmental Psychology, 44,* 117–126.

Wald, A., Langenberg, A. G., & Krantz, E. (2005). The relationship between condom use and herpes simplex virus acquisition. *Annals of Internal Medicine, 143,* 707–713.

Walker, D. D., Roffman, R. A., Stephens, R. S., Wakana, K., & Berghuis, J. (2006). Motivational enhancement therapy for adolescent marijuana users: A preliminary randomized controlled trial. *Journal of Consulting and Clinical Psychology, 74,* 628–632.

Walker, D. R., & Milton, G. A. (1966). Memory transfer vs. sensitization in cannibal planarians. *Psychonomic Science, 5,* 293–294.

Walker, H. (2008). *Breaking free: My life with dissociative disorder.* New York: Simon & Schuster.

Walker, L. E. A. (2009). *The battered woman syndrome* (3rd ed.). New York: Springer.

Walker, L. J., & Frimer, J. A. (2011). The science of moral development. In M. K. Underwood & L. H. Rosen (Eds.), *Social development.* New York: Guilford. (in press)

Waller, E. A., Bendel, R. E., & Kaplan, J. (2008). Sleep disorders and the eye. *Mayo Clinic Proceedings, 83,* 1251–1261.

Wallerstein, R. S. (1989). The psychotherapy research project of the Menninger Foundation: An overview. *Journal of Consulting and Clinical Psychology, 57,* 195–205.

Walter, K. H., Horsey, K. J., Palmieri, P. A., & Hobfoll, S. E. (2010). The role of protective self-cognitions in the relationship between childhood trauma and later resource loss. *Journal of Traumatic Stress, 23,* 264–273.

Wampold, B. E. (2001). *The great psychotherapy debate: Models, methods, and findings.* Mahwah, NJ: Erlbaum.

Wampold, B. E., & Brown, G. S. (2005). Estimating variability in outcomes attributable to therapists: A naturalistic study of outcomes of managed care. *Journal of Consulting and Clinical Psychology, 73,* 914–923.

Wamsley, E. J., Perry, K., Djonlagic, I., Reaven, L. B., & Stickgold, R. (2010). Cognitive replay of visuomotor learning at sleep onset: Temporal dynamics and relationship to task performance. *Sleep, 33,* 59–88.

Wanat, M. J., Sparta, D. R., Hopf, F. W., Bowers, M. S., Melis, M., & Bonci, A. (2009). Strain specific synaptic modifications on ventral tegmental area dopamine neurons after ethanol exposure. *Biological Psychiatry, 65,* 646–653.

Wang, L., Li, C. C., Wang, G. W., & Cai, J. X. (2009). The effects of centrally administered fluorocitrate via inhibiting glial cells on working memory in rats. *Science in China. Series C, Life Sciences, 52,* 701–719.

Wang, S.-H., & Morris, R. G. M. (2010). Hippocampal-neocortical interactions in memory formation, consolidation, and reconsolidation. *Annual Review of Psychology* (vol. 61). Palo Alto, CA: Annual Reviews.

Wangberg, S. C., Gammon, D., & Spitznogle, K. (2007). In the eyes of the beholder: Exploring psychologists' attitudes towards the use of e-therapy in Norway. *CyberPsychology and Behavior, 10,* 418–423.

Ward, J. (2010). *The student's guide to cognitive neuroscience* (2nd ed.). New York: Psychology Press.

Ward, J., Jonas, C., Dienes, Z., & Seth, A. (2010). Grapheme-colour synaesthesia improves detection of embedded shapes, but without pre-attentive "pop-out" of synaesthetic color. *Proceedings: Biological Sciences.* (in press)

Ward, T. B. (2007). Creative cognition as a window on creativity. *Methods, 42,* 28–37.

Wardlaw, G. M., & Smith, A. M. (2011). *Contemporary nutrition* (8th ed.). New York: McGraw-Hill.

Warnecke, R. B., Morera, O., Turner, L., Mermelstein, R., Johnson, T. P., Parsons, J., Crittenden, K., Freels, S., & Flay, B. (2001). Changes in self-efficacy and readiness for smoking cessation among women with high school or less education. *Journal of Health and Social Behavior, 42,* 97–109.

Warren, G., Schertler, E., & Bull, P. (2009). Detecting deception from emotional and unemotional cues. *Journal of Nonverbal Behavior, 33,* 59–69.

Warren, J. I., Stein, J. A., & Grella, C. E. (2007). Role of social support and self-efficacy in treatment outcomes among clients with co-occurring disorders. *Drug and Alcohol Dependence, 89,* 267–274.

Wasserman, D., Wasserman, J., & Sokolowski, M. (2010). Genetics of HPA-axis, depression, and suicidality. *European Psychiatry.* (in press)

Watanabe, H., & Mizunami, M. (2007). Pavlov's cockroach: Classical conditioning of salivation in an insect. *PloS One, 6,* e529.

Watson, A., El-Deredy, W., Bentley, D. E., Vogt, B. A., & Jones, A. K. (2006). Categories of placebo response in the absence of site-specific stimulation of analgesia. *Pain, 126,* 115–122.

Watson, D. (2001). Positive affectivity: The disposition to experience pleasurable emotional states. In C. R. Snyder & S. J. Lopez (Eds.), *Handbook of positive psychology.* New York: Oxford University Press.

Watson, D. (2009). Differentiation of mood and anxiety disorders. *Annual Review of Clinical Psychology* (vol. 5). Palo Alto, CA: Annual Reviews.

Watson, D., & Clark, L. A. (1997). Extraversion and its positive emotional core. In R. Hogan, J. A. Johnson, & S. R., Briggs (Eds.), *Handbook of personality psychology* (pp. 767–793). San Diego: Academic.

Watson, D., & Naragon, K. (2009). Positive affectivity: The disposition to experience positive emotional states. In S. J. Lopez & C. R. Snyder (Eds.), *Oxford handbook of positive psychology* (2nd ed., pp. 207–215). New York: Oxford University Press.

Watson, J. B., & Rayner, R. (1920). Conditioned emotional reactions. *Journal of Experimental Psychology, 3,* 1–14.

Waugaman, R. M. (2005). Substance abuse and borderline personality disorder. *American Journal of Psychiatry, 162,* 1759.

Wayment, H. A., & O'Mara, E. M. (2008). The collective and compassionate consequences of downward social comparisons. In H. A. Wayment & J. J. Bauer (Eds.), *Transcending self-interest: Psychological explorations of the quiet ego* (pp. 159–169). Washington, DC: American Psychological Association.

Weaver, K., Garcia, S. M., Schwarz, N., & Miller, D. T. (2007). Inferring the popularity of an opinion from its familiarity: A repetitive voice can sound like a chorus. *Journal of Personality and Social Psychology, 92,* 821–833.

Webb, W. B. (2000). Sleep. In A. Kazdin (Ed.), *Encyclopedia of psychology.* Washington, DC, & New York: American Psychological Association and Oxford University Press.

Weber, S., Habel, U., Amunts, K., & Schneider, F. (2008). Structural brain abnormalities in psychopaths—A review. *Behaviorial Sciences and the Law, 26,* 7–28.

Webster, J. M., Smith, R. H., Rhodes, A., & Whatley, M. A. (1999). The effect of a favor on public and private compliance: How internalized is the norm of reciprocity? *Basic and Applied Social Psychology, 21,* 251–260.

Wechsler, H., Lee, J. E., Kuo, M., & Lee, H. (2000). College binge drinking in the 1990s—A continuing health problem: Results of the Harvard University School of Public Health 1999 College Alcohol Study. *Journal of American College Health, 48,* 199–210.

Wechsler, H., Lee, J. E., Kuo, M., Seibring, M., Nelson, T. F., & Lee, H. (2002). Trends in college binge drinking during a period of increased prevention efforts: Findings from 4 Harvard School of Public Health college alcohol study surveys: 1993–2001. *Journal of American College Health, 50,* 203–217.

Wecker, L., & others. (2010). *Brody's human pharmacology* (5th ed.). London: Elsevier.

Weerda, R., Muehlhan, M., Wolf, O. T., & Thiel, C. M. (2010). Effects of acute psychosocial stress on working memory related brain activity in men. *Human Brain Mapping.* (in press)

Wegener, D. T., Clark, J. K., & Petty, R. E. (2006). Not all stereotyping is created equal: Differential consequences of thoughtful versus non-thoughtful stereotyping. *Journal of Personality and Social Psychology, 90,* 42–59.

Weiner, B. (2006). Social motivation, justice, and the moral emotions: An attributional approach. Mahwah, NJ: Erlbaum.

Weiner, I. B. (2004). Rorschach assessment: Current status. In M. Hersen (Ed.), *Comprehensive handbook of psychological assessment* (vol. 2). New York: Wiley.

Weinstein, T. A. R., Capitanio, J. P., & Gosling, S. D. (2008). Personality in animals. In O. P. John, R. W. Robins, & L. A. Pervin (Eds.), *Handbook of personality theory and research* (3rd ed., pp. 328–350). New York: Guilford.

Weir, W. (1984, October 15). Another look at subliminal "facts." *Advertising Age,* 46.

Weis, C. O., & others. (2010). Relationships of cardiac, pulmonary, and muscle reserves and frailty to exercise capacity in older women. *Journals of Gerontology A: Biological Sciences and Medical Sciences, 65A,* 287–294.

Weismiller, D. G. (2009). Menopause. *Primary Care, 36,* 199–226.

Weiss, B., & Feldman, R. S. (2006). Looking good and lying to do it: Deception as an impression management strategy in job interviews. *Journal of Applied Social Psychology, 36,* 1070–1086.

Weissman, M., & Olfson, M. (1995). Depression in women: Implications for health care research. *Science, 269,* 99–801.

Weissman, M. M. (2009). Teenaged, depressed, and treatment resistant: What predicts self-harm? *American Journal of Psychiatry, 166,* 385–387.

Wellen, M. (2010). Differentiation between demoralization, grief, and anhedonic depression. *Current Psychiatry Reports, 12,* 229–233.

Wellman, H. M., & Woolley, J. D. (1990). From simple desires to ordinary beliefs: The early development of everyday psychology. *Cognition, 35,* 245–275.

Wenzel, M. (2009). Social identity and justice: Implications for intergroup relations. In S. Otten, K. Sassenberg, & T. Kessler (Eds.), *Intergroup relations.* New York: Psychology Press.

Werner, J. M., & Bolino, M. C. (1997). Explaining U.S. courts of appeals decisions involving performance appraisal: Accuracy, fairness, and validation. *Personnel Psychology, 50,* 1–24.

Werner, K., & Gross, J. J. (2010). Emotion regulation and psychopathology: A conceptual framework. In A. M. Kring & D. M. Sloan (Eds.), *Emotion regulation and psychopathology: A transdiagnostic approach to etiology and treatment* (pp. 13–37). New York: Guilford.

Wesson, M. J., & Gogus, C. I. (2005). Shaking hands with a computer: An examination of two methods of organizational newcomer orientation. *Journal of Applied Psychology, 90,* 1018–1026.

West, R. (2005). Time for a change: Putting the transtheoretical (stages of change) model to rest. *Addiction, 100,* 1036–1039.

Westen, D., Gabbard, G. O., & Soto, C. J. (2008). Psychoanalytic approaches to personality. In O. P. John, R. W. Robins, & L. A. Pervin (Eds.) *Handbook of personality theory and research* (3rd ed., pp. 61–113). New York: Guilford.

Weyers, P., Muhlberger, A., Kund, A., Hess, U., & Pauli, P. (2009). Modulation of facial reactions to avatar emotional faces by nonconscious competition priming. *Psychophysiology, 46,* 328–335.

Wheeler, D. S., & Miller, R. R. (2008). Determinants of cue interactions. *Behavioral Processes, 78,* 191–203.

Whiffen, V. E., & Demidenko, N. (2006). Mood disturbances across the lifespan. In J. Worell & C. D. Goodheart (Eds.), *Handbook of girls' and women's health: Gender and well-being across the lifespan.* New York: Oxford University Press.

Whitaker, R. (2002). Mad in America: Bad science, bad medicine, and the mistreatment of the mentally ill. Cambridge, MA: Perseus.

White, J. W., & Frabutt, J. M. (2006). Violence against girls and women: An integrative developmental perspective. In J. Worell & C. D. Goodheart (Eds.), *Handbook of girls' and women's psychological health: Gender and well-being across the lifespan* (pp. 85–93). New York: Oxford University Press.

White, R. C., & Aimola Davies, A. (2008). Attention set for numbers: Expectation and perceptual load in inattentional blindness. *Journal of Experimental Psychology: Human Perception and Performance, 34,* 1092–1107.

White, R. W. (1992). Exploring personality the long way: The study of lives. In R. A. Zucker, A. I. Rabin, J. Aronoff, & S. J. Frank (Eds.), *Personality structure in the life course: Essays on personology in the Murray tradition* (pp. 3–21). New York: Springer.

Whorf, B. L. (1956). *Language, thought, and creativity.* New York: Wiley.

Widiger, T. A. (2009). Neuroticism. In M. R. Leary & R. H. Hoyle (Eds.), *Handbook of individual differences in social behavior* (pp. 129–146). New York: Guilford.

Wiebe, R. P. (2004). Delinquent behavior and the Five Factor model: Hiding in the adaptive landscape? *Individual Differences Research, 2,* 38–62.

Wiedeman, R. (2008, March 25). Digital man. *Boston Globe.* http://www.boston.com/news/education/higher/articles/2008/03/25/digital_man/

Wiegand, B., & others. (2010). Efficacy of a comprehensive program for reducing stress in women: A prospective, randomized trial. *Current Medical Research and Opinion, 26,* 991–1002.

Wiegand, D. M., & Geller, E. S. (2004). Connecting positive psychology and organizational behavior management: Achievement motivation and the power of positive reinforcement. *Journal of Organizational Behavior Management, 24,* 3–24.

Wiersma, D., Nienhuis, F. J., Slooff, C. J., & Giel, R. (1998). Natural course of schizophrenic disorders: A 15-year follow up of a Dutch incidence cohort. *Schizophrenia Bulletin, 24,* 75–85.

Wiese, H., & Schweinberger, S. R. (2010). Accessing semantic person knowledge: Temporal dynamics of nonstrategic categorical and associative priming. *Journal of Cognitive Neurosceince.* (in press)

Wigfield, A., Eccles, J. S., Schiefele, U., Roeser, R. W., & Davis-Kean, P. (2006). Development of achievement motivation. In W. Damon & R. Lerner (Eds.), *Handbook of child psychology* (6th ed.). New York: Wiley.

Wijesiri, L. (2005, October 21). Meditation's effect on the brain. *Ceylon Daily News.* http://www.maithri.com/links/articles/meditation_effect_brain.htm (accessed April 23, 2010)

Wijnen, V. J., & van Boxtel, G. J. (2010). The continuing problem of diagnosing unresponsive patients: Searching for neuropsychological correlates of consciousness. *Clinical Neurophysiology.* (in press)

Wildman, J. L., Bedwell, W. L., Salas, E., & Smith-Jentsch, K. A. (2010). Performance measurement at work: A multilevel perspective. In S. Zedeck (Ed.), *APA handbook of industrial and organizational psychology.* Washington, DC: APA. (in press)

Wilfley, D. E., Friedman, M. A., Dounchis, J. Z., Stein, R. I., Welch, R. R., & Ball, S. A. (2000). Comorbid psychopathology in binge eating disorder: Relation to eating disorder severity at baseline and following treatment. *Journal of Consulting and Clinical Psychology, 68,* 641–649.

Wilkowski, B. M., & Robinson, M. D. (2010). Associative and spontaneous appraisal processes

independently contribute to anger elicitation in daily life. *Emotion, 10,* 181–189.

Willcox, D. C., Willcox, B. J., He, Q., Wang, N. C., & Suzuki, M. (2008). They really are that old: A validation study of centenarian prevalence in Okinawa. *Journals of Gerontology A: Biological Sciences and Medical Sciences, 63,* 338–349.

Willenbockel, V., & others. (2010). Does face inversion change spatial frequency tuning? *Journal of Experimental Psychology: Human Perception and Performance, 36,* 122–135.

Willert, M. V., Thulstrup, A. M., & Hertz, J. (2009). Changes in stress and coping from a randomized controlled trial of a three-month stress management intervention. *Scandinavian Journal of Work and Environmental Health, 35,* 145–152.

Williams, K. D. (2007). Ostracism. *Annual Review of Psychology* (vol. 58). Palo Alto, CA: Annual Reviews.

Williams, L. M. (1995). Recovered memories of abuse in women with documented child sexual victimization histories. *Journal of Traumatic Stress, 19,* 257–267.

Williams, L. M. (2003). Understanding child abuse and violence against women: A life-course perspective. *Journal of Interpersonal Violence, 18,* 441–451.

Williams, L. M. (2004). Researcher-advocate collaborations to end violence against women. *Journal of Interpersonal Violence, 19,* 1350–1357.

Williams, R. B. (2001). Hostility (and other psychosocial risk factors): Effects on health and the potential for successful behavioral approaches to prevention and treatment. In A. Baum, T. A. Revenson, & J. E. Singer (Eds.), *Handbook of health psychology.* Mahwah, NJ: Erlbaum.

Williams, R. B. (2002). Hostility, neuroendocrine changes, and health outcomes. In H. G. Koenig & H. J. Cohen (Eds.), *The link between religion and health.* New York: Oxford University Press.

Williams, S. K., & Davidson, K. W. (2009). Psychological distress and cardiovascular disease with emphasis on acute coronary syndromes. *Journal of the American College of Cardiology, 53,* 1339.

Willis, J., & Todorov, A. (2006). First impressions: Making up your mind after a 100-ms exposure to a face. *Psychological Science, 17,* 592–598.

Willis, S. L., & Schaie, K. W. (2005). Cognitive trajectories in midlife and cognitive functioning in old age. In S. L. Willis & M. Martin (Eds.), *Middle adulthood.* Thousand Oaks, CA: Sage.

Wilsey, B., Marcotte, T., Tsodikov, A., Millman, J., Bentley, H., Gouaux, B., & Fishman, S. (2008). A randomized, placebo-controlled, crossover trial of cannabis cigarettes in neuropathic pain. *Journal of Pain, 9,* 506–521.

Wilson, A., & Godin, J. J. (2010). Boldness and intermittent locomotion in the bluegill sunfish, *Lepomis macrochirus. Behavioral Ecology, 21,* 57–62.

Wilson, G. T., Grilo, C. M., & Vitousek, K. M. (2007). Psychological treatment of eating disorders. *American Psychologist, 62,* 199–216.

Wilson, J. F. (2007). Posttraumatic stress disorder needs to be recognized in primary care. *Annals of Internal Medicine, 146,* 617–620.

Wilson, R. S., Mendes de Leon, D. F., Bienias, J. L., Evans, D. A., & Bennett, D. A. (2004). Personality and mortality in old age. *Journals of Gerontology: Psychological Sciences and Social Sciences, 59B,* 110–116.

Wilt, J., & Revelle, W. (2009) Extraversion. In M. Leary & R. Hoyle (Eds.), *Handbook of individual differences in social behavior* (pp. 27–45). New York: Guilford.

Wiltermuth, S. S., & Heath, C. (2009). Synchrony and cooperation. *Psychological Science, 20,* 1–5.

Winecoff, A., Labar, K. S., Madden, D. J., Cabeza, R., & Huettel, S. A. (2010). Cognitive and neural contributors to emotion regulation in aging. *Social Cognitive and Affective Neuroscience.* (in press)

Winer, R. L., Hughes, J. P., Feng, Q., O'Reilly, S., Kiviat, N. B., Holmes, K. K., & Koutsky, L. A. (2006). Condom use and the risk of genital human papilloma virus infection in young women. *New England Journal of Medicine, 354,* 2645–2654.

Wingo, A. P., Fani, N., Bradley, B., & Ressler, K. J. (2010). Psychological resilience and neurocognitive performance in a traumatized community sample. *Depression and Anxiety.* (in press)

Winner, E. (1996). *Gifted children: Myths and realities.* New York: Basic.

Winner, E. (2000). The origins and ends of giftedness. *American Psychologist, 55,* 159–169.

Winner, E. (2006). Development in the arts. In W. Damon & R. Lerner (Eds.), *Handbook of child psychology* (6th ed.). New York: Wiley.

Winter, D. G. (2005). Measuring the motives of political actors at a distance. In J. M. Post (Ed.), *The psychological assessment of political leaders: With profiles of Saddam Hussein and Bill Clinton* (pp. 153–177). Ann Arbor: University of Michigan Press.

Wirtz, P. H., Redwine, L. S., Ehlert, U., & von Kanel, R. (2009). Independent association between lower level of social support and higher coagulation activity before and after acute psychosocial stress. *Psychosomatic Medicine, 71,* 30–37.

Wirtz, P. H., Siegrist, J., Schuhmacher, A., Hoefels, S., Maier, W., & Zobel, A. W. (2010). Higher overcommitment to work is associated with higher plasma cortisol but not ACTH responses in the combined dexamethasone/CRH test in apparently healthy men and women. *Psychoneuroendocrinology, 35,* 536–543.

Wiseman, R., & Watt, C. (2006). Belief in psychic ability and the misattribution hypothesis: A qualitative review. *British Journal of Psychology, 97,* 323–338.

Witelson, S. F., Kigar, D. L., & Harvey, T. (1999). The exceptional brain of Albert Einstein. *Lancet, 353,* 2149–2153.

Witelson, S. F., Kigar, D. L., Scamvougeras, A., Kideckel, D. M., Buck, B., Stanchev, P. L., Bronskill, M., & Black, S. (2008). Corpus callosum anatomy in right-handed homosexual and heterosexual men. *Archives of Sexual Behavior, 37,* 857–863.

Woike, B. A. (2001). Working with free response data: Let's not give up hope. *Psychological Inquiry, 12,* 157–159.

Woike, B. A. (2008). The state of the story in personality psychology. *Social and Personality Psychology Compass, 2,* 434–443.

Woike, B. A., & Matic, D. (2004). Cognitive complexity in response to traumatic experiences. *Journal of Personality, 72,* 633–657.

Woike, B. A., Mcleod, S., & Goggin, M. (2003). Implicit and explicit motives influence accessibility to different autobiographical knowledge. *Personality and Social Psychology Bulletin, 29,* 1046–1055.

Wojtczak, M., & Oxenham, A. J. (2009). Pitfalls in behavioral estimates of basilar-membrane compression in humans. *Journal of the Acoustical Society of America, 125,* 270–281.

Wolf, A. (2000). Emotional expression online: Gender differences in emoticon use. *CyberPsychology & Behavior, 3,* 827–833.

Wolf, R., Matzke, K., Paelchen, K., Dobrokolny, H., Goverts, B., & Schwegler, H. (2010). Reduction of prepulse inhibition (PPI) after neonatal excitotoxic lesion of the ventral thalamus in pubertal and adult rats. *Pharmacopsychiatry.* (in press)

Wolitzky, K. B., & Telch, M. J. (2009). Augmenting in vivo exposure with fear antagonistic actions: A preliminary test. *Behavior Therapy, 40,* 57–71.

Wolkove, N., Elkholy, O., Baltzan, M., & Palayew, M. (2007). Sleep and aging: 1. Sleep disorders commonly found in older people. *Canadian Medical Association Journal, 176,* 1299–1304.

Wolkowitz, O. M., Epel, E. S., Reus, V. I., & Mellon, S. H. (2010). Depression gets old fast: Do stress and depression accelerate cell aging? *Depression and Anxiety, 27,* 327–338.

Wolpe, J. (1963). Behavior therapy in complex neurotic states. *British Journal of Psychiatry, 110,* 28–34.

Wong, A. C., Jobard, G., James, K. H., James, T. W., & Gauthier, I. (2009). Expertise with characters in alphabetic and non-alphabetic writing systems engage overlapping occipito-temporal areas. *Cognitive Neuropsychology, 26* (1), 111–127.

Wong, Y. J., Kim, S. H., & Tran, K. K. (2010). Asian Americans' adherence to Asian values, attributions about depression, and coping strategies. *Cultural Diversity and Ethnic Minority Psychology, 16* (1), 1–8.

Wood, A. H., & Eagly, A. H. (2010). Gender. In S. Fiske, D. Gilbert, & G. Lindzey (Eds.), *Handbook of social psychology.* New York: Oxford University Press.

Wood, D., Harms, P., & Vazire, S. (2010). Perceiver effects as projective tests: What your perceptions of others say about you. *Journal of Personality and Social Psychology, 99* (1), 174–190.

Wood, R. L., & Liossi, C. (2006). Neuropsychological and neurobehavioral correlates of aggression following traumatic brain injury.

Journal of Neuropsychiatry & Clinical Neurosciences, 18, 333–341.

Woolf, N. J., & Butcher, L. L. (2010). Cholinergic systems media action from movement to higher consciousness. *Behavioural Brain Research.* (in press)

World Health Organization (WHO). (2009). *Suicide rates per 100,000 by country.* http://www.who.int/mental_health/prevention/suicide_rates/en/index.html (accessed April 20, 2010

World Health Organization (WHO). (2010). *Health through safe drinking water and basic sanitation.* http://www.who.int/water_sanitation_health/mdg1/en/index.html (accessed May 6, 2010)

Worthington, R. L., Navarro, R. L., Savoy, H. B., & Hampton, D. (2008). Development, reliability, and validity of the Measure of Sexual Identity Exploration and Commitment (MoSIEC). *Developmental Psychology, 44,* 22–33.

Wortman, C. B., & Boerner, K. (2007). Reactions to death of a loved one: Beyond the myths of coping with loss. In H. S. Friedman & R. C. Silver (Eds.), *Foundations of health psychology.* New York: Oxford University Press.

Wright, R. G. (2008). Sex offender post-incarceration sanctions: Are there any limits? *Criminal and Civil Confinement, 34,* 17–50.

Wright, T. A., & Cropanzano, R. (2000). Psychological well-being and job satisfaction as predictors of job performance. *Journal of Occupational Health Psychology, 5,* 84–94.

Wright, T. A., & Staw, B. M. (1999). Affect and favorable work outcomes: Two longitudinal tests of the happy–productive worker thesis. *Journal of Organizational Behavior, 20,* 1–23.

Wrzesniewski, A. (2003). Finding positive meaning in work. In K. S. Cameron, J. E. Dutton, & R. E. Quinn (Eds.), *Positive organizational scholarship: Foundations of a new discipline* (pp. 296–308). San Francisco: Berrett-Koehler.

Wrzesniewski, A., Dutton, J. E., & Debebe, G. (2003). Interpersonal sense-making and the meaning of work. In R. M. Kramer, M. Roderick, & B. M. Staw (Eds.), *Research in organizational behavior: An annual series of analytical essays and critical reviews* (vol. 25, pp. 93–135). Oxford: Elsevier.

Wrzesniewski, A., McCauley, C. I., Rozin, P., & Schwartz, B. (1997). Jobs, careers, and callings: People's relations to their work. *Journal of Research in Personality, 31,* 21–33.

Wykes, T., Brammer, M., Mellers, J., Bray, P., Reeder, C., Williams, C., & Corner, J. (2002). Effects on the brain of a psychological treatment: Cognitive remediation therapy: Functional magnetic resonance imaging in schizophrenia. *British Journal of Psychiatry, 181,* 144–152.

 X

Xu, H., Kotak, V. C., & Sanes, D. H. (2010). Normal hearing is required for the emergence of long-lasting inhibitory potentiation in the cortex. *Journal of Neuroscience, 30,* 331–341.

Y

Yalom, I. D., & Leszcz, M. (2006). *Theory and practice of group psychotherapy* (5th ed.). New York: Basic.

Yamada, M., & Decety, J. (2009). Unconscious affective processing and empathy: An investigation of subliminal priming on the detection of painful facial expressions. *Pain, 143,* 71–75.

Yamanishi, T., & others. (2009). Changes after behavior therapy among responsive and non-responsive patients with obsessive-compulsive disorder. *Psychiatry Research, 172,* 242–250.

Yamazaki, Y., Yokochi, H., Tanaka, M., Okanoya, K., & Iriki, A. (2010). Potential role of monkey inferior parietal neurons coding action semantic equivalences as precursors of parts of speech. *Social Neuroscience, 5,* 105–117.

Yamin, S., & Vaddadi, K. (2010). Are we using excessive neuroleptics? An argument for systematic neuroleptic dose reduction in stable patients with schizophrenia with specific reference to clozapine. *International Review of Psychiatry, 22,* 138–147.

Yang, H., & others. (2010). Residual sleep disturbance and risk of relapse during the continuation/maintenance phase treatment of major depressive disorder with the selective serontoin reuptake inhibitor fluoxetine. *Annals of General Psychiatry, 9,* 10.

Yang, Y. (2008). Social inequalities in happiness in the United States, 1972–2004: An age-period-cohort analysis. *American Sociological Review, 73,* 204–226.

Yang, Y., Glenn, A. L., & Raine, A. (2008). Brain abnormalities in antisocial individuals: Implications for the law. *Behavioral Sciences & the Law, 26,* 65–83.

Yang, Y., & Raine, A. (2009). Prefrontal structural and functional brain imaging findings in antisocial, violent, and psychopathic individuals: A meta-analysis. *Psychiatry Research, 174,* 81–88.

Yang, Y., Raine, A., Lencz, T., Bihrle, S., LaCasse, L., & Colletti, P. (2005). Volume reduction in prefrontal gray matter in unsuccessful criminal psychopaths. *Biological Psychiatry, 57,* 1103–1108.

Ye, C. Q., Poo, M. M., Dan, Y., & Zhang, X. H. (2010). Synaptic mechanisms of direction selectivity in primary auditory cortex. *Journal of Neuroscience, 30,* 1861–1868.

Yen, C. F., Chen, C. C., Lee, Y, Tang, T. C., Ko, C. H., & Yen, J. Y. (2009). Association between quality of life and self-stigma, insight, and adverse effects of medication in patients with depressive disorders. *Depression and Anxiety, 26* (11), 1033–1039.

Yeshurun, Y., & Sobel, N. (2010). An odor is not worth a thousand words: From multidimensional odors to unidimensional objects. *Annual Review of Psychology* (vol. 61). Palo Alto, CA: Annual Reviews.

Yi, Y., Driesen, N., & Leung, H. (2009). Behavioral and neural correlates of memory selection and interference resolution during a digit working memory task. *Cognitive, Affective & Behavioral Neuroscience, 9,* 249–259.

Yip, T., Kiang, L., & Fuligni, A. J. (2008). Multiple social identities and reactivity to daily stress among ethnically diverse young adults. *Journal of Research in Personality, 42,* 1160–1172.

Yordanova, J., Kolev, V., & Verleger, R. (2009). Awareness of knowledge or awareness of processing? Implications for sleep-related memory consolidation. *Frontiers in Human Neuroscience, 3,* ARTID 40.

Young, L. J. (2009). Being human: Love: Neuroscience reveals all. *Nature, 457,* 148.

Young, S. G., & Claypool, H. M. (2010). Mere exposure has differential effects on attention allocation to threatening and neutral stimuli. *Journal of Experimental Social Psychology, 46,* 424–427.

Young, T. (1802). On the theory of light and colors. *Philosophical Transactions of the Royal Society of London, 92,* 12–48.

Ystad, M., Eichele, T., Lundervold, A. J., & Lundervold, A. (2010). Subcortical functional connectivity and verbal episodic memory in healthy elderly—a resting state fMRI study. *NeuroImage.* (in press)

Yuan, J., Luo, Y., Yan, J. H., Meng, X., Yu, F., & Li, H. (2009). Neural correlates of the female's susceptibility to negative emotions: An insight into gender-related prevalence of affective disturbances. *Human Brain Mapping, 30,* 3676–3686.

Yuan, Y., Zhang, Z., Bai, F., You, J., Yu, H., Shi, Y., & Liu, W. (2010). Genetic variation in apolipoprotein E alters regional gray matter volumes in remitted late-onset depression. *Journal of Affective Disorders, 121,* 273–277.

Z

Zajonc, R. B. (1965). Social facilitation. *Science, 149,* 269–274.

Zajonc, R. B. (1968). Attitudinal effects of mere exposure. *Journal of Personality and Social Psychology, 9,* 1–27.

Zajonc, R. B. (1984). On the primacy of affect. *American Psychologist, 39,* 117–123.

Zajonc, R. B. (2001). Mere exposure: A gateway to the subliminal. *Current Directions in Psychological Science, 10,* 224–228.

Zedeck, S. (Ed.). (2010). *APA handbook of industrial and organizational psychology.* Washington, DC: APA. (in press)

Zeidan, F., Gordon, N. S., Merchant, J., & Goolkasian, P. (2010). The effects of brief mindfulness meditation training on experimentally induced pain. *Journal of Pain, 11,* 199–209.

Zhang, L.-F., & Sternberg, R. J. (2009). Learning in a cross-cultural perspective. In T. Husén & T. N. Postlethwaite (Eds.), *International encyclopedia of education* (3rd ed.), *Learning and cognition.* Oxford, U.K.: Elsevier.

Zhang, Y., & others. (2010). Serotonin (5-HT) receptor 5A sequence variants affect human plasma triglyceride levels. *Physiological Genomics.* (in press)

Zhang, Z., Ilies, R., & Arvey, R. D. (2009). Beyond genetic explanations for leadership: The moderating role of the social environment. *Organizational Behavior and Human Decision Processes, 110,* 118–128.

Zhao, H., Seibert, S. E., & Lumpkin, G. T. (2010). The relationship of personality to entrepreneurial intentions and performance: A meta-analytic review. *Journal of Management, 36,* 381–404.

Zhao, F., Manchiaiah, V. K., French, D., & Price, S. M. (2010). Music exposure and hearing disorders: An overview. *International Journal of Audiology, 49,* 54–64.

Zhou, X., Tang, W., Greenwood, T. A., Guo, S., He, L., Geyer, M. A., & Kelsoe, J. R. (2009a). Transcription factor SP4 is a susceptibility gene for bipolar disorder. *PLoS ONE, 4,* e5196.

Zhou, Z., Zhen, J., Karpowich, N. K., Law, C. J., Rith, M. E., & Wang, D. N. (2009). Antidepressant specificity of serotonin transporter suggested by three LeuT-SSRI structures. *Nature Structure and Molecular Biology, 16,* 652– 657.

Zhu, B., & others. (2010). Individual differences in false memory from misinformation: Personality characteristics and their interactions with cognitive abilities. *Personality and Individual Differences, 48,* 889–894.

Zhu, D. C., Zacks, R. T., & Slade, J. M. (2010). Brain activation during interference resolution in young and older adults: An fMRI study. *NeuroImage, 50,* 810–817.

Zietsch, B. P., Morley, K. I., Shekar, S. N., Verweij, K. J. H., Keller, M. C., Macgregor, S., Wright, M. J., & Zilney, L. A. (2011). *Drugs.* Upper Saddle River, NJ: Prentice-Hall.

Zimbardo, P. (2007). *The Lucifer effect: Understanding how good people turn evil.* New York: Random House.

Zimmer-Gembeck, M. J., Hunter, T. A., Waters, A. M., & Pronk, R. (2009). Depression as a longitudinal outcome and antecedent of preadolescents' peer relationships and peer-relevant cognitions. *Development and Psychopathology, 21,* 555–557.

Ziol-Guest, K. M. (2009). Child custody and support. In D. Carr (Ed.), *Encyclopedia of the life course and human development.* Boston: Cengage.

Zou, L., & others. (2010). Proliferation, migration, and neuronal differentiation of the endogenous neural progenitors in hippocampus after fimbria fornix transaction. *International Journal of Neuroscience, 120,* 192–200.

Zou, Y., Misri, S., Shay, J. W., Pandita, T. K., & Wright, W. E. (2009). Altered states of telomere deprotection and the two-stage mechanism of replicative aging. *Molecular and Cellular Biology, 29* (9), 2390–2397.

Zucker, K. J. (1999). Intersexuality and gender identity differentiation. *Annual Review of Sex Research, 10,* 1–69.

Zurron, M., Pouso, M., Lindin, M., Galdo, S., & Diaz, F. (2009). Event-related potentials with the Stroop color-word task: Timing of semantic conflict. *International Journal of Psychophysiology, 72,* 246–252.

Zwanzger, P., & others. (2009). Effects of the GABA-reuptake inhibitor tiagabine on panic and anxiety in patients with panic disorder. *Pharmacopsychiatry, 42,* 266–269.

CREDITS

Text and Line Art Credits

Section 2

Figure 3.1: From Laura King, *Experience Psychology*, 1st ed. Copyright © 2010 The McGraw-Hill Companies, Inc. Reproduced with permission of The McGraw-Hill Companies.

pp. 35–36: "Satisfaction with Life Scale." Ed Diener, Robert A. Emmons, Randy J. Larson, Sharon Griffin, U. Illinois at Urbana-Champaign, *J. of Personality Assessment,* 1985, 49, 1, p. 72.

Figure 4.2: From Laura King, *Experience Psychology*, 1st ed. Copyright © 2010 The McGraw-Hill Companies, Inc. Reproduced with permission of The McGraw-Hill Companies.

Section 3

Figure 6.1: From Laura King, *Experience Psychology*, 1st ed. Copyright © 2010 The McGraw-Hill Companies, Inc. Reproduced with permission of The McGraw-Hill Companies.

Figure 6.3: From R. Lewis, *Life*, 3rd ed. Copyright © 1998 McGraw-Hill Companies, Inc. Reproduced with permission of The McGraw-Hill Companies.

Figure 6.4: From R. Lewis, *Life*, 3rd ed. Copyright © 1998 McGraw-Hill Companies, Inc. Reproduced with permission of The McGraw-Hill Companies.

Figure 6.6: From *Mapping the Mind* by Rita Carter, 1998. Reprinted by permission of Moonrunner Design, Ltd.

Figure 7.4: From *Brain, Mind, and Behavior* by Floyd Bloom, Charles A. Nelson, Arlyne Lazerson. Copyright ©1985, 1988, 2001 by Educational Broadcasting Corporation. Used with permission of Worth Publishers.

Figure 7.9: From *Brain, Mind, and Behavior* by Floyd Bloom, Charles A. Nelson, Arlyne Lazerson. Copyright ©1985, 1988, 2001 by Educational Broadcasting Corporation. Used with permission of Worth Publishers.

Figure 7.10: From Laura King, *Experience Psychology*, 1st ed. Copyright © 2010 The McGraw-Hill Companies, Inc. Reproduced with permission of The McGraw-Hill Companies.

Figure 7.11: From Laura King, *Experience Psychology*, 1st ed. Copyright © 2010 The McGraw-Hill Companies, Inc. Reproduced with permission of The McGraw-Hill Companies.

Figure 7.12: From Laura King, *Experience Psychology*, 1st ed. Copyright © 2010 The McGraw-Hill Companies, Inc. Reproduced with permission of The McGraw-Hill Companies.

Section 4

Figure 9.1: From Laura King, *Experience Psychology*, 1st ed. Copyright © 2010 The McGraw-Hill Companies, Inc. Reproduced with permission of The McGraw-Hill Companies.

Figure 9.2: From Laura King, *Experience Psychology*, 1st ed. Copyright © 2010 The McGraw-Hill Companies, Inc. Reproduced with permission of The McGraw-Hill Companies.

Figure 10.10: Reproduced from *Ishihara's Tests for Colour Deficiency*, published by Kanehara Trading Inc., Tokyo, Japan. But tests for color deficiency cannot be conducted with this material. For accurate testing, the original plates should be used. Used with permission.

Figure 10.11: From Atkinson/Hilgard/Smith/Hoeksema/Frederickson. *Atkinson and Hilgard's Introduction to Psychology*, 14E. © 2003 Wadsworth, a part of Cengage Learning. Reproduced by permission. www.cengage.com/permissions.

Figure 10.18: From James J. Gibson, *The Perception of the Visual World.* © 1950 Wadsworth, a part of Cengage Learning. Reproduced by permission. www.cengage.com/permissions.

Figure 11.1: From *Brain, Mind and Behavior* by Floyd Bloom, Charles A. Nelson, and Arlyne Lazerson. Copyright © 1985, 1988, 2001 by Educational Broadcasting Corporation. Used with permission of Worth Publishers.

Section 5

Figure 14.5: From H. P. Roffwarg, J. N. Muzio, and W. C. Dement, "Ontogenetic Development of Human Dream-Sleep-Cycle," *Science* 152, 604–609. Copyright ©1966 American Association for the Advancement of Science.

p. 163, Psychological Inquiry: From *Brain, Mind, and Behavior*, by Floyd Bloom, Charles A. Nelson, Arlyne Lazerson. Copyright ©1985, 1988, 2001 by Educational Broadcasting Corporation. Used with permission of Worth Publishers.

p. 170, Psychological Inquiry: From Laura King, *Experience Psychology*, 1st ed. Copyright © 2010 The McGraw-Hill Companies, Inc. Reproduced with permission of The McGraw-Hill Companies.

Figure 15.3: (line art) From Laura King, *Experience Psychology*, 1st ed. Copyright © 2010 The McGraw-Hill Companies, Inc. Reproduced with permission of The McGraw-Hill Companies.

Figure 15.4: (line art) From Laura King, *Experience Psychology*, 1st ed. Copyright © 2010 The McGraw-Hill Companies, Inc.

Reproduced with permission of The McGraw-Hill Companies.

Figure 15.5: From Laura King, *Experience Psychology*, 1st ed. Copyright © 2010 The McGraw-Hill Companies, Inc. Reproduced with permission of The McGraw-Hill Companies.

Section 6

Figure 18.2: From Laura King, *Experience Psychology*, 1st ed. Copyright © 2010 The McGraw-Hill Companies, Inc. Reproduced with permission of The McGraw-Hill Companies.

Section 7

Figure 22.4: From Laura King, *Experience Psychology*, 1st ed. Copyright © 2010 The McGraw-Hill Companies, Inc. Reproduced with permission of The McGraw-Hill Companies.

Figure 23.5: From John Santrock, *Life-Span Development*, 11th ed. Copyright © 2008 The McGraw-Hill Companies, Inc. Reproduced with permission of The McGraw-Hill Companies.

p. 247, Psychological Inquiry: Copyright © 1974 From *Human Memory: Theory and Data*, by B. Murdock, Jr. Reproduced by permission of Lawrence Erlbaum Associates, Inc. a division of Taylor & Francis Group.

Figure 25.2: © Exploratorium, www.exploratorium.edu. Used with permission.

Section 8

Figure 27.1: (line art) From Laura King, *Experience Psychology*, 1st ed. Copyright © 2010 The McGraw-Hill Companies, Inc. Reproduced with permission of The McGraw-Hill Companies.

Figure 28.4: From Laura King, *Experience Psychology*, 1st ed. Copyright © 2010 The McGraw-Hill Companies, Inc. Reproduced with permission of The McGraw-Hill Companies.

p. 283, Psychological Inquiry: From John Santrock, *Children*, 7th ed. Copyright © 2003 The McGraw-Hill Companies, Inc. Reproduced with permission of The McGraw-Hill Companies.

Figure 29.4: From "The Increase in IQ Scores from 1932–1997," by Ulric Neisser. Used with permission.

Figure 30.2: From John Santrock, *Educational Psychology*. Copyright © 2001 The McGraw-Hill Companies, Inc. Reprinted with permission of The McGraw-Hill Companies.

Section 9

Figure 32.2: From Laura King, *Experience Psychology*, 1st ed. Copyright © 2010 The McGraw-Hill Companies, Inc. Reproduced

with permission of The McGraw-Hill Companies.

Figure 32.5: From John Santrock, *A Topical Approach to Life-Span Development*, 2002. Copyright © The McGraw-Hill Companies, Inc. Reprinted by permission of The McGraw-Hill Companies.

Figure 32.8: (line art) From John Santrock, *Life-Span Development*, 9th ed. Copyright © The McGraw-Hill Companies, Inc. Reproduced with permission of The McGraw-Hill Companies.

Figure 33.1: From John Santrock, *Life-Span Development*, 11th ed. Copyright © 2008 The McGraw-Hill Companies, Inc. Reproduced with permission of The McGraw-Hill Companies.

p. 333, Psychological Inquiry: From John Santrock, *Life-Span Development*, 8th ed. Copyright © 2002 The McGraw-Hill Companies, Inc. Reproduced with permission of The McGraw-Hill Companies.

Figure 34.3: From John Santrock, *Life-Span Development*, 8th ed. Copyright © 2002 The McGraw-Hill Companies, Inc. Reproduced with permission of The McGraw-Hill Companies.

Section 10

Figure 37.1: From Laura King, *Experience Psychology*, 1st ed. Copyright © 2010 The McGraw-Hill Companies, Inc. Reproduced with permission of The McGraw-Hill Companies.

Figure 37.3: From Laura King, *Experience Psychology*, 1st ed. Copyright © 2010 The McGraw-Hill Companies, Inc. Reproduced with permission of The McGraw-Hill Companies.

p. 377, Psychological Inquiry: From Laura King, *Experience Psychology*, 1st ed. Copyright © 2010 The McGraw-Hill Companies, Inc. Reproduced with permission of The McGraw-Hill Companies.

Section 11

Figure 38.3: From J. M. Tanner et al., in *Archives of Diseases in Childhood* 41, 1966. Reproduced with permission from BMJ Publishing Group, Ltd.

Figure 39.1: From John Santrock, *Child Development*, 10th ed., Figure 13.3. Copyright © 2008 The McGraw-Hill Companies, Inc. Reprinted with permission of The McGraw-Hill Companies.

p. 403, Psychological Inquiry: From R. D. Clark & E. Hatfield. (1989). "Gender Differences in Receptivity to Sexual Offers." *Journal of Psychology & Human Sexuality*, 2(1), 39-55. doi:10.1300/J056v02n01_04. Reprinted by permission of Taylor & Francis Ltd. http://www.tandf.co.uk/journals.

p. 414, **Psychological Inquiry:** From *Sex in America* by Robert T. Michael, John H. Gagnon, Edward O. Laumann, and Gina Kolata. Copyright © 1994 by Robert T. Michael, John H. Gagnon, Edward O. Laumann, and Gina Kolata. By permission of Little Brown & Company and Brockman, Inc.

Figure 42.2: From Laura King, *Experience Psychology*, 1st ed. Copyright © 2010 The McGraw-Hill Companies, Inc. Reproduced with permission of The McGraw-Hill Companies.

Section 13

Figure 54.1: (text) This figure was published in "Types of Identity" by K. Deaux in *Encyclopedia of Women and Gender: Sex Similarities and Differences and the Impact of Society and Gender,* 2 volume set, edited by Judith Worell. Copyright © 2001 Elsevier USA. Reprinted by permission.

Figure 54.2: "Attiudes Toward the Out-Group Following Competitive and Cooperative Activities." From M. Sherif, O. J. Harvey, B. J. White, W. E. Hood, and C. W. Sherif, "The Robber's Cave Experiment: Intergroup Conflict and Cooperation." Copyright © 1988 by Muzafer Sherif and reprinted by permission of Wesleyan University Press. www.wesleyan.edu/wespress.

Section 15

Figure 60.1: From *Annual Review of Neuroscience, Online,* Vol. 20, by Annual Review. Copyright ©1997 by Annual Reviews, Inc. Reproduced with permission of Annual Reviews, Inc. in the format Textbook via Copyright Clearance Center. www.annualreviews.org.

p. 563, **Psychological Inquiry:** From Weissman and Olfson, *Science* 269, p. 779, Figure 1. Copyright © 1995 American Association for the Advancement of Science. Reprinted with permission from AAAS.

Figure 60.4: From Laura King, *Experience Psychology*, 1st ed. Copyright © 2010 The McGraw-Hill Companies, Inc. Reproduced with permission of The McGraw-Hill Companies.

p. 574, **Psychological Inquiry:** © Irving I. Gottesman, 2004. Used by permission.

p. 580: (text) From Laura King, *Experience Psychology*, 1st ed. Copyright © 2010 The McGraw-Hill Companies, Inc. Reproduced with permission of The McGraw-Hill Companies.

p. 581: From Laura King, *Experience Psychology*, 1st ed. Copyright © 2010 The McGraw-Hill Companies, Inc. Reproduced with permission of The McGraw-Hill Companies.

Section 16

Figure 65.2: From Laura King, *Experience Psychology*, 1st ed. Copyright © 2010 The McGraw-Hill Companies, Inc. Reproduced with permission of The McGraw-Hill Companies.

p. 600, **Psychological Inquiry:** From Laura King, *Experience Psychology*, 1st ed. Copyright © 2010 The McGraw-Hill Companies, Inc. Reproduced with permission of The McGraw-Hill Companies.

p. 601: (bottom) From A. T. Beck, A. J. Rush, B. F. Shaw, G. Emery, *Cognitive Ther-*

apy of Depression. 1979, pp. 145–146. Reprinted with permission of The Guilford Press.

Figure 65.3: Adapted from A. Freeman and M.A. Reinecke, "Cognitive Therapy" in A. S. Gurman, ed., *Essential Psychotherapies.* Adapted with permission of The Guilford Press.

Figure 65.4: Copyright © 1999, American Psychological Association.

Figure 65.5: From Laura King, *Experience Psychology*, 1st ed. Copyright © 2010 The McGraw-Hill Companies, Inc. Reproduced with permission of The McGraw-Hill Companies.

p. 607, **Psychological Inquiry:** Reprinted with permission of Michael J. Lambert, professor of Psychology, Brigham Young University.

Figure 65.6: From "A Survival Analysis of Clinically Significant Change in Outpatient Psychotherapy" by Anderson & Lambert from *Journal of Clinical Psychology,* 57, 875–888. Copyright © 2010 Wiley Periodicals, Inc., A Wiley Company.

Section 17

Figure 67.1: From Laura King, *Experience Psychology*, 1st ed. Copyright © 2010 The McGraw-Hill Companies, Inc. Reproduced with permission of The McGraw-Hill Companies.

p. 631, **Psychological Inquiry:** From Laura King, *Experience Psychology*, 1st ed. Copyright © 2010 The McGraw-Hill Companies, Inc. Reproduced with permission of The McGraw-Hill Companies.

Figure 69.1: Figure, "Hans Selye's General Adaptation Syndrome," from *The Stress of Life,* 2nd ed., by Hans Selye, p. 476, 1976. New York: McGraw-Hill. Reprinted by permission of The McGraw-Hill Companies.

Figure 69.2: Copyright © 1998, American Psychological Association.

Figure 69.4: This article was published in *Journal of Psychosomatic Research,* Vol. 29, S. C. Kobasa, S. R. Maddi, M. C. Puccette, and M. A. Zola, pp. 525–533. Copyright © 1985, Elsevier. Used with permission.

p. 641, **Psychological Inquiry:** From John Santrock, *Life-Span Development,* 11th ed. Copyright © 2008 The McGraw-Hill Companies, Inc. Reproduced with permission of The McGraw-Hill Companies.

Figure 70.2: From Laura King, *Experience Psychology*, 1st ed. Copyright © 2010 The McGraw-Hill Companies, Inc. Reproduced with permission of The McGraw-Hill Companies.

Figure 70.5: From Laura King, *Experience Psychology*, 1st ed. Copyright © 2010 The McGraw-Hill Companies, Inc. Reproduced with permission of The McGraw-Hill Companies.

Figure 70.6: From John Santrock, *Life-Span Development,* 11th ed. Copyright © 2008 The McGraw-Hill Companies, Inc. Reproduced with permission of The McGraw-Hill Companies.

Photo Credits

Frontmatter

p. i © Image Source/Getty Images; p. ii: © Image Source/Getty Images; p. vi: Courtesy of Laura King; p. vii: © PhotoAlto/Punch-

Stock; p. xxi: © Stockbyte/Getty Images; p. xxii: © Jae Rew/Photonica/Getty Images; xxvi: © Burke/Triolo/Brand X Pictures/Jupiterimages; p. xxvi: © The McGraw-Hill Companies, Inc./Ken Karp photographer; p. xxvii: © PhotoAlto/PunchStock; p. xxix: © RubberBall Productions; p. xxxi: © Fly Fernandez/Corbis.

Section 1

Opener: © Michael Blann/Digital Vision/ Getty; **p. 4 (inset):** © GlowImages/Alamy; **p. 4:** © Brand X Pictures/PunchStock; **p. 7:** AP Photo/Carolyn Kaster; **p. 8:** © Bettmann/Corbis; **p. 9:** © Bettmann/Corbis; **p. 10:** © Michele Burgess/Corbis; **p. 11:** AP Photo; **p. 12:** © Time & Life Pictures/Getty; **p. 13:** © Kevin Dodge/Corbis; **p. 17:** Courtesy of Richard Davidson, University of Wisconsin, Madison. Photo by Jeff Miller; **p. 18:** Courtesy of Carol S. Dweck, Stanford University; **p. 19 (top left):** © Atlantide Phototravel/Corbis; **p. 19 (top middle):** © Chip Somodevilla/Getty; **p. 19 (top right):** © Peter Foley/Reuters/Corbis; **p. 19 (bottom left):** © Dennis MacDonald/PhotoEdit; **p. 19 (bottom right):** © David McNew/ Getty; **p. 21:** Courtesy of the Suicide Prevention Center; **p. 22:** © artpartner-images. com/Alamy; **p. 24:** © Ryan McVay/Getty.

Section 2

Opener: © Dimitri Vervitsiotis/Photographer's Choice RF/Getty; **p. 28 (top):** © Creatas/Punchstock; **p. 28 (bottom):** © George Doyle & Ciaran Griffin/Stockbyte/ Getty; **p. 29 (left):** © Stockdisc/Punch-Stock; **p. 29 (right):** © Masterfile/Royalty Free; **p. 30:** © Peter Ciresa Cires/Index Stock/Photolibrary; **p. 32:** © Stockbyte/ Punchstock; **p. 34:** © The McGraw-Hill Companies, Inc./John Flournoy, photographer; **p. 35 (top):** © Photographers Choice RF/SuperStock; **p. 35 (bottom):** © Bettmann/Corbis; **p. 37:** © Photodisc/Punch-Stock; **p. 38 (yawn):** © Doug Menuez/ Getty Images; **p. 38 (tired student):** © BananaStock/JupiterImages; **p. 38 (library):** © Veer; **p. 38 (friends):** © Stockbyte/ Punchstock; **p. 39:** © Tony Savino/Corbis; **p. 40:** AP Photo/Richard Vogel; **p. 42:** © Stockbyte/Getty; **p. 44:** Image courtesy of The Advertising Archives; **p. 45:** © Visions of America, LLC/Alamy; **p. 47 (left):** © Peter Arnold/Photolibrary; **p. 47 (right):** © Elsa/Staff/Getty; **p. 48 (left):** © Michael Nichols/National Geographic/Getty; **p. 48 (right):** Courtesy of Barbara Fredrickson, University of North Carolina; **p. 50:** AP Photo/Ted S. Warren; **p. 51:** © RF@PPS/ Alamy; **p. 53:** © Josef Lindau/Corbis; **p. 55:** © age fotostock/SuperStock; **p. 56:** © CBS/ Photofest; **p. 58 (top):** Courtesy of James W. Pennebaker, University of Texas. Photo by Marsha Miller; **p. 58 (bottom):** © Brand X Pictures.

Section 3

p. T1-1: © Chad Baker/Thomas Northcut/ Stone/Getty Images; **Opener:** © Hybrid Medical/Photo Researchers; **p. 62 (left):** © Amana Productions, Inc./Getty; **p. 62 (right):** © Digital Vision/Getty; **p. 63:** Press Association via AP Images; **p. 64:** © RubberBall Productions; **p. 67:** AP Photo/Kevin

Ferguson; **p. 70:** Centers for Disease Control; **p. 73:** © PhotoAlto/PunchStock; **p. 74:** © Lennart Nilsson/Albert Bonniers Forlag AB; **p. 76:** © Jonathan Nourok/PhotoEdit; **p. 77:** © Blend Images/Alamy; **p. 78:** © Peter Arnold, Inc./Alamy; **p. 79:** © Lennart Nilsson/Albert Bonniers Forlag AB; **p. 83 (top):** © John Whiley, California Institute of Technology, estate of James Olds; **p. 83 (bottom):** © A. Glauberman/Photo Researchers, Inc; **p. 84:** From: H. Damasio, T. Grabowski, R. Frank, A. M. Galaburda, and A. R. Damasio: The return of Phineas Gage: Clues about the brain from the skull of a famous patient. *Science* 264: 1102–1105, 1994. Departments of Neurology and Image Analysis Facility, University of Iowa; **p. 85:** Courtesy of Michael J. Tarr, Ph.D.; **p. 91:** © Yann Arthus-Bertrand/Corbis; **p. 93:** © Riccardo Cassiani-Ingoni/Photo Researchers; **p. 96:** © Rick Rickman; **p. 97:** © Punchstock/BananaStock; **p. 98:** © Enrico Ferorelli; **p. 99:** © Joe Murphy/NBAE via Getty.

Section 4

p. T2-1: © Jae Rew/Photonica/Getty Images; ; **Opener:** © Brand New Images/ Stone/Getty; **p. 107:** © Ariel Skelley/Riser/ Getty; **p. 108 (owl):** © Ron Austing; Frank Lane Picture Agency/Corbis; **p. 108 (rabbit):** © Image Source/Punchstock; **p. 108 (eye:** © Barbara Penoyar/Getty Images; **p. 108 (ear):** © The McGraw-Hill Companies, Inc./Eric Wise, photographer; **p. 108 (foot):** The McGraw-Hill Companies, Inc./ Jill Braaten, photographer; **p. 108 (smelling):** © ZenShui/Sigrid Olsson/Getty; **p. 108 (eating):** © istockphoto.com/Zorani; **p. 109:** © Stockbyte/PunchStock; **p. 110 (top):** © Photodisc; **p. 110 (bottom):** © Stockdisc; **p. 116:** © Jose Luis Pelaez, Inc./ Blend Images/Corbis; **p. 121:** Courtesy of X-Rite, Inc.; **p. 122:** © Frank S. Werblin; **p. 123:** © Editorial Image, LLC/Alamy; **p. 124:** © RubberBall Productions/Getty; **p. 125:** © Silver Screen Collection/Hulton Archives/Getty; **p. 128:** © Erich Lessing/Art Resource, NY; **p. 129:** © Steve Allen/Getty; **p. 135:** © Mary Kate Denny/PhotoEdit; **p. 142:** © Chip Simons; **p. 144:** © Dominic Rouse/The Image Bank/Getty; **p. 144 (inset):** © Lennart Nilsson/Albert Bonniers Forlag AB.

Section 5

Opener: © hana/Datacraft/Getty; **p. 150:** © Comstock/Alamy; **p. 154:** © Newscom; **p. 157:** © Philip Lee Harvey/Getty; **p. 158 (top):** © Frank Greenaway/Getty; **p. 158 (bottom):** © Royalty Free/Corbis; **p. 159:** © Will and Deni McIntyre/Photo Researchers, Inc.; **p. 160:** © J. Allan Hobson & Hoffman La Roche, Inc.; **p. 162:** © Rubberball/ Alamy; **p. 163:** © Steve Cole/Getty; **p. 166:** © Thinkstock/PunchStock; **p. 170:** © PhotoAlto/PictureQuest; **p. 171:** © Ingram Publishing/Alamy; **p. 172 (top):** © George Doyle/Stockbyte/Getty; **p. 172 (bottom):** © Royalty-Free/Corbis; **p. 173:** © Ingram Publishing/SuperStock; **p. 175 (top):** © Image Source/Getty; **p. 179:** AP Photo/ Reed Saxon; **p. 182:** © Stanford News Service; **p. 185:** © Erin Koran/McGraw-Hill; **p. 186:** © Jules Frazier/Getty.

Post. Photo by Gerald Martineau; **p. 572:** © Grunnitus/Photo Researchers, Inc.; **p. 576 (both):** © Bettmann/Corbis; **p. 578:** © WoodyStock/Alamy; **p. 582:** Courtesy of Sheila Hollingsworth.

Section 16

Opener: © Symphonie/Iconica/Getty; **p. 586:** © Science & Society Picture Library/Getty; **p. 589:** © Compassionate Eye Foundation/Jetta Productions/Photodisc/Getty;

p. 591: © Will McIntyre/Photo Researchers, Inc.; **p. 597:** © Perfect Picture Parts/Alamy; **p. 599:** © BananaStock/PictureQuest; **p. 601 (top):** © Bettmann/Corbis; **p. 601 (bottom):** © Leif Skoogfors/Woodfin Camp & Associates; **p. 606:** © Ralph Mercer/The Image Bank/Getty; **p. 608:** © Andrea Morini/Getty Images; **p. 612:** © Frank Pedrick/The Image Works; **p. 614:** © Gerald Martineau/The Washington Post/Getty; **p. 615:** © Photofusion Picture Library/

Alamy; **p. 617:** © By Ian Miles-Flashpoint Pictures/Alamy.

Section 17

Opener: © Flint/Corbis; **p. 622:** © Andre Jenny/Alamy; **p. 625:** © Photodisc/Punch-Stock; **p. 628:** © Wang Zhide/ChinaFoto-Press/Getty; **p. 629:** © Justin Sullivan/Getty; **p. 630 (top):** © M. Taghi/zefa/Corbis; **p. 630 (bottom):** © Manchan/Digital Vision/Getty; **p. 631:** © Jim West/Alamy;

p. 636 (top): © Eye of Science/Photo Researchers, Inc.; **p. 636 (bottom):** © image100 Ltd; **p. 638:** © John Lund/Tiffany Schoepp/Blend Images/Corbis; **p. 640:** Courtesy of Colin M. Bloor; **p. 641:** © Stockbyte/PunchStock; **p. 642 (left):** © Reed Kaestner/Corbis; **p. 642 (right):** © Stockbyte/PunchStock; **p. 645:** © Mike Schroeder/Peter Arnold.

NAME INDEX

Maier, W., 542
Maisto, S. A., 171
Maitlis, S., 537
Major, B., 500, 503
Mak, A., 634
Makioka, S., 109
Malamuth, N. M., 489, 490
Malcarne, V. L., 163
Malcolm, K. T., 444
Malcolm-Smith, S., 167
Maldonado, R., 645
Malhotra, R. K., 162
Mallach, N., 627
Malur, C., 591
Mamelak, A. N., 242
Mamo, D. C., 588
Manchanda, R., 568
Manchiaiah, V. K., 146
Manci, L., 451
Mancini, A. D., 559
Mancini, F., 370
Mandara, J., 334
Mandell, D. L., 375
Mander, B. A., 158
Manderscheid, R. W., 613
Mandisodza, A. N., 472
Mandler, G., 240
Maner, J. K., 483
Manganotti, P., 79
Manhart, L. E., 419
Manini, T. M., 640
Mann, D. M., 622
Manning, J. T., 408
Manson, J. E., 337, 644
Manstead, A. S. R., 623
Mantonakis, A., 247
Mantzoros, C. S., 360
Maramis, A., 559
March, J., 589
March, J. S., 561
Marcia, J. E., 332, 333, 334
Marcotte, T., 179
Marcus, E. C., 504
Marcus, G. F., 241, 268
Marcus, S. C., 587, 588, 594
Margolin, G., 604
Margolskee, R. F., 141
Margoob, M. A., 591
Margrett, J. A., 17
Maril, A., 230, 258
Marine, A., 469
Marini, A., 294
Marin-Martinez, F., 599
Mariottini, C., 251
Maris, R. W., 566
Markesbery, W. R., 32, 39
Markessis, E., 109
Markey, C. N., 331
Markham, H. J., 5
Markides, K. S., 39
Markon, K. E., 457
Markowitsch, H. J., 264
Markowitz, J. C., 559
Markowitz, S., 589
Marks, I., 594
Markus, H. R., 22
Marlatt, M. W., 338
Marlow, A., 199
Marlowe, F., 484, 485
Marois, R., 78
Marom, M., 292
Maron, E., 556
Marques, J. K., 422
Marrazzo, J. M., 415
Marsh, E. J., 249

Marsh, R. L., 258
Marshall, D. A., 638
Marshall, D. S., 416
Marshall, G., 198
Marshall, M., 575
Marshall, R. D., 559
Martelli, S., 294
Marti, C. N., 363, 628
Martin, C., 444
Martin, C. E., 414
Martin, C. L., 18, 387, 396
Martin, D., 614
Martin, D. K., 151
Martin, F., 313
Martin, G. L., 211
Martin, G. R., 71
Martin, J., 577
Martin, L. L., 381
Martin, L. R., 466
Martin, M., 575
Martin, N. G., 406, 578
Martin, P. P., 334, 500
Martinez, M. E., 228
Marting, M. O., 399
Martin-Garcia, E., 645
Martin-Joy, J., 337
Martinko, M. J., 462
Martino, S., 93
Martinovich, Z., 561, 607
Martin-Soelch, C., 71
Martinussen, M., 332, 334
Maruyama, Y., 141
Marx, R. F., 569
Mascaro, N., 631
Masheb, R. M., 364
Maslach, C., 493
Maslow, A. H., 12, 45, 352, 353, 438
Mason, C., 621
Mason, H. R., 542
Mason, K. A., 96, 107
Mason, S., 532
Mason, T. B., 165
Massey, C., 308
Massimini, F., 345
Masten, A. S., 310, 377, 564
Master, A., 221
Masters, W. H., 415
Masul, Y., 466
Mate, J., 246
Mathew, A., 568
Mathew, K. L., 561
Matic, D., 463
Matis, G., 153
Matlin, M. W., 259
Matschinger, H., 478
Matsumoto, D., 374, 376
Mattes, K., 472
Matthews, K., 13, 543
Matthews, K. A., 337, 468
Matthews, P. M., 77
Matthews, R. A., 542
Matusch, A., 591
Matz, D. C., 501
Matzel, L. D., 229
Matzke, K., 76
Maurer, T. J., 526
Maxwell, C. A., 542
May, F. B., 289
May, M., 119, 123, 146, 147
May, P. J., 137
Mayans, D., 614
Mayans, L., 614
Mayberg, H., 158
Mayberry, E. J., 84
Mayer, J. D., 288, 435
Mayer, K. H., 415

Mayer, R., 271
Mayer, R. E., 191, 350
Mayes, T. L., 589
Mayeux, R., 265
Mayo Foundation, 591
Mazziotta, J. C., 564
McAdams, D. P., 18, 45, 250, 264, 342, 447, 448
McAfee, R. B., 518
McAndrew, F. T., 487
McAuley, P., 640
McBride-Chang, C. A., 292, 388
McBurney, D. H., 28
McCabe, J., 416
McCarthy, M. M., 389
McCarthy, P. M., 484
McCauley, C., 494
McCauley, C. I., 533
McCaulley, M. H., 462
McClain, J. A., 171
McClay, J., 577
McClearn, G. E., 97
McClelland, J. L., 241
McClelland, M. M., 451
McClintock, S., 591
McClintock, S. M., 591
McCollum, V., 615
McConnell, A. R., 478
McConnell, J., 230
McCorkle, B. H., 613
McCorkle, R., 617
McCormack, J. P., 645
McCormick, N., 206
McCrae, R. R., 441, 442, 444, 458, 461
McCulloch, K. C., 240
McCullough, J. L., 337
McCullough, M. E., 7, 381, 444, 631
McDaniel, B., 329, 483, 485, 491
McDaniel, M. A., 259
McDermott, M., 508, 539
McDermott, R., 276
McDonald, K. L., 335
McDonald, S. D., 31
McDonel, E. C., 478
McDowell, N. K., 475
McElhaney, K. B., 210
McElreath, R., 484, 485
McFadden, D., 408
McFadden, K. E., 48
McFadden, S. H., 310
McFarlane, A. C., 558, 559
McFatter, R. M., 469
McGettigan, C., 236
McGhee, K. E., 445
McGinnis, M. Y., 487
McGlashan, T. H., 578
McGlave, P. B., 508
McGregor, D. M., 529
McGue, M., 98, 285, 535
McGuffin, P., 97
McGugin, R. W., 85
McGuire, H., 587
McGuire, M. T., 643
McGuire, T. R., 146
McGuire, W. J., 478, 481
McHale, S. M., 331
McIntosh, A. R., 244
McIntosh, W. D., 381
McIntyre, L. L., 212
McKay, K. M., 608
McKellar, S., 626
McKibbin, W. F., 402
McKie, S., 368
McKone, E., 85
McLaren, D., 161
Mcleod, S., 463

McLeskey, J., 552
McMahon, C. G., 422
McMahon, D. B., 124
McMahon, K. L., 284
McMain, S., 604
McManus, F., 557
McManus, M. A., 521
McMillan, B., 466, 591
McMillan, J. H., 5, 35
McNamara, P., 161
McNamara, T. P., 240
McNaughton, N., 456
McNeil, D. G., 267
McNiel, J. M., 469
McNulty, S., 589
McQueeny, T., 78
McRae, K., 239, 302
McRobbie, H., 645
McVay, J. C., 152
McWhirter, R. M., 469
Meade, C. S., 301
Means, B., 278
Mecklinger, A., 246
Medendorp, W. P., 84
Medland, S. E., 408, 556
Medley-Rath, S. R., 413
Medoff, D. R., 631
Medvec, V. H., 27
Meece, J. L., 357
Meehan, S. K., 87
Meehl, P., 574
Meeren, H. K., 374
Meeus, W. H., 334, 458
Mehl, M. R., 295
Mehra, A., 163
Meier, D., 165
Meier-Ewert, H. K., 158
Meinhardt, J., 196, 599
Meints, J. O., 458, 466
Meissner, C. A., 253
Meissner, W. W., 596
Meister, I. G., 183
Mejia-Arauz, R., 220
Melendez-Ferro, M., 71
Melis, M., 171
Mellers, J., 606
Mellerup, E., 457
Mello, J. A., 528
Mellon, S., 623
Mellon, S. H., 338
Melton, L., 264, 265
Meltzer, L. J., 161
Meltzoff, A. N., 321
Memmi, J. M., 128
Mendel, G., 96, 97
Mendes, W. B., 497
Mendes de Leon, D. F., 466
Mendoza, S. A., 503
Meng, X., 562
Menn, L., 292, 299
Menon, S., 531
Menzel, R., 243
Menzer, M. M., 327
Mercer, C. H., 415
Mercer, V. E., 638
Merchant, J., 185, 435
Merckelbach, H., 251, 252
Merenakk, L., 457
Merkl, A., 591
Merkle, H., 241
Merlino, G., 163
Mermelstein, R., 467
Mermi, O., 558
Merskey, H., 568
Mertens, I., 578
Mervielde, I., 441

Salas, E., 512, 525, 526
Saleem, M., 490
Salminen, N. H., 137
Salomons, T. V., 185
Salovey, P., 288
Salter, N., 628
Salters, K., 376
Salthouse, T. A., 340
Salvia, J., 282
Salzman, C. D., 11, 83, 91
Sameroff, A., 285
Samochowiec, J., 363
Sampaio, A. S., 558
Sampaio, C., 153
Sampson, S., 591
Samuelson, L. K., 293
Sanberg, P. R., 71
Sanchez, D., 477
Sanchez, J. L., 530
Sanchez-Burks, J., 500
Sanchez-Meca, J., 599
Sanchez-Padilla, J., 71
Sand, S., 621
Sandberg, L. S., 595
Sanders, A. R., 573
Sanderson, C. A., 265
Sandler, I., 16, 309
Sandnabba, N. K., 402
Sandoval, M., 614
Sanes, D. H., 106
Sanfey, A., 17
Sanislow, C., 578
Santomauro, J., 117
Santos-Victor, J., 269
Santtila, P., 402
Saper, C. B., 167
Saphire-Bernstein, S., 72
Sapolsky, R. M., 101, 224
Sapp, S., 630
Sar, V., 568, 569
Saracbasi, O., 542
Sarkar, U., 451, 467
Sarma, K., 566
Saroglou, V., 444
Sarpal, D., 573
Sarrazin, P., 111
Sartor, C. E., 97
Sartorius, N., 581
Sasaki, Y., 111
Sass, H., 444
Sass, S. M., 114
Satir, D. A., 363
Sato, W., 372
Saucier, D. A., 410
Sauer, H., 204, 550
Sauer, J., 480
Saul, S., 164
Saunders, F. W., 462
Saurer, T. B., 197
Sauter, D. A., 374
Sava, F. A., 601, 603, 604
Savage, J., 487, 489, 490
Savage, P. D., 640
Savic, I., 407
Savin-Williams, R., 331, 402, 405, 410
Savoy, H. B., 409
Sawalani, G. M., 401
Sawyer, M. G., 549
Sawyer, P. J., 503
Saxe, L., 368
Saxon, J. L., 381
Sayal, K., 313
Scally, M., 458
Scamvougeras, A., 407
Scardamalia, M., 272
Scarmeas, N., 158, 265

Scarr, S., 284, 309
Schaal, B., 401, 487
Schachter, S., 370, 371
Schacter, D. L., 228, 230, 239, 244, 258, 259
Schaefer, A., 556
Schaie, K. W., 307, 310, 339, 340
Schaller, M., 352, 484
Schank, R., 241
Schankler, C., 243
Scharf, M. J., 185
Scharrer, E., 489
Scheepers, C., 374
Scheffler, K., 81
Scheibe, S., 310
Scheid, T. L., 549
Scheier, M. F., 356, 467, 637
Scheiffele, P., 70
Scherer, K. R., 366
Schermer, J. A., 457
Scherrer, J., 173
Schertler, E., 367
Schiefele, U., 357
Schieffelin, B., 296
Schienle, A., 556
Schiff, W. J., 543, 642
Schillinger, D., 451
Schira, M. M., 122
Schkade, D. A., 380
Schlaepfer, T. E., 591
Schlaug, G., 77
Schleicher, A., 77
Schlosser, R. G., 204
Schmader, T., 477
Schmahl, C., 568
Schmeichel, B. J., 456
Schmidt, A. M., 511
Schmidt, B. L., 141
Schmidt, F. L., 521
Schmidt, J., 468
Schmidt, N. B., 556, 604
Schmidtke, J. I., 455
Schmiedek, F., 257
Schmitt, K. C., 170
Schmukle, S. C., 429
Schnall, E., 631
Schnall, S., 484
Schneider, D. W., 257
Schneider, F., 577
Schneider, K. J., 440, 597
Schneiderman, N., 617, 631
Schnepf, B., 165
Schnyder, U., 408
Schoen, L. S., 223
Schoenberger, Y., 626
Schoenfelder, E., 16, 309
Schomerus, G., 478
Schooler, J. W., 249, 251, 252, 381
Schott, L. L., 337
Schoueri, P., 595
Schraw, G. J., 261
Schredl, M., 161, 164, 166
Schroeder, S. A., 645
Schuckit, M. A., 173
Schuhmacher, A., 542
Schulenberg, J. E., 169, 170, 171, 172, 174, 177, 178, 336
Schulter, G., 90, 377
Schultheiss, O. C., 463
Schultz, J., 468
Schultz, W., 83, 204, 217, 239
Schultz, W. T., 448
Schultz-Hardt, S., 497, 498
Schulz, D., 205
Schulz, E., 575
Schulz, R., 635

Schulz-Stubner, S., 183
Schumacher, J., 91, 185
Schuman, E. M., 242
Schumann, A., 626
Schumm, J. S., 288
Schumm, L. P., 342
Schunk, D. H., 214, 216, 271, 354, 357, 451
Schur, E. A., 363
Schutzwohl, A., 402
Schuz, B., 627
Schwabe, L., 249
Schwartz, B., 278, 533
Schwartz, J. E., 466
Schwartz, J. H., 242
Schwartz, J. M., 564
Schwartz, M., 437, 462, 463
Schwartz, M. D., 198
Schwartz, S., 166, 549
Schwartzbaum, J. A., 165
Schwartz-Mette, R. A., 401
Schwarz, J. M., 389
Schwarz, N., 474, 489
Schwarzer, R., 466, 627
Schwegler, H., 76
Schweinberger, S. R., 240
Schweinsburg, A. D., 78
Schweizer, S., 561, 562, 636
Schwerdtner, J., 196, 599
Schwiezer, H. R., 182
Schyns, P. G., 374
Scollon, C. K., 448
Scott, C., 7, 566
Scott, G., 534
Scott, R. S., 243
Scott, S. K., 165, 374
Scott-Phillips, T. C., 292
Scott-Sheldon, L. A. J., 425
Sczesny, S., 396
Seacat, J. D., 476
Seal, B. N., 423
Sealfon, S. C., 178
Sears, D. O., 502
Sears, R. R., 487
Sedikides, C., 475
Seeman, T. E., 72
Segal, D. L., 460
Segal, M., 65
Segal, M. E., 494
Segal, S. K., 389
Segal, Z., 605
Segall, L. A., 157
Segerstrom, S. C., 378, 467, 468, 637
Seguin, J. R., 401, 487
Seibert, S. E., 444
Seibring, M., 172
Seibt, J., 158
Seidi, K. N., 372
Seidman, L. J., 389
Seifert, C. M., 367
Seifritz, E., 81
Seilacher. A., 79
Seim, H. C., 364
Sekiguchi, T., 110
Selby, E. A., 566, 578
Seligman, D. A., 606, 607
Seligman, M. E. P., 8, 196, 205, 219, 224, 271, 467, 562, 591
Selin, C. E., 564
Sellbom, M., 461
Sellers, R. M., 334, 500
Selye, H., 633
Sen, A., 399
Senecal, C., 628
Senghas, A., 373
Sergent, C., 150

Serra, C., 469
Serrador, J. M., 158
Serretti, A., 185, 363, 588
Sershen, H., 174
Sesardic, N., 285
Sessa, B., 179
Seth, A., 109
Seto, M. C., 402, 421, 422
Severe, J., 589
Sewell, R. A., 179
Seymour, K., 124
Seymour, T. L., 367
Sforza, L., 97
Sgobio, C., 243
Shackelford, T. K., 402
Shackman, A., 370
Shadbolt, N. R., 115
Shafto, M. G., 367
Shakir, S. A., 645
Shallice, T., 248, 274
Shamay-Tsoory, S. G., 577
Shanks, D. R., 12, 17
Shapiro, C. M., 425, 426
Shapiro, J. R., 502
Shapiro, S. J., 608
Shariff, A., 536
Sharma, A., 65
Sharma, P. S. V. N., 568
Sharma, V., 568
Sharma, Y. S., 397
Sharp, E. S., 444
Sharpes, K. M., 271
Shattuck, D. W., 284
Shaver, P., 18
Shaw, D., 206
Shaw, D. S., 564
Shaw, H., 363, 628
Shay, J. W., 337, 338
Shea, M. T., 578
Shea, N., 270
Shear, J., 186
Sheehan, T., 613
Sheese, B. E., 322
Shekar, S. N., 406
Sheldon, K. M., 12, 30, 353, 354, 355, 357, 380, 381
Sheldon, M. S., 629
Shelton, J., 42
Shelton, R. C., 360, 561, 592
Shen, B. J., 617
Shen, K., 70
Sher, K. J., 172
Sheridan, J. F., 91, 185
Sherif, C. W., 504
Sherif, M., 504
Sherman, D., 167
Sherman, D. K., 475
Sherman, F. T., 591
Sherman, R. A., 452
Sherman, S. J., 478
Sherwood, A. R., 179
Shetty, A. K., 92
Shevell, S. K., 124
Shi, Y., 561
Shibata, S. B., 134
Shibuya, A., 490
Shields, B., 552
Shields, S. A., 375
Shier, D. N., 65
Shiffman, S., 466, 629
Shiffrin, R. M., 233, 246
Shigemune, Y., 244
Shih, M., 183, 477
Shimai, S., 377
Shimanouchi, S., 641
Shimizu, H., 227

SUBJECT INDEX

Note: Page references in bold refer to definitions. Page references followed by "*f*" refer to figures.

identity, social, 500–501, 501*f*
identity formation, 334–335
identity status, 333–334, 333*f*
identity *vs.* identity confusion, **332–333**
illusions, perceptual, 107*f*, 130*f*
imagery, 230–232
imitation (observational learning), 191, 214–215, 215*f*
immune system
classical conditioning and, 197
meditation and, 185
sleep and, 163
stress and, 634–636, 635*f*, 636*f*
implementation intentions, **628**
Implicit Associations Test (IAT), 502–503
implicit learning, 217
implicit memory, 237*f*, **239**–240, 244
implicit racism, 502–503
improvement, stress and, 224
inattentional blindness, 114
income disparity, crime rates and, 489
incremental theory, 221
incubation, 153
independent variables, **41**
individualistic cultures, 22, 329, 354, 614
individual psychology, **436**
induction illusion, 130*f*
inductive reasoning, **274**, 274*f*
industrial and organizational psychology (I/O psychology)
Americans with Disabilities Act, 520, 520*f*, 581
best places to work, 514, 515*f*
Civil Rights Act, 522, 522*f*, 538
employee commitment, 531–533
employee development, 524
employee selection, 521–523, 521*f*, 522*f*
ergonomics, 513
Hawthorne studies, 513–514
human relations approach, 514
job analysis, 517–521, 518*f*, 519*f*, 520*f*
job satisfaction, 530–531
leadership, 534–536
management approaches, 528–530, 530*f*
meaning of work, 533–534
organizational culture, 536–540, 539*f*
performance appraisals, 525–527
personality psychology and, 462, 535
scientific management in, 512–513
sexual harassment, 538–539, 539*f*
stress at work, 542–544
study of, 18
training, 523–524
workplace aggression, 539–540
infant attachment, **322**–323, 323*f*
infants and babies
attachment in, **322**–323, 323*f*
brain in, 315–316, 315*f*, 316*f*
gender in, 393
imitation by, 191
inhibition in, 322
motor and perceptual skills in, 314–315, 315*f*
preference for attractive faces by, 315
preterm infants, 313
reflexes in, 314, 314*f*
sudden infant death syndrome, 165
temperament in, 322
inferential statistics, **53**
infinite generativity, **292**
informational social influence, **493**

information processing, 12
informed consent, 54, 56
in-groups/out-groups, 501, 503
inhibition, in infants, 322
inner ear, 133*f*, **134**–135, 134*f*
inoculation, 481
insight learning, 217–**218**, 218*f*
insight therapies, 598–600, 599*f*, 600*f*
insomnia, 163, 164
instinct, **350**
instinctive drift, 218–**219**, 219*f*
institutional review board (IRB), 54–55
instrumental conditioning. *See* operant conditioning
instrumentality, 388
insulin, 74, 359–360
integrative therapy, 604–**605**
integrity tests, **521**
integrity *vs.* despair, 342
intellectual disability, 287–288
intelligence, 281
crystallized and fluid, 339–340
cultural bias in tests, 283–284, 284*f*
g (general ability), 281
genetic and environmental influences on, 284–286, 286*f*
giftedness, 286–287
intellectual disability, 287–288
IQ tests, 282*f*, 283–284, 283*f*, 284*f*
theories of multiple intelligences, 288–290
intelligence quotient (IQ), 281–284, **282**, 282*f*, 283*f*, 284*f*
interference theory, **257**, 258*f*
intergroup relations, 500–507, 501*f*, 504*f*
internal locus of control, 451
internal validity, **43**
Internet
cybertherapy, 594
job ads on, 521
O*NET, 513
online support groups, 613–614
interpretation, **596**
intersex conditions, 390
interval schedules, 207
interviewer illusion, 522
interviews, 34–35, 522–523
intimacy motive, 448
intimacy *vs.* isolation, 341
intrinsic motivation, 30, **354**–355, 628
introspection, 9
intuitive processing, 275
Inuit people, 36, 294
investment model, **506**–507
in vitro fertilization, 93
ion channels, 67–68
I/O psychology. *See* industrial and organizational psychology
iPods, 146
IQ (intelligence quotient), 281–284, **282**, 282*f*, 283*f*, 284*f*
IQ tests, 282*f*, 283–284, 283*f*, 284*f*
IRB (institutional review board), 54–55
iris, 120, 121*f*
Islets of Langerhans, 74

J

James-Lange theory, **368**–369, 369*f*, 373
"Japanese" management style, 528–529, 530*f*
jet lag, 157
jigsaw classroom, 504

Jim twins, 98
job analysis, **517**–521, 518*f*, 519*f*, 520*f*
job crafting, 534
jobs. *See* employment
job satisfaction, **530**–531
job stress, **542**–544
journal keeping, 39, 58–59, 381
justice perspective, 329
just noticeable difference, 110–111

K

Katrina, Hurricane, 502, 585
kinesthetic senses, **143**–144, 144*f*
The Kinsey Reports, 414
KSAOs (or KSAs), **517**, 519, 521
Ku Klux Klan, 496*f*, 497

L

labia, 387
language, **292**
basic properties of, 292–293
biological influences on, 295–296
brain and, 296
Broca's area and, 87, 87*f*
deafness and, 135
environmental influences on, 296–297
gender differences in, 295
learning second languages, 238, 238*f*, 300
left hemisphere and, 87, 87*f*
over the life span, 298*f*, 299–300, 299*f*
people-first, 553
role in cognition, 293–294
sign, 135
somniloquy, 164
Wernicke's area and, 87, 87*f*
latency period, 434
latent content, **166**, 596
latent learning, **217**
lateral hypothalamus, 360
lateralization, 339, 339*f*
law of effect, **201**–202, 202*f*
leadership, 534–536
learned helplessness, **205**, 224
learning, **190**. *See also* classical conditioning; operant conditioning
animal models of stress, 223
breaking habits, 196
cultural influences, 220, 503
expectancy learning and information, 216–217
fears, 196, 196*f*
insight, 217–218, 218*f*
instinctive drift, 218–219, 219*f*
latent, 217
mindset and, 220–221
observational, 191, 214–215, 215*f*, 450
overlearning, 352, 524
placebo effect, 196–197, 216
preparedness, 219–220
second languages, 238, 238*f*, 300
study of, 17
study tips, 261–262
taste aversion, 197–198, 219
types of, 190–191, 191*f*
left-brained, 90
leisure, **542**–543, 543*f*
lens, 120–121, 121*f*
leptin, 360, 360*f*
lesbian women. *See* sexual orientation

levels of processing, **229**, 230*f*
lexical approach, 441
lie detectors, 367–368, 368*f*
life changes. *See* health psychology
life span. *See also* aging; longevity
development and, 345–346
language development over, 298*f*, 299–300, 299*f*
sleep over, 161–162, 161*f*
life story approach, 448–449
Lifestraw, 267
life themes, 308, 345–346
light, 119, 120*f*, 121*f*
limbic system, **81**–82, 244
linear perspective, 127, 128*f*
linguistic relativity hypothesis, 293–294
lithium, **588**
lobotomies, 592
locked-in syndrome, 149
loneliness, 508
longevity
conscientiousness and, 466
happiness and, 39–40, 367–368
obesity and fitness and, 644
personal control and, 466
physical activity and, 641, 641*f*
quitting smoking and, 643, 643*f*
religion and, 631
vacations and, 543, 543*f*
longitudinal design, **39**–40
longitudinal studies, 307
long-term memory, **237**
components of, 237–240, 237*f*, 238*f*, 239*f*
explicit memory, 237–239, 237*f*, 238*f*, 244
implicit memory, 237*f*, 239–240, 244
location of stored memories, 242–244, 244*f*
organization of, 240–242
smell and, 243
long-term potentiation, 242–243
loudness, 132
love, 505–506
LSD (lysergic acid diethylamide), 177–179

M

MA (mental age), **282**
Maasai people, 36
magnetic resonance imaging (MRI), 77–78
Maier string problem, 272, 273*f*
maintenance stage, 624*f*, 626
major depressive disorder (MDD), **560**. *See also* depression/depressive disorders
major histocompatibility complex (MHC), 143
majority influence, 499
management approaches, 528–530, 530*f*
mania, 563, 565*f*
manifest content, **166**, 596
Man's Search for Meaning (Frankl), 345
MAO inhibitors, 587, 590
marijuana, 177, 179
marriage, 5, 310, 341, 410–411
Maslow's hierarchy of needs, **352**–353, 353*f*
masturbation, 416
maturation, 331
MBTI (Myers-Briggs Type Indicator), 461, 462

Thematic Apperception Test (TAT), 447–448, **463,** 463*f*
theory, **28,** 30–31
theory of mind, 154
theory of mind mechanism (TOMM), 154
theory of planned behavior, **623**–624
theory of reasoned action, **623**–624
Theory X managers, **529,** 530*f*
Theory Y managers, **529,** 530*f*
therapeutic alliance, **608**
therapies
    for alcoholism, 196, 613
    behavior therapies, 598–600, 599*f*, 600*f*
    brain changes from, 606
    client participation in, 608
    cognitive-remediation therapy, 606
    cognitive therapies, 600–604, 602*f*, 604*f*
    community mental health, 614
    comparison of, 605*f*
    cybertherapy, 594
    drug therapy, 586–590, 587*f*, 590*f*
    effectiveness of, 606–608, 607*f*, 608*f*
    electroconvulsive therapy, 590–591, 591*f*
    ethnicity and, 615
    family and couples therapy, 612–613
    gender and, 615
    group therapy, 611
    humanistic therapies, 597–598
    hypnosis in, 183
    integrative therapy, 604–605
    prevention and, 617
    psychodynamic therapies, 594–597
    psychosurgery, 592
    self-help support groups, 613–614
    therapeutic alliance in, 608
    types of mental health professionals, 595*f*
    well-being therapy, 617–618
thermoreceptors, **140,** 140*f*
theta waves, 159, 160*f*
thinking, **270**
    artificial intelligence, 268*f*, 269
    biases and heuristics, 275–277, 276*f*
    concepts, 270–271
    convergent *vs.* divergent, 279
    creative, 279
    critical, 5, 31–33, 277–279
    decision making, 274–275
    emotions and, 278
    health and wellness and, 301–302
    intuitive processing in, 275
    problem solving, 271–273, 273*f*, 302*f*
    reasoning, 274–275, 274*f*
    role of language in, 293–294
third force psychology, 438
third variable problem, **37**
Thorndike's puzzle box, 201–202, 202*f*
thought disorder, 572
"three faces of Eve," 569–570, 569
360-degree feedback, **525**–526, 526*f*

thresholds
    absolute, 68, 109–110, 110*f*
    difference, 110–111
    subliminal perception, 111–112, 111*f*
timbre, 132
time and motion studies, 512
time-out, 209
tip-of-the-tongue (TOT) phenomenon, **258**
TMS (transcranial magnetic stimulation), 78
tobacco use
    health effects of, 174, 175*f*, 643, 643*f*
    nicotine, 174, 175*f*, 645
    reinforcement of, 211
    smoking cessation, 467, 643, 643*f*, 645
tolerance, to psychoactive drugs, **169**
TOMM (theory of mind mechanism), 154
top-down processing, **106**–107
TOT (tip-of-the-tongue) phenomenon, **258**
touch, 108–109, 108*f*, 110*f*, 139
training, 523–**524**
trait theories, **441**–445, 442*f*
tranquilizers, **173,** 586
transactional leaders, **534**
transcendence, 626
transcranial magnetic stimulation (TMS), 78
transference, **596**
transformational leaders, **534**–536
transgender individuals, **391**–392
transvestic fetishes, 420, 421*f*
traumatic memories, 58–59, 250–251, 558–559
treatment. *See* therapies
triarchic theory of intelligence, **289**
trichromatic theory, 124–**125,** 126*f*
tricyclics, 587
TV violence, 489
twin studies
    on bipolar disorder, 563, 563*f*
    fraternal *vs.* identical twins in, 97–98
    Jim twins, 98
    on leadership, 535
    on obesity, 361
    on personality, 457–458
    on physical aggression, 486
    on schizophrenia, 574*f*
    on sexual orientation, 407
2D:4D ratio, 408
two-factor theory of emotion, **370**–372, 371*f*
Type A/Type B behavior patterns, **468,** 635

U

umami, 141–142
unconditional positive regard, **439,** 598

unconditioned response (UCR), **193,** 193*f*
unconditioned stimulus (UCS), **193,** 193*f*
unconscious thought, **153**–154

V

vacations, 542–543, 543*f*
valence, 376
validity, 42–44, **282,** 282*f*
values, in research, 55
varenicline, 645
variable-interval schedules, 207
variable-ratio schedules, 207
variables, **28,** 41
ventral tegmental area (VTA), 170, 170*f*, 171
ventromedial hypothalamus, 360
vestibular sense, **144,** 144*f*
vicarious punishment, 215
vicarious reinforcement, 214
video games, 485, 490
vigilance, 229
violence. *See also* aggression
    alcohol use and, 171
    media, 489–490
    in pornography, 489–490
    workplace, 539–540
virginity, 413
virtual lesions, 78
virtue, organizational, 537
vision
    binding, 123–124
    blindness, 114, 124, 157, 349
    blind spot in, 122, 123*f*
    color perception, 124–125, 125*f*, 126*f*
    depth perception, 126–128
    eye structure and, 119–122, 121*f*, 122*f*
    illusions, 107*f*, 130*f*
    light and, 119, 120*f*, 121*f*
    motion perception, 128–129
    nutrition and, 146
    occipital lobes and, 83–85
    parallel processing in, 123
    perceptual constancy, 129, 129*f*
    photoreception in, 108–109, 108*f*
    shape perception, 125–126
    threshold for, 110, 110*f*
    visual processing in the brain, 122–124, 123*f*, 124*f*
visual cortex, 122–123
visuospatial working memory, 236, 236*f*
volley principle, **136**
voyeurism, 420, 421*f*
VTA (ventral tegmental area), 170, 170*f*, 171

W

waigawa system, **529**
wavelength, 119, 120*f*
WBT (well-being therapy), **618**

Weber's law, **110**–111
weight. *See* obesity
weight loss
    community support for, 621
    exercise and, 642
    motivation in, 360–361
    stages of change model in, 624–626, 624*f*
    success of strategies for, 643, 643*f*
well-being therapy (WBT), **618**
wellness
    cognitive appraisal and, 301–302
    good life and, 647
    human development and, 345–346
    job stress and, 542–544
    meditation and, 185–186
    memory and, 264–265
    mind and body in, 24–25
    motivation, emotion, and, 380–381
    personality and, 466–469
    scientific method and, 58–59
    sensation and perception and, 146–147
    sexual behavior and, 425–426
    social psychology and, 508
    stigma of psychological disorders, 580–582, 580*f*, 581*f*
    stress and, 101–102, 223–224
    therapies and, 617–618
    writing about traumas and, 58–59
Wernicke's area, 87, 87*f*
Williams syndrome, 294
windigo, 550*f*
wisdom, **340**
women and girls. *See also* gender differences; pregnancy
    brain in, 295, 389
    Freud on, 430–431
    maturation age in, 331
    menopause in, 337
    psychology of, 18
    self-objectification in, 475–476
    sex organs of, 387, 387*f*
    sexual harassment of, 538–539, 539*f*
    in violent pornography, 489–490
"word salad," 572
working memory, **235**–236, 236*f*, 246
workplace. *See* employment
workplace aggression, 539–540
work samples, 515, 521, 523
work settings, 16, 16*f*
writing, healing power of, 58–59

X

X rays, 76–77

Y

Yerkes-Dodson law, **351**–352, 352*f*

Z

Zyban, 645